Human Rights Law in the UK

This book offers a rich analysis of many aspects of human rights law in the UK and the European legal framework while also including critiques of human rights and the varying conceptions of rights. This book has the advantage of engaging with Strasbourg case law, domestic jurisprudence and academic scholarship. The issues covered include the right to life, the prohibition of torture, inhuman or degrading treatment, abortion and assisted dying, modern slavery and human trafficking, terrorism, immigration, privacy, hate speech, protest, religion, equality and non-discrimination.

Kirsty Hughes is an associate professor at the University of Cambridge Faculty of Law, Director of the Centre for Public Law, and a member of Blackstone Chambers Academic Panel. She is joint General Editor of the *European Human Rights Law Review* and Deputy Editor of *Public Law*. Her research has been awarded the Wedderburn Prize and has been cited by the Supreme Court of Canada, the Court of Appeal in England and Wales and parliamentary committees. She has also given oral evidence in the House of Lords. She has been the recipient of numerous research fellowships including at UNSW, EUI, Universidad Autónoma de Madrid and Harvard Law School. She has also lectured at universities in Poland, the Czech Republic, Slovakia and Hungary. In 2023 she was shortlisted for the Postgraduate Research Supervisor of the year award.

Stevie Martin is a college assistant professor at Fitzwilliam College, University of Cambridge, though aspects of the book were written while she was a senior lecturer at the T. C. Beirne School of Law (University of Queensland). She is also joint General Editor of the *European Human Rights Law Review*. Her research into human rights and medical law has been relied upon in courts nationally and internationally and she has given oral evidence to the Joint Committee on Human Rights. Her doctoral thesis was awarded the Yorke Prize and her research has been referred to in media reports on end-of-life issues.

Stephanie Palmer has taught for many years at the University of Cambridge Faculty of Law and also at Harvard Law School. She is a barrister at Blackstone Chambers, a joint General Editor of the *European Human Rights Law Review*, a Fellow of Girton College and the Lauterpacht Centre, Cambridge. She assisted with training the judiciary prior to the implementation of the Human Rights Act 1998. She is a member of the Alliance for Lawyers at Risk, and on the Advisory Board of the pro bono organisation, the Law Corner. Her published work on official secrecy and freedom of information has been translated into French, Spanish, Ukrainian and Russian. She has given advice to the Parliament of Ukraine on constitutional issues.

'This book does more than its title promises. As well as human rights law in the UK, it provides a good account of the foundations of human rights internationally and detailed accounts of how international bodies elucidate and apply human rights law in relation to specific, often intractable, conflicts and disputes. Within the UK, it places the issues in the context of domestic law and practice and shows how and how successfully – alongside Parliament, government and courts – other officials and institutions contribute to securing respect for and sometimes compliance with human rights. The authors thereby bring the subject to life in a rich, multifaceted way, and their expertise and experience make the book a reliable, thought-provoking guide. Readers will find illumination and stimulating new ideas on every page, as I have.'

Professor David Feldman KC, FBA, FRSA

'This is the right book, at the right time, in the right place with the right focus. The quality of the democracies which govern us, and the solidity of the rule of law which necessarily underpins effective democracies, can be assessed via the degree of respect for human rights in a given jurisdiction. By focusing on substantive topics instead of individual Convention rights, and via the choice of those topics, the authors illustrate this point extremely well. It is a point too often lost in modern debates about human rights but one which is becoming startlingly real (in courts across the globe) in the turbulent times in which we are living.'

Judge Síofra O'Leary, former President of the European Court of Human Rights

'Comprehensive, rigorous and deeply insightful, this book's illuminating examination of critical issues within human rights law in the UK is urgently needed and masterfully executed. It will be a vital resource for students, scholars and practitioners of human rights law in the UK and beyond.'

Professor Natasa Mavronicola

'This book is a must for any human rights lawyer, academic or activist. I am impressed by the excellent review of the European Court of Human Rights' case law, as well as by the thorough analysis of the most delicate domestic law issues that have been impacted by that case law. Ultimately, this book demonstrates with rigorous but simultaneously simple language that the time of constitutional parochialism is over in Europe. In the era of multilevel constitutionalism, the European Convention on Human Rights is a constitutional instrument of European public order, and thus prevails over constitutional provisions and interests of the Contracting Parties. The authors have successfully shown that the old-fashioned distinction between monist and dualist constitutional orders has become irrelevant, and domestic jurisdictions only have to gain when they leave the misleading comfort of a narrow-minded, parochial understanding of human rights law and embrace an open-minded, multifaceted, cosmopolitan interpretation of that law.'

Judge Paulo Pinto de Albuquerque, former Judge of the European Court of Human Rights

'A vital, necessary, meticulous and magisterially accessible account of human rights law in Britain, more important than ever – a first point of reference in times of uncertainty and threat to the basic rights of all individuals and groups.'

Professor Phillipe Sands KC, FBA, FRSL

Human Rights Law in the UK

Themes and Principles

Kirsty Hughes
University of Cambridge

Stevie Martin
University of Cambridge

Stephanie Palmer
University of Cambridge

CAMBRIDGE
UNIVERSITY PRESS

CAMBRIDGE
UNIVERSITY PRESS

Shaftesbury Road, Cambridge CB2 8EA, United Kingdom

One Liberty Plaza, 20th Floor, New York, NY 10006, USA

477 Williamstown Road, Port Melbourne, VIC 3207, Australia

314–321, 3rd Floor, Plot 3, Splendor Forum, Jasola District Centre, New Delhi – 110025, India

103 Penang Road, #05–06/07, Visioncrest Commercial, Singapore 238467

Cambridge University Press is part of Cambridge University Press & Assessment, a department of the University of Cambridge.

We share the University's mission to contribute to society through the pursuit of education, learning and research at the highest international levels of excellence.

www.cambridge.org
Information on this title: www.cambridge.org/highereducation/isbn/9781316515006

DOI: 10.1017/9781009091749

When citing this work, please include a reference to the DOI 10.1017/9781009091749

First published 2026

Cover image: Heritage Images / Hulton Fine Art Collection / Getty Images

A catalogue record for this publication is available from the British Library

Library of Congress Cataloging-in-Publication Data
Names: Hughes, Kirsty Elizabeth, author. | Martin, Stevie, author. | Palmer, Stephanie, author.
Title: Human rights law in the UK : themes and principles / Kirsty Hughes, University of Cambridge; Stevie Martin, University of Cambridge; Stephanie Palmer, University of Cambridge.
Description: Cambridge, United Kingdom ; New York, NY : Cambridge University Press, 2025. | Includes bibliographical references and index. | Summary: "This book offers a unique and detailed analysis of human rights law from the perspective of both domestic UK law and ECHR law. It will be of invaluable use for undergraduate and graduate students studying and researching human rights law. It will also be of significant interest to human rights practitioners and judges"–Provided by publisher.
Identifiers: LCCN 2025016417 (print) | LCCN 2025016418 (ebook) | ISBN 9781316515006 (hardback) | ISBN 9781009095457 (paperback) | ISBN 9781009091749 (epub)
Subjects: LCSH: Human rights–Great Britain. | Human rights–Europe. | Civil rights–Great Britain. | Political rights–Great Britain. | Convention for the Protection of Human Rights and Fundamental Freedoms (1950 November 5)
Classification: LCC KD4080 .H84 2025 (print) | LCC KD4080 (ebook) | DDC 342.4108/5–dc23/eng/20250507
LC record available at https://lccn.loc.gov/2025016417
LC ebook record available at https://lccn.loc.gov/2025016418

ISBN 978-1-316-51500-6 Hardback
ISBN 978-1-009-09545-7 Paperback

CONTENTS

FOREWORD

What? Another book on Human Rights Law? Is this the right time? Is this the right place? And aren't there enough of them already?

It is very much the right time and place. The human rights project has been under serious attack, both at home and abroad, in recent times. In this country, government ministers have threatened to disobey court orders which they do not like. They have promoted laws to restrict the rights of people to complain that the actions of government are unlawful. They have threatened to repeal the Human Rights Act and replace it with a British Bill of Rights which would have severely curtailed the protection given to human rights in UK law. They have even threatened to withdraw from the European Convention on Human Rights. More insidiously, but more shockingly, they have promoted laws which restrict the human rights of people they do not like. They have denied the fundamental principle that human rights are universal – that everyone has them simply by virtue of being human. They have promoted laws which are inconsistent with the international treaties to which the United Kingdom is a party and obliged by international law to observe. They have vilified the lawyers who are trying to protect the rights of people they do not like and the Judges who make decisions which they do not like.

Ah yes, it might be said. But that was the previous Government. We now have a Government led by a prime minister who used to be a human rights lawyer (and a very good one too). He has brought in an attorney-general to repair the damage, to reassert the Government's commitment to the rule of law, to reaffirm that the United Kingdom would not withdraw from the European Court of Human Rights or refuse to comply with its judgments. Yet we read that ministerial colleagues have accused him of blocking critical legislation out of undue deference to international law, that the Attorney-General's Office is now known as the 'anti-government office'. We have even seen the Prime Minister express his disagreement with a judgment he did not like. Somehow or other, the view seems to have crept into the minds of some politicians that the rule of law, whether nationally or internationally, must take second place to the wishes of a Government with a large majority in Parliament.

Yet the purpose of all human rights instruments – going back at least as far as the revolutionary movements of the late eighteenth century – is to say that there are certain things that any Government cannot do, whether or not it has a large majority. There are certain rights which every person has, simply by virtue of their humanity, however unpopular they may be with the majority. That is why the Safety of Rwanda (Immigration and Asylum) Bill of 2023–2024 was attacked so fiercely in the House of Lords – the unelected Upper House standing up for the right of outsiders to have their claims properly considered by an independent and impartial judiciary. The strength and persistence of that opposition – from peers of many different political persuasions and none – gave me hope that the human rights project was still alive among the powers-that-be in this country.

It is certainly still alive amongst the young. I go to a lot of events for students – especially students of law and politics. Many, even most, of the law students want to be human rights lawyers, although they realise that they may have to settle for the more lucrative and reliable work of a transactional or commercial lawyer. They see the excitement and the value in fighting for the rights of the marginalised, the disadvantaged, the unpopular.

But do they need another book? There are plenty of good books about European human rights law. These explain the structure and mechanisms of the Human Rights Act and then go through the articles of the European Convention on Human Rights one by one. Nothing wrong with that. This book too has some introductory chapters on the theory of human rights, the protection of human rights in UK law, and the protection of human rights under the European Convention on Human Rights. But it takes a different approach to the detailed discussion of the substance of those rights. It does not go through the individual Convention rights one by one. You will not find, for example, chapters on the right to liberty or the right to a fair trial. But this is because the aim is to look at how certain particularly hot topics are dealt with, not only in Convention law, but also in UK law (and they do mean UK law – not just the law of England and Wales). So there are chapters on the right to life and the prohibition of torture and inhuman or degrading treatment or punishment. But there are also chapters on, for example, the beginning of life and end of life, human trafficking, terrorism, migration, protests, hate speech and equality. On some of these topics, such as terrorism and protests, there is a great deal of UK law. On some, such as the beginning and end of life, there is perhaps surprisingly little, so the interplay between UK and Convention law becomes more prominent.

This comprehensive approach – and on the topics covered it is indeed comprehensive – enables the authors – and the readers – to draw out the issues for thought and discussion much more realistically than a simple concentration on the individual Convention rights would do. It does mean that certain topics have to be left out; I would, for example, have liked to see a chapter on human rights and the welfare state – but with a comprehensive approach like this there is not room for everything.

The contextual approach also draws out the developing issues in Convention jurisprudence. In many contexts, such as freedom of speech, freedom of religion and belief, freedom of assembly, there will be more than one Convention right in play and they will often be in conflict: how to balance the conflicting rights is a recurring theme. Another recurring theme is the evolution of positive obligations. The early hate speech cases, for example, were about whether the interference with freedom of expression could be justified; later cases began to recognise that there might be a positive obligation to protect certain people from the harm caused by hate speech. And a third recurring theme is the margin of appreciation. When will the matter be left entirely to the Member State to decide, when will the Strasbourg Court confine itself to checking whether the Member State has conducted the right evaluative exercise, and when will the Strasbourg Court step in to say that the Member State has got it wrong? There are signs that the Strasbourg Court has drawn back a little in recent years in the face of pushback from Member States, not least the United Kingdom.

There are also signs that it is not only the UK Government and Parliament which have drawn back in the protection of human rights in the United Kingdom. The appellate committee of the House of Lords has held that there are circumstances in which the courts have the constitutional competence to develop the Convention rights even though Strasbourg would regard it as within the margin of appreciation.[1] It is the job of the courts to be particularly vigilant, for example, in cases of alleged discrimination in the enjoyment of the Convention rights. The Supreme Court of the United Kingdom has also held that the courts have the constitutional competence to decide whether an absolute ban on assisting suicide is incompatible with the Convention rights even though this is clearly within the margin of appreciation.[2] But more recently the Supreme Court has held that if the matter is within the margin of appreciation left to the Member States, then there is no breach of the Convention rights, and deciding upon the UK's approach must be left to Parliament.[3] Apparently, this is so even if the matter is not governed by Act of Parliament, so the courts could put it right.

[1] *In re G (Adoption: Unmarried Couple)* [2008] UKHL 38, [2009] 1 AC 173. See Lord Hoffmann, para 37, Lord Hope, para 48, Lady Hale, paras 119–120, Lord Mance paras 126–130. Clearly essential to the decision that the restriction of adoption to married couples in article 14 of the Adoption (Northern Ireland) Order 1987 could be disregarded.

[2] By a majority but clearly *obiter* in *R (Nicklinson)* v. *Ministry of Justice* [2014] UKSC 38, [2015] AC 657.

[3] *R (Elan-Cane)* v. *Secretary of State for the Home Department* [2021] UKSC 56, [2023] AC 559. Observations in *In re G (*above*)* are 'best regarded as obiter'.

This makes it all the more important to have a book which can explore the interaction between Convention law and UK law in detail and in depth, provoking, one hopes, the liveliest of discussions and debates. It follows that no reader, and that includes me, is likely to agree with all the views expressed. But it also follows that every reader, and that too includes me, will have learned a lot.

Brenda Hale
Formerly President, Supreme Court of the United Kingdom

PREFACE

One of the many challenges that we have faced while writing this book is the pace of change. This book was written against a backdrop of constant flux in human rights law. It would be naïve to regard this as a uniquely contemporary phenomenon, but it is nonetheless important to recognise that in recent years calls to repeal the Human Rights Act 1998 (HRA) and threats to withdraw from the European Convention on Human Rights (ECHR) have been especially heightened. During the period in which we were writing this book it was not at all guaranteed that the HRA would still be in force by the time that the book appeared in print; 2021–2022, in particular, was spent writing and then rewriting the book to reflect the changing tides. Moreover, while calls to repeal the HRA and threats to withdraw from the ECHR pose the most obvious challenge to human rights law in the United Kingdom, recent years have seen the enactment of a significant body of legislation that has eroded rights. This has been particularly prevalent in relation to immigration, modern slavery and human trafficking, and the law of protest. Many of these developments have given rise to important legal challenges.

In writing this book we have thus been writing and rewriting to reflect developments in real time, often in the face of ongoing uncertainty. Broadly speaking, this edition examines human rights law as of May 2025. The manuscript was initially completed in the summer of 2024, however, we have been able to include some material and developments while the book was in production. We updated the manuscript to reflect the change of Government in July 2024 and to include major cases handed down between April 2024 and May 2025. The change of Government in the summer of 2024 has meant that existential threats to the HRA and ECHR currently seem to be in abeyance, but considerable uncertainty remains. It is not clear what will happen in respect of much of the rights-corrosive legislation and policies that emerged during the previous Governments. We wait to see what new policies and legislation will transpire concerning such matters as assisted dying, immigration law and the Northern Ireland Troubles (Legacy and Reconciliation) Act 2023. This book is destined (as all human rights law books are) to reflect a particular moment.

The perspective that we have offered as to the state of human rights law in 2025 may appear pessimistic. Yet, while many developments might be characterised as moves to restrict rights, there have also been moments where rights have been extended. For instance, climate litigation has illustrated how human rights can be used to protect populations from environmental degradation by imposing obligations on Governments. The European Court of Human Rights (ECtHR) has also extended the protection accorded to victims of human trafficking, including in some circumstances imposing obligations of non-prosecution of victims. Meanwhile in the UK, Parliament and domestic courts have expanded the protections afforded to reproductive autonomy, which is in stark contrast to the trend we have seen internationally in recent years.

The aim of this book is to shed light on key issues by examining human rights law from the perspective of both UK and ECHR law. In deciding which topics to cover, we have drawn on comments from students and colleagues in Cambridge and beyond involved in the study, research and practice of human rights law in the UK. The resulting structure of the book is as follows. The first part explores the nature and critiques of human rights before setting out the human rights frameworks in the UK and Europe (including the ECHR). This is followed by chapters on the Right to Life, Freedom from Torture or Inhuman or Degrading Treatment or Punishment, Assisted Dying and Abortion, Modern Slavery and Human Trafficking, Terrorism, Migrants' Rights, Privacy, Hate Speech, Protest, Religion and Equality. Chapters 1 and 3 were co-authored by Kirsty Hughes, Stevie Martin and Stephanie Palmer; Chapters 2 and 14 were written by Stephanie Palmer; Chapters 4, 5, 6 and 8 were written by Stevie Martin; and Chapters 7, 9, 10, 11, 12 and 13 were written by Kirsty Hughes. Anyone familiar with human rights law will appreciate that a comprehensive account of any one of these topics would be a sizable book, and decisions regarding scope and focus have therefore been made in rendering the book manageable. There are, of course, other issues that we would have liked to examine within each of these chapters, as well as many other chapters that we would have wished to include in the book. We may well do so in a future edition.

One of the many benefits of considering this array of rights in a single book, as opposed to a book dedicated to simply one of these rights, is that several interlocking themes have emerged. The first two, autonomy and dignity, connect to the overarching theme of vulnerability. In addition, two further themes – the function and legitimacy of the courts, and the efficacy of human rights law – permeate each chapter.

Vulnerability is a concept that runs throughout the book, appearing to varying extents in the issues addressed in each of the chapters. Much has been written on the notion of vulnerability, how to conceptualise it within human rights law, how to identify vulnerable individuals or classes of people, and whether vulnerability should be the threshold for state action. Critics have argued that 'vulnerability is neither conceptually straightforward nor as morally and politically neutral as its popularity may suggest.'[1] The role of vulnerability is thus neither inevitable nor uncontested; it is, however, present.

Vulnerability intersects with another theme of autonomy, which plays a central role in deliberations on abortion, assisted dying, religion and privacy, among others. Vulnerability also relates to the theme of dignity. Often, a threat to a person's dignity gives rise to concerns regarding their vulnerability and, inversely, a person's vulnerability may make them especially susceptible to interferences with their dignity.[2] Dignity features prominently in some chapters, particularly those examining migrants' rights, modern slavery and human trafficking, domestic abuse, abortion and assisted dying, hate speech and equality. Yet dignity is also a concept that arises in circumstances in which vulnerability is not at play, thus (as acknowledged above) calling into question whether vulnerability is the right lens for human rights law.

In addition to these themes, we examine the role and function of the courts in relation to the delivery of human rights protection. Concerns with respect to legitimacy and institutional competence are evident in the jurisprudence of both the domestic courts and the ECtHR across the issues examined in this book. The domestic courts have relied heavily on the practice of deference to the Government or legislature in cases involving topics that are morally, politically and ethically contentious. For example, courts have refrained from deciding on issues such as assisted dying, citing concerns regarding institutional competence to justify leaving the issue to Parliament. Likewise, the ECtHR has given States a considerable margin of appreciation in issues such as abortion and assisted dying. Each of the themes examined here raises questions about the function of human rights and the efficacy of rights as a means of securing the autonomy, equality and dignity of individuals.

As we noted at the outset, such questions and the potential limitations of the human rights protections do not warrant their abandonment. But anyone concerned with the future of human rights should carefully consider these limitations and the ways in which human rights could be developed to improve their efficacy and strengthen the protection they offer. That is no small function of this book; as academics researching and teaching human rights law in the UK, we are attuned to the limitations and the potential of rights. We hope that this book not only offers a useful resource to others teaching, learning, researching and practising human rights law in the UK but that is also meaningfully contributes to the continued refinement and improvement of human rights law in the UK and in Europe.

[1] Amalia Gilodi, Isabelle Albert and Birte Nienaber, 'Vulnerability in the Context of Migration: A Critical Overview and a New Conceptual Model' (2024) 7 *Human Arenas* 620, p.621.

[2] It is, perhaps, unsurprising that concerns regarding vulnerability and dignity feature prominently in the ECtHR's Article 4 ECHR jurisprudence (see, for instance, *Chowdury* v. *Greece* [2017] ECHR 300).

We are grateful for the support and encouragement of Cambridge University Press in bringing this book to life, and to our indexer Kate McIntosh and copy editor Ian Pickett, who were outstanding in getting it across the finish line. We would also like to thank Clare College, Fitzwilliam College and Girton College for generously assisting with the cost of indexing this book. We had the privilege of being able to craft this book over many years while teaching human rights law at the University of Cambridge. We would therefore like to thank the following colleagues for their support and comments on various drafts: Alex Allen-Franks, Rebecca Freund, Lewis Graham, Lady Brenda Hale, Lena Holzer, Vandita Khanna, Conor McCormick, Judge Paulo Pinto de Albuquerque, Darren Peterson, Nathalie Prouvez, Shona Wilson Stark and Leslie Turano. We would especially like to thank the students who have studied human rights law at the University of Cambridge and who have read earlier versions of these chapters. They have contributed significantly to the shape of this book and helped us to refine our approach and ideas. Most of all we would like to thank our families for all their love and support, and especially our children, for whom we hope that human rights law will continue to offer protection and possibilities.

TABLE OF CASES

TABLE OF STATUTES

1 The Nature of Rights and Critiques of Human Rights

CONTENTS

1.1 INTRODUCTION

The European Convention on Human Rights (ECHR) primarily provides protection for civil and political human rights; rights akin to those found in bills of rights and/or constitutional documents in many contemporary Western democracies. Given this confluence, it is understandable that one might assume that these rights are universally accepted and most deserving of protection. Such a view is, however, too simplistic. There is disagreement (sometimes considerable) about the scope and content of these civil and political rights and whether their effective enjoyment requires recognition and protection of social and economic rights (and if so, *which* social and economic rights). More existential questions abound, also, including whether human rights are useful or desirable at all or whether they are themselves part of the problem.

Underpinning this book is a belief in the role of human rights in securing the dignity, autonomy and bodily integrity of all individuals, particularly the most vulnerable in society. We accept the importance of human rights – civil, political, social and economic – but we also acknowledge their limits and weaknesses. Improvements can and should be made, but suggestions that the existing human rights system, whether in the UK or at the ECHR level, should be dismantled ought to be approached with considerable caution, not least as those most likely to be affected by the diminution of rights are often unrepresented (or at least underrepresented) in debates over the future of human rights.

1.2 PHILOSOPHICAL UNDERSTANDINGS OF HUMAN RIGHTS

What rights are recognised and protected as *human* rights and why do these rights have this status whilst other rights and interests do not receive the same level of recognition or protection? Are human rights simply the result of political agreements or do they exist as natural or moral rights that we have simply by virtue of being human? These are complex questions with no definitive answers. Yet, without an accepted theoretical basis, it can be difficult to identify the origins of (and, thus, the justifications for) human rights, as well as the standards against which human rights law and practice should be judged.

Broadly speaking, there are two primary schools of philosophical thought when it comes to the normative foundation of rights: the 'orthodox' or moral view and the political view. Theorists who favour a moral view posit that the meanings and existence of human rights are independent of the outcomes of political and legal processes, with the origins of rights being found in religious or secular values.[1] Conversely, those of a positivist persuasion regard the content of rights as no more or no less than what results from the political and legal process. In this vein Martti Koskenniemi asserts: '[w]e do not know our rights, we create them through our political processes'.[2]

These different understandings of the origins of rights affect perceptions of the role of the courts in interpreting and enforcing rights. As George Letsas notes:

> How law should be interpreted, and what legal rights individuals have, is taken to be an important question of political morality that is both capable and in need of principled justification. Judges have a responsibility to justify their decision and cite the reasons that led them to it. In doing so they cannot help but engage, either directly or indirectly, with the above normative questions. This should be even more so in the case of the ECHR, a human rights instrument that has brought together all European states and has an important effect on both domestic law and culture.[3]

[1] Michael Addo, *The Legal Nature of International Human Rights* (Nijhoff, 2010); James Griffin, *On Human Rights* (Oxford University Press, 2008); John Tasioulas, 'Taking Rights out of Human Rights' 120(4) Ethics 647–678.

[2] Martti Koskenniemi, *The Politics of International Law* (Hart, 2011), p.35.

[3] George Letsas, *A Theory of Interpretation of the European Convention on Human Rights* (Oxford University Press, 2009), pp.4–5.

In his focus on questions concerning the nature of human rights, Samuel Moyn turns to history and observes that moral understandings of rights have 'old roots' dating back centuries:

It is well known that at the most abstract level – including the foundational claim that individuals have moral entitlements that in turn implicate duties of protection to be borne by others – philosophers historically gave most attention to 'human rights' in natural law traditions of early modern or even medieval vintage.[4]

Moral understandings of rights are not, however, homogeneous; they draw on multiple ontological sources to justify the existence (and scope) of rights. As John Tasioulas aptly puts it:

Some philosophers echo contemporary human rights instruments by presenting human dignity as the foundation [of human rights], others appeal to a schedule of basic human needs or universal interests, yet others to the value of personhood or some combination of these factors. And of course there are still those who insist, against all secular doctrines of the kind just listed, that a compelling grounding of human rights is inescapably theistic in character.[5]

In James Griffin's view '[t]he secularized notion that we were left with at the end of the Enlightenment is still our notion today. . .'.[6] Griffin, an important proponent of the Orthodox approach, posits that human rights 'can be seen as protections of our human standing or . . . personhood'.[7] Cental to our 'personhood', according to Griffin, is 'agency': to be an 'agent', individuals must 'choose [their] own path through life' ('call it "autonomy"') and that choice 'must be real; one must have at least certain minimum education and information'.[8] Having 'chosen', 'one must then be able to act' which requires the 'minimum provision of resources and capabilities' and, fundamentally, individuals need 'liberty' to pursue what one perceives to be a 'worthwhile life'.[9]

Insight into the moral characterisations of rights is also offered by Steven Wheatley who explains that:

Arguments for natural rights invariably depend on a two-stage process of analytical reasoning. First, moral philosophers explain what they see as the distinctive nature of human existence, often without reference to insights from anthropology, biology, psychology or sociology. Second, they proceed, by a process of deductive reasoning, to explain the natural rights necessary to protect those essential qualities.[10]

[4] Samuel Moyn, 'Human Rights in Heaven' in Adam Etinson (ed), *Human Rights: Moral or Political?* (Oxford University Press, 2018), p.69.

[5] John Tasioulas, 'On the Foundations of Human Rights' in Rowan Cruft, Matthew S. Liao and Massimo Renzo (eds), *Philosophical Foundations of Human Rights* (Oxford University Press, 2015), p.45. See also Addo (n 1).

[6] Griffin (n 1), p.2. [7] Ibid, p.33. [8] Ibid. [9] Ibid, pp.47 and 159.

[10] Steven Wheatley, *The Idea of International Human Rights Law* (Oxford University Press, 2019), pp.22–23.

As Freeman observes, it is difficult to argue that we should prefer the theoretical justification of one philosopher to another, or the position of moral philosophy to the actual practice of human rights. Freeman concludes: 'Unfortunately there are no uncontested philosophical foundations of human rights.'.[11]

The 'orthodox' or moral idea of rights – whatever their ontological starting point – can be contrasted with political understandings of rights. The difference, as James Nickel puts it, is that '[p]olitical conceptions of human rights assign one or more constitutive political functions to human rights, frequently at an international level'.[12] They look to relationships between individuals or, more generally, between individuals and the State, indeed '[t]he objective [of the political view] is to explain the proper relationship between the government and the individual in terms of rights'.[13] In contrast, '[o]rthodox [or moral] conceptions are more closely associated with the natural rights tradition, which holds that the justification of at least some political and legal rights is based on analogous moral rights, refuses to limit the roles of human rights to the political realm, and is not adverse to philosophical theories of human rights that rely on controversial values such as autonomy or equality' or, indeed, suffering.[14]

Neither the orthodox, moral view of human rights nor the political conceptualisation is without criticism. Moral views of rights may fail to demonstrate why human rights are a subclass of moral rights, thus rendering the concept of moral rights redundant.[15] Political understandings have a potential to 'other' non-citizens, with their focus on the relationship between subject and State (thus leaving non-citizens/non-subjects without protection). The emphasis on the function of rights within the political sphere has the potential to cause indeterminacy. As Andrea Sangiovanni has observed:

> Imagine someone is tortured in Pakistan. And imagine that any criticism or other international action (whether sovereignty-overriding or not) would severely destabilize the region such that it would not be justified. According to the Political view, while there is certainly a moral right that has been violated, it is not a human right. But now imagine that international circumstances change enough that international action (whether sovereignty-overriding or not) becomes justifiable. Has the person tortured acquired a human right in the process – a right that they previously lacked? Can we gain and lose our human rights in virtue of shifting international circumstances?[16]

[11] Michael Freeman, 'The Philosophical Foundations of Human Rights' (1994) 16 Human Rights Quarterly 491, p. 511.

[12] James Nickel, 'Assigning Functions to Human Rights' in Etinson (ed), *Human Rights* (n 4), p.145.

[13] Wheatley (n 10), p.25. [14] Ibid.

[15] See, for instance, Andrea Sangiovanni, 'Beyond the Political-Orthodox Divide' in Etinson (ed), *Human Rights* (n 4), p.176.

[16] Ibid, p.182.

According to Sangiovanni, the orthodox and political debates are misguided in their focus on distilling a 'master list' of rights 'that will both reveal the moral unity underlying all of human rights practice and serve as a standard for its criticism'.[17] Such a list is a chimera. Instead, Sangiovanni offers an alternative view – termed the 'Broad View' – which posits that 'human rights are not those moral rights possessed by virtue of our humanity, but those moral rights whose systematic violation ought to be of universal moral, legal, and political concern'.[18]

Rainer Forst suggests that this alternative view is too broad. While it is an important contribution to the wider project of promoting philosophical debate on the basis of human rights beyond the orthodox/political divide, it lacks clarity as to how contextual conceptions and interpretations are connected.[19]

Human rights law is a specific manifestation of human rights, and there may not be direct correspondence between one's understanding of what human rights are on the one hand and what human rights law is on the other. This means that 'perhaps not all (moral) human rights are well suited for legal protection' and that not all 'legal human right[s]' necessarily have a 'direct moral counterpart'.[20] This divergence between the normative, moral foundations of human rights and the legal codification of rights may 'complicate the task of evaluating human rights law'.[21] Measuring the efficacy of human rights law is not just a matter of seeing how well it conforms to human rights morality. One should not assume that the metric being employed in a specific instance is an uncontroversial one.

A pragmatic acceptance of rights as laid out in human rights treaties, without further analysis, is perhaps a tempting solution. Sionaidh Douglas-Scott, however, finds such a solution troubling 'for the existence and identifications of human rights are bound up with the very justifications we use for them'.[22] Pragmatism may also lead to utilitarian thinking and an inclination towards suspending rights when it seems in the public interest to do so, with the attendant risks that poses for marginalised groups.[23]

Ultimately, regardless of whether human rights are moral rights, purely legal rights, or occupy some middle point between the two, they have normative content. In this respect John Tasioulas argues that a 'crude, legalistic reduction of human rights fails on its own terms, since the human rights laws it invokes typically pre-suppose an extra-legal conception of human rights,

[17] Ibid, p.175. [18] Ibid, p.186. Emphasis in original.

[19] Rainer Forst, 'Human Rights in Context: A Comment on Sangiovanni' in Etinson (ed), *Human Rights* (n 4), p.201.

[20] Adam Etinson, 'Introduction' in Etinson (ed), *Human Rights* (n 4), p.3. [21] Ibid, p.4.

[22] Sionaidh Douglas-Scott, *Law after Modernity* (Hart, 2020), p.292.

[23] Ibid. See also, Michael Ignatieff, *The Lesser Evil: Political Ethics in the Age of Terror* (Princeton University Press, 2004).

one that is a bench mark against which the laws themselves are to be assessed.'[24] Mark Elliott similarly observes '[h]owever feasible and realistic it may be to express rights in legalistic, rather than moralistic terms, it is impossible to explore their content and limits without regard to the morality in which they are founded. Consequently the meaning and nuances of any right can be determined only by locating it within precisely that framework of morality from [which] it sprang in the first place.' [25] Some consensus between the seemingly opposed points of view is perhaps not surprising; indeed, David Feldman has suggested that 'certain natural law and positivist approaches to rights are complementary rather than in conflict'.[26] He highlights the fact that 'those parts of positive law which consist of statements of proper or desired behaviour, backed by a reward or sanction, presuppose the rightness of those forms of behaviour' and '[s]uch ideas of rightness can be derived only from a system of social or moral values operating independently of law'.[27]

There is considerable debate as to the foundation of human rights, with neither the orthodox, moral view nor the political view offering, on its own, a convincing or complete account. Indeed, the debate merely serves to highlight the complexity of the subject matter. Nevertheless, theorising about human rights must draw on both natural law and positive approaches to reach any coherent account of the basis of human rights.[28]

1.3 CRITIQUES OF RIGHTS

Human rights law has been attacked from all points on the political spectrum. Some reject the very idea of human rights law, while others seek to expand its scope. When considering such critiques, it is useful to distinguish between criticisms of the institutionalisation and juridification of rights and ideological criticisms of human rights themselves. In this respect Tom Campbell, Keith Ewing and Adam Tomkins suggest that institutional critiques focus 'on the mechanisms that are associated with contemporary human rights law, particularly those that diminish the role of parliaments and extend the political role of courts, which are considered to be illegitimate and ineffective'; whilst ideological critiques range 'from rejection of the very idea of human rights to doubts about politically biased content of much human rights law'.[29] We consider these critiques below.

24 John Tasioulas, 'Towards a Philosophy of Human Rights' (2012) 1 Current Legal Problems 2.

25 Mark Elliott, *The Constitutional Foundations of Judicial Review* (Hart, 2001), p.223.

26 David Feldman, *Civil Liberties and Human Rights* (2nd ed) (Oxford University Press, 2002), p.28.

27 Ibid.

28 See, for instance, Corina Heri, 'Deference, Dignity and "Theoretical Crisis": Justifying ECtHR Rights Between Prudence and Protection' (2024) 24 Human Rights Law Review 1.

29 Tom Campbell, Keith Ewing and Adam Tomkins, 'Introduction' in Tom Campbell, K. D. Ewing and Adam Tomkins (eds), *The Legal Protection of Human Rights: Sceptical Essays* (Oxford University Press, 2011), p.4.

1.3.1 Are Rights Legal or Political?

In the late twentieth century, academics were divided 'deeply and fiercely about who should protect rights in a democracy'.[30] In one corner were writers such as Ronald Dworkin who 'portrayed judges as Herculean heroes in a "forum of principle", valiantly defending our most basic liberties against the inevitable encroachments of a rights-infringing legislature'.[31] In the other corner, academics such as Jeremy Waldron valorised the legislature, opposing the courts as the protectors of rights on the basis that judicial review of rights entailed the courts 'riding roughshod over the principle of political equality, and foisting their elite views on the unwilling masses in a deeply disrespectful and disempowering manner'.[32] While the Dworkin/Waldron debate dominated the wider discussion about which branch of the State should protect human rights (i.e., legislature or judiciary or neither or both), each academic's theorising suffered from a similar tendency to 'airbrush out' the wrinkles of their chosen enforcer. As Aileen Kavanagh puts it, 'either way we are ruled by philosopher-kings problematically detached from the fundamental determinants of institutional role'.[33] Further, each seems to pit the judiciary against the legislature – as if it is one or the other when it comes to rights protection. But that is not how it works in practice. Indeed a binary framing is not the most conducive approach to securing rights: '[i]n order to protect rights in a constitutional democracy, we need both courts and legislatures to play different roles whilst working alongside each other in multiple ways'.[34] As David Dyzenhaus observes:

> That parliaments, on occasion, engage admirably in moral debate is to be welcomed. But just as advocates of strong judicial review might romanticize the judiciary, so constitutional positivists are prone to romanticize their favored institution, one whose reputation among the people often seems rather low these days, if only because of the popular perception that legislatures act as rubber stamps for powerful governments. Far from being reason debating forums, they often fail even to be reason-demanding forums.[35]

In contrast to Dyzenhaus (or, perhaps, in illustration of his point), Grégoire Webber and Paul Yowell criticise the tendency amongst human rights lawyers and academics to overlook the central role that legislation plays in securing rights, particularly in the UK.[36] According to Webber and Yowell, Dworkin's majoritarian conception of the legislature ought to be rejected as it fails to

[30] Aileen Kavanagh, 'Keeping It Real in Constitutional Theory' (2023) 1 Comparative Constitutional Studies 2, 246.

[31] Ibid, referring to Ronald Dworkin, A Matter of Principle (Harvard University Press, 1985), 33.

[32] Ibid, referring to Jeremy Waldron, The Dignity of Legislation (Cambridge University Press, 1999).

[33] Ibid, p.248. [34] Ibid.

[35] David Dyzenhaus, 'Are Legislatures Good at Morality? Or Better at It Than the Courts?' (2009) 7 Issues in Constitutional Law 1, 50.

[36] Grégoire Webber and Paul Yowell, 'Introduction: Securing Rights through Legislation' in Grégoire Webber et al. (eds), *Legislated Rights: Securing Human Rights through Legislation* (Cambridge University Press, 2018).

appreciate the nuance of the legislative process.[37] They emphasise that it is through legislation that specificity is given to general rights instruments such as the ECHR and it is through legislation that rights can most legitimately (and effectively) be secured.[38] That is not to suggest that it is only through legislation that rights can be secured, but that legislation is critical to provide content to the otherwise broadly defined rights set out in instruments such as the ECHR: '[w]ithout positive action by legislation, and positive law more generally, many human rights would fail to be realised. That is true not only for what some refer to as "positive" rights (such as the right to state provision of primary and secondary education), but also of the more classical, "negative" rights.'[39] Webber and Yowell may well be correct that, in many instances, 'the legislature is well placed to secure and promote human rights, providing specified legal form to the broad, goal-oriented standards of instruments such as the … European Convention [on Human Rights]'.[40] Yet, there can be little doubt that robust and effective rights protection depends upon the three branches of the State working symbiotically, rather than competing against each other.

It is in this respect that dialogic theories take on particular relevance. Such theories focus on the ways in which the judiciary and the legislature/executive communicate with each other. One facet of the dialogue approach to rights review posits that courts 'calibrate' or moderate the intensity with which they review a rights issue depending on a number of factors including, for instance, institutional competence, the nature of the right engaged (e.g., is it 'a right "of high constitutional importance"'?[41]), the subject-matter of the dispute (e.g. does it involve questions of public policy or economic spending which are, traditionally, issues for the elected branches?), and whether there is a need 'for democratically legitimate decision making on broad, controversial questions of policy'.[42] The notion that courts can communicate with the legislative and executive branches and temper (or not as the case may be) the degree of scrutiny they apply to rights disputes offers a pragmatic counterpoint to the binary, legal-versus-political debate foregrounded by Dworkin and Waldron. Indeed, the courts' calibrated review can be observed in domestic rights jurisprudence. For instance, in cases involving assisted suicide and determinations as to whether there is a state of public emergency, where courts have moderated the degree of scrutiny they apply based on factors including institutional competence, the polycentric nature of the dispute and the importance of the rights in issue.[43] In addition to the courts actively moderating their

[37] Ibid, p.5. [38] Ibid, p.14. [39] Ibid, p.19. [40] Ibid, p.21.

[41] Aileen Kavanagh, *The Collaborative Constitution* (Cambridge University Press, 2023), p.278.

[42] Ibid, p.279.

[43] Aileen Kavanagh argues that the approach of the majority UKSC in *R (Nicklinson and Anor) v. Ministry of Justice* [2014] UKSC 38, [2015] AC 657 (which is discussed in greater detail in

review, dialogue entails a corresponding response by the State. Thus, according to Schauer:

> The term 'dialogue' has . . . been used . . . because it is often thought that the process of formal legislative reaction to judicial action can be understood as one step in an iterative dialogue between the legislative and judicial branches of government. The legislature enacts a law, and if the judiciary invalidates it, or issues a declaration of incompatibility, then the legislature can subsequently consider the merits of the judicial action and thereafter choose to persist with the same law, or accept the judiciary's action, or modify the statute. In the last of these options, especially, the judiciary can then consider the modified statute and issue another ruling, which the legislature can then take into account in determining what actions to take thereafter. And so on. The process, so it is said, is one in which the courts and the legislature are engaged in a continuous dialogue about the meaning and effect of the constitution or of the quasi-constitutional rights-protecting document.[44]

Dialogue is not limited to the domestic context and the metaphor has been drawn upon to describe the function of supranational courts such as the European Court of Human Rights (ECtHR). According to Robert Spano (former President of the ECtHR), while criticism of the ECtHR is not 'without some foundation, the Court has, when one analyses the case-law closely, attempted to engage in a constructive conversation with national judiciaries'.[45] This will indeed become apparent as issues such as abortion, assisted dying, migrants' rights and privacy – and the relevant jurisprudence of the ECtHR on such topics – are discussed throughout the ensuing chapters of this book. Further, as discussed in Chapter 3, the ECtHR employs a range of jurisprudential devices as part of that dialogue (e.g. interim measures, the margin of appreciation, the pilot judgment procedure).

Dialogue theories are not, however, without their own limitations. In particular, there is a risk that not having a clear sense of which branch is, ultimately, responsible for enforcing rights may result in a lacuna in protection. As Jeff King has observed 'equivocation over who has the last word in rights disputes puts rights at substantial risk' and 'the dialogue metaphor pays insufficient attention to the need for finality and authoritative resolutions of law'.[46] To counteract such risks (and criticism) academics have generated more nuanced

Chapter 6) exemplifies calibrated judicial review and reflects the benefits of a collaborative approach to rights protection: Kavanagh (n 41). See, also, the approach of the majority in *A and Ors* v. *Secretary of State for the Home Department* [2004] UKHL 56, [2005] 2 AC 68 as discussed in Chapters 2 and 8.

44 Frederick Schauer, 'Dialogue and Its Discontents' in Geoffrey Sigalet, Grégoire Webber and Rosalind Dixon (eds), *Constitutional Dialogue: Rights, Democracy, Institutions* (Cambridge University Press, 2019), p.424.

45 Robert Spano, 'The European Court of Human Rights and National Courts: A Constructive Conversation or a Dialogue of Disrespect?' (2015) 33 Nordic Journal of Human Rights 1, 1.

46 Jeff King, 'Dialogue, Finality and Legality' in Sigalet, Webber and Dixon (eds), *Constitutional Dialogue: Rights, Democracy, Institutions* (Cambridge University Press, 2019), p.187.

conceptualisations of dialogue including, for instance, Rosalind Dixon who has highlighted the centrality of deference and proposed 'responsive judicial review' as a means of securing rights while not compromising democracy. Responsive judicial review requires that courts 'be guided by the presence, or absence, of various forms of democratic dysfunction both in determining the proper scope of judicial review, and calibrating its intensity'.[47] Further, courts are only *one* means of protection when it comes to rights; '[T]here are a range of constitutional institutions that can play an important role in protecting democratic norms and processes – including a range of independent "fourth branch" or "guarantor" institutions, such as electoral and human rights commissions, and transnational legal and political bodies.'[48]

Moreover, not everyone is convinced that there is a dialogue. In this respect Tom Campbell et al. contend that:

> 'dialogue' is not the name of the game. The metaphor of dialogue fails to capture the dynamics of a process that is more a mixture, in different proportions, of unpredicted consequences, little or no reasoned interaction between the branches of government, routine judicial inaction, and, where courts do intervene, a de facto transfer of political power which weakens the role of parliaments in holding executives to account.[49]

It is clear, then, that no theory comprehensively, or entirely satisfactorily, addresses the question of which institution – or branch of the State – is best placed to protect rights. What does seem clear is that no one branch should have absolute control over the conferral and enforcement of rights. Whether it is characterised as 'dialogue' between courts and the executive/legislature or between domestic and supranational courts, there needs to be some form of community of protection whereby the State as a whole works towards the fulfilment of rights, and where one branch fails, the other(s) step in to provide that protection.

1.3.2 Institutional Critiques of the ECtHR

Institutional challenges arise in respect of both the ECtHR (where the concern is often one of State sovereignty) and domestic courts (where there is disquiet that rights adjudication illegitimately expands the powers of unelected judges). Such criticisms are considered in more detail in Chapters 2 and 3. For now, it is sufficient to note that two main lines of institutional critique have been directed at the ECtHR. One is that is it has adopted a conservative approach to human rights and is overly deferential to States. The second is that

[47] Rosalind Dixon, *Responsive Judicial Review* (Oxford University Press, 2023), p.95.

[48] Rosalind Dixon, 'In Defense of Responsive Judicial Review' [2022] University of New South Wales Law Research Series 11, p.1.

[49] Campbell et al. (n 29), p.4.

the ECtHR is an undemocratic institution and, therefore, its adjudication amounts to an incursion into State sovereignty.

With regard to the first strand of criticism, Costas Douzinas argues that '[o]fficial thinking and action on human rights has been entrusted in the hands of triumphalist column writers, bored diplomats and rich international lawyers in New York and Geneva, people whose experience of human rights violations is confined to being served a bad bottle of wine'.[50] He despairs that 'in the process, human rights have been turned from a discourse of rebellion and dissent into that of state legitimacy'.[51] Màrie-Bénédicte Dembour suspects that 'Douzinas may have been ready to mention Strasbourg alongside New York and Geneva.'[52] In this respect she observes that many of her '"protest" friends objected to [her] selection of the European Convention to probe the meaning and significance of the human rights concept, urging [her] to look at the action of NGOs instead'.[53] Yet she comments that her research visits to Strasbourg 'have made [her] aware that individuals who work at the European Court of Human Rights, either as judges or as members of the Registry, often do not fit Douzinas's description'.[54] She notes that '[t]hey believe in human rights ... and they want to make a difference by carving routes through the law of the Convention which can then be used, notably, by applicants'.[55] She concludes that '[t]hrough persuasion, logic and sometimes, of course, diplomacy, they achieve small victories; but they would not deny that the greater battle continues. The victories need to be acknowledged as forcefully as the failures of the Convention.'[56]

The second strand to the institutional critique of the ECtHR questions the democratic legitimacy and competence of the Court, in particular the relationship between the Court, the national courts and member States. Relatedly, concerns relating to the expansion of the Convention rights through the Court's 'living instrument' approach to the Convention have been voiced by some academics and politicians.[57] According to Richard Ekins, 'for the past

[50] Costas Douzinas, *The End of Human Rights: Critical Legal Thought at the Turn of the Century* (Hart, 2000) p.7.

[51] Ibid.

[52] Marie-Bénédicte Dembour, *Who Believes in Human Rights? Reflections on the European Convention* (Cambridge University Press, 2006), p.13.

[53] Ibid. [54] Ibid. [55] Ibid, pp.13–14. [56] Ibid.

[57] Nicolas Bratza, 'The Relationship between the UK Courts and Strasbourg' (2011) European Human Rights Law Review 505; Janneke Gerards, 'The Prism of Fundamental Rights' (2012) 8 European Constitutional Law Review 2; Jack Straw, *Aspects of Law Reform: An Insider's Perspective* (2012), Ch. 2; Ed Bates, 'British Sovereignty and the European Court of Human Rights' (2012) 128 Law Quarterly Review 382; Jean-Paul Costa, 'On the Legitimacy of the European Court of Human Rights' Judgments' (2011) 7 European Constitutional Law Review 2; Ed Bates, 'Strasbourg's Integrationist Role, or the Need for Self-restraint?' (2020) 1 European Convention on Human Rights Law Review 1; Angelika Nussberger, 'The European Court of Human Rights at Sixty: Challenges and Perspectives' (2020) 1 European Convention

four decades [the ECtHR] has merrily departed from the terms the UK agreed in 1950' by conceiving of the ECHR as a living instrument.[58] Ekins further contends that the ECtHR 'routinely subverts the terms of the Convention which the UK and other member states agreed in 1950 (and in successive Protocols) . . . by taking the ECHR to be a "living instrument", with the effect that the Court reshapes the meaning and effect of the Convention as it pleases'.[59]

In 2011, former President of the European Court of Human Rights Nicolas Bratza firmly refuted some of the criticism levelled at the Court:

> The vitriolic – and I am afraid to say, xenophobic – fury directed against the judges of my Court is unprecedented in my experience, as someone who has been involved with the Convention for over 40 years. We are as a Court, not unused to criticism by Governments who think we have gone too far, by unsuccessful applicants and by NGOs who think we have not gone far enough, and by certain sections of the media that miss no opportunity to attack the Court, often in intemperate and inaccurate terms. But the scale and tone of the current hostility directed towards the Court, and the Convention system as a whole, by the press, by members of the Westminster Parliament and by senior members of the Government has created understandable dismay and resentment among the judges in Strasbourg.[60]

In this respect George Letsas observes that while we will not all agree on the moral foundations of rights, States have agreed (for now at least) to accept Strasbourg determination of issues of moral principle:

> We must not of course hold the naïve view that we will one day all agree (public, politicians, judges, academics) on the moral foundations of rights and on how they should be interpreted by courts. To be sure, courts (and the European Court of Human Rights in final instance) have the difficult task to make decisions that are controversial and affect the lives of so many people. But their decisions must be reasoned and well-founded and their views are shaped and influenced by a public dialogue in which we can and should all participate. Our European institutional practice already commits us to the view that the European Court should have the final say on matters of human rights interpretation and it is not an open question for us whether judges will decide such important issues of moral principle – they should; until states decide to abolish

on Human Rights Law Review 1; Colm O'Cinneide, 'What Has the ECHR Ever Done for Us?': The Particular and Specific Importance of the Convention in Protecting Rights across a Democratic Europe' (2023) **7** The Irish Judicial Studies Journal 2; Richard Ekins, *Human Rights and the Rule of Law* (Policy Exchange, April 2024).

[58] Richard Ekins, 'The Balance of the Constitution' (2022) **67** The American Journal of Jurisprudence 2, p.216.

[59] Richard Ekins, *The Limits of Judicial Power: A Programme of Constitutional Reform* (Policy Exchange, 2022), p.10, policyexchange.org.uk/wp-content/uploads/2022/10/The-Limits-of-Judicial-Power.pdf.

[60] Bratza (n 57), pp.505–506.

the right of individual application or the binding nature of the European Court's judgments we must accept and honor that commitment.[61]

In addition to institutional critiques, human rights law is subject to myriad ideological critiques; notwithstanding the large degree of consensus in the content of national, supranational and international rights instruments, there is considerable debate as to the form, scope and application of the rights enshrined therein.

1.3.3 Ideological Critiques

There are many different, competing and overlapping understandings of human rights.[62] Are human rights concrete and fixed, or are they evolving and fluid? Are they determinative, or are they aspirational? Are they legal, political, ethical, social or some other type of construct?[63] At the heart of this is a tension between those who regard the rights as concrete enforceable entitlements and those who perceive human rights as aspirational claims that are pursued and fought for but may never be fully realised. For example, Jacques Ranicere argues that 'human rights are needed to demand rights which we do not currently have'.[64] Similarly, the political, rebellious, revolutionary and visionary character of human rights is emphasised by Douzinas who warns that 'the end of human rights comes when they lose their utopian end'.[65] These notions of human rights suggest that the task of identifying their content may not only be impossible, but may also be undesirable as it is contrary to the raison d'être of human rights to finalise, and therefore restrict, their content. Some of the differences stem from distinct uses of human rights, in particular between human rights as political or cultural concepts and human rights as law. Yet, whilst context is important, it does not explain all the differences; there are also important ideological distinctions.

[61] Letsas (n 3), p.xvii.

[62] Dembour (n 52), ch.8. Dembour has conveniently identified four schools of thought on human rights. There are those that regard human rights as given (the natural school), those that conceive human rights as agreed upon (the deliberative school), those that perceive human rights as fought for (the protest school), and those that believe that human rights are talked about (the discourse school).

[63] For a useful introduction to the different meanings of human rights, see Mark Goodale and Sally Engle Merry, *The Practice of Human Rights: Tracking Law Between the Global and Local* (Cambridge University Press, 2007).

[64] For discussion of the role of human rights and the relationship with humanitarian intervention, see Jacques Rancière, 'Who Is the Subject of the Rights of Man?' (2004) 103 South Atlantic Quarterly 297.

[65] Douzinas (n 50), p.380.

While increasing attention has been paid to human rights, there is no shortage of sceptics.[66] There are three primary lines of challenge to the concept of human rights and the human rights movement:

1. Human rights fail to provide sufficient (or, indeed, any) protection for certain rights;
2. Human rights are inherently biased (in that they are based on the interests of Western, white men) and, accordingly, fail to protect groups of people on the basis of their race, gender, sexuality, class and so on;
3. The human rights movement has failed to achieve its objectives and, instead, has enabled the ever-growing disparity between the 'haves' and the 'have-nots'.

Accordingly, these challenges emphasise: (i) gaps in rights protection; and, (ii) gaps in terms of who is protected; both of which ultimately lead critics to ask whether the human rights movement is fundamentally flawed.

1.3.3.1 *Gaps in Rights Protection*

An important critique of human rights focuses upon what is and is not protected, in particular the limited protection accorded to economic, social and cultural (ESC) rights within domestic and international rights instruments. In 1948, the Universal Declaration of Human Rights (UDHR) was proclaimed by the General Assembly amidst political and ideological differences after the Second World War. Subsequently, two milestone human rights treaties were drafted and, in 1966, the International Covenant on Civil and Political Rights (ICCPR) and the International Covenant on Economic, Social and Cultural Rights (ICESCR) were adopted by the General Assembly. The decision to embody rights in two separate instruments was a pragmatic response to the existing political situation. Thus, the debate surrounding whether ESC rights 'should' be included in rights instruments has obtained since the birth of modern human rights. As Ellie Palmer has observed:

> it is now generally conceded that, during the Cold War when the international normative framework for the protection of human rights was in the process of negotiation by the UN, ideological perceptions about differences between the two sets of rights were allowed to undermine the persuasive logic of their unitary moral and existential foundations.[67]

[66] See Charles R. Beitz, *The Idea of Human Rights* (Oxford University Press, 2011); Dembour (n 52); Samuel Moyn, *Not Enough: Human Rights in an Unequal World* (Harvard University Press, 2018); Stephen Hopgood, *The End Times of Human Rights* (Cornell University Press, 2015); Eric Posner, *The Twilight of Human Rights* (Oxford University Press, 2014).

[67] Ellie Palmer, 'Protecting Socio-economic Rights through the European Convention on Human Rights: Trends and Developments in the European Court of Human Rights' (2009) 2 Erasmus Law Review 397, 400.

Indeed, this cleft between what are considered to be political or negative rights – for instance, the right to life, the right to freedom from torture or inhuman or degrading treatment, the freedom of speech and so on – and ESC or positive rights – for instance, the right to adequate housing, the right to food and so on – was also evident in the debates attending the formulation and enactment of the ECHR.

One of the original drafters of the Convention, Pierre-Henri Teitgen – a former senior French Resistance leader and Minister who had been interned in Gestapo prisons during the war – foresaw it as 'a complete code of all the freedoms and fundamental rights; all the individual freedoms and rights, and all the so-called social freedoms and rights'.[68] However, the substantive rights contained in Articles 2–11 of the ECHR are not, at least ostensibly, ESC rights. As another drafter of the Convention Sir David Maxwell-Fyfe (a former British Conservative MP, Law Officer, and Deputy Chief Prosecutor at the Nuremberg war crimes trials) observed at the time of the ECHR's inception:

> Our list, it is true, contains none of the so-called economic or social rights which appear in the U.N.O. Declaration. Such rights would, in my view, be too controversial and difficult [for] enforcement even in the changing state of social and international development in Europe, and their inclusion would jeopardise the acceptance of the Convention. Examples, on which I need not expatiate, are the right to free choice of employment, and the right, unknown to you, I am sure, Mr. President, of rest or leisure.[69]

The question arises, however, as to what is meant by ESC rights, given that many are essential for the true enjoyment of 'political' or 'civil' rights. Of what value is the right to life if a person does not have a right to food or safe shelter? According to Virginia Mantouvalou:

> Social rights are conventionally understood as rights to the meeting of basic needs that are essential for human welfare. Although we need to deepen our understanding of the justification for social rights, this definition serves to highlight the point that social rights are entitlements to the avoidance of severe deprivation, not rights to the satisfaction of individual preferences more generally. They incorporate a safeguard against poverty and not provision of a life in luxury. They are claims with some urgency representing vital interests of the individual to avoid harm. They do not guarantee access to the goods that we each might desire to possess, so as to live a fulfilling life; they are preconditions for the pursuance of a good life.[70]

[68] *Collected Edition of the 'Travaux Préparatoires'*, Vol I (Martinus Nijhoff, 1975) cited in Alastair Mowbray, *Cases, Materials, and Commentary on the European Convention on Human Rights* (Oxford University Press, 2012), p.2.

[69] Ibid, p.6.

[70] Virginia Mantouvalou, 'The Case for Social Rights' in Conor Gearty and Virginia Mantouvalou, *Debating Social Rights* (Hart, 2010), p.3.

As Maxwell-Fyfe observed, the UDHR does contain economic and social rights. These include, for instance:

- the right to own property (Article 17);
- the right to 'social security' and the 'economic, social and cultural rights' that are 'indispensable to [a person's] dignity' (Article 22);
- the right to work (Article 23), the right to 'rest and leisure' (Article 24), and,
- the right to 'a standard of living adequate for the health and well-being of himself and his family, including food, clothing, housing and medical care' (Article 25).

In addition, the ICESCR is a dedicated United Nations (UN) treaty on ESC rights and includes rights to self-determination (Article 1), fair wages and safe working conditions (Article 7(a)(i) and 7(b)), of mothers to paid leave and adequate social security benefits (Article 10(2)), to education (Article 13) and to take part in cultural life (Article 15(1)(a)).

While the ECHR does not, itself, contain such rights, the First Protocol to the Convention does. It enshrines, inter alia, the rights to property (Article 1) and education (Article 2). Much case law (both domestic and ECtHR) has been dedicated to distilling the content and scope of the protections afforded by Article 1 of Protocol 1 ECHR.[71] For now, it is sufficient to note that the Council of Europe has sought to fill some of the lacunae when it comes to the protection of ESC rights through the enactment of the Protocols. Further, as the issues canvassed in several of the ensuing chapters reveal, the ECtHR has interpreted some of the civil and political rights contained in the ECHR itself to provide protections for ESC rights. This has been achieved, in many cases, through the imposition of positive obligations on States.

In addition to the ECHR and its Protocols, there is the European Social Charter – a Council of Europe treaty that protects (via its original text of 1961, its revised version in 1996 and several Protocols[72]) a swathe of ESC rights, including:

- the right to work (including fair and safe working conditions);
- the right to social security;
- the right to medical assistance;
- the right to housing.

Thus, insofar as we are concerned with the ECHR, what at first blush appears to be a significant gap in the protections afforded to human rights may not be

[71] European Court of Human Rights, *Guide on Article 1 of Protocol No. 1 to the European Convention on Human Rights*, 29 February 2024.

[72] The collated documents are available here: https://rm.coe.int/CoERMPublicCommonSearchServices/DisplayDCTMContent?documentId=090000168048b059.

as problematic as it seems. However, it is unsatisfactory that a system for protecting ESC rights should depend on the ad hoc addition of rights through the ratification of Protocols to the main rights document and on the judicial arm of the organisation construing existing rights in the main treaty document in an expansive manner. Further, while the European Social Charter (revised) provides protection for many ESC rights and has been ratified by thirty-six of the Member States,[73] it is not enforceable in the same way as the ECHR (i.e., via individual or State complaint to the ECtHR). Rather, the European Committee of Social Rights (ESCR) supervises States' compliance with the Charter. While there is a collective complaints procedure, through which certain non-governmental organisations can lodge collective complaints, only sixteen Member States have ratified the Protocol recognising the competence of the Committee to hear such complaints.[74] Another means of supervision is via State reports. Twenty-three Member States have ratified the Turin Protocol, which sets out the reporting requirements and the role of the Committee in respect of same.[75]

Accordingly, while there are mechanisms through which ESC rights are protected at the supranational level, the UK has not ratified the revised European Social Charter. For those States that have ratified the Charter and the attendant Protocols, the enforcement mechanisms are limited when compared with the enforcement of the ECHR through the individual complaints procedure.

There have been notable developments in the sphere of ESC rights protection in the devolved jurisdictions in the UK. In 2015, Wales introduced the Well-being of Future Generations (Wales) Act 2015 that 'requires public bodies in Wales to think about the long-term impact of their decisions, to work better with people, communities and each other, and to prevent persistent problems such as poverty, health inequalities and climate change'.[76] And there have been proposals to insert a 'right to food' into Scots Law, though such proposals are yet to be translated into domestic legislation.[77] According to a Consultation document, the 'right to food' is conceived of as:

[73] European Social Charter (revised) (ETS No. 163), Chart of signatures and ratifications, www.coe.int/en/web/conventions/full-list?module = signatures-by-treaty&treatynum = 163.

[74] Additional Protocol to the European Social Charter Providing for a System of Collective Complaints (ETS No. 158), www.coe.int/en/web/conventions/full-list?module = treaty-detail& treatynum = 158.

[75] Protocol amending the European Social Charter (ETS No. 142), www.coe.int/en/web/conventions/full-list?module = signatures-by-treaty&treatynum = 142.

[76] Future Generations Commissioner for Wales, 'Well-being of Future Generations (Wales) Act 2015', www.futuregenerations.wales/about-us/future-generations-act/.

[77] Elaine Smith MSP, 'Proposed Right to Food (Scotland) Bill: A Proposal for a Bill to Incorporate the Human Right to Food in Scots Law', 23 June 2020, https://webarchive.nrscotland.gov.uk/20240327011030/https://archive2021.parliament.scot/parliamentarybusiness/Bills/115201.aspx. While MSP Elaine Smith secured the right to introduce a bill on the right to food in 2021, time ran out before the end of the Session to do so. In 2024, permission was once again

both a negative and positive right. The negative right to obtain food by one's own actions, and the positive right to be supplied with food if one is unable to access it. The negative right entails inaction by authorities in some areas: in simple terms governments should not inflict conditions upon individuals which mean that they cannot acquire their own food. A positive right, by contrast, requires governments to take action to ensure a right is maintained and protected.[78]

The House of Lords has also interpreted civil and political rights to secure base levels of necessity. In *R (Limbuela)* v. *Secretary of State for the Home Department*,[79] the Court held that withdrawing support from 'asylum seekers' under s.55 of the Nationality, Immigration and Asylum Act 2002, thereby leaving them without any financial support (as they were legally precluded from seeking paid employment), constituted treatment reaching the minimum level of severity in violation of Article 3 ECHR. In the absence of any support, the claimants were forced to sleep in the open (or were at risk of having to do so). They were left seriously hungry and unable to satisfy even the most basic requirements of hygiene, including sanitary products. This was both inhuman and degrading treatment in violation of Article 3 ECHR.

There has also been significant development in the protection of economic and social rights in other jurisdictions. The Inter-American Court of Human Rights has made impressive headway in this respect through its expansive interpretation of the right to life in Article 4 of the American Convention on Human Rights, which the Court has held includes the right to a 'vida digna' (a dignified life). As Thomas Antkowiak has observed:

> With its innovative judgments, the Inter-American Court has recognized that the fundamental right to life will never be meaningful and effective without nutrition, water, health care, housing, education, and ancestral lands. By establishing that these elements are indivisible from life, the Court also justified its expansion of remedies to safeguard the lives and dignity of many individuals and communities at risk. While States originally did not draft this right to a dignified life, they have permitted it to develop in the Inter-American System, as it aligns with their emphasis – at least in principle – on human dignity and respectable living conditions.[80]

Cultural rights specifically are also frequently overlooked. Again, the Inter-American Court has been instrumental in securing protection of such rights. In several recent decisions, the Court has confirmed that Article 26 of the American Convention on Human Rights (which is the centrepiece of the Convention's protections of economic, social and cultural rights) not only protects

secured to introduce a right to food bill: Proposed Right to Food, 21 February 2024, www.parliament.scot/bills-and-laws/proposals-for-bills/session-6-right-to-food-scotland-bill.

[78] Consultation document accompanying the 2020 Bill; Smith, ibid, p.6.

[79] *R (Limbuela)* v. *Secretary of State for the Home Department* [2005] UKHL 66, [2006] 1 AC 396.

[80] Thomas Antkowiak, 'A "Dignified Life" and the Resurgence of Social Rights' (2020) 18 Northwestern Journal of Human Rights 1, p.4.

the right to self-determination of Indigenous peoples,[81] it also encompasses a right to no contact which is particularly important for Indigenous communities who are living in voluntary isolation.[82] Article 26 has also proven instrumental in attempts to redress the disproportionate impacts of climate change on Indigenous populations and cultural minorities. In the case of *Indigenous Communities Members of the Lhaka Honhat Association* v. *Argentina*, the Court:

> analyzed the rights to a healthy environment, adequate food, water and cultural identity autonomously from Article 26 of the American Convention [which is directed at securing the 'full realization of the rights implicit in the economic, social, educational, scientific, and cultural standards'], ordering specific measures of reparation for the restitution of those rights, including actions for access to water and food, for the recovery of forest resources and for the recovery of indigenous culture.[83]

Consistent with the approach of the Inter-American Court, the UN Human Rights Committee (HRC) (the body responsible for monitoring the implementation of the ICCPR, including by way of individual complaints) has recently stated that:

> The duty to protect life implies that States [P]arties should take appropriate measures to address the general conditions in society that may eventually give rise to direct threats to life or prevent individuals from enjoying their right to life with dignity. These general conditions may include high levels of criminal and gun violence, . . . pervasive traffic and industrial accidents, . . . degradation of the environment, . . . deprivation of land, territories and resources of indigenous peoples, . . . the prevalence of life threatening diseases, . . . extensive substance abuse, widespread hunger and malnutrition and extreme poverty and homelessness . . . The measures called for addressing adequate conditions for protecting the right to life include, where necessary, measures designed to ensure access without delay by individuals to essential goods and services such as food, . . . water, shelter, health-care, . . . electricity and sanitation, and other measures designed to promote and facilitate adequate general conditions such as the bolstering of effective emergency health services, emergency response operations (including fire-fighters, ambulances and police forces) and social housing programs.[84]

[81] *Pueblos Rama y Kriol* v. *Nicaragua*, Inter-American Court of Human Rights, 1 April 2024, www.corteidh.or.cr/docs/casos/articulos/seriec_522_esp.pdf.
Article 26 of the American Convention states:

> The States Parties undertake to adopt measures, both internally and through international cooperation, especially those of an economic and technical nature, with a view to achieving progressively, by legislation or other appropriate means, the full realization of the rights implicit in the economic, social, educational, scientific, and cultural standards set forth in the Charter of the Organization of American States as amended by the Protocol of Buenos Aires.

[82] *Pueblos Indígenas Tagaeri y Taromenane* v. *Ecuador*, Inter-American Court of Human Rights, 4 September 2024, https://jurisprudencia.corteidh.or.cr/es/vid/1049684937.

[83] I-ACtHR, Press Release, corteidh.or.cr/docs/comunicados/cp_24_2020_eng.pdf.

[84] Human Rights Committee, 'General Comment No. 36 (2018) on article 6 of the International Covenant on Civil and Political Rights, on the right to life', CCPR/C/GC/36, 30 October 2018 at [26]. References omitted.

Indeed, in 2022 the HRC found that Australia's failure to adopt adequate adaptation measures to address the flooding and other impacts of climate change on low-lying islands in the Torres Strait region had violated several of the applicants' rights in the ICCPR, including Article 27. Specifically, Australia had failed 'to protect the authors' collective ability to maintain their traditional way of life, to transmit to their children and future generations their culture and traditions and use of land and sea resources' and this violated 'the State party's positive obligation to protect the authors' right to enjoy their minority culture'.[85]

Despite these 'advancements', many remain troubled by the lack of adequate protection for ESC rights. Others contend that human rights are not the sphere for protecting such interests; that they are inherently political issues and should be left to the executive and/or parliament to resolve. Virginia Mantouvalou described the competing positions on social and economic rights in the following way:

> In contrast to debates about civil and political rights, debates about social and economic rights are far from settled. The practical implementation of social rights in particular remains deeply controversial amongst activists, academic scholars, lawyers and judges alike. Some activists view social rights as worth fighting for, and employ the language of rights and their alleged violation as an all-encompassing rhetorical device to advance claims on injustice stemming from economic need. Other activists hold the view that there is little chance that social change will come about through 'rights talk'; what we really need is action, not 'vacuous rhetoric'.[86]

1.3.3.2 *Who Is Protected?*

In addition to the lacuna in the rights protected, there are significant gaps in those who 'benefit' from human rights. These gaps arise in myriad ways, including where the relevant rights document does not apply in that area/jurisdiction or the temporal scope of the rights instrument is limited.[87] Gaps may also arise as a result of the inherent bias of the rights instruments themselves. Given that most rights instruments constituting the modern human rights law corpus are based on Western, liberal conceptualisations of rights as liberties, many fail to protect groups of people on the basis of their race, gender, sexuality, class and so on. It was only in 2009 that the ECtHR

[85] Human Rights Committee, 'Views adopted by the Committee under article 5 (4) of the Optional Protocol, concerning communication No. 3624/2019', CCPR/C/135/D/3624/2019, 22 September 2022 at [8.14].

[86] Mantouvalou (n 70), p.2.

[87] For examples of such situations, see the revocation of citizenship of Shamima Begum discussed at length in Chapters 8 and 9 and limitations on the application of the ECHR in domestic law to events taking place during 'The Troubles' (as discussed in Chapter 4).

held that a State could be liable for a violation of the right to life (Article 2) by failing to put in place a system punishing domestic violence and protecting victims and that the failure to put in place such a system was discriminatory as women were the primary victims of domestic violence.[88] Another example of a gap includes the lack of a right to marriage for same-sex couples under the ECHR. Certainly, the ECtHR has been instrumental in extending the rights in the ECHR to provide some degree of protection for vulnerable groups such as those belonging to the LGBTQI+ community. It has found, for instance, that laws criminalising forms of intercourse between two men violated Article 8 (the right to respect for private life),[89] and that, under the same Article, States need to ensure some degree of legal recognition for change of gender[90] and provide a mechanism for same-sex couples to have their relationship legally recognised.[91] Nevertheless, while progress has been made in the context of LGBTQI+ rights, there still remain gaps in protection, including within the domestic legal framework. For instance, domestic courts have rejected claims of a legal right of transgender parents to have their legal gender registered on their child's birth certificate[92] or of a non-gender marker (such as an 'X') in a passport.[93]

Another deficiency in protection stems from the anthropocentric focus of rights; they are, after, all 'human' rights. The consequence of this has been a deficit in the protection of the environment. Certainly, it is possible to fit the implications of climate change within the existing rights rubric as was demonstrated by the Grand Chamber (GC) in *Verein Klimaseniorinnen Schweiz and Ors* v. *Switzerland*.[94] Climate change, after all, raises a number of issues including, for instance, rising sea waters leading to dispossession, health issues stemming from pollution, increasing temperatures and so on, which could fit within the existing rights protection regime (for instance, a failure to put in place a system that deters threats to life or the right to respect for private life). However, few rights instruments recognise a distinct right to a healthy environment (contrast the finding of the Inter-American Court in *Indigenous*

[88] *Opuz* v. *Turkey* (2010) 50 EHRR 28. In the earlier decision of *Kontrova* v. *Slovakia* [2007] ECHR 419 the Court found a violation of the regulatory and protective obligations under Article 2 in the context of domestic abuse, but it did not consider Article 14. For a more detailed discussion of domestic abuse and the ECHR, see Chapter 4.

[89] *Dudgeon* v. *the United Kingdom* [1981] 4 EHRR 149.

[90] *Christine Goodwin* v. *the United Kingdom* [2002] 35 EHRR 447.

[91] *Fedotova and Ors* v. *Russia* [GC] [2023] ECHR 55.

[92] *R (on the application of McConnell)* v. *Registrar General for England and Wales* [2020] EWCA Civ 559, [2021] Fam. 77.

[93] *R (on the application of Elan-Cane) (Appellant)* v. *Secretary of State for the Home Department* [2021] UKSC 56, [2023] AC 559. See further discussion in Chapter 14.

[94] *Verein Klimaseniorinnen Schweiz and Ors* v. *Switzerland* [GC] (2024) 79 EHRR 1. See the discussion of this case in Chapters 3 and 4.

Communities Members of the Lhaka Honhat Association v. *Argentina* discussed above with the observations of the Supreme Court of Ireland in *CLG* v. *Government of Ireland*[95]).

In addition to the issues raised by the anthropocentric focus of modern human rights law, such rights tend to be highly individualised, potentially neutering the efficacy of rights for those cultures for whom group rights are of equal or greater importance than the rights of individuals. As Makau Matua has observed:

> Another problem of the liberal tradition, which has been inherited by the human rights movement, is its unrelenting focus on individualism. This arises from liberalism's focus on formal equality and abstract autonomy. The human rights corpus views the individual as the center of the moral universe, and therefore denigrates communities, collectives, and group rights. . . . This is a particularly serious problem in areas of the world where group and community rights are deeply embedded both in the cultures of the peoples, and exacerbated by the multinational nature of the postcolonial state.[96]

1.3.3.3 *Is the Human Rights Movement Fundamentally Flawed?*

The modern human rights movement has been the subject of normative critique since its inception.[97] Central to this critique is the question of whether human rights achieve what they set out to or if they are, in fact, part of the growing inequality present in contemporary society.

A well-known proponent of the latter view is Samuel Moyn who argues that human rights have failed to secure the basic needs of individuals and have, if not facilitated neoliberalism and its attendant inequality, failed miserably to offer protections against it. Human rights, he says, have failed to stop 'the crisis of national welfare, the stagnation of middle classes, and the endurance of global hierarchy' and no amount of change to the rights rubric will suffice.[98] Rather, to bridge the widening gap between the haves and have-nots, it is necessary to adopt an entirely different approach. According to Moyn '[t]he truth is that local and global economic justice requires redesigning markets or at least redistributing from the rich to the rest, something that naming and shaming ["the chief tools of the human rights movement"] are never likely to achieve, even when supplemented by novel forms of legal activism'.[99]

[95] *CLG* v. *Government of Ireland* [2020] IECS 49 at [9.5].

[96] Makau Mutua, 'Human Rights and Powerlessness: Pathologies of Choice and Substance' (2008) 56 Buffalo Law Review 1027, 1029.

[97] See Karl Marx, 'On the Jewish Question' in J. Waldron (ed), *Nonsense upon Stilts: Bentham, Burke and Marx on the Rights of Man* (Methuen, 1987), who pointed out that law can corrupt rights and lead to the misuse of rights.

[98] Moyn (n 66), p.xii.

[99] Ibid, p.218.

This presents a damning critique of the efficacy of rights as a means of securing basic needs and equality. Posner is similarly critical, contending that 'human rights law has failed to accomplish its objective' and there is 'little evidence that human rights treaties, on the whole, have improved the well-being of people, or even resulted in respect for the rights in those treaties'.[100]

Other critiques have focused on the normative deficiencies from specific viewpoints. According to the feminist legal critique, human rights:

> are a product of the dominant male half of the world, framed in their language, reflecting their needs and aspirations. Whereas the 'rights of man' as originally conceived by the great liberal thinkers were not intended to include women, today's 'universal human rights' still overlook them as a matter of fact. The feminist critique of human rights thus basically argues for the inclusion of women in the human rights protection system. Feminists of all strands advance various means to realize this aim.[101]

Stephanie Palmer identifies an affinity between feminist ideas and human rights, as both operate as ideals containing utopian elements with their commitment to progressive social change and emancipatory possibilities. Any excavation of the relationship between law and feminism exposes paradoxes: who is the universal 'woman'? Nevertheless, there is an opportunity for feminist engagement with human rights and new ground for theorising and strategy making. The challenge lies in giving meanings to rights that are consistent with feminist values and that are responsive to the reality of women's lives.[102] Given the authority of law and 'the immense political power of a rights-oriented framework', feminists should not discard rights so easily.[103] Patricia Williams, referring to the Black struggle for civil rights, acknowledges the symbolic power of rights claims:

> 'Rights' feel so new in the mouths of most black people. It is still so deliciously empowering to say. It is a sign for and a gift of selfhood that is very hard to contemplate restructuring . . . at this point in history. It is the magic wand of visibility and invisibility, of inclusion and exclusion, and of power and no power.[104]

While feminist critiques of human rights are by no means homogeneous, many emphasise the 'false dichotomy' between the public and private sphere

[100] Posner (n 66), p.7.

[101] Eva Brems, 'Enemies or Allies? Feminism and Cultural Relativism as Dissident Voices in Human Rights Discourse' (1997) 19 Human Rights Quarterly 136, 137.

[102] Stephanie Palmer, 'Feminism and the Promises of Human Rights: Possibilities and Paradoxes' in Susan James and Stephanie Palmer (eds), *Visible Women: Possibilities and Paradoxes* (Hart, 2002).

[103] Ibid, p.97.

[104] Patricia Williams, 'Alchemical Notes: Reconstructed Ideal from Reconstructed Rights' (1987) Harvard Civil Rights–Civil Liberties Law Review 401, 431. See also, Patricia Williams, *The Alchemy of Race and Rights* (Harvard University Press, 1991).

in human rights, which has the effect of perpetuating gender roles.[105] This, in turn, leads to a hierarchy of rights, which acts to the detriment of women since 'private rights' sit lower on the scale than 'public rights', and women are the primary beneficiaries of the former. For instance, cases involving abortion are, generally, dealt with under Article 8 ECHR which protects the right to respect for private life. This disadvantage is exacerbated by other factors such as race and sexuality.

The inherently Western nature of the rights documents (i.e., the UDHR, ICCPR, and ICESCR) also raises issues in terms of the epistemic foundations of human rights law.[106] The American Anthropological Association argued at the time the UDHR was being drafted that:

> Human rights were an expression of value conflicts rather than consensus. Further, owing to the Western origins of human rights, such universalistic articulation of values was nonrepresentative. In the distinct language of sociological legitimacy, the Association argued that the declaration:
>
> [. . .]will not be convincing to the Indonesian, the African, the Indian, the Chinese, if it lies on the same plane as like documents of an earlier period. The rights of Man in the Twentieth Century cannot be circumscribed by the standards of any single culture.[107]

It is indisputable that there are normative limitations within human rights law. It is undeniable that they need to be rectified in order for rights to function in a meaningful way. But, should these limitations lead to human rights being assigned to the dustbin of history? It is perhaps salutary to end with the realism proffered by Malcolm Langford:

> Critics of human rights also need to face the question of alternatives. The rise of both left-wing and right-wing populism with strains of authoritarianism raises real questions as to the role and value of critique. From Poland to the United States, the Philippines to South Africa, human rights are the object of direct challenge and not simply benign neglect. The human rights project might be a partial cause of these developments – if it did encourage neglect of social equality and inclusion. But is a full-throttled critique of human rights productive in these circumstances, and can transformation occur without it?[108]

[105] Vedika Luthra, 'Aliens No More? Addressing Feminist Critiques to Human Rights with Regard to Sexual Violence in the West' (2019) 11 Journal of Gender and Power 1, 10.

[106] That is not to suggest that there are not provisions that protect collective interests or cultural rights. (See, for instance, Article 27 of the ICCPR discussed above.) Indeed, the ICESCR is specifically intended to cover social and cultural rights.

[107] American Anthropological Association, 'Statement on Human Rights submitted to the Commission on Human Rights, United Nations by the Executive Board, American Anthropological Association' (1947) 49(4) American Anthropologist 539. For discussion see Malcolm Langford, 'Critiques of Human Rights' (2018) 14 Annual Review of Law and Social Science 69, pp.72–73.

[108] Ibid, p.83.

1.4 CONCLUSION

According to Douzinas, '[h]uman rights are the necessary and impossible claim of law to justice'.[109] As this chapter has demonstrated, there is much to support this contention. There are many flaws in the human rights machine (at least insofar as the Western, neoliberal system of human rights is concerned) and no shortage of critics. The juridification of rights is accompanied by its own complexities and disappointments. However, as Lynn Hunt suggests: 'Human rights are our only bulwark' against the evil of dehumanising crimes.[110] The human rights framework, with its bodies, courts and conventions, might be 'exasperating in its slowness to respond or repeated inability to achieve its ultimate goals, but there is no better structure available for confronting these issues'.[111] Our sense remains that rights are an unfinished project and one that still promises a hopeful future. The language of rights provides an avenue to challenge the dominant narrative and to confront discourses that marginalise and exclude the most vulnerable in society. It provides a framework to challenge indignity and suffering. The practice of human rights can instil ethical values into the heart of decision-making. It can guide the policy-making of those in power and, in some circumstances, it has successfully imposed controls on the exercise of power. Yet as Gearty has observed, 'there is no certainty of a happy ending'.[112]

Human rights remain an enigma, and perhaps Douzinas is right that they do constitute 'the impossible claim'. But, as the chapters in this book demonstrate, there are many examples of the ways in which human rights have influenced and developed our law and society in a positive fashion. There are also numerous instances where the practice of human rights has led to frustration and disappointment.

It might be that human rights are the 'necessary' or perhaps even the only way to inject moral and ethical principles into the legal system and to keep alive the hope that change for the better is always possible. Certainly, we should be slow to abandon the entire human rights project without first attempting to address its shortcomings.

[109] Douzinas (n 50), p.380.

[110] Lynne Hunt, *Inventing Human Rights* (W.W. Norton, 2007), p.212.

[111] Ibid, p.213.

[112] Conor Gearty, *Can Human Rights Survive?* (Cambridge University Press, 2006), p.1.

2 The Human Rights Law Framework in the UK

CONTENTS

2.1 INTRODUCTION

While many countries have long had specific rights instruments, in the UK it was often argued that the unwritten constitution provided a sufficient means of protection against abuse of power. Dicey, the influential nineteenth-century constitutional theorist, was sceptical about rights. In his view, the common law system, with its system of remedies, was a far superior safeguard against tyranny or arbitrary government than a written statement of rights.[1] The traditional view in the UK was that it was unnecessary to give special protection to fundamental rights through codification.[2] Instead, it was thought that it was sufficient to have a system in which individuals were free to do anything not expressly proscribed by law, subject to the proviso that a sovereign Parliament could restrict such freedoms, or civil liberties, with little or no domestic constraints. In this constitutional framework there was heavy reliance on political accountability to ensure that any impingement on domestic rights was limited and imposed solely for necessary democratic purposes. But scepticism grew over the efficacy of political controls to protect liberties or rights as, increasingly during the twentieth century, these political mechanisms proved incapable of restraining a powerful and determined executive.[3] The Westminster system allows the political party with the majority of seats in the House of Commons to form the Government and this in turn may, and indeed has, limited effective legislative scrutiny in Parliament. Following the Second World War, the many international human rights treaties to which the UK became a party were a catalyst for increased concern about civil liberties and human rights and renewed debate about the best way to protect rights and freedoms in the UK. With the enactment of the Human Rights Act 1998 (HRA) and the 'bringing home' of the European Convention on Human Rights (ECHR), the UK has seen the proliferation of domestic rights jurisprudence. As this chapter will demonstrate, the evolution of rights protection in the UK has involved a delicate balance between legal and political constitutionalism, with the juridification of rights (and the attendant role of the domestic courts and the ECtHR) never far from scrutiny and criticism.

[1] Albert V. Dicey, *Introduction to the Study of the Law of the Constitution* (8th ed) (Macmillan, 1915), pp.123–125.

[2] Instruments of importance, such as Magna Carta (1215) and the Bill of Rights (1689), protect interests (usually of powerful groups) and controlled abuse of monarchical power.

[3] See, for instance, Keith Ewing and Conor Gearty, *Freedom under Thatcher: Civil Liberties in Modern Britain* (Oxford University Press, 1990).

2.2 THE PROTECTION OF RIGHTS PRIOR TO THE HUMAN RIGHTS ACT 1998

2.2.1 Civil Liberties

Although there was ambivalence in the United Kingdom to legal instruments enumerating rights, during the twentieth century individual freedom was highly valued. A significant means through which an individual's freedoms were protected was by way of liberties. In essence, liberty is the freedom that exists when an area of life is not restricted by law: it entails non-interference with an individual's freedom of choice and action. In the words of Isaiah Berlin, citizens enjoyed freedom from harms rather than rights to goods.[4] As Browne-Wilkinson LJ explained, '[t]hese fundamental freedoms therefore are not positive rights but an immunity from interference by others'.[5] Parliament was, however, expected to pass legislation that did not unduly restrict freedom and as a public authority only has such powers as are conferred by law,[6] the courts would interpret law as far as possible to ensure liberties were not impinged. What, then, are 'civil liberties'? Helen Fenwick observes that '[l]iberties are termed "civil liberties" in the UK because they refer to freedoms of citizens within the civic state"';[7] civil liberties thus attach to people by virtue of their citizenship of a State as opposed to their membership of the human race.[8] Yet, while this provides some insight into the distinction between civil liberties and other liberties, as David Feldman points out there is no agreed way of separating the two categories of liberties. In his view, describing something as a *civil* liberty indicates that 'the state has a special obligation to protect one against interference with it, either as a matter of political morality or as a matter of law'.[9] A civil liberty thus implies that a particular liberty has significance as it allows 'people to participate as a citizen in the functioning of the state, such as freedom of expression' or 'the liberty is particularly significant in defining the relationship between the state and its citizens, such as freedom from arbitrary or discriminatory treatment'.[10] A liberty of particular significance is usually described as 'fundamental' or as a 'constitutional right'. Such labels raise questions as to whether these

[4] Isaiah Berlin, *Four Essays on Liberty* (Oxford University Press, 1969), pp.122–123.

[5] *Wheeler* v. *Leicester City Council* [1985] UKHL 6, [1985] AC 1054, 1065.

[6] *Entick* v. *Carrington* (1765) 19 St Tr 1030; *R* v. *Somerset City Council, Ex parte Fewings (Quantock Staghounds)* [1995] EWCA Civ 24, [1995] 1 WLR 1037.

[7] Helen Fenwick, *Fenwick on Civil Liberties* (Routledge, 2017), p.13.

[8] For a further discussion of the contested philosophical foundation of rights, see Chapter 1.

[9] David Feldman, *Civil Liberties and Human Rights* (2nd ed) (Oxford University Press, 2002), p.5. See also, Keith Ewing and Conor Gearty, *The Struggle for Civil Liberties: Political Freedom and the Rule of Law in Britain, 1914–1945* (Oxford University Press, 2000).

[10] Feldman (n 9), p.4.

liberties or rights have some greater protected status and, if so, what that means in a system based on parliamentary sovereignty in which, at least on the orthodox view, Parliament can make or unmake any law it wishes.

2.2.2 Principle of Legality

In a constitution premised upon parliamentary sovereignty, the common law principle of legality plays a fundamental role. This principle was clearly articulated by Lord Steyn in the House of Lords judgment in *Pierson*:[11]

> Parliament does not legislate in a vacuum. Parliament legislates for a European liberal democracy founded on the principles and traditions of the common law and the courts may approach legislation on this initial assumption. But this assumption only has prima facie force. It can be displaced by a clear and specific provision to the contrary.[12]

Pierson concerned the statutory power of the Home Secretary to fix a tariff on those sentenced to mandatory life imprisonment.[13] The tariff decision of the Home Secretary determined the first review date of the prisoner's sentence and, therefore, the earliest possible date of release. In this case, the Home Secretary had decided retrospectively to increase the tariff of the prisoner. Lord Steyn concluded that the statutory power was broad enough to allow the Home Secretary to fix a tariff but not so wide as to permit an increase of it retrospectively. In his view, 'common law and statute law coalesce in one legal system'[14] and 'a general power to increase tariffs duly fixed is in disharmony with the deep rooted principle of not retrospectively increasing lawfully pronounced sentences'.[15] Thus, Parliament is presumed not to have intended to alter the general system of law without openly expressing its intention to do so. Lord Steyn specifically linked his analysis to the rule of law and assumed that Parliament would also exercise its sovereignty consistently with the rule of law, in the 'spirit of legality'.[16] Lord Hoffmann further elaborated on this doctrine, placing it within the UK constitutional framework:

> Parliamentary sovereignty means that Parliament can, if it chooses, legislate contrary to fundamental principles of human rights. ... The constraints upon its exercise are ultimately political, not legal. But the principle of legality means that Parliament must squarely confront what it is doing and accept the political cost. Fundamental rights cannot be overridden by general or ambiguous words. ... In the absence of express language or necessary implication to the contrary, the courts therefore presume that

[11] *R* v. *Secretary of State for the Home Department; Ex parte Pierson* [1997] UKHL 37, [1998] AC 539.

[12] Ibid at [587].

[13] The Home Secretary can no longer exercise this sentencing power. See *Stafford* v. *the United Kingdom* [GC] (2002) 35 EHRR 32.

[14] *Pierson* (n 11), p.589. [15] Ibid, p.590. [16] Ibid, pp.587–588 and 591–592.

even the most general words were intended to be subject to the basic rights of the individual. In this way the courts of the United Kingdom, though acknowledging the sovereignty of Parliament, apply principles of constitutionality little different from those which exist in countries where the power of the legislature is expressly limited by a constitutional document.[17]

In this respect 'fundamental principles of human rights' are drawn upon in interpreting legislation.

2.2.3 Common Law Rights

There is a significant body of jurisprudence from the English courts concerning common law rights. Indeed, some of the rights protected in modern bills of rights, and in the ECHR itself, originated in the common law. Those rights include the right of access to justice, which is arguably one of the most significant of the common law rights.[18] Common law rights are also reflected in the tort of false imprisonment and the writ of habeas corpus, each safeguarding liberty, whilst the right to life is protected through the criminal law relating to murder and manslaughter. The torts of assault, battery and false imprisonment along with the criminal law also safeguard the right to personal liberty and security of the person. Trespass to land protects property and the integrity of the home.[19] Meanwhile the fundamental right to freedom of expression has been used to develop the common law of defamation,[20] and in *DPP* v. *Jones*, the common law was utilised to conclude that holding a peaceful protest on the highway is not trespassory.[21]

Yet, whilst the common law has long protected some constitutional or fundamental rights, a degree of ambiguity remains as to which rights are protected by the common law. As Lady Hale has observed, 'no two lists of common law rights would be the same'.[22] In contrast to the HRA and the ECHR, which explicitly set out the protected rights, 'there is no comparable

[17] *R* v. *Secretary of State for the Home Department; Ex parte Simms* [1999] UKHL 33, [2000] 2 AC 115, 131. See T. R. S. Allan, *The Sovereignty of Law: Freedom, Constitution, and Common Law* (Oxford University Press, 2013), pp.90–93.

[18] See *Raymond* v. *Honey* [1983] 1 AC 1, [1982] 2 WLR 465. Se-shauna Wheatle, 'Access to Justice: From Judicial Empowerment to Public Empowerment' in Mark Elliott and Kirsty Hughes (eds), *Common Law Constitutional Rights* (Hart, 2020). See also, *R (Anufrijeva)* v. *Secretary of State for the Home Department* [2003] UKHL 36, [2004] 1 AC 604 at [26], per Lord Steyn: 'the right of access to justice . . . is a fundamental and constitutional principle of our legal system'.

[19] *Entick* (n 6).

[20] *Derbyshire City Council* v. *Times Newspapers Ltd and Ors* [1993] UKHL 18, [1993] AC 534.

[21] *Director of Public Prosecutions* v. *Jones* [1999] UKHL 5, [1999] 2 AC 240, 257.

[22] Lady Hale, 'UK Constitutionalism on the March?' [2014] JR 201, 201.

definitive statement of common law rights'.[23] The authors of *De Smith's* have developed a helpful list based on existing case law, though it may not be conclusive.[24] Those rights include: right to life; liberty of the person; right to justice in public; right to a fair hearing; prohibition on the retrospective imposition of criminal penalty; freedom of expression; rights of access to legal advice and to communicate confidentially with a legal adviser; limitations on searches of premises and seizure of documents, including a presumption against general warrants; prohibition on the use of evidence obtained by torture; a fundamental right of British citizens to live in, or return to, that part of the King's territory of which they are a citizen; presumption against the deprivation of property rights without compensation; privilege against self-incrimination; a duty on the State to provide subsistence to asylum seekers; and freedom of movement within the UK.

In addition to ambiguity as to the range of rights which exist within the common law (and whether they are fundamental or not), there are also limits on the extent to which the common law protects such rights. Public authorities, such as the police, could also take advantage of the concept that there is liberty to act provided it is not prohibited by law. In *Malone*, Sir Robert Megarry V-C dismissed an action which arose out of a 'telephone tap' and recordings of confidential telephone conversations.[25] He stated: 'If the tapping of telephones by the Post Office at the request of the police can be carried out without any breach of the law, it does not require any statutory or common law power to justify it: it can lawfully be done simply because there is nothing to make it unlawful.'[26] There was no infringement of any law as there was no trespass on the plaintiff's premises. Furthermore, there was no cause of action that could address the wrong as the plaintiff had no right to property in the telephone line or the conversation: as the judge surmised, the ear cannot be guilty of trespass.[27] Moreover, at that time, the common law did not recognise an actionable right to privacy.[28]

Many common law liberties, rights and freedoms are 'residual'; they exist only if they are not limited or overridden by legal provisions. Indeed, Parliament has frequently intervened by enacting primary legislation which did not respect common law fundamental rights, thereby curtailing (or removing) the ability of the judiciary to give effect to such rights. As noted above, the principle of legality requires that Parliament clearly indicate its intention

[23] Roger Masterman and Se-Shauna Wheatle, 'A Common Law Resurgence in Rights Protection?' [2015] 1 EHRLR 57, 59.

[24] *De Smith's Judicial Review* (9th ed) (Sweet & Maxwell, 2023) at [6-076].

[25] *Malone* v. *Metropolitan Police Commissioner* [1979] Ch 344, [1979] 2 WLR 700.

[26] Ibid, p.367. [27] Ibid, p.369.

[28] Ibid, p.366. Exemplifying the limitations of the common law, the ECtHR found a violation of Article 8. *Malone* v. *the United Kingdom* (1985) 7 EHRR 14.

to legislate contrary to rights but, due to its sovereignty, there is nothing precluding Parliament from so legislating. In the 1980s and 1990s, there was increasing concern about the erosion of civil liberties by virtue of legislation that disregarded or severely impinged upon liberties, especially during the Miners' Strike in 1984–85.[29] While the courts could employ principles of statutory interpretation to mitigate the effect of such legislation, in practice, Parliament had the power to remove rights at common law if it chose to do so.

Another drawback of the common law was that the grounds for judicial review were not broad enough to enable the judiciary to protect rights fully. The courts were unable to review the substance of the decision except on the restricted basis of irrationality or *Wednesbury* unreasonableness. Lord Bingham in *Smith*, a judicial review application concerning individuals who were discharged from the army due to the implementation of a policy against participation of homosexuals in the armed forces, developed an approach of increased intensity of review, referred to as 'anxious scrutiny', given its implications for the interests of the individuals concerned.[30] But even this more intensive review did not lead the Court of Appeal to find that the public authority had acted unlawfully. Indeed, the ECtHR ultimately found that the State had violated Article 8 ECHR (the right to respect for private life), illuminating the yawning gap between the protection afforded by the common law and that of the standards applied by the ECtHR.[31] The ECtHR also found a breach of Article 13 (the right to an effective remedy) due to the inadequacy of the standard of judicial review.[32]

More fundamentally there were also concerns with the underlying structure of justice found in the common law and who and what judges would protect. In this respect Conor Gearty was highly critical of the role of the common law and its record of rights protection prior to the HRA.[33] He pointed to an historical acceptance of racial and religious subjugation in the common law through slavery and penal laws; seditious libel laws being used to silence political critics; whilst freedom of assembly protected organisations such as the Salvation Army, a charity with a Protestant ethos,[34] but not political dissidents, such as suffragettes,[35] striking miners[36] or nuclear disarmament protestors.[37] He also highlighted the use of private nuisance law to curtail freedom of association during

[29] Ewing and Gearty (n 3). See also, Broadcasting Act 1981, s.29(3) (media ban on a lawful political party) and Public Order Act 1986.

[30] *R* v. *Ministry of Defence; Ex parte Smith* [1996] QB 517, [1996] 2 WLR 305.

[31] *Smith and Grady* v. *the United Kingdom* (2000) 29 EHRR 548.

[32] Ibid at [138].

[33] Conor Gearty, *Fantasy Island* (Oxford University Press, 2016).

[34] *Beatty* v. *Gillbanks* (1882) 9 QBD 308, [1882] All ER 559.

[35] *Despard* v. *Wilcox* (1910) 22 Cox 258.

[36] *Thomas* v. *National Union of Mineworkers* [1986] Ch 20, [1985] 2 WLR 1081.

[37] *Kent* v. *Commissioner of Police of the Metropolis*, *The Times*, 15 May 1981.

the miners' strike,[38] failure to prevent ill-treatment of the Irish Republican Army (IRA) prisoners[39] and inadequate protection of journalists' sources.[40]

2.2.4 International Law

Although the UK had been a signatory to the ECHR since 1950, the ECHR as an international treaty had no legal status in domestic UK law. The UK has a dualist constitutional system and international law and domestic law 'operate in independent spheres'.[41] Thus, in domestic legal proceedings, it was not possible to rely directly on the rights set out in the ECHR. The accession of the UK to the ECHR in 1953 played a crucial role in increasing the awareness and influence of human rights thinking and once the right of victims to petition the European Human Rights Commission under Article 25 came into effect from 1966, the UK was regularly found to have infringed Convention rights.[42] As there was no legislation making the ECHR part of UK law, individuals were unable to obtain a remedy based on Convention rights in domestic law unless there was an existing cause of action on which they could rely. If not, the only alternative was to turn to the Strasbourg system.

Yet, whilst the ECHR was not incorporated into domestic law, it still had an indirect legal influence. The principles of statutory interpretation include a presumption that Parliament intends to comply with the UK's international obligations; any ambiguity in the language of a statute is resolved by choosing a meaning that is consistent with the international treaty obligation.[43] It also informed the exercise of discretionary power.[44] Before the enactment of the HRA, this presumption applied to the ECHR. The courts also tried to develop, as far as possible, the common law to conform with ECHR principles.[45] Between 1964 and July 1999, the ECHR was referred to in over 650 domestic legal decisions.[46]

[38] *Thomas* (n 36); *Mersey Dock & Harbour Co* v. *Verrinder* [1982] IRLR 152.

[39] *Ireland* v. *the United Kingdom* (1979–80) 2 EHRR 25.

[40] *Attorney General* v. *Mullholland* [1963] 2 QB 477, [1963] 2 WLR 658; *Secretary of State of Defence* v. *Guardian Newspapers Ltd* [1985] AC 339, [1984] 3 WLR 986.

[41] *R (On the application of Miller)* v. *Secretary of State for Exiting the European Union* [2017] UKSC 5, [2018] AC 6, at [55].

[42] See Andrew Z. Drzemczewski, *European Human Rights Convention in Domestic Law: A Comparative Study* (OUP, 1985); Joanna Dawson and Allwell Uwazuruike, 'UK Cases at the European Court of Human Rights Since 1975', 23 July 2024, https://researchbriefings.files.parliament.uk/documents/CBP-8049/CBP-8049.pdf.

[43] *Salomon* v. *Customs and Excise Commissioners* [1967] 2 QB 116, [1966] 3 WLR 1223.

[44] *R* v. *Secretary of State for the Home Department; Ex parte Brind* [1991] 1 AC 696, [1991] 2 WLR 588.

[45] *Raymond* v. *Honey* [1983] 1 AC 1, [1982] 2 WLR 465; *Derbyshire CC* v. *Times Newspapers Ltd* [1990] 1 AC 109, [1992] 3 WLR 28.

[46] Murray Hunt, *Using Human Rights Law in English Courts* (Hart Publishing, 1997), Appendix 1.

Recent decisions have reaffirmed the dualist nature of the UK Constitution.[47] The issue that arose in *R (SC)* v. *Secretary of State for Work and Pensions* concerned the status in domestic law of unincorporated treaties, which are often referred to and indeed relied upon by the ECtHR in its jurisprudence. According to Lord Reed, the only treaty to which the HRA gives effect in domestic law is the ECHR.[48] He states:

> the European court has not treated provisions of international treaties as if they were directly incorporated into the Convention itself, so as to impose specific obligations on the contracting states via the Convention. Nor does it refer to international materials for the purpose of determining whether contracting states have complied with their obligations under unincorporated international treaties, recognising that it possesses no jurisdiction to make such a determination.[49]

In the past, the UK courts have been more receptive to the values and standards in treaties such as the UNCRC[50] but according to Lord Reed, there is no basis 'for any departure from the rule that our domestic courts cannot determine whether this country has violated its obligations under unincorporated international treaties'.[51]

Principles of customary international law is another source used to develop the common law and fundamental rights. This form of law is developed by identifiable State practice combined with *opinio juris sive necessitatis* – a sense of legal obligation under international law to comply with that practice.[52] As the law has developed through State practice, it is not contained in treaties. The courts have given effect to these rules of international law through the common law without the need for an Act of Parliament.[53] However, in circumstances where Parliament has legislated, the courts have refused to import international rules that would impinge upon the limits set by Parliament.[54]

[47] *R (On the application of SC, CB and 8 children)* v. *Secretary of State for Work and Pensions* [2021] UKSC 26, [2022] AC 223 at [76]–[78]; *Local Authority* v. *JB* [2021] UKSC 52, [2022] AC 1322 at [120]; Lewis Graham, 'The Supreme Court's Recent Approach to Unincorporated Treaties' [2024] 1 EHRLR 1, 49.

[48] *SC* (n 47) at [79]. [49] Ibid at [83].

[50] See e.g. *R (On the application of SG)* v. *Secretary of State for Work and Pensions* [2015] UKSC 16, [2015] 1 WLR 1449 at [83], per Lord Reed.

[51] *SC* (n 47) at [84].

[52] Olivier De Schutter, *International Human Rights Law* (3rd ed) (CUP, 2019), p.60.

[53] *Trendtex Trading Corporation* v. *Central Bank of Nigeria* [1977] QB 529, 554, [1977] 2 WLR 356. See also, *R (On the application of Freedom and Justice Party and others)* v. *Secretary of State for Foreign and Commonwealth Affairs and Anor* [2018] EWCA Civ 1719, [2019] QB 1075 at [15]–[16].

[54] *R (On the application of Keyu)* v. *Secretary of State for Foreign and Commonwealth* Affairs [2015] UKSC 69, [2016] AC 1355 at [111]–[113], per Lord Neuberger and at [151], per Lord Mance.

Customary international law contains some norms in the field of human rights. Indeed the role of customary international law in the common law is exemplified by the prohibition of torture. The House of Lords considered whether evidence obtained by torture is admissible in an English court or tribunal in *A and Ors* v. *Secretary of State for the Home Department (No 2)*.[55] This decision is considered in Chapter 8. For the purposes of this chapter, it should be noted that the decision was decided largely on common law grounds, including norms of customary international law. The House of Lords unanimously held that evidence obtained by torture is not admissible and that the prohibition of the use of evidence obtained by way of torture is a norm of *ius cogens,* that is part of the body of international law that comprises peremptory norms which permit of no derogation.[56] A further example of the potential of customary international law to protect human rights is the decision in the *European Roma Rights Centre* case.[57] The facts arose out of the practice of UK immigration officers stationed at Prague Airport who would question and refuse applications from Czech citizens seeking to come to the UK who appeared to be of Roma origin: nearly all Czech asylum seekers were Roma. This practice was found to be an example of direct race discrimination based on ethnic origins.[58] The House of Lords concluded that there was a breach of s.19B Race Relations Act 1976 but in addition their Lordships also found that the immigration officers contravened a norm of customary international law. According to Lord Steyn, '[t]he moral norm [the prohibition of racial discrimination] has ripened into a rule of customary international law. It is binding on all states.'[59]

2.3 THE HUMAN RIGHTS ACT 1998

2.3.1 Enactment of the Human Rights Act 1998

For many years before the enactment of the HRA, the UK was becoming far more rights-conscious than it had been traditionally and there was growing demand to provide greater protection of human rights in domestic law. Non-Governmental Organisations (NGOs) such as Liberty and JUSTICE actively campaigned for a Bill of Rights.[60] In the 1990s, judges also began to make

[55] *A and Ors* v. *Secretary of State for the Home Department* [2004] UKHL 56, [2005] 2 AC 68.

[56] Ibid at [33], per Lord Bingham. See also, *R* v. *Bow Street Metropolitan Stipendiary Magistrate; Ex parte Pinochet Ugarte (No 3)* [1999] UKHL 17, [2000] 1 AC 147 at [197]–[199].

[57] *R (On the application of European Roma Rights Centre)* v. *Secretary of State for the Home Department* [2004] UKHL 55, [2005] 2 AC 1.

[58] See Chapter 14 for further details of discrimination on race or ethnicity.

[59] *European Roma Rights* (n 57) at [46] and [98], per Lady Hale.

[60] See, for example, Liberty, *A People's Charter: Liberty's Bill of Rights* (Liberty, 1991).

public statements about the need to incorporate the ECHR into domestic law. Lord Bingham famously stated: 'The ability of English judges to protect human rights in this country . . . is inhibited by the failure of successive governments over many years to incorporate into United Kingdom law the [ECHR].'[61] Meanwhile Lord Woolf argued that it was unacceptable that 'our citizens should be able to obtain a remedy which the Government will honour in the European Court of Human Rights, [but] which they cannot obtain from the courts in this country' and asserted that 'a British Bill of Rights would avoid the difficulty which exists at present in protecting some of our basic rights. It would enable us to play our part in the development of human rights jurisprudence internationally.'[62]

In 1994, Tony Blair was elected leader of the Labour Party and made plans for a large constitutional reform programme, which included protecting Convention rights within domestic law.[63] In 1997, the Labour Party won the general election by a landslide majority and, upon forming a new Government, Blair quickly introduced a White Paper, 'Rights Brought Home: the Human Rights Bill' setting out the case for reform.[64] The Human Rights Bill was introduced into the House of Lords in 1997.[65] During the debates in Parliament on the Bill, the Lord Chancellor, Lord Irvine, expounded on the primary reasons for the Government's decision to introduce it:

> [The Bill] occupies a central position in our integrated programme for constitutional change. It will allow British judges for the first time to make their own distinctive contribution to the development of human rights in Europe. . . . This Bill will bring rights home. People will be able to argue for their rights and claim their remedies under the Convention in any court or tribunal in the United Kingdom. Our courts will develop human rights throughout society. A culture of awareness of human rights will develop . . . there will have to be close scrutiny of all legislation before it goes forward.[66]

The HRA received the Royal Assent on 9 November 1998 and, after a programme of education and preparation by both government departments and the judiciary, it came into force in 2000. Human rights took effect in Scotland,

[61] Tom H. Bingham, 'The European Convention on Human Rights: Time to Incorporate' (1993) 109 LQR 390, 390.

[62] Lord Woolf, 'Droit Public: English Style' [1995] PL 57.

[63] Jack Straw and Paul Boateng, 'Bringing Rights Home: Labour's Plans to Incorporate the European Convention on Human Rights into UK Law' (Labour Party, 1996), reprinted [1997] EHRLR, 71–80. Incorporation had become official Labour Party policy in September 1993; see *A New Agenda for Democracy: Labour's Proposals for Constitutional Reform* (Labour Party, 1993).

[64] Home Office, *Rights Brought Home: The Human Rights Bill*, Cm 3782, (October 1997).

[65] For further details see Francesca Klug, *Values for a Godless Age: The Story of the United Kingdom's New Bill of Rights* (Penguin, 2000).

[66] Hansard, HL, vol.582, col.1227, 3 November 1997.

Wales and Northern Ireland before it did so in England due to the devolution legislation that was enacted in 1998. The three devolution statutes of 1998 restricted the legislative and executive competences of the respective devolved legislatures and governments by providing that their devolved powers could not be exercised in a manner contrary to a Convention right, as defined in the HRA.[67]

2.3.2 Relationship between the Human Rights Act 1998, the Northern Ireland Belfast /Good Friday Agreement and the Windsor Framework

Under the 2015–2024 Conservative Government, Ministers increasingly threatened to withdraw from the ECHR and there was immense speculation about the UK's continued membership of the Council of Europe. In respect of Northern Ireland, withdrawal from the ECHR and the Council of Europe would not be straightforward because of domestic constitutional factors and other international legal obligations.[68] Indeed, the HRA has a constitutional function in Northern Ireland that is unique in the UK.[69] After decades of violent conflict in Northern Ireland, a period that is euphemistically known as 'The Troubles', the Belfast/Good Friday Agreement ('the Agreement') was a political deal intended to bring peace to the country.[70] The Agreement was reached on 10 April 1998 and approved by referendums in Northern Ireland and the Republic of Ireland on 22 May 1998.[71] The Agreement formed the basis of a new constitutional settlement for Northern Ireland and is founded on the concept of consociationalism, a mechanism designed to facilitate political stability in deeply divided communities. To this end a novel power-sharing arrangement was established that included an Executive and Assembly with devolved competence.[72] The Agreement is multi-dimensional: on the one hand it is the peace settlement between opposing factions in Northern Ireland after decades of conflict[73] and, on the other, it comprises a bilateral treaty between

[67] Scotland Act 1998, Government of Wales Act 1998 and Northern Ireland Act 1998.

[68] Frederick Cowell, 'Locking in Human Rights: An Exploration of the Barriers to ECHR Withdrawal' [2024] 5 ECHRLR 1. Domestic constitutional complications would arise because of the devolution agreements with Scotland and Wales.

[69] See, QUB Human Rights Centre, 'Response to the Ministry of Justice's Consultation Paper on Human Rights Act Reform', March 2022 at [100]–[108], www.qub.ac.uk/research-centres/human-rights-centre/news/QUBHumanRightsCentreRespondstoMoJConsultationonHumanRightsActReform.html.

[70] The Belfast Agreement: An Agreement Reached at the Multi-Party Talks on Northern Ireland, Cm. 3883 (10 April 1998). It is also known as the Good Friday Agreement.

[71] Note Chapters 4, 5 and 8 also cover human rights issues arising in Northern Ireland.

[72] There was a previous history of devolution in Northern Ireland, which sets it apart from Scotland and Wales.

[73] See Colin Harvey, 'The 1998 Agreement: Context and Status' in Christopher McCrudden (ed), *The Law and Practice of the Ireland–Northern Ireland Protocol* (Cambridge University Press,

the UK and the Republic of Ireland.[74] The HRA forms a seminal part of that constitutional settlement and is 'integral to the rebuilding of trust in public institutions in Northern Ireland after the Troubles'.[75]

The Agreement guarantees the protection of human rights in several interrelated ways.[76] First, it embodies a commitment to political self-determination of the people of Northern Ireland.[77] Second, the Agreement required the establishment of the Northern Ireland Human Rights Commission (NIHRC)[78] and an Equality Commission 'to monitor a statutory obligation to promote equality of opportunity ... and to investigate individual complaints against public bodies'.[79] Third, against the background of the recent history of communal conflict, the parties affirmed their commitment to a number of civil and religious liberties: the right of free political thought; the right to freedom and expression of religion; the right to pursue democratically national and political aspirations; the right to seek constitutional change by peaceful and legitimate means; the right to freely choose one's place of residence; the right to equal opportunity in all social and economic activity, regardless of class, creed, disability, gender or ethnicity; the right to freedom from sectarian harassment; and the right of women to full and equal political participation.[80] Fourth, referring to the then proposed Human Rights Bill, the Agreement provided that the British Government would complete incorporation of the ECHR into the law of Northern Ireland, including the power for the courts to overrule Assembly legislation on grounds of inconsistency.[81] Finally, 'safeguards' were imposed on the new democratic institutions 'to ensure that all sections of the community can participate and work together successfully' in their operation, including: 'the ... ECHR and any Bill of Rights for Northern

2022), ch.2; Christopher McCrudden, 'Northern Ireland, the Belfast Agreement, and the British Constitution' in Jeffery Jowell and Dawn Oliver (eds), *The Changing Constitution* (5th ed) (Oxford University Press, 2004), p.207 and Brice Dickson, 'Devolution: Northern Ireland' in Jeffery Jowell and Colm O'Cinneide, *The Changing Constitution* (9th ed) (Oxford University Press, 2019), ch.9.

[74] The British–Irish Agreement is the formal name of the international law treaty between the UK and Ireland. The Belfast/Good Friday Agreement (n 70), includes a copy of the text of the Treaty as an annex and the text of the Agreement reached in the Multi-Party Talks is included in Annex 1 of the Treaty.

[75] See letter from Sir Robert Buckland, Chair Northern Ireland Affairs Committee to the Secretary of State for Northern Ireland, 24 May 2024, https://committees.parliament.uk/publications/45010/documents/223298/default/. See also, Colin Harvey, 'Building Bridges? Protecting Human Rights in Northern Ireland' (2001) 1 HRLR 243–264.

[76] Jack Beatson et al., *Human Rights: Judicial Protection in the United Kingdom* (Sweet and Maxwell, 2008) at 8-155.

[77] Northern Ireland Act 1998, s.1.

[78] The Agreement, 'Strand One: Democratic Institutions in Northern Ireland' (n 70) at [5(b)].

[79] Ibid at [5(e)].

[80] The Agreement, 'Rights, Safeguards and Equality of Opportunity' (n 70) at [1].

[81] Ibid at [2].

Ireland supplementing it, which neither the Assembly nor public bodies can infringe'.[82] The Northern Ireland Act 1998 (NIA) thus partially implements the Agreement,[83] and the HRA and the NIA mutually reinforce each other. More broadly, human rights continue to play a crucial role in maintaining the peace in Northern Ireland.

The UK's decision to leave the European Union (EU) in 2016 provoked uncertainty in Northern Ireland in respect of many issues including the border between the Republic of Ireland and Northern Ireland, the position of Northern Ireland within the UK, and the effect withdrawal would have on the protection of human rights in the region.[84] Promises concerning human rights protection were therefore made as part of the EU withdrawal process. Any interference with the efficacy of human rights in NI would thus result in acute complexities in respect of EU relations and could undermine the political gains and the peace settlement in Northern Ireland. The Brexit withdrawal negotiations led to the creation of the Withdrawal Agreement's Protocol on Ireland/Northern Ireland[85] ('the Protocol'), which left Northern Ireland in the EU customs union and some parts of the EU single market whilst the remainder of the UK left the EU.[86]

Owing to unforeseen (and arguably foreseen) practical challenges relating to the implementation of the Protocol on Ireland/Northern Ireland, the EU and the UK agreed a new solution to these difficulties that resulted in a political agreement known as the Windsor Framework (WF).[87] The WF concerns new arrangements in relation to both the EU single market and, importantly for our purposes, the protection of human rights.[88] In particular, Article 2(1) of the WF embodies a UK Government commitment to ensure that '*no diminution of rights*, safeguards or equality of opportunity, as set out in [the relevant part of the Belfast/Good Friday] Agreement, results from the UK's withdrawal from

[82] The Agreement, 'Strand One: Democratic Institutions in Northern Ireland' (n 70) at [5] and [5(b)].

[83] See Conor McCormick, 'The Amendability of the Agreement' (2023) Fortnight 489 https://fortnightmagazine.org/articles/the-amendability-of-the-agreement/.

[84] Lisa Claire Whitten, *Brexit and the Northern Ireland Constitution* (Oxford University Press, 2023); Federico Fabbrini (ed), *The Law and Politics of Brexit: Volume IV: The Protocol on Ireland/Northern Ireland* (Oxford University Press, 2022); Conor J. Kelly and Etain Tannam, 'The Future of Northern Ireland: The Role of the Belfast/Good Friday Agreement Institutions' (2023) **94** The Political Quarterly 85–94.

[85] See s.7A European Union (Withdrawal Agreement) Act 2018 as amended by the European Union (Withdrawal Agreement) Act 2020. Both of these Acts have led to amendments of the Northern Ireland Act 1998.

[86] The Withdrawal Agreement and the accompanying Protocol on Ireland/Northern Ireland were signed on 24 January 2020.

[87] Joint Declaration (EU and UK) No. 1/2023 of 24 March 2023. See also, the Windsor Framework (Democratic Scrutiny) Regulations 2024.

[88] Anurag Deb and C. R. G. Murray, 'Article 2 of the Ireland/Northern Ireland Protocol: A New Frontier in Human Rights Law?' [2023] EHRLR 608–625.

the [European] Union'.[89] This is a strong statement of the UK's commitment to the rights set out in the Agreement which 'applies to everyone subject to Northern Ireland law – irrespective of whether such law has been passed by the Northern Ireland legislature or Westminster'.[90] Moreover, it has the potential to disapply inconsistent primary legislation and automatically update the law of Northern Ireland to reflect changes in EU law.[91]

2.3.3 Which Rights Are Protected?

It is often stated that the HRA has incorporated the ECHR into domestic law, but this is not technically correct: the HRA does not make the Convention rights a substantive part of UK law. The Long Title to the HRA states that it is designed to 'give further effect to' Convention rights and the provisions of the HRA establish mechanisms whereby the Convention rights are given effect in certain ways in domestic law. These mechanisms are set out in detail below. They include a principle of statutory interpretation which requires that all legislation is to be read and given effect in a manner compatible with Convention rights, so far as it is possible to do so, and a legal duty which is imposed on public authorities to act in a manner compatible with Convention rights. Further, victims of a violation are entitled to a remedy. Another important element of the HRA is that it does not directly impact the doctrine of parliamentary sovereignty; Parliament remains free to pass legislation which is incompatible with Convention rights and the courts do not have the power to strike down or disapply any provision in primary legislation that is incompatible with the relevant ECHR rights. Instead, the HRA scheme provides for a declaration of incompatibility. All of these provisions are considered in further detail below.

Pursuant to s.1(1) HRA 'Convention rights' means the rights and fundamental freedoms set out in Articles 2 to 12 and 14 of the Convention, Articles 1 to 3 of the First Protocol, and Article 1 of the Thirteenth Protocol as read with Articles 16 to 18 of the Convention. These Articles are to have effect subject to any designated derogation or reservation.[92] The rights themselves are set out

[89] The Withdrawal Agreement and the accompanying Protocol on Ireland/Northern Ireland, Article 2. Emphasis added.

[90] Ibid at [8].

[91] See, for instance, the High Court's judgment in *Re Dillon & Ors* [2024] NIKB 11 concerning the (in)compatibility of aspects of the Northern Ireland (Troubles and Reconciliation) Act 2023 with Article 2 ECHR and the subsequent confirmation by the Northern Ireland Court of Appeal in *Re Dillon & Ors* [2024] NICA 59. See also, the discussion in Kirsty Hughes, Stevie Martin and Stephanie Palmer, 'Editorial' (2024) 3 EHRLR 195. Note also that in *In the Matter of an Application by the NIHRC for Judicial Review* [2024] NIKB 35 the High Court of Northern Ireland held that provisions of the Illegal Migration Act 2023 breached the Withdrawal Agreement because of the diminution of rights, and the offending provisions were disapplied.

[92] Sections 14–17 HRA 1998.

in schedule 1 to the HRA. It notably does not include Articles 1 (obligation to respect human rights) and 13 ECHR (right to an effective remedy).[93]

2.3.4 Section 2 HRA 1998: Taking Account of Strasbourg Jurisprudence

Section 2(1) HRA requires that a court or tribunal determining a question which has arisen in connection with a Convention right must take into account any 'judgment, decision, declaration or advisory opinion' of the ECtHR. The section is an important link between the jurisprudence of the ECtHR and the protection and enforcement of Convention rights in the UK. Both the Joint Committee on Human Rights and the Independent Review of the Human Rights Act set up by the Government concluded that s.2 HRA was of importance to the 'judicial dialogue' between UK courts and the ECtHR.[94] It enables them to speak the same language and it ensures that the ECtHR understands the UK context and the reasoning adopted by the domestic courts in applying Convention rights.

However, the meaning of the phrase 'take into account' has led to some uncertainty. It is clear that the courts are not bound by this jurisprudence; it is persuasive but not binding on domestic courts. As the purpose of the HRA is to protect Convention rights in the UK and to obtain remedies for any breaches, the domestic courts usually adopt the level of human rights protection that would be offered by the ECtHR. It is a sensible approach to treat the ECtHR's definition of a right as setting the minimum floor of its interpretation, as this ensures that rights will be protected and avoids the need for unnecessary and costly litigation in Strasbourg.[95] The interpretation of Convention rights can only be understood by considering the ECtHR's jurisprudence.

As Lord Slynn stated:

> Although the Human Rights Act 1998 does not provide that a national court is bound by these decisions it is obliged to take account of them so far as they are relevant. In the absence of some special circumstances it seems to me that the court should follow any clear and constant jurisprudence of the ECtHR. If it does not do so, there is at least a possibility that the case will go to that court, which is likely in the ordinary case to follow its own constant jurisprudence.[96]

[93] For further details see Feldman (n 9), pp. 82–83; Jack Beatson et al., *Human Rights: Judicial Protection in the United Kingdom* (Sweet & Maxwell, 2008), pp. 30–33.

[94] Joint Committee on Human Rights, Third Report of Session 2021–2022 – The Government's Independent Review of the Human Rights Act, HC 89/HL 31, 8 July 2022, ch 3. See also, the discussion of dialogic theories in Chapter 1.

[95] Joint Committee on Human Rights, Thirteenth Report of Session 2021–2022 – Human Rights Act Reform, HC 1033/HL Paper 191, 13 April 2022, 30; The Government's Independent Review of the Human Rights Act (n 94), ch. 3.

[96] *R* v. *Secretary of State for the Environment, Transport and Regions, ex p. Alconbury Developments Ltd* [2001] UKHL 23, [2003] AC 295 at [26].

The position might appear to be relatively straightforward where there is Strasbourg jurisprudence on the matter in hand, but circumstances have arisen where the Strasbourg court has not yet addressed a situation, has misunderstood some part of domestic law, or where the domestic courts consider there is no clear line of authority from the ECtHR. The cases dealing with s.2 HRA thus illustrate the complexities that may arise when trying to regulate public authorities in domestic law through the lens of an international legal system. Section 2 HRA has also been criticised by those who oppose the influence in domestic law of the ECtHR's jurisprudence, in particular the influence of the living instrument doctrine. Indeed, the extent to which domestic courts are bound by Strasbourg jurisprudence lies at the heart of opposition to the HRA.

In order to address the s.2 HRA requirement to 'take into account' ECtHR case law, Lord Bingham developed an approach that became known colloquially as the 'mirror principle' or the *Ullah* principle. He reasoned in *R (on the application of Ullah)* v. *Special Adjudicator* that as Convention rights could only be authoritatively expounded by the ECtHR, the domestic UK courts should mirror the interpretation of Convention rights adopted by the ECtHR:

> [A] national court subject to a duty such as that imposed by section 2 should not without strong reason dilute or weaken the effect of the Strasbourg case law. . . . It is of course open to member states to provide for rights more generous than those guaranteed by the Convention, but such provision should not be the product of interpretation of the Convention by national courts, since the meaning of the Convention should be uniform throughout the states party to it. The duty of national courts is to keep pace with the Strasbourg jurisprudence as it evolves over time: *no more, but certainly no less.*[97]

In 2009, in *Secretary of State for the Home Department* v. *AF*, Lord Roger observed, when considering ECtHR jurisprudence relating to restrictions on participation in judicial proceedings (discussed further in Chapter 8): 'Even though we are dealing with rights under a United Kingdom statute, in reality, we have no choice . . . Strasbourg has spoken, the case is closed.'[98] Whilst providing weaker protection than that guaranteed by the ECtHR might be regarded as unacceptable (although as we will see below the position on even this issue has become more complex), it is not so obvious that providing greater protection than the existing Strasbourg jurisprudence should be restricted.[99] A domestic court's interpretation of Convention rights does not

[97] *R (on the application of Ullah)* v. *Special Adjudicator* [2004] UKHL 26, [2004] 2 AC 323 at [20]. Emphasis added.

[98] *Secretary of State for the Home Department* v. *AF and Ors* [2009] UKHL 28, [2010] 2 AC 269 at [98].

[99] A State would not have the standing to challenge a more generous interpretation of the Convention rights. See *R (Al-Skeini)* v. *Secretary of State for Defence* [2007] UKHL 26, [2008] 1 AC 153, per Lord Brown who observed that the *Ullah* principle might equally have been 'no less, but certainly no more' at [106].

apply outside of the UK, thus such an interpretation would not replace the ECtHR's authoritative role. Moreover, the Strasbourg jurisprudence develops through the living instrument doctrine and includes examining the approach to rights across the Member States of the Council of Europe. If UK domestic courts are unwilling to go beyond the existing Strasbourg jurisprudence, their capacity to contribute to the development of Convention rights will be seriously weakened.[100]

More recently, the Supreme Court in *Shamima Begum*[101] again restated the orthodox view. Shamima Begum is a British-born woman who in 2015, at the age of fifteen, entered Syria to join the Islamic State. In 2019, the Home Secretary stripped her of her British citizenship, citing national security concerns. The Supreme Court refused permission for leave to appeal, stating that the grounds of appeal did not raise an arguable point of law. The Supreme Court expressed wariness of 'developing the law under the Convention well beyond the principles established by the European Court'.[102] In their view, an extension of the Convention rights along the lines suggested by the appellant must be decided by the ECtHR 'as the authoritative interpreter of the ECHR'.[103]

In circumstances where the European Court has not considered the issue, the domestic courts remain cautious about developing Convention rights. In *R (Elan-Cane)* v. *Secretary of State for the Home Department,* the appellant, Christie Elan-Cane, challenged the Government's policy not to issue non-gender specific 'X' passports to non-gendered, non-binary and other trans persons who do not identify as either male or female. The Supreme Court restated the orthodox view: 'Since the rights have the same content at the domestic level as at the international level, it follows that the relevant articles of the Convention should in principle receive the same interpretation in both contexts.'[104] The Supreme Court also expressed concerned about encroaching

[100] Some commentators have encouraged the Supreme Court to depart from Strasbourg decisions in appropriate cases: for example, Nicholas Bratza, 'The Relationship between the UK Courts and Strasbourg' [2011] EHRLR 505; Philip Sales, 'Strasbourg Jurisprudence and the Human Rights Act: A Reply to Lord Irvine' [2012] PL 253 and Richard Clayton, 'Smoke and Mirrors: The Human Rights Act and the Impact of Strasbourg Case Law' [2012] PL 639; Nuno Ferreira, 'The Supreme Court in a Final Push to Go beyond Strasbourg' [2015] PL 367 and Paul Mahoney, 'The Relationship between the Strasbourg Court and the National Courts' (2014) 130 LQR 568. Of the UK judges, the strongest advocate for this approach was Lord Kerr: 'The UKSC: The Modest Underworker of Strasbourg?' (Clifford Chance Lecture, 25 January 2012).

[101] *Shamima Begum* v. *SSHD*, UKSC 2024/0096 (Permission to appeal decision). The case is discussed in greater detail in Chapters 7 and 8.

[102] Ibid at [7]. [103] Ibid.

[104] *R (on the application of Elan-Cane)* v. *Secretary of State for the Home Department* [2021] UKSC 56, [2023] AC 559 at [87], per Lord Reed PSC (with whom Lord Lloyd-Jones, Lady Arden, Lord Sales and Lady Rose JJSC agreed). The European Court had not considered the position of individuals who identified as non-gendered [30] and [63] and there was no

on parliamentary sovereignty if it were to venture beyond lines which have been clearly drawn by Strasbourg.[105] But Lord Reed did suggest that 'the protection of Convention rights under the Human Rights Act can go beyond the situations previously considered by the European court, where the principles established by that court enable such a step to be taken'.[106]

Some important modifications to the *Ullah* 'mirror principle' have emerged in domestic court judgments. Going beyond the Strasbourg jurisprudence may be possible in some circumstances. For example, where the domestic court is unable to identify a clear and constant line of authority from Strasbourg,[107] or where there is no clear authority as the ECtHR has not had the opportunity to address a specific issue at hand, it may then be legitimate for the domestic courts to decide the matter. For example, in *Rabone* v. *Penine Care NHS Foundation*, the appeal concerned the positive duty on states imposed by Article 2 ECHR to take preventative operational measures to safeguard an individual's life. This case is discussed in Chapter 4 (Right to Life). The ECtHR had determined that the positive duty applied to involuntary psychiatric patients at risk of suicide. The Supreme Court extended the duty to voluntary psychiatric patients. As Lord Brown opined in *Rabone*: '[i]f ... the domestic court is content ... to decide a Convention challenge against a public authority and believes such a conclusion to flow naturally from existing Strasbourg case law (albeit that it could be regarded as carrying the case law a step further), then in my judgment it should take that further step'.[108] Thus in circumstances when Strasbourg is silent and a decision would move beyond the jurisprudence of the ECtHR, domestic courts should only adopt a position on Convention rights that 'flow[s] naturally'[109] from the existing law. In any case, the domestic courts should only take the law to the point that it predicts the ECtHR would itself allow.[110]

The second modification is where Strasbourg has considered the matter but found no breach. Although cases such as *Nicklinson* and *Re G* indicated that domestic courts might be willing to go further than the ECtHR in circumstances where the ECtHR found no breach of the Convention due to the

consensus among Council of Europe States that passports should be issued with an 'X' marker [59]. See also Chapter 14.

105 Ibid at [88–93]. 106 Ibid at [101].

107 See *Moohan* v. *Lord Advocate* [2014] UKSC 67, [2015] AC 901 at [104]–[105]; *R (on the application of Keyu)* v. *Secretary of State for Foreign and Commonwealth Affairs & Secretary of State for Defence* [2015] UKSC 69, [2016] AC 1355 at [234]–[235], per Lord Kerr.

108 See *Rabone* v. *Penine Care NHS Foundation* [2012] UKSC 2, [2012] 2 AC 72, per Lord Brown at [112]. See also, the discussion of Lewis Graham, 'Taking Strasbourg Jurisprudence into Account' [2022] EHRLR 2, 163–172.

109 *R (Maguire)* v. *HM Senior Coroner* [2020] EWCA Civ 738, [2021] QB 409, [2020] 3 WLR 1268 at [99].

110 *R (AB)* v. *Secretary of State for Justice* [2021] UKSC 28, [2022] AC 487 at [59].

application of the margin of appreciation,[111] the Supreme Court in *Elan-Cane* retreated from this.[112] According to Lord Reed, 'it has generally been accepted that the domestic application of Convention rights under the Human Rights Act has to be based on the principles established in the case law of the European court, rather than upon a distinct domestic interpretation of Convention rights'.[113] Accordingly, where the ECtHR has found no breach of rights in a given situation, even when it does so on the basis of the margin of appreciation, it seems domestic courts must follow.

The final modification is where Strasbourg has considered the issue and found a breach. In certain rare circumstances, the domestic courts have exercised a discretion to refuse to apply Strasbourg case law.[114] A decision of Strasbourg may not be followed where the decision is considered flawed due to some fundamental misunderstanding relating to the UK's domestic law.[115] According to Lord Philips:

> There will . . . be rare occasions where this court has concerns as to whether a decision of the Strasbourg Court sufficiently appreciates or accommodates particular aspects of our domestic process. In such circumstances it is open to this court to decline to follow the Strasbourg decision, giving reasons for adopting this course. This is likely to give the Strasbourg Court the opportunity to reconsider the particular aspect of the decision that is in issue, so that there takes place what may prove to be a valuable dialogue between this court and the Strasbourg Court.[116]

Thus, an ECtHR decision may not be followed where it is 'inconsistent with some fundamental substantive or procedural aspect of [UK] law'.[117] To date, the ECtHR has accepted the (re)interpretations of its judgments by UK courts. For example, the ECtHR has considered the question of whether whole life tariffs are compatible with Article 3 ECHR and established that domestic law should provide some prospect of release and a possibility of review. As discussed in Chapter 5 (freedom from torture or inhuman or degrading treatment or punishment), in *Vinter* v. *the United Kingdom*[118] the ECtHR found a lack of clarity in the whole life sentence arising from the discrepancy within the domestic system between the applicable law and the published official policy. One year later in *Hutchinson* v. *the United Kingdom*,[119] the Grand

[111] See e.g. *R (Nicklinson)* v. *Ministry of Justice* [2014] UKSC 38, [2015] AC 657 at [70] (per Lord Neuberger) and [299] (per Lady Hale); *Re G (A Child) (Adoption: Unmarried Couple)* [2008] UKHL 38, [2009] 1 AC 173 at [31] (per Lord Hoffmann) and [120] (per Lady Hale).

[112] *Elan-Cane* (n 104), per Lord Reed [102]–[107]. [113] Ibid at [101].

[114] See Lewis Graham, 'The Modern Mirror Principle' [2021] PL 523.

[115] *R* v. *Horncastle* [2009] UKSC 14, [2010] 2 AC 373. [116] Ibid at [11].

[117] *Manchester City Council* v. *Pinnock* [2011] UKSC 6 at [48], [2011] 2 WLR 220. *R (Chester)* v. *Secretary of State for Justice* [2013] UKSC 63, [2014] AC 271 at [27].

[118] *Vinter* v. *the United Kingdom* (2016) 63 EHRR 1.

[119] *Hutchinson* v. *the United Kingdom* [GC], App. No. 57592/08, 17/01/2017.

Chamber accepted that the UK Court of Appeal[120] had dispelled their concerns as outlined in *Vinter*, and there was no violation of Article 3 ECHR.

After analysing the jurisprudence on s.2 HRA, Lewis Graham made the worrying observation that 'UK courts are much more comfortable with departing from Strasbourg case law which identifies, or increases the scope of, obligations upon public bodies; by contrast, they are much more likely to mirror Strasbourg case law which limits the scope of a Convention right, or grants more leeway to public bodies. This is an unsatisfying prospect.'[121]

2.3.5 Section 3 HRA 1998: The Interpretation of Legislation

Another important mechanism for giving effect to Convention rights in domestic law is the interpretative duty imposed by s.3 HRA. The obligation to read and give effect to all legislation in a Convention-compatible manner, so far as it is possible to do so, applies to all courts and tribunals and in all proceedings. A public authority need not be a party to the proceedings. Prior to the enactment of the HRA, the courts would protect rights through interpretation in two limited circumstances: where the right at issue raised a common law constitutional right or when the right concerned a Convention right and the domestic legislation in question was ambiguous.[122] The interpretative duty under s.3 HRA is far broader; it applies to all Convention rights given effect in domestic law through the HRA and does not depend upon any finding of ambiguity.

The landmark s.3 HRA decision is *Ghaidan* v. *Godin-Mendoza.*[123] It concerned the interpretation of provisions of the Rent Act 1977, which provided for succession to a statutory tenancy. The legislation stated that where a statutory tenant dies, 'a person who was living with the original tenant as his or her wife or husband shall be treated as the spouse of the original tenant' and would thus become the 'statutory tenant'.[124] Statutory tenants are protected against eviction. Godin-Mendoza had cohabited with his same-sex partner for eighteen years and his partner, the 'original tenant', had died, following which the claimant landlord wished to evict Godin-Mendoza from his property. The legal question in *Ghaidan* turned on whether Godin-Mendoza, relying upon Articles 8 (right to respect for private life) and 14 (non-discrimination) ECHR, could become the statutory tenant. For this to

[120] *Re Attorney General's Reference (No. 69 of 2013)* [2014] EWCA Crim 188, [2014] 1 WLR 3964.

[121] Graham (n 108), pp.163–164.

[122] *R* v. *Secretary of State for the Home Department, ex p. Brind* [1991] 1 AC 696, [1991] 2 WLR 588.

[123] *Ghaidan* v. *Godin-Mendoza* [2004] UKHL 30, [2004] 2 AC 557.

[124] Rent Act 1977, Sch1. para 2.

happen, the relevant provisions in the Rent Act – 'living with the original tenant as his or her wife or husband' – would need to be read as applying to same-sex couples;[125] this was difficult because, at the time, marriage was only available to heterosexual couples.

The House of Lords found that if the provisions in the Rent Act 1977 were given their natural meaning, Godin-Mendoza could not be considered a statutory tenant – a conclusion that would breach his Convention rights. Consequently, the Court had to decide whether it was 'possible' to interpret the legislation in a Convention-compatible manner. Lord Nicholls noted that s.3 HRA is of an 'unusual and far-reaching character' which 'may require a court to depart from the unambiguous meaning the legislation would otherwise bear'.[126] As further explained by Lord Nicholls, the interpretation of legislation usually 'involves seeking the intention reasonably to be attributed to Parliament in using the language in question'. Section 3 HRA, however, may 'require the court to depart from this legislative intention, that is, depart from the intention of the Parliament which enacted the legislation'.[127] In order to find a Convention-compliant interpretation, the Court may be required to read in words which change the meaning of primary and secondary legislation.[128] Nevertheless, Lord Nicholls accepted that the s.3 HRA interpretative duty was not without limits: 'Parliament, however, cannot have intended that in the discharge of this extended interpretative function the courts should adopt a meaning inconsistent with a fundamental feature of legislation.'[129] Lord Roger made a similar point, stressing that the words implied must 'go with the grain of legislation'.[130] Thus, any interpretation adopted must not conflict with the 'essential principles' of the legislation or it would cross 'the boundary between interpretation and amendment of the statute' and go beyond the proper role of the judiciary under s.3 HRA.[131] For the majority, the 'underlying thrust' of the Rent Act 1977 was to protect the rental interests of survivors of stable relationships, regardless of sexuality. The Court proceeded to use the interpretative obligation in s.3 HRA to read the legislative provision in a way that brought same-sex partners within its protective scope.

Lord Millett delivered a strong dissenting judgment. He agreed with Lord Nicholls' analysis of the interpretative duty and commented: '[s.3] can do considerable violence to the language [of a statute] and stretch it almost (but not quite) to breaking point. The court must "strive to find a *possible* interpretation compatible with Convention rights" . . . But it is not entitled to give it

[125] See also, discussion in Chapter 14.

[126] *Ghaidan* (n 123) at [30]. This paragraph was cited with approval by Lord Reed (with whom Lords Hodge, Lloyd-Jones, Sales and Stephens agreed) in *In re United Nations Convention on the Rights of the Child (Incorporation) (Scotland) Bill* [2021] UKSC 42, [2021] 1 WLR 5106 at [25]–[26], [2021] 1 WLR 5106.

[127] Ibid. [128] Ibid at [32]. [129] Ibid at [33]. [130] Ibid at [121]. [131] Ibid.

an impossible one, however much it would wish to do so.'[132] For him, s.3 HRA does not authorise the courts to supply words which are inconsistent with a fundamental feature of the legislation.[133] His disagreement with the majority in this case concerned the 'fundamental features' of the Rent Act 1977. In his view, its fundamental feature was to provide protection to surviving spouses from different-sex relationships. He focused on the use of gender-specific language throughout all the changes to the statutory provision and concluded that these issues raised 'questions of social policy which should be left to Parliament'.[134]Lord Millett's interpretation of the fundamental feature of the Act focused far more on the wording used by the legislature than the majority and he expressed concern about the separation of powers. These different perspectives on what is 'fundamental' highlight that the inherent flexibility of language leaves the 'fundamental feature' test a potential site of contention.

There are clearly limits as to what is 'possible' under s.3 HRA and the courts will not always be able to use the interpretative duty; this reflects the fact that parliamentary sovereignty is specifically preserved in the HRA.[135] As we shall see below, the HRA also provides for declarations of incompatibility and remedial acts, which would be ineffectual if all inconsistent matters could be dealt with through the interpretative duty. Where the proposed interpretation is contrary to the fundamental feature of the legislation, the courts will not use the s.3 HRA power.[136] A further limitation is where the consequence of the interpretation is not predictable.[137] An example of where interpretation could not resolve the incompatibility is *Bellinger* v. *Bellinger.*[138] The question before the Court was whether the parties were lawfully married. The petitioner was assigned male at birth but underwent gender reassignment treatment. In 1981 she had married Michael Bellinger (who was assigned male at birth); however, s.11(c) of the Matrimonial Causes Act 1973 states that a marriage is void unless the parties are 'respectively male and female'. Lord Nicholls found that it was not possible to interpret s.11(c) so as to give effect to the petitioner's rights under Articles 8 and 12 (right to marry) ECHR which would recognise her as a woman and the marriage as valid. Lord Nicholls explained that using s.3 HRA in this way would 'represent a major change in the law, having far reaching ramifications'. These issues required extensive enquiry and wide public consultation and were 'ill-suited for determination by courts and court procedures'.[139] Moreover, Parliament had indicated that it was preparing

[132] Ibid at [67]. [133] Ibid at [68]. [134] Ibid at [101]. [135] Section 3(2)(b) and (c) HRA.

[136] See e.g., *Re S (Care Order: Implementation of Care Plan)* [2002] UKHL 10, [2002] 2 AC 291.

[137] See *R (Anderson)* v. *Secretary of State for the Home Department* [2002] UKHL 46, [2003] 1 AC 837 and Alison Young, 'Ghaidan v. Godin-Mendoza: Avoiding the Deference Trap' [2005] PL 23, pp.25–26.

[138] *Bellinger* v. *Bellinger* [2003] UKHL 21, [2003] 2 AC 467. [139] Ibid at [37].

comprehensive primary legislation on this subject. The Court thus issued a declaration of incompatibility under s.4 HRA.

There has been a lively academic debate about the extent of the power under s.3 HRA and the section itself provides little guidance about how it should be exercised. Some commentators have expressed concern that the s.3 HRA duty transgresses the separation of powers by providing the courts with too much power.[140] According to critics, it allows the courts to rewrite legislation and to adopt interpretations that fall outside the original intentions of the democratically elected legislature. In contrast, Trevor Allan argues that s.3 HRA is consistent with the primary role of the courts which is to protect fundamental constitutional values, including human rights.[141]

2.3.6 Section 4 HRA 1998: Declarations of Incompatibility

If a court is unable to provide an interpretation consistent with the ECHR, it may issue a declaration of incompatibility (DOI) under s.4 HRA. As the judiciary has no power to strike down primary legislation, if a compatible interpretation is impossible, a DOI is the only option available under the HRA. Whilst as noted above, there is some ambiguity as to how far the courts should go in striving to find a Convention-compatible interpretation, it is evident that where such an interpretation is possible, the court must interpret the provisions accordingly and s.4 HRA is only applicable where a compatible reading is not possible. The Supreme Court has thus described a DOI as 'a measure of last resort'.[142]

The power to issue a DOI is limited to certain higher courts, which include the High Court, the Court of Appeal (in England, Wales and Northern Ireland), the High Court of Justiciary and the Court of Session (in Scotland), the Judicial Committee of the Privy Council and the Supreme Court.[143] Two cases provide some understanding of the scope of s.4 HRA.

As discussed in Chapters 3 (European Framework) and 8 (Terrorism), following the 9/11 terrorist attacks in New York in 2001, the British

[140] Geoffrey Marshall, 'The Lynchpin of Parliamentary Intention: Lost, Stolen, or Startled?' [2003] PL 236, p.248; Philip Sales and Richard Ekins, 'Rights-consistent Interpretation and the Human Rights Act 1998' (2011) 127 LQR 217; Richard Ekins, 'Legislative Freedom in the United Kingdom' (2017) 133 LQR 582.

[141] Trevor Allan, 'Parliament's Will and the Justice of the Common Law: The HRA in Constitutional Perspective' (2006) 59 Current Legal Problems 27. See also, Aileen Kavanagh, 'Statutory Guidance and Human Rights After Anderson: A More Contextual Approach' (2006) 26 OJLS 179; and Young (n 137).

[142] *A and Ors* (n 55) at [44]; cited with approval by Lady Simler in *Secretary of State for Business and Trade* v. *Mercer* [2024] UKSC 12, [2024] WLR(D) 165 at [112].

[143] Section 4(5) HRA. The High Court of Justiciary cannot issue a DOI when sitting as a trial court.

Government passed the Anti-Terrorism, Crime and Security Act 2001 (ATCSA) which provided for indefinite detention without trial of non-nationals in specific circumstances. As noted in Chapter 8, such detention was not compatible with Article 5 ECHR. Consequently, on 11 November 2001, the Secretary of State made a derogation order pursuant to the HRA which set out the terms of a proposed notification to the Secretary General of the Council of Europe of a derogation from Article 5 ECHR. Several individuals subject to detention under the ATCSA challenged its lawfulness (including the lawfulness of the derogation) with the case coming before the House of Lords in 2004.[144] A majority of the Law Lords considered that the provision permitting indefinite detention did not fall within the exception to the general right of liberty set out in Article 5(1)(f) ECHR. The question, then, was whether the derogation was valid, with the House of Lords finding for the reasons canvassed in Chapter 8 that it was not.

As a declaration of incompatibility under the HRA does not alter the validity of the law and is not binding on the parties to the domestic litigation, the applicants' success in the House of Lords led neither to their immediate release nor to the payment of compensation for unlawful detention. The applicants subsequently filed a complaint before the ECtHR which is considered in Chapter 3 (European Framework) and the ensuing establishment of the control order regime is discussed in Chapter 8 (Terrorism).

It is important to note that there is no obligation to issue a DOI under s.4 HRA. It is unusual for the courts to decline to exercise their discretionary s.4 HRA power where they have found a violation of the ECHR, but they have done so in the past. For instance, in *Nicklinson*[145] the Supreme Court was required to consider whether the Suicide Act 1961, which makes it a crime to encourage or assist suicide, was incompatible with Article 8 ECHR (the right to respect for private life). Nicklinson was severely paralysed after a stroke and only able to move his head and eyes. He wished to end his own life but would not be able to do so without assistance. Only two of the nine justices were willing to consider fully the question of compatibility and would have issued a DOI. Four members of the majority – Lords Clarke, Sumption, Hughes and Reed – concluded that this issue was not suitable for a DOI. The case raised 'controversial and complex questions of fact arising out of moral and social dilemmas' and was 'a classic "polycentric problem"'.[146] Parliament has access to expertise and experience and is better able to consider the interests of unrepresented or insufficiently represented groups who were not before the courts. Thus, in their view, the Parliamentary process is a better way of resolving these issues.

[144] *A and Ors* (n 55). [145] *Nicklinson* (n 111). See also, *Re Ewart* [2020] NIQB 33.

[146] Ibid at [232], per Lord Sumption. These cases are discussed in greater detail in Chapter 6.

Three other members of the majority – Lords Neuberger, Mance and Wilson – considered that while the Court *could* make a DOI in relation to this subject matter, it would be 'institutionally inappropriate at this juncture' because of the sensitivity of the issue and as Parliament was due to debate the issue in the near future.[147] In a sentiment emblematic of the dialogic theories discussed in Chapter 1, Lord Neuberger stated that mechanisms for 'collaboration' between the courts and Parliament under s.4 HRA can be conveyed with firmness but there are times 'when an indication, rather than firm words are more appropriate and can reasonably be expected to carry more credibility'.[148] He concluded that this was such a case.

The dissenting justices, Lady Hale and Lord Kerr, took the view that the law was incompatible with Convention rights and would have issued a DOI. Lady Hale stated:

> I see little to be gained, and much to be lost, by refraining from making a declaration of incompatibility. Parliament is then free to cure that incompatibility, either by a remedial order under section 10 of the Act or (more probably in a case of this importance and sensitivity) by Act of Parliament, or to do nothing. It may do nothing, either because it does not share our view that the present law is incompatible, or because, as a sovereign Parliament, it considers an incompatible law preferable to any alternative.[149]

Lord Kerr's position was that when a court issues a declaration of incompatibility, they remit it 'to Parliament for a political decision, informed by the court's view of the law'. This does not involve the court 'making a moral choice which is properly within the province of the democratically elected legislature'.[150] In a later decision, Lord Kerr commented that: 'The circumstances in which such self-restraint should be exercised have not been comprehensively catalogued. This is understandable. Different considerations may favour reticence. Others may call for a declaration to be made.'[151]

The concerns raised by some of the judges in *Nicklinson* that a DOI could unduly influence the Parliamentary debate are puzzling.[152] After all, the DOI has no effect in law and remits the issue to Parliament for its consideration. There is no legal duty placed on the Government or Parliament to respond to a DOI. However, as discussed below, a DOI may still exert political pressure.

Shona Wilson Stark contends that the judicial approach to s.4 HRA is unsatisfactory and unduly deferential to the executive.[153] In her view, the

[147] Ibid at [116], per Lord Neuberger. [148] Ibid at [117]. [149] Ibid at [300].

[150] Ibid at [344]. [151] *R (Steinfeld)* v. *SSID* [2018] UKSC 32, [2020] AC 1 at [57].

[152] Mark Elliott and Robert Thomas, *Public Law* (4th ed) (Oxford University Press, 2020), pp.791–794. Stevie Martin, 'Declaratory Misgivings: Assisted Suicide in a Post-*Nicklinson* Context' (2018) 2 PL 209.

[153] Shona Wilson Stark, 'Facing Facts: Judicial Approaches to Section 4 of the Human Rights Act 1998' (2017) 133 LQR 631–655.

courts have shown reluctance and confusion in exercising their novel DOI power. She suggests that in contrast to the interpretative power under s.3 HRA, the courts should be willing to look more broadly, beyond the instant case, when deciding whether to issue a DOI.[154] She persuasively argues that the HRA does not demand that there is a victim before s.4 HRA can be used, especially as s.4 HRA provides no remedy for an applicant.[155] Consequently, she concludes that 'the courts have conflated the rationale of s.4 with the rationale of ss.3 and 6–8'.[156] In contemplating this judicial reluctance, it is important to reiterate that a DOI has no effect on 'the validity, continuing operation or enforcement of the provision'.[157] Nor is it binding on the parties to the proceedings in which it is made.[158] Given the limited legal effect of a DOI, it is unsurprising that s.3 HRA is seen as the primary remedial remedy.

A DOI has only one legal effect, namely that it may trigger the power of the executive to issue remedial orders under s.10 HRA.[159] Section 10 HRA permits a government to enact secondary legislation amending the incompatible provision. A further trigger for s.10 HRA arises where it appears to a Minister that UK legislation is incompatible with the ECHR by virtue of a decision of the ECtHR.[160] In these circumstances, the Minister can exercise a discretion where 'he considers that there are compelling reasons' for doing so, to make such amendments to the legislation as he considers necessary to remove the incompatibility.[161] Thus s.10 HRA enables the Executive, by way of secondary legislation, to amend primary legislation which is not compatible with the ECHR.[162]

Public oversight of DOIs is through the Parliamentary Joint Committee on Human Rights. The Committee notes all decisions involving the issuing of a DOI and the response of the Government. There is, therefore, an expectation that the Government will respond to a DOI and it has certainly done so in the past. One reason why the Government responds to DOIs is that if the incompatibility is not removed, an application to the ECtHR could be expected. It is also highly likely that the ECtHR would agree with senior courts in the UK and find a breach of the ECHR. Such a finding of a violation by the ECtHR would legally bind the UK in international law to implement the judgment. A DOI may have no legal effect, but it can exert a powerful political one. During the

[154] Ibid at [631].

[155] Note also, *Re Northern Ireland Human Rights Commission's Application for Judicial Review* [2018] UKSC 27, [2019] 1 All ER 173, and see the discussion of this decision in Chapter 6.

[156] Wilson Stark (n 153), p.654. [157] HRA, s.4(6)(a). [158] HRA, s.4(6)(b).

[159] Elliott and Thomas (n 152), p.787. [160] HRA, s.10(1)(b).

[161] HRA, s.10(2) and Schedule 2.

[162] This is an example of the exercise of a Henry VIII power. Lord Irvine, during debates on the HRA, argued that remedial orders under the HRA do not represent a threat in constitutional terms as the power is only invoked to protect rights and not to interfere with them. Hansard, HL, vol.582, col.1231 (3 November 1997).

debates in Parliament on the Human Rights Bill, Jack Straw described a DOI as an 'unexploded bomb' landing in a Minister's room.[163]

Since the HRA came into force in 2000 until the end of July 2023, forty-seven DOIs have been issued. Of these, forty-four have been addressed: eleven by remedial orders, sixteen by primary or secondary legislation, five related to provisions that had already been amended by primary legislation at the time of the DOI, whilst twelve were overturned on appeal.[164] From August 2022 to July 2023 the Government responded to the JCHR in relation to its responses to DOI in seven cases.[165] It made legislative changes through remedial orders in three cases to remove the incompatibility and announced its intention to address an inconsistency through a remedial order in a fourth. The Supreme Court set aside the DOI in one case[166] and the Northern Ireland Court of Appeal did so in another.[167] The Government is still considering its response in the seventh case. Since the publication of the 2023 report, DOIs have been issued in relation to provisions in some highly controversial legislation including, the Illegal Migration Act 2023,[168] the Northern Ireland Troubles (Legacy and Reconciliation) Act 2023[169] and the Criminal Justice and Public Order Act 1994.[170]

2.3.7 Section 6 HRA 1998: Acts of Public Authorities and the HRA

2.3.7.1 Public Authorities

Section 6(1) of the HRA states: 'it is unlawful for a public authority to act in a way which is incompatible with a Convention right'. This is subject to two exceptions set out in s.6(2) HRA the effect of which is that the duty under s.6 (1) HRA will not apply where primary legislation requires them to act in an incompatible manner or the authority is acting to give effect to or enforce

[163] HL Select Committee on the Constitution, Judicial Appointments Process (Oral and Written Evidence) Q. 133 (2011). See also, Wilson Stark (n 153).

[164] Ministry of Justice: Responding to Human Rights Judgments 2022–2023, CP 958 (November 2023), Annex A: All Declarations of Incompatibility.

[165] Ministry of Justice: Responding to Human Rights Judgments 2022–2023: CP 958, 34.

[166] *R* v. *Marks, Morgan, Lynch and Heaney* [2023] UKSC 14, [2024] AC 130.

[167] *In the matter of an application by JR123 for judicial review* [2023] NICA 30, but the Northern Ireland Minister of Justice plans to introduce changes to the system by way of secondary legislation in light of the concerns of the court at first instance.

[168] *In the Matter of an Application by the NIHRC for Judicial Review* (n 91).

[169] See both the High Court and Court of Appeal judgments in *Re Dillon & Ors* (n 91). Sections were also found to be incompatible with Article 2 of the Windsor Framework and pursuant to s.7A European Union (Withdrawal) Act 2018 and they were disapplied. See Chapter 4 for a discussion of some of the problematic aspects of the Act and the judgment of the Northern Ireland courts.

[170] *R (Smith)* v. *Secretary of State for the Home Department* [2024] EWHC 1137 (Admin).

provisions which cannot be read compatibly under the HRA.[171] Section 6 HRA is thus a key provision of the HRA as it places a legal obligation on public authorities, including the courts, to ensure that all decisions and administrative acts are compliant with Convention rights. In this way, human rights have influenced and affected innumerable decisions and acts of public authorities since the HRA was enacted.

Pursuant to s.6 HRA, Convention rights can be directly enforced against public authorities: a new statutory right of action founded on breach of a Convention right has been established. Judicial review proceedings can also be brought against public authorities and acts and decisions can be quashed (provided s.6(2) HRA is not applicable) if found to be incompatible with rights. Section 6 HRA has thus extended the judicial review powers of the courts and provided for more intensive review as a result of the proportionality standard that applies in respect of the ECHR.

The term 'public authority' is not defined in the HRA, but some insight can be gleaned from s.6(3) HRA which specifically excludes 'either House of Parliament or a person exercising functions in connection with proceedings in Parliament' from the obligation under s.6(1) HRA. While s.6(6) HRA states that a failure to introduce in, or lay before, Parliament a proposal for legislation or to make any primary legislation or remedial order is not included. In contrast to the provisions exempting Parliament, s.6(3) HRA expressly provides that courts and tribunals *are* public authorities for these purposes, as well as 'any person certain of whose functions are functions of a public nature' (unless the nature of the impugned act is private – per s.6(5) HRA).

Thus s.6 HRA creates two categories of public authority. The first comprises the 'core' or 'pure' public authorities, such as government departments, local authorities, the police and the armed forces – all their actions must be compatible with human rights and there is no need to decide whether acts are public or private. The second category comprises 'hybrid' bodies that perform a mixture of public and private functions. Their acts will only fall under s.6 HRA if the function in issue is of a public nature. In contrast to core public authorities, hybrid ones also have Convention rights and can bring claims under the HRA.[172]

The issue of 'core' and 'hybrid' public authorities was first addressed by the House of Lords in *Aston Cantlow*.[173] Mr and Mrs Wallbank, the defendants, were the proprietors of a farm. Under an archaic rule, the Parochial Church Council (PCC) served a notice on the defendants to meet the substantial costs of repair to the chancel of the local church. The defendants contended that this

[171] Section 6(2)(a) and (b) HRA.

[172] *Aston Cantlow and Wilmcote with Billesley Parochial Church Council* v. *Wallbank* [2003] UKHL 37, [2004] AC 546, per Lord Nicholls at [11].

[173] Ibid.

demand breached Article 1 of Protocol 1 ECHR (the protection of property) but, to rely on this Convention right, it was necessary to demonstrate that the PCC was a public authority for the purposes of s.6 HRA. According to Lord Nicholls, a public authority is a body 'whose nature is governmental in a broad sense of that expression . . . Behind the instinctive classification of these organisations as bodies whose nature is governmental lie factors such as the possession of special powers, democratic accountability, public funding in whole or in part, an obligation to act only in the public interest, and a statutory constitution.'[174] In determining a 'hybrid' public authority, Lord Nicholls noted that there was no universal test but he suggested factors which may be taken into account would include 'the extent to which in carrying out the relevant function the body is publicly funded, or is exercising statutory powers, or is taking the place of central government or local authorities, or is providing a public service'.[175]

In *Aston Cantlow*, the House of Lords concluded that the PCC was not a 'core' public authority but a hybrid public authority as it provided some public services, for example church services, weddings and funerals. As discussed above the impact of s.6(5) HRA is that a hybrid public authority is not bound by s.6(1) HRA when engaged in private acts. The Court concluded that in 'seeking to enforce a civil debt' – the liability for chancel repairs – the PCC was acting in a private capacity.[176] Thus on the facts, the PCC was not a public authority pursuant to s.6 HRA and the defendants were unable to reply upon Convention rights to dispute their liability.

2.3.7.2 *Contracting Out and Privatisation*

The 'hollowing out of the State'[177] and the delegation of governmental power to private parties has become a common feature of governance. The performance of important governmental functions and essential public services are increasingly trusted to private actors such as charities, corporations and associations. This delegation takes many different forms. One common form of privatisation in the UK is the transfer of Government assets to private companies or actors.[178] In other circumstances, privatisation is achieved through outsourcing by the Government of certain functions, although the responsibility for the delivery of those functions is maintained. Examples include residential care for the elderly, foster placements of children and

174 Ibid at [7]. 175 Ibid at [12].

176 Ibid at [16], per Lord Nicholls and [64], per Lord Hope.

177 See R. Rhodes, 'The Hollowing Out of the State: The Changing Nature of the Public Service in Britain' [1994] 65(2) Political Quarterly 138.

178 Utilities, such as gas and electricity, have been transferred to private companies and competition between them is encouraged and regulatory oversight has been established.

adoption agencies. Prisons and immigration centres have also been privatised.[179] Difficult issues have arisen when the performance of a function is moved to the private sphere through privatisation and contracting out. In commenting on the tangled inter-relationship between public and private bodies, Paul Craig argued that '[i]t is difficult to see why the nature of a function should alter if it is contracted out, rather than being performed in house. If it is a public function when undertaken in house, it should equally be so when contracted out.'[180] The courts, however, have not accepted this straightforward understanding.

The courts have considered the nature of hybrid public authorities, contracting out and s.6 on a number of occasions.[181] In *Donoghue* v. *Poplar Housing* (*Poplar*)[182] the issue was whether a housing association – a registered charity that had been created and assisted by a local authority to take over a publicly funded service – was carrying out a public function. The association sought to evict one of its tenants who argued that her rights under Article 8(1) ECHR – right to respect for private life, family and home – would be breached if she were evicted. Lord Woolf suggested that in order to make an otherwise private act a public one, there must be 'a feature or a combination of features which impose a public character or stamp on the act'.[183] Such public characteristics may include statutory authority for the task carried out; the degree of control exercised by the public body; and how closely the acts in question are 'enmeshed in the activities of the public body'. On the facts of this case, the Court found that the housing association was a hybrid public authority exercising a public function because of its close association with the local authority.

YL v. *Birmingham City Council*[184] illustrates how difficult it is to draw this public/private distinction. YL was eighty-four years old and suffering from Alzheimer's disease. The National Assistance Act 1948 imposes an 'essential duty on the State to provide care and accommodation for the needy'. In order to discharge its statutory duty, Birmingham City Council contracted with Southern Cross Healthcare Ltd for the care of YL and she moved into one of their care homes. The accommodation of the care home was paid largely at public expense. After a dispute with her family, Southern Cross decided to terminate the contract and evict YL from the care home. The appellant argued

[179] Daphne Barak-Erez, 'The Private Prison Controversy and the Privatization Continuum' (2011) 5 Law and Ethics of Human Rights 138. See also, *LW & Ors v. Sodexo Ltd* [2019] EWHC 367 (Admin), [2019] 1 WLR 5654.

[180] Paul Craig, 'Contracting Out, the Human Rights Act and the Scope of Judicial Review' (2002) 118 LQR 551, at 556.

[181] Stephanie Palmer, 'Public Functions and Private Services: A Gap in Human Rights Protection' (2008) 6 International Journal of Constitutional Law 3–4.

[182] *Donoghue* v. *Poplar Housing* (*Poplar*) [2001] EWCA (Civ) 595, [2002] QB 48.

[183] Ibid at [65].

[184] *YL* v. *Birmingham City Council* [2007] UKHL 27, [2008] 1 AC 95.

that the termination of the contract was a breach of Article 8 ECHR. For this argument to succeed, it had to be shown that Southern Cross was exercising a public function. By a slim 3:2 majority, the House of Lords decided that a privately owned care home, operating on a for-profit commercial basis and acting pursuant to a contract with a local authority, could not be deemed to be a hybrid public authority under s.6(3)(b) HRA. The majority and minority judges disagreed on the nature of the function that was being performed. In determining whether a function is 'public' within the meaning of s.6(3)(b) HRA, Lord Neuberger commented that these words 'are so imprecise in their meaning that one searches for a policy as an aid to interpretation'.[185] The majority judges adopted the classical liberal distinction between public (state) and private (economically self-interested individuals). They were not persuaded by the argument that the care was being paid for out of public funds. While this might be a *necessary* condition for activities classified as public functions, it was not itself a decisive factor and could only be given limited weight.[186] Lord Mance (with whom Lords Scott and Neuberger concurred) distinguished between the statutory duty of a local authority to arrange care and accommodation and a private company delivering the services on a commercial basis after contracting with the local authority. He commented that 'the actual provision, as opposed to the arrangement, of care and accommodation' is not an inherently governmental function.[187]

Lady Hale, in dissent, described this distinction as 'artificial and legalistic', given that the State had assumed responsibility for both meeting needs and arranging care.[188] According to Lord Bingham (also dissenting), the detailed contractual arrangements between the parties were 'a matter of little or no moment'.[189] Both minority judges placed emphasis on the context and policy of social welfare in the UK: while private arrangements could be made for the delivery of care and accommodation, this function should still be considered public when 'performed pursuant to statutory arrangements'.[190] As Lord Bingham observed, the HRA is intended to give effective protection to Convention rights in domestic law and it is therefore 'appropriate to give a generously' wide expression to 'public function' in s.6(3)(b) HRA.[191] Lady Hale had no doubt that Parliament intended that this function carried out under 'statutory arrangements, at public expense and in the public interest' should be covered by s.6(3)(b) HRA.[192]

The *YL* decision was widely criticised.[193] Following the decision, Parliament amended the law, which effectively reversed the decision in relation to care

[185] Ibid at [141]. [186] Ibid at [142] and [148]. [187] Ibid at [115]. [188] Ibid at [66].

[189] Ibid at [16]. [190] Ibid at [66], per Lady Hale. [191] Ibid at [4]. [192] Ibid at [73].

[193] Joint Committee on Human Rights, Legislative Scrutiny: Health and Social Care Bill, HC 46/ HL 303, 2007–2008; Palmer (n 181), Alex Williams, 'A Fresh Perspective on Hybrid Public

homes.[194] In many other situations, where services have been contracted-out, the *YL* decision remains the leading authority.

2.3.8 Obligations under the HRA and Private Parties

The rights set out in the ECHR are not expressed to apply only in relation to the State, and the Convention case law imposes positive obligations on States to ensure that Convention rights are respected. Thus, on many occasions the ECtHR has recognised that private individuals as well as agents of the State are capable of infringing Convention rights.[195] There are also broader considerations that suggest Convention rights apply between private parties. Article 1 ECHR requires States to secure to everyone within their jurisdiction their rights and freedoms under the Convention. It would not be possible to secure the effective exercise of rights if there is no protection from interference by other individuals.

When the HRA was enacted, there was thus considerable debate as to whether the Convention rights would be applied directly in cases concerning private parties. The debate exposed varying ideas about the ECHR and its relationship with the State and highlighted some of the complexities that arise when interweaving an international treaty into domestic law. As Elliott and Thomas have observed,[196] for some commentators, Convention rights would only be effective vertically under the HRA[197] while at the other end of the spectrum, Wade argued that the HRA would confer full horizontal effect on Convention rights.[198] Wade's argument centred on the fact that s.6(3) includes 'courts and tribunals' as public authorities and therefore they are required by s.6(1) to act in a Convention-compliant way *in all cases*. Hunt and Phillipson adopted a more nuanced approach. Hunt posited that all existing law, including the common law, must be applied in a way to give effect to Convention rights but it does not require the courts to fill any lacuna by creating new causes of action.[199] Phillipson suggested that whilst the Convention rights would not have full horizontal effect, the

Authorities under the Human Rights Act 1998; Private Contractors, Rights Stripping and "Chameleonic" Horizontal Effect' [2011] PL 139.

194 Health and Social Care Act 2008, s.145; Care Act 2014, s.73.

195 See, for instance, the discussion of the obligation to put in place regulatory frameworks deterring violations by private persons in Chapters 4 (Right to Life) and 7 (Modern Slavery).

196 Elliott and Thomas (n 152), pp.801–802.

197 Richard Buxton, 'The Human Rights Act and Private Law' (2000) 116 LQR 48. See also, *R (on the application of Weaver)* v. *London and Quadrant Housing Trust* [2009] 4 All ER 865, [2010] 1 WLR 363.

198 William Wade, 'Horizons of Horizontality' (2000) 116 LQR 217.

199 Murray Hunt, 'The "Horizontal Effect" of the Human Rights Act' [1998] PL 423.

law should be developed in cases between private parties to reflect ECHR values and principles.[200]

Today it is evident that claims can only be brought directly under the HRA against public authorities. It is not possible for private individuals or organisations to bring proceedings pursuant to s.6 HRA against other private parties alleging a breach of their Convention rights. This is because s.6 HRA makes it unlawful for public authorities to act incompatibly with Convention rights. A person who qualifies as a victim, who claims a breach of s.6(1) may bring proceedings against a public authority under the HRA or by relying on Convention rights in any legal proceedings, as set out under s.7(1)(a) and (b) HRA. Although an action pursuant to the HRA for a Convention breach by a private party cannot be brought directly against a private individual or organisation, there are circumstances in which the Convention rights will be applicable in cases between private parties.

2.3.8.1 *Private Parties and Legislative Obligations*

If the dispute is governed by statute, private parties can use the s.3 HRA interpretative power which operates even if a public authority is not a party to the proceedings. This obligation requires all legislation to be read and given effect, so far as it is possible to do so, compatibly with the Convention rights. The *Ghaidan* case,[201] which was discussed above, provides a good example of how Convention rights can be relevant in a dispute between private parties. The Supreme Court interpreted the Rent Act 1977 in a way to ensure that the Article 8 ECHR rights of the tenant were guaranteed as against landlords.

2.3.8.2 *Private Parties and the Common Law*

Second, the HRA affects the relations between private parties through s.6 HRA, which requires all public authorities, including the courts and tribunals, to uphold Convention rights.[202] This shapes the development of the common law where courts are entitled to have regard to the Convention, even where they are not obliged to apply the Convention in disputes between private parties. There are limits to this as s.6(2) HRA provides that it is not unlawful for a public authority, including courts and tribunals, to act incompatibly with Convention rights where this is required by either primary legislation or where it is necessary to give effect to primary legislation. Consequently, the courts will still have to decide whether a particular course, and the requirement to

[200] Gavin Phillipson, 'The Human Rights Act, "Horizontal Effect" and the Common Law: A Bang or a Whimper (1999) 62 MLR 824.

[201] *Ghaidan* v. *Godin-Mendoza* (n 123).

[202] HRA, s.6(3)(a).

grant or refuse relief, is one that is open to them to take. The courts must still consider their constitutional role even when acting under s.6 HRA.[203]

This indirect effect is not an entirely new occurrence. Even before the HRA came into force there were examples of the courts using Convention rights to develop the common law, albeit not in a consistent way.[204] In the decades that have followed the coming into force of the HRA it is evident that whilst the Convention rights are not directly applicable against private parties there are some contexts, such as the law of misuse of private information, where the common law has evolved in a manner that largely replicates the Convention rights.[205] Thus, Convention principles and values can profoundly influence the way courts develop or interpret the law between private parties.

2.3.9 Who May Bring Proceedings? The 'Victim' Requirement

Section 7 of the HRA sets out who is entitled to claim under s.6 HRA that a public authority has acted, or proposes to act, in a way which is incompatible with Convention rights. The test is drawn from the requirements for standing under the ECHR. Article 34 ECHR states that a 'victim' (an individual who is directly affected by behaviour which is not Convention compliant) is entitled to bring a claim for a breach of Convention rights, and the HRA mirrors this formulation. As discussed further in Chapter 3 (European Framework), Article 34 has been interpreted broadly by the Strasbourg organs.[206] Article 34 ECHR also provides that claims can be made by individuals, NGOs or groups of individuals.[207]

The courts are directed by the HRA to adopt the same meaning of 'victim' as that applied by the ECtHR.[208] A 'victim' may bring proceedings in the appropriate court or rely upon Convention rights in any legal proceedings, or where a Convention issue is raised on appeal.[209] Different rules of standing apply with respect to the Equality and Human Rights Commission (EHRC) and the NIHRC which have the power to institute and intervene in legal proceedings whether for judicial review or other proceedings.[210]

[203] See, e.g., *Re S(Children) (Care Order: Implementation of Care Plan)* [2002] UKHL 10, [2002] 2 AC 291.

[204] See, e.g., *Derbyshire City Council* v. *Times Newspapers Ltd.* [1992] QB 770 (CA); *Attorney General* v. *Guardian Newspapers* [1987] UKHL 13, [1987] 1 WLR 1248; *Middlebrook Mushrooms* v. *TGWU* [1993] ICR 612; *Rantzen* v. *MGN* [1994] QB 670.

[205] See discussion in Chapter 10. See also *Abbasi v. Newcastle upon Tyne NHS Foundation Trust* [2025] UKSC 15; [2025] 2 WLR 815 at [88]–[94].

[206] David Harris, Michael O'Boyle, Ed Bates and Carla M. Buckley, *Harris, O'Boyle and Warbrick: Law of the European Convention on Human Rights* (5th ed) (OUP, 2023), p.88.

[207] See, also the discussion of the standing of groups in climate litigation discussion in Chapter 4 (Right to Life).

[208] HRA, s.7(7).

[209] HRA, s.7(1) and s.7(3).

[210] Equality Act 2006, s.30 (EHRC); NIA 1998, ss.69, 70 and 71 (NIHRC).

The standing requirement under the HRA is narrower than the 'sufficient interest' standard applied in judicial review.[211] Thus there are now two different standing tests in domestic law and there is some illogicality with this position.[212] Complaints under s.6 HRA are limited to 'victims'. But other complainants who bring judicial review claims buttressed by ss.3 or 4 HRA or common law rights may rely on the more liberal 'sufficient interest' test.[213] There is no apparent restriction on standing where a claimant relies on s.3 or s.4 HRA.[214] The 'victim test' is premised on the idea that an individual claimant will be best placed to argue the case,[215] although this may not always be the situation. In contrast, it is suggested that the law of judicial review often involves wider values and policy interests including holding Government accountable and safeguarding the rule of law rather than a focus on an individual.[216] Yet HRA cases may also raise these wider public law issues, which makes it harder to justify the more limited test. During parliamentary debates, Lord Lester of Herne Hill stated that the wider test adopted in judicial review proceedings 'has the advantage of enabling all relevant matters at issue to be determined together at an early stage in order to clarify whether there has been a misuse of public powers, including an abuse involving a violation of human rights. I am not aware of any instances of abuse that would justify excluding such public interest proceedings in human rights cases.'[217] The rationale for the exclusion of public interest challenges under the HRA appears to lie in the fear that campaign groups would use the HRA to challenge the policies of public authorities.

2.3.10 Remedies

Article 13 ECHR, which confers a right to an effective remedy, is not one of the Convention rights listed in s.1 HRA. During the progress of the HR Bill through

[211] Supreme Court Act 1981, s.31(3).

[212] Joanna Miles, 'Standing under the Human Rights Act 1998: Theories of Rights Enforcement and the Nature of Public Law Adjudication' (2000) **59** CLJ 133 at 143. Neil Garnham, 'A Sufficient Victim? Standing and the Human Rights Act' (1998) **4**(1) JR 39.

[213] Elliott and Thomas (n 152), p. 806. See also *R (Rusbridger)* v. *Her Majesty's Attorney General* [2003] UKHL 38, [2004] 1 AC 357 at [21].

[214] Though note the majority's findings with respect to the NIHRC's standing in ss.3 and 4 HRA cases in *In the Matter of an Application by the Northern Ireland Human Rights Commission for Judicial Review (Northern Ireland)* [2018] UKSC 27, [2018] HRLR 14. Parliament subsequently sought to confirm that the NIHRC *could* bring proceedings under ss.3 and 4 without the need for an actual victim by amending s.71(2B) of the NIA to explicitly refer to 'proceedings which rely on section 7(1)(b) of the Human Rights Act 1998'.

[215] See e.g. *Ghaidan* v. *Godin-Mendoza* (n 123) discussed in Section 2.3.5. Note also Ronah McQuigg, 'The Victim Test under the Human Rights Act 1998 and Its Implications for Domestic Violence Cases' (2011) EHRLR **294**.

[216] Beatson et al. (n 93), p.334.

[217] Hansard, HL Vol. 583, col 823 (November 24, 1997).

Parliament, its omission was explained by the Lord Chancellor: s.8 HRA would provide an effective domestic remedy for breaches of Convention rights and thus there was no need for this right to be included.[218]

Pursuant to s.8 HRA, '[i]n relation to any act (or proposed act) of a public authority which the court finds is (or would be) unlawful, it may grant such relief or remedy, or make such order, within its powers as it considers just and appropriate'. In addition to the usual powers possessed by courts in judicial review proceedings (including, for instance, quashing orders and declarations),[219] a court also has the specific interpretive power in s.3 HRA and can make declarations regarding the interpretation to be given to a specific provision(s).[220] Additionally, a DOI under s.4 HRA is itself a remedy, though note that the ECtHR has held that a DOI is not an effective remedy for the purposes of the requirement in Article 34 ECHR that domestic remedies must be exhausted before an application can be made to the ECtHR.[221] A court may also make an award of damages against a public authority,[222] though there are specific limitations to compensation awards set out in s.8 and s.9 HRA, the effect of which are summarised in *De Smith's* as follows:

(1) Damages may only be awarded by a court which has the power to do so in civil proceedings;
(2) The award of damages must be necessary to afford just satisfaction to the claimant. In determining whether an award is necessary, the court will have regard to the availability of alternative remedies.
(3) The court is required to take into account the principles applied by the ECtHR in awarding compensation under Article 41.[223]
(4) The court should not award exemplary or punitive damages. The court may award damages for psychological damages, anxiety and distress. The ECtHR will award damages for proven pecuniary losses, but will generally make no award for the loss of an opportunity.
(5) Domestic courts have begun to rely more on tortious scales of damages on the basis that the injury for which recovery is sought is frequently the same (for example to bodily integrity or liberty) whether the claim is brought in tort or under the HRA. Under this approach, now widely

[218] HL Official Report, 18 November 1997, vol. 583, col.475 cited in Feldman (n 9), p.102.

[219] In respect of which, see *De Smith's Judicial Review* (n 24) at 18-001.

[220] See *Ghaidan* v *Godin-Mendoza* (n 123).

[221] *Burden* v. *the United Kingdom* (2008) 27 EHRR 38 at [40].

[222] As Lord Kerr observed in *Commissioner of Police of the Metropolis* v. *DSD and Anor* [2018] UKSC 11, [2019] AC 196 at [2], '[t]he combined effect of [ss.7 and 8 HRA] (so far as [a case for compensation] is concerned)... is to allow a person who claims that a public authority has acted in a way which is incompatible with their rights under the [ECHR] to bring proceedings against the public authority and to be awarded damages'.

[223] In respect of which, see Chapter 3.

followed, tortious principles form the starting point and the Strasbourg doctrine is used merely as a check to ensure that recovery under the HRA does not become completely out of step with the approach of the ECtHR.[224]

2.3.11 Human Rights and Parliamentary Procedure: Statements of Compatibility and the Joint Committee on Human Rights

Section 19 HRA introduced a new parliamentary procedure to provide additional protection for human rights. As primary legislation remains valid even if incompatible with Convention rights, Parliament must give careful consideration to any issues of compatibility. This section requires a Minister in charge of presenting a bill to Parliament to make a statement, before the bill's second reading, as to whether it is compatible with human rights. The purpose of this procedure is 'to make the human rights implications of proposed Government legislation more transparent'.[225] Even if a Minister declares that a bill is compatible with the HRA, this is no guarantee that it is so and the judiciary can still assess whether the legislation is incompatible with protected rights.[226] Section 19 HRA also provides for the possibility that a positive statement on compatibility cannot be provided. In these circumstances a Minister must explain to Parliament why they are unable to provide a statement of compatibility to ensure that the human rights implications are debated. The Minister will indicate that despite being unable to issue a positive statement, the Government nevertheless wishes to proceed with the bill.[227] Thus, Parliament should be fully aware of any potential violation, such that it cannot inadvertently enact incompatible legislation.

One of the first occasions on which the Government introduced a bill without a positive statement of compatibility concerned the Communications Act 2003 and restrictions on political advertising. The Government explained to Parliament why it had decided to balance the right to free speech in Article 10 ECHR and other interests in a particular way. When the legislation was challenged in the House of Lords, weight was accorded to the judgement of Parliament:

> Parliament has resolved, uniquely since the 1998 [HRA] came into force . . ., that the prohibition of political advertising on television and radio may possibly, although improbably, infringe article 10 but has nonetheless resolved to proceed under section 19(1)(b) of the Act. It has done so, while properly recognising the interpretative supremacy of the European Court, because of the importance which it attaches to

224 *De Smith's Judicial Review* (n 24) at 19-080. For a guide as to the range of compensation for breaches of particular rights, see ibid at 19-082 to 19-096.

225 Home Department, *Rights Brought Home: The Human Rights Bill*, HMSO 1997 Cm.3782.

226 *R* v. *A* [2001] UKHL 25, [2001] 1 AC 45 at [69], per Lord Hope.

227 HRA, s.19(1)(b).

maintenance of this prohibition. The judgment of Parliament on such an issue should not be lightly overridden.[228]

When the ECtHR subsequently considered this it also attached 'considerable weight' to the 'exacting and pertinent reviews' conducted by both Parliament and domestic judicial bodies and found no violation of the Convention.[229] A thorough parliamentary debate and careful consideration by domestic courts thus insulated the legislation against a successful challenge in Strasbourg. More recently, the 2015–2024 Conservative Government introduced highly controversial legislation – the Illegal Migration Act 2023 and the Safety of Rwanda (Asylum and Immigration) Act 2024 – without providing a positive statement of compatibility. These Acts of Parliament disapplied large sections of the HRA and, as a consequence, would have been far more vulnerable to a successful Strasbourg challenge. On 30 January 2025, the Labour Government introduced into Parliament the Border Security, Asylum and Immigration Bill that will repeal the Safety of Rwanda (Asylum and Immigration) Act 2024 and most (but not all) of the provisions of the Illegal Migration Act 2023.

The Joint Committee on Human Rights also scrutinises all Government bills to ensure compatibility with human rights commitments.[230] The Committee's reports make an important contribution to the upholding of human rights standards. The Committee may take (and has done so) a different view from that of the Minister about the compatibility of a bill's provisions and this ensures that Members of Parliament will be cognisant of contrary viewpoints. A further factor which emphasises the value of the Joint Committee's work is that their reports are considered and taken into account by the courts.[231]

2.3.12 Proposed Repeal/Reform of HRA 1998

Under the 2015–2024 Conservative Government, there were repeated attempts to curtail rights including a proposal that the HRA be repealed and replaced with a British Bill of Rights.[232] The rights contained in the proposed British Bill of Rights were, in fact, largely the same as those contained in the ECHR. The only additional right proposed was a right to a jury trial. There was no mention of including any other rights such as socio-economic rights. Yet, whilst it

[228] *R (Animal Defenders International)* v. *Secretary of State for Culture, Media and Sport* [2009] UKHL 15, [2009] 1 AC 908 at [33], per Lord Bingham.

[229] *Animal Defenders International* v. *the United Kingdom* [2013] 57 EHRR 21 at [116].

[230] See David Feldman, 'Parliamentary Scrutiny of Legislation and Human Rights' [2002] PL 232.

[231] See e.g. *A and Ors* v. *Secretary of State for the Home Department* [2004] UKHL 56, [2005] 2 AC 68 at [22], [24] and [26].

[232] Bill of Rights Bill 2022.

included the same rights, the proposed Bill of Rights offered less protection to those rights. The Conservative Government's stated purpose was to 'make sure a proper balance is struck between individuals' rights, personal responsibility, and the wider public interest'.[233] The proposals thus sought to recast the relationship between the courts, Parliament, the Executive and the ECtHR.

Ultimately, following several changes of Prime Minister, the Bill of Rights Bill was withdrawn. There could be no doubt, however, that the Conservative Government remained committed to curtailing rights, as evidenced by numerous pieces of legislation, which are discussed in the ensuing chapters.[234] Following its success at the 2024 General Election, the Labour Party has reaffirmed its commitment to human rights, including the ECHR and has undertaken to repeal some of the more problematic statutes, including the Northern Ireland Troubles (Legacy and Reconciliation) Act 2023.[235]

2.4 COMMON LAW RIGHTS SINCE THE HRA

Common law rights did not cease to exist after the HRA came into force and they have continued to evolve alongside the HRA though, since the enactment of the HRA, applicants have tended to focus primarily on Convention rights rather than the common law. Yet, in the 2010s, common law rights enjoyed 'something of a resurgence'[236] which may, at least partly, have been a judicial response to the 2010 Conservative Party pledge to repeal and replace the HRA with a British Bill of Rights.[237] The Supreme Court began to focus explicitly upon the common law as a vehicle to protect rights and fundamental values.[238] The Independent Human Rights Act Review (IHRAR) also recommended increasing the prominence of the common law.[239]

This development led Lady Hale to suggest 'UK constitutionalism' is 'on the march' as 'there is emerging a renewed emphasis on the common law and distinctively UK constitutional principles as a source of legal inspiration'.[240]

In 2010 in *Kennedy*, in relation to the applicant's decision to base an argument about the Charity Commissioner's refusal to disclose information in the HRA rather than the common law, Lord Toulson stated:

[233] The Lord Chancellor, Mr D. Raab, HC. vol. 705, col. 915, 14 December 2021.

[234] See, for instance, the Illegal Migration Act 2023, the Northern Ireland Troubles (Legacy and Reconciliation) Act 2023 and the Safety of Rwanda (Asylum and Immigration) Act 2024.

[235] *Change*, Labour Party Manifesto 2024.

[236] *De Smith's Judicial Review* (n 24) at 6-056.

[237] *Invitation to Join the Government of Britain*, The Conservative Manifesto 2010.

[238] Mark Elliott, 'Beyond the European Convention on Human Rights and the Common Law' (2015) **68** Current Legal Problems 1, 92.

[239] IHRAR at [185]–[200].

[240] Lady Hale, 'UK Constitutionalism on the March?' [2014] JR 201, 201.

The growth of the state has presented the courts with new challenges to which they have responded by a process of gradual adaptation and development of the common law to meet current needs. This has always been the way of the common law and it has not ceased on the enactment of the Human Rights Act 1998, although since then there has sometimes been a baleful and unnecessary tendency to overlook the common law. It needs to be emphasised that it was not the purpose of the Human Rights Act that the common law should become an ossuary.[241]

Indeed, it was suggested that litigants should turn *first* to the common law before considering Convention rights. As Lord Mance indicated: '[T]he natural starting point in any dispute is to start with domestic law, and it is certainly not to focus exclusively on the Convention rights, without surveying the wider common law scene.'[242]

Access to justice continues to be strongly protected by the common law post-HRA. In 2017, the Supreme Court delivered an important judgment on access to justice in *R (Unison)* v. *Lord Chancellor*, a case which concerned fees for the bringing and continuing of claims in the Employment Tribunals.[243] The evidence indicated that the fees resulted in a 'dramatic and persistent fall' in the number of people taking their cases to the Employment Tribunals and it was argued that this impeded access to justice.[244] The Supreme Court found that the Order was unlawful. The Court used the presumption in favour of access to justice to interpret the legislation and concluded that individuals must have unimpeded access to courts and tribunals in order to be able effectively to enforce their rights. Lord Reed stated:

When Parliament passes laws creating employment rights, for example, it does so not merely in order to confer benefits on individual employees, but because it has decided that it is in the public interest that those rights should be given effect. It does not envisage that every case of a breach of those rights will result in a claim before an [Employment Tribunal]. But the possibility of claims being brought by employees whose rights are infringed must exist, if employment relationships are to be based on respect for those rights.[245]

The rule of law also requires that judicial review be available to provide redress in cases in which the executive deviates from the law.[246] As a consequence, access to justice is inherent in the rule of law. According to Lord Reed:

Courts exist in order to ensure that the laws made by Parliament, and the common law created by the courts themselves, are applied and enforced. That role includes ensuring that the executive branch of government carries out its functions in accordance with the law. In order for the courts to perform this role people must in principle have unimpeded access to them. Without such access, laws are liable to become a dead letter, the work done by Parliament may be rendered nugatory and the democratic

[241] *Kennedy* v. *Information Commissioner* [2014] UKSC 20, [2015] AC 455 at [133].
[242] Ibid at [46]. [243] *R (Unison)* v. *Lord Chancellor* [2017] UKSC 51, [2020] AC 869.
[244] Ibid at [39]. [245] Ibid at [70]–[72]. [246] Ibid at [61].

election of Members of Parliament may become a meaningless charade. That is why the courts do not merely provide a public service like any other.[247]

These principles were confirmed in *R (Privacy International)* v. *Investigatory Powers Tribunal*[248] where Lord Carnwath stated:

I see a strong case for holding that, consistently with the rule of law, binding effect cannot be given to a clause which purports wholly to exclude the supervisory jurisdiction of the High Court to review a decision of an inferior court or tribunal, whether for excess or abuse of jurisdiction, or error of law.[249]

The relationship between common law rights and the ECHR was specifically considered in *R (Jalloh)* v. *Secretary of State for the Home Department.*[250] The Supreme Court declined to accept the Secretary of State's argument that the common law notion of 'imprisonment' for the purposes of the tort of false imprisonment should be aligned with Article 5(4) ECHR. It held that the concept of 'deprivation of liberty' adopted by the ECtHR is different from that developed in the common law. Imprisonment for the purpose of false imprisonment could be very short whereas several factors had to be considered in determining whether there was a deprivation of liberty pursuant to Article 5 ECHR. As Lady Hale stated:

what [counsel for the Secretary of State] is asking this Court to do is not to develop the law but to make it take a retrograde step: to restrict the classic understanding of imprisonment at common law to the very different and much more nuanced concept of deprivation of liberty under the ECHR. ... There is no need for the common law to draw such a distinction and every reason for the common law to continue to protect those whom it has protected for centuries against unlawful imprisonment.[251]

The courts have, however, displayed reticence in expanding the common law. *R (Elgizouli)* v. *Secretary of State for the Home Department*[252] concerned a challenge to the UK sharing information with the USA about suspected terrorists, without receiving the usual assurances that the information given would not facilitate the imposition of the death penalty. The majority rejected the existence of such a principle under the common law. Lord Reed emphasised that the common law develops by 'building on [existing principles] incrementally rather than making more dramatic changes which are the prerogative of the legislature'.[253] He also commented on the existence of

[247] Ibid.

[248] *R (Privacy International)* v. *Investigatory Powers Tribunal* [2019] UKSC 22, [2020] AC 491.

[249] Ibid at [144].

[250] *R (Jalloh)* v. *Secretary of State for the Home Department* [2020] UKSC 4, [2021] AC 262.

[251] Ibid at [33].

[252] *R (Elgizouli)* v. *Secretary of State for the Home Department* [2020] UKSC 10, [2021] AC 937.

[253] Ibid at [170]. The UKSC was, nevertheless, unanimous in finding that sharing the information was unlawful under the Data Protection Act 2018.

constraints on judicial law-making due to 'procedural and institutional limitations which restrict the ability of litigation before the courts to act as an engine of law reform'.[254]

Mark Elliott has questioned whether common law rights provide the same level of protection as Convention rights. He measured common law rights and the HRA against three separate criteria: 'the normative reach of the system, the rigour with which it equips courts to uphold rights, and the degree of constitutional resilience that rights exhibit in the face of adverse legislative or administrative action'.[255] In doing so, Elliott concluded that 'if the common law has been invigorated by the [HRA], then that, at least in part, is because the Act has served to highlight the capacity of the common law'.[256] More recently, Elliott and Hughes have expressed scepticism about the operation of common law rights. They point to both 'significant limitations to the way that common law constitutional rights have functioned in the past and the way that they operate today' and thus concluded that the 'overall picture that emerges ... is of a patchy and limited framework for rights protection'.[257]

2.5 CONCLUSION

The HRA protects fundamental rights through a legally unentrenched statute which does not formally disrupt the traditional constitutional underpinnings of the UK constitution. In particular, it leaves undisturbed the doctrine of parliamentary sovereignty. Parliament remains free to legislate contrary to Convention rights, and the judiciary may not strike down primary legislation. Although the HRA does not legally limit parliamentary sovereignty, it has imposed constraints on what a Government can achieve. Thus, in practice, the operation of the HRA has affected the political scope for legislative interference with rights, by making the ECHR the standard for assessment by the judiciary. Significant political pressure can be placed on the Government through a DOI, if the judiciary have found that the ECHR has been violated. In the past the Government has responded positively to a DOI, although in some circumstances, especially during the prisoner voting saga, the Government has taken years to comply.[258]

[254] Ibid at [105] and [142]. Lord Kerr dissented and relied upon six factors to support the recognition of such a principle. See also, the discussion of institutional critiques in Chapter 1.

[255] Elliott (n 238), p.85.

[256] Ibid, p.117.

[257] Mark Elliott and Kirsty Hughes (eds), *Common Law Constitutional Rights* (Hart, 2020), p.16.

[258] Minstry of Justice, 'Responding to human rights judgments: 2022 to 2023', 13 November 2023, https://assets.publishing.service.gov.uk/media/654cf01c014cc9000d677371/responding-human-rights-judgments-2022_2023.pdf. See also, Conall Mallory and Hélène Tyrrell, 'Discretionary Space and Declarations of Incompatibility' (2021) 32 King's Law Journal 3.

In this way, the HRA has affected the dynamic between the political and legal constitution. For example, in the HRA s.4, Parliament has invited the judiciary 'to tell it that it has acted wrongly by legislating incompatibly with a Convention right'.[259] The extension of judicially protected rights has moved the judiciary into a new arena and led to an increase in legal constitutionalism. Although the HRA does not give the courts the power to strike down Acts of Parliament, it has effectively placed a subtle political restraint on the orthodox understanding of the concept of parliamentary sovereignty. Until recently, no Government has sought to pass legislation which is specifically non-Convention compliant without reasoned grounds for doing so. This changed when the Conservative Government introduced into Parliament what would become the Illegal Migration Act 2023 and the Safety of Rwanda (Asylum and Immigration) Act 2024. The Conservative Government was willing to use primary legislation to remove the opportunity for the judiciary to assess the Convention compatibility of its policies, thereby interrupting the relationship between legal and political concepts of constitutionalism which had developed since the HRA came into force.

The HRA never resolved the tension between the binding nature of ECHR rights in international law and the constitutional freedom of the sovereign UK Parliament to override human rights as a matter of domestic law. The HRA system is reliant upon a political commitment to preserve human rights, and this political will depends upon the Government of the day. In recent years there have been developments which called into question the previous Conservative Government's commitment to human rights and its political willingness to remain a member of the Council of Europe. The UK now has a new Labour Government which claims to support the Convention and the UK's membership of the Council of Europe. Although human rights perhaps appear to be on a more secure footing for the moment in the UK, human rights guarantees remain precarious and the future of the ECHR as a seminal part of the UK's Constitution still remains uncertain and subject to fluctuating political intentions.

[259] Feldman (n 9), p.91.

3 The European Human Rights Framework

CONTENTS

3.1 INTRODUCTION

In this chapter we examine the history and operation of European Human Rights law. This chapter provides insight into how the ECHR and the ECtHR emerged, how they have evolved and how this relates to the different conceptions of the role of Human Rights law considered in Chapter 1. This chapter thus examines how the ECtHR processes cases and how it interprets rights, as the way in which the ECtHR approaches those tasks is fundamental to the relationship between the ECtHR and States. Indeed, it is the interpretation of rights and the processing of cases that have been the focus of reform of the Convention system. The various reform measures adopted are intended to ensure the effective operation of an institution that has seen its workload grow exponentially and to preserve the continuing participation of States. The processes for derogating from rights and the suspension, expulsion and withdrawal from the ECtHR are further important aspects of the relationship between the Court and the Contracting States which are considered in this chapter.

3.2 HISTORICAL DEVELOPMENT OF THE COUNCIL OF EUROPE AND THE EUROPEAN CONVENTION ON HUMAN RIGHTS

3.2.1 International Origins of the Council of Europe and the European Convention on Human Rights

The origins of the Council of Europe and the ECHR can be traced to the post-Second World War period and the growth of interest in international human rights law.[1] In 1948, the United Nations sought to respond to the atrocities that had been committed both during and prior to the war by identifying fundamental rights and freedoms. This resulted in the proclamation of the UDHR in Paris on 10 December 1948 'as the common standard of achievement for all peoples and all nations'.[2] The UDHR set out fundamental human rights to be universally protected, but it was not a legally binding treaty and it had no direct enforcement mechanism. It was, however, an essential moment in a process of transforming aspirations into law, and later years saw many of the rights identified in the UDHR translated into treaties.[3] Today, the UDHR 'has inspired more than 80 international human rights treaties and declarations, a great number of regional human rights conventions, domestic human rights bills, and constitutional provisions'.[4]

[1] On the origins and history of the ECHR, see Ed Bates, *The Evolution of the European Convention on Human Rights: From Its Inception to the Creation of a Permanent Court of Human Rights* (Oxford University Press, 2020); Steven Greer and Lewis Graham, 'Europe' in Daniel Moeckli et al., *International Human Rights Law* (4th ed) (Oxford University Press, 2024); D. J. Harris et al., *Harris, O'Boyle and Warbrick Law of the European Convention on Human Rights* (5th ed) (Oxford University Press, 2023); Bernadette Rainey et al., *The European Convention on Human Rights* (8th ed) (Oxford University Press, 2020), ch. 1; Alistair Mowbray, *Cases, Materials and Commentary on the European Convention on Human Rights* (3rd ed) (Oxford University Press, 2012), ch. 1; and Mark W. Janis et al., *European Human Rights Law* (Oxford University Press, 2018), chs. 1–3. For the history of human rights law, see Ed Bates, 'History' in Daniel Moeckli et al., *International Human Rights Law* (4th ed) (Oxford University Press, 2024). On the Council of Europe, see Ganna Yudkivska, 'Council of Europe' in Anne van Aaken (ed), *The Oxford Handbook of International Law in Europe* (Oxford University Press, 2024) and Robert Blackburn, 'The Institutions and Processes of the Convention' in Robert Blackburn and Jörg Polakiewicz (eds), *Fundamental Rights in Europe* (Oxford University Press, 2001). On the role of Human Rights in Europe, see Başak Çali, 'Human Rights Ideas, Law and Institutions in Europe' in Anne van Aaken (ed), *The Oxford Handbook of International Law in Europe* (Oxford University Press, 2024).

[2] United Nations General Assembly Resolution 217 A, A/RES/3/217 A, 10 December 1948.

[3] United Nations International Covenant on Civil and Political Rights, adopted 16 December 1966 by United Nations General Assembly Resolution 2200A (XXI), entry into force 23 March 1976, United Nations International Covenant on Economic, Social and Cultural Rights, adopted 16 December 1966 by United Nations General Assembly Resolution 2200A (XXI), entry into force 3 January 1976.

[4] United Nations Universal Declaration of Human Rights: The Foundations of International Human Rights Law, www.un.org/en/about-us/udhr/foundation-of-international-human-rights-law#:~:text=Foundation%20for%20Our%20Common%20Future,rights%20are%20expressed%20and%20guaranteed.

3.2.2 Creation and Structure of the Council of Europe

The Council of Europe was created in the same period and was formally established in 1949 by the Statute of the Council of Europe.[5] At the time, there were ten members: Belgium, Denmark, France, Ireland, Italy, Luxembourg, Netherlands, Norway, Sweden and the United Kingdom. Greece and the Republic of Turkey (today Türkiye)[6] joined shortly thereafter in August 1949. Over the decades since then, the Council has expanded significantly and at the time of writing there are forty-six Member States, all of which have signed up to the European Convention on Human Rights. (It is a condition of Council of Europe membership that States ratify the ECHR.) Until 2022, there were forty-seven members, but, as discussed below, Russia has recently left the Council of Europe following its military aggression in Ukraine. In addition to members, there are six Observer States (Canada, Holy See, Israel, Japan, Mexico and the United States of America). Any State may be granted observer status if it is willing to accept the principles of (i) democracy; (ii) the rule of law; (iii) the enjoyment by all persons within its jurisdiction of human rights and fundamental freedoms; and (iv) if it is willing to co-operate with the Council of Europe.[7] The Council of Europe has developed a vast body of human rights treaties, including the European Convention on Human Rights, the European Social Charter, the Council of Europe Convention on Violence against Women and Domestic Violence, and the Council of Europe Convention on Action against Trafficking in Human Beings.

Governance of the Council of Europe primarily comprises the Committee of Ministers, Parliamentary Assembly, and the Congress of Local and Regional Authorities. The Committee of Ministers consists of the ministers of foreign affairs from each Member State or their permanent diplomatic representatives in Strasbourg. They determine the Council of Europe's policy and approve its budget and programme of activities. The Parliamentary Assembly is made up of over 300 Members of Parliament from the Member States of the Council of Europe. Amongst other things, the Parliamentary Assembly elects the Secretary General and Deputy Secretary General, the Human Rights Commissioner and the judges of the ECtHR. The Secretary General and Deputy Secretary General are each elected for five-year terms,

[5] For further discussion of the development of the Council of Europe, see (n 1).

[6] In 2022 following an official letter submitted to the United Nations by the Republic of Türkiye, the country's name was officially changed to Türkiye at the UN. The European Court of Human Rights has also used the official name Türkiye since 2022. See European Court of Human Rights Country Press File, *Türkiye*, January 2025.

[7] Council of Europe Statutory Resolution (93) 26 on Observer Status adopted by the Committee of Ministers on 14 May 1993 at its 92nd Session. See also Conor Gearty, 'The Council of Europe and Israel' [2024] EHRLR 104–111.

and are responsible for leading and representing the organisation, strategic planning and direction. The Human Rights Commissioner is responsible for: fostering the effective observance of human rights, and assisting Member States in the implementation of Council of Europe human rights standards; promoting education in and awareness of human rights in Council of Europe Member States; identifying possible shortcomings in the law and practice concerning human rights; facilitating the activities of national ombudsperson institutions and other human rights structures; and providing advice and information regarding the protection of human rights across the region.[8] The Commissioner fulfils that mandate by engaging in country-specific visits to Member States, thematic work and awareness raising. In 2022, the Commissioner, Dunja Mijatović, visited the UK and reported that 'both the overall system for protecting human rights, and the rights of specific groups, are currently under pressure in the United Kingdom'.[9] In particular, she raised concerns about freedom of assembly, the rights of travelling communities, refugees, asylum seekers, migrants, the trans community and children's rights, particularly socio-economic rights and child poverty. The Commissioner also raised grave concerns in respect of Northern Ireland, including the implications of the Legacy and Reconciliation legislation, the security of the Belfast/Good Friday Agreement, concerns about the safety of journalists, and the failure to ensure sexual and reproductive health rights.[10] In her 2023 Report, she published a letter sent to the Speakers of the House of Commons and the House of Lords warning that what was then the 'Illegal Migration Bill' creates 'clear and direct tension with well-established and fundamental human rights safeguards'[11] and expressing grave concern that preventing irregular migrants from claiming asylum 'would strip away one of the essential building blocks of the protection system'.[12] In 2025 the current Commissioner, Michael O'Flaherty, focused on child poverty and expressed concern about 'the management of irregular migration, restrictions on the right to protest, the situation of trans people, and the legacy of the Troubles in Northern Ireland.[13]

[8] Council of Europe Resolution (99) 50 on the Council of Europe Commissioner for Human Rights, entry into force 07/05/1999. According to this resolution, the Commissioner is mandated to promote education in, awareness of and respect for human rights.

[9] Council of Europe, *Commissioner for Human Rights of the Council of Europe, Report Following Her Visit to the United Kingdom from 27 June to 1 July 2022* (Strasbourg, 18 November 2022), CommDH (2022)27.

[10] Ibid.

[11] Council of Europe, *Commissioner for Human Rights of the Council of Europe, Dunja Mijatović, Annual Activity Report 2023* (Strasbourg, 22 January 2024), CommHR(2024)3, p.13.

[12] Ibid.

[13] Council of Europe, *Visit to United Kingdom: tackling poverty is crucial to protect children's human rights; a number of other areas call for attention.(Strasbourg, 8 July 2025).*

3.2.3 Creation of the European Convention on Human Rights and the Focus on Civil and Political Rights

Although the Council of Europe is portrayed in some quarters of the press, and by some politicians, as an institution that has been foisted upon the UK, in fact the UK was one of the 'founding fathers' of the Council of Europe. Winston Churchill was at the forefront of its creation declaring at the time that in the aftermath of the Second World War:

> The dangers threatening us are great but great too is our strength, and there is no reason why we should not succeed in achieving our aims and establishing the structure of this united Europe whose moral concepts will be able to win the respect and recognition of mankind, and whose physical strength will be such that no one will dare to hold up its peaceful journey towards the future.[14]

A core component of that 'peaceful journey' was the development of the ECHR which the UK, represented by Sir David Maxwell-Fyfe, was highly involved in drafting.[15] When the ECHR opened for signature in Rome on 1 November 1950, the UK was an early signatory and was the first State to ratify it in March 1951.[16] The ECHR came into force in 1953. It was the first instrument to give binding legal effect to some of the rights stated in the UDHR.

The original Convention rights were the right to life; prohibition on torture and inhuman and degrading treatment or punishment; prohibition on slavery, servitude, forced or compulsory labour; right to liberty; right to a fair trial; right to private life, family life, home and correspondence; right to freedom of expression; right to freedom of association and assembly; right to freedom of religion and belief; right to marry and the right of non-discrimination. The ECHR was subsequently supplemented by additional protocols, such as the protocols abolishing the death penalty.[17] As we will discuss later in this chapter, and as you will see throughout the book, an essential feature of the ECHR is the ECtHR's living instrument approach to interpretation as this has enabled the ECtHR to interpret the original Convention rights in line with

[14] Council of Europe, *Winston Churchill and the Council of Europe*, Winston Churchill attends the First Session of the Consultative Assembly, transcript of 12 August 1949, www.coe.int/en/web/documents-records-archives-information/winston-churchill-and-the-ce (last accessed 12 August 2024).

[15] On the drafting of the Convention, see chapters 3 and 4 in Bates, *Evolution of the European Convention* (n 1).

[16] A. W. B. Simpson, *Human Rights and the End of Empire* (Oxford University Press, 2001), p.2.

[17] Council of Europe – Protocol No. 6 to the Convention for the Protection of Human Rights and Fundamental Freedoms concerning the Abolition of the Death Penalty (ETS No. 114) abolishing the death penalty in peacetime, entered into force on 01/03/1985. Council of Europe – Protocol No. 13 to the Convention for the Protection of Human Rights and Fundamental Freedoms concerning the Abolition of the Death Penalty in all circumstances (ETS No. 187), entered into force on 01/07/2003.

contemporary values. Consequently, rights such as Article 8 ECHR – the right to respect for private life, family life, home and correspondence – have been interpreted to provide protection to same-sex relationships and gender recognition that would not be possible on an originalist interpretation of the text.[18]

Yet, as discussed in Chapter 1, whilst the ECHR rights have evolved significantly, it is important to emphasise that the text of the Convention focused upon civil and political rights and did not include the social, economic and cultural rights that had featured in the UDHR. One possible explanation for that omission is that the drafters of the ECHR thought that social rights were non-justiciable or that they were secondary compared to civil and political rights.[19] A further explanation, advanced by Marco Duranti, is that it was the very presence of the United Kingdom Conservative politicians in the drafting of the Convention which led to the focus on civil and political rights and exclusion of social and economic rights, in contradiction to the European focus at the time upon the developing welfare state.[20]

Since its enactment, the civil and political focus of the ECHR has remained strong, but there have been significant developments in the case law in respect of socio-economic rights. Indeed, as long ago as 1979 the ECtHR recognised that:

> Whilst the Convention sets forth what are essentially civil and political rights, many of them have implications of a social or economic nature. The Court therefore considers, like the Commission, that the mere fact that an interpretation of the Convention may extend into the sphere of social and economic rights should not be a decisive factor against such an interpretation; there is no water-tight division separating that sphere from the field covered by the Convention.[21]

This dictum was proclaimed long before the HRA 1998 was enacted.[22] Yet the expansion of the Convention rights remains controversial as some regard this as overreach on the part of the ECtHR into matters that remain within the purview of the democratically accountable institutions within States. Others take the view that there is a core element to socio-economic rights that is a legitimate part of the ECtHR's role in protecting the most vulnerable in Europe.[23]

[18] *Smith and Grady* v. *the United Kingdom* (1999) 29 EHRR 493.

[19] Simpson (n 16), p.483.

[20] Marco Duranti, 'Curbing Labour's Totalitarian Temptation: European Human Rights Law and British Postwar Politics' (2012) 3 Humanity: An International Journal of Human Rights, Humanitarianism, and Development 3, 362.

[21] *Airey* v. *Ireland* (1979–80) 2 EHRR 305 at [26]. The ECtHR in its Admissibility Decision repeated this dicta in *Stec* v. *United Kingdom* (2005) 41 EHRR SE18 295 at [52].

[22] For analysis of *Airey* and its significance see chapter 8 in Bates, *Evolution of the European Convention* (n 1) in which he highlights the 'groundbreaking' role of *Airey* in the development of a Court in the 1970s which 'unequivocally rejected a dogmatic view that the human rights protected by the Convention must always be negative rights with no possible financial implications, or with no duty on the State's part to do anything except abstain from harmful acts', p.346.

[23] See, for example, Ingrid Leijten, *Core Socio-Economic Rights and the European Court of Human Rights* (CUP, 2018).

3.3 THE OPERATION OF THE EUROPEAN COURT OF HUMAN RIGHTS

Of crucial importance to the success of the ECHR are the mechanisms for examining alleged violations.[24] Three institutions were initially tasked with implementing the ECHR: the European Commission of Human Rights, the European Court of Human Rights and the Committee of Ministers of the Council of Europe. The European Court of Human Rights was established in 1959 and it delivered its first judgment in 1960 in *Lawless* v. *Ireland*.[25] States were not, however, obliged to allow for the right of individual petition and the jurisdiction of the Court was optional. In fact, it was not until 1990 that all Contracting States had accepted the jurisdiction of the ECtHR. Following the entry into force of Protocol No. 11 in 1998, the Commission and the Court were merged into a single permanent Court (hereafter ECtHR). Today over 25,000 judgments and 30,000 decisions have been delivered. Judgments are binding on the State concerned, but as we will discuss further below, non-compliance is a major concern.

3.3.1 Composition and Structure of the Court

The ECtHR is comprised of forty-six judges, one from each Member State,[26] and each judge is elected to a single non-renewable term of nine years. Hugh Mercer KC has recently been elected as the United Kingdom judge. The electoral process is set out in Article 22 ECHR, which provides that the Parliamentary Assembly elects a judge from a list of three candidates nominated by the High Contracting Party. Since 2004, the Parliamentary Assembly of the Council of Europe has required States' lists of potential judges to contain at least one candidate from the sex that is underrepresented on the Court at the time;[27] however, in 2020 Keller and colleagues observed that whilst initially the number of female judges at the Court rapidly rose, today, there are still fewer women on the Strasbourg bench than men and the number of female judges is now declining.[28]

[24] For an overview of the operation and structure of the ECtHR, see also Harris et al. (n 1), ch.3; Rainey et al. (n 1), ch. 2; Pieter van Dijk et al., *Theory and Practice of the European Convention on Human Rights* (5th ed) (Intersentia, 2018); and Janneke Gerards, *General Principles of the European Convention on Human Rights* (2nd ed) (Cambridge University Press, 2023), ch.2.

[25] *Lawless* v. *Ireland* (1979) 1 EHRR 1.

[26] Article 20 ECHR.

[27] Parliamentary Assembly of the Council of Europe, 'Candidates for the European Court of Human Rights,' Resolution 1366 (2004), as modified by Resolutions 1426 (2005), 1627 (2008), 1841 (2011), and 2002 (2014).

[28] Helen Keller et al., 'Fifty Years of Women at the European Court of Human Rights: Successes and Failures of the Council of Europe's Gender Agenda' in Freya Baetens (ed), *Identity and Diversity on the International Bench: Who Is the Judge?* (Oxford University Press, 2020).

The Parliamentary Assembly can reject the list provided by the High Contracting Party, and it has done so on occasion.[29] One of the forty-six judges serving on the ECtHR is elected by the plenary Court as President of the ECtHR for a period of three years; at the time of writing, the President is Marco Bošnjak (Slovenia) who replaced Síofra O'Leary (Ireland) on 2 July 2024.

A crucial component of the entire operation of the ECtHR is the Registry, which provides vast legal and administrative support.[30] Its primary function is to process applications lodged before the ECtHR. There are thirty-three case-processing divisions and the lawyers in the Registry prepare the files and notes for the judges. The Registry consists of over 600 legal, administrative, technical staff and translators. It is overseen by the Registrar and the Deputy Registrar, who are elected to those roles by the ECtHR. Each of the Sections of the ECtHR are also assisted by a Section Registrar and Deputy Section Registrar.

The ECtHR operates in different formations depending upon the stage of proceedings. Cases that are manifestly inadmissible can be dealt with by a single judge. This was introduced by Protocol 14 to help clear the backlog of cases.[31] A single judge can thus declare a case inadmissible or strike it out. A single judge cannot, however, declare a case admissible. Consequently, potentially admissible cases have to be referred to a Committee (three judges) or a Chamber (seven judges).[32] Committees have the power to declare cases inadmissible or strike out cases. Following the Protocol 14 reforms, Committees can also consider the merits of repetitive cases, declare them admissible and render judgment if there is well-established case law.[33] Beyond these situations, decisions on both admissibility and the merits are taken by a Chamber (seven judges) or in certain circumstances by the Grand Chamber (seventeen judges).

In addition to these various formations, the ECtHR has a priority policy for processing cases with a view to speeding up the system and concentrating

[29] See Nobert Engel, 'More Transparency and Governmental Loyalty for Maintaining Professional Quality in the Election of Judges to the European Court of Human Rights' (2013) HRLJ **448**. On the process of electing judges, see also, Koen Lemmens, '(S)electing Judges for Strasbourg: A (Dis)appointing Process?' and David Kosař, 'Selecting Strasbourg Judges: A Critique' in Michal Bobek (ed), *Selecting Europe's Judges: A Critical Review of the Appointment Procedures to the European Courts* (Oxford University Press, 2015) and Harris et al. (n 1), pp.113–118.

[30] Under Article 24 ECHR, the task of the Registry is to provide legal and administrative support to the Court in the exercise of its judicial functions. On the role of the Registry see Harris et al. (n 1), ch.3, in particular at p.119.

[31] Council of Europe, Protocol No. 14 to the Convention for the Protection of Human Rights and Fundamental Freedoms, amending the control system of the Convention (Strasbourg, 13. V.2004), Council of Europe Treaty Series No. 194.

[32] Articles 26 and 27 ECHR. [33] Article 28 ECHR.

resources on the most important cases. This triage system was adopted in 2009 and was revised in 2017. The list of priorities is as follows:[34]

I. **Urgent** applications (in particular risk to life or health of the applicant, the applicant deprived of liberty as a direct consequence of the alleged violation of his or her Convention rights, other circumstances linked to the personal or family situation of the applicant, particularly where the well-being of a child is at issue, application of Rule 39 of the Rules of Court)
II. Applications raising questions capable of having an **impact on the effectiveness of the Convention system** (in particular a structural or endemic situation that the Court has not yet examined, pilot-judgment procedure) or applications raising an **important question of general interest** (in particular a serious question capable of having major implications for domestic legal systems or for the European system)
III. Applications which on their face raise as main complaints issues under **Articles 2, 3, 4 or 5 § 1** of the Convention ("core rights"), irrespective of whether they are repetitive, and which have given rise to direct threats to the physical integrity and dignity of human beings
IV. Potentially well-founded applications based on other Articles
V. Applications raising issues already dealt with in a pilot/leading judgment ('well-established case-law cases')
VI. Applications identified as giving rise to a problem of admissibility
VII. Applications which are manifestly inadmissible

When cases are considered by a Chamber, a Judge Rapporteur is nominated by the President of the Section. It is often the case that the judge from the respondent State is appointed as the Judge Rapporteur, on the basis that they will have the greatest understanding of the domestic legal framework, but the Court may choose not to make the national judge the Rapporteur in politically sensitive cases.[35] The Judge Rapporteur is responsible for presenting the application to the Chamber. Cases are then communicated to the respondent State and the respondent State is invited to submit observations. Once the State's observations are received, the applicant is given an opportunity to respond, following which the State is given a further opportunity to make submissions before the case is considered by the Chamber. The Chamber will typically examine the admissibility and the merits together.

At the apex of the ECtHR is the Grand Chamber, which consists of seventeen judges and hears only the most important cases. There are two processes by which cases arrive at the Grand Chamber. The first is where a Chamber relinquishes a case to the Grand Chamber before giving judgment.[36] The

[34] See European Court of Human Rights, 'The Court's Priority Policy', available at www.echr.coe.int/documents/d/echr/Priority_policy_ENG (last accessed 12 August 2024).

[35] Helen Keller and Corina Heri, 'Deliberation and Drafting: European Court of Human Rights (ECtHR)' (last updated May 2018) in A. Peters and R. Wolfrum (eds), *The Max Planck Encyclopedia of Public International Law* (Oxford University Press, 2008–), www.mpepil.com (last accessed 12 August 2024).

[36] Article 30 ECHR.

second is where a Chamber has given judgment but one of the parties requests a referral to the Grand Chamber.[37] Upon receipt of a referral, the Grand Chamber convenes a panel of five judges in order to determine whether to accept or reject the request by reference to whether it raises a 'serious question affecting the interpretation or application of the Convention or the Protocols thereto, or a serious issue of general importance'.[38] To date, the Grand Chamber has delivered approximately 500 judgments and its case law spans across the rights.

3.3.2 Who Can Bring Proceedings?

There are two types of applications which can be lodged with the ECtHR. *Inter-State applications* are cases in which one contracting State party alleges breaches by one of the other State parties to the Convention. *Individual applications* may be made by individuals, non-governmental organisations or a group of individuals with victim status.

3.3.2.1 Inter-State Applications

Inter-State applications are relatively rare compared to the tens of thousands of individual applications, but they are of fundamental and growing importance.[39] As a former judge, Judge Spielmann has observed the inter-State application is of 'intrinsic importance' as it 'casts the European Court of Human Rights in the very important role of guarantor of the peaceful public order in the greater Europe'. This is particularly so where action is brought by one or more States 'seeking to uphold the rights that are the benchmark of the modern democratic state'.[40]

Inter-State applications are governed by Article 33 ECHR which provides that any High Contracting Party may refer to the ECtHR any alleged breach of the provisions of the Convention by another State party to the Convention.

[37] Article 43 ECHR.

[38] Article 43 ECHR. See also, Council of Europe, Registry of the European Court of Human Rights, *Practice followed by the Panel of the Grand Chamber when deciding on Requests for Referral under Article 43 of the Convention* (2021); this is prepared by the Registry and is not binding on the Court.

[39] On inter-State applications, see further, Isabella Risini and Tim Eicke, 'Inter-state Applications under the European Convention on Human Rights: Situating the Instrument in the Current Human Rights Landscape' (2024) 13 International Human Rights Law Review 41–73; and Isabella Risini, *The Inter-state Application under the European Convention on Human Rights: Between Collective Enforcement of Human Rights and International Dispute Settlement* (Brill, 2018).

[40] Dean Spielmann, 'The European Court of Human Rights as Guarantor of a Peaceful Public Order in Europe', Speech to Gray's Inn, 12 November 2014, available at www.echr.coe.int/documents/d/echr/Speech_20141107_Spielmann_GraysInn (last accessed 12 August 2024).

When the ECHR was first enacted, neither the right of individual petition, nor the jurisdiction of the ECtHR were mandatory, but States were obliged to accept inter-State applications to the Commission. The Commission would report to the Committee of Ministers and the Committee could issue binding decisions. The first inter-State application was brought by Greece in 1956 against the UK.[41] It concerned practices in Cyprus of whipping, arbitrary arrest, detention and deportation, breaking into houses and censorship of correspondence.[42]

Former Judge of the ECtHR Dean Spielmann has suggested that inter-State cases tend to come in waves, and that certainly seems to be true at present. In recent years there has been a vast rise in the number of inter-State applications.[43] Indeed, as of April 2025 there are fifteen inter-State applications pending before the ECtHR.[44] An application was lodged by Ireland against the UK in January 2024.[45] The scale of the pending cases is evident if we compare the number of pending cases with the fact that only twenty-three inter-State applications have been completed by the ECtHR since 1956.[46]

Almost all inter-State applications stem from conflict situations and often raise numerous complex issues. The 2024 GC judgment in *Ukraine* v. *Russia (re Crimea)* found a multitude of breaches of Convention rights.[47] Russia invaded Crimea in 2014 and Ukraine claimed the Russian occupation led to a systemic campaign of repression, which included: disappearances; ill-treatment; unlawful detention; impossibility to opt out of Russian citizenship; suppression of Ukrainian media and of the Ukrainian language in schools;

[41] *Greece* v. *the United Kingdom*, App. No. 176/56, 02/06/1956.

[42] See Simpson (n 16), pp.924–987.

[43] On the rise of inter-State applications and the challenges this poses, see Risini and Eicke (n 39); Philip Leach, 'On Inter-state Litigation and Armed Conflict Cases in Strasbourg' [2021] ECHRLR 27; and Kanstantsin Dzehtsiarou and Vassilis P. Tzevelekos, 'The Aggression against Ukraine and the Effectiveness of Inter-state Cases in Case of War' [2022] ECHRLR 165.

[44] The European Court of Human Rights provides a list of pending and completed inter-State applications on its website, www.echr.coe.int/inter-state-applications (last accessed 15 April 2025). Recent cases include *Azerbaijan* v. *Armenia*, App. No. 47319/20, lodged on 27/10/20; *Azerbaijan* v. *Armenia (II)*, App. No. 39912/22, lodged on 18/08/22; *Armenia* v. *Azerbaijan*, App. No. 42521/20, lodged on 27/09/20; *Armenia* v. *Azerbaijan (II)*, App. No. 33412/21, lodged on 29/06/21; *Armenia* v. *Azerbaijan (III)*, App. No. 42445/21, lodged on 24/08/21; *Armenia* v. *Azerbaijan (IV)*, App. No. 15389/22, lodged on 24/03/22; *Ukraine and the Netherlands* v. *Russia*, App. Nos. 8019/16, 43800/14 and 28525/20, lodged on 25/01/2023; The GC handed down its judgment on the merits on (9 July, 2025). *Ukraine* v. *Russia (VIII)*, App. No. 55855/18, lodged on 29/11/18; *Ukraine* v. *Russia (IX)*, App. No. 10691/21, lodged on 19/02/21; *Armenia* v. *Türkiye*, App. No. 43517/20, lodged on 04/10/20; *Liechtenstein* v. *the Czech Republic*, App. No. 35738/20, lodged on 19/08/20; *Ireland* v. *the United Kingdom (III)*, App. No. 1859/24, lodged on 17/01/2024; and *Slovakia* v. *Belgium*, App. No. 6187/25, lodged on 27/02/25.

[45] *Ireland* v. *the United Kingdom (III)*, App. No. 1859/24, lodged on 17/01/2024.

[46] ECtHR list of inter-State applications (n 44).

[47] *Ukraine* v. *Russia (re Crimea)* [GC], App. Nos. 20958/14 and 38334/18, 25/06/2024.

pre-trial detention in overcrowded conditions; prosecution and conviction on fabricated charges without a fair trial in reprisal for any pro-Ukrainian stance. A further inter-State application arising from a conflict situation is the *Ireland* v. *the United Kingdom* proceedings,[48] lodged in 1971, in respect of the actions of the UK in Northern Ireland during the period that is euphemistically known as 'The Troubles'.[49] We will examine this case further in Chapter 5, but in sum it concerned the use of five interrogation techniques by the UK in Northern Ireland, namely: hooding, stress position, white noise, sleep deprivation and deprivation of food and water. In 1978, the ECtHR held that these practices violated Article 3 ECHR as they constituted inhuman and degrading treatment, but that they did not constitute torture. A request for revision of that judgment in 2018 was dismissed by six votes to one (the Irish judge dissented).[50] The 2024 *Ireland* v. *the United Kingdom* application also relates to that conflict. In particular, it concerns the Northern Ireland Troubles (Legacy and Reconciliation) Act 2023 the stated purpose of which is to address the legacy of 'The Troubles' and promote reconciliation.[51] The Irish Government argued that certain provisions of the Act are incompatible with the Convention, in particular, Articles 2, 3, 6, 13, and 14. In July 2024, the newly elected UK Government announced that it is committed to repealing and replacing the 2023 legislation and is hoping to find a way of dealing with this issue leading to a withdrawal of the inter-State case brought by Ireland.[52] Further examples of the inter-State application in the context of conflict include Turkey's military operations in northern Cyprus in 1974,[53] armed conflict between Georgia and Russia in 2008,[54] hostilities between Azerbaijan and Armenia,[55] and Russia's ongoing military operations in Ukraine.[56]

[48] *Ireland* v. *the United Kingdom*, App. No. 5310/71, Commission, 01/10/1972 and *Ireland* v. *the United Kingdom*, App. No. 5310/71, Court, 18/01/1978.

[49] A conflict in Northern Ireland that lasted from the late 1960s to 1998. See Brice Dickson, *The European Convention on Human Rights and the Conflict in Northern Ireland* (Oxford University Press, 2010).

[50] *Ireland* v. *the United Kingdom*, App. No. 5310/7, 20/03/2018.

[51] *Ireland* v. *the United Kingdom* (2024) (n 45).

[52] Hilary Benn, Secretary of State for Northern Ireland, Hansard Vol. 752, Cols. 657–658, 24 July 2024. In December 2024 the Government proposed a Remedial Order to amend the Northern Ireland Troubles (Legacy and Reconciliation Act) 2023. In February 2025 the Joint Committee on Human Rights issued its report in which it welcomed the proposed Remedial Order whilst also identifying three areas where the Government should make improvements before it proceeds.

[53] *Cyprus* v. *Turkey*, App. Nos. 6780/74 and 6950/75, 26/05/1975.

[54] *Georgia* v. *Russia (No.II)* [GC], App. No. 38263/08, 21/01/2021.

[55] Pending cases: *Azerbaijan* v. *Armenia*, App. No. 47319; *Armenia* v. *Azerbaijan*, App. No. 42521/20; *Armenia* v. *Turkiye*, App. No. 43517/20. Armenia alleges Türkiye provided assistance to Azerbaijan during hostilities.

[56] *Ukraine* v. *Russia (VIII)*, App. No. 55855/18 concerns the Kerch Strait naval incident in 2018; *Ukraine and the Netherlands* v. *Russia*, App. Nos. 8019/16, 43800/14 and 28525/20, 30/11/2022 concerning events in Eastern Ukraine and the shooting down of Malaysian Airlines

The former President of the ECtHR, Siofra O'Leary, has spoken of the 'strains which inter-State and conflict cases place on the overall effectiveness of the Convention system'.[57] These strains flow from the pressure on expertise and the limited resources. At present, many of the inter-State cases involve Russia which has ceased to cooperate with the Court since its expulsion, adding a further layer of complexity. President O'Leary notes, however, that the increase in pending cases, reflects 'the faith placed by individuals and States in that system'.[58] Thus, whilst the Court appears to be under-equipped to deal with the increasing number of inter-State conflict issues, this is arguably where it is most needed.

Although most inter-State cases arise from conflict, it is important to note that the process can be used in other contexts. For, example in *Latvia* v. *Denmark*, Latvia complained that Denmark would be in breach of Articles 3, 5 and 8 ECHR if they extradited to South Africa a Latvian national detained in Denmark.[59] On that occasion, the case was struck out after the national was returned to Latvia, but it provides insight into the circumstances in which the application may be used. The inter-State application cannot, however, be used to circumvent the limits of the individual application. This was evident when the ECtHR rejected an inter-State application in respect of debts owed by Croatian companies to a Slovenian bank on the basis that the bank had no standing to lodge an individual application and Slovenia could not get round this by invoking the inter-State application.[60]

3.3.2.2 *Individual Applications*

In contrast to the inter-State mechanism, thousands of individual applications are lodged every year. Article 34 ECHR provides that the ECtHR may receive such petitions from any person, NGOs or group of individuals claiming to be a victim.[61] It also provides that the High Contracting Parties undertake not to hinder, in any way, the effective exercise of this right. 'Victim' for these purposes has an autonomous Convention meaning. In general, this means that the applicant is someone that is directly affected, albeit the ECtHR has indicated that this should not be applied in a 'rigid, mechanical and inflexible way'.[62]

flight MH17; The GC handed down its judgment on the merits on (9 July, 2025). *Ukraine* v. *Russia*, App. No. 10691/21 concerning allegations of Russian Federation, State-authorised targeted assassination operations against opponents of the Russian Federation in Russia and in other States, including other Member States of the Council of Europe.

[57] Síofra O'Leary, 'Challenges to the European Human Rights Protection System' (Third International Human Rights Forum, 25/05/2023).

[58] Ibid, p.5. [59] *Latvia* v. *Denmark*, App. No. 9717/20 (struck off the list on 16/06/2020).

[60] *Slovenia* v. *Croatia* [GC], App. No. 54155/16, 18/11/2020.

[61] For further details on victim status, see European Court of Human Rights, *Practical Guide on Admissibility Criteria* (31 August 2023), pp.9–20.

[62] *Centre for Legal Resources on behalf of Valentin Câmpeanu* v. *Romania* [GC], App. No. 47848/08, 17/07/2014 at [96].

A significant limitation is that the ECtHR will not accept *actio popularis*, as its task is not to review law and practice *in abstracto* but rather to determine whether the way that the law and practice was applied to, or affected, the applicant led to a violation of the Convention.[63] A victim, who is not directly affected by a national law, cannot complain about such a measure simply because they consider it may contravene the Convention.[64] There are, however, some contexts in which the ECtHR has had to be flexible. For example, in *Klass* v. *Germany* it was impossible to know whether the applicants had been subject to the regime of secret surveillance and so the ECtHR allowed the applicants to challenge the regime itself.[65] The ECtHR also held that women of child-bearing age could claim to be victims in a case concerning a prohibition in Ireland of the dissemination of information about abortion facilities available outside of Ireland.[66] Two types of potential victim status have thus been evidenced in the case law. First, the Court may accept the existence of victim status where applicants contend that a law breaches their rights, if they belong to a class of people who risk being directly affected by the legislation, or if they are required either to modify their conduct or risk being prosecuted.[67] Second are those persons who argue that they may be affected at some future point. In theory, the Court will not examine a violation until that violation has occurred. However, in highly exceptional circumstances, an applicant may claim to be a victim of a violation of the Convention owing to the risk of a future violation.[68]

The Convention is given wider protection by the ECtHR's consistent recognition that 'Article 34 concerns not just the direct victim or victims of the alleged violation, but also any indirect victims to whom the violation would cause harm or who would have a valid and personal interest in seeing it brought to an end.'[69] The ECtHR thus allows family members to bring proceedings in respect of alleged violations of the right to life of close relatives.[70] The ECtHR also allows for family members to bring proceedings where allegations of ill-treatment are closely linked to the death or disappearance of relatives.[71] Family members of persons who have been detained or vulnerable persons are also able to bring

[63] *Roman Zakharov* v. *Russia* [GC] (2016) 63 EHRR 17 at [164].

[64] *Aksu* v. *Turkey* [GC] (2013) 56 EHRR 4 at [50]–[51].

[65] *Klass and Others* v. *Germany* (1978) 2 EHRR 214 at [34].

[66] *Open Door and Dublin Well Woman* v. *Ireland* (1993) 15 EHRR 244 at [44].

[67] *Tănase* v. *Moldova* [GC], App. No. 7/08, 27/04/2010 at [104].

[68] *Berger-Krall and Others* v. *Slovenia*, App. No. 14717/ 04, 12/06/2014 at [258].

[69] *Vallianatos and Others* v. *Greece* [GC] (2014) 59 EHRR 12 at [47].

[70] *Van Colle* v. *the United Kingdom* (2013) 56 EHRR 23 at [86]; *Tsalikidis and others* v. *Greece*, App. No. 73974/14, 16/11/2016 at [64].

[71] *Khayrullina* v. *Russia*, App. No. 29729/09, 19/12/2017 at [91]–[92] and [100]–[107]; *Açış* v. *Turkey*, App. No. 7050/05, 01/02/2011 (in French) at [36] and [51]–[54].

proceedings.[72] Moreover, if the original applicant dies before the ECtHR decides their case, then their heirs may be able to continue proceedings.[73]

Groups of individuals and NGOs can lodge applications under Article 34 ECHR provided that they are directly affected by the impugned provision or measure. There are also circumstances in which NGOs can bring proceedings on behalf of an affected individual as their representative.[74] In cases where applicants choose to be represented under Rule 36(1) of the Rules of Court, they are required by Rule 45(3) to produce a written authority to act. Representatives thus have to demonstrate that they have received instructions from the alleged victim. An exception to this arose in *Centre for Legal Resources on Behalf of Valentin Câmpeanu* v. *Romania* where an NGO was permitted to bring proceedings on behalf of the deceased without having received instructions from him whilst he was alive. The ECtHR observed that the deceased was a young Roma man with severe mental disabilities who had HIV and spent his entire life in the care of the State authorities; he had died in hospital, allegedly as a result of neglect. Indeed, having accepted the standing of the NGO, the Grand Chamber ultimately found violations of both the substantive and procedural aspects of Article 2 ECHR.[75] In *Suprun* v. *Russia*, the NGO applicant, International Memorial, was liquidated in 2022 by the Russian authorities, but the Court nevertheless allowed the Chairman and executive director to have standing to pursue the application.[76]

The ECtHR has had to give special consideration to how to approach standing in the context of climate change. In the landmark case of *Verein KlimaSeniorinnen Schweiz* v. *Switzerland*, the Grand Chamber considered a complaint bought by a non-profit association 'established to promote and implement effective climate protection on behalf of its members' (who were women (the majority over seventy years of age) living in Switzerland), and four women who were members of the association and who claimed to have suffered ill-health that they argued was due to climate change-induced heatwaves.[77] The GC addressed the question of standing in climate-change cases as follows:

> [E]veryone may be, one way or another and to some degree, directly affected, or at a real risk of being directly affected, by the adverse effects of climate change ... [T]he fact remains that potentially a huge number of persons could claim victim status under

[72] See *Janowiec and others* v. *Russia* [GC] (2014) 58 EHRR 30 at [177] and also [178]–[181] and *Belli and Arquier Martinez* v. *Switzerland*, App. No. 65550/13, 11/12/2018 at [97].

[73] *Varnava* v. *Turkey* [GC], App. No. 16064/90, 18/09/2009 at [112] and [200].

[74] For case law on representation, see ECtHR (n 61) at [73]–[83].

[75] *Centre for Legal Resources on Behalf of Valentin Câmpeanu* v. *Romania* (n 62) at [104]–[114].

[76] *Suprun* v. *Russia*, App. Nos. 58029/12, 29440/19, 12396/21, 61350/21 and 25390/22, 18/06/2024 at [67]–[68].

[77] *Verein KlimaSeniorinnen Schweiz* v. *Switzerland*, App. No. 53600/20 [GC], 9/04/2024. See also Corina Heri, 'KlimaSeniorinnen and Its Discontents: Climate Change at the European Court of Human Rights' (2024) 4 EHRLR 317 and Kantstantsin. Dzehtsiarou, 'KlimaSeniorinnen Revolution: The New Approach to Standing' (2024) ECHRLR 5(4) 423–431.

the Convention on this basis .... [I]t would not sit well with the exclusion of *actio popularis* from the Convention mechanism and the effective functioning of the right of individual application to accept the existence of victim status in the climate-change context without sufficient and careful qualification.[78]

The Court concluded that for an applicant to claim victim status in the context of claims concerning harm, or risk of harm, because of a State's failure to combat climate change, a victim needs to show that he or she was personally and directly affected by the State's failures.

The ECtHR thus identified that the following must be established by an individual applicant in these types of cases:

1. The applicant is 'subject to high intensity of exposure to the adverse effects of climate change'. The level and severity of the adverse consequences (or risk thereof) of governmental (in)action must be significant; and,
2. Due to the absence or inadequacy of any reasonable measures to reduce harm, there must be a 'pressing need to ensure the applicant's individual protection'.[79]

The Court acknowledged that 'the threshold for fulfilling these criteria is especially high'.[80]

The Court also set out new requirements, tailored for an association to be given standing, in climate change cases. In particular, an association must:

1. Be lawfully established in the State concerned or have standing to act there;
2. Pursue 'a dedicated purpose in accordance with its statutory objectives in the defence of the human rights of its members or other affected individuals within the jurisdiction concerned, whether limited to or including collective action for the protection of those rights against the threats arising from climate change';
3. Demonstrate that it is a 'genuinely qualified representative to act on behalf of members or other affected individual within the jurisdiction who are subject to specific threats or adverse effects of climate change on their lives, health or well-being as protected under the Convention'.[81]

The majority was not satisfied that the individual applicants met the requisite criterion,[82] whereas the association satisfied the newly formulated standing requirements and the GC then addressed the merits of the claim.[83]

[78] Ibid at [483]. [79] Ibid at [487]. [80] Ibid at [488].

[81] Ibid at [502]. Judge Eicke, partly concurring and partly dissenting, criticised the expansion of standing as creating a basis for *actio popularis* complaints, at [45]. See also *Carême* v. *France*, [GC], App. No. 7189/21, 09/04/2024 at [83]–[84].

[82] Ibid at [485]. [83] Ibid at [521]–[535].

3.3.2.3 *Third-Party Interventions*

Article 36 ECHR allows for third-party interventions in proceedings. Article 36 (1) ECHR provides that in any case where the applicant is a national of a High Contracting Party, the High Contracting Party has the right to submit written comments and to take part in hearings. In addition to this, Article 36(2) ECHR and Article 3 of Protocol 16 ECHR (advisory opinions) provide that the President of the ECtHR may invite any High Contracting Party that is not a party to the proceedings, or any person concerned who is not the applicant, to submit written comments or to take part in the hearings. In these cases, there is no right to intervene; this is granted at the discretion of the ECtHR and is only granted if the Court is satisfied that it would be 'in the interest[s] of the proper administration of justice'.[84] In 2023, a new Practice Direction on Third-Party Interventions sought to clarify the manner in which third parties can intervene in cases.[85] As explained in the Practice Direction, the role of third-party interventions is to put before the ECtHR, as impartially and objectively as possible, legal or factual points capable of assisting it in resolving the matters in dispute before it on a more enlightened basis.[86] Consequently, third parties are not entitled to express support directly for one or the other party, make requests as regards the procedures before the Court, seek a remedy from the Court, participate in friendly-settlement negotiations between the parties, or seek the relinquishment or referral of a case to the Grand Chamber.[87] Interventions can be made with leave by third party States, persons who are implicated by the facts other than the applicant and NGOs.[88] In high-profile cases, it is not unusual to see a large number of interventions by third parties. An example of this is *Verein KlimaSeniorinnen Schweiz* v. *Switzerland* where numerous third-party comments were received from organisations and other entities.[89]

3.3.3 How Are Cases Processed?

In 2023, there were over 68,000 applications pending before the ECtHR and faced with such a daunting caseload it is essential that the procedures of the Court are efficient.[90] The system developed for processing the ECtHR's case law has been the subject of reform aimed at enabling the ECtHR to clear the backlog. For example, the pilot judgment procedure was developed to deal

[84] Practice Directions, *Third-party intervention under Article 36 § 2 of the Convention or under Article 3, second sentence, of Protocol No. 16* (March 2023).

[85] Ibid. [86] Ibid at [2]. [87] Ibid.

[88] For further examples, see Harris et al. (n 1), pp.161–164.

[89] *Verein KlimaSeniorinnen Schweiz* v. *Switzerland* (n 77).

[90] Council of Europe, *Annual Report 2023 of the European Court of Human Rights* (Council of Europe, 2024).

with the problem of numerous repetitive complaints. Moreover, the ECtHR works together with the Contracting States, who carry the primary responsibility for upholding the values of the Convention. This notion of 'shared responsibility' between the ECtHR and State authorities is reinforced through the principle of subsidiarity which has been prominent at the high-level conferences and is discussed below.[91] Subsidiarity is explicitly included in the Preamble of the Convention and linked to the margin of appreciation.[92] Yet, whilst many aspects of the reforms have been welcomed by States, the Court continues to face challenges from those that allege that it still fails to respect adequately the principle of subsidiarity, especially in relation to the granting of interim measures (see discussion at Section 3.3.5.1 Interim Measures and the UK's Rwanda Agreement).

3.3.4 Admissibility Requirements

When an application is lodged, the ECtHR will determine whether it complies with the admissibility criteria established under Article 35 ECHR.[93] Many of the admissibility requirements are procedural in nature, but some require an assessment of the merits of the case.

An important admissibility requirement provided for by Article 35(1) ECHR is that all domestic remedies must have been exhausted.[94] The intention behind this is to give the State, primarily the national courts, the opportunity to resolve the matter in line with the ECtHR's subsidiary role. Article 35(1) ECHR also establishes a time limit for lodging the application after the final decision is taken by the contracting State. This used to be six months, but in 2022 it was reduced to four months by Protocol 15 ECHR.

Article 35(2) ECHR provides that the ECtHR shall not deal with any application that is (a) anonymous or (b) substantially the same as another matter that has already been examined by the Court or has already been submitted to another procedure of international investigation or settlement and contains no relevant new information.[95]

Meanwhile, Article 35(3) ECHR provides that the ECtHR will declare inadmissible any application if it considers that:

[91] See European Court of Human Rights, *High Level Conference on the Future of the European Court of Human Rights: Brighton Declaration* (2012).

[92] Council of Europe, Protocol 15 ECHR amending the Convention on the Protection of Human Rights and Fundamental Freedoms, Council of Europe Treaty Series – No.213. Strasbourg 24. VI.2013, entered into force 01/08/2021.

[93] On admissibility, see ECtHR (n 61).

[94] See, e.g., *Duarte Agostinho and Ors* v. *Portugal and Ors* [GC], App. No. 39371/20, 9/04/2024.

[95] See case law discussed in ECtHR (n 61), pp.50–51.

(a) the application is incompatible with the provisions of the Convention or the Protocols thereto, manifestly ill-founded, or an abuse of the right of individual application; or
(b) the applicant has not suffered a significant disadvantage, unless respect for human rights as defined in the Convention and the Protocols thereto requires an examination of the application on the merits and provided that no case may be rejected on this ground which has not been duly considered by a domestic tribunal.

The latter was introduced by Protocol No.14 ECHR and stems from the Brighton Declaration. The Court has sought to steer clear of providing a definitive definition of 'significant disadvantage', but it has stated that it means that a violation should attain a minimum level of severity, and that violations that are purely technical and insignificant do not warrant consideration.[96] It has also observed that:

> The assessment of this minimum level is relative and depends on all the circumstances of the case ... The severity of a violation should be assessed by taking into account both the applicant's subjective perceptions and what is objectively at stake in a particular case ... However, the applicant's subjective perception cannot alone suffice to conclude that he/she suffered a significant disadvantage. The subjective perception must be justified on objective grounds ... A violation of the Convention may concern important questions of principle and thus cause a significant disadvantage regardless of pecuniary interest.[97]

One use of this provision is to dismiss financial cases where the sum involved is relatively small (e.g. 1–500 euros)[98] or there has been a delay in the payment of a small sum.[99]

As Harris and colleagues note, whilst historically the ECtHR has sought to 'give a more favourable interpretation to rules such as the obligation to exhaust domestic remedies for the benefit of applicants', in recent years 'the trend has been towards a stricter application of the admissibility criteria'.[100] They suggest that this reflects the ECtHR's policy since 2014, as well as the fact that 'the Convention now forms part of domestic law in [that] many of the contracting parties and litigants are able to rely directly and specifically on its provisions in their domestic courts'.[101]

96 See *Shefer* v. *Russia*, App. No. 45175/04, 13/03/2012 at [27]–[28], *Avellone and others* v. *Italy*, App. No. 6561/10, 09/07/2020 at [35], *Anthony France and others* v. *the United Kingdom*, App. No. 25357/16, 26/09/2017.

97 *Sylka* v. *Poland*, App. No. 19219/07, 03/06/2014 at [27].

98 See *Korolev* v. *Russia*, App. No. 25551/05, 01/07/2010; *Burov* v. *Moldova*, App. No. 38875/03, 14/06/2011. See further, cases cited in (n 61) at [392].

99 *Gururyan* v. *Armenia*, App. No. 11456/05, 24/01/2012.

100 Harris et al. (n 1), p.47.

101 Ibid, p.48.

3.3.4.1 *Strike Out Powers*

In addition to the admissibility requirements, Article 37 ECHR provides that the ECtHR may strike out a case at any stage. The Court may strike out a case if: (a) the applicant does not intend to pursue the application; (b) the matter has been resolved; or (c) for any other reason established by the Court it is no longer justified to continue the examination of the application. Under Article 37(2) ECHR, the Court may decide to restore an application to its list of cases if it considers that the circumstances justify such a course.

3.3.4.2 *Pilot Judgment Procedure*

The pilot judgment procedure set out in Article 46 ECHR is a means of dealing with large groups of identical cases.[102] When faced with such applications, the ECtHR may decide to select one or more cases for priority treatment and freeze the others. In a pilot judgment, the Court aims to: (i) determine whether there has been a violation of the Convention in the particular case; (ii) identify the dysfunction under national law that is at the root of the violation; (iii) give clear indications to the Government as to how it can eliminate this dysfunction; (iv) bring about the creation of a domestic remedy capable of dealing with similar cases (including those already pending before the Court awaiting the pilot judgment), or at least to bring about the settlement of all such cases pending before the ECtHR. The Court delivered its first pilot judgment in 2004 in the *Bug River* cases from Poland, which led to new legislation and the settlement of other cases.[103] These cases concerned a legislative scheme which enabled discounted purchases of land by those who had lost land due to the redrawing of the eastern border of Poland after the Second World War. A more recent example is *Tunikova* v. *Russia* where the Court set out in detail the steps that Russian authorities must take to comply with the ECHR in the context of domestic abuse.[104]

[102] See Rule 61 of the Rules of Court, Pilot Judgment Procedure. See also The Pilot- Judgment Procedure, Information Note issued by the Registrar. For analysis of the pilot judgment procedure see Lize R. Glas, 'The Functioning of the Pilot-Judgment Procedure of the European Court of Human Rights in Practice' (2016) **34**(1) NQHR 41.

[103] *Broniowski* v. *Poland* [GC] (2005) 40 EHRR 21. See also *Broniowski* v. *Poland* (friendly settlement) [GC] (2006) 43 EHRR 1. See *Hutten-Czapska* v. *Poland* [GC] (2007) 45 EHRR 4 at [231]–[234]; *E.G.* v. *Poland and 175 other Bug River Applications*, App. No. 50425/99, 23/09/2008.

[104] *Turnikova* v. *Russia*, App. No. 55974/16, 14/12/2021 at [153]–[159]. See also, *Walesa* v. *Poland*, App. No. 50849/21, 23/11/2023.

3.3.5 Interim Measures

Interim measures are an important, and controversial, tool in the ECHR toolkit.[105] Rule 39(1) of the Rules of Court provides that the Court may 'in exceptional circumstances, whether at the request of a party or of any other person concerned, or of its own motion, indicate to the parties any interim measure which it considers should be adopted'.[106] It provides that such measures are applicable in cases of imminent risk of irreparable harm which would not be susceptible to reparation, restoration or adequate compensation in the interests of the parties or of the proper conduct of the proceedings. Interim measures are thus urgent measures granted on an exceptional basis. The ECtHR typically receives a couple of thousand applications for interim measures each year, most of which are rejected.[107] For example, in 2023, sixty-four requests were made for interim measures in respect of the UK, of which one was granted.[108] The ECtHR examines each request on an individual and priority basis through a written procedure. Such measures are decided without prejudicing any subsequent admissibility decision or the merits of the case. There is, however, no right to appeal a refusal to grant an interim measure.

In the context of some ambiguity in the case law as to the threshold for an interim measure, Rule 39 was amended in November 2023 and specifies that the threshold is one of 'imminent risk of irreparable harm'. Even before the adoption of the new wording in Rule 39, it was evident that interim measures are exceptional, and that the threshold is a demanding one. In *Rackete* v. *Italy*, the applicants who had been rescued in international waters within the Libyan Search and Rescue region, applied to the Court requesting to be permitted to disembark in Italy from their rescue ship.[109] The Court decided not to indicate to the Italian Government an interim measure. It reasoned that as vulnerable passengers had already disembarked, there were not any exceptionally serious and exigent reasons justifying the application of the urgent measures.[110]

[105] For further information on interim measures, see European Court of Human Rights, *Factsheet: Interim measures* (March 2024).

[106] Press Release ECHR 308 (2023). The judges who deal with interim measures will now be named.

[107] See European Court of Human Rights, *Analysis of Statistics 2023* (Council of Europe, January 2024), p.4. In 2023, the total number of decisions on interim measures (2,634) decreased by 15 percent in comparison to 2022, which has been attributed to a decrease in applications from Russia, Türkiye, Serbia and Greece.

[108] The Court has made available online statistics concerning interim measures; see Council of Europe, *Analysis of Statistics 2023 on Interim Measures*, www.echr.coe.int/documents/d/echr/stats_art_39_01_eng-1 (last accessed 12 August 2024).

[109] *Rackete* v. *Italy*, App. No. 32969/19, 25/06/2019.

[110] Ibid.

Most interim measures relate to requests to suspend expulsion or extradition where it is alleged that Article 2 or Article 3 ECHR would be violated if the expulsion/extradition takes place.[111] Interim measures are thus an important safety valve to protect a potential victim and to ensure that a claim is fully considered, even if ultimately the victim does not succeed. An example of this can be seen in an interim measure indicated against the UK in July 2021 concerning Jonah Horne who was resisting his extradition to the United States in relation to a charge of second-degree murder with a firearm.[112] The interim measure was granted to stay his extradition for the duration of the proceedings before the Court.[113] In 2024, the Court declared the application inadmissible as, in their view, there was no risk that extradition to the United States would violate Article 3 ECHR, and the application of Rule 39 was discontinued. The ECtHR has also considered applications in respect of other potential rights violations relating to deportation/extradition, including Article 6,[114] Article 8[115] and Article 10 ECHR.[116]

Interim measures may also be sought in other contexts. For example, the ECtHR has issued an interim measure in respect of withdrawal of treatment. This was applicable in *Lambert* v. *France* where the ECtHR indicated that France should stay execution of the judgment of *Conseil d'État* that life-sustaining medical treatment should be withdrawn whilst the Grand Chamber considered an application that had been made by family members opposing the withdrawal of treatment.[117] Similarly in *Evans* v. *the United Kingdom*, the ECtHR indicated under Rule 39 that the UK should prevent the applicant's embryos from being destroyed prior to the ECtHR considering the application.[118] Interim measures have also been considered in cases where children are to be

[111] See (n 105), p.2. See also, *I.A.* v. *France*, App. No. 40788/23, 28/11/23.

[112] *Jonah Horne* v. *the United Kingdom*, App. No. 34392/21, 13/02/2024. [113] Ibid at [32].

[114] For example, in *Soering* v. *the United Kingdom* (1989) 11 EHRR 439 and *Othman* v. *the United Kingdom* (2012) 55 EHRR 1, the ECtHR indicated to the UK under Rule 9 an interim measure until it examined the application alleging that extradition/expulsion would violate Article 6 ECHR. See also, *Wróbel* v. *Poland*, App. No. 6904/22, 08/02/2022 in which the ECtHR indicated an interim measure asking that Poland ensure that the lifting of a Supreme Court judge's judicial immunity comply with Art. 6(1) requirements; and *Raczkowski* v. *Poland*, App. No. 33082/22, 12/07/2022 in which an interim measure was indicated concerning the lifting of judicial immunity of a military judge.

[115] *Amrollahi* v. *Denmark*, App. No. 56811/00, 11/07/2002 in which it was argued that deportation to Iran would sever family life and that Rule 39 applied until the ECtHR could consider the matter.

[116] *Novaya Gazeta and others* v. *Russia*, App. No. 11884/22, 08/03/2022 in which the ECtHR indicated to Russia that it should abstain from actions and decisions aimed at blocking or terminating the activities of a newspaper and television company and depriving them of rights guaranteed under Article 10 ECHR.

[117] *Lambert* v. *France* [GC] (2016) 62 EHRR 2. The ECtHR held that there would be no violation of Article 2 in the event of implementing the judgment of the *Conseil d'Etat*.

[118] *Evans* v. *the United Kingdom* [GC] (2008) 46 EHRR 34.

taken into care or returned to another jurisdiction.[119] Moreover, during COVID-19, the ECtHR received numerous requests for interim measures relating to persons in detention in prison and immigration centres. Most of these applications were rejected, but some interim measures were issued in respect of 'very vulnerable persons' (unaccompanied minors, persons with serious medical conditions and pregnant persons, in particular).[120]

It is important to note that the receiving State is obliged to comply where an interim measure is indicated. This was confirmed by the Grand Chamber in *Mamatkulov* v. *Turkey* in which it held that failure to comply with an interim measure constitutes a failure to comply with the States' obligations under Article 34 ECHR not to hinder applicants in the exercise of their right of individual application.[121] The Grand Chamber reiterated this in *Paladi* v. *Moldova*, once more finding a violation of Article 34 ECHR.[122] There are numerous other cases in which a Chamber of the ECtHR has found a violation of Article 34 ECHR on the same basis.[123]

3.3.5.1 *Interim Measures and the UK's Rwanda Agreement*

The fact that States are obliged to comply with interim measures is one of the reasons why they have proved so controversial, particularly where they relate to immigration. An infamous example of this is the 2022 interim measure in respect of removals to Rwanda, which led to renewed threats that the UK would withdraw from the ECHR. The background to the measure was the the UK–Rwanda Asylum Partnership Arrangement[124] which provided that Rwanda would receive asylum seekers from the UK and process their asylum applications through the Rwandan domestic asylum system.[125] Following the signing of the agreement, the first deportation flight was scheduled for 14 June 2022. After the domestic courts had declined to issue an injunction,[126] a last-minute application was made to the ECtHR which resulted in the granting of interim measures.[127] The ECtHR ruled that an Iraqi man, known as KN, should be permitted to remain

[119] See *Soares de Melo* v. *Portugal*, App. No. 72850/14, 16/02/2016 (interim measure discussed in judgment); *Eskinazi and Chelouche* v. *Turkey*, App. No. 14600/05, 06/12/2005 (interim measure discussed in judgment).

[120] ECtHR, Factsheet on interim measures (n 105) pp.13–14.

[121] *Mamatkulov* v. *Turkey* [GC] (2005) 41 EHRR 25 at [128].

[122] *Paladi* v. *Moldova* [GC] (2008) 47 EHRR 15 at [88]–[92].

[123] ECtHR (n 107).

[124] Home Office, *Factsheet: Migration and Economic Development Partnership* (April 2022).

[125] Home Office, *Memorandum of Understanding between the government of the UK of Great Britain and Northern Ireland and the government of the Republic of Rwanda for the provision of an asylum partnership arrangement*, 14 April 2022.

[126] *R (NSK (Iraq))* v. *Secretary of State for the Home Department*, Supreme Court, Permission to Appeal, Case ID: the UKSC 2022/0090, 14/06/2022.

[127] *KN* v. *the United Kingdom*, App. No. 28774/22, 14/06/2022.

in the UK for three weeks after legal options were exhausted. The ECtHR's decision to issue an interim measure led to emergency applications from the five remaining passengers seeking interim measures to halt their removal. Two were successful and their removal was stayed until 20 June 2022 for their requests to be considered.[128] Two requests were rejected because domestic remedies had not been exhausted.[129] The final request was withdrawn before any decision could be taken because the Home Office withdrew the applicant's removal directions. Consequently, by the time the plane was due to leave there were no asylum seekers that could be taken to Rwanda. The decision of the ECtHR to issue interim measures was met with vociferous anger by the UK Government. Then Prime Minister, Boris Johnson, accused the lawyers acting for the asylum-seekers of 'effectively … abetting the work of criminal gangs'[130] and of undermining the Government's efforts to support safe and legal routes for people to come to the UK and to oppose illegal and dangerous routes. His interventions prompted widespread concern amongst legal practitioners and, in a joint statement, the Bar Council and the Law Society warned that:

> Legal challenges ensure government is acting lawfully, following laws agreed by parliament. It is misleading and dangerous for the Prime Minister to suggest lawyers who bring such legal challenges are doing anything other than their job and upholding the law. Anyone at risk of a life-changing order has a right to challenge its legality with the assistance of a lawyer, who has a duty to advise their client on their rights.[131]

Yet whilst those were the views of the legal profession, s.55 of the Illegal Migration Act 2023 was later enacted, which gave Ministers legislative permission to ignore interim measures indicated by the ECtHR.[132] It also provided that where a Minister decides to ignore an interim measure, the Upper Tribunal and the courts are prevented from having regard to interim measures when considering proceedings challenging removal under the Act.[133] The Joint Committee on Human Rights cautioned that ignoring 'an interim measure of the ECtHR would be a breach of the UK's legal obligations'.[134] The legal

[128] *RM* v. *the United Kingdom*, App. No.29080/22, 20/06/2022 and *HN* v. *the United Kingdom*, App. No.29084/2, 20/06/2022.

[129] *Abdollahi* v. *the United Kingdom*, App. No. 29081/22, 20/06/2022 and *Shokri* v. *the United Kingdom*, App. No. 29082/22, 20/06/2022.

[130] Bar Council, *Prime Minister must stop attacks on legal professionals, say Bar Council and Law Society*, 14 June 2022.

[131] Ibid. In the Supreme Court proceedings, Lord Reed stated that 'the appellant's lawyers were performing their proper function of ensuring that their clients are not subjected to unlawful treatment at the hands of the Government'. *R (NSK (Iraq))* v. *Secretary of State for the Home Department* (n 126).

[132] Section 55(1)–(4). [133] Section 55(6)–(7).

[134] House of Commons and House of Lords, Joint Committee on Human Rights, *Legislative Scrutiny: Illegal Migration Bill*, Twelfth Report of Session 2022–23, HC 1241 HL Paper 208, Published on 11 June 2023.

challenges to the Rwanda Agreement itself are considered in greater detail in Chapter 5 (Freedom from Torture and Inhuman and Degrading Treatment and Punishment), but for now it is important to note that in November 2023, the Supreme Court in *R (AAA and Others)* v. *Secretary of State for the Home Department* delivered a unanimous judgment declaring the Government's 'Rwanda plan' unlawful.[135] In response to this decision, The Safety of Rwanda (Asylum and Immigration) Act 2024 was enacted which sought to circumvent the Supreme Court's judgment in *AAA* in a number of respects. The point that is relevant here is that the 2024 Act confirmed that only a Government Minister can decide whether to comply with an interim measure issued by the ECtHR. According to the Home Office:

> The Bill makes it unambiguously clear that the UK Parliament is sovereign, and the validity of any Act of Parliament is unaffected by international law. Ministers will be able to retain the decision on whether to comply with interim measures from the European Court of Human Rights, for example, a Rule 39 injunction.[136]

The Border Security, Asylum and Immigration Bill which is currently before Parliament will, if enacted, repeal both the Safety of Rwanda (Asylum and Immigration) Act 2024 and most of the Illegal Migration Act 2023, including s.55.

3.4 MERITS JUDGMENTS OF THE EUROPEAN COURT OF HUMAN RIGHTS

If a case is considered admissible, the ECtHR will issue a judgment on the merits. It is at this stage that the Court will consider whether any rights have been violated and will issue reasons for its decision. We will examine the structure of the Convention rights and how the Court interprets those rights shortly, however, before we do so, it is worth noting a number of other important features about the way in which the ECtHR operates at the merits stage.

3.4.1 The Court Decides Which Rights to Consider

The ECtHR frequently states that it is the 'master of the characterisation to be given in law to the facts of a case' and thus it is not bound by the characterisation given by the applicant or the Government in a given case.[137]

[135] *R (AAA and Others)* v. *Secretary of State for the Home Department* [2023] the United Kingdom SC 42, [2023] 1 WLR 4433 at [36], [73] and [105].

[136] Home Office, *Rwanda Bill to become Law in major illegal migration milestone*, Press Release (23 April 2024).

[137] See, e.g., *Yüksel Yalçinkaya* v. *Türkiye* [GC], App. No. 15669/20, 26/09/2023 at [217], *Vavřička* v. *Czech Republic* [GC], App. No. 47621/13, 08/04/2021 at [169] and *S.M.* v. *Croatia* [GC] (2021) 72 EHRR 1.

Consequently, in *S.M.* v. *Croatia*, the Court elected to consider the matter under Article 4 ECHR even though the application had focused on other rights.[138] Moreover, where an applicant alleges violations of multiple rights, the ECtHR may decide not to consider particular rights where it has already found a violation of another right in respect of the same facts; the Court may also decline to consider different challenges under the same article on the basis of the same facts (e.g. violations of substantive as opposed to procedural rights, or vice versa).[139]

3.4.2 No Doctrine of Precedent

There is no doctrine of binding precedent and so the ECtHR is able to depart from its own previous interpretations. Thus, whilst Chambers are expected to follow the Grand Chamber, they may depart from previous Chamber decisions if there are cogent reasons. The Grand Chamber is always free to depart from one of its own previous judgments if there are convincing reasons for doing so; such a departure might, for example, be warranted in order to ensure that the interpretation of the Convention reflects societal changes and remains in line with present-day conditions, or to correct a misunderstanding of the domestic law in question by the ECtHR.[140] In practice, the ECtHR rarely departs from its earlier decisions in the interests of legal certainty, foreseeability and equality before the law. An example of changing conditions leading to a different interpretation is provided by the judgment in *Goodwin* v. *the United Kingdom* concerning the lack of legal recognition of a transgender person.[141] The ECtHR found that 'the situation, as it has evolved, no longer falls within the United Kingdom's margin of appreciation'.[142] The judgment was given prospective effect thus mitigating the effect on legal certainty.

3.4.3 Single Judgment, Separate Concurring and Dissenting Opinions

The ECtHR issues a single authoritative judgment and Article 45 ECHR provides that reasons shall be given for judgments. Consequently, all statements within a judgment carry the same significance as there is no distinction within the judgment between *ratio decidendi* and *obiter dicta*. Article 45(2) ECHR provides that if the judgment does not represent, in whole or in part, the

[138] Ibid.

[139] See, e.g., *Lăcătuş* v. *Switzerland*, App. No. 14065/15, 19/01/2021, *Adamčo* v. *Slovakia (no. 2)*, App. No. 55792/20, 12/12/2024, partly dissenting opinion of Judge Serghides. For discussion, see Alan Greene, 'Allegation-Picking and the European Court of Human Rights: A Pervasive Court Practice Hiding in Plain Sight?' Strasbourg Observers, 25 February 2025.

[140] See, e.g., *Z* v. *the United Kingdom* (2002) 34 EHRR 3 at [100]; *Stafford* v. *the United Kingdom* (2002) 35 EHRR 32 at [36].

[141] *Goodwin* v. *the United Kingdom* [GC] (2002) 35 EHRR 18.

[142] Ibid at [120].

unanimous opinion of the judges, then any judge is entitled to deliver a separate opinion. Individual judges or groups of judges often do provide separate concurring opinions, as well as dissenting opinions. Concurring opinions do not form part of the judgment but may contain a greater level of discussion on particular issues than the judgment itself and can thus be of significant interest.

3.5 WHAT HAPPENS WHEN A VIOLATION IS FOUND?

3.5.1 Just Satisfaction

Article 41 ECHR provides that if the ECtHR has found a violation of the Convention or the Protocols thereto, and if the internal law of the High Contracting Party concerned allows only partial reparation to be made, the Court shall, if necessary, afford just satisfaction to the injured party. In these circumstances, a sum of money to compensate for damage can be awarded. The purpose of the award is not to punish the contracting State or any other party responsible. Where damages are contemplated this can include pecuniary and non-pecuniary damages. On occasions, the Court concludes that the finding of a violation constitutes sufficient just satisfaction for any non-pecuniary damage sustained by the applicants.[143] Costs and expenses may also be awarded. Time-limits and other formal requirements for submitting claims for just satisfaction are laid down in Rule 60 of the Rules of Court.

3.5.2 Binding Force and Execution of Judgments

Article 46(1) ECHR provides that the High Contracting Parties undertake to abide by the final judgment of the Court in any case to which they are parties. Once a judgment is final, then Article 46(2) ECHR provides that it should be transmitted to the Committee of Ministers, which shall supervise its execution. According to Article 46(3) ECHR, if the Committee of Ministers considers that the supervision of the execution of a final judgment is hindered by a problem of interpretation of the judgment, it may refer the matter to the Court for a ruling on the question of interpretation. A referral decision shall require a majority vote of two-thirds of the representatives entitled to sit on the committee.

[143] See, e.g., *Hirst* v. *the United Kingdom (No. 2)* [GC] (2006) 42 EHRR 41 at [93]–[94]. See also European Court of Human Rights *Practice Direction: Just Satisfaction Claims (Article 41 of the Convention)*, Practice direction issued by the President of the Court in accordance with Rule 32 of the Rules of Court on 28 March 2007 and amended on 9 June 2022.

What happens though if a State refuses to comply? In such circumstances, Article 46(4) ECHR provides that the Committee of Ministers may, after serving formal notice on that State and by decision adopted by a majority vote of two-thirds of the representatives entitled to sit on the Committee, refer to the Court the question of whether that party has failed to fulfil its obligation. Following which, Article 46(5) ECHR provides that if the ECtHR finds a violation of Article 46(1) ECHR, then it shall refer the case to the Committee of Ministers for consideration of the measures to be taken. If the Court finds no violation, it shall refer the case to the Committee of Ministers, which shall close its examination of the case.

3.5.3 How Effective Is Enforcement?

Until 2022, even States that persistently violated the ECHR remained contracting parties.[144] Indeed, as Philip Leach has observed: 'States such as Turkey and Azerbaijan have been in frequent, flagrant violation of the ECHR, over many years, without any decisive response from the Council of Europe'.[145] The military aggression by the Russian Federation on Ukraine in 2022 led to its expulsion from the Council of Europe. Yet for many years prior to this, the lack of enforcement of Strasbourg judgments in Russia was deeply problematic, not least since the Russian Constitutional Court held in 2015 that Strasbourg judgments that conflict with the Russian Constitution are unenforceable.[146] As Leach notes, the absence of effective enforcement mechanisms led to 'a disastrous failure to double down on judgments highlighting the state authorities' alarmingly increasingly repressive measures'.[147] This includes 'unregulated surveillance of mobile phones by the security services, the widespread suppression of peaceful protest, the repeated detention and prosecution of opposition politicians, the poisoning of dissidents, and the death of 330 people in the aftermath of the Beslan school siege in 2004'.[148] Yet whilst this highlights the very real limits of the ECtHR, the ECHR and the Court offered a means of shedding international light on the plight of victims in Russia. It was as such, despite its many limitations, a beacon of hope for many. Some insight into the sense of continuing significance for Russian citizens was

[144] On the problem of non-execution of judgments, see also Fiona de Londras and Kanstantsin Dzehtsiarou, 'Mission Impossible? Addressing Non-execution through Infringement Proceedings in the European Court of Human Rights' (2017) **66** ICLQ 2.

[145] Philip Leach, 'A Time of Reckoning? Russia and the Council of Europe' [2022] 3 EHRLR **219**, p.226.

[146] Resolution of the Constitutional Court of the Russian Federation No. 21-P of July 14, 2015, on the Matter of Verifying the Constitutionality of Provisions of Article 1 of the Federal Law on Ratification of the Convention on Human Rights and Fundamental Freedoms, Rossiiskaia Gazeta (RG) (official publication) (27 June 2015) (in Russian).

[147] Leach (n 145), p.226. [148] Ibid.

evident in the sheer number of applications lodged before the Court; indeed in 2021, almost a quarter of the Court's judgments concerned Russia.

On occasions, the UK has also shown itself unwilling to conform, a famous example of which was its refusal to comply with the ECtHR finding that the UK's blanket ban on prisoner voting violated Article 3 of Protocol 1 ECHR.[149] There was a lengthy political backlash as successive governments refused to address the incompatibility, whilst the ECtHR continued to find that the legislation violated the Convention.[150] The Prime Minister at the time, David Cameron, famously declared that it made him 'physically ill even to contemplate having to give the vote to anyone who is in prison'.[151] Two years later, while still resisting a change to the domestic law, he stated: 'I have always believed that when someone is sent to prison they lose certain rights, and one of those rights is the right to vote. Crucially I believe that it should be a matter for Parliament to decide and not a foreign court.'[152] He was not the only one who believed that Strasbourg had overreached in this respect and the stand-off became symbolically connected to wider contestation about State sovereignty. Eventually in November 2017, the Secretary of State for Justice proposed that prisoners on temporary licence would be allowed to vote, but that otherwise there would be no change, and in December 2017 the Council of Europe agreed to these proposals as an acceptable compromise. The case was finally closed in September 2018.

3.6 THE CONVENTION RIGHTS

After an examination of formation of the ECtHR and the admissibility process, it is now time to examine the Convention rights themselves. Many of the rights are considered in detail in later chapters in this book. However it is important to note at the outset that the rights have different structures which encapsulate important conceptual distinctions and calibrate the role of the ECtHR and the State accordingly. The ECtHR also draws upon several important doctrines in interpreting those rights, and those doctrines are also fundamental to the relationship between the ECtHR and the State.

[149] *Hirst* v. *the United Kingdom (No.2)* (n 143).

[150] *Greens and MT* v. *the United Kingdom* (2011) 53 EHRR 21, *Firth and others* v. *the United Kingdom*, App. No. 47784/09, 12/08/2014, *McHugh* v. *the United Kingdom and 1,014 other applicants*, App. No. 50987/08, 22/09/2014, *Millbank* v. *the United Kingdom*, App. No. 44417/14, 30/06/2016.

[151] David Cameron, *Official Report*, House of Commons Debates, Vol. 517 col. 921 (3 November 2010).

[152] David Cameron, *Official Report*, House of Commons Debates, Vol. 545 col. 1127 (23 May 2012).

3.6.1 Categories of Convention Rights

3.6.1.1 Absolute Rights

An absolute right is one that can never be interfered with in any circumstances. These rights cannot be balanced against other competing rights or the public interest. Nor can they be subject to derogation under Article 15 ECHR in times of emergency. Very few ECHR rights are absolute. The text of the Convention suggests that Article 3 ECHR (the prohibition of torture and inhuman and degrading treatment and punishment), Article 4(1) ECHR (the prohibition of slavery and servitude), Article 7 ECHR (no punishment without law) and Article 9 ECHR (the right to hold a belief) are absolute rights. Yet in practice, as we will see in later chapters, questions arise as to whether any of the rights are absolute in their operation. In particular, we will examine in Chapter 5 whether Article 3 ECHR – the prohibition on torture and inhuman and degrading treatment and punishment – is truly 'absolute'.

3.6.1.2 Limited Rights

Limited rights are ECHR rights which, unlike qualified rights, cannot be balanced against the needs of other individuals or against the public interest in normal circumstances but are subject to specific exceptions or limits. Unlike absolute rights, they may also be subject to derogation in times of emergency under Article 15 ECHR. Limited rights include Article 2 ECHR (the right to life), Article 4(2) ECHR (the prohibition of forced or compulsory labour), Article 5 ECHR (the right to liberty) and Article 6 ECHR (the right to a fair trial).

3.6.1.3 Qualified Rights

A further important category of ECHR rights is that of qualified rights. These are rights where States can justify interfering with the right in pursuit of a competing public interest or the rights of others, provided that certain criteria are met. The texts of some of the Convention rights provide a framework for evaluating these competing rights and interests, namely that the interference must be prescribed by law (legality), it must pursue a legitimate aim (those aims are set out in the text of the Convention right itself) and the interference must be necessary in a democratic society (proportionality). If you look at the structure of Articles 8–11 ECHR, you will see that they all have the same two-part structure setting out the right in the first paragraph followed by the qualification provision in the second paragraph. Yet whilst these rights are subject to a proportionality analysis, the degree of scrutiny that attaches to that analysis can vary significantly in practice.

3.6.1.4 *Non-discrimination: An Ancillary Right*

Article 14 ECHR, the non-discrimination provision, states that the enjoyment of the rights and freedoms set forth in this Convention shall be secured without discrimination on any ground such as sex, race, colour, language, religion, political or other opinion, national or social origin, association with a national minority, property, birth or other status. As discussed in Chapter 14, the ECtHR has interpreted this right as a parasitic right, meaning that it must operate in conjunction with another right. Often, but certainly not exclusively, this is with Article 8 ECHR, the right to respect for private and family life. Although Article 14 ECHR does not follow the two-paragraph structure of the qualified rights discussed above, the ECtHR has held that 'Article 14 does not prohibit differences in treatment which are founded on an objective assessment of essentially different factual circumstances and which, being based on the public interest, strike a fair balance between the protection of the interests of the community and respect for the rights and freedoms safeguarded by the Convention.'[153] Consequently, the ECtHR will also consider whether the alleged discrimination had a legitimate aim and whether 'there was reasonable relationship of proportionality between the means employed and the aim sought to be realised'.[154] The principle of non-discrimination and Article 14 ECHR are discussed further in Chapter 14.

3.6.2 Interpretation of Rights: Key ECHR Doctrines

There are a number of key doctrines that the ECtHR draws upon in interpreting and applying the Convention rights. As a Treaty, the ECHR must be guided in its interpretation by the Vienna Convention on the Law of Treaties 1969.[155] In particular, the ECtHR has relied upon the principle set out in Article 31(1) Vienna Convention on the Law of Treaties which requires that a treaty be 'interpreted in good faith in accordance with the ordinary meaning to be given to the terms of the treaty in their context and in the light of its object and purpose'.[156] The ECtHR has thus stated that it seeks to 'ascertain the ordinary meaning to be given to the terms of these provisions in their context and in the

[153] *Ünal Tekeli* v. *Turkey*, App. No. 29865/96, 16/11/2004 at [51].

[154] See, e.g., *Molla Sali* v. *Greece* [GC], App. No. 20452/14, 19/12/2018 at [135].

[155] United Nations, *Treaty Series*, vol. 1155, 331. See *Golder* v. *the United Kingdom* (1979–80) 1 EHRR 524 at [29] where the ECtHR stated that Articles 31 to 33 of the Vienna Convention should guide the Court in its interpretation.

[156] Ibid. For further discussion of the Vienna Convention principles in this context, see chapter 4 of Rainey et al. (n 1); Geir Ulfstein, 'Interpretation of the ECHR in Light of the Vienna Convention on the Law of Treaties' (2020) 24(7) International Journal of Human Rights 917 and Steven Wheatley, 'Interpreting the ECHR in Light of the Increasingly High Standards Being Required by Human Rights: Insights from Social Ontology' (2024) 24(1) HRLR 1.

light of their object and purpose'.[157] In *Soering* v. *the United Kingdom*, the ECtHR articulated two principles to give effect to the object and purpose of the Convention.[158] First, Convention rights should be 'interpreted and applied so as to make its safeguards practical and effective', and second, they should be interpreted to be consistent with 'the general spirit of the Convention, an instrument designed to maintain and promote the ideals and values of a democratic society'.[159] Thus, it is the nature of the Convention as a human rights treaty that underpins the interpretation adopted by the Court. Consequently, whilst there are cases where a reading of the ordinary meaning has led to a restricted interpretation, such examples are rare.[160]

3.6.2.1 *Living Instrument*

One of the most important, and contentious, of the interpretation doctrines is the living instrument approach to the Convention.[161] The living instrument doctrine reflects the notion that the Convention did not crystalise at the point at which it was enacted in the 1950s, but is open to interpretation in line with changes in social needs.[162] Convention rights are given an evolutive or dynamic interpretation which is constantly developing in response to events in the world,[163] evolving moral and social structures,[164] and scientific and medical developments.[165] The ECtHR will look to see whether there is consensus across States as to values and rights when considering how to interpret the ambit of a Convention right.[166] It will therefore consider whether a consistent pattern emerges across the Contracting States in respect of a given issue. The evolutive approach to interpretation has led the ECtHR to expand the substantive content and meaning of Convention rights, to change the assessment of what is 'necessary' in a democratic society, to adjust what constitutes a fair balance and to constrain the scope of the State's margin of appreciation. The living instrument approach thus enables the ECtHR to interpret the

[157] *Loizidou* v. *Turkey* (1997) 23 EHRR 513 at [73] and [89].

[158] *Soering* v. *the United Kingdom* (n 114). [159] Ibid at [87].

[160] In *Johnston* v. *Ireland* (1987) 9 EHRR 203 at [51] and [53], the Court concluded that the ordinary meaning of the words 'right to marry' in Article 12 could not be expanded to cover a guarantee of a right to divorce. While in *Pretty* v. *the United Kingdom* (2002) ECHR 427, the right to life in Article 2 could not be read as including a right to die.

[161] On the living instrument, see George Letsas, 'The ECHR as a Living Instrument: Its Meaning and Legitimacy' in Andreas Føllesdal et al., *Constituting Europe: The European Court of Human Rights in a National, European and Global Context* (CUP, 2013).

[162] *Tyrer* v. *the United Kingdom*, App. No. 5856/72, 25/04/1978 at [31].

[163] *Chahal* v. *the United Kingdom* [GC] (1997) 23 EHRR 413, *S.M.* v. *Croatia* (n 137).

[164] *Smith and Grady* v. *the United Kingdom* (n 18).

[165] *Goodwin* v. *the United Kingdom* (n 141) at [100].

[166] *A, B and C* v. *Ireland* [GC] (2011) 53 EHRR 13, *Mortier* v. *Belgium* [2022] ECHR 764, *Dániel Karsai* v. *Hungary* [2024] ECHR 516.

Convention rights in ways that would not have been foreseen or intended by the drafters of the Convention.[167] It is this aspect of the Convention that has, for example, enabled the ECtHR to offer protection to the LGBTQI+ community.[168]

The Strasbourg jurisprudence has thus largely sidestepped the issue of 'originalism' that has afflicted interpretation of the Constitution of the United States.[169] Reference to the meaning of the text at the time of its signing cannot be decisive as the meaning of the Convention is subject to dynamic interpretation.[170] Nevertheless, the ECtHR has not avoided the accusation of applying an 'activist interpretation'.[171] The Grand Chamber in *Verein KlimaSeniorinnen Schweiz*, a case concerning climate change, found that Switzerland breached the positive obligation under Article 8 by failing to put in place a relevant legislative and administrative framework designed to provide effective protection of human health and life.[172] Judge Eicke, in his partly concurring and partly dissenting opinion, stated that in doing so the ECtHR created a new right through evolutive interpretation:

> As is clear from the historic refusal of the Contracting Parties to the Convention to respond positively to the repeated calls by the Parliamentary Assembly of the Council of Europe for the adoption of an additional protocol to the Convention which would provide for (and give the Court jurisdiction to ensure the observance of) a right to a clean and healthy environment ... even if this issue was not, perhaps, considered at the time of the drafting of the original Convention, the omission from the Convention as it stands today of such a right was not coincidental.[173]

This was in stark contrast to the judgment of the Court which observed that:

> The Court has consistently held that the Convention should be interpreted, as far as possible, in harmony with other rules of international law ... Moreover, a failure by the Court to maintain a dynamic and evolutive approach would risk rendering it a bar to reform or improvement.[174]

[167] *Handyside* v. *the United Kingdom* (1979) 1 EHRR 737 at [49].

[168] *Smith and Grady* (n 18). See Kanstantsin Dzehtsiarou, *European Consensus and the Legitimacy of the European Court of Human Rights* (CUP, 2015).

[169] On the Court's interpretative approach, see Carl Emilio Lewis, 'The European Court of Human Rights and its Search for Common Values' (2023) 4(2) European Convention on Human Rights Law Review 179.

[170] Article 32 Vienna Convention permits recourse to preparatory material in limited circumstances.

[171] See, e.g., Paul Mahoney, 'Judicial Activism and Judicial Self-Restraint in the European Court of Human Rights: Two Sides of the Same Coin' [1990] 11 HRLJ 57.

[172] *Verein KlimaSeniorinnen Schweiz* (n 77) at [538]. [173] Ibid at [19].

[174] Ibid at [455]. References omitted. The Court has also been criticised for failing 'to adopt an evolutive approach to the right to liberty [that] has resulted in significant gaps in rights protection'. Sabina Garahan, *Detention and the Right to Liberty* (Taylor and Francis, 2025), p.3.

Determining the limits of the living instrument approach is thus challenging, not least because this is closely connected to perceptions on the proper role of the ECtHR and the relationship between the ECtHR and States.[175]

3.6.2.2 *Effective Interpretation*

The ECtHR has often declared that the Convention is intended to guarantee rights that are practical and effective and not theoretical or illusory.[176] The effective interpretation principle is integral to the approach of the ECtHR.[177] In practice, the Court will not construe rights in a narrow and legalistic way as this would hinder giving effect to the purpose and object of the Convention.[178] Nor will the Court adopt an interpretation that undermines the 'essence' of a right that would render it 'theoretical or illusory'.[179] Judge Serghides thus describes the principle of effectiveness as 'the fuel of the Convention engine'.[180] He considers that the living instrument doctrine derives from this principle of effectiveness,[181] without which 'the Convention cannot evolve, advance or be enriched'.[182]

A striking example of making the Convention rights 'practical and effective' can be seen in *Airey* v. *Ireland*, where the Court held that in some civil cases an individual has a right to legal representation without cost.[183] An effective right to access to court or a fair trial before a court, pursuant to Article 6, required legal representation in complex legal proceedings. An applicant's right to represent herself was not an adequate solution for this indispensable right.[184]

The principle that the guaranteed rights in the Convention must be practical and effective has supported the development of important doctrines by the ECtHR. These include, positive obligations,[185] autonomous Convention concepts[186] and implied rights.[187] The ECtHR has adopted a generous approach to interpretation

175 See discussion in Chapter 1.

176 See, e.g., *Goodwin* v. *the United Kingdom* (n 141) at [75]; *Andrejeva* v. *Latvia* [GC] (2010) 51 EHRR 28 at [98].

177 Some academics contend that 'effectiveness' is the core role of human rights institutions. Beth A. Simmons, *Mobilizing for Human Rights: International Law in Domestic Politics* (Cambridge University Press, 2009); Gráinne de Búrca, *Reforming Human Rights in a Turbulent Era* (Oxford University Press, 2021).

178 *Golder* v. *the United Kingdom* (n 155) at [29]–[36].

179 *Winterwerp* v. *Netherlands* (1979) 2 EHRR 387 at [75]; *Ashingdane* v. *the United Kingdom* (1985) 7 EHRR 528 at [57].

180 Georgios Serghides, *The Principle of Effectiveness and Its Overarching Role in the Interpretation and Application of the European Convention on Human Rights* (Strasbourg, 2022) (self-published).

181 Ibid, p.406. 182 Ibid. 183 *Airey* v. *Ireland* (n 21). 184 Ibid at [26].

185 See, e.g., *Marckx* v. *Belgium* (1979) 2 EHRR 330 at [45]; *X and Y* v. *Netherlands* (1985) 8 EHRR 235 at [23]–[24], [27]; *M.C.* v. *Bulgaria* (2005) 40 EHRR 20 at [150].

186 *Chassagnou* v. *France* (2000) 29 EHRR 615 at [100].

187 See *Golder* v. *the United Kingdom* (n 155) at [35].

which follows from the need to give effect to the object and purpose of the Convention and to promote the values which underlie human rights.

3.6.2.3 *Autonomous Meaning of Convention Rights*

The Court has held that some terms in the ECHR have a meaning which differs from either the same or similar terms used in the domestic law of any member State. These specific terms are given what is referred to as an 'autonomous meaning' and are also referred to as 'autonomous concepts'. This independent classification of terms by the ECtHR is justified to ensure uniformity of treatment among the contracting States and to prevent States from denying the Convention protections by interpreting or categorising issues in a way that the rights guarantees are avoided. This is particularly important in the context of 'legality' which has an independent Convention meaning that is not determined by whether the State purports to have a domestic legal provision in place.[188] Legality for the purposes of the Convention means that it must have the quality of law as understood in the Convention context. This is self-evidently important to ensure that States cannot render the Convention rights redundant. Some further examples of terms with an autonomous meaning are, 'peaceful' in Article 11, which has an autonomous meaning, regardless of the definition given in domestic law;[189] and 'civil rights and obligations' and 'criminal charge' in Article 6.[190] Autonomous meanings will be discussed further as they arise in relation to substantive rights.

3.6.2.4 *Non-Convention Sources When Interpreting and Applying Convention Rights*

The ECtHR will also look to other international human rights treaties as well as specialist instruments from the Council of Europe in respect of a given issue. For example, in *Kurt* v. *Austria*, a case concerning domestic violence, the Grand Chamber drew upon the Istanbul Convention (The Council of Europe Convention on preventing and combating violence against women and domestic violence),[191] the UN Convention on the Elimination of All Forms of Discrimination against Women,[192] the UN Convention on the Rights of the Child[193] and material from the European Union.[194] Similarly in its human trafficking case law, the Court has drawn upon the UN Protocol to Prevent, Suppress and Punish Trafficking in Persons, Especially Women and Children

[188] *J.N.* v. *the United Kingdom*, App. No. 37289/12, 19/05/2016 at [77].

[189] *Cissé* v. *France*, App. No. 51346/99, 09/04/2002.

[190] *Engel and others* v. *The Netherlands* (1976) 1 EHRR 647.

[191] *Kurt* v. *Austria* (2022) 74 EHRR 6 at [75]–[86]. [192] Ibid at [91]–[93]. [193] Ibid at [94].

[194] Ibid at [95]–[98].

(Palermo Protocol) and the Council of Europe Convention on Action against Trafficking in Human Beings (ECAT).[195]

The ECtHR has also stated that it 'must endeavour to interpret and apply the Convention in a manner which is consistent under international law delineated by the International Court of Justice'.[196]

In *Verein KlimaSeniorinnen Schweiz* v. *Switzerland*, the Grand Chamber examined an extensive range of materials outside the ECHR.[197] This included, inter alia, the United Nations Framework Convention on Climate Change, the Kyoto Protocol, the Paris Agreement, COP26, COP27 and COP28, and opinions of the Human Rights Committee, the Committee on the Convention on the Elimination of All Forms of Discrimination Against Women and the Committee on the Rights of the Child. The Aarhus Convention, which the Grand Chamber noted had been ratified by a large majority of Council of Europe Member States, accepts NGO standing in environmental cases, and this was influential in the decision to extend the standing requirements in the climate change case. The Grand Chamber found a European consensus on this concept of associational standing by drawing on the Aarhus Convention.[198]

3.6.3 Scope of Rights: Negative and Positive Obligations

The classic conception of a human right is that it sets limits on what a State can do, such that it requires the State to refrain or abstain from doing certain things to an individual. For example, Article 3 ECHR prohibits the State from torturing an individual. This is a negative obligation.

This contrasts with positive obligations which require the State to do something to ensure that the individual can effectively enjoy his or her rights.[199] It is, however, important to note that the ECtHR frequently states that

> [t]he boundaries between the State's positive and negative obligations under Article 8 do not lend themselves to precise definition. The applicable principles are nonetheless similar. In particular, in both instances regard must be had to the fair balance which has to be struck between the competing interests; and in both contexts the State enjoys a certain margin of appreciation.[200]

[195] *S.M.* v. *Croatia* (n 137).

[196] *Hasan* v. *the United Kingdom* [GC], App. No. 29750/09, 16/09/2014 at [77] and [102]. In *Ukraine* v. *Russia (re Crimea)* [GC] (n 47) at [918], the GC determined that Russia functioned as an occupying power in Crimea and therefore, that International Humanitarian Law should be taken into account when determining the Convention.

[197] *Verein Klimaseniorinnen Schweiz* v. *Switzerland* (n 77).

[198] Ibid at [491].

[199] See Vladislava Stoyanova, *Positive Obligations under the European Convention on Human Rights: Within and Beyond Boundaries* (Oxford University Press, 2023), ch.1 and more generally, Sandra Fredman, *Human Rights Transformed: Positive Rights and Positive Duties* (Oxford University Press, 2009).

[200] *Evans* (n 118) at [75] and *Odievre* v. *France* (2004) 38 EHRR 43 at [40].

Positive obligations can arise as a means of giving effect to Article 1 ECHR, which requires contracting States to 'secure to everyone within their jurisdiction' the rights and freedoms set out in the Convention and contribute to making them practical and effective. Positive rights have also been drawn expressly from the text of the Convention right, but others have been implied by the ECtHR from the Convention text. There are many different types of positive obligations, some of which are procedural,[201] whilst others are substantive.[202] In the early jurisprudence of the Court, steps were taken to ensure that legal mechanisms were in place to safeguard the effective realisation of Convention rights.[203] Thus, the Court found that Article 8 ECHR imposes a positive duty on the State to provide full legal recognition to the gender of post-operative transgender individuals.[204] Some positive obligations require the State to protect the individual from the actions of private actors. In these circumstances, the State is required to impose obligations and penalties on third parties in order to secure the enjoyment of the guaranteed right, such as the positive obligations applied to the prohibition of slavery or forced labour.[205]

A further category of positive obligation requires the State to put in place not only legal mechanisms but to take positive operational or regulatory steps to secure individual rights. This obligation has been extended to a wide variety of situations. For example, the right to life under Article 2 has been interpreted to ensure that procedures are established so that apposite care is taken when assessing the absolute necessity for taking life.[206] State responsibility has arisen under Article 8 in environmental cases from a failure to regulate adequately private industry[207] and an omission 'to collect, process and disseminate such information' about environmental hazards.[208] In relation to climate change, the Court has stated: 'the State's primary duty is to adopt, and to effectively apply in practice, regulations and measures capable of mitigating the existing and potentially irreversible, future effects of climate change'.[209] The Court concluded that Switzerland had failed to fulfil the positive obligation required by Article 8 to devise an adequate regulatory framework.[210] Other cases have dealt with requiring a reasonable level of

201 See, e.g., *Buckley* v. *the United Kingdom* (1997) 23 EHRR 101 at [76] in relation to Article 8.

202 See, e.g., *Osman* v. *the United Kingdom* (1998) 29 EHRR 245.

203 See, e.g., *Marckx* v. *Belgium* (n 185) at [31].

204 *Goodwin* v. *the United Kingdom* (n 141) at [85].

205 *Siliadin* v. *France* (2005) 43 EHRR 16 at [89].

206 *McCann, Farrell and Savage* v. *the United Kingdom* [GC] (1996) 21 EHRR 97.

207 *Hatton and Others* v. *the United Kingdom* [GC] (2003) 37 EHRR 28 at [98]; and *Lopez-Ostra* v. *Spain* (1995) 20 EHRR 277.

208 *Guerra* v. *Italy* [GC] (1998) 26 EHRR 357 at [52].

209 *Verein KlimaSeniorinnen Schweiz* v. *Switzerland* (n 77) at [545].

210 Ibid at [562] and [572].

policing protection for individuals whose personal safety is threatened,[211] instituting care proceedings to protect children,[212] and guaranteeing pursuant to Article 11 ECHR, that appropriate measures are taken to enable lawful demonstrations to take place peacefully.[213] In an important development, this positive obligation was extended to situations of domestic violence.[214]

The ECtHR has also developed significant jurisprudence that requires a State, in certain circumstances, to conduct an effective and independent investigation into alleged violations of Article 2 and Article 3 ECHR.[215] Such investigations are needed to ensure that the substantive Convention right is practical and effective.[216] This obligation is also aimed at improving public confidence in the action of authorities.[217]

The ambit and potential expansion of positive obligations is a further aspect of the Convention that is controversial and is closely connected to perspectives as to the proper role of the ECtHR, and the limits to that role.

3.6.3.1 *Proportionality*

The ECtHR often refers to the doctrine of proportionality.[218] It is an essential aspect of the reasoning advanced in the qualified rights case law when determining whether a measure was necessary in a democratic society; in these cases the ECtHR is asking whether the interference was proportionate to the legitimate aim pursued. In *Dudgeon* v. *the United Kingdom*, the Court stated:

> the notion of 'necessity' is linked to that of a 'democratic society'. According to the Court's case-law, a restriction on a Convention right cannot be regarded as 'necessary in a democratic society' – two hallmarks of which are tolerance and broadmindedness – unless, amongst other things, it is proportionate to the legitimate aim pursued.[219]

The notion of 'necessary in a democratic society' was clarified in *Sunday Times* v. *the United Kingdom (No 1)* where the Court explained that 'whilst the adjective "necessary", within the meaning of Article 10 (2) …, is not synonymous with "indispensable", neither has it the flexibility of such

[211] *Osman* v. *the United Kingdom* (n 202); *RR and Others* v. *Hungary*, App. No. 19400/11, 04/12/2012 at [32].

[212] *Z* v. *the United Kingdom* (2002) 34 EHRR 3 at [73].

[213] *Plattform Artzte fur das Leben* v. *Austria* (1991) 13 EHRR 204 at [32].

[214] *Opuz* v. *Turkey* (2010) 50 EHRR 28 and *Kurt* v. *Austria* (n 191).

[215] *McCann* (n 206); *Aydin* v. *Turkey* (1998) 25 EHRR 251.

[216] *McCann* (n 206) at [161]; *Nachova* v. *Bulgaria* [GC] (2005) 42 EHRR 933 at [110].

[217] *Armani Da Silva* v. *the United Kingdom* [GC] (2016) 63 EHRR 12 at [232].

[218] Different accounts have been offered by scholars as to the role currently served by proportionality and whether there should be a role for proportionality. For insight into the debate, see Jeremy Letwin, 'Proportionality, Stringency and Utility in the Jurisprudence of the European Court of Human Rights' (2023) 2 HRLR 3.

[219] *Dudgeon* v. *the United Kingdom* (1981) 4 EHRR 149 at [53].

expressions as "admissible", "ordinary", "useful", "reasonable" or "desirable" and that it implies the existence of a "pressing social need"'.[220] The 'pressing social need' relates to the weight and importance of the aims pursued.

The proportionality test as applied by the Court is flexible, but broadly the Court asks:

1. Whether there is a pressing social need for any interference with a protected right. There must be a legitimate aim that is sufficiently important to justify limiting the right.
2. Is the measure designed to meet the legitimate aim rationally connected to it and directed at the pressing social need?
3. Is the measure proportionate to the aim it pursues? Are the means employed disproportionate to the objective?[221]

The Court balances the nature and extent of the interference against the reasons for the interference. The greater the interference with the right, the higher the demand for the State to provide weighty justifications: an interference must never injure the essence or substance of a right.[222] A further element of the proportionality test is whether the limitation on the right is the 'least restrictive means' of achieving the relevant public interest. The Court will sometimes ask whether it would have been possible to achieve the aim by less intrusive means.[223] In practice, the Court often focuses on the conduct of the State rather than whether a less restrictive alternative could have been adopted.[224] After all, the States are given a margin of appreciation by the Court to decide between different courses of conduct, but it will depend on the breadth of the margin of appreciation in the specific instance. A factor that can thus influence the ECtHR's determination of whether the measure was 'necessary in a democratic society' is the extent to which the measure has been scrutinised domestically by the legislature[225] or national courts.[226]

Proportionality will be addressed further in the chapters looking at the specific Convention rights. The sophisticated concept of proportionality has been developed by the Court through its jurisprudence. It is an important doctrine as it provides a structure and a methodology which should in

[220] *Sunday Times* v. *the United Kingdom (No 1)* (1979) EHRR 245 at [59].

[221] Jack Beatson et al., *Human Rights: Judicial Protection in the UK* (Sweet and Maxwell, 2008), pp.169–170.

[222] *Golder* v. *the United Kingdom*, App. No. 4451/70 at [38].

[223] See *Mouvement Raëlien Suisse* v. *Switzerland* [GC] (2013) 56 EHRR 14 at [75].

[224] On the use of the least restrictive means test, see Eva Brems and Laurens Lavrysen, '"Don't Use a Sledgehammer to Crack a Nut": Less Restrictive Means in the Case Law of the European Court of Human Rights' (2015) 15 HRLR 1.

[225] *Animal Defenders International* v. *the United Kingdom* (2013) 57 EHRR 21 at [114]–[116].

[226] Ibid.

principle give priority to the protected Convention right, albeit that this is not always the case in practice.[227]

Moreover, it is also important to observe that whilst the term 'proportionality' typically refers to the assessment that takes places within the context of the qualified rights, the notion that the degree of interference needs to be evaluated against competing rights and interests is also evident elsewhere within the Convention, with different standards applying in different contexts. For example, where there is a clash of rights, the ECtHR considers whether a 'fair balance' has been struck.[228] The concept of a fair balance also appears in respect of Article 1 of Protocol No. 1 ECHR (protection of property);[229] a standard which is:

> less stringent than the test of 'necessary in a democratic society' found in Convention Articles 8 to 11 ECHR. It requires the State to show it has struck a fair balance between the person's right and the public interest. That will not be achieved if the individual (or company) has to bear an excessive burden, or where he or she has no or few procedural avenues to challenge the deprivation.[230]

It has also been suggested at times that the notion of a fair balance is one that is 'inherent in the whole of the Convention'.[231] This reflects the fact that human rights place limits on what States can do in pursuit of competing rights and public interest. Proportionality can thus be seen in relation to Article 14 ECHR, the non-discrimination principle,[232] even though there is no express reference to proportionality in the text of the right.[233]

Although the principle of proportionality is the seminal interpretive tool applied by the ECtHR, the multiple and varying uses of the principle mean that Christofferson is right to conclude that 'we know a lot about the principle of proportionality, but there is also quite a bit that we do not know. The interaction between the principle of proportionality , the margin of appreciation, and the ordinary canons of interpretation remains a partial mystery.' [234]

[227] See Chapter 9, Article 8 ECHR and Immigration.

[228] See Chapter 10, Privacy and Freedom of Expression.

[229] See, e.g., *Ališić and Others* v. *Bosnia and Herzegovina, Croatia, Serbia, Slovenia and the former Yugoslav Republic of Macedonia* [GC], App. No. 60642/08, 16/07/2014 at [101]; and *Beyeler* v. *Italy* [GC] (2001) 33 EHRR 52 at [107].

[230] Council of Europe Toolkit, Article 1 of Protocol No.1, www.coe.int/en/web/echr-toolkit/protocole-1 (last accessed 12 August 2024).

[231] This statement appeared in some of the earlier case law; see *Sporong Lönnroth* v. *Sweden* [1983] 5 EHRR 35 at [69]. For analysis of the case law in respect of 'fair balance' and its role in the Convention, see Alistair Mowbray, 'A Study of Fair Balance in the Jurisprudence of the European Court of Human Rights' (2010) 10(2) HRLR 289.

[232] See, e.g., *Thlimmenos* v. *Greece* (2001) 31 EHRR 411. See Chapter 14, Non-discrimination and Equality.

[233] Jonas Christoffersen, *Fair Balance: Proportionality, Subsidiarity and Primarity in the European Convention on Human Rights* (Brill/Nijhoff, 2009), p.69.

[234] Ibid, p.1.

3.6.3.2 *Margin of Appreciation*

Having observed the role of proportionality reasoning in limiting States, as alluded to above, it is important to observe the role of the margin of appreciation in conferring latitude on States. The margin of appreciation or area of discretionary judgment is an essential doctrine in the ECHR case law. It reflects the subsidiary role of the ECtHR vis-à-vis States, namely the idea that States have primary responsibility for protecting rights and that the ECtHR should not intervene prematurely.[235] Its primary purpose is to delineate the areas of competence of the ECtHR and domestic or national authorities in securing Convention rights. The Preamble of the Convention was amended by Protocol No. 15 with the addition of a new recital, referring to the principle of subsidiarity and the margin of appreciation. The Explanatory Report on Protocol No. 15 stated that this recital 'is intended to enhance the transparency and accessibility of these characteristics and to be consistent with the doctrine of the margin of appreciation as developed by the Court in its case law'.[236]

In *Handyside* v. *the United Kingdom*, the ECtHR first explained the rationale for the doctrine as follows: 'By reason of their direct and continuous contact with the vital forces of their countries, State authorities are in principle in a better position than the international judge to give an opinion on the exact content.'[237] It is, however, for the ECtHR to set the limits in which States may act. Thus in *Handyside*, the ECtHR went on to state that States do not have 'an unlimited power of appreciation'.[238] It observed that the Court 'is responsible for ensuring the observance of those States' engagements' and thus the margin of appreciation 'goes hand in hand with a European supervision'.[239] It concluded that 'it follows from this that it is in no way the Court's task to take the place of the competent national courts but rather to review under Article 10 ... the decisions they delivered in the exercise of their power of appreciation'.[240]

The area of discretionary judgment is often relied upon when deciding whether an interference of qualified rights (Articles 8–11 ECHR) is justified on any of the permitted grounds set out in paragraph (2) of the relevant

[235] See Steven Greer, 'The Interpretation of the European Convention on Human Rights: Universal Principle or Margin of Appreciation?' (2010) 3 UCL Law Review 1; Yutaka Arai-Takahashi, *The Margin of Appreciation Doctrine and the Principle of Proportionality in the Jurisprudence of the ECHR* (Intersentia, 2002); Jan Kratochvil, 'The Inflation of the Margin of Appreciation by the European Court of Human Rights (2011) 29 NQHR 324, Dean Spielman, 'Allowing the Right Margin: The European Court of Human Rights and the National Margin of Appreciation Doctrine – Waiver or Subsidiarity of National Review? (2012) 14 Camb.Y.B. Eur. Legal Studies 318.

[236] Council of Europe, Protocol No. 15 amending the Convention for the Protection of Human Rights and Fundamental Freedoms (CETS No. 213) Explanatory Report.

[237] *Handyside* v. *the United Kingdom* (n 167) at [48]. [238] Ibid at [49]. [239] Ibid at [49].

[240] Ibid at [50].

Article,[241] or when determining whether the State has adequately complied with positive obligations.[242] The margin of appreciation is important in the application of Article 15 ECHR, when determining the existence of a public emergency and whether the measures taken are 'strictly required by the exigencies of the situation'. Harris and colleagues comment that the Articles which are linked to the margin of appreciation 'largely coincide with those to which the principle of proportionality applies, the point being that in assessing the proportionality of the State's acts, the margin of appreciation doctrine is the vehicle relied upon to give a certain degree of deference to the judgment of national authorities when they weigh competing public and individual interests in view of their local knowledge and the principle of subsidiarity'.[243]

There is a degree of ambiguity surrounding the scope and application of the margin of appreciation accorded to States, as the ECtHR expands or contracts the 'width' of the margin in line with a number of factors. One of which is the importance of the right at stake and the context in which it is being invoked, but other factors include the existence, or absence, to which there is consensus across States on the issue. It will therefore consider whether a consistent pattern emerges in respect of a given issue. There is also considerable uncertainty as to how much consensus is needed, and the ECtHR is arguably not very consistent itself as to its approach to this matter.[244] As noted above in respect of proportionality, a further factor which the ECtHR takes into account is the extent to which the matter has been considered at the domestic level by the executive, legislature and the judiciary.[245]

A broader margin is attributed in matters concerning national security, or economic and social policy, although the ECtHR will still intervene if the policy leads to discrimination on a 'suspect' ground.[246] States are considered to be in a better position than international judges to assess the best interests of the public in relation to economic and social issues. The ECtHR usually respects legislative policy choices unless they are 'manifestly without reasonable foundation'.[247] The margin of appreciation is not so wide to enable States to take measures which impair the very essence of the right in question.[248]

241 See, e.g., *Evans* v. *the United Kingdom* (n 118) at [77]–[82]. 242 Ibid at [75]–[76].

243 Harris et al. (n 1), p.16.

244 See Panos Kapotos and Vassilis P. Tzevelekos, *Building Consensus on European Consensus: Judicial Interpretation of Human Rights in Europe and Beyond* (Cambridge University Press, 2019).

245 *Animal Defenders International* v. *the United Kingdom* (n 225) at [114]–[116].

246 *Stec* v. *the United Kingdom* [GC] (2006) 43 EHRR 47 at [52].

247 *Andrejeva* v. *Latvia* [GC] (2010) 51 EHRR 28.

248 See, e.g., *Verein KlimaSeniorinnen Schweiz* v. *Switzerland* (n 77) at [638]; *Naït-Liman* v. *Switzerland* [GC], App. No. 51357/07, 15/03/2018 at [114]; *Baka* v. *Hungary*, App. No. 20261/12, 23/06/2016 at [120]. See also Sébastien Van Drooghenbroeck and Cecilia

If an issue raises highly sensitive political, moral and ethical matters and there is no degree of European consensus, the ECtHR will grant States a margin of appreciation. In *A, B and C* v. *Ireland*, however, the Grand Chamber decided that although there was 'a consensus amongst a substantial majority of the Contracting States of the Council of Europe towards allowing abortion on broader grounds than accorded under Irish law', this could not replace Ireland's margin of appreciation in these circumstances.[249]

In *Verein Klimasenioinnen Schweiz* v. *Switzerland*, the Grand Chamber adopted differing margins of appreciation within the same judgment.[250] The Grand Chamber held that to comply with their climate obligations, domestic authorities were required to adopt measures and to take action to mitigate the effects of climate change and, on this point, the margin of appreciation is narrow. States, however, were given a wide margin of appreciation regarding the choices of objectives, methods and measures to deal with the climate emergency. The Grand Chamber also went on to set out specific criteria for determining whether that margin had been exceeded.[251]

The Strasbourg judgments do not always seem to consistently follow their own criteria. For example, in *Hirst (No 2)*, concerning voting rights for prisoners, the ECtHR disregarded the lack of consensus in Europe and observed that 'even if no common European approach to the problem can be discerned, this cannot of itself be determinate of the issue'.[252] According to the ECtHR, the 'general, automatic and indiscriminate restriction on a vitally important Convention right' was 'outside any acceptable margin of appreciation, however wide that margin may be'.[253] Even though the lack of consensus across Europe would suggest that the State has a wide margin of appreciation, a State is not free to adopt any legal measure without consideration of the balance to be struck.

The ECtHR has been criticised for this ambiguity by both those that would prefer the ECtHR to accord a wider margin of appreciation to States and those that wish to see the ECtHR adopting a less deferential role.[254] As indicated above and discussed further below, Protocol No.15 was introduced in order to allay some of these criticisms.[255]

Rizcallah, 'The ECHR and the Essence of Fundamental Rights: Searching for Sugar in Hot Milk?' (2019) 20 German Law Journal 904.

[249] *A, B and C* v. *Ireland* [GC] (2011) 53 EHRR 13.

[250] *Verein KlimaSeniorinnen Schweiz* v. *Switzerland* (n 77). [251] Ibid at [550].

[252] *Hirst* v. *the United Kingdom (No 2)* (n 143) at [81]. [253] Ibid.

[254] On the criticisms levelled at the margin of appreciation, see Yutaka Arai-Takahashi, 'The Margin of Appreciation Doctrine: A Theoretical Analysis of Strasbourg's Variable Geometry' in Andreas Føllesdal et al., *Constituting Europe: The European Court of Human Rights in a National, European and Global Context* (Cambridge University Press, 2013).

[255] See Section 3.6.3.4.

3.6.3.3 *Substantive or Procedural Review*

We have already seen that the ECtHR uses proportionality in a number of contexts in order to determine whether an intrusion into a right is justified. Thus far we have been considering this as a substantive mode of protecting the right where the ECtHR considers whether the intrusion (i.e., the measure or action) is proportionate. The degree of protection that is afforded using this approach is calibrated by reference to the intensity of the proportionality standard and the width of the margin of appreciation. There is, however, another form of review that has emerged within the case law, namely procedural review. Using this mode of analysis, the ECtHR focuses upon the process that was used by the domestic authorities in determining to adopt a measure or engage in conduct that interfered with the right. This is commonly referred to as the 'procedural turn' in human rights law and we will see the role that it has played in a number of contexts in this book.[256]

3.6.3.4 *Subsidiarity*

Closely connected to the procedural turn and the margin of appreciation is the idea of subsidiarity.[257] Protocol No.15 entered into force on 1 February 2022. Article 1 of Protocol 15 amended the preamble to the Convention to add the following new recital affirming the subsidiary role of the ECtHR:

> Affirming that the High Contracting Parties, in accordance with the principle of subsidiarity, have the primary responsibility to secure the rights and freedoms defined in this Convention and the Protocols thereto, and that in doing so they enjoy a margin

[256] On procedural review and the procedural turn, see Janneke Gerards and Eva Brems, *Procedural Review in European Fundamental Rights Cases* (Cambridge University Press, 2017); Oddny Mjöll Arnardóttir,'The "Procedural Turn" under the European Convention on Human Rights and Presumptions of Convention Compliance' (2017) 15(1) ICON 9–35; Peter Cumper and Tom Lewis, 'Blanket Bans, Subsidiarity, and the Procedural Turn of the European Court of Human Rights' (2019) 68(3) ICLQ 611–638; Robert Spano, 'The Future of the European Court of Human Rights: Subsidiarity, Process-Based Review and the Rule of Law' (2018) 18 HRLR 473; Thomas Kleinlein, 'The Procedural Approach of the European Court of Human Rights: Between Subsidiarity and Dynamic Evolution' (2019) 68 ICLQ 91; Patricia Popelier, 'Procedural Rationality Review after Animal Defenders International: A Constructively Critical Approach' (2019) 15 European Constitutional Law Review 272; Miles Jackson, 'Judicial Avoidance at the European Court of Human Rights: Institutional Authority, the Procedural Turn and Docket Control' (2022) 20(1) ICON 112–140.

[257] On subsidiarity, see Robert Spano, 'Universality or Diversity of Human Rights? Strasbourg in the Age of Subsidiarity' (2015) 14 HRLR 487; Dean Spielmann. 'Allowing the Right Margin: The European Court of Human Rights and the National Margin of Appreciation Doctrine: Waiver or Subsidiarity of European Review?' (2012) Cambridge Yearbook of European Legal Studies 381–418; Marisa Iglesias Vila, 'Subsidiarity, Margin of Appreciation and International Adjudication within a Cooperative Conception of Human Rights' (2017) 15(2) ICON 393–413.

of appreciation, subject to the supervisory jurisdiction of the European Court of Human Rights established by this Convention.

The Explanatory Report accompanying the Protocol explained that this was 'intended to enhance the transparency and accessibility of these characteristics of the Convention system and to be consistent with the doctrine of the margin of appreciation as developed by the Court in its case law'.[258] It went on to explain that the ECtHR's jurisprudence makes it clear that State Parties enjoy a margin of appreciation, 'that the Convention system is subsidiary to the safeguarding of human rights at national level and that national authorities are in principle better placed than an international court to evaluate local needs and conditions'.[259] Consequently, 'the role of the Court is to review whether decisions taken by national authorities are compatible with the Convention, having due regard to the State's margin of appreciation'.[260]

3.7 DEROGATION FROM RIGHTS

Article 15 ECHR allows States to derogate from some of the Convention rights in exceptional circumstances, in a limited and supervised manner. Article 15 (1) ECHR thus provides that in times of war or other public emergency threatening the life of the nation, any High Contracting Party may take measures derogating from its obligations under the Convention to the extent strictly required by the exigencies of the situation, provided that such measures are not inconsistent with its other obligations under international law.[261] This means that States can derogate where there is (a) a state of war or other emergency and (b) it is necessary to derogate, but Article 15(1) ECHR also limits measures that can be taken during a derogation. Derogation is not permitted from Articles 3, 4(1) and 7 ECHR.[262] Derogation from Article 2 ECHR is also not permitted, with the exception of deaths resulting from lawful acts of war.[263] Article 15(3) ECHR provides that any High Contracting Party availing itself of this right of derogation shall keep the Secretary General

[258] Council of Europe, Protocol No. 15 amending the Convention for the Protection of Human Rights and Fundamental Freedoms (CETS No. 213) Explanatory Report at [7.] See discussion in House of Lords and House of Commons Joint Committee on Human Rights, *Fourth Report – Protocol 15 to the European Convention on Human Rights – Human Rights Joint Committee* HL Paper 71, HC 837 (26/02/2014) Ch.3.

[259] Council of Europe, Protocol No. 15 Explanatory Report (n 236) at [9].

[260] Ibid. See also the discussion of the Brighton Declaration below.

[261] The Human Rights Committee has elaborated on the phrase 'exigencies of the situation' in the context of the ICCPR and confirms that it encompasses both necessity and proportionality requirements; United Nations, ICCPR, General Comment No 29, States of Emergency (Article 4), CCPR/C/21/Rev.1/Add.11, 31 August 2001.

[262] Article 15(2) ECHR. [263] Ibid.

of the Council of Europe fully informed of the measures which it has taken and the reasons therefore. It shall also inform the Secretary General of the Council of Europe when such measures have ceased to operate and the provisions of the Convention are again being fully executed.[264]

The ECtHR has never been called upon to define the meaning of 'war' within Article 15 ECHR. Emergencies short of war have led to derogations relying on the second limb of Article 15(1) ECHR, 'a public emergency threatening the life of the nation'. In circumstances where an applicant alleges that his or her rights were violated during a derogation period, the Court will first assess whether the measures taken can be justified under the substantive Convention articles. If the measures cannot be justified, then the Court will go on to determine whether the derogation was a valid one.[265] According to the Court in *Lawless* v. *Ireland*, a public emergency threatening the life of the nation is 'an exceptional situation of crisis or emergency which affects the whole population and constitutes a threat to the organised life of the community of which the State is composed'.[266] It is clear that the crisis, as well as actual, must be exceptional or imminent but there is no need to wait for a terrorist attack before taking necessary measures.[267] It is also important to note that the Court has accepted that the emergency may affect only a particular area of a State in this respect there have been derogations in Northern Ireland and in South-East Türkiye.[268] Although Article 15 ECHR requires that there must be exceptional circumstances, the Courts have accepted that such circumstances can continue for a long period. Nevertheless, the key characteristic of any emergency regime remains its *temporary* character.[269]

The Convention organs have generally deferred to the assessment of the State by giving it a wide margin of appreciation. According to the Court in *Ireland* v. *the United Kingdom*:

> It falls in the first place to each Contracting State, with its responsibility for 'the life of [its] nation', to determine whether that life is threatened by a 'public emergency' and, if so, how far it is necessary to go in attempting to overcome the emergency. By reason of their direct and continuous contact with the pressing needs of the moment, the

[264] Natasha Holcroft-Emmess, 'Notified Derogations and Their Absence: Conditions for Valid Derogation and Measures Restricting Rights in Conflicts and Crises' [2024] 2 EHRLR 147.

[265] *A and others* v. *the United Kingdom* [GC] (2009) 49 EHRR 29 at [161]; *Ireland* v. *the United Kingdom* (ECtHR) (n 48) at [191].

[266] *Lawless* v. *Ireland* (n 25) at [28].

[267] *A* v. *SSHD* [2004] the United Kingdom HL 56, [2005] 2 AC 68 at [119] and *A and others* v. *the United Kingdom* (n 265) at [177]. See also Section 3.7.1.

[268] *Brannigan and McBride* v. *the United Kingdom* (1994) 17 EHRR 539 and *Aksoy* v. *Turkey* (1997) 23 EHRR 553 at [70].

[269] Venice Commission, *Turkey Opinion: On Emergency Decree Laws Nos 667–676 Following the Failed Coup of 15 July 2016*, CDL-AD(2016) 037 (Strasbourg, 12 December 2016) at [78].

national authorities are in principle in a better position than the international judge to decide both on the presence of such an emergency and on the nature and scope of derogations necessary to avert it.[270]

Although the State is given a wide margin of appreciation, this deference is still subject to European supervision. In *Ireland* v. *the United Kingdom*, it was accepted by all that the crisis in Northern Ireland had reached the threshold required to be a public emergency.[271] The Court noted that: 'Up to March 1975 ... over 1,100 people had been killed, over 11,500 injured and more than £140,000,000 worth of property destroyed during the recent troubles in Northern Ireland. This violence found its expression in part in civil disorders, in part in terrorism, that is organised violence for political ends.'[272] In *Ireland* v. *the United Kingdom*, the Court concluded that the Government was 'reasonably entitled to consider that normal legislation offered insufficient resources ... and that recourse to measures outside the scope of the ordinary law, in the shape of extrajudicial deprivation of liberty, was called for'.[273] The Court's assessment is not retrospective but considers the conditions and circumstances as they existed when the decision was originally applied.[274]

In circumstances where the Court accepts the existence of a public emergency, the Court will still assess whether the State has gone beyond 'the extent strictly required by the exigencies of the situation'.[275] This aspect of Article 15 ECHR usually attracts more intense judicial scrutiny than whether or not a public emergency exists.[276] An example is provided by *Yalçinkaya* v. *Türkiye*.[277] After a failed coup attempt in Türkiye in July 2016, Türkiye gave notice of a derogation pursuant to Article 15 ECHR indicating that a state of emergency has been declared in order to tackle the threat posed to the life of the nation by the severe dangers resulting from the attempted military coup and other terrorist acts.[278] The Court accepted that a state of emergency existed but found the measures taken were not strictly required by the exigencies of the situation. The emergency measures taken by Türkiye included excessive recourse to detention: over 150 journalists had been placed in pretrial detention, and over 130,000 people including judges, civil servants, teachers, police officers and soldiers were also purged from their employment,

[270] *Ireland* v. *the United Kingdom* (n 48) at [207]. Note also *Denmark, Norway, Sweden and the Netherlands* v. *Greece* ('The Greek Case'), App. No. 3325/67, 5/11/1969, conditions for the application of Article 15 of the Convention were not met.

[271] *Ireland* v. *the United Kingdom* (n 48) at [205]. [272] Ibid at [11]–[12]. [273] Ibid at [212].

[274] Ibid at [214].

[275] See European Court of Human Rights, *Guide on Article 15 European Convention on Human Rights* (31 August 2023), which summarises at [24] the issues considered by the Court.

[276] See Alan Greene, 'Separating Normalcy from Emergency: The Jurisprudence of Article 15 of the European Convention on Human Rights' (2011) 12(10) German Law Journal 1764.

[277] *Yalçinkaya* v. *Türkiye*, App. No. 15669/20, 26/09/2023. [278] Ibid at [211].

or arrested and convicted of various offences.[279] When considering the derogation requirements, the ECtHR found that Türkiye had satisfied the conditions for the exercise of the exceptional right of derogation but the Court did not find that the measures taken were strictly proportionate to the exigencies of the situation.[280]

European supervision is essential in Article 15 ECHR cases as illustrated by *Dareskizb Ltd* v. *Armenia*, where the ECtHR reviewed a derogation and concluded that it failed to satisfy the requirements of Article 15(1) ECHR.[281] The State had imposed a ban on the publication of a newspaper due to protests following a disputed Presidential election in February 2008. The ECtHR addressed whether the conditions laid down in Article 15 ECHR for the exercise of the right of derogation were satisfied in this case. In the Court's view,

> the Government failed to demonstrate convincingly and to support with evidence their assertion that the opposition demonstrations – which, moreover, were apparently confronted by heavy-handed police intervention – could be characterised as a public emergency 'threatening the life of the nation' within the meaning of Article 15 of the Convention.[282]

Normal measures of control must be inadequate before States can derogate from their Convention obligations. Having considered the operation of Article 15 ECHR in general we now turn to consider the use of derogation in two particular contexts: (i) terrorism and (ii) public health.

3.7.1 Terrorism and Derogation

As discussed in Chapter 8 (Terrorism), following the 9/11 terrorist attacks in New York in 2001, the British Government passed the ATCSA which provided for indefinite detention without trial of non-nationals in specific circumstances. As noted in Chapter 8, such detention was not compatible with Article 5 ECHR. Consequently, on 11 November 2001, the Secretary of State made a derogation order pursuant to the HRA 1998 which set out the terms of a proposed notification to the Secretary General of the Council of Europe of a derogation from Article 5 ECHR.[283] Several individuals subject to detention under the ATCSA challenged its lawfulness (including the lawfulness of the

[279] Tom Ruys and Emre Turkut, 'Turkey's Post-Coup "Purification Process": Collective Dismissals of Public Servants under the European Convention on Human Rights' (2018) 18(3) HRLR 539, 539.

[280] See, e.g., *Mehmet Hasan Altan* v. *Türkiye*, App. No. 13237/17, 20/03/2018; *Aydin Sefa Akay* v. *Türkiye*, App. No. 59/17, 23/04/24. See also, Alan Greene, 'Yalçinkaya v. Türkiye: A Chocolate-Box Judgment or a Victory for Human Rights?' (2024) 5 EHRLR 5.

[281] *Dareskizb Ltd* v. *Armenia*, App. No. 61737/08, 21/09/2021.

[282] Ibid at [62].

[283] Section 14 of the Human Rights Act 1998; see discussion in *A and Others* v. *the United Kingdom* (n 265) at [11].

derogation) with the case coming before the House of Lords in 2004.[284] A majority of the Law Lords considered that the ATCSA did not fall within the exception to the general right of liberty set out in Article 5(1)(f) of the Convention.[285] A majority also determined that the derogation was unlawful as it was discriminatory and 'not strictly required by the exigencies of the situation'.[286] The applicants took their case to Strasbourg, and the ECtHR, amongst other matters, addressed the Article 15 ECHR derogation.[287] Unusually, the Government sought to challenge the decision of the House in Lords concerning the proportionality of the derogation measures. It contended that the judgment was problematic and further guidance was needed from the Court.[288] The ECtHR agreed to address this issue.

Initially, the ECtHR considered whether the detentions were lawful under Article 5(1)(f) ECHR and concluded, agreeing with the House of Lords, that the applicants were deprived of their liberty in breach of Article 5 ECHR. This then raised the question of the validity of the derogation order. The ECtHR reiterated that it falls to each Member State to determine whether 'the life of the nation' is being threatened by a 'public emergency'. In their view, the domestic authorities and not an international court are best placed to decide whether an emergency exists and the nature and scope of a derogation. In other words, the State is given a wide margin of appreciation in assessing the threat.[289] Nevertheless, the domestic margin is also accompanied by European supervision. Given the careful consideration given by the highest domestic courts, 'the Court consider[ed] that it would be justified in reaching a contrary conclusion only if satisfied that the national court had misinterpreted or misapplied Article 15 or the Court's jurisprudence under that Article or reached a conclusion which was manifestly unreasonable'.[290]

The applicants argued that there had been 'no emergency threatening the life of the nation' which would justify the derogation measures in the UK. In their view, the emergency was neither actual nor imminent, it was not of a temporary nature and other States had not issued derogations.[291] Given the evidence available at the time, the ECtHR chose not to criticise the decision of the UK government for fearing that an attack could be imminent. In particular, the ECtHR observed that '[t]he requirement of imminence cannot be interpreted so narrowly as to require a State to wait for disaster to strike before taking measures to deal with it'.[292] They added that the ECtHR's jurisprudence has never explicitly required that an emergency be temporary, although the duration of the emergency may be part of the proportionality assessment.[293] The ECtHR found it 'striking' that no other European State had lodged a

[284] *A* v. *SSHD* (n 267). [285] See, for instance, Lady Hale ibid at [222].
[286] Ibid at [231], per Lady Hale. [287] *A and Others* v. *the United Kingdom* (n 265).
[288] Ibid at [157]. [289] Ibid at [173]. [290] Ibid at [174]. [291] Ibid at [175].
[292] Ibid at [177]. [293] Ibid at [178].

derogation after 9/11, but the ECtHR placed weight on the decisions of the Government, Parliament and the views of the domestic courts.[294] The ECtHR therefore accepted that there had been a public emergency threatening the life of the nation.

The ECtHR then turned to consider whether the derogating measures were 'strictly required by the exigencies of the situation'. The Government challenged the House of Lords' finding that the detention of the applicants was disproportionate. First, they argued that the domestic courts had afforded the State too narrow a margin of appreciation. The ECtHR explained: 'The doctrine of the margin of appreciation has always been meant as a tool to define relations between the domestic authorities and the Court. It cannot have the same application to the relations between the organs of State at the domestic level.'[295] Importantly, the ECtHR agreed with the House of Lords, that the question of proportionality is a judicial question and especially so in these circumstances where the applicants had been deprived of their liberty for a long period of time. The Government also submitted that the House of Lords had examined 'the legislation in the abstract rather than considering the applicants' concrete cases'.[296] The ECtHR gave this argument short shrift. According to the ECtHR, the approach under Article 15 ECHR focuses on the general situation, and both domestic and international courts are required to weigh the adopted derogation measures against the threat posed by the emergency. Where, as in these circumstances, the House of Lords found that the measures were disproportionate to the threat and discriminatory in their operation, there is no need to examine the 'concrete' case of each applicant. The Government also took issue with the House of Lords' approach concerning the comparison between non-national and national suspected terrorists. The ECtHR strongly supported the House of Lords' decision that the detention powers were not immigration measures, where distinctions between nationals and non-nationals are accepted as legitimate. The ECtHR stated:

> The choice by the Government and Parliament of an immigration measure to address what was essentially a security issue had the result of failing adequately to address the problem, while imposing a disproportionate and discriminatory burden of indefinite detention on one group of suspected terrorists.[297]

The ECtHR thus accepted that the national authorities enjoyed a wide margin of appreciation in assessing the threat based on the known facts. In their view, weight had to attach to the judgment of the executive and Parliament and, *specifically*, to the views of the national courts, who were better placed than the ECtHR to assess the relevant evidence. The weight attached to the national courts was thus crucial here as the ECtHR observed that it would only

[294] Ibid at [180]. [295] Ibid at [184]. [296] Ibid at [185]. [297] Ibid at [186].

intervene if Article 15 ECHR was misinterpreted or misapplied by domestic courts or that a manifestly unreasonable conclusion had been reached. The ECtHR thus found that the derogating measures were disproportionate.[298]

3.7.2 Derogation and Public Health

An important question that arose during the COVID-19 pandemic, during which States put in place various measures that impacted upon Convention rights, was whether States should derogate from the Convention. Albania, Armenia, Estonia, Georgia, Latvia, North Macedonia, Moldova, Romania, San Merino and Serbia all declared states of emergency and notified the Council of Europe of derogation,[299] but other States including the UK did not declare a state of emergency.

Scholars differed as to whether the UK should have declared a state of emergency and derogated from rights. Alan Greene argued that the UK should have derogated as this was the 'closest we shall get to an "ideal state of emergency" – the very situation it was designed for'.[300] He argued that the real risk of emergency powers is their 'propensity to become permanent' and that this is 'amplified by failure to declare a de jure state of emergency'.[301] In particular, he asserted that failure to utilise Article 15 ECHR could result in human rights provisions being recalibrated downwards. Moreover, that 'the quarantining effect of a de jure state of emergency [would be] lost' and we would be with 'a de facto state of emergency that enables the same powers but lacking the transparency, additional oversight and supervision that should accompany a de jure state of emergency'.[302] In particular, he considered the ramifications of this for Article 5 and Article 14 ECHR. This was challenged by Kanstantsin Dzehtsiarou who argued that the 'quarantining effect' was presented by reference to military emergencies and that health emergencies are substantively different such that direct parallels were inappropriate.[303] He also argued that the Convention rights have a 'natural quarantining effect' and that Article 15 ECHR derogations do not significantly change the ECtHR's approach.[304] He thus concluded that Greene had overestimated the impact of Article 15 ECHR derogations.[305]

> What derogations under art.15 really do is that they slightly increase the margin of appreciation of the Contracting Parties to the Convention, in the circumstances when

[298] Ibid at [190]. [299] Council of Europe Treaty Office, Derogations Covid-19.

[300] Alan Greene, 'Derogating from the European Convention on Human Rights in Response to the Coronavirus Pandemic: If Not Now, When?' (2020) 3 EHRLR 262, 262.

[301] Ibid. [302] Ibid at [266].

[303] Kanstantsin Dzehtsiarou, 'Article 15 Derogations: Are They Really Necessary during the Covid-19 Pandemic?' [2020] 4 EHRLR 359, 360.

[304] Ibid. [305] Ibid.

> the state's margin of appreciation is already quite wide due to the lack of European consensus and the magnitude of the crisis. Therefore, the benefits of derogating under art.15 in securing human rights are hypothetical and hardly supported by practice; its benefits to the Contracting Parties to the Convention in adopting measures that are supposed to prevent spreading the disease are only marginal and can be seen in very narrow borderline cases. At the same time its symbolic and political cost might be quite substantive.[306]

Greene wrote a rebuttal to this, arguing that Dzehtsiarou fell into what Greene termed the '"objectivity trap" of emergencies', which had led Dzehtsiarou to believe that emergency powers may be quarantined to the duration of the pandemic without the need for Article 15 ECHR.[307]

A further perspective on the issue was provided by Tom Hickman.[308] He argued that the UK did not need to derogate to ensure that the lockdown laws were compatible with Article 5 ECHR because such laws fell within Article 5(1)(e) ECHR, which already imposes constraints of legality and proportionality. He thus argued that by framing the COVID-19 measures within the rights regime the UK Government was acting in accordance with its obligations under Article 15 ECHR, which required it to only derogate when and to the extent that this is strictly required. Moreover, he felt that derogation would have reduced and complicated the oversight of both domestic courts and the ECtHR and thus the decision not to derogate was therefore both sound and welcome. Greene responded to this by publishing a further rejoinder in which he argued for a narrow interpretation of Article 5 (1)(e) ECHR and rejected the suggestion that requiring derogation waters down the definition of a 'public emergency threatening the life of the nation' in Article 15 ECHR.[309] Finally, he asserted that his argument was premised upon how law *ought* to be interpreted and that this should be the focus of legal analysis, as opposed to simply focusing on predicting what courts may decide.

Given these differences of opinion it is perhaps noteworthy that in its September 2020 report the Joint Committee on Human Rights commented as follows:

> It is welcome that a derogation from the UK's human rights obligations has not been necessary so far in the pandemic, since the current the UK measures in response to the crisis are capable of being compatible with Convention rights, so the question of

306 Ibid at 371.

307 Alan Greene, 'On the Value of Derogations from the ECHR in Response to the Covid-19 Pandemic: A Rejoinder' (2020) 5 EHRLR 526–532.

308 Tom Hickman, 'The Coronavirus Pandemic and Derogation from the ECHR' (2020) 6 EHRLR 593–609.

309 Alan Greene, 'Derogations, Deprivation of Liberty and the Containment Stage of Pandemic Responses' (2021) 4 EHRLR 389–402.

derogation does not arise. It is important that the Government and Parliament remain vigilant to ensure that if the criteria for a derogation are met and if a derogation becomes necessary, that the correct procedures are followed.[310]

The issue of non-derogation arose before the ECtHR in *Communauté Genevoise d'Action Syndicale (CGAS)* v. *Switzerland.*[311] The case concerned restrictions on public gatherings during the pandemic in circumstances in which Switzerland had not derogated from the Convention. The applicant alleged that the measures violated Article 11 ECHR.

> The applicant association added that the Government had taken advantage of a power, which it described as unlimited, in order to enact measures which in substance amounted, in its view, to a derogation from a fundamental right guaranteed by the Convention, without observing any of the conditions imposed by Article 15. It considered that, given the intensity of the restriction on guaranteed rights, [the Swiss measure] did not constitute a sufficient legal basis to justify the interference with the rights enshrined in Article 11.[312]

A Chamber of the ECtHR held in March 2022 by a 4:3 majority that the claim was admissible, and that the measures fell outside of Article 11(2) ECHR. Natasha Holcroft-Emmess suggests that the Chamber appears to have held that the measures were, in effect, non-notified derogation measures.[313] The case was, however, subsequently referred to the Grand Chamber, which delivered judgment in November 2023.[314] A majority of the Grand Chamber (12:5) found the case to be inadmissible, reversing the Chamber decision on admissibility.[315] As Holcroft-Emmess notes in the light of this conclusion, the Grand Chamber majority did not express any view on the merits of the case, nor on the potential relevance of the derogation clause.[316]

[310] Joint Committee on Human Rights, *The Government's Response to Covid 19: Human Rights Implications*, Seventh Report of Session 2019–21 HC 265, HL Paper 125, printed on 21 September 2020 at [14].

[311] *Communauté Genevoise d'Action Syndicale (CGAS)* v. *Switzerland* (Court), App. No. 21881/20, 15/03/2022 and *Communauté Genevoise d'Action Syndicale (CGAS)* v. *Switzerland* [GC], App. No. 21881/20, 27/11/2023. For discussion, see Holcroft-Emmess (n 264).

[312] Ibid at [63].

[313] For discussion of the Chamber judgment in *CGAS*, covering both admissibility and merits, see Natasha Holcroft-Emmess, 'Communaute genevoise d'action syndicale (CGAS) v. Switzerland: Proportionate Limitation or (Non-notified) Derogation? A Chamber Divided Over Covid-19 Pandemic Restrictions' (2023) 5 EHRLR 482–496.

[314] *Communauté Genevoise d'Action Syndicale (CGAS)* v. *Switzerland* [GC] (n 311).

[315] The main ground for the Grand Chamber majority's conclusion of inadmissibility was a failure to exhaust domestic remedies; *Communauté Genevoise d'Action Syndicale (CGAS)* v. *Switzerland* [GC] (n 311) at [147]–[164].

[316] Holcroft-Emmess (n 264).

3.8 EUROPEAN SOCIAL CHARTER

The unity and indivisibility of fundamental rights, including civil and political rights on the one hand and social and economic rights on the other hand, has been recognised since the adoption in 1948 of the UDHR. This led to the adoption of the International Covenant on Civil and Political Rights and its two optional protocols, and the International Covenant on Economic, Social and Cultural Rights. Similarly at the European level, when it came to giving binding legal force to the rights in the Universal Declaration, the Council of Europe first adopted the ECHR and in 1961 it adopted the European Social Charter.

The 1961 European Social Charter (ESC) guarantees fundamental social and economic rights related to employment, housing, health, education, social protection and welfare.[317] It emphasises the importance of the protection of particular persons such as elderly people, children, people with disabilities, women and migrants, and it requires that enjoyment of the rights to be guaranteed without discrimination.[318] The Revised European Social Charter (RESC)[319] adopted in 1996 embodies in a single instrument all the rights guaranteed by the 1961 Charter, its Additional Protocol of 1988[320] as well as new rights and amendments adopted by the Parties.[321] It was adopted to take account both of developments in social and economic rights as reflected in other international instruments and in the legislation of States and also of social problems not covered by the other international instruments in force.

317 See further, The Academic Network on the European Social Charter and Social Rights (eds), *The European Social Charter: A Commentary* (Brill (Volume I, June 2022), (Vol. II, March 2023), (Vol III, January 2024)).

318 See Council of Europe, the European Social Charter, www.coe.int/en/web/european-social-charter (last accessed 12 August 2024).

319 For an article-by-article commentary of the RESC, see Karin Lukas, *The Revised European Social Charter* (Edward Elgar Publishing, 2021).

320 The 1988 Additional Protocol extends the protection of social and economic rights to give all workers: (i) the right to equal opportunities and equal treatment in matters of employment and occupation without discrimination on the grounds of sex; (ii) the right to be informed and consulted; and (iii) the right to participate in the determination and improvement of working conditions and the working environment. In addition, the elderly are given the right to social protection. Council of Europe, European Treaty Series – No.128, Additional Protocol to the European Social Charter, Strasbourg 5.V.1988.

321 New rights include: right to protection against poverty and social exclusion; right to housing; right to protection in cases of termination of employment; right to protection against sexual harassment in the workplace and other forms of harassment; rights of workers with family responsibilities to equal opportunities and equal treatment; rights of workers' representatives in undertakings. Amendments included reinforcement of the principle of non-discrimination; improvement of gender equality in all fields covered by the treaty; better protection of maternity and social protection of mothers; better social, legal and economic protection of employed children; better protection of persons with disabilities.

Furthermore, all amendments were to be made bearing in mind the need to ensure equal treatment of men and women.

Forty-three of the Council of Europe Member States are parties to either the 1961 Charter or the Revised Charter (RESC).[322] Only Liechtenstein, Monaco, San Marino and Switzerland have not ratified either of these treaties. The the UK ratified the ESC in 1962 and has accepted sixty of the seventy-two paragraphs of the ESC.[323] It has signed but not ratified the RESC. Nor has it signed the 1988 Additional Protocol to the European Social Charter. In 2005, the Parliamentary Joint Committee on Human Rights recommended that the UK ratify the RESC, but the UK has not done so.[324]

The Revised Charter is seen as the 'Social Constitution of Europe' and 'represents an essential component of the continent's human rights architecture'.[325] Even though the development of the normative systems relating to civil and political rights on the one hand and social and economic rights on the other hand, has followed a different tempo and brought some substantial differences to the monitoring mechanisms set up by both treaties, they are complementary and interdependent.

Many of the rights protected under the Convention and its Protocols are also regulated, sometimes with greater detail, under the 1961 Charter, its Additional Protocol of 1988 and the Revised Charter, adopted in 1996. This is the case as regards trade unions' rights,[326] the rights to life and to protection from inhuman or degrading treatment,[327] the protection of health and of the

[322] Thirty-five states are party to the RESC and twenty-seven to the ESC.

[323] Note, however, that as per Article 22 of the ESC, the Committee of Ministers can ask States to send reports at appropriate intervals relating to provisions of the Charter which they did not accept at the time of their ratification or approval or in a subsequent notification. The implementation of this provision became effective after a 2002 decision of the Committee of Ministers, following which States having ratified the RESC must report on the non-accepted provisions every five years after the date of ratification. See Council of Europe, Social Rights, *Procedure on Non-accepted Provisions of the European Social Charter*, www.coe.int/en/web/european-social-charter/accepted-of-provisions (last accessed 12 August 2024).

[324] Joint Committee on Human Rights, *Seventeenth Report* (Session 2004–2005) 23 March 2005 at [44].

[325] Council of Europe, Social Rights, *The European Social Charter*, www.coe.int/en/web/european-social-charter (last accessed 12 August 2024).

[326] These rights are generically protected as freedom of assembly and association under Article 11 of the Convention, but find a more specific identification of positive obligations to be fulfilled under Articles 5 and 6 of the 1961 Charter and Article 28 of the Revised Charter.

[327] These rights covered by Articles 2 and 3 of the Convention are also taken into account in several provisions of the 1961 Charter and Revised Charter, dealing for example with concrete measures to be implemented in the work place to preserve the life and health of workers, including in relation to maternity or in respect of young workers or workers with disability (Articles 3, 7, 8, 15), the protection of women against domestic violence (Article 16), the right to emergency social and medical assistance to anybody in need (Article 13), as well as in relation to sexual or moral harassment (Article 26 of the Revised Charter).

environment,[328] the prohibition of slavery and forced labour,[329] or the right to education.[330] It is also the case for the prohibition of discrimination[331] and for procedural rights relating to liberty and security, to fair trial and to the lawfulness of sanctions,[332] and the effectiveness of remedies.

Some further connections also exist in relation to respect for private and family life,[333] the right to property,[334] rights related to freedom of movement and expulsion from the territory of a State[335] and freedom of thought, conscience and religion and freedom of expression.[336] While the ECHR protects under its Article 12 the right to marry and under Article 5, Protocol No. 7, equality between spouses, the rights and obligations of spouses are covered by Article 16 of the 1961 Charter and Revised Charter.

The ECSR[337] monitors compliance of all State Parties with the ESC or the RESC through a reporting system. All State Parties to the ESC or the RESC

328 Under the case law developed by the ECtHR, this right has been covered mainly under Articles 2 and 3 or Article 8, but enjoys specific protection under Article 11 of the 1961 Charter and Revised Charter.

329 This prohibition, set forth by Article 4 of the Convention, is also covered by Article 1 of the 1961 Charter and Revised Charter.

330 This right set forth by Article 2 of Protocol No. 2 to the Convention is developed in detail in Articles 7, 9, 10, 15 and 19 of the 1961 Charter and Revised Charter.

331 This prohibition set forth by Article 14 of the Convention and in its Protocol No. 12 is also provided in specific provisions of the 1961 Charter and Revised Charter that ensure explicit protection against discrimination based on property status (Article 13), disability (Article 15), nationality (Article 19), sex and age (Article 1 of the Additional Protocol of 1988 to the 1961 Charter and and Article 20 of the Revised Charter), as well as family status (Article 27 of the Revised Charter). Furthermore, the prohibition of discrimination is specifically ensured by virtue of Article E of the Revised Charter.

332 These rights covered by Articles 5, 6 and 7 of the Convention are taken into account by Article 17 of the 1961 Charter as regards the treatment of young offenders, and by Article 19 as regards the expulsion of migrant workers.

333 Several aspects falling under Article 8 of the Convention (respect for private and family life) form the object of specific rights and concrete positive obligations under the 1961 Charter and Revised Charter, for example as regards workers' right to privacy under Article 1, the status of children born out of wedlock under Article 17, or the placement of children under Article 16.

334 The right to protection of property, covered by Article 1 of Protocol No. 1 to the Convention, is also covered by many provisions of the 1961 Charter and Revised Charter dealing for example with salary, benefits, etc. (Articles 4 and 12 of 1961 Charter and Revised Charter), as well as with housing evictions (Article 31 of the Revised Charter).

335 Certain rights in this regard are covered by Articles 2, 3 and 4 of Protocol No. 4 to the Convention, Article 1 of Protocol No. 7 to the Convention and by Articles 18 and 19 of the 1961 Charter and Revised Charter.

336 These rights are taken into account in the Charter's normative system, for example, with regard to the right to be informed on health risks, workers' rights to information or migrant workers' rights to education in their own language (1961 Charter, Additional Protocol to the 1961 Charter and the Revised Charter).

337 The ECSR is composed of fifteen independent, impartial members elected by the Council of Europe's Committee of Ministers for a period of six years, renewable once.

must submit regular reports to the ECSR providing information on how they are complying with the Charter. Following consideration of State party reports, the Committee issues conclusions that must be respected by the State concerned.[338] With regard to the UK, the Committee has indicated in its conclusions a number of areas where domestic law is not in conformity with the ESC.[339]

The implementation of the conclusions is supervised by the Committee of Ministers of the Council of Europe through the follow up procedure. If the ECSR finds a breach of the ESC in its conclusions, the State concerned must provide information on the measures taken to give effect to these conclusions when submitting its next national report.[340]

In 1995, a new Additional Protocol to the RESC was adopted. The aim was the introduction of a collective complaints procedure to increase the effectiveness, speed and impact of the implementation of the Charter. The procedure has strengthened the role of the social partners and NGOs by enabling them to directly apply to the ESCR for rulings on possible non-implementation of the Charter in the countries concerned, namely those States which have accepted its provisions and the complaints procedure.[341] The the UK is not party to the 1995 Protocol.

Because of their collective nature, complaints should raise questions in general, concerning non-compliance of a State's law or practice with one or more of the provisions of the Charter. Complaints about individual situations

[338] The ECSR conclusions can be found at European Social Charter HUDOC Database. See also, Council of Europe, *Digest of the Case Law of the European Committee of Social Rights* (Council of Europe, June 2022).

[339] Ibid.

[340] At the end of each supervision cycle, the Committee of Ministers will adopt a resolution based on the proposals made by the Governmental Committee, containing individual guidance for the State Party concerned. If the State Party concerned has failed to take action, the Committee of Ministers will then issue a recommendation, based on the proposals of the Governmental Committee, asking that the State change the situation in law and/or in practice. On 27 September 2022, the Committee of Ministers adopted a reform package aimed at modernising the European Social Charter system (CM(2022)114-final). The ultimate goal is to assist States Parties in ensuring respect for social rights in line with their commitments. For this purpose, emphasis is placed on the need for enhanced dialogue between the ESCR, the Council of Europe Governmental Committee, States Parties as well as all relevant stakeholders (national human rights institutions, national equality bodies, trade unions and other civil society organisations). In operational terms, several aspects of the monitoring process are evolving with a view to increasing the effectiveness of the European Social Charter system as a whole, and further emphasis is placed on recommendations, which may include appropriate technical meetings, exchanges of good practices, and cooperation projects.

[341] Sixteen States have accepted the collective complaints procedure. For decisions adopted by the ESCR, see the European Social Charter Caselaw Database (HUDOC Charter).

may not be submitted. Complaints may be lodged without exhausting domestic remedies and without the complainant organisation necessarily being a victim of the alleged violation.

Following examination of a collective complaint, the ESCR adopts a decision which must be implemented by the State concerned. The implementation of the decision is supervised by the Committee of Ministers of the Council of Europe, which may adopt a resolution or address a recommendation to the State concerned. The Committee's jurisprudence (decisions and conclusions) represents an authoritative interpretation of the Charter's provisions. States Parties have an obligation to cooperate with the Committee that arises from the application of the principle of good faith to the observance of all treaty obligations.

The collective complaints procedure complements the judicial protection provided for civil and political rights under the Convention. The connections between the Convention and Charter normative systems are taken into account by the ECtHR and the ECSR in their assessment of the cases submitted to them, and the criteria applied are very similar: both the ECtHR and the Committee assess the implementation in practice of the protected rights. Through their ever-developing case law, the ECtHR and the Committee ensure that all human rights – be they civil, political, social or economic rights – are effectively protected in a complementary and progressive way.

3.9 COUNCIL OF EUROPE/ECHR REFORM

3.9.1 Introduction and the Interlaken Process

As the Council of Europe is an intergovernmental organisation, all States have equal rights and take turns chairing the Committee of Ministers, the organisation's decision-making body, for a period of six months. During Switzerland's Chairmanship of the Committee of Ministers (November 2009 to May 2010), Switzerland organised a High-Level Conference on the Future of the European Court of Human Rights in Interlaken. During this Conference, the high number of applications brought before the ECtHR and the growing backlog of cases were noted with grave concern. It was feared that this situation was damaging the effectiveness and credibility of the Convention and was also a threat to the authority of the Court and the quality and consistency of its case law.[342] It was emphasised that the effective implementation of the Convention is the shared responsibility of the Member States and the ECtHR. At this Conference, the

[342] Council of Europe, '*High Level Conference on the Future of the European Court of Human Rights*', Interlaken, 18–19 February 2010 at p.119.

Ministers of Justice of the Member States adopted a declaration, which formally charged the Committee of Ministers with the reform of the Court. This reform was named the Interlaken Process and was a direct response to the ECtHR's struggle to cope with the growing number of applications.[343] This ten-year process led to necessary reforms, including the introduction of the pilot procedure, more effective filtering of applications and the expeditious handling of repetitive cases. The Interlaken reform process together with Protocol 14, which entered into force at the same time, led to significant advances and the increased efficiency of the ECtHR but the backlog of cases remained stubbornly high. It was also recognised that the Convention system must continue to be provided with sufficient resources.[344] The influence of the Interlaken Process was incremental rather than transformative.[345] While the courts ability to filter and process applications improved significantly, the specific proposals concerning the functioning of the courts were never implemented.[346]

3.9.2 Brighton Declaration

During the UK's Chairmanship of the Committee of Ministers (November 2011 to May 2012), the UK Government set out its priorities for the period of its Chairmanship.[347] This included dealing with the large and growing backlog of applications to the ECtHR. Despite the various reforms initiated by the Interlaken Process, the system was still struggling to deal with the huge application numbers. The the UK Government announced that it would seek consensus on, amongst other matters, the following issues:

- **A set of efficiency measures**, which will enable the Court to focus quickly, efficiently and transparently on the most important cases that require its attention;
- **Strengthening the implementation of the Convention at national level**, to ensure that national courts and authorities are able to assume their primary role in protecting human rights;

[343] Council of Europe, *The Interlaken Process: Measures Taken from 2010 to 2019 to Secure the Effective Implementation of the European Convention on Human Rights* (Council of Europe, November 2020).

[344] Ibid.

[345] Ibid. See also Lize R. Glas, 'From Interlaken to Copenhagen: What Has Become of the Proposals Aiming to Reform the Functioning of the European Court of Human Rights?' (2020) 20 HRLR 121, 148.

[346] Glas, ibid, p.147.

[347] *United Kingdom Chairmanship of the Council of Europe: Priorities and Objectives* (7 November 2011), CM/Inf (2011) 41.

- Measures to **strengthen subsidiarity** – new rules or procedures to help ensure that the Court plays a subsidiary role where Member States are fulfilling their obligations under the Convention.[348]

The Government sought to have new measures agreed at a high-level conference held in Brighton in April 2012. The antagonistic attitude towards the ECHR by some British politicians, triggered by concerns over loss of sovereignty, the prisoners' voting crisis and judgments on immigration, led to fears that the UK Government may use this opportunity to promote measures to diminish the role of the ECtHR.[349] The compromise reached at the Brighton conference ensured that this did not eventuate.

The Brighton Declaration, reflecting the political agreement of the States, includes the commitment in principle to amend the Convention in five specific areas:

1. to add a reference to the principle of subsidiarity and the doctrine of the margin of appreciation to the Preamble to the Convention;
2. to change the rules on the age of judges of the Court, to ensure that all judges are able to serve the full nine-year term;
3. to remove the right of parties to a case before the Court to veto the relinquishment of jurisdiction in a case before a Chamber in favour of the Grand Chamber;
4. to reduce the time limit for applications to the Court from six months to four months; and
5. to tighten the admissibility criteria to make it easier for the Court to reject trivial applications.

Protocol No. 15 gives legal effect to these changes.

While many of these changes were welcomed, others were subject to criticism. There were fears that the changes to 'the admissibility criteria' may affect the practical and effective access to the ECtHR.[350] Although these reforms are made on the basis of the need to increase efficiency (the more restrictive the admissibility criteria, the reduced number of cases that the ECtHR will have to decide on the merits), they may hinder the effective exercise of the right to individual petition, especially for potentially vulnerable claimants. The commitment to the right of individual application was confirmed as a cornerstone of the Convention system in the Brighton Declaration, and it was accepted that it should be 'practically realisable, and States Parties must ensure that they do not hinder in any way the effective exercise of this

[348] *Ministers' Deputies*, Information documents CM/INF (2011)41 (27 October 2011).

[349] House of Lords and House of Commons Joint Committee on Human Rights, *Fourth Report – Protocol 15* (n 258) at [3.3].

[350] See Nikos Vogiatzis, 'The Admissibility Criterion Under Article 35(3)(b) ECHR: A "Significant Disadvantage" to Human Rights Protection' (2016) 65 ICLQ 185–211.

right'.[351] Restricting the time limit to make a claim in Strasbourg will undoubtedly be detrimental to some, perhaps many, claimants but it is difficult to assess. The Declaration also affirmed that the ECtHR should adopt 'a strict and consistent approach' in rendering applications inadmissible under Article 35(3)(a) ECHR unless a 'serious question concerning the interpretation or application of the Convention' is raised.[352] Raising the admissibility threshold was to prevent the ECtHR having to deal with trivial matters. The ECtHR is left with a discretion to link the absence of any significant disadvantage to the applicant to the merits of a case. The Joint Committee on Human Rights thus concluded:

> we consider that the amended Convention will still enable the Court to strike the right balance between not having to consider trivial matters and ensuring that victims of human rights violations are not deprived of their right of access to a court to have their claim determined.[353]

The concept of subsidiarity underscored the negotiations in Brighton and was of particular interest to the UK Government. This principle broadly reflects the idea that States have the initial responsibility to protect Convention rights domestically and the ECtHR should only intervene where domestic authorities fail to protect such rights.[354] The most significant agreement at the Conference was that 'for reasons of transparency and accessibility, a reference to the principle of subsidiarity and the doctrine of the margin of appreciation as developed in the Court's case law should be included in the Preamble to the Convention'.[355] Protocol No. 15 gives legal effect to this change and inserts into the Preamble of the Convention, specific references to subsidiarity and the margin of appreciation. Human rights NGOs were concerned that these two doctrines have been singled out to be included in the body of the ECHR while other seminal principles, such as 'the principle of proportionality, the doctrine of the Convention as a living instrument and the principle of dynamic and evolutive interpretation; the principle that rights must be practical and effective rather than theoretical and illusory; and the principle that the very essence of a right must never be impaired' have not been mentioned.[356] Nevertheless, Article 1 of Protocol No. 15 specifically recognises the supervisory judgment of the ECtHR and therefore it 'remains the sole institution empowered to

[351] Brighton Declaration at [2], [13] and [31].

[352] Ibid at [15d]. Note also Article 5 of Protocol No. 15 ECHR.

[353] House of Lords and House of Commons Joint Committee on Human Rights, *Fourth Report – Protocol 15* (n 258) at [4.25].

[354] Brighton Declaration at [3]. [355] Ibid at [12b].

[356] Joint NGO Statement: 'Protocol 15 to the ECHR must not result in a weakening of human rights protection' (24 June 2013). Available at www.hrw.org/sites/default/files/related_material/2013_Europe_Joint%20NGO%20Statement%20ECHR.pdf (last accessed 12 August 2024).

define, develop and apply tools of judicial interpretation such as the margin of appreciation doctrine'.[357]

The express reference to the principle of subsidiarity and the doctrine of margin of appreciation in the Preamble has not obviously led to a radical change in the approach of the ECtHR.[358] These concepts are already well established principles of interpretation and prior to inclusion in the Preamble, the ECtHR has used them in developing its jurisprudence.[359] Moreover, the accompanying Explanatory Report to Protocol No. 15 clarifies the drafters' intention that the reference to the margin of appreciation is to be consistent with the doctrine 'as developed by the Court in its case-law'.[360] The Parliamentary Joint Committee on Human Rights observed that subsidiarity and the margin of appreciation are not concerned with the primacy of domestic law over the Convention system. They explained:

> The Convention system is subsidiary, not to the political will of the national authorities, but to the national system for safeguarding human rights. Where that national system is well developed, and has led to detailed and reasoned assessment of a law or policy by the national authorities in light of the Convention and the principles in the Court's case-law, the assessment of the national authorities is likely to be within the State's margin of appreciation (depending on the nature of the right).[361]

Arguably, this change has reinforced the concept that national authorities are primarily responsible for protecting human rights, subject to the supervisory jurisdiction of the ECtHR. Preventing the ECtHR from being overwhelmed by the sheer number of applications is critical to ensuring its long-term survival and legitimacy. An effective national implementation of the ECHR and protection of rights at domestic level is thus an important strategy to achieve this aim.

It was also agreed at Brighton to invite the Committee of Ministers to draft a new Optional Protocol concerning an extension to the advisory opinion mechanism which is now set out in Protocol No. 16.[362] The Preamble of the Protocol specifically mentions that this 'will further enhance the interaction between the Court and national authorities … in accordance with the principle of subsidiarity'.

[357] Ibid, p.2.

[358] See, e.g., Helga Molbaek-Steensig, 'Subsidiarity Does Not Win Cases: A Mixed Methods Study of the Relationship between Margin of Appreciation Language and Deference at the European Court of Human Rights' (2023) **36** Leiden Journal of International Law 83–107. Note also Speech by Dean Spielmann, President of the European Court of Human Rights, 'Whither the Margin of Appreciation?' Current Legal Problems Lecture (20 March 2014).

[359] See, e.g., *Animal Defenders International* v. *the United Kingdom* (n 225).

[360] Council of Europe, Protocol No. 15 Explanatory Report (n 236) at [7].

[361] House of Lords and House of Commons Joint Committee on Human Rights, *Fourth Report – Protocol 15* (n 258) at [3.11].

[362] Brighton Declaration at [12d].

3.9.3 Reykjavík Summit

The Council of Europe has organised summits of the Heads of State and Government of its Member States on only four occasions during the seventy-five-year history of the Council of Europe. The most recent was held at Reykjavík in May 2023. In response to Russia's invasion of Ukraine, systemic threats posed by creeping authoritarianism, democratic backsliding and the climate emergency, a High Level Reflection Group was set up by the Secretary General of the Council of Europe in June 2022.[363] Their report setting out the myriad and extraordinary challenges to be faced was the catalyst for the call for the fourth Summit in Reykjavík.

The Reykjavík Summit focused not on the ECtHR alone but on the entire Council of Europe with the aim to renew 'the conscience of Europe'.[364] There were four overarching issues: (i) ensuring accountability for Russia's crimes in Ukraine, (ii) reviving commitment to the ECHR control system, (iii) reiterating fundamental principles of democracy, and (iv) advancing the agenda of human rights and the environment. In the Reykjavík Declaration, the forty-six Heads of State and Government affirmed support for all of these issues.[365] It was decided to establish a Register of damage caused by the Russian Federation's aggression against Ukraine and a declaration on the situation of the children of Ukraine was adopted. The Declaration also affirmed principles of democracy, firmly recommitted to the ECHR and to developing tools to tackle the emerging climate crisis.[366]

In relation to the Convention system, the Declaration reaffirmed its unwavering commitment stating that: as 'a mechanism to promote peace and stability in Europe and the Council of Europe's core values of human rights, democracy and the rule of law'; to the right of individual application to the Court; to ensure the full, effective and prompt execution of the final judgments of the Court; 'reaffirm also the principle of subsidiarity and the fact that respondent States remain free to choose the means by which they discharge the obligation'; and to ensure the allocation of 'sufficient and sustainable resources to enable the Court to exercise its judicial functions effectively and to deal with its workload expeditiously'.[367]

In relation to the operation of the ECtHR, the States translated their political support for the ECHR system and its values into the provision of more sustainable financing.

[363] Council of Europe, *Report of the High Level Reflection Group of the Council of Europe* (October 2022).

[364] See Special Issue of the European Human Rights Law Review (2023(2)) 'The Road to Reykjavik and Beyond'.

[365] Council of Europe, *United Around Our Values: Reykjavík Declaration* (2023). [366] Ibid.

[367] Ibid at Appendix 4, pp.18 and 19.

3.10 SUSPENSION, EXPULSION AND WITHDRAWAL OF STATES

Article 58 ECHR provides that a High Contracting Party may denounce the Convention after the expiry of five years from the date on which it became a party to it and after six months' notice is given to the Secretary General of the Council of Europe. Denunciation does not have the effect of releasing the High Contracting Party concerned from its obligations under the Convention in respect of any act which, being capable of constituting a violation of such obligations, may have been performed by it before the date at which the denunciation became effective. Article 58(3) ECHR also provides that '[a]ny High Contracting Party which shall cease to be a member of the Council of Europe shall cease to be a Party to this Convention under the same conditions'. This needs to be examined together with Article 8 of the Statute of the Council of Europe which provides that any member of the Council of Europe which has seriously violated Article 3 may be suspended from its rights of representation and may be requested by the Committee of Ministers to withdraw. If the State does not comply with that request, the Committee may decide that the State has ceased to be a member of the Council with effect from a date determined by the Committee.

3.10.1 Greece

Greece denounced the Convention in 1970 and ceased to be a High Contracting State Party on 31 December 1970. This pre-empted a decision by the Committee of Ministers that would have expelled Greece following widespread violations of the Convention by the Greek military dictatorship government that occupied Greece at the time. In 1974, after the fall of the Greek junta, Greece acceded once more to the Statute of the Council of Europe.

3.10.2 Russia

Following the Russian invasion of Ukraine on 24 February 2022, the Committee of Ministers decided on the 25 February 2022, following an exchange of views with the Parliamentary Assembly, to launch the procedure provided by Article 8 of the Statute and suspend the Russian Federation from the Council of Europe. On 15 March 2022, the Parliamentary Assembly unanimously adopted an Opinion which considered that the Russian Federation could no longer be a Member State of the Organisation.[368] On the same day, the Government of the Russian Federation informed the Secretary General of its withdrawal from the Council of Europe in accordance with the Statute of the

[368] Council of Europe Parliamentary Assembly, *Consequences of the Russian Federation's aggression against Ukraine*, Opinion 300 (2022).

Council of Europe and of its intention to denounce the European Convention on Human Rights.

On 16 September 2022, Russia thus ceased to be a party to the European Convention on Human Rights. This will undoubtedly have profound and potentially catastrophic consequences for individuals for whom the Convention system, including the oversight of the ECtHR, has been the only means by which they can secure their human rights. Indeed, in 2021 alone, of the 1,105 judgments delivered by the Court, 232 involved the Russian Federation (and in almost 95 per cent of those cases, at least one violation was found).[369] In addition to the sheer volume of findings of violations, the severity of those violations is striking; there were eighty-three violations of the prohibition of torture and inhuman or degrading treatment under Article 3, ninety-six violations of the right to liberty (Article 5) and nineteen violations of the right to life (Article 2).[370] That 85 per cent of the violations concerned the most fundamental rights protected by the Convention – namely, the rights to life, liberty and bodily integrity – demonstrates just how profoundly important the Convention, and the Court's oversight, is for those who are the victims of serious rights violations by Russian authorities. The enforcement of Strasbourg judgments in Russia has, however, long been deeply problematic, not least since the Russian Constitutional Court held in 2015 that Strasbourg judgments that conflict with the Russian Constitution are unenforceable. Moreover, it has been reported that in June 2022 a law entered into force in Russia stating that, 'because of the "procedurally incorrect exclusion" of the Russian Federation from the Council of Europe ... judgments of the [ECtHR] which became final after 15 March 2022 shall not be enforced, nor shall they serve as a ground for the reopening of proceedings'.[371] It has also been reported that over 2 billion euros is outstanding from Russia in respect of Just Satisfaction awards.[372]

3.10.3 Belarus

On 17 March 2022, the Committee of Ministers suspended all relations with Belarus authorities due to its participation in the Russian Federation's military aggression against Ukraine. At the same time, the Committee decided to maintain and enhance relations with Belarusian civil society and the

[369] European Parliament, *Russia's war on Ukraine: Russia ceases to be a member of the Council of Europe*, 8 March 2022. See also European Court of Human Rights, Press Country Profile, Russia (last update July 2024).

[370] Ibid.

[371] European Court of Human Rights, 'Binding Force: Institutional Dialogue between the ECHR and the Committee of Ministers under Article 46 of The European Convention on Human Rights', Speech by Clare Ovey, Strasbourg, 23 March 2023.

[372] Ibid.

opposition in exile.[373] In November 2022 the first meeting of the Belarus Contact Group opened its aim to provide support and expertise to strengthen Belarusian democratic society in line with Council of Europe core values and according to the activities for human rights, rule of law and democracy. The 2023 Council of Europe Reykjavík Summit Declaration underlined the need for co-operation and the commitment to pursue the work of the Contact Group.

3.10.4 UK Threats to Withdraw from the European Convention on Human Rights

In recent years, several Conservative politicians have expressly called for, or hinted at the possibility that, the UK will withdraw from the ECHR if the ECtHR finds violations in respect of certain the UK policies and legislation, most notably the Rwanda asylum agreement. These issues have been considered in further detail in the previous chapter, which examines the current system for protecting rights, the HRA and the role of the HRA within the UK Constitution. The the UK's membership of the Council of Europe is likely to be secure for the next few years as since July 2024 the UK has a new Government that supports membership of the Council of Europe.

3.11 CONCLUSION

The Council of Europe has reached its seventy-fifth anniversary and it remains as significant today as it was for the original ten Member States who signed the Statute of the Council of Europe in London in 1949. One of the primary means of achieving greater unity and safeguarding the common heritage of Member States was and remains the ECHR.[374] The ECHR has undoubtedly established a highly successful regional human rights system with its innovative mechanism for the collective enforcement of individual rights. Since its establishment, the ECtHR has dealt with over one million applications and handed down over 27,000 judgments. Its numerous achievements deserve to be celebrated. Yet we cannot ignore the enormous challenges that the system faces as acknowledged at the Reykjavík Summit in 2023. There are increasing fears of creeping authoritarianism, democratic erosion and a lack of respect for the rule of law in some States. Europe is once again witnessing armed conflict and devastation between Ukraine and the Russian Federation. This conflict has

[373] Council of Europe, 1429th meeting, 17 March 2022, 2.5 *Relations between the Council of Europe and Belarus*, Reference document, SG/Inf(2022)10.

[374] President's Statement on the 75th Anniversary of the Council of Europe, ECHR 121, 2024 (17/05/2024).

led to the Russian Federation ceasing to be a member of the Council of Europe and with it a loss to the thousands of individuals who saw the Strasbourg system as a beacon of hope. There has also been conflict between Armenia and Azerbaijan, Georgia and Russia, which together with the invasion of Ukraine has generated almost 8,850 pending applications.[375]

A concern for the future of the Court has been the vast increase in the number of applications which, unless stemmed, threatened to overwhelm the system. In this respect the Court's procedural reforms have increased the efficiency of the Court. This includes the Court's priority policy for processing cases with a view to speeding up the system and concentrating resources on the most important cases, pilot judgments and the practice of considering similar complaints against the same State in one judgment.[376] On 1 July 2024, the number of pending applications before the ECtHR was 64,200, a decrease of 4,250 applications from 2023.[377] Approximately three quarters of applications come from the same few countries: Türkiye, the Russian Federation, Ukraine, Romania and Greece.[378] As the Russian Federation is no longer a member, there are no new applications from that State, however, the ECtHR is still dealing with many cases from the Russian Federation by virtue of the residual jurisdiction conferred by Article 58 (2) and (3), if the violation occurred prior to 16 September 2022. Recent significant cases involving the Russian Federation have included the inter-State judgment of *Ukraine* v. *Russia (Crimea)*[379] and just as this book was about to go to print in July 2025, the Grand Chamber handed down its decision on Ukraine and Netherlands v. Russia, encompassing four inter State applications.[380] Russia was found to have committed grave violations of human rights.

The last decade has seen a marked increase in the number of inter-State cases brought before the Court. There are currently fifteen pending inter-State cases. These cases are highly complex and require considerable resources. Judge Bošnjak has commented that: 'It is worth reiterating that the Court is the only international tribunal dealing with human rights issues related to the ongoing war in Ukraine. It is the only international court which is examining, at the merits stage, events in Ukraine dating back to 2014 including the invasion in 2022.'[381] The inter-State cases suggest a continued faith and confidence in the role of the Court even in the face of conflict. Victims of conflict, including States and individuals, can seek a public statement of an

[375] European Court of Human Rights, Keynote Speech by Marko Bošnjak, '2024 Help Network Conference' Strasbourg, 4/07/2024, p.2.

[376] See, e.g., *Suprun* v. *Russia* (n 76).

[377] ECtHR, Statistical Reports, https://prd-echr.coe.int/web/echr/statistical-reports (last accessed 12 August 2024).

[378] Ibid.

[379] *Ukraine* v. *Russia (Crimea)* (n 47).

[380] *Ukraine and Netherlands* v. *Russia* (n 56).

[381] Bosnjak (n 375), p.2.

international law violation and judicial decisions can contribute to the establishment of historical and factual truth.[382]

The Reykjavík Summit also committed to advancing the agenda of human rights and the environment. The Court had already developed a rich jurisprudence on environmental issues concerning the right to private and family life, access to court, right to property and freedom of information. The important decision concerning climate change of *Verein KlimaSeniorinnen* only confirms the relevance and importance of the Court's supervisory role.[383] At the same time, the idea of subsidiarity remains present, as seen in *Verein KlimaSeniorinnen* itself, as well as the two additional climate change cases that were heard simultaneously.[384]

Over the last few decades, the political support of the ECtHR in the UK has diminished. During the fourteen years of Conservative government in the UK, the ECtHR's legitimacy has been increasingly questioned, with particular consternation levied at the Court's interim judgments regarding the Rwanda asylum plan, its judgments on prisoner voting rights, and its use of the living instrument doctrine in its interpretation of the Convention. This dissatisfaction has led to threats that the UK will leave the ECHR and the Council of Europe. The immediate threat to the UK's future in the ECHR has abated for the moment with the election of a new Government in July 2024.

This is important as the Strasbourg system needs the cooperation and goodwill of Member States in order to succeed in its role. It is not solely the function of the ECtHR to sustain the legitimacy of the Convention and its judicial machinery. As the Brighton Declaration noted, it is the 'shared responsibility' of both Member States and the ECtHR, and, without the cooperation of both, it will not be possible to ensure respect for human rights.

382 European Court of Human Rights, Speech by Siofra O'Leary, 'Why the European Convention on Human Rights Still Matters', University of Liechtenstein, 17/06/2024, p. 4.

383 *Verein KlimaSeniorinnen* (n 77), see especially at [420].

384 *Carême* v. *France* (n 81) and *Duarte Agostinho and Ors* v. *Portugal and Ors* (n 94). See also, Heri (n 77), pp.326–327.

4 The Right to Life

CONTENTS

4.1 INTRODUCTION

The inherent value of human life is a common thread running through most, if not all, of the world's major religions and is a consistent theme throughout centuries of Western philosophical thought.[1] This emphasis on life's

[1] For a comprehensive discussion of the value attributed to human life by the major faiths and philosophies, see Elizabeth Wicks, *The Right to Life and Conflicting Interests* (Oxford University Press, 2010), ch 2.

sanctity or inherent value has found reflection in the core human rights documents enacted over the last century,[2] including the ECHR.[3] Indeed, it is often said that '[t]he most fundamental of the rights protected by the European Convention is the right to life' and that, together with Article 3 ECHR (see Chapter 5), it 'enshrines one of the most basic values of the democratic societies making up the Council of Europe'.[4] The common law similarly attributes considerable value to human life.[5] In fact, there is within the common law a presumption in favour of preserving life, though this is not irrebuttable; other factors including, for instance, the individual's own wishes and their quality of life may weigh more heavily in a given case.[6] Given that without life all other rights are nugatory,[7] the relative ubiquity of the protection of the right to life is unsurprising. Indeed, the right to life has been characterised as a peremptory norm of international law (jus cogens); a fundamental, overriding international law principle.[8]

However, to contend that the 'right to life' is the 'fundamental right' enshrined in the ECHR begs more questions than it answers. Whose life is protected by Article 2 ECHR? What does the right to life guarantee (i.e. just protection from arbitrary killing, or does it protect access to food, shelter and so on)? Why is killing a human (at least in most instances) murder, but killing an animal is not? At what point is the 'right to life' conferred: at conception, when a 'foetal heartbeat' is detected, at the point of viability, or upon birth? What happens when the right to life of individuals conflict; whose right to life

[2] See, for instance, The United Nations Declaration of Human Rights (1948) (Article 3), The International Covenant on Civil and Political Rights (1966) (Article 6(1)), United Nations Convention on the Rights of the Child (1989) (Article 6), United Nations Convention on the Rights of Persons with Disabilities (2007) (Article 10).

[3] The ECHR is not the only regional human rights document to foreground and protect the right to and sanctity of life. See, for instance, the Charter of Fundamental Rights of the European Union (2000) (Article 2), the American Convention on Human Rights (1969) (Article 4) and the African Charter on Human and Peoples' Rights (1986) (Article 4).

[4] *Giuliani and Gaggio* v. *Italy* [GC] (2012) 54 EHRR 10 at [174].

[5] See, for instance, *R (B)* v. *Cambridge Health Authority* [1995] EWCA Civ 49, [1995] 1 WLR 898, 905, per Sir Thomas Bingham MR. See also, Natasa Mavronicola's discussion of the common law's protection of bodily integrity in 'The Mythology and the Reality of Common Law Constitutional Rights to Bodily Integrity' in Mark Elliott and Kirsty Hughes (eds), *Common Law Constitutional Rights* (Hart Publishing, 2020), ch 2.

[6] See, for instance, *An NHS Trust & Ors* v. *Y & Anor* [2018] UKSC 46, [2019] AC 978. See also, the discussion in Chapter 6.

[7] 'Article 2 [is] one of the most fundamental provisions of the Convention. . . . It safeguards the right to life, without which enjoyment of any of the other rights and freedoms of the Convention is rendered nugatory' (*Pretty* v. *the United Kingdom* (2002) ECHR 427 at [37]).

[8] See the discussion in Stuart Casey-Maslen, *The Right to Life under International Law: An Interpretive Manual* (Cambridge University Press, 2021), ch 1. For more on the role of international law within domestic law, see Chapter 2.

prevails? And, who should decide these difficult questions, which have many and varied legal, medical, political, ethical, philosophical and religious implications? These issues are considered throughout this and other chapters of this book including Chapter 6, which examines abortion, withdrawal/refusal of medical treatment and assisted dying.

We begin this chapter by considering the protection afforded by the common law to the right to life. The focus then shifts to the ECHR, commencing with an examination of when 'life' begins for the purposes of Article 2 ECHR. The various obligations that States have under Article 2 ECHR are then considered. As will be seen, there is significant overlap in the principles applicable to these obligations in respect of Articles 2, 3 (see Chapter 5) and 4 ECHR (see Chapter 7).

Inquiries such as those into the fire at Grenfell Tower – a block of residential flats in London – and the Manchester Arena bombing, provide useful insights into the scope and application of the State's positive and procedural obligations under Article 2 ECHR. The Grenfell Tower inquiry also illuminates an issue that permeates this book, namely the efficacy of the ECHR in the context of socio-economic rights, such as the right to adequate housing. The UK Government's response to the COVID-19 pandemic, particularly in terms of care homes, and the implications for Article 2 ECHR is also considered as is the ECtHR nascent climate change jurisprudence.

4.2 THE RIGHT TO LIFE AND THE COMMON LAW

The common law undoubtedly recognises a right to life. Thus, in *Bugdaycay*[9] – a decision predating the enactment of the HRA by more than a decade – Lord Bridge observed that '[t]he most fundamental of all human rights is the individual's right to life'.[10] Indeed, such was the importance of that right that Lord Bridge considered that decisions which could put an individual's life at risk must 'surely call for the most anxious scrutiny'.[11] Nevertheless, as Natasa Mavronicola has noted, 'while the right to life has been given the label of common law constitutional right by some, it is unclear to what extent this rhetoric is reflected in judicial practice, what content we can convincingly ascribe to this right, and what its demands are in particular situations'.[12] Citing case law involving medical treatment (in respect of which, see Chapter 6), Mavronicola suggests that domestic courts have, at least in those

[9] *R (Bugdaycay)* v. *Secretary of State for the Home Department* [1986] UKHL 6, [1987] 1 AC 514.

[10] Ibid, 531. [11] Ibid. [12] Mavronicola (n 5), p.31.

contexts, moved away from framing the issue as a matter of the right to life, instead adopting the concept of the 'sanctity of life' – a 'value or principle' as distinct from a legal entitlement.[13] Lord Reed's reasons in the 2020 UK Supreme Court judgment in *R (Elgizouli)*[14] appear to provide support for Mavronicola's view. As Lord Reed observed, in the context of a claim that the common law precluded the sharing of information by authorities in the UK with their US counterparts given the risk that such proceedings could culminate in the imposition of the death penalty:

> authorities do not vouch the existence of a right [to life] in the sense in which that term is used in the law of obligations, and the idea that there might be a right of that character is absent from leading cases concerned with questions of life and death, such as *Airedale NHS Trust v Bland* [1993] AC 789, *R v Cambridge Health Authority, Ex p B* [1995] 1 WLR 898, *In re A (Children) (Conjoined Twins: Surgical Separation)* [2001] Fam 147 and *R (Nicklinson) v Ministry of Justice (CNK Alliance Ltd intervening)* [2014] UKSC 38; [2015] AC 657. Nevertheless, the authorities support the recognition of what might more aptly be described as a value to which the courts attach great significance when exercising their supervisory jurisdiction.[15]

That said, Lord Reed (citing *Bugdaycay*) noted that '[j]udicial recognition of the right to life, understood in that sense, can have an important influence on adjudication'.[16] Accordingly, the right to life – whether formulated as a right in the sense of an obligation or a value to which great importance is attached – continues to affect the degree of scrutiny with which courts will review decisions.

It seems clear, then, that the common law recognises and gives effect to the 'right to life' even if this is primarily through an increased level of scrutiny during public law review. Further, as Lady Hale observed in *Michael*,[17] there is 'no doubt that the police owe a positive duty ***in public law*** to protect members of the public from harm caused by third parties' which would, presumably, extend to lethal harm.[18] Whether such a duty does or should find reflection in private law – particularly in the tort of negligence – is a separate and enduring question,[19] and one which divided the Supreme

[13] Ibid, p.32.

[14] *R (Elgizouli)* v. *Secretary of State for the Home Department* [2020] UKSC 10, [2021] AC 937.

[15] Ibid at [175]. [16] Ibid at [176].

[17] *Michael and Ors* v. *the Chief Constable of South Wales Police and Anor* [2015] UKSC 2, [2015] 1 AC 1732.

[18] Ibid at [195]. Emphasis added.

[19] See, for instance, *Van Colle* v. *Chief Constable of Herts Police, Smith* v. *Chief Constable of Sussex Police* [2008] UKHL 50, [2009] 1 AC 225, especially at [137]–[138], per Lord Brown. See also, the findings of the UKSC in *Smith and Ors* v. *Ministry of Defence* [2013] UKSC 41, [2014] 1 AC 52 regarding the existence (or not) of a duty of care owed to soldiers engaged in active combat.

Court in *Michael*,[20] though there has been a degree of evolution in the jurisprudence in this respect in recent years.[21]

Michael centred on the culpability of the Welsh police under both common law (negligence) and the HRA for the death of Joanna Michael who was brutally murdered by her former partner after she had called the police and told the call handler that he was aggressive, had turned up at her house and found her with another man, had already assaulted her (bitten her ear) and had threated to return to kill her (the latter was disputed by the handler who subsequently claimed she heard the deceased say 'hit' rather than 'kill'). The call was initially graded to require an immediate response by police, though when the call handler spoke to police in Michael's area and summarised the call, the police downgraded it as requiring a response within sixty minutes (no mention was made of a threat to kill). Michael subsequently called the emergency line again and police were dispatched immediately, arriving at the house shortly after to find her deceased, having been stabbed multiple times by her former partner. Michael's parents and children brought proceedings against the police under both the HRA and the common law (tort of negligence). While the HRA claim (based on Article 2) was permitted to go to trial, a majority of the Supreme Court declined to find that a duty of care could arise in circumstances such as those attending Michael's death. For the majority, Lord Toulson rejected the contention that the tort of negligence should evolve to reflect the liability of state agents under the HRA (in particular, Article 2). Lord Toulson cited several public policy reasons for not finding a duty of care akin to the operational obligation under Article 2,[22] including the potentially significant financial implications and the lack of a public interest in police priorities being 'affected by the risk of being sued'.[23] Lady Hale and Lord Kerr dissented; each considered that a duty of care in negligence could arise in circumstances such as those surrounding Michael's death. As Lady Hale observed, the policy reasons said to preclude such a duty were diminished by the fact that the authorities already owe a public law duty of care and in light of the obligations on authorities under Article 2 ECHR.[24] Lord Kerr (with whom Lady Hale

[20] *Michael* (n 17).

[21] See, *Robinson* v. *Chief Constable of West Yorkshire* [2018] UKSC 4, [2018] AC 736 (though in this case, the conduct of the police officers was characterised as an act, rather than an omission or failure to protect) and *Poole Borough Council* v. *GN and another* [2019] UKSC 25, [2020] AC 780 (which was concerned with an alleged failure to protect).

[22] See Section 4.3.2.4.

[23] *Michael* (n 17) at [121]–[124]. Such policy justifications found less favour with a differently constituted Supreme Court in *Poole* (n 21).

[24] *Michael* (n 17) at [195]–[196].

agreed) considered that the proximity necessary to create a duty of care could be established where:

> sufficient information has been conveyed to or is otherwise available to the police to alert them to the urgent need to take action which it is within their power to take. That the information be specific and the threat imminent are prerequisites of the proximity relationship.[25]

As such factors were present in Michael's case, Lord Kerr concluded that a duty of care *had* arisen and the Court ought to confront what a refusal to find such a duty would mean:

> To find that no duty arises on the facts of the present case requires us to squarely confront the consequence of such a finding. If the police force had not negligently downgraded the urgency of Ms Michael's call, on the facts as they are known at present, it is probable that she would still be alive. While the police are not responsible for the actions of her murderer, if the allegations made against them are established, police played a direct, causative role in her death as a result of their negligence. If they were to be found liable for such negligence, would this be so different from the liability of the doctor of a patient who fails to provide life-saving drugs to prevent an aggressive condition in the necessary time? The police have been empowered to protect the public from harm. They should not be exempted from liability on the general common law ground that members of the public are not required to protect others from third party harm; such protection of autonomy for individuals is not appropriate for members of a force whose duty it is to provide precisely the type of protection from the harm that befell Ms Michael. This is the essential and critical obligation of the police force. Any other professional would be liable for inaction with such grievous consequences. So also should be the police.[26]

Since *Michael*, the Supreme Court has evinced a greater willingness to find that authorities owe a duty of care in tort to protect individuals from the actions of third parties, though there remains a differentiation between culpability in tort and that which arises under Article 2.[27]

The common law (again through the tort of negligence) also has the potential to afford individuals recourse – 'on appropriate facts' – in cases in which the HRA does not have territorial application for instance, where individuals are killed by British armed forces in a region that is outside of the control of the UK.[28]

[25] Ibid at [168], per Lord Kerr. [26] Ibid at [181], per Lord Kerr.

[27] This has been justified on the basis of the different objectives of civil proceedings in negligence *viz* proceedings under the HRA: 'Whereas civil actions are designed essentially to compensate claimants for losses, Convention claims are intended to uphold minimum human rights standards and to vindicate those rights' (*Michael* (n 17) at [127], per Lord Toulson).

[28] As was recognised by Lord Bingham in *Secretary of State for Defence* v. *Al-Skeini & Ors* [2007] UKHL 26, [2008] 1 AC 153 at [26], citing *Bici* v. *Ministry of Defence* [2004] EWHC 786 (QB).

While there is a basis in the common law for reliance on a right to life (including when the HRA has reached its territorial limits), outside of medical treatment cases (and, indeed, even within such contexts[29]), the ECHR has taken precedence, with Article 2 (the right to life) 'taking the demands made of the state substantially beyond what was otherwise required under domestic common law and statute'.[30] Accordingly, Article 2 is the focus of the remainder of this chapter.

4.3 THE RIGHT TO LIFE UNDER THE ECHR

4.3.1 What Is Meant by 'Life' in Article 2 ECHR?

Pursuant to Article 4 of the American Convention on Human Rights, '[e]very person has the right to have his life respected. This right shall be protected by law and, in general, *from the moment of conception*'.[31] The same is not true of Article 2(1) ECHR, which refers only to 'life' and does not define it in any way. As discussed in greater detail in Chapter 6, the ECtHR has, on a number of occasions, considered whether Article 2 extends to zygotes/embryos or foetuses or is confined to life as exists following birth. To date, the ECtHR has held that 'the unborn child is not regarded as a "person" directly protected by Art. 2 of the Convention'[32] though States can (and some do) confer rights,

[29] See Chapter 6. [30] Mavronicola (n 5), p.32.

[31] Emphasis added. The Inter-American Court of Human Rights has interpreted Article 4 with an emphasis on 'in general'. It has determined that embryos are *not* persons with rights and do not have an absolute right to life (e.g., *Artavia Murillo* et al. *("In Vitro Fertilization")* v. *Costa Rica* [2012], IACtHR, Ser. C No. 257). Rather, the right to life is 'gradual and incremental according to its development' (*Artavia Murillo* et al. at [264]). Indeed, the Inter-American Commission drew the ire of pro-life Senators in the US for its statements to Member States encouraging them to repeal blanket bans on abortion: 'The Commission also underscores that laws criminalizing abortion in all circumstances have a negative impact on women's dignity and their rights to life, to personal integrity, and to health, as well as on their general right to live free from violence and discrimination. The absolute criminalization of abortion, including in cases where the woman's life is at risk and when the pregnancy results from a rape or incest, imposes a disproportionate burden on the exercise of women's rights and creates a context that facilitates unsafe abortions and high rates of maternal mortality' (Inter-American Court of Human Rights Press Release, 'IACHR Urges All States to Adopt Comprehensive, Immediate Measures to Respect and Protect Women's Sexual and Reproductive Rights', 23 October 2017, https://mailchi.mp/dist/iachr-urges-all-states-to-adopt-comprehensive-immediate-measures-to-respect-and-protect-womens-sexual-and-reproductive-rights?e = 07a43d57e2. See discussion of Ligia De Jesús Castaldi, 'Partial U.S. sanctions on Inter-American Commission on Human Rights', Oxford Human Rights Hub, 2 August 2019, https://ohrh.law.ox.ac.uk/partial-u-s-sanctions-on-inter-american-commission-on-human-rights/).

[32] *Vo* v. *France* [GC] (2005) 40 EHRR 12 at [80]. See also the Grand Chamber's judgment in *Evans* v. *the United Kingdom* [GC] (2008) 46 EHRR 34.

including the right to life, on foetuses. In terms of the ending of life, an issue that is also canvassed in greater detail in Chapter 6, withdrawing life-sustaining treatment and permitting assisted suicide and/or euthanasia in accordance with clear regulatory guidelines does not violate Article 2.[33] Accordingly, unless domestic law provides otherwise, Article 2 does not confer a right to life on the unborn and it does not compel the preservation of life at all costs.

4.3.2 State Obligations under Article 2 ECHR

Article 2 imposes three distinct but overlapping duties/obligations on the State:

1. A duty not to take life, save in the limited circumstances provided for in Article 2(2) (the negative duty);
2. A duty to conduct an effective investigation into deaths where the State may be responsible or where there is evidence to suggest that a person's Article 2 right to life has been violated (a positive procedural obligation); and,
3. A positive duty to protect lives in certain circumstances which, in turn, requires:
   a. the putting in place of a legislative and administrative framework that effectively deters threats to life; and,
   b. protecting individuals from the criminal acts of third parties where the authorities knew or ought to have known at the time of the existence of a real and immediate risk to the life of an identified individual or individuals.

Before we consider those obligations in more detail, something should be said of victim status given that it is often the case that the victim of a violation of Article 2 cannot bring proceedings on their own behalf. This presents a difficulty since, pursuant to Article 34 ECHR, only victims of violations can bring proceedings before the ECtHR. However:

> [a]n exception is made to this principle where the alleged violation or violations of the Convention are closely linked to a death or disappearance in circumstances allegedly engaging the responsibility of the State. In such cases the Court has recognised the standing of the victim's next-of-kin to submit an application.[34]

Accordingly, 'the next-of-kin of a person whose death allegedly engages the responsibility of the State may claim to be victims of a violation of Article 2 of the Convention'.[35]

[33] *Lambert and Ors* v. *France* [GC] (2015) 62 EHRR 2. [34] Ibid at [90]. [35] Ibid at [115].

4.3.2.1 *The Prohibition on the Intentional Taking of Life*

Article 2(1) prohibits the intentional deprivation of life. A State will not violate Article 2 if its authorities use force which results in the death of a person (or persons) provided the force used is no more than is absolutely necessary for one of the three listed exceptions in Article 2(2), namely: (i) the protection of a person from unlawful violence; (ii) the effectuation of a lawful arrest or to prevent a person who has been lawfully detained from escaping; or (iii) action taken lawfully to quell an insurrection or riot. Given the importance of the right to life, these exceptions are 'strictly construed'.[36]

The negative obligation under Article 2 can be engaged in near-death scenarios[37] and may arise in extradition and deportation cases.[38] However, by far the most common scenario in which a complaint that the negative obligation in Article 2 has been violated arises as a result of the use of lethal force by State authorities.

4.3.2.1.1 *Use of Force by State Authorities*

In its landmark judgment in *McCann and Ors* v. *the United Kingdom*,[39] the Grand Chamber set out the principles applicable when considering whether the use of lethal force by State authorities violated the negative obligation in Article 2. The case concerned the fatal shooting of three Irish nationals in Gibraltar – Daniel McCann, Mairead Farrell and Sean Savage – by soldiers in the Special Air Service (SAS) (a special forces unit of the British Army). The three individuals had been the subject of surveillance in the days leading up to their deaths following intelligence that the IRA were planning an attack in Gibraltar. It was believed that the suspects intended to plant a car bomb in a crowded area and that they would be carrying a concealed detonator, allowing them to detonate the bomb away from the site. As it transpired, that intelligence was incorrect. The suspects were followed throughout the day in question and soldiers reported a suspected car bomb. While the soldiers were given orders to arrest the suspects, the three were shot multiple times and killed prior to arrest after one of the soldiers thought he had been recognised. The soldiers involved alleged that movements by, and communication among, the suspects led them to believe that they were likely to use a remote detonator to set off a car bomb. In fact, the car which was thought to contain a bomb did not and none of the suspects were in possession of a remote detonator or armed with

[36] See, for instance, *Giuliani and Gaggio* (n 4) at [177].

[37] See, for instance, *Makaratzis* v. *Greece* [GC] (2005) 41 EHRR 49 at [49].

[38] See the discussion of the death penalty in Section 4.3.2.1.5 and the discussion of removal in cases involving medical illness in Chapter 5.

[39] *McCann and Ors* v. *the United Kingdom* [GC] (1996) 21 EHRR 97.

any weapons. A subsequent search did, however, reveal a second car containing explosives, though the timers had not yet been set. A jury at the coroner's inquest returned a verdict of lawful killing and a subsequent application by family members of the deceased for leave to apply for judicial review challenging the lawfulness of the operation was unsuccessful.

The family members subsequently filed a complaint with the European Commission of Human Rights alleging a violation of Article 2. The Commission declared the application admissible and found (by eleven votes to six) that there was no violation of Article 2 ECHR.[40] The case was subsequently considered by a Grand Chamber of the ECtHR. It held by an incredibly slim majority (ten votes to nine) that there *had been* a violation of Article 2. The majority emphasised that force causing death (however unintentional) had to be 'absolutely necessary' which means:

> a *stricter and more compelling test of necessity* must be employed from that normally applicable when determining whether State action is 'necessary in a democratic society' under paragraph 2 of Articles 8 to 11 of the Convention. In particular, the force used must be *strictly proportionate* to the achievement of the aims set out in subparagraphs 2(a), (b) and (c) of Article 2.[41]

Significantly, the majority held that:

> In keeping with the importance of this provision in a democratic society, the Court must, in making its assessment, subject deprivations of life to *the most careful scrutiny,* particularly where deliberate lethal force is used, *taking into consideration not only the actions of the agents of the State who actually administer the force but also all the surrounding circumstances including such matters as the planning and control of the actions under examination.*[42]

Thus, the ECtHR considered not only the shooting of the three suspects, but also the planning that went into the operation. The majority rejected the applicants' contention that the killings were premeditated,[43] but it found that the planning and control of the operation had fallen short of what is required by Article 2. While the conduct of the soldiers themselves did not give rise to a violation as the killings were 'based on an honest belief which [was] perceived, for good reasons, to be valid at the time but which subsequently turn[ed] out to be mistaken',[44] there were several significant deficiencies in the planning and control of the operation which indicated that the use of force was not absolutely necessary. For instance, the authorities could have had the suspects stopped at the border and precluded from travelling into Gibraltar.

[40] *McCann and Ors* v. *the United Kingdom*, Report of the Commission, adopted 4 March 1994.

[41] *McCann and Ors* v. *the United Kingdom* (n 39) at [149]. Emphasis added.

[42] Ibid at [150]. Emphasis added. [43] Ibid at [184]–[185]. [44] Ibid at [200]–[201].

The authorities also failed to make sufficient allowances for the possibility of inaccuracies in their intelligence. Consequently, the killing of the three suspects 'constituted the use of force which was . . . more than absolutely necessary in defence of persons from unlawful violence within the meaning of Article 2(2)(a) of the Convention'.[45]

McCann was subject to significant criticism by the UK Government and the then Deputy Prime Minister Michael Heseltine described it as 'incomprehensible' and 'ludicrous'. Threats were also made that the UK would withdraw its recognition of the ECtHR's jurisdiction.[46] It is notable that despite the Government's consternation, the decision of the ECtHR very clearly recognised that an 'unrealistic burden' should not be placed on the State and its law-enforcement personnel. Hence the finding that the fatal use of force by authorities may be justified where there is an 'honest belief which is perceived, for good reasons, to be valid at the time but which subsequently turns out to be mistaken'.[47] Further, despite the finding of a violation of Article 2, the Grand Chamber determined not to award damages given that 'the three terrorist suspects who were killed had been intending to plant a bomb in Gibraltar'.[48]

The ECtHR has applied this 'honest belief' standard in a number of subsequent cases in which authorities have used lethal force on the basis of information that has subsequently been found to be unreliable or incorrect. In doing so, it has consistently reaffirmed the importance of not imposing a disproportionate or unrealistic burden on authorities. The Court has recognised that, when considering cases in which authorities have resorted to lethal force it is necessarily 'detached from the events at issue' and, accordingly, 'it cannot substitute its own assessment of the situation for that of an officer who was required to react in the heat of the moment to avert an honestly perceived danger to his life'.[49] This was evident in *Giuliani and Gaggio* v. *Italy*,[50] a case in which a *carabinieri* shot and killed a man embroiled in violent clashes with police and the *carabinieri* during demonstrations surrounding the G8 summit in Genoa in 2001. In that case a majority of the Grand Chamber found that the *carabinieri* had an 'honest belief' that the use of lethal force was absolutely necessary. The context was that the victim had been seen lifting a fire extinguisher in a manner which suggested he would use it as a 'blunt instrument' to attack three *carabinieri* trapped in a Jeep amidst a large crowd of violent protestors. The back window of the Jeep had been smashed and the

[45] Ibid at [202]–[213].

[46] Sarah Joseph, 'Denouement of the Deaths on the Rock: The Right to Life of Terrorists' (1996) 14 Netherlands Quarterly of Human Rights 1, 6. See also, Stephanie Palmer, 'Death on the Rock and the European Convention on Human Rights' (1996) 55 CLJ 1.

[47] *McCann and Ors* v. *the United Kingdom* (n 39) at [200].

[48] Ibid at [219].

[49] *Bubbins* v. *the United Kingdom* (2005) 41 EHRR 24 at [139].

[50] *Giuliani and Gaggio* v. *Italy* (n 4).

carabinieri who fired the lethal shot was crouched in the back 'protecting himself on one side with a riot shield' and suffering from the effects of the tear gas that had been discharged earlier.[51] Before firing his weapon, the *carabinieri* had 'displayed his gun and clearly warned the demonstrators, shouting at them to leave unless they wanted to be killed'.[52] Accordingly, there had been no violation of the negative obligation not to arbitrarily take life.[53]

In contrast, in *Gül* v. *Turkey*[54] Gül was fatally shot by police officers wielding automatic weapons whilst he was opening the door to the home he shared with his wife and children. The police fired approximately fifty to fifty-five shots at the door and later claimed that they did so in response to a shot being fired from inside. There was, however, no reliable evidence that Gül (who was suspected of harbouring members of the PKK) had fired any shots at the police. While statements were taken from the police who fatally killed Gül and those who attended afterwards indicating that two weapons and a spent shell casing had been located, those statements were inconsistent and there was no supporting evidence, such as photographs or forensic evidence. The ECtHR concluded that, in those circumstances, the use of force was 'grossly disproportionate' and could not be regarded as absolutely necessary.[55]

What constitutes 'honest belief' was further considered by the Grand Chamber in *Da Silva* v. *the United Kingdom*.[56] The Court was presented with the argument that the subjective 'honest belief' had to be objectively reasonable. The events that formed the subject of the complaint in *Da Silva* took place in the weeks after a series of terrorist attacks on London transport on 7 July 2005. The police misidentified Brazilian Jean Charles de Menezes as a suspected suicide bomber and, having followed him onto the London Underground, shot him several times in the head thinking he was going to detonate an explosive device. The Metropolitan Police were convicted under the Health and Safety Act 1974 and ordered to pay a fine of almost £200,000. The deceased's family also settled claims in negligence against the authorities.[57] However, as none of the individual officers involved were prosecuted,

[51] Ibid at [23].

[52] Ibid, joint partly dissenting opinion of Judges Tulkens, Zupančič, Gyulumyan and Karakas at [1].

[53] For a different perspective, see the joint partly dissenting opinion of Judges Tulkens, Zupančič, Gyulumyan and Karakas at [3]–[5]. In particular, they note that the *carabinieri* shot indiscriminately (raising questions about whether he had in fact seen the applicant's son with the fire extinguisher) and did not fire a warning shot into the air.

[54] *Gül* v. *Turkey* (2000) 54 EHRR 278.

[55] Ibid at [82]–[83].

[56] *Armani Da Silva* v. *the United Kingdom* [GC] (2016) 63 EHRR 12. For a discussion of the domestic proceedings, see 4.3.2.2.1.

[57] Jan Hessenbruegge, 'ECtHR Armani Da Silva v. UK: Unreasonable Police Killings in Putative Self-Defence?', *EJIL:Talk!*, 14 April 2016, www.ejiltalk.org/ecthr-armani-da-silva-v-uk-unreasonable-police-killings-in-putative-self-defence/.

the deceased's cousin brought proceedings alleging a violation of the obligation to carry out an effective investigation as required by Article 2. The complaint (which is considered below in respect of the investigative obligation) was unsuccessful, with the Grand Chamber observing that:

> in applying the *McCann and Others* test the principal question to be addressed is whether the person had an honest and genuine belief that the use of force was necessary. In addressing this question, the Court will have to consider whether the belief was *subjectively reasonable*, having full regard to the circumstances that pertained at the relevant time. If the belief was not subjectively reasonable (that is, it was not based on subjective good reasons), it is likely that the Court would have difficulty accepting that it was honestly and genuinely held.[58]

There is, then, no objective element to the honest belief test; it is based purely on the subjective belief of the individual who used the force. Mavronicola has suggested that this conflates individual criminal responsibility (in respect of which the purely subjective honest belief standard is relevant) with the State's responsibility under Article 2 (where the objective absolutely necessary standard is relevant), with the effect that the right to life is not being adequately protected. She calls upon the ECtHR to reinstate a robust approach to safeguarding the right to life by decoupling the negative obligation under Article 2 ECHR from takings of life which ought to attract criminal liability under domestic law.[59] In the latter, '[s]ubjectivity [including honest belief], can be central ... to delimiting the criminal liability of individuals involved'. However, when it comes to *State* responsibility under Article 2, Mavronicola espouses a return to the 'objective, rigorously applied' 'no more than absolutely necessary test'.[60]

4.3.2.1.2 *State Responsibility for Acts Carried Out by Authorities in Their 'Private' Capacity*

While State responsibility under the negative limb of Article 2 is, in the main, confined to instances in which force has been employed by those acting in their official capacity, there are limited circumstances in which the State may be liable for the private actions of its agents. The threshold for responsibility in such circumstances is very high:

> it [must] be convincingly demonstrated that, by their actions, the ... [State] not only 'approved' and 'endorsed' the impugned acts ... but also 'clearly and unequivocally' 'acknowledged' and 'adopted' these acts 'as their own' within the meaning of those

[58] *Armani Da Silva* v. *the United Kingdom* (n 56) at [248]. Emphasis added.

[59] Natasa Mavronicola, 'Taking Life and Liberty Seriously: Reconsidering Criminal Liability Under Article 2 of the ECHR' (2017) 80 MLR 6, p.1050.

[60] Ibid.

terms, as they are interpreted and applied under international law. In other words, they require that the ... authorities 'acknowledge' and 'adopt' them as acts perpetrated by the State ... thus directly and categorically assuming responsibility for [the impugned acts].[61]

The case of *Makuchyan and Minasyan* v. *Azerbaijan and Hungary*[62] illuminates just how difficult it is for this threshold to be met. In that case an Azerbaijani army officer beheaded an Armenian officer and attempted to kill another, while he was attending a language course organised by NATO which was being held in Hungary. The Azerbaijani officer was convicted of murder and sentenced to life imprisonment in Hungary. After eight years, pursuant to an agreement between Azerbaijan and Hungary, he was returned to Azerbaijan where it was understood by the Hungarian authorities he would serve the remainder of his sentence in prison. Instead, 'he received a hero's welcome. He was released, pardoned, promoted and awarded salary arrears for the period spent in prison, as well as the use of a state apartment in the capital. Many high-ranking Azerbaijani officials expressed their approval of [the officer's] conduct and pardon.'[63] Notwithstanding what appeared to be official endorsement of the officer's conduct, the ECtHR concluded that the Azerbaijani authorities had not 'clearly and unequivocally' acknowledged and adopted these acts as their own. Unsurprisingly, this decision has been the subject of significant criticism.[64]

The position of the officer in *Makuchyan and Minasyan* can be contrasted with the culpability of the Russian State for the murder of Alexander Litvinenko, discussed in detail below (see Section 4.3.3.1).[65] Russia argued before the ECtHR that it was not responsible for the acts of Lugovoy and Kovtun. In rejecting this contention, the ECtHR noted that when Lugovoy and Kovtun murdered Litvinenko they were not acting on their own initiative, but on the direction of the FSB and/or President Putin. Neither had any motive to kill Litvinenko 'and it was not plausible that, if acting on their own behalf, they would have had access to the rare radioactive isotope used to poison him'.[66] The means of Litvinenko's murder, thus, pointed to State involvement. So, too, did the motive. The ECtHR stressed the finding of the inquiry in the UK which, having 'carefully reviewed and discarded several theories as to the entities which might have wished Mr Litvinenko dead', concluded that 'there

[61] *Makuchyan and Minasyan* v. *Azerbaijan and Hungary* [2020] ECHR 336. [62] Ibid.

[63] Marko Milanović, 'Makuchyan and Minasyan v Azerbaijan and Hungary' (2021) 115 American Journal of International Law 2, p.294.

[64] See, for instance, ibid, and Kushtrim Istrefi and Cedric Rynhaert, '*Makuchyan and Minasyan* v. *Azerbaijan and Hungary*: Novel Questions of State Responsibility, Presidential Pardon, and Due Diligence of Sentencing Transfer Meet in a Rare Case of the Right to Life' (2021) 3 ECHRLR 2.

[65] *Carter* v. *Russia* [GC] [2021] ECHR 766. [66] Ibid at [163].

existed a strong probability that when poisoning Mr Litvinenko, Mr Lugovoy and Mr Kovtun were acting under the direction of the Russian security service'.[67] Thus, Litvinenko's death was attributable to the Russian State.[68]

4.3.2.1.3 *Standard and Burden of Proof*

As noted above, the ECtHR applies a stricter level of scrutiny when considering the necessity of the use of force under Article 2 than is employed when considering whether an interference with a qualified right is 'necessary in a democratic society' and the use of force must be *strictly* necessary to one of the three listed aims. However, the ECtHR has recognised that the context in which use of force occurs may affect the level of scrutiny. Thus, in *Tagayeva and Ors* v. *Russia*, which concerned the authorities' response to the Beslan hostage crisis, the ECtHR held that '[t]he absolute necessity test formulated in Article 2 is bound to be applied with different degrees of scrutiny, depending on whether and to what extent the authorities were in control of the situation and other relevant constraints inherent in operative decision-making in this sensitive sphere'.[69]

In terms of the standard of proof, although the ECtHR employs the standard of beyond reasonable doubt when resolving factual disputes, proof may flow from 'the coexistence of sufficiently strong, clear and concordant inferences or of similar unrebutted presumptions of fact'.[70]

In terms of the burden of proof, while in principle it rests on the applicant to establish that the use of force was more than strictly necessary, which party bears the burden depends on the specific facts. Accordingly:

> [w]here the events in issue lie wholly, or in large part, within the exclusive knowledge of the authorities, as in the case of persons within their control in custody, strong presumptions of fact will arise in respect of injuries and death occurring during such detention. Indeed, the burden of proof may be regarded as resting on the authorities to provide a satisfactory and convincing explanation.[71]

The impact of shifting the burden is exemplified in cases involving forced disappearances.

4.3.2.1.4 *Disappeared Persons*

The ECtHR has found violations of Article 2 where a person was taken into custody or detained by State agents but has then disappeared. In such cases, the ECtHR must first reach a conclusion (referred to in the case law as a

[67] Ibid at [164]. [68] Ibid at [169].

[69] *Tagayeva and Others* v. *Russia* [2017] ECHR 354 at [481]. [70] Ibid at [586].

[71] *Salman* v. *Turkey* [GC] (2000) 34 EHRR 425 at [100].

'presumption'), beyond reasonable doubt, that the individual who has disappeared is dead.[72] The Court has emphasised that '[t]his presumption of death is not automatic and is only reached on examination of the circumstances of the case, in which the lapse of time since the person was seen alive or heard from is a relevant element'.[73] In cases:

> where it is possible to establish that a person entered a place under the authorities' control and has not been seen since, the *onus is on the Government* to provide a *plausible and satisfactory explanation* as to what happened at that place, and to show that the person concerned was not detained by the authorities, but left the premises without subsequently being deprived of his or her liberty.[74]

Once the ECtHR has made a finding that the disappeared person is to be presumed dead, unless the State can demonstrate that one of the three exceptions in Article 2(2) applies, liability for the individual's presumed death will be attributable to the State and a violation of the negative aspect of Article 2 will follow.[75]

It is also worth noting at this juncture that where a person is presumed to be dead following their disappearance at the hands of the State, in addition to the negative obligation not to take life, the positive obligation to protect life may also arise. In such cases, the State may be held to have violated its positive obligation to protect under Article 2 *in addition to* its negative obligation not to arbitrarily take life if:

- there is evidence of a real and immediate risk to an individual's life; and
- the authorities failed to 'act rapidly and decisively'; and
- the authorities did not take 'operative measures within the scope of their powers which, judged reasonably, might have been expected to avoid risking the missing [person's] life'.[76]

Likewise, where a person is presumed dead following their disappearance and the State is found to be responsible, the procedural obligation to conduct an effective investigation (discussed in greater detail below) will arise.[77] It is also possible that a State may be found to have violated its procedural obligation to conduct an effective investigation despite being found not to have violated the negative obligation in Article 2 (for instance, because there is insufficient evidence to find, beyond reasonable doubt, that the individual was deprived of their life by State agents).[78] This is because the procedural obligation 'has its own distinct application which can operate independently from the

[72] See, for instance, *Varnava and Ors* v. *Turkey* [GC] [2009] ECHR 1313. [73] Ibid at [143].
[74] *Turluyeva* v. *Russia* [2013] ECHR 566 at [83]. Emphasis added.
[75] See, for instance, ibid at [88]. [76] This occurred in *Turluyeva* v. *Russia* (n 74).
[77] See, for instance, *Varnava and Ors* v. *Turkey* (n 72).
[78] Such findings were made in *Shafiyeva* v. *Russia* [2012] ECHR 809.

substantive limb of Article 2'.[79] The procedural obligation to investigate in the case of a disappeared person arises 'where individuals, last seen in the custody of agents of the State, subsequently disappeared in a life-threatening context'.[80]

4.3.2.1.5 *The Death Penalty*

As discussed in Chapter 5 (Article 3), as initially drafted, the carrying out of the death penalty – where it was provided for in law and was imposed by a court following a criminal conviction – did not violate Article 2(1). Since the ECHR came into force, however, practice amongst the States has significantly changed, leading to the adoption of the Sixth Protocol in 1983, which provided for the abolition of the death penalty in peacetime.[81] Subsequently, the Thirteenth Protocol entered into force in 2003 abolishing the death penalty even in times of war.[82] The ECtHR has since held that, given the near unanimous ratification of the Sixth and Thirteenth Protocols, Article 2 has been amended to remove the exception permitting the death penalty.[83]

While the prohibition on the death penalty carried out *within* the jurisdiction of Contracting States falls squarely within the negative obligation, there is also the question of whether a State can be liable under Article 2 in cases involving the deportation or extradition of a person to a country where they may face the death penalty. In these cases, the ECtHR has determined that where 'substantial grounds have been shown for believing there to be a real risk [the person being returned would be] subjected to the death penalty' in the receiving state, Article 2 imposes an obligation not to deport or extradite.[84] In such cases, 'in so far as any liability under the Convention is or may be incurred, it is liability incurred by the Contracting State, by reason of its having taken action which has as a direct consequence the exposure of an individual to the risk of [death]'.[85] That is, it is the State's negative obligation that is engaged.

In the domestic decision of *R (Elgizouli)* v. *Secretary of State for the Home Department*,[86] the UK Supreme Court considered whether the common law

79 *Varnava and Ors* v. *Turkey* (n 72) at [136].

80 Ibid at [181].

81 All State Parties to the ECHR bar Russia (which ceased being a State Party in 2022) have ratified the Sixth Protocol.

82 All State Parties have ratified Protocol 13 bar Azerbaijan, which signed the Protocol in 2023 but is yet to ratify it.

83 *Al-Saadoon and Mufdhi* v. *the United Kingdom* [2010] ECHR 282 at [120].

84 See, for instance, ibid at [123]. For a discussion of the early ECtHR removal cases (e.g., *Soering* v. *the United Kingdom* (1989) 11 EHRR 439), see Chapter 5.

85 *Saadi* v. *Italy* [GC] (2009) 49 EHRR 30 at [126] and *Al-Saadoon and Mufdhi* v. *the United Kingdom* (n 83) at [124].

86 *Elgizouli* (n 14).

prohibited the sharing of information with US authorities in circumstances where that information was going to be used to prosecute the claimant's son for capital offences, without obtaining assurances from the US authorities that the death penalty would not be imposed. The claimant argued that, in light of the UK's ratification of the Sixth and Thirteenth Protocols and its consistent refusal to extradite individuals where there is a real risk that they will be subjected to the death penalty, 'the UK has maintained a firm policy of refusing extradition or deportation to countries that impose the death penalty'.[87] It was further argued that 'this is not "just some alien obligation imposed on us by the European Court", on the contrary, the UK has taken that stance as a legal principle and it now forms part of the common law of this country'.[88] A difficulty confronting the claimant was that Strasbourg has not held that providing information in such circumstances violates Article 2 (though it has not expressly rejected that contention either). Thus, the claimant had to argue that the common law should 'outstrip' the limits of the ECHR. A majority of the Supreme Court rejected that argument, though the Court was unanimous in its finding that the sharing of the information was unlawful as it breached the Data Protection Act 2018.[89] In contrast, Lord Kerr would have accepted that there was 'a common law right not to have one's trial in a foreign state facilitated [through the sharing of information] where there is a prospect that such a trial would lead to the death penalty being carried out'.[90]

4.3.2.2 Procedural Obligation

In addition to the negative obligation, Article 2 also obliges the State to investigate when an individual has been killed.[91] This procedural obligation extends not only to deaths involving State agents,[92] but also to deaths caused by private persons and persons unknown.[93] 'The essential purpose of such an investigation is to secure the effective implementation of the domestic laws safeguarding the right to life and, in those cases involving State agents or bodies, to ensure their accountability for deaths occurring under their responsibility'.[94]

The procedural obligation does not require, in all cases, a criminal investigation. It may be satisfied by way of an effective civil law system. What is

[87] Ibid at [62], per Lord Kerr. [88] Ibid. [89] See, for instance, ibid at [230], per Lord Hodge.

[90] Ibid at [141], per Lord Kerr.

[91] *Nachova and Ors* v. *Bulgaria* [GC] (2005) 42 EHRR 933 at [110].

[92] See Chapter 5 for a discussion of the analogous obligation under Article 3 and its extension beyond those cases involving State agents.

[93] See, for instance, *Paul and Audrey Edwards* v. *the United Kingom* [GC] (2002) 35 EHRR 487 (involving violence between individuals who were incarcerated) and *Opuz* v. *Turkey* (2010) 50 EHRR 28 (involving domestic violence).

[94] *Nachova and Ors* v. *Bulgaria* (n 91) at [110].

required for the procedural obligation to be met in a given case depends on the specific circumstances. As the ECtHR observed in *Traskunova* v. *Russia* which involved the death of the applicant's daughter during a clinical trial of a new drug:

> The procedural obligation of Article 2 in the context of health care requires States to set up an effective and independent judicial system so that the cause of death of patients in the care of the medical profession, whether in the public or the private sector, can be determined and those responsible made accountable. In some exceptional situations, where the fault attributable to the healthcare providers went beyond a mere error or medical negligence, the Court has considered that compliance with the procedural obligation must include recourse to criminal law. In all other cases where the infringement of the right to life or to personal integrity is not caused intentionally, the procedural obligation imposed by Article 2 does not necessarily require the provision of a criminal-law remedy ... That obligation will be satisfied if the legal system affords victims a remedy in the civil courts, either alone or in conjunction with a remedy in the criminal courts, enabling any responsibility of the doctors concerned to be established and any appropriate civil redress to be obtained. Disciplinary measures may also be envisaged.[95]

'When an intentional taking of life is alleged, the mere fact that the authorities are informed that a death had taken place gives rise *ipso facto* to an obligation under Article 2 to carry out an effective official investigation.'[96] In the context of negligence resulting in (unintentional) death, the procedural obligation may be engaged upon the institution of civil proceedings by the deceased's relatives.[97]

As for the characteristics required of an investigation for the procedural obligation under Article 2 to be met, the ECtHR has repeatedly affirmed that:

- The persons responsible for carrying it out must be independent and impartial both in practice and in law, though Article 2 does not require 'complete hierarchical or institutional disconnection'[98] between those conducting the investigation and the subjects of it;
- Where a person died as a result of the use of force, the investigation must be capable of leading to a determination of whether the force used was or was not justified in the circumstances;
- The investigation must be capable of leading to the identification of those responsible and the holding of them to account. In certain cases, this may require a criminal-law remedy, though not all cases necessitate recourse to

95 *Traskunova* v. *Russia* [2022] ECHR 631 at [81]. See also, *Lopes de Sousa Fernandes* v. *Portugal* [GC] (2018) 66 EHRR 28 at [214]–[215].

96 *Šilih* v. *Slovenia* [GC] (2009) 49 EHRR 37 at [156].

97 See, for instance, ibid, and *Lopes de Sousa Fernandes* v. *Portugal* (n 95) at [220].

98 *R (McQuillan, McGuigan and McKenna)* [2021] UKSC 55, [2022] AC 1063 at [110].

criminal law; civil law remedies, inquests or inquiries may be sufficient, as may disciplinary proceedings;

- The authorities must have taken reasonable steps to secure the evidence including eyewitness testimony and forensic evidence;
- The conclusions must be based on thorough, objective and impartial analysis of all relevant elements;
- The investigation must be prompt;
- There must be sufficient public scrutiny of the investigation or its results to secure accountability in theory and in practice, maintain public confidence in the authorities' adherence to the rule of law and prevent any appearance of collusion in or tolerance of unlawful acts. While the degree of scrutiny necessary will vary from case to case, in all cases the victim's next of kin must be involved to secure their legitimate interest.[99]

What these requirements mean in practice is best illustrated by reference to specific cases and issues.

4.3.2.2.1 *Jean Charles de Menezes*

In *Armani Da Silva*[100] – which was discussed above in the context of the negative obligation under Article 2 – the Grand Chamber considered whether the domestic investigations complied with the procedural obligation. In particular, the decision not to prosecute any of the officers involved in the shooting of Jean Charles de Menezes. By a majority of 13:4, the ECtHR held that there had been *no* violation of the procedural obligation. The Court emphasised that there had been internal investigations and proceedings before the criminal courts against the police service as an entity and there had been an inquest. The family had also commenced civil proceedings which had been settled. In the dissenting judgments (which considered that there had been a violation of the procedural obligation), emphasis was placed on the fact that the criminal proceedings could not lead to the identification and punishment of the individual officers involved. There were also issues with the promptness of the investigations.

4.3.2.2.2 *Deaths Occurring during 'The Troubles' and the 'Genuine Connection' Test*

Patrick Finucane, a lawyer, was shot dead in his home in North Belfast in front of his wife and three children in February 1989. The incident has been

[99] *Nachova and Ors* v. *Bulgaria* (n 91) at [110]–[113], *Ramsahai and Ors* v. *Netherlands* [GC] (2008) 46 EHRR 43 at [322], *Anguelova* v. *Bulgaria* (2004) 38 EHRR 31 at [140] and *Traskunova* v. *Russia* (n 95) at [81].

[100] *Armani Da Silva* v. *the United Kingdom* (n 56).

described as 'one of the most notorious of what are euphemistically called "the Northern Ireland troubles"'.[101] It transpired that Finucane was murdered by self-described loyalists and there had been collusion between the murderers and members of the British security forces. Various investigations (including several inquiries) were conducted but none led to the identity of those members of the security services who colluded with the murderers, nor to the nature of that collusion. In 2019, the UK Supreme Court determined that there had been a failure to carry out an Article 2 compliant investigation into Finucane's death:

> An article 2 compliant inquiry involves providing the means where, if they can be, suspects are identified, and, if possible, brought to account. It should also provide the opportunity to recognise, if possible, the lessons to be learned so that a similar event can be avoided in the future.[102]

Finucane was murdered in 1989: over ten years before the HRA came into force in the UK (which occurred on 2 October 2000). The question arises, then, as to how the State could be responsible for breaches of the HRA in respect of events that took place *before* the HRA came into force, particularly as it has no retrospective effect. This has been an enduring issue in the context of the violence in Northern Ireland, with the UK Government resisting responsibility on the basis that the HRA was not in force at the relevant times. While the House of Lords initially agreed with the Government,[103] the Grand Chamber subsequently held in *Šilih* v. *Slovenia* that Article 2 entails an *autonomous* procedural obligation which may be invoked in respect of events that occur *before* a State has ratified the ECHR or granted individuals the right of individual petition to the ECtHR.[104] The ECtHR has, however, repeatedly held that the substantive obligations under Article 2 *do not* apply to events that took place prior to the State Party acceding to the ECHR or recognising the right of individual petition (whichever took place later).[105]

[101] *Re Finucane's Application for Judicial Review* [2019] UKSC 7, [2019] 3 All ER 191 at [1], per Lord Kerr.

[102] Ibid at [134].

[103] *Re McKerr's Application for Judicial Review* [2004] UKHL 12, [2004] 1 WLR 807.

[104] *Šilih* v. *Slovenia* (n 96) at [159]: 'Although it is triggered by the acts concerning the substantive aspects of Article 2 it can give rise to a finding of a separate and independent "interference" . . . In this sense it can be considered to be a detachable obligation arising out of Article 2 capable of binding the State even when the death took place before the critical date.' This was subsequently confirmed by the Grand Chamber in *Janowiec and Ors* v. *Russia* [GC] (2014) 58 EHRR 30. In light of the decision in *Šilih* (n 96), the UKSC subsequently held that investigations regarding 'shoot to kill' deaths in Northern Ireland in the 1990s had to comply with Article 2 despite the events taking place before the HRA 1998 was enacted: *Re McCaughey's Application for Judicial Review* [2011] UKSC 20, [2012] 1 AC 725.

[105] *Šilih* v. *Slovenia* (n 96).

Consequently, whilst the death might take place prior to the enactment of the HRA such that the substantive obligations are *not* engaged, the procedural obligation to investigate is separate and *can arise and persist* in respect of pre-HRA deaths. This occurs in one of two situations. Either:

1. there is a 'genuine connection' between the 'triggering event[s]' (for instance, the killing of the relevant individual(s)) and the coming into force of the HRA (referred to as the 'critical date' in the ECtHR case law); or,
2. there is a need to ensure that the Convention values are protected (referred to as the 'Convention values' test).

For a 'genuine connection' to arise, the period between the triggering event and the critical date (i.e. the enactment of the HRA) should not normally be greater than ten years.[106] And, for the State's procedural obligation to arise in such cases, 'a major part of the investigation must have been carried out, or ought to have been carried out, *after* the entry into force [of the Convention in domestic law]'.[107]

As for the 'Convention values' test, this applies in 'extraordinary situations' which do not meet the 'genuine connection' test and is satisfied:

> if the triggering event was of a larger dimension than an ordinary criminal offence and amounted to the negation of the very foundations of the Convention. This would be the case with serious crimes under international law, such as war crimes, genocide or crimes against humanity, in accordance with the definitions given to them in the relevant international instruments.[108]

Finucane is notable because the murder of Finucane (the 'triggering event') took place eleven years and eight months before the HRA came into force. This, however, did not stop a unanimous Supreme Court concluding that the State's procedural obligation had been violated, resulting in a breach of s.6(1) HRA. Lord Kerr, giving the lead judgment, held that determining whether there was a genuine connection requires a multi-factorial analysis such that whilst the length of time between the triggering event and critical date is a relevant factor, it is not an immutable requirement that no more than ten years has passed.[109]

In its subsequent judgment in *McQuillan*,[110] the UK Supreme Court revisited the investigative duty under Articles 2 and 3[111] in respect of the shooting of Jean Smyth during The Troubles and the ill-treatment of the 'Hooded Men'

[106] *Janowiec and Ors* v. *Russia* (n 104) at [146]–[147]. [107] Ibid at [148]. Emphasis added.

[108] Ibid at [150]. [109] *Re Finucane* (n 101) at [108]. [110] *R (McQuillan)* (n 98).

[111] As discussed in Chapter 5, the procedural obligation under Article 3 to investigate arises 'where there is a reasonable suspicion that a person has been subjected to torture or inhuman or degrading treatment' and the relevant principles are largely analogous to those developed in respect of Article 2: *R (McQuillan)*, ibid at [109(iii)].

who were the subject of the proceedings in *Ireland* v. *the United Kingdom.*[112] The latter is discussed in detail in Chapter 5 in the context of Article 3. A central issue in *McQuillan* was whether the 'critical date' for the purposes of a claim under s.6(1) HRA is the date that the HRA came into force (2 October 2000) or whether it is the date that the UK granted individuals the right to directly petition the ECtHR (14 January 1966). The Supreme Court concluded that the 'critical date' is 2 October 2000, citing the fact that the HRA gives the relevant ECHR rights distinct effect in domestic law. The Supreme Court summarised the distinction between the HRA and the ECHR and the implications for the procedural obligation in respect of events occurring before the critical event in the following terms:

> Under the HRA, the substantive right under article 2 has no application before 2 October 2000, by contrast with the substantive right under article 2 of the Convention. Under the Convention, the substantive right under article 2 has no relevant application in relation to the United Kingdom before 1966. In both cases the same issue arises, as to when a death which occurred before the inception of the relevant right under article 2 can trigger an investigative obligation under article 2 which is capable of recognition and enforcement by a domestic court or the Strasbourg Court, respectively. For the purposes of application of the genuine connection test, the 'critical date' is the date of inception of the relevant right under article 2. In the case of the Convention, so far as concerns the United Kingdom, it is 14 January 1966; and different dates are relevant for other contracting states, depending on the date of inception of the right under article 2 for them. In the case of the HRA, applying the same principle, the critical date is 2 October 2000.[113]

In obiter, the Court in *McQuillan* clarified that the 'normal ten year limit' that the ECtHR has established in respect of the 'genuine connection' test may be extended by a further two years *only* if:

> there are compelling reasons to allow such an adjustment constituted by circumstances that (a) any original investigation into the triggering death can be seen to have been seriously deficient and (b) the bulk of such investigative effort which has taken place post-dates the relevant critical date.[114]

The Supreme Court revisited the scope of the 'genuine connection' again in *Dalton.*[115] The case centred on the death of Sean Dalton during The Troubles. Dalton was killed after a bomb exploded on 31 August 1988 – that is, just over twelve years before the HRA 1998 entered into force. An initial inquest held in

[112] *Ireland* v. *the United Kingdom* (1979–80) 2 EHRR 25. [113] *R (McQuillan)* (n 98) at [164].

[114] Ibid at [144].

[115] *Re Dalton's Application for Judicial Review (Northern Ireland)* [2023] UKSC 36, [2023] 3 WLR 671. For a discussion of the case, see Helen Jennings, 'Looking Ourselves in the Mirror: Troubles-Related Legacy Litigation and the Article 2 Investigative Obligation in Light of Dalton [2023] UKSC 36' [2025] 2 EHRLR 194–213.

December 1989 concluded that Mr Dalton died from injuries suffered in the explosion. Dalton's family subsequently requested a fresh inquest into his death, in particular to take account of findings made by the Police Ombudsman of Northern Ireland. That request was refused, and subsequent challenges to the refusal before the courts in Northern Ireland were met with varying success. The case made its way to the Supreme Court, where the central issue was whether Dalton's death occurred outside of the temporal scope of the HRA. The Court unanimously held that *it was outside the temporal scope*, though there was a significant division in the Court in terms of the nature and scope of the 'genuine connection' test.

The majority – Lords Reed, Leggatt and Burrows and Dame Siobhan Keegan – considered that both *Finucane* and *McQuillan* were correctly decided. In contrast, according to Lords Hodge and Sales and Lady Rose, *Finucane* and *McQuillan* were wrong to suggest that the temporal scope of the procedural obligation could extend past ten years prior to the critical date. Thus, as it stands in the UK, the procedural obligation to investigate may arise with respect to a death that occurred between ten and twelve years before the coming into force of the HRA provided there are 'compelling reasons', that is, where the original investigation was 'seriously deficient' and where 'the bulk of [the] investigative effort' has taken place after the critical date.[116]

In the context of the long line of cases both before the domestic courts and the ECtHR concerning violations of the ECHR stemming from violence taking place during The Troubles,[117] the UK Parliament enacted the Northern Ireland Troubles (Legacy and Reconciliation) Act 2023. The Act created a new independent body – the Independent Commission for Reconciliation and Information Recovery (ICRIR) – to investigate deaths and very serious injuries resulting from conduct associated with The Troubles.[118] The Act raised many challenges for the UK's compliance with the ECHR,[119] and the Committee of Ministers expressed concern about the legislation prior to its enactment.[120] Indeed, Ireland lodged an inter-State application against the UK challenging a

[116] Ibid at [332].

[117] The Committee of Ministers continues to monitor the UK's compliance with a number of judgments of the ECtHR finding violations of the procedural obligation to investigate deaths occurring during the Troubles. See, for instance, Council of Europe, Committee of Ministers, 'H46-32 McKerr group v the United Kingdom (Application No. 28883/95)', 1443rd Meeting, 20–22 September 2022 (DH), https://search.coe.int/cm?i=0900001680a7f588.

[118] Northern Ireland Troubles (Legacy and Reconciliation) Act, Part 2.

[119] See, for instance, Joint Human Rights Committee, 'Legislative Scrutiny: Northern Ireland Troubles (Legacy and Reconciliation) Bill', Sixth Report of Session 2022–23, 19 October 2022, Summary (see also, [11] (noting submissions highlighting the then-Bill's potential to breach human rights standards)).

[120] Committee of Ministers, 'H46-32 McKerr group' (n 117) at [8]–[9].

number of especially problematic aspects of the Act under several Articles of the ECHR including Article 2.[121] As discussed in greater detail below, proceedings were also brought before the courts in Northern Ireland by the next of kin of persons killed or injured during The Troubles challenging the lawfulness of the Act, including under the HRA. Shortly after its election (and consistent with its electoral manifesto[122]), the UK Labour Government indicated its intention to repeal the Act (which was enacted during the previous Conservative Government's period of office). At the time of writing, the Act remains in force and it appears the plan is to retain the ICRIR,[123] though a draft remedial order has been laid before Parliament under s.10 HRA which would, if approved, remove certain provisions including those relating to immunities and bars on civil proceedings which have been the subject of successful challenges before the lower courts (see below).[124] Whatever the outcome with respect to the Act, the criticisms (both judicial and otherwise) of its provisions are nevertheless illuminating in terms of the nature of the procedural obligation under Article 2. Particularly given that the UK Supreme Court has recently granted permission to the State to appeal certain of the Northern Ireland Court of Appeal's findings, notably for instant purposes, those relating to disclosure and family involvement (issues relevant to the operation of the ICRIR which, as noted above, the Government intends to retain).[125]

Pursuant to Part 3 of the Act, 'criminal investigations (other than those referred by the ICRIR to the prosecutor), police complaints, civil proceedings and inquests/inquiries arising out of the Troubles' that are commenced after the Act came into force or, in some cases, after the first reading of the bill, are prohibited.[126] Much emphasis is, thus, placed on the ICRIR as the mechanism by which the State's procedural obligation under Article 2 can be met and concerns have been expressed about the ICRIR's capacity to fulfil that function.[127]

Another significant issue posed by the Act is the *duty* imposed on the ICRIR to grant immunities to individuals who participated in The Troubles where

[121] *Ireland* v. *the United Kingdom*, Inter-State Application No. 1859/24, 17 January 2024.

[122] *Change: Labour Party Manifesto 2024*, pp.113, https://labour.org.uk/wp-content/uploads/2024/06/Labour-Party-manifesto-2024.pdf.

[123] See, for instance, House of Commons, *Northern Ireland: Legacy of the Troubles*, 4 December 2024, vol 758, col 419.

[124] See, for instance, the discussion of the draft remedial order by the Joint Human Rights Committee, 'Proposal for a Draft Northern Ireland Troubles (Legacy and Reconciliation) Act 2023 (Remedial) Order 2024', HC 569/HL Paper 88, 28 February 2025.

[125] *In the matter of an application by Martina Dillon, John McEvoy, Brigid Hughes and Lynda McManus for Judicial Review*, UKSC/2025/0013, Permission to Appeal application granted, 7 April 2025.

[126] Northern Ireland Human Rights Commission, 'Legislative Scrutiny: NI Troubles (Legacy and Reconciliation) Bill', June 2022 at [4.1], https://nihrc.org/publication/detail/briefing-on-the-ni-troubles-legacy-and-reconciliation-bill.

[127] Joint Human Rights Committee (n 119), Summary.

certain criteria are met, in particular where the individual's disclosures before the ICRIR would tend to expose them '(a) to a criminal investigation of, or (b) to prosecution for, one or more particular serious or connected Troubles-related offences'.[128]

This power was successfully challenged under Articles 2 and 3 of the ECHR before the Northern Ireland High Court in February 2024.[129]

In finding that the legislation was incompatible with Article 2, the High Court considered the ECtHR case law on amnesties, concluding that 'the ECtHR has articulated strong opposition to the granting of amnesties in the context of articles 2/3'.[130] As the High Court noted, 'the procedural obligations under articles 2 and 3 . . . are clearly undermined by the prospect of immunity from prosecution under the 2023 Act'.[131] Significantly, the High Court rejected the Government's claim that the immunities were aimed at facilitating enduring peace: 'there is no evidence that the granting of immunity under the 2023 Act will in any way contribute to reconciliation in Northern Ireland, indeed, the evidence is to the contrary'.[132]

Both the applicants and the Secretary of State for Northern Ireland appealed aspects of the High Court's judgment to the Northern Ireland Court of Appeal. While the Secretary of State subsequently abandoned its challenge to the trial judge's finding that the immunity provisions were incompatible with the ECHR, the Court of Appeal nevertheless indicated that it would have dismissed the challenge and set out its reasons for so finding.[133] The appellate court agreed with the trial judge's assessment of the ECtHR's case law on immunities and the likely manner in which the Strasbourg court would decide the case.[134] According to the Court of Appeal, 'the Strasbourg jurisprudence was not on the [Secretary of State's] side in this appeal. ... We are confident that the ECtHR has set its face against amnesties and immunity in a fashion which would result in the 2023 Act being held to be incompatible with the Convention.'[135] The Court of Appeal went further than the High Court, however, and held that the 2023 Act was also incompatible with Article 2 ECHR because there was no obligation for next of kin to be involved in the ICRIR's reviews and there were limitations on the ICRIR's disclosure obligations, both of which undermined the effectiveness (as that term is used in respect of investigations under Article 2 ECHR) of the ICRIR's reviews.[136] The State has appealed against these findings (amongst others). At the time of publication, the Supreme Court had just granted the State permission for leave to appeal, the outcome of which could have significant implications for the operation of the ICRIR if it is retained as currently proposed.

[128] Northern Ireland Troubles (Legacy and Reconciliation) Act 2023, s.19.
[129] *Re Dillon & Ors* [2024] NIKB 11. [130] Ibid at [183]. [131] Ibid at [186].
[132] Ibid at [187]. [133] *Re Dillon & Ors* [2024] NICA 59. [134] Ibid at [164].
[135] Ibid at [172]. [136] Ibid at [218], [232]–[237] and [311(ii)].

Given that, according to Government data, the Police Service of Northern Ireland 'has a caseload of over 900 cases involving nearly 1,200 deaths' relating to The Troubles, the Act would, if it were to remain in force, have profound and far-reaching consequences for victims and their families and their rights under Article 2 (and 3) ECHR.[137] In light of the significant litigation that has attended (and is likely to attend) the Act, whatever the future of the legislation, its implications will be felt for years to come.

4.3.2.2.3 *Inquests and Public Inquiries*

Inquests and public inquiries fulfil important, albeit distinct, functions in terms of the State's procedural obligation to investigate deaths. A coronial inquest must be conducted into violent or unnatural deaths, deaths where the cause is unknown, or deaths that take place while the person is in custody or state detention.[138] The purpose of an inquest is to ascertain who died, how they died, when they died and where.[139] A coroner – or a jury – will make a determination at the end of the inquest regarding those issues. Where there is an arguable case that one or more of the State's substantive Article 2 obligations have been breached in relation to the death, the question of the wider circumstances in which the individual died is added to the list of factors for determination.[140] This is known as a *Middleton* inquest[141] and it entails asking 'by what means and in what circumstances' the deceased came to die.[142] Significantly, this cannot be framed in such a way as to determine criminal or civil liability.[143] *Middleton* inquests can, however, provide a valuable insight into any failings by the State in respect of their obligations under Article 2. Indeed, *Middleton* inquests are not infrequent in cases involving domestic abuse. For instance, in the case of Susan Nicholson, a *Middleton* inquest conducted after her former partner was convicted of her murder revealed significant shortcomings in the response of the police and indicated potential violations of the positive obligation to protect under Article 2. It is notable that the coroner initially declined to reopen the inquest following the conviction of Nicholson's former partner for her murder. The High Court subsequently ordered 'an article 2 compliant inquest into [her] death'.[144] Similarly, a second inquest into the death of Kellie Sutton was conducted as

[137] Northern Ireland Troubles (Legacy and Reconciliation) Bill, Explanatory Memorandum at [2].

[138] Coroners and Justice Act 2009 (CJA), s.1. [139] CJA, s.5. [140] CJA, s.5(2).

[141] *R (Middleton)* v. *West Somerset Coroner* [2004] UKHL 10, [2004] 2 AC 182.

[142] See, for instance, *R (Grice)* [2020] EWHC 3581 (Admin) at [56] and *R (Letts)* v. *Lord Chancellor* [2015] EWHC 402 (Admin), [2015] 1 WLR 4497 at [71]–[75].

[143] CJA, s.10(2).

[144] *Skelton* v. *Senior Coroner for West Sussex* [2020] EWHC 2813 (Admin), [2021] 2 WLR 413 at [125].

a *Middleton* inquest (the first inquest had concluded that Sutton died by suicide), and the jury concluded that Sutton had, in fact, been unlawfully killed as a result of the domestic abuse she had been subjected to in the lead up to her death (the jury also made critical findings about the actions of the police preceding Sutton's death).[145]

Inquests may also be conducted in cases involving medical treatment that (potentially) engage the State's positive obligation (as discussed below). This may be the case where, for instance, the individual was deprived of their liberty under the Mental Capacity Act 2005, though as the decision of the Supreme Court in *Maguire* makes clear, the 'enhanced procedural obligation', which a *Middleton* inquest is designed to meet, is not automatically required in cases involving deprivations of liberty (such as where an individual resides in a care home or other residential facility).[146]

The utility of *Middleton* inquests as a means of securing the rights protected by Article 2 is exemplified by the inquests that took place following the Hillsborough stadium disaster. On 15 April 1989:

> as thousands of fans were preparing to watch the FA Cup semi-final between Liverpool and Nottingham Forest, a crush developed in the central pens of the Leppings Lane terrace. 96 men, women and children lost their lives as a result. Hundreds more were injured, and many were left traumatised.[147]

The initial inquest into the deaths of the ninety-six victims[148] commenced in April 1989 and ran until March 1991. The jury returned verdicts of 'accidental death', notwithstanding the finding that 'the main reason for the disaster was the failure of police control'[149] expressed by Lord Justice Taylor who was conducting a public inquiry into the disaster and had published an interim report which was known to the jury. It is notable that the jury at the initial inquest were expressly confined to the question of 'when' and 'where' each individual had died. They were told not to consider the question of 'how' they died because of ongoing investigations into the events. Significantly, the

[145] Bhatt Murphy, 'Press Release: Jury Concludes that Kellie Sutton was Unlawfully Killed in Self Inflicted Death Following Domestic Abuse', 6 July 2023, https://bhattmurphy.co.uk/wp-content/uploads/2023/07/Sutton-press-release-conclusion.pdf.

[146] *R (Maguire)* v. *His Majesty's Senior Coroner for Blackpool & Fylde and Anor* [2023] UKSC 20, [2023] 3 WLR 103.

[147] Home Secretary Theresa May, 'Determinations and findings of the Hillsborough inquests', 27 April 2016, www.gov.uk/government/speeches/determinations-and-findings-of-the-hillsborough-inquests.

[148] In 2021, the ninety-seventh victim died as a result of injuries sustained during the disaster: David Conn and Robyn Vinter, 'Liverpool fan's death ruled as 97th of Hillsborough disaster', *The Guardian*, 28 July 2021, www.theguardian.com/football/2021/jul/28/liverpool-fans-death-ruled-as-97th-victim-of-hillsborough-disaster.

[149] *Attorney General* v. *Coroner of South Yorkshire* [2012] EWHC 3782 (Admin) at [3].

coroner imposed a 'cut off' period so that the inquest was confined to a consideration of events that took place before 3:15pm. This precluded an examination of the adequacy of the rescue efforts and ignored medical evidence that a significant number of the victims may still have been alive at and after 3:15pm.[150]

In 2012, following publication of the Hillsborough Independent Panel's report[151] and its 'shocking conclusions',[152] the Attorney General successfully applied to the High Court to have the initial inquest verdicts quashed, and new inquests ordered.[153] The Court noted that the new inquests would have to conform with the requirements set out in *Middleton*:

> The interests of justice must be served. Within the limits of the coronial system, the facts must be investigated and reanalysed in a fresh inquest when, however distressing or unpalatable, the truth will be brought to light. In this way the families of those who died in this disaster will be vindicated and the memory of each victim will be properly respected.[154]

The new inquests began in March 2014 and concluded in April 2016 – the longest running in British history.[155] The jury concluded that the ninety-six victims were unlawfully killed and, significantly, that in all bar one case, the time of death bracket ran beyond the 3:15pm cut-off set by the Coroner at the original inquest, and acts and omissions on the part of the authorities, including police and ambulance services, contributed to the loss of lives.[156]

As the Hillsborough stadium disaster demonstrates, inquests and inquiries are important means by which the State can fulfil its procedural obligation under Article 2. In the UK, public inquiries can be either statutory or non-statutory, though since the 2005 Inquiries Act was passed, non-statutory inquiries have become less common.[157] Notable non-statutory inquiries include the initial inquiry into the Hillsborough stadium disaster, the inquiry into the war in Iraq (known as the Chilcot Inquiry), and an inquiry into the abduction, rape and murder of Sarah Everard by an off-duty Metropolitan Police officer (the Angiolini Inquiry) is ongoing, its terms of reference having

[150] Ibid at [17].

[151] *The Report of the Hillsborough Independent Panel,* 12 September 2012, HC 581, https://assets.publishing.service.gov.uk/media/5a7c9e4840f0b65b3de0a0ff/0581.pdf.

[152] Home Secretary Theresa May, 'Determinations and findings' (n 147).

[153] *Attorney General* v. *Coroner of South Yorkshire* (n 149). [154] Ibid at [29].

[155] Home Secretary Theresa May, 'Determinations and findings' (n 147).

[156] *Attorney-General* v. *Coroner of South Yorkshire* (n 149) at [20].

[157] See, for instance, House of Commons Library, 'Public Inquiries: Non-statutory public inquires', 7 March 2022, https://commonslibrary.parliament.uk/research-briefings/sn02599/. See also, Home Office Press Release, 'Inquiry launched into issues raised by Couzens conviction', 5 October 2021, www.gov.uk/government/news/inquiry-launched-into-issues-raised-by-couzens-conviction.

been expanded to, inter alia, include an examination of wider issues in policing in respect of protection of women.[158]

Statutory public inquiries are usually, though not exclusively, conducted under the Inquiries Act 2005 which, together with the Inquiry Rules 2006, provide a detailed framework for the establishment and conducting of statutory inquiries. Whether statutory or non-statutory, public inquiries serve a multitude of functions including: establishing the facts; learning from events; providing an opportunity for reconciliation and resolution; rebuilding public confidence; accountability, blame and retribution; and, serving a wider political agenda.[159]

While inquiries can serve an important function in ensuring the State complies with its obligations under Article 2 in the context of major accidents or disasters, or 'when something goes seriously wrong within a government or a public body',[160] the ability of an inquiry to satisfy the State's procedural obligations very much depends on the nature of the inquiry, its scope, the evidence that is adduced and the people involved. Shortcomings in a number of inquiries into deaths related to The Troubles, including delays, the failure to reach conclusions or to make conclusions public, the lack of adequate reasons and so on, have led domestic courts and the ECtHR to conclude that they have not satisfied the procedural obligations under Article 2.[161]

Judicial review proceedings were brought by survivors of the Manchester Arena bombing challenging their exclusion from the list of 'core participants' in the statutory Manchester Arena Inquiry. Core participant status affords individuals, inter alia, the right to provide oral evidence, the right to ask questions of witnesses and the right to be legally represented.[162] The applicants claimed that Articles 2 and/or 3 mandated that they be granted core participant status. This argument was rejected by the High Court which

[158] The Angiolini Inquiry, *Terms of Reference*, www.angiolini.independent-inquiry.uk/. The report from Part 1 of the Inquiry was published in 2024, making sixteen recommendations including with respect to recruitment and vetting to 'prevent those unsuitable for policing from joining the policing profession': The Angiolini Inquiry, Part 1 Report, February 2024, Recommendation 8, https://iipcv-prod.s3.eu-west-2.amazonaws.com/E02740018_Angiolini-Inquiry.pdf.

[159] Geoffrey Howe, 'The Management of Public Inquiries' (1999) **70** The Political Quarterly 3, cited in Cowie (n 158) at [1.1].

[160] Graeme Cowie, 'Statutory public inquiries: the Inquiries Act 2005', Commons Library Research Briefing, 14 March 2022, Summary.

[161] See, for instance, *McKerr* v. *the United Kingdom* (2002) 34 EHRR 20 and *McKerr* v. *the United Kingdom*, App. No. 28883/95, 19 March 2009, Committee of Ministers, Interim Resolution CM/ResDH(2009)44, *Finucane* v. *the United Kingdom* (2003) 37 EHRR 29 and *Re Finucane* (n 101).

[162] Inquiries Rules 2006, rr.5–10.

emphasised the distinction between liability under s.6(1) HRA and the UK's compliance with its international obligations under the ECHR. The applicants were relying on s.6(1) HRA to argue that the Chairperson's refusal to grant them core participant status was a breach of the ECHR and, thus, unlawful under the HRA. However, as the High Court observed, the Chairperson derived his powers from the Terms of Reference. Those Terms did not confer any separate investigative powers in respect of survivors and, accordingly, there was no entitlement to core participant status for survivors under either Article 2 or 3 of the ECHR *in respect of this particular inquiry*: '[i]t was not designed to cover every aspect of the United Kingdom's Convention obligations arising out of the Manchester Arena bombing. It was not designed as the vehicle by which the United Kingdom might discharge Convention obligations owed to the survivors'.[163]

Another notable public inquiry was that into the Grenfell Tower fire, which concluded in September 2024. On 14 June 2017, fire engulfed the Grenfell Tower, a twenty-four-storey residential building in West London. The fire started in a freezer in one of the residences and quickly spread throughout the building, primarily via the cladding on the outside. Seventy-two people were killed and hundreds more affected both physically and psychologically. The building was owned by the Royal Borough of Kensington and Chelsea and managed by the Royal Borough of Kensington and Chelsea Tenant Management Organisation (which was unaffiliated with either the council or the Borough). The property provided a significant number of individuals and families with social housing.[164] Given their dependence on the authorities for the provision of housing and their limited ability to relocate from the tower, notwithstanding concerns regarding fire safety, such individuals were particularly vulnerable.[165]

After the fire, a statutory public inquiry was established. The Grenfell Tower Inquiry, chaired by a retired Court of Appeal judge, had a number of terms of reference including to 'examine': 'the immediate cause or causes of the fire and the means by which it spread to the whole of the building'; the scope and

[163] *R (EA and BT)* v. *The Chairman of the Manchester Arena Inquiry* [2020] EWHC 2053 (Admin) at [45] and [49].

[164] Grenfell Tower Inquiry, *Phase I Report: Report of the Public Inquiry into the Fire at Grenfell Tower on 14 June 2017*, HC 489-I, October 2019, Vol 1 at [3.6].

[165] For further discussion of the intersection between race, inequality and the fire, see Tracy Shildrick, 'Lessons from Grenfell: Poverty Propaganda, Stigma and Class Power' (2018) 66 The Sociological Review 4. See also, Jessie Hohmann, 'The Elements of Adequate Housing: Grenfell as Violation' (2019) 5 QMHRR 2, Colm O'Cinneide, 'Grenfell and the Limited Reach of Equality within the UK Constitutional Order' (2019) 5 QMHRR 2 and Daniela Nadj, 'Deregulation, the Absence of the Law and the Grenfell Tower Fire' (2019) 5 QMHRR 2.

adequacy of the relevant regulatory system and whether it was complied with; and, the response of the London Fire Brigade.[166] There was a significant list of core participants, with survivors of the fire, all residents of the Tower at the time of the fire and the families of those who died or were injured and unable to participate in the Inquiry, automatically qualifying for core participant status.[167]

The Inquiry was conducted in two stages. The first stage – Phase 1 – examined what happened on 14 June 2017 including where and how the fire started and spread, and the response of the emergency services, in particular the fire department. The report was published in October 2019 and set out a number of preliminary recommendations.[168] Then Prime Minister Boris Johnson wrote to the Inquiry to confirm that the Government accepted the recommendations made in the Phase 1 Report, though it remains to be seen whether these recommendations will be implemented effectively.

Phase 2 of the Inquiry concluded in November 2022, and the final report was published in September 2024. The focus of Phase 2 was on justifications for the use of certain materials (which were found in Phase 1 to have been the primary cause of the spread of the fire) on a high-rise residential building. Findings made during Phase 1 also necessitated further examination of failings within the London Fire Brigade both on the night of the fire and more generally, particularly in light of what appears to have been a failure to learn from past experiences of residential fires. Concerns were also raised regarding the training offered to members of the Fire Brigade and to its management.[169]

Many (if not all) of the terms of reference of the Inquiry have implications from an Article 2 perspective. In particular, issues surrounding the effectiveness of fire safety and building regulations,[170] a lack of compliance with any such regulations, the failure to respond to concerns raised by residents regarding fire hazards and inadequacies in the response of the London Fire Brigade, individually and cumulatively raise issues in terms of the State's positive obligation to put in place (and enforce) an *effective* regulatory system

[166] Grenfell Tower Inquiry, 'Terms of Reference', 15 August 2017, www.grenfelltowerinquiry.org.uk/about/terms-of-reference.

[167] Grenfell Tower Inquiry, 'Update on Core Participants', 20 October 2017, www.grenfelltowerinquiry.org.uk/news/update-core-participants.

[168] Grenfell Tower Inquiry, *Phase I Report* (n 164), Part V. [169] Ibid at [34.5].

[170] A separate review into the regulation of high-rise and complex buildings found significant failings and determined that the existing regulations were not 'fit for purpose' and that there was evidence of a 'system failure' driven by, amongst other things, 'indifference', 'lack of clarity' and 'inadequate regulatory oversight': Ministry of Housing, Communities and Local Government, *Independent Review of Building Regulations and Fire Safety: Final Report*, 17 May 2018, www.gov.uk/government/publications/independent-review-of-building-regulations-and-fire-safety-final-report.

deterring threats to life as well as the positive obligation to take preventive operational measures (see Section 4.3.2.3 below). The Phase 2 Report is especially pertinent in this respect. The Report notes that prior to the fire at Grenfell Tower, 'there were many opportunities for the government to identify the risks posed by the use of combustible cladding panels and insulation, particularly to high-rise buildings, and to take action in relation to them'.[171] In fact, the relevant Government department was 'well aware of those risks, but failed to act on what it knew', which included a warning in 1999 from the Environment and Transport Select Committee that 'it should not take a serious fire in which people were killed before steps were taken to minimise the risks posed by some external cladding systems'.[172] Such systemic failings suggest a breach of the State's regulatory and operational obligations under Article 2. There is also evidence of systemic failings within the London Fire Brigade, including a failure to learn from previous fires and deficiencies in training,[173] which go beyond one-off instances of negligence and are likely to engage the State's obligations under Article 2.

The Inquiry goes some way to meeting the State's Article 2 procedural obligation to investigate. However, more will need to be done for the State to comply fully with its investigative obligation – particularly given that the Inquiry cannot ensure that those who may be criminally responsible are held accountable. To that end, the Metropolitan Police Service is conducting an investigation into the fire with a view to determining whether any criminal offences have been committed by, inter alia, those who were responsible for the design, maintenance and/or construction of the building. Individual coronial inquests into the deaths of residents during the fire have been suspended pending the outcomes of the public inquiry and the police investigation.

4.3.2.3 *Positive Obligation to Protect: Regulatory Obligation*

The State's positive obligation to protect under Article 2(1) comprises two distinct (but related) duties:

1. putting in place a legislative and administrative framework that effectively deters threats to life; and,

[171] Grenfell Tower Inquiry, *Phase II Report: Report of the Public Inquiry into the Fire at Grenfell Tower on 14 June 2017*, September 2024, HC 19–1, Volume 1 at [2.5].

[172] Ibid.

[173] Grenfell Tower Inquiry, *Phase II Report: Report of the Public Inquiry into the Fire at Grenfell Tower on 14 June 2017*, September 2024, HC 19–1, Volume 5, Part 8. See also, Grenfell Tower Inquiry, *Phase II Report Overview: Report of the Public Inquiry into the Fire at Grenfell Tower on 14 June 2017*, September 2024 at [2.90]–[2.98].

2. protecting individuals from threats to life, including by the criminal acts of third parties or from the individuals themselves, where the authorities knew or ought to have known at the time of the existence of a real and immediate risk to the life of an identified individual or individuals.[174]

The duty to put in place a legislative and administrative framework that deters threats to life requires: (i) effective criminal laws that deter the commission of life-threatening acts (e.g., murder and manslaughter) and proportionate sanctions for those crimes (e.g., imprisonment);[175] (ii) civil laws and professional standards regulating the provision of healthcare which prevent systematic instances of negligence causing death;[176] and (iii) that activities that may pose a threat to life must be sufficiently regulated.[177]

The requirement of effective criminal laws has been considered by the ECtHR in a number of cases concerning domestic abuse, particularly involving Russia when it was still a party to the ECHR. Indeed, the Court utilised its pilot judgment procedure pursuant to Article 46 in this context in *Tunikova and Ors* v. *Russia*.[178] The pilot judgment procedure allows the Court to identify systemic human rights violations and to provide clear indications to the Member State of the types of remedial measures necessary to resolve the issue.[179] In *Tunikova*, the ECtHR held that:

> In view of the continued absence of legislation addressing the issue of domestic violence at national level and the urgency of the matter concerning, as it does, the possibility for victims to live a life free from violence, the Court considers that the Government's obligations under the Convention compel it to introduce legislative and other changes without further delay. The need for such amendments is all the more pressing as large numbers of people affected by violations of a fundamental Convention right have no other choice but to seek relief through time-consuming international litigation. This situation is at odds with the principle of subsidiarity, which is prominent in the Convention system.[180]

Notably, the Court held that to remedy the systemic issues the authorities had to, inter alia, ensure that 'all acts of domestic violence, including battery and forms other than injuries' were criminalised and 'punishable by appropriate penalties'.[181]

[174] See, for instance, *Rabone* v. *Pennine Care NHS Foundation Trust* [2012] UKSC 2, [2012] 2 AC 72 at [12].

[175] See, for instance, *Mastromatteo* v. *Italy* [GC] [2002] ECHR 694 at [67] and *Kurt* v. *Austria* [GC] (2022) 74 EHRR 6 at [157].

[176] See, for instance, *Lopes de Sousa Fernandes* v. *Portugal* (n 95).

[177] See, for instance, *Öneryildiz* v. *Turkey (No 2)* (2005) 41 EHRR 20.

[178] *Tunikova and Ors* v. *Russia* (2022) 75 EHRR 1.

[179] European Court of Human Rights: Press Unit, 'Pilot Judgments', November 2023, www.echr.coe.int/documents/fs_pilot_judgments_eng.pdf.

[180] *Tunikova and Ors* v. *Russia* (n 178) at [150]–[151].

[181] Ibid at [154].

4.3.2.3.1 *Regulation of Medical Treatment*

The Grand Chamber clarified the nature of the regulatory obligation in the context of medical treatment in *Lopes de Sousa Fernandes* v. *Portugal.*[182] In that case, the ECtHR held that the obligation is not limited to the making of 'regulations compelling hospitals, whether private or public, to adopt appropriate measures for the protection of patients' lives'.[183] Rather, it extends to ensuring 'the effective functioning of that regulatory framework. The regulatory duties thus encompass necessary measures to ensure implementation, including supervision and enforcement.'[184] That said, the Court went on to emphasise that a deficiency in the regulatory system will not give rise to a violation of Article 2 without evidence that it has deleteriously affected a specific individual.[185] The State was found to have violated the regulatory obligation in *Sarishvili-Bolkvadze* v. *Georgia,*[186] a case in which the applicant's son had died as a result of medical treatment provided by unlicensed and unqualified doctors. In that case, although the domestic regulatory framework included supervision of compliance with the relevant licensing requirements, the Government failed to adduce evidence demonstrating how those protections were ensured in practice.[187] The ECtHR has also found that the State's obligations under Article 2 include ensuring that individuals obtaining treatment are made aware of any risks that the treatment carries and that regulations are in place providing for doctors to obtain informed consent.[188]

In addition to the obligation to put in place an adequate regulatory framework, there are two 'exceptional circumstances' in which the State may be found liable under the substantive limb of Article 2 for the acts or omissions of health care professionals:

1. Where an individual's life is *knowingly* put in danger by denial of access to life-saving emergency treatment; or
2. Where a *systemic or structural dysfunction* in hospital services results in the patient being deprived of life-saving treatment. For State responsibility to arise in such a case, there must be evidence that the authorities knew or ought to have known about the risk and failed to take necessary measures to prevent the risk from materialising.[189]

In *Lopes de Sousa Fernandes* v. *Portugal* the Court further clarified what is required for a State to be liable in the second, exceptional circumstance. Specifically, the

[182] *Lopes de Sousa Fernandes* v. *Portugal* (n 95).

[183] States are 'expected to make adequate provision for securing high professional standards among health professionals', ibid at [168].

[184] *Lopes de Sousa Fernandes* v. *Portugal* (n 95) at [166] and [189].

[185] Ibid at [188].

[186] *Sarishvili-Bolkvadze* v. *Georgia* [2018] ECHR 628.

[187] Ibid at [76]–[77].

[188] See, for instance, *Traskunova* v. *Russia* (n 95) at [70].

[189] *Lopes de Sousa Fernandes* v. *Portugal* (n 95) at [191]–[192].

acts or omissions of the healthcare providers must go beyond mere error or negligence; the dysfunction must be 'objectively and genuinely identifiable as systemic or structural', there must be a link between the dysfunction and the harm suffered and the dysfunction must have resulted from a failure of the State to meet its obligation to provide a regulatory framework.[190] The threshold for State liability for medical treatment is, thus, very high and it is unsurprising that the Court has found very few instances of Article 2 violations in this context.[191]

4.3.2.3.2 *Regulation of Dangerous Activities*

The landmark Grand Chamber decision in *Öneryildiz* v. *Turkey*[192] set out what States must do to comply with their substantive obligation under Article 2 in terms of regulating dangerous activities. According to the Court, regulations governing the 'licensing, setting up, operation, security and supervision of the [dangerous] activity and [which] make it compulsory for all those concerned to take practical measures to ensure the effective protection of citizens whose lives might be endangered by the inherent risks' are required.[193] Dangerous activities include clinical medical trials[194] and industrial activities such as refuse tips.[195] Thus, there had been a violation of the substantive Article 2 obligation in *Öneryildiz* as a result of the State's failure to properly regulate the municipal refuse tip which bordered the slum in which the applicant's nine family members lived and who had been killed following a landslide stemming from an explosion due to an accumulation of methane gas at the tip. Similarly, in *Budayeva*, the ECtHR found that Russia had violated its positive obligation under Article 2 after authorities failed to take any steps to prevent the materialisation of the threat to life posed by a succession of mudslides which the authorities had been notified were at risk of occurring.[196]

4.3.2.4 *Positive Obligation to Take Preventive Operational Measures*

While the State is, ordinarily, not responsible for the private actions of individuals, the ECtHR has found States liable where:

[190] Ibid at [194]–[196].

[191] For examples of cases in which the Court has found a violation, see, for instance, *Mehmet Senturk and Bekir Senturk* v. *Turkey* (2015) 60 EHRR 4 (violation because individual patient's life is knowingly put in danger by denial of access to life-saving emergency treatment) and *Asiye Genc* v. *Turkey* [2015] ECHR 78 (violation because systemic or structural dysfunction in hospital services results in the patient being deprived of life-saving treatment).

[192] *Öneryildiz* v. *Turkey (No 2)* (n 177).

[193] Ibid at [90]. See also, *Budayeva* v. *Russia* (2014) 59 EHRR 2 at [129]–[132]. An equivalent obligation can arise under Article 8.

[194] For a recent example, see *Traskunova* v. *Russia* (n 95).

[195] See, for instance, *Fadeyeva* v. *Russia* [2005] ECHR 376.

[196] *Budayeva* v. *Russia* (n 193).

(i) the authorities knew or ought to have known of a real and immediate risk to the life of an identified individual/s from the criminal acts of a third party; *and*
(ii) they failed to take measures within the scope of their powers which, judged reasonably, might have avoided that risk.[197]

This is known as the '*Osman* test' after the case in which it was first formulated.[198] The ECtHR has emphasised, however, that an 'impossible or disproportionate burden must not be imposed on the authorities'; and that 'operational choices ... must be made in terms of priorities and resources'.[199]

The threshold for establishing a 'real and immediate risk' is high, although where a person dies while within the State's control or custody, 'the burden of proof may be regarded as resting on the authorities to provide a satisfactory and convincing explanation'.[200] In this regard, the ECtHR has found violations of the obligation to protect in cases of deaths of individuals who are subject to conscription or mandatory military service.[201] The ECtHR has also held that 'persons in custody are in a vulnerable position' and '[i]t is incumbent on the State to account for any injuries suffered in custody, which obligation is particularly stringent where that individual dies'.[202] Applying this standard, the ECtHR determined that the UK had violated the obligation to protect Christopher Edwards from being killed by 'a dangerous, mentally ill prisoner, Richard Linford' who was placed in Edwards' cell.[203] The ECtHR found failings in the screening of Linford and shortcomings in the sharing of information between agencies which ought to have alerted them to the real and immediate risk posed by Linford.

Applying the *Osman* test, the domestic courts have found breaches of the positive obligation to protect in cases involving patients who are being treated both on an involuntary and voluntary in-patient basis for mental illness and who subsequently died by suicide either while on leave or having escaped from the hospital or facility they were being treated in.[204] And, in the case of *Safi and Ors* v. *Greece*[205] – which is discussed in greater detail in the context of Article 3 and border pushbacks in Chapter 5 – the Court held that the Greek authorities had violated the positive obligation to protect in the manner in which it carried out the rescue of the boat on which the applicants and their families were travelling. The boat sunk off the coast of Greece and there was

[197] *Osman* v. *the United Kingdom* (1998) 29 EHRR 245 at [116] and *Kurt* (n 175) at [158].
[198] *Osman* (n 197). [199] Ibid at [116]. [200] *Fanziyeva* v. *Russia* (2018) 67 EHRR 33 at [49].
[201] See, for instance, *Petrosyan* v. *Armenia*, App. No. 51448/15, 09/01/2025.
[202] *Paul and Audrey Edwards* v. *the United Kingom* (n 93) at [56]. [203] Ibid at [57].
[204] *Savage* v. *South Essex Partnership NHS Foundation Trust* [2008] UKHL 74, [2009] AC 681 (patient being treated on an involuntary basis) and *Rabone* (n 174) (patient being treated on a voluntary basis).
[205] *Safi and Ors* v. *Greece* [2022] ECHR 559.

evidence both of a lack of promptness in the authorities' response, despite being aware that the boat – which was carrying twenty-seven people, including women and children – was sinking, and of deficiencies in the response itself (while the Court did not make a finding, there was evidence that the use of a speedboat to tow the sinking vessel could have contributed to its sinking). While the Court accepted that authorities cannot be expected to rescue every person who is at risk of dying at sea, the authorities in this case were well aware of the danger faced by the applicants and their families and failed to take the measures that were reasonably available to them to protect them. There had, thus, been a violation of the positive obligation to protect under Article 2.[206]

Outside of the context of domestic abuse (which is considered below), the ECtHR has not provided much guidance as to what constitutes a 'real and immediate' risk. It has, however, said that 'real' requires 'the existence of a serious, genuine and sufficiently ascertainable threat to life' and the 'imminence' of 'such a risk entails an element of physical proximity of the threat ... and its temporal proximity'.[207]

The UK Supreme Court characterised the 'real and immediate' standard in similar terms, with Lady Hale observing that a 'real' risk is one which is 'substantial or significant' and not 'remote or fanciful' and an 'immediate' risk is one which is 'present and continuing'.[208]

While the obligation to protect as conceptualised in *Osman* refers to 'identified individual[s]', the ECtHR has also held that the positive obligation to protect can extend to the 'public at large' where the authorities are aware of an individual who poses a real and immediate risk of harm. Thus, when organising and operating a system of early release or leave for prisoners, a positive obligation to protect those that are likely to come into contact with the releasee may arise.[209]

4.3.3 Extraterritorial Scope of the Right to Life

4.3.3.1 Territorial Scope of Article 2 ECHR and the ECtHR

Pursuant to Article 1 ECHR, Member States must secure to everyone *within their jurisdiction* the rights set out in the ECHR. 'Jurisdiction' under Article 1 is a 'threshold criterion'; '[t]he exercise of jurisdiction is a necessary condition for a Contracting State to be ... held responsible for acts or omissions

[206] Ibid at [157]–[167]. The Court also found a violation of the procedural obligation under Article 2. Criminal proceedings against members of the coastguard had been discontinued despite very significant issues with interpretations provided of the applicants' statements and failings in ensuring the applicants were able to meaningfully participate in the proceedings: ibid at [121]–[128].

[207] *Verein KlimaSeniorinnen Schweiz and Ors* v. *Switzerland* [GC] (2024) 79 EHRR 1 at [512].

[208] *Rabone* (n 174) at [37]–[38].

[209] See, for instance, *Mastromatteo* v. *Italy* (n 175).

imputable to it which give rise to an allegation of the infringement of rights and freedoms set forth in the Convention'.[210] While jurisdiction is primarily determined by reference to a State's physical territory, in exceptional cases the ECtHR has found that a State has had jurisdiction outside its territorial boundaries.[211] Specifically:

- Where acts of the State's agents 'produce effects outside of its own territory'. Thus, acts of diplomatic and consular agents 'may amount to an exercise of jurisdiction when these agents exert authority and control over others';
- When, 'through the consent, invitation or acquiescence of the Government of the overseas territory', the Member State 'exercises all or some of the public powers normally ... exercised by that Government';
- When the use of force by a State's agents acting overseas brings an individual within the 'control of the State's authorities'. This can occur, for instance, where a State's agents take individuals into custody. The key in such cases is that the individuals are under the 'authority and control' of the Member State's agents. Examples of such control include the detention of Iraqi nationals in British-controlled military prisons during the Iraq War and the interception in international waters of a foreign flagged ship by French agents. In such cases '[w]hat is decisive ... is the exercise of physical power and control over the person in question';
- Where, 'as a consequence of lawful or unlawful military action, a Contracting State exercises effective control of an area outside that national territory'. In such cases, the primary factor is the 'strength of the State's military presence in the area'. Other relevant factors include the extent of the State's military, economic and political support for the local administration.[212]

A recent example of the extraterritorial scope of the obligations under Article 2 is the murder, in the UK, of Alexander Litvinenko, a Russian and British national and former member of the Russian FSB, by agents of the Russian state.[213] In *Carter* v. *Russia*, the ECtHR held that Russia (which was, at that time, still a Contracting State to the ECHR) had, through the conduct of the two men who had murdered Litvinenko, exercised 'State agent authority and control' such that Russia's obligations under the ECHR extended to Litvinenko. After being granted asylum in the UK, Litvinenko 'involved himself in a wide range of activities, mainly focused on exposing corruption in Russian intelligence services and their links with organised crime', and there was evidence

[210] *Güzelyurtlu and Ors* v. *Cyprus and Turkey* [GC] [2019] ECHR 100 at [178]. [211] Ibid.

[212] These examples are drawn from *Al-Skeini and Ors* v. *the United Kingdom* [GC] [2011] ECHR 1093, (2011) 53 EHRR 18 at [133]–[137].

[213] *Carter* v. *Russia* (n 65).

that he was 'consulting for British intelligence services on Russian organised crime in Europe' and conducting private security work. On several occasions between October and November 2006, Litvinenko met with two Russian citizens – Andrei Lugovoy and Dmitry Kovtun – in London. Litvinenko subsequently became critically unwell and ultimately died. The post-mortem revealed that he had been poisoned with radioactive polonium 210. Police inquiries into Litvinenko's death resulted in Lugovoy and Kovtun (who had returned to Russia prior to Litvinenko's death) being charged with murder, and a request was made by the UK authorities for their extradition, which was refused.

An inquest and a statutory public inquiry were conducted in the UK into Litvinenko's murder. The inquiry – which was able to consider closed material evidence not available to the inquest – found, to the criminal standard of proof, that Litvinenko had been fatally poisoned by polonium 210 by Lugovoy and Kovtun who had acted on behalf of the Russian State (specifically, the FSB and President Putin). Litvinenko's wife brought a complaint before the ECtHR alleging that the murder of her husband by individuals acting on behalf of the State constituted a violation of the negative obligation in Article 2 and that the subsequent 'investigation' conducted by the Russian authorities violated the procedural obligation under Article 2. As the ECtHR observed, a central issue with respect to the allegation of a violation of the negative obligation was the fact that:

> At the time he was poisoned Mr Litvinenko was in the United Kingdom and therefore not present in an area over which the Russian State exercised 'effective control'. It remains therefore to be established whether the Russian State can be held accountable for the alleged violation of his right to life under the personal concept of jurisdiction.[214]

In finding that the Russian State *was* accountable under Article 2 for Litvinenko's death, the ECtHR held that 'the assassination of Litvinenko amounted to the exercise of physical power and control over his life in a situation of proximate targeting' and 'it was carried out by individuals acting as State agents'.[215] The ECtHR subsequently found that both the substantive and procedural obligations under Article 2 had been violated and ordered Russia to pay Litvinenko's widow €100,000 in non-pecuniary damages.

While Russia's responsibility for Litvinenko's murder emanated from the control exercised by Russian State agents over Litvinenko, the Grand Chamber in *Georgia* v. *Russia (II)* also had cause to consider Russia's responsibility for violations of the ECHR as a result of its territorial control over Abkhazia and South Ossetia in the context of armed conflict between Georgia and the

[214] Ibid at [149]. [215] Ibid at [150], [161] and [166].

Russian Federation in August 2008.[216] Georgia argued that during the active phase of hostilities and in the aftermath, referred to as the 'occupation phase', Russian forces and separatist forces under the control of Russia had engaged in indiscriminate and disproportionate attacks that had resulted in hundreds of civilians being killed, injured, detained and disappeared, and thousands of civilians had their property and homes destroyed, while 300,000 people were forced to flee. As a result, it was submitted, Russia had violated Article 2. A central issue before the Grand Chamber was whether Russia had jurisdiction over Abkhazia and South Ossetia for the purposes of Article 1.

A majority of the Grand Chamber concluded that, during the active phase of hostilities, Russia did *not* have 'effective control' over the relevant territory such as to engage its responsibility under the substantive provisions in the ECHR. According to the majority:

> in the event of military operations – including, for example, armed attacks, bombing or shelling – carried out during an international armed conflict one cannot generally speak of 'effective control' over an area. The very reality of armed confrontation and fighting between enemy military forces seeking to establish control over an area in a context of chaos means that there is no control over an area. This is also true in the present case, given that the majority of the fighting took place in areas which were previously under Georgian control.[217]

A majority was, however, satisfied that during the 'occupation phase' of hostilities, Russia *was* in 'effective control' of Abkhazia and South Ossetia and the 'buffer zone' which bordered Abkhazia and South Ossetia in undisputed Georgian territory such that its obligations under the ECHR (and the relevant Additional Protocols) did arise. According to the majority, there was ample evidence of extensive economic, military and political support to those regions, and this reflected a relationship of dependency and a position of 'effective control' by the Russian Federation over those regions.[218] Having established that the Russian Federation's jurisdiction extended to Abkhazia and South Ossetia and the 'buffer zone' during the 'occupation phase' of hostilities, the majority Grand Chamber subsequently held that Russia had violated its substantive and procedural obligations under Article 2 as a result of the 'systematic campaign of killing civilians' and the failure of the Russian authorities to carry out an effective investigation into these events.

Notably, the majority concluded that the breach of the procedural obligation extended to a failure to conduct an effective investigation into events that took place during the active phase of hostilities (which, as noted above, the majority held fell outside Russia's jurisdiction). The apparent inconsistency in the majority's findings has been the subject of academic criticism.[219]

[216] *Georgia* v. *Russia (II)* [GC] [2021] ECHR 58. [217] Ibid at [126]. [218] Ibid at [166]–[175].

[219] See the separate, dissenting judgments of Judges Yudkivska, Pinto de Albuquerque, Wojtyczek, Lemmens and Chanturia. See also, Kanstantsin Dzehtsiarou, 'Georgia v. Russia

A 'jurisdictional link' under Article 1 in relation to the procedural obligation under Article 2 in respect of a death (or deaths) occurring outside of the State's territorial jurisdiction will arise where: (1) the 'Contracting State had instituted an investigation or proceedings in accordance with its domestic law'; or (2) there were 'special features' in the case that warranted a finding of a jurisdictional link.[220] In the case of the hostilities between Georgia and Russia, there were 'special features' which justified extending Russia's jurisdiction under Article 1 to encompass a procedural obligation under Article 2 to investigate deaths occurring during the active phase of hostilities.[221] Those 'special features' included the fact that Russia was accused of committing war crimes during the active phase of hostilities, the Russian authorities had established effective control over the territories in question shortly after the active phase of hostilities and 'given that all the potential suspects among the Russian service personnel were located either in the Russian Federation or in territories under the control of the Russian Federation, Georgia was prevented from carrying out an adequate and effective investigation into the allegations'.[222]

4.3.3.2 *Territorial Scope of the HRA*

The domestic courts were called upon to consider the territorial reach of the HRA in several cases involving the British armed forces during the war in Iraq. In *Al-Skeini*,[223] the issue was whether the HRA applied to the deaths of the claimants' relatives, Iraqi civilians killed in Basra. Each of the deceased was killed by British armed forces (five were killed either by British patrols or during a raid, whereas the sixth was killed while detained by British forces) and their relatives argued before the domestic courts that there had been an inadequate investigation into the deaths in violation of Article 2 ECHR in breach of s.6 HRA. The central issue was whether the HRA applied extraterritorially. A majority of the House of Lords held that, in exceptional circumstances, the HRA *could* apply extraterritorially. In dissent, Lord Bingham

(II)' (2021) 115 American Journal of International Law 2, 292, Jessica Gavron and Philip Leach, 'Damage Control after *Georgia* v. *Russia (II)* – Holding states responsible for human rights violations during armed conflict', *Strasbourg Observers*, 8 February 2021 https://strasbourgobservers.com/2021/02/08/damage-control-after-georgia-v-russia-ii-holding-states-responsible-for-human-rights-violations-during-armed-conflict/, Marko Milanovic, 'Georgia v. Russia No. 2: The European Court's Resurrection of Bankovic in the Contexts of Chaos', *EJIL:Talk!*, 25 January 2021, www.ejiltalk.org/georgia-v-russia-no-2-the-european-courts-resurrection-of-bankovic-in-the-contexts-of-chaos/. The Grand Chamber also found that Russia was in 'effective control' of Crimea in 2014/2015 based on 'the technical, tactical, military and qualitative superiority and conduct of the Russian military forces, who had "boots on the ground" [in Crimea] without the consent of Ukraine' (*Ukraine* v. *Russia (re Crimea)* [GC] [2024] ECHR 569 at [864]).

220 *Georgia* v. *Russia (II)* (n 216) at [330]. 221 Ibid at [329]–[330]. 222 Ibid at [331].

223 *Al-Skeini & Ors* (n 28).

concluded that the HRA had no extraterritorial application, citing the presumption of territorial application of domestic legislation and the lack of evidence of an intention on the part of Parliament for the HRA to apply outside UK territory:

> It cannot of course be supposed that in 1997–1998 Parliament foresaw the prospect of British forces being engaged in peacekeeping duties in Iraq. But there can be relatively few, if any, years between 1953 and 1997 in which British forces were not engaged in hostilities or peacekeeping activities in some part of the world, and it must have been appreciated that such involvement would recur. This makes it the more unlikely, in my opinion, that Parliament could, without any express provision to that effect, have intended to rebut the presumption of territorial application so as to authorise the bringing of claims, under the [HRA], based on the conduct of British forces outside the UK and outside any other contracting state. Differing from the courts below, I regard the statutory presumption of territorial application as a strong one, which has not been rebutted.[224]

In contrast, a majority of the House of Lords found that the HRA could have extraterritorial application. As Lord Brown observed, 'the central purpose' of ss.6 and 7 HRA is to 'provide a remedial structure in domestic law for the rights guaranteed by the Convention'.[225] Accordingly, the HRA should be interpreted as applying wherever the UK has jurisdiction under Article 1 ECHR. Citing the ECtHR's authority on Article 1, the majority concluded that the HRA could have extraterritorial application where, inter alia, the UK was in 'effective control' of an area or through the conduct of its diplomatic or consular agents.[226] Having regard to the specific facts surrounding the deaths of the claimants' relatives, the majority House of Lords determined that Article 1 did not extend to the first five claimants as the UK was not in effective control of Basra. In contrast, the sixth claimant's relative was killed while in the custody of British forces in a British military detention unit. He was, thus, within the control and authority of UK agents at the time of his death and the HRA accordingly applied extraterritorially to him.[227] The sixth claimant's case was remitted for rehearing, while the first five claimants' appeals were dismissed.

The claimants (together with the father of a teenager who had died after being arrested by British forces and who had settled a civil claim against the Ministry of Defence[228]) subsequently brought complaints before the ECtHR in *Al-Skeini* v. *the United Kingdom* alleging a violation of the procedural obligation under Article 2 (see Section 4.3.2.2 for a discussion of this obligation). The Grand Chamber held, contrary to the arguments on behalf of the respondent State (and the findings of the domestic courts), that *all* of the applicants'

224 Ibid at [24].
225 Ibid at [56], per Lord Rodger. For a discussion of ss.6 and 7 HRA see Chapter 2.
226 Ibid at [109(4)], per Lord Brown.
227 Ibid at [107], per Lord Brown. This was not challenged by the Secretary of State.
228 *Al-Skeini* (n 212) at [55]–[62].

relatives fell within the jurisdiction of the UK for the purposes of Article 1 ECHR (and, thus, the procedural obligation in Article 2 was applicable to their deaths). In reaching that conclusion, the Grand Chamber noted that 'jurisdiction' under Article 1 is 'primarily territorial' though there are exceptions, as set out above.[229] In the case of the six applicants, the UK had jurisdiction over the deaths of their family members either because they were under the direct control of British forces at the time or because, contrary to the findings of the domestic courts, the Grand Chamber considered that the UK (together with the US) had 'assumed authority and responsibility for the maintenance of security in south-east Iraq' at the time the applicants' relatives were killed.[230] The applicants' relatives thus fell within the jurisdiction of the UK at the time of their deaths. Having reached that conclusion, the Grand Chamber went on to consider whether there had been a breach of the Article 2 investigative obligation, finding that there had been in respect of the first to fifth applicants given the lack of independence of the investigations into the deaths.[231] At the time of the Grand Chamber's judgment, a public inquiry into the death of the sixth applicant's son was ongoing and it was accepted that the sixth applicant could no longer claim to be a victim of a violation of the procedural obligation under Article 2.[232]

4.3.4 Normative Justifications for the State's Obligations under Article 2 ECHR: Dignity and Effectiveness

While it is evident from the right to life jurisprudence of the domestic courts and the ECtHR that life is considered to be inherently valuable, it is not immediately clear *why* this is the case. Is it the very fact of life that is being protected by Article 2 and similar provisions in other rights instruments? This seems improbable given the existence of exceptions for some forms of force that result in death (for instance, the use of force where absolutely necessary to protect a third party or third parties). Similarly, as considered in Chapter 6, the right to life does not preclude the withdrawal of life-sustaining treatment. If the ECHR protected life at all costs, such treatment would be obligatory, regardless of the consequences for the individual's bodily integrity, dignity and autonomy. So *why do* we ascribe such importance to the right to life?

Many judgments of the ECtHR make reference to the concept of 'dignity'.[233] It has been suggested that the Court uses this concept not only to 'develop the scope of Convention rights, but also to signal to respondent states just how serious a violation is and to nudge them toward better compliance'.[234] Courts

[229] Ibid at [131]. [230] Ibid at [149].

[231] Ibid at [169]–[175]. See, also, the discussion of the nature of the procedural investigation in Section 4.3.2.2.

[232] Ibid at [176].

[233] Veronika Fikfak and Lora Izvorova, 'Language and Persuasion: Human Dignity at the European Court of Human Rights' (2022) 22 HRLR 3.

[234] Ibid, p.1.

in England and Wales similarly turn to concepts such as dignity when confronted with cases involving the right to life including, for instance, whether continued life-sustaining treatment is in a patient's best interests.[235] Yet, despite its increasing presence in right to life jurisprudence, 'dignity' is a contested concept. The Canadian Supreme Court has suggested that 'it is ... an abstract and subjective notion that ... [can] ... become confusing and difficult to apply'.[236] Further, it is an inherently relativistic notion which has been given different meanings by different courts, and by different judges within the same courts.[237] Thus, while dignity may be proffered as a normative justification for the right to life, it is not always clear why dignity in a given case requires the course of action being proposed.

While principles such as dignity and bodily integrity can provide some justification for a positive obligation to protect life and to conduct effective investigations into the deprivation of it, there is a further possible justification for such positive obligations: the principle of effectiveness, which applies to all of the substantive Convention rights.

According to Judge Serghides of the ECtHR, the principle of effectiveness is 'an overarching and ubiquitous Convention principle' and 'the foundation stone, source or matrix of positive obligations'.[238] It operates as a method of interpretation and as a norm of international law and, in both respects, its function is to ensure that rights are given full effect.[239] To be effective, the ECHR – including the right to life – must be interpreted in a manner that ensures that individual rights are given full and complete protection and prevents 'perforation of or leakage from the protective shield' of the right.[240]

The evolution of positive obligations is intimately related to the notion that the ECHR is a 'living instrument' which is to be interpreted in light of present-day conditions.[241] The idea that the ECHR is a 'living instrument' is intimately related to the principle of effectiveness, and both principles provide a foundation for the positive obligations imposed on Member States. As the ECtHR observed in *Goodwin*:

> It is of crucial importance that the Convention is interpreted and applied in a manner which renders its rights practical and effective, not theoretical or illusory. A failure by the Court to maintain a dynamic and evolutive approach would indeed risk rendering it a bar to reform or improvement.[242]

[235] See, for instance, Monique Jonas and Samantha Ryan, 'The Discourse of Dignity in the Charlie Gard, Alfie Evans and Isaiah Haastrup Cases' (2020) 29 Medical Law Review 1. See also, Chapter 6.

[236] As recognised by the Canadian Supreme Court in *R* v. *Kapp* [2008] 2 SCR 483 at [22].

[237] See, for instance, Filip Horak, 'Human Dignity in Legal Argumentation: A Functional Perspective' (2022) 18 European Constitutional Law Review 2.

[238] *Traskunova* v. *Russia* (n 95), separate opinion of Judge Serghides at [6]. [239] Ibid at [3].

[240] Ibid at [5]. [241] *Tyrer* v. *the United Kingdom* (1978) 2 EHRR 1 at [31]. See also, Chapter 3.

[242] *Christine Goodwin* v. *the United Kingdom* [GC] [2002] 35 EHRR 447 at [74].

4.4 CURRENT ISSUES AND THE RIGHT TO LIFE

4.4.1 Climate Change Litigation and Environmental Pollution

The Grand Chamber in *Öneryildiz* v. *Turkey*[243] set out what States must do to comply with their substantive obligation under Article 2 in terms of regulating dangerous activities.[244] *Öneryildiz* arose from the State's failure to properly regulate a municipal refuse tip, resulting in an explosion and subsequent landslide which killed a number of people. The judgment is a key component of the ECtHR's case law concerning State responsibility for environmental damage causing harm.[245] The right to life has also featured in environmental cases before UK domestic courts. For example, in *R (Richards)* v. *The Environment Agency*, it was argued that the authorities' alleged failure to address environmental pollution in the form of excessive (and harmful) levels of hydrogen sulphide emanating from a landfill site violated the right to life.[246] The claimant, the mother of a five-year-old boy, Mathew, who had a lung condition, brought proceedings alleging that the agency responsible for regulating landfill sites had violated Mathew's Article 2 and Article 8 ECHR rights due to its alleged failure to take all reasonable steps within its powers to address the levels of hydrogen sulphide emissions. Although the Court of Appeal found no violation on the facts, it was accepted by the trial judge, and not challenged on appeal, that the emissions posed a real and immediate risk to Mathew's life as there was a substantial and significant risk that Mathew would develop heart disease as a result of the exposure to the hydrogen sulphide. The claim was, however, unsuccessful as the Court of Appeal rejected the contention that the authorities had failed to take reasonable measures to address that risk. In particular, the agency was monitoring the level of emissions and had taken steps to reduce them.[247] The agency was, thus, not in breach of its positive operational obligation under Article 2 at the relevant time. An application for leave to appeal to the Supreme Court was refused in February 2022.[248]

The ECtHR has 'repeatedly stressed' that there is 'no Article of the Convention designed to provide protection of the environment as such'.[249] States may, however, be responsible for environmental harms that have been 'deemed to *affect* the Convention rights of individuals, particularly Article

[243] *Öneryildiz* v. *Turkey (No 2)* (n 177). [244] See Section 4.3.2.3.2.

[245] See, also, *Fadeyeva* v. *Russia* (n 195) and *Budayeva* v. *Russia* (n 193). In such cases, there is a 'nexus between a source of harm and those affected by the harm, and the requisite mitigation measures may be identifiable and available to be applied at the source of the harm': *Verein KlimaSeniorinnen Schweiz* (n 207) at [415].

[246] *R (Richards)* v. *Environment Agency* [2022] EWCA Civ 26, [2022] 1 WLR 2593 at [4].

[247] Ibid at [90]. [248] *R (Richards)* v. *Environment Agency* [2022] 2 WLUK 646.

[249] *Verein KlimaSeniorinnen Schweiz* (n 207) at [445].

8 [the right to respect for private and family life]'.[250] Thus, the Convention has been found to apply in cases involving environmental harms,[251] including pollution and dangerous industrial activities.[252] The positive obligation to protect has also been found to arise in the context of natural disasters, such as mudslides and earthquakes.[253] Moreover, while it seems unlikely that the ECtHR will find a right to a healthy environment in Article 8 (or any other Article) in the near future, it has not ruled out doing so if there is a corresponding development in 'the international-law context in which the Court assesses Convention issues'.[254]

Whilst it is evident that Convention rights, including the right to life, may be engaged by some environmental harms (e.g. pollution), in recent years questions have arisen as to the applicability of the Convention, including Articles 2 and 8 to the specific issue of climate change. Such cases raise complex questions regarding institutional competency, causation, damage and foreseeability which, until April 2024, had not been considered by the ECtHR.

There has been a proliferation in climate change litigation both domestically and before supranational courts which, given the vast body of evidence concerning the catastrophic implications of climate change, is not surprising.[255] Such litigation has relied on various lines of argument, including the right to life. Indeed, in the landmark decision of *Urgenda,*[256] the Dutch Supreme Court confirmed that both the State's general positive obligation to protect and its operational preventive obligation were engaged by climate change, and the State accordingly had a responsibility to reduce its emissions by at least 25 per cent by 2020 (compared to 1990 levels). Notably, the Supreme Court held that the State was liable notwithstanding the fact that climate change is a global problem, based on the 'no harm' principle employed elsewhere in international law 'which entails that countries must not cause each other harm'.[257] The decision in *Urgenda* has been relied upon in subsequent proceedings in the Netherlands including in a case against the oil company Shell.[258]

[250] Ibid at [446]. Emphasis in original.

[251] See, for instance, *Fadeyeva* v. *Russia* (n 195), *Öneryildiz* v. *Turkey (No 2)* (n 177), *Budayeva* v. *Russia* (n 193).

[252] See, for instance, *Öneryildiz* (n 177) and *Brincat and Others* v. *Malta* [2014] ECHR 836.

[253] *Budayeva* v. *Russia* (n 193) and *M. Özel and Ors* v. *Turkey* [2015] ECHR 1024.

[254] *Verein KlimaSeniorinnen Schweiz and Ors* v. *Switzerland* (n 207) at [448]–[449].

[255] See, for instance, Intergovernmental Panel on Climate Change, 'Climate Change 2021: The Physical Science Basis', AR6 report (7 August 2021), www.ipcc.ch/report/ar6/wg1/downloads/report/IPCC_AR6_WGI_Full_Report.pdf.

[256] *The State of the Netherlands* v. *Stichting Urgenda*, ECLI:NL:HR:2019:2007, 13 January 2020.

[257] Ibid at [5.7.5].

[258] *Milieudefensie et al.* v. *Royal Dutch Shell plc*, ECLI:NL:RBDHA:2021:5339, 26 May 2021, https://linkeddata.overheid.nl/front/portal/document-viewer?ext-id = ECLI:NL:

Prior to the Dutch Supreme Court's decision, the Inter-American Court of Human Rights (I-ACtHR) had expressed the opinion that climate change threatened the right to life (as protected by Article 4 of the American Convention on Human Rights).[259] In its Advisory Opinion, the I-ACtHR considered in detail the 'interrelationship between human rights and the environment', noting 'the existence of an undeniable relationship between the protection of the environment and the realization of other human rights, in that environmental degradation and the adverse effects of climate change affect the real enjoyment of human rights'.[260] The Court went on to discuss the nature of the right to life in the context of environmental damage, and observed that States have a number of obligations under Article 4 in respect of climate change including a positive obligation to put in place an effective legal system deterring threats to life and 'safeguard[ing] the right of access to the conditions that ensure a decent life'. Notably, '[a]mong the conditions required for a decent life, the Court has referred to access to, and the quality of, water, food and health . . . The Court has also included environmental protection as a condition for a decent life.'[261] '[E]nvironmental pollution may affect an individual's health' and, thus, may violate the right to life in Article 4.[262]

The HRC also considered the implications of climate change for the right to life as protected by Article 6 ICCPR in its 2022 opinion against Australia (*Daniel Billy and Ors* v. *Australia*). In a complaint brought by members of the Indigenous population and residents of the Torres Strait Islands against Australia, the HRC observed that 'both it and regional human rights tribunals have established that environmental degradation can compromise effective enjoyment of the right to life, and that severe environmental degradation can adversely affect an individual's well-being and lead to a violation of the right to life'.[263] Notably, however, a majority of the HRC considered that while there was evidence that if steps were not taken to address climate change an Article 6 (right to life) violation *might* arise in ten to fifteen years, there was evidence that Australia *was* taking steps to reduce emissions and combat the consequences of climate change in the relevant areas.[264] This finding raises questions about the efficacy of rights protection as it tends to suggest that

RBDHA:2021:5339. While the Court of Appeal overturned the decision, it did so on the basis that a specific reduction amount could not be imposed on the company, it did not disagree that Shell has an obligation to counter dangerous climate change: *Milieudefensie et al.* v. *Royal Dutch Shell plc*, ECLI:NL:GHDHA:2024:2100, 12 November 2024 at [1], https://uitspraken.rechtspraak.nl/details?id=ECLI:NL:GHDHA:2024:2100

259 Inter-American Court of Human Rights, Advisory Opinion, OC-23/17, 15 November 2017, www.corteidh.or.cr/docs/opiniones/seriea_23_ing.pdf.

260 Ibid at [47]. 261 Ibid at [109]. 262 Ibid at [110].

263 UN Human Rights Committee, *Daniel Billy and Ors* v. *Australia*, Communication No. 3624/19, CCPR/C/135/D/3624/2019, 22 September 2022 at [8.7].

264 Ibid at [8.8].

individuals must wait until their right to life has been violated or is very likely to be in the near future which seems antithetical to the effective enjoyment of the right to life (which includes the right to live with dignity).[265] Indeed, it is notable that several members of the HRC dissented with respect to the Article 6 claim. Committee Member Duncan Laki Muhumuza was 'convinced that there is a violation of Article 6'.[266] Citing *Urgenda*, Committee Member Muhumuza noted that 'the State Party is tasked with an obligation to prevent a foreseeable loss of life from the impacts of climate change, and to protect the authors' right to life with dignity' and concluded that Australia had failed to take 'any measures to reduce greenhouse gas emissions and cease the promotion of fossil fuel extraction and use'.[267] Similarly, Committee Members Marcia V. J. Kran and Arif Bulkan considered that there had been a violation of Article 6 and criticised the majority for interpreting Article 6 – and, in particular, the 'real and foreseeable risk' standard – too restrictively.[268] More specifically, while the majority considered that evidence of adverse health impacts was necessary to prove a real and foreseeable risk to life, the separate opinion writers were of the view that the applicants' evidence of 'significant loss of food sources' and livelihood was sufficient evidence of a 'real and foreseeable risk' to life for the purposes of Article 6.[269] It bears noting that the HRC *did* find a violation of Article 17 ICCPR, the equivalent to Article 8 ECHR, on the basis that Australia had failed to take adaptation measures to reduce the impact of climate change. In particular, there was evidence that rising sea levels (and temperatures) had led to 'reduction of marine resources used for food and the loss of crops and fruit trees on the land on which the [applicants] live and grow crops' and:

> their lives have been adversely affected by flooding and inundation of their villages and ancestral burial lands; destruction or withering of their traditional gardens through salinification caused by flooding or seawater ingress; and decline of nutritionally and culturally important marine species and associated coral bleaching and ocean acidification.[270]

[265] See also, Committee on the Rights of the Child, *Saachi et al.* v. *Argentina*, Communication No. 104/2019, CRC/C/88/D/104/2019, 8 October 2021 at [10.6].

[266] *Daniel Billy* (n 263), individual opinion by Committee Member Duncan Laki Muhumuza at [2].

[267] Ibid at [10].

[268] Ibid, joint opinion by Committee Members Marcia V. J. Kran and Arif Bulkan (partially dissenting) at [2].

[269] Ibid at [3] and [5].

[270] *Daniel Billy* (n 263) at [8.12]. The Committee also found a violation of Article 27 of the ICCPR which, 'interpreted in the light of the United Nations Declaration on the Rights of Indigenous Peoples, enshrines the inalienable right of Indigenous Peoples to enjoy the territories and natural resources that they have traditionally used for their subsistence and cultural identity': ibid at [8.13].

Similar issues with respect to damage and causation, which pervaded the majority HRC's opinion in *Billy*, featured in the ECtHR Grand Chamber's landmark judgment, *Verein KlimaSeniorinnen Schweiz*,[271] which was delivered together with another two climate change judgments in April 2024.

Verein KlimaSeniorinnen Schweiz centred on a complaint brought by a non-profit association 'established to promote and implement effective climate protection on behalf of its members' who were women living in Switzerland (most of whom were over seventy years of age) and four women who were members of the association and claimed to have suffered ill-health as a result of heatwaves which they said were caused by climate change.[272] The applicants alleged that the Swiss authorities' failure to take adequate mitigative steps and adopt adapatation measures[273] in response to climate change violated its positive obligations under Articles 2 and 8.[274]

Recognising that the nature of climate change is such that its 'various adverse effects and future risks' means that the 'number of persons affected ... is indefinite', the Grand Chamber developed a 'special approach to victim status' that applies in climate change cases.[275] Such an approach reflects the fact that *actio popularis* claims are not permitted under the ECHR and the nature of the Court's function is 'by definition reactive rather than proactive'.[276] Noting its existing case law on potential victims, the Court considered that that did not apply in climate change cases as 'this could cover virtually anybody and would therefore not work as a limiting criterion'.[277] Instead, in order to claim victim status for harm or risk of harm emanating from alleged failures by a State to combat climate change, individuals need to show that they are personally and directly affected by those alleged failures. In particular, the ECtHR will need to be satisfied that:

1. The applicant is 'subject to a high intensity of exposure to the adverse effects of climate change'. That is, the level and severity of the adverse consequences (or risk thereof) of governmental (in)action must be significant; and,

[271] *Verein KlimaSeniorinnen Schweiz and Ors* v. *Switzerland* (n 207). [272] Ibid at [10]–[21].

[273] The Grand Chamber referred to 'mitigation measures' as those aimed at reducing greenhouse gas emissions and 'adaptation measures' as those necessary to 'adapt to climate change and reduce its impacts': ibid at [478].

[274] They also alleged a violation of Article 6 ECHR on the basis of a lack of effective access to court, which was upheld by the Grand Chamber.

[275] *Verein KlimaSeniorinnen Schweiz and Ors* v. *Switzerland* (n 207) at [479]. Though the ordinary approach to victim status pertains when an individual/individuals claim to have suffered specific harm as a result of conduct on the part of the State. See also, Chapter 3.

[276] Ibid at [481]. [277] Ibid at [485].

2. Due to the absence or inadequacy of any reasonable measures to reduce harm, there must be a 'pressing need to ensure the applicant's individual protection'.[278]

The threshold for establishing individual victim status in climate change cases is 'especially high' and the Court will have regard to considerations including the 'actuality/remoteness and/or probability of the adverse effects of climate change in time', the 'scope of the risk (localised or general)', 'and the nature of the applicant's vulnerability'.[279]

The Court also developed specific principles with respect to the standing of associations to bring complaints in the context of climate change litigation. As the Court recognised, recourse to associations may be the only means by which individuals are able to defend their interests effectively.[280] Given the importance of intergenerational burden-sharing, collective action through associations/other interest groups may be one of the only means through which 'the voice of those at a distinct representational disadvantage [i.e. future generations] can be heard'.[281] As with the victim status of individuals, the majority judges in the Grand Chamber enunciated a number of factors relevant to a determination of whether an association has *locus standi* under Article 34 in climate change cases. In particular, the association must:

1. Be lawfully established in the State concerned or have standing to act there;
2. Pursue 'a dedicated purpose in accordance with its statutory objectives in the defence of the human rights of its members or other affected individuals within the jurisdiction concerned, whether limited to or including collective action for the protection of those rights against the threats arising from climate change';
3. Demonstrate that it is 'genuinely qualified and representative to act on behalf of members or other affected individuals within the jurisdiction who are subject to specific threats or adverse effects of climate change on their lives, health or well-being as protected under the Convention'.[282]

Notably, in climate change cases, standing of associations will *not* be dependent on proving that those whom it represents would themselves have victim status under Article 34.[283]

Turning to the substantive rights, drawing on its environmental harm jurisprudence the majority observed that 'in order for a positive obligation [under Article 2] to arise . . ., a threat to the right to life must be at stake'.[284] And, 'complaints concerning the alleged failures of the State to combat climate change most appropriately fall into the category of cases concerning an activity which is, by its very nature, capable of putting an individual's life

[278] Ibid at [487]. [279] Ibid at [488]. [280] Ibid at [489]. [281] Ibid. [282] Ibid at [502].
[283] Ibid. [284] Ibid at [508].

at risk'.[285] Specifically, in order for Article 2 to arise in the context of an alleged threat to life caused by State (in)action in response to climate change, there must be a real and immediate risk to life. However:

> such a risk to life in the climate-change context must be understood in the light of the fact that there is a grave risk of inevitability and irreversibility of the adverse effects of climate change, the occurrences of which are most likely to increase in frequency and gravity.[286]

The Court appears to have diluted somewhat the 'real and imminent risk' test as it applies in climate change cases, holding that it 'may be understood as referring to a serious, genuine and sufficiently ascertainable threat to life, containing an element of temporal proximity of the threat to the harm complained of by the applicant'.[287] Significantly, the ECtHR went on to find that 'it would be possible to assume that a serious risk of a significant decline in a person's life expectancy owing to climate change ought also to trigger the applicability of Article 2'.[288]

As for Article 8 (right to respect for private and family life) the Grand Chamber held that it encompasses a right to effective protection from 'serious adverse effects of climate change on . . . life, health, well-being and quality of life'.[289] However, for that right to be engaged, 'general deterioration of the environment is not sufficient'; there must be an 'actual interference' with, or a 'relevant and sufficiently serious risk' to, the individual's private or family life.[290] In deciding whether such an interference or risk is present, the Court stated that the criteria set out for determining victim status will be 'determinative'.[291]

Ultimately, the Grand Chamber determined that it was 'unnecessary to analyse . . . the issues pertinent to the threshold of applicability of Article 2', having noted that it was 'questionable' whether the shortcomings in the State's response to climate change has 'such life-threatening consequences as could trigger the applicability of Article 2'.[292] It did, however, consider the applicability of Article 8, first finding that the association – Verein KlimaSeniorinnen Schweiz – had standing, whilst the four individual women did *not* meet the criteria for victim status. In respect of the four individuals, the Grand Chamber noted that while they had provided evidence that heatwaves affected their quality of life, it was 'not apparent from the available materials that they were exposed to the adverse effects of climate change, or were at risk of being exposed at any relevant point in the future, with a degree of intensity giving rise to a pressing need to ensure their individual protection'.[293] In contrast, the association *did* have standing.[294]

285 Ibid. 286 Ibid at [513]. 287 Ibid. 288 Ibid. 289 Ibid at [519].
290 Ibid at [520]. 291 Ibid. 292 Ibid at [536]. 293 Ibid at [533]. 294 Ibid at [524].

As for the merits of the Article 8 claim by the association, and notwithstanding its finding that it need not consider Article 2, the majority Grand Chamber observed that the principles developed under Article 2 are 'to a very large extent ... similar to those under Article 8' and 'provide a useful basis for defining the overall approach to be applied in the climate-change context under both provisions'.[295] Significantly, the Court found that States have a positive obligation under Article 8 to ensure effective protection of those within their jurisdiction 'from serious adverse effects on their life, health, well-being and quality of life arising from the harmful effects and risks caused by climate change'.[296] The State's obligation under Article 8 in this context is 'to do its part', with the 'primary duty [being] to adopt, and to effectively apply in practice, regulations and measures capable of mitigating the existing and potentially irreversible, future effects of climate change'.[297] Specifically, Article 8 requires each State to 'undertake measures for the substantial and progressive reduction of their respective [greenhouse gas] emission levels, with a view to reaching net neutrality within, in principle, the next three decades'.[298]

In assessing whether a State has complied with this obligation, the Grand Chamber will consider a number of factors including whether the State has specified a target timeline for achieving carbon neutrality and the remaining carbon budget (or equivalent) for the same time period, and whether it has set out intermediate greenhouse gas emissions reduction targets and pathways that are 'capable' of meeting the reduction targets within the specific period.[299]

In assessing whether the State has met these requirements, the Court will adopt an 'overall' approach, meaning that a failure to comply with one factor will not, necessarily, result in a finding that the State has 'overstepped' its margin of appreciation.[300] States also have an obligation to put in place 'adaptation measures aimed at alleviating the most severe or imminent consequences of climate change' as well as procedural obligations.[301]

Applying the above to the position in Switzerland, the Grand Chamber (by a majority of 16:1) concluded that the State *had* violated the Article 8 rights of the association. In reaching that conclusion, the Court observed that there were some 'critical lacunae in the Swiss authorities' process of putting in place the relevant domestic regulatory framework' to mitigate the adverse effects of climate change. While the Court reiterated multiple times that 'the measures and methods of determining the details of the State's climate policy fall within its wide margin of appreciation' where, as was the case here, there is such a deficiency in the State's regulatory response, there will be a violation of

[295] Ibid at [537]. [296] Ibid at [544]. [297] Ibid at [545]. [298] Ibid at [548].
[299] Ibid at [550]. [300] Ibid at [551]. [301] Ibid at [553]–[554].

Article 8.[302] The association made no claim for damages and none were ordered. Academic commentary surrounding the case prior to the judgment's delivery correctly predicted that the Court would need to adopt innovative approaches to standing and the rights in the ECHR if the litigation were to be a success.[303] And, as many have observed, the case is likely to provide fodder for academic debate and analysis for years to come.[304]

There was a single dissent in the Grand Chamber. The British representative, Judge Eicke, disagreed with each of the majority's substantive findings (save for the finding of a violation of Article 6). Judge Eicke's 'disagreement' with the majority was of a:

> fundamental nature and, at least in part, goes to the very heart of the role of the Court within the Convention system and, more generally, the role of a court in the context of the unique and unprecedented challenges posed to humanity (including in but also across our societies) by anthropogenic climate change.[305]

For Judge Eicke, the Court had deviated from its usual 'careful, cautious and gradual approach to the evolutive interpretation of the Convention'.[306] In doing so, it had created a new right under Article 8 ('and, possibly, Article 2') which did not have 'any basis in Article 8 or any other provision of or Protocol to the Convention' and the Court had 'unnecessarily expanded the concept of "victim" status/standing'.[307] Judge Eicke was at pains to make clear that his disagreement did not emanate from a dispute as to the 'nature or magnitude of the risks and challenges' posed by climate change, but, rather centred on his view of the role the Court should play in addressing those risks and challenges.[308] In addition to his critique of the majority's approach to standing, he concluded that, if there is a causal connection between failures of the State to combat climate change and threats to an individual's life, it is 'plainly too remote to be capable of engaging Article 2'.[309] He also concluded that there was no basis in Article 8 for the right which the majority found. For the dissenting judge, the Court 'clearly "tried to run before it could walk" and,

302 Ibid at [572]–[573].

303 See, for instance, Vassilis P. Tzevelekos and Kanstantsin Dzehtsiarou, 'Climate Change: The World and the ECtHR in Unchartered Waters' (2022) 3 ECHRLR 1, Jaques Hartmann and Marc Willers, 'Protecting Rights through Climate Change Litigation before European Courts' (2022) 13 Journal of Human Rights and the Environment 1, Christina Voight, 'The Climate Change Dimension of Human Rights: Due Diligence and States' Positive Obligations' (2022) 13 Journal of Human Rights and the Environment 152–171, Helen Keller and Viktoriya Gurash, 'Expanding NGOs' Standing: Climate Justice through Access to the European Court of Human Rights' (2023) 14 Journal of Human Rights and the Environment 2.

304 See, for instance, Corina Heri, 'KlimaSeniorinnen and its Discontents: Climate Change at the European Court of Human Rights' (2024) 4 EHRLR 317.

305 *Verein KlimaSeniorinnen Schweiz and Ors* v. *Switzerland* (n 207), partly concurring and partly dissenting opinion of Judge Eicke at [2].

306 Ibid at [3]. 307 Ibid at [4]. 308 Ibid at [5]. 309 Ibid at [59].

thereby, went beyond what was legitimate for this Court'.[310] Judge Eicke had further concerns that the majority's findings 'will prove an unwelcome and unnecessary distraction for the national and international authorities, both executive and legislative' as there is 'a significant risk that they will now be tied up in litigation about whatever regulations and measures they have adopted (whether as a result or independently) or how those regulations and measures have been applied in practice'.[311] It bears recalling the majority's emphasis that States have a choice as to the means by which they develop and implement mitigation measures; the key being that they actually develop and implement such measures which, as Judge Eicke himself observed, are 'being undertaken as we speak'.[312] It is also notable that the dissenting judge made only a passing reference[313] to the inter-generational burdens that climate change imposes, and the role that human rights litigation can play in securing 'inter-generational justice' which the majority discussed at length. Extra-judicial writings by Judge Eicke on the issue of climate litigation before the ECtHR are notable in light of his dissent.[314]

Verein KlimaSeniorinnen Schweiz was one of three judgments delivered contemporaneously regarding State liability for climate change. The other two cases – *Duarte Agostinho and Ors* v. *Portugal*[315] and *Carême* v. *France*[316] – involved similar challenges to State (in)action in the face of the climate crisis. The six applicants in *Duarte Agostinho* were Portuguese children who alleged 'the existing, and serious future, impacts of climate change imputable to the respondent States, and specifically those in relation to heatwaves, wildfires and smoke from wildfires, which affected their lives, well-being, mental health and the amenities of their home, were in breach of their rights under Articles 2, 3, 8 and 14'.[317] The complaint was brought against Portugal and thirty-two other Member States, including the UK. The Grand Chamber unanimously declared the complaint inadmissible on two bases. First, while the territorial jurisdiction of Portugal could be established, the applicants' complaints against the other States did not correspond to any of the circumstances in earlier cases in which extraterritorial jurisdiction had been found. The applicants' attempt to formulate a new test of jurisdiction, based on 'control over the applicants' Convention interests' was not accepted

310 Ibid at [68]. 311 Ibid at [69]. 312 Ibid at [69].

313 'Of course, I also, in principle, perfectly understand (and share) the majority's desire to ensure inter-generational justice': ibid at [42].

314 See, for instance, Tim Eicke, 'Human Rights and Climate Change: What Role for the European Court of Human Rights?' (2021) 3 EHRLR 262–273 and Tim Eicke, 'Climate Change and the Convention: Beyond Admissibility' (2022) 3 ECHRLR 1.

315 *Duarte Agostinho and Ors* v. *Portugal and Ors*, Grand Chamber, App. No. 39371/20, 9/04/2024.

316 *Carême* v. *France*, Grand Chamber, App. No. 7189/21, 9/04/2024.

317 *Duarte Agostinho and Ors* v. *Portugal and Ors* (n 315) at [66].

by the Court, which noted that reliance on 'such a criterion for establishing the State's extraterritorial jurisdiction would lead to a critical lack of foreseeability of the Convention's reach'.[318] Thus, the complaint was declared inadmissible in respect of all respondent States, bar Portugal. The complaint against Portugal was declared inadmissible on the basis of a failure to exhaust domestic remedies; the applicants had not pursued their complaints via any legal avenue in Portugal, and there were mechanisms available to the applicants to do so under Portuguese law.[319] The finding of inadmissibility in *Duarte Agostinho* was not unexpected, particularly given the failure of the applicants to exhaust domestic remedies.[320]

The third case, *Carême* v. *France*, was also declared inadmissible. The applicant, the former mayor of a region in Dunkirk, France which is 'particularly exposed to the risks of climate change', complained that the French authorities had failed to take adequate steps to prevent climate change which constituted a violation of his Article 2 and Article 8 rights given the risk of 'climate-change-induced flooding' in the region in which he had lived and been mayor.[321] A unanimous Grand Chamber declared the complaint inadmissible as being incompatible *ratione personae* as the applicant had subsequently relocated to Brussels and had no continuing link to the region. As the Court observed:

> having regard to the fact that the applicant has no relevant links with [the region] and ... he currently does not live in France, the Court does not consider that for the purposes of any potentially relevant aspect of Article 8 ... he can claim to have victim status under Article 34 of the Convention as regards the alleged risks linked to climate change threatening that municipality ... The same considerations apply as regards the applicant's complaint under Article 2 of the Convention.[322]

The Grand Chamber's trio of climate change judgments joins a growing body of national and supra/international jurisprudence examining the rights dimensions of State responses to climate change, including the implications for the right to life. We are likely to see more such cases before the domestic courts and the ECtHR in the coming years, though the potential for the right to life as protected by Article 2 in such cases remains uncertain given the Grand Chamber's refusal to engage with that right in *Verein KlimaSeniorinnen.*

4.4.2 COVID-19

The COVID-19 pandemic had significant implications for the right to life. To varying extents, decisions by States regarding border closures, 'lockdown'

[318] Ibid at [206]. [319] Ibid at [217] and [219].

[320] Helen Keller and Corina Heri, 'The Future Is Now: Climate Cases Before the ECtHR' (2022) **40**(1) Nordic Journal of Human Rights 153–174 and Ole W. Pedersen, 'Any Role for the ECHR When It Comes to Climate Change' (2022) 3 ECHRLR 1.

[321] *Carême* v. *France* (n 316) at [56]. [322] Ibid at [83].

measures, travel restrictions, mandatory vaccination policies and medical equipment procurement all impacted the lives of citizens. Several aspects of the UK Government's response to the pandemic serve to illuminate the difficult issues that arise when States are required to balance the right to life against other human rights.

One such instance is the controversy over the provision of Personal Protective Equipment (PPE) to key workers and vulnerable members of the population, such as residents of care homes. Given the State's positive obligation to protect life from a 'real and immediate' threat of which it was aware or ought to have been aware, it is arguable that 'this duty included prioritising the provision of available PPE to healthcare staff, other frontline workers, and persons most vulnerable to the virus such as those in care homes'.[323] Further, as the JCHR observed in its report on the Government's response to the pandemic:

> It is also arguable that when it became clear that black, Asian and minority ethnic communities were suffering disproportionately from the effects of Covid-19, the right to life (Article 2 ECHR) read together with the right to non-discrimination in the enjoyment of the substantive ECHR rights (Article 14 ECHR) should have required the prioritisation of the allocation of PPE to (for instance) BAME doctors and nurses. We have received evidence that in some cases the reverse has in fact been the case.[324]

Protection of care home residents from the virus also raised issues under Article 2. The mortality rates of people living in care homes during the pandemic were significantly higher than for those outside of care homes of the same age.[325] In its report, the JCHR commented that 'the very high number of deaths from Covid-19 in care homes is a matter of deepest concern to us and engages the operational duty to secure life (Article 2 ECHR)'.[326] The JCHR went on to say that '[t]he causes behind it are complex and we have not been able to devote the necessary time and attention to address them fully in the context of this report. It is, however, imperative that they be interrogated thoroughly in order to meet the state's procedural obligations under Article 2'.[327] Thus, the Government's management of care homes during the pandemic may well implicate more than one aspect of Article 2, though the High Court's decision in *Gardner*[328] significantly limits the likelihood of such an argument succeeding. In *Gardner*, the High Court rejected the claim that the State 'had a positive

[323] Joint Committee on Human Rights, 'The Government's response to COVID-19: Human rights implications', Seventh Report of Session 2019–21, HC 265/HL Paper 125, 21 September 2020 at [68], https://committees.parliament.uk/publications/2649/documents/26914/default/.

[324] Ibid at [69]. [325] Ibid at [95]. [326] Ibid at [97]. [327] Ibid.

[328] *R (Gardner & Anor)* v. *Secretary of State for Health and Social Care & Ors* [2022] EWHC 967 (Admin), [2022] WLR(D) 188.

obligation to take appropriate steps to safeguard the lives of those within England and do all that could have been required to prevent life from being avoidably put at risk'.[329] In dismissing the complaint under Article 2, the High Court noted that:

> [t]here is no authority of the Strasbourg court which has gone as far as holding that a State is under an operational duty to take all reasonable steps to avoid the real and immediate risk to life posed by an epidemic or pandemic to as broad and undefined a sector of the population as residents of care homes for the elderly. There is no clear and consistent line of Strasbourg authority which indicates that such a duty exists and we cannot be at all confident – indeed we gravely doubt – that the ECtHR would be willing to declare that it does. We should keep pace with the Strasbourg jurisprudence, but not run past it and disappear into the distance. The Defendants did not, in our view, owe the Article 2 operational duty for which the Claimants contend.[330]

Complaints before the ECtHR challenging state responses to the pandemic under Article 2 have been similarly unsuccessful. For instance, in *Le Mailloux* v. *France*, the ECtHR declared the complaint inadmissible *ratione personae*.[331] While the ECtHR did not foreclose the possibility that a State's response to the pandemic *could* engage its positive obligations under Article 2, the complainant in *Le Mailloux* failed to demonstrate that *his* Article 2 rights had been violated.

4.4.3 The ECtHR's Approach to Domestic Abuse: Effectiveness in Action?

Domestic abuse is a global health crisis which primarily, though not exclusively, affects women.[332] In the period March 2021 to March 2023, there were

[329] Ibid at [151]. [330] Ibid at [252].

[331] *Le Mailloux* v. *France*, App. No. 18108/20, 05/11/2020.

[332] According to the latest data from the Office for National Statistics, in the year ending March 2024, an estimated 2.3 million people (1.6 million women and 712,000 men) aged sixteen years and over in England and Wales experienced domestic abuse, which is defined by reference to s.1 of the Domestic Abuse Act 2021: Office for National Statistics, 'Domestic abuse prevalence and trends, England and Wales: year ending March 2024', 27 November 2024. Of the domestic abuse-related crimes recorded by police in the year ending March 2024, 72.5 per cent of victims were female and of the sexual offences that were recorded as domestic abuse-related crimes, 92.1 per cent of victims were female: Office for National Statistics, 'Domestic abuse prevalence and victim characteristics, England and Wales: year ending March 2024', www.ons.gov.uk/peoplepopulationandcommunity/crimeandjustice/bulletins/domesticabuseinenglandandwalesoverview/november2024. Globally, about one in three women have been subjected to either physical and/or sexual intimate partner violence or non-partner sexual violence in their lifetime: World Health Organisation, 'Violence Against Women', 25 March 2024, www.who.int/news-room/fact-sheets/detail/violence-against-women.

353 domestic homicides[333] in England and Wales.[334] Of those killed, 231 were female and of those, almost 75 per cent were killed by a male partner or ex-partner (whereas for the majority of male victims of domestic homicides, the suspect was a male family member).[335] As discussed in greater detail in Chapter 5 in respect of Article 3 and in Chapter 14 in respect of Article 14, domestic abuse potentially raises a number of human rights issues, including the State's positive obligation to put in place and enforce an effective regulatory system deterring such abuse and its obligation to take preventive operational measures in specific cases under Articles 2, 3 and 8 (read alone, or together with the prohibition on discrimination in Article 14). It is also not uncommon for domestic abuse cases before the ECtHR to involve allegations of a failure by State authorities to conduct effective investigations as required by Articles 2 and 3 (again, taken alone, or read together with Article 14). As discussed above, domestic abuse has also given rise to proceedings before the domestic courts in the UK under both the HRA and based (albeit unsuccessfully) on the tort of negligence.[336]

While prior to the Grand Chamber's 2021 landmark decision in *Kurt* v. *Austria*,[337] the ECtHR had found violations of the procedural and operational obligations under Article 2 in cases involving domestic abuse,[338] the need for immediacy of risk as required by the *Osman* test (discussed in Section 4.3.2.4) proved problematic for victims and survivors given the unique cumulative nature of domestic abuse. As also discussed in Chapter 5, following *Kurt*, authorities are required to conduct an 'autonomous, proactive and comprehensive assessment' through which 'the reality and immediacy of the risk [of deadly violence] must be assessed taking due account of the particular context of domestic violence cases'.[339] In order to be 'autonomous and proactive', the authorities (primarily the police) must investigate allegations of

[333] A homicide (an umbrella term covering murder, manslaughter or infanticide) is classified as 'domestic' by the Office of National Statistics 'where the relationship between a victim aged 16 years and over and the perpetrator falls into one of the following categories: spouse, common-law spouse, cohabiting partner, boyfriend or girlfriend, ex-spouse, ex-cohabiting partner or ex-boyfriend or girlfriend, adulterous relationship, son or daughter (including step and adopted relationships), parent (including step and adopted relationships), brother or sister, other relatives': Office for National Statistics, 'Domestic abuse prevalence and trends, England and Wales: year ending March 2024', 27 November 2024 at [7].

[334] Office for National Statistics, 'Domestic abuse victim characteristics, England and Wales: year ending March 2023', Table 22b, 24 November 2023.

[335] Ibid, Table 23. [336] See Section 4.3.3.2. [337] *Kurt* v. *Austria* (n 175).

[338] See, for instance, *Kontrová* v. *Slovakia* [2007] ECHR 419, *Opuz* v. *Turkey* (n 93), *Branko Tomasic and Ors* v. *Croatia* [2009] ECHR 79, *Durmaz* v. *Turkey* [2014] ECHR 1213, *Talpis* v. *Italy* [2017] ECHR 224 and *Tërshana* v. *Armenia* (2021) 72 EHRR 13.

[339] *Kurt* v. *Austria* (n 175) at [190].

domestic abuse 'of their own motion' and must do so by 'proactively collecting and assessing information on all relevant risk factors and elements of the case'.[340] In terms of comprehensiveness, while the use of standardised risk assessments is not necessary, the Court nevertheless recommended that such assessments be used given they 'indicate specific risk factors and have been developed on the basis of sound criminological research and best practices in domestic violence cases, [and] can contribute to the comprehensiveness of the authorities' risk assessment'.[341]

While the Grand Chamber in *Kurt* did not dispose of the 'immediacy' requirement entirely in domestic abuse cases, it significantly curtailed its application, holding that:

> the application of the immediacy standard ... should take into account the specific features of domestic violence cases, and the ways in which they differ from incident-based situations such as that in *Osman* ... The Court reiterates that consecutive cycles of domestic violence, often with an increase in frequency, intensity and danger over time, are frequently observed patterns in that context ... The Explanatory Report to Article 52 of the Istanbul Convention ... clarifies that the term 'immediate danger' in that provision refers to any situations of domestic violence in which harm is imminent or has already materialised and is likely to happen again. The Court has observed in numerous other cases that a perpetrator with a record of domestic violence posed a significant risk of further and possibly deadly violence ... Based on what is known today about the dynamics of domestic violence, the perpetrator's behaviour may become more predictable in situations of a clear escalation of such violence. This general knowledge of domestic violence and the comprehensive research available in this area must duly be taken into account by the authorities when they assess the risk of a further escalation of violence, even after the issuance of a barring and protection order.[342]

It is debateable whether, following *Kurt*'s explicit recognition of the specific and unique characteristics of domestic abuse, the concept of 'immediacy' continues to serve any function in the context of domestic abuse, particularly if we consider that Article 52 of the Istanbul Convention[343] defines 'immediate danger' in the context of violence against women and domestic violence as that which is 'imminent' *or* 'likely to happen again'. Given that, as the Court itself recognised, '"immediate" does not lend itself to a precise definition', its utility as a means of assessing the State's protective duty in this context is questionable. Nevertheless, it remains an aspect of the test applicable when determining whether the authorities ought to have taken reasonable measures to protect a victim of domestic abuse.

[340] Ibid at [170]. [341] Ibid at [171]. [342] Ibid at [175].

[343] Council of Europe Convention on preventing and combating violence against women and domestic violence (CETS No.210, 1/8/14). The Istanbul Convention entered into force in the UK in November 2022.

If a person is murdered (or suffers life-threatening injuries) as a result of domestic abuse, the procedural obligation to investigate will arise.[344] The requirements for an investigation to be effective are set out above and they apply equally in cases involving domestic abuse. Notably, the ECtHR has, on several occasions, found that States have violated the procedural obligation under Article 2, read in conjunction with Article 14 of the ECHR which prohibits discrimination. A violation of the procedural obligation under Article 2, taken together with Article 14, will occur where there was 'general and discriminatory judicial [or police] passivity [creating] a climate that was conducive to domestic violence'.[345] As the ECtHR has observed:

> Without a strict approach from the law enforcement authorities, prejudice-motivated crimes would unavoidably be treated on an equal footing with ordinary cases without such overtones, and the resultant indifference would be tantamount to official acquiescence to or even connivance with hate crimes.[346]

4.5 CONCLUSION

The right to life is one of the most fundamental of human rights and is protected both under the common law in the UK and via Article 2 ECHR. In this chapter, we have focused on Article 2 and the obligations it imposes on States. While the most obvious obligation is the negative duty on State authorities not to take life save in the limited circumstances listed in Article 2(2), this duty is not as simple as it may seem. For example, questions arise as to State culpability for the private acts of members of the security forces, there has been considerable evolution in the law regarding the imposition of the death penalty and its implications under Article 2, and States may be liable for a violation of Article 2 in extradition and deportation cases despite the risk to life emanating from a third country (which may or may not be a party to the ECHR). Beyond the negative obligation not to arbitrarily take life, States also have positive obligations and procedural obligations under Article 2. In respect of the former, States have a general duty to put in place regulatory systems which effectively deter threats to life and to enforce those regulations as well as a specific positive obligation to take preventive operational measures where the authorities knew or ought to have known of a real and immediate risk to life. This chapter has considered the ways in which domestic courts and the ECtHR have framed these obligations in specific contexts. In particular, the evolution of the positive operational investigative duty in

[344] See, for instance, *Tkhelidze* v. *Georgia* [2021] ECHR 614 at [50]. [345] Ibid at [51].

[346] Ibid at [60]. See, further, the discussion of Article 14 in the context of domestic abuse in Chapter 14.

cases involving domestic abuse was examined and the nature of the procedural obligation was considered through the lens of The Troubles in Northern Ireland, paying particular attention to the decisions of the UK Supreme Court in *Finucane, McQuillan* and *Dalton*. The implications of climate change for the right to life were also explored, having regard to litigation before the domestic courts in the UK, the ECtHR, the Inter-American Court of Human Rights and the Human Rights Committee. The Grenfell Tower Fire provided an insight in the myriad ways that the State's obligations under Article 2 can intersect as well as the potential limitations of rights as a means of providing effective protection for society's most vulnerable members.

The capacity for Article 2's protective reach to expand and contract has both positive and negative consequences. As the discussion of the ECtHR's response to domestic abuse illustrates, this flexibility can ensure that the rights enshrined in the ECHR including the right to life are rendered effective. However, the Court's restrictive approach in other circumstances, including, for instance, when determining whether States are responsible for the private acts of security forces and/or whether investigations into lethal force by security forces have been effective, can significantly undermine the effectiveness of the right.

5 Freedom from Torture or Inhuman or Degrading Treatment or Punishment

CONTENTS

5.1 INTRODUCTION

This chapter examines the right not to be subject to torture or inhuman or degrading treatment or punishment (which is referred to collectively throughout this chapter as 'ill-treatment'). As the Grand Chamber observed in *Gäfgen* v. *Germany*, this right – which finds reflection in Article 3 of the ECHR – 'enshrines one of the most fundamental values of democratic societies'.[1] Indeed, unlike most other rights in the ECHR, 'Article 3 makes no provision for exceptions and no derogation from it is permissible under Article 15 § 2 even in the event of a public emergency threatening the life of the nation'.[2] Consequently, the ECtHR has held that 'even in the most difficult circumstances, such as the fight against terrorism and organised crime, the Convention prohibits in absolute terms torture or inhuman or degrading treatment or punishment, irrespective of the conduct of the person concerned'.[3]

At least textually, then, the prohibition on ill-treatment is absolute: there is no scope for legitimate interferences with the right nor are there exceptions such as we see in the context of, for instance, Articles 2 and 5 ECHR. In terms of drafting, Article 3 is as simple as it gets: 'No one shall be subjected to torture or to inhuman or degrading treatment or punishment.' Such simplicity, however, belies the complexity of the debate surrounding the 'absoluteness' of the right, what constitutes 'treatment', what is meant by 'torture', 'inhuman' and 'degrading', and the extent to which Article 3 compels the State to take positive steps to protect individuals from ill-treatment.

The prohibition on torture is considered to be a peremptory norm of international law.[4] Unsurprisingly, then, a number of international treaties contain similar prohibitions to that set out in Article 3,[5] and there is a dedicated Convention Against Torture and Other Cruel, Inhuman or Degrading Treatment or Punishment (CAT) which was ratified by the UK in 1988.

While, objectively, torture is clearly antithetical to the rule of law and inconsistent with the core principles of dignity, bodily integrity and autonomy which underpin the ECHR, the question of what conduct constitutes ill-treatment for the purposes of Article 3 has proven divisive. This chapter examines the meaning of the various elements of Article 3 and considers the

[1] *Gäfgen* v. *Germany* [GC] (2011) 52 EHRR 1 at [87]. [2] Ibid. [3] Ibid.

[4] See, for instance, *Questions Relating to the Obligation to Prosecute or Extradite (Belgium* v. *Senegal), Judgment*, ICJ Reports 2012 and *A and Ors* v. *Secretary of State for the Home Department (No 2)* [2005] UKHL 71, [2005] 2 AC 221 at [33].

[5] See, for instance: the United Nations Declaration of Human Rights (1948), Article 5; the International Covenant on Civil and Political Rights, Article 7; the United Nations Convention on the Rights of the Child (1989), Article 37(a); the United Nations Convention on the Rights of Persons with Disabilities (2006), Article 15.

obligations it imposes on States, including in cases involving deportation or extradition, extraordinary rendition, domestic abuse and border pushbacks. Before doing so, however, the prohibition on ill-treatment under the common law is considered.

5.2 ILL-TREATMENT AND THE COMMON LAW

In addition to being a peremptory norm of international law,[6] torture is 'totally repugnant to the fundamental principles of English law'.[7] In *A and Ors* v. *Secretary of State for the Home Department*,[8] the House of Lords was called upon to determine whether evidence which had (or may have been) procured by way of torture inflicted by officials in a foreign state could be received in appeal proceedings before the Special Immigration Appeals Commission (SIAC). In finding that such evidence was inadmissible, the House of Lords cited the common law's longstanding prohibition on the admission of evidence that may have been procured by way of torture. As Lord Carswell observed:

> I am satisfied that, whether or not it has ever been affirmatively declared that the common law declines to allow the admission of evidence obtained by the use of torture, it is quite capable now of embracing such a rule. If that is any extension of the existing common law, it is a modest one, a necessary recognition of the conclusions which should be drawn from long established principles.[9]

Likewise, Lord Bingham considered that the common law's 'condemnation' of the use of torture to acquire evidence was a 'constitutional principle' with a very long tradition: 'the English common law has regarded torture and its fruits with abhorrence for over 500 years, and that abhorrence is now shared by over 140 countries which have acceded to the [CAT]'.[10] While the focus of the judgment in *A and Ors* was torture, it has been suggested that the same considerations also apply to inhuman or degrading treatment or punishment.[11]

6 See, for instance, *A and Ors* v. *Secretary of State* (n 4) at [33].

7 Ibid at [12], per Lord Bingham.

8 *A and Ors* v. *Secretary of State* (n 4).

9 Ibid at [122].

10 Ibid at [51].

11 See, for instance, Natasa Mavronicola's discussion of the common law's protection of bodily integrity in 'The Mythology and the Reality of Common Law Constitutional Rights to Bodily Integrity' in Mark Elliott and Kirsty Hughes (eds), *Common Law Constitutional Rights* (Hart Publishing, 2020), p.34. Though note Lord Mance in *Belhaj* v. *Straw* [2017] UKSC 3, [2017] AC 964 appears to have limited the *jus cogens* prohibition to torture, observing at [107(i)]:

> The analogy of *jus cogens* would suggest that a domestic court would be able to adjudicate upon an allegation that its national government connived in a serious violation of the claimant's rights by a foreign government, but would be required to abstain from adjudicating

Subsequent authorities have reaffirmed the common law's 'condemnation' of torture. Thus, in *Belhaj* v. *Straw*,[12] which 'concern[ed] the alleged complicity of United Kingdom authorities and officials in various torts, allegedly committed by various other states in various overseas jurisdictions' (i.e. extraordinary rendition[13]), the Supreme Court rejected the respondent's reliance on the doctrines of State immunity and foreign act of state to avoid culpability.[14] As Lord Sumption observed, 'English law's rejection of torture ... is an essential feature of our constitutional order'.[15] Similarly, Lord Mance stated 'torture has long been regarded as abhorrent by English law' and 'individuals are unquestionably entitled to be free of deliberate physical *mistreatment* while in the custody of state authorities'.[16] Lord Mance's use of the term 'mistreatment' is notable given it suggests the common law prohibits (at least of those detained by the State) inhuman and degrading treatment and punishment, as well as torture.

Accordingly, the common law provides a degree of protection against ill-treatment. Indeed, as was discussed in the context of the right to life (Chapter 4), the common law also recognises and imposes certain public law obligations on authorities including investigative obligations. In *DSD & NBV* v. *Commissioner of Police for Metropolis*,[17] a central issue was the scope of the investigative obligation under Article 3 ECHR. The nature of the dispute (which is considered in greater detail below) necessitated a consideration of the scope of any analogous investigative obligation under the common law. At trial, Mr Justice Green observed that an obligation on the part of the State to investigate instances of ill-treatment, even where State agents were not complicit in the treatment itself, was not 'heretical to the common law' given that:

> The duty on the police to investigate effectively is a bare minimum safeguard in any civilised State. In the course of argument I asked Mr Johnson QC whether he accepted, on behalf of the Commissioner, that there was in domestic law a duty to investigate. He accepted that there was and, most helpfully, provided me with authority to support the proposition. He cited by way of authority a number of sources for this wholly unsurprising proposition. In *Rice v Connolly* [1966] 2 QB 414, Lord Parker CJ referred to the duty to 'detect crime' and 'to bring offenders to justice':
>
> > It is part of the obligations and duties of a police constable to take all steps which appear to him to be necessary for keeping the peace, for preventing crime or for

upon a less serious violation, such as 'mere' unlawful detention or cruel or inhuman treatment not amounting to torture.

[12] *Belhaj* v. *Straw*, ibid. [13] In respect of which, see Section 5.3.3.2.

[14] *Belhaj* v. *Straw* (n 11) at [1], per Lord Mance. [15] Ibid at [272], per Lord Sumption.

[16] Ibid at [98], per Lord Mance. Emphasis added.

[17] *DSD & NBV* v. *Commissioner of Police for Metropolis* [2014] EWHC 436 (QB).

> protecting property from criminal injury. There is no exhaustive definition of the powers and obligations of the police but they are at least these and they would further include the duty to detect crime and to bring offenders to justice.
>
> In *R v Commissioner of Police of the Metropolis ex parte Blackburn* [1968] 2 QB 118 Lord Denning MR referred to the duty of the Commissioner '… to post his men that crimes may be detected'.[18]

That the common law recognises the prohibition of torture and an obligation to investigate effectively alleged acts of torture seems plain. It is, however, less clear whether the same degree of protection attaches to the prohibition of inhuman or degrading treatment/punishment. Further, as the proceedings in *DSD* make clear (and as was discussed in the context of the right to life in Chapter 4), the ability to translate those protections into justiciable claims against the State is not straightforward. While public law challenges, including on the basis of rationality, may be open to an individual who has been subject to (or is at risk of being subject to) ill-treatment (whether by State agents or private persons), there are similar limitations in the application of the law of negligence in such circumstances as were canvassed in Chapter 4, though it bears noting that the UK Supreme Court has recognised the potential for public authorities to owe a duty of care to protect from ill-treatment those for whom they have assumed responsibility (such as children who are under the care of the authorities).[19]

While authorities such as *A and Ors* indicate a recognition by the common law of the *prohibition* of torture, they do not 'represent the recognition of a robust right not to be tortured or ill-treated at common law'.[20] In response to the question of whether the common law could provide the same protections afforded by the HRA and Article 3 ECHR, Mavronicola states:

> allusions to the idea that protection from torture and ill-treatment is constitutionally embedded appear thin and shaky in comparison to the explicit protection of the right under the HRA, coupled with the wealth of principles and concrete findings that have emerged out of hundreds of ECtHR judgments on Article 3 ECHR, building up a body of jurisprudence which has been treated widely as *res interpretata*.[21]

Given the potential limitations in the common law's protection against ill-treatment (including the extent to which it protects against inhuman or degrading treatment/punishment), the remainder of this chapter concentrates

[18] Ibid at [230].

[19] *Poole Borough Council* v. *GN and another* [2019] UKSC 25, [2020] AC 780.

[20] Natasa Mavronicola, 'Facilitating (Further) Inhumanity: On the Prospect of Losing Article 3 ECHR, a Vital Guarantee for the Under-Protected' (2024) 5 ECHRLR 1, p.111.

[21] Ibid, p.110.

on the prohibition of ill-treatment as contained in Article 3 ECHR, paying particular attention to the ways in which the HRA has functioned to secure the right within domestic law.

5.3 ILL-TREATMENT AND THE ECHR: THE CONSTITUTIVE ELEMENTS OF ARTICLE 3

Save in cases where the ECtHR has held that there is a strong presumption that the conduct is contrary to Article 3 ECHR (for instance, where a detainee has less than 3 square metres of personal space in a multi-occupancy cell[22]), the individual alleging a violation of Article 3 bears the burden of proof and must provide evidence sufficient to satisfy the Court beyond reasonable doubt that ill-treatment has taken place.[23] The ECtHR has, however, held that such proof may 'follow from the coexistence of sufficiently strong, clear and concordant inferences or of similar unrebutted presumptions of fact'.[24] For instance, where an individual is taken into police custody in good health but has sustained injuries by the time of release, it is incumbent upon the State to provide a 'plausible explanation' for the injuries and, if it fails to do so, a 'clear issue' will arise under Article 3 ECHR.[25] Proof of the injuries must still be provided by the applicants.[26]

As to the meaning that has been attributed to the various components of Article 3 ECHR, there is no single definition of any of the constituent elements. As the ECtHR has repeatedly emphasised, the assessment of whether a person has been subject to ill-treatment which is covered by Article 3 ECHR 'is relative; it depends on all the circumstances of the case'.[27] Nevertheless, as the ensuing demonstrates, the Court has sought to provide guidance in determining whether treatment is covered by Article 3 ECHR.

5.3.1 'Inhuman' vs. 'Degrading'

The ECtHR has found treatment to be inhuman because, '*inter alia*, it was premeditated, was applied for hours at a stretch and caused either actual bodily injury or intense physical and mental suffering'.[28] In contrast:

> [t]reatment has been considered 'degrading' when it was such as to arouse in its victims feelings of fear, anguish and inferiority capable of humiliating and debasing

[22] See, for instance, *Muršić* v. *Croatia* [GC] [2016] ECHR 927 at [105].

[23] See, for instance, *Gäfgen* (n 1) at [92] and *Ireland* v. *the United Kingdom* [2018] ECHR 247 at [41].

[24] See, for instance, *Bouyid* v. *Belgium* [GC] [2015] ECHR 819 at [82].

[25] *Gäfgen* (n 1) at [92].

[26] See, for instance, *Panayotopoulos and Others* v. *Greece* [2025] ECHR 25.

[27] See, for instance, *Muršić* (n 22) at [97].

[28] *Jalloh* v. *Germany* [GC] (2007) 44 EHRR 32 at [68].

> them and possibly breaking their physical or moral resistance . . . or when it was such as to drive the victim to act against his will or conscience.[29]

Treatment may also be 'degrading' because it was inflicted for the purpose of humiliating or debasing the person concerned, although the absence of such a purpose does not render degrading treatment compatible with Article 3 ECHR.[30]

The meanings developed by the ECtHR for inhuman and degrading treatment, in particular their reference to bodily injury or physical or mental suffering and feelings of humiliation, debasement, fear and compulsion, are reflective of the concepts of bodily integrity, dignity and autonomy which are central to the ECHR.[31] As the Grand Chamber observed in *Bouyid*, 'the prohibition of torture and inhuman or degrading treatment or punishment is a value of civilisation closely bound up with respect for human dignity'.[32]

Recognising the potential for policing and other facets of the criminal justice system to be significantly curtailed by Article 3 ECHR, the Grand Chamber has emphasised that:

> In order for a punishment or treatment associated with it to be 'inhuman' or 'degrading', the suffering or humiliation involved must in any event go beyond that *inevitable* element of suffering or humiliation connected with a given form of *legitimate* treatment or punishment.[33]

What is meant by 'legitimate' punishment is considered below.

While 'inhuman' and 'degrading' lack precise definitions, this elasticity is necessary if Article 3 ECHR is to achieve its objectives. As noted above, central to Article 3 ECHR are the principles of bodily integrity and dignity and attributing comprehensive and exhaustive definitions to the terms in Article 3 ECHR would inevitably result in the exclusion of some individuals whose bodily integrity and dignity have been violated. The position adopted by the ECtHR recognises the context-specific nature of the inquiry – what is humiliating or debasing for one person may not be for another – and Article 3 ECHR must be flexible enough to accommodate those differences.[34]

That is not to say, however, that every instance of humiliation, debasement, physical or mental suffering and so on, will constitute a violation. To engage Article 3 ECHR, the impugned treatment must reach the 'minimum level of severity'.

[29] Ibid. [30] Ibid.

[31] *Bouyid* (n 24) at [81] and [87]; *Tyrer* v. *the United Kingdom* (1979–80) 2 EHRR 1 at [33].

[32] Ibid at [81]. [33] Ibid. Emphasis added.

[34] *Bouyid* (n 24) at [87]. For a discussion of this case, see Natasa Mavronicola, 'Bouyid and dignity's role in Article 3 ECHR', *Strasbourg Observers*, 8 October 2015, https://strasbourgobservers.com/2015/10/08/bouyid-and-dignitys-role-in-article-3-echr/.

5.3.2 The Minimum Level of Severity

As Mavronicola has observed, 'Article 3 proscribes certain forms of absolute *wrongs*, including wrongs that result in significant suffering and other forms of harm. The minimum level of severity does not, contrary to misconceptions, refer to a certain scale of *harm*; rather, it concerns the gravity of the wrong committed.'[35] Whether the minimum level of severity has been met 'depends on all the circumstances of the case' including, for instance, the characteristics of the victim as well as 'the purpose for which the treatment was inflicted together with the intention or motivation behind it . . ., [and the] context, such as an atmosphere of heightened tension and emotions'.[36]

It is also possible for a 'threat of conduct prohibited by Article 3' to reach the minimum level of severity so as to constitute ill-treatment 'provided [the threat of such treatment] is sufficiently real and immediate'.[37] This was the case in *Gäfgen*[38] in which the Grand Chamber held that subjecting the applicant – who was suspected of abducting an eleven-year-old boy – to the threat of violence for the purpose of extracting information constituted inhuman treatment.[39] That was so even though the conduct of the police officers, including the threat of violence, resulted in Gäfgen confessing to abducting and killing the boy and revealing the location of the young boy's body.[40]

As *Gäfgen* demonstrates, whether treatment reaches the minimum level of severity and, if so, whether it is inhuman, degrading or torture, is fact specific. It also highlights the significance which the ECtHR ascribes to the environment in which the impugned treatment takes place. Indeed, the Grand Chamber has elsewhere held that:

> in respect of a person who is deprived of his liberty, or, more generally, is confronted with law-enforcement officers, any recourse to physical force which has not been made strictly necessary by his own conduct *diminishes human dignity* and is, in principle, an infringement of the right set forth in Article 3.[41]

The finding of a violation in *Gäfgen* notwithstanding the motivation (to locate a missing child) and the consequence (a confession and the location of pivotal physical evidence) is reflective of the fact that:

> the prohibition on ill-treatment of a person applies irrespective of the conduct of the victim or the motivation of the authorities. Torture, inhuman or degrading treatment

[35] Natasa Mavronicola, '*Bouyid* v. *Belgium*: The "Minimum Level of Severity" and Human Dignity's Role in Article 3 ECHR' (2020) 1 ECHRLR 2, p.120. Emphasis in original.

[36] *Jalloh* (n 28) at [68]. [37] *Gäfgen* (n 1) at [91]. [38] Ibid. [39] Ibid at [108].

[40] Ibid. A separate issue in *Gäfgen* was whether the admission of the evidence acquired as a result of the applicant's ill-treatment in his trial violated Article 6 of the ECHR which protects the right to a fair trial. The Chamber had held that there had been no violation of Article 6 because the applicant had confessed again at the trial and this was what was used against him, together with the evidence obtained at the scene which was used to corroborate that second confession. The Grand Chamber reaffirmed this finding (at [180]).

[41] *Bouyid* (n 24) at [88]. Emphasis added.

> cannot be inflicted even in circumstances where the life of an individual is at risk ... The philosophical basis underpinning the absolute nature of the right under Article 3 does not allow for any exceptions or justifying factors or balancing of interests, irrespective of the conduct of the person concerned and the nature of the offence at issue.[42]

Ostensibly, such absoluteness is at odds with the fact that the ECtHR has held that, when determining whether the minimum level of severity has been met, reference may be had to the 'purpose' for which the treatment has been inflicted.[43] The two positions are reconcilable because whilst purpose may *elevate* conduct so that it reaches the minimum level of severity, purpose *can never* be used to *reduce the severity* of what would otherwise breach Article 3. This was confirmed by Lord Kerr in *The Northern Ireland Abortion Case*[44] wherein he observed that the Article 3 ECHR case law 'confine[s] the issue of motivation or purpose to a relatively narrow compass', namely 'an assessment of whether treatment which might otherwise not meet the standard set by Article 3 crosses the threshold by reason of that motivation or purpose'.[45] Nevertheless, the contention – that purpose cannot be relied upon to transform treatment that would otherwise violate Article 3 ECHR into Convention-compatible treatment – sits uncomfortably with several lines of authority from the ECtHR, as illuminated by the Court's decision in *Y. P.* v. *Russia*.[46]

Y.P. involved a young woman who had been sterilised without her consent following an emergency caesarean section when she was in her third trimester of pregnancy. The applicant had experienced complications with her pregnancy and her unborn child was in significant distress. The applicant signed a form which clearly stated that she consented to the caesarean section *but not sterilisation*. During the caesarean section, doctors discovered that her uterus had ruptured, and a panel was convened to discuss whether the uterus should be removed or whether it should be sutured, with the panel deciding on the latter. Notwithstanding the fact that it was not medically necessary, the doctors also decided that the applicant's right fallopian tube should be ligated. As the applicant had previously suffered an ectopic pregnancy and had had her left fallopian tube removed as a result, the measure taken in respect of the right tube rendered her sterile. Doctors did not explain to her that she had been sterilised and so, it was with some shock that she discovered several years later, when she and her husband had been having trouble conceiving, that she

[42] *Gäfgen* (n 1) at [107].

[43] See, for instance, *Jalloh* (n 28) at [68] which refers to 'the purpose for which the treatment was inflicted together with the intention or motivation behind it'.

[44] *In the matter of an application by the Northern Ireland Human Rights Commission for Judicial Review (Northern Ireland)* [2018] UKSC 27, [2019] 1 All ER 173 (*Northern Ireland Abortion Case*).

[45] Ibid, per Lord Kerr at [217]–[218]. See also, Stephanie Palmer, 'A Wrong Turning: Article 3 ECHR and Proportionality' (2006) **65** CLJ 2, 438–451.

[46] *Y.P.* v. *Russia* [2022] ECHR 722.

had been subjected to tubal ligation without her consent. Civil proceedings brought against the doctors and hospital by the applicant were rejected by the domestic courts.

Before the ECtHR, the applicant argued that her sterilisation, in addition to being performed without her consent – and, in fact, contrary to her express indication that she did *not* consent to sterilisation – was not medically necessary, and this constituted a violation of both Articles 3 and 8 (right to respect for private and family life) ECHR. In response, the Government argued that ligation of the fallopian tube was necessary because if she were to get pregnant again in the future, there was a heightened risk of the applicant's uterus rupturing and that could be life threatening. The Government also argued that the applicant's sterilisation had no 'medical or physiological consequences'[47] and the applicant could still undergo *in vitro fertilisation* as she had retained her uterus.

In what Judge Pavli in dissent described as a judgment capable of causing 'irreparable harm',[48] a majority of the ECtHR concluded that the minimum level of severity for Article 3 ECHR was *not* met in this case. While there are several troubling aspects of the majority's judgment, of significance for instant purposes is the emphasis it placed on the lack of malicious intent on the part of the doctors in deciding that the applicant's forced sterilisation did not constitute inhuman or degrading treatment. This sits uncomfortably with the Court's repeated contention that the purpose of ill-treatment (which, one might reasonably consider, includes the motivation behind its infliction) cannot render ill-treatment reaching the minimum level of severity nevertheless compliant with Article 3 ECHR. The fact that Gäfgen was suspected (correctly, as it transpired) of kidnapping an eleven-year-old boy did not justify the *threat* of violence by police in an attempt to obtain intelligence with the aim of rescuing the child.[49] The fact that a person is suspected of being involved in terrorist activity does not permit a State to facilitate that individual's rendition and/or torture by the CIA.[50] Following that logic, the fact that a person with full capacity *may*, in the future, exercise their bodily autonomy to get pregnant with the possible risk of placental rupture, should not permit a State to sterilise the individual contrary to their express wishes. It smacks of a paternalism that is inconsistent with the Convention's emphasis on autonomy and dignity.

Given the judgment's arguble inconsistency with the ECtHR's established Article 3 ECHR jurisprudence, it is unsurprising that Judge Elósegui in her separate, concurring opinion in *Y.P.* was at pains to emphasise that the decision in this case should not be taken as authority for the general proposition that the absence of a malicious intent or purpose renders Article 3 ECHR

[47] Ibid at [32]. [48] Ibid, partly dissenting opinion of Judge Pavli at [10]. [49] *Gäfgen* (n 1).

[50] See, for instance, *Al Nashiri* v. *Poland* (2015) 60 EHRR 16.

inapplicable.[51] It is, however, difficult to see why the finding that the complaint was inadmissible *ratione materiae* because of the lack of *mala fides* ought not have the same application (with the same outcome) in a case such as *Gäfgen*. Indeed, this dissonance is exacerbated by the majority's finding that the applicant's forced sterilisation *did* violate her right to private life under Article 8 ECHR. The majority found that the doctors had taken 'an intrusive and paternalistic attitude, treating the applicant as if she were a minor incapable of making her own decisions' and had 'permanently deprived [her] of her reproductive capacity' thereby causing 'serious damage to her health' and 'grossly affect[ing] her physical integrity' in a manner 'incompatible with the requirement of respect for human freedom and dignity' in violation of Article 8 ECHR.[52] The majority nevertheless concluded that Article 3 ECHR – at the centre of which is the protection of a person's dignity and bodily integrity – was not engaged because the doctors acted without malice. Not only do the Court's findings with respect to Article 8 ECHR vis-à-vis Article 3 ECHR appear inherently inconsistent, they also suggest that, contrary to the contention that ill-treatment *cannot* be justified, there are situations in which the absence of a malicious purpose will render ill-treatment Article 3 ECHR compliant. As Judge Pavli noted, such a conclusion has the potential to cause 'irreparable harm'.

5.3.3 Torture

Whereas the CAT explicitly defines 'torture',[53] the ECHR does not, and the ECtHR has not developed a single definition, preferring instead to characterise torture as an aggravated form of inhuman treatment. In *Gäfgen*, the Court stated that:

> it appears that it was the intention that the Convention should … attach a special stigma to deliberate inhuman treatment causing very serious and cruel suffering … In addition to the severity of the treatment, there is a purposive element to torture

[51] *Y.P.* (n 46), separate concurring opinion of Judge Elósegui at [17].

[52] Ibid at [51], [56] and [57], and the separate concurring opinion of Judge Elósegui at [3].

[53] United Nations Convention Against Torture and Other Cruel, Inhuman or Degrading Treatment and Punishment, Article 1(1):

> For the purposes of this Convention, the term 'torture' means any act by which severe pain or suffering, whether physical or mental, is intentionally inflicted on a person for such purposes as obtaining from him or a third person information or a confession, punishing him for an act he or a third person has committed or is suspected of having committed, or intimidating or coercing him or a third person, or for any reason based on discrimination of any kind, when such pain or suffering is inflicted by or at the instigation of or with the consent or acquiescence of a public official or other person acting in an official capacity. It does not include pain or suffering arising only from, inherent in or incidental to lawful sanctions.

[namely] . . . intentional infliction of severe pain or suffering with the aim, *inter alia*, of obtaining information, inflicting punishment or intimidating.[54]

Given that torture involves a purposive element, it is perhaps unsurprising that many of the cases in which the ECtHR has found that conduct constitutes torture involve ill-treatment of individuals who are being detained (lawfully or otherwise) by the authorities. For example, the following instances of ill-treatment were found by the ECtHR to amount to torture:

- Subjecting prisoners to '*falaka*' (whipping of the soles of the feet) or severe beatings to all parts of the body to extract confessions or other information;[55]
- Subjecting a detainee to 'Palestinian hanging' (being stripped naked and then being suspended by the arms which are tied behind the back), leading to long-term paralysis in both arms;[56]
- Dragging a prisoner along by his hair, making him run along a corridor with police officers positioned on either side to trip him up, making him kneel in front of a young woman, exposing him to a police officer's penis, urinating on him, and threatening him with a blowlamp and then a syringe;[57]
- Force-feeding a prisoner in the absence of medical necessity and where the prisoner had been handcuffed and his mouth held open with a mouth-widener and a tube inserted into his oesophagus with a funnel on the end through which food was poured;[58]
- Keeping a prisoner in solitary confinement for years in a badly ventilated cell without natural light.[59]

Given these examples of torture, the finding of the ECtHR in *Ireland* v. *the United Kingdom* (colloquially known as the 'Hooded Men' case) that the 'interrogation techniques' did not constitute torture is perplexing. As the next subsection will demonstrate, the Court's finding hinged on the concept of 'special stigma' which the Court first developed in that case and, ultimately, utilised to insulate the United Kingdom from a finding of torture.

5.3.3.1 *Ireland* v. *the United Kingdom* and The 'Special Stigma' of Torture

The original complaint stemmed from treatment by soldiers from the UK of alleged IRA suspects[60] during The Troubles.[61] Ireland argued that while the suspects (referred to colloquially as the 'Hooded Men' as they had been forced

[54] *Gäfgen* (n 1) at [90]. [55] *Bati* v. *Turkey* (2006) 42 EHRR 37.

[56] *Aksoy* v. *Turkey* (1997) 23 EHRR 553. [57] *Selmouni* v. *France* [GC] (2000) 29 EHRR 403.

[58] *Nevmerzhitsky* v. *Ukraine* (2006) 43 EHRR 32.

[59] *Ilascu* v. *Moldova and Russia* [GC] (2005) 40 EHRR 46.

[60] Short for the Irish Republican Army or the Provisional Irish Republican Army, the names used by paramilitary groups on the island of Ireland.

[61] A term euphemistically employed to describe decades of civil unrest on the island of Ireland.

to wear hoods by security personnel during their detention and ill-treatment) had been detained by British authorities they had been subject to five specific methods of ill-treatment to extract confessions and other intelligence: being kept hooded; deprived of sleep; deprived of fluids and food; exposed to excessive noise; and forced to stand against a wall in a spreadeagled and painful posture for prolonged periods. At first instance, the Commission found that the infliction of the five techniques constituted torture, holding that:

> the systematic application of the techniques for the purpose of inducing a person to give information shows a clear resemblance to those methods of systematic torture which have been known over the ages. Although the five techniques ... might not necessarily cause any severe after effects the Commission sees in them a modern system of torture falling into the same category as those systems which have been applied in previous times as a means of obtaining information and confessions.[62]

The Irish government subsequently exercised its right to refer the case to the ECtHR, asking it to confirm the finding of torture, *which the UK did not contest*, as well as examine other alleged breaches.[63] Notwithstanding the acceptance by the respondent State of the finding of torture, the ECtHR found that the detainees had been subjected to inhuman and degrading treatment but rejected the Commission's finding that that ill-treatment constituted torture. In reaching that conclusion, the ECtHR observed:

> Although the five techniques, as applied in combination, undoubtedly amounted to inhuman and degrading treatment, although their object was the extraction of confessions, the naming of others and/or information and although they were used systematically, they did not occasion suffering of the particular intensity and cruelty implied by the word torture as so understood.[64]

The Court's conclusion that the ill-treatment of the men did not constitute torture sits at odds with its recognition that a finding of torture fulfils an important role of stigmatising State misconduct. It was accepted by the ECtHR that the five techniques constituted inhuman and/or degrading treatment and were inflicted upon individuals *for the purpose of extracting intelligence.* The State itself did not dispute the Commission's finding of torture before the ECtHR and, based on subsequent case law involving findings of torture, it seems clear that the treatment fits the ECtHR's current conceptualisation of

[62] *Ireland* v. *the United Kingdom*, App. No. 5310/71, Commission decision, 25/1/1976 at [402].

[63] The Commission's findings, which were not made public as was standard at the time, were not binding in the same way that a judgment of the ECtHR was (and is). Thus, a referral by a State such as Ireland which recognised the compulsory jurisdiction of the Court would result in a judicial determination (as opposed to the report of the Commission) which *would* be binding on the parties. See, Deirdre E. Donahue, 'Human Rights in Northern Ireland: Ireland v. the United Kingdom' (1980) 2 Boston College International and Comparative Law Review 385.

[64] *Ireland* v. *the United Kingdom* [1978] 2 ECHR 25 at [167].

torture. Indeed, in the subsequent decision of *Selmouni*, the Grand Chamber noted that had *Ireland* v. *the United Kingdom* been decided today, the Court may well have confirmed the Commission's finding of torture:

> having regard to the fact that the Convention is a 'living instrument which must be interpreted in the light of present-day conditions' . . . the Court considers that certain acts which were classified in the past as 'inhuman and degrading treatment' as opposed to 'torture' could be classified differently in future. It takes the view that the increasingly high standard being required in the area of the protection of human rights and fundamental liberties correspondingly and inevitably requires greater firmness in assessing breaches of the fundamental values of democratic societies.[65]

It has been suggested that the ECtHR's decision in *Ireland* v. *the United Kingdom*, particularly the ECtHR's invocation of the notion of 'special stigma' as a means of demarcating torture in fact 'accommodated British imperial torture'.[66] As Farrell has observed, '[t]he Court introduced the phrase ["stigma"] in a case in which it found no stigma. The Court produced this language to remove the stigma from the specific acts in question. In doing so, the Court saved the UK from stigmatisation.'[67] The ECtHR in *Ireland* also placed significant emphasis on the lack of any enduring injuries in concluding that this was not torture. This focus on physical injury persisted for years, though as cases such as *Aydin*[68] and, more recently, *Diri*[69] indicate, there has been a shift in the ECtHR's perspective to include a consideration of the emotional and psychological consequences of ill-treatment and the intention behind the infliction of the ill-treatment.

Almost forty years after its initial decision, the ECtHR was presented with the opportunity to revisit its findings in *Ireland*. In 2014, the Irish Government notified the ECtHR that documents had been discovered that might have changed the decision of the Court in 1978 had they been known at that time. The Irish Government subsequently requested a revision of the 1978 judgment pursuant to Rule 80 of the Rules of Court which was refused by the ECtHR. The evolution in understanding of what constitutes torture referred to in *Selmouni* had occurred *after* the initial judgment and 'the Court ha[d] to make its assessment [of the State's application for revision] in the light of the case-law on Article 3 of the Convention *as it stood at the time*'.[70] From that point-of-view, the ECtHR in 2018 concluded that the requirements of Rule 80 had not been made out and rejected the application. Accordingly, while '[i]t is likely that the deplorable treatment to which the Hooded Men were subjected

65 *Selmouni* v. *France* (n 57) at [101].

66 Michelle Farrell, 'The Marks of Civilisation: The Special Stigma of Torture' (2022) 22 HRLR 1, p.2.

67 Ibid. 68 *Aydin* v. *Turkey* [GC] (1998) 25 EHRR 251.

69 *Diri* v. *Turkey* [2007] ECHR 683.

70 *Ireland* v. *the United Kingdom* [2018] ECHR 247 at [125]. Emphasis added.

at the hands of the security forces would be characterised today ... as torture',[71] the ECtHR was not convinced that the new evidence would have resulted in such a finding in 1978. The ECtHR's decision, which has been the subject of significant criticism,[72] is perplexing for several reasons, not least given that the Commission had – *at the time* – reached a conclusion that the five techniques constituted torture, *without the benefit of the further evidence.* As Judge O'Leary observed in her dissent in the 2018 judgment:

> In 1978, the Court decided not to draw certain inferences from what was alleged but could not then be proved as being the conduct of the respondent State. In 2018, a majority of the chamber has decided to ignore the bigger picture now available to it on the grounds that the principle of legal certainty must prevail. However, it is difficult to see in what way legal certainty was endangered in a case where a violation of Article 3 had in any event been found, where the respondent State did not contest the Commission finding of torture and where the revision request sought not to call into question the legal principles established but rather their application in the circumstances, now properly demonstrated, of the original case.
>
> In my view, *it was the Court and the Convention system and not the respondent State which was primarily under scrutiny in the context of this revision request.* I regret that my colleagues in Chamber were not able or willing to see this. Revision must remain exceptional and requests should, where appropriate, be defeated by the very legitimate and fundamental principle of legal certainty. However, in the present case it is difficult to avoid the impression that it is the Court which has sought to shelter itself behind that principle. By doing so it risked damaging the authority of the case-law which that principle seeks to safeguard and overlooking its own responsibilities.[73]

Both the 1978 judgment and the 2018 decision concerning ill-treatment at the hands of British security forces at the peak of The Troubles reflect a troubling dilution of the protective potential of Article 3. While inhuman and degrading treatment was found, a finding of torture would not only have served a normative function (by correctly labelling the treatment), it is also important that rights are fully operationalised if they are to be truly effective. Instead, the decisions have arguably operated to shelter the UK from the stigma that, insofar as that term is employed by the ECtHR, ought to be attached to British imperial torture.[74]

As noted, the concept of torture carrying a special stigma was first proposed by the ECtHR in *Ireland* v. *the United Kingdom.* It has since become a fixture of the Court's Article 3 jurisprudence, including in cases involving extraordinary rendition.

[71] *In the Matter of an Application by Margaret McQuillan* [2021] UKSC 55, [2022] AC 1063 at [186] citing Lords Bingham and Hoffmann in *A and Ors* v. *Secretary of State* (n 4) at [53] and [97].

[72] Including by Judge O'Leary who wrote a powerful dissent.

[73] *Ireland* v. *the United Kingdom* (n 70) at [76]–[77], separate dissenting opinion of Judge O'Leary. Emphasis added.

[74] Farrell (n 66).

5.3.3.2 *Extraordinary Rendition*

'Extraordinary rendition' involves 'the extra-judicial transfer of persons from one jurisdiction or State to another, for the purposes of detention and interrogation outside the normal legal system, where there [is] a real risk of torture or cruel, inhuman or degrading treatment'.[75] It was used by US intelligence agents as part of the US's 'War on Terror' following the 9/11 terrorist attacks and the subsequent wars in Afghanistan and Iraq.[76] It is relevant for instant purposes as US operatives used several sites in Council of Europe States to detain, interrogate and move people who had been subject to extraordinary rendition. And, in many of those cases, the relevant States knew (or ought to have known) that individuals within their jurisdiction were being (or were at risk of being) subject to ill-treatment contrary to Article 3 ECHR as part of the US's extraordinary rendition programme.

State responsibility under Article 3 ECHR for the extraordinary rendition practices of the US has arisen primarily in two scenarios. The first involves cases where individuals are being extradited or deported to the US and there is a real risk that they will be subject to extraordinary rendition by US officials. The second involves cases where State authorities knew or ought to have known that individuals within their jurisdiction were being subject to ill-treatment by US officials as part of their extraordinary rendition practices.

In *Babar Ahmad and Ors* v. *the United Kingdom*,[77] the applicants (three British nationals and another man who had been deprived of his British citizenship) sought to resist their extradition from the UK to face trial in the US on terrorism charges on the basis, inter alia, of an alleged real risk that they would be subject to extraordinary rendition. Both the domestic courts and the ECtHR rejected that claim. As the ECtHR observed in its decision on admissibility:

> It would be incompatible with a Contracting State's obligations under the Convention if it were to extradite or otherwise remove an individual from its territory in circumstances where that individual was at real risk of extraordinary rendition. To do so would be to collude in the violation of the most basic rights guaranteed by the Convention.[78]

The Court was, however, satisfied that the assurance provided by US authorities that the applicants would be tried before federal courts with the 'full panoply of rights and protections that would otherwise be available to a defendant' ameliorated any such risk.[79] Any extraordinary rendition before trial would be inimical to that assurance. And, according to the ECtHR, it was

[75] *Babar Ahmad and Ors* v. *the United Kingdom* (2010) 51 EHRR SE6 at [113].

[76] See, for instance, *El-Masri* v. *The Former Yugoslav Republic of Macedonia* [GC] (2013) 57 EHRR 25.

[77] *Babar Ahmad and Ors* v. *the United Kingdom* (n 75). [78] Ibid at [114]. [79] Ibid.

the 'clear intention' of the US authorities that, should the applicants be convicted, they would serve any custodial sentence in a federal prison and, if acquitted, 'it was equally clear' they would be returned to the UK.[80]

Within the second subset of extraordinary rendition cases – those involving allegations of ill-treatment *within* a Council of Europe's jurisdiction – there have been several decisions finding culpability on the part of the State for violations of Article 3 (including findings of torture). Perhaps the most notable decision is the Grand Chamber's judgment in *El-Masri*.[81] The case involved ill-treatment both by Macedonian authorities and then by US authorities on Macedonian territory. The Court found that the applicant had been subject to inhuman and degrading treatment by the Macedonian authorities while being held, incommunicado, for over twenty days in a hotel in Skopje. He was then transferred to an airport where he was 'beaten severely', 'stripped and sodomised with an object'. He was then forcibly marched to a CIA aircraft 'which was surrounded by Macedonian security agents', where he was 'thrown to the floor, chained down and forcibly tranquillised' and, while in that position, transferred to Kabul via Iraq[82] The Court found the State responsible for the actions of the 'special CIA rendition team', concluding that 'the acts complained of were carried out in the presence of officials of the respondent State and within its jurisdiction'.[83] The Government failed to provide any justification for the measures used against the applicant and that, coupled with the fact that they were 'used in combination and with premeditation, the aim being to cause severe pain or suffering in order to obtain information, inflict punishment or intimidate the applicant', led to a finding of torture by the ECtHR which had noted the 'special stigma' that attached to such ill-treatment.[84] The Court also found that the State had exposed the applicant to a real risk of ill-treatment contrary to Article 3 ECHR upon removal from its jurisdiction by transferring him to the US authorities.

Similar findings were made in *Al Nashiri* v. *Poland*.[85] The applicant had been detained for six months in a CIA 'black site' that had been established in Poland, with the State's knowledge and assistance. During that time, he was subjected to various interrogation 'techniques'. This included two mock executions; '[t]he first one was with the use of an unloaded pistol being "cocked" to his head while he was shackled in a sitting position, the second with a power drill while he was forced to stand naked and hooded in his cell'.[86] The applicant was also subjected to 'potentially injurious stress positions'.[87] In finding that the applicant's treatment carried the 'special stigma' of torture, the Court noted that it was premeditated, deliberate and part of a programme 'designed to elicit information or confessions or to obtain intelligence from

[80] Ibid. [81] *El-Masri* v. *The Former Yugoslav Republic of Macedonia* (n 76).
[82] Ibid at [200]–[205]. [83] Ibid at [206]. [84] Ibid at [191] and [211].
[85] *Al Nashiri* v. *Poland* (n 50). [86] Ibid at [511]. [87] Ibid.

captured terrorist suspects'.[88] As with the State in *El-Masri*, the Court found Poland responsible for such treatment under Article 3 ECHR given that it 'knew of the nature and purposes of the CIA's activities on its territory at the material time and cooperated in the preparation and execution of the CIA rendition, secret detention and interrogation operations on its territory'.[89]

5.3.4 'Treatment'

At first blush, whether something constitutes 'treatment' seems relatively straightforward. But, beyond the paradigm examples of a person physically doing something to another – for instance, police officers extracting information through physical violence – what constitutes 'treatment' for the purposes of Article 3 ECHR becomes a little murkier.

As discussed further in Chapter 6, in *Pretty*,[90] Diane Pretty argued that the refusal of the Director of Public Prosecutions to undertake not to prosecute her husband if he were to assist her to die by suicide constituted treatment by the State which violated Article 3 ECHR. The House of Lords firmly rejected that contention:

> the absolute and unqualified prohibition on a member state inflicting the proscribed treatment requires that 'treatment' should not be given an unrestricted or extravagant meaning. It cannot, in my opinion, be plausibly suggested that the Director or any other agent of the United Kingdom is inflicting the proscribed treatment on Mrs Pretty, whose suffering derives from her cruel disease.[91]

The ECtHR was similarly unreceptive to the claim that the UK had subjected Pretty to 'treatment'.[92] In the absence of something done to Pretty to exacerbate her medical condition – as would be the case if, for instance, she was placed in a prison cell that was not equipped for specialist medical equipment[93] or was deported to a country where she would receive inadequate medical care for her condition[94] – there was no 'treatment' attributable to the State (or anyone for that matter).

The approach of the House of Lords and the ECtHR in *Pretty* may be contrasted with the reasons (albeit in obiter dicta) of Lady Hale and Lord Kerr (with whom Lord Wilson agreed) in the *Northern Ireland Abortion Case*.[95] In that case, Lady Hale considered that the risk of prosecution of pregnant

88 Ibid at [515]–[516]. 89 Ibid at [517].

90 *R (Pretty)* v. *Director of Public Prosecutions* [2001] UKHL 61, [2002] 1 AC 800.

91 Ibid at [13]. 92 Ibid at [54]–[55].

93 As occurred in *Price* v. *the United Kingdom* (2002) 34 EHRR 53.

94 In respect of which, see *D* v. *the United Kingdom* (1997) 24 EHRR 423 and, more recently, the UKSC decision in *AM (Zimbabwe)* v. *Secretary of State for the Home Department* [2020] UKSC 17, [2021] AC 633.

95 *Northern Ireland Abortion Case* (n 44). See discussion in Chapter 6.

women and those assisting them in procuring illegal abortions in Northern Ireland constituted 'treatment' by the State. According to Lady Hale '[i]t is the state which is subjecting [the pregnant woman who wants to obtain an abortion in cases of rape, incest or fatal foetal abnormality] to the agonising dilemma' of either procuring an illegal abortion in Northern Ireland or travelling to Great Britain to obtain one.[96] Further, in Lady Hale's opinion, such treatment would reach the minimum level of severity for 'some women' so as to be 'inhuman or degrading'.[97] Lord Kerr similarly observed that:

> At present, a girl or woman who obtains an abortion in circumstances other than those narrowly prescribed by the 1861 and 1945 Acts commits a criminal offence and is liable to prosecution. *That constitutes ill-treatment in so far as imposing that sanction on women amounts to a breach of art.3.* Likewise, requiring a woman to carry to term a foetus who is doomed to die, or a foetus who is the consequence of rape or incest, when the impact on the mother *is inhuman or degrading is, in every sense, treatment to which the woman is subjected by the state.* It is, moreover, treatment which because of its inhumanity or degrading effect, is in violation of article 3.[98]

Further, as with Lady Hale, Lord Kerr (with Lord Wilson) was of the view that the threat of prosecution of those assisting a pregnant woman to obtain an abortion illegally in Northern Ireland constituted treatment of the pregnant woman by the State authorities.[99]

The takeaway from the *Northern Ireland Abortion Case* – at least for instant purposes – is that the concept of 'treatment' as used in Article 3 ECHR may be broader than the House of Lords and ECtHR in *Pretty* were willing to countenance. Abortion, withdrawal/withholding of treatment and assisted dying are examined further in Chapter 6.

The complexity of the concept of 'treatment' is further illuminated in the context of deportation and extradition which are discussed below.

5.3.5 'Punishment'

Article 3 ECHR also prohibits inhuman or degrading *punishment*. A functional legal system, under both its criminal and civil limbs, invariably entails some degree of legitimate punishment (for instance, imprisonment following conviction for a criminal offence). Article 3 ECHR does not preclude these forms of punishment. Rather, the ECtHR has found violations in cases where a person (typically a prisoner) has been subjected to punishment causing suffering or humiliation 'beyond that inevitable element . . . connected with a given form of legitimate . . . punishment'.[100] Whether something is a 'legitimate' form of

[96] Ibid at [33]. [97] Ibid. [98] Ibid at [231], per Lord Kerr. Emphasis added.

[99] Ibid at [232], per Lord Kerr. [100] *Jalloh* v. *Germany* (n 28) at [68].

punishment depends on the circumstances. As the ECtHR observed in *Tyrer* v. *the United Kingdom*:

> It would be absurd to hold that judicial punishment generally, by reason of its usual and perhaps almost inevitable element of humiliation, is 'degrading' within the meaning of Article 3. Some further criterion must be read into the text. Indeed, Article 3 . . ., by expressly prohibiting 'inhuman' and 'degrading' punishment, implies that there is a distinction between such punishment and punishment in general.[101]

While 'judicial punishment generally' may not constitute inhuman or degrading punishment, some forms of 'punishment' are never permitted. For instance, measures of restraint are never to be used as a means of punishment (as opposed to being used to prevent self-harm or serious danger to others).[102] Other forms of disciplinary punishment of detainees, such as solitary or other disciplinary confinement, are not necessarily inherently incompatible with Article 3 ECHR. Rather, the Court will consider the proportionality of the imposition and conditions of the confinement.[103] Consistent with the approach taken by the ECtHR, the UK Supreme Court has rejected the contention that solitary confinement of a minor (i.e. a person under the age of eighteen years) per se violates Article 3 ECHR.[104]

As discussed below, a particular issue that has arisen in the context of Article 3 ECHR has been the imposition of what are said to be grossly disproportionate sentences. While the question of whether a term of imprisonment is appropriate tends to fall within a State's margin of appreciation, where the sentence is grossly disproportionate, it may constitute inhuman or degrading punishment at the moment of its imposition.[105]

5.3.6 Examples of Inhuman and Degrading Treatment and Punishment

After an examination of the constitutive elements of Article 3 ECHR, it is useful to consider some examples of inhuman or degrading treatment or punishment. It is important to emphasise that the following overview of the case law is non-exhaustive and that the circumstances in which Article 3 ECHR is engaged are context-specific. It is also important to observe that whilst the ECtHR has, as discussed above, offered some insights into the meaning of 'inhuman' and 'degrading', the Court does not always identify which is applicable in determining whether there is a violation of Article 3 ECHR and does in fact sometimes simply refer to treatment being 'inhuman and degrading' jointly.

[101] *Tyrer* v. *the United Kingdom* (n 31) at [30].

[102] See, for instance, *Tali* v. *Estonia* [2014] ECHR 294.

[103] See, for instance, *Ramishvili and Kokhreidze* v. *Georgia* [2009] ECHR 153.

[104] *R (AB)* v. *Secretary of State for Justice* [2021] UKSC 28, [2022] AC 487.

[105] See, for instance, *Harkins* v. *the United Kingdom* [GC] (2012) 55 EHRR 19.

5.3.6.1 *Policing*

Many of the cases on inhuman or degrading treatment or punishment have centred on conduct by police. One especially contentious issue is the use of handcuffs; while handcuffing a person will not, per se, contravene Article 3 ECHR, it has been held to be degrading in several cases. For example, in *Erdoğan Yağiz* v. *Turkey* it was held that placing the applicant in handcuffs in a public car park at his place of work and later transporting him to his work and home in handcuffs was degrading as there was no risk of the applicant absconding, causing injury or damaging/supressing evidence.[106] Likewise in *Kashavelov* v. *Bulgaria* it was held that the routine handcuffing of the applicant over many years every time he left his prison cell was degrading.[107] Moreover, consistent with the principle of dignity in Article 3 ECHR, the ECtHR has found that handcuffing the applicant, an asylum seeker living in a transit zone with his family, and attaching him to a leash while he accompanied his pregnant wife to hospital appointments 'diminished his human dignity and [was] . . . degrading'.[108]

Use of force by police during arrest (or while a person is in their custody or otherwise under their control) also raises the possibility of a violation of Article 3 ECHR, particularly where excessive force is used.[109] A slap across the face by a police officer while being held in a police station was found *not* to constitute inhuman treatment because the applicants suffered only minor bodily injuries and had not undergone serious physical or mental suffering. It did, however, amount to degrading treatment. The physical force had not been made strictly necessary by their conduct, thereby diminishing their dignity.[110] This was compounded in the case of the first applicant by the fact that he was a minor at the time and was, thus, especially vulnerable.

5.3.6.2 *Conditions of Detention*

Article 3 ECHR has also frequently featured in cases challenging conditions of detention (which includes prisons but is broader covering, for instance, immigration detention). In one case, the confinement for almost four months of a

[106] *Erdoğan Yağiz* v. *Turkey*, App. No. 27473/02, 06/03/2007.

[107] *Kashavelov* v. *Bulgaria* (2015) 61 EHRR 34.

[108] *H.M. and Ors* v. *Hungary* [2022] ECHR 408.

[109] See, for instance, *Rehbock* v. *Slovenia* [2000] ECHR 645 (Admissibility decision), though contrast with *Berlinski* v. *Poland* [2002] ECHR 505.

[110] *Bouyid* v. *Belgium* (n 24). According to Smet, *Bouyid* demonstrates that the interpretation of Article 3 depends on 'interrelated circumstances of control, powerlessness and vulnerability (Stijn Smet, 'Gäfgen v. Germany: Some Reflections, Ten Years On' *Strasbourg Observers*, 15 April 2020, https://strasbourgobservers.com/2020/04/15/blog-symposium-strasbourg-observers-turns-ten-3-gafgen-v-germany-some-reflections-ten-years-on/.

pregnant woman and her children to the section in a transit zone in which their temporary accommodation was located while they were seeking asylum was such as to cause 'anxiety and psychological disturbance' reaching the minimum level of severity such as to violate Article 3 ECHR.[111] The ECtHR has also held that placing a woman with physical disabilities who used a wheelchair in a cell that was not equipped for her needs, resulting in her not being able to use the toilet and having to sleep in her wheelchair, constituted inhuman treatment.[112]

The forced feeding of prisoners who are on a hunger strike where the medical evidence 'convincingly' shows that such action is necessary to preserve life will not violate Article 3 ECHR. However, the manner by which the prisoner is force fed must not surpass the minimum level of severity.[113] In contrast, the forced administration of an emetic through a nasogastric tube to secure the expulsion of a bag of cocaine while being held down by police officers for the purpose of procuring evidence of a crime as opposed to medical necessity constituted inhuman and degrading treatment.[114]

Generally, there is a presumption of inhuman and degrading treatment when the personal space available to a detainee falls below 3 square metres in multi-occupancy accomodation. The State bears the burden of displacing this presumption and can do so by demonstrating that there were factors capable of compensating for the lack of personal space, such as access to outside areas.[115]

Several cases before the ECtHR have centred on the alleged conditions in 'supermax' prisons in the US. In *Babar Ahmad and Others* v. *the United Kingdom*,[116] the applicants alleged that their detention in a supermax prison in the US would result in ill-treatment such that their extradition would violate Article 3 ECHR. In considering the applicants' complaint, the ECtHR noted that States 'must ensure that a person is detained under conditions which are compatible with respect for his human dignity' and, in the particular context of solitary confinement (a feature of supermax prisons), 'complete sensory isolation, coupled with total social isolation, can destroy the personality and constitutes a form of inhuman treatment which cannot be justified by the requirements of security or any other reason'.[117] In less extreme cases of solitary confinement, Article 3 ECHR may nevertheless be engaged,

[111] *R.R. and Ors* v. *Hungary* [2021] ECHR 173 at [63]. Note that the ECtHR did not specify whether this was inhuman or degrading. This is not uncommon; the Court often finds a violation of Article 3 without specifying whether the treatment is inhuman or degrading or both.

[112] *Price* v. *the United Kingdom* (2002) 34 EHRR 53.

[113] See, for instance, *Ciorap* v. *Moldova* [2007] ECHR 502 at [77].

[114] *Jalloh* v. *Germany* (n 28).

[115] See, for instance, *Muršić* v. *Croatia* (n 22) at [106].

[116] *Babar Ahmad and Ors* v. *the United Kingdom* (n 75).

[117] Ibid at [202] and [206].

however this ‘depends on the particular conditions, the stringency of the measure, its duration, the objective pursued and its effects on the person concerned’.[118] Similarly, access to recreational facilities and outdoor exercise may be relevant to the Court’s assessment of the conditions of detention and their compliance with Article 3 ECHR.[119] In finding that detention in a specific supermax prison in the US would *not* violate Article 3 ECHR in the applicants’ cases, the ECtHR noted that while they would be subject to isolation it would be ‘partial and relative’ and there was no evidence that the psychiatric services available in the supermax prison would be unable to treat the mental health conditions with which the applicants had been diagnosed. Their extradition would, thus, not violate Article 3 ECHR.

5.3.6.3 *Examples of the Wider Application of Article 3 ECHR*

The preceding examples are perhaps what one would expect in terms of the application of Article 3 ECHR in the policing and detention contexts, but Article 3 ECHR has a much wider scope. Thus, the deliberate destruction of people’s homes, carried out without warning and without regard to their safety or welfare and thereby depriving them of their livelihood and shelter, constituted inhuman treatment.[120] The ECtHR has also held that withdrawing support from asylum seekers thereby leaving them without any financial support (as they were legally precluded from seeking paid employment) constitutes treatment reaching the minimum level of severity in violation of Article 3 ECHR.[121] In the absence of any support, the claimants were forced to sleep in the open (or were at risk of having to do so), they were left seriously hungry and unable to satisfy even the most basic hygiene requirements, including sanitary products. This was both inhuman and degrading treatment in violation of Article 3 ECHR.

In terms of *punishment* reaching the Article 3 ECHR threshold, the Court held that forcing a conscript to perform 350 knee bends – notwithstanding his known medical issues – leading to his collapse and necessitating medical treatment, constituted inhuman punishment.[122] And, the infliction of corporal punishment (the striking of naked buttocks with birch) on a student while being held by two police officers constituted degrading punishment.[123]

The variability in the forms of ill-treatment found to constitute inhuman or degrading treatment or punishment is reflective of the flexibility of Article 3

[118] Ibid at [209]. [119] Ibid at [213]–[214].

[120] *Selçuk and Asker* v. *Turkey* (1998) 26 EHRR 477.

[121] *R (Adam and Ors)* v. *Secretary of State for the Home Department* [2005] UKHL 66, [2006] 1 AC 396.

[122] *Chember* v. *Russia* [2008] ECHR 591. [123] *Tyrer* v. *the United Kingdom* (n 31).

ECHR. It is also demonstrative of the changing nature of the ECHR. The litigation involving the 'Hooded Men' in *Ireland* v. *the United Kingdom* (considered above) is a further example of the evolving conceptualisation of Article 3 and a useful demonstration of both the potential and the limitations of the ECHR as a means of protecting individuals vulnerable to mistreatment by security personnel.

Having considered the meaning, scope and limitations of the substantive elements of Article 3 ECHR, the next section will examine the nature of the State's obligations under the Article.

5.4 STATE OBLIGATIONS UNDER ARTICLE 3 ECHR

As with other rights in the ECHR (see Article 2 discussed in Chapter 4 and Article 4 which is canvassed in Chapter 7), Article 3 ECHR not only imposes a negative obligation on the State not to subject individuals within its territory to ill-treatment; Article 3 ECHR, when read together with Article 1, also imposes positive obligations on the State to take steps to deter ill-treatment and, in certain circumstances, to protect individuals from ill-treatment perpetrated by third parties. As with Articles 2 and 4 ECHR, States have a duty under Article 3 ECHR to conduct an effective investigation into alleged ill-treatment. This secion considers these obligations in greater detail, culminating in an examination of how they have evolved and are applied in the contexts of domestic abuse and border pushbacks.

5.4.1 Negative Obligation

The negative obligation is deceptively simple: States must not subject individuals to torture or to inhuman or degrading treatment or punishment. Yet as Section 5.3 of this chapter revealed, what constitutes torture, or inhuman or degrading treatment or punishment is not always clear and reasonable people can and do disagree as to the scope and meaning of the substantive components of Article 3 ECHR. Moreover, there is also the question of whether the prohibition is, in fact, absolute. The preceding section necessarily included a discussion of conduct that would violate the State's negative obligation under Article 3 ECHR (the prototypical being the infliction of serious physical injury upon a person by security forces for the purposes of extracting evidence). In the ensuing section, the State's negative obligation not to expose individuals to a real risk of ill-treatment at the hands of a third party via deportation or extradition is considered. As will be discussed, the ECtHR's jurisprudence in this context suggests that, contrary to the ECtHR's contentions in *Gäfgen*, the protections in Article 3 ECHR may not be absolute.

5.4.1.1 *Extradition/Deportation*

Deportation and extradition cases are different to those considered above in the sense that they involve allegations of potential ill-treatment *in a third-party State*, often one that is not a Member State of the Council of Europe. That is, it is not the sending State that is (or will be) directly inflicting ill-treatment upon the individual (for instance, the death penalty, or a lack of adequate medical treatment). However, the ECtHR has found that Article 3 ECHR operates to preclude the removal of individuals where there are substantial grounds for believing that there is a real risk that they will be subject to ill-treatment contrary to Article 3 in the receiving state (see above discussion of this obligation in the context of extraordinary rendition). Given that the ECHR does not apply beyond the jurisdiction of a Contracting State, the imposition of Convention standards and obligations in the context of deportation and extradition has been the subject of heated debate before the domestic courts and the ECtHR and in academic writing on the topic.[124]

This section considers the issues that arise in removal cases in two specific contexts. These specifc examples illuminate the legal principles and the wider normative implications of removal of individuals from Contracting States for the alleged absoluteness of Article 3 ECHR and the universality (or not) of human rights. The first issue concerns the law as it pertains to removal where, because of the medical condition of the individual being removed, there are 'substantial grounds for believing' that there is a 'real and immediate risk' of ill-treatment contrary to Article 3 ECHR. The second example centres on the law as it pertains to extradition of individuals where there are substantial grounds for believing that they will be sentenced to life imprisonment without the prospect of parole. In recent years, the Grand Chamber has clarified (or at least sought to clarify) the legal principles applicable in both scenarios. There are, of course, many other situations involving removal that may engage Article 3 ECHR[125] but these two scenarios provide a useful insight into the contradictory approaches taken by the domestic courts and the ECtHR in such cases.

5.4.1.1.1 *The General Principles Applicable to Deportation and Extradition Cases*

Significant confusion (both in the jurisprudence and the academic literature) has surrounded the legal principles and standards applicable to cases

[124] See, for instance, Natasa Mavronicola and Francesco Messineo, 'Relatively Absolute? The Undermining of Article 3 ECHR in *Ahmad v UK*' (2013) **76** MLR 3.

[125] Including, for instance, where characteristics of the individual being removed (such as their ethnicity, gender, sexuality, religion and so on) are said to expose them to the real risk of ill-treatment upon their return (for example, *Khasanov and Rakhmanov* v. *Russia* [GC] [2022] ECHR 331). See Section 5.3.3.2 above in the context of extraordinary rendition.

involving removal where there are substantial grounds for believing that the person being removed will face ill-treatment that would, if inflicted in the sending State, reach the minimum level of severity under Article 3 ECHR. This is particularly so in cases involving the possibility of the returnee being subjected to a 'grossly disproportionate' prison sentence, which is usually a term of imprisonment without the prospect of parole (also known as 'whole life sentences'). To understand such cases however, it is necessary to briefly summarise the evolution of the law in the context of removal and Article 3 ECHR and the general principles enunciated by the ECtHR.

In the landmark decision of *Soering* v. *the United Kingdom*,[126] the ECtHR was confronted with the question of whether the UK, in agreeing to extradite the applicant to Virginia (United States) where there were substantial grounds for believing that he would be sentenced to the death penalty following his conviction for murder, would violate Article 3 ECHR. The Court held that extraditing the applicant *would* violate Article 3 ECHR. At this point in time, Protocol No.6 (which prohibits the death penalty during peacetime) had not been enacted and, as a result, no issue arose under Article 2 ECHR.[127] However, the ECtHR accepted evidence of what was termed the 'death row phenomenon' in the US, which referred to the likely long delay of many years between the passing of a sentence of death and the execution of the sentence. This, the ECtHR accepted, would expose the applicant to 'anguish and mounting tension of living in the ever-present shadow of death' which, when taking into account the applicant's youth at the time of the killings (he was eighteen years old) and his 'impaired mental responsibility' for the acts, 'would expose him to a real risk of treatment going beyond the threshold set by Article 3'.[128] In reaching that conclusion the ECtHR outlined the principles applicable in such cases:

> In sum, the decision by a Contracting State to extradite a fugitive may give rise to an issue under Article 3, and hence engage the responsibility of that State under the Convention, *where substantial grounds have been shown for believing that the person concerned, if extradited, faces a real risk of being subjected to torture or to inhuman or degrading treatment or punishment in the requesting country.* The establishment of such responsibility inevitably involves an assessment of conditions in the requesting country against the standards of Article 3 of the Convention. Nonetheless, there is no question of adjudicating on or establishing the responsibility of the receiving country, whether under general international law, under the Convention or otherwise. *In so far as any liability under the Convention is or may be incurred, it is liability incurred by the extraditing Contracting State by reason of its having taken action which has as a direct consequence the exposure of an individual to proscribed ill-treatment.*[129]

[126] *Soering* v. *the United Kingdom* (1989) 11 EHRR 439.

[127] For more on the evolution of Article 2 in the context of the death penalty, see Chapter 4.

[128] *Soering* v. *the United Kingdom* (n 126) at [106], [108] and [111].

[129] Ibid at [91]. Emphasis added.

Consistent with *Soering*, the ECtHR held in *Al-Saadoon and Mufdhi* v. *the United Kingdom*[130] that to return the applicants to Iraq where there were substantial grounds to believe that they were at a real risk of being subjected to the death penalty would violate Article 3 ECHR. This is because '[w]hatever the method of execution, the extinction of life involves some physical pain. In addition, the foreknowledge of death at the hands of the State must inevitably give rise to intense psychological suffering'.[131] Recalling that at the time of *Soering*, the death penalty was not inconsistent with Article 2 ECHR, by the time of *Al-Saadoon* developments in State practice regarding the death penalty (in particular, the ratification of Protocol No.13 (the abolition of the death penalty in times of war) by almost all Member States) led the ECtHR to conclude that Article 2(1) ECHR had been amended to prohibit the death penalty in all circumstances and, as a result, Article 2 did not 'act as a bar' to a finding that the death penalty itself constituted inhuman or degrading treatment.[132]

As cases such as *Soering* and *Al-Saadoon* illuminate, the State removing the individual is 'not being held responsible for the acts of another state but [rather] for the facilitation, through the process of extradition [or deportation], of a denial of the applicant's rights by another state'.[133] It is for this reason that the returning or deporting State can discharge its obligation under Article 3 ECHR by securing assurances from the receiving State that the individual will not be subject to ill-treatment reaching the Article 3 ECHR threshold upon their return.[134] However, while it may seem as though we are discussing a State's positive protective obligation in such cases – that is, the State's duty to protect an individual from being subjected to ill-treatment at the hands of a third party, about which see below – the ECtHR has clarified that in removal cases, we are in fact discussing the sending State's *negative* obligation not to subject an individual to the *risk* of ill-treatment.[135]

Beyond the early death penalty cases, the ECtHR has also held States responsible for violations of Article 3 ECHR in the context of removals where there were substantial grounds for believing that there was a real risk that the individual would be exposed to physical or other forms of ill-treatment which would meet the minimum level of severity.[136] Several of those cases involved the UK. Thus, in *Chahal* v. *the United Kingdom*,[137] the Grand Chamber held that removal of the first

[130] *Al-Saadoon and Mufdhi* v. *the United Kingdom* (2010) 51 EHRR 9.

[131] Ibid at [115]. See also, *Chahal* v. *the United Kingdom* [GC] (1997) 23 EHRR 413.

[132] *Al-Saadoon and Mufdhi* v. *the United Kingdom* (n 130) at [120].

[133] James O'Reilly (ed), *Human Rights and Constitutional Law: Essays in Honour of Brian Walsh* (Round Hall Press, 1992), p.97.

[134] See, for instance, *Othman (Abu Qatada)* v. *the United Kingdom* (2012) 55 EHRR 1 at [189].

[135] *Paposhvili* v. *Belgium* [GC] [2016] ECHR 1113 at [188].

[136] See, for instance, *Chahal* v. *the United Kingdom* (n 131), *MSS* v. *Belgium and Greece* [GC] (2011) 53 EHRR 2, *Saadi* v. *Italy* [GC] (2009) 49 EHRR 30, *Aswat* v. *the United Kingdom* (2014) 58 EHRR 1, *Al Nashiri* v. *Poland* (n 50), *N* v. *Sweden*, App. No. 23505/09, 20/07/2010.

[137] *Chahal* v. *the United Kingdom* (n 131).

applicant would violate Article 3 ECHR as there was evidence that, because of his political and religious activities in the UK (he was a leading figure in the Sikh community), he was at a real risk of being subject to ill-treatment if returned to India. Notably, the Court rejected the UK Government's argument that Article 3 ECHR applied in an attenuated form in removal cases, where the individual's removal was for the purposes of protecting national security (as it was alleged to be necessary in respect of the first applicant). The Court noted that 'the activities of the individual in question, however undesirable or dangerous, cannot be a material consideration' when determining whether their removal would violate Article 3 ECHR; there is no 'room for balancing the risk of ill-treatment against the reasons for expulsion in determining whether a State's responsibility under Article 3 . . . is engaged'.[138]

A central issue in *Chahal* was whether the provision of assurances by authorities in India that the applicant would not be subject to ill-treatment was sufficient for the UK to meet its Article 3 ECHR obligations should it proceed with the applicant's removal. The Grand Chamber was 'not persuaded that the assurances would provide Mr Chahal with an adequate guarantee of safety' and his removal would, thus, violate Article 3 ECHR.[139]

The question of assurances also featured heavily in the ECtHR's decision in *Othman (Abu Qatada)* v. *the United Kingdom*.[140] In that case, the ECtHR held that the assurances provided by the Jordanian authorities *were* sufficient to discharge the UK's Article 3 ECHR obligations in removing the applicant. Significantly, the ECtHR set out several factors that are relevant to the Court's assessment of 'the quality of assurances given and, second, whether, in light of the receiving State's practices they can be relied upon'.[141] These factors are:

- Whether the terms of the assurance(s) have been disclosed to the Court and whether they are specific or vague/ambiguous;
- Whether the person giving the assurances can bind the receiving State;
- Whether local authorities can be expected to comply with any assurances given by the central government in the receiving State;
- The legality under the domestic law of the receiving State of any treatment which is the subject of the assurance(s);
- Whether the receiving State is a Contracting State;
- The 'length and strength' of the bilateral relationship between the sending and receiving States, including the receiving State's record in complying with similar assurances;
- Whether the receiving State's compliance with the assurances can be objectively verified;
- Whether there is an 'effective system of protection against torture' in the receiving State;

[138] Ibid at [80]–[81]. [139] Ibid at [105].

[140] *Othman (Abu Qatada)* v. *the United Kingdom* (n 134). [141] Ibid at [189].

- Any evidence that the applicant has previously been ill-treated in the receiving State;
- Whether the domestic courts/authorities have examined the reliability of the assurances.[142]

As noted, having regard to those factors, the ECtHR was satisfied that the assurances offered by the Jordanian authorities were sufficient for the UK to discharge its Article 3 ECHR obligations in extraditing the applicant.

The function of assurances or agreements with receiving States was relevant to proceedings before the UK Supreme Court in *AAA* in respect of the former Government's Rwanda asylum policy.[143] The background to *AAA* was that the Conservative Government had entered into an agreement with Rwanda that would see the latter take individuals who had had their asylum claims deemed inadmissible in the UK on the basis that they had had the opportunity to apply for asylum in a safe third country but had not done so. Under UK law such individuals could be removed to the safe third country where the opportunity arose (if that country was willing to accept them), or to any other safe third country which agreed to accept the individuals. The Rwanda policy was premised upon the designation of Rwanda as a safe third country which had agreed to accept such individuals. The legality of the policy was thus contingent on whether Rwanda was in fact a 'safe third country' for these purposes and this was what was at issue in *AAA*. In this respect the applicants cited evidence – including from the United Nations High Commissioner for Refugees (UNHCR) – that they argued demonstrated 'substantial grounds for believing that a person, if relocated to Rwanda, would face a real risk of treatment that is likely to be contrary to article 3' (i.e. refoulement).[144] The Supreme Court unanimously agreed that this evidence was of 'particular significance' due to the status, role, expertise and experience of the UNHCR in Rwanda, and the fact that its evidence was 'essentially uncontradicted by any cogent evidence to the contrary'.[145] The Supreme Court unanimously held that there *were* substantial grounds for believing that individuals sent to Rwanda would be at a real risk of refoulement, notwithstanding the undertakings that had been made by the Rwandan authorities in the Memorandum of Understanding that was entered into between the two countries. Given the hostility which successive Governments have demonstrated towards the ECHR and the ECtHR in recent years, it is notable that the Supreme Court emphasised that:

> The principle of non-refoulement is . . . given effect not only by the ECHR but also by other international conventions to which the United Kingdom is party. It is a core

[142] Ibid.

[143] *R (On the application of AAA and others)* v. *Secretary of State for the Home Department* [2023] UKSC 42, [2023] 1 WLR 4433.

[144] Ibid at [3] and [6].

[145] Ibid at [64] and [70].

principle of international law, to which the United Kingdom government has repeatedly committed itself on the international stage, consistently with this country's reputation for developing and upholding the rule of law.[146]

Despite a robust judgment from the Supreme Court this was not the end of the matter.[147] The agreement between the UK and Rwanda was made into a treaty, and the Safety of Rwanda (Asylum and Immigration) Act 2024 ('Safety of Rwanda Act') enacted which compelled all decision makers (including judicial bodies reviewing immigration decisions) to treat Rwanda as a safe country. The Safety of Rwanda Act also prohibited courts and tribunals from considering any claim or complaint that Rwanda would or might violate the principle of non-refoulement.[148] The Safety of Rwanda Act also disapplied the key provisions of the HRA 1998 and it conferred a discretion on Ministers as to whether they complied with an interim measure issued by the ECtHR.[149] The Act clearly raised significant concerns for the UK's compliance with the ECHR. In particular, transposing the Memorandum of Understanding into a treaty did not address the evidence that the Supreme Court cited in finding that Rwanda was not a safe country. Such concerns may well be moot with the Labour Government appearing to make good on its vow to 'scrap' the Rwanda plan[150] though, as currently drafted, the Border Security, Asylum and Immigration Bill will repeal the Safety of Rwanda Act in its entirety.

In terms of the burden and standard of proof in cases involving removal, the applicant bears the initial burden of 'adduc[ing] evidence capable of demonstrating that there are substantial grounds for believing that, if the measure complained of were to be implemented [for instance, deportation], they would be exposed to a real risk of being subjected to treatment contrary to Article 3'.[151] Given the inherently speculative nature of such risks, the evidential obligation does *not* require of applicants that they provide 'clear proof . . . that they will be exposed to proscribed treatment'.[152] Once the applicant has adduced sufficient evidence, the burden shifts to the State to 'dispel any doubts raised by it':

The risk alleged must be subjected to close scrutiny . . . in the course of which the authorities in the returning State must consider the foreseeable consequences of removal for the individual concerned in the receiving State, in the light of the general

[146] Ibid at [26].

[147] See Chapter 2 (The Human Rights Law Framework in the UK) for further discussion.

[148] Safety of Rwanda (Asylum and Immigration) Act 2024, s.2.

[149] Ibid, ss.4 and 5. See Chapter 2 for a discussion of the HRA 1998 and Chapter 3 for a discussion of interim measures.

[150] Labour Party Manifesto, 'Change', https://labour.org.uk/wp-content/uploads/2024/06/Labour-Party-manifesto-2024.pdf, p.17.

[151] *Paposhvili* v. *Belgium* (n 135) at [186]. [152] Ibid.

> situation there and the individual's personal circumstances . . . The assessment of the risk . . . must therefore take into consideration general sources such as reports of the World Health Organisation or of reputable non-governmental organisations and the medical certificates concerning the person in question.[153]

Evidence should be assessed at the time of removal (or, if the individual is still in the Contracting State, at the time of the ECtHR's consideration of the issue).[154]

Having considered the principles applicable generally in cases involving removal, the next section examines how such principles have been applied in cases where there is evidence that an individual will not receive adequate medical treatment in the receiving country and in cases where the individual being extradited faces the real risk of being sentenced to life without the prospect of parole.

5.4.1.1.2 *Extradition and Deportation of Persons with Medical Conditions*

The UK Supreme Court considered whether a person cannot be returned because of a medical condition in *AM (Zimbabwe).*[155] The Court held that a person opposing removal on the grounds of serious illness must adduce evidence which demonstrates 'substantial' grounds for believing that it is a 'very exceptional' case because of a 'real risk' of being subjected to inhuman treatment.[156] The obligation on the applicant is to 'raise a "prima facie case" of potential infringement of article 3. This means a case which, if not challenged or countered, would establish the infringement.'[157] In reaching that conclusion, the Court had to consider the implications of *Paposhvili* v. *Belgium*[158] in which the Grand Chamber held that a State may violate Article 3 ECHR in:

> situations involving the removal of a seriously ill person in which substantial grounds have been shown for believing that he or she, *although not at imminent risk of dying*, would face a *real risk*, on account of the *absence of appropriate treatment* in the receiving country *or the lack of access to such treatment*, of *being exposed to a serious, rapid and irreversible decline* in his or her state of health *resulting in intense suffering or to a significant reduction in life expectancy.*[159]

In contemplating what is meant by 'significant reduction in life expectancy' in *AM,* Lord Wilson (with whom the rest of the Supreme Court agreed) held:

> Like the skin of a chameleon, the adjective ['significant'] takes a different colour so as to suit a different context. Here the general context is inhuman treatment; and the

[153] Ibid at [187]. References omitted.

[154] *Al-Saadoon and Mufdhi* v. *the United Kingdom* (n 130) at [125] and *Sanchez-Sanchez* v. *the United Kingdom* [GC] (2023) 76 EHRR 16 at [88].

[155] *AM (Zimbabwe)* (n 94). [156] Ibid at [32]. [157] Ibid.

[158] *Paposhvili* v. *Belgium* (n 135). [159] Ibid at [183]. Emphasis added.

> particular context is that the alternative to 'a significant reduction in life expectancy' is 'a serious, rapid and irreversible decline in . . . health resulting in intense suffering'. From these contexts the adjective takes its colour. The word 'significant' often means something less than the word 'substantial'. In context, however, it must in my view mean substantial. Indeed, were a reduction in life expectancy to be less than substantial, it would not attain the minimum level of severity which article 3 requires. Surely the Court of Appeal was correct to suggest, albeit in words too extreme, that a reduction in life expectancy to death in the near future is more likely to be significant than any other reduction. But even a reduction to death in the near future might be significant for one person but not for another. Take a person aged 74, with an expectancy of life normal for that age. Were that person's expectancy be reduced to, say, two years, the reduction might well – in this context – not be significant. But compare that person with one aged 24 with an expectancy of life normal for that age. Were his or her expectancy to be reduced to two years, the reduction might well be significant.[160]

The Supreme Court also outlined the procedural obligations on returning States in cases involving serious illness where the applicant had met the burden of adducing evidence 'capable of demonstrating that there are substantial grounds for believing' that, if removed, they would be exposed to a real risk of subjection to treatment contrary to Article 3 ECHR.[161]

Following *AM*, the Grand Chamber confirmed in *Savran*[162] the principles enunciated in *Paposhvili* and reaffirmed in *AM*, namely that the *negative* obligation on States not to expose individuals to a real risk of ill-treatment in a receiving State by deporting or extraditing them is not confined to cases where the individual is close to death. Rather, the obligation not to remove an individual due to their medical condition can arise in 'very exceptional cases' where the individual is 'seriously ill' and where there is a real risk that the individual will, given the absence of appropriate treatment, be exposed to a 'serious, rapid and irreversible decline in his or her state of health resulting in intense suffering or to a significant reduction in life expectancy'.[163] Indeed, in *Savran* the Grand Chamber confirmed that these principles apply to individuals suffering from a mental illness, though in that case a majority of the ECtHR held that the applicant's deportation would not violate Article 3 ECHR as the risk of the applicant, who had been diagnosed with paranoid schizophrenia, relapsing and the resulting 'significantly higher risk of offences against the person of others' did not constitute 'intense suffering' for the applicant.[164] The Court, did, however find that the applicant's exclusion from Denmark violated Article 8 ECHR.[165]

[160] *AM (Zimbabwe)* (n 94) at [31]. [161] Ibid at [23].

[162] *Savran* v. *Denmark* [GC] [2021] ECHR 1025. [163] Ibid at [133]–[136].

[164] Ibid at [137]–[144]. [165] See Chapter 9 for a discussion of the Article 8 findings.

While the issues considered thus far have not, at least overtly, challenged the absoluteness of Article 3 ECHR, the ECtHR's case law regarding extradition to face whole life sentences (or sentences of life imprisonment without the prospect of parole) raises doubts as to whether Article 3 ECHR is, in all instances, absolute.

5.4.1.1.3 *Extradition and 'Grossly Disproportionate' Sentences*

As noted at the outset of this section, confusion has historically surrounded the principles applicable in cases involving extradition to face trial (or following trial) where there is a real risk the individual will be subjected to a 'grossly disproportionate' sentence. In November 2022, the Grand Chamber, in a unanimous judgment in *Sanchez-Sanchez* v. *the United Kingdom*,[166] clarified the relevant principles.

The facts of *Sanchez-Sanchez* can be briefly stated: the US authorities sought the extradition of the applicant to face federal charges relating to serious drug trafficking offences.[167] If convicted, there was a possibility that the applicant would be sentenced to life without parole. The High Court held that the applicant's extradition would not violate Article 3 ECHR as there were avenues for release, in particular clemency or compassionate release. In rejecting the applicant's appeal, the Divisional High Court detailed the existing domestic and ECtHR jurisprudence in this area, determining that the current position is that extradition to face a term of imprisonment without the prospect of parole does not violate Article 3 ECHR provided the sentence is de jure and de facto reducible. It held that in the case of federal whole life sentences in the US (such as that faced by the applicant) this is satisfied as there is the prospect of presidential clemency.

To fully understand the implications of the decision in *Sanchez-Sanchez*, it is necessary to consider the cases that preceded the judgment as they provide important insights into the alleged absoluteness of Article 3 ECHR. The evolution of the case law in this context is significant for several reasons. First, it illuminates the dialogical nature of the relationship between the domestic courts and the ECtHR (in respect of which, see Chapters 2 and 3). Second, the jurisprudence – in both the domestic courts and the ECtHR, at least prior to *Sanchez-Sanchez* – espouses principles which appear to contradict the purported absoluteness of Article 3 ECHR.

The line of authority leading to *Sanchez-Sanchez* starts in earnest with the ECtHR's judgment in *Kafkaris* in which it held that a life sentence was not, per se, incompatible with Article 3 ECHR but an irreducible one *could* raise an issue under Article 3 ECHR. In this regard, the Court stated that '[t]he question whether a sentence was irreducible depended on whether a life prisoner had

[166] *Sanchez-Sanchez* v. *the United Kingdom* (n 154).

[167] *Sanchez* v. *Government of the United States of America* [2020] EWHC 508 (Admin).

any prospect of release. If the sentence was de facto and de jure reducible, that would satisfy Art.3. The mere fact that such a sentence might be served in full did not make it irreducible.'[168] The House of Lords had cause to consider *Kafkaris* shortly after its delivery, in the case of *Wellington*[169] which concerned an application by the State of Missouri for the extradition of Wellington to face charges of murder. The penalties for the charges under Missouri law at the time were death or imprisonment for life without the prospect of parole. The Missouri authorities gave an undertaking that the applicant would not face the death penalty if convicted and, on that basis, the Home Secretary ordered his extradition. The issue before the House of Lords was whether the risk of a term of imprisonment without the prospect of parole (save for clemency of the Governor) was such that the UK could not extradite Wellington without violating its negative obligation under Article 3 ECHR.

In rejecting Wellington's appeal, a majority of the House of Lords held that, unlike in other cases involving Article 3 ECHR (and in direct contradiction to the supposedly absolute nature of the right), in cases involving punishment in a different country, Article 3 ECHR applies in an 'attenuated form'.[170] Thus, 'even if the sentence is irreducible and might therefore contravene article 3 *if imposed in the United Kingdom*, there remains the question of whether it would contravene article 3 as interpreted in the context of extradition'.[171] In such cases, according to the majority, an issue under Article 3 ECHR arises *only* if the 'sentence was likely, on the facts of the case, to be clearly disproportionate'.[172] In justifying this approach, Lord Hoffmann observed that '[a] *relativist approach* to the scope of article 3 seems to me *essential* if extradition is to continue to function'.[173]

In contrast to Lord Hoffmann's 'relativist approach' (i.e. an approach that takes into account the importance of extradition and the diplomatic and political importance of sustaining a cooperative relationship with other countries – i.e. the purpose of the ill-treatment), Lords Brown and Scott adopted an 'absolutist approach' holding that treatment which would violate Article 3 ECHR if imposed in a domestic context violates Article 3 ECHR even if it takes place in a third party country.[174] As Lord Scott observed:

> It is accepted that the absolute nature of the Article 3 bar on torture would bar extradition to a country where the extradited person would face torture and that that which would constitute torture for Article 3 purposes in Europe would constitute torture for those purposes everywhere. But it is suggested that treatment or

[168] *Kafkaris* v. *Cyprus* [GC] (2009) 49 EHRR 35 at [38].

[169] *R (Wellington)* v. *Secretary of State for the Home Department* [2008] UKHL 72, [2009] AC 335.

[170] Ibid at [28], per Lord Hoffmann. [171] Ibid at [35], per Lord Hoffmann. Emphasis added.

[172] Ibid. [173] Ibid at [28], per Lord Hoffmann. Emphasis added.

[174] Ibid at [39], per Lord Scott (agreeing with Lord Brown).

punishment that might for Article 3 purposes be inhuman or degrading in Europe would not necessarily need to be so categorised if it were treatment or punishment likely to be faced in the requesting country by a person faced with extradition to that country for crimes committed there. *But, if that is so, how can it be said that Article 3 rights not to be subjected to inhuman or degrading treatment are absolute rights? If, in an extradition context they can be 'relativist' rights, why should they not also be 'relativist' rights in other contexts where the public interest were equally engaged and would be advanced by the removal to his home country of the individual in question? This might often be so in immigration or deportation cases.*[175]

As Lord Scott further noted, 'the language of the Article provides no basis at all for distinguishing between that which would qualify as sufficiently inhuman or degrading, and therefore prohibited by Article 3, in an extradition context and that which would be prohibited by Article 3 in a domestic context'.[176]

While both Lords Brown and Scott adopted an 'absolutist approach', they nevertheless concluded that an irreducible sentence is not, per se, incompatible with Article 3. Rather, if the sentence was 'so grossly disproportionate to the circumstances of the crime as to offend ordinary notions of fairness and justice' it would violate Article 3.[177] That was not the case in respect of Wellington.

The ECtHR was given the opportunity to clarify whether the relativist approach espoused in *Wellington* was compatible with Article 3 ECHR in *Harkins* v. *the United Kingdom.*[178] UK authorities had agreed to a request that the applicants be extradited to the US where they faced murder charges. Given assurances from the US authorities that the death penalty would not be sought, the maximum penalty the applicants faced if convicted was life imprisonment without parole. The applicants complained that the relativist approach taken by the domestic courts was incompatible with Article 3 ECHR and that life imprisonment without the prospect of parole, subject only to commutation by the authorities, was grossly disproportionate and therefore violated Article 3 ECHR. In finding that there was no violation, the ECtHR held that in a case of extradition where there is a real risk of a discretionary or mandatory sentence of life imprisonment without parole, an issue under Article 3 ECHR will arise if it can be shown either:

(a) That the sentence is, at the time it is imposed (or likely to be imposed), grossly disproportionate to the crime (alleged to have been) committed; or,
(b) that the applicant's continued imprisonment can no longer be justified on any legitimate penological grounds (such as punishment, deterrence, public protection or rehabilitation) *and* the sentence is irreducible de facto and de jure.[179]

[175] Ibid at [40], per Lord Scott. Emphasis added. [176] Ibid at [42], per Lord Scott.
[177] Ibid at [45], per Lord Scott. [178] *Harkins* v. *the United Kingdom* (n 105).
[179] Ibid at [137] and [138].

As there was the prospect of commutation of a sentence of life imprisonment without parole and given the severity of the crimes with which the applicants were charged, neither ground was made out. Consequently, extradition of the applicants would not violate Article 3 ECHR.

Harkins is also notable for what the ECtHR said in respect of the relativist approach adopted in *Wellington.* While the ECtHR reiterated that the conduct of the person being removed from a Contracting State could not factor in the assessment of whether there was a real risk of ill-treatment in the receiving State,[180] it nevertheless expressly endorsed Lord Brown's reasoning in *Wellington* 'that the absolute nature of Article 3 does not mean that any form of ill-treatment will act as a bar to removal from a Contracting State.'[181] The ECtHR subsequently confirmed the relativist approach in removal contexts in the case of *Babar Ahmad and Ors* v. *the United Kingdom* wherein the Court held that:

> treatment which might violate Article 3 because of an act or omission of a Contracting State might not attain the minimum level of severity which is required for there to be a violation of Article 3 in an expulsion or extradition case. For example, a Contracting State's negligence in providing appropriate medical care within its jurisdiction has, on occasion, led the Court to find a violation of Article 3 but such violations have not been so readily established in the extra-territorial context.[182]

While not an extradition case, the Grand Chamber's subsequent decision in *Vinter* provided further clarification of when a whole life sentence would be considered reducible de facto and de jure. *Vinter* involved a challenge to the UK's own 'whole life sentences' regime. Under the legislation as it then was, a prisoner who was subject to a whole life sentence had no right to apply/be considered for parole; the only way their sentence could be reduced was via the discretionary power given to the Secretary of State via s.30(1) of the Crime (Sentences) Act 1997 which empowered the Secretary to order the release of the prisoner on 'compassionate grounds'. The ECtHR reiterated that Article 3 ECHR required 'reducibility of the sentence' and where 'domestic law does not provide any mechanism or possibility for review of a whole life sentence, the incompatibility with Article 3 ... *arises at the moment of the imposition of the sentence*'.[183] Accordingly, provided there is some form of review which allows the 'domestic authorities to consider whether any changes in the life prisoner are so significant, and such progress towards rehabilitation has been made ... as to mean that continued detention can no longer be justified on legitimate penological grounds', there would be no violation of Article 3

[180] As made clear in *Chahal* v. *the United Kingdom* (n 131) and *Saadi* v. *Italy* (n 136).

[181] *Harkins* v. *the United Kingdom* (n 105) at [129]. See also, Mavronicola and Messineo (n 124).

[182] *Babar Ahmad and Ors* v. *the United Kingdom* (n 75) at [177].

[183] *Vinter* v. *the United Kingdom* [GC] (2016) 63 EHRR 1 at [122]. Emphasis added.

ECHR.[184] The Grand Chamber listed several other requirements for a whole life regime *within* a Contracting State to be compatible with Article 3 ECHR including that there must be a dedicated mechanism guaranteeing a review of the sentence no later than twenty-five years after its imposition, with further periodic review thereafter.[185]

The Grand Chamber ultimately found that the UK's whole life order regime *did* violate Article 3 ECHR since the Secretary of State's discretionary power did not satisfy the requirement that the life sentence should be de facto reducible. This was because the Government had issued guidance indicating that 'compassionate grounds' were limited to prisoners who were terminally ill or physically incapacitated. The Court was, thus, not satisfied that a whole life sentence was reducible where the detention could no longer be justified on legitimate penological grounds.[186]

In a marked example of the dialogical nature of the relationship between the domestic courts and Strasbourg,[187] the domestic courts subsequently rejected the Grand Chamber's findings in *Vinter*. In *McLoughlin*,[188] the Court of Appeal held that s.30(1) of the Crime (Sentences) Act 1997 *was* sufficient to inform the prisoner – at the time of sentence – of the approach to be taken to have their sentence reduced. Given that the Secretary of State was bound by law to act compatibly with the prisoner's ECHR rights (by virtue of s.6 of the HRA) and the Secretary of State's decision under s.30(1) could be subject to scrutiny by judicial review, the domestic courts concluded that whole life orders did *not* violate Article 3 ECHR.

In the subsequent case of *Hutchinson*,[189] the ECtHR reconsidered its decision in *Vinter* in light of the Court of Appeal's judgment in *McLoughlin*. The ECtHR concluded that 'it is not its task to prescribe whether [the review necessary for a whole life sentence to be compatible with Article 3 ECHR] should be judicial or executive, having regard to the margin of appreciation that must be accorded to contracting states'.[190] Accordingly, having regard to the clarification proffered by the Court of Appeal in *McLoughlin*, the ECtHR determined that the discretionary power of the Secretary of State *did not* violate Article 3 ECHR.

From *Kafkaris* to *Hutchinson*, then, it seemed as though there was broad agreement between the domestic courts and the ECtHR on two key issues. The first was that a relativist approach to Article 3 ECHR in removal cases was acceptable and the second was that, provided there was scope for a whole life/life without parole sentence to be reduced in law and in fact, whether by executive order or judicial decree, no issue would arise under Article 3 ECHR.

[184] Ibid at [119]. [185] Ibid at [120]. [186] Ibid at [130].

[187] See the discussion of dialogue in Chapter 1.

[188] *R* v. *McLoughlin* [2014] EWCA Crim 188, [2014] 1 WLR 3964.

[189] *Hutchinson* v. *the United Kingdom* [GC] [2017] ECHR 65. [190] Ibid at [45].

Then, however, the ECtHR delivered judgment in the matter of *Trabelsi* v. *Belgium*[191] which caused considerable consternation within both the Government and the judiciary in the UK. In *Trabelsi* the ECtHR held that the prospect of Presidential clemency in the US was *insufficient* to satisfy the requirement that the sentence be de jure and de facto reducible since the evidence of the avenues of reduction was too vague. While that finding in and of itself was the subject of subsequent criticism by the domestic courts,[192] it was the ECtHR's contention that there should be no differentiation between conduct taking place in a Contracting State and conduct carried out by a non-contracting receiving State which caused the greatest furore. Indeed, in stark contrast to the relativist approach adopted by the domestic courts in *Wellington* and endorsed by the ECtHR in *Harkins*, the ECtHR in *Trabelsi* stated:

> The fact that the ill-treatment is inflicted by a non-Convention State is beside the point ... In such cases Article 3 implies an obligation not to remove the person in question to the said country, even if it is a non-Convention State. The Court draws no distinction in terms of the legal basis for removal; it adopts the same approach in cases of both expulsion and extradition.[193]

This approach led the ECtHR in *Trabelsi* to apply principles that had been developed in the context of considering whole life sentences in Contracting States (e.g., the requirement of review after no more than twenty-five years) to cases involving the imposition of whole life sentences in third party States.[194] It was this aspect of the *Trabelsi* Court's reasoning that drew the heaviest criticism.

The applicant in *Harkins* subsequently sought to reopen proceedings before the UK courts challenging his extradition based on what was submitted to be a change in the legal principles following *Trabelsi*. The High Court rejected this application holding that *Trabelsi* was wrong insofar as it 'purport[ed] to lift the *Vinter* principles [which apply to domestic sentencing practices] and apply

[191] *Trabelsi* v. *Belgium* (2014) 60 EHRR 21.

[192] See, for instance, *Hafeez* v. *Government of the United States* [2020] EWHC 155 (Admin), [2020] 1 WLR 1296.

[193] *Trabelsi* v. *Belgium* (n 191) at [116]. See also, *Khasanov and Rakhmanov* v. *Russia* [GC] [2022] ECHR 331 at [94]:

> In the case of an extradition, a Contracting State finds itself under an obligation to cooperate in international criminal matters. However, that obligation is subject to the same State's obligation to respect the absolute nature of the prohibition under Article 3 of the Convention. Therefore, any claim of a real risk of treatment contrary to Article 3 in the event of extradition to a certain country *must be subjected to the same level of scrutiny regardless of the legal basis for the removal.* (Emphasis added.)

[194] As set out in *Vinter* v. *the United Kingdom* (n 183).

them wholesale to the extradition context'.[195] Further, the ECtHR's judgment was, according to the High Court, wholly unreasoned in terms of the consideration of the review scheme in the US. The Supreme Court refused leave to appeal, and the ECtHR similarly declared inadmissible a subsequent complaint lodged by Harkins on the basis that it was 'substantially the same' as his earlier complaint and developments in the ECtHR's case law including *Vinter* and *Trabelsi* did not amount to 'relevant new information' such as to make the second application admissible.[196]

Given that long and complex jurisprudential history, it is unsurprising that the Grand Chamber in *Sanchez-Sanchez* was called upon to clarify the principles that are applicable in cases of extradition where there are substantial grounds to believe that, in the event of conviction, there is a real risk that the individual will face a sentence of life imprisonment without the prospect of parole. Notably, the Grand Chamber held that the principles in *Vinter*, particularly the standards of review required for whole life sentences to be compatible with Article 3 ECHR,[197] are applicable to 'domestic cases' and an 'adapted approach is called for in the extradition context'.[198]

This adapted approach asks two questions. The first – a preliminary question – asks whether 'the applicant has adduced evidence capable of proving that there are substantial grounds for believing that, in the event of conviction, there is a real risk of a sentence of life imprisonment without parole'.[199] If yes, the second question is whether there 'exists in the requesting state a mechanism of sentence review which allows the competent authorities there to consider whether any changes in the life prisoner are so significant, and such progress towards rehabilitation has been made in the course of the sentence, as to mean that continued detention can no longer be justified on legitimate penological grounds'.[200] According to the Grand Chamber, it is for the authorities to demonstrate that there are such grounds for review.[201] If there is no de jure and/or de facto basis for review, the imposition of the sentence will be incompatible with Article 3 ECHR. It is at the 'moment of sentencing' that there must be 'a review mechanism in place allowing the domestic authorities to consider the prisoner's progress towards rehabilitation or any other ground for release based on his or her behaviour or other relevant personal

[195] *R (Harkins)* v. *Secretary of State for Home Department (Rev 1)* [2014] EWHC 3609 (Admin), [2015] 1 WLR 2975 at [120].

[196] *Harkins* v. *the United Kingdom* (n 105).

[197] Including a requirement of 'the institution of a dedicated mechanism guaranteeing a review no later than twenty-five years after the imposition of a life sentence, with further periodic reviews thereafter' (*Murray* v. *the Netherlands* [GC] [2016] ECHR 408 at [99] citing *Vinter* v. *the United Kingdom* (n 183)).

[198] *Sanchez-Sanchez* v. *the United Kingdom* (n 154) at [95]. [199] Ibid. [200] Ibid at [97].

[201] Ibid at [96].

circumstance'.[202] As the Chamber in *Trabelsi* did not address the first, preliminary question (and it applied the *Vinter* criteria in their entirety), the decision was erroneous and it was, to that extent, overruled by the Grand Chamber.[203]

Finally, the Grand Chamber seemingly put to rest the *Wellington/Harkins* relativist approach to Article 3 ECHR, stating at [99] that:

> the prohibition of Article 3 ill-treatment remains absolute. In this regard, it does not consider that any distinction can be drawn between the minimum level of severity required to meet the Article 3 threshold in the domestic context and the minimum level required in the extra-territorial context (compare *Harkins* and *Edwards*, cited above, §§ 124–131). Furthermore, nothing in the preceding paragraphs undermines the now well-established position that the extradition of a person by a Contracting State will raise problems under Article 3 of the Convention where there are serious grounds to believe that he would run a real risk of being subjected to treatment contrary to Article 3 in the requesting State. [Underlined emphasis added]

While that seems to suggest that the relativist approach espoused in *Wellington* and adopted in *Harkins* is no longer accurate, it should be recalled that the Grand Chamber considered that an 'adapted approach' to the *Vinter* criteria is necessary in extradition cases, which could well be considered relativist.[204]

5.4.1.2 *Is the Ban on Torture or Inhuman or Degrading Treatment or Punishment Really 'Absolute'?*

Cases such as *Y.P.* v. *Russia* and the line of decisions stretching from *Kafkaris* to *Harkins* (with *Trabelsi* situated as an outlier) throw doubt on the claim that the prohibition on ill-treatment in Article 3 ECHR is, in fact, absolute. Certainly, the significance which the majority ECtHR placed on the doctors' intention and purpose in *Y.P.* and the adoption of an 'adapted' approach to extradition cases in *Sanchez-Sanchez* is hard to square with Article 3 ECHR prohibiting ill-treatment in all its forms and in all circumstances.

Debate has also waged as to whether it *should* be absolute. The decision in *Gäfgen* prompted significant academic discussion as to whether Article 3 ECHR could and/or should give way in cases involving potential conflicts of rights. In a series of articles following *Gäfgen*, Steven Greer and Natasa Mavronicola debated whether the case involved a conflict of purported absolute rights (namely, the right to life of eleven-year-old Jakob von Metzler and the right to freedom from ill-treatment of Magnus Gäfgen).

[202] Ibid at [97]. [203] Ibid at [98].

[204] For a critique of the Grand Chamber's judgment, see Lewis Graham, 'Life Sentences and Article 3 ECHR in the Extradition Context: *Sanchez-Sanchez* v. *United Kingdom*' (2023) 1 EHRLR 40–47.

Greer argued that it did involve such a conflict and the resolution of this conflict was 'fundamentally a moral rather than a legal matter'.[205] Greer further postulated a 'narrow *Gäfgen* thesis' and a 'broad *Gäfgen* thesis'. Pursuant to the narrow thesis (which arises in the quintessential 'ticking time bomb' scenario) where there is a conflict of rights, the authorities should choose the option that causes the least suffering. When lives are at stake, it is argued, the application of ill-treatment to a suspect to extricate information may well be the lesser of two evils. The broad *Gäfgen* thesis builds upon this and posits that, once it is accepted that the lesser of two evils should be adopted, that constitutes an exception to the 'absolute' prohibition in Article 3 ECHR and this single exception is enough for the prohibition to lose its absolute status generally.

In reply, Mavronicola highlighted the important distinction between whether treatment violating Article 3 ECHR is *morally* defensible and whether it can be *legally* justified.[206] By failing to properly delineate between these two distinct issues (and, thus, by relying on examples of moral 'acceptability' to refute legal absoluteness), Greer 'ma[de] a straw man of legal absoluteness'.[207] Mavronicola also posited that the focus ought properly be on the obligations owed by the State and, through that prism, there are two different legal obligations in play (if at all): Gäfgen's right not to be subjected to ill-treatment reaching the Article 3 ECHR threshold (which is an 'absolute', negative obligation) and the State's positive obligation to protect Jakob von Metzler's life (which is *not* absolute and which requires the State to take 'reasonable steps').[208] Subjecting a person to torture or inhuman or degrading treatment in violation of the State's negative obligation could not be considered a 'reasonable step'.

The proposition that torture (and other forms of ill-treatment) may be morally justified but should nevertheless remain legally prohibited has been the subject of a considerable body of academic work. As Jeremy Letwin observed, the view that 'torture is sometimes morally justifiable, but should nonetheless be absolutely prohibited in law' 'is based on the contention that even if the moral costs of torture may sometimes be lower than its benefits, the moral costs of institutionalising torture are always higher than its benefits'.[209] While it may be argued, as Greer purported to, that 'the right not to be tortured

[205] Steven Greer, 'Should Police Threats to Torture Suspects Always Be Severely Punished? Reflections on the *Gäfgen* Case' (2011) 11 HRLR 1.

[206] Natasa Mavronicola, 'In the Prohibition Against Torture and Cruel, Inhuman and Degrading Treatment Absolute in International Human Rights Law? A Reply to Steven Greer' (2017) 17 HRLR 3.

[207] Ibid, p.481. [208] Ibid, pp.483–484.

[209] Jeremy Letwin, 'A Utilitarian Account of Article 3 ECHR' (2022) 3 ECHRLR 350, p.368.

should nonetheless be generally limitable' so as to accommodate scenarios such as that which arose in *Gäfgen*, such an approach invites abuse:

> The danger is especially pronounced in relation to torture, because any scenario in which the question of whether to torture seriously arises is likely to be an emergency; the potential torturer who does not have clear strict rules to apply and who must weigh up all the considerations for themselves is likely, in an emergency, incorrectly to weigh these considerations by focusing excessively on the immediate dangers and the immediate benefits.[210]

The debate that has waged over *Gäfgen* and the absoluteness (or not) of Article 3 ECHR has concentrated on the extreme margins of policing; genuine 'ticking time bomb' scenarios are relatively rare. That is not to say that the issues which the Grand Chamber's decision raised and the academic discourse surrounding it are not relevant to Article 3 ECHR more generally. But greater attention needs to be given to more 'mundane' cases, including the long line of authorities regarding extradition and deportation and cases such as *Y.P.* v. *Russia*. For these are the cases that have the potential to fundamentally undermine the effectiveness of the protections in Article 3 ECHR. These are not cases that can be labelled 'one-offs' like *Gäfgen* may be. The willingness of the ECtHR in such cases to adopt a relativist approach to Article 3 ECHR and to make reaching the minimum level of severity dependant on the presence of malicious intent or purpose carries the real risk of fundamentally (and permanently) eroding the protective potential of Article 3 ECHR.[211]

5.4.2 Positive Procedural Obligation

As with Articles 2[212] and 4 ECHR,[213] Article 3 ECHR requires that the State conduct an effective investigation into 'arguable claims of infliction of [treatment contrary to Article 3]'.[214] The purpose of such an investigation is 'to establish the facts of the case and identify and, if appropriate, punish those responsible'.[215] Nevertheless, it is an obligation of means, not result. Accordingly, there is no absolute obligation for all investigations to result in prosecutions nor that all prosecutions result in convictions, and the ECtHR 'is not concerned with allegations of errors or isolated omissions in the investigation: it cannot replace the domestic authorities in the assessment of the facts of the case, nor can it decide on the alleged perpetrators' criminal

[210] Ibid, p.363.

[211] See, for instance, the discussion of the role of the principle of effectiveness in Judge Serghides' dissenting opinion in *Y.P.* v. *Russia* (n 46).

[212] See Chapter 4. [213] See Chapter 7.

[214] *X and Ors* v. *Bulgaria* [GC] [2021] ECHR 93 at [178]. [215] Ibid at [184].

responsibility'.[216] As with the equivalent obligation under Articles 2 and 4 ECHR, for an investigation into alleged ill-treatment to be effective for the purposes of Article 3 ECHR, it must:

- Establish the circumstances of the case;
- Be carried out by institutions and persons who are independent from its subjects. Such independence requires both a lack of institutional connection and practical independence;
- Be carried out promptly and with reasonable expedition;
- Ensure that the victim can participate effectively;
- Base its conclusions on thorough, objective and impartial analysis of all the relevant information.[217]

In addition to these general requirements, the specific characteristics of the victim may require additional components of the investigation for it to be sufficiently effective. Thus, in the context of child victims, their best interests must be a primary consideration.[218]

The nature of the investigative obligation under Article 3 ECHR was at the centre of the domestic proceedings in *DSD*,[219] which concerned the 'legion of sexual offences' perpetrated on women by black cab driver John Worboys and the allegation of egregious failings on the part of the police in investigating complaints made against Worboys who was able to continue to attack women. A central issue was whether the duty to investigate under Article 3 ECHR only arose when the State was otherwise responsible for, or in some way complicit in, the ill-treatment which the individual was alleged to have suffered. In rejecting this argument, Mr Justice Green at first instance surveyed the relevant ECtHR jurisprudence, distilling thirteen 'main propositions' regarding the procedural obligation under Article 3 ECHR.[220] Those propositions include the characteristics of an effective investigation set out above, but further provide that:

- The duty to investigate arises under Article 3 ECHR *in its own right* and, thus, does not depend on Article 1 ECHR (which is the generic obligation on all states to secure the rights set out in Section I ECHR to everyone within their jurisdiction and which is not included in the list of rights in Schedule 1 HRA);[221]

[216] Ibid at [186]. [217] Ibid at [187]–[190]. [218] Ibid at [192].

[219] The proceedings culminated in a judgment of the UKSC in 2018: *Commissioner of Police of the Metropolis* v. *DSD and Anor* [2018] UKSC 11, [2019] AC 196.

[220] *DSD* (n 17) at [211]–[224].

[221] The respondent had sought to argue that the investigative obligation under Article 3 arose because of Article 1 which obliges states to 'secure to everyone within their jurisdiction the rights and freedoms' set out in Section I of the Convention (which includes Article 3). Since Article 1 is not included in the list of rights given domestic effect under the HRA, the respondent argued that the procedural obligation under Article 3 did not arise in domestic law.

- The duty to investigate is *not* dependent upon the State being guilty, directly or indirectly of ill-treatment itself;[222]
- The duty is triggered where there is a 'credible or arguable' claim by the victim (or a third party) of ill-treatment reaching the minimum level of severity under Article 3 ECHR;[223]
- Since not all crimes perpetrated against an individual fall within Article 3 ECHR, the procedural obligation does not arise in all cases involving allegations of crimes against an individual. Rather, 'a credible allegation of a grave or serious crime' (such as '[r]ape and serious sexual assault') will trigger the obligation;[224] and,
- '[N]ot every failing attracts liability.' Thus, an 'operational failing which, had it not occurred, would not have been "capable" of leading to the apprehension and prosecution of an offender is … not actionable. Police are only liable for failing to meet an operational standard that is capable of leading to the apprehension and prosecution of an offender.'[225]

There was some disagreement between the courts as to whether operational failings would be sufficient to trigger the State's liability or whether only systematic failings would attract State responsibility.[226] Ultimately, a majority of the Supreme Court agreed with the trial judge that 'serious failures which are purely operational [i.e. failings on the part of individual police officers responsible for conducting the specific investigation] will suffice to establish a claim that an investigation carried out pursuant to an article 3 (or indeed an article 2) duty infringed that duty'.[227] Notwithstanding the disagreement on this issue, the trial judge and the appellate courts all found that there *had* been a violation of the State's positive procedural obligation under Article 3 ECHR as a result of the numerous failings in the police investigation of Worboys (including failures to 'conduct proper searches, conduct proper interviews of Worboys, [and] to follow up CCTV evidence'[228]).

5.4.3 Positive Obligation to Protect

5.4.3.1 Obligation to Put in Place an 'Effective Legal Framework'

A State must have in place a legal framework which provides 'adequate protection', including by way of deterrence, against ill-treatment by State agents and private persons.[229] While the State has a margin of appreciation in formulating the relevant legal framework, the limits of that margin are

[222] *DSD* (n 17) at [213]. [223] Ibid at [214]. [224] Ibid at [215]–[216].

[225] Ibid at [221]. Underlined emphasis in original.

[226] *The Commissioner of Police of the Metropolis* v. *DSD and NBV & Ors* [2015] EWCA Civ 646, [2015] 3 WLR 966.

[227] *DSD* (UKSC) (n 219) at [82], [85]. [228] *DSD* (Court of Appeal) (n 226) at [76].

[229] See, for instance, *M.C.* v. *Bulgaria* (2005) 40 EHRR 20 at [149]. See also, *A* v. *the United Kingdom* (1999) 27 EHRR 611 and *O'Keeffe* v. *Ireland* [GC] (2014) 59 EHRR 15.

circumscribed by the ECHR, which is to be interpreted in light of 'the changing conditions within Contracting States'.[230] As the Grand Chamber has observed:

> The positive obligation under Article 3 of the Convention necessitates in particular establishing a legislative and regulatory framework to shield individuals adequately from breaches of their physical and psychological integrity, particularly, in the most serious cases, through the enactment of criminal-law provisions and their effective application in practice.[231]

Accordingly, in *MC* v. *Bulgaria*, the ECtHR found that the State had violated its obligation to establish and effectively apply a criminal-law system punishing all forms of rape and sexual abuse because, inter alia, the authorities applied an overly rigid approach to the prosecution of the applicant's rape, including by placing considerable weight on the absence of proof of resistance.[232] As discussed below, the Court has also found violations of this obligation in cases involving domestic abuse (read alone or together with the parasitic prohibition on discrimination in Article 14) because the State has failed to criminalise acts of violence within the domestic context and the 'toolbox of legal and operational measures' available to police in responding to allegations and incidents of domestic abuse has been inadequate to effectively 'shield' individuals from such ill-treatment.[233]

In addition to putting in place an effective legal system, States also have a positive obligation, in specific circumstances, to take preventive operational measures to protect specific individuals from the real and immediate threat of ill-treatment from third parties (this is akin to the operational obligation discussed in the context of Article 2 ECHR in Chapter 4).

5.4.3.2 *Obligation to Take Preventive Operational Measures*

The 'test' for whether the positive obligation to protect has arisen in the context of Article 3 ECHR is an adapted version of the *Osman* test[234] which was outlined in Chapter 4 in the context of Article 2 ECHR. It requires that there is a 'real and immediate risk of ill-treatment of which the authorities knew or ought to have known' and obliges the State to take 'reasonable measures' to protect against it.[235] The burden is on the applicant (in most cases[236]) and the threshold is high; it has been interpreted by the domestic courts as requiring that there is a present and continuing risk that is neither fanciful nor negligible.[237]

230 *M.C.* v. *Bulgaria*, ibid at [155]. 231 *X and Ors* v. *Bulgaria* (n 214) at [179].

232 *M.C.* v. *Bulgaria* (n 229).

233 See, for instance, *Tunikova and Ors* v. *Russia* (2022) 75 EHRR 1 at [95]–[100].

234 *Osman* v. *the United Kingdom* (2000) 29 EHRR 245.

235 See, for instance, *Volodina* v. *Russia* [2019] ECHR 539 at [77(b)]. 236 See Section 5.3.

237 See, for instance, *Savage* v. *South Essex Partnership NHS Foundation Trust* [2008] UKHL 74, [2009] AC 681 at [41].

As with the equivalent obligation under Article 2 ECHR, the operational obligation in Article 3 ECHR 'must be interpreted in a way which does not impose an impossible or disproportionate burden on the authorities, bearing in mind the difficulties in policing modern societies, the unpredictability of human conduct and the operational choices which must be made in terms of priorities and resources'.[238] Nevertheless, as the ensuing section on domestic abuse demonstrates, there is a limit to the latitude afforded to authorities in respect of decisions involving policing.

The cases in which a breach of the positive obligation has been found by the ECtHR vary significantly in their facts. A number involve domestic abuse which is considered separately in the next section. Two cases will be considered here to demonstrate how the obligation has been characterised in other contexts.

In *Z* v. *the United Kingdom*,[239] the Grand Chamber found a violation of the positive obligation to protect as a result of the failure of the local authorities to take steps to protect four children from abuse by their parents. Multiple State agencies (e.g. police and social services) had reported concerns about the children's care and the authorities also had reports of concerns from medical professionals, teachers and neighbours. The children were reported as raiding bins at school to find food to eat, their living conditions were 'appalling', they were 'ill-kempt' and dirty and they were clearly emotionally and psychologically traumatised. Notwithstanding all of the evidence from various parties, the local authority took years to finally take the children into care (and then only at the mother's insistence). The children subsequently commenced proceedings in negligence against the local authority. Those proceedings were, ultimately, unsuccessful as English law at the time did not recognise a duty of care in the specific circumstances. Before the ECtHR, the children argued that the inertia on the part of the local authority violated the positive obligation to protect under Article 3 ECHR. The Grand Chamber accepted that argument, noting that the Government did not dispute that 'the neglect and abuse suffered by the four applicant children reached the threshold of inhuman and degrading treatment'.[240] While the Court was attuned to 'the difficult and sensitive decisions facing social services and the important countervailing principle of respecting and preserving family life' the evidence that was put before the local authorities over a number of years demonstrated a 'failure of the system to protect these applicant children from serious, long-term neglect and abuse'.[241]

The positive obligation to protect was also a key facet of domestic proceedings brought by Kate Wilson against the Metropolitan Police Service as a result of ill-treatment by an undercover police officer. Mark Kennedy had been tasked with infiltrating the Sumac Centre in Nottingham, a 'vibrant, self-organised social

[238] *Mamazhonov* v. *Russia* (2017) 64 EHRR 26 at [174].

[239] *Z and Others* v. *the United Kingdom* [GC] [2001] 34 EHRR 3.

[240] Ibid at [74].

[241] Ibid.

space . . . frequented by a range of political activists'.[242] There he met Kate Wilson, a political activist, and they commenced a sexual relationship which persisted for several years. When Wilson discovered that Kennedy was, in fact, a police officer, she and two other women who also had sexual relationships with undercover operatives, issued a claim for damages in tort and under the HRA 1998. In respect of the latter, the claimants argued, inter alia, that the respondents had failed to protect them from ill-treatment contrary to Article 3 ECHR. More specifically, Wilson argued that the respondents, including the Commissioner of Police of the Metropolis, had failed to take reasonable measures to obviate the real and immediate risk that Kennedy (and other undercover officers) would enter sexual relationships with women who were unaware that they were undercover operatives. The Metropolitan Police Service conceded that there had been a breach of the positive obligation to protect under Article 3 ECHR because 'the decision to deceive [Wilson] into a long-term intimate and sexual relationship amounted to inhuman and degrading treatment' and 'the Respondents were in breach of their positive obligations under Art[icle] 3 . . . in that [Kennedy's] principal cover officer failed in his duty to supervise [Kennedy]'.[243]

However, the respondents disputed the claim that there was a further violation of the positive obligation to protect under Article 3 ECHR by virtue of the lack of sufficient training and monitoring by superior officers. In finding against the respondents, the Tribunal held that the training that Kennedy received was 'grossly inadequate and failed to meet the Respondents' positive obligations under Article 3.'[244] There was 'simply no evidence of the Respondents thinking about, planning, or taking any steps to mitigate the obvious risk of [Kennedy's] entering into sexual relationships with activists'.[245] Consequently, there had been a further violation of Article 3 ECHR.

5.5 STATE OBLIGATIONS UNDER ARTICLE 3 ECHR IN RESPONSE TO DOMESTIC ABUSE

Domestic abuse[246] raises issues that intersect with a range of ECHR rights including the right to life,[247] the freedom from torture or inhuman or degrading treatment and the right to private life, as well as freedom from

[242] *Wilson* v. *The Commissioner of Police of the Metropolis, National Police Chiefs' Council* [2021] UKIPTrib IPT_11_167_H at [8].

[243] Ibid at [14]. [244] Ibid at [193]. [245] Ibid at [233].

[246] The phrase 'domestic abuse' is used instead of 'domestic violence' as it more accurately covers the spectrum of abusive behaviours including non-violent forms of abuse such as coercive and controlling behaviour.

[247] See, in this respect, the discussion in Chapter 4, Section 4.4.3.

discrimination. We know that the State has a positive obligation to protect individuals from ill-treatment and a procedural obligation to ensure that cases involving potential instances of Article 3 ECHR ill-treatment are effectively investigated and, yet, in cases of domestic abuse, both of these obligations are often unmet in the UK[248] and the broader Council of Europe community.[249]

While the ECtHR's case law regarding domestic abuse remains in its relative infancy given that it was only in the 2000s that the Court first recognised that the State owed individuals positive obligations to prevent and protect them from domestic abuse, there is a growing body of case law in which it has found violations of Articles 2, 3 and 8 ECHR (alone and together with Article 14) as a result of State responses (or the lack thereof) to domestic abuse.[250] Such

[248] The Domestic Abuse Commissioner reported in 2023 that '[d]omestic abuse crimes remain high in England and Wales, yet no significant improvements in criminal justice system outcomes are being made', indeed:

> criminal justice outcomes for domestic abuse are getting worse. Compared with data from four years ago, fewer referrals of domestic abuse offences are being made to the CPS, fewer charges are taking place, fewer prosecutions are completed, and fewer convictions are achieved.
>
> This amounts to fewer perpetrators of domestic abuse being held accountable, and fewer victims and survivors being protected.

(Domestic Abuse Commissioner, 'Domestic Abuse Commissioner responds to latest domestic abuse crime statistics', 20 October 2023, https://domesticabusecommissioner.uk/domestic-abuse-commissioner-responds-to-latest-criminal-justice-statistics/).

In Scotland, the HM Inspectorate of Prosecution carried out an in-depth review of the prosecution of domestic abuse cases at sheriff summary level and concluded that failures of communication and a lack of 'ownership' of cases by prosecutors has resulted in delays and poor outcomes: HM Inspectorate of Scotland, 'The prosecution of domestic abuse at sheriff summary level', April 2024, p.4, www.prosecutioninspectorate.scot/media/h30hqpbr/the-prosecution-of-domestic-abuse-cases-at-sheriff-summary-level.pdf.

[249] Indeed, in the year ending March 2024 in England and Wales, while police recorded 851,062 domestic abuse-related *crimes*, only 72,641 (i.e. 8.5 per cent) were referred to the CPS for charging. Ultimately, there were 51,183 domestic abuse-related prosecutions which, if considered in light of referrals, is a relatively high percentage, but when one considers that there were over 850,000 domestic abuse-related crimes in the same period, the number of prosecutions is comparatively miniscule (just over 6 per cent of recorded domestic abuse-related crimes result in prosecution): Office for National Statistics, 'Domestic Abuse in England and Wales overview: November 2024', 27 November 2024, www.ons.gov.uk/peoplepopulationandcommunity/crimeandjustice/bulletins/domesticabuseinenglandandwalesoverview/november2024.

[250] See, for instance, *Kontrová* v. *Slovakia* [2007] ECHR 419; *Bevacqua and S* v. *Bulgaria* [2008] ECHR 498; *E.S. and Others* v. *Slovakia* [2009] ECHR 1282; *Opuz* v. *Turkey* (2010) 50 EHRR 28; *A* v. *Croatia* [2010] ECHR 1506; *Hajduova* v. *Slovakia* [2010] ECHR 1908; *Kalucza* v. *Hungary* [2012] ECHR 756; *Valiuliene* v. *Lithuania* [2013] ECHR 240; *Eremia and Others* v. *Republic of Moldova* (2014) 58 EHRR 2; *B.* v. *Republic of Moldova* [2013] ECHR 684; *Mudric* v. *Republic of Moldova* [2013] ECHR 685; *N.A.* v. *Republic of Moldova* [2013] ECHR 860; *T.M. and C.M.* v.

violations have stemmed from, inter alia, failings of the State's regulatory system to adequately deter domestic abuse, including by way of effective punishment,[251] failures by the authorities to take reasonable measures to protect specific individuals from domestic abuse[252] and ineffective investigations into domestic abuse.[253] The Court has summarised the State's obligations under Article 3 in the context of domestic abuse as follows, noting the particular vulnerability of the victims and the need for active State involvement in their protection:

> Those positive obligations, which often overlap, consist of: (a) the obligation to take reasonable measures designed to prevent ill-treatment of which the authorities knew or ought to have known and (b) the (procedural) obligation to conduct effective official investigation where an individual raises an arguable claim of ill-treatment … In addition, the Court has held that States have a positive obligation to establish and apply effectively a system punishing all forms of domestic violence and to provide sufficient safeguards for the victims.[254]

It is quite clear that Article 2 ECHR is engaged when a person has been killed as a result of domestic abuse or where there is a real and immediate risk to life as a result of domestic abuse.[255] However, the Court has also grappled with the applicability of other rights in respect of non-fatal forms of domestic abuse. In early cases, Article 8 ECHR and the right to private life which protects bodily integrity, featured quite prominently.[256] More recently, the ECtHR has recognised that non-fatal forms of abuse, including coercive and controlling behaviour, can in fact constitute ill-treatment contrary to Article 3 ECHR.[257] Given that Article 3 ECHR covers treatment which causes 'intense physical and mental suffering'[258] and/or arouses 'feelings of fear, anguish and inferiority capable of humiliating and debasing [victims] and possibly breaking their physical or moral resistance,[259] it is entirely appropriate that the Court would

Republic of Moldova [2014] ECHR 81; *M.G.* v. *Turkey* [2016] ECHR 295; *Balsan* v. *Romania* [2017] ECHR 468; *Talpis* v. *Italy* [2017] ECHR 224; *Volodina* v. *Russia* (n 235); *Kurt* v. *Austria* [GC] (2022) 74 EHRR 6; *Tunikova and Ors* v. *Russia* (n 233); *Tkhelidze* v. *Georgia* [2021] ECHR 614; *Y and Ors* v. *Bulgaria* [2022] ECHR 249; *Landi* v. *Italy* [2022] ECHR 308; *A.E.* v. *Bulgaria* [2023] ECHR 428; *Luca* v. *the Republic of Moldova* [2023] ECHR 797. See also, Ronagh McQuigg, *The Istanbul Convention, Domestic Violence and Human Rights* (Routledge, 2017), pp.60–67.

[251] See, for instance, *Volodina* v. *Russia* (n 235).

[252] See, for instance, *Tunikova and Ors* v. *Russia* (n 233); *Tkhelidze* v. *Georgia* (n 250); *Y and Ors* v. *Bulgaria* (n 250).

[253] See, for instance, *Volodina* v. *Russia* (n 235).

[254] *Balsan* v. *Romania* (n 250) at [57].

[255] See the discussion in Chapter 4, Section 4.3.2.4.

[256] See, for instance, *Bevacqua and S* v. *Bulgaria* (n 250).

[257] See, for instance, *Tunikova and Ors* v. *Russia* (n 233) and *Volodina* v. *Russia* (n 235).

[258] *Jalloh* v. *Germany* (n 28) at [68].

[259] Ibid.

apply Article 3 ECHR to cases of non-fatal forms of domestic abuse. Yet, while the Court has found that the minimum threshold of severity has been met in several domestic abuse cases, it has been inexplicably reluctant to find that such treatment has reached the threshold of torture. Judge Pinto de Albuquerque addressed this in his separate opinion in *Volodina* indicating that he would have labelled this abuse torture:

> In my view, the applicant's ordeal as described in this judgment meets all the criteria for being identified as torture. The majority refer to feelings of fear, anxiety and powerlessness, as well as being subjected to controlling and coercive behaviour, which trigger the application of Article 3. This summary is a tame expression of what the applicant endured. She was subjected to multiple and persistent instances of extreme domestic violence, including a punch to her stomach, which in fact led to medical advice that she should induce the abortion of her unborn baby. She was further psychologically taunted through the publication of private photographs, the finding of what was believed to be a GPS tracker inside her purse, threats to kill her – which S. attempted to substantiate by damaging her car – and abduction from her city of residence.[260]

There is much to be said for Judge Pinto de Albuquerque's argument that such treatment ought to have been characterised as torture. Not only did the victim deserve to have the ill-treatment she was subjected to appropriately characterised to properly vindicate her rights (including in terms of the quantification of non-pecuniary damages), but it is also important for holding States to account that the severity of the violations for which they are responsible are recognised. It is also a vital component of the wider recognition of the importance of identifying and preventing domestic abuse: there can be little dispute that States need to prevent torture and to protect individuals from it.

One of the issues that has confronted victims and survivors of domestic abuse in the context of the positive obligation to protect has been the need, under the existing *Osman* test (as discussed in Chapter 4 in respect of the right to life), to prove that the risk to life or of ill-treatment contrary to Article 3 is 'real and *immediate*'.[261] This standard is problematic in the context of domestic abuse since:

> A 'real and immediate risk' in the context of domestic violence infers that the risk, namely the batterer, is already in the direct vicinity of the victim and about to strike the first blow. Were the test to be applied in such a manner, two concerns arise. Firstly, any protective action offered by the State would be too late and secondly, the State would have a legitimate excuse for not acting in a timely manner, since it is implausible to assume that the victim will be constantly accompanied by a State agent who

[260] *Volodina* v. *Russia* (n 235), separate opinion of Judge Pinto de Albuquerque at [6]–[7]. Footnote references omitted.

[261] *Osman* v. *the United Kingdom* (n 234) at [116]. Emphasis added.

may jump in to help. Hence, the 'immediacy' of the *Osman* test does not serve well in the context of domestic violence.[262]

Concerns about the immediacy requirement in the context of domestic abuse were expressed from within the Court as early as 2013,[263] but it was not until 2021 that the Grand Chamber finally recognised that the *Osman* test needed to be adapted to reflect the particular nature of domestic abuse. In the judgment of *Kurt* v. *Austria*,[264] a unanimous Grand Chamber held that in order for States to comply with their obligations under Article 2 ECHR in the context of domestic abuse, particularly in terms of the positive preventive obligation, the authorities must immediately respond to allegations of abuse and must conduct an autonomous, proactive and comprehensive assessment of the reality and immediacy of the risk, taking due account of the particular domestic violence context.[265]

While *Kurt* was concerned with Article 2 ECHR, the principles enunciated by the Grand Chamber have been applied in subsequent cases involving domestic abuse which have been considered under Article 3 ECHR[266] and Article 8 ECHR (in the context of cyberviolence).[267]

5.6 BORDER PUSHBACKS

In May 2024, the BBC released the findings of its investigation into pushbacks at sea by Greek authorities.[268] The term 'pushbacks' refers to the:

> various measures taken by States, sometimes involving third countries or non-State actors, which result in migrants, including asylum seekers, being summarily forced back, without an individual assessment of their human rights protection needs, to the country or territory, or to sea, whether it be territorial waters or international waters, from where they attempted to cross or crossed an international border.[269]

The BBC reported that '[t]he Greek coastguard has caused the deaths of [43] migrants in the Mediterranean over a three-year period' with witnesses reporting nine individuals being deliberately thrown into the water.[270] There was also video 'footage of 12 people being loaded into a Greek coastguard

[262] *Volodina* v. *Russia* (n 235), separate opinion of Judge Pinto de Albuquerque at [12].

[263] *Valiuliene* v. *Lithuania* (n 250). [264] *Kurt* v. *Austria* (n 250). [265] Ibid at [190].

[266] See, for instance, *Tunikova and Ors* v. *Russia* (n 233).

[267] *Volodina* v. *Russia (No 2)* [2021] ECHR 745.

[268] Lucile Smith and Ben Steele, 'Greek coastguard threw migrants overboard to their deaths, witnesses say', *BBC News*, 17 June 2024, https://www.bbc.co.uk/news/articles/c0vv717yvpeo.

[269] Special Rapporteur on the Human Rights of Migrants, *Report on means to address the human rights impact of pushbacks of migrants on land and at sea*, A/HRC/47/30 (2021), p.4.

[270] Smith and Steele (n 268).

boat, and then abandoned on a dinghy'.[271] Greece is by no means the only Council of Europe State to engage in pushbacks,[272] and not all pushbacks occur at sea; it is a practice that occurs at land borders as well.[273] While the issue of collective removals is specifically dealt with under Article 4 of Protocol No. 4,[274] pushbacks can (and do) also raise issues under other articles in the ECHR, in particular Articles 2 and 3 ECHR (as has been argued in recent cases before the Grand Chamber[275]). In terms of Article 3 ECHR, State agents may violate the negative obligation as a result of their treatment of individuals being 'pushed back'. Pushbacks might also violate the prohibition on refoulement if there are substantial grounds for believing that there is a real and immediate risk that the individual could be exposed to ill-treatment in the receiving country or where there is a risk of 'chain-refoulement' which refers to the possibility that a person may be returned to a seemingly 'safe' third country only to then be removed without an assessment of the risks faced.[276]

Such issues were at the centre of the Grand Chamber's decision in *Ilias and Ahmed* v. *Bulgaria*.[277] The application was brought by two Bangladeshi individuals who had been held in the Röszke transit zone (located on Hungarian territory at the border between Hungary and Serbia). They submitted asylum requests on the day they arrived at the transit zone, which were rejected the same day. The authorities relied on the fact that the applicants had travelled through Serbia, which was considered a safe third country and where the applicants could have made their asylum claims. Legal challenges to the rejection of the asylum claims were, ultimately, unsuccessful and the applicants were escorted out of the transit zone and into Serbia in circumstances which led the applicants to believe they were being threatened by Hungarian police.[278] In finding that the Hungarian authorities had breached their procedural obligations under Article 3 ECHR in removing the applicants to Serbia,

[271] Ibid.

[272] See, for instance, cases involving Cyprus (*M.A. and Z.R.* v. *Cyprus* [2024] ECHR 785) and Spain (*N.D. and N.T.* v. *Spain* [GC] [2020] ECHR 142).

[273] See, for instance, *Ilias and Ahmed* v. *Hungary* [GC] (2020) 71 EHRR 6 and *D.A. and Ors* v. *Poland* [2021] ECHR 615. Indeed, three cases heard by the Grand Chamber in February 2025 all concerned alleged pushbacks occurring at a land border: *C.O.C.G. and Others* v. *Lithuania*, App. No. 17764/22, Grand Chamber hearing 12/02/2025; *H.M.M. and Others* v. *Latvia*, App. No. 42165/21, Grand Chamber hearing 12/02/2025; *R.A. and Others* v. *Poland*, App. No. 42120/21, Grand Chamber hearing 12/02/2025. For a discussion of the cases, see Aleksandra Ancite-Jepifánova, 'From the EU-Belarus Border to Strasbourg', *Verfassungsblog*, 3 March 2025, https://verfassungsblog.de/eu-belarus-border-migrant-instrumentalisation/.

[274] In respect of which, see Chapter 9.

[275] *C.O.C.G. and Others* v. *Lithuania* (n 273), *H.M.M. and Others* v. *Latvia* (n 273) and *R.A. and Others* v. *Poland* (n 273).

[276] *Hirsi Jamaa and Ors* v. *Italy* [GC] (2012) 55 EHRR 21 at [147].

[277] *Ilias and Ahmed* v. *Hungary* (n 273).

[278] Ibid at [40].

the Grand Chamber clarified the principles applicable under Article 3 ECHR in cases involving pushbacks, specifically in cases involving removal to allegedly safe third countries. The Court reiterated that while States have 'the right, as a matter of well-established international law and subject to their treaty obligations, including the Convention, to control the entry, residence and expulsion of aliens',[279] they also have an obligation not to expose individuals to a real risk of treatment contrary to Article 3 ECHR. In the context of removal of individuals claiming asylum to third party States, the Grand Chamber noted that 'where a Contracting State seeks to remove the asylum seeker to a third country without examining the asylum request on the merits, the State's duty not to expose the individual to a real risk of treatment contrary to Article 3 is discharged in a manner different from that in cases of return to the country of origin'.[280] Whereas in cases involving removal to the country of origin, the State will discharge its duty under Article 3 ECHR by examining whether the applicant's claim for asylum is well-founded, in the case of removal to a third party State, the removing country must ascertain whether the individual will have access to an adequate asylum procedure in the receiving State.[281] The differing duties arise because in removal without consideration cases (i.e. pushback cases) 'the removing country acts on the basis that it would be for the receiving third country to examine the asylum request on the merits, if such a request is made to the relevant authorities of that country'.[282]

While it is permissible under the ECHR for States to remove individuals seeking asylum to a third party state without considering the merits of their asylum claim, States have a procedural obligation under Article 3 ECHR 'to examine thoroughly whether that country's asylum system could deal adequately with those claims'.[283] The Grand Chamber in *Ilias and Ahmed* clarified what is required of a State to discharge this procedural duty. Specifically, it must 'conduct a thorough examination of the relevant conditions in the third country concerned and, in particular, the accessibility and reliability of its asylum system'.[284] In conducting this examination, the principles relevant to an assessment of whether an individual's country of origin is safe for them to be removed to also apply.[285] The Court also made clear that in these cases – that is, pushback cases – where the merits of the asylum claim have not been considered by the domestic authorities, it is not the role of the Court to consider the merits. Rather:

[279] Ibid at [125]. [280] Ibid at [130]. [281] Ibid at [131].

[282] Ibid. The Court also observed that 'where the alleged risk of being subjected to treatment contrary to Article 3 concerns, for example, conditions of detention or living conditions for asylum seekers in a receiving third country, that risk is also to be assessed by the expelling State' (ibid).

[283] Ibid at [138]. [284] Ibid at [139]. [285] Ibid at [140].

> the Court must examine: 1) whether [the domestic] authorities took into account the available general information about [the third party State] and its asylum system in an adequate manner and of their own initiative and, 2) whether the applicants were given sufficient opportunity to demonstrate that [the third party state] was not a safe third country in their particular case.[286]

Applying those principles to the decision of the Hungarian authorities to remove the applicants without considering the merits of their asylum claims, the Court concluded that there had been a breach of the procedural obligation under Article 3 ECHR. The authorities proceeded on a presumption contained in domestic law that Serbia was a safe third country. While there is nothing in the ECHR preventing States from adopting such presumptions, they 'must be sufficiently supported at the outset by an analysis of the relevant conditions in that country and, in particular, of its asylum system'.[287] In this instance, the Court was not satisfied that the authorities had regard to the risk of chain-refoulement:

> it does not appear that the authorities took sufficient account of consistent general information that at the relevant time asylum-seekers returned to Serbia ran a real risk of summary removal to the Republic of North Macedonia and then to Greece and, therefore, of being subjected to conditions incompatible with Article 3 in Greece.[288]

This, coupled with the fact that the Hungarian authorities compounded those risks by compelling the applicants to enter Serbia illegally, rather than 'negotiating an orderly return', led the Court to conclude that the Hungarian authorities had failed to discharge the State's procedural obligation under Article 3 ECHR.

A similar issue was at the core of the domestic proceedings in *AAA* (discussed in Section 5.4.1.1.1), namely: '[w]hether asylum seekers removed to Rwanda would have access to an adequate asylum procedure'.[289] In finding that they would not, the UK Supreme Court placed significant weight on the evidence of the UNHCR regarding failings in the asylum system in Rwanda and a history of removal of individuals to their countries of origin, without adequate consideration of their claims for asylum, and notwithstanding assurances with other States that this would not occur. As noted above, the UK Supreme Court concluded that there were substantial grounds for believing that there was a real risk of refoulement (either direct or indirect) if those seeking asylum were sent to Rwanda.[290] While the Secretary of State placed significant emphasis on the potential reform of the Rwandan asylum system, as the Supreme Court observed at [102] 'intentions and aspirations do not necessarily correspond to reality: the question is whether they are achievable

[286] Ibid at [148]. [287] Ibid at [152]. [288] Ibid at [158]. [289] *AAA* (n 143) at [24].
[290] Ibid at [105].

in practice' and, as the evidence stood at the relevant time, there were significant doubts as to whether Rwanda's undertakings to comply with, inter alia, the principle of non-refoulement were achievable in practice. As noted above, the Government responded to the Supreme Court's judgment by enacting legislation compelling decision-makers, including courts, to treat Rwanda as a safe third country.[291] Notably, under the Safety of Rwanda (Asylum and Immigration) Act 2024, even the narrow exception permitting decision-makers to consider an individual's circumstances on the basis of 'compelling evidence' is limited by s.4(2) which prohibits a consideration of whether there is a risk of refoulement. Clearly, there is a strong argument that the legislation is not compliant with the UK's obligations under Article 3 ECHR, in particular the procedural obligation set out in *Ilias*. As noted above, legislation is currently being considered by Parliament which will, if enacted, repeal the Safety of Rwanda Act.[292]

While *Ilias* was a pushback case involving a risk of chain-refoulement (or indirect refoulement), an earlier judgment of the Grand Chamber involving pushbacks to an allegedly unsafe third country concerned risks of both direct and indirect refoulement. The applicants in *Hirsi Jamaa and Ors* v. *Italy*[293] – Eritrean and Somali nationals – were part of a group of about two hundred individuals who left Libya on three vessels headed for the Italian coast. They were intercepted off the Italian coast (within the 'Maltese Search and Rescue Region') by Italian authorities and were transferred onto Italian military ships and returned to Libya. The applicants alleged that they were at risk of ill-treatment in Libya (direct refoulement) and of being returned to their countries of origin where they also faced a real risk of ill-treatment (indirect or chain-refoulement). The Grand Chamber unanimously agreed with the applicants, holding that Italy had violated Article 3 ECHR both because there was a real risk of ill-treatment in Libya and there was a real risk of refoulement from Libya to their countries of origin.

In terms of the allegation of direct refoulement, the Court reiterated the principles from its removal jurisprudence (discussed above). In this case, the applicants relied on evidence that 'irregular migrants' from Somalia and Eretria were held in inhuman and degrading conditions in Libya. In reply, the Government cited a bilateral treaty it had entered into with Libya concerning the return of individuals who were intercepted on the seas. In stark parallels to the UK's treaty with Rwanda and the UK Government's arguments in the *AAA* litigation (discussed in Section 5.4.1.1.1), Italy relied on the fact that its treaty with Libya 'made specific reference to compliance with the provisions of international human rights law and other international conventions to which

[291] Safety of Rwanda (Asylum and Immigration) Act 2024.

[292] Border Security, Asylum and Immigration Bill, cl 37.

[293] *Hirsi Jamaa and Ors* v. *Italy* (n 276).

Libya was party'.[294] In rejecting Italy's reliance on that treaty as proof of its compliance with Article 3 ECHR, the Grand Chamber observed:

> that the existence of domestic laws and the ratification of international treaties guaranteeing respect for fundamental rights are not in themselves sufficient to ensure adequate protection against the risk of ill-treatment where, as in the present case, reliable sources have reported practices resorted to or tolerated by the authorities which are manifestly contrary to the principles of the Convention...
>
> ... Italy cannot evade its own responsibility by relying on its obligations arising out of bilateral agreements with Libya. Even if it were to be assumed that those agreements made express provision for the return to Libya of migrants intercepted on the high seas, the Contracting States' responsibility continues even after their having entered into treaty commitments subsequent to the entry into force of the Convention or its Protocols in respect of these States.[295]

There was an abundance of evidence of the risks of ill-treatment of individuals such as the applicants in Libya, including from the UNHCR. Italy, thus, knew or ought to have known that the applicants, as irregular migrants, would be (or were at real risk of being) exposed to ill-treatment contrary to Article 3 ECHR upon their return to Libya.[296] Pushing the applicants back to Libya thus constituted direct refoulement in violation of Article 3 ECHR.

In terms of the risk of chain/indirect refoulement, the Court in *Hirsi Jamaa* held that 'Italy is not exempt from complying with its obligations under Article 3 ... because the applicants failed to ask for asylum or to describe the risks faced as a result of the lack of an asylum system in Libya. It reiterates that the Italian authorities should have ascertained how the Libyan authorities fulfilled their international obligations in relation to the protection of refugees.'[297] As the Italian authorities had not done so, they had violated Article 3 ECHR when returning the applicants to Libya.

Before we conclude this discussion of pushbacks and Article 3 ECHR, the case of *Safi and Others* v. *Greece*[298] ought to be considered. The case involved the sinking of a fishing boat carrying twenty-seven foreign nationals in the Aegean Sea off the coast of a Greek island. The sinking of the vessel resulted in the deaths of the applicants' relatives (eight children and three women), and the applicants claimed that the boat sunk as a result of its being towed at very high speeds by a Greek coastguard vessel which was attempting to push it back towards the Turkish coast. While the focus of the application was Article 2 ECHR,[299] the Court also had regard to Article 3 ECHR in the context of complaints of ill-treatment by the applicants at the hands of the coastguard during their subsequent arrest and detention. In particular, applicants, who

[294] Ibid at [127]. [295] Ibid at [128] and [129]. [296] Ibid at [131]. [297] Ibid at [157].
[298] *Safi and Ors* v. *Greece* [2022] ECHR 559. [299] As discussed in Chapter 4.

were incredibly vulnerable having just survived a shipwreck and lost loved ones, were strip-searched in full view of others. The Court considered that body-searches may be necessary in some circumstances, but in the instant case the applicants were 'forced to undress at the same time and in the same place, in front of at least thirteen people' and were 'exceedingly vulnerable'.[300] The Greek Government failed to demonstrate that the searches were based on 'a compelling security need or a need to prevent disorder or crime' and, accordingly, the searches were degrading in violation of the negative obligation under Article 3 ECHR.[301]

5.7 CONCLUSION

While the right to life may well be the most fundamental of the rights enshrined in the ECHR,[302] the right to live one's life free from torture or inhuman or degrading treatment or punishment must surely be of equal, or very nearly equal, importance. Indeed, the lack of any express limitations to the prohibition of ill-treatment is a testament to the significance of the protections afforded by Article 3 ECHR. As with the right to life, Article 3 ECHR imposes not only a negative obligation on States not to subject individuals within their juridiction to ill-treatment which reaches the minimum level of severity, but it also imposes positive and procedural obligations. This chapter has examined each of these obligations in detail, drawing on contemporary issues to illuminate both the protective potential of Article 3 ECHR and to demonstrate problematic approaches to rights protection adopted by the ECtHR. Central to a consideration of the obligations which Article 3 ECHR imposes on States is an appreciation of what the substantive terms mean. Accordingly, this chapter has considered the definitions attributed by the domestic courts and the ECtHR to 'torture', 'inhuman', 'degrading', 'treatment' and 'punishment'. The evolution of the ECtHR's understanding of what constitutes torture was considered, paying particular attention to both the original judgment in *Ireland* v. *the United Kingdom* and to the 2018 application to revisit the 1979 judgment in light of new evidence. The ECtHR's reluctance to properly characterise forms of domestic abuse as torture when they so clearly meet the threshold (including by virtue of the presence of an intention or purpose to debase, humiliate or otherwise erode the human dignity and integrity of the victim or survivor), has also been considered, and suggests that the protective potential of Article 3 ECHR is unmet in some cases involving especially vulnerable victims. In addition to these issues with

[300] *Safi and Ors* v. *Greece* (n 298) at [196].
[301] Ibid at [197]–[198].
[302] As suggested by Lady Hale in *R (Elgizouli)* v. *Secretary of State for the Home Department* [2020] UKSC 10, [2021] AC 937 at [14].

classification of treatment, this chapter has also examined a concerning willingness on the part of the ECtHR (and the domestic courts) to dilute the absoluteness of Article 3 ECHR in certain contexts, most notably in cases involving deportation and extradition.

At the core of the prohibition of torture or inhuman or degrading treatment or punishment is respect for and protection of human dignity. While few people would dispute the importance of human dignity not only to Article 3 ECHR but to the ECHR more generally, the case law of the ECtHR and the academic commentary regarding Article 3 ECHR reveals a complex and, at times, contradictory approach to the prohibition of ill-treatment. The approach of domestic courts and the ECtHR in cases involving the removal of individuals has, on a number of occasions, called into question the alleged absoluteness of the prohibition in Article 3 ECHR, which suggests that human dignity may be offset against State interests. While the approach taken by the ECtHR in cases involving extradition and deportation may be explained (at least in part) by reference to the complexities of modern society and the realities of globalisation, the willingness of the domestic courts and the ECtHR to (at least arguably) dilute the absoluteness of the right in Article 3 ECHR is deeply troubling in terms of the right's effectiveness and the effectiveness of the ECHR more generally.

6 Human Rights at the Beginning and End of Life: Abortion, Withdrawal/Refusal of Treatment and Assisted Dying

CONTENTS

6.1 INTRODUCTION

As discussed in Chapter 4 (The Right to Life), there is no European consensus as to when 'life' begins, and States have a margin of appreciation when it comes to affording rights to an embryo/foetus under the ECHR. The ECtHR has also stopped short of finding that the ECHR confers a right to access abortion, leaving it to States to determine whether to permit such access. Likewise, there is no consensus as to whether individuals should be permitted to access assistance in dying though, again, States have a margin of appreciation when it comes to affording individuals the right to die with assistance. This chapter considers the rights issues that have arisen in the specific contexts of abortion and end-of-life treatment with a view to highlighting key themes and the implications for various rights as protected both under the common law and the ECHR. As will become apparent, autonomy and dignity feature heavily in both contexts, with Article 8 ECHR (the right to respect for private life) being the primary basis upon which cases have been brought before the ECtHR in these contexts. The right to life (Article 2 ECHR) and freedom from inhuman or degrading treatment (Article 3 ECHR) have also been regularly referenced in such cases.

It is perhaps trite to observe that issues such as abortion and assisted dying[1] raise complex moral, ethical, philosophical, medical and political considerations. The legal implications – particularly in terms of human rights – are no less multifaceted. For instance, the cases on abortion that have been considered by both the domestic courts in the United Kingdom and the ECtHR have demonstrated that the permissibility of abortion raises difficult questions in respect of identifying what and whose rights and interests are at stake and how they can (or should) be balanced. Likewise, as the few cases on permitting access to assisted dying that have been considered by domestic courts and the ECtHR highlight, this issue not only raises questions in terms of the rights of those who would access assistance if they could; there are potential implications for the rights of others and wider societal interests that need to be considered. This complexity, coupled with a lack of European consensus in respect of these issues, has resulted in the ECtHR affording a very wide margin of appreciation to States in regulating the start and end of life. That is not to say, however, that State decision-making in these areas is unbounded. Several key cases considered in this chapter demonstrate that the ECtHR retains supervisory oversight in terms of the ECHR implications of the regulation of abortion and end-of-life treatment. Such cases present an opportunity to consider wider themes that

[1] Unless stated otherwise, 'assisted dying' is an umbrella term used in this chapter to refer to assisted suicide and voluntary active euthanasia.

permeate this book, including the ECtHR's use of vulnerability to justify its decision-making and the function of the margin of appreciation in sustaining the legitimacy of the Court as a supranational rights-enforcement entity.

6.2 ABORTION AND THE ECHR

6.2.1 The Beginning of 'Life' and Abortion

Article 4 of the American Convention on Human Rights provides that the right to life applies 'from the moment of conception'.[2] This can be contrasted with Article 2 ECHR which refers only to 'life' and does not proceed to qualify it in any way. In both contexts, the judicial bodies responsible for interpreting the relevant rights document have played a significant role in clarifying the scope and application of the provisions to the antenatal context. The Inter-American Court of Human Rights has determined that embryos are not persons with rights and do not have an absolute right to life.[3] Rather, the right to life (and the degree of its protection) is 'gradual and incremental according to its development'.[4] Indeed, the Inter-American Commission on Human Rights drew the ire of pro-life Senators in the United States[5] for its statements to Member States encouraging them to repeal blanket bans on abortion, including that:

> laws criminalizing abortion in all circumstances have a negative impact on women's dignity and their rights to life, to personal integrity, and to health, as well as on their general right to live free from violence and discrimination. The absolute criminalization of abortion, including in cases where the woman's life is at risk and when the pregnancy results from a rape or incest, imposes a disproportionate burden on the exercise of women's rights and creates a context that facilitates unsafe abortions and high rates of maternal mortality.[6]

[2] The inclusion of this phrase 'not found in any other human rights treaty' was, according to Cecilia Medina Quiroga and Valeska David Contreras, driven by religious motivations and intended to 'prohibit all types of abortion': Cecilia Medina Quiroga and Valeska David Contreras, *The American Convention on Human Rights: Critical Rights and Their Theory and Practice* (3rd ed) (Intersentia, 2022), pp.198–199.

[3] *Artavia Murillo et al. ('In Vitro Fertilization')* v. *Costa Rica* [2012], IACtHR, Ser. C No. 257.

[4] Ibid at [264].

[5] The US is a founding member of the Organisation of American States but has not ratified the American Convention on Human Rights.

[6] Inter-American Commission of Human Rights, 'IACHR Urges All States to Adopt Comprehensive, Immediate Measures to Respect and Protect Women's Sexual and Reproductive Rights', 23 October 2017, https://mailchi.mp/dist/iachr-urges-all-states-to-adopt-comprehensive-immediate-measures-to-respect-and-protect-womens-sexual-and-reproductive-rights?e=07a43d57e2. See discussion of Ligia De Jesús Castaldi, 'Partial U.S. sanctions on Inter-American Commission on Human Rights', Oxford Human Rights Hub, 2 August 2019, https://ohrh.law.ox.ac.uk/partial-u-s-sanctions-on-inter-american-commission-on-human-rights/.

That such statements would be received with hostility in some quarters in the US is not surprising given that, following the overturning by the Supreme Court of the United States[7] of the landmark decision of *Roe* v. *Wade*,[8] there has been a proliferation of blanket (or near-complete) bans on abortion in many US states.[9] The Inter-American Commission's comments reflect the issues that have arisen in the cases that have been considered by UK courts and the ECtHR concerning similarly restrictive approaches to abortion. Before considering such cases, it is necessary to examine the approach taken by the domestic and Strasbourg courts to the meaning of 'life' in Article 2 ECHR.

6.2.2 The Unborn and the Right to Life under Article 2 ECHR

In several cases, the ECtHR has considered whether Article 2 ECHR extends to embryos and/or foetuses or is confined to life following birth. In *Vo* v. *France*,[10] the ECtHR observed that:

> in the circumstances examined to date by the Convention institutions – that is, in the various laws on abortion – the unborn child is not regarded as a 'person' directly protected by Art.2 of the Convention and . . . if the unborn do have a 'right' to 'life', it is implicitly limited by the mother's rights and interests. The Convention institutions have not, however, ruled out the possibility that in certain circumstances safeguards may be extended to the unborn child. That is what appears to have been contemplated by the Commission in considering that 'Article 8 § 1 cannot be interpreted as meaning that pregnancy and its termination are, as a principle, solely a matter of the private life of the mother' and by the Court in . . . *Boso* [*v. Italy* [2002] ECHR 846] . . . It is also clear from an examination of these cases that the issue has always been determined by weighing up various, and sometimes conflicting, rights or freedoms claimed by a woman, a mother or a father in relation to one another or vis-à-vis an unborn child.

According to Lord Kerr sitting in the UK Supreme Court (with whom Lord Wilson agreed), 'the proper construction to be placed on *Vo* is that contracting

[7] *Dobbs* v. *Jackson Women's Health Organisation*, 597 US 66 (2022).

[8] *Roe* v. *Wade*, 410 US 113 (1973). The decision had recognised a constitutional right to abortion.

[9] 'State bans on abortion throughout pregnancy', *Guttmacher*, 7 July 2025, www.guttmacher.org/state-policy/explore/state-policies-abortion-bans, Human Rights Watch, 'Human Rights Crisis: Abortion in the United States After Dobbs', 18 April 2023, www.hrw.org/news/2023/04/18/human-rights-crisis-abortion-united-states-after-dobbs, Nigel Madden et al., 'Post-Dobbs Abortion Restrictions and the Families They Leave Behind' (2024) **114** American Public Health Association 10. For a more general assessment of the impact of *Dobbs* on 'abortion law and politics', see Rachel Rebouché and Mary Ziegler, 'Fracture: Abortion Law and Politics After *Dobbs*' (2023) **76** SMU Law Review 27.

[10] *Vo* v. *France* [GC] (2005) 40 EHRR 12. In 2024, France amended its constitution to enshrine the 'guaranteed freedom' to terminate a pregnancy. For a discussion of the amendment, see Eleonora Bottini, Margaux Bouaziz and Stephanie Hennette-Vauchez, 'Enshrining Abortion Rights in the French Constitution', *Verfassungsblog*, 9 March 2024, https://verfassungsblog.de/enshrining-abortion-rights-in-the-french-constitution/.

states enjoy a margin of appreciation in deciding when human life begins but that this does not afford protection to the foetus under article 2'.[11]

As a result of the margin of appreciation afforded to States to determine when life begins and what rights, if any, to confer on embryos and foetuses, laws placing consent restrictions on in vitro fertilisation have been found to be compatible with Articles 2 and 8 ECHR (even though the consequence is that the embryo will be destroyed)[12] and States can prohibit the donating of embryos to science on the basis of protecting the potential 'life' of the embryo.[13]

That there may be competing considerations in cases involving access to abortion services was apparent in several of the earlier decisions of the ECtHR concerning access to abortion services in Ireland. Prior to its amendment following a referendum in 2018,[14] the Constitution of Ireland had provided (in Article 40.3.3) that '[t]he State acknowledges the right to life of the unborn and, with due regard to the equal right to life of the mother, guarantees in its laws to respect, and as far as practicable, by its laws to defend and vindicate that right'. In *Open Door Counselling*,[15] the Grand Chamber considered the compatibility with Article 10 ECHR (freedom of expression) of injunctions preventing the claimants (counselling organisations in Ireland) from giving clients information regarding abortion services available in England. The Grand Chamber accepted that the injunctions were necessary, inter alia, to protect morals (which is an explicit aim in Article 10(2) ECHR). In particular, the Grand Chamber acknowledged that the 'protection of morals' in Ireland included (as evidenced by Article 40.3.3 of the Constitution) protection of the

[11] *In the matter of an application by the Northern Ireland Human Rights Commission for Judicial Review (Northern Ireland)* [2018] UKSC 27, [2019] 1 All ER 173 (*'Northern Ireland Abortion Case'*) at [305]. See also *Paton* v. *the United Kingdom* (1981) 3 EHRR 408 and *Re MB (Medical Treatment)* [1997] EWCA Civ 3093, [1997] 2 FLR 426.

[12] *Evans* v. *the United Kingdom* [GC] [2006] ECHR 200.

[13] *Parrillo* v. *Italy* [GC] [2015] ECHR 755. Though it is worth noting that in *Jennings* v. *Human Fertilisation and Embryology Authority* [2022] EWHC 1619 (Fam), [2023] 1 FLR 476, the High Court found that it would be a disproportionate interference with Mr Jennings' Article 8 ECHR right to respect for private life to require the written consent of his late wife (Ms Choya) to use an embryo they had created together. Jennings wished to use the embryo to have a child via a surrogate; however, there was no valid written consent from Choya to that course of action. The Court held that a requirement of written consent in all of the circumstances (which, the Court found, indicated that Choya *would* have agreed to the embryo being implanted in a surrogate) would be a disproportionate interference with Jennings' Article 8 ECHR rights.

[14] For a discussion of the backstory to the referendum, and the referendum itself, see Louise Maguire and Fiona Murphy, 'Putting Abortion in the Frame: The Success of the Campaign to Repeal the 8th Amendment in Ireland' (2023) 12 Social Sciences 9.

[15] *Open Door Counselling Ltd and Dublin Well Woman Centre & Ors* v. *Ireland* (1993) 15 EHRR 244.

right to life of the unborn.[16] Nevertheless, the injunction (especially given its absolute and perpetual nature) constituted a disproportionate interference with the claimants' Article 10 ECHR rights.[17] The Grand Chamber further noted that the injunction 'created a risk to the health of those women who are now seeking abortions at a later stage in their pregnancy, due to lack of proper counselling, and who are not availing themselves of customary medical supervision after the abortion has taken place'.[18] These were factors 'to take into consideration in assessing the proportionality of the restriction'.[19]

Almost two decades after *Open Door* was delivered, the Grand Chamber again considered restrictions on access to abortion services in Ireland. *A, B and C* v. *Ireland* centred on whether the ban in Ireland on abortion in all cases, bar those involving a real and substantial risk to the life of the pregnant woman, violated the applicants' right to respect for private life in Article 8 ECHR.[20] The facts of this case are considered in greater detail below. For now, it is sufficient to note that the State had argued that the interferences with the applicants' Article 8 ECHR rights[21] pursued the legitimate aims of 'the protection of morals and the rights and freedoms of others including the protection of pre-natal life'.[22] While the applicants in *A, B and C* challenged the State's contention that the legislation reflected the moral views of the Irish people, the Grand Chamber reiterated its finding in *Open Door Counselling* that 'the impugned restriction ... pursued the legitimate aim of the protection of morals of which the protection in Ireland of the right to life of the unborn was one aspect'.[23] The majority's approach was not without criticism, with the dissenting judges stating:

> it is the first time that the Court has disregarded the existence of a European consensus [of permitting abortion on more expansive grounds] on the basis of 'profound moral views'. Even assuming that these profound moral views are still well embedded in the conscience of the majority of Irish people, to consider that this can override the European consensus, which tends in a completely different direction, is a real and dangerous new departure in the Court's case-law.[24]

[16] Ibid at [63]. [17] Ibid at [73]–[74]. [18] Ibid at [77]. [19] Ibid.

[20] *A, B and C* v. *Ireland* [GC] (2011) 53 EHRR 13. The ECtHR determined that the applicants' claims under Article 3 ECHR were manifestly ill-founded because the minimum level of severity required to engage Article 3 ECHR had not been reached.

[21] The Grand Chamber noted that while Article 8 ECHR cannot 'be interpreted as conferring a right to abortion, the Court finds that the prohibition in Ireland of abortion where sought for reasons of health and/or well-being about which the first and second applicants complained, and the third applicant's alleged inability to establish her eligibility for a lawful abortion in Ireland, come within the scope of their right to respect for their private lives and accordingly Article 8' (ibid at [214]).

[22] Ibid at [181]. [23] Ibid at [227].

[24] Ibid, joint partly dissenting opinion of Judges Rozakis, Tulkens, Fura, Hirvelä, Malinverni and Poalelungi at [9].

Reliance on protection of morals was less successful in the *Northern Ireland Abortion Case*[25] which is considered in greater detail below. In that case, Lady Hale observed that 'there is no evidence that the profound moral views of the people of Northern Ireland are against allowing abortion in the three situations under discussion here [namely, where the pregnancy arose as a result of rape or incest or there was a fatal foetal abnormality]. Quite the reverse. There is a remarkably consistent series of public opinion polls showing majority support for abortion in these circumstances.'[26] Thus, while Lady Hale accepted – in line with *Vo*, *Open Door* and *A, B and C* – that 'the community undoubtedly does have a moral interest in protecting the life, health and welfare of the unborn', it is also the case that the:

> community . . . has an interest in protecting the life, health and welfare of the pregnant woman – that interest also underlies the regulation of assisted reproduction, of midwifery and of the termination of pregnancy. And pregnant women are undoubtedly rights-holders under both the Convention and domestic law with autonomy as well as health and welfare rights. The question, therefore, is how the balance is to be struck between the two.[27]

How the domestic courts and Strasbourg have struck that balance is the focus of the next section.

6.2.3 A 'Right' to Abortion?

While the unborn are not recognised as persons for the purposes of the right to life in Article 2 ECHR, that does not mean that there is a general right under the ECHR to access abortion services. Certainly, there is a strong European consensus that abortion should be permitted,[28] and a European consensus,

[25] *Northern Ireland Abortion Case* (n 11). [26] Ibid at [24]. [27] Ibid at [21].

[28] As was recognised fifteen years ago in *A, B and C* (n 20) at [112]: 'Abortion is available on request (according to certain criteria including gestational limits) in some 30 Contracting States. An abortion justified on health grounds is available in some 40 Contracting States and justified on well-being grounds in some 35 such States. Three Contracting States prohibit abortion in all circumstances (Andorra, Malta and San Marino). In recent years, certain States have extended the grounds on which abortion can be obtained (Monaco, Montenegro, Portugal and Spain).' And the ECtHR recognised in 2011 that 'there is indeed a consensus amongst a substantial majority of the Contracting States of the Council of Europe towards allowing abortion and that most Contracting Parties have in their legislation resolved the conflicting rights of the foetus and the mother in favour of greater access to abortion' (*R.R.* v. *Poland* (2011) 53 EHRR 31 at [186]). See, more recently, *Northern Ireland Abortion Case* (n 11) at [305]: '[there is a] consensus across the vast majority of contracting states as to the right to abortion in cases of rape, incest and fatal foetal abnormality. While the laws of those states vary in terms of gestational limits, all apart from Ireland, Liechtenstein, Malta, San Marino and Andorra are unanimous in permitting abortion in those circumstances.' In a report, the Centre for Reproductive Rights noted that '[a]bortion on request is legal in Austria, Belgium, Bulgaria, Croatia, Cyprus, Czech Republic, Denmark, Estonia, France, Finland, Germany, Greece, Hungary, Ireland, Italy, Latvia, Lithuania,

usually, narrows the margin of appreciation within which a State may regulate conduct.[29] However, the ECtHR has, to date, declined to find a right to access abortion within any of the articles of the ECHR. It thus remains within the State's margin of appreciation to determine how it will regulate abortion, which includes, it seems, completely prohibiting abortion.[30] The inverse, however, should also hold true: it remains within a State's margin of appreciation to permit abortion on unlimited grounds.[31] The approach in England, Scotland and Wales is considered in Section 6.3 below. Given the significant rights implications, the ECtHR's case law on abortion has tended to focus on States whose regulation of abortion sits at the other (more restrictive) end of the spectrum. In addition to the cases involving Ireland referred to above, several cases have centred on the regulation of abortion in Poland. For ease of reference, the cases have been thematically grouped under the rights in issue.

6.2.4 Abortion and the 'Right to Life' Whilst Pregnant

We have already seen that the right to life has been invoked (albeit without success) in cases *challenging* laws permitting abortion.[32] A further context in which the right to life has been invoked has been in support of the argument that a failure to ensure access to abortion in cases in which the pregnant woman's life is at risk raises issues in terms of the State's obligations under Article 2 ECHR.[33] It is arguable that if a State criminalises abortion in *all* cases,

Luxembourg, Netherlands, Portugal, Romania, Slovakia, Slovenia, Spain and Sweden' (Centre for Reproductive Rights, 'European Abortion Laws: A Comparative Overview', September 2023, https://reproductiverights.org/wp-content/uploads/2023/09/European-Abortion-Laws-A-Comparative-Overview-new-9-13-23.pdf.

29 See, for instance, *A, B and C* v. *Ireland* (n 20), joint partly dissenting opinion of Judges Rozakis, Tulkens, Fura, Hirvelä, Malinverni and Poalelungi at [5].

30 Certainly, when the Court last examined this issue in detail in *A, B and C* v. *Ireland* (ibid), it noted that three states completely prohibited abortion without indicating that such a position would be contrary to the ECHR.

31 Again, the Court did not appear to take issue with the relatively broad grounds upon which abortion was permitted in a significant number of Member States in *A, B and C* v. *Ireland* (ibid) (though note that this issue – i.e., whether broad rights to abortion are compatible with the Convention rights of others – has not been the subject of proceedings before the ECtHR, though the domestic courts have considered it recently as is discussed below).

32 See Section 6.2.2.

33 The overwhelming majority of people who conceive identify as women. (See, for instance, Daphna Stroumsa et al., 'Pregnancy Outcomes in a US Cohort of Transgender People' (2023) JAMA 21, 1879–1881.) It is, then, unsurprising that the case law, international material and academic commentary on reproductive issues such as abortion tend to refer to 'pregnant *women*'. It must, however, be acknowledged that not all individuals who conceive identify as women. Recognising this diversity is especially important if we are to ensure that reproductive rights are effective, not least given evidence of impediments to accessing quality health care for transgender, nonbinary and gender-expansive people (see, for instance, Elizabeth Kukura,

it is putting the lives of some pregnant people at risk in violation of its positive obligation to put in place an adequate regulatory framework that deters threats to life (in respect of which, see Chapter 4 (Life)). Indeed, a system that permits abortion but only on the basis of a threat to life of the pregnant person may violate the State's regulatory obligation under Article 2 where the law is unclear or is not adequately implemented, exposing pregnant people to very grave risks. An example of such a case is that of Savita Halappanavar, who died in an Irish hospital aged thirty-one years after she developed septicaemia following a miscarriage when she was seventeen weeks pregnant. Halappanavar had been refused an abortion despite the fact that she was miscarrying and reporting being in pain.[34] The basis for refusing the abortion was not clear, though the clinical midwife manager admitted during the subsequent inquest to stating that 'this is a Catholic country'.[35] The coronial inquest revealed significant failings in the treatment of Halappanavar including a failure to review her blood test results which indicated infection and a failure to conduct adequate observations.[36] Whether such failings were reflective of a systematic issue such as to engage the State's Article 2 ECHR obligations in the context of medical care[37] is not clear. However, it was conceded by the Irish Government at the time that there was 'legal confusion' which had led to 'the type of difficulties' that had resulted in Halappanavar's death[38] which lends support to the argument that the regulatory system relating to abortions that was in effect in Ireland at the time was deficient, in violation of Article 2 ECHR.

Similarly, it could be argued that a system that compels pregnant people to obtain illegal abortions because of the restrictive nature of its regulations, thereby exposing them to the risk of significant injury or potential death,[39]

'Reconceiving Reproductive Health Systems: Caring for Trans, Nonbinary, and Gender-Expansive People during Pregnancy and Childbirth' (2022) 50 Journal of Law, Medicine and Ethics 3). When referring to specific cases, international material or commentary, this chapter uses the terminology employed therein. Where, however, normative issues regarding reproductive rights and access to reproductive services are discussed, we endeavour to use the more inclusive 'pregnant person' or 'pregnant people' in recognition that not all persons who conceive identify as women.

[34] Muiris Houston, 'Investigations Begin into Woman Who Was Refused an Abortion' (2012) BMJ 345.

[35] Muiris Houston, 'Coroner Identifies Two Failings in Care of Woman Who Died after Being Refused an Abortion' (2013) BMJ 346.

[36] Ibid. [37] See Chapter 4 (Life). [38] Houston (n 34).

[39] See, for instance, Terry McGovern, Ira Memaj and Samantha Garbers, 'US Abortion Restrictions Are Causing Widespread Harm' (2024) BMJ 386 and UNHCR, 'United States: Abortion bans put millions of women and girls at risk, UN experts say', 2 June 2023, https://www.ohchr.org/en/press-releases/2023/06/united-states-abortion-bans-put-millions-women-and-girls-risk-un-experts-say#:~:text=GENEVA%20(2%20June%202023)%20%E2%80%93,%2C%20UN%20experts*%20said%20today.

also demonstrates a failure to comply with the positive obligation to put in place a regulatory framework that deters threats to life.[40]

6.2.5 Abortion and Freedom from Torture or Inhuman or Degrading Treatment

Article 3 ECHR prohibits torture or inhuman or degrading treatment or punishment.[41] Just as a foetus does not have a distinct right to life under the ECHR, nor does it have an absolute right to freedom from torture or inhuman or degrading treatment. There is, however, no doubt that pregnant people have rights under Article 3 ECHR. Given the breadth of the meaning of inhuman and degrading,[42] it is unsurprising that Article 3 ECHR has featured prominently in several of the abortion cases before the ECtHR (and in the *Northern Ireland Abortion Case* before the UK Supreme Court) and the ECtHR has found a violation of Article 3 ECHR in cases involving abortion access (or, more specifically, the lack thereof).[43]

In *RR* v. *Poland*,[44] the applicant had been denied access to genetic tests in order to confirm preliminary diagnostic testing which suggested that the foetus she was pregnant with had a serious malformation (Turner Syndrome). The applicant was prevented from accessing such testing – which was available to her (and, indeed, which domestic law obliged authorities to ensure unimpeded access to in such cases) – due to significant failings on the part of various medical professionals including 'procrastination, confusion and a failure to provide her with proper counselling and information'.[45] This resulted in the applicant eventually having the diagnosis confirmed *after* the date at which she was permitted to obtain an abortion under domestic law (twenty-four weeks). The ECtHR found that, as a result of the inaction on the part of health professionals, the applicant 'had to endure weeks of painful uncertainty' and 'suffered acute anguish'.[46] This constituted degrading treatment under Article 3 ECHR, for which the State was responsible. While the Court did not explicitly clarify the basis on which Article 3 ECHR was engaged, it is likely that the State's responsibility arose because of systemic failings in the medical system that resulted in the applicant being denied access to genetic testing which domestic law required she have unimpeded access to.[47]

A violation of Article 3 ECHR was also found in *P and S* v. *Poland*.[48] The case concerned a minor who became pregnant as a result of a sexual assault.

[40] See Chapter 4 (Life). [41] See Chapter 5 (Ill-Treatment). [42] Ibid.

[43] The ECtHR rejected the applicants' claim in *A, B and C* v. *Ireland* (n 20), and the applicant's claim in *Tysiac* v. *Poland* (2007) 45 EHRR 42, that the minimum level of severity had been met in order to engage Article 3 ECHR.

[44] *R.R.* v. *Poland* (n 28). [45] Ibid at [153]. [46] Ibid at [159].

[47] On a State's responsibility for systemic failings in the medical context, see Chapter 4 (Life).

[48] *P and S* v. *Poland* [2012] ECHR 1853.

In such circumstances, domestic law permitted abortion and the applicant, with her mother, attempted to access such services. However, as with *RR* v. *Poland*, the 'approach of the authorities was marred by procrastination, confusion and lack of proper and objective counselling and information', with doctors attempting to 'exert pressure' on the applicant.[49] In all, the applicant 'was treated by the authorities in a deplorable manner' and her suffering reached the minimum level of severity under Article 3 ECHR (though the Court did not specify the type of ill-treatment).[50] Again, it is not clear whether the State's responsibility was based on the its positive or negative obligations under Article 3 ECHR, though the reference to the applicant being 'treated by the authorities' suggests it could be a breach of the negative obligation under Article 3 ECHR.

In another decision again involving Poland, the ECtHR described being forced to travel abroad for an abortion as 'psychologically arduous'.[51] However, and notwithstanding that the applicant – who was prevented from accessing an abortion on the basis of a Constitutional Court ruling which the ECtHR found not to be 'in accordance with the law' as required by Article 8(2) ECHR – 'suffered emotional and mental pain', the Court found that the minimum level of severity was not met.[52]

Finally, in *SFK* v. *Russia*,[53] the ECtHR found a violation of both the negative and the procedural aspects of Article 3 ECHR. At the instigation of her parents, the applicant was subjected to an abortion which she did not consent to and which was carried out 'in breach of all the applicable medical rules'.[54] The minimum level of severity was clearly met as:

> forced abortion undergone in these circumstances was contrary to the applicant's human dignity. It was an egregious form of inhuman and degrading treatment which not only resulted in a serious immediate damage to her health – that is the loss of her unborn child – but also entailed long-lasting negative physical and psychological effects.[55]

The abortion was carried out at a public hospital by medical professionals who were employed by the State. On that basis, the ECtHR (by majority) concluded that the State bore 'direct responsibility under Article 3'.[56] Judges Roosma and Lobov disagreed with the finding regarding the State's negative obligation, noting that:

> according to the Court's settled case-law, a Contracting State will be responsible under the Convention for violations of human rights caused by acts of its agents carried out in the performance of their duties. Where the behaviour of a State agent is unlawful,

[49] Ibid at [167]. [50] Ibid at [168]. [51] *M.L.* v. *Poland* [2023] ECHR 1009 at [84].
[52] Ibid. [53] *S.F.K.* v. *Russia* [2022] ECHR 807. [54] Ibid at [81]. [55] Ibid.
[56] Ibid at [80].

the question of whether the impugned acts can be imputed to the State requires an assessment of the totality of the circumstances and consideration of the nature and circumstances of the conduct in question.[57]

In the instant case, the abortion 'was the result of the concerted actions of the applicant's parents and the relevant medical personnel of a public hospital. More specifically, the medical personnel concerned subjected the applicant to inhuman treatment in the context of their criminal venture with the applicant's parents rather than as a patient admitted to the hospital in a regular manner.'[58] In those circumstances, the dissenting judges suggested that the case ought to have been approached as one involving domestic abuse which engaged the State's *positive* obligation to protect.[59]

6.2.6 Abortion and Private Life

As with other rights in the ECHR,[60] Article 8 ECHR imposes both negative and positive obligations on the State and regulations restricting access to abortion services can engage both.[61] Ultimately, it may not matter which lens the obligation in the case is examined through, since:

> The boundaries between the State's positive and negative obligations under [Article 8] do not lend themselves to precise definition. The applicable principles are nonetheless similar. In both the negative and positive contexts regard must be had to the fair balance that has to be struck between the competing interests of the individual and of the community as a whole; and in both contexts the State enjoys a certain margin of appreciation ... While the State regulations on abortion relate to the traditional balancing of privacy and the public interest, they must – in case of a therapeutic abortion – be also assessed against the positive obligations of the State to secure the physical integrity of mothers-to-be.[62]

There are several ways in which a State's regulation of abortion access can engage (and violate) its obligations under Article 8 ECHR, although 'not every regulation of the termination of pregnancy constitutes an interference with the right to respect for the private life of the mother'.[63] Thus, it is not a given in a case involving access to abortion services that Article 8 ECHR will be engaged. The ECtHR has, however, also found that 'private life' in Article 8 ECHR is a 'broad concept' which 'encompasses, inter alia, the right to

[57] Ibid, partly dissenting opinion of Judges Rooma and Lobov at [7]. [58] Ibid.

[59] Ibid at [8]. See, in this respect, Chapter 4 (Life).

[60] See, for instance, the right to life (as discussed in Chapter 4), the right to freedom from ill-treatment (Chapter 5) and prohibition of slavery and forced labour (Chapter 7).

[61] In terms of the negative obligation, see *A, B and C* v. *Ireland* (n 20), and *M.L.* v. *Poland* (n 51). In terms of the positive obligations, see *Tysiac* v. *Poland* (n 43), *R.R.* v. *Poland* (n 28) and *P and S* v. *Poland* (n 48).

[62] *R.R.* v. *Poland* (n 28) at [189]. [63] *A, B and C* v. *Ireland* (n 20) at [216].

personal autonomy', 'personal development' and 'physical and psychological integrity'[64] such that restrictions on access to abortion may constitute an interference with the right to private life. Indeed, in the most recent abortion cases before the Court, it has found that Article 8 ECHR was engaged, with the focus being on whether such interferences were justified under Article 8(2) ECHR 'namely whether the interference was "in accordance with the law" and "necessary in a democratic society" for one of the "legitimate aims" specified in Article 8 of the Convention'.[65]

A significant takeaway from the Court's abortion jurisprudence is that while there is no right to abortion under Article 8 ECHR, where the State elects to regulate abortion – including where it provides for abortion in limited circumstances – it must ensure effective access to such services. This includes providing access to relevant information and appropriate medical treatment to enable pregnant people to make informed decisions and, if eligible, to exercise their right under domestic law to access abortion services.[66] Nevertheless, the State retains a not insignificant margin of appreciation in determining how such regulations should be framed.

In *A, B and C* v. *Ireland*, a majority Grand Chamber found that the Irish regulatory system, which limited abortion to cases involving a real and substantial risk to the life of the pregnant woman, was proportionate to the legitimate aim of protection of morals, such that in the cases of A and B, who sought abortions on bases other than a 'real and substantial risk' to life (namely, on 'health and well-being grounds'[67]), there had been no violation. The Grand Chamber was, however, unanimous that there had been a violation of Article 8 ECHR in the case of C who had a rare form of cancer and had been treated with chemotherapy in the three years before her pregnancy. She became pregnant unintentionally and was unaware of her pregnancy when she underwent several tests for cancer which were contraindicated during pregnancy. She was unable to obtain sufficient information from her doctors regarding the impact of her pregnancy on her health and life and of the prior tests on the foetus. Nor was she able to ascertain whether she would be eligible for an abortion. She travelled to England to obtain an abortion though upon returning, she suffered complications including prolonged bleeding and infection.

The Grand Chamber concluded in respect of C that Article 8 imposes positive obligations on the State which include the provision of an 'accessible and effective procedure by which [C] could have established whether she qualified for a lawful abortion'.[68] While pregnant women in Ireland were

[64] *M.L.* v. *Poland* (n 51) at [91] and [154]. [65] Ibid at [155].

[66] See, for instance, Stephanie Palmer, 'Abortion and Human Rights' [2014] 6 EHRLR 596 at 603.

[67] As so characterised by Lady Hale in the *Northern Ireland Abortion Case* (n 11) at [23].

[68] *A, B and C* v. *Ireland* (n 20) at [267].

constitutionally entitled to an abortion where the pregnancy posed a real and substantive risk to their life, there was a 'striking discordance between the theoretical right to a lawful abortion in Ireland on grounds of a relevant risk to a woman's life and the reality of its practical implementation'.[69]

A similar approach was taken in *Tysiac* v. *Poland*.[70] In that case, the pregnant woman had significantly compromised vision before becoming pregnant and, being concerned that the pregnancy could lead to further deterioration in her eyesight, sought advice from medical professionals. Under Polish law in effect at the time, abortion was permitted where the pregnancy posed a threat to the pregnant woman's life or health. All the experts agreed that there was a risk to the claimant's eyesight as a result of the pregnancy, but they refused to recommend that the pregnancy be terminated, despite the claimant's requests. While the claimant was able to secure a recommendation for termination from a GP, doctors at the hospital refused to perform the abortion. The claimant gave birth and her eyesight deteriorated considerably, and she faced the prospect of going blind. Domestic proceedings against the hospital and specific doctors found no wrongdoing.

The ECtHR by majority (with only one judge dissenting) concluded that there *had* been a violation of Article 8 ECHR. The majority held that 'effective enjoyment of the rights guaranteed by [Article 8 requires] that the relevant decision-making process [with respect to access to abortion services] is fair and such as to afford due respect to the interests safeguarded by [Article 8]'.[71] The Court built upon the decision in *A, B and C*, holding that there is also a need for procedural safeguards which secure access to a therapeutic abortion as provided for in domestic law. Such procedural safeguards include a right to be heard, to have one's views considered by an independent competent authority which can resolve any disagreements between patients and their practitioners or between practitioners.[72] There were no such procedural guarantees under Polish law at the time and, as a result, there had been a violation of Article 8 ECHR.

In a subsequent decision, also against Poland, the ECtHR found that the failure to provide timely access to diagnostic services to enable a decision to be made regarding termination of a pregnancy (which was permitted in specific circumstances under domestic law) in which the foetus had a very serious chromosomal abnormality (Turner Syndrome) violated Article 8 ECHR.[73] A violation of Article 8 ECHR was also found in *P and S* v. *Poland*[74] as a result of the failure of domestic authorities (including public health facilities) to provide effective access to abortion services for a minor who had become pregnant as a result of sexual assault (there being a right to abortion in such

[69] Ibid at [264]. [70] *Tysiac* v. *Poland* (n 43). [71] Ibid at [113]. [72] Ibid at [116]–[117].
[73] *R.R.* v. *Poland* (n 28). [74] *P and S* v. *Poland* (n 48).

circumstances under domestic law at the time). As a majority of the Court observed, in terms almost identical to those employed in respect of the applicant C in *A, B and C* v. *Ireland*:

> the uncertainty which arose in the present case despite a background of circumstances in which under [the relevant domestic law] there was a right to lawful abortion resulted in a striking discordance between the theoretical right to such an abortion on the grounds referred to in that provision and the reality of its practical implementation.[75]

In another case against Poland, the ECtHR was confronted with an Article 8 ECHR challenge to the significant curtailment of Poland's abortion laws by the domestic Constitutional Court. The argument was that, given the ECtHR's earlier finding (in separate, unrelated cases) that the Constitutional Court was not a 'tribunal established by law', the amendments to the abortion regulations which significantly curtailed abortion access were not compatible with the rule of law and the interference with the claimant's rights (who was forced to travel overseas to obtain an abortion) were 'not in accordance with the law' as required by Article 8(2) ECHR.[76] In finding that Article 8 had, indeed, been violated, a majority of the Court observed that 'the interference with the applicant's rights cannot be regarded as lawful in terms of Article 8 of the Convention because it was not issued by a body compatible with the rule of law requirements'.[77]

In *Boso* v. *Italy*,[78] the ECtHR rejected a father's claim that a mother's decision to have an abortion – in conformance with domestic law – without consulting him violated *his* right to respect for family and private life under Article 8 ECHR. As the Court observed, 'the potential father's right to respect for his private and family life cannot be interpreted so widely as to embrace the right to be consulted or to apply to a court about an abortion which his wife intends to have performed on her'.[79]

6.3 ABORTION REGULATION AND RIGHTS: THE DOMESTIC CONTEXT

6.3.1 Abortion in England, Scotland and Wales

In England, Scotland and Wales, it is lawful for a registered medical practitioner to perform an abortion if two medical practitioners are of the opinion ('formed in good faith') that one (or more) of the following conditions is met:

[75] Ibid at [111]. [76] *M.L.* v. *Poland* (n 51). [77] Ibid at [175].
[78] *Boso* v. *Italy*, App. No. 50490/99, 05/09/2002.
[79] Ibid at [2]. See also, *Paton* v. *the United Kingdom* (n 11).

- In a pregnancy of no more than twenty-four weeks gestation, that 'the continuance of the pregnancy would involve risk, greater than if the pregnancy were terminated, of injury to the physical or mental health of the pregnant woman or any existing children of her family';
- In a pregnancy of any gestation:
  - Where the termination is necessary to prevent 'grave permanent injury to the physical or mental health of the pregnant woman';
  - Where continuing the pregnancy would 'involve risk to the life of the pregnant woman, greater than if the pregnancy were terminated'; or
  - Where 'there is a substantial risk that if the child were born it would suffer from such physical or mental abnormalities as to be seriously handicapped'.[80]

While not unbounded, the eligibility criteria to exercise the 'right'[81] to abortion conferred by domestic statute in three of the four countries comprising the UK is broader than many other jurisdictions in the Council of Europe.[82]

6.3.2 Abortion in Northern Ireland

The Northern Ireland context is somewhat more complex, with a significant and recent jurisprudential intervention from the UK's Supreme Court as well as legislation from Parliament in Westminster culminating in a profound change in the law regulating abortion in Northern Ireland. Under the devolution settlement in the UK, Northern Ireland remains competent to legislate with respect to abortion and historically had done so in a far more restrictive manner than that which applied elsewhere in the UK. More specifically, until recently, abortion was only permissible in Northern Ireland if there was a risk to the pregnant woman's life or of serious long-term or permanent injury to their physical or mental health. Procuring an abortion on any other ground was a criminal offence. In 2018 the Committee on the Elimination of Discrimination Against Women (CEDAW Committee) published a report in which it found that the UK had violated a number of provisions of the Convention on the Elimination of All Forms of Discrimination Against Women as a result of the restrictive abortion laws in Northern Ireland.[83]

[80] Abortion Act 1967, s.1.

[81] As so characterised by the Court of Appeal in *R (Crowter & Ors)* v. *Secretary of State for Health and Social Care* [2022] EWCA Civ 1559, [2023] WLR 989 at [1].

[82] In particular, it would seem that England, Wales and Scotland allow for termination on request at the latest stage of gestation – twenty-four weeks – amongst most European countries: Christian Fiala et al., 'Abortion: Legislation and Statistics in Europe' (2022) **27** The European Journal of Contraception and Reproductive Health Care 4.

[83] CEDAW, 'Inquiry concerning the United Kingdom of Great Britain and Northern Ireland under article 8 of the Optional Protocol to the Convention on the Elimination of All Forms of

These violations were both 'grave' and 'systematic' given that the law in Northern Ireland (as it then stood) 'compel[led] women in cases of severe fetal impairment, including fatal fetal abnormality, and victims of rape or incest to carry pregnancies to full term, thereby subjecting them to severe physical and mental anguish, constituting gender based violence against women' and 'compel[led] women to carry pregnancies to full term, to travel outside Northern Ireland to undergo legal abortion or to self-administer abortifacients'.[84]

Following the publication of the CEDAW Committee's report, the NIHRC brought proceedings before the courts in Northern Ireland challenging the compatibility of Northern Ireland's abortion law with the ECHR (in particular, Articles 3 and 8 ECHR, alone and together with Article 14 ECHR (freedom from discrimination)). After mixed success before the lower courts, the NIHRC's case was heard by the UK Supreme Court which held, by a majority, that the Commission lacked standing to bring the challenge.[85] Nevertheless, a differently composed majority of the Court proceeded to set out its findings (albeit in obiter dicta) on the substantive question of compatibility (and, in turn, on the issue of whether Article 8 ECHR confers a right to abortion in cases of rape, incest and fatal foetal abnormality).

Five of the justices considered that the lack of access to abortion in cases of fatal foetal abnormality violated Article 8 ECHR. Lady Hale and Lords Kerr, Mance and Wilson went further, stating that the lack of access to abortion in cases of rape and incest was also incompatible with Article 8 ECHR. Lords Kerr and Wilson also considered the issue from the perspective of Article 3 ECHR, which is discussed below.

The five justices (Ladies Hale and Black and Lords Kerr, Mance and Wilson) considered that the ban pursued the legitimate aim of protecting moral interests, namely the life, health and welfare of the unborn child. However, as noted above, Lady Hale also observed that the community has an interest in protecting the life, health and welfare of the pregnant woman and confirmed that 'the unborn are not the holders of rights under the Convention' (citing *Vo*).[86]

Despite pursuing a legitimate aim and being in accordance with law, Ladies Hale and Black and Lords Kerr, Mance and Wilson concluded that the interference with the Article 8 ECHR right to respect for private life (and, in particular, reproductive autonomy) was disproportionate in cases of fatal foetal abnormality because there was no community interest in obliging the

Discrimination against Women', C/OP.8/GBR/1, 6 March 2018, https://digitallibrary.un.org/record/1480026?ln=en&v=pdf.

[84] Ibid at [83].

[85] The Commission's standing to bring such challenges was subsequently confirmed by the Government through legislative amendment.

[86] *Northern Ireland Abortion Case* (n 11) at [21]. See also, Lord Kerr at [366].

person to carry such a pregnancy to term if they did not wish to do so. As Lady Black observed:

> Where the unborn child cannot survive, in contrast to the other categories of pregnancy with which we are concerned, there is no life outside the womb to protect. In those circumstances, even if allowance is made for the intrinsic value of the life of the foetus, the moral and ethical views of society cannot, it seems to me, be sufficient to outweigh the intrusion upon the autonomy of the pregnant woman, and her suffering, if she is obliged to carry to term a pregnancy which she does not wish to continue.[87]

As for cases involving rape and incest, Lady Hale and Lords Kerr, Mance and Wilson considered that the interference was disproportionate and that 'the autonomy rights of the pregnant woman should prevail over the community's interest in the continuance of the pregnancy'.[88] Lord Mance observed in the case of rape that forcing a person to continue with the pregnancy against their will was an invasion of the fundamental right to bodily integrity.[89] In the case of incest, Lady Hale and Lord Mance referred to the fact that 'typical' cases of incest involve an abusive relationship with younger female relatives and forcing a person to bear a child conceived in those circumstances could not be justified.[90] Given the majority's conclusion regarding the NIHRC's standing (or lack thereof), these observations regarding compatibility with the ECHR were obiter dicta and no declaration of incompatibility was issued under the HRA 1998, s.4.

Following the *Northern Ireland Abortion Case,* the Northern Ireland High Court heard an application arguing that the ban on abortion in Northern Ireland in cases of fatal foetal abnormality violated Article 8 ECHR. The applicant, Sarah Ewart, had been compelled to travel to England to obtain an abortion after discovering that the foetus she was pregnant with suffered from an abnormality that would be fatal either before or shortly after birth.[91] Ewart's claim was successful, though the Northern Ireland High Court[92] declined to issue a declaration of incompatibility under s.4 HRA[93] as the UK Parliament was in the process of drafting legislation to amend the law in Northern Ireland[94] to bring it in line with the CEDAW Committee's report.

The UK Parliament subsequently voted to require the Secretary of State for Northern Ireland to make regulations permitting abortion at the least in cases: (i) where there is a threat to the pregnant woman's physical or mental health without conditionality of 'long-term or permanent' effects; (ii) involving rape and incest; and (iii) involving severe foetal impairment. While abortion would

[87] Ibid at [371], per Lady Black. [88] Ibid at [27], per Lady Hale.

[89] Ibid at [127]. See also, [25], per Lady Hale.

[90] Ibid at [27], per Lady Hale and [132], per Lord Mance. [91] *Re Ewart* [2019] NIQB 88.

[92] *Re Ewart* [2020] NIQB 33 at [4]–[5]. [93] See Chapter 2 (Domestic Framework).

[94] Specifically, ss.58 and 59 of the Offences Against the Person Act 1861.

ordinarily be a devolved matter, at the time the UK Parliament passed the legislation requiring the Secretary of State to take such steps Stormont was not sitting.[95] Pursuant to the Abortion (Northern Ireland) (No. 2) Regulations 2020, abortion is permitted in Northern Ireland on the following bases:

- Upon request in a pregnancy of up to twelve weeks gestation by a registered medical professional who is of the opinion 'formed in good faith' that the pregnancy has not exceeded twelve weeks; or
- In a pregnancy of up to twenty-four weeks gestation, where two registered medical professionals are of the opinion (formed in good faith) that continuing the pregnancy 'would involve risk of injury to the physical or mental health of the pregnant woman which is greater than if the pregnancy were terminated'; or
- In all cases regardless of gestation, where:
  - a registered medical professional is of the opinion (formed in good faith) that it is immediately necessary to save the life of, or prevent 'grave permanent injury to the physical or mental health, of the pregnant woman';
  - two registered medical professionals are of the opinion (formed in good faith) that 'termination is necessary to prevent grave permanent injury to the physical or mental health of the pregnant woman' or 'the continuance of the pregnancy would involve risk to the life of the pregnant woman which is greater than if the pregnancy were terminated'; or
  - two registered medical professionals are of the opinion (formed in good faith) that there is a 'substantial risk' that the condition of the foetus is such that its death is likely before, during or shortly after birth or, if the child were born, it would suffer from such physical or mental impairment as to be 'seriously disabled'.[96]

It should be noted that the imposition of such regulations on Northern Ireland by the Westminster Parliament was not without resistance.[97]

Notwithstanding the significant expansion, *in law*, of the bases upon which abortion is permissible in Northern Ireland, access to such services has continued to be limited. As a report by Amnesty International from December 2023 observed:

Access to existing abortion services in Northern Ireland is largely limited to those whose pregnancies have not advanced past nine weeks and six days. Each trust

[95] For more information, see House of Commons Library, 'Abortion and same-sex marriage in Northern Ireland: Do Westminster votes undermine devolution?', 10 July 2019, https://commonslibrary.parliament.uk/parliament-and-elections/devolution/abortion-and-same-sex-marriage-in-northern-ireland-do-westminster-votes-undermine-devolution/.

[96] Abortion (Northern Ireland) (No. 2) Regulations 2020, regs 3–7.

[97] See, for instance, House of Commons Library, 'Research Briefing: Abortion in Northern Ireland: Recent changes to the legal framework', 19 February 2025, https://commonslibrary.parliament.uk/research-briefings/cbp-8909/.

currently offers early medical abortion services until that point in pregnancy. After that, women's ability to access care depends on their address or postcode.[98]

These limitations in access, coupled with a refusal of the Northern Irish Executive to take the necessary steps to ensure access to abortions in public health facilities led to the creation of further secondary legislation by the Secretary of State for Northern Ireland to facilitate access.[99] Judicial proceedings have also challenged the Northern Ireland Executive's inertia,[100] while separate proceedings also, unsuccessfully, challenged the lawfulness of regulations and directives which conferred powers on the Secretary of State for Northern Ireland to take the steps necessary to secure access to abortion services in Northern Ireland.[101]

Limited access to abortion services was also noted by the UK Supreme Court in its judgment in *Abortion Services (Safe Access Zones).*[102] As the Court observed:

> Currently, the provision of abortion services in public health facilities in Northern Ireland remains very limited. The changes to the law which were designed to enable such services to be provided, in compliance with [the recommendations of the] CEDAW report, have been largely frustrated.[103]

As discussed in Chapter 12 (Protest), one such way that compliance with the CEDAW Committee's report had been frustrated was through the failure to protect those using abortion services and those working within facilities providing such services from harassment by anti-abortion protestors. That has been remedied – at least in law – through the Abortion Services (Safe Access Zones) (Northern Ireland) Act 2023. That Act and its scope it discussed in greater detail in Chapter 12.

6.3.3 Abortion and the Right to Life under the Human Rights Act 1998

As discussed above, the right to life has featured prominently in the case law concerning abortion access. This has tended to be in terms of an alleged competing right of the unborn which, as noted, is not conferred by the

[98] Amnesty International, 'Legal but not local: Barriers to accessing abortion services in Northern Ireland', December 2023, p.5, https://www.amnesty.org.uk/resources/legal-not-local-barriers-accessing-abortion-services-northern-ireland.

[99] As discussed in *Re Abortion Services (Safe Access Zones)* [2022] UKSC 32, [2023] AC 505 ('*Safe Access Zones*') at [73]–[78].

[100] *Re Northern Ireland Human Rights Commission (Abortion Services)* [2021] NIQB 91.

[101] *Re SPUC Pro-Life Ltd's Application for Judicial Review* [2022] NIQB 9. For a more complete overview of that complicated political and legal trajectory, see *Safe Access Zones* (n 99) at [73]–[78].

[102] *Safe Access Zones* (n 99).

[103] Ibid at [79].

ECHR. This was one of the bases upon which the applicants in *R (Crowter & Anor)*[104] sought to challenge the compatibility of the UK's abortion law under s.4 HRA. In *Crowter*, two of the three applicants had Down Syndrome and their case was that the Abortion Act 1967 (UK), which permits abortion at any stage of gestation where two medical professionals are of the opinion that there is a 'substantial risk that if the child were born it would suffer from such physical or mental abnormalities as to be seriously handicapped'[105] (which includes Down Syndrome), was incompatible with Articles 2, 3, 8 and 14 ECHR.

In terms of Article 2 ECHR, counsel for the applicants argued that the legislation 'places in danger the life of a disabled unborn child ... at a time when it is both viable and sentient, by permitting abortion in circumstances where, and at a time at which, it would not be permitted in the case of a non-disabled child'.[106] Counsel specifically focused on the period post-viability in making the Article 2 ECHR argument.

In rejecting that argument, the Divisional Court (as implicitly supported by the Court of Appeal's refusal to grant leave to appeal on the Article 2 ECHR ground), observed that the ECtHR has 'never decided that a foetus, even one post-viability, is the bearer of Convention rights, including Article 2'.[107] As the Court noted, the ECtHR's case law was such that while 'there may be circumstances in which the foetus has *interests* which the State is entitled to protect [this] does not lead to the proposition that it enjoys *rights* under Article 2'.[108]

6.3.4 Abortion and Inhuman or Degrading Treatment under the Human Rights Act 1998

In *Crowter*, the applicants also argued that termination when the 'disabled unborn child' is 'fully developed and sentient' poses a 'serious risk' of 'death, along with the absence of any protection against the concomitant pain and suffering' in violation of the Article 3 rights of the foetus.[109] In rejecting that argument, the Divisional Court noted again that there was no ECtHR authority deciding that a foetus has Article 3 ECHR rights.[110] Leave to appeal against the Article 3 ECHR finding was refused.[111]

In the *Northern Ireland Abortion Case,* Lord Kerr (with whom Lord Wilson agreed) – again in obiter dicta – considered whether the criminalisation of abortion in cases of rape, incest and fatal foetal abnormality violated the Article 3 ECHR rights of *a pregnant woman.* In concluding that it did, their Lordships observed, firstly, that the criminalisation of abortion in these specific

[104] *R (Crowter & Ors)* v. *Secretary of State for Health and Social Care* [2021] EWHC 2536 (Admin), [2022] 1 WLR 2513; *R (Crowter & Ors)* (Court of Appeal) (n 81).

[105] Abortion Act 1967, s.1(1). [106] *R (Crowter & Ors)* (High Court) (n 104) at [51].

[107] Ibid at [62]. [108] Ibid. Emphasis in original. [109] Ibid at [73]. [110] Ibid at [80].

[111] *R (Crowter & Ors)* (Court of Appeal) (n 81) at [26].

circumstances (and the attendant risk of prosecution) constituted 'treatment' for the purposes of Article 3 ECHR.[112] While not all pregnant women will experience trauma or suffer to the same extent if they are denied an abortion in the three circumstances that the Court was considering, 'it is undeniable that some will suffer profound psychological trauma' and '[t]hat circumstance is sufficient to give rise to a violation of article 3 where proper safeguards to mitigate the risk of such trauma are not put in place'.[113] It would seem, then, that Lords Kerr and Wilson were considering the Article 3 ECHR case from the perspective of the positive obligation to protect[114] (including by virtue of an effective regulatory system and a medical system free from systemic issues impeding access to appropriate healthcare). In concluding that the law in Northern Ireland violated its positive obligation to protect under Article 3, Lord Kerr observed that 'it is plainly humiliating to require a girl or woman to continue a pregnancy when she knows that the foetus she carries will die or where she finds that pregnancy abhorrent because it is the consequence of rape or incest'.[115] While Lord Mance was not persuaded that a finding with respect to Article 3 ECHR could be made generally or in abstraction (i.e. without a specific victim in respect of whom the Court could make an assessment of their particular experiences and trauma), he nevertheless observed that:

> that does not mean that the Northern Ireland authorities' treatment of a pregnant woman, with a foetus with a fatal abnormality or the result of rape or incest (or, indeed, in other cases) may not on particular facts achieve that level of severity that justifies a conclusion of breach of article 3. It means only that the legislation by itself cannot axiomatically be regarded as involving such a breach.[116]

Similarly, while Lady Hale did not consider it necessary to express a concluded view on the issue of Article 3 ECHR, she had 'little doubt that there will be some women whose suffering on being denied a lawful abortion in Northern Ireland, in the three situations under discussion here, will reach the threshold of severity required to label the treatment "inhuman or degrading"'.[117]

While the CEDAW is not directly enforceable in domestic law,[118] it is nevertheless binding upon the UK on the international plane and the CEDAW Committee's report regarding the effects of the abortion law in Northern Ireland[119] were instrumental in the subsequent legislative amendments made

[112] *Northern Ireland Abortion Case* (n 11) at [231]. A conclusion with which Lady Hale agreed at [33].

[113] Ibid at [235].

[114] For a discussion of the various obligations imposed on States under Article 3, see Chapter 5.

[115] *Northern Ireland Abortion Case* (n 11) at [237]. See also [261].

[116] Ibid at [103].

[117] Ibid at [33].

[118] In this respect, see Chapter 2 (Domestic Framework).

[119] Report of the inquiry concerning the United Kingdom of Great Britain and Northern Ireland (n 83).

expanding eligibility. In the report, the Committee concluded that the legislative framework then in effect in Northern Ireland:

> affecting only women, preventing them from exercising reproductive choice and resulting in women being forced to carry almost every pregnancy to full term, involves mental or physical suffering constituting violence against women and potentially amounting to torture or cruel, inhuman and degrading treatment…
>
> … The mental anguish suffered is exacerbated when women are forced to carry to term a non-viable fetus (in cases of fatal fetal abnormality) or where the pregnancy results from rape or incest.[120]

In reaching that conclusion, the CEDAW Committee cited several decisions of the Human Rights Committee in which it had found that restrictive abortion laws (including as then existed in the Republic of Ireland) constituted ill-treatment in violation of Article 7 ICCPR[121] and several reports of the Committee Against Torture (which oversees the implementation of and adherence to the CAT), which similarly highlighted that restrictive abortion laws (including, again, as then existed in the Republic of Ireland), could amount to cruel and inhuman treatment.[122]

6.3.5 Abortion and Private Life: A Domestic Perspective

As noted above, five of the seven justices of the Supreme Court in the *Northern Ireland Abortion Case* found, albeit in obiter dicta, that the ban on abortion in cases of fatal foetal abnormality was inconsistent with the Article 8 ECHR right to private life of pregnant women; a further four of those five justices considered that the ban on abortion in cases of rape and incest was also incompatible with Article 8 ECHR. For those five justices, the balance between the community's moral interest in protecting the 'life, health and welfare of the unborn' and the 'life, health and welfare of the pregnant woman … [who is] undoubtedly a rights-holder […] under the Convention and domestic law with autonomy as well as health and welfare rights' had not been appropriately struck.[123] In finding that the law in Northern Ireland violated Article 8 ECHR in cases of rape, incest and fatal foetal abnormality, Lady Hale and Lords Kerr, Mance and Wilson clearly indicated that there is a right to abortion in those instances. As also noted above, however, access to abortion services remains significantly limited in Northern Ireland, raising issues with respect to the UK's compliance with the positive obligations under Article 8 ECHR also discussed above.

[120] Ibid at [65].

[121] *Whelan* v. *Ireland* (CCPR/C/119/D/2425/2014) and *Mellet* v. *Ireland* (CCPR/C/116/D/2324/2013).

[122] CAT/C/PER/CO/5-6 and CAT/C/IRL/CO/1.

[123] *Northern Ireland Abortion Case* (n 11) at [21], per Lady Hale.

A different Article 8 ECHR claim arose in *Crowter* where it was argued that permitting abortion on the basis of serious 'handicap' (to use the outdated nomenclature of the Abortion Act 1967) created negative stereotypes about people with disabilities and, consequently, violated 'the rights to identity and personal development, to establish and develop relationships with other human beings and the outside world, and to dignity and autonomy, which are inherent within the concept of "private life" in Article 8'.[124] The Divisional Court dismissed the claim that the 1967 Act perpetuated and reinforced negative stereotypes to the detriment of people with disabilities.[125] There was, then, no interference with the applicants' Article 8 ECHR right to private life. That decision has been the subject of both academic and judicial scepticism.[126]

Notwithstanding its finding that there was no interference with the applicants' Article 8 ECHR rights, the Divisional Court went on to consider whether – in the event it was wrong as to the issue of interference – such an interference was proportionate. In finding that it was, the Court noted the wide margin of appreciation afforded to States in this area and observed that there are compelling arguments on both sides of the debate, such that: '[t]his is just one example of the intensely difficult issues which are better debated in Parliament, which can take account of different interests and viewpoints, rather than in litigation'.[127] The applicants' appeals – which proceeded on the basis of Articles 8 and 14 ECHR – were unsuccessful.[128] It bears noting, however, that while Justice Jackson in the Court of Appeal agreed that the appeal ought to be dismissed, he was not willing to accept, as the Divisional Court had done, that s.1(1)(d) of the Abortion Act 1967 did not contribute to negative stereotypes of people with disabilities. Indeed, he was 'inclined to accept that section 1(1)(d) plays its part in contributing to discriminatory public attitudes'.[129] However, '[n]ot every adverse circumstance amounts to an interference with Convention rights and in ... the impact of the legislation on these Appellants is not so serious as to amount to an interference'.[130]

[124] *R (Crowter & Ors)* (High Court) (n 104) at [93]. [125] Ibid at [102].

[126] See, for instance, Zoe Tongue, '*Crowter* v. *Secretary of State for Health and Social Care* [2021] EWHC 2536: Discrimination, Disability, and Access to Abortion' (2022) **30** Medical Law Review 1, pp.177–187 and Heloise Robinson, 'Discrimination in Abortion Law and the Message the Law is Sending: *R (Crowter)* v. *Secretary of State for Health and Social Care*' (2024) **87** MLR 1, pp.218–230. As for judicial scepticism, see *Re SPUC Pro Life* [2023] NICA 35 at [86]–[88].

[127] *R (Crowter & Ors)* (High Court) (n 104) at [130]. See further the discussion regarding institutional critiques of rights adjudication in Chapter 1 and of the approach taken by the domestic courts to rights disputes in Chapter 2 (Domestic Framework).

[128] *R (Crowter & Ors)* (Court of Appeal) (n 81). [129] Ibid at [130(3)]. [130] Ibid at [129].

6.3.6 The Criminalisation of Abortion in Great Britain: Recent Developments

The Abortion Act 1967 permits the obtaining and provision of abortion services in a comparatively expansive range of circumstances when compared with other jurisdictions, including those within the Council of Europe. It is, nevertheless, important to remember that the Abortion Act 1967 did not decriminalise abortions in all circumstances; it only provided an exception to criminal liability for those procuring and/or providing abortions in accordance with s.1. Outside of the situations falling within s.1, abortion remained illegal for those obtaining such services and those providing them (though there has been a very significant shift in this area recently, as discussed below). While historically, prosecutions were rare, there has been a recent uptick in rates of investigation and prosecution of offences stemming from 'illegal abortions'.[131] According to one news report, between 1861 and November 2022 only 'three women in Great Britain were convicted of an illegal abortion'.[132] Yet, in the period between December 2022 and November 2023, one woman was convicted and six women were charged with offences.[133]

One such woman, who was charged with an offence of administering poison with intent to procure her own miscarriage contrary to s.58 of the Offences Against the Person Act 1861, was convicted (on a plea of guilty) and sentenced to twenty-eight months' imprisonment (the maximum sentence being life imprisonment). Carla Foster was forty-four years old at the time of sentence. She had three children (the youngest of whom was ten at the relevant time) with her long-term partner, and became pregnant in late 2019 after a brief separation during which she had had relationships with other men as a result of which she became pregnant. She moved back in with her former partner at the beginning of the COVID-19 pandemic but concealed the pregnancy. Foster obtained abortifacient drugs from a registered provider after giving false information that indicated that the foetus was under ten weeks' gestation (the evidence that was available to Foster suggested she was, in fact,

[131] See, for instance, Sally Sheldon and Jonathan Lord, 'Guest Editorial: Care Not Criminalisation; Reform of British Abortion Law Is Long Overdue' (2023) **49** JME 523–524. See also, Zoe L. Tongue, 'The Increasing Investigations and Prosecutions for Illegal Abortion in Britain: A Case for Decriminalisation' (2024) **20** Clinical Ethics 1.

[132] Zoe Williams, 'The women being prosecuted in Great Britain for abortions: "Her confidentiality was completely destroyed"', *The Guardian*, 10 November 2023, www.theguardian.com/world/2023/nov/10/the-women-being-prosecuted-in-great-britain-for-abortions-her-confidentiality-was-completely-destroyed. See also, Maya Oppenheim and Lydia Patrick, 'UK faces sharp rise in abortion convictions', *Independent*, 28 February 2024, www.independent.co.uk/news/uk/home-news/abortions-women-investigations-prosecutions-rise-b2496958.html.

[133] Ibid. In April 2025, news outlets reported on the trial of another woman charged with unlawfully administering to herself a poison or other noxious thing with intent to procure a miscarriage (see, for instance, 'Woman denies self-medicating to induce miscarriage', *BBC News*, 25 April 2025, www.bbc.com/news/articles/cwy639j97j2o).

approximately twenty-eight weeks' pregnant). After taking the tablets, Foster began labour and paramedics were called to her house where she delivered a baby girl (subsequently named Lily) who was stillborn. Subsequent medical investigations estimated that Lily was between thirty-two and thirty-four weeks' gestation and that her cause of death was 'a combination of stillbirth and maternal use of abortifacients'.[134]

It was only as a result of subsequent admissions by Foster to medical staff and police that the cause of Lily's death became known.[135] Following a police investigation, Foster was charged. Ultimately, a period of almost three years passed between the date of Foster taking the abortifacients and her sentencing. Foster successfully appealed her sentence. In reducing the sentence to fourteen months, wholly suspended, the Court of Appeal made several significant observations including that 'in cases of this nature, there will often be substantial personal mitigation to balance against the seriousness of the charge; and that an immediate custodial sentence in such cases is unlikely to provide a just outcome. And this was precisely the case here.'[136]

Following Foster's case – which garnered a significant amount of media attention within the UK – the Royal College of Obstetricians and Gynaecologists (RCOG)[137] published guidelines recommending that healthcare professionals do not report people to police following an abortion, pregnancy loss or unattended delivery, save in very limited circumstances (for instance, where there are concerns for the person's safety).[138] In introducing the guidance, the president of the RCOG stated '[w]e firmly believe it is never in the public interest to investigate and prosecute women who have sought to end their own pregnancy. These women should be treated with care and compassion, without judgement or fear of imprisonment.'[139]

An argument such as that which found favour before Lords Kerr and Wilson (i.e., that criminalisation of abortion in cases of rape, incest and fatal foetal abnormality violates Article 3 ECHR) has not yet been considered by the ECtHR. The ECtHR did, however, find that having to travel overseas to obtain

[134] *Foster* v. *R* [2023] EWCA Crim 1196 at [9]–[10]. [135] Ibid at [11]. [136] Ibid at [28].

[137] Together with several other agencies.

[138] Royal College of Obstetricians and Gynaecologists, 'Involvement of the Police and External Agencies following Abortion, Pregnancy Loss and Unexpected Delivery: Guidance for Healthcare Staff', www.rcog.org.uk/media/s3rf2brq/liaison-with-police-guideline-for-nhs-staff-in-womens-health-2.pdf.

[139] Royal College of Obstetricians and Gynaecologists, 'RCOG issues guidance for healthcare professionals on involving the police following abortion and pregnancy loss', 22 January 2024, https://www.rcog.org.uk/news/rcog-issues-guidance-for-healthcare-professionals-on-involving-the-police-following-abortion-and-pregnancy-loss/.

an abortion, notwithstanding the emotional toll that entailed, *did not* reach the minimum level of severity in *M.L. v Poland.*[140] It is, then, questionable whether the ECtHR would reach the same conclusion as Lords Kerr and Wilson if presented with the same arguments. Insofar as the UK is concerned, recent developments may well remove the need for resort to such arguments, at least for those who use abortion services.

As this book was going to press, an overwhelming majority of MPs in the House of Commons voted in favour of an amendment to the Crime and Policing Bill which provides that for the purposes of the law relating to abortion 'no offence is committed by a woman acting in relation to her own pregnancy' (cl 191). Specifically, the clause disapplies sections 58 (administering drugs or using instruments to procure an abortion) and 59 (procuring drugs etcetera to cause abortion) of the Offences Against the Person Act 1861 and the Infant Life (Preservation) Act 1929, in respect of a pregnant woman acting in relation to her own pregnancy. While undoubtedly significant, particularly in light of the increasing number of prosecutions relating to abortion, the amendment does not alter s.1 of the Abortion Act 1967 insofar as it specifies the eligibility criteria for accessing and providing abortion services depending on gestational length.

6.4 THE ENDING OF LIFE

In this section, we move to the other end of the lifespan, examining the role of rights (both under the ECHR and the common law) at the end of life. This involves a consideration of:

- The role of Articles 2 and 8 ECHR and the common law principle of the sanctity of life in cases involving the withdrawal/withholding of life-sustaining medical treatment;
- The role of Articles 2, 3 and 8 ECHR in the context of assisted suicide and voluntary active euthanasia[141] (collectively referred to as 'assisted dying').

State responsibility for deaths under Article 2 ECHR was explored in detail in Chapter 4. In this chapter, we are particularly concerned with how the domestic and Strasbourg courts have framed (and considered) the rights implications

[140] *M.L.* v. *Poland* (n 51).

[141] Defined by the NHS as 'where a person makes a conscious decision to die and asks for help to do so', NHS, *Euthanasia and Assisted Suicide*, www.nhs.uk/conditions/euthanasia-and-assisted-suicide/.

of end-of-life practices (including assisted dying). Such issues, like abortion, have been the subject of extensive legal, medical, political, moral, ethical and philosophical debate and the ECtHR has confirmed that there is no European consensus as to whether assisted dying should be permitted. That being the case, States have a wide margin of appreciation when it comes to regulating end-of-life care:

> in this sphere concerning the end of life, as in that concerning the beginning of life, States must be afforded a margin of appreciation, not just as to whether or not to permit [certain end-of-life practices] and the detailed arrangements governing [them], but also as regards the means of striking a balance between the protection of patients' right to life and the protection of their right to respect for their private life and their personal autonomy.[142]

However, as always, the ECtHR retains supervisory jurisdiction and has, on a number of occasions, heard cases challenging domestic laws relating to end-of-life treatment, including assisted dying.

6.4.1 Withdrawal of Life-Sustaining Treatment: The Domestic Context

If the right to life is, indeed, 'absolute' – subject to the limited exceptions set out in Article 2(1) ECHR – and '[e]veryone's right to life shall be protected by law', then does withdrawing/withholding life-sustaining treatment where the inevitable consequence is the person's death violate Article 2 ECHR? The issue is especially acute in cases involving incapacitous patients (i.e. those who cannot make decisions regarding their continued medical treatment).[143]

This question was confronted – from a common law point of view – in the House of Lords decision in *Bland*.[144] Mr Bland was left in a persistent vegetative state after the Hillsborough tragedy.[145] His family and doctors were agreed that it was not in his best interests to continue to receive artificial nutrition and hydration (ANH). If, however, that was ceased, he would die. The hospital sought a ruling from the domestic courts regarding whether it would be lawful to cease ANH. Ultimately, the House of Lords held that while 'a profound respect for the sanctity of human life is embedded in our law and our

[142] *Gard* v. *the United Kingdom* [2004] ECHR 103 at [84].

[143] Under English law, capacitous patients can refuse treatment and any attempt by medical staff to force it upon them will be unlawful: *Re B (Withdrawal of Treatment)* [2002] EWHC 429 (Fam), [2002] 2 All ER 449.

[144] *Airedale NHS Trust* v. *Bland* [1993] UKHL 17, [1993] AC 789.

[145] This refers to the 1989 crowd crush at the Hillsborough football stadium in Sheffield (UK) in which hundreds of spectators were injured or killed. See Chapter 4 (Life) for a discussion of the tragedy.

moral philosophy', it is not absolute.[146] There will be cases where it is not in the patient's best interests to receive life-sustaining treatment such as ANH and, in such cases, it would not be unlawful for doctors to cease such treatment (indeed, in such cases – i.e. where treatment is not considered to be in the patient's best interests – it would be unlawful for doctors to continue to provide it). That, under the common law, the sanctity of life is of considerable importance but is not absolute has been reaffirmed on a number of occasions, including by the UK Supreme Court in the 2019 case of *Re Y*.[147]

In *Re Y*, the Supreme Court held that treating practitioners and those 'with an interest in the welfare' of an incapacitous patient who is receiving life-sustaining treatment do not need to obtain court approval prior to the cessation of such treatment where the parties are in agreement that continued treatment is not in the patient's best interests. (Likewise, they do not need approval not to administer such treatment where there is such agreement.) Greater controversy has attended cases where there is such dispute, particularly when the patient concerned is a child. There have been several cases in recent years before the domestic courts involving this particularly devastating issue – namely, whether life-sustaining treatment of very young children should be continued. These cases[148] have confirmed that while the sanctity of life is important, 'the sole principle is that the best interests of the child must prevail and that must apply even to cases where parents, for the best of motives, hold on to some alternative view [to that held by the medical professionals and experts involved]'.[149] This extends to situations where parents disagree with the withdrawal of treatment on the basis of their religious beliefs.[150]

6.4.2 Withdrawal of Life-Sustaining Treatment: The ECtHR Context

The ECtHR has also confirmed that Article 2 ECHR does not preclude the withdrawal or withholding of life-sustaining treatment and in *Re Y*, the UK Supreme Court concluded that neither the common law *nor* the ECHR required prior court approval of withdrawal of treatment where doctors and those

146 *Bland* (n 144), p.808. 147 *An NHS Trust* v. *Re Y* [2018] UKSC 46, [2019] AC 978.

148 See, for instance, *Yates & Anor* v. *Great Ormond Street Hospital for Children NHS Foundation Trust* [2017] EWCA Civ 410, [2018] 4 WLR 5, *Kings College Hospital NHS Foundation Trust* v. *Haastrup (Withdrawal of Medical Treatment)* [2018] EWHC 127 (Fam), [2018] 2 FLR 1028, *Raqeeb* v. *Barts NHS Foundation Trust* [2019] EWHC 2531 (Admin), [2020] 1 FLR 1298, *Guy's and St Thomas' NHS Foundation Trust* v. *A & Ors* [2022] EWHC 2422 (Fam).

149 *Yates and Anor* (n 148) at [112].

150 See, for instance, *Fixsler & Anor* v. *Manchester University NHS Foundation Trust* [2021] EWCA Civ 1018, [2021] 4 WLR 123.

concerned with the patient's welfare are agreed.[151] In the leading decision of *Lambert* v. *France*,[152] the Grand Chamber held that when considering whether there had been a violation of Article 2 ECHR in the context of withdrawing/withholding life-sustaining treatment, 'reference should be made . . . to Article 8 of the ECHR and to the right to respect for private life and the notion of personal autonomy which it encompasses'.[153] In other words, life is not protected purely for life's sake. Rather, considerations of quality of life, which are ordinarily the remit of Article 8 ECHR, come into play in such cases. That said, 'Article 2 requires the State to take appropriate steps to safeguard the lives of those within its jurisdiction [and] in the public-health sphere, these positive obligations require States to make regulations compelling hospitals, whether private or public, to adopt appropriate measures for the protection of patients' lives'.[154] In determining whether the State has complied with its positive obligations under Article 2 ECHR in the context of withdrawal/withholding of treatment, the ECtHR will take into account:

- the existence in domestic law and practice of a regulatory framework compatible with the requirements of Article 2 ECHR;
- whether account had been taken of the applicant's previously expressed wishes and those of the persons close to him or her, as well as the opinions of other medical personnel;
- the possibility to approach the courts in the event of doubts as to the best decision to take in the patient's interests.[155]

The ECtHR found that the UK's regulatory system complied with the first requirement in the 2003 decision of *Glass*.[156] The ECtHR also had cause to consider the UK's compliance with the other requirements in the case of *Gard*[157] which involved the withdrawal of life-sustaining treatment from a very young child, Charlie. While the case on behalf of Charlie centred on an alleged right under Article 2 ECHR to access experimental treatment,[158] the ECtHR also considered whether the domestic courts' approach complied with the second and third requirements set out by the Grand Chamber in *Lambert*. Having found that the domestic proceedings *did* comply with such requirements and 'in view of the

[151] *Re Y* (n 147) at [102], citing *Lambert* v. *France* [GC] (2016) 62 EHRR 2.

[152] *Lambert* v. *France* (ibid). [153] Ibid at [142].

[154] Ibid at [140]. For more on State responsibility under Article 2 for the effective running of medical systems, see Chapter 4.

[155] *Lambert* v. *France* (n 151) at [143]. [156] *Glass* v. *the United Kingdom* (2004) 39 EHRR 15.

[157] *Gard* v. *the United Kingdom* (n 142).

[158] Ibid at [85]–[98]. The complaint was dismissed as manifestly ill-founded, with the Court observing that it had previously concluded that 'Article 2 of the Convention cannot be interpreted as requiring access to unauthorised medicinal products for the terminally ill to be regulated in a particular way': ibid at [78] and [87].

margin of appreciation left to the authorities'[159] in such cases, the Court declared the complaint under Article 2 ECHR inadmissible.

In addition to raising potential Article 2 ECHR issues, withdrawal and withholding of treatment cases also involve questions of autonomy and, in some instances, religious freedom both of which are protected under the ECHR.[160] As the Grand Chamber observed in *Lambert*, States have a 'margin of appreciation' when it comes to 'striking a balance between the protection of patients' right to life and the protection of their right to respect for their private life and their personal autonomy'[161] though this remains subject to the Court's oversight, as demonstrated by the judgment in *Lambert* itself.

Another area of significant controversy in the context of end-of-life treatment is that of assisted dying and it is here that questions of autonomy, dignity and sanctity of life not only come directly to the fore, but also, at least as articulated in the case law, potentially conflict.

6.4.3 Assisted Suicide and Euthanasia: The Domestic Context

Euthanasia – which derives from the Greek *eu* meaning good and *thanatos* meaning death – refers to a third party deliberately ending another person's life. Some definitions include reference to an intention to relieve suffering, though this is by no means a unanimously accepted aspect of euthanasia. Euthanasia is unlawful in England and Wales because it constitutes murder.

Assisted suicide is unlawful pursuant to s.2 Suicide Act 1961 (though suicide was itself decriminalised by that Act).[162] Section 2 prohibits the doing of acts 'capable of encouraging or assisting the suicide or attempted suicide of another'. The maximum sentence is imprisonment for fourteen years, though prosecution cannot take place without the consent of the Director of Public Prosecutions.

On its face, the domestic law prohibiting assisted dying seems to comply with Article 2 ECHR which, as has been noted, provides that '[e]veryone's right to life shall be protected by law'. Yet, as discussed, withdrawing/withholding

[159] Ibid at [98].

[160] See, for instance, the discussion of autonomy in Chapters 5 (Ill-treatment) and 10 (Privacy) and religious freedom in Chapter 13.

[161] *Lambert* v. *France* (n 151) at [84].

[162] While the Suicide Act 1961 applies to England and Wales, the same prohibition has been extended to Northern Ireland by virtue of Criminal Justice (Northern Ireland) Act 1966, s.13. In Scotland '[i]t is not a crime "to assist" another to commit suicide. However, if a person does something which he knows will cause the death of another person, he will be guilty of homicide if his act is the immediate and direct cause of the person's death' (*Ross* v. *Lord Advocate* [2016] CSIH 12, 2016 SCLR 764 at [29] per Lord Carloway). Euthanasia – insofar as it constitutes murder or unlawful homicide – is unlawful in all of the jurisdictions comprising the UK.

life-sustaining treatment from patients is lawful, even where that will inevitably lead to their deaths. How do we reconcile this apparent tension? The short answer is with some difficulty, as the case law demonstrates.

6.4.3.1 *Pretty* v. *DPP*

Diane Pretty – who had motor neurone disease, a terminal, neurodegenerative condition – was the first person to challenge the compatibility of s.2 Suicide Act 1961 with the then-recently enacted HRA. Before the domestic courts, Pretty argued that the refusal of the Director of Public Prosecutions (DPP) to undertake not to charge her husband with an offence under s.2 if he were to assist her in dying (Pretty being physically unable to take her own life) and/or the ban itself violated Articles 2, 3, 8 and 9 ECHR alone, or taken together with Article 14 ECHR.

The House of Lords rejected each of her claims.[163] In respect of Article 3 ECHR, the Court considered that there was no 'treatment' by the State since Pretty's suffering stemmed from her medical condition and there was no suggestion that the palliative care that was available to her was deficient.[164] The House of Lords also rejected the argument that Article 8 ECHR was engaged, holding that the ban (or, more specifically, the refusal of the DPP to undertake not to prosecute Pretty's husband) did not interfere with her private or family life.

As to the Article 2 ECHR claim, Pretty argued the right to life also protects the inverse: namely, the right to die. The House of Lords rejected that contention as 'untenable':

> The article protects the right to life and prevents the deliberate taking of life save in very narrowly defined circumstances. An article with that effect cannot be interpreted as conferring a right to die or to enlist the aid of another in bringing about one's own death...
>
> It is true that some of the guaranteed Convention rights have been interpreted as conferring rights not to do that which is the antithesis of what there is an express right to do ... It cannot however be suggested (to take some obvious examples) that articles 3, 4, 5 and 6 confer an implied right to do or experience the opposite of that which the articles guarantee. Whatever the benefits which, in the view of many, attach to voluntary euthanasia, suicide, physician-assisted suicide and suicide assisted without the intervention of a physician, these are not benefits which derive protection from an article framed to protect the sanctity of life.[165]

[163] *R (Pretty)* v. *Director of Public Prosecutions* [2001] UKHL 61, [2002] 1 AC 800.

[164] The argument is made in Chapter 5 (Ill-treatment), by reference to the reasoning of Lady Hale and Lords Kerr and Wilson, that 'treatment' under Article 3 may well extend to the criminalisation of assisted dying. See also, Stevie Martin, *Assisted Suicide and the ECHR* (Routledge, 2021), ch 3.

[165] *R (Pretty)* v. *Director of Public Prosecutions* (n 163) at [5]–[6], per Lord Bingham.

Pretty subsequently lodged a complaint with the ECtHR alleging violations of Articles 2, 3, 8, 9 and 14 ECHR.[166] The ECtHR found no violations in respect of any of those articles, *but* it did hold that the ban on assisted suicide could constitute an interference with Pretty's right to private life:

> The applicant in this case is prevented by law from exercising her choice to avoid what she considers will be an undignified and distressing end to her life. The Court is not prepared to exclude that this constitutes an interference with her right to respect for private life as guaranteed under Article 8(1) of the Convention.[167]

This was a very significant development in the assisted dying case law – it was the first time the ECtHR held that Article 8 ECHR could cover the right to choose to avoid an 'undignified and distressing end' to life. Yet, the ECtHR found that any such interference with Pretty's Article 8 ECHR rights was proportionate to the legitimate aim of protecting the rights of vulnerable individuals who might feel compelled to take their lives if assisted dying were permitted. Further, the ECtHR noted that:

> flexibility is provided for in individual cases by the fact that consent is needed from the DPP to bring a prosecution and by the fact that a maximum sentence is provided, allowing lesser penalties to be imposed as appropriate.[168]

There have been several attempts at reform of the Suicide Act 1961, with the most recent bill (which would, if enacted, permit assisted suicide for terminally ill adults with six months or less to live) passing its Third Reading and moving to the House of Lords as this book went to print.[169] However, at this point in time, the Suicide Act 1961 continues to criminalise the assisting and encouraging of suicide. This has resulted in several post-*Pretty* legal challenges to the ban's compatibility with the ECHR under the HRA. The most notable being that of *Nicklinson*.[170]

6.4.3.2 *Nicklinson*

Paul Lamb and Tony Nicklinson – both of whom had locked-in syndrome – argued that the ban violated their Article 8 ECHR right to respect for private life (more specifically, the right to choose the manner and timing of their deaths as articulated by the ECtHR in *Pretty*). Following *Pretty* v. *the United Kingdom*, it was accepted that s.2 Suicide Act 1961 interfered with the appellants' right to respect for private life, though a majority of the UK Supreme

[166] *Pretty* v. *the United Kingdom* (2002) ECHR 427. [167] Ibid at [67]. [168] Ibid at [76].

[169] In June 2025, a Private Member's Bill passed its Third Reading and will, if enacted, amend the Suicide Act 1961 to permit assisted suicide for capacitous, terminally ill adults with six months or less to live: Terminally Ill Adults (End of Life) Bill 2024–25.

[170] *R (Nicklinson and Anor)* v. *Ministry of Justice & Ors* [2014] UKSC 38, [2015] 1 AC 657.

Court declined to consider whether such an interference was proportionate. Each of the nine members of the *Nicklinson* Supreme Court delivered separate reasons:

- Lords Neuberger, Mance and Wilson determined that while the Court *could* consider the ban's compatibility with the ECHR, 'it was such a controversial issue' that it was institutionally inappropriate to issue a declaration of incompatibility without first giving Parliament the opportunity to (re)consider the issue, particularly as Parliament was then considering potential amendments to the Suicide Act 1961;[171]
- Lords Sumption, Clarke, Reed and Hughes considered that the nature of the subject matter and, in particular, its moral complexity, rendered it 'institutionally [in]appropriate' for the Court to consider the compatibility of the ban with the ECHR. Though, arguably, Lords Clarke and Reed did not exclude the possibility of the Court ruling on the question of compatibility in the future;[172] and, finally,
- Lady Hale and Lord Kerr determined that the matter was justiciable and proceeded to examine the compatibility of s.2 Suicide Act 1961 with Article 8 ECHR. Having done so, they each determined that the blanket ban was incompatible and would have issued declarations to that effect under s.4 HRA.

Pursuant to Article 8(2) ECHR an interference must be in accordance with the law, in pursuit of a legitimate aim, and necessary in a democratic society. Lady Hale and Lord Kerr accepted that the ban pursued a legitimate aim (i.e a sufficiently important legislative objective) of protecting the rights of others – namely, protecting individuals vulnerable to pressure from feeling compelled to die with assistance. Lady Hale rejected, however, the contention that the ban was also necessary to protect morals – namely, the sanctity of life – observing that:

> Respect for individual autonomy and human dignity are also important moral principles. The very complexity of the moral argument, amply demonstrated in the

[171] Lord Neuberger, 'The Supreme Court and the Rule of Law' (The Conkerton Lecture, Liverpool, October 2014), https://supremecourt.uk/uploads/speech_141009_lord_neuberger_4000bc552b.pdf.

[172] Lord Reed observed at [298] that 'it is not . . . inconceivable that the position could alter in the future' so as to warrant a finding of incompatibility and Lord Clarke noted that, 'If Parliament chooses not to debate these issues, I would expect the court to intervene' (at [293]: *Nicklinson* (n 170). Indeed, as Elizabeth Wicks has identified, it is arguable that Lord Sumption referred to the possibility of the Court having a role to play should Parliament 'abdicate' its responsibility (at [233]): Elizabeth Wicks, 'The Supreme Court Judgment in Nicklinson: One Step Forward on Assisted Dying; Two Steps Back on Human Rights' (2015) 23 Medical Law Review 144, pp.147–148.

material before this court, tells against relying upon [the sanctity of life as a manifestation of the protection of morals] as the legitimate aim of the legislation.[173]

As for whether the interference was 'necessary in a democratic society', this required a determination of whether it pursued a pressing social need and was proportionate to that aim.[174] When determining whether an interference is proportionate, the domestic courts have developed the following 'test' which largely mirrors that adopted by the ECtHR in cases involving qualified rights:

(a) is the legislative objective sufficiently important to justify limiting a fundamental right?; (b) are the measures which have been designed to meet it rationally connected to it?; (c) are they no more than are necessary to accomplish it?; and (d) do they strike a fair balance between the rights of the individual and the interests of the community?[175]

Applying this test to s.2 Suicide Act 1961, Lady Hale and Lord Kerr concluded that the *blanket* ban was more than was necessary to achieve the aim of protecting individuals vulnerable to undue pressure and, accordingly, the ban failed to strike a fair balance. For Lady Hale, the blanket ban, which permitted of no exception, was not the least restrictive means possible of securing the aim of protecting the vulnerable. There was an alternative:

It would not be beyond the wit of a legal system to devise a process for identifying those people, those few people, who should be allowed help to end their own lives. There would be four essential requirements. They would firstly have to have the capacity to make the decision for themselves. They would secondly have to have reached the decision freely without undue influence from any quarter. They would thirdly have had to reach it with full knowledge of their situation, the options available to them, and the consequences of their decision . . . And they would fourthly have to be unable, because of physical incapacity or frailty, to put that decision into effect without some help from others. I do not pretend that such cases would always be easy to decide, but the nature of the judgments involved would be no more difficult than those regularly required in the Court of Protection or the Family Division [referring to withdrawal/refusal of treatment cases].[176]

Such a procedure would be 'more than sufficient to protect those vulnerable people whom the present universal prohibition is designed to protect' since those individuals would not qualify for assistance.[177]

In addition to finding that the ban was disproportionate, Lord Kerr also queried whether there was a rational connection between s.2 and its objective of protecting vulnerable individuals:

One needs to have a clear view of the nature of the susceptibility of the vulnerable in this area and how it can be said to be increased by making assisted suicide (provided

[173] *Nicklinson* (n 170) at [311].

[174] See, for instance, *The Sunday Times* v. *the United Kingdom* (1979) 2 EHRR 245.

[175] *Nicklinson* (n 170) at [336]–[337] (Lord Kerr). [176] Ibid at [314]. [177] Ibid at [316].

that it is accompanied by appropriate safeguards) available. It is reasonable to assume that this 'vulnerable class of persons' is composed of persons who are physically able to commit suicide. Why should they feel more vulnerable because those who cannot do so are enabled to bring their lives to an end? One can understand that those who consider themselves to be a burden might feel constrained to consider suicide because it no longer attracts the opprobrium that it once did. But why should they be more disposed to do so because of a law which permits those who want to, but cannot, commit suicide to avail of human assistance to bring about their desire? The two situations are not linked in any logical way. On that account I do not consider that it has been demonstrated that there is the necessary rational connection between the aim of the legislation and the interference with the article 8 right.[178]

However, as noted above, Lady Hale and Lord Kerr were in the 'minority' in the sense that they were the only two judges to complete the full proportionality assessment. While they would have issued a declaration under s.4 HRA that the ban was incompatible with Article 8 ECHR, the majority determined not to do so. Accordingly, no declaration was issued. Nor did Parliament pass the Assisted Dying Bill 2014 which Lord Neuberger referred to in his reasons. Tony Nicklinson subsequently died of pneumonia, having refused food, hydration and medical treatment.

Following his death, Nicklinson's widow lodged a complaint with the ECtHR.[179] Significantly, Jane Nicklinson did not ask the ECtHR to revisit *Pretty* and determine whether s.2 Suicide Act 1961 violates Article 8 ECHR. Rather, she argued that the failure of the majority of the Supreme Court to fulsomely consider the issue of the ban's compatibility with Article 8 ECHR violated her husband's (and her own) procedural rights under Article 8 ECHR. The ECtHR rejected this contention as manifestly ill-founded; it was satisfied that the Supreme Court had dealt with the substance of Nicklinson's claim.[180]

6.4.3.3 *Post-Nicklinson* Challenges to Section 2

More recent challenges to s.2 Suicide Act 1961 before the domestic courts have been similarly unsuccessful. Noel Conway sought to challenge the ban's compatibility on more limited grounds than those run in *Nicklinson*. In particular Conway, who had motor neurone disease, challenged the lack of access to assisted dying for individuals who are terminally ill and have a life expectancy of six months or less to live.[181] In line with Lady Hale's reasons in *Nicklinson*, Conway also proposed a system that could operate as an

[178] Ibid at [350]. See also, Lord Neuberger who considered that 'the rational connection between the aim and effect of section 2 is fairly weak' (at [111]).

[179] *Nicklinson* v. *the United Kingdom* (2015) 61 EHRR 97. [180] Ibid at [85].

[181] *R (Conway)* v. *Secretary of State for Justice* [2017] EWHC 2447 (Admin), [2018] 2 WLR 322, *R (Conway)* v. *Secretary of State for Justice* [2018] EWCA Civ 1431, [2018] 3 WLR 925.

alternative to the blanket ban which he argued demonstrated that there was a less restrictive means available to achieve a fairer balance between the competing interests. Notwithstanding the more narrow grounds of challenge, Conway was unsuccessful, with the domestic courts emphasising the fact that Parliament was the more appropriate forum to determine the balance that should be struck between 'the interests of the wider community and the interests of people in the position of Conway'.[182] In dismissing the application (and Conway's subsequent appeals) the domestic courts put much weight on the fact that Parliament, in rejecting the proposed amendments to the Suicide Act 1961 which were under consideration at the time of *Nicklinson*, had clearly determined how the balance should be struck. It is also notable that in the *Conway* proceedings the courts expanded the list of legitimate aims which the ban was said to pursue. As noted above, Lady Hale in *Nicklinson* considered that the ban had one legitimate aim: to protect the rights of others (namely, the right of vulnerable individuals not to be subject to undue pressure). In *Conway*, the domestic courts added two further legitimate aims: protecting the doctor–patient relationship and protecting the sanctity of life. This is significant given the issues with relying on the sanctity of life as a legitimate aim as identified by Lady Hale and because it expands the bases upon which the State can justify the interference that s.2 Suicide Act 1961 poses to Article 8 ECHR.

Another attempt to challenge the ban in *Newby* – this time inviting the courts to engage in a more fulsome analysis of the evidence available – was also unsuccessful.[183] Paul Lamb (who had previously been an applicant in the *Nicklinson* proceedings) was also unsuccessful in a subsequent attempt to challenge the ban on the basis of Article 14 ECHR (prohibition of discrimination), taken together with Article 8 ECHR.[184] It seems, therefore, that judicial challenges to the compatibility of the Suicide Act 1961 with the ECHR (by way of the HRA) reached their zenith in *Nicklinson* and efforts to reinvigorate that debate before the courts are likely to be met with limited success. Indeed, in declining permission to apply for judicial review in Lamb's latter challenge, Lord Justice Dingemans stated:

> I can see no prospect, however the legal argument is framed or presented, and it has been framed with conspicuous skill by . . . his legal team, of the legal answer to the claim being other than that the assessment of the justifications for any interference with rights under Article 8 of the European Convention on Human Rights or assessment of the justifications for any discrimination under Article 14, when read

[182] *R (Conway)* (Court of Appeal) (ibid) at [206]. See also, the discussion of the domestic courts' approach to rights adjudication in Chapter 2 (Domestic Framework).

[183] *R (Newby)* v. *Secretary of State for Justice* [2019] EWHC 3118 (Admin).

[184] *R (Lamb)* v. *Secretary of State for Justice* [2019] EWHC 3606 (Admin).

with Article 8 of the European Convention on Human Rights, is a matter for Parliament.[185]

Parliament has considered the issue by way of various committees in recent years[186] and the Isle of Man and Jersey (Crown Dependencies) have moved forward with assisted dying legislation, with other neighbouring jurisdictions (including Scotland[187]) also considering permitting assisted dying which suggests that there may be a political resolution to the issue in England and Wales in the near future. Indeed, at the time of publication, Kim Leadbeater MP's Private Members' Bill – Terminally Ill Adults (End of Life) Bill, had passed its Third Reading and moved to the House of Lords for consideration, which is the closest England and Wales have come to legalising assisted suicide. If enacted, the legislation would decriminalise assisted suicide for capacitous, terminally ill adults with a life expectancy of six months or less. The Bill contains a number of safeguards including, perhaps most notably, the establishment of specialist multidisciplinary panels which will consider all requests for assistance in dying (which is limited to physician-assisted suicide) to determine whether the eligibility criteria have been met *prior* to a person being assisted to die.[188]

If the Terminally Ill Adults (End of Life) Bill does become law, England and Wales will join an increasing number of permissive jurisdictions (those in which assisted dying is lawful). Beyond the commonly cited Benelux jurisdictions, Colombia, Austria, Spain, Portugal, Canada, New Zealand, all states in Australia, and ten US States (plus the District of Colombia) permit some form of assisted dying. The Italian Constitutional Court and the German Constitutional Court have also declared that their country's respective prohibitions on assisted suicide are unconstitutional in certain circumstances.[189]

[185] Ibid at [32].

[186] House of Commons Health and Social Care Committee, 'Assisted dying/assisted suicide', Second Report of Session 2023–24, 20 February 2024, https://publications.parliament.uk/pa/cm5804/cmselect/cmhealth/321/report.html; UK Parliament Joint Committee on Human Rights, 'Human rights and assisted dying', Oral evidence, 24 May 2023, https://committees.parliament.uk/work/7355/human-rights-and-assisted-dying/publications/.

[187] The Assisted Dying for Terminally Ill Adults (Scotland) Bill was introduced into Scotland's Parliament in March 2024 with Members of the Scottish Parliament voting in favour of the general principles of the Bill in May 2025. At the time of publication, the Bill had moved to Stage 2.

[188] Terminally Ill Adults (End of Life) Bill, https://bills.parliament.uk/bills/3774. See the discussion of the Bill in Ruthie Jeanneret and Stevie Martin, 'Prospective Approval in Assisted Dying Legislation: Safety over Access?' (2025) BMJ **389**:e083604.

[189] Constitutional Court of Italy, Decision No. 242 of 22 November 2019, www.cortecostituzionale.it/documenti/download/doc/recent_judgments/Sentenza_n_242_del_2019_Modugno_en.pdf; Constitutional Court of Germany (BVerfG) Judgment of the Second Senate of 26 February 2020 – 2 BvR 2347/15, https://www.bundesverfassungsgericht.de/SharedDocs/Entscheidungen/EN/2020/02/rs20200226_2bvr234715en.html.

While jurisdictions permitting assisted dying are still in the minority, the increasing number of permissive jurisdictions is notable.

6.4.4 Assisted Suicide and Euthanasia: The ECtHR Context

As discussed in Section 6.4.3.1, *Pretty* v. *the United Kingdom* was significant for its finding that the right to private life enshrined in Article 8 protects the right to choose to 'avoid what [an individual] considers will be an undignified and distressing end to [their] life'.[190] In subsequent case law concerning assisted dying, this has been framed as the right to 'choose the time and manner of' one's death, provided the individual is acting of their own free will.[191] While a number of cases have come before the ECtHR concerning State regulation of assisted dying, the Court has maintained that this is an area in which States have a wide margin of appreciation.[192] That margin is not, however, unbounded.

In *Koch* v. *Germany*,[193] the ECtHR held that there had been a violation of the applicant's Article 8 ECHR rights as a result of the domestic courts' refusal to consider his complaint challenging the decision of the relevant domestic authority not to authorise a prescription of sodium pentobarbital to his wife. The applicant's wife had total sensorimotor quadriplegia and wanted to end her life; accordingly, she sought permission to obtain medication that would enable her to die by suicide at home. After permission was refused the applicant's wife travelled to Switzerland where she was assisted to die. The applicant unsuccessfully sought to continue the proceedings he and his wife had jointly commenced prior to her death challenging the refusal to permit her to access the medication. Before the ECtHR the applicant complained of a violation of his own Article 8 rights (as well as a violation of his wife's Article 8 rights[194]). In finding that there had been a violation of the applicant's *procedural* Article 8 rights, the ECtHR held that the domestic courts had an obligation to consider the merits of the applicant's claim, which they had failed to do.[195]

In *Haas* v. *Switzerland*,[196] the ECtHR rejected the complaint that a failure to facilitate access to medication necessary to die by suicide violated Article 8 ECHR. The applicant challenged a refusal of the domestic authorities to permit him to obtain sodium pentobarbital without a prescription. The applicant, who

190 *Pretty* v. *the United Kingdom* (n 166) at [67].

191 See, for instance, *Haas* v. *Switzerland* (2011) 53 EHRR 33 at [60].

192 See, for instance, *Mortier* v. *Belgium* [2022] ECHR 764 at [142]–[143].

193 *Koch* v. *Germany* (2012) 56 EHRR 6.

194 This aspect of the complaint was dismissed as inadmissible *ratione materiae* with the Convention as the wife's Article 8 rights were non-transferrable.

195 *Koch* v. *Germany* (n 193) at [71]–[72].

196 *Haas* v. *Switzerland* (n 191).

suffered from bipolar disorder, wanted to suicide by way of a lethal dose of that medication but had been unsuccessful in obtaining a prescription for it. The applicant alleged before the domestic authorities and the ECtHR that the failure to provide him access to the medication violated Article 8 ECHR. In finding that there had been no violation of Article 8 ECHR, the ECtHR noted the 'considerable' margin of appreciation States enjoy when determining how to regulate assisted dying and held that the Swiss regulations which required a prescription in order to obtain sodium pentobarbital were a proportionate means of securing the legitimate aims of 'protecting everybody from hasty decisions and preventing abuse'.[197]

In *Gross* v. *Switzerland*,[198] a violation of Article 8 was found by a Chamber of the Court on the basis that whilst Swiss law provided for the possibility of obtaining a lethal dose of sodium pentobarbital on medical prescription it did not 'provide sufficient guidelines ensuring clarity as to the extent of this right'.[199] This is consistent with the jurisprudence on abortion discussed above (i.e. if a State determines to permit abortion or, here, assisted dying, access cannot be impeded by a lack of transparency within the regulatory framework). What was particularly interesting in *Gross*, however, was that it was subsequently discovered that the applicant had successfully procured a prescription of sodium pentobarbital and died by suicide *prior* to the application being heard by the Chamber and that steps had been taken to keep this information from legal representatives and, consequently, the ECtHR. As a result, when the case went to the Grand Chamber it held (by a very slim majority of 9:8) that the applicant had abused the right of individual application and declared the complaint inadmissible under Article 35(3)(a) ECHR.[200] Thus, the Chamber's ruling is not authority for the procedural requirements of Article 8 ECHR in the context of assisted suicide regulation.

In its recent assisted dying judgment, *Dániel Karsai* v. *Hungary*, the ECtHR confirmed that a blanket ban on assisted dying will not, at least at this point in time, violate the Article 8 ECHR rights of those who would access assistance were it available.[201] The case involved a challenge to Hungary's ban on assisted dying, brought by Dániel Karsai (a Hungarian lawyer suffering from a terminal neurodegenerative condition). Karsai argued, inter alia, that the State had a *positive obligation* under Article 8 ECHR to provide him with access to assistance in dying. Karsai submitted that less restrictive means than a complete ban on assisted dying were available which could better balance the competing rights of people seeking access to assistance in dying and those vulnerable to undue pressure. While the ECtHR (by majority) rejected the claim that States owe a positive obligation to individuals to provide access to

[197] Ibid at [55]–[56]. [198] *Gross* v. *Switzerland* [GC] (2013) 58 EHRR 197.

[199] *Gross* v. *Switzerland*, App. No. 67810/10, 14/05/2013 at [67].

[200] *Gross* v. *Switzerland* [GC] (n 198). [201] *Dániel Karsai* v. *Hungary* [2024] ECHR 516.

assistance in dying, it made several important observations. First, it recognised 'that a certain trend is currently emerging towards decriminalisation of medically assisted suicide, especially with regard to patients who are suffering from incurable conditions'.[202] Second, having regard to the fact that the Convention is a living instrument which must be interpreted and applied in light of present-day conditions, the Court highlighted '[t]he need for appropriate legal measures [relating to end-of-life care] [to] be kept under review, having regard to the developments in European societies and in the international standards on medical ethics in this sensitive domain'.[203]

In his partly concurring, partly dissenting judgment, Judge Wojtyczek disagreed with the majority regarding the scope of Article 8 ECHR in cases involving assisted dying. In particular, Judge Wojtyczek strongly disagreed with the Court's erstwhile assisted dying jurisprudence, arguing instead that, in light of the right to life in Article 2 ECHR, Article 8 ECHR does not protect the right to choose the manner and timing of one's death:

> Personal autonomy is a very precious freedom and an important pre-condition for a happy and self-fulfilling life, and must be effectively protected; however, given the clear letter of Article 2, its scope under the Convention cannot encompass decisions about one's own life and death. The very notion of 'private life' – which first and foremost presupposes life – does not extend to the choice of death by means of medically assisted suicide or euthanasia.[204]

In stark contrast, Judge Felici considered that Hungary's failure to provide a system of assisted dying for Dániel Karsai violated Article 8 ECHR, alone and together with Article 14 ECHR. In his dissent, Judge Felici referred to 'European and non-European' developments in the legalisation of assisted dying, and suggested that:

> If we take account of the considerable attention currently being paid to the issue of access to active end-of-life treatment in public debate, essentially at a global level, it is indisputable that the magnitude of a trend in favour of recognising at least some forms of PAD [physician-assisted dying] cannot be questioned.[205]

Rejecting the Government's arguments regarding the difficulties in regulating assisted dying and the need to protect vulnerable individuals, Judge Felici suggested that 'the risk of abuse of legal instruments does not in itself represent a legal argument. It is assumed that the State, understood as the guarantor of the protection of citizens and their fundamental rights, as established in various constitutional charters, must have the necessary tools to prevent any abuse.'[206] Judge

[202] Ibid at [143]. [203] Ibid at [167].

[204] Ibid, partly concurring, partly dissenting judgment of Judge Wojtyczek at [4].

[205] Ibid, dissenting opinion of Judge Felici at [5].

[206] Ibid, dissenting opinion of Judge Felici at [8].

Felici similarly rejected the Government's arguments regarding the adequacy of palliative care, citing expert evidence before the Court of the inability to treat existential suffering of the type which the applicant had described experiencing himself.[207] Finally, Judge Felici accepted that the distinction in Hungarian law (present also in the UK and many other jurisdictions) between 'terminally-ill patients who do not require life-saving treatment and therefore do not have access to [the possibility of bringing about their death by the withdrawal of life-sustaining treatment] (such as ALS patients) and those who do require life-saving treatment and can therefore choose to end their suffering through [refusal or withdrawal of life-sustaining treatment]' was discriminatory in violation of Article 14 ECHR, taken together with Article 8 ECHR.[208] The majority had avoided determining whether physician-assisted dying and withdrawal of treatment are 'inherently different acts'[209] as, even assuming the acts were analogous for the purposes of Article 14 ECHR, the differential treatment was justified (for the same reasons there was no violation of Article 8 ECHR). Judge Felici in contrast considered that 'subordination of the decision to take one's life to whether one is dependent on life-saving treatment represents an unnecessary reduction of the protection of the right to life and an interference in private life, understood as the individual's capacity for self-determination'.[210]

In addition to Article 8 ECHR, the ECtHR has also considered other rights in the context of assisted dying including Articles 2 and 10 ECHR. The applicant in *Lings* v. *Denmark*[211] argued that his conviction and prison sentence for the provision of advice to specific individuals on how to die by suicide violated his right to freedom of expression under Article 10 ECHR. The applicant – who had been a physician – was charged with offences relating to the assisting of suicide. He was convicted on one count of assisted suicide and one count of attempting to assist suicide and was sentenced to sixty days' imprisonment, which was suspended. The applicant argued that his conviction and sentence violated Article 10 ECHR because he had merely provided oral information (which was permitted, if it was published online under Danish law) and '[s]uch an interference with his right to freedom of expression, which did not relate to the actual subject of the expression or information but rather to how and to whom it was provided, could not be considered proportionate'.[212] While it was accepted that the applicant's conviction and sentence constituted an interference with his right to freedom of expression, the Court found no violation. The Court accepted the domestic courts' findings, including that the applicant had provided specific, tailored advice as opposed to the sort of general information that

[207] Ibid, dissenting opinion of Judge Felici at [9].

[208] Ibid, dissenting opinion of Judge Felici at [11].

[209] Ibid, Court's judgment at [174].

[210] Ibid, dissenting opinion of Judge Felici at [13].

[211] *Lings* v. *Denmark* [2022] ECHR 314.

[212] Ibid at [36].

would be permitted to be published online. In those circumstances, and given that States have an obligation under Article 2 ECHR to 'protect vulnerable persons, even against actions by which they endanger their own lives, [which] also obliges the national authorities to prevent an individual from taking his or her own life if the decision has not been taken freely and with full understanding of what is involved',[213] the interference was proportionate.

The ECtHR has also considered whether States which permit assisted dying are violating Article 2 ECHR. In *Mortier* v. *Belgium*,[214] the applicant argued that the Belgian assisted dying system violated his mother's right to life as protected by Article 2 ECHR. The applicant's mother had been assisted to die in accordance with the Belgian requirements (which permits individuals who are suffering intolerably as a result of psychiatric illness – as the applicant's mother was – to be assisted to die). The applicant's challenge was on the basis that the State failed in its positive obligations to protect the life of his mother given alleged procedural failings in the system regulating assisted dying in Belgium.[215] The majority in *Mortier* made a number of significant findings in terms of the rights implications of assisted dying. In particular, it noted that human dignity and freedom are the 'very essence' of the ECHR and, in a time of 'growing medical sophistication and increased life expectancy', many people fear that they will be forced to live a life that sits at odds with the perception they have of themselves.[216]

Perhaps most significantly, the majority found that, while it may not be possible to deduce a right to die from Article 2 ECHR, the right to life cannot be interpreted in such a way as to per se prohibit the decriminalisation of euthanasia.[217] The ECtHR has, however, made it clear that in order to be compatible with Article 2 ECHR, a system which permits assisted dying must have in place sufficient guarantees and safeguards that are directed at avoiding abuses.[218] In *Mortier*, the majority held that there had been a violation of this obligation because the inability of members of the Federal Commission for the Control and Evaluation of Euthanasia (which reviews all instances of reported assisted dying) to recuse themselves meant that a doctor who had participated in an assisted death could sit on the Commission that reviewed compliance with the regulations *in that specific case*.[219] Indeed, such was the case in respect of the applicant's mother's death; the doctor who had provided the assistance sat on the Commission that considered whether her death (and the decisions leading up to it) had complied with the regulations. As the Court held, this framework failed to ensure the independence required for such a posteriori control of assisted dying to comply with Article 2 ECHR.

[213] Ibid at [49], citing *Haas* v. *Switzerland* (n 191) at [54]. [214] *Mortier* v. *Belgium* (n 192).
[215] Ibid at [85]. [216] Ibid at [124] and [136]. [217] Ibid at [138]. [218] Ibid at [139].
[219] Ibid at [171]–[176].

Judges Elósegui and Serghides both authored partly dissenting opinions, with the former finding that the Belgian system failed to provide adequate protection to vulnerable individuals and the latter arguing that given that Article 2 ECHR requires states to *protect* life, the legalisation of assisted dying can never be compatible with Article 2 ECHR.[220]

The finding of the majority in *Mortier* that the right to life does not, in and of itself, prohibit assisted dying was subsequently affirmed in *Dániel Karsai* v. *Hungary*[221] and the Grand Chamber rejected a request for referral in *Karsai*.[222] Accordingly, at this point in time it would seem that the position under the ECHR is that: the right to choose the manner and timing of one's death *is* protected by Article 8 ECHR; permitting assisted dying is not, per se, incompatible with Article 2 ECHR but States must put in place sufficient safeguards; and, there is no obligation on States to provide access to assistance in dying.

Thus, while the ECtHR has not found that the ECHR confers a right to be assisted to die, the Court's rulings in the context of assisted dying, especially *Mortier* and *Karsai*, confirm that the ECHR (including Article 2 ECHR) does not preclude States from legalising assisted dying, subject to strict controls.

6.5 CONCLUSION

In this chapter we have considered the application of human rights (both under the common law and the ECHR) to both ends of the lifespan. What becomes abundantly apparent from the survey of that case law is that there is a great deal of similarity not only in terms of the issues that arise, but also the rights involved and there is significant consistency in the domestic courts' and the ECtHR's approach to the rights disputes involving these issues. References to the sanctity of life, vulnerability, autonomy and dignity, as well as institutional considerations such as competence and legitimacy, abound and have played a central role in the courts' reasoning in both the abortion and assisted dying contexts. Notably, notwithstanding the not insignificant corpus of case law both on abortion and assisted dying, there is no right to either under the ECHR. Such cases that have found success under the ECHR (either before the domestic courts or the ECtHR) have done so either because the domestic courts have moved past Strasbourg (as arguably occurred in the *Northern Ireland Abortion Case*) or

[220] For a more detailed analysis of this case, see Stevie Martin, 'The Right to Life at the End of Life: A Note on *Mortier* v. *Belgium* App No. 78017/17, 4 October 2022' (2024) **24** Medical Law International 2.

[221] *Dániel Karsai* v. *Hungary* (n 201) at [145].

[222] *Dániel Karsai* v. *Hungary*, App. No. 32312/23, Grand Chamber Panel Decision, 2 September 2024.

because, no matter how wide the margin of appreciation afforded to States in a given area, the ECtHR retains a supervisory function and will step in where States have failed to ensure that the way in which they regulate a practice is compliant with the ECHR.

At a domestic level, there is a stark contrast in the approach the UK Supreme Court has taken to the issue of abortion on the one hand and assisted dying on the other. In respect of the former, the Court took a robust approach to the question of whether Northern Ireland's then very restrictive eligibility criteria for abortion was compatible with the ECHR. In contrast, a majority of the Court took a very hands-off approach to the question of whether the ban on assisted suicide in England and Wales is compatible with the ECHR, preferring to leave it to Parliament to resolve. Of course, the Court's task in the *Northern Ireland Abortion Case* was made somewhat easier by the fact that, under both domestic law and the ECHR, a foetus does not have 'rights' and there is, then, no need to balance competing rights in the context of abortion. In contrast, one of the core aims of the ban on assisted suicide in England and Wales is to protect the lives of individuals vulnerable to undue pressure – with such individuals undoubtedly having rights under the ECHR which require consideration and balancing against the right of individuals to choose the manner and timing of their deaths (providing they are acting of their own free will).

Further, while both abortion and assisted dying raise complex legal, social, medical, philosophical, moral, and ethical questions, there is a general consensus amongst Council of Europe States that abortion should be permitted in specific circumstances. In contrast, in the end-of-life context, '[o]pinions and legal responses ... among States Parties to the Convention are very diverse'.[223] In such circumstances, it is perhaps understandable that both the domestic courts and the ECtHR are reluctant to enter into what is considered to be more (institutionally) appropriately the sphere of politics. Nevertheless, this does run the risk that rights violations go unremedied if a State's political body is unable or unwilling to address such issues. Indeed, the margin afforded to States in both contexts, coupled with the absence of either a right to abortion or to assisted dying, means that States can roll back protections previously granted, raising questions about the effectiveness and universality of rights.

[223] *Mortier* v. *Belgium* (n 192) at [142].

7 Modern Slavery and Human Trafficking

CONTENTS

7.1 INTRODUCTION

Slavery was abolished in the UK by the Slave Trade Abolition Act 1807 and the Slavery Abolition Act 1833,[1] yet almost two centuries later various forms of exploitation persist in the form of modern slavery and human trafficking. These pernicious practices are prevalent in industries such as nail bars, car washes, agriculture, manufacturing of clothing, sex work and the drug trade, as well as domestic exploitation such as au pairs and housekeepers, particularly in diplomatic households. Those might be the most well-known locales of exploitation, but it is also believed that modern slavery and human trafficking exist throughout many settings, and it is often said that it is hidden in plain sight.

Some insight into the scale of the problem is provided by statistics. For example, it is estimated that there are at least 100,000 victims of modern slavery and human trafficking in the UK.[2] Moreover, in 2010 the UN estimated that the annual flow of *new* victims into Europe for *sexual exploitation* alone was in the region of 70,000.[3] A horrifying figure and yet one that reflects only a subset of those trafficked, not accounting for those already within Europe, nor those trafficked for other purposes. Indeed, while trafficking for sexual exploitation is a major part of the trafficking industry the UN reported in 2024 that 'victims trafficked for forced labour now account for the biggest share of all victims around the world, overtaking those who are trafficked for sexual exploitation'.[4] In this regard it is also worth observing that, while there are a number of

[1] On the history of the abolition of slavery, see Jenny Martinez, *The Slave Trade and the Origins of International Human Rights Law* (Oxford University Press, 2012).

[2] House of Commons Home Affairs Committee, *Human Trafficking*, First Report of Session 2023–2024, HC124 at [2].

[3] United Nations Office on Drugs and Crime, Trafficking in Persons to Europe for Sexual Exploitation (2010).

[4] United Nations Office on Drugs and Crime, Global Report on Trafficking in Persons (2024), p.3.

driving forces behind these practices, armed conflict and climate change are significant factors and therefore it is antcipated that the number of victims of human trafficking will grow.[5]

This chapter examines the role of human rights law, in particular Article 4 ECHR, in tackling these forms of abuse and exploitation. We begin with the conceptual ambit of Article 4 ECHR which expressly prohibits slavery, servitude and forced or compulsory labour, examining how those concepts are defined by the ECtHR, as well as the expansion of Article 4 ECHR to include human trafficking. We then consider States' obligations in respect of Article 4 ECHR observing that while a framework of positive obligations is evolving there are considerable areas of uncertainty as to how far human rights law will go in protecting victims, an issue that is especially contentious where immigration is involved. Finally, we look at how the UK seeks to satisfy its international human rights obligations through the National Referral Mechanism (NRM) and the Modern Slavery Act 2015 (MSA), examining the operation of those systems and highlighting their strengths and weaknesses. In particular we will see that amendments made by the Nationality and Borders Act 2022 (NBA) and the Illegal Migration Act 2023 (IMA) starkly expose tensions over, and resistance to, human rights law where it gives rise to obligations to those that have crossed a State's border. Overall, this chapter thus highlights fundamental differences between the direction of travel in domestic law as compared with the direction of travel on the international plane in respect of modern slavery and human trafficking.

7.2 OVERVIEW OF THE HUMAN RIGHTS FRAMEWORK

7.2.1 Article 4 ECHR

Article 4 ECHR provides as follows:

Article 4 ECHR Prohibition of Slavery and Forced Labour

1. No one shall be held in slavery or servitude.
2. No one shall be required to perform forced or compulsory labour.
3. For the purpose of this Article the term 'forced or compulsory labour' shall not include:
   (a) any work required to be done in the ordinary course of detention imposed according to the provisions of Article 5 of this Convention or during conditional release from such detention;

[5] Ibid, p.19.

(b) any service of a military character or, in case of conscientious objectors in countries where they are recognised, service exacted instead of compulsory military service;
(c) any service exacted in case of an emergency or calamity threatening the life or well-being of the community;
(d) any work or service which forms part of normal civic obligations.

Article 4 ECHR expressly prohibits slavery, servitude and forced or compulsory labour. Article 4(1) ECHR (which prohibits slavery and servitude) is an absolute right, there are no exceptions, and it cannot be derogated from under Article 15 ECHR. Article 4(2) ECHR, which prohibits forced or compulsory labour, is limited by Article 4(3) ECHR and is subject to derogation under Article 15 ECHR.[6] The ECtHR has also read into Article 4 ECHR a prohibition on human trafficking.[7] In addressing human trafficking, it has been influenced by two other treaties: the UN Protocol to Prevent, Suppress and Punish Trafficking in Persons, especially Women and Children (Palermo Protocol) and the Council of Europe Convention on Action against Trafficking in Human Beings (ECAT).

7.2.2 UN Protocol to Prevent, Suppress and Punish Trafficking in Persons, Especially Women and Children (The Palermo Protocol)

The Palermo Protocol was the first legally binding global instrument with an agreed definition of trafficking in persons. This definition is important, not least because the Grand Chamber of the ECtHR has adopted it for the concept of human trafficking that it has identified within Article 4 ECHR.[8]

Article 3(a) Palermo Protocol

'Trafficking in persons' shall mean the recruitment, transportation, transfer, harbouring or receipt of persons, by means of the threat or use of force or other forms of coercion, of abduction, of fraud, of deception, of the abuse of power or of a position of vulnerability or of the giving or receiving of payments or benefits to achieve the consent of a person having control over another person, for the purpose of exploitation. Exploitation shall include, at a minimum, the exploitation of the prostitution of others or other forms of sexual exploitation, forced labour or services, slavery or practices similar to slavery, servitude or the removal of organs.

The text of the Article 3(a) Palermo Protocol definition is lengthy, but it can be broken down to three elements, all of which must be present to constitute human trafficking, namely: the act (what is done); the means (how it is done); and the purpose (why it is done).

[6] For a discussion of the power to derogate under Article 15 ECHR, see Chapter 3.

[7] *Rantsev* v. *Cyprus and Russia* (2010) 51 EHRR 1.

[8] *SM* v. *Croatia*, Chamber judgment (2019) 68 EHRR 7, *SM* v. *Croatia*, Grand Chamber judgment (2021) 72 EHRR 1.

- **Act** = recruitment, transportation, transfer, harbouring or receipt of persons
- **Means** = threat or use of force or other forms of coercion, of abduction, of fraud, of deception, of the abuse of power or of a position of vulnerability or of the giving or receiving of payments or benefits to achieve the consent of a person having control over another person
- **Purpose** = for the purpose of exploitation, which includes as a minimum the exploitation of the prostitution of others or other forms of sexual exploitation, forced labour or services, slavery or practices similar to slavery, servitude or the removal of organs.

7.2.3 Convention on Action against Trafficking in Human Beings (ECAT)

The Council of Europe Convention on Action against Trafficking in Human Beings (ECAT) entered into force on 1 February 2008. The definition of trafficking under ECAT is identical to that contained in the Palermo Protocol,[9] and, by extension, Article 4 ECHR. However, ECAT, as a specialist Convention, is far more detailed than Article 4 ECHR. It specifies rights such as the right to be identified as a victim, the right to be protected and assisted, an entitlement to a recovery and reflection period, a renewable residence permit, and a right to receive compensation. ECAT is frequently referred to by both the ECtHR and domestic courts when considering the obligations under Article 4 ECHR, which raises the question as to what extent ECAT obligations form part of the positive obligations inherent in Article 4 ECHR. ECAT is not subject to oversight by the ECtHR but is instead overseen by a two-pillar monitoring system: GRETA (Group of Experts on Action against Trafficking in Human Beings) monitors the extent to which States are fulfilling their obligations by carrying out State visits and publishing country reports, while the Committee of the Parties makes recommendations to States based on GRETA reports.

Sadly, a significant impetus for the UK signing up to ECAT was the tragic death in 2004 of twenty-three Chinese nationals employed as cockle pickers in Morecambe Bay.[10] This led to a Joint Committee on Human Rights inquiry into human trafficking which reported that the UK was a destination country for human trafficking, and that the problem was far worse than previously thought.[11] The Joint Committee found that existing domestic attempts to tackle matters were not going far enough and thus called upon the UK to sign and ratify

[9] Article 4(a) ECAT.

[10] Mike Stevens, 'Morecambe Bay cockling tragedy victims remembered 20 years on', *BBC News*, 5 February 2024, www.bbc.co.uk/news/uk-england-lancashire-68191697.

[11] House of Lords and House of Commons Joint Committee on Human Rights, *Human Trafficking*, Twenty-Sixth Report of Session 2005–2006, HL Paper 245-I, HC 117-I (13 October 2006).

ECAT. They rejected the Government's argument that doing so would make it a pull factor for migration into the UK.[12] The UK thus ratified ECAT in 2008 and it entered into force in 2009. The UK has developed various mechanisms aimed at ensuring compliance with ECAT. These include the NRM and the MSA. GRETA's third report in 2021 highlighted significant shortcomings with the NRM and the MSA and made recommendations for improvement.[13] Those recommendations were subsequently incorporated into recommendations by the Committee of the Parties, however, as we will see throughout this chapter, many of those recommendations have not been addressed.[14] A fourth GRETA report is expected in 2025.

7.3 CONCEPTUAL FRAMEWORK OF ARTICLE 4 ECHR

There are relatively few Article 4 ECHR cases compared with the case law in respect of other Convention rights.[15] At one time, the sparse nature of the case law was such that a leading scholar declared Article 4 ECHR 'largely irrelevant in modern European democracies'.[16] She went on to state that the problem derives from 'its restrictive wording [as] it has not proved possible to interpret Art[icle] 4 in such a way as to allow it to cover rights unthought of when it was conceived'.[17] Certainly, the lack of case law is striking given the prevalence of modern slavery and human trafficking amongst contracting States, however, since the mid 2000s the ECtHR has sought to interpret the provision in a manner that renders it highly relevant to 'modern European democracies'. We are therefore seeing a rise in Article 4 ECHR cases and it is likely that this will continue in the future.

In respect of the conceptual framework of Article 4 ECHR, there are four forms of exploitation expressly included in the text of the Convention right, namely slavery, servitude and forced or compulsory labour, while further concepts such as human trafficking have been read into the right by the ECtHR. One view of Article 4 ECHR is that the express concepts 'represent a continuum from most to least abusive, with slavery forming the gravest abuse,

[12] Ibid, pp.25–27, 73.

[13] Council of Europe, Group of Experts on Action against Trafficking in Human Beings (GRETA), *Evaluation Report United Kingdom*, Third Evaluation Round (20 October 2021) GRETA (2021).

[14] Committee of the Parties to the Council of Europe Convention on Action against Trafficking in Human Beings Recommendation CP/Rec(2021)07 on the implementation of the Council of Europe Convention on Action against Trafficking in Human Beings by the United Kingdom adopted at the 29th meeting of the Committee of the Parties on 17 December 2021.

[15] For an overview of the Article 4 case law, see also the European Court of Human Rights, *Guide on Article 4* of the *European Convention on Human Rights* and David Harris et al., *Law of the European Convention on Human Rights* (5th ed) (Oxford University Press, 2023), ch.7.

[16] Helen Fenwick, *Civil Liberties and Human Rights* (Routledge, 2007), p.50.

[17] Ibid.

servitude less so, and forced labour by comparison the least abusive'.[18] This view is, however, contested by Stoyanova who observes that this is not an entirely accurate picture as although Article 4 ECHR 'is based on such a gradation model ... this gradation model must be assessed as inadequate, given that it fails to cover some of the distinguishing features of slavery'.[19] Moreover, she suggests that the distinctions between the concepts are important and that they should not simply be collapsed into each other as there are important differences between them which may lead to different obligations and different levels of compensation.[20] These are issues to keep in mind as we contemplate how the ECtHR has interpreted each of the components of Article 4 ECHR.

7.3.1 Slavery

Article 4(1) ECHR provides for an absolute prohibition on slavery. To date, there are no cases in which the ECtHR has found a violation of this provision, perhaps because none of the contracting States allow for the lawful ownership of another person. This has given rise to an important question namely whether 'slavery' for the purposes of Article 4 ECHR is limited to the classic conception in which the power of 'legal ownership' is exercised or whether de facto ownership also triggers the right. There is no clear answer to this question in the case law at present, indeed to the extent that there are dicta on this issue there are conflicting signs from the ECtHR.[21]

A conception of slavery based on legal ownership can be seen in *Siliadin* v. *France*.[22] The facts in that case were that Henriette Akofa Siliadin, a Togolese national was brought to France at around fifteen years of age by a French national of Togolese origin (Mrs D). Henriette's family had agreed with Mrs D that Henriette would work at Mrs D's home until the cost of the air ticket had been reimbursed, whilst Mrs D would attend to Henriette's immigration status and find her a place at school. This did not happen; instead, Henriette became an unpaid housemaid, and her passport was taken from her. Moreover, some months later, Mrs D 'lent' Henriette to Mr and Mrs B so that Henriette could assist the pregnant Mrs B with housework. After Mrs B had her baby, she told Henriette that she 'had decided to keep' Henriette. Henriette thus remained with Mr and Mrs B, working seven days a week from 7.30am–10.30pm and sleeping on a mattress on the floor in the baby's room; she was not paid. After two years she tried to escape but was compelled to return by an uncle.

[18] Vladislava Stoyanova, *Human Trafficking and Slavery Reconsidered* (Cambridge University Press, 2017), p.285.

[19] Ibid. [20] Stoyanova (n 18), p.290.

[21] For further discussion of international definitions of slavery and de jure and de facto slavery, see Stoyanova (n 18), ch.6.

[22] *Siliadin* v. *France* (2006) 43 EHRR 16 at [122].

Eventually after four years, the police raided the home, Mr and Mrs B were prosecuted for various offences, but were ultimately acquitted on appeal.[23]

This led to *Siliadin* v. *France* in which it was argued that France had violated Article 4 ECHR by failing to have adequate criminal-law provisions punishing treatment contrary to Article 4 ECHR.[24] In contemplating whether there had been a violation, the Court had to first establish whether Henriette's situation fell within Article 4 ECHR.[25] In this respect it held, by reference to the International Labour Organisation (ILO) Forced Labour Convention, that at the very least Henriette's exploitation constituted forced labour,[26] following which it went on to consider whether her exploitation also constituted slavery or servitude.[27] In determining that it did not constitute slavery, the Court drew upon the 1926 Slavery Convention and held that 'slavery is the status or condition of a person over whom any or all of the powers attaching to the right of ownership are exercised'.[28] It observed that this 'definition corresponds to the "classic" meaning of slavery as it was practised for centuries'.[29] Applying this to the facts, the ECtHR determined that Henriette was not 'held in slavery in the proper sense' as Mr and Mrs B had not 'exercised a genuine right of *legal ownership* over her ... reducing her to the status of an "object"'.[30] The Court's narrow approach to slavery has been criticised for rendering the slavery provision redundant,[31] with scholars arguing that a de facto, as well as a de jure, approach is necessary.[32]

Elsewhere in the case law there are some indications that the Court may be open to a de facto approach.[33] *M* v. *Italy and Bulgaria* concerned three Bulgarian nationals of Roma ethnic origin (a mother, father and their seventeen-year-old daughter)[34] who travelled to Italy to work for a Roma man of Serbian nationality. It is alleged that shortly thereafter the daughter was forced to marry the nephew of the man they were working for, and that a

[23] Ibid at [9]–[45]. [24] Ibid at [102]. [25] Ibid at [113]. [26] Ibid at [120].

[27] Ibid at [121]. [28] Ibid at [122]. [29] Ibid. [30] Ibid. Emphasis added.

[31] Ryszard Piotrowicz, 'States' Obligations under Human Rights Law towards Victims of Trafficking in Human Beings: Positive Developments in Positive Obligations' (2012) 24 International Journal of Refugee Law 2, p.189, Valentina Milano, 'The European Court of Human Rights' Case Law on Human Trafficking in Light of *L.E.* v. *Greece*: A Disturbing Setback?' (2017) 17 HRLR 4, p.704.

[32] Jean Allain, *Slavery in International Law* (Brill, 2013), p.121. Note, however, that Stoyanova (n 18) at p.246 suggests that '[a]lthough very strained in light of the text of the judgment, an alternative interpretation [of *Siliadin*] is also possible'. In this respect she goes on to suggest that '[o]ne might highlight the expression "reducing her to the status of an 'object'" and argue that the ECtHR interprets slavery as a de facto form of gross and egregious objectification of a person'.

[33] See concurring opinion of Judge Pinto de Albuquerque, joined by Judge Tsotsoria in *J* v. *Austria*, App. No. 58216/12, 17/01/2017 at [40]; see also discussion by Stoyanova in (n 18), pp.245–248.

[34] *M* v. *Italy and Bulgaria* (2013) 57 EHRR 29.

sum of money was paid to her father in connection with the marriage. Following the marriage the daughter was beaten, raped and forced to participate in robberies which gave rise to a number of arguments before the ECtHR, some of which led to findings of violations of the Convention. A number of the facts were contested but the issue that is relevant here is the question of whether the daughter was held in slavery on the basis that her father received money in respect of the purported marriage. In contemplating this argument, the Court observed that a 'genuine right of ownership' needed to be established, but it made no mention of '*legal* ownership'.[35] It went on to find that there was insufficient evidence of a genuine right of ownership, determining that a monetary contribution in respect of marriage cannot be considered to amount to a price attached to the transfer of ownership such as to bring into play the concept of slavery as such payments can reasonably be accepted as representing a gift from one family to another, a tradition that is common to many different cultures.[36] The point that is relevant here is that although the ECtHR found no violation of the slavery provision the fact that it engaged in this enquiry at all may be read as suggesting that 'legal ownership' is not essential and that de facto ownership (if it had been established on the facts) would have sufficed.[37]

7.3.2 Servitude

Article 4(1) ECHR also prohibits servitude, and in the absence of a textual definition we must again look to the case law to see how it has been interpreted. The leading case is *Siliadin,* as after the ECtHR determined that Henriette had not been held in slavery, it went on to consider whether she had been held in servitude.[38] It defined servitude as a 'particularly serious form of denial of freedom', which includes 'in addition to the obligation to perform certain services for others ... the obligation ... to live on another person's property and the impossibility of altering [this] condition'.[39] It observed that servitude is an obligation to provide one's services imposed by the use of coercion.[40] Applying this to the facts, the Court determined that Henriette *had* been held in servitude.[41] It emphasised that: she was required to work almost fifteen hours a day, seven days per week; she had been brought to France by a relative and had not chosen to work for Mr and Mrs B; as a minor, she had no resources, was vulnerable and

35 Ibid at [149].

36 Ibid at [161]. It is worth reflecting on this approach in the light of research by the UN Office on Drugs and Crime highlighting the complexity of identifying trafficking in the context of forced marriage, UNODC, *Interlinkages between Trafficking in Persons and Marriage: Issues Paper* (Vienna, 2020).

37 *M* v. *Italy and Bulgaria* (n 34) at [161]. See also, discussion in Stoyanova (n 18), p.248 in which she suggests that the ECtHR 'opened up the possibility of applying the concept of slavery to contemporary forms of abuses' in this case.

38 *Siliadin* v. *France* (n 22) at [123]. 39 Ibid. 40 Ibid at [123]–[124]. 41 Ibid at [129].

isolated; she had no means of living elsewhere; she was completely dependent on Mr and Mrs B and entirely at their mercy as her passport had been confiscated and whilst she had been promised that her immigration status would be regularised this never occurred, consequently, she was afraid of being arrested; she had no freedom of movement and no free time and as she had not been sent to school, she could not hope that her situation would improve.[42]

In *C.N. and V* v. *France*,[43] the ECtHR examined the difference between servitude and forced labour and observed that what distinguishes them is that a victim of servitude feels that their situation is permanent.[44] The applicants (C.N. and V) were two sisters. Following the civil war in Burundi during which their parents had been killed, the sisters were brought to France by an aunt. At the time they were sixteen and ten years of age respectively. The girls were housed in a poorly heated, unconverted basement and were made to do housework for Mr and Mrs M and their seven children. They had limited access to a bathroom, were not allowed to eat with the family, and were given limited food. Only V attended school, whilst C.N. remained at home to complete housework and look after her disabled cousin. During this time C.N. was hospitalised three times under a cousin's name. Eventually, after five years, the sisters escaped following the intervention of a child welfare organisation.

In examining Article 4 ECHR, the ECtHR held that C.N. had been held in servitude.[45] It emphasised that she had believed that she could not escape without the risk of becoming an illegal immigrant, a feeling that had been reinforced by being hospitalised under a false name. The fact that she did not attend school and had no training meant that she had no hope of finding paid work, and with no days off and no leisure activities there was no possibility for her to meet people whom she might ask for help. The ECtHR accordingly considered that C.N. had felt that her condition was permanent, especially as it lasted four years and that it had commenced when she was still a minor and continued after she reached adulthood.[46] The ECtHR reached a different conclusion, however, in respect of the younger sister.[47] V had attended school and was not confined to the home, she had learned French, had time to do her homework and was less isolated (which is what enabled her to confide in a school nurse, thereby starting the process of the sisters' escape from the home). The ECtHR accordingly held that she was not kept in servitude.[48] In fact, the Court concluded that Article 4 ECHR was not applicable to her at all.[49]

Central to the ECtHR's approach to servitude is thus the question of whether the victim feels that their situation is permanent. This has been criticised by scholars such as Stoyanova.[50] She argues that the ECtHR should discard this approach and instead focus on whether there was a particularly serious form

[42] Ibid at [126]–[127]. [43] *C.N. and V* v. *France*, App. No. 67724/09, 11/10/2012. [44] Ibid.
[45] Ibid at [94]. [46] Ibid at [92]. [47] Ibid at [93]. [48] Ibid. [49] Ibid at [94].
[50] Stoyanova (n 18), p.255.

of denial of freedom; and whether there was an obligation to perform certain services that was imposed by the use of coercion.[51]

7.3.3 Forced or Compulsory Labour

Article 4(2) ECHR provides that 'no one shall be required to perform forced or compulsory labour'. In terms of the meaning of 'forced or compulsory labour', the ECtHR frequently cites the ILO definition which states that forced labour is 'all work or service which is exacted from any person under the menace of any penalty and for which the said person has not offered himself voluntarily'.[52] The Court considered the concept of a 'penalty' in *C.N. and V* observing that whilst it may involve physical violence or restraint, it can also take subtler forms of coercion, such as threats to denounce victims to the police or immigration authorities.[53] The ECtHR has also stated that '[t]he term "forced labour" brings to mind the idea of physical or mental coercion'[54] and that the ECHR aims to protect against instances of 'serious exploitation'.[55] The emphasis accorded to 'serious exploitation' means that, although the ECtHR draws upon the ILO definition which refers to '*all* work or service', not *all* work exacted under the threat of a 'penalty' is 'forced or compulsory labour' for the purposes of Article 4 ECHR. We must instead consider the type and volume of work and whether it amounts to a 'disproportionate burden'.[56] Consequently, in *Van der Mussele* v. *Belgium* the Court held that requiring a lawyer to act pro bono does not constitute compulsory labour.[57] Other unsuccessful forced or compulsory labour cases concern obligations to engage in pro bono work,[58] obligations to work overtime[59] or outside ordinary hours,[60] and obligations to obtain and accept work by reducing benefits if there is a refusal to do so.[61] Stoyanova thus suggests that 'although the ILO definition is a starting point, more complex tools, namely contextualization and a form of proportionality assessment, have to be introduced and made operational for determining whether abuses amount to forced labour under the ECHR'.[62]

[51] Ibid, pp.255–259. [52] ILO Forced Labour Convention, 1930 (No. 29).

[53] *C.N. and V* v. *France* (n 43) at [77]. [54] *Zoletic* v. *Azerbaijan* (2022) 75 EHRR 10 at [147].

[55] Ibid at [148]. [56] *Van der Mussele* v. *Belgium* (1984) 6 EHRR 163 at [39].

[57] Ibid at [40].

[58] Ibid, see also, *Graziani-Weiss* v. *Austria* (2014) 58 EHRR 22 regarding an obligation to act as a legal guardian and *X* v. *Germany*, App. No. 8410/78, 13/12/1979 where a notary was required to receive reduced fees when acting for non-profit making organisations and *Danoiu* v. *Romania*, App. No. 54780/15, 25/01/2022 where officially appointed lawyers acting in criminal proceedings had their fees reduced by the courts.

[59] *Tibet Mentes* v. *Turkey* (2018) 67 EHRR 13.

[60] *Adigüzel* v. *Turkey*, App. No. 7442/08, 13/02/2018.

[61] *Schuitemaker* v. *Netherlands* (dec.), App. No. 15906/08, 04/05/2010.

[62] Stoyanova (n 18), p.268.

A further important limitation is that Article 4(3) ECHR provides that forced or compulsory labour shall not include:

(a) any work required to be done in the ordinary course of detention imposed according to the provisions of Article 5 of [the] Convention or during conditional release from such detention;
(b) any service of a military character or, in case of conscientious objectors in countries where they are recognised, service exacted instead of compulsory military service;
(c) any service exacted in case of an emergency or calamity threatening the life or well-being of the community;
(d) any work or service which forms part of normal civic obligations.[63]

The exclusion of 'work required to be done in the ordinary course of detention' from the protection accorded by Article 4 ECHR raises questions about labour obligations on prisoners. It was argued in 2011 in *Stummer* v. *Austria* that prison work should no longer be regarded as work required to be done in the ordinary course of detention.[64] This was rejected by the Grand Chamber on the basis that there was insufficient consensus.[65] Judge Tulkens dissented, arguing that Article 4(3) ECHR 'must be interpreted in the light of the present-day situation':

> [C]an it really still be maintained in 2011, in the light of current standards in the field of social security, that prison work without affiliation to the old-age pension system constitutes work that a person in detention may *normally* be required to do? I do not think so. This, in my view, is the fundamental point. Nowadays, work without adequate social cover can no longer be regarded as normal work. It follows that the exception provided for in Article 4 § 3 (a) of the Convention is not applicable in the present case. *Even a prisoner cannot be forced to do work that is abnormal.*[66]

It is worth noting that as it has now been over a decade since the Grand Chamber rejected *Stummer* it is possible that the ECtHR may come to a different view today.[67]

In contemplating Article 4(2) ECHR, it is important to observe that because slavery and servitude both require a sense of permanency, the forced or compulsory labour provisions come to the fore where a situation is temporary. This was evident in *Chowdury* v. *Greece* where seasonal agricultural workers were forced to pick strawberries for twelve hours a day, supervised by armed

63 For discussion of the role of Article 4(3), see Stoyanova (n 18), pp.262–266.

64 *Stummer* v. *Austria* [GC] (2012) 54 EHRR 11. 65 Ibid at [131]–[132].

66 Ibid, dissenting opinion of Judge Tulkens at [8]. Emphasis in original.

67 For discussion of the structural injustice that arises from unpaid work in prison, see Virginia Mantouvalou, *Structural Injustice and Workers' Rights* (Oxford University Press, 2023), ch.4. See also, Council of Europe, *Guidance Document on the European Prison Rules* (Council of Europe, 2023).

guards, and were living in shacks, without toilets or running water.[68] They had been promised abysmally low wages, but were in fact not paid, and when they collectively demanded payment, armed guards opened fire at them, seriously injuring some of the workers. The ECtHR determined that this was not servitude because the applicants as seasonal workers could not have felt that their situation was permanent, but it *was* forced labour.[69] The forced labour provision was thus deployed to ensure that one of the major domains of exploitation (seasonal agricultural work) was brought within the ambit of Article 4 ECHR.[70] The same approach was applied to migrant construction workers in *Zoletic* v. *Azerbaijan*.[71]

In *Chowdury* and *Zoletic*, the Court also considered the relevance of 'consent' to 'forced labour'. It observed in *Chowdury* that 'where an employer abuses his power or takes advantage of the vulnerability of his workers in order to exploit them, they do not offer themselves for work voluntarily'.[72] It thus stressed that '[t]he prior consent of the victim is not sufficient to exclude the characterisation of work as forced labour' and that '[t]he question whether an individual offers himself for work voluntarily is a factual question which must be examined in the light of all the relevant circumstances of a case'.[73] It adopted the same approach in *Zoletic* stating that even if at the point of recruitment 'the applicants had offered themselves for work voluntarily and believed in good faith that they would receive their wages', the situation subsequently changed as a result of their employer's conduct.[74] In this respect it highlighted 'allegations of forced excessively long work shifts, lack of proper nutrition and medical care, and the general picture of the coercive and intimidating atmosphere'.[75]

7.3.4 Human Trafficking

7.3.4.1 Bringing Human Trafficking into Article 4 ECHR

An important development for Article 4 ECHR was the ECtHR's determination in *Rantsev* v. *Cyprus and Russia*[76] that human trafficking falls within its scope. The facts in *Rantsev* were that the applicant's daughter (Rantseva) arrived in Cyprus on a 'cabaret-artiste' visa (a type of visa which is reported to have been commonly used in Cyprus for the sex trade) and that she disappeared shortly thereafter. To understand the sequence of events that followed it is important to note how the visa scheme operated. The 'cabaret-

[68] *Chowdury* v. *Greece* [2017] ECHR 300. [69] Ibid at [99].

[70] For discussion, see Vladislava Stoyanova, 'Sweet Taste with Bitter Roots: Forced Labour and Chowdury v. Greece' (2018) 1 EHRLR 67–75.

[71] *Zoletic* v. *Azerbaijan* (n 54). [72] *Chowdury* v. *Greece* (n 68) at [96]. [73] Ibid.

[74] *Zoletic* v. *Azerbaijan* (n 54) at [167]. [75] Ibid. [76] *Rantsev* v. *Cyprus and Russia* (n 7).

artiste' visa scheme required managers to provide a bank guarantee in connection with the visa, they were also obliged to advise the immigration office if an artiste failed to show up for work. If an artiste did not show up for work and the manager failed to notify the authorities, then the guarantee deposited would be forfeited. Consequently, after Rantseva went missing from work her employer searched for her, found her and took her to the police asking them to detain her.[77] The police contacted the immigration authorities who gave instructions that Rantseva should be released to the employer and that the employer should bring her to the immigration office the next morning.[78] Tragically, the following morning Rantseva was found dead in the street below her employer's apartment.[79] An inquest took place in Cyprus which concluded that Rantseva died attempting to escape but found no evidence of foul play,[80] Russia's own autopsy found that conclusion unsatisfactory,[81] but Cyprus refused to carry out additional investigations and no further steps were taken by Russia.

Rantseva's father lodged proceedings with the ECtHR alleging various violations of the Convention, following which the Cypriot authorities made a declaration acknowledging violations, offering to pay compensation, and advising that independent experts had been appointed to investigate.[82] This did not placate the ECtHR which held that it must examine the case in view of the serious nature of the allegations, the acute problem of trafficking and sexual exploitation in Cyprus and the paucity of Article 4 ECHR case law.[83] The Court thus seized upon Rantsev as an opportunity to examine and develop Article 4 ECHR.

Contemplating the applicability of Article 4 ECHR, the Court observed that the provisions of the Convention are not the sole framework of reference for the interpretation of the rights enshrined therein.[84] It also noted that the absence of an express reference to trafficking in Article 4 ECHR was unsurprising given that the UDHR upon which the Convention is based does not refer to trafficking[85] and that the Convention is a living instrument which must be interpreted in the light of present-day conditions.[86] In this respect, it noted that human trafficking has increased significantly globally in recent years and the Palermo Protocol and ECAT demonstrate 'increasing recognition at [the] international level of the prevalence of trafficking and the need for measures to combat it';[87] all of which led the ECtHR to declare that 'there is no doubt that human trafficking is not compatible with the values expounded in the Convention'[88] and that, as the Convention must be interpreted in the light of present-day conditions, human trafficking falls within the scope of Article 4 ECHR.[89]

[77] Ibid at [18]–[19]. [78] Ibid at [20]. [79] Ibid at [25]. [80] Ibid at [30]–[41].
[81] Ibid at [51]. [82] Ibid at [201]. [83] Ibid at [199]–[202]. [84] Ibid at [273].
[85] Ibid at [277]. [86] Ibid. [87] Ibid at [278]. [88] Ibid at [282]. [89] Ibid at [277].

This expansion of Article 4 ECHR was not universally welcomed by scholars.[90] Some argued that it lacked conceptual clarity and that the Court should have used the express terms of Article 4 ECHR instead of introducing human trafficking.[91] There was also concern that no clear definition of human trafficking was provided, and that the Court's description of trafficking seemed to depart from the international definition established by the Palermo Protocol.[92] This criticism has not deterred the ECtHR as, since *Rantsev*, it has consistently held that human trafficking falls within Article 4 ECHR.[93] It has, however, as we will now see in *SM* v. *Croatia,* addressed the definitional question as to what constitutes 'human trafficking'.

7.3.4.2 The Definition of Human Trafficking

The facts in *SM* v. *Croatia* were that a young Croatian woman (SM) was forced into sex work by another Croatian national (TM).[94] After she escaped and lodged a complaint with the police, TM was indicted on charges of forcing another into prostitution, SM was recognised as a victim of human trafficking, but the investigation into TM was limited and the authorities neglected various lines of enquiry. This ultimately led to his acquittal as whilst it was determined that he had recruited SM into prostitution, it was not established that he had forced her and, as he had only been indicted for the offence of forcing another into prostitution, he could not be convicted of the basic offence of organising prostitution. Proceedings were subsequently lodged with the ECtHR alleging that Croatia had violated the Convention.

SM was considered first by a Chamber and subsequently by the Grand Chamber of the ECtHR. Both found that Croatia had violated Article 4 ECHR, but they took different approaches to the definition of human trafficking. The Chamber took a very broad approach declaring that 'trafficking itself *as well as exploitation of prostitution* ... fall within the scope of Article 4' (emphasis added).[95] Judge Koskelo in her dissent objected that:

> neither the Palermo Protocol nor the Anti-Trafficking Convention purport to ban the 'exploitation of prostitution' as a phenomenon distinct from its place as an element of the 'purpose' component of human trafficking, nor is it defined in those instruments.

[90] For discussion of these issues, see Jean Allain, '*Rantsev* v. *Cyprus and Russia*: The European Court of Human Rights and Trafficking as Slavery' (2010) 10 HRLR 3 and Vladislava Stoyanova, 'Dancing on the Borders of Article 4 ECHR: Human Trafficking and the European Court of Human Rights in the *Rantsev* Case' (2012) 30 NQLR 2. See also, Stoyanova (n 18), ch.7. On the importance of the definition of human trafficking and not conflating different concepts see also concurring opinion of Judge Pinto de Albuquerque, joined by Judge Tsotsoria in *J* v. *Austria* (n. 33).

[91] Ibid. [92] Ibid.

[93] See, for example, the Grand Chamber's analysis in *SM* v. *Croatia* (n 8).

[94] *SM* v. *Croatia* (n 8). [95] *SM* v. *Croatia* (Chamber) (n 8) at [54].

By considering now that the 'exploitation of prostitution' – whatever is meant by it – falls within the prohibition enshrined in Article 4, the majority introduce an enlargement of the scope of that Article that is both significant and obscure.[96]

When the case went to the Grand Chamber, it responded to that criticism by declaring that exploitation of prostitution only constitutes human trafficking if all the constituent elements of the international definition of human trafficking are met.[97] This clarified the definition of human trafficking. Yet, whilst the Grand Chamber resolved the definition of human trafficking, it also went on to state that 'forced prostitution' is something that may give rise to a 'separate issue' within Article 4 ECHR.[98] This raised questions as to the meaning and location of 'forced prostitution' within Article 4 ECHR (akin to the way in which *Rantsev* prompted such questions vis-à-vis human trafficking a decade earlier).[99] This is perhaps unsurprising given that the separate opinions provided in *SM* evidence clearly diverging views amongst the judges as to the scope of Article 4 ECHR.[100] In this respect it is interesting to observe that in the subsequent case of *Krachunova* v. *Bulgaria*, the ECtHR did not treat forced prostitution as a separate 'phenomenon' under Article 4 ECHR but, rather, applied the full human trafficking definition to a situation of forced prostitution when determining that obligations arose in respect of Article 4 ECHR.[101]

7.3.4.3 *Vulnerability and Human Trafficking*

Finally, in contemplating the definition of trafficking it is worth observing the contexts in which the ECtHR has recognised and emphasised the vulnerability of applicants when applying the international definition. For example, in *I.C.* v. *Republic of Moldova*, the Court observed that the applicant was 'an intellectually disabled woman' who had been abandoned at birth and had been in State care her entire life. [102] At the time of the events I.C. was residing in a State asylum (a residential neuropsychiatric institution) when the asylum was approached by a couple who asked for a resident to be placed into their care as a suitable 'bride' for an employee on their farm.[103] Following which I.C. moved to the farm where it is alleged that she was subjected to labour exploitation and sexual abuse.[104] When an application was lodged before the ECtHR in

[96] Ibid, dissenting opinion of Judge Koskelo at [18].

[97] *SM* v. *Croatia* (GC) (n 8) at [290]. See also *I.C.* v. *Republic of Moldova*, App. No. 36436/22, 27/02/2025 at [138] and [143], *F.M.* v. *Russia*, App. Nos. 71671/16 and 40190/18, 10/12/2024.

[98] *SM* v. *Croatia* (GC) (n 8) at [302]–[303].

[99] Kirsty Hughes, 'Human Trafficking, SM v. Croatia and the Conceptual Evolution of Article 4 ECHR' (2022) 85 MLR 4, p.1044.

[100] Ibid.

[101] *Krachunova* v. *Bulgaria*, App. No. 18269/18, 28/11/2023 at [145]–[157].

[102] *I.C.* v. *Republic of Moldova* (n 97).

[103] Ibid at [8].

[104] Ibid at [9]–[18].

which it was argued that Moldova had violated a number of Convention rights (including Article 4 ECHR) the Moldovan Government sought to argue that Article 4 ECHR was not applicable to the facts.[105] The ECtHR thus had to consider whether I.C. had made an arguable claim or whether there was prima facie evidence that she had been subjected to treatment prohibited by Article 4 ECHR.[106] In making that assessment the ECtHR emphasised that the applicant's 'intellectual disability and gender, set against the background of her lifelong institutionalisation – undoubtedly suggested that she belonged to a vulnerable group', whilst the couple's role as 'carers suggested that they were capable of assuming a dominant position over her and abusing her vulnerability for the purpose of exploitation'.[107] It connected this with the 'means' component of the trafficking definition observing that

> the applicant's disability and lifelong institutionalisation, combined with the apparent lack of a support network after her deinstitutionalisation and the various more subtle forms of coercion used, provided the context for the "means" element of trafficking (abuse of vulnerability). The same can be said of the applicant's situation whereby she apparently had no real alternative accommodation.[108]

In coming to that conclusion, the ECtHR also noted that GRETA reports indicate that persons with disabilities are in a situation of particular vulnerability and at an increased risk of human trafficking and that there is an increasing trend in the number of persons with disabilities being targeted for recruitment for exploitation.[109] Thus after determining that the act, means and purpose components of the human trafficking definition were present, the Court concluded that I.C. had made an arguable claim that she had been subjected to treatment contrary to Article 4 of the Convention, namely human trafficking, as well as potentially servitude.[110] Indeed, the Court ultimately found that there had been a violation of Article 4 ECHR.[111]

The vulnerability of the applicants was also emphasised in *F.M.* v. *Russia*, a case which concerned female migrant workers from Kazakhstan and Uzbekistan who were victims of human trafficking and labour exploitation lasting from several months to ten years at convenience stores in the Golyanovo district of Moscow.[112] In concluding that there was 'ample evidence to conclude that all the constituent elements of the international definition of human trafficking'[113] were present, the ECtHR observed that 'the applicants were vulnerable individuals on account of their gender and economic need'.[114] The ECtHR also recognised the vulnerability of the applicants in *B.B.* v. *Slovakia* where the ECtHR emphasised the applicant's 'applicant's young age' and the fact that she came from a 'disadvantaged social and

[105] Ibid at [86]. [106] Ibid at [146]–[151]. [107] Ibid at [149]. [108] Ibid at [149].
[109] Ibid at [124] and [149]. [110] Ibid at [150]. [111] Ibid at [166] and [177].
[112] *F.M.* v. *Russia* (n 97). [113] Ibid at [272]. [114] Ibid at [271].

economic background'.[115] The vulnerability of the applicant was also emphasised in *T.V.* v. *Spain* where the ECtHR found that the applicant's alleged personal situation 'undoubtedly pointed to her having been in a position of extreme vulnerability' (T.V. had been trafficked as a child for prostitution and there were signs of mental health problems).[116]

7.4 STATES' OBLIGATIONS IN RESPECT OF ARTICLE 4 ECHR

Having considered the various forms of exploitation prohibited by Article 4 ECHR we now consider States' obligations in respect of Article 4 ECHR. There are both negative and positive obligations. The negative obligation precludes the State from engaging in the prohibited forms of exploitation; however, as exploitation is often carried out by private actors, the positive obligations are also of vital importance.[117] When the ECtHR first examined positive obligations in *Siliadin* it held that States must adopt and apply criminal-law provisions which penalise the practices referred to in Article 4 ECHR.[118] The initial focus was thus upon punishing offenders, this changed in *Rantsev* where the Court drew upon the 'comprehensive approach to combat [ting] trafficking' advocated in the Palermo Protocol and ECAT.[119] It accordingly declared that the 'duty to penalise and prosecute trafficking is only one aspect of member States' general undertaking to combat trafficking' and that 'the positive obligations arising under Article 4 must be considered within this broader context'.[120] These obligations include 'measures to prevent trafficking and to protect victims, in addition to measures to punish traffickers'.[121] The Court also observed parallels with Articles 2 and 3 ECHR which require States 'to take operational measures to protect victims' and a 'procedural obligation to investigate'.[122] Consequently, in *Rantsev* the ECtHR identified four obligations:

- An obligation to put in place an appropriate legislative and administrative framework;[123]
- An obligation to take protective measures where the State was aware, or ought to have been aware of circumstances giving rise to credible suspicion of human trafficking;[124]

[115] *BB.* v. *Slovakia*, App. No. 48587/21, 24/10/2024 at [86].

[116] *T.V.* v. *Spain*, App. No. 22512/21, 10/10/2024 at [92].

[117] For detailed discussion of earlier case law in respect of positive obligations in this context, see (n 18), ch.8.

[118] *Siliadin* v. *France* (n 22) at [92].

[119] *Rantsev* v. *Cyprus and Russia* (n 7) at [285].

[120] Ibid at [285].

[121] Ibid.

[122] Ibid at [288]. See, in respect of Articles 2 and 3, Chapters 2 and 3.

[123] *Rantsev* v. *Cyprus and Russia* (n 7) at [285].

[124] Ibid at [286].

- A procedural obligation to investigate trafficking;[125]
- A duty to co-operate with other States in cross-border cases.[126]

Subsequent case law has affirmed and refined this framework of obligations. The positive obligations are, however, still evolving in this context. Thus, prior to examining each of the obligations further, it is worth noting that the ECtHR articulated in *Krachunova* v. *Bulgaria* what guides its interpretation of the positive obligations.[127] The specific question that arose in *Krachunova* was whether States are obliged under Article 4 ECHR to enable victims of human trafficking to claim compensation from their traffickers in respect of lost earnings. In determining that there is such an obligation and that this had been violated on the facts,[128] the ECtHR set out the general principles which guide the Court's approach to interpreting Article 4 ECHR.[129] In particular, it identified the three 'canons of interpretation that normally guide it' when considering the scope of Article 4 ECHR.[130] First, the ECtHR observed that the object and purpose of the Convention requires that its provisions are 'interpreted in a way that renders the rights that they guarantee practical and effective'.[131] In contemplating the object and purpose, the ECtHR observed that it is not decisive that Article 4 ECHR is silent as to a specific positive obligation, that there 'are strong arguments in favour of construing Article 4 in much the same manner as Article 2' and Article 3 of the Convention, and that 'redress for the victim should be the overarching consideration from a human rights perspective'.[132] Indeed, in respect of redress, the ECtHR observed that it cannot 'be seen as a secondary consideration; it must be considered an essential part of the integrated State response to trafficking required under Article 4' ECHR.[133] Applying this to compensation in *Krachunova*, the ECtHR emphasised that compensation 'would go a considerable way ... towards upholding their dignity, assisting their recovery, and reducing the risks of their falling victim again to traffickers'.[134] The second canon of interpretation is that the Convention 'should as far as possible be construed in harmony with the other rules of international law, of which they form a part'.[135] In this respect the ECtHR went on to emphasise 'that it must construe Article 4 of the Convention in the light of the Anti-Trafficking Convention, and that in so doing it ought to be guided by the way that Convention has been interpreted by GRETA'.[136] The third canon of interpretation is that the 'Court may have regard to developments in domestic legal systems that indicate a uniform or common approach or a developing consensus between the Contracting States in a given area'.[137] In developing and applying the obligations in future cases,

[125] Ibid at [288]. [126] Ibid at [289]. [127] *Krachunova* v *Bulgaria* (n 101).
[128] Ibid at [177]. See discussion below at Section 7.5.7. [129] Ibid at [162]–[165].
[130] Ibid at [162]. [131] Ibid at [163]. [132] Ibid at [166]–[168]. [133] Ibid at [171].
[134] Ibid. [135] Ibid at [164]. [136] Ibid. [137] Ibid at [165].

we may therefore expect to see the ECtHR referring to these three 'canons of interpretation'.

7.4.1 Legislative and Administrative Framework

The first obligation is that States must have a legislative and administrative framework that prohibits and punishes the exploitation prohibited by Article 4 ECHR.[138] States should also have a legislative and administrative framework which protects victims;[139] this includes regulation of businesses and immigration.[140] A further facet of the legal and administrative framework obligation is that States are required to provide relevant training for law enforcement and immigration officials.[141] The ECtHR found various breaches of the framework obligations in *Siliadin* v. *France*,[142] *C.N. and V.* v. *France*,[143] *C.N.* v. *the United Kingdom*,[144] *Rantsev* v. *Cyprus and Russia*[145] and *F.M.* v. *Russia*.[146] Moreover, in *I.C.* v. *Moldova* (discussed above), the ECtHR held that whilst the criminal legal framework was adequate, there were a number of weakenesses 'as regards the legal and administrative framework and the adequacy of the Moldovan deinstitutionalisation policy in relation to persons who have an intellectual disability and have been deprived of their legal capacity'.[147] The ECtHR thus found that this aspect of the legal framework 'did not afford the applicant practical and effective protection against trafficking and/or other forms of treatment contrary to Article 4 of the Convention.'[148]

7.4.2 Obligation to Take Protective Measures

There are various obligations that fall under the umbrella of the obligation to take protective measures. In developing these obligations, the ECtHR has been influenced by Articles 2 and 3 ECHR, ECAT and practices in Contracting States. It should be observed, however, that while the ECtHR has developed the obligation to protect so that it extends beyond immediate operational measures (e.g. non-prosecution of victims and compensation) it has not considered issues such as whether victims receive adequate accommodation and support. It is therefore possible that the ECtHR will need to consider whether the obligation to protect extends further to encompass other

[138] *Rantsev* (n 7) at [285]. See also *C.N.* v. *the United Kingdom* (2013) 56 EHRR 24 at [66]; *Siliadin* v. *France* (n 22) at [112]; *C.N. and V.* v. *France* (n 43) at [105]. For further discussion and analysis of the relationship between human rights law and criminal law in this context, see Stoyanova (n 18), ch.8.

[139] *V.C.L. and A.N.* v. *the United Kingdom* (2021) 73 EHRR 9 at [151].

[140] *Rantsev* v. *Cyprus and Russia* (n 7) at [284].

[141] Ibid at [87].

[142] *Siliadin* v. *France* (n 22) at [148].

[143] *C.N. and V.* v. *France* (n 43) at [108].

[144] *C.N.* v. *the United Kingdom* (n 138) at [76].

[145] *Rantsev* v. *Cyprus and Russia* (n 7).

[146] *F.M.* v. *Russia* (n 97).

[147] *I.C.* v. *Moldova* (n 97) at [155].

[148] Ibid at [157].

protective measures. One way of addressing this would be to develop the obligation to protect in line with the obligations under Chapter III of ECAT, but it is difficult to gauge how far the ECtHR may be willing to go in this respect.[149] It is also important to note the relationship with Article 2 and 3 ECHR as those rights may be applicable in circumstances in which the State wishes to return someone to the country in which they were initially trafficked or whether they may face other forms of exploitation contrary to Article 3 ECHR.[150]

7.4.2.1 *Operational Duty*

Article 4 ECHR, like Articles 2 and 3 ECHR, may in certain circumstances require a contracting State to take operational measures to protect potential victims.[151] This obligation is triggered when authorities are aware, or ought to be aware, of circumstances giving rise to a *credible suspicion*[152] that an identified individual has been, or is at real and immediate risk of being subjected to treatment in breach of Article 4 ECHR.[153] Once that obligation arises they must take appropriate measures, within the scope of their powers, to remove the individual from that situation or risk.[154] As with Articles 2 and 3 ECHR, the obligation is considered against the backdrop of the difficulties involved in policing and the operational choices that must be made in terms of priorities and resources. The obligation to take operational measures must therefore be interpreted in a way which does not impose an impossible or disproportionate burden on the authorities.[155] The ECtHR found violations of this obligation in *Rantsev* as the police had failed to take measures to protect Rantseva after she was brought to the police station.[156] The ECtHR also found a violation in *Chowdury* as the authorities were aware of the situation and had failed to take adequate measures to prevent trafficking and to protect the applicants.[157] Conversely, in *V.F.* v. *France*, the Court held that the evidence did not demonstrate that the police authorities knew or ought to

[149] *V.C.L. and A.N.* v. *the United Kingdom* (n 139).

[150] See, for example, *Ould Barar* v. *Sweden*, App. No. 42367/98, 19/01/1999 in which the ECtHR observed that 'the expulsion of a person to a country where there is an officially recognised regime of slavery might, in certain circumstances, raise an issue under Article 3 of the Convention'.

[151] *Rantsev* v. *Cyprus and Russia* (n 7) at [286]; *C.N.* v. *the United Kingdom* (n 138) at [67].

[152] Articles 2 and 3 ECHR require that the authorities 'knew or ought to have known of a real and immediate risk'. See Chapters 3 and 4.

[153] *V.C.L. and A.N.* v. *the United Kingdom* (n 139) at [152].

[154] Ibid.

[155] *C.N.* v. *the United Kingdom* (n 138) at [68]; *Rantsev* v. *Cyprus and Russia* (n 7) at [287].

[156] *Rantsev* v. *Cyprus and Russia* (n 7) at [298].

[157] *Chowdury* v. *Greece* (n 68) at [111]–[115].

have known that the applicant was the victim of trafficking when they decided to deport her.[158]

Since then, a number of violations of the operational duty have been found in recent cases. For instance, in *I.C.* v. *Moldova*, the ECtHR concluded that the deficiencies in the placement process and in the support provided by the authorities before and after the applicant's placement (on the farm), in circumstances which gave rise to a credible suspicion that she might be trafficked or exploited, resulted in a failure by the Moldovan authorities to take measures to protect the applicant.[159] Whilst in *F.M.* v. *Russia*, where the applicants had been trafficked for labour exploitation, a violation of the operational duty was found on the basis that 'the Russian authorities did not take any of the steps which could reasonably have been expected of them in the given circumstances',[160] 'their response ignored the gravity and urgency' of the situation,[161] and there was 'passivity and indifference' from the State's law enforcement authorities.[162]

7.4.2.2 *Preventative Measures*

Preventative measures include strengthening coordination at the national level between the various anti-trafficking bodies and discouraging the demand for all forms of exploitation of persons.[163]

7.4.2.3 *Identification and Assistance in Recovery*

Protective measures include facilitating the identification of victims by qualified persons and assisting victims in their physical, psychological and social recovery.[164]

7.4.2.4 *Non-prosecution of Victims*

A major development in respect of the obligation to protect occurred in *V.C.L. and A.N.* v. *the United Kingdom.*[165] V.C.L. and A.N. were two teenage boys who had been trafficked from Vietnam to work on cannabis farms. The boys were discovered working on two different and unrelated cannabis farms in 2009. VCL was found alone in a house in Cambridge, which was used for cultivating cannabis. AN had been locked up in a disused factory in which the windows were bricked up and the doors were bolted. VCL was discovered during a police raid, whilst AN was discovered by the police after burglars

158 *V.F.* v. *France* (dec.), App. No. 7196/10, 29/11/2011.
159 *I.C.* v. *Republic of Moldova* (n 97) at [165]. 160 *F.M.* v. *Russia* (n 97) at [299].
161 Ibid. 162 Ibid at [304]. 163 *V.C.L. and A.N.* v. *the United Kingdom* (n 139) at [153].
164 Ibid. 165 Ibid.

smashed the wall of the factory down. Both children were charged with drug offences and advised by their legal advisers to plead guilty, following which they were imprisoned. It took more than a decade for their cases to reach the ECtHR, but when they did the ECtHR determined that in certain circumstances prosecuting a *victim* of human trafficking may violate Article 4 ECHR as it is at odds with the duty to take operational measures to protect.[166] The Court established the following principles:

(i) First, that early identification of potential victims of trafficking is of paramount importance. Consequently, as soon as the authorities are aware, or ought to be aware, of circumstances giving rise to credible suspicion the potential victim must be assessed promptly by individuals trained and qualified to deal with victims of trafficking.[167]

(ii) Second, as an individual's status may affect whether there is sufficient evidence to prosecute and whether it is in the public interest to do so, any decision on whether or not to prosecute should – insofar as possible – only be taken once a trafficking assessment has been made by a qualified person.[168]

(iii) Third, that once a trafficking assessment has been made by a qualified person, any subsequent prosecutorial decision has to take that assessment into account, and whilst the decision is not binding, the prosecutor needs clear reasons which are consistent with the international law definition of trafficking.[169]

Applying those principles in *V.C.L. and A.N.*, the Court found a violation as (i) no trafficking assessment had taken place prior to prosecution, (ii) the prosecution had not given clear reasons consistent with the international law definition of human trafficking for reaching a different conclusion to that of the competent authority, and (iii) the Court of Appeal had failed to advance reasons consistent with international law in rejecting the appeal.[170] The authorities had therefore failed to take adequate measures to protect the boys and had violated Article 4 ECHR.[171]

It is important to emphasise that while *V.C.L. and A.N.* extends the duty to protect into new territory, namely non-prosecution of victims, it does not preclude prosecution. Indeed in the subsequent case of *G.S.* v. *the United Kingdom*, the ECtHR held that it *was* satisfied that the Court of Appeal, in refusing to grant an adult victim leave to appeal a conviction, had considered the extent to which she had been compelled to commit the offence and concluded that it did not extinguish her culpability.[172] It distinguished *G.S.* from *V.C.L. and A.N.* on the basis that for adult victims the non-prosecution

[166] Ibid at [159]. [167] Ibid at [160]. [168] Ibid at [161]. [169] Ibid at [162].

[170] Ibid at [172] and [181]. [171] Ibid at [174] and [183].

[172] *G.S.* v. *the United Kingdom* (dec.), App. No. 7604/19, 23/11/2021.

obligation under Article 26 ECAT only applies if they were compelled to engage in unlawful activities (whereas compulsion is not necessary for child victims).[173]

7.4.2.5 Repatriation

The State's obligations in respect of those trafficked *out* of its jurisdiction were recently considered by our domestic courts in the context of the Shamima Begum proceedings.[174] Shamima Begum, a UK national, left the UK in 2015, at the age of fifteen and travelled to Syria with two friends, ostensibly with the view to marry an ISIL fighter. Ten days after arriving in Syria, Shamima Begum was married to a twenty-one-year-old ISIL fighter, following which she gave birth in Syria to three children, all of whom died in infancy. In 2019 Shamima Begum, then aged nineteen, was located in a camp in Syria and interviewed by reporters, whilst she was nine months pregnant with her third child. She was interviewed again shortly after the birth. Those interviews were published and broadcast, following which her UK citizenship was revoked. Less than three weeks later her third child died in the camp in Syria. Shamima Begum's citizenship deprivation and the legal proceedings that have followed are considered in further detail in Chapter 8 (Terrorism). For present purposes we will focus on the Article 4 ECHR aspect of her challenge to the deprivation order, noting that her challenges have thus far been unsuccessful. There have been two sets of legal proceedings. In the first set of proceedings Shamima Begum sought leave to enter the UK to challenge the deprivation order; this was rejected by the Supreme Court.[175] The second set of proceedings concerned the substantive challenge to the deprivation order.[176] The aspect of the deprivation challenge which is relevant to this chapter are the arguments that Shamima Begum is a victim of human trafficking whom the UK failed to protect and that this affects the legitimacy of the deprivation order.

The relevant facts are as follows. In September 2014, Shamima Begum entered Year 11 at Bethnal Green Academy. She was predicted to attain A/A* grades in most of her GCSE subjects. In the autumn of 2014 Shamima Begum's school friend, Sharmeena Begum (no relation), was following the blog of Aqsa Mahmood who had travelled to Syria earlier in 2014 and was encouraging others to follow her. Sharmeena tweeted Aqsa Mahmoud asking her to message her directly via Twitter. Sharmeena was a close friend of Shamima and of the two other girls who were in due course to travel as a group to Syria. Around the same time another girl from the borough, known as 'B', was also planning to travel to Syria via Istanbul but was taken off the

[173] Ibid at [23]. [174] *Shamima Begum* v. *SSHD* [2024] EWCA Civ 152 at [81].

[175] *R (on the application of Begum)* v. *SIAC and SSHD* [2021] UKSC 7.

[176] *Shamima Begum* v. *SSHD* (n 174).

plane at the last moment. B's case came before the Family Division on 21 August 2015 where Hayden J observed that there were a:

> number of other cases within the Borough of Tower Hamlets, each of which involves intelligent young girls, highly motivated academically, each of whom has, to some and greatly varying degrees, been either radicalised or exposed to extreme ideology. . . . In each of these cases . . . young women . . . have been captured, seduced, by a belief that travelling to Syria to become what is known as 'Jihadi brides' is somehow romantic and honourable both to them and their families. There is no doubt, to my mind, that young women have been specifically targeted, in addition to young men of course, but for different purposes. The reality is that the future for such girls as we know, holds only exploitation, degradation and risk of death; in other words these children with whose future I have been concerned, have been put at risk of really serious harm and as such the State is properly obligated to protect them.[177]

On 5 December 2014, Sharmeena travelled from Gatwick Airport to Istanbul and then to Syria. On a date between 5 and 10 December 2014, police officers visited Shamima Begum's school and spoke to seven girls, including Shamima and her two friends. The police concluded that Shamima was not at risk, although the SIAC later observed that this conclusion may be thought to be 'somewhat myopic'.[178] Shamima Begum's school had considered that Shamima was at risk, but had allowed the police assessment to overrule their concerns. On 5 February 2015 police officers returned to the school and handed letters to Shamima Begum and her friends in the expectation that the girls would give the letters to their parents, the letters sought parental consent to the police interviewing the girls. Unsurprisingly, the girls did not give the letters to their parents and less than two weeks later Shamima Begum and her two friends left for Syria. The police later apologised for not sending the letters to the parents directly.

In her legal challenge to the deprivation order, Shamima Begum argued that she was trafficked to Syria and that the UK had various obligations to prevent her from being trafficked and to protect her as a victim of human trafficking.[179] Her argument as to the relevance of those obligations to the deprivation order shifted somewhat during the proceedings. Initially she argued that there had been a breach of Article 4 ECHR but by the time the matter was considered by the Court of Appeal her argument was that the Secretary of State (SofS) had failed to take into account a possible breach of Article 4 ECHR by the UK authorities.[180] In this regard, Shamima Begum argued that it was necessary for the SofS to take into account any possible breaches of Article 4 ECHR as part of his assessment of whether the deprivation was conducive to

177 As discussed in *Shamima Begum* v. *SSHD* (n 174) at [15].

178 *Shamima Begum* v. *SSHD* SC/163/2019, 22/02/2023 at [83].

179 *Shamima Begum* v. *SSHD* (n 174) at [52].

180 Ibid at [55].

the public good pursuant to the statutory provision which governs the SofS's power to issue a deprivation order.[181] The SofS argued that in circumstances where the statute did not identify what considerations were to be taken into account (which this legislation did not), it was necessary to define the test for determining what needed to be taken into account, and that this was a matter for the SofS subject to the *Wednesbury* irrationality test.[182] The Court of Appeal agreed with the SofS.

> The question for us is whether the credible suspicion that Ms Begum was trafficked (and the possible breaches of Article 4 consequent upon that suspicion), taken alone or together, amounted to an obviously material consideration for the Secretary of State in the assessment of whether to deprive Ms Begum of her citizenship, according to the Wednesbury irrationality test.[183]

The Court of Appeal acknowledged that there was a credible suspicion that Shamima Begum was at risk of being trafficked and there was an arguable case that the police, school and/or local authority had failed to take reasonable preventative measures as required by the State's operational duty under Article 4 ECHR.[184] Crucially, however, it held that this was only arguable, and that the passage of time and the lack of any causal link were fatal to the argument that the UK authorities now owed Shamima Begum a protective duty.[185] In other words, whilst the State may have failed to take preventative measures prior to her being trafficked this did not mean that they now owed her a *protective* duty which precluded the SofS from depriving her of her citizenship. Thus, it could not be said that the 'possibility of the existence of such a duty should have been taken into account: there was nothing in this regard for the Secretary of State to take into account, let alone something obviously material.'[186]

The Court of Appeal also considered the recovery component of the Article 4 ECHR operational duty. In respect of the UK's *recovery* duty, it held that there is no Strasbourg or domestic decision which supports the proposition that a State has an obligation, as part of the recovery duty, to repatriate a former victim of trafficking in order that they can receive support and protection within the jurisdiction.[187] The Court of Appeal also rejected the argument that Article 16 ECAT assisted Shamima Begum with this argument.[188] They held that Article 16 ECAT does not flesh out Article 4 ECHR, nor does the SofS's policy in respect of ECAT limit the application of the SofS's power to issue a deprivation order.[189]

A further argument advanced by Shamima Begum was that the *non-punishment* principle developed in *VCL and AN* was broad enough to include

[181] Ibid at [56]. [182] Ibid at [58]. [183] Ibid at [62]. [184] Ibid at [75]–[77].
[185] Ibid at [78]. [186] Ibid at [78]. [187] Ibid at [79]. [188] Ibid at [80]–[81].
[189] Ibid at [80]–[81].

non-repatriation.[190] This was rejected by the Court of Appeal which found no authority for this in either domestic or Strasbourg case law.[191] It thus declined to extend the non-punishment principle as this would be an extension of the Strasbourg case law which was more than an incremental development.[192] Consequently, as the non-punishment principle was not engaged, there was nothing which the Secretary of State was required to take into account.[193]

In addition to her arguments based on the operational duty, Shamima Begum also argued that the *investigative obligation* was applicable.[194] This was rejected by the Court of Appeal for the following reasons.[195] First, there was no operational duty to repatriate and thus it would be surprising if the investigative duty obligation provided a means of procuring that outcome.[196] Second, Shamima Begum had not been allowed to enter to participate in her own deprivation proceedings and so it would be surprising if she were allowed to enter to participate in proceedings against others.[197] Third, the duty is only to take reasonable steps to investigate and repatriation of someone who has been assessed as posing a national security threat would exceed what could be regarded as reasonable.[198]

The final component of Shamima Begum's Article 4 ECHR argument was that where there is a breach of an ECHR obligation, the State is under an obligation to restore the individual to the position they would have been in if the breach had not occurred.[199] The Court of Appeal rejected this.[200] First, it held that no breach had been established and that a possible or arguable breach was insufficient to trigger the restitutionary duty.[201] Second, even if a breach were established, States have latitude in determining how reparation is to be assessed.[202] Third, the alleged breach occurred 'four years before the deprivation decision and before many of the events which gave rise to it' and the Court was 'shown no authority to support the proposition that a restitutionary duty consequent on the breach of the protective duty could exist so long after the event giving rise to that breach, and despite supervening events which supported the adverse national security assessment'.[203]

Consequently, the Court of Appeal concluded that there was no obligation under the ECHR to repatriate Shamima Begum in 2015 or 2019 and there is none now.[204] The Supreme Court subsequently refused permission to appeal.[205] In respect of the Article 4 ECHR ground of appeal, the panel of the Supreme Court determined that the argument was based on submissions

[190] Ibid at [82]. [191] Ibid at [82]. [192] Ibid at [82]. [193] Ibid at [82].

[194] Ibid at [83]–[86]. [195] Ibid at [85]. [196] Ibid. [197] Ibid. [198] Ibid.

[199] Ibid at [87]. [200] Ibid at [88]–[91]. [201] Ibid at [88]. [202] Ibid at [89].

[203] Ibid at [89]. [204] Ibid at [91].

[205] Permission to Appeal decision in the matter of *Shamima Begum (Appellant)* v. *SSHD (Respondent)* UKSC 2024/0096, 7 August 2024.

which appear to the panel to go well beyond the existing case law of the European Court of Human Rights, or the incremental development of the principles established by that case law: for example, that the non-punishment principle extends to a decision to deprive a person of her citizenship on grounds of national security, that the recovery duty applies to persons outside the State's jurisdiction, and that the restitutionary obligation can give rise to an obligation to repatriate.[206]

Consequently, the panel determined that the Court of Appeal was right to reject the Article 4 ECHR arguments.[207] In this regard, it observed that

Whether the Convention law should be developed as the Appellant argues is a matter which can only appropriately be decided by the European court, as the authoritative interpreter of the ECHR. It is not the role of this court to develop the law under the Convention well beyond the principles established by the European court.[208]

It will be interesting to see how the ECtHR approaches the Article 4 ECHR obligations if it is faced with a case of this nature.

7.4.2.6 *Compensation*

As noted above, a further development in *Krachunova* v. *Bulgaria* was the recognition that States have a positive obligation to enable trafficking victims to claim compensation from their traffickers for lost earnings.[209] In developing this obligation the ECtHR in *Krachunova* observed that 'investigation and punishment' does not 'wipe away the material harm suffered by the victims of trafficking that has already taken place' nor does it 'practically assist their recovery'[210] and that similar issues arise in respect of compensation to those that it had considered in *V.C.L. and A.N.*[211]

The possibility for them to seek compensation in respect of lost earnings, especially earnings withheld from them by their traffickers, would constitute one means of ensuring *restitutio in integrum* for those victims by making good the full extent of the harm suffered by them. It would also go a considerable way (by providing them with the financial means to rebuild their lives) towards upholding their dignity, assisting their recovery, and reducing the risks of their falling victim again to traffickers. This cannot therefore be seen as a secondary consideration; it must be considered an essential part of the integrated State response to trafficking required under Article 4 of the Convention. Moreover, redress for the victim should be the overarching consideration from a human-rights perspective.[212]

Applying this to the facts, the ECtHR held that Bulgaria had failed to comply with this obligation when it dismissed the applicant's claim for lost earnings on the basis that she had obtained those earnings through sex work.[213]

[206] Ibid at [6]. [207] Ibid. [208] Ibid at [7]. [209] *Krachunova* v. *Bulgaria* (n 101) at [169].
[210] Ibid at [169]. [211] Ibid at [170]. [212] Ibid at [171]. [213] Ibid at [183]–[199].

7.4.3 Procedural Obligation to Investigate

In *Rantsev*, it was stated that the obligation to investigate arises where 'the State authorities *were aware, or ought to have been aware*, of circumstances giving rise to a *credible suspicion* that an identified individual *had been, or was at real and immediate risk* of being subjected to treatment in breach of Article 4 of the Convention'.[214] The threshold was lowered in *SM*, where it was held that the obligation is triggered where the applicant makes an 'arguable claim' or there is prima facie evidence.[215] This brings the trigger for the procedural obligation to investigate under Article 4 ECHR in line with that which applies in respect of Articles 2 and 3 ECHR.[216] It is, however, important to note that there was disagreement amongst the judges on this issue. Judges O'Leary and Ravarani opposed the lowering of the threshold on the basis that whilst in Article 2 and 3 ECHR cases there will generally be 'physical evidence', in Article 4 ECHR cases the evidence is likely to be different in nature.[217] Consequently, they argued that the lower threshold is inappropriate as it is not clear what an arguable Article 4 ECHR claim looks like, nor what will constitute prima facie evidence.[218] In many ways those concerns are inherently connected to their understanding of human trafficking itself. Indeed, Judges O'Leary and Ravarani declared that 'the reality of the applicant's case was that the facts she presented did not appear to match the constituent elements of human trafficking': an assertion that contradicted both the official recognition of SM as a victim of human trafficking in Croatia, and the ECtHR's own analysis.[219] This underscores the challenges in recognising human trafficking and the arguable need for a threshold which is not tied to perceptions of the credibility of potential victims of human trafficking.[220] This is significant, because as we will see later in this chapter, the UK system has recently been amended to put a greater emphasis on credibility.

Having lowered the trigger for the obligation, the Grand Chamber in *SM* also elaborated on the nature of the obligation once it is triggered. It observed first that the requirements are similar regardless of whether the treatment has been inflicted by State agents or private individuals.[221] Second, that an investigation must be capable of leading to the establishment of the facts and of identifying and – if appropriate – punishing those responsible.[222] Third, that it is vital that the authorities act of their own motion once the matter has

[214] *Rantsev* v. *Cyprus and Russia* (n 7) at [286] (emphasis added).

[215] *SM* v. *Croatia* [GC] (n 8) at [324]. [216] Ibid.

[217] Ibid, joint concurring opinion of Judges O'Leary and Ravarani. [218] Ibid. [219] Ibid.

[220] Kirsty Hughes, 'Human Trafficking, *SM* v. *Croatia* and the Conceptual Evolution of Article 4 ECHR' (2022) **85**(4) Modern Law Review 1044. For discussion of the problems with the focus on credibility in the ECtHR's case law prior to *SM*, see Stoyanova (n 18), ch.8.

[221] *SM* v. *Croatia* (n 8) at [312]. [222] Ibid at [313].

come to their attention and that they do not leave it to the initiative of the victim to take responsibility for the conduct of any investigatory procedures.[223] Fourth, that the obligation is a requirement of means and not of results and thus there is no absolute right to obtain the prosecution or conviction of any particular person where there were no culpable failures in seeking to hold perpetrators of criminal offences accountable.[224] Consequently, the fact that an investigation ends without concrete, or with only limited, results is not indicative of any failings as such.[225] The authorities must, however, take whatever reasonable steps they can to collect evidence and elucidate the circumstances of the case.[226] Fifth, that the procedural obligation must not be interpreted in such a way as to impose an impossible or disproportionate burden on the authorities.[227] Finally, it held that the investigation's conclusions must be based on thorough, objective and impartial analysis of all relevant elements.[228] Failing to follow an obvious line of inquiry undermines to a decisive extent the investigation's ability to establish the circumstances of the case and the identity of those responsible,[229] however, 'possible defects must amount to significant flaws in order to raise an issue under Article 4'.[230] Consequently, 'the Court is not concerned with allegations of errors or isolated omissions but only significant shortcomings in the proceedings and the relevant decision making process . . . namely those that are capable of undermining the investigation's capability of establishing the circumstances of the case or the person responsible'.[231] Applying this in *SM*, the Grand Chamber held that the authorities had failed to follow up on major lines of inquiry and had violated Article 4 ECHR. The Court also found violations of this obligation in *Rantsev*,[232] *Chowdury*,[233] *Zoletic*,[234] *T.V.*,[235] *B.B.*,[236] *I.C.*[237] and *F.M.*[238]

7.4.4 Cross-border Duty

In addition to the obligation to conduct domestic investigations, contracting States must also cooperate effectively with other States.[239] It appears that this duty was breached in *Zoletic* v. *Azerbaijan* within the context of a general failure to investigate.[240]

[223] Ibid at [314]. [224] Ibid at [315]. [225] Ibid at [315]. [226] Ibid at [316].
[227] Ibid at [315]. [228] Ibid at [316]. [229] Ibid. [230] Ibid at [320]. [231] Ibid at [320].
[232] *Rantsev* v. *Cyprus and Russia* (n 7). [233] *Chowdury* v. *Greece* (n 68).
[234] *Zoletic* v. *Azerbaijan* (n 54). [235] *T.V.* v. *Spain* (n 116). [236] *B.B.* v. *Slovakia* (n 115).
[237] *I.C.* v. *Republic of Moldova* (n 97). [238] *F.M.* v. *Russia* (n 97).
[239] *Rantsev* v. *Cyprus and Russia* (n 7) at [289] and *Zoletic* v. *Azerbaijan* (n 54) at [191].
[240] *Zoletic* v. *Azerbaijan* (n 54).

7.5 THE UK'S NATIONAL REFERRAL MECHANISM

Having considered the international framework, we now turn to consider how this is addressed in domestic law. The NRM governs the identification of victims in the UK. It was created in 2009 to meet the UK's international obligations, but the former Independent Anti-Slavery Commissioner has deemed it a 'dysfunctional' system that is 'failing victims'[241] and GRETA has identified numerous areas in which improvement is needed.[242]

In 2024, 19,125 potential victims were referred into the NRM system.[243] This is the highest number of referrals made in a year, overtaking the record from the previous year and is more than five times as many as the 3,263 referrals that were made in 2015 when the Modern Slavery Act was passed.[244] It is, however, estimated that there are in fact at least 100,000 victims in the UK.[245] The most common nationality referred in 2024 were UK nationals, followed by Albanian and Vietnamese nationals.[246] In 2024, 31 per cent of all referrals related to potential child victims;[247] 78 per cent of which were boys, the majority of whom had been criminally exploited.[248] That figure is partially driven by 'county lines' drug cases, reflecting the fact that a high proportion of modern slavery and human trafficking involves UK nationals,[249] and that 75 per cent of the UK nationals referred into the NRM system are children.[250] These figures are horrifying; however, the House of Commons Home Affairs Committee concluded in December 2023 that 'there is still likely to be under-reporting of the true number of victims'.[251]

Many regard increased use of the NRM system as an indication of the scale of the problem, others, however, such as the former Home Secretary, Suella Braverman, interpret it as evidence that 'modern slavery laws are being abused by people gaming the system'.[252] The suggestion that the system is flooded with false claims is arguably contradicted by the number of positive NRM decisions. Between January and March 2022, 89 per cent of Reasonable Grounds and 92 per cent of Conclusive Grounds decisions were positive.[253] Since then there has been a considerable decline in the rate of positive

[241] Independent Anti-Slavery Commissioner's Annual Report 2021–2022, foreword.

[242] GRETA (n 13).

[243] Home Office National Referral Mechanism and Duty to Notify Statistics UK, End of Year Summary 2024 (6 March 2025).

[244] Ibid. [245] House of Commons Home Affairs Committee, *Human Trafficking* (n 2) at [2].

[246] Home Office National Referral Mechanism Statistics (n 243). [247] Ibid. [248] Ibid.

[249] Ibid. [250] Ibid.

[251] House of Commons Home Affairs Committee, *Human Trafficking* (n 2), p.4.

[252] Suella Braverman Speech to Conservative Party Conference (4/10/2022).

[253] Modern Slavery: National Referral Mechanism and Duty to Notify Statistics UK, Quarter 1 2022 – January to March (12 May 2022).

decisions as in 2024 only 53 per cent of Reasonable Grounds decision were positive and 56 per cent of Conclusive Grounds decisions were positive.[254] This fall in the rate of positive NRM decisions probably reflects the changes that have been made to the system which as we will see in this chapter have made it harder for victims to obtain a positive NRM decision. It should also not be assumed that when a negative decision is issued that the application was false. There are many reasons why a negative decision may be issued, and it is not infrequent that negative NRM decisions are flawed as evidenced by the role of judicial review in correcting such decisions. Moreover, whilst Braverman suggests that 'people are gaming the system' the fact that first responders are identifying a sizable cohort of potential victims that do not want to enter the NRM, strongly contradicts this claim.[255]

Political concerns about illegal immigration led to the enactment of the NBA which amended the NRM system. The NBA made significant amendments that were widely opposed by those working directly with survivors, as well as the former Independent Anti-Slavery Commissioner who cautioned that it will make the 'identification of victims of modern slavery harder and ... create[s] additional vulnerabilities'.[256] The NBA is now in force and in this chapter we will examine the changes that it has made to the NRM. An additional contentious development in respect of the NRM was the introduction of the Slavery and Human Trafficking (Definition of Victim) Regulations 2022 which set out a definition of human trafficking that is narrower than the international definition. This has given rise to further concerns about obstacles to victim identification and support.[257]

Finally, it is important to observe that at the time of writing the IMA purports to impose a duty on the SofS to remove people that have travelled through a safe third country en route to the UK who require leave to enter or remain and do not have it.[258] To facilitate this duty, the IMA purports to disapply the SofS's obligations in respect of leave to remain (unless there are 'compelling circumstances') for victims of modern slavery or human trafficking, as well as support for such victims.[259] The Chair of the Joint Committee on Human Rights cautioned when it scrutinised the Bill that:

[254] Home Office National Referral Mechanism Statistics (n 243).

[255] Ibid, p.5. Duty to Notify reports that in 2024 the Home Office received 5,598 reports of adult potential victims who had refused to enter the NRM system via the Duty to Notify process (compared to 4,929 in the previous year). The number received in 2024 was the highest in a year since the NRM began, overtaking the record from the previous year.

[256] Independent Anti-Slavery Commissioner's Letter to Priti Patel (6 May 2021).

[257] Jason Hayes, 'Regressing from the Gold Standard: The UK's Slavery and Human Trafficking Regulations and the Narrowing of Victim Protection' (2024) 45 Statute Law Review 1.

[258] Section 2 of the Illegal Migration Act 2023.

[259] Sections 22–25 IMA 2023.

Again, the weight of evidence we received was overwhelmingly clear that this would be in breach of the UK's obligations under the Council of Europe Convention Against Trafficking (ECAT) and Article 4 of ECHR (prohibition of slavery). Removing protections from VOTs and VOSs is a response to what the Home Secretary has described as 'abuse' of our modern slavery laws. Many have disputed this claim that the system is being abused, including former Prime Minister Theresa May MP who has said that there is no evidence to support this claim.[260]

The IMA provisions were not brought into force upon enactment. Instead the Act provided that the provisions could be brought into effect by Regulation by the SofS, however, the former Conservative Government indicated that it would not bring the provisions into effect prior to the Supreme Court's ruling on the legality of the Rwanda policy. The Supreme Court subsequently held in *AAA* v. *SSHD* that the Rwanda policy was unlawful, which led to the enactment of the Safety of Rwanda (Asylum and Immigration) Act 2024.[261] Alongside these developments legal challenges were brought in respect of the IMA in Northern Ireland, where the Northern Ireland Human Rights Commission argued that the IMA is in breach of the UK's domestic and international human rights obligations under Article 2(1) of the Windsor Framework, 1951 Refugee Convention and the ECHR.[262] The High Court of Northern Ireland found numerous provisions of the IMA to be incompatible with the Convention rights (including Aricle 4 ECHR) and issued declarations of incompatibility.[263] The Government appealed the ruling and a hearing was scheduled for spring 2025. However, in the interim a new Labour Government came to power in July 2024 and it now appears that the Safety of Rwanda (Asylum and Immigration) Act 2024 as well as some aspects of the Illegal Migration Act (including the duty to remove) will be repealed by the Border Security, Asylum and Immigration Bill which is currently before Parliament. Consequently, in February 2025 the Court of Appeal in Northern Ireland stayed the Government's appeal against the IMA ruling on the basis that legislation currently before Parliament will render the case academic.[264] It is, however, important to note that in its current form the Border Security, Asylum and Immigration Bill will not repeal the NBA provisions, nor will it repeal all of the IMA provisions including provisions which disqualify victims of modern slavery and human trafficking from support.

[260] Joint Committee on Human Rights, *Legislative Scrutiny Illegal Migration Bill* (11 June 2023), p.9.

[261] [2023] UKSC 42, [2023] 1 WLR 4433, [2024] 1 All ER 1.

[262] Northern Ireland Human Rights Commission Illegal Migration Act Challenge Factsheet (7 December 2023).

[263] *Northern Ireland Human Rights Commission's Application and JR295's Application In the matter of The Illegal Migration Act 2023* [2024] NIKB 35 at [229] and [259].

[264] BBC News, 'Illegal Migration Act Appeal Paused by NI Court', *BBC News*, 18 February 2025, www.bbc.co.uk/news/articles/cz7v3qd4x2vo.

7.5.1 Entering the NRM System

The NRM is governed by both statute (NBA) and statutory guidance (*Modern Slavery Statutory Guidance for England and Wales under s 49 of the Modern Slavery Act 2015*, or non-statutory guidance for Scotland and Northern Ireland). The system functions on the basis that if a first responder suspects that a person is a potential victim of modern slavery and/or human trafficking, they should notify the competent authority which then determines whether the person should be recognised as a victim. First responders include organisations such as Health and Social Care Trusts, the police, the Salvation Army, Barnardo's and the National Society for the Prevention of Cruelty to Children. Adult potential victims must consent to being referred to the NRM and there has been a significant rise in the number of adults refusing to consent to referral.[265] One of the reasons why non-British nationals may be refusing to enter the NRM system is that the 'competent authority' which determines NRM applications resides within the Home Office.[266] The fact that the body tasked with identifying victims resides within an organisation tasked with immigration is concerning. Such concerns were heightened following the revelation in 2022 that the Home Office removed modern slavery from the official list of responsibilities of the safeguarding minister, and reclassified it as a component of the 'illegal immigration and asylum' brief of the immigration minister.[267] Both the Organisation for Security and Cooperation in Europe (OSCE) and the House of Commons Home Affairs Committee urged the Government to withdraw modern slavery and human trafficking from the Minister for Immigration and reinstate the full remit of human trafficking and modern slavery policy to the Minister for Safeguarding.[268]

Once a referral is made to the competent authority there are two stages in the NRM process; these are known as the Reasonable Grounds decision and the conclusive determination. We will look at each of these in turn.

7.5.2 Reasonable Grounds Decision

The Reasonable Grounds decision is an initial filter. It should, where possible, be made within five working days of the referral being received, and emergency support may be available whilst awaiting a determination. Until recently, the threshold for a Reasonable Grounds decision was that the competent authority 'suspect[s] but cannot prove the person *may be* a victim of

[265] House of Commons Home Affairs Committee, *Human Trafficking* (n 2) at [221].

[266] Ibid at [219].

[267] Emily Dugan, 'Home Office reclassifies modern slavery as illegal immigration issue', *The Guardian*, 13 October 2022, www.theguardian.com/world/2022/oct/13/home-office-reclassifies-modern-slavery-as-immigration-issue.

[268] House of Commons Home Affairs Committee, *Human Trafficking* (n 2) at [32].

modern slavery which includes human trafficking or slavery, servitude, or forced or compulsory labour' (emphasis added). Section 60 NBA amended this to the competent authority 'suspect[s] but cannot prove the person *is* a victim' (emphasis added). The shift from 'may' to 'is' raises the threshold, which could in turn reduce the number of persons identified as victims, and/or result in a longer timeframe for decisions.

In addition to the NBA amendment, the SofS for the Home Department published new Statutory Guidance in January 2023. This required potential victims to produce *objective evidence* of their trafficking. It stated that 'a decision maker must base their decision on objective factors to have real suspicion and therefore meet the RG threshold' and that a 'victim's own account, by itself, would not be sufficient absent objective factors to have real suspicion'. Following the entry into force of this Guidance, Home Office statistics indicated that there was a significant drop in positive Reasonable Grounds decisions from 88 per cent in 2022 to 50 per cent in the first quarter of 2023.[269] Judicial review proceedings were thus initiated in which it was to be argued that the Guidance was unlawful because it induced breaches of Article 4 ECHR, it was irrational at common law, undercut the statutory provisions of the MSA and was procedurally unfair.[270] This prompted the SSHD to revise the statutory guidance. The revised policy states that decision makers should consider 'whether it is reasonable in all the circumstances' to expect supporting evidence or corroborating information'.[271] Yet in December 2023, the House of Commons Home Office Affairs Committee reported that despite this change 'between July and September 2023 only 52% of all Reasonable Grounds decisions were positive'.[272] The Committee also reported that 'between July and September 2023, the Home Office started reporting on decisions that were "reconsidered" by the competent authorities; receiving 314 reconsideration requests in that quarter. Of these, 51% of Reasonable Grounds decisions and 67% of Conclusive Grounds decisions were reconsidered to be positive, supporting the concern that the Home Office may have been incorrectly rejecting cases following these changes.'[273] The Committee thus recommended an independent review of the implementation of modern slavery provisions in the NBA and a pause of any requirement to provide third

[269] Matrix Chambers, 'SSHD Withdraws New Evidential Test for "Reasonable Grounds" Decisions in Modern Slavery Statutory Guidance' (27 June 2023), www.matrixlaw.co.uk/news/sshd-withdraws-new-evidential-test-for-reasonable-grounds-decisions-in-modern-slavery-statutory-guidance/#:~:text=The%20Secretary%20of%20State%20for,to%20receive%20a%20positive%20reasonable.

[270] Ibid.

[271] *Modern Slavery: Statutory Guidance for England and Wales (under s49 of the Modern Slavery Act 2015) and Non-Statutory Guidance for Scotland and Northern Ireland* at [14.55].

[272] House of Commons, Home Affairs Committee, *Human Trafficking* (n 2) at [122].

[273] Ibid at [122].

party evidence at the Reasonable Grounds stage until such an independent review has been concluded and has determined that the new requirements are not unduly burdensome.[274]

If a negative Reasonable Grounds decision is issued then it should be reviewed by a second caseworker. At one time it was Government policy that only first responders could request reconsideration, but this was successfully challenged as an abdication of the State's responsibilities to identify victims,[275] and the Home Office updated its guidance accordingly.[276]

If a positive Reasonable Grounds decision is made, then this triggers a recovery and reflection period. This stems from Article 13 ECAT which requires each State to provide a recovery period of at least thirty days. Until recently the recovery period was provided for by statutory guidance, but it was placed on a legislative footing by s.64 NBA. At the same time the recovery period was reduced from what was previously forty-five days to thirty days.[277] It is important to note, however, that if a decision has not been made after thirty days (which is frequently the case), then the recovery period must continue until a decision has been made.[278] This is significant because the reality is that victims often wait years for a decision. Indeed, in April 2022 the Independent Anti-Slavery Commissioner reported that the 'average number of days for a conclusive grounds decision was 568 days' and that there were '24,499 cases awaiting decisions'.[279]

A further change made by s.63 NBA is that the duty to provide support ceases entirely if the competent authority determines that the person is disqualified. Consequently, whilst the general rule is that potential victims cannot be removed from the UK during the recovery period (s.61(2) NBA), they may be removed if the competent authority determines that the person is a threat to public order or has claimed to be a victim in bad faith (s.63(1) NBA). In 2024 there were 276 disqualification requests (95 per cent (262 requests) were on grounds of public order and 5 per cent (fourteen requests) were on grounds of bad faith; 255 of those requests were confirmed of which 95 per cent (242 disqualifications) were on grounds of public order and 5 per cent (thirteen disqualifications) were on grounds of bad faith.[280] It is important to observe that if it is brought into force, s.29 of the IMA 2023 would further amend this provision from 'may' to 'must', that is, obliging the competent authority to determine that the victim is disqualified if they have determined that the person is a threat to public order or has claimed to be a victim in bad faith. Section 29(4) IMA 2023 would also

[274] Ibid at [215]–[216].

[275] *R (on the application of DS)* v. *SSHD* [2019] EWHC 3046 (Admin) at [72].

[276] *Modern Slavery: Statutory Guidance* (n 271) at [14.216] and [14.219].

[277] Section 61(3) NBA. [278] Section 61(3)(b)(ii) NBA.

[279] Independent Anti-Slavery Commissioner's Annual Report 2021–2022 at [1.3.4].

[280] Home Office National Referral Mechanism Statistics (n 243) at [4.2].

expand the scope of the 'threat to public order' ground for disqualification to include any person who is not a British citizen who is convicted in the UK of an offence and has been sentenced to a period of imprisonment for the offence. At the time of writing, it appears that the Border Security, Asylum and Immigration Bill will retain both the NBA disqualification provisions and the s.29 IMA expansion of those provisions. Consequently section 29 IMA was scrutinised again by the Joint Committee on Human Rights during its legislative scrutiny of the Border Security, Asylum and Immigration Bill. It determined that s.29 IMA is not compatible with the UK's obligations under ECAT and Article 4 ECHR, and thus recommended that it be repealed.[281]

Another restriction brought about by the NBA is that a person who has previously been identified as a potential victim and benefitted from a recovery period may not be entitled to a further recovery period if they bring forward additional grounds based on matters that occurred before the previous decision.[282] In such cases the victim may not receive support and may be removed from the UK whilst the Conclusive Grounds decision is being made (s.62(2) NBA). This change reflects a presumption that the failure to provide the information earlier was driven by some form of mala fides. A stance that fails to appreciate the impact of trauma, the fact that victims of modern slavery and/or human trafficking may not recognise that they are victims, and that they may not appreciate that information is relevant.

If the recovery period applies, then support may include access to relevant legal advice, accommodation, protection and independent emotional and practical help. This is provided through the Modern Slavery Victim Care Contract and is determined by risk- and needs-based assessments. Victims are also entitled to financial support, but in practice many have received no or reduced financial support and the Home Office has had to launch a scheme to compensate those who had funding withheld unlawfully.[283] The House of Commons Home Affairs Committee has also reported that there is a shortage of appropriate safe housing for victims whilst they are within the Modern Slavery Victim Care Contract.[284]

7.5.3 Conclusive Grounds Decision

During the recovery period, the competent authority is expected to gather further information and make a conclusive decision. It must take into account

[281] Joint Committee on Human Rights, *Legislative Scrutiny: Border Security, Asylum and Immigration Bill, Fourth Report of Session 2024-2025* at [114].

[282] Section 62 NBA, Explanatory Memorandum at [619].

[283] Home Office, *Modern Slavery: Back-pay for incorrect financial support reductions* (16 February 2022).

[284] House of Commons, Home Affairs Committee, *Human Trafficking* (n 2) at [78].

expert reports and objective country of origin information as well as other published information from trusted sources,[285] but an interview with the potential victim is not normally held.[286]

One of the key differences between the Reasonable Grounds stage and the Conclusive Grounds stage is that a higher threshold applies in respect of the latter. At the Conclusive Grounds stage, the competent authority must determine whether, on the *balance of probabilities*, the individual *has been* a victim of modern slavery or human trafficking. This contrasts with the Reasonable Grounds stage which requires a determination of whether there are reasonable grounds *to suspect* that a person *is* a victim. In *R (on the application of MN and IXU)* v. *SSHD (AIRE Centre and Anti-Slavery International Intervening)*, it was argued that the balance of probabilities test is incompatible with ECAT.[287] The High Court and the Court of Appeal rejected that argument. They held that there is no particular standard mandated by ECAT, and the balance of probabilities is an appropriate standard well recognised in domestic law. The Court further held that there is no point in having a two-stage process unless the stages are distinct, and it makes sense that the Conclusive Grounds decision is subject to a higher threshold. Section 60(4) NBA has since placed the 'balance of probabilities' threshold on a legislative footing.

The new provisions on credibility are amongst the most controversial aspects of the NBA. Sections 58–59 NBA empower the SofS to oblige potential victims to provide information by a specified date, coupled with a mandate that failure to meet that deadline damages credibility (unless there are 'good reasons' for delay). When these provisions were enacted, the Independent Anti-Slavery Commissioner at the time cautioned that 'there is a very real risk' that these provisions 'will result in a failure to identify vulnerable victims'.[288]

If a negative Conclusive Grounds decision is issued it used to be reviewed by a multi-assurance panel, which could make a non-binding recommendation. This has however recently been removed and now there is only the possibility of review by a second caseworker or manager (referred to as a second pair of eyes in the current guidance).[289] The multi-assurance panel process was removed because of pressures on the time taken to make NRM decisions. The Home Affairs Committee noted, however, in December 2023 that 'there is no publicly available data on the extent to which [the second pair of eyes process] is being used and whether any negative decisions were subsequently

[285] *Modern Slavery: Statutory Guidance* (n 271) at [14.92]–[14.93]. [286] Ibid at [14.94].

[287] *R (on the application of MN and IXU)* v. *SSHD (AIRE Centre and Anti-Slavery International Intervening)* [2020] EWCA Civ 1746, [2021] 1 WLR 1956.

[288] Independent Anti-Slavery Commissioner (n 279) at [6.1.6].

[289] *Modern Slavery: Statutory Guidance* (n 271) at [14.163].

overturned with the "internal second pair of eyes"'.[290] It thus recommended that the Home Office either reinstate the multi-agency assurance process or establish a similar quality assurance process.[291]

Those not recognised as victims receive nine working days moving-on support following which all support will cease.[292] The ending of support after nine days was challenged in *R (on the application of MN and IXU)* v. *SSHD (AIRE Centre and Anti-Slavery International Intervening)* on the basis that if there are still reasonable grounds to believe that the applicants are victims then they should continue to receive support in accordance with Article 12 ECAT.[293] The Court of Appeal rejected this argument.[294] The position was recently considered by GRETA. It agreed that ending support did not breach ECAT, but it went on to state that 'a more cautious approach is required when significant gaps are found in the identification process, and when, on the basis of an individual assessment, reasonable doubts remain'.[295] This suggests that a more nuanced approach is needed.

7.5.4 Challenging Negative NRM Decisions

Judicial review is the only independent process for challenging a negative NRM decision and resolving errors. As errors are frequently made, it is of vital importance.[296] It is, however, a fraught process, the time limits are short, and cases can be complex. The systemic failings of the legal aid system compound problems,[297] with 'legal aid deserts' prevalent, especially outside of London.[298] Thus judicial review may be inaccessible in practice. It is also important to recall that even if a negative NRM decision is quashed, this will not necessarily result in a positive NRM decision. With those caveats in mind we consider the ways in which NRM decisions have been challenged by way of judicial review.

First, it is well established that if a public authority fails to follow its own guidance that this may constitute an error of law. The relevance of this was evident in *R (on the application of SF (St Lucia))* v. *SSHD* in which it was observed that it '[i]s incumbent on those reaching "Conclusive Grounds" to

[290] House of Commons, Home Affairs Committee, *Human Trafficking* (n 2) at [199].
[291] Ibid at [201]. [292] *Modern Slavery: Statutory Guidance* (n 271) at [8.27].
[293] *R (on the application of MN and IXU)* v. *SSHD (AIRE Centre and Anti-Slavery International Intervening)* (n 287).
[294] Ibid at [99]. [295] GRETA (n 13) at [279].
[296] See Anti-Trafficking and Labour Exploitation Unit's Submission to the Independent Review of Administrative Law (27 October 2020).
[297] Anti-Trafficking Sector Joint Response Immigration Legal Aid: A Consultation on New Fees for New Services (21 September 2022).
[298] Ibid, pp.3–4. The House of Commons Home Affairs Committee has made a number of recommendations in respect of legal aid including expanding its provision and increasing the rate paid to practitioners (n 2) at [241]–[242].

pay regard to the Guidance and it is trite law that a failure by a public authority to follow its own established policy without good reason can be an error of law'.[299] The courts have also held that as the Guidance purports to give effect to ECAT, it should be interpreted compatibly with it and that failure to do so is a justiciable error of law.[300] The High Court explained in *R (on the application of KTT)* v. *SSHD* that this derives from the fact that compatibility is the stated policy of the Home Office and that this does not amount to the courts directly enforcing the international obligations themselves.[301]

Decisions have also been quashed where the decision-maker failed to consider relevant evidence. For example, in *R (on the application of NS)* v. *SSHD* the competent authority failed to consider all the claimant's documents.[302] Equally, in *AB* v. *SSHD*, the decision-maker failed to engage with medical, psychiatric and trafficking reports.[303] The judge explained that although the reports did not bind the decision-maker they could not fail to engage with them entirely, particularly as the importance of these reports was emphasised in the Guidance. The role of expert evidence was also considered in *R (on the application of MN and IXU)* v. *SSHD (AIRE Centre and Anti-Slavery International Intervening)* where the Court stated that 'decision-makers should in each case assess whether and to what extent any particular expert evidence relied on by an applicant supports their case as a matter of rational analysis'.[304] The Court of Appeal recognised that there may be cases in which there are reasons to qualify 'the value to be given to a particular piece of evidence', but this 'is not a reason for excluding it altogether: if it has some weight it must go into the overall assessment'.[305] Indeed, whilst it is generally up to the competent authority to determine what weight should be accorded to evidence, in *R (on the application of NS)* v. *SSHD* it was held that in circumstances in which contemporaneous, unchallenged documentary evidence supported the claimant's account, it could not be said that no weight could be attached to that evidence.[306] The competent authority had therefore failed to carry out a balanced assessment and their approach to credibility was flawed.

NRM decisions can also be challenged if the competent authority fails to apply the appropriate definition of human trafficking. For example, in *R (on the application of NS)* v. *SSHD* it was held that the competent authority's

[299] See also, *R (on the application of FK)* v. *SSHD* [2016] EWHC 56 (Admin).

[300] This was evident in *R (on the application of Atamewan)* v. *SSHD* [2013] EWHC 2727, [2014] 1 WLR 1959 at [55].

[301] *R (on the application of KTT)* v. *SSHD* [2021] EWHC 2722 (Admin), [2022] 1 WLR 1312.

[302] *R (on the application of NS)* v. *SSHD* [2019] EWHC 861 (Admin).

[303] *AB* v. *SSHD* [2015] EWHC 1490 (Admin).

[304] *R (on the application of MN and IXU)* v. *SSHD (AIRE Centre and Anti-Slavery International Intervening)* (n 287).

[305] Ibid at [123].

[306] *R (on the application of NS)* (n 302).

determination that the 'act' criteria was not satisfied in respect of her transportation to the UK was perverse and unsustainable.[307]

Finally, decisions may be challenged as irrational. Accordingly, a decision was quashed in *R (on the application of EK)* v. *SSHD* on the ground that it was based on the erroneous conclusion that there were inconsistencies in the victim's account when there were none.[308] The Court held that the decision failed to evidence the rigorous standard of scrutiny required, failed to have regard to factors supporting the credibility of the claimant's account and was, accordingly, irrational. In *R (on the application of Alnoor)* v. *SSHD*, Fordham J explained that an 'anxious scrutiny' standard applies to the reasonableness review in this context, observing that this 'means the reviewing court has to do more; and also, the reviewing court needs more ... The idea of the reviewing court needing more recognises that "the starting point must be in the standard of reasoning required in the decision itself".'[309] Applying this to the facts he found that the decision he was reviewing could not withstand reasonableness review with anxious scrutiny.[310]

7.5.5 Support for Those Positively Identified as Victims

Having considered the consequences of a negative NRM decision, we now consider what happens if a positive Conclusive Grounds decision is made. Those identified as victims at the Conclusive Grounds stage are entitled to at least another forty-five days' moving-on support. Unlike the earlier recovery period, this has not been placed on a legislative footing and thus remains governed by statutory guidance.[311] The current entitlement is an improvement on previous policies, as prior to 1 February 2019 support only continued for fourteen days. In October 2018 the SofS announced that it would be extended to forty-five days, but that it would automatically cease after forty-five days. Automatic cessation of support after forty-five days was challenged in *NN* v. *SSHD* where it was argued that automatically ending support carries a serious risk of irreparable harm which breaches ECAT.[312] Knowles J granted permission to challenge the rule by way of judicial review,[313] following which the Government conceded that the policy should be amended. Consequently, the current policy states that 'victims receive a guaranteed *minimum* of

[307] Ibid. See also *SAC v Secretary of State for the Home Department* [2025] EWHC 1400 (Admin) where the High Court held at [76] that 'the Defendant's approach to the definitions of human trafficking and forced labour was too narrow, unduly restrictive and characterised by excessive rigidity which was not provided for in the statutory guidance.'

[308] *R (on the application of EK)* v. *SSHD* [2019] EWHC 1696 (Admin).

[309] *R (on the application of Alnoor)* v. SSHD [2025] EWHC 922 (Admin), at [28].

[310] Ibid at [33].

[311] *Modern Slavery: Statutory Guidance* (n 271) at [8.27].

[312] *NN* v. *SSHD* [2019] EWHC 1003 (Admin).

[313] Ibid.

45 calendar days of move-on support' (emphasis added).[314] The Government also committed in 2021 to providing a minimum of twelve months' support for confirmed victims of human trafficking who have ongoing support needs, however, this has not been delivered in practice and Ministers have said the commitment is now under review.[315] The House of Commons Home Affairs Committee has thus observed that there is an absence of support for victims once they exit the statutory support provided and that this is in part because the process is ineffective in assessing and meeting the needs of victims within forty-five days following a positive Conclusive Grounds decision.[316] They called for the Conservative Government to deliver on its commitment of twelve months' support for all victims with a positive Conclusive Grounds decision by the end of 2024.[317]

7.5.6 Leave to Remain

Unfortunately, for many victims the ordeal does not end at the point at which they escape their traffickers or are identified as victims. Leave to remain is vital as, without it, irregular immigration status renders victims vulnerable to further abuse in the UK and, if they are returned to the country from which they were originally trafficked, there is a risk of re-trafficking. For these reasons there have been calls for leave to be automatically granted to identified victims. Automatic leave to remain has, however, been firmly resisted by the Government, and ECAT does not require an automatic right of leave to remain for all victims. Article 14 ECAT provides that a renewable residence permit should be issued if the competent authority considers the stay necessary owing to the victim's personal situation or for the purpose of their co-operation with the investigation or criminal proceedings. In the UK this was previously addressed by statutory guidance, the impact of which was that whilst public authorities were not directly bound by ECAT, they were required to comply where the relevant obligations were incorporated into their own policies and guidance.[318]

A major development in respect of leave to remain occurred in *R (on the application of KTT)* v. *SSHD* in which the High Court held that it was the SofS's policy to make decisions on leave in accordance with ECAT and that pursuing an asylum claim based on fear of re-trafficking constitutes a relevant 'personal circumstance' for the purposes of Article 14 ECAT.[319] In *R (on the*

[314] *Modern Slavery: Statutory Guidance* (n 271) at [8.27].

[315] House of Commons, Home Affairs Committee, *Human Trafficking* (n 2) at [247].

[316] Ibid.

[317] Ibid at [248].

[318] See, for instance, *O* v. *Aberdeen City Council* [2017] CSOH 9, 2017 SLT 181 and *R (on the application of BG)* v. *SSHD* [2016] EWHC 786 (Admin).

[319] *R (on the application of KTT)* v. *SSHD* [2021] EWHC 2722, [2022] 1 WLR 1312.

application of SSA (Ethiopia)) v. *SSHD*, the Upper Tribunal held that the impact of *KTT* is that victims of human trafficking should be granted leave to remain whilst their asylum claim is pending where there is a fear of re-trafficking. The SSHD had sought to argue that leave to remain was only necessary where the claim was 'substantially' based on fear of re-trafficking but this was rejected by the Upper Tribunal, which held that 'fear of trafficking' is sufficient. In December 2023 however, it was reported that the Government has refused to implement this and has thus denied leave to remain to 1,600 victims of trafficking.[320]

It is also important to observe that since then, leave to remain has been put on a legislative footing by the NBA. Consequently, s.65(2) NBA now provides that the SofS must grant limited leave to remain if they consider it necessary for the purpose of: (a) assisting the person in their recovery from any physical or psychological harm arising from the relevant exploitation; (b) enabling the person to seek compensation in respect of the relevant exploitation; or, (c) enabling the person to co-operate with a public authority in connection with an investigation or criminal proceedings in respect of the relevant exploitation. Yet whilst many welcomed the fact that leave to remain was put on a statutory footing, the NBA narrowed the grounds for granting leave in several respects, which has raised concerns about the risk of non-compliance with international obligations. First, s.65(4)(a) NBA provides that leave is not necessary for the purpose of assisting a person in their recovery if the SofS considers that this assistance can be met in a country or territory of which the person is a national or citizen or is one to which the person may be removed in accordance with an agreement between that country/territory and the UK. Second, s.65(4)(b) NBA states that leave for the purposes of seeking compensation does not need to be provided if the SofS considers that: (i) the person is capable of seeking compensation from outside the United Kingdom; and, (ii) it would be reasonable for the person to do so in the circumstances. Third, s.65(6)–(7) NBA provide that the SofS is not required to grant leave (and if leave has been granted it may be revoked) if the SofS is satisfied that: (a) the person is a threat to public order; [321] or, (b) the person has claimed to be a victim of slavery or human trafficking in bad faith. Finally, s.65(8) NBA

[320] Diane Taylor, 'Patel and Braverman accused of secret policy to deny trafficking victims leave to remain', *The Guardian*, 1 December 2023, www.theguardian.com/uk-news/2023/dec/01/patel-and-braverman-accused-of-denying-trafficking-victims-leave-to-remain-in-uk.

[321] If s.29(4) IMA 2023 is brought into force it will also expand the scope of the 'threat to public order' ground in respect of disqualification from leave to remain to include any person who is not a British citizen who is convicted in the UK of an offence and has been sentenced to a period of imprisonment for the offence. Section 29(4) IMA 2023 (not currently in force) amends the definition of public order in s.63 NBA 2022, which by virtue of s.63(2)(b) NBA 2022 applies to the leave to remain provision under s.65 NBA 2022. At the time of writing it appears that the Border Security, Asylum and Immigration Bill will retain both the s.65(6)–(7)

provides that leave may also be revoked in such other circumstances as may be prescribed in immigration rules. In contemplating these changes, it is important to observe that, even prior to the NBA, leave to remain permits were rarely granted and those that were granted were for a short duration.[322] Consequently, GRETA has urged the UK to ensure that all those who are eligible under Article 14 ECAT receive a permit and to collect data and investigate the reasons for the low number of residence permits granted.[323]

Challenging a removal order and seeking leave to remain may involve a complex interface between asylum law, ECHR obligations and public law. It is beyond the scope of this book to provide a full account of the asylum system, but it is important to note that some victims of human trafficking may seek asylum in the UK. Indeed the Upper Tribunal held in *HD (Trafficked women) Nigeria CG* that a real risk of being trafficked constitutes a 'real risk of being persecuted' for the purposes an asylum application.[324] Yet whilst the evidence in HD's case was sufficient to demonstrate that she would be at 'real risk' of being re-trafficked, numerous cases have failed on the basis of insufficient evidence of a 'real risk' and/or a finding that relocation is possible.[325]

A further possible legal route is to challenge removal on the basis that it breaches Articles 2, 3 or 8,[326] or Article 4 ECHR on the basis that States are obliged not to expose a person to real risk of treatment contrary to the Convention in a third country. In respect of the latter, the burden of proof is on the applicant and again the burden is high as the appellant must show not only that there is a real risk of being re-trafficked, but also that the requesting State is not in a position to provide appropriate protection.[327]

A further question that arises concerns the extent to which the obligations under ECAT take effect through the positive obligations of Article 4 ECHR. The Supreme Court was faced with this in *MS (Pakistan)* v. *SSHD*.[328] On that occasion Lady Hale observed that '[i]t would be of much greater help if a failure to observe the requirements of ECAT were also a violation of article 4 of the ECHR'.[329] However, it was not necessary to determine in *MS (Pakistan)*

NBA 2022 disqualification provision and the s.29(4) IMA 2023 expansion of those provisions.

322 GRETA (n 13) at [309]. 323 Ibid at [313]–[314].

324 *HD (Trafficked women) Nigeria CG* [2016] UKUT 454 (IAC).

325 See, for instance, *Nguyen (Anti-Trafficking Convention: respondent's duties)* [2015] UKUT 170 (IAC); *EK (Article 4 ECHR: Anti-Trafficking Convention) Tanzania* [2013] UKUT 00313 (IAC); *HC & RC (Trafficked women) China CG* [2009] UKAIT 00027.

326 For further discussion, see Chapters 3, 4 and 8.

327 *Olga C* v. *The Prosecutor General's Office of the Republic of Latvia* [2016] EWHC 2211 (Admin) at [10]. Emphasis added.

328 *MS (Pakistan)* v. *SSHD* [2020] UKSC 9, [2020] 1 WLR 1373. 329 Ibid at [21].

whether all the obligations in ECAT are incorporated into the State's positive obligations under Article 4 ECHR and thus the issue was not pursued further.[330] The Court of Appeal has since reiterated in *R (on the application of MN and IXU)* v. *SSHD (AIRE Centre and Anti-Slavery International Intervening)*[331] that obligations under ECAT are directly enforceable where they correspond to a positive obligation under Article 4 ECHR.[332] The question nevertheless, remains as to *which* obligations in ECAT correspond with positive obligations under Article 4 ECHR, something which neither the domestic courts, nor Strasbourg have pinned down.[333] SIAC thus observed in *Begum* that, 'the extent to which the specific requirements of ECAT feed into and/or supplement those of Article 4 of the ECHR is debatable'.[334] It was also recognised by both SIAC and the Court of Appeal in *Begum* that the domestic courts would be unwilling to flesh out Article 4 ECHR by reference to ECAT in the absence of Strasbourg case law to this effect.[335]

Victims may also be able to argue that the SofS has failed to comply with the SofS's own policy when denying leave. This was important in *Re EK (Article 4 ECHR: Anti-Trafficking Convention: Tanzania)* v. *SSHD* a case in which the applicant had been trafficked to the UK as an unpaid domestic worker, fed food scraps and forced to sleep on the floor.[336] She had been refused medical treatment and, ultimately, contracted tuberculosis and suffered irreparable lung damage. The Upper Tribunal found that the SofS's decision to remove her was unlawful because it had been made *without considering* the link between a breach of the UK's protective obligations and the state of her health, and *without considering* Articles 12, 14 and 16 ECAT.[337] Similarly in *R (on the application of FM)* v. *SSHD* the Court found that a removal decision was unlawful as the SofS had not referred the matter to the police for investigation, nor had they had regard to the fact that the applicant was part-way through medical treatment.[338] It observed that Article 12(1) ECAT imposes a duty to assist in the victim's recovery and the Home Office's published Guidance stated that discretionary leave to remain 'should

[330] Ibid at [27].

[331] *R (on the application of MN and IXU)* v. *SSHD (AIRE Centre and Anti-Slavery International Intervening)* (n 287).

[332] Ibid at [85]. Emphasis added.

[333] Note, however, the discussion in *Krachunova* v. *Bulgaria* (n 101) about the ECtHR's approach to the interpretation of the positive obligations under Article 4 ECHR, see Section 7.4.

[334] *Begum* (n 178) at [177].

[335] *Begum* (n 178) at [231] and *Shamima Begum* v. *SSHD* (n 174) at [81]. See discussion at Section 7.4.2.5 above.

[336] *Re EK (Article 4 ECHR: Anti-Trafficking Convention: Tanzania)* v. *SSHD* [2013] UKUT 313 (IAC).

[337] Ibid at [60], [66]–[68].

[338] *R (on the application of FM)* v. *SSHD* [2015] EWHC 844 (Admin).

be granted to allow a victim to finish a course of treatment that would not be readily available in his or her home country'.[339]

A final important point to observe is that if removal stems from a negative NRM decision then it may be possible to contest the NRM decision during the legal challenge to the removal decision. The Supreme Court in *MS (Pakistan)* confirmed that immigration tribunals are not bound by negative NRM decisions as this is a question of fact and the tribunals must determine factual issues for themselves, albeit that they must give proper consideration to the NRM decision.[340] The non-binding nature of the NRM decision is important as survivors would be unlikely to engage in the NRM process if a negative decision was determinative.

7.5.7 Compensation

An important right provided by ECAT is the right to compensation and legal redress (Article 15 ECAT). This includes compensation from both the perpetrators and States. As GRETA observed in its report, 'compensation plays a crucial role in the fight against human trafficking not only as an instrument of restorative justice, but also by way of prevention and recognition by States of their failure to meet their human rights obligations'.[341]

In the UK, there are, in principle, various routes through which survivors can seek compensation,[342] but in practice very few survivors receive compensation.[343] Survivors often wait years for compensation, and it is reported that some have given up due to the length of time taken to deal with their application.[344] GRETA has therefore urged the UK 'to make additional efforts

[339] Ibid at [46]. [340] *MS (Pakistan)* (n 328) at [11]–[14]. [341] GRETA (n 13) at [110].

[342] In England and Wales, survivors may seek compensation: (i) under the Sentencing Act 2020; (ii) under s.8 Modern Slavery Act 2015 (Slavery Reparation Order); (iii) civil proceedings, including claims through employment tribunals; and (iv) the Criminal Injuries Compensation Authority. Although in respect of the latter, note that victims with unspent criminal convictions are not eligible for compensation from the Criminal Injuries Compensation Authority – *A and B* v. *Criminal Injuries Compensation Authority* [2021] UKSC 27, [2021] 1 WLR 3746. In Scotland, there is no specific human trafficking reparation order hence compensation should be dealt with under the Criminal Procedure (Scotland) Act 1995, although there is no evidence that compensation has been awarded in criminal proceedings in Scotland. It is also possible for survivors to bring civil claims, including employment tribunal proceedings. The Criminal Injuries Compensation Authority that applies to England and Wales is also applicable in Scotland. In Northern Ireland, the Human Trafficking and Exploitation Act 2015 enables the Crown Court to impose a reparation order. In its third report, GRETA reported that the Public Prosecution Service had confirmed that it was not aware of any compensation being awarded to victims in criminal proceedings. As with the other jurisdictions, victims can also seek civil remedies, including through the employment tribunals. They may claim compensation from the Northern Ireland Criminal Injuries Compensation Scheme.

[343] GRETA (n 13) at [132]. [344] GRETA (n 13).

to guarantee effective access to compensation for all victims'.[345] It has also repeatedly called upon the UK to develop a system for recording compensation claims and awards.[346]

One means of seeking redress is through the employment tribunals in respect of unpaid wages and unfair working conditions. An important case in this regard is *Hounga* v. *Allen* in which the Supreme Court held that the defence of illegality did not defeat a claim for discrimination.[347] The claimant in that case Hounga was fourteen years old when she illegally entered the UK from Nigeria with the assistance of the defendant, Allen, in order to provide domestic help for Allen and her family. Over a period of eighteen months Hounga lived in Allen's home and looked after Allen's children, during which time Hounga was unpaid and she was subjected to serious physical abuse by Allen. Allen also threatened Hounga that if she left the home she would be imprisoned due to her illegal immigration status in the UK. In July 2008, Allen forcibly evicted Hounga from the home and dismissed her from employment. A number of claims and complaints were subsequently brought by Hounga against Allen in the Employment Tribunal which Allen sought to defend by relying on the illegality defence.

The Employment Tribunal held that the illegality defence precluded all of the claims except unlawful discrimination relating to her dismissal; in respect of which it ordered Allen to pay compensation of £6,187 to Hounga for the resultant injury to her feelings. That decision was upheld by the Employment Appeal Tribunal,[348] however, on appeal the Court of Appeal determined that upholding the discrimination claim would be to condone the illegality.[349] The case thus went to the Supreme Court, which allowed the appeal against the Court of Appeal decision. Lord Wilson (with whom Lady Hale and Lord Kerr agreed) observed that the Court of Appeal had previously held that the defence of illegality can only succeed where there is an inextricable link between the complaint and the claimant's illegal conduct.[350] Consequently they observed that if the inextricable link test applied then there was no such link between the illegal conduct and the abuse on the facts of this case.[351] They went on, however, to consider whether the inextricable link test was applicable, observing that the defence of illegality rests upon the foundation of public policy and that it is thus necessary to first ask what aspect of public policy founds the defence and second whether there is another aspect of public policy to which the application of the defence would run counter.[352] In respect of the first question, they found that the considerations of public policy in favour of

[345] Ibid at [132]. [346] Ibid at [133].

[347] *Hounga* v. *Allen* [2014] UKSC 47, [2014] 1 WLR 2889.

[348] UKEAT/0327/10/LA, UKEAT/0329/10/LA. [349] [2012] EWCA Civ 609, [2012] IRLR 685.

[350] *Hounga* v. *Allen* (n 347) at [40]. [351] Ibid. [352] Ibid at [41]–[42].

applying the defence to defeat this claim scarcely existed.[353] In respect of the second question they observed, having examined the Palermo definition on human trafficking that it is 'hard to resist the conclusion that Mrs Allen was guilty of trafficking'[354] and that 'if Miss Hounga's case was not one of trafficking on the part of Mrs Allen and her family, it was so close to it that the distinction will not matter for the purpose of what follows'.[355] Following which it determined that as the UK authorities are striking to combat trafficking and protect victims that upholding Allen's illegality defence would run 'strikingly counter to this prominent strain of current public policy'.[356] They thus concluded that 'public policy in support of the application of that defence, to the extent that it exists at all, should give way to the public policy to which its application is an affront; and Miss Hounga's appeal should be allowed'.[357]

A further critical question that has arisen in this context is whether foreign diplomats are able to rely upon diplomatic immunity in respect of such claims. Sadly, as the Supreme Court recently observed, 'exploitation of migrant domestic workers by foreign diplomats is a significant problem'.[358] In fact, evidence advanced by Kalayaan, a charity devoted to advising and supporting migrant domestic workers, suggests that the proportion of domestic workers that are victims of trafficking is considerably higher in diplomatic households than in other households.[359] They suggest that this is largely because perceived immunity leads diplomats to consider that they can exploit with impunity.[360] The Supreme Court has heard two cases concerning the scope of diplomatic immunity in the context of human trafficking and modern slavery. In *Al-Malki* v. *Reyes*, the Court considered whether diplomatic immunity persisted after the end of a diplomatic posting.[361] The background to that case was that, Reyes, a Phillipine national, had been employed by Mr and Mrs Al-Malki as a domestic servant in their residence in London, during which time it is alleged that their treatment of her amounted to human trafficking. At the relevant time, Mr Al-Malki was a member of the diplomatic staff of the embassy of Saudi Arabia in London. Consequently, when Reyes began proceedings in the Employment Tribunal alleging direct and indirect race discrimination, unlawful deduction from wages and failure to pay her the national minimum wage, it was argued that the Tribunal had no jurisdiction because Mr Al-Malki was entitled to diplomatic immunity. This raised questions about whether diplomatic immunity could apply to allegations of human trafficking. The Supreme Court did not need to answer this question

[353] Ibid at [43]–[45]. [354] Ibid at [49]. [355] Ibid. [356] Ibid at [52]. [357] Ibid.

[358] *Wong* v. *Basfar* [2022] UKSC 20, [2023] AC 33 at [5].

[359] See evidence reported in *Al-Malki* v. *Reyes* [2017] UKSC 61, [2019] AC 735 at [59].

[360] Ibid. [361] Ibid.

as Mr Al-Malki's diplomatic post had already come to an end. It thus held that once a diplomatic posting ends, immunity is limited to acts performed in the exercise of official functions, and employment of a domestic servant is not an official function. In that case, Lord Sumption expressed the view that Al-Malki would have been entitled to immunity if he had still been in post,[362] a stance that was doubted, but left undetermined, by other members of the Court.

The Supreme Court returned to the question of diplomatic immunity whilst in post in *Wong* v. *Basfar*, where it was alleged that Wong had been kept in servitude in the London house of a member of the diplomatic staff of Saudi Arabia.[363] On this occasion it held that diplomatic immunity does not apply to holding someone in servitude as this is a 'commercial activity' and commercial activities are a stated exception to diplomatic immunity under the Vienna Convention on Diplomatic Relations 1961.[364] Consequently, diplomatic immunity could not prevent Wong from bringing a claim in the employment tribunal.

7.6 MODERN SLAVERY ACT 2015

The MSA is the other major component of the domestic legal framework. When it was enacted, Theresa May, then Home Secretary, claimed it would send 'the strongest possible signal to criminals that if you are involved in this vile trade you will be arrested, you will be prosecuted and you will be locked up' and that it would signal to victims that 'you are not alone – we are here to help you'.[365] Yet the evidence to date suggests the MSA has failed to achieve those goals. Reviewing the first three years of the Act, Virginia Mantouvalou found that the MSA had failed to increase prosecutions or to provide adequate remedies for victims, its heavy reliance on criminal law failed to address structural factors, and that it is too weak in tackling modern slavery by businesses in their supply chains.[366] She highlighted considerable scope for improvement in identifying and prosecuting individuals and addressing structural factors that create vulnerability to exploitation.[367]

[362] Ibid. [363] *Wong* v. *Basfar* (n 358). [364] Ibid at [26].

[365] Theresa May, 'Historic Law to End Modern Slavery Passed' (26 March 2015), www.gov.uk/government/news/historic-law-to-end-modern-slavery-passed#:~:text=A%20landmark%20Bill%20to%20help,today%20(Thursday%2026th%20March).&text=The%20Modern%20Slavery%20Act%202015,trafficking%20in%20the%2021st%20century.

[366] Virginia Mantouvalou, 'The UK Modern Slavery Act 2015: Three Years On' (2018) 81(6) MLR 1017–1045.

[367] Ibid.

7.6.1 Offences

The MSA consolidated the various offences, and the two main offences in the Act are s.1 which concerns slavery, servitude and forced or compulsory labour and s.2 which deals with human trafficking. Since then, there have been convictions in respect of many types of modern slavery and human trafficking, including county lines drug trafficking,[368] a criminal gang that have coached and exploited teenage girls into a UK-wide shoplifting scam,[369] human trafficking within the construction industry,[370] exploitation of a disabled victim in his own home by live-in carers,[371] and in a landmark case in May 2023 offences in respect of organ trafficking.[372] Yet whilst a core intention behind the legislation was to ensure that perpetrators are prosecuted, the number of prosecutions remains strikingly low when compared to the number of NRM referrals.[373] In this regard, GRETA has observed that '[c]uts to the criminal justice system and [a] lack of resources contribute to low prosecution and conviction rates of perpetrators'.[374] The '[l]ack of sustainable support for victims is another factor which impacts the UK authorities' ability to prosecute traffickers'.[375]

A further intention behind the MSA was that it would lead to enhanced sentencing which would have a deterrent effect. Consequently, s.5(1) provides that the s.1 and s.2 offences carry a sentence of up to life imprisonment. The courts have reflected on the rationales for higher sentences. In *R* v. *Iyamu (Josephine)* it was observed that:

> Offending of this gravity requires condign sentencing. It also requires that persons be deterred from engaging in offending of this kind. Mr Benson suggested that those in Nigeria or elsewhere will not be deterred by severe sentences imposed by the courts in England and Wales. We are unmoved by that. Those who are within the reach of the jurisdiction of the courts of England and Wales should expect severe sentencing in this context. Those who engage in vicious, ruthless and heartless human trafficking of this

[368] CPS, 'Organised Crime Gang sentenced for drug and modern slavery offences' (23 August 2023), www.cps.gov.uk/cymruwales/news/organised-crime-gang-sentenced-drug-and-modern-slavery-offences.

[369] Fiona Hamilton, '"Fagin" used girls for county lines shoplifting spree', *The Times*, 11 February 2022, www.thetimes.com/uk/law/article/fagin-used-girls-for-county-lines-shoplifting-spree-p5vfhd6v0.

[370] CPS, 'CPS reports on conviction of an organised crime family for human trafficking', *Lexis Nexis, LNB News 02/12/2021 91* (2 December 2021).

[371] CPS, 'Wife and carer jailed after enslaving disabled victim in his own home' (14 July 2023), www.cps.gov.uk/south-east/news/wife-and-carer-jailed-after-enslaving-disabled-victim-his-own-home-1.

[372] CPS, 'Senior Nigerian politician jailed over illegal UK organ-harvesting plot' (5 May 2023), www.cps.gov.uk/cps/news/updated-sentence-senior-nigerian-politician-jailed-over-illegal-uk-organ-harvesting-plot.

[373] Mantouvalou (n 366). [374] GRETA (n 13) at [157]. [375] Ibid at [157].

particular kind are playing for high stakes. They need to know that the courts will show no mercy when their criminality is exposed.[376]

A victim-focused rationale was also articulated in *R* v. *David Zielinski*:

> Sentences in this class of case must make clear, not merely that the statutory minimum wage should not be undermined, but much more important, that every vulnerable victim of exploitation will be protected by the criminal law, and they must also emphasise that there is no victim, so vulnerable to exploitation, that he or she somehow becomes invisible or unknown to or somehow beyond the protection of the law. Exploitation of fellow human beings in any of the ways criminalised by the legislation represents deliberate degrading of a fellow human being or human beings. It is far from straight forward for them even to complain about the way they are being treated, let alone to report their plight to the authorities so that the offenders might be brought to justice. Therefore when they are, substantial sentences are required, reflective, of course, of the distinctions between enslavement, serfdom, and forced labour, but realistically addressing the criminality of the defendants.[377]

Yet while the courts have reflected on the rationales for higher sentences, no life sentences have been conferred thus far, and in fact the Sentencing Council,[378] and the Independent Anti-Trafficking Commissioner,[379] have raised concerns that the duration of sentences has remained very similar to those conferred prior to the MSA. This prompted the Sentencing Council to issue detailed sentencing guidelines, but at the time of writing it is too early to tell what impact this will have.

7.6.2 Reparation Orders

When the MSA was drafted, the Home Office emphasised the importance of reparation orders. This was reflected in ss.8–10 which provide the courts with the power to issue a slavery and trafficking reparation order obliging the perpetrator to pay compensation. To date, however, it appears that few reparation orders have been issued.[380]

7.6.3 Prevention and Risk Orders

As part of the preventative approach, the MSA provides for Slavery and Trafficking Prevention Orders (STPO)[381] and Slavery and Trafficking Risk

[376] *R* v. *Iyamu (Josephine)* [2018] EWCA Crim 2166 at [51].

[377] *R* v. *David Zielinski* [2017] EWCA Crim 758 at [18].

[378] Sentencing Council, *Modern Slavery Offences (Consultation)* October 2020.

[379] Independent Anti-Slavery Commissioner Annual Report 2021–2022 (April 2022) at [2.3.6].

[380] In April 2022, the Independent Anti-Slavery Commissioner's policy paper suggested that eight reparation orders have been issued since 2015; see Independent Anti-Slavery Commissioner, *IASC Policy Paper: Access to Compensation and Reparation for Survivors of Trafficking* (April 2022).

[381] Sections 14–22 MSA.

Orders (STRO).[382] An STPO is predominantly issued post-conviction, whilst the STRO is applied when criminal justice proceedings do not ensue or prior to conviction. Both orders restrict the activities of those subject to the order.

Under an STPO, an individual can be prohibited from doing anything anywhere provided that such restrictions are necessary for the purposes of protecting persons generally, or particular persons, from the physical or psychological harm which would be likely to occur if the defendant committed a slavery or human trafficking offence. This may last for a fixed period of five years or until further order. It may prohibit travel and in such cases the offenders have to surrender passports. Necessity applies not only to the making of an order, but to the individual terms, which have to be both reasonable and proportionate. Each of the defendants in *R* v. *David Zielinksi*[383] and *R (on the application of McNiece) and Anor* v. *Criminal Injuries Compensation Authority*[384] were subject to STPOs.

An STRO can be issued by a magistrates court on an application by a chief officer of police, immigration officer or the Director General of the National Crime Agency.[385] An STRO may be issued if the court is satisfied that the defendant acted in a way which means that there is a risk that the defendant will commit a slavery or human trafficking offence, and it is necessary to make the order for the purpose of protecting persons generally, or particular persons, from the physical or psychological harm which would be likely to occur if the defendant committed such an offence.[386] There is no requirement for the subject of the STRO to have been convicted or cautioned. The effect of the STRO is to prohibit the defendant from doing anything listed in the order, but the only prohibitions that may be included are those which the court is satisfied are necessary for the purpose of protecting persons generally, or particular persons, from the physical or psychological harm which would be likely to occur if the defendant committed a slavery or human trafficking offence. As with slavery and trafficking prevention orders, STROs can apply to activities outside the UK and can prohibit foreign travel. An STRO can last for at least two years or until further order and it is an offence to do anything contrary to an STRO.[387]

Reviews of the use of STPOs and STROS have repeatedly found that these orders are under used. In 2019, the Chair of the Independent Review of the Modern Slavery Act (2019) reported that 'too few Slavery and Trafficking Prevention and Risk Orders are in place to restrict offender activity'.[388]

[382] Sections 23–29 MSA. [383] *Zielinski* (n 377).

[384] *R (on the application of McNiece) and Anor* v. *Criminal Injuries Compensation Authority* [2017] EWHC 2 (Admin).

[385] Section 23(1) MSA. [386] Section 23(2) MSA. [387] Section 23(2) MSA.

[388] Frank Field MP, Maria Miller MP and Baroness Butler-Sloss (2019), 'Independent Review of the Modern Slavery Act 2015: Final Report', www.gov.uk/government/publications/independent-review-of-the-modern-slavery-act-final-report.

In 2022, the Independent Anti-Slavery Commissioner carried out a further review and reported that although there had been an increase in their use,[389] 'STROs remain under-utilised particularly while criminal investigations are being progressed or where criminal justice proceedings may not ensue.'[390] She suggested that '[d]espite previous recommendations, the lack of standard procedures to actively monitor individuals subject to STPOs and STROs remains a significant weakness' and that a national approach is clearly required'.[391] As of February 2022, there were 168 STPOs and 78 STROs live across UK regions.[392] In a subsequent report in December 2024 the House of Lords Modern Slavery Committee concluded once more that 'STROs and STPOs are potentially powerful tools in tackling modern slavery which have been underused'.[393] The Committee recommended the introduction of legislation to facilitate wider use of STROs and STPOs.[394]

7.6.4 Independent Anti-Slavery Commissioner

Throughout this chapter, we have encountered references to the Independent Anti-Slavery Commissioner. This role was established by the MSA in order to encourage good practice in prevention, detention, investigation and prosecution.[395] This includes producing reports, making recommendations and providing information, education or training.[396] The Commissioner is supposed to be an independent office, however, the first Independent Anti-Slavery Commissioner resigned in May 2018 stating that 'independence has felt somewhat discretionary from the Home Office, rather than legally bestowed'.[397] In 2021, GRETA also observed that 'despite being physically located outside of the Home Office, the Commissioner still sits under the control of the Home Office and must consult with Government Ministers on her work plans'.[398] Following the retirement of Dame Sara Thornton in 2022, there was no Independent Anti-Slavery Commissioner from April 2022 to December 2023. The House of Commons *Home Office Affairs Committee* declared this 'unacceptable' and, at least in spirit, a breach of the statutory

[389] Independent Anti-Slavery Commissioner, *The Use of Modern Slavery Risk and Prevention Orders* (March 2022), p.6, https://antislaverycommissioner.co.uk/media/nosgdfwl/iasc-review-risk-and-prevention-orders-report-march-2022.pdf.

[390] Ibid. [391] Ibid. [392] Ibid at [2.3.7].

[393] House of Lords Modern Slavery Act 2015 Committee, The Modern Slavery Act 2015: Becoming world-leading again, Report of Session 2024–2025, HL Paper 8 at [137].

[394] Ibid at [138]. [395] Section 41(1) MSA. [396] Section 41(3) MSA.

[397] Lizzie Dearden, 'UK's first Independent Anti-Slavery Commissioner resigns citing government interference', *The Independent*, 17 May 2018, www.independent.co.uk/news/uk/politics/modern-slavery-uk-commissioner-resigns-interference-kevin-hyland-government-a8356601.html.

[398] GRETA (n 13) at [23].

duty, particularly as during this period 'key legislative changes have been made and levels of public discourse around modern slavery have been high'.[399] A new Commissioner was appointed in 2023 but questions were raised as to whether the incoming Commissioner, Eleanor Lyons, a former special advisor to Boris Johnson, was suitably independent and experienced for the role. The previous Commissioners were Dame Sara Thornton, a former chief constable and Kevin Hyland, a former Detective Inspector who had led the Metropolitan police's human trafficking unit.

7.6.5 Non-prosecution of Victims

One of the most important components of the MSA is the s.45 MSA defence. This provision may provide a defence where a victim of modern slavery or trafficking faces prosecution for offences committed as a consequence of their exploitation. The impetus for s.45 MSA is Article 26 ECAT which obliges States to provide for the possibility of not imposing penalties. It will be recalled that neither Article 26 ECAT, nor Article 4 ECHR, absolutely prohibit prosecution. There are two versions of the s.45 MSA defence depending upon the age of the survivor.

For an **adult** the defence is applicable where:

(i) the defendant was compelled to do the act;
(ii) the compulsion was attributable to slavery or relevant exploitation; *and*,
(iii) a reasonable person in the same situation and with the same relevant characteristics would have no reasonable alternative to carrying out the offence.

For a **child** the defence is applicable where:

(i) the act is a direct consequence of slavery or relevant exploitation; *and*,
(ii) a reasonable person in the same situation as the person and having the person's relevant characteristics would do that act.

The difference is thus that no element of compulsion is required if the defendant was under the age of eighteen at the time of the offence. In those circumstances, it suffices that the defendant committed the offence as a 'direct consequence' of being, or having been, a victim of slavery or relevant exploitation.[400]

[399] House of Commons, Home Affairs Committee, *Human Trafficking* (n 2) at [49]. See also House of Lords Modern Slavery Act 2015 Committee, Chapter 6 (n 393).

[400] In *R* v. *NHF* [2022] EWCA Crim 859, a conviction was quashed where the recorder had misdirected the jury as to the elements of the s.45(4) MSA defence for those under eighteen. He had directed that a reasonable person in the defendant's position had to have had 'no realistic alternative but to do the act' when there was no requirement to show compulsion where a defendant was under eighteen years old.

A point of contention has been where the burden of proof lies. The CPS has sought to argue that the defendant must prove each element of the defence, but this was rejected by the Court of Appeal in *R* v. *MK*.[401]

An important limitation is that s.45 MSA is not applicable to all offences as over 100 offences are excluded from its ambit by Schedule 4.[402] One of the consequences of this is that the courts have had to consider whether the mechanisms relied upon prior to the MSA (i.e. the common law defence of duress; prosecutorial discretion; or staying prosecution for abuse of process) persist post-MSA in respect of the excluded offences.[403] Initially it was determined in *R* v. *DS* that the power to stay proceedings for abuse of process no longer applies and thus cannot be invoked where the alleged offence is excluded from the s.45 MSA defence by Schedule 4.[404] The Court of Appeal reasoned in *R* v. *A* that the special abuse of process jurisdiction was displaced by s.45 MSA and the limits of the legislation cannot be circumvented.[405] However, this was overturned by the Court of Appeal in *R* v. *AAD, AAH and AAI* in which it held that abuse of process remains open to victims of trafficking, whether or not the matter is a Schedule 4 case.[406] The Court observed that s.45 MSA was intended to provide enhanced protection for victims and there is nothing to indicate 'that the previously established availability of an abuse of process jurisdiction in this context was designed to be removed or significantly curtailed by the 2015 Act'.[407] The Court found no risk of the floodgates opening as 'cases of abuse of process will be (as they always should have been) very rare in this context and can arise in only very limited circumstances'.[408]

The operation of s.45 MSA also needs to be examined in the light of *V.C.L. and A.N.* v. *the United Kingdom*. In this regard it is important to recall that in *V.C.L. and A.N.* the ECtHR established that Article 4 ECHR requires:

(i) that States must as soon as they are aware or ought to be aware of circumstances giving rise to credible suspicion ensure that the potential victim is assessed promptly by individuals trained and qualified to deal with victims;

401 *R* v. *MK* [2018] EWCA Crim 667, [2019] QB 86 at [45].

402 Karl Laird, 'Evaluating the Relationship between Section 45 of the Modern Slavery Act 2015 and the Defence of Duress: An Opportunity Missed?' (2016) 6 *Criminal Law Review* 396. See also House of Lords Modern Slavery Act 2015 Committee (n 393) at [149] which recommended that the Government review and consider removing the offences in Schedule 4 to extend the protection applied by the non-punishment principle, including to those who have committed modern slavery offences.

403 *R* v. *Joseph (Verna Sermafure) and Ors* [2017] EWCA Crim 36, [2017] 1 WLR 3153 at [2]; see also, *R* v. *N* [2012] EWCA Crim 189, [2013] QB 379.

404 *R* v. *DS* [2020] EWCA Crim 285, [2021] 1 WLR 303.

405 *R* v. *A* [2020] EWCA Crim 1408, [2021] 4 WLR 16.

406 *R* v. *AAD, AAH and AAI* [2022] EWCA Crim 106, [2022] 1 WLR 4042 at [142]; see also [140].

407 Ibid at [143]. 408 Ibid at [143].

(ii) that any decision on whether to prosecute should only be taken once a trafficking assessment has been made by a qualified person;
(iii) that once a trafficking assessment has been made that any subsequent prosecutorial decision has to take that assessment into account and whilst the decision is not binding the prosecutor needs clear reasons consistent with the international law definition of trafficking.

It will also be recalled that the UK was found to have breached those obligations in *V.C.L. and A.N.* One might assume that as *V.C.L. and A.N.* related to events that took place prior to the enactment of the MSA, that the s.45 MSA defence, coupled with the NRM system for identifying victims, now ensures that the UK satisfies the non-prosecution obligations. Certainly, this was the view of the UK Government, which reported to the Committee of Ministers that no 'further legislative change is required to implement the judgment'[409] and any further action taken will be through policy and operational changes.[410] Many of those working with survivors are not, however, content that this is adequate. The AIRE (Advice on Individual Rights in Europe) centre has argued that the NRM 'does not go far enough to ensure the identification of trafficking victims at the earliest possible opportunity by trained and qualified personnel'.[411] There is also concern that domestic legislation, policy guidance and judgments do not clearly reflect the requirement in *V.C.L.* that the 'prosecutor needs to have clear reasons consistent with the definition of human trafficking to prosecute someone that has been identified as a victim of trafficking'.[412] Indeed, s.45 MSA 'does not specifically provide for how prosecutors justify disagreeing with trafficking assessments and pursue prosecutions'.[413] Moreover, domestic case law since *V.C.L. and A.N.* arguably deviates from the threshold established by the ECtHR.

To understand the issues that have arisen in the domestic case law, it is important to first consider the role of NRM decisions in criminal proceedings, as whilst one might assume that a positive Conclusive Grounds decision establishes that a defendant was a victim for the purpose of the s.45 MSA defence, this is not necessarily the case. The role of the NRM decision in criminal proceedings arose in *R* v. *DS* as the trial judge had relied on the positive Conclusive Grounds determination in order to stay proceedings as an abuse of process.[414] This was successfully challenged on appeal on the basis that he 'was wrong to hold that the CPS and the court, should have "abided by" the decision of the Authority' as it was in fact 'open to the Crown to seek to challenge it'.[415] The Court of Appeal held that whilst the CPS should *take into account* a positive NRM decision, the prosecutor is entitled to challenge a

[409] DH-DD (2022) 39E, p.8. [410] Ibid. [411] AIRE DH-DD (2022) 950E at [12].
[412] *V.C.L. and A.N.* (n 139). [413] AIRE DH-DD (n 411) at [21]. [414] *R* v. *DS* (n 404).
[415] Ibid at [30].

Conclusive Grounds decision and invite the jury to come to a different conclusion.[416] Consequently, whilst the NRM decision should be considered, *it is not binding*. What was not determined in *R* v. *DS* was whether the NRM decision is admissible at all before a jury. It was observed by the Court of Appeal that although this question had been briefly canvassed it would not be right for it to express a view as it was outside the scope of issues that it could properly decide on appeal.[417]

The opportunity to consider admissibility arose shortly thereafter in the case of *DPP* v. *M* in which it was determined that a positive NRM decision *is admissible* as evidence for the purposes of the s.45 MSA defence.[418] In that case, the High Court held that 'the full minute of the SCA decision, the evidence of the police officers and the admitted facts – was sufficient to satisfy the evidential burden'.[419] This did not render the decision determinative such that a positive Conclusive Grounds decision would automatically lead to an acquittal, but the NRM decision was admissible before the Court as evidence. The evidential use of NRM decisions was, however, subsequently challenged in *R* v. *Brecani* in which the Court of Appeal determined that Conclusive Grounds decisions *are not in fact admissible* at trial and nor can a competent authority's case worker give expert evidence of their findings.[420] *Brecani* was a seventeen-year-old Albanian national on trial for conspiracy to supply cocaine, although a Conclusive Grounds decision had positively identified him as a victim, the prosecution subsequently obtained evidence that completely discredited his account. The Court of Appeal thus concluded that 'the content of the appellant's phone coupled with cell site evidence completely undermined his defence under section 45 of the 2015 Act'.[421] The decision that NRM decisions are inadmissible at trial was upheld by the Court of Appeal in *R* v. *AAD, AAH and AAI,* which set out further guidance.[422] First, that while Conclusive Grounds decisions are not admissible at trial, they are admissible on appeal when considering whether a conviction is safe.[423] Second, experts can give evidence at trial, but only if they are instructed to address questions that are outside the knowledge of the jury 'for instance as to the defendant's psychiatric or psychological state or the detailed mores of people trafficking gangs operating in countries that are outside the court's own knowledge and experience'.[424] They cannot address questions of fact for the jury such as the vulnerability of the defendant or whether the facts meet the definition of human trafficking.[425]

[416] Ibid at [41] and [42]. [417] Ibid at [43].

[418] *DPP* v. *M* [2020] EWHC 3422, [2021] 1 WLR 1669 (Admin). [419] Ibid at [14].

[420] *R* v. *Brecani* [2021] EWCA Crim 731, [2021] 1 WLR 5851. [421] Ibid at [38].

[422] *R* v. *AAD, AAH and AAI* [2022] EWCA Crim 106, [2022] 1 WLR 4042. [423] Ibid at [87].

[424] Ibid. [425] Ibid at [86].

Following *Brecani* and *ADD*, practitioners have argued that the inadmissibility of NRM decisions will make matters difficult for defendants, particularly in cases where the defendants are reluctant to given evidence themselves. Concerns have also been raised as to whether *Brecani* is compatible with *V.C.L. and A.N.* It is important to recall here that the third limb of *V.C.L. and A.N.* provides that although a decision on victim status is not binding, the 'prosecutor needs clear reasons consistent with the international law definition of trafficking' in order to proceed with prosecution. This arguably sits uneasily with the approach taken by the Court of Appeal in *Brecani* in which it stated that the CPS is not bound by a trafficking assessment, but it needs 'a good reason to disagree with it'.[426] The problem being that whilst a 'good reason' may well include reasons that are consistent with the international law definition, it may also be interpreted to include other reasons as well. This is arguably a different standard to that set out in *V.C.L. and A.N.*

Concerns about the potential ambit of this 'good reasons' approach are given some credence by the fact that the Court in *Brecani* sought to distinguish *Brecani* from *V.C.L. and A.N.* on the basis that the CPS in *Brecani* had considered the Conclusive Grounds decision and provided evidence for why its conclusions were incorrect, whereas the CPS had offered 'no substantial reason' in *V.C.L. and A.N.*[427] Indeed, the AIRE Centre in its submission to the Committee of Ministers has cautioned that this 'diminishes the weight intended to be attributed to the trafficking status assessment as provided for in *V.C.L. and A.N.*',[428] an approach that was arguably replicated in *R* v. *ADD and others.*[429] Perhaps it is not surprising then that in December 2023, the House of Commons Home Office Affairs Committee found that victims are continuing to be prosecuted for criminal acts they were compelled to commit, which 'is mainly due to an insufficient understanding amongst investigators, prosecutors, judges, and defence lawyers of the statutory defence available to such victims, and when or how that defence should be applied'.[430]

7.6.6 Transparency of Supply Chains

The final element of the MSA is its provisions concerning the transparency of supply chains. Section 54 MSA provides that commercial organisations with an annual turnover of £36 million or more should ensure transparency in their supply chain. This is a weak duty as there is no penalty for non-disclosure. The SoS can apply for an injunction to compel compliance and to impose penalties, but there have been no penalties imposed against organisations to date.[431]

[426] *Brecani* (n 420) at [35]. [427] Ibid at [10]. [428] AIRE DH-DD (n 411) at [37].

[429] *R* v. *AAD, AAH and AAI* (n 422) at [38].

[430] House of Commons, Home Affairs Committee, *Human Trafficking* (n 2) at [166].

[431] House of Commons, Home Affairs Committee, *Human Trafficking* (n 2) at [71].

This soft law approach has been roundly criticised as inadequate and ineffective.[432] In September 2020, the Government introduced a Modern Slavery Statement Registry intended to make it easier for consumers and investors to locate statements and compare businesses, publishing statements in the registry is, however, currently voluntary.

In January 2021, following growing concerns about human rights abuses in Xinjiang, China, the UK Government stated it would introduce new financial penalties for non-compliance. This was intended to form part of a package of measures announced in the face of 'mounting evidence from a variety of credible sources that the Uyghur population has been the subject of systematic human rights violations, including slave labour, sanctioned by the Government of the People's Republic of China'.[433] In March 2021 the Business, Energy and Industrial Strategy Committee recommended that the Government accelerate these proposals,[434] and in May 2022 the Queen's Speech indicated that legislation would be forthcoming which would introduce civil penalties for non-compliance. At the time of writing this has yet to take place.[435]

7.7 CONCLUSION

We began this chapter by considering the pernicious nature of modern slavery and human trafficking and the scale of the problem. Although it took a long time for the ECtHR to activate Article 4 ECHR, there are clear signs that the ECtHR is striving to address this and is developing the case law on States' obligations. Those obligations are being shaped by reference to equivalent obligations within the rich body of Articles 2 and 3 ECHR case law and by drawing upon the specialist trafficking treaties. Thus far this has led to the recognition of protective obligations such as non-prosecution of victims and compensation. It is therefore possible that we will see further case law in respect of Article 4 ECHR and that further obligations may be developed.

In the UK, it was intended that the NRM and MSA would provide a robust framework for identifying and protecting victims, and prosecuting and imprisoning those that exploit them. Sadly, the evidence thus far is that these systems are failing to achieve those ambitions. In this respect, GRETA and the

432 Ibid.

433 House of Commons, Business, Energy and Industrial Strategy Committee, *Uyghur forced labour in Xinjiang and UK Value Chains*, HC 241, 17 March 2021.

434 Ibid.

435 Prime Minister's Office, *The Queen's Speech 2022: Background Briefing Notes*, 10 May 2022. See also House of Lords Modern Slavery Act 2015 Committee (n 393) which concluded at [198] that '[t]here are many options for enforcing the supply chain requirements of the Modern Slavery Act, but the current approach of no enforcement is not one of them'.

Committee of Ministers have made a number of recommendations for reform. Yet while recommendations are being made on the international plane, the domestic political environment has been pulling in the opposite direction. Concerns about immigration and the 'small boat crisis' led to the enactment of both the NBA and the IMA which significantly limit the protections accorded to victims. In this regard, it is noteworthy that the House of Commons Home Affairs Committee concluded in respect of the last Government that 'the fight against human trafficking is, in practice, no longer a priority for the UK Government, notwithstanding the Government's claims to the contrary'.[436] It highlighted the 'prioritisation of irregular migration policies over those concerning human trafficking, claims of migrants 'abusing the system', the lack of outputs from the Home Office modern slavery unit, the lack of an updated modern slavery strategy, and the eighteen-month delay in appointing a new Independent Anti-Slavery Commissioner, as indicative of 'a disappointing lack of commitment on the part of the Home Office for tackling human trafficking in the UK'.[437] Indeed, these developments also raise serious questions as to whether the UK is complying with its international obligations. It therefore seems likely that there will be further litigation in respect of the UK's human rights obligations to victims of modern slavery and human trafficking.

[436] House of Commons, Home Affairs Committee, *Human Trafficking* (n 2) at [4].
[437] Ibid at [4].

8 Terrorism

CONTENTS

8.1 INTRODUCTION

In this chapter we examine the human rights implications of the UK's response to terrorism. Whereas other chapters have considered specific rights, terrorism – and how a State responds to it – cuts across myriad human rights, including those enshrined in ECHR. It is obvious that some terrorist acts violate the right to life and freedom from ill-treatment, and States have positive obligations to protect lives and bodily integrity. In attempting to identify and fight terrorism, States may also impinge upon rights. Many of the rights involved are protected both under the common law and the ECHR though the domestic jurisprudence concerning the rights implications of the State's response to terrorism has centred on the ECHR. This chapter will, then, consider the UK's response to terrorism primarily through the prism of the ECHR, though where the common law has featured, that will also be discussed. As for the relevant ECHR rights, these include the right to life (Article 2 ECHR) and the prohibition on torture or inhuman or degrading treatment or punishment (Article 3 ECHR), as well as the rights to liberty (Article 5 ECHR), fair trial (Article 6 ECHR), respect for private and family life (Article 8 ECHR), freedom of thought, conscience and religion (Article 9 ECHR), freedom of expression (Article 10 ECHR), freedom of association (Article 11 ECHR), the right to property (Article 1, Protocol 1 ECHR) and freedom from discrimination (Article 14 ECHR).[1] In respect of the qualified rights (bar Article 9 ECHR), national security is a legitimate aim that may justify interfering with the right. Cases involving terrorism can also raise issues under Article 17 ECHR – the abuse of rights clause – which may preclude an individual from relying upon their Convention rights.[2] And, in extreme situations, terrorism may give rise to a

[1] For an indication of the breadth of the European Court of Human Rights' (ECtHR) case law involving terrorism, see ECtHR, 'Factsheet – Terrorism and the ECHR', February 2024, www.echr.coe.int/documents/d/echr/FS_Terrorism_ENG.

[2] For a discussion of the operation of Article 17 ECHR, see Chapter 10.

state of emergency that justifies the State derogating from almost all[3] of the Convention rights (Article 15 ECHR).

Terrorism and the State's response to it raise several complex, ideological and institutional issues including, perhaps most controversially, what *is* 'terrorism' and who decides? This is crucial because once the terrorism label is attached, the protection that is (or at least ought to be) otherwise accorded by human rights is often quickly eroded. This chapter examines such issues, particularly insofar as they engage human rights. Before doing so, however, it is necessary to say something of the phenomena that is terrorism, its evolution, and its current manifestations, with a particular focus on the UK.

While the attacks in the US on 9 September 2011 ('9/11') brought terrorism into stark focus for many throughout the Western world, the UK had long been dealing with its own sectarian conflict. During 'The Troubles',[4] various pieces of primary and secondary legislation were passed to deal with the violence, including laws permitting internment of individuals for extended periods without charge. As discussed in Chapter 5 (Ill-Treatment), the first case involving the UK to be heard by the ECtHR – *Ireland* v. *the United Kingdom* – concerned ill-treatment of individuals detained by British security forces in Northern Ireland during this time.[5]

Thus, when the 9/11 terrorist attacks took place, the UK already had a rather extensive 'counter-terrorism toolkit'. Indeed, one of the principal statutes relating to terrorism – the Terrorism Act 2000 – was enacted *prior* to the 9/11 attacks. Nevertheless, following 9/11, and the '7/7 attacks' in London (which refer to the bombing of public transport in London on 7 July 2005, killing fifty-two people and injuring hundreds more), Parliament enacted a swathe of terrorism-related legislation. In recent years, there has been an evolution in the forms of terrorism the State is having to respond to including, most notably, the proliferation of extreme right-wing (XRW) terrorism. Indeed, seven out of

[3] Some rights are non-derogable, such as Articles 3, 4(1) and 7 ECHR (see Chapter 3 (European Framework) for a discussion of the power of derogation under Article 15 ECHR). Article 15(2) permits derogation from Article 2 but only 'in respect of deaths resulting from lawful acts of war'.

[4] 'The Troubles' is a euphemism referring to decades of violent conflict between *soi-disant* loyalists (who wanted Northern Ireland to remain part of the United Kingdom) and republicans who wanted Northern Ireland to (re)unify with the Republic of Ireland. This occurred in the context of the establishment in 1922 of the Irish Free State via the Anglo-Irish Treaty, which ended a five-year struggle for independence from Britain (see, for instance, *Re Finucane* [2019] UKSC 7, [2019] 3 All ER 191 at [1]–[2]. The enduring implications of The Troubles have been considered in other chapters, including Chapters 4 (Life) and 5 (Ill-Treatment).

[5] *Ireland* v. *the United Kingdom* (1979–1980) 2 EHRR 25. See [13]–[19] for an outline of the conflict, and the legislative and policy responses of the UK.

the last ten organisations to be proscribed[6] under the Terrorism Act 2000 (TA 2000), have been XRW organisations (including the Terrogram collective, which was the first online group to be proscribed).[7] The intersection between XRW terrorism and other highly problematic ideologies including, for instance, inceldom,[8] is the subject of a growing body of research, which highlights significant limitations in the traditional conceptualisation of terrorism and questions the efficacy of State responses to novel forms of violence, particularly given many groups operate predominantly online.[9] There has also been a notable diversification in the demographics of people found to have engaged in terrorism, with a growing number of children (those under the age of eighteen) being prosecuted for terrorism offences (many of which relate to XRW ideologies).

Significant attention has also been dedicated to the various methods of direct action employed by climate change activists including XR/Extinction Rebellion and Just Stop Oil in recent years. 'Eco-terrorism' or environmental terrorism is not a new issue, though conduct that might be characterised as terrorism in response to, and as a result of, climate change is likely to assume far greater significance in the coming years given the worsening climate crisis and the political and geographical instability it has caused, and will continue to cause.[10] The fact that most instances of direct action which are motivated by

[6] Proscription refers to the power conferred by Part II of the Terrorism Act 2000 on the Secretary of State to ban any organisation which they believe is concerned in terrorism. The effects of proscription are significant and include the criminalisation of a range of activities including, for instance, being a member, support or funder of the organisation. Proscription is discussed in greater detailed below in Section 8.3.1.1.

[7] Schedule 2 Terrorism Act 2000.

[8] 'Involuntary celibates or "Incels" are a group of men who believe that the world we live in is a feminist gynarchy. This system unfairly favours attractive men and women to the extent that unattractive men are unable to find romantic and sexual partners': Shannon Zimmerman, 'The Ideology of Incels: Misogyny and Victimhood as Justification for Political Violence' (2024) **36** Terrorism and Political Violence 2, p.1.

[9] See, for instance, Gavin Hart and Antoinette Raffaela Huber, 'Five Things We Need to Learn About Incel Extremism: Issues, Challenges and Avenues for Fresh Research' (2023) Studies in Conflict & Terrorism 1–7; Yi Ting Chua and Lydia Wilson, 'Beyond Black and White: The Intersection of Ideologies in Online Extremist Communities' (2023) **29** European Journal on Criminal Policy and Research 337–354; Intelligence and Security Committee of Parliament, 'Extreme Right-Wing Terrorism', HC 459, 13 July 2022 at [73]–[76], https://isc.independent.gov.uk/wp-content/uploads/2022/07/E02710035-HCP-Extreme-Right-Wing-Terrorism_Accessible.pdf; and Intelligence and Security Committee of Parliament, 'Annual Report', HC 257, 5 December 2023, https://isc.independent.gov.uk/wp-content/uploads/2023/12/ISC-Annual-Report-2022-2023.pdf.

[10] 'Climate change has provoked protest activism in many countries and there has been some speculation that this may have the potential to spill over into extremism and terrorism': Andrew Silke and John F. Morrison, 'Gathering Storm: An Introduction to the Special Issue on Climate Change and Terrorism' (2022) **34** Terrorism and Political Violence 5, p.888.

'environmentally related ideology' do not result in fatalities (or, indeed, injuries) illuminates the complexity inherent in defining 'terrorism' and determining how States should respond to it.[11]

Accordingly, while the UK's counter-terrorism machinery has a long history, questions abound as to whether it is fit for purpose in the face of changing terrorist ideologies and forums. This chapter will consider these issues, including the appropriateness of how 'terrorism' is defined, before turning to examine the legislative response to terrorist threats, with a view to highlighting the human rights implications of such responses. This chapter is not intended to provide a comprehensive account of UK counter-terrorism law; rather, key issues have been selected to illuminate the human rights implications of the UK's response to terrorism.

8.2 WHAT IS 'TERRORISM'?

According to Lord David Anderson KBE KC, the former Independent Reviewer of Terrorism Legislation (IRTL):

> The very word [terrorism] has such magnetic qualities that ordinary compasses are not to be trusted anywhere near it. It might have been preferable if it had never found its way into the law. For our more juridical purposes, something more prosaic – politically motivated violent crime, perhaps – might have been more suitable. But it is too late for that. The concept is now considered to be a legal one, for better or worse. We need to shield our compasses and try to work out how (if at all) these special laws are to be justified.[12]

It is notoriously difficult to distil a single, comprehensive definition of 'terrorism'. On the international plane there is no universally accepted definition. Work at the UN level on a Draft Comprehensive Convention on International Terrorism has been taking place since 1996, but States differ significantly in their views of what constitutes terrorism and in particular whether States can commit acts of terrorism. In the absence of an agreed definition, the UN has published numerous resolutions which attempt to characterise terrorism.[13] The lack of a single definition is not simply an academic concern; as those heading the key security services have emphasised 'having specific terminology ... is essential'.[14]

[11] Ibid, p.889.

[12] David Anderson, 'Shielding the Compass: How to Fight Terrorism Without Defeating the Law' (2013) 3 EHRLR 233, p.245.

[13] See, for instance, UNSC, S/RES/1566 (2004) at [3].

[14] Intelligence and Security Committee of Parliament (n 9) at [18].

At the domestic level, the TA 2000 defines 'terrorism' for the purposes of that Act and, as will be discussed, a range of other legislative and regulatory instruments in the UK. Section 1 of the TA 2000 provides:

(1) In this Act "terrorism" means the use or threat of action where–
   (a) the action falls within subsection (2),
   (b) the use or threat is designed to influence the government or an international governmental organisation or to intimidate the public or a section of the public, and
   (c) the use or threat is made for the purpose of advancing a political, religious, racial or ideological cause.
(2) Action falls within this subsection if it–
   (a) involves serious violence against a person,
   (b) involves serious damage to property,
   (c) endangers a person's life, other than that of the person committing the action,
   (d) creates a serious risk to the health or safety of the public or a section of the public, or
   (e) is designed seriously to interfere with or seriously to disrupt an electronic system.
(3) The use or threat of action falling within subsection (2) which involves the use of firearms or explosives is terrorism whether or not subsection (1)(b) is satisfied.
(4) In this section–
   (a) "action" includes action outside the United Kingdom,
   (b) a reference to any person or to property is a reference to any person, or to property, wherever situated,
   (c) a reference to the public includes a reference to the public of a country other than the United Kingdom, and
   (d) "the government" means the government of the United Kingdom, of a Part of the United Kingdom or of a country other than the United Kingdom.
(5) In this Act a reference to action taken for the purposes of terrorism includes a reference to action taken for the benefit of a proscribed organisation.

In summary, s.1 TA 2000 requires the following elements to be present for conduct to constitute terrorism:

ACTION – there is an action (or threat of action) that falls within the meaning set out in s.1(2);

INTENTION – the action/threat is designed to influence the government (including international governments and international governmental organisations) *or* is designed to intimidate the public (or a section thereof) (*unless* the use of firearms or explosives is involved in which case it will be considered terrorism regardless of intention); and,

PURPOSE – the action/threat is for the purpose of advancing a political, religious, racial or ideological cause.

8.2.1 Is the Definition of 'Terrorism' in Section 1 TA 2000 Too Wide?

The definition in s.1 TA 2000 is extremely broad. Indeed, all three components – action, intention and purpose – have given rise to concerns, as they can result in the definition of terrorism attaching to circumstances which many might not consider to be terrorism (for instance, non-violent forms of direct action by protestors).

In respect of the intention component, the former IRTL Lord Anderson proposed that s.1(1)(b) be amended to read: 'designed to *compel, coerce or undermine* the government or an international organisation' in place of 'designed to *influence* the government or an international organisation'.[15] Adam Tomkins similarly argues that by using the standard of influencing the Government (as opposed to a higher threshold such as intimidation or coercion) whilst also extending the reach of terrorism beyond the most serious violence, the definition 'dangerously blurs the former distinction between terrorism and criminal activity governed by regular public order law'.[16]

The purposive component of the definition is also controversial, not least because it is clearly open to interpretation by authorities and the courts. Further, as noted by Anderson 'from an operational point of view, it is difficult to see why [purpose] should be relevant' as the counter-terrorism legislation 'is justified, if at all, by the potentially lethal effects of terrorism rather than by the mental element behind it'.[17]

In practice, the approach of the Joint Terrorism Analysis Centre (JTAC) – which analyses and assesses intelligence relating to international terrorism, and sets threat levels and issues warnings of threats and other terrorist-related subjects – is to cluster particular types of ideologies as follows:[18]

- Islamist Terrorism (incorporating Sunni extremist terrorism and State-sponsored Shia terrorism);

[15] David Anderson, 'The Terrorism Acts in 2013: Report of the Independent Reviewer on the Operation of the Terrorism Act 2000 and Part 1 of the Terrorism Act 2006' (TSO, 2014) [10.35]–[10.43], cited in Alan Greene, 'Defining Terrorism: One Size Fits All?' (2017) **66** ICLQ 2, p.435. Emphasis added.

[16] Adam Tomkins, 'Legislating against Terror: The Anti-Terrorism, Crime and Security Act 2001' (2002) PL (Summer) **205**, pp.211–212.

[17] Anderson (n 12), p.243.

[18] Joint Terrorism Analysis Centre, www.mi5.gov.uk/joint-terrorism-analysis-centre. This categorisation is referred to in Intelligence and Security Committee of Parliament (n 9) at [15].

- Right Wing Terrorism (incorporating offences motivated by both so-called Far Right and XRW ideologies);
- Left-Wing, Anarchist and Single-Issue Terrorism;
- Ethno-nationalist/Separatist Terrorism (including Sikh terrorism, Basque separatists);
- Northern Ireland-Related Terrorism;
- Hostile State Activity;
- The Cyber Threat; and
- Nuclear Proliferation.[19]

In addition to these comparatively 'organised' ideologies, there is an increasing awareness of the threat posed by 'mixed, unstable and unclear ideolog[ies]'.[20] This is particularly apparent on the far right where there has been a 'proliferation and confusion of ideologies' which has been referred to as 'salad-bar' extremism.[21] This 'confusion' of ideologies may, however, 'be down to novelty and the time required for practitioners to catch up ... Unfamiliarity does not equate to incoherence.'[22]

A further critique of s.1 TA 2000 is that it adopts a single definition for a wide range of activity. As Alan Greene argues, 'the decision to take a "one-size fits all" approach to defining terrorism was taken without much consideration of alternatives and there has been little appetite for questioning this approach'.[23] It is perhaps inevitable that a definition purporting to cover a concept as heterogeneous as terrorism is overly broad as such a definition must 'accommodate the lowest common denominator'.[24] Greene argues that such breadth 'confers extensive discretion on decision makers which is applied in an inconsistent and unclear manner, undermining the principle of legality as reflected in British constitutional law, and the [ECHR]'.[25]

Notwithstanding these issues, the definition in s.1 TA 2000 is the cornerstone of terrorism-related legislation in the UK. Its breadth is particularly pronounced when one considers (as we will) the consequences of a finding that a person has been or is engaged in terrorism-related activities (e.g. the imposition of a Terrorism Prevention and Investigation Measure (TPIM) and, more recently,

[19] Intelligence and Security Committee of Parliament (2022) (n 9) at [13] and Intelligence and Security Committee of Parliament (2023) (n 9) at Annex A.

[20] Jonathan Hall, 'The Terrorism Acts in 2021: Report of the Independent Reviewer of Terrorism Legislation on the Operation of the Terrorism Acts 2000 and 2006, and the Terrorism Prevention and Investigation Measures Act 2011', 12 March 2023 at [11.16], https://assets.publishing.service.gov.uk/government/uploads/system/uploads/attachment_data/file/1140911/E02876111_Terrorism_Acts_in_2021_Accessible.pdf.

[21] Ibid. [22] Ibid at [11.17]–[11.18]. [23] Greene (n 15), p.411. [24] Ibid.

[25] Ibid, p.412.

the imposition of fourteen-year minimum prison sentences with the possibility of twenty-five-year licence periods for 'serious terrorism offences').

8.2.2 Can States Fall within the Definition of 'Terrorism' in Section 1 TA 2000?

While the definition in s.1 TA 2000 does not expressly provide that States or Governments cannot be the perpetrators of terrorism, it appears that actions by States are not regarded as 'terrorism' under this Act. This is contested by Conor Gearty who observes that, '[h]istorically, it has been states that have been the most extreme in their deployment of political terror'.[26] He explains that '[t]errorism' was (and, arguably, remains) a type of violence, not a type of person and when it is conceived of in this manner – that is, as a technique – it is clear that it can be used by 'any player on the political or international scene'.[27] Gearty goes on to observe, however, that 'terrorism nowadays has a strong connotation of the subversive about it' and, as a result, no longer comfortably accommodates acts by States, no matter how violent or terrorising.[28] This constriction in the use and, consequently, meaning of 'terrorism' – to apply only to the subversive who opposes the established order – means that States/the established order are now always the 'counter-terrorist' no matter 'how violent they themselves are or how much more brutal and terror-inducing they are than those they oppose'.[29] This change has arisen in no small part because a 'moral judgment has insinuated itself into the language of terrorism' such that what the 'terrorist' does is always wrong and what the counter-terrorist is compelled to do in response is invariably right'.[30]

A separate but related issue is whether all 'governments' fall within s.1(1)(b) TA 2000 or whether there are some governments which, because of their conduct, are precluded. The defendant in *R* v. *F*[31] was charged with offences contrary to s.58(1)(b) TA 2000, having been found in possession of documents detailing how to construct bombs and establish terrorist cells. The defendant had intended to travel to Libya (having previously fled the country and been granted asylum in the UK) to join the resistance to the Gaddafi-led Government. The defendant argued that the terrorism legislation should not apply to governments constituted by a dictatorship, military junta, uprising/invading power and so on. The courts rejected that argument, holding that s.1 TA 2000 was unambiguous: there was no qualification on what constituted a Government and no list of 'proscribed' or otherwise 'unrecognised' Governments for the purposes of s.1. It seems, then, that no matter how disdainful or, indeed, unlawful the conduct of a government, resistance to it

[26] Conor Gearty, 'Terrorism and Morality' [2003] 4 EHRLR 377, p.378. [27] Ibid.
[28] Ibid, p.379. [29] Ibid, p.380. [30] Ibid.
[31] *R* v. *F* [2007] EWCA Crim 243, [2007] 3 WLR 164.

which otherwise falls within the definition of s.1 will constitute 'terrorism' for the purposes of the TA 2000 (and other terrorism-related legislation).

8.2.3 Contemporary Forms of Terrorism

8.2.3.1 Extreme Right-Wing Terrorism

While far right-wing ideology has been present in British society for decades,[32] there has been a marked increase in the number of individuals charged with terrorism offences relating to XRW ideology in recent years. As of December 2024, of the 257 individuals in custody in Great Britain for 'terrorism and terrorism-connected offences', seventy-eight (i.e. 30 per cent) were identified as adhering to XRW ideologies.[33] Interestingly, of the ten people in custody for such offences in Scotland, seven were identified as having an XRW ideology. There are many and varied definitions of far right and XRW ideologies. Unless otherwise specified, the terms 'far right' and 'extreme right-wing'/XRW are used in this chapter to encompass ideologies that can be broadly charactersed as: cultural nationalism; white nationalism; and white supremacism.

A particular feature of recent convictions for XRW terrorism offences is the centrality of online forums. This is by no means a unique feature of XRW terrorism but it is notable that of the most recently proscribed XRW organisations, two are based primarily online (e.g., Sonnenkrieg Division and Feuerkrieg Division (FKD)) and the Terrorgram collective is based entirely online.[34] These groups tend to communicate primarily via closed channels and 'attract young or very young members'.[35] For example, the British 'head' of the FKD was sixteen years old when he was sentenced for terrorist publication offences (which took place when he was fourteen years old), and one of his 'recruits' was convicted for offences committed when he was also sixteen.[36]

[32] 'The British Far Right can trace its roots back to the 1930s and the emergence of Sir Oswald Mosley and his party, the British Union of Fascists': Intelligence and Security Committee of Parliament (n 9) at [23].

[33] Home Office, 'Operation of police powers under the Terrorism Act 2000: quarterly update to December 2024: Annual data tables', 13 March 2025, Table P.01: Number of persons in custody for terrorism-related offences, by ideology, www.gov.uk/government/statistics/operation-of-police-powers-under-tact-2000-to-december-2024.

[34] Jonathan Hall, 'The Terrorism Acts in 2020: Report of the Independent Reviewer of Terrorism Legislation on the Operation of the Terrorism Acts 2000 and 2006, and the Terrorism Prevention and Investigation Measures Act 2011', April 2022 at [3.6], https://terrorismlegislationreviewer.independent.gov.uk/wp-content/uploads/2022/04/Terrorism-Acts-in-2020.pdf. See also, UK Government, 'Terrorgram added to list of proscribed terrorist organisations', 22 April 2024, www.gov.uk/government/news/terrorgram-added-to-list-of-proscribed-terrorist-organisations.

[35] Ibid. [36] Ibid and *R* v. *Dunleavy* [2021] EWCA Crim 39.

The utilisation of online modes of organisation and communication by XRW terrorist groups (amongst others) raises questions about the utility and applicability of existing terrorism legislation. As the current IRTL Jonathan Hall KC has observed:

> the online age could see proscription becoming of less relevance in countering domestic terrorism. In the past, physical coordination between likeminded individuals was required in the form of meetings, weapons training, and the generation of printed material, in order to disseminate terrorist tradecraft, capability, and inspiration. Proscription of groups was an effective means of reducing this type of activity, as it has been for some online groups. But the decentralised nature of the internet and the ease of user-generated content means that individuals can find all the inspiration and tradecraft they need without joining or even interacting with any identifiable group.[37]

'Online radicalisation' has also garnered increasing attention in recent years, especially with the rising number of children arrested for terrorism offences as a result of their online activity.[38] While according to the current IRTL, '[i]t is doubtful that all of [the children arrested on account of their online behaviour] are really terrorists in any meaningful sense', the role of the internet in radicalisation, particularly of children, cannot be disregarded.[39]

The Online Safety Act 2023 (OSA) which was enacted in 2023 is likely to prove significant in this context, particularly given that one of its primary objectives is to minimise access to 'illegal content' and content that is harmful to children.[40] 'Illegal content' includes content that amounts to an offence under a number of provisions of the TA 2000 and the Terrorism Act 2006 (TA 2006) and 'content that is harmful to children' includes content that encourages, promotes or provides instructions for an act of serious violence against a person.[41] There are difficulties with the Act, including that it relies on offences under the TA 2000 and other terrorism legislation to define 'terrorism content' which amounts to an offence under the OSA and, as the current IRTL has observed '[i]dentifying whether online conduct amounts to a terrorism offence is not always straightforward as a matter of law'.[42]

8.2.3.2 *'Inceldom'*

Violence, often fatal, perpetrated predominantly against women by men who identify as involuntarily celibate ('incels') has increased in recent years, particularly in the US and Canada, though the UK has also seen instances of lethal

[37] Hall (n 34) at [3.12]. [38] Hall (n 20) at [5.8]. [39] Ibid at [11.11].

[40] See, for instance, Online Safety Bill, Explanatory Notes, Bill 4-EN at [1], https://publications.parliament.uk/pa/bills/cbill/58-03/0004/en/220004en.pdf. See, also, Online Safety Act 2023, s.1(2).

[41] Online Safety Act 2023, ss.59, 60, 62(4) and Schedule 5. [42] Hall (n 20) at [12.89].

violence by incels.[43] While some instances of incel violence have been classified as terrorism (including in Scotland[44]), there is considerable resistance to labelling violence perpetrated by men who identify as incels as terrorism. In fact, the current IRTL criticised '[a] new form of social pressure' to apply terrorism legislation 'more liberally'.[45] Writing in the context of the shootings of five people by a man in Plymouth in 2021 who was linked with incel ideology,[46] Hall suggested that attempts to label such violence as terrorism was motivated by a desire to 'gain status or legitimacy or resources' and 'risk[ed] inconsistency, discrimination and perverse outcomes'.[47] While those concerns must be taken seriously, we must also be careful not to diminish the very real threat individuals who identify as incels – which has been described as an 'overtly extreme manifestation of misogynistic, homophobic, racist, classist and ableist ideas and beliefs'[48] – pose to the community. Moreover, the link between incel ideology and XRW terrorism is also increasingly being recognised.[49]

Much debate attends whether incel-related violence meets the ideology requirements of s.1(1)(c) TA 2000. In response to the Plymouth murders, the deputy senior national coordinator for Counter Terrorism Policing stated that 'Incel in and of itself is not a terrorist ideology'.[50] This seems to overlook the

[43] See, for instance, the shooting of four members of the public and his mother by Jake Davison who then shot himself. Davison's mother had referred her son to the counter-terrorism PREVENT programme several years earlier, and before he had acquired a gun licence: Steven Morris, 'Mother of Plymouth shooter reported him to Prevent anti-terror scheme', *The Guardian*, 15 March 2022, www.theguardian.com/uk-news/2022/mar/15/mother-of-plymouth-shooter-reported-him-to-prevent-anti-terror-scheme.

[44] A jury in the trial of Gabrielle Friel, who was charged with a number of terrorism offences following discovery of a machete, ballistic vest, a high-powered crossbow and metal bolts with pointed steel tips for use in same, found the charge that he was motivated by incel ideology not proven: BBC News, 'Gabrielle Friel: Man guilty of weapons haul terrorism charge', *BBC News*, 15 December 2020, www.bbc.co.uk/news/uk-scotland-edinburgh-east-fife-55317874. For academic work on whether inceldom is terrorism, see, for instance, Bruce Hoffman, Jacob Ware and Ezra Shapiro, 'Assessing the Threat of Incel Violence' (2020) 43 Studies in Conflict & Terrorism 7, pp.565–587.

[45] Hall (n 34) at [1.4].

[46] See, for instance, BBC News, 'Plymouth shooting: Jake Davison was licensed gun holder', *BBC News*, 13 August 2021, www.bbc.co.uk/news/uk-england-devon-58197414.

[47] Hall (n 34) at [1.4].

[48] Lisa Sugiura, *The Incel Rebellion: The Rise of the Manosphere and the Virtual War against Women* (Emerald Publishing Limited, 2021), p.70.

[49] See, for instance, Kyler Ong, 'Ideological Convergences in the Extreme Right' (2020) 12 Counter-Terrorist Trends and Analyses 5, pp.1–7; Stephane Baele, Lewys Brace and Debbie Ging, 'A Diachronic Cross-Platforms Analysis of Violent Extremist Language in the Incel Online Ecosystem' (2024) 36 Terrorism and Political Violence 3, pp.383–405.

[50] See, for instance, Maria Norris, 'Dismissing the ideology of incels like the Plymouth shooter is shortsighted and dangerous', *The Independent*, 29 September 2021, www.independent.co.uk/voices/incel-terrorism-plymouth-shooting-b1929162.html.

fact that there is clear evidence that 'multiple elements of the incel culture are highly misogynistic and favorable toward violence against women, indicating that this subculture may be at risk for [committing] future [acts of] violence' and '[t]he risk of violence stemming from incel communities and their online operational practices suggests they may resemble other ideologically motivated extremist groups'.[51] Indeed, the Government in its most recent iteration of the CONTEST strategy seems to acknowledge that inceldom *could* satisfy the act and intention requirements of s.1 TA 2000 in its observation that 'violent adherents to movements and subcultures, such as . . . Incels . . ., could meet the threshold of terrorist intent or action, should the threat or use of serious violence be used to influence the government, or to intimidate the public'.[52] Though the Government did appear to stop short of recognising that inceldom could be an ideology for the purpose requirement in s.1(1)(c).

While he may have cautioned against extending the application of s.1 TA 2000 too far, the current IRTL has recognised that incel violence *may* constitute terrorism for the purposes of that section:

> [t]he definition [in s.1] does not require the authorities to identify a group of ideas that may be said to form an 'ideology', a label that superficially at least might suggest a degree of internal coherence. The issue in the statutory definition is whether the person is advancing an ideological (or political, or religious, or racial) *cause.*[53]

Citing research into the nature of incel-based violence, Hall recognised that the definition in s.1 is 'sufficiently broad to capture modern phenomena such as incel violence' though he also noted that 'an overambitious use of terrorism legislation could go beyond what society at large understood as "terrorism", so that the public might come to wonder whether harsher measures were being deployed than were really warranted. This might be reflected in a jury refusing to convict'.[54] The case of Gabrielle Friel is notable here (not least as it provides a counterpoint to Hall's concerns), as while Friel was acquitted by the jury of a charge under s.5 TA 2006 (preparing to commit terrorist acts), he was found guilty of possession of articles for terrorist purposes (s.57 TA 2000) and was

[51] Roberta Liggett O'Malley, Karen Holt and Thomas J Holt, 'An Exploration of the Involuntary Celibate (Incel) Subculture Online' (2020) 37 Journal of Interpersonal Violence 7–8, NP4984.

[52] HM Government, 'CONTEST: The United Kingdom's Strategy for Countering Terrorism 2023', CP 2023, July 2023 at [24], https://assets.publishing.service.gov.uk/media/650b1b8d52e73c000d54dc82/CONTEST_2023_English_updated.pdf.

[53] Jonathan Hall, 'The Terrorism Acts in 2019: Report of the Independent Reviewer of Terrorism Legislation on the Operation of the Terrorism Acts 2000 and 2006, and the Terrorism Prevention and Investigation Measures Act 2011', March 2021 at [2.60], https://assets.publishing.service.gov.uk/government/uploads/system/uploads/attachment_data/file/972261/THE_TERRORISM_ACTS_IN_2019_REPORT_Accessible.pdf#page23 (Emphasis in original).

[54] Ibid at [2.62]. See also, BBC News (n 44).

subsequently sentenced to ten years' imprisonment.[55] Friel was found in possession of a crossbow, arrows, a machete and a ballistics vest and had carried out research online into '"incel" (involuntary celibate) ideology, weapons, and mass murderers, including those who had been motivated by the "incel" ideology, and had said that he could relate to such individuals.'[56]

8.2.3.3 Overseas Conflicts and the Scope of 'Terrorism'

In recent years, an increasing number of conflicts in foreign countries have seen UK nationals and residents travelling to join the fighting. While the UK does not (generally) have jurisdiction in such countries, issues can arise with respect to criminal culpability under UK law when those individuals return. In *R* v. *Gul*,[57] the UK Supreme Court had to determine whether attacks by non-State actors (i.e. individuals not part of a State's armed forces) on national or international forces could constitute terrorism for the purposes of s.1 TA 2000. In holding that the definition encompassed such acts, the Court noted that while there might be popular support for acts of insurgents or 'freedom fighters', that did not justify reading down s.1 TA 2000. Significantly, the Court expressed (albeit in obiter dicta) its concerns regarding the breadth of the definition:

> While acknowledging that the issue is ultimately one for Parliament, we should record our view that the concerns and suggestions about the width of the statutory definition of terrorism which Mr Anderson [then the IRTL] has identified in his two reports merit serious consideration. *Any legislative narrowing of the definition of 'terrorism', with its concomitant reduction in the need for the exercise of discretion under section 117 of the 2000 Act, is to be welcomed*, provided that it is consistent with the public protection to which the legislation is directed.[58]

The difficulty with labelling the actions of non-State actors as terrorism arose in the context of hostilities undertaken by Islamic State/ISIL fighters in Syria and neighbouring countries. Several Britons were investigated for terrorism-related offences after returning from fighting with the Kurdish YPG militia. The YPG was a chief component of the Syrian Democratic Forces (SDF), a US-backed entity which formed to fight against the Islamic State/ISIL.[59] Neither the YPG nor

[55] Crown Office and Procurator Fiscal Service, 'Terrorism Prosecutions in Scotland', 26 April 2024, www.copfs.gov.uk/crime-info/terrorism-prosecutions-in-scotland/.

[56] Ibid. [57] *R* v. *Gul* [2013] UKSC 64, [2014] AC 1260. [58] Ibid at [62]. Emphasis added.

[59] See, for instance, Ruby Mellen, 'A brief history of the Syrian Democratic Forces, the Kurdish-led alliance that helped the US defeat the Islamic State', *The Washington Post*, 7 October 2019, www.washingtonpost.com/world/2019/10/07/brief-history-syrian-democratic-forces-kurdish-led-alliance-that-helped-us-defeat-islamic-state/, and Congressional Research Service, 'Armed Conflict in Syria: Overview and U.S. Response', 27 July 2020, p.7, https://sgp.fas.org/crs/mideast/RL33487.pdf.

the SDF were proscribed under the TA 2000. It is perhaps for that reason that several of the terrorism-related charges against individuals who fought with the SDF and/or YPG were dropped by the CPS and/or led to acquittals.[60]

One of the more well-known cases of returned YPG/SDF fighters involved UK national Aidan James. He had travelled to Syria, through Iraq, with the help of the PKK (which *is* a proscribed organisation under Schedule 2 TA 2000) to join the YPG. Upon arriving in Iraq, he stayed in a refugee camp that was controlled by the PKK and he attended weapons training conducted by the PKK. It was in respect of that training that he was charged (and convicted) of attending at a place where terrorist training in weapons was being delivered (s.8 TA 2006). The case is notable for the way in which James' involvement with the YPG was treated. In particular, James was acquitted of terrorism offences relating to his training by the YPG because:

> The jury was not satisfied that the YPG had any political or religious cause beyond fighting against ISIS for which this training camp was delivering weapons training. This activity was not, on the jury's verdict 'noble cause terrorism': at least for present purposes, it was not terrorism at all. The force for which [James was] being trained was defensive force against a lethal and genocidal threat from ISIS. The prosecution has not sought to prove otherwise, and no jury has found otherwise.[61]

The sentencing judge considered that it was 'not irrelevant to the proper classification of that YPG activity that it was supporting the policy of the United Kingdom and other allies by fighting ISIS'.[62]

8.3 THE LEGAL RESPONSE TO TERRORISM IN THE UK

As the former IRTL observed, 'it is no disrespect to [the] victims or their relatives [of the 9/11 and 7/7 attacks] to point out that . . . despicable as these major attacks were, all were criminal acts under the ordinary law. Their existence, and the public reaction to them, cannot justify the tearing up of longstanding freedoms and protections'.[63] Indeed, those individuals involved in the most heinous crimes which fall within the definition in s.1 TA 2000 are frequently charged with existing criminal offences. For instance, the man who killed Sir David Amess MP was convicted of his murder,[64] the man who killed

[60] See, for instance, Daniel De Simone, 'Father and son "left in limbo" by failed terror case', *BBC News*, 3 July 2020, www.bbc.co.uk/news/uk-53270896.

[61] *R* v. *Aidan James*, Central Criminal Court, Sentencing Remarks of Mr Justice Edis, 7 November 2019, p.2, www.judiciary.uk/wp-content/uploads/2019/11/SENTENCING-REMARKS.pdf.

[62] Ibid. [63] Anderson (n 12), p.235.

[64] BBC News, 'Sir David Amess murder: Ali Harbi Ali given whole-life sentence', *BBC News*, 14 April 2022, www.bbc.com/news/uk-england-61094059.

Jo Cox MP was found guilty of her murder,[65] the men who stabbed Lee Rigby to death were convicted of his murder,[66] one of the men responsible for the Manchester Arena bombing was found guilty of twenty-two counts of murder,[67] and the man who drove his van into a crowd of people outside a mosque in Finsbury Park was found guilty of one count of murder.[68] That the perpetrators of the most egregious terrorism-related crimes are charged with and convicted of 'general' or 'non-terrorism' criminal offences is something to keep in mind as we move through the considerable corpus of terrorism-specific legislation: if those crimes can be dealt with under the existing criminal justice system, is terrorism-specific legislation needed?

One of the rationales for the terrorism label is that it justifies 'defending further up the field' than ordinary criminal law permits. It both criminalises actions that would not otherwise be unlawful and it legitimises the use of State powers that would otherwise not be permissible, for instance surveillance, deprivation of liberty, departures from fair trial processes, and deprivations of assets.

The question that needs to be considered in this context is whether human rights law sets limits on the use of such measures or whether it normalises exceptional measures and, consequently, legitimises the dilution of human rights. We will return to this question at the end of this chapter. In the next section we examine key pieces of terrorism-related legislation in the UK. The legislation will be considered by reference to what it does, namely:

1. The creation of new offences and the corresponding introduction of specific sentences for those offences;
2. Restrictions on a person's rights:
   a. Deprivations of liberty, including detention and Terrorism Prevention and Investigation Measures (TPIMS);
   b. Stop and search powers (including at the borders);
   c. Deprivation of a person's British nationality and refusal to repatriate;
   d. Deprivation of assets; and,
   e. Restrictions on access to material in judicial proceedings.

[65] See, for instance, Ian Cobain and Matthew Taylor, 'Far-right terrorist Thomas Mair jailed for life for Jo Cox murder', *The Guardian*, 23 November 2016, www.theguardian.com/uk-news/2016/nov/23/thomas-mair-found-guilty-of-jo-cox-murder.

[66] See, for instance, Vikram Dodd and Josh Halliday, 'Lee Rigby murder: Michael Adebolajo and Michael Adebowale found guilty', *The Guardian*, 19 December 2013, www.theguardian.com/uk-news/2013/dec/19/lee-rigby-murder-michael-adebolajo-adebowale-guilty.

[67] See, for instance, Greater Manchester Police, 'A man who conspired with his brother to carry out a terror attack that killed 22 people at the Manchester Arena has been convicted', 17 March 2020, https://www.gmp.police.uk/news/greater-manchester/news/news/2020/march/a-man-who-conspired-with-his-brother-to-carry-out-a-terror-attack-that-killed-22-people-at-the-manchester-arena-has-been-jailed/.

[68] See, for instance, *BBC News*, 'Darren Osborne guilty of Finsbury Park mosque murder', 1 February 2018, www.bbc.co.uk/news/uk-42910051.

8.3.1 Terrorism Offences

There are numerous terrorism offences under the TA 2000 and the TA 2006. These include:

TA 2000

- Section 11 – membership of a proscribed organisation;
- Section 13 – wearing, carrying or displaying an item of clothing or an article in support of a proscribed organisation;
- Sections 15 to 18 – fundraising offences;
- Section 54 – providing and receiving weapons training;
- Section 57 – possession of articles for a terrorist purpose;
- Section 58 – collection/possession/accessing of information likely to be useful to a person committing or preparing an act of terrorism.

TA 2006

- Section 1 – encouraging terrorism;
- Section 2 – dissemination of terrorist publications;
- Sections 5 – preparation for acts of terrorism;
- Sections 6 and 8 – providing and receiving 'terrorism training'.

The intention behind these offences is to empower the State to address terrorism at the earliest possible point, and prior to an attack being carried out. In addition to the specific terrorism offences outlined above, certain criminal law offences which are found to have a 'terrorist connection' can result in longer sentences.[69]

We will now consider several of these terrorism-specific offences in greater detail, including their interactions with human rights, in particular freedom of expression and freedom of assembly as protected by Articles 10 and 11 ECHR respectively.[70]

8.3.1.1 Membership of a Proscribed Organisation (Section 11 TA 2000)

For the purposes of s.11 TA 2000 (membership of a proscribed organisation), the list of proscribed organisations is contained in Schedule 2 and includes: The IRA; The Ulster Freedom Fighters; The Ulster Volunteer Force; Al-Qa'ida; The Kurdistan Workers' Party (PKK); Boko Haram; and National Action. The latter of these – National Action – was the first far-right organisation to be proscribed under the TA 2000. In February 2020, Sonnenkrieg Division – a National Action offshoot – was proscribed and in July 2020, Feuerkrieg Division became the third Neo-Nazi organisation to be proscribed. In April

[69] See, for instance, Counter-Terrorism Act 2008, sch.2 and the Counter-Terrorism and Sentencing Act 2021.

[70] For more on these rights, see Chapter 12.

and May 2021, two further neo-Nazi organisations were added: Atomwaffen Division (including National Socialist Order) and The Base. In April 2024, the Terrorgram collective (an XRW group that 'subscribes to militant accelerationist and neo-fascist ideologies, notably pursuing the collapse of the Western world and a 'Race War' through violent acts of terrorism, and often seeks to target young individuals to adopt their ideology'[71]) was proscribed and in July 2025 two further neo-Nazi groups (Maniacs Murder Cult and Russian Imperialist Movement) were added to Schedule 2.

The power to proscribe organisations is set out in s.3 TA 2000. Pursuant to s.3(4), the Secretary of State may exercise the power only if they 'believe' that the organisation is 'concerned in terrorism'. 'Concerned in terrorism' is further defined in s.3(5) and involves committing or participating in acts of terrorism, preparing for terrorism, promoting or encouraging terrorism[72] or, 'is otherwise concerned in terrorism'.

Proscription has clear implications for the rights of members (and, where relevant, the entities proscribed), in particular freedom of expression and freedom of association, not least given that proscription feeds into several terrorism offences including offences relating to expression.[73]

It is, however, evident from the ECHR case law that States can proscribe terrorist organisations and that where this interferes with Articles 10 and 11, such measures will be justified. In fact, terrorist organisations may well be precluded from relying upon Convention rights entirely by virtue of Article 17 ECHR.[74] Of course, the ECtHR will have to consider whether the State is invoking national security concerns to simply suppress its opponents, but otherwise a wide margin of appreciation is accorded to States in this context.

The issue of the compatibility of proscription with Article 11 ECHR was considered recently in a complaint brought against Germany – *Humanitäre Hilfsorganisation Internationale E.* v. *Germany*.[75] The applicant, a non-profit organisation, was proscribed on the basis of its association with the Islamic Society and, consequently, Hamas. The judgment, which found no violation of Article 11 ECHR, interpreted in light of Article 17 ECHR, is notable for several reasons, including the fact that the proscription arose as a result of the organisation's link with a terrorist organisation in a different, non-Member State. The Court's observation that the legitimate aim of 'protecting the rights and freedoms of others' extends to protecting the right to life of individuals outside the State's jurisdiction is especially significant.[76] Another important

[71] UK Government (n 34). [72] See the further clarification provided in ss.3(5A)–(5C) TA 2000.

[73] For more on freedom of association, see Chapter 12.

[74] In respect of the scope and function of Article 17, see Chapter 11 (Hate Speech).

[75] *Internationale Humanitäre Hilfsorganisation e.V.* v. *Germany* [2023] ECHR 776. See also, the discussion of the case in Chapter 12.

[76] Ibid at [75]–[76].

aspect of the decision was the Court's finding that prior notice of proscription and the opportunity to remedy shortcomings were not required.[77]

8.3.1.2 *Disseminating Terrorist Publications (Section 2 TA 2006)*

The scope of the offence under s.2 TA 2006 is very broad; dissemination covers a wide range of activities (s 2(2)) and what constitutes a 'terrorist publication' is broadly defined. While there is a mens rea element (which may be satisfied by recklessness), this offence clearly has the potential to interfere with freedom of expression which is protected both under the common law and by Article 10 ECHR. It is, then, unsurprising that there is a defence to a charge under s.2 if the defendant can show that the publication neither expressed their views nor had their endorsement *and* that this was clear in all the circumstances of the conduct (s.2(9)).

In *R* v. *Faraz*, the Court of Appeal considered the offence in considerable detail.[78] The appellant, a manager of an Islamic bookshop, had been convicted of a number of offences under s.2. During his trial, the prosecution tendered expert evidence to the effect that the material that formed the subject of the charges had been found in the possession of 'suspected terrorists' in 26 per cent of terrorist investigations.[79] The prosecution also adduced evidence that named terrorist offenders had had the material in question (or similar material) in their possession.[80] In allowing the appeal, the Court of Appeal emphasised that the offence under s.2 could be committed whether or not a person had actually been encouraged to commit acts of terrorism. Evidence that a person had been so encouraged was admissible only insofar as it was relevant to the jury's consideration of the likely effect of the publication on its readers and to support the prosecution's case that they were likely to be encouraged to commit such acts. In the instant case, there was no *direct* evidence that the persons who had possession of the publications had been encouraged as a result of them and an inference that they had been so encouraged could not be drawn merely from the possession of the material. There was also further risk of the jury ascribing guilt by association. The convictions were, thus, unsafe and quashed.

Notably, the appellant also argued that the trial judge's description of the nature of the s.2 offence to the jury violated his right to freedom of speech in Article 10 ECHR. In rejecting that contention, the Court of Appeal observed:

> It was perfectly obvious to the jury that they could not convict the defendant merely because his publication expressed a religious or political view, controversial or not. We do not consider it arguable that a publication which to the knowledge of the

[77] Ibid at [100]. [78] *R* v. *Faraz (Ahmed Raza)* [2012] EWCA Crim 2820, [2013] 1 WLR 2615.
[79] Ibid at [47]. [80] Ibid at [4].

defendant carried a real risk that it would be understood by a significant number of readers as encouraging the unlawful commission of terrorist offences . . . is entitled to exemption (in consequence of article 10) merely because it expressed political or religious views.[81]

The Court of Appeal further considered the interplay between s.2 TA 2006 and Article 10 ECHR in *R* v. *Ali*.[82] The defendant was convicted of, inter alia, dissemination offences under s.2 TA 2006 following the sharing in a group chat of videos supportive of the Islamic State. He argued on appeal that the trial judge should have read down s.2 to comply with Article 10 ECHR. In rejecting that argument, the Court of Appeal emphasised that s.2 TA 2006 does not prevent a person holding 'offensive views or personally supporting a terrorist cause'.[83] Rather, what s.2 prohibits 'is the intentional or reckless dissemination of a terrorist publication where the effect of an offender's conduct is a direct or indirect encouragement to the commission, preparation or instigation of acts of terrorism'.[84] The trial judge had made it clear to the jury that they could not convict the defendant based purely on his views. To convict, the jury had to be satisfied that the defendant had 'overstepped the permissible line [of holding views supportive of Islamic State] and committed criminal acts'.[85] Based on the trial judge's summing up, the Court of Appeal was 'amply satisfied' that the defendant's Article 10 ECHR rights had not been violated.[86]

The number of charges under s.2 TA 2006 increased significantly in 2015/2016 and has remained relatively consistent since.[87] Indeed, it was the most charged offence in 2023 (twenty-five people were charged with s.2 offences) and the second most charged offence in 2024 (together with offences under ss.12 and 58 TA 2000) which may be explicable, at least in part, by reference to the rise in XRW terrorism and the increasing role of the internet. For instance, seventeen-year-old Harry Blake Vaughan was convicted of, inter alia, offences under s.2 TA 2000 relating to posts he had made on online forums in which he shared material relating to XRW ideologies.[88] Similarly, eighteen-year-old Malakai Wheeler was convicted of, inter alia, offences under s.2 TA 2000 following his 'active member[ship of] an extreme right-wing online chat group'.[89] The content shared was 'racist, antisemitic and included information on how to create weapons and explosives' and he was given an extended sentence of seven years.[90]

[81] Ibid at [54]. [82] *R* v. *Ali* [2018] EWCA Crim 547, [2018] 1 WLR 6105. [83] Ibid at [17].
[84] Ibid. [85] Ibid at [19]. [86] Ibid at [20]. [87] Home Office (n 33), Table A.05a.
[88] See, for instance, Daniel De Simone, 'Harry Vaughan: Neo-Nazi teenager sentenced', *BBC News*, 2 November 2020, www.bbc.co.uk/news/uk-england-london-54782394.
[89] CPS, 'Student Malakai Wheeler sentenced for sharing terror documents', 3 November 2023, www.cps.gov.uk/cps/news/student-malakai-wheeler-sentenced-sharing-terror-documents.
[90] Ibid.

8.3.1.3 *Collection/Possession of Material Useful to a Terrorist (Section 58 TA 2000)*

Pursuant to s.58 TA 2000, it is an offence to possess a document 'of a kind likely to be useful to a person committing or preparing an act of terrorism'. It is also an offence under s.58(1)(c) if a person views or otherwise accesses a document containing such information. It is a defence under s.58(3A) if the person has possession of the information for, inter alia, the purposes of carrying out work as a journalist or academic research.

In recent years, offences under s.58 have (together with offences under s.2 TA 2006) been the most charged offences[91] under terrorism legislation (nine persons were charged with a s.58 offence in the year ending December 2024 and 206 charges have been made under that provision in Great Britain since 11 September 2001).[92] This contrasts with what had been a considerable drop in the number of charges for offences under s.5 TA 2006 (which relate to preparation for terrorist acts).[93] In 2024, however, there was a notable rise in the number of charges under s.5 – twelve persons charged (which was the highest number of charges for a terrorism offence).[94] It is not apparent from the data published by the Government or from the information provided by the CPS what has caused the sudden increase in charges under s.5.

Several recent cases involving s.58 have concerned XRW ideology. For instance, Charles Cannon was convicted of offences under s.58 based on documents and images on his laptop and phone of an extreme right-wing nature along with homemade explosive manuals.[95] A man was convicted of an offence under s.58 following an investigation that revealed he had participated in an XRW online chat group and was found in possession of a copy of 'The Anarchist's Cookbook'.[96] And a nineteen-year-old pleaded guilty to five offences under s.58 (and five offences under s.2 TA 2006) after he was found to be the 'administrator of a Telegram channel which shared far right extremist, antisemitic and racist views, as well as manuals on bomb building and how to 3D print firearms'.[97]

[91] There was a marked increase in charges under s.5 TA 2006 (preparation for terrorist acts) in 2024 (12 persons were charged, in contrast to 5 in 2023): Home Office (n 33), Table A.05a.

[92] Ibid. [93] Ibid. [94] Ibid.

[95] *BBC News*, 'Lab technician Charles Cannon sentenced for terrorism offences', *BBC News*, 2 February 2024, https://www.bbc.co.uk/news/uk-england-hampshire-68182944.

[96] Counter Terrorism Policing, 'Leicester man sentenced for possessing terrorist document', 24 June 2025, https://www.counterterrorism.police.uk/leicester-man-sentenced-for-possessing-terrorist-document/.

[97] CPS, 'Teenage Neo-Nazi convicted of possessing synagogue attack plan', 26 April 2024, www.cps.gov.uk/cps/news/teenage-neo-nazi-convicted-possessing-synagogue-attack-plan.

8.3.1.4 *Wearing, Carrying or Displaying an Item of Clothing or an Article in Support of a Proscribed Organisation (Section 13 TA 2000)*

Pursuant to s.13 TA 2000, it is an offence to wear an item of clothing or wear, carry or display an article in a public place in such a way or in such circumstances as to arouse 'reasonable suspicion' that the person supports or is a member of an organisation proscribed under s.3 TA 2000. This includes items such as flags (discussed below), jewellery[98] and t-shirts[99] connected to proscribed organisations.

In *Barr* v. *DPP* the defendant was charged with wearing an 'item of clothing, namely a beret, sunglasses, a scarf, camouflage jacket, military style jumper and trousers, boots and gloves, in such a way or in such circumstances as to arouse reasonable suspicion that he was a member of a proscribed organisation'.[100] The defendant challenged the charge, arguing that it was defective as it failed to specify *which* proscribed organisation the clothing was likely to arouse reasonable suspicion he was a member of. This was rejected by the Court which held that the circumstances aroused suspicion that Barr was a member of the IRA and that if the legislation required precision in relation to factions this would render it impossible to charge. It was also noted that as the legislation sought to target activity that generated a reasonable suspicion of support for or participation in prohibited groups, and since in the specific context of Northern Ireland 'the internal workings of these [proscribed] organisations cannot be known by observation alone', it would be wrong to require specificity in the charges as that would prevent the legislation from achieving its purpose.[101]

In *Pwr* v. *DPP*,[102] the Supreme Court was asked to determine whether s.13 requires intention (mens rea) or whether it is a strict liability offence. The section is silent as to intention and there is a presumption, at common law, that mens rea is an ingredient of a statutory offence unless it has clearly been excluded by Parliament. The appellants – who had been convicted of s.13 offences – had participated in a demonstration in central London in January 2018. Each carried a flag of the PKK (Kurdistan Workers' Party) which is a proscribed organisation under s.3 and Schedule 2 of the TA 2000. The appellants argued that if the offence was one of strict liability, it represented a

[98] *Rankin* v. *Murray* [2004] SLT 1164.

[99] *Maguire* v. *the United Kingdom*, App. No. 58060/13, 03/03/2015.

[100] *Barr* v. *DPP* [2020] NICA 46 at [2].

[101] Ibid at [36]. For a discussion of the decision, see Neil Parpworth, 'Uniforms and Proscribed Organisations: Does a Proscribed Organisation Need to be Named in a s 13 Charge?: *Barr v Public Prosecution Service* [2020] NICA 46' (2021) **85** The Journal of Criminal Law 2.

[102] *Pwr* v. *DPP* [2022] UKSC 2, [2022] 1 WLR 789.

disproportionate interference with Article 10 ECHR (freedom of expression). The Divisional High Court held that s.13 *is* a strict liability offence and the Supreme Court unanimously agreed, holding that there is a limited mental element in that the wearing, carrying or displaying of the relevant article must be deliberate – a police officer carrying a flag that they have confiscated would, thus, not be caught by the provision – but there is no further mental element.[103] Accordingly, it was irrelevant that the defendants did not intend to express support for a proscribed organisation.

As for Article 10 ECHR, the Supreme Court concluded that while the offence constitutes an interference with freedom of expression, such an interference is proportionate to the legitimate aims of safeguarding national security and ensuring order. The appellants had argued that for the interference to be justified, there would need to be evidence that the impugned expression included an incitement to violence. This was rejected by the Supreme Court which endorsed the lower court's finding that there is no unequivocal statement from the ECtHR to the effect that 'a restriction on freedom of expression can only be justified where expression includes an incitement to violence'.[104]

Following recent protests in the UK against the war in Gaza, several people have been charged with and/or convicted of offences under s.13 based on their 'carrying or displaying an article, namely an image displaying a paraglider' such as 'to arouse reasonable suspicion that they are supporters of a proscribed organisation, namely Hamas'.[105]

8.3.1.5 *Recent Amendments to Terrorism Legislation*

Following terrorist attacks in London in 2019 and 2020,[106] new legislation imposing mandatory minimum sentences for 'serious terrorism offences' and

[103] Ibid at [26] and [58].

[104] Ibid at [74]. For more in respect of hate speech, incitement to violence and freedom of expression, see Chapter 11.

[105] CPS, 'CPS authorises charges against two women following protest in London', 3 November 2023, www.cps.gov.uk/cps/news/cps-authorises-charges-against-two-women-following-protest-london#:~:text=The%20Counter%20Terrorism%20Division%20is,secrets%20cases%2C%20piracy%20and%20hijacking. In terms of conviction, see CPS, 'Man who wore Hamas headband to central London rally is convicted', 25 April 2024, www.cps.gov.uk/cps/news/man-who-wore-hamas-headband-central-london-rally-convicted.

[106] For more information, see HH Judge Lucraft QC, *Inquests Arising from the Deaths in Fishmongers' Hall Terror Attack: Regulation 28 Report on Action to Prevent Future Deaths*, 3 November 2021, www.judiciary.uk/wp-content/uploads/2021/11/Fishmongers-Hall-Inquests-Prevention-of-future-deaths-report-2021-0362_Published-by-Chief-Coroner.pdf and IOPC, 'IOPC statement following the conclusion of inquest into the death of Sudesh Amman in Streatham', 20 August 2021, www.policeconduct.gov.uk/news/iopc-statement-following-conclusion-inquest-death-sudesh-amman-streatham.

other offences with a 'terrorist connection' was introduced,[107] as was legislation terminating the automatic release on licence of individuals convicted of terrorist or terrorism-related offences after they had served half of their sentence.[108] The latter legislation – the Terrorist Offenders (Restriction of Early Release) Act 2020 (TORER) – was the subject of an unsuccessful HRA challenge relying on Articles 5, 7 and 14 ECHR.[109] Key to the Court's finding with respect to Article 7 ECHR (which prohibits retrospective punishment) was the conclusion that changes to arrangements for early release do not amount to an imposition of a heavier penalty; the penalty remains the same.[110] Interestingly, a challenge to the same legislation on the basis of, inter alia, Article 7 ECHR *was* successful before the Northern Ireland Court of Appeal, though the Supreme Court subsequently overturned that decision.[111]

More recently, the National Security Act 2023 (NSA) was enacted. The Act is primarily concerned with espionage offences. However, Part 5 of the Act 'make[s] changes restricting both the award of damages (i.e. financial remedies in legal proceedings) in respect of those who have been involved in terrorist activity and the grant of legal aid to those with a terrorism-related conviction'.[112] As the IRTL (Hall KC) observed, this could be applied 'in a contract claim between two private parties before the County Court' but, in practice, it is likely such powers are intended to be available to the High Court in cases involving a terrorist suspect, 'for example a claim in which a convicted terrorist is applying for damages against the intelligence

[107] Counter-Terrorism and Sentencing Act 2021. For information on the Act when it was in bill form, see Jonathan Hall, 'Note on Counter-Terrorism and Sentencing Bill: Sentencing Reforms (1)', 1 June 2020 at [2]–[4], https://terrorismlegislationreviewer.independent.gov.uk/wp-content/uploads/2020/06/Note-1-on-Sentencing-Reforms-1.pdf.

[108] Terrorist Offenders (Restriction of Early Release) Act 2020. For more information, see Nicola Padfield KC, 'New Legislation: Statute Terrorist Offenders (Restriction of Early Release) Act 2020 (c.3)', *Criminal Law Week* (Issue 8, 4 March 2020). As the current IRTL (Hall KC) has observed in respect of TORER: 'Care must . . . be taken . . . to avoid a cliff-edge, where a defendant is released not on licence but at the very end of his sentence. After Fishmongers' Hall, the Terrorist Offenders (Restriction of Early Release) Act 2020 increased the possibility of this cliff-edge' (Hall, 'Response to Independent Sentencing Review Dated 12.12.24', 12 December 2024 at [5], https://terrorismlegislationreviewer.independent.gov.uk/wp-content/uploads/2024/12/IRTSL-to-sentencing-review.pdf.

[109] *R (Khan)* v. *Secretary of State for Justice* [2020] EWHC 2084 (Admin), [2020] 1 WLR 3932.

[110] Ibid at [104]–[105].

[111] *R* v. *Morgan Seamus & Ors* [2021] NICA 67 and *Morgan & Ors* v. *Ministry of Justice (Northern Ireland)* [2023] UKSC 14, [2024] AC 130.

[112] Joint Committee on Human Rights, 'Legislative Scrutiny: National Security Bill – Report Summary', 19 October 2022, https://publications.parliament.uk/pa/jt5803/jtselect/jtrights/297/summary.html.

agencies'.[113] The Joint Committee on Human Rights (JCHR) also noted that such powers have 'the potential to undermine effective enforcement of human rights and to interfere with the ECHR rights to an effective remedy under Article 13 ECHR and to respect for property under Article 1 Protocol 1 ECHR'.[114] Furthermore, according to the IRTL, the power goes further than is necessary and 'also risks the impression that if the government is sued, it will have a special advantage in keeping hold of monies which is not available to other unsuccessful parties in civil proceedings'.[115]

Finally, the Terrorism (Protection of Premises) Act 2025, commonly known as 'Martyn's Law' after one of the victims of the Manchester Arena bombing, received Royal Assent in April 2025 (though the Government has foreshadowed an implementation period of at least twenty-four months before the Act comes into force[116]). The Act creates a scheme 'under which publicly accessible venues and events would be required to take certain steps to reduce risk [of terrorist attacks], such as terrorism protection training, risk assessment and mitigation, and maintaining security plans'.[117] Not all venues or events are covered by the Act; they must be 'qualifying premises' (which is defined in s.2) or 'qualifying events' (which is defined in s.3).

8.3.2 Prevent Duty

The 'Prevent duty' was introduced via the Counter-Terrorism and Security Act 2015 (CTSA). Pursuant to s.26 CTSA, '[a] specified authority must, in the exercise of its functions, have due regard to the need to prevent people from being drawn into terrorism'. Specified authorities are listed in Schedule 6 and include local governments, governors of prisons in England and Wales, police officers of specified ranks, NHS trusts and educational institutions including, for instance, universities. The duty is part of the Government's 'Prevent strategy' which, in turn, forms part of the Government's counter-terrorism

[113] Jonathan Hall, 'Note on terrorism clauses in the National Security Bill', 23 May 2022 at [7]–[8], https://terrorismlegislationreviewer.independent.gov.uk/wp-content/uploads/2022/05/NS-Bill-Pt-3-Note.pdf.

[114] Joint Committee on Human Rights, 'Legislative Scrutiny: National Security Bill', HC297/HL Paper 73, 19 October 2022 at [146], https://committees.parliament.uk/publications/30344/documents/175399/default/.

[115] Hall (n 113) at [13].

[116] Home Office in the media, 'Martyn's law factsheet', 3 April 2025, https://homeofficemedia.blog.gov.uk/2025/04/03/martyns-law-factsheet/.

[117] House of Commons Library, 'Research Briefing: Draft Terrorism (Protection of Premises) Bill', 16 October 2023, https://commonslibrary.parliament.uk/research-briefings/cbp-9799/#:~:text=The%20draft%20Terrorism%20(Protection%20of,the%20public%20from%20terrorist%20attacks.

strategy which is known as CONTEST. There are four strands to CONTEST: *Pursue* (to stop terrorist attacks); *Prevent* (to stop people from becoming terrorists or supporting violent extremism); *Protect* (to strengthen protection against terrorist attack); and, *Prepare* (where an attack cannot be stopped, to mitigate its impact).[118]

The Prevent duty requires the specified authorities take steps to safeguard people from being drawn into terrorism. According to the most recent duty guidance document, the Prevent strategy has three objectives: (i) tackle the ideological causes of terrorism; (ii) intervene early to support people susceptible to radicalisation; and (iii) enable people who have already engaged in terrorism to disengage.[119] In the year ending March 2024, there were over 6,900 referrals to the Prevent programme, with the highest number coming from the education sector (40 per cent).[120] Notably, for the fourth year running, the number of referrals for XRW concerns was greater than referrals for Islamist concerns, though the category 'Vulnerability present but no ideology or [counter terrorism] risk' accounted for the largest proportion of referrals.[121]

In acknowledgement of the potential impact on free speech in educational institutions (in particular universities), s.31 CTSA specifically refers to the need to have regard to freedom of speech and 'the importance of academic freedom' when fulfilling the Prevent duty. Similarly, when issuing guidance under s.29, the Secretary of State must have regard to freedom of speech and academic freedom (per s.31). A specific Prevent guidance document for higher education bodies had previously been issued by the Secretary of State under s.29 CTSA and was subject to a partially successful legal challenge.[122] This higher education-specific guidance has since been replaced by the most recent Prevent duty guidance document.[123] Notably, the current guidance document provides that when deciding whether to host a particular speaker, education

[118] Jonathan Hall, 'The Terrorism Acts in 2018: Report of the Independent Reviewer of Terrorism Legislation on the operation of the Terrorism Acts 2000 and 2006, and the Terrorism Prevention and Investigation Measures Act 2011', March 2020 at [1.7], https://terrorismlegislationreviewer.independent.gov.uk/wp-content/uploads/2020/03/Terrorism-Acts-in-2018-Report.pdf.

[119] Home Office, 'Prevent duty guidance' (2023) at [17], www.gov.uk/government/publications/prevent-duty-guidance/revised-prevent-duty-guidance-for-england-and-wales.

[120] Home Office, 'Official Statistics: Individuals referred to and supported through the Prevent Programme, April 2023 to March 2024', 5 December 2024, https://www.gov.uk/government/statistics/individuals-referred-to-prevent-to-march-2024/individuals-referred-to-and-supported-through-the-prevent-programme-april-2023-to-march-2024.

[121] Ibid.

[122] *Butt* v. *The Secretary of State for the Home Department* [2019] EWCA Civ 256, [2019] 1 WLR 3873.

[123] Ibid at [1].

settings are recommended to 'undertake their own due diligence to understand any risks around a particular speaker', having regard to whether the views likely to be expressed will 'encourage people into participating in or supporting terrorism, or are shared by terrorist groups'.[124] Given the evolving nature of terrorism discussed above, the scope of the obligations on education settings in respect of assessing risks are not immediately apparent and further guidance will likely be necessary as issues inevitably arise.

8.3.3 Investigatory Powers

In this section, we examine the powers conferred on the police and other authorities to investigate terrorism, in particular the power to detain a person without charge and the power to stop and search a person. We will consider the implications of such powers for the rights to liberty as protected by Article 5 ECHR and the right to respect for private life (Article 8 ECHR). Powers directed at 'preventing' or 'controlling' terrorist suspects are considered separately.[125]

8.3.3.1 Stop and Search Powers

Previously, ss.44–46 TA 2000 empowered a police officer to stop individuals and vehicles in a specified area for the purposes of searching for articles that could be used in connection with terrorism, regardless of whether the police officer had reasonable grounds for believing such articles would be present on the person or in the vehicle. The lack of any requirement of 'reasonable suspicion' was extremely problematic and statistics revealed a disproportionate use of s.44 powers against people belonging to minority ethnicities.[126]

Section 44 was the subject of a successful challenge before the ECtHR in the case of *Gillan and Quinton* v. *the United Kingdom*.[127] The two applicants (a journalist and a protestor) – who had been stopped by police on their way to a demonstration against an arms fair – alleged that s.44 violated Article 8 ECHR. The ECtHR held that the stop and search power constituted an interference with private life and that the breadth of s.44 meant that it was not 'in accordance with law' as required by Article 8(2) ECHR. The fact that there

[124] Home Office, 'Prevent duty guidance' (n 119) at [191].

[125] See, Sections 8.3.2 (Prevent Duty) and 8.3.4.2 (Control Orders and Terrorism Prevention and Investigation Measures).

[126] *Gillan and Quinton* v. *the United Kingdom* (2010) 50 EHRR 45 at [86]. See also, Equality and Human Rights Commission, 'Stop and think: A critical review of the use of stop and search powers in England and Wales', March 2010, www.equalityhumanrights.com/sites/default/files/ehrc_stop_and_search_report.pdf.

[127] *Gillan and Quinton* (n 126).

was not even a suspicion requirement for the exercise of the power meant that there was a clear risk of arbitrariness and discrimination.

It is worth noting that the applicants in *Gillan and Quinton* had also alleged violations of Articles 5 and 10 ECHR. In respect of Article 5 ECHR, the UK argued that the applicants, who had been stopped for no more than thirty minutes,[128] had not been deprived of their liberty. The ECtHR rejected this contention. It did not matter that the applicants had been stopped for no more than thirty minutes; during this period the applicants were completely deprived of any freedom of movement: '[t]hey were obliged to remain where they were and submit to the search and if they had refused they would have been liable to arrest, detention at a police station and criminal charges. This element of coercion [was] indicative of a deprivation of liberty within the meaning of art.5(1)'.[129] As it transpired, given the finding with respect to Article 8 ECHR, the ECtHR did not consider it necessary to finally determine the Article 5 ECHR claim.

Following *Gillan and Quinton*, the s.44 power was repealed. Currently, the stop and search powers in the TA 2000 are as follows (in the context of suspected terrorism offences[130]):

1. Section 43: a power to stop and search a person reasonably suspected to be a terrorist to discover whether they have in their possession anything which may constitute evidence that they are a terrorist;[131]
2. Section 43A: a power to stop and search a vehicle which is reasonably suspected of being used for terrorism (and to search anyone in the vehicle), to discover whether there is evidence that the vehicle is being used for the purposes of terrorism;
3. Section 47A: a suspicion-less power that can only be used in extremely limited circumstances.[132]

In terms of s.47A TA 2000, an officer of a specific rank can grant authority for suspicion-less stops and searches in specific areas. The power to search extends to pedestrians, vehicles and the occupants thereof. The search can only be for the purpose of discovering evidence that the vehicle is being used for terrorism or that the person is a 'terrorist' as defined in s.40 TA 2000. And the authorising officer must reasonably suspect that an act of terrorism will

[128] There was a dispute between the parties as to whether one of the applicants had been stopped for five minutes or thirty minutes.

[129] *Gillan and Quinton* (n 126) at [57].

[130] Different provisions apply in the context of policing more generally. See, for instance, s.60 Criminal Justice and Public Order Act 1994 and ss.10 and 11 Public Order Act 2023.

[131] The latest data indicates that seventy-one persons were stopped and searched under s.43 in the year ending December 2024 which resulted in ten arrests: Home Office (n 33), Table S.01.

[132] Note also the suspicion-less stop and search power contained in s.11 Public Order Act 2023 as discussed in Chapter 12.

take place and that the authorisation is necessary to prevent that act (s.47A(1), TA 2000). The power has not been used since 2017.[133]

8.3.3.2 Port and Border Controls

Schedule 7 TA 2000[134] empowers police officers to 'examine' (i.e. stop and question) members of the public at ports and borders for the purpose of determining whether they are terrorists. Police are also empowered to search individuals, detain them, compel them to turn over their electronic devices (including for copying), and to take their biometric data. Refusal to comply is a criminal offence. Significantly, no reasonable suspicion is required to exercise the power.

The Schedule 7 powers have been the subject of several significant legal challenges, including proceedings based on the ECHR. As Schedule 7 has since been amended, the cases will not be considered in detail, but reference to them ought to be made given their role in the current formulation of the powers.

The appellant in *Miranda*[135] was the spouse of a journalist (Glenn Greenwald) and, to assist Greenwald in his journalistic activity, the appellant transported computer drives containing encrypted data provided by US National Security Agency (NSA) whistleblower Edward Snowden. The data was stolen by Snowden from the US NSA and revealed the use of mass surveillance by US authorities and was subsequently published by Greenwald and other journalists.[136] Miranda was stopped and detained under Schedule 7 by the Metropolitan Police at Heathrow Airport. While detained at the airport, he was questioned and items in his possession including encrypted storage devices were taken from him. He argued, inter alia, that the powers in Schedule 7 were disproportionate to any legitimate aim and violated Article 10 ECHR (which protects, amongst other things, the right to receive information). He ran a number of arguments with respect to Article 10 ECHR, with only one being successful, namely that the Schedule 7 power – at least insofar

[133] Home Office, Operation of police powers under TACT 2000, to December 2024, 13 March 2025 at [5], www.gov.uk/government/statistics/operation-of-police-powers-under-tact-2000-to-december-2024/operation-of-police-powers-under-the-terrorism-act-2000-and-subsequent-legislation-arrests-outcomes-and-stop-and-search-great-britain-quarterly-u.

[134] Similar powers are set out in the Counter-Terrorism and Border Security Act 2019, sch.3. These powers relate to individuals engaged in hostile activities on the behalf of third party States. Accordingly, these powers are not strictly related to terrorism.

[135] *R (Miranda)* v. *Secretary of State for the Home Department* [2016] EWCA Civ 6, [2016] 1 WLR 1505.

[136] Glenn Greenwald, Ewen MacAskill and Laura Poitras, 'Edward Snowden: The whistleblower behind the NSA surveillance revelations', *The Guardian*, 11 June 2013, www.theguardian.com/world/2013/jun/09/edward-snowden-nsa-whistleblower-surveillance.

as it was used in respect of journalistic material – was not in accordance with law. The argument – akin to that which had been successful before the ECtHR in *Gillan and Quinton* – was that the lack of safeguards meant that there was a risk that the Schedule 7 power would be arbitrarily exercised. The defects of the Schedule 7 power in this context were the absence of any express obligation on authorities to consider or take account of the right to freedom of expression and there was no provision for authorisation by a court or independent and impartial decision-making body in a case involving journalistic material.

In *Beghal* v. *the United Kingdom*,[137] the applicant – a French national ordinarily resident in the UK – was stopped upon arriving in the UK on a flight from Paris, where she and her three children had visited her husband who was being held in custody in relation to terrorist offences. She was taken to an examination room and her luggage was searched. The applicant was given an opportunity to speak with her lawyer on the phone, though the police would not delay her questioning in order for her lawyer to be present. She was asked a number of questions all of which she refused to answer. The questioning lasted approximately thirty minutes. Beghal was subsequently charged with several offences including two stemming from her failure to answer the officers' questions, and she ultimately pleaded guilty to wilfully failing to comply with a duty under Schedule 7 TA 2000 for which she was sentenced to a conditional discharge. She appealed alleging that there had been an abuse of process based on a violation of her rights under Articles 5, 6 (right to a fair trial) and 8 ECHR. The High Court rejected the applicant's appeal as did the Supreme Court (by a majority, with Lord Kerr dissenting).[138]

Beghal then applied to the ECtHR. The ECtHR held that the Schedule 7 power was not subject to adequate safeguards. It concluded that, 'while . . . the absence of any requirement of "reasonable suspicion" [was not] alone . . . fatal to the lawfulness of the regime', there had been a violation of Article 8 ECHR when the lack of those safeguards were:

> considered together with the fact that the examination could continue for up to nine hours, during which time the person would be compelled to answer questions without any right to have a lawyer present, and the possibility of judicially reviewing the exercise of the power would be limited.[139]

The Anti-Social Behaviour, Crime and Policing Act 2014 and the Counter-Terrorism and Border Security Act 2019 subsequently amended Schedule 7 to introduce certain safeguards addressing the shortcomings identified in

[137] *Beghal* v. *the United Kingdom* (2019) 69 EHRR 28.

[138] *Beghal* v. *Director of Public Prosecutions* [2015] UKSC 49, [2016] AC 88.

[139] *Beghal* v. *the United Kingdom* (n 137) at [109].

Miranda and *Beghal*.[140] However, the Nationality and Borders Act 2022 further amended Schedule 7 to extend the powers to stop and search to individuals who are not physically present at a port or border area but who have arrived in the UK by sea within the previous five days and have been arrested or detained under the Immigration Acts.[141] In July 2022, the Home Office issued a new Code of Practice which takes into account the amendments made by the Nationality and Borders Act 2022.[142] Notably, the Code of Practice directs examiners and reviewers that:

> It is not appropriate for race, ethnic background, religion and/or other 'protected characteristics' (whether separately or together) to be used as criteria for selection except to the extent that they are used in association with considerations that relate to the threat from terrorism.[143]

The current IRTL has observed that the Schedule 7 examination powers – which were exercised in respect of 2,401 people in the year ending December 2024[144] – are 'valuable and justified counter-terrorism power[s]' which enable 'authorities to detect and deter terrorist activity within and outside the UK'.[145] Nevertheless, as *Miranda* and *Beghal* demonstrate, such powers may be incompatible with the ECHR where there are inadequate safeguards in place. Indeed, even with the safeguards inserted following those cases, there are still instances of questionable uses of the Schedule 7 powers, as illustrated by the stop and search of Ernest Moret which has been subject to criticism.[146] Moret, a publisher from France, was stopped at St Pancras station as part of 'a planned intelligence-led stop based, in summary, on information that Mr Moret may be associated with violent extremism or terrorism overseas'.[147] As Hall KC observed in his report as IRTL into Moret's examination under Schedule 7:

[140] For instance, reducing the maximum period of examination from nine to six hours (and if officers wish to examine a person for longer than one hour, they must formally detain them under Schedule 7 which ensures access to legal advice).

[141] Nationality and Borders Act 2022, Explanatory Memorandum at [738].

[142] Home Office, 'Examining Officers and Review Officers under Schedule 7 to the Terrorism Act 2000: Code of Practice', July 2022, Part 5, https://assets.publishing.service.gov.uk/government/uploads/system/uploads/attachment_data/file/1088709/Schedule_7_Code_of_Practice_-_July_2022.pdf. As this book was going to print, a new code of practice was being discussed by the Government in respect of Schedule 7. That draft contains a similarly worded provision with respect to the need for authorities to act in accordance with the Equality Act 2010 (Home Office, 'Draft revised Schedule 7 Code of Practice: July 2025', 9 July 2025, https://www.gov.uk/government/publications/codes-of-practice-for-officers-using-examination-powers-at-ports/draft-revised-schedule-7-code-of-practice-july-2025-accessible).

[143] Ibid at [30]. [144] Home Office (n 33), Table S_03.a.

[145] Jonathan Hall, 'Report on the use of Schedule 7 powers against Ernest Moret', 21 July 2023 at [14], https://terrorismlegislationreviewer.independent.gov.uk/wp-content/uploads/2023/07/IRTL-Moret-Report.pdf.

[146] Ibid. [147] Ibid at [33].

> [i]t is clear that the substance of the questioning was directed entirely towards establishing whether Mr Moret was involved in violent demonstrations. As part of this, he was asked about his political views and those of his associates.[148]

Hall KC ultimately concluded that '[i]t has never been the case that terrorism powers should be exercised merely because it is possible to use them' and 'based on the information provided, police both *could* have decided not to exercise the power, and *should* have decided not to exercise the power'.[149] The alleged suspicion regarding Moret arose because of his potential involvement in anti-Government protests in France which had turned violent. But, as the IRTL recognised '[t]he rights of free expression and protest are too important in a democracy to allow individuals to be investigated for potential terrorism merely because they may have been involved in protests that have turned violent'.[150]

8.3.4 Detention and Liberty

This section considers the powers conferred upon police and other authorities to detain or restrict the movement of individuals suspected of being engaged in (or connected to) terrorism.

8.3.4.1 Pre-charge/No-Charge Detention

Perhaps the most notorious power exercised by the authorities when investigating terrorism is the power to detain without charge. Given the significance that both the common law and Article 5 ECHR place on individual liberty,[151] it is unsurprising that the UK's response to terrorism via pre-charge detention has been the subject of considerable domestic and Strasbourg jurisprudence.

Article 5 ECHR protects the right to liberty and security of the person. Only in the explicitly listed circumstances in Article 5(1)(a)–(f) ECHR can a person be legitimately deprived of their liberty. The ECtHR has held that the exceptions outlined in Article 5(1)(a)–(f) ECHR are exhaustive; if the deprivation is not for one of the listed reasons, it will violate Article 5 ECHR.[152] For the reasons set out below, it is significant to note that Article 5 does not permit indefinite detention without charge. For those individuals who fall within one of the exceptions, there are express protections in Article 5(2)–(5) ECHR

148 Ibid at [55]. 149 Ibid at [56]. Emphasis in original.

150 Ibid at [57]. The IRTL's observations regarding the use of Schedule 7 powers in respect of Moret prompted a specific provision in the proposed new code of practice which provides that 'Schedule 7 powers should not be used for the purpose of public order policing' (Draft revised Schedule 7 Code of Practice (n 142) at [9]).

151 For an exposition, see Lady Hale's reasons in *R (Jalloh)* v. *Secretary of State for the Home Department* [2020] UKSC 4, [2021] AC 262.

152 See, for instance, *Austin* v. *the United Kingdom* [GC] (2012) 55 EHRR 14, which concerned the kettling by police of protestors and those caught up with them.

including a requirement that they be 'promptly informed . . . of the reasons for [their] arrest and of any charge' (Article 5(2) ECHR) and that they be entitled to bring proceedings before a court to determine the lawfulness of their detention (Article 5(4) ECHR).

8.3.4.1.1 *Pre-charge Detention under Terrorism Legislation*

Since the 9/11 terrorist attacks, the period during which a person can be detained without charge in the context of investigating terrorism has fluctuated considerably. Under the TA 2000 as enacted, police officers could arrest and detain for up to forty-eight hours a person reasonably suspected of being concerned in the commission, preparation or instigation of acts of terrorism (s.41). Thereafter, a judicial authority could extend the period of detention for up to a further five days (i.e. seven days in total). This period was extended to a maximum fourteen days in 2003 (via the Criminal Justice Act 2003), then to twenty-eight days in 2006 (per s.23 TA 2006). The Government had sought a ninety-day period, but this was defeated in the House of Commons. The TA 2006 included a sunset clause such that the pre-charge detention period would revert to a maximum of fourteen days after a year, unless renewed. In 2012 the Protection of Freedoms Act 2012 (s.57) confirmed that the period was fourteen days (the provision increasing it to twenty-eight days having lapsed).[153]

Outside of s.41 TA 2000, pre-charge detention is covered by the Police and Criminal Evidence Act 1984 (PACE) which allows for detention of up to ninety-six hours. According to the most recent data, the overwhelming majority of individuals arrested for terrorism-related offences are detained under non-terrorism arrest powers (such as PACE).[154] For those individuals who are detained under s.41 TA 2000 and for whom data was available, all were held for eight days or less.[155]

The ECtHR has considered UK legislation authorising pre-charge detention on several occasions. In *Brogan* v. *the United Kingdom*[156] the four applicants were arrested based on their suspected involvement with the IRA. They were detained for between four and six days. Under the relevant legislation, the power to detain was limited to an initial forty-eight-hour period though after that a senior police officer could (subject to authorisation by the Secretary of State for Northern Ireland) extend the detention up to a total of seven days. While detained, none of the applicants were brought before a judge or other appropriately authorised officer for the purposes of considering the lawfulness of their detention and none of the applicants were charged. The ECtHR held that there had been a violation of Article 5(3) ECHR which requires that where

[153] House of Commons Library, 'Pre-Charge Detention in Terrorism Cases', SN/HA/5634, 15 March 2012, https://researchbriefings.files.parliament.uk/documents/SN05634/SN05634.pdf.

[154] Home Office (n 33), Table A.01.

[155] Ibid, Table A.02.

[156] *Brogan* v. *the United Kingdom* (1989) 11 EHRR 117.

individuals have been arrested or detained for the purposes of bringing them before a competent legal authority on reasonable suspicion of having committed an offence (as is permitted under Article 5(1)(c) ECHR), they must be brought promptly before a judge or appropriately authorised officer. Even the shortest period of detention –four days and six hours – fell 'outside the strict constraints as to time permitted' by the requirement of 'promptness' in Article 5(3) ECHR.[157]

Following *Brogan,* the UK derogated from Article 5(3) ECHR under Article 15 ECHR[158] and, in *Brannigan* v. *the United Kingdom,*[159] the ECtHR found that derogation to be valid given the ongoing sectarian violence in Northern Ireland. There were, however, several strongly worded dissents which questioned the bona fides of the derogation, in particular whether it was truly a response to a public emergency threatening the life of the nation or whether it was a mechanism to get around *Brogan.*[160] In the years following *Brannigan* the nature of terrorism changed and so did the UK's response to it. It was in that context that *Belmarsh*[161] was decided.

8.3.4.1.2 *No-Charge Detention:* Belmarsh

Following the 9/11 attacks, the UK Parliament enacted the Anti-terrorism, Crime and Security Act 2001 (ATCSA). One of the core provisions of this statute was the power vested in the Secretary of State under Part 4 (specifically s.23) to issue a certificate authorising the indefinite detention without charge of a non-national who the Secretary of State reasonably believed posed a risk to national security by being in the UK and was a 'terrorist'. 'Terrorist' was defined in s.21(2) by reference to affiliation with international terrorism (i.e. the ATCSA did not cover individuals involved in domestic terrorism). The purported need to detain indefinitely and without charge arose as these individuals could not be deported under existing immigration legislation because to do so would put them at risk of torture or inhuman or degrading treatment contrary to Article 3 ECHR.[162] There was also insufficient evidence to charge them with criminal offences relating to terrorism.

Not only is indefinite detention without charge or trial 'anathema in any country which observes the rule of law',[163] it is also incompatible with Article 5 ECHR. Under Article 5(1)(f) ECHR, a person may be detained where 'action is being taken with a view to deportation or extradition' but that was not the case in respect of 'non-national suspected terrorists' detained under s.23 ATCSA: they could not be deported. Exercise of the detention power under s.23 ATCSA would, thus, violate Article 5. However, Article 5 ECHR is a

[157] Ibid at [62]. [158] For more on derogations, see Chapter 3 (European Framework).

[159] *Brannigan and McBride* v. *the United Kingdom* (1994) 17 EHRR 539.

[160] See, in particular, the dissenting opinions of Judge Pettiti and Judge De Meyer, ibid.

[161] *A and Ors* v. *Secretary of State for the Home Department* [2004] UKHL 56, [2005] 2 AC 68.

[162] See the discussion of refoulement in Chapter 5.

[163] *A and Ors* (n 161) at [74], per Lord Nicholls.

'derogable' right pursuant to Article 15 ECHR; as discussed in Chapter 3 (European Framework) in times of war or public emergencies threatening the life of the nation, States can take measures – to the extent strictly required by the exigencies of the situation – that would otherwise violate certain ECHR rights. Accordingly, the Secretary of State issued a derogation order[164] in respect of Article 5(1)(f) ECHR following the enactment of ATCSA.

The appellants in *Belmarsh* – all of whom had been certified as suspected foreign terrorists and subsequently detained in Belmarsh Prison under s.23 ATCSA – challenged the lawfulness of the derogation order and, relatedly, the lawfulness of their detention without charge: if the derogation order was invalid, then their detention violated Article 5 ECHR. The question for the House of Lords was whether the derogation was lawful which required a consideration of the requirements under Article 15 ECHR.

The appellants argued that the derogation was unlawful as there was no state of emergency and thus the threshold test for Article 15 ECHR had not been met. The House of Lords held by eight judges to one that a state of emergency existed. Lord Hope assessed the evidence and considered: '[i]t is an emergency which is constituted by the threat that these attacks will be carried out. It threatens the life of the nation because of the appalling consequences that would affect us all if they were to occur here. But it cannot yet be said that these attacks are imminent.'[165] Although Lord Bingham had misgivings, he was persuaded that the question of whether there was a state of emergency was 'very much at the political end of the spectrum', observing that it is 'the function of political and not judicial bodies to resolve political questions'.[166] Lord Hoffmann famously disagreed with the majority judges on this assessment of an emergency which in his opinion had to threaten 'our institutions of government or our existence as a civil community' and, based on that standard, he concluded that the Government had not established the existence of an emergency. In his view:

> The real threat to the life of the nation, in the sense of a people living in accordance with its traditional laws and political values, comes not from terrorism but from laws such as these. That is the true measure of what terrorism may achieve. It is for Parliament to decide whether to give the terrorists such a victory.[167]

As Article 15(3) ECHR requires that a State should not take any measures in a derogation which go beyond that which is 'strictly required by the exigencies of the situation', the majority went on to assess the detention scheme. The Government had forcefully submitted that it was for the executive and Parliament, and not the judiciary, to decide on the actions needed to protect public security when (as the majority had accepted) there was a state of emergency. The majority, however, rejected this

[164] Pursuant to the power vested by s.14 HRA, the Secretary of State issued the Human Rights Act 1998 (Designated Derogation) Order 2001.

[165] *A & Ors* (n 161) at [119]. [166] Ibid at [29]. [167] Ibid at [97].

contention. They determined for three reasons that the measures did not rationally address the terrorism threat and it was a disproportionate response. First, the scheme applied only to non-nationals even though some nationals were also suspected of being a threat.[168] The Government failed to provide a satisfactory explanation of why it was necessary to detain indefinitely one group of people but not the other, even though they share the same characteristics and pose the same potential threat.[169] In fact, the Government considered that it would be a draconian step to lock up nationals which could not be justified at this stage. Lady Hale concluded: 'if it is not necessary to lock up the nationals it cannot be necessary to lock up the foreigners. It is not strictly required by the exigencies of the situation.'[170] Further evidence of the disproportionate effect of the s.23 power was located in the fact that suspected foreign terrorists were not prohibited from leaving the UK of their own volition.[171] While the State could not deport or otherwise remove them because of concerns regarding the risk of ill-treatment, there was nothing stopping those individuals who were detained from deciding that they would leave the UK (as some, in fact, did). This was a 'the central complaint made by the appellants', namely that:

> the choice of an immigration measure to address a security problem had the inevitable result of failing adequately to address that problem (by allowing non-UK suspected terrorists to leave the country with impunity and leaving British suspected terrorists at large) while imposing the severe penalty of indefinite detention on persons who, even if reasonably suspected of having links with Al-Qaeda, may harbour no hostile intentions towards the United Kingdom.)[172]

Finally, the legislation was inconsistent with the UK's other obligations under international law from which there had been no derogation, in particular Article 14 ECHR (freedom from discrimination). The legislation failed to treat like cases alike: non-nationals and nationals posed the same risk, and yet they were treated differently, on the basis of the protected characteristic of nationality.[173] As Lady Hale so eloquently put it:

> Democracy values each person equally. In most respects, this means that the will of the majority must prevail. But valuing each person equally also means that the

168 Ibid at [54], per Lord Bingham.

169 See, for instance, ibid at [53]–[54], per Lord Bingham.

170 Ibid at [231].

171 As Lord Hope observed '[t]here is no safe country to which they can be extradited, but they are free to leave the United Kingdom at any time if they wish and can find another safe country to which they can go' (ibid at [123]).

172 Ibid at [43], per Lord Bingham.

173 As Lady Hale observed, non-national suspected international terrorists 'are just like a British national who cannot be deported. The relevant circumstances making the two cases alike for this purpose are the same three which constitute the problem: a suspected international terrorist, who for a variety of reasons cannot be successfully prosecuted, and who for a variety of reasons cannot be deported or expelled': ibid at [235].

will of the majority cannot prevail if it is inconsistent with the equal rights of minorities.

...

No one has the right to be an international terrorist. But substitute 'black', 'disabled', 'female', 'gay', or any other similar adjective for 'foreign' before 'suspected international terrorist' and ask whether it would be justifiable to take power to lock up that group but not the 'white', 'able-bodied', 'male' or 'straight' suspected international terrorists. The answer is clear.[174]

Having determined that the derogation order was disproprtionte, the House of Lords granted a quashing order in respect of the derogation order and made a declaration of incompatibility under s.4 HRA in respect of s.23 ATCSA. The appellants' subsequent complaint to the ECtHR was discussed in Chapter 3 (European Framework), though it is worth noting that the State sought to reargue the legitimacy (specifically, the proportionality) of the derogation before the ECtHR which, consistent with the House of Lords, found that it was disproportionate on the basis that the measures discriminated unjustifiably between nationals and non-nationals.[175] The ECtHR also found a violation of the ECHR on the basis of the use of closed material proceedings which is discussed further below.

While the House of Lords' judgment in *Belmarsh* could be labelled a 'success' for rights protection,[176] the Government and Parliament responded to the decision by introducing control orders and, subsequently, Terrorism Prevention and Investigation Measures (TPIMs) which, as the ensuing section reveals, are profoundly limiting in terms of the liberty and other rights and interests of the individuals who are subjected to them.

8.3.4.2 Control Orders and Terrorism Prevention and Investigation Measures

8.3.4.2.1 Control Orders

The control order 'scheme' was introduced via the Prevention of Terrorism Act 2005 (PTA). Under the PTA, the Secretary of State was permitted to make non-derogating control orders[177] if they had 'reasonable grounds for suspecting

[174] Ibid at [237]–[238], per Lady Hale.

[175] *A and Ors* v. *the United Kingdom* [GC] (2009) 49 EHRR 29 at [190].

[176] For a summary of that argument, and an articulation of the counterpoint, see Conor Gearty, 'Human Rights in the Age of Counter-Terrorism: Injurous, Irrelevant or Indispensible?' (2005) 58 *Current Legal Problems* 1.

[177] The Prevention of Terrorism Act 2005 also introduced derogating control orders – which could only be made by the court (upon the application of the Secretary of State). But no derogation order under s.14 of the HRA was ever made for the purposes of such orders being issued (Lord Carlile of Berriew CBE KC, 'Sixth Report of the Independent Reviewer Pursuant to Section 14(3) of the Prevention of Terrorism Act 2005', 3 February 2011 at [13], https://assets.publishing.service.gov.uk/media/5a789afa40f0b62b22cbb53e/lord-carlile-sixth-report.pdf.

that the individual is or has been involved in terrorism-related activity' and they considered it 'necessary, for the purposes connected with protecting members of the public from a risk of terrorism' (s.2(1) PTA). The orders could be made in respect of non-nationals *and* nationals (in contrast to the detention power in s.23 ATCSA that was the subject of *Belmarsh*). A non-derogating control order had effect for twelve months, though it could be renewed for a further twelve months if the same conditions set out in s.2(1) were met (s.2(4) PTA). There was no statutory limit on the conditions that could be set with a control order, though s.1(4) PTA detailed various obligations that could be imposed. Perhaps the most significant mechanism of control was restricting a person's ability to leave their home. Some of the early control orders required a person to remain in their residence for up to eighteen hours each day. This, it must be recalled, was imposed in circumstances where the UK had not derogated from Article 5 ECHR. Moreover, the exceptions to the right to liberty listed in Article 5(1) ECHR are *exhaustive* – that is, if a person is deprived of their liberty and the reason does not fit within one of those exceptions, the deprivation will violate Article 5 ECHR (unless there has been a valid derogation). As was made very clear by the House of Lords in *Belmarsh*, neither the common law nor Article 5 ECHR permits the indefinite detention of a person without charge. It is, then, perhaps unsurprising that a number of the early control orders were found by the courts to violate Article 5 ECHR.

The six respondents in *JJ*[178] were subject to control orders under the PTA, which confined them to their respective one-bedroom flats for eighteen hours per day. All bar one of the respondents had been forced to relocate. When permitted to leave their flat (between 10am and 4pm), there were further restrictions on where they could go. Visitors to their residences had to be approved beforehand by the Home Office and they were not permitted to meet anyone who did not have clearance. Their homes were subject to searches by the police and their movements were monitored by way of electronic tags. They were not allowed access to the internet. On appeal before the House of Lords, a 3:2 majority held that they had been deprived of their liberty in violation of Article 5 ECHR (there being no suggestion of the deprivation falling within one of the limited exceptions in Article 5 ECHR). Having regard to the concrete circumstances of each of the respondents, Lady Hale concluded that '[u]ndoubtedly, these people were deprived of their liberty during the curfew hours'.[179] The fact that they were permitted out for six hours each day made no difference; '[t]he reality is that every aspect of their lives was severely controlled'.[180] Indeed, 'in several respects a prisoner might be better off'.[181]

[178] *Secretary of State for the Home Department* v. *JJ and Ors* [2007] UKHL 45, [2008] AC 385.
[179] Ibid at [61], per Lady Hale. [180] Ibid at [62]. [181] Ibid.

In a subsequent case involving a sixteen-hour curfew,[182] the Supreme Court again held that the appellant had been deprived of his liberty under Article 5 ECHR. In reaching that conclusion, the Court emphasised that a curfew of sixteen hours or less would not, *per se*, constitute a deprivation of liberty. Rather, other conditions imposed would have to be 'unusually destructive of the life that the controlee might otherwise have been living' in order for them to be deprived of their liberty.[183] In this case, the particularly isolating effects of the control order (the controlee was relocated to the Midlands, 150 miles away from his family in London which had the effect that his mother could not visit him) were such that this aspect of the order violated Article 5 ECHR.

The courts' response to the control order regime, including the decisions of the House of Lords and Supreme Court outlined above, played no small part in the repeal of the regime. However, according to Helen Fenwick, the finding that control orders *could* be (and *were*) compatible with Article 5 ECHR in specific circumstances allowed Parliament to 'transmute[. . .] the [control order regime] into a modified version of itself in 2011 that came close to achieving ... compatibility' with the 'attenuated' version of Article 5 ECHR that the courts had developed in the control order case law.[184]

8.3.4.2.2 *Terrorism Prevention and Investigation Measures (TPIMs)*

In 2011 control orders were repealed and Terrorism Prevention and Investigation Measures (TPIMs) were introduced.[185] TPIMs:

> are anticipatory, in that they seek to forestall future terrorist harm but require some proof of involvement in terrorism-related activity. As with the former control order regime, their greatest drawback is that morally culpable behaviour is addressed outside the criminal process and subject to closed procedures from which the TPIM subject is excluded.[186]

Under the Terrorism Prevention and Investigation Measures Act 2011 (TPIMA) the Secretary of State is empowered to impose a TPIM on a person if they reasonably believe that an individual is, or has been, involved in 'terrorism-related activity' (s.3(1) TPIMA).[187] Terrorism-related activity is defined in s.4 by reference to the definition of terrorism in s.1 TA 2000.[188] The Secretary of State must also reasonably consider it necessary, 'for purposes connected with

[182] *Secretary of State for the Home Department* v. *AP* [2010] UKSC 24, [2011] 2 AC 1.

[183] Ibid at [4].

[184] Helen Fenwick, 'Terrorism and the Control Orders/TPIMs Saga: A Vindication of the Human Rights Act Or a Manifestation of "Defensive Democracy"?' [2017] PL 609, p.614.

[185] Terrorism Prevention and Investigation Measures Act 2011.

[186] Hall (n 34) at [8.2].

[187] The standard was reduced from the balance of probabilities via the Counter Terrorism and Sentencing Act 2021.

[188] Per s.30(1) TPIMA.

protecting members of the public from a risk of terrorism', for a TPIM to be imposed and for the specific TPIM to be imposed on the individual (ss.3(3) and (4) TPIMA). The Secretary of State must obtain the court's permission to impose a TPIM unless the Secretary of State reasonably considers that the urgency of the case requires the imposition of the TPIM (s.3(5) TPIMA).

Whereas the conditions that could be imposed under a control order were unlimited, the same is not true of TPIMs. Schedule 1 of the TPIMA sets out the measures that can be imposed which include a requirement that the individual live in a specific residence and that they stay in that residence during specific hours. In their initial iteration a generalised relocation power was not a included under the TPIMA. This changed in 2015 with the CTSA which removed a number of the restrictions on the relocation power in Schedule 1. Pursuant to s.1(3A) of Schedule 1 relocation can be over 200 miles away from where the individual was residing at the time the TPIM is imposed (provided the residence is in 'an agreed locality'). Zedner has characterised such forcible relocation as a form of 'internal exile' and has queried the efficacy of such restrictions as counter-terrorism measures given that they may well 'exacerbate [the individual's] sense of alienation', thereby *increasing* the risk such individuals may pose to national security.[189] Previously, individuals subject to TPIMs could only be required to remain in their residences 'overnight' (the Government distinguished this from control orders which could require a person to remain in their residence for 'up to 16 hours').[190] However, following the enactment of the CTSA 2021, the Secretary of State can specify 'the hours' during which a person is required to stay at home (Schedule 1, s.1(2)(c)).[191]

TPIMs have effect for an initial period of one year (s.5 TPIMA), though (subject to certain requirements) a TPIM notice can be extended on up to four occasions (i.e. resulting in a total five-year period). Safeguards include an ongoing duty on the Secretary of State to review the continuing necessity of the TPIM, reporting requirements (s.19 TPIMA) and a duty on the Secretary of State, prior to imposing a TPIM, to consult with police regarding the

[189] Lucia Zedner, 'Curtailing Citizenship Rights as Counterterrorism' in Benjamin Goold and Liora Lazarus (eds), *Security and Human Rights* (2nd ed.) (Hart Publishing, 2019), pp.113–114.

[190] ECHR Memorandum by the Home Office, *Terrorism Prevention and Investigation Measures (TPIM) Bill* at [17], https://assets.publishing.service.gov.uk/government/uploads/system/uploads/attachment_data/file/98372/echr-memorandum.pdf.

[191] Given the findings of the UKSC in the cases concerning control orders, it seems unlikely that such periods will extend beyond sixteen hours. Indeed, as recognised in the Explanatory Memorandum accompanying the relevant amendments to the TPIMA: 'This period could be longer than overnight if considered necessary in a particular case (subject to the overriding restrictions on length of curfews established by caselaw relating to Article 5 of the European Convention on Human Rights)' (Counter Terrorism and Sentencing Bill, Explanatory Memorandum at [231], https://publications.parliament.uk/pa/bills/cbill/58-01/0129/en/20129en.pdf).

availability of evidence that 'could realistically be used for the purposes of prosecuting the individual for an offence related to terrorism' (s.10(2) TPIMA). While this is clearly an important safeguard, the IRTL has found that both the Secretary of State and their officials see the consultation requirement as nothing more than a 'tick in the box'.[192] According to the current IRTL, '[the title of TPIMs] is something of a misnomer: no measures are imposed specifically for the purpose of investigation. There is merely a duty to keep the question of prosecution for terrorism-related activity under review.'[193] And, as a former IRTL observed, 'it is in the public interest for the conventional charge and trial process to be used whenever possible, rather than control orders [and, today, TPIMs]'.[194]

While there may be greater safeguards under the TPIMA than under the PTA (which introduced control orders), that does not mean that they do not violate the rights of those subjected to them. In *DD*[195] the High Court was asked to determine whether a TPIM violated a man's right to freedom from inhuman or degrading treatment under Article 3 ECHR as the requirements of the TPIM were exacerbating the symptoms of his 'mental illness which [were] [post-traumatic stress disorder], and either paranoid schizophrenia or a schizoaffective disorder, depressive type'.[196] Mr Justice Ouseley determined that Article 3 ECHR was *not* violated because of the reason for the imposition of the TPIM. As discussed in Chapter 5, the prohibition on ill-treatment in Article 3 ECHR is absolute; the purported justification cannot transform ill-treatment that is contrary to Article 3 ECHR into Article 3-compliant treatment. Unsurprisingly, that determination was appealed and the Divisional Court held that the minimum level of severity *had* been met in DD's case and the monitoring element of the TPIM was quashed. In reaching that conclusion, Mr Justice Collins stated '[i]t seems that it was believed that Ouseley J had indicated that even if the effect of the TPIM was to breach Article 3 the interest of national security could prevail. He did not so indicate *nor would it have been a correct application of the law if he had*'.[197] TPIMs are, thus, not immune from challenge under the HRA based on violations of the ECHR.

[192] Hall (n 118) at [8.22]. [193] Ibid at [8.4] referring to s.10 TPIMA.

[194] Lord Carlile (n 177) at [6].

[195] *DD* v. *Secretary of State for the Home Department* [2014] EWHC 3820 (Admin), [2015] 1 WLR 2217.

[196] Ibid at [112].

[197] *DD* v. *Secretary of State for the Home Department* [2015] EWHC 1681 (Admin) at [10]. Emphasis added. For a more fulsome discussion of the case, see Stevie Martin, 'The role of legitimacy and proportionality in the (supposedly absolute) prohibition on inhuman and degrading treatment: The United Kingdom's High Court decisions in DD v. Secretary of State', *EJIL:Talk!*, 22 December 2015, www.ejiltalk.org/the-role-of-legitimacy-and-proportionality-in-the-supposedly-absolute-prohibition-on-inhuman-and-degrading-treatment-the-united-kingdoms-high-court-decisions-in-dd-v-secretary-of-state/.

TPIMs – like control orders – are 'seriously resource intensive' for both the individual and the Home Office, police and MI5.[198] Data from the most recent reporting period reveals that there were three TPIMs in force (two were existing, and one new TPIM was issued), with each subject being a British citizen and two subjects being relocated.[199] Notably, in 2022, 'for the first time, a TPIM notice was served on an individual believed to be involved in [XRW] Terrorism'.[200] Not only do such measures have the potential to significantly impact the rights of the individuals subject to them (as well as their families),[201] but breach of a TPIM carries criminal sanctions and can lead to individuals being imprisoned. The risk that neurodivergent individuals and those with mental health issues (as was the case in *DD*) are being subjected to TPIMs, with the attendant potential of breaching 'the numerous and detailed requirements' imposed by them has been noted by the current IRTL who has also observed that 'TPIM subjects should avoid being set up to fail. Otherwise a TPIM is not really a tool for managing risk in the community, but a speedy route to prison.'[202] In the most recent report of the IRTL, Hall noted his 'impression of the resource-intensive and humane approach taken by officials and police to TPIM subjects ... experiencing poor mental health'.[203]

8.3.5 Citizenship and Exclusion

The efflux of British nationals to Syria and Iraq and their subsequent return and/or detention in Kurdish-run camps in Syria raised significant issues in terms of the UK's obligations under domestic human rights law and international humanitarian and human rights law. From 2013, approximately '900 UK-linked individuals of national security concern' travelled to engage in the Syrian conflict.[204] While 25 per cent are believed to have been killed, approximately 360 returned to the UK. As at March 2023, fourteen returners had been

[198] Hall (n 118) at [8.23].

[199] UK Parliament House of Commons, 'Terrorism Prevention and Investigation Measures (1 December 2024 to 28 February 2025)', Statement UIN HCWS604, 25 April 2025, https://questions-statements.parliament.uk/written-statements/detail/2025-04-25/hcws604.

[200] Jonathan Hall, 'The Terrorism Acts in 2022: Report of the Independent Reviewer of Terrorism Legislation on the Operation of the Terrorism Acts 2000 and 2006, and the Terrorism Prevention and Investigation Measures Act 2011', 28 November 2024 at [8.11], https://assets.publishing.service.gov.uk/media/674848622ac8a6da30723942/E03236791_-_IRTL_Annual_Report_2022_Accessible.pdf.

[201] See, for instance, the description of the restrictions imposed on one individual under a TPIM in Hall (n 34) at [8.4] (for a full discussion of that particular situation, see *Secretary of State for the Home Department* v. *JM and LF* [2021] EWHC 266 (Admin)).

[202] Hall (n 20) at [8.27].

[203] Hall (n 200) at [8.24].

[204] Hall (n 20) at at [2.23].

convicted of Islamist terrorist offences in relation to their conduct in Syria or based on documents seized in the UK after their departure or upon their return.[205] Travel to conflict zones has continued to present an issue for the UK's security services, with the current IRTL observing 'contemporary conflicts are becoming increasingly transnational in nature' and '[e]merging destinations include the Sahel in Africa (especially Mali), while post-US withdrawal Afghanistan has resurrected fears about terrorist safe havens'.[206] An additional mechanism that has been employed to address the purported risk posed by UK nationals/dual nationals who have travelled to participate in an overseas conflict has been to place restrictions on their right to return to the UK.

While restrictions on citizens' rights of movement are not a new tactic in countering terrorism, '[c]urtailing citizens' rights of freedom of movement has become a key aspect of UK security policy' in recent years.[207] One way in which this is achieved is by 'shutting out' individuals who have a right to reside and are seeking to return to the UK where they have been deemed to be a threat to national security. This is achieved primarily through the imposition of Temporary Exclusion Orders which are discussed in this section. Another, more draconian mechanism by which the UK has sought to preclude individuals from returning (particularly those who travelled to Syria and Iraq to align with ISIS) is through the deprivation of British citizenship. This too is discussed in the ensuing section.

8.3.5.1 Deprivation of Citizenship

Under s.40(2) British Nationality Act 1981 (BNA), the Secretary of State has the power to deprive a person of their citizenship if the deprivation is 'conducive to the public good'.[208] A person cannot be deprived of their British citizenship if it would render them stateless (per s.40(4) BNA). 'Stateless' for the purposes of s.40 BNA means that the person is 'not considered as a national by any state under the operation of its law'.[209] It is de jure statelessness – which is a 'binary question'.[210] While this is superficially a relatively simple issue, a number of cases before the domestic courts have illuminated the difficulties in ascertaining whether a person is considered a national by

[205] Ibid at [2.23] and [2.25] (for the data up to October 2021).

[206] Hall (n 200) at [1.23] and [1.25]. Footnote references omitted.

[207] Zedner (n 189), p.106.

[208] The Nationality and Borders Act 2022 amended the BNA to enable the Secretary of State to deprive a person of their citizenship without prior notification (s.40(5A) BNA).

[209] *Pham* v. *Secretary of State for the Home Department* [2015] UKSC 19, [2015] WLR 1591.

[210] Ibid at [21]; *Begum* v. *Secretary of State for the Home Department* [2024] EWCA Civ 152, [2024] WLR 4269 at [100].

operation of another country's law.[211] Such issues have been at the forefront of the Shamima Begum litigation which has received considerable press coverage and will be considered in some detail as it provides insights into the UK's response to alleged threats posed by individuals who have travelled to participate (in some form) in the hostilities in Syria and who now wish to return to the UK.

Begum's parents were born in what would become Bangladesh though they both moved to the UK in the 1970s/1980s. Her father was subsequently granted indefinite leave to remain and her mother became a naturalised British citizen. Begum was born in the UK and, as a result of her parents' leave to remain/naturalised citizenship, was automatically considered a British citizen. Both of her parents were Bangladeshi citizens at the time of Shamima's birth. In 2015, at the age of fifteen, Shamima travelled to Syria with two friends, with the view to marrying an ISIS fighter. The SIAC has subsequently found that 'there is a credible suspicion that Ms Begum was recruited, transferred and then harboured for the purpose of sexual exploitation'.[212] She is currently detained by the SDF in the Al-Roj camp in Syria. Shamima was located by journalists in February 2019 in a camp run by the Autonomous Administration of North and East Syria and she expressed a desire to return to the UK. She had given birth to two children while in Syria, both of whom had died. Another baby subsequently born in the Al-Roj camp (where conditions were described as 'squalid' and 'wretched'[213]) also died.

In February 2019, the Secretary of State served a notice on Shamima's family in the UK under s.40 BNA, depriving Shamima of her British citizenship. MI5 had determined that she had travelled to Syria and aligned with the Islamic State and, thus, posed a threat to national security. Shamima's substantive challenges to the deprivation decision – including the argument that it would leave her stateless – were largely unsuccessful. Her application for leave to enter the UK to participate in the review of the deprivation order was also refused and her challenge to that refusal was, ultimately, dismissed by the Supreme Court in 2021. The procedural history leading to the Supreme Court's judgment is complex and not directly relevant. For instant purposes, it is sufficient to note that a central issue before the SIAC, the Court of Appeal and, ultimately, the Supreme Court was whether Shamima could effectively

[211] See, for instance, *Al-Jedda* v. *Secretary of State for the Home Department* [2013] UKSC 62, [2014] 1 AC 253.

[212] *Begum* v. *Secretary of State for the Home Department*, SIAC, Appeal No. SC/163/2019, 22 February 2023 at [219]. See, also, the discussion of this case in Chapter 7 (Modern Slavery and Human Trafficking).

[213] *Begum* v. *Secretary of State for the Home Department*, SIAC, Appeal No. SC/163/2019, 7 February 2020 at [15].

participate in the proceedings and whether the Secretary of State had departed from his extra-territorial human rights policy in making the deprivation order.

Of particular importance are the contrasting findings of the Court of Appeal and the Supreme Court. The Court of Appeal held that the 'options' which the SIAC had proffered – namely staying the proceedings or continuing without meaningful involvement – failed to remedy the unfairness that stemmed from her inability to participate meaningfully and effectively. As Singh LJ said 'it is difficult to conceive of any case where a court or tribunal has said we cannot hold a fair trial, but we are going to go on anyway'.[214] Similarly, the indefinite staying of Shamima's appeal was 'wrong in principle' and 'would in effect render her appeal against an executive decision to deprive her of her British nationality meaningless for an unlimited period of time'.[215] It also ignored the fact that she was 'being detained by the SDF in [a] camp [the conditions of which, the SIAC accepted, would violate Article 3 if it applied to that territory] and [did] nothing to address the foreseeable risk if she is transferred to Iraq or Bangladesh, which is that in either of those countries she would be unlawfully killed or suffer mistreatment'.[216]

With the conclusion that none of the options identified by the SIAC addressed the unfairness of Shamima's inability to participate in the appeal, the question arose for the Court of Appeal as to what *should* be done to remedy the unfairness? The answer reached by the Court was to allow the appeal in respect of the refusal of the application for leave to enter, thereby enabling Shamima to return to the UK (subject to the provision of the requisite temporary entry documents) to participate in the appeal concerning the deprivation of her nationality. In reaching this conclusion, the Court of Appeal was 'acutely conscious of the national security issues' though it highlighted that the 'seriousness' of Shamima's conduct was at the lower end, particularly given that her decision to travel to Syria had been made when she was a child.[217] The Court of Appeal also noted the options available to the authorities upon Shamima's return to minimise any risk she may pose to public security including charging her with a terrorism offence and remanding her in custody or subjecting her to a TPIM.[218]

The Secretary of State successfully appealed to the Supreme Court.[219] The Supreme Court considered that the Court of Appeal 'overlooked the limitations to its competence, both institutional and constitutional, to decide questions of national security'.[220] The Supreme Court was also critical of the purported findings of fact made by the Court of Appeal including, notably, the risk of

[214] *Begum* v. *Special Immigration Appeals Commission & Ors* [2020] EWCA Civ 918, [2020] 1 WLR 4267 at [113].

[215] Ibid at [117]. [216] Ibid at [116]. [217] Ibid at [119]–[120]. [218] Ibid at [120].

[219] *R (Begum)* v. *Special Immigration Appeals Commission* [2021] UKSC 7, [2021] AC 765.

[220] Ibid at [109].

Shamima being transferred to Iraq or Bangladesh and the level of risk she posed to national security, given that at that stage of the proceedings there had been no findings of fact by the lower courts upon which the Court of Appeal could base its assessment.[221]

As Shamima was in Syria at the time the deprivation decision was made and Syria was not under the control of UK authorities, Articles 2 and 3 ECHR did not directly apply to her. Yet, the Secretary of State has adopted a policy which required him to decide 'whether there are substantial grounds for believing' that the relevant individual 'would be exposed to a real risk of mistreatment or loss of life as a result of being deprived of her British nationality'.[222] A significant issue in the proceedings was thus the effect of the Secretary of State's policy concerning the extra-territorial application of human rights. While the SIAC accepted that conditions in the various camps in which Shamima had been held would violate Article 3 ECHR *if* it was applicable,[223] the Article only applied by analogy as a result of the policy.[224] And while the policy was a relevant consideration to be taken into account when deciding whether or not to deprive Shamima of her citizenship, there was evidence that the Secretary of State *had* considered the policy and determined that there were not substantial grounds for believing that she would be at a real risk of mistreatment or loss of life as a result of the deprivation. Consequently, Shamima could not point to any grounds on which the Secretary of State's consideration of the policy could be challenged.[225] It should be noted that 'the same decision [to deprive Shamima of her citizenship] could no longer be made, because with the loss of Ms Begum's Bangladeshi citizenship when she reached her 21st birthday, a decision to deprive her of her British citizenship now would render her stateless (contrary to s 40(4))'.[226]

Following the Supreme Court judgment, evidence emerged suggesting that Shamima was the victim of human trafficking.[227] This was a central

[221] Ibid at [107]–[111]. For an analysis of the case, see Stevie Martin, 'Deference, "Fairness" and Accountability in the National Security Context" (2021) **80** CLJ 209.

[222] *Begum* (n 213) at [131]. [223] Ibid at [130]. [224] Ibid. [225] Ibid at [138]–[139].

[226] *Begum* v. *Secretary of State for the Home Department* [2024] EWCA Civ 152, [2024] WLR 4269 at [30]. A central issue before the courts was whether Shamima had Bangladeshi citizenship by virtue of her parents' citizenship of that country. While Shamima argued that she did not (such that the deprivation decision rendered her de jure stateless), the courts ultimately concluded that she did: *Begum* (n 213).

[227] The SIAC accepted that there is a 'credible suspicion' that Shamima was trafficked (*Begum* (SIAC) (n 213) at [165]). The Special Rapporteur on contemporary forms of slavery, including its causes and consequences, separately observed the possibility that women and girls had been trafficked to Syria 'for the purpose of sexual exploitation at the hands of members of the Islamic State in Iraq and Levant': Report of the Special Rapporteur on contemporary forms of slavery to the Human Rights Committee, *Nexus between Displacement and Contemporary Forms of Slavery,* A/HRC/48/52, 26 July 2021 at [43].

component of her subsequent appeal against the deprivation decision before the SIAC where it was argued that as a victim of trafficking, the State had a positive obligation to protect her under Article 4 ECHR,[228] and that not only did it fail to do that, inter alia, by preventing her travel to Syria, it compounded that failure through its deprivation of her citizenship (argued to be a form of punishment not permitted under Article 4 ECHR, as interpreted through the lens of the ECAT).[229] The SIAC determined that there was credible suspicion that Shamima was a victim of trafficking until she was detained in Syria.[230] Ultimately, however, the SIAC rejected Shamima's appeal. To succeed in the investigative obligation argument, she would have to prove that there was a corresponding repatriation obligation under Article 4 (which the SIAC rejected, having surveyed the relevant ECtHR jurisprudence). And the positive obligation argument hinged on the claim that the deprivation order constituted punishment as prohibited by Article 26 ECAT which also failed based on the existing ECtHR case law. It is, however, notable that the SIAC observed that 'there were State failures, and possible violations of the corollary protective duty, between December 2014 and February 2015 [the period before and during Shamima's travel to Syria]. There is force in the submission that these could be investigated.'[231]

Shamima's subsequent appeal to the Court of Appeal was similarly unsuccessful.[232] The decision is discussed in greater detail in Chapter 7 as much of the appeal turned on the issues with respect to trafficking, so for instant purposes it will only be canvassed in brief. There were five grounds of appeal before the Court of Appeal, with Shamima and the Secretary of State each challenging aspects of the decision. Two of the grounds related to trafficking (both of which failed) and, for discussion of those grounds, readers are directed to Chapter 7. The other three grounds related to arguments regarding de facto statelessness, procedural unfairness and breach of the public sector duty under the Equality Act 2010. The Secretary of State was successful in challenging the SIAC's finding that fairness required that Shamima be given the opportunity to make representations before a deprivation order was made. According to the Court of Appeal, the existence of a right of appeal from a deprivation decision under the Special Immigration Appeals Commission Act 1997, coupled with 'the risk of pre-emptive action by the appellant if prior notice is given', meant the SIAC fell into error in deciding that procedural fairness required the making of prior representations.[233] Nevertheless, the Court of Appeal agreed with the SIAC's ultimate conclusion (challenged by Shamima) that nothing turned on that finding as the outcome would not have been different 'had [Shamima] been

[228] See Chapter 7 (Modern Slavery). [229] *Begum* (n 212) at [181] and [219].
[230] Ibid at [219]. [231] Ibid at [224]. [232] *Begum* (n 226). [233] Ibid at [112]–[113].

offered the opportunity to make submissions' either because she could only put forward the basic facts which were already known to the Secretary of State or because 'examining the matter at the date of SIAC's judgment, the outcome would have been the same anyway'.[234]

In terms of the public sector equality duty (PSED) under the Equality Act 2010 (EqA 2010),[235] Shamima argued that in making the deprivation decision the Secretary of State failed 'to have due regard to whether the exercise of deprivation powers: (i) is disproportionately applied to British Muslims of certain ethnic minorities (engaging s.149(1)(a) EqA 2010); and/or (ii) impacts detrimentally upon the relations between members of Muslim communities and others (engaging s.149(1)(c) EqA 2010)'.[236] In support of this argument, statistical evidence was tendered:

> showing that deprivation powers have been used almost exclusively against Muslims, mainly of South Asian, Middle Eastern, and African heritage, and highlights the concerns raised by prominent British Muslims that the use of deprivation powers has created what is seen as a 'second class' category of British citizenship defined by race and religion.[237]

The Court of Appeal considered that such data needed to be 'treated with caution' given that the deprivation power cannot be used against those who only have British citizenship or those with dual British and Irish citizenship.[238] Though it found that the PSED was engaged by the deprivation decision, the SIAC ultimately rejected Shamima's challenge based on the PSED, finding that the exception in s.192 EqA 2010 applied. Section 192 EqA 2010 provides that '[a] person does not contravene this Act only by doing, for the purpose of safeguarding national security, anything it is proportionate to do for that purpose'. The challenge before the Court of Appeal hinged on the meaning of 'doing . . . anything'. It was argued on behalf of Shamima that it must refer to the breach of an obligation under the EqA 2010. The Court of Appeal, like the SIAC, concluded that it 'refers to *any* exercise of functions or powers, rather than being restricted to the breach of duties or obligations imposed by the [EqA] 2010'.[239] The Court of Appeal further confirmed the SIAC's finding that the s.192 EqA 2010 exemption applied on the facts of Shamima's case.[240]

Finally, on the statelessness challenge, it had been argued on behalf of Shamima that the Secretary of State failed to take account of the fact that the deprivation order would render her de facto stateless.[241] This was swiftly rejected by the Court of Appeal. It was clear from the material that the Secretary of State was aware that Shamima could not realistically go to

[234] Ibid at [115]. [235] For more on this duty, see Chapter 14. [236] *Begum* (n 226) at [124].
[237] Ibid at [125]. [238] Ibid. [239] Ibid at [131]. Emphasis in original. [240] Ibid at [135].
[241] Ibid at [101].

Bangladesh and, thus, 'had nowhere else to go'.[242] There was, however, no error of law on the part of the Secretary of State in nevertheless deciding to deprive Shamima of her citizenship. As the Court of Appeal observed:

> Despite knowing that she had nowhere else to go, in all practicality, the Secretary of State nonetheless decided that to deprive her of her British citizenship on grounds that to do so was conducive to the public good and in the interests of national security. He took that matter into account. The decision cannot be impugned on the basis that he did not do so.[243]

Shamima's subsequent application for permission to appeal to the Supreme Court was refused in August 2024[244] and in May 2025, the Supreme Court – in the context of an appeal by a woman who had been deprived of her British citizenship after she travelled to Syria with her husband and children to live in ISIL-controlled territory – reiterated the limited function of the SIAC when hearing challenges to deprivation decisions and to refusals of leave to enter:

> SIAC's function, in this context, differs from the usual judicial function. The assessment of a risk to national security, and a decision that it is sufficient to justify a deprivation decision or the refusal of leave to enter the UK, involve the exercise of judgment. Unlike the Parole Board assessing the risk of a prisoner's re-offending, SIAC is not the primary decision-maker. Responsibility for assessing whether a person presents such a risk to national security that a deprivation decision or the refusal of entry clearance is justified has been given by Parliament to the Secretary of State, subject to a right of appeal to SIAC. Furthermore, the Secretary of State is also exercising a discretion. Under section 40(2) of the 1981 Act, the Secretary of State "may" deprive a person of citizenship if satisfied that deprivation is conducive to the public good. Similarly, under section 3 of the 1971 Act, the decision whether to grant leave to enter the UK to a person who is not a British citizen is likewise discretionary. SIAC's role in this context is therefore to review the Secretary of State's exercise of his or her discretion, based on an evaluative judgement of the risk to national security.
>
> . . .where the assessment of a risk to national security is based on an evaluation of a body of evidence, the issue SIAC has to decide is not whether the assessment is based on facts that have been established on a balance of probabilities. Rather, the central question is whether the evidence, viewed as a whole, provides a rational basis for the Secretary of State's decision, applying principles of administrative law.[245]

242 Ibid at [102]. 243 Ibid.

244 *Permission to Appeal decision in the matter of Shamima Begum (Appellant)* v. *Secretary of State for the Home Department (Respondent)*, UK Supreme Court, UKSC 2024/0096, 7 August 2024, https://supremecourt.uk/news/pta-decision-shamima-begum. The reasons for permission being refused are discussed in greater detail in Chapter 7 (Modern Slavery and Human Trafficking).

245 *U3* v. *Secretary of State for the Home Department* [2025] UKSC 19, [2025] 2 WLR 1041 at [63] and [87].

This decision (not least as it involves a mother whose three British children have been repatriated to the UK[246]), and Shamima's case, illuminate in stark detail the implications of citizenship deprivation for an individual's rights, and such consequences are further apparent when one considers the judgment of the Grand Chamber in *H.F.* v. *France.*[247]

8.3.5.2 Denial of Repatriation

H.F. v. *France* involved a challenge brought by families of four French nationals (two women and their children) who were being held in SDF-controlled camps in Syria. They alleged, inter alia, that the failure of the French authorities to repatriate the women and their children violated Article 3 ECHR as it exposed them to inhuman or degrading treatment and it breached their right to enter the territory of a State of which they are nationals as guaranteed by Article 3(2) of Protocol No. 4 ECHR. It is notable that, in contrast to Shamima Begum, the women in *H.F.* had *not* been deprived of their French citizenship.

The Grand Chamber unanimously held that the complaint under Article 3 ECHR was inadmissible given that the women and their children did not fall within the jurisdiction of France. In this respect it observed that 'the mere fact that decisions taken at national level have had an impact on the situation of persons residing abroad is not such as to establish the jurisdiction of the State concerned over them outside its territory'.[248] Further, the fact that criminal proceedings had been commenced in France against the applicants' daughters (and civil proceedings had been commenced by the applicants in France) was insufficient to trigger France's jurisdiction.[249] Finally, the operational capacity to repatriate was not enough to constitute a form of 'control or authority' that would trigger France's jurisdiction.[250]

In respect of Article 3(2) of Protocol No. 4 ECHR, however, the Grand Chamber held that there had been a violation. Unlike Article 3 ECHR, the right to enter:

> inherently implies that the right guaranteed thereby will apply to the relationship between a State and its nationals when the latter are outside its territory or a territory over which it exercises effective control. If the right to enter secured by that provision were limited to nationals already in the territory of that State or under its effective control, the right would be rendered ineffective.[251]

There were also several 'special features' of the cases before the Court that were sufficient to trigger France's jurisdiction under Article 3(2) of Protocol

[246] Ibid at [4]. [247] *H.F. and Ors* v. *France* [GC] [2022] ECHR 678.
[248] Ibid at [200]. See also the discussion of extraterritoriality in Chapter 4 (Life).
[249] Ibid at [193]–[195]. [250] Ibid at [199]. [251] Ibid at [209].

No. 4 ECHR. Those features included: the repeated requests made of the French authorities to repatriate the women and children; the fact that they 'were facing a real and immediate threat to their lives and physical well-being, on account both of the living conditions and safety concerns in the camps'; the health of the family members and the extreme vulnerability of the children; the fact that they were 'not able to leave the camps, or any other place where they may be held incommunicado, in order to return to France without the assistance of the French authorities'; and, the fact that the Kurdish authorities had repeatedly affirmed a willingness to facilitate the return of female detainees with French nationality and their children.[252]

The Grand Chamber made several notable findings with respect to the nature of the right protected by Article 3(2) of Protocol No. 4 ECHR. In particular, that the right:

- only applies to nationals;
- it applies to individuals who have left the national territory voluntarily and to individuals born overseas who have nationality;
- it prohibits only the expulsion of nationals, not their extradition; and,
- while it is expressed in absolute terms 'there may be room for implied limitations, where appropriate, in the form of exceptional measures that are merely temporary' such as the restrictions on travel imposed during the COVID-19 pandemic.[253]

Significantly, in terms of the issues raised in Shamima Begum's litigation, the Grand Chamber noted that it has not been ruled out that deprivation of nationality 'could be problematic under this provision'.[254] Though for Shamima herself, the Protocol could not offer assistance as it has not been ratified by the UK.

As to whether Article 3(2) of Protocol No. 4 ECHR conferred a positive obligation on France to repatriate the applicants' family members, the Grand Chamber noted that the ECHR must be interpreted in a manner which renders its 'safeguards practical and effective'. However, there is no obligation under international treaty law or customary international law for States to repatriate their nationals and Article 3(2) of Protocol No. 4 ECHR could not be read as conferring such a right.[255] Nevertheless, Article 3(2) of Protocol No. 4 ECHR *does* impose on States positive obligations to ensure that their nationals' right to enter is practical and effective.[256]

While the Grand Chamber did not 'delineate in broad terms the nature of those positive obligations', it did conclude that such obligations require that the decision-making process regarding repatriation is 'surround[ed] … by

[252] Ibid at [213]. [253] Ibid at [245]–[248]. [254] Ibid at [249]. [255] Ibid at [259].
[256] Ibid at [260].

appropriate safeguards against arbitrariness'.[257] In the instant case, such safeguards were absent. Given the 'humanitarian emergency' in Syria, Article 3(2) of Protocol No. 4 ECHR obliged the authorities to conduct 'individual examination[s] of their requests'. However, the applicants received nothing in response to their repeated requests to indicate that they had been considered by the authorities.[258] Further, the domestic courts determined that they could not review the decisions of the authorities which meant that the applicants did not have 'access to a form of independent review of the tacit decisions to refuse their repatriation requests by which it could be ascertained that there were legitimate and reasonable grounds, devoid of arbitrariness, to justify those decisions'.[259] In those circumstances, there had been a violation of Article 3(2) of Protocol No. 4.[260] The separate, concurring opinion of Judges Pavli and Schembri Orland provides a succinct encapsulation (and critique) of the reasoning of the majority.[261]

While *H.F.* v. *France* is a very significant decision, its reach is limited in terms of the UK given that, as noted above, it is one of four states that have not ratified Protocol No. 4 ECHR. This is deeply problematic for the women and children with British citizenship who are currently being held in camps in Syria. In 2019, three British children were repatriated from Syria (while their mother, who had been deprived of her British citizenship was denied leave to enter the UK).[262] In October 2022, the first British woman was repatriated to the UK from Syria with her child and it was reported in December 2023 that another woman and five children were to be repatriated.[263] Data regarding the numbers of women and children currently held in SDF-controlled camps is elusive, and attempts to secure such information through formal channels (e.g. by way of a request under the Freedom of Information Act 2000) have been unsuccessful on the basis of national security.[264] One informal estimate suggests that twenty to twenty-five women or families with British nationality are in Syrian camps.[265] In a submission to the Special Rapporteur on

257 Ibid, separate concurring opinion of Judges Pavli and Schembri Orland at [2].

258 *H.F and Ors v. France* (n 247) at [277]–[279]. 259 Ibid at [281]. 260 Ibid at [283].

261 Ibid, separate concurring opinion of Judges Pavli and Schembri Orland at [2].

262 *U3* v. *Secretary of State for the Home Department* (n 245).

263 Dan Sabbagh, 'First British woman and her child repatriated to UK from Syrian camp', *The Guardian*, 13 October 2022, www.theguardian.com/politics/2022/oct/13/british-woman-and-her-child-repatriated-from-syrian-detention-camp-in-uk-first#:~:text=It%20is%20estimated%20about%2060,Syria%20when%20she%20was%2015. Dan Sabbagh, 'Britain to repatriate woman and five children from Syrian camps', *The Guardian*, 12 December 2023, www.theguardian.com/politics/2023/dec/12/britain-to-repatriate-woman-and-five-children-from-syrian-camps.

264 *Rights & Security International* v. *Information Commissioner* [2024] UKFTT 296.

265 'Evidence Submission by the All-Party Parliamentary Group (APPG) on Trafficked Britons in Syria to the Foreign Affairs Committee's Inquiry into the UK's International Counter-Terrorism Policy', June 2023 at [2], https://committees.parliament.uk/writtenevidence/122003/pdf/; Sabbagh, 'Britain to repatriate woman and five children' (n 263).

contemporary forms of slavery, including its causes and consequences, Reprieve stated that it:

> has had sight of the decision letters in respect of seven women, where the UK government has refused to repatriate them. Far from considering requests for assistance on a case-by-case basis, the UK Government uses identical language in each letter, providing no evidence that the individual circumstances of each woman have been considered, and using the same stock phrase in each letter, that 'The Government assesses that [X] is a threat to national security having travelled of her own volition to join a proscribed terrorist organisation'.[266]

If the UK had ratified Protocol No. 4 ECHR, then there might have been an argument based on the findings of the Grand Chamber in *H.F.* that the UK authorities' approach to repatriation requests failed to comply with the positive obligations imposed under Article 3(2) of Protocol No. 4 ECHR. However, as the UK has not ratified the Protocol this leaves those British citizens in camps in Syria with limited recourse under the ECHR and, in light of recent case law from the High Court, the common law appears unlikely to provide any additional protection for such individuals.

In 2022, the High Court rejected applications for habeas corpus brought by two women with British citizenship[267] (both of whom had young children) who were being held in a refugee camp in Syria, having travelled to Syria to join ISIS.[268] As the Court of Appeal subsequently noted, '[c]onditions in the camp are unsafe and unhealthy and are wholly inappropriate for the detention of adults, let alone children'.[269] While the Divisional High Court observed that the writ of habeas corpus is a 'flexible remedy which must adapt to changing circumstances',[270] it was not satisfied that the relevant Minister had the requisite control to procure the release of the applicants. While the Autonomous Administration of North and East Syria (AANES) which controls the camp had indicated its willingness to facilitate the return of individuals such as the applicants, that was insufficient to demonstrate that the Minister has 'custody or control of the custody' of the applicants as is required for the writ which 'is a means of securing the release of a person who is being detained unlawfully' and may be issued 'against the person who has custody

[266] Special Rapporteur on contemporary forms of slavery, including its causes and consequences, *Call for Input: The Nexus between Forced Displacement and Contemporary Forms of Slavery*, Submission of Reprieve, p.4, www.ohchr.org/sites/default/files/Documents/Issues/Slavery/SR/ReportHRC48/CSOs/PRIV_Mondern_slavery_input.docx.

[267] Both had been deprived of their citizenship under s.40 BNA but that was overturned on appeal by SIAC on the basis that it rendered them both stateless: *C3 & Anor* v. *The Secretary of State for Foreign, Commonwealth & Development Affairs* [2023] EWCA Civ 444, [2023] 3 WLR 529 at [5].

[268] *C3 & C4* v. *Secretary of State for Foreign, Commonwealth & Development Affairs* [2022] EWHC 2772 (Admin).

[269] *C3 & Anor* (Court of Appeal) (n 267) at [1].

[270] *C3 & C4* (High Court) (n 268) at [88].

of the individual being detained'.[271] Significantly, a reading of the separate reasons of Lord Justice Lewis could be taken to signify to the applicants that the better course would be judicial review of the:

> lawfulness of any refusal by the Secretary of State to make an official request to the AANES for the release of the applicants, or any refusal to issue emergency travel documents or to deliver those documents to the applicants in the camp in North East Syria. It may, perhaps, even involve consideration of any failure of the Secretary of State to make, or participate in, the necessary arrangements for repatriation of the applicants to the United Kingdom . . . The lawfulness of any action or failure to act by the Secretary of State would be determined by reference to established principles of public law including those governing the circumstances in which judicial review is available to review decisions concerning the provision of assistance to British nationals abroad or decisions involving the conduct of foreign relations.[272]

Indeed, on appeal to the Court of Appeal (which upheld the High Court's decision on the habeas corpus claim), Lord Justice Underhill appeared to reiterate the observations of Lord Justice Lewis:

> The Applicants' current situation is indeed dire, however much it may be the result of their own choices; and it is made worse that it is shared by their innocent children. There may be – though we are not in a position to form a view – a powerful case that neither the difficulties about the repatriation arrangements described by [the Government] nor (which appears to be the essential point) the Foreign Secretary's concerns about the risk that the Applicants pose to national security can justify his refusal to take steps to secure their release and repatriation.[273]

But as the Secretary of State did not have control over the applicants and a habeas corpus claim was, thus, not available to them,such a case could only be brought via a claim for judicial review of the lawfulness of the Secretary of State's refusal of assistance.[274] Given the significant degree of deference demonstrated by the courts towards the Government in the *Begum* proceedings, particularly in respect of the Government's assessment of national security, it is questionable how successful such judicial review proceedings would be.

8.3.5.3 Temporary Exclusion Orders

The CTSA 2015 empowers the Secretary of State of the Home Department to impose a Temporary Exclusion Order (TEO) on a British citizen who is outside of the UK. The purpose of a TEO is to 'control the manner of an individual's return to the United Kingdom, and to provide a limited measure of control over that individual thereafter'.[275] In this sense, the term TEO is a misnomer: TEOs

[271] Ibid at [106] and [108]. [272] Ibid at [109].
[273] *C3 & Anor* (Court of Appeal) (n 267) at [59]. [274] Ibid. [275] Hall (n 118) at [8.33].

'are not about exclusion, but about managing return, typically when there is some indication that the individual intends to travel to the UK'.[276] Section 2 CTSA sets out five conditions that must be met before the Secretary of State can 'impose' a TEO, including that they reasonably suspect that the individual (who must have a right of abode in the UK) is, or has been, involved in terrorism-related activity outside of the UK and that they reasonably consider that it is necessary to protect members of the public from a risk of terrorism for a TEO to be imposed. Permission is generally required from the High Court for a TEO to be imposed, though in 'urgent' circumstances, one may be imposed without prior approval (s.2(7) and s.3 CTSA). A TEO lasts for a maximum of two years, though there is nothing preventing the Secretary of State from imposing back-to-back TEOs (s.4(3) and (8) CTSA). Upon the issuing of a TEO, a person's British passport is invalidated (s.4(9) CTSA). A person who is subject to a TEO can apply for permission to return to the UK (s.5 CTSA). Upon returning, the individual can be subject to the same reporting and attending conditions as imposed via TPIMs (s.9 CTSA) and failure to comply with a TEO or with any conditions imposed under s.9 is an offence (s.10 CTSA).

According to the current IRTL:

> The typical profile [of a person subject to a TEO] is a British mono-national who has travelled to Syria and spent time in Da'esh controlled areas . . . TEOs are considered to be particularly appropriate for returning women. Despite the relatively limited obligations that may be imposed (compared to the broader TPIM power) . . . the Home Office consider that TEOs are an effective response for a range of individuals returning from Syria and Iraq, especially in the absence of a criminal justice response. I have seen one file where a decision to impose a TEO was taken for an individual with dual nationality.[277]

Data from the Home Office indicates that no TEOs were imposed in 2016 (the first year they were in force); nine were imposed in 2017 (three males, six females); sixteen were imposed in 2018 (fourteen males and two females); four were imposed in 2019 (two males and two females); one was imposed in 2020 (one male); five were imposed in 2021 (four males and one female); two were imposed in 2022 (two males); and one was imposed in 2023 (the gender is unknown).[278]

[276] Hall (n 34) at [8.42]. [277] Hall (n 118) at [8.44].

[278] Home Office, *HM Government Counter-Terrorism Disruptive Powers Report 2023*, 28 November 2024 at [3.10]; Home Office, *HM Government Counter-Terrorism Disruptive Powers Report 2022*, 26 October 2023 at [3.9]; Home Office, *HM Government Counter-Terrorism Disruptive Powers Report 2021*, 19 January 2023 at [3.9]; Home Office, *HM Government Transparency Report: Disruptive Powers 2020*, 3 March 2022 at [4.8]; and Home Office, *Transparency Report: Disruptive Powers 2018–2019*, CP212, March 2020, p.21.

8.3.5.4 *Can Restrictions on Citizenship and Mobility be Justified?*

Scholars such as Zedner ask whether it is 'just to limit mobility so radically, to curtail citizenship rights, or to render someone stateless, whatever danger they pose?'[279] The case of Shamima Begum serves to illustrate just how profound the consequences of such actions can be. Indeed, the Australian High Court[280] recently concluded that an equivalent power to that contained in s.40 of the BNA is a form of punishment; citizenship confers 'rights of "fundamental importance" to the relationship between the individual and the Commonwealth' and a removal of citizenship serves a punitive purpose, a form of 'retribution for conduct deemed so reprehensible as to be "incompatible with the shared values of the Australian community"'.[281] The same could be said of s.40 BNA and its use in respect of Shamima Begum. Indeed, it is difficult to see how the deprivation order is not punishment. Nevertheless, as discussed in Chapter 7 (Modern Slavery and Human Trafficking) in greater detail, this argument has been rejected by the domestic courts, at least insofar as the concept of 'punishment' is utilised in the ECAT. Whether or not deprivation is punishment, as Zedner has observed, the effect of measures such as TEOs and the power to deprive a person of their citizenship under s.40 BNA is to 'render citizenship and its attendant rights more precarious and more easily lost than was once the case',[282] and the Grand Chamber's judgment in *H.F.* v. *France* and the domestic cases discussed above highlight the profound implications of the loss of the rights that are attendant upon citizenship.

8.3.6 Asset Freezing

The power to restrict a person's access to their property, including income, can have profound implications for their human rights. In addition to Article 1 of Protocol 1 ECHR (which protects the qualified right to peaceful enjoyment of one's property), placing limitations on the access a person can have to their assets may have a significant impact upon the designated individual's private and family lives (Article 8 ECHR).[283]

The history of the current asset freezing regime in the UK is complex and there were successful legal challenges to the early regime[284] which resulted in legislative changes, and there were further changes following the UK's withdrawal from the European Union. Currently, the Sanctions and Anti-

[279] Zedner (n 189), p.118. [280] The Australian equivalent to the UK Supreme Court.

[281] *Alexander* v. *Minister for Home Affairs & Anor* [2022] HCA 19 at [74].

[282] Zedner (n 189), p.117.

[283] See, for instance, Daley J. Birkett, 'Asset Freezing at the European and Inter-American Courts of Human Rights: Lessons for the International Criminal Court, the United Nations Security Council and States' (2020) 20 HRLR 3, 502–525.

[284] *HM Treasury* v. *Ahmed & Ors* [2010] UKSC 2, [2010] 2 WLR 378.

Money Laundering Act 2018 (SAMLA) governs asset freezing.[285] In essence, the SAMLA (through regulations), permits the designating of individuals for the purposes of, inter alia, imposing financial sanctions upon them, including freezing funds or economic resources owned or controlled by designated persons and preventing funds or economic resources from being made available to or for the benefit of designated persons. While previously, a person could not be designated unless, amongst other things, the Treasury had 'reasonable grounds to suspect that the person' is or has been involved in terrorist activity,[286] amendments made to the regulations in 2025 (which were pending at the time of writing) retained the reasonable grounds requirement for designations under the 'standard procedure' but removed it for designations occurring under the newly established 'urgent procedure'[287] (see regulation 5A).[288] 'Terrorist activity' is defined in regulation 6(3) of the Counter-Terrorism (Sanctions) (EU Exit) Regulations 2019 and includes 'being responsible for, engaging in or providing support for, the commission, preparation or instigation of acts of terrorism'.

An 'appropriate Minister' oversees designation under the regulations created pursuant to SAMLA: the Minister can vary or revoke designations (s.22) and a designated person can request a variation or revocation pursuant to s.23 (the request being made to the Minister). There are additional requirements for reviews of regulations that have a counter-terrorism purpose (s.31 SAMLA). The IRTL reviews the asset-freezing provisions in the Counter-Terrorism (International Sanctions) (EU Exit) Regulations 2019 (CTIS Regs) and the domestic sanctions regime provided for in the Counter-Terrorism (Sanctions) (EU Exit) Regulations 2019 (CTS Regs).

The current IRTL has likened the impact of designation for the relevant individual's rights to the impact of TPIMs:

> the impact of financial sanctions [especially those provided for in the CTIS Regs] is comparable to some extent, in terms of degree, to the impact of Terrorism Prevention and Investigation Measures (TPIMs) which lie at the sharper end of terrorist risk countermeasures.[289]

[285] More specifically, the Counter-Terrorism (Sanctions) (EU Exit) Regulations 2019 and the Counter-Terrorism (International Sanctions) (EU Exit) Regulations 2019 which were made under the SAMLA.

[286] The Counter-Terrorism (Sanctions) (EU Exit) Regulations 2019, reg 6.

[287] 'Through which the Secretary of State can mirror designations made by certain allied countries (specified in the regulations)': The Sanctions (EU Exit) (Miscellaneous Amendments) Regulations 2025, Explanatory Memorandum at [5.3].

[288] The Sanctions (EU Exit) (Miscellaneous Amendments) Regulations 2025, reg 9.

[289] Jonathan Hall, 'Independent review of the operation of the Counter-Terrorism (International Sanctions) (EU Exit) Regulations 2019', 18 December 2023 at [4.1], https://www.gov.uk/government/publications/review-of-the-operation-of-the-counter-terrorism-international-sanctions-eu-exit-regulations-2019.

Moreover, 'the mere fact of UK-designation, unless welcomed as a badge of honour, or experienced within a non-Western state which has scant regard for UK interventions, could have harsh consequences for reputation, privacy, and relationships (financial and personal)'.[290]

8.3.7 Closed Proceedings and Article 6 ECHR

A further controversial aspect of the UK's counter-terrorism strategy is the use of the closed material procedure (CMP). Under Part 2 of the Justice and Security Act 2013 (JSA), courts seised of 'relevant civil proceedings may make a declaration that [they] are proceedings in which a closed material application may be made to the court' (s.6(1) JSA). Under the CMP, evidence and other material can be withheld from a non-Government party and their lawyers. The material is, instead, given to 'special advocates' who are only permitted limited contact with the individuals once they have seen the material. The function of the special advocates is to:

> test the executive's case for non-disclosure (the disclosure function) and to represent the 'interests' of the person in the proceedings (the representative function), although they are not formally responsible to, and can have only limited contact with their 'client' once they have seen the closed material; but who can make submission to the SIAC on their behalf.[291]

Two conditions must be met in order for a declaration under s.6 JSA to be made: (i) that without the declaration, a party to the proceedings would be required to disclose 'sensitive material' (or would otherwise be required to disclose such material were it not for one of the exceptions referred to in s.6(4)(b)); and, (ii) that it is in the interests of the fair and effective administration of justice to make a declaration (s.6(4)–(5) JSA). 'Sensitive material' is defined as 'material the disclosure of which would be damaging to the interests of national security' (s.6(11) JSA). A separate statutory instrument provides for the use of the CMP in SIAC proceedings.[292] The CMP may also be used when granting TPIMs.[293]

The human rights implications of the CMP are considered in the light of two landmark decisions, namely, the Grand Chamber judgment in *A & Ors* v. *the*

[290] Ibid at [4.3].

[291] Eva Nanopoulos, 'European Human Rights Law and the Normalisation of the "Closed Material Procedure": Limit or Source?' (2015) **78** MLR 6, p.916.

[292] Special Immigration Appeals Commission (Procedural) Rules 2003, r.37. Notably, 'closed material' is defined more broadly in these Rules than in the JSA (r.37(1)).

[293] Civil Procedure Rules (Part 80), specifically r.80.24 deals with the CMP in TPIM proceedings.

United Kingdom[294] and the subsequent House of Lords decision in *Secretary of State for the Home Department* v. *AF (No 3)*.[295]

A & Ors v. *the United Kingdom*[296] involved eleven applicants who had challenged the indefinite detention scheme under ATCSA which was the subject of the proceedings in *Belmarsh.*[297] Of particular relevance is the Grand Chamber's discussion of Articles 5 (right to liberty) and 6 (right to a fair trial) ECHR in the context of the use of the CMP in the SIAC.

By way of background, the applicants' challenge to their indefinite detention was heard by the SIAC using the CMP. The applicants argued that this violated both Articles 5 and 6 ECHR. In relation to Article 5 ECHR, it was contended that Article 5(4) ECHR incorporates certain minimum standards for a fair trial. The Grand Chamber agreed but considered that 'there may be restrictions on the right to a fully adversarial procedure where strictly necessary in the light of strong countervailing public interest, such as national security'.[298] Significantly, however, 'there will not be a fair trial … unless any difficulties caused to the defendant by a limitation on his rights are sufficiently counterbalanced by the procedures followed by the judicial authorities'.[299]

In concluding that the CMP used by the SIAC violated Article 5(4) ECHR, the Grand Chamber made the following observations. First, that the lengthy – possibly indefinite – deprivation of the applicants' liberty had a dramatic impact on their fundamental rights and, consequently, Article 5(4) ECHR 'must import substantially the same fair trial guarantees as art.6(1) in its criminal aspect'.[300] Second, that 'it was essential that as much information about the allegations and evidence against each applicant was disclosed as was possible without compromising national security or the safety of others'. Where full disclosure of the material was not possible, each applicant was still required to have the possibility of effectively challenging the allegations against him.[301] Third, that SIAC – a fully independent court – was 'best placed to ensure that no material was unnecessarily withheld from the detainee' and the special advocate could provide 'an important, additional safeguard'.[302] Fourth, that while the special advocate could put arguments on behalf of the detainee during the closed hearings, this function could not be performed 'in any

[294] *A and Ors* v. *the United Kingdom* (n 175).

[295] *Secretary of State for the Home Department* v. *AF and Anor* [2009] UKHL 28, [2010] 2 AC 269.

[296] *A and Ors* v. *the United Kingdom* (n 175).

[297] *A and Ors* v. *Secretary of State for the Home Department* (n 161). See discussion in Section 8.3.4.1.2.

[298] *A and Ors* v. *the United Kingdom* (n 175) at [205]. [299] Ibid. [300] Ibid at [217].

[301] Ibid at [218]. [302] Ibid at [219].

meaningful way unless the detainee was provided with sufficient information about the allegations against him to enable him to give effective instructions to the special advocate'.[303] Fifth, that even where 'all or most of the underlying evidence [against the detainee] remained undisclosed, if the allegations contained in the open material were sufficiently specific' it should be possible for the detainee to give effective instructions to the special advocate in the manner required by Article 5(4) ECHR.[304] Finally, that where 'the open material consisted purely of general assertions and SIAC's decision to uphold the certification and maintain the detention was based solely or to a decisive degree on closed material, the procedural requirements of art.5(4) would not be satisfied'.[305]

In the case of *A & Ors*, several applicants had had available to them open material which included 'detailed allegations about, for example, the purchase of specific telecommunications equipment, possession of specific documents linked to named terrorist suspects and meetings with named terrorist suspects with specific dates and places' and, as a result, those applicants had been able to effectively challenge the allegations.[306] However, for two of the applicants who were said to have been involved in fundraising for Al-Qaeda, the open material did not disclose the apparent link between money transfers/raising money and terrorism. These applicants were, thus, not in a position to effectively challenge the allegations against them and there had been a violation of Article 5(4) ECHR.[307] For two other applicants who were accused, in general terms, of being members of Islamist groups linked to Al-Qaeda, the open evidence was 'insubstantial and ... the evidence on which [SIAC] relied [in finding] against them was largely to be found in the closed material'. As a result, those applicants were not in a position to effectively challenge the allegations against them, and there had been a violation of Article 5(4).[308] The Grand Chamber did not proceed to consider the arguments under Article 6 ECHR, in light of its findings in respect of Article 5(4) ECHR.

Following the Grand Chamber's judgment in *A & Ors v. the United Kingdom*, the House of Lords was called upon to consider whether the procedure that resulted in the making of non-derogating control orders against the three appeallants in *AF*[309] satisfied each appellant's right to a fair hearing as guaranteed by Article 6 ECHR. Each of the appellants argued that Article 6 ECHR had been violated because the judge making the order relied on material that was received in closed hearings and, thus, not disclosed to the appellant.

The decision of the Grand Chamber in *A & Ors* v. *the United Kingdom* was delivered shortly before the commencement of the appeal proceedings before

[303] Ibid at [220]. [304] Ibid. [305] Ibid. [306] Ibid at [222]. [307] Ibid at [223].
[308] Ibid at [224]. [309] *Secretary of State for the Home Department* v. *AF and Anor* (n 295).

the House of Lords in *AF*. In light of that decision, the appellants argued that '[w]here there was a closed hearing the special advocate could not [effectively challenge the allegations] on behalf of his client in any useful way unless provided with sufficient information about the allegations against him to enable him to give effective instructions to the special advocate'.[310] Lord Phillips, having regard to *A & Ors* v. *the United Kingdom*, concluded that:

> [T]he controlee must be given sufficient information about the allegations against him to enable him to give effective instructions in relation to those allegations ... Where ... the open material consists purely of general assertions and the case against the controlee is based solely or to a decisive degree on closed materials the requirements of a fair trial will not be satisfied, however cogent the case based on the closed materials may be.[311]

Given the 'low threshold' required for the imposition of a control order (i.e. reasonable grounds for *suspecting* involvement in terrorism-related activity), Lord Phillips concluded that there are 'bound to be cases where the closed evidence is so cogent that the judge can rightly form the conclusion that there is no possibility that the controlee would be able, if this evidence were disclosed to him, to dispel the reasonable suspicion'.[312] Nevertheless, '[t]here are ... strong policy considerations that support a rule that a trial procedure can never be considered fair if a party to it is kept in ignorance of the case against him'.[313] Accordingly, given the finding of the Grand Chamber in *A & Ors*, the House of Lords determined that the PTA 2005 should be read down such that 'the judge will have to consider not merely the allegations that have to be disclosed in order to place in the open sufficient to satisfy the requirements laid down by the Grand Chamber, but whether there is any other matter whose disclosure is essential to the fairness of the trial'.[314]

The same principle – namely, that a person must be provided with sufficient evidence to enable them to effectively challenge the case against them – applies in cases involving applications for TPIMs under the TPIMA.

8.3.8 Normalisation of Exceptionalism and a Dilution of Human Rights?

Having examined the array of counter-terrorism legislation that has been, and currently is, in force in the UK, we return to consider whether terrorism-specific legislation is necessary and the impact that it has had on rights protection. More specifically, has there been a 'normalisation of exceptionalism' to the detriment

[310] Ibid at [46]. [311] Ibid at [59]. [312] Ibid at [62]. [313] Ibid at [63].

[314] Ibid at [68]. Following *AF* (n 295), the Court of Appeal held that the disclosure requirements set out in *AF* arose when the Secretary of State decided to impose a non-derogative control order and not, as the Government has sought to argue, only once there was a refusal to disclose: *AN* v. *Secretary of State for the Home Department* [2010] EWCA Civ 869.

of rights? Have we seen a dilution of rights as society grows increasingly more accustomed to what are touted as 'emergency' and 'temporary' measures such as TPIMs?

8.3.8.1 *Is Terrorism-Specific Legislation Necessary?*

As the former IRTL Lord Anderson has observed, '[m]any advanced countries managed until recently without special terrorism laws of any kind. The terror label – evocative as it is – risks distorting anything to which it is attached by its sheer emotional power'.[315] Consequently, '[t]he case for terrorism-specific powers should be approached with a measure of scepticism'.[316] Anderson proposed four 'partial justifications' for terrorism-specific legislation:

1. Terrorism is a 'uniquely great threat to our lives and wellbeing';
2. Terrorism poses an 'existential threat';
3. '[O]nly the terror label will do to mark public revulsion at a particularly unpleasant offence';
4. 'New terrorism' characterised by 'transnational networks, suicide bombers who strike without warning and the deliberate causing of mass civilian causalities' required 'an enhanced international response'.[317]

None of these 'justifications' is entirely persuasive. The sectarian violence in Northern Ireland was dealt with without the huge corpus of terrorism-specific legislation that proliferated post-9/11. The 'terror label' is applied to increasingly peripheral acts (e.g. one of the most commonly charged terrorism-related offences is possession of material useful to a terrorist (s.58 TA 2000)), while the most heinous of the offences related to terrorism – murder – is treated as just that: murder. 'New terrorism' is not so 'new': bombings were (and remain) a prominent feature of the conflict in Northern Ireland. Indeed, Guy Fawkes Night celebrates a foiled bombing of Parliament from the seventeenth century. And 'new' forms of terrorism struggle to be identified as such (see, for instance, the tepid response of counter-terrorism authorities to inceldom) and, thus, are not caught by the counter-terrorism framework.[318]

Anderson proposed two 'operational justifications' for terrorism-specific legislation: the perceived need to 'defend further up the field' and the need to rely on intelligence that cannot be disclosed. Both justifications play out in the corpus of counter-terrorism law we have considered above. There is a whole array of provisions under the TA 2000 and TA 2006 which defend further up the field. Similarly, TPIMs are clearly directed at preventing terrorism-related activities from taking place, as are the 'stop and search'

[315] Anderson (n 12), p.234. [316] Ibid. [317] Ibid, pp.235–236.

[318] See the discussion in Section 8.2.

powers discussed in Section 8.3.3.1 and the restrictions on citizenship canvassed in Section 8.3.5. The indefinite detention scheme successfully challenged in *Belmarsh* could be said to epitomise the idea of 'defending further up the field'. Finally, the Prevent statutory duty is the 'ultimate example of defending further up the field, indeed so far up the field as to be outside the criminal justice context altogether'.[319]

The second operational justification is based on the need to rely on intelligence that cannot be disclosed. We see this justification borne out in the use of the CMP in proceedings concerning control orders and TPIMs. While *A and Ors* v. *the United Kingdom* and *AF* made clear that individuals who are subject to such measures must be provided with sufficient evidence to enable them to effectively challenge them, the CMP is still extremely restrictive, particularly when one considers the implications of a TPIM on a person's liberty. This is all the more so given the lowered standard of proof for the imposition of TPIMs and the possibility of indefinite TPIMs.[320]

Much, if not all, of the terrorism-specific legislation that we have discussed can thus be linked to one or both of the operational justifications proffered by Anderson. However, the mere fact that there may be a 'justification' for the measure does not mean that 'each measure operates in a just or acceptable manner'.[321] Indeed, it is perhaps telling that some of the most significant cases involving terrorism-related legislation have involved measures that have pushed these justifications beyond the limits demarcated by human rights law. Thus, the indefinite detention of foreign suspected international terrorists was not lawful,[322] nor was the unbounded power to stop and search individuals.[323] Likewise, confining individuals to their homes for eighteen hours each day – and significantly limiting their movements when they were outside their homes – was too defensive.[324]

It seems, then, that there may be justifications for terrorism-specific legislation including, in particular, the need to prevent terrorist attacks by 'defending further up the field' and, thus, criminalising conduct that would not otherwise fit within the criminal concept of inchoate offences (e.g. attempting, assisting or encouraging). But such justifications do not permit unbridled executive and legislative action. As we have seen, a balance must be struck between community interests (including the rights of others) and the rights of individuals who are suspected of having engaged in activities that are related to terrorism. To date, the primary enforcers of that balance have been the courts (both domestic and Strasbourg). While UK courts are well versed in checking executive overreach, in a constitutional framework based around the sovereignty of Parliament, the HRA has provided the domestic courts

[319] Anderson (n 12), p.238. [320] See, Section 8.3.4.2. [321] Anderson (n 12), p.240.
[322] See, Section 8.3.4.1.2. [323] See, Section 8.3.3.1. [324] See, Section 8.3.4.2.1.

with significant traction in response to Parliamentary excess in the counter-terrorism context. Indeed, the 'dialogue' between the domestic and Strasbourg courts has been profoundly important in maintaining the balance between community and individual interests. (See, in particular, *A and Ors* v. *the United Kingdom* and *AF*.) However, to suggest that the courts have steadfastly maintained rights protection in the counter-terrorism context would be naïve. As the next section will suggest the balancing exercises undertaken by the domestic courts has arguably led to a dilution of fundamental rights, including liberty.

8.3.8.2 Diluting Rights

One way of looking at *Belmarsh*[325] and control order and TPIM cases such as *JJ* and *DD*[326] is as examples of courts protecting human rights. After all, in these cases the courts held that the extremely restrictive measures imposed by the State in the name of counter-terrorism violated the right to liberty and the right to freedom from inhuman or degrading treatment. There is, however, a flip side to that coin, particularly in the context of control orders/TPIMs. While being restricted to one's residence for eighteen hours was 'too long' in the context of control orders, sixteen hours was not, and forced relocation was permissible so long as it did not lead to the destruction of family life. Thus, 'significant interferences with liberty without trial – although *not* of the extensive nature demanded by the initial iteration of the [control measure] scheme – had been accepted by the courts as compatible with Article 5' and these interferences could, thus, be seen as having received a 'judicial imprimatur'.[327]

Similarly, the judgments in *A & Ors* v. *the United Kingdom* and *AF*, while on one view are examples of judicial assertiveness by the domestic and Strasbourg courts in favour of rights, can also be seen as judicial acceptance of significant encroachment on the rights of individuals to a fair trial. Even with evidence of the 'gist' of the case against them, individuals who are subject to the CMP (including in cases involving significant restrictions on liberty and asset-freezing orders) are limited in the ways in which they can engage with the special advocates who have, in turn, expressed concerns regarding their ability to effectively challenge the State's objection to disclosure of evidence.[328]

The enduring use of the CMP in a multitude of contexts, not just those involving allegations against individuals of terrorism-related activity,[329] has

[325] Discussed in Section 8.3.4.1.2. [326] Discussed in Section 8.3.4.2.

[327] Helen Fenwick, 'Terrorism and the Control Orders/TPIMs Saga: A Vindication of the Human Rights Act Or a Manifestation of "Defensive Democracy"?' (2017) 4 PL 609, p.614.

[328] See, Lady Hale's judgment in *AF* (n 295) at [104].

[329] See, for example, the judgment of the Divisional Court in *Reprieve and Ors* v. *the Prime Minister* [2020] EWHC 1695 (Admin). The case involved an application for permission to

been described by Eva Nanopoulos as 'symptomatic of a deeper interrelationship between human rights law and the preservation of states' security interests, which renders the former inherently unsuitable for dealing with security phenomena'.[330] According to Nanopoulos, 'there is a temptation to view arrangements such as the CMP as responses to the terrorist emergency that gradually become normalised'.[331] This links back to Anderson's description of the 'existential threat' justification of terrorism-specific legislation, as well as the two, alternative, operational justifications he offered. The expansion of the situations in which the CMP can be used reflects the normalisation of the 'tool' and, consequently, 'there is a natural risk of abuse, as the stigma with which its use is traditionally associated dissipates'.[332] Much like the judicial imprimatur given to control orders and, subsequently, TPIMs, arguably the Grand Chamber's judgment in *A & Ors* v. *the United Kingdom* endorsed the use of the CMP. It did so by finding that, provided the individual is given evidence sufficient to enable them to effectively challenge the measure, the CMP will be compliant with Article 5(4) ECHR (and, arguably (since the Grand Chamber did not expressly rule on it), Article 6 ECHR). That conclusion, couched as it was in human rights nomenclature 'opened the door to an institution [the CMP] which would have been previously legally unthinkable'.[333] The same could be said of the control order/TPIM regime.

The continued contortion of rights such as the right to liberty and the right to a fair trial – fundamental rights both under the ECHR and at common law – to enable human rights law to embrace various counter-terrorism measures has arguably 'not only failed to protect individuals against the excess of state authority but [has] positively contributed to creating a new space that power can legally occupy and in which it will naturally grow'.[334] The same could be said about the proceedings involving Shamima Begum. Having concluded that she could not effectively participate in the appeal against the decision to strip her of her British citizenship, the SIAC nevertheless upheld the refusal of her application for leave to enter the UK. That the Supreme Court took such a deferential approach to the Government's assessment of what is necessary in the interests of national security, notwithstanding the profound encroachment upon the rule of law's requirement of access to justice has given rise to concerns. This is all the more so given subsequent evidence to credibly suggest that Shamima may have been the victim of human trafficking. From this perspective the courts' displacement of the apparently fundamental right to natural justice

judicially review a decision not to conduct a public inquiry into allegations of the involvement of UK intelligence services in the torture, mistreatment and rendition of detainees following 9/11. The CMP applied as the State relied on 'sensitive material' to oppose the application.

330 Nanopoulos (n 291), p.913. 331 Ibid, p.914. 332 Ibid, p.921. 333 Ibid, p.925.

334 Ibid, p.931.

appears consistent with criticism levied by Nanopoulos at the courts in the context of the proliferation of the CMP, namely that they have potentially made further space for excessive state authority to grow.

The risk of normalisation highlighted by Fenwick and Nanopoulos lends support to the contention that, at least from a rights perspective, it is better for the State to derogate from rights than to have the courts dilute and contort rights to fit counter-terrorism measures. When a State derogates from the ECHR via Article 15 ECHR,[335] it is expressly acknowledging that measures it will take would otherwise violate human rights. And derogations are time-limited: they pertain for only so long as the 'state of emergency' exists. Once the necessity for the otherwise rights-incompatible measure(s) has passed (i.e. the exigencies of the situation no longer warrant the derogation), the law reverts to the status quo: there is no lingering dilution of rights. In a 2018 article, Helen Fenwick and Daniel Fenwick observed the recent trend of limited use of derogations in State responses to terrorism, noting that much of the terrorist threat today presents from citizens who cannot, in most cases, be excluded from the State. This, in turn, has 'prompted the search for counter-terrorism measures that can be used to control their activities' which, in turn, 'tend to be in tension with domestic and international human rights law, but they have often been presented as reconcilable with them, via downgrading recalibrations of human rights, as was necessitated by control orders, and similar measures, which have recently spread from the UK to other contracting states'.[336]

Beyond the impact on the content and protections offered by rights, the re-interpretation of rights to accommodate counter-terrorism measures which have significant implications for liberty, dignity, privacy and natural justice has profound normative implications: 'Minimising human rights via reinterpretation, rather than openly departing from them via a derogation, implies that a re-balancing between societal needs and individual rights *should occur*, in effect emptying the right of part of its content'.[337] That is, the rebalancing signifies that the balance *should* be struck in favour of the State, to the detriment of rights. Beyond the minimisation of rights, several recent measures employed by the UK effectively circumvent ECHR protections, including the use of TEOs. Such measures effectively deprive a British national of the protections of the ECHR if they are in a non-ECHR country at the time the TEO is imposed. Thus, the State can avoid the protections afforded by the ECHR without needing to derogate and without the courts even grappling with the rights implications of the measure.[338] Indeed, stripping individuals of their

[335] See Chapter 3 (European Framework).

[336] Helen Fenwick and Daniel Fenwick, 'The Case for a More Ready Resort to Derogations from the ECHR in the Current "War on Terror"' (2018) 4 EHRLR 303, p.304.

[337] Ibid, pp.304–305. Emphasis added.

[338] Ibid, p.305.

citizenship in circumstances in which they are likely to remain in conditions that would be contrary to the Convention if they took place within the Contracting State, epitomises the power States wield in the name of counter-terrorism and national security and the fragility of rights in response.

8.4 CONCLUSION

There is an 'irresolvable tension between the role of the State as the primary source of security and, at the very same time, as [a] potential threat to citizens' rights'.[339] Many facets of the UK's current counter-terrorism strategy serve to illuminate this tension. That is not to suggest that the authorities do not have a formidable task in addressing the threat posed by terrorism, but as the former IRTL Lord Anderson observed over a decade ago, the mere reference to 'terrorism' has the potential to distort our perception of the appropriateness (or not) of executive conduct. One could add to Lord Anderson's observation that, by ascribing such significance to 'terrorism', we run the risk that by *not* affixing the label to certain ideologies and/or conduct, we implicitly deem them to be less serious. Indeed, this has been the case with respect to violence perpetrated by self-defined 'incels'. The reluctance of authorities to designate such conduct as terrorism implicitly (if not explicitly) suggests that such violence – which is predominantly directed at women – is not as serious as other forms of terrorism. Such inconsistency is but one example of the issues with the definition of 'terrorism' in s.1 TA 2000.

The changing nature of terrorism including the proliferation of online modes of communication and 'lone wolf' attacks also serves to highlight the limitations of the existing counter-terrorism armoury. Although this certainly does not inevitably lead to the conclusion that *more* options need to be added to that arsenal. Indeed, the rise in XRW terrorism and the novel issues it poses for authorities (particularly in terms of restrictions on speech and online activity) 'should be used as an opportunity to re-evaluate the effectiveness and propriety of all counterterrorism' measures.[340]

This chapter has considered the limitations within the existing counter-terrorism regime in the UK and highlighted the extraordinary breadth of the definition of terrorism in s.1 TA 2000 and the extent to which context drives the interpretation of that provision in a manner that lacks conceptual consistency. This is evident when comparing the approach taken to the definition when examining individuals travelling to Iraq and Syria to fight *against* ISIS vis-à-vis individuals travelling to *join* ISIS. The malleability of the definition

[339] Zedner (n 189), p.119.

[340] Kent Roach, 'Counterterrorism and the Challenges of Terrorism from the Far Right' (2021) 50 Common Law World Review 1, p.3.

confers vast power upon the State to determine whether or not an individual is brought within the terrorism framework, a decision which, as this chapter has also discussed, has profound rights implications.

In a Western liberal democracy grounded in the rule of law, one might expect the courts to provide a degree of protection against such excesses. Particularly as 'we have . . . seen the re-emergence of nationalism and xenophobia, a hardening of attitudes towards migrants, and a dramatic increase in Islamophobia'.[341] While decisions such as *Belmarsh* and the early control order cases suggested that the domestic courts would 'provide a brake on the worst excesses of security populism',[342] recent jurisprudence from the domestic courts including the Supreme Court's judgment in *Begum* suggest otherwise.

[341] Liora Lazarus and Benajmin Goold, 'Finding a Language of Resilience and Inclusion' in Goold and Lazarus (n 189), p.20.

[342] Ibid.

9 Article 8 ECHR and Immigration

CONTENTS

9.1 INTRODUCTION TO MIGRANTS' RIGHTS

Immigration is one of the most politically charged aspects of human rights law, as border control is regarded as fundamental to State sovereignty. Yet whilst it may seem that sovereignty is inherent to the notion of the State, it is worth recalling that this conception of borders is something that largely emerged in the twentieth century. As Çali et al. explain, it was in this period that European States abandoned their earlier 'permissive view of migration and began to see borders as important sites for reifying homogenous nation-states'.[1] Law started 'to exert its authority on migration' and 'become the key site for demarcating the rules of inclusion and exclusion of migrants'.[2] International law followed suit in initially adopting the permissive view and later deferring to States' domestic law.[3] Today, international law, including human rights law, establishes obligations on States in respect of migration, but it would, as we will see in this chapter, be vastly overstating matters to suggest that the tide has turned away from deference to States.

The Convention was not drafted with migration in mind and obligations to permit non-nationals to enter or to remain in a State are thus sometimes seen as extending the Convention and the role of the ECtHR far beyond what States agreed. Yet whilst the protection of migrants was clearly not the impetus for the ECHR, it was 'always accepted that it would apply to anyone who found themselves under the jurisdiction of a Contracting State'.[4] This followed from the fact that the Convention was intended to confer rights on *humans* and not just citizens. There were, however, distinctions. First, the Convention did not

[1] Başak Çali (ed), *Migration and the European Convention on Human Rights* (Oxford University Press, 2021), p.3.

[2] Ibid.

[3] Ibid, p.4. Although for contrasting views on the history of international law and customary international law in this respect, see James A. Nafziger, 'The General Admission of Aliens under International Law' (1983) **77**(4) AJIL 804 and Vincent Chetail (ed), *International Law and Migration Volume I* (Edward Elgar, 2016).

[4] Marie-Bénédicte Dembour, *When Humans Become Migrants* (Oxford University Press, 2015), p.21.

automatically extend to all of the territories for whose international relations the signatory States was responsible.[5] Consequently, colonial subjects were perceived as having been othered from the outset.[6] The Convention also drew a distinction between nationals and non-nationals in Article 16 ECHR which provides that nothing in Articles 10, 11 and 14 ECHR precludes the High Contracting Parties from imposing restrictions on the political activities of aliens.[7] The continuing presence of Article 16 ECHR is indicative of the enduring significance of nationality despite the declaration of universal human rights.[8]

More generally, we see throughout the ECHR case law that it is often the impact of borders and nationality that creates the crucible from which rights violations emerge. There are multiple contexts in which the ECtHR has considered the application of human rights to cases concerning migration, and it has drawn upon a range of rights in doing so. The volume of cases facing the

[5] Article 56 ECHR. In respect of the UK, see A. W. Brian Simpson, *Human Rights and the End of Empire* (Oxford University Press, 2004), ch.16. See also, the continuing legacy of Article 56 ECHR in *Chagos Islanders* v. *the United Kingdom*, App. No. 35622/04, 11/12/2012.

[6] On the history of the colonial clause, see Dembour (n 4), ch.3.

[7] There are few references to Article 16 ECHR in the case law but a noteworthy case is *Piermont* v. *France*, App. Nos. 15773/89 and 15774/89, 27/04/1995, in which the ECtHR held that Article 16 ECHR did not authorise the State to restrict the applicant's rights under Article 10 ECHR. Piermont was a German citizen, a Member of the European Parliament, an environmentalist and a pacifist who was expelled by the French Government from French Polynesia and banned from re-entering the territory after she took part in a public demonstration in which she denounced the continuation of nuclear testing and French presence in the Pacific. Piermont argued that this violated a number of Convention rights including Article 10 ECHR and the Government contested this in part by arguing that Article 16 ECHR was applicable (at [60]). The ECtHR rejected the Government's argument on the ground that 'Piermont's possession of the nationality of a member State of the European Union and . . . her status as a member of the European Parliament do not allow Article 16 (art. 16) of the Convention to be raised against her' (at [64]). In their joint partly dissenting opinion, Mr Ryssdal, Mr Matscher, Sir John Freeland and Mr Jungwiert stated that Piermont was 'indubitably an alien in the eyes of French law, notwithstanding her status as a member of the European Parliament' (at [4]). Consequently they reasoned that Article 16 ECHR 'has to be regarded as at least of some relevance: its reference to "aliens" is unambiguous and without express exception; and convincing grounds would be required for an exception to be inferred' (at [4]). Having identified the need for convincing grounds they went on to observe that such grounds did not exist. Article 16 ECHR was thus applicable. Yet whilst they were of the opinion that Article 16 ECHR applied, they went on to state that it does not follow that 'any restriction at all, at the unfettered discretion of the host State, may justifiably be imposed on the political activity of an alien without contravention of Article 10' ECHR (at [5]). In particular they observed that given 'the increased internationalisation of politics in modern circumstances' and the interest that 'an MEP may legitimately have in the affairs of a Community territory' that 'limits may have to be admitted to the restrictions on the political activity of aliens permissible under Article 16' ECHR (at [5]).

[8] Preamble of the European Convention on Human Rights.

ECtHR led to the establishment of a thematic immigration committee (the first thematic committee of its kind) which operates as a panel of three judges in order to deal with cases falling within the Court's well-established case law; cases falling outside this category continue to be heard by Chambers of seven judges.

Earlier chapters of this book examined Articles 2 and 3 ECHR, observing both their roles in protecting migrants from expulsion as well as the significant limits that apply. Rights that are not considered in detail in this book are those contained in Protocol No. 4 ECHR which includes several rights specific to migration, such as the right to freedom of movement, a prohibition on the expulsion of nationals and the prohibition on collective expulsion of aliens. Article 1 of Protocol No. 7 ECHR also provides for procedural safeguards relating to the expulsion of aliens. To date, neither of those protocols has been ratified by the UK, but significant case law has emerged from the ECtHR in respect of the provisions, including in relation to push-backs at sea or at land borders.[9] In particular there have been important findings of violations of Article 4 of Protocol No. 4 ECHR[10] as well as Articles 2 and 3 ECHR in relation to interceptions and border control operations.[11] Another right that is not considered in detail here is Article 5 ECHR, the right to liberty. Article 5(1)(f) ECHR permits the detention of persons who do not have permission to enter the Contracting State as well as the detention of persons against whom action is being taken with a view to deportation or extradition. Controversially, Article 5(1)(f) ECHR does not require States to establish a maximum period of detention, and there is currently no maximum period of detention in the UK.[12] Nor does Article 5(1)(f) ECHR oblige States to demonstrate that detention is necessary.[13] Detention cannot,

[9] Protocol No. 4 to the Convention for the Protection of Human Rights and Fundamental Freedoms, securing certain rights and freedoms other than those already included in the Convention and in the first Protocol thereto (ETS No. 046).

[10] See for example, *A.R.E.* v. *Greece*, App. No. 15783/21, 07/01/2025; *M.A. and Z.R.* v. *Cyprus*, App. No. 39090/20, 08/10/2024, *M.D. and others* v. *Hungary*, App. No. 60778/19, 19/09/2024; *Sherov and others* v. *Poland*, App. No. 54029/17, 04/04/2024; *S.S. and others* v. *Hungary*, App. No. 56417/19, 12/10/2023; *J.A. and others* v. *Italy*, App. No. 21329/18, 30/03/2023; *Hirsi Jamaa and Others* v. *Italy* [GC] (2012) 55 EHRR 21. Note, however, that in *N.D. and N.T.* v. *Spain*, App. No. 8675/15, 13/02/2020, the Grand Chamber stated at [200] that 'the applicant's own conduct is a relevant factor in assessing the protection to be afforded under Article 4 of Protocol No. 4' ECHR. For a critique see Paulo Pinto de Albuquerque and Guillaume Dartigue, 'Children of a Lesser God: The Rights of Migrants and Refugees under the European Convention on Human Rights' (2023) 3 EHRLR 217, 232.

[11] *Hirsi Jamaa and Others* v. *Italy* (n 10); *Safi and Others* v. *Greece*, App. No. 5418/15, 07/07/2022; *Alkhatib and Others* v. *Greece*, App. No. 3566/16, 16/01/2024; *Alhowais* v. *Hungary*, App. No. 59435/17, 02/02/2023; *A.R.E.* v. *Greece* (n 10).

[12] *JN* v. *the United Kingdom*, App. No. 37289/12, 19/05/2016.

[13] *Chahal* v. *the United Kingdom* [GC] (1997) 23 EHRR 413 at [112].

however, be arbitrary,[14] whilst, in cases involving children or adults with specific vulnerabilities, their detention may not be justified under Article 5(1)(f) ECHR if the aim pursued could be achieved by other less coercive measures.[15] It is also important to note that the conditions of detention may violate Article 3 ECHR.[16] In this respect serious questions arose from the UK's use of Bibby Stockholm, a floating barge, to detain migrants in Dorset, where there was an outbreak of legionella, a suspected suicide, and allegations of severely overcrowded conditions.[17] A non-statutory inquiry has also begun in respect of alleged mistreatment of asylum seekers at the Manston processing centre where some people were placed in tents in November 2022.[18] Finally we should note that arguments have also been advanced in respect of Articles 9 and 14 ECHR where migrants face being returned to a country in which they face religious persecution, although thus far the ECtHR has been reluctant to accord protection under Article 9 ECHR if the threshold for Article 3 ECHR is not met.[19] Article 14 ECHR also raises issues where the applicant alleges that they have been

[14] *Saadi* v. *the United Kingdom* [GC] (2008) 47 EHRR 17 at [73]–[74] stated that to avoid being branded as arbitrary, 'detention must be carried out in good faith; it must be closely connected to the purpose of preventing unauthorised entry of the person to the country; the place and conditions of detention should be appropriate, bearing in mind that "the measure is applicable not to those who have committed criminal offences but to aliens who, often fearing for their lives, have fled from their own country"; and the length of the detention should not exceed that reasonably required for the purpose pursued'.

[15] See, for example, *Popov* v. *France*, App. No. 39472/07, 19/01/2012 at [119].

[16] On the conditions of immigration detention in general see, for example, *Khlaifia and Others* v. *Italy* [GC], App. No. 16483/12, 15/12/2016 at [159]–[177] and 196; *Georgia* v. *Russia (I)* [GC], App. No. 13255/07, 03/07/2014 at [192]–[205]; *M.S.S.* v. *Belgium and Greece* [GC] (2011) 53 EHRR 2 at [216]–[234]; *Sakir* v. *Greece*, App. No. 48475/09, 24/03/2016 at [50]–[58]; *S.Z.* v. *Greece*, App. No. 66702/13, 21/06/2018 at [36]–[42]. On detention of migrant children, see ECHR-KS Key Theme, *Immigration, Detention of Migrant Children* (31/08/2023) which discusses the case law in respect of Articles 3, 5 and 8 ECHR. See also, Pinto de Albuquerque and Dartigue (n 10).

[17] The barge arrived in July 2023 and asylum seekers were moved on to the barge in August 2023. In July 2024 the Home Office announced that the contract for Bibby Stockholm would not be renewed past January 2025 and the barge was subsequently removed in January 2025. Diane Taylor, 'People on Bibby Stockholm treated like 'cattle', former workers say', *The Guardian*, 14 May 2024, www.theguardian.com/uk-news/article/2024/may/14/people-on-bibby-stockholm-treated-like-cattle-former-workers-say; Diane Taylor, 'Family of man who died on Bibby Stockholm say Government should be held responsible', *The Guardian*, 19 March 2024, www.theguardian.com/uk-news/2024/mar/19/family-of-leonard-farruku-who-died-on-bibby-stockholm-say-government-should-be-held-responsible; Diane Taylor, 'Deadliest legionella strain found onboard Bibby Stockholm', *The Guardian*, 8 September 2023, www.theguardian.com/uk-news/2023/sep/08/legionella-found-onboard-the-bibby-stockholm-is-most-deadly-strain.

[18] Home Office Guidance, *Manston Independent Inquiry: terms of reference* (12 February 2025), www.gov.uk/government/publications/independent-inquiry-into-manston-short-term-holding-facility/manston-independent-inquiry-terms-of-reference.

[19] *Z and T* v. *the United Kingdom*, App. No. 27034/05 (dec.), 28/02/2006.

discriminated against on grounds of their immigration status,[20] or where they have been discriminated on other grounds in an immigration-related context.[21]

Following contemplation of some of the ways in which immigration policies and practices raise issues across the Convention, the focus of this chapter will rest on the role of Article 8 ECHR, the right to respect for private life, family life, home and correspondence. This right is used in cases where migrants face deportation and where family members seek entry to the Contracting State. Article 8 ECHR has a vastly broader remit than Articles 2 and 3 ECHR, as the threshold for engaging Article 8 ECHR is far lower. In fact, if an individual resides within the Contracting State, then Article 8 ECHR will almost certainly be applicable if the State seeks to expel them. Article 8 is also applicable where core members of the applicant's family reside in the Contracting State. Consequently, Article 8 ECHR brings almost all deportation cases into the human rights law framework, and it is this that is contentious. Yet the mere fact that Article 8 ECHR is engaged does not mean that the applicant will succeed in resisting expulsion. Unlike Articles 2 and 3 ECHR, Article 8 ECHR is a qualified right and so States can (and often do) justify interfering with it. Thus in practice few applicants succeed in using Article 8 ECHR to resist deportation even in cases where they were born or lived almost their entire life in the Contracting State. This has led to the criticism that the ECtHR prioritises State sovereignty over and above the rights that it purports to confer on migrants, rendering the rights virtually meaningless and legitimising States' practices.[22] There is also a colonial context to many of the cases, giving rise to questions about who benefits from human rights law.[23] Yet whilst the limits of the case law are decried by many, an opposing perspective arises from institutional critiques in which the ECtHR is regarded as too interventionist. From this perspective the process of having to justify deportation (in many cases of convicted criminals) to a court (and especially to an international human rights court) is regarded as an incursion into State sovereignty that exceeds the limits of the ECtHR's role.

Similar issues arise in respect of the case law on family reunification. These are often cases in which family members separated by borders seek to rely on the positive obligations in Article 8 ECHR to be reunited in the Contracting State. They involve spouses forced to live apart, children seeking to be reunited with their parents, and adult children trying to bring elderly parents to the State in which they live and work in order to care for them during the later

[20] *Anakomba Yula* v. *Belgium*, App. No. 45413/07, 10/03/2009; *Bah* v. *the United Kingdom*, App. No. 56328/07, 27/09/2011; *Ponomarayov* v. *Bulgaria*, App. No. 5335/05, 10/02/2009; *Hode and Abdi* v. *the United Kingdom*, App. No. 22341/09, 06/11/2012; *MT* v. *Sweden*, App. No. 22105/18, 20/10/2022.

[21] *Biao* v. *Denmark* [GC] (2017) 64 EHRR 1; *Abdulaziz, Cabales and Balkandali* v. *the United Kingdom* (1985) 7 EHRR 471; *Kiyutin* v. *Russia* (2011) 53 EHRR 26; *Pajić* v. *Croatia* (2018) 67 EHRR 12; *Taddeucci and McCall* v. *Italy*, App. No. 51362/09, 30/06/2016.

[22] Dembour (n 4). [23] Ibid, ch.3.

stages of life. In some cases, family members were separated due to hardship and/or conflict in the State from which they originate and have waited years to be reunited. In other cases, citizens of the Contracting State are denied the prospect of living with their family in their own country; as Wray observes, in these circumstances '[c]itizens see living with their loved ones in their own country as central to their belonging, but governments do not'.[24] The impact of this is that while 'a citizen refused family reunification has not lost the formal attributes of citizenship . . . they experience a deeper and more personal disenfranchisement',[25] as denying entry often means that applicants will either never reside with their family, or will never do so in their own country. In other cases, family members have lived apart for a period but shifting needs mean that they now need to be closer together in order to provide support. There are also cases in which the family is not separated but is living together in the Contracting State with an irregular status and is asking the State to regularise their residence. Denial of residency in these circumstances perpetuates vulnerabilities, leaving families open to exploitation as well as the prospect of separation.[26]

The rationales advanced by States for denying entry are often different to their reasons for deportation. Deportation is routinely an additional punishment following a criminal conviction, but in family reunification cases there is often no criminality,[27] instead borders are invoked to exclude those who are seen as a burden to the State. There are very few cases in which applicants have succeeded in convincing the ECtHR that the Contracting State is obliged to allow entry; where cases have succeeded, they usually involve children, but it is important to note that even they are not guaranteed entry. Meanwhile, the prospects for elderly parents are non-existent. As Wray observes:

> This pain is not felt equally by all but is distributed according to wider patterns of racial, gender and class disadvantage, and it often reproduces older patterns of colonial domination and exclusion.[28]

The family reunification case law has thus led to criticism that the ECtHR allows State sovereignty to trump the needs of migrants and that it is averting its eyes to

[24] Helena Wray, *Article 8 ECHR, Family Reunification and the UK's Supreme Court: Family Matters?* (Hart, 2023), p.9.

[25] Ibid.

[26] See Francesca Ippolito and Carmen Pérez González, '"Handle with Care" in Strasbourg – The Effective Access of Vulnerable Undocumented Migrants to Minimum Socio-Economic Rights' in Çali (ed) (n 1) in which they argue that the ECtHR, despite the limited scope of protection for undocumented migrants enshrined in the ECHR and the Court's resistance to impose impossible or disproportionate burdens on States has contributed to the consolidation of a minimum standard of socio-economic rights for undocumented migrants.

[27] There are cases in which the applicant has already entered the Contracting State as an irregular migrant, has overstayed, or otherwise committed an immigration-related offence.

[28] Wray (n 24), p.10.

the hardship and suffering this creates. Yet as noted above, the ECtHR is simultaneously criticised by those that regard the recognition of *any* obligations in respect of *entry of non-nationals* as vastly beyond the realm of the ECtHR's legitimate function. Difficult questions thus arise as to whether the ECtHR has overextended or is at risk of overextending human rights law, or conversely whether it has failed to protect migrants such that they are pushed to the margins of human rights law, a stance that challenges the notion of the universality of rights.

The final part of this chapter examines the ways in which Article 8 ECHR has both shaped and been shaped by domestic immigration law. The enactment of the Human Rights Act 1998 (HRA) meant that public authorities, including the Home Office and the courts were bound by s.6 HRA to act compatibly with Article 8 ECHR. In the early case law, the domestic courts regarded the question of whether a deportation order was compatible with Article 8 ECHR to be one that was firmly within the judicial realm.[29] This prompted a political backlash which resulted in legislation prescribing how Article 8 ECHR should be applied by the courts, tipping the scales heavily towards deportation by stipulating the weight that should be accorded to the public interest. In respect of family reunification, enactment of the HRA also meant that immigration officials were bound by Article 8 ECHR when determining entry. The provisions in respect of entry are set out in Immigration Rules and were substantially amended in 2012 to reflect the Government's desire to reduce net migration. Those amendments dramatically curtailed prospects of family reunification by erecting significant entry requirements, coupled with onerous thresholds for exceptions in cases where those requirements cannot be met.[30] The provisions in respect of deportation, as well as those in respect of family reunification, have prompted legal challenges in which it has been argued that the provisions are incompatible with Article 8 ECHR. To date, these cases have been largely unsuccessful as both the domestic courts and the ECtHR have upheld the legality of these provisions and adopted a deferential approach in respect of the UK's calibration of Article 8 ECHR. This chapter thus offers insight into the ways in which the Convention right has been shaped both domestically and internationally and the driving forces behind the interpretation and application of rights.

9.2 IMMIGRATION AND ARTICLE 8 ECHR

Article 8 – Right to Respect for Private and Family Life

1. Everyone has the right to respect for his private and family life, his home and his correspondence.

[29] See 9.3.1.1 below. [30] See 9.3.1 and 9.3.2 below.

2. There shall be no interference by a public authority with the exercise of this right except such as is in accordance with the law and is necessary in a democratic society in the interests of national security, public safety or the economic wellbeing of the country, for the prevention of disorder or crime, for the protection of health or morals, or for the protection of the rights and freedoms of others.

9.2.1 Article 8 ECHR and Deportation

Applicants facing deportation are usually able to rely upon either the right to respect for family life or the right to respect for private life in Article 8 ECHR. Occasionally there have been references to the right to respect for the home, but this has not been developed or considered independently of the other two rights.[31] Yet whilst Article 8 ECHR is often applicable, it is common practice for States to seek to expel non-nationals who commit criminal offences. As Çali and Cunningham observe, States 'see deportation as the default legal policy treating those who violate domestic laws as outstaying their welcome, despite the length of time spent in the host state'.[32] This practice extends to non-nationals who were born in the Contracting State as well as those who have lived almost their entire lives in the Contracting State.[33] Thus, while nationals who commit criminal offences are subject to the criminal justice system, non-nationals may face being sent to countries in which they have never resided or in which they have few ties. The legitimacy of this has long been contested. In fact, the Parliamentary Assembly of the Council of Europe opposed it almost twenty-five years ago in Recommendation 1504 (2001) observing that the application of expulsion measures to long-term immigrants 'seems both disproportionate and discriminatory'.[34] The Assembly thus pronounced that '[u]nder no circumstances should expulsion be applied to people born or brought up in the host country or to under-age children'.[35] It also recommended limiting expulsion to 'highly exceptional cases' where 'it has

[31] This is interesting as 'respect for the home' of the applicant may have focused the ECtHR's attention on the place of residence, whereas the invocation of 'private life' has extended the focus to 'the totality of social ties between settled migrants and the community in which they are living'. As we will see, this has allowed the ECtHR to consider to what extent the applicant is 'integrated' into the Contracting State, a development that raises difficulties in cases where applicants have ties with other States. It is, however, possible that such factors could have also been introduced under the umbrella of the right to respect for the home.

[32] Başak Çali and Stewart Cunningham, 'The European Court of Human Rights and Removal of Long-term Migrants: Entrenched Statism with a Human Voice?' in Çali (n 1), p.60.

[33] *Azerkane* v. *Netherlands*, App. No. 3138/16, 02/06/2020 *Z* v. *Switzerland*, App. No. 6325/15, 22/12/2020.

[34] Parliamentary Assembly of the Council of Europe Recommendation 1504 (2001) *Non-expulsion of long-term immigrants*, 14 March 2001 at [3].

[35] Ibid at [7].

been proven, with due regard to the presumption of innocence, that the person concerned represents a real danger to the state'.[36] Those recommendations were, however, rejected by the ECtHR in *Üner* v. *Netherlands* where it observed that an absolute right not to be expelled cannot be derived from Article 8 ECHR, and that the position of non-nationals 'cannot be equated with that of a national when it comes to the above-mentioned power of the Contracting States to expel aliens'.[37] Thus, almost twenty-five years after the Parliamentary Assembly Recommendation, the ECtHR continues to find that expulsion is compatible with the ECHR in circumstances far broader than those suggested by the Assembly and continues to permit the expulsion of those who were born or brought up in the Contracting State.[38]

9.2.1.1 *Article 8(1) ECHR and Family Life*

Acknowledging that expulsion of the applicant may lead to families being separated, the ECtHR has recognised that 'removal of a person from a country where close members of his family are living may amount to an infringement of the right to respect for family life as guaranteed by Article 8 (1)'.[39] The ECtHR's reference to 'close' family members is significant as family life is strictly limited in the immigration context to the nuclear or core family, that is, spouses and child dependents.[40] Spouses includes heterosexual and homosexual partnerships,[41] including both married and de facto relationships. In respect of spouses, the ECtHR has made it clear that Article 8 ECHR does not oblige the State to recognise a child marriage, thus the Court accepted that a State did not have to recognise a marriage contracted by a fourteen year old.[42] With regard to de facto partnerships, the ECtHR has indicated that in deciding whether a couple can be said to have 'family life' the relevant factors include 'whether the couple live together, the length of their relationship and whether they have demonstrated their commitment to each other by having children together or by any other means'.[43] In respect of children that have yet to come of age, there is usually family life between a parent and child, regardless of whether the parents were married and regardless of whether the parent and child cohabit, albeit that ties may not be recognised where there are 'exceptional circumstances'.[44] There is, however, no family life with other adult family members such as siblings, grandparents or nieces and

[36] Ibid at [10]. [37] *Üner* v. *Netherlands* (2007) 45 EHRR 14 at [56].

[38] Parliamentary Assembly of the Council of Europe Recommendation 1504 (n 34).

[39] *Al-Nashif* v. *Bulgaria* (2003) 36 EHRR 37. [40] *Slivenko* v. *Latvia* (2004) 39 EHRR 24.

[41] *Pajić* v. *Croatia* (n 21). [42] *Z.H. and R.H.* v. *Switzerland* (2017) 65 EHRR 30.

[43] *Al-Nashif* v. *Bulgaria* (n 39) at [112].

[44] *Boughanemi* v. *France* (1996) 22 EHRR 228 at [35].

nephews unless there are 'more than the normal emotional ties', which means that a high level of dependency must be shown.[45]

This narrow focus on the nuclear family has been heavily criticised by scholars who have emphasised that this does not reflect the true nature of family ties and that it imposes a particular Western view on families that may have different cultural notions and traditions.[46] Indeed this practice is indicative of the phenomenon that scholars have emphasised, namely, that the very concept of 'family' is 'construed socially and politically in ways that intersect crucially with constructions of ethnicity, race, nation and belonging'.[47] This is evident not only at the Article 8(1) ECHR stage where the ECtHR determines where the right to respect for family life is applicable, but also, as we will see later in this chapter, in the Article 8(2) ECHR analysis where there is an assessment of whether there was 'real and genuine family life' and the 'solidity of family ties'.[48]

A question that has arisen from this approach is whether adult children can rely upon family ties with their parents when opposing deportation. The early case law was mixed, in some cases family ties were recognised,[49] while in others it was determined that adult children no longer had ties to their parents,[50] but it now appears that family ties will only be recognised where the adult child has not yet formed their own family and there is the requisite degree of dependency.[51] The need for dependency and the high threshold attached to it was evident in the Grand Chamber's judgment in *Savran* v. *Denmark*.[52] The facts in Savran (which was discussed in Chapter 5 in the context of Article 3 ECHR) were that the applicant, who was receiving treatment for paranoid schizophrenia, was expelled from Denmark and made the subject of an entry ban following conviction for a serious criminal offence. He opposed this on account of his condition, relying on Articles 3 and 8 ECHR. As discussed in Chapter 5, the ECtHR held that the threshold set by Article

45 *Pormes* v. *Netherlands*, App. No. 25402/14, 28/07/2020 at [47].

46 Dembour (n 4) and Yaël Ronen, 'The Ties that Bind: Family and Private Life as Bars to the Deportation of Immigrants' (2012) International Journal of Law in Context 283, Wray (n 24), p.6. On adult children and elderly parents, see Carmen Draghici, 'Adult Children and Elderly Parents in Strasbourg Proceedings: A Misconstrued Approach to "Family Life"' (2018) 32 International Journal of Law, Policy and the Family 42–62.

47 Saskia Bonjou and Laura Cleton, 'Co-constructions of Family and Belonging in the Politics of Family Migration' in Emma Carmel et al. (eds), *Handbook on the Governance and Politics of Migration* (Edward Elgar Publishing Limited, 2021). See also, Joe Turner, *Bordering Intimacy: Postcolonial Governance and the Policing of Family* (Manchester University Press, 2020).

48 See discussion at Section 9.2.1.3 below.

49 *Bouchelkia* v. *France* (1998) 25 EHRR 686, *Boujlifa* v. *France* (2000) 30 EHRR 419 and *Maslov* v. *Austria* [GC], App. No. 1638/03, 23/06/2008.

50 *Onur* v. *the United Kingdom* (2009) 49 EHRR 38 and *A W Khan* v. *the United Kingdom* (2010) 50 EHRR 47.

51 *Samsonnikov* v. *Estonia*, App. No. 52178/10, 3/07/2012.

52 *Savran* v. *Denmark*, App. No. 57467/15, 07/12/2021.

3 ECHR was not met. In relation to Article 8 ECHR, the applicant argued that the measures violated his right to respect for family life and his right to respect for private life. In respect of the family life provision, he argued that he had very close ties with his mother and siblings as well as his niece and nephew, and that due to his condition, he was dependent on them. This was rejected by the Grand Chamber. In determining that he could not rely on the right to family life, the ECtHR emphasised that the applicant 'had often lived in foster care and institutional settings',[53] a stance that clearly restricts the right for some of the most vulnerable members of society. The ECtHR also went on to state that his illness was not 'sufficient evidence of his dependence'.[54] In particular, it determined that it had not been demonstrated that his 'health condition incapacitated him to the extent that he was compelled to rely on their care and support in his daily life'.[55] Nor was he financially dependent as he was supported by a disability pension.[56] This suggests that family ties are only established where there is extensive physical and financial dependency. Indicating that the ECtHR approaches dependency as if something akin to an infantile relationship within a stable family set-up is required. A further point to observe is the way in which the ECtHR pointed to the applicant's disability pension as a reason to deny family ties. This is also problematic, not least because it determines what constitutes a 'family' and therefore the ambit of the right by reference to the State's own policies. The overall impression is thus that the ECtHR has gone down a route in which it determines the ambit of family life by reference to factors that do not accord with the complexity of emotional attachments and the plurality of family life. The ECtHR's refusal to recognise family ties was firmly criticised by Judge Ivana Jelić who emphasised the vulnerability of the applicant. She argued that

> the specific meaning of the family in respect of vulnerable persons should be taken into consideration, since they are unable to establish their own nuclear families, a factor which consequently has an impact on the meaning of their right to respect for family life. In the instant case, the standard metric should not have been applied to the applicant when assessing whether he had family ties in Denmark. In the concrete circumstances of the case, the extended notion of family and family life should have been accepted.[57]

Although Jelić's approach is more generous than the ECtHR's, there are problems with this vulnerability approach. First, the ECtHR should be cautious about assuming that mental illness renders a person unable to establish their own nuclear family. Second, this approach perpetuates the notion that a 'nuclear' family is the end goal for all and that the natural progression is for a child to be born into a nuclear family, to have a brief period of time as an

[53] Ibid at [177]. [54] Ibid at [177]. [55] Ibid at [178]. [56] Ibid at [178].

[57] Ibid, separate opinion by Judge Ivana Jelić.

adult where they are in between nuclear families, before establishing their own nuclear family as an adult.

Having highlighted the ECtHR's narrow approach to family life, we have to consider whether this is significant given that (as we will see below) applicants facing deportation are usually able to rely upon the right to respect for private life. Indeed, Savran was ultimately successful in arguing that there had been a violation of his right to respect for private life.[58] Yet whilst Savran succeeded due to the particular circumstances of his case, others will struggle because even if applicants are able to rely upon the right to respect for private life to engage Article 8(1) ECHR, a finding of no violation at the Article 8(2) ECHR stage remains likely if there are no family ties. In this respect, Alan Desmond suggests that what may appear to be an innocuous distinction between family and private life is in fact insidious.[59]

9.2.1.2 *Article 8(1) ECHR and Private Life*

In stark contrast to family ties, which as we have seen is subject to a narrow definition, the concept of private life or personal ties is very broad and there is no fixed set of criteria. The factors that the ECtHR considers include the length of time and integration into the State, through for example, language, relationships and employment.[60] Although these are relevant factors, it is important to emphasise that there are very few cases where the ECtHR assesses personal ties at the Article 8(1) ECHR stage and it has hardly ever determined that an applicant has failed to establish such ties. A rare case in which it did so was *Auad* v. *Bulgaria*, but in that case the applicant had been in the host state for less than a month.[61] The breadth of the provision is thus such that the ECtHR frequently declares that 'it will be a rare case where a settled migrant will be unable to demonstrate that his or her deportation would interfere with his or her private life as guaranteed by Article 8'.[62]

We have already seen that the right to respect for private life is crucial where the ECtHR does not recognise family ties. The private life provision is also vital where the entire family faces expulsion. In these circumstances, the family will not be separated, hence there will be no intrusion into family life. This situation arose in *Slivenko* v. *Latvia* a case in which the Latvian Government sought to deport a mother and her daughter.[63] The reason for their expulsion was that the husband/father had been a member of the Russian military and following

[58] Ibid at [178].

[59] Alan Desmond, 'The Private Life of Family Matters: Curtailing Human Rights Protection for Migrants under Article 8 of the ECHR?' (2018) 29 EJIL 261–279.

[60] *AA* v. *the United Kingdom*, App. No. 8000/08, 20/09/2011; *Slivenko* v. *Latvia* (n 40).

[61] *Auad* v. *Bulgaria*, App. No. 46390/10, 11/10/2011.

[62] *Samsonnikov* v. *Estonia* (n 51) at [81].

[63] *Slivenko* v. *Latvia* (n 40).

Latvia's independence a treaty required the removal of Russian military from Latvia. The mother and daughter objected to their expulsion on the basis that their ties to Latvia existed independently of their ties to their husband/father as the mother had lived there since she was one month old, while the daughter had been born there. Realising that family life would not assist, the ECtHR observed that it 'must be accepted that the totality of social ties between settled migrants and the community in which they are living constitutes part of the concept of "private life"'.[64] This has been described as a 'sea change' moment in the case law as it was 'the first time the ECtHR relied exclusively on the private life of the applicants as a bar to deportation not only in describing the facts but also in defining the right violated under Article 8'.[65]

The ECtHR's use of the private life provision has received mixed responses. One perspective is that moving from family life to private life shifts the ECtHR's focus from a status-based analysis to a rights-based analysis which benefits migrants with no family ties.[66] Yet while this has expanded the right, it has not led to the rights-based approach recommended by the Parliamentary Assembly Resolution namely, that long-term immigrants should only be expelled where there are particularly serious offences affecting state security of which they have been found guilty; and that migrants who are born or raised in the country and their children should not be expelled under any circumstances.[67] Moreover, the focus on private life has brought with it an emphasis upon 'integration'. This affects the way in which the right is evaluated at the Article 8(2) ECHR stage, where the ECtHR emphasises factors such as whether the individual has learnt the language and whether they have severed ties with their home community. This may adversely affect migrants where there is limited social integration or where they have retained strong ties to their country of origin or culture. The way in which this plays out forces us to confront the way in which plurality may be more readily accepted when migrants are ethnically and culturally closer to the host state.

9.2.1.3 *Justifying an Interference under Article 8(2) ECHR*

Regardless of whether the private life or family life provision is engaged, States can justify expulsion if they satisfy the three elements required by Article 8(2) ECHR:

(i) Legal framework governing expulsion;
(ii) Expulsion is in pursuit of a legitimate aim; and
(iii) Expulsion is necessary in a democratic society (i.e. a proportionate response).

[64] Ibid. [65] Ronen (n 46). [66] Ibid.

[67] Parliamentary Assembly of the Council of Europe Recommendation 1504 (n 34).

There are cases in which the ECtHR has held that deportation violates Article 8 ECHR,[68] but there are also many cases in which States have justified expulsion, including cases where applicants have lived their entire lives in the Contracting State.[69]

9.2.1.3.1 *Legal Safeguards*

The first requirement of Article 8(2) ECHR is that the State must demonstrate that deportation was governed by national law and that the legal framework has the quality of law. In many cases this is straightforward, but the ECtHR will scrutinise the adequacy of the domestic process and whether there are sufficient legal safeguards. For example, in *Liu* v. *Russia*, the ECtHR found that the legal provisions did not provide for the adequate degree of protection against arbitrary interference.[70] In *CG and others* v. *Bulgaria*, the ECtHR found a violation as there was a discrepancy in the reasons provided for the deportation.[71] Whilst in *Al-Nashif* v. *Bulgaria*, the ECtHR found a violation where the grounds for the decision were not made known to the applicant, nor to his lawyer, and there was no opportunity to challenge the decision in legal proceedings.[72]

9.2.1.3.2 *Legitimate Aim*

The applicable legitimate aims are specified in Article 8(2) ECHR. In many cases, the State will rely upon protection of public order, national security or prevention of disorder or crime. The Grand Chamber has also accepted that immigration control typically serves the general interests of the economic wellbeing of the country and that this is a legitimate aim.[73] Thus, while States must identify a legitimate aim, this aspect of Article 8(2) ECHR is usually straightforward.

9.2.1.3.3 *Necessary in a Democratic Society: Proportionality*

The core question in most cases is whether the interference is necessary in a democratic society. The ECtHR has identified a non-exhaustive list of factors

[68] In *Omojudi* v. *the United Kingdom*, App. No. 1820/08, (2010) 51 EHRR 10, a Nigerian national could not be expelled following convictions for theft, conspiracy to defraud and sexual assault and in *A. W. Khan* v. *the United Kingdom* (n 50), the ECtHR held that a Pakistani national convicted of drug-trafficking could not be expelled. In those cases the ECtHR recognised the particular difficulties that Omojudi's family would have faced in relocating to Nigeria, and the fact that Khan had been living in the UK since infancy.

[69] *Azerkane* v. *Netherlands* (n 33), *Z* v. *Switzerland* (n 33).

[70] *Liu* v. *Russia*, App. No. 42086/05, 06/12/2007.

[71] *CG and others* v. *Bulgaria* (2008) 47 EHRR 51.

[72] *Al-Nashif* v. *Bulgaria* (n 39).

[73] *Biao* v. *Denmark* (n 21).

that the domestic authorities must consider in determining whether deportation is necessary in a democratic society and provided the State has done so, the ECtHR will generally not intervene. Many of these factors were identified in *Boultif* v. *Switzerland* and are known as the *Boultif* factors.[74]

Boultif was an Algerian national living in Switzerland when he was convicted of robbery. After he was released from prison his residence permit was withdrawn. As he was married to a Swiss national, this violated his right to respect for family life, thus the question for the ECtHR was whether this was necessary in a democratic society. The Court observed that it needed to 'establish guiding principles in order to examine whether the measure in question was necessary in a democratic society'.[75] It then went on to identify the following criteria:

> the nature and seriousness of the offence committed by the applicant; the duration of the applicant's stay in the country from which he is going to be expelled; the time which has elapsed since the commission of the offence and the applicant's conduct during that period; the nationalities of the various persons concerned; the applicant's family situation, such as the length of the marriage; other factors revealing whether the couple lead a real and genuine family life; whether the spouse knew about the offence at the time when he or she entered into a family relationship; and whether there are children in the marriage and, if so, their age. Not least, the Court will also consider the seriousness of the difficulties which the spouse would be likely to encounter in the applicant's country of origin, although the mere fact that a person may face certain difficulties in accompanying her or his spouse cannot in itself preclude expulsion.[76]

Applying this to the facts, the ECtHR concluded that there was a real impediment to family life as it was practically impossible for Boultif to continue family life outside Switzerland.[77] Consequently, as 'he presented only a comparatively limited danger to public order' the interference was not proportionate to the aim pursued.[78]

The *Boultif* criteria were developed for cases where 'the main obstacle to expulsion was that it would entail difficulties for the spouses to stay together and, in particular, for one of them and/or the children to live in the other's country of origin'.[79] However, since then they have become the foundation for the balancing exercise in *all* deportation cases regardless of whether the right to family life is engaged. An important development in this respect was the recognition in *Üner* v. *Netherlands* that the *Boultif* criteria were not sufficiently comprehensive to 'render them suitable for application in all cases concerning the expulsion and/or exclusion of settled migrants following a criminal conviction'.[80] The ECtHR thus held that the 'solidity of social and cultural ties with the host country' should be added to the *Boultif* factors;[81]

[74] *Boultif* v. *Switzerland* (2001) 33 EHRR 1179. [75] Ibid at [48]. [76] Ibid at [48].
[77] Ibid at [55]. [78] Ibid. [79] Ibid at [48]. [80] *Üner* v. *Netherlands* (n 37) at [59].
[81] Ibid at [58]–[60].

also observing that this gives weight to the ties that applicants may have with the Contracting State if they have lived there for most or all their lives and that it is important to recognise these ties, as not all long-term migrants will have family life in the host country.[82]

The subsequent case law has confirmed that the *Boultif* and *Üner* criteria must be considered in all cases regardless of whether the right to respect for private life or family life applies.[83] The Grand Chamber in *Savran* v. *Denmark* (discussed above) also observed that this is a non-exhaustive list of requirements and that other factors may be considered.[84] Thus the Court noted the medical implications of expulsion had to be taken into account, although on the facts it was found that the domestic authorities had done so.[85] Six judges dissented from this, arguing that medical needs should not be considered under Article 8 ECHR in cases where those needs have been held to be insufficient in respect of Article 3 ECHR.[86] They argued that this causes serious problems for the interface between the Convention rights.[87] We may therefore see further case law on the relationship between Articles 3 and 8 ECHR.

Another factor that the ECtHR considers in determining whether there has been a violation of Article 8 ECHR is the duration of any re-entry ban. As the Grand Chamber observed in *Savran* the ECtHR has found 'a ban to be disproportionate on account of its unlimited duration, whilst in other cases it has considered the limited duration of the exclusion measure to be a factor weighing in favour of its proportionality'.[88] In this regard it noted that it will accept an expulsion measure as proportionate in a situation where, in spite of the indefinite duration of that measure, possibilities remain for the applicants to enter the returning State.[89] Conversely, where a temporary re-entry ban is in effect a permanent ban as the prospect of the applicant being readmitted is purely theoretical then the temporary status of the ban cannot be attributed decisive weight as a factor capable of rendering an applicant's expulsion compatible with Article 8 ECHR.[90] This was significant in *Sharafane* v. *Denmark* where the applicant, an Iraqi national, was born in Denmark, had no criminal past, had never received a warning of the risk of expulsion, and had never been to Iraq prior to being expelled and subject to a six year re-entry ban.[91] Although

[82] Ibid at [59].

[83] *Unuane* v. *the United Kingdom* (2021) 72 EHRR 24 at [74] and *Savran* v. *Denmark* (n 52) at [183].

[84] *Savran* v. *Denmark* (n 52) at [183].

[85] Ibid at [191].

[86] Ibid, dissenting opinion of Judges Kjølbro, Dedov, Lubarda, Harutyunyan, Kucsko-Stadlmayer and Poláčková.

[87] Ibid, dissenting opinion at [16].

[88] *Savran* v. *Denmark* (n 52) at [199].

[89] Ibid.

[90] *Sharafane* v. *Denmark*, App. No. 5199/23, 12/11/2024 at [73].

[91] Ibid. For cases where no violation was found see *Al-Habeeb* v. *Denmark*, App. No. 14171/23, 12/11/2024; *Savuran* v. *Denmark*, App. No. 3645/23, 12/11/2024; *Winther* v. *Denmark*, App. No. 9588/21, 12/11/2024.

the re-entry ban was limited to six years, it amounted de facto to a permanent ban, since the prospect of his re-entering Denmark remained purely theoretical.[92] He had no partner or children or relevant education which could justify an application for a residence permit. Moreover, in respect of applying for a short-term visa, as an Iraqi national he belonged to a group for whom visas were granted only in very exceptional circumstances, for example if a close family member in Denmark was terminally ill or had died. This meant that the exceptional circumstances where a visa could be granted were in reality the same as for a person who was subject to a re-entry ban.[93] The statistics provided by the Government confirmed that no nationals of countries in this visa group had been granted a visa between 2019 and 2024.[94] In these circumstances the ECtHR held that the domestic authorities could not attribute decisive weight to the fact that the re-entry ban was limited to six years in determining whether the applicant's expulsion compatible with Article 8 ECHR.[95] The measures were thus disproportionate and violated Article 8 ECHR.[96]

The *Boultif* and *Üner* criteria do not tell us how the factors will be evaluated and thus the outcome can be difficult to predict, which is perhaps not surprising given the number of issues that need to be considered. Nevertheless, the general trend is that few cases result in the finding of a violation.[97] In this regard, the dissenting judges in *Savran* suggested that a violation may be found where: (i) the criminal offence was less serious or the punishment less severe; (ii) there were very special circumstances; (iii) the applicant was still a minor at the time of the decision on expulsion; (iv) the applicant was a minor when the crimes were committed and they were of a less serious nature typical of 'juvenile delinquency'; or (v) the applicant had retained no ties with the country of origin.[98]

Certainly, one of the factors that seems to weigh heavier in the balancing exercise is whether the applicant was a juvenile. The significance of this was evident in *Maslov* v. *Austria* where the Grand Chamber declared that:

> for a settled migrant who has lawfully spent all or the major part of his or her childhood and youth in the host country very serious reasons are required to justify expulsion. This is all the more so where the person concerned committed the offences underlying the expulsion measure as a juvenile.[99]

[92] Ibid at [72]. [93] Ibid at [68]. [94] Ibid at [70]. [95] Ibid at [74].

[96] Ibid at [75]. [97] Dembour (n 4), ch. 6, fn.83.

[98] *Savran* v. *Denmark* (n 52), dissenting opinion of Judges Kjølbro, Dedov, Lubarda, Harutyunyan, Kucsko-Stadlmayer and Poláčková at [11].

[99] *Maslov* v. *Austria* (n 49). The UK Supreme Court considered in *Sanambar* v. *SSHD* [2021] UKSC 30, [2021] 1 WLR 3847 at [46] whether *Maslov* creates an additional threshold. It determined that it does not establish a threshold, but reflects the fact that 'the weight that should be given to those criteria will depend upon the circumstances' and that '[u]nsurprisingly children are treated differently from adults'.

When it comes to adults, the ECtHR is far less sympathetic. Consequently, although the balancing criteria include according weight to 'social and cultural ties' and the 'duration of the applicant's stay in the country', it is questionable whether much weight is accorded to them given that there are cases in which even those who have lived their entire life in the Contracting State have been expelled.[100] It is also important to observe that whilst family ties are emphasised such that an adult applicant is unlikely to succeed without family ties, this is no guarantee of success either.[101] In fact, the ECtHR frequently downplays the difficulties that applicants and their families would face if the applicant is removed from the Contracting State by suggesting that they can stay in contact by the telephone and internet.[102]

9.2.1.4 *Margin of Appreciation*

An important feature of *Boultif* was that the ECtHR would itself assess the competing interests by reference to the *Boultif* factors and thus determine whether the measure was necessary. However, in the later case law, the ECtHR has adopted a far more subsidiary role. Indeed, part of the reason for the low levels of success for applicants is the wide margin of appreciation accorded to States. The contemporary case law makes it clear that having identified the criteria that the domestic authorities must consider, the role of the ECtHR is to ensure that the domestic authorities act in accordance with those criteria, and beyond this it is reluctant to intervene. It thus accords a wide margin of appreciation to the States in applying those criteria. This was evident in *Ndidi* v. *the United Kingdom* where it explained that provided an independent and impartial domestic court has carefully examined the facts and applied the proportionality criteria, the ECtHR will need 'strong reasons' in order to carry out a fresh assessment of the balancing exercise.[103] This threshold was not met in *Ndidi* and so no violation was found. The ECtHR further explained its role in *Unuane* v. *the United Kingdom.*

> The requirement for 'European supervision' does not mean that in determining whether an impugned measure struck a fair balance between the relevant interests, it is necessarily the Court's task to conduct the Article 8 proportionality assessment afresh. On the contrary, in Article 8 cases the Court has generally understood the margin of appreciation to mean that, where the independent and impartial domestic courts have carefully examined the facts, applying the relevant human rights standards consistently with the Convention and its case-law, and adequately balanced the applicant's personal interests

[100] *Pormes* v. *Netherlands* (n 45), *Azerkane* v. *Netherlands* (n 33), *Z* v. *Switzerland* (n 33).

[101] *Otite* v. *the United Kingdom*, App. No. 18339/19, 27/09/2022.

[102] Ibid at [54], *Salem* v. *Denmark*, App. No. 77036/11, 01/12/2016 at [81]; *Külekci* v. *Austria*, App. No. 30441/09, 01/06/2017 at [49].

[103] *Ndidi* v. *the United Kingdom*, App. No. 41215/14, 14/09/2017.

> against the more general public interest in the case, it is not for it to substitute its own assessment of the merits (including, in particular, its own assessment of the factual details of proportionality) for that of the competent national authorities. The only exception to this is where there are shown to be strong reasons for doing so.[104]

On the facts of *Unuane*, the threshold for intervention *was* met as the Upper Tribunal had not conducted a separate balancing exercise. It therefore fell to the ECtHR to apply the criteria and having done so, it found that deportation would be disproportionate.[105] The Grand Chamber affirmed this approach to the ECtHR's role in *Savran* v. *Denmark,* while emphasising that '[d]omestic courts must put forward specific reasons' for their decisions and that where 'the reasoning of domestic decisions is insufficient, without any real balancing of the interests in issue' this will violate Article 8 ECHR.[106] The ECtHR has since stated in *Otite* v. *the United Kingdom* that the domestic authorities must make explicit reference to the case law of the ECtHR when carrying out the balancing exercise and if they do not then it will fall 'to the Court, in exercise of its supervisory jurisdiction, to give the final ruling on whether the applicant's expulsion would be reconcilable with that Article 8'.[107] Yet whilst this ensures that the domestic authorities follow the ECHR case law, they retain considerable latitude in striking the balance between Article 8 ECHR and the public interest, and as we will see later in this chapter, this has been of fundamental importance in UK immigration law.

Having identified the threshold for intervention it is worth noting that one case in which that threshold was recently met is *P.J. and R.J.* v. *Switzerland.*[108] In that case a violation was found on the basis that the national courts had not satisfactorily applied the ECtHR's case-law, in particular they had failed to give due weight to the applicant's low level of culpability, the fact that his sentence was suspended, his lack of a criminal record, the fact that he no longer posed a threat to public safety, his status as a long-term immigrant and the adverse effect of the expulsion on the members of his family.[109] Two judges dissented on the ground that the national authorities had carefully examined the facts, adequately balanced the interests at stake in the light of the relevant criteria and based their decisions on relevant and sufficient reasons. Thus in their opinion there were no strong reasons for the ECtHR to interveve as the respondent State did not overstep the margin of appreciation afforded to it under the Convention.[110]

[104] *Unuane* v. *the United Kingdom* (n 83) at [76]. [105] Ibid at [89].

[106] *Savran* v. *Denmark* (n 52) at [188].

[107] *Otite* v. *the United Kingdom* (n 101) at [45]. Note, however, that whilst the ECtHR carried out the balancing exercise for itself, it ultimately concluded that deportation was justified and thus there was no violation at [46].

[108] *P.J. and R.J.* v. *Switzerland*, App. No. 52232/20, 17/09/2024. [109] Ibid at [55].

[110] Joint dissenting opinion of Judges Schukking and Arnardóttir, ibid at [6].

9.2.2 Article 8 ECHR and Family Reunification

The ECtHR is clear that Article 8 ECHR does not 'guarantee the right of a foreign national to enter or to reside in a particular country'[111] and that it 'cannot be considered to impose on a State a general obligation to respect the choice by married couples of the country of their matrimonial residence and to authorise family reunion in its territory'.[112] Indeed, the ECtHR recently observed in *B.F.* v. *Switzerland* that even for refugees 'it has so far not recognised an absolute and unconditional right to family reunification'.[113] Yet alongside those demarcations of the limits of Article 8 ECHR, the ECtHR also recognises that States do sometimes have 'obligations to admit to its territory relatives of persons residing there'.[114] The applicable Article 8 ECHR right can, as Costello explains, be seen as one of 'insider privilege' as the right vindicated is the right of the insider who has 'already established themselves in the host country or are citizens thereof'.[115] It is, however, important not to overstate the extent of 'insider privilege' as although the insider is privileged over and above the outsider, the insider is also frequently denied family reunification in the Contracting State. As Costello goes on to note, 'the Strasbourg jurisprudence does not vindicate the right of residence of insiders as it permits States to require even their own citizens and long-settled denizens to live elsewhere in order to enjoy family life with foreigners'.[116]

The family reunification case law involves a complex array of situations including cases in which entry is sought as well as cases in which someone with an irregular migration status seeks to remain in the State's territory. Where permission to enter is sought, this would appear to invoke the State's *positive* obligation, whereas resisting deportation suggests that it is the *negative* obligation that is applicable. The ECtHR has, however, avoided drawing such distinctions by asserting that:

> the boundaries between the State's positive and negative obligations under [Article 8] do not lend themselves to precise definition. The applicable principles are nonetheless similar. In both cases, regard must be had to the fair balance that has to be struck between the competing interests of the individual and of the community as a whole; and in both contexts the State enjoys a certain margin of appreciation.[117]

Consequently, the ECtHR does not amend the structure of its family reunification analysis depending upon whether the migrant is within or outside the State. What this means in practice is that in none of the family reunification

[111] *M.A.* v. *Denmark* [GC], App. No. 6697/18, 09/07/2021 at [131]. See also (n 39) at [114].

[112] *M.A.* v. *Denmark*, ibid at [132], and *Al-Nashif* v. *Bulgaria* (n 39) at [114].

[113] *B.F.* v. *Switzerland* (2024) 78 EHRR 14 at [103].

[114] *M.A.* v. *Denmark* (n 111) at [132].

[115] Cathryn Costello, *The Human Rights of Migrants and Refugees in European Law* (Oxford University Press, 2015), p.106.

[116] Ibid, p.110.

[117] *Jeunesse* v. *Netherlands* (2015) 60 EHRR 17 at [106].

cases does the ECtHR follow the structured approach to proportionality that one might expect where the negative obligation is at play. In general, within the Article 8 ECHR framework when the negative obligation is applicable, the State should justify the interference under Article 8(2) ECHR which requires demonstrating that the interference is proportionate to the legitimate aim pursued. The default position presented by the structure of the text of the Convention right is thus that Article 8 ECHR will be upheld unless the interference is justified under Article 8(2) ECHR. The situation is different where there are competing qualified rights at stake, for example where, as we will see in the next chapter, Article 8 ECHR clashes with Article 10 ECHR. In such cases a balance will need to be struck as neither right takes priority over the other. However, where there is no competing right, but there is only a competing public interest, the proportionality model prescribed by Article 8(2) ECHR should apply. This is not, however, the approach in the immigration context. In the immigration context, what emerges is a process of balancing between the Article 8 ECHR right of the applicant and the 'competing interests of the community as a whole'.[118] As many scholars have noted, this derives from the State sovereignty assumption that dominates the ECtHR's case law.[119] In these cases, the sovereignty of the State is elevated to the position of something akin to a collective right which must be balanced against the applicant's Article 8 ECHR right, as opposed to a competing public interest that would only be regarded as justifying an interference where it was strictly necessary.[120] We see this in both the family reunification case law and, as we have just seen, in the deportation case law where the ECtHR structures its approach around whether the State has 'struck a fair balance between the relevant interests, namely the individual's rights protected by the Convention on the one hand and the community's interests on the other'.[121] Thus in both contexts a balancing approach is used even where the State's negative obligation is clearly at play.

The origins of the family reunification case law can be traced to *Abdulaziz, Cabales and Balkandali* v. *the United Kingdom* (*ACB*) an important case which established that the right to family life was applicable, but prioritised State sovereignty.[122] This set out the principles that continue to govern the case law today. The background to *ACB* was that following a report in 1968 which stated that 1,676 male Commonwealth citizens had been admitted to the UK for marriage, a political backlash led to new restrictions on the admission of husbands and fiancés. The applicants were three women lawfully settled in the UK who had married men from their countries of origin who had been refused entry based on the new restrictions. The applicants argued that this violated

118 Ibid. 119 Dembour (n 4). 120 Wray (n 24), pp.13–16.

121 *Savran* v. *Denmark* (n 52) at [187].

122 *Abdulaziz, Cabales and Balkandali* v. *the United Kingdom* (1985) 7 EHRR 471.

Article 8 ECHR, while the UK Government argued that the family life provision did not apply as the applicants had never established homes with their partners and there were no obstacles to the couples living in their countries of origin. The ECtHR rejected the UK's argument that there was no family life. It held that marriage established family life even if they had not set up home together; it also observed that all three couples had cohabited, and that one of the couples had a son. Yet while it accepted that there was family life, it agreed with the UK that Article 8 ECHR does not impose 'a general obligation on the part of a Contracting State to respect the choice by married couples of the country of their matrimonial residence and to accept the non-national spouses for settlement in that country'.[123] Consequently, it held that the refusals did not violate Article 8 ECHR.[124]

If we examine this from the perspective of State sovereignty then the ECtHR's refusal to find that the UK was obliged to permit entry was not surprising. The ECtHR's stance is, however, challenged by the colonial critique. Dembour reflects on what the ECtHR could have done:

> Had the Court been so inclined, it could have drawn out the implications of the inequality of this phenomenon and scrutinised admission refusals. This would have chimed well with a postcolonial critique of imperialism which reminds us that we prefer not to recall that the colonial powers of yesteryear were happily relying on the idea that circulation in the world should be free. It would also have recognised that the transformation of the world from which European states have benefited and significantly engineered may, or even should, give rise to special responsibilities on their part towards people originating from the regions they colonised in the past or are occupying or waging wars in today. However, such a morally ambitious agenda was not pursued at Strasbourg.[125]

This was not, however, the road taken by the ECtHR, and the principles established in *ACB* continue to apply today.[126] Consequently, as the Grand Chamber recently affirmed in *M.A.* v. *Denmark*,[127]

[123] Ibid at [68].

[124] It is important to observe that in *Abdulaziz, Cabales and Balkandali*, the ECtHR was also asked whether the restrictions violated Article 8 coupled with Article 14 ECHR on the grounds of sex and race discrimination. It held that the scheme discriminated based on sex, as it only applied to husbands seeking entry and not to wives seeking entry, but it found no violation in respect of race discrimination. Consequently, the UK remedied the sex discrimination by making it equally difficult for wives to enter. Resolution 9214/80 9473/81 9474/81. See discussion of *Abdulaziz, Cabales and Balkandali* in Chapter 14. See also Judge Pinto de Albuquerque's critique of the case in his concurring opinion in *Biao* v. *Denmark* (n 21).

[125] Dembour (n 4), ch.4.

[126] See Judge Pinto de Albuquerque's concurring opinion in *Biao* v. *Denmark* (n 21) in which he lamented the approach adopted by the ECtHR to family reunification and stated that '[t]he day will come, hopefully sooner rather than later, when the Court will take the simple but courageous step of concluding, in an unequivocal manner, that the right to family life does warrant family reunification' at [30].

[127] *M.A.* v. *Denmark* (n 111) at [131]–[132].

in a case which concerns family life as well as immigration, the extent of a State's obligations to admit to its territory relatives of persons residing there will vary according to the particular circumstances of the persons involved and the general interest, and is subject to a fair balance that has to be struck between the competing interests involved.[128]

In family reunification cases, the ECtHR thus considers (i) whether family life is applicable and (ii) whether the State has an obligation to admit given the competing interests involved and the need to strike a fair balance.

9.2.2.1 *Is the Right to Family Life Applicable?*

In determining whether the right to family life applies, the ECtHR uses the same concept of the 'core family' that we saw in the deportation context, that is, spouses and partners[129] and parents and children that have not come of age.[130] Beyond the core family, it is highly unlikely that an applicant will be able to establish family ties, even in cases of considerable dependency. We saw in *Savran* the restrictive approach that the ECtHR takes to dependency, but the severity of the dependency threshold was already evident in the family reunification case law in the earlier case of *Senchishak* v. *Finland.*[131] *Senchishak* was a case in which an elderly woman who had suffered a stroke was refused residency in Finland with her daughter, her only surviving relative.[132] In determining that there was no family life, the ECtHR emphasised that the mother and daughter had not lived together for over twenty years. In considering dependency, it held that even if the mother was 'dependent on outside help in order to cope with her daily life, this does not mean that she is necessarily dependent on her daughter who lives in Finland, or that care in Finland is the only option'.[133] Consequently, it determined that there were no 'additional factors of dependence other than normal ties of affection' and thus no family life within the meaning of Article 8 ECHR.[134]

128 Ibid.

129 *Abdulaziz, Cabales and Balkandali* (n 122) 'lawful and genuine marriage' at [62], *Al-Nashif* v. *Bulgaria* (n 39) '"family life" encompasses families based on marriage and also *de facto* relationships' at [112], *Pajić* v. *Croatia* (n 21) – if heterosexual partners are recognised, then it is contrary to Arts. 8 and 14 ECHR not to recognise homosexual partners.

130 *Gül* v. *Switzerland* (1996) 22 EHRR 93: 'child born of a marital union is ipso jure part of that relationship; hence, from the moment of the child's birth and by the very fact of it, there exists between him and his parents a bond amounting to "family life" . . . which subsequent events cannot break save in exceptional circumstances' at [32]; *Boughanemi* v. *France* (n 44): 'concept of family life on which Article 8 (art. 8) is based embraces, even where there is no cohabitation, the tie between a parent and his or her child, regardless of whether or not the latter is legitimate' at [35].

131 *Senchishak* v. *Finland*, App. No. 5049/12, 18/11/2014.

132 Ibid.

133 Ibid at [57].

134 Ibid at [57].

The impact of *Senchishak* is that it is very difficult for adult children that have emigrated to bring their elderly parents to them if they need care later in life. This has been the subject of considerable criticism, including in *Senchishak* itself, where Judges Bianku and Kalaydjieva declared:

> A time comes when elderly parents do need the loving care of their adult children and actually receive it as a matter of moral duty and preserved feelings of affection. To deny this is to hold that once an individual comes of age, the emotional ties with his or her parents are to be considered once and for all *de facto* and *de jure* severed and that for this reason neither a moral nor a legal duty to provide care may be said to exist between them. In our understanding this is incorrect in both legal and moral terms.[135]

The ECtHR's approach also fails to capture the broader understanding of family life prevalent in some of the Contracting States.[136]

The role of dependency was discussed further in two cases concerning family reunification between adult relatives in the Netherlands. In *Kumari* v. *the Netherlands* the ECtHR found no family life between Ms Kumari (who was in her fifties) and her adult son on the ground that '"additional elements of dependency, involving more than the normal emotional ties" between the applicant and her eldest son, have not been shown to exist'.[137] The ECtHR observed that Kumari had mainly cited health issues commonly associated with age, which were not of such seriousness that she had been in need of constant care and support.[138] It also observed that there was no indication that she could not get by on the medical care and support available to her India.[139] The ECtHR also declined to find family life on the basis that Kumari was providing emotional support to her son who was grieving the loss of his prematurely born daughter. On this issue the ECtHR observed that while the son was being treated for post-traumatic stress disorder, his level of anxiety had decreased, and he was no longer suffering from flashbacks.[140] Consequently, although the ECtHR accepted that the 'death of his daughter has caused a great impact on his mental well-being' there was 'no evidence before it which would suggest that his condition was so severe as to entirely incapacitate him'.[141] It thus declared, by a majority, the application inadmissible.[142]

Conversely, in *Martinez Alvarado* v. *the Netherlands*[143] the ECtHR found that there was family life between an adult man (who had an intellectual disability which meant that he functioned at the level of an eight-year-old

[135] Ibid.

[136] *Slivenko* v. *Latvia* (n 40). Judge Kovler in *Slivenko* highlighted the fact that the extended family is a central feature of life in some European countries which enjoys constitutional recognition.

[137] *Kumari* v. *the Netherlands*, App. No. 44051/20, 19/11/2024 at [54].

[138] Ibid at [49].

[139] Ibid at [50].

[140] Ibid at [47].

[141] Ibid at [48].

[142] Ibid at [55].

[143] *Martinez Alvarado* v. *the Netherlands*, App. No. 4470/21, 10/12/2024.

child)[144] and his adult sisters. The ECtHR observed that Martinez Alvarado relied entirely on the care and support in his daily life of his four sisters, who all lived in the Netherlands, and that although he had previously been cared for by his parents in Peru since their deaths he had been taken to the Netherlands by his eldest sister.[145] The ECtHR found that due to his dependency the relationship between the siblings amounted to family life under the Convention.[146] On this occasion the ECtHR stated that while the threshold is one of 'additional elements of dependency other than normal emotional ties', this does not mean that 'exclusive dependency' is required.[147] This arose from the fact that the national authorities had concluded that Article 8 ECHR was not applicable on the basis that the applicant had a brother in Peru and thus was not exclusively dependent on his sisters. The ECtHR, having determined that Article 8 ECHR was applicable, observed that while 'the presence of family members who can provide care – or other viable alternatives – in the country of origin or where the person requiring care and support lives' may be of relevance, 'the weight to be accorded to this element is relative and depends on the other facts and specific circumstances of the case'.[148] In this regard it went on to state that it cannot be derived from the case-law 'that "exclusive dependency" is always required in order to find that "family life" exists.'[149] On the facts it found that the applicant had substantiated that his brother, who was the only remaining family member in Peru, was unable to provide the necessary daily care.[150] Consequently it held that there had been a violation of Article 8 ECHR as the national authorities had erred in focusing primarily on the fact that his sisters had not been involved in his daily care prior to their parents' deaths[151] and that the State had not established that there were viable alternatives in Peru where persons such as the applicant tended to be cared for by their relatives.[152] The national authorities had thus carried out their analysis in a manner which was not consistent with the principles outlined in the Convention.[153]

9.2.2.2 *Factors That the ECtHR Considers in Determining Whether There Is an Obligation*

Even if an applicant is able to establish family ties, they will still need to convince the ECtHR that a State is under a duty under Article 8 of the Convention to grant the family reunification which has been requested.[154] The Grand Chamber in *M.A.* v. *Denmark* reviewed the case law and applicable

[144] Ibid at [47]. [145] Ibid at [48]. [146] Ibid at [150]. [147] Ibid at [49]–[50].
[148] Ibid at [49]. [149] Ibid at [49]. [150] Ibid at [50]. [151] Ibid at [48].
[152] Ibid at [50]. [153] Ibid at [55]. [154] Ibid.

principles and observed that the ECtHR is reluctant to find an obligation if *one or more* of the following apply:

i. Family life was created at a time when the persons involved were aware that the immigration status of one of them was precarious. In such a situation, it is likely only to be in exceptional circumstances that the removal of the non-national family member will constitute a violation of Article 8.
ii. The person requesting family reunification had limited ties to the host country, which is usually the case if they have only stayed there for a short time, or stayed there illegally.
iii. There were no insurmountable obstacles in the way of the family living in the country of origin of the person requesting family reunification.
iv. The person requesting family reunification could not demonstrate that they have sufficient independent and lasting income, not being welfare benefits, to provide for the basic cost of subsistence of family members.[155]

Family reunification is thus likely to be denied if family life was created when immigration status was precarious, the applicant has limited ties to the host State, there are no insurmountable obstacles to living in the country of origin, or the applicant is economically dependent on the State. In fact, precarity of immigration status will almost certainly be fatal unless there are truly exceptional circumstances.[156] The same is true in respect of economic dependency.[157] Both the precarity and the economic dependency arguments align

[155] *M.A.* v. *Denmark* (n 111) at [134]. [156] See Section 9.2.2.3.3.

[157] This was evident in *Haydarie and others* v. *Netherlands*, App. No. 8876/04, 20/10/2005 in which the ECtHR held that an income requirement was reasonable and that there was no violation when the applicant's three children could not join her in the Netherlands. Note, however, that in *B.F.* v. *Switzerland* (n 113) it was observed that whilst States have a margin of appreciation in relation to requiring non-reliance on social assistance before enabling family reunification in respect of refugees, this margin is not unlimited, the requirement of non-reliance needs to be applied with sufficient flexibility and refugees 'should not be required to "do the impossible" in order to be granted family reunification' at [105]. Applying this to the facts, the ECtHR found violations in relation to several applications where the applicants had done all that could reasonably be expected of them. The scope of the margin that is accorded to states in this context was considered further in *Dabo* v. *Sweden*, App. No. 12510/18, 18/01/2024 where the ECtHR stated at [105] that

> the Court considers that the member States should be afforded a wide margin of appreciation in deciding that, after being exempted from any maintenance requirement for three months, refugees should have to satisfy such a condition when subsequently seeking family reunification. A refugee will most likely stay permanently in the host country, which will have taken and will take various measures to secure successful integration, including the granting of family reunification without any maintenance requirement during the first three months after the sponsor is granted refugee status. The Court does not consider it unreasonable that, subsequently, in order to be granted family reunification, a refugee sponsor should be required to demonstrate that he or she has a sufficient independent and

with the immigration tropes that migrants are trying to play the system by creating family relationships to obtain residency, and/or that they are moving to States to obtain benefits. These arguments are challenged by those that highlight the ways in which immigration law creates and prolongs precarious immigration status; as well as colonial critiques which underline the role of colonialism in both creating precarious immigration statuses and in creating the wealth of the State that the migrant is precluded from accessing.[158]

Having contemplated the factors that will deny an obligation, we thus need to consider when an obligation will be found. In *M.A.*, the ECtHR stated that it might be prepared to find an obligation if *several* of the following circumstances are *cumulatively present*:

i. The person requesting family reunification had achieved a settled status in the host country or had strong ties with that country.
ii. Family life was already created, when the requesting person achieved settled status in the host country.
iii. Both the person requesting family reunification, and the family member concerned, were already staying in the host country.
iv. Children were involved, since their interests must be afforded significant weight.
v. There were insurmountable or major obstacles in the way of the family living in the country of origin of the person requesting family reunification.

For an obligation to arise, there should therefore be strong ties to the State, and family life should have been created prior to the conferral of the applicant's settled status, but not in circumstances in which there was precarious immigration status. Those who are likely to be successful are thus those in stable situations, whilst those who are poor and whose immigration situation is more precarious are more likely to fall within the exclusionary criteria highlighted above. The fourth and fifth of the *M.A.* criteria provide some hope for those with children and for those for whom a return to the country of origin is impossible but the threshold for finding an obligation is very high.

In respect of children, the position adopted by the ECtHR is that 'in all decisions concerning children, their best interests must be paramount',[159] but this does not mean that their interests will be a trump card. Indeed, provided

stable income, without recourse to welfare benefits, in order to meet the basic living expenses of the family members with whom he or she seeks reunification.

On the facts the ECtHR thus found that that a fair balance had been struck which was within the State's margin of appreciation. For further applications of these principles which have become known as the 'Dabo principles' see *Okubamichael Debru* v. *Sweden*, App. No. 49755/18, 25/07/2024; *D.H.* v. *Sweden*, App. No. 34210/19, 25/07/2024; and *S.F.* v. *Finland*, App. No. 35276/20, 08/10/2024.

[158] Nadine El-Enany, *(B)ordering Britain: Law, Race and Empire* (Manchester University Press, 2018), pp.17–18.

[159] *I.A.A.* v. *the United Kingdom* (2016) 62 EHRR SE19 at [39]–[41].

the domestic authorities have placed the child's best interests at the heart of their reasoning and put forward relevant and sufficient reasons for declining entry, the Court remains unlikely to intervene.[160] The fact that children's best interests are not determinative is reflected in the numerous cases in which the ECtHR has refused to find that a State is obliged to allow children to join their parents. In such cases the ECtHR often indicates that the parent/s can return to their country of origin, or family life can continue from a distance. Thus, in *Gül* v. *Switzerland* the ECtHR refused to find that Switzerland was obliged to allow a child to join his parents even though his parents had been given residents' permits on humanitarian grounds.[161] The ECtHR found no obligation to admit the child as family life could either continue from a distance or they could return to Turkey.[162] This 'return home or live apart' approach was also evident in *Ahmut* v. *Netherlands* when the applicant, a Dutch national of Moroccan origin, sought to bring his Moroccan children to the Netherlands following the death of their mother.[163] In a similar fashion to *Gül*, the ECtHR found that the father could return to Morocco or continue family life apart. Several judges dissented, including Judge Valticos, who observed that:

> The father had acquired Netherlands nationality, and in any country, a national is entitled to have his son join him, even if the son does not have the same nationality. How does it come about that in the present case this right was refused him? I cannot think that it is because the Dutch father was called 'Ahmut'. However, the suspicion of discrimination must inevitably lurk in people's minds.

A further contentious issue in respect of children is the ECtHR's approach to the age of a child when determining whether there is an obligation. Essentially, the ECtHR assumes that teenage children need their parents less than younger children and thus do not need to be with their parents. This was evident in *Chandra* v. *Netherlands*[164] and *I.A.A.* v. *the United Kingdom*.[165] The

[160] This was evident in *Ghatet* v. *Switzerland*, App. No. 56971/10, 08/11/2016 at [46] in which the ECtHR observed that if the domestic authorities had done this then the Court would have considered that they had struck a fair balance, but as they had failed to consider this, there had been a violation of Article 8.

[161] *Gül* v. *Switzerland* (n 130).

[162] Ibid, dissenting opinion of Judge Martens, approved by Judge Russo at [12].

[163] *Ahmut* v. *Netherlands* (1997) 24 EHRR 62.

[164] *Chandra* v. *Netherlands*, App. No. 53102/99, 13/05/2003. Chandra, a Dutch national of Indonesian origin, moved to the Netherlands following separation from her husband; her children remained in Indonesia while she sought custody. Once she obtained custody she applied for residency for her children. The ECtHR agreed with the Dutch Government that the children had strong links with the linguistic and cultural environment of their home country. It also emphasised that as the children were now teenagers (fifteen and thirteen years) they needed less care and this could be provided by relatives in Indonesia or Chandra could return to Indonesia.

[165] *I.A.A.* v. *the United Kingdom* (n 159). In finding no violation, the ECtHR emphasised that the children were now twenty-one, twenty, nineteen, fourteen and thirteen, they had grown up

assumption that teenage children need less care is an erroneous one for which there seems to be no empirical basis. Moreover, the ECtHR's approach to the passage of time is highly detrimental to migrants where their circumstances are such that one family member must move before the others are able to do so. Such families are often compelled to experience a period of separation and it is inevitable that in the interim the children will age, and that they will grow up living with other family members in the cultural and linguistic environment of the country in which they reside. Giving weight to these factors renders a finding of no violation somewhat inevitable.

9.2.2.3 *Cases in Which the Court Has Found a Violation*

Given consideration of the limits of the family reunification case law, it is important to note that Article 8 ECHR is not entirely redundant, as there are some exceptional cases in which the ECtHR has found a violation. The rare cases that have been successful have involved children, albeit that as we have already seen the involvement of children is no guarantee of success.

9.2.2.3.1 *Child Permitted to Join Parents with Lawful Residence*

There are several cases in which the ECtHR has found that a State was obliged to allow children to join their parents. One of those cases is *Sen* v. *Netherlands* which concerned Turkish nationals whose child had remained in Turkey while they settled in the Netherlands and had two other children in the Netherlands.[166] The ECtHR commented that while the applicants had elected to leave their child behind, this could not be regarded as an irrevocable decision. Moreover, there were major obstacles to the family returning to Turkey as the two other children had always lived in the Netherlands, and had very few links with Turkey. Consequently, the ECtHR held that reunification in the Netherlands was the most appropriate way to establish family life and that the State had failed to strike a fair balance between the interests of the applicants and its own interest.

A violation of Article 8 ECHR was also found in *Tuquabo-Tekle* v. *Netherlands*.[167] Tuquabo-Tekle, a refugee, had fled Ethiopia following the death of her husband, leaving her child in the care of her grandmother and uncle in Eritrea. She had two further children in the Netherlands, but her first

in the cultural and linguistic environment of their country of origin before living in Ethiopia, had never been to the UK and had not lived with their mother for more than eleven years. The ECtHR emphasised that the mother could relocate to Ethiopia or Somalia.

[166] *Sen* v. *Netherlands* (2003) 36 EHRR 7 (available in French). See also, the Legal Summary of the European Court of Human Rights.

[167] *Tuquabo-Tekle* v. *Netherlands*, App. No. 60665/00, 01/12/2005.

child was refused entry. Before the ECtHR, the Netherlands sought to argue that she had left the child behind of her own free-will, but this was doubted by the Court as she had fled during civil war.[168] Moreover, the ECtHR reiterated its reasoning in *Sen*, namely that applicants who leave children behind while they settle abroad cannot be assumed to have irrevocably decided that those children are to remain in the country of origin permanently and to have abandoned any idea of family reunion.[169] The ECtHR also emphasised that Tuquabo-Tekle was lawfully residing in the Netherlands, had obtained Dutch nationality and had further children in the Netherlands.[170] In this respect it held that the case was similar to *Sen.* There was, however, one factor that potentially distinguished the two cases, namely the age of the child. In *Sen* the child was aged nine, whereas in Tuquabo-Tekle the child was aged fifteen. In contemplating the age of the child the ECtHR observed that it had rejected other cases on the basis that the child was now of an age that they no longer needed the same care as a young child.[171] It went on, however, to consider the applicant's argument that her daughter's age made it even more pertinent for her to be allowed to join her family in the Netherlands. This was because, in accordance with Eritrean custom, the child's grandmother had taken her out of school, and the child had reached an age where she could be married off. Tuquabo-Tekle objected to this, but was unable to do anything while her daughter was living in Eritrea.[172] In considering this the ECtHR was at pains to point out that these circumstances did not mean that the State was obliged to allow entry. It was, however, willing to accept that in this particular case the child's age should not 'lead it to assess the case differently from that of *Şen*'.[173] Moreover, the ECtHR observed that, albeit not decisive, it was noteworthy that when Tuquabo-Tekle had lodged the application her daughter was roughly the same age as Sen.[174] The ECtHR thus held that the Netherlands had failed to strike the right balance, whilst limiting the potential ambit of its reasoning for future cases.[175]

9.2.2.3.2 *Parent Permitted to Remain with Child with Lawful Residence*

Thus far we have considered cases in which children are joining their parents, but there are also cases in which parents seek permission to join their children. *Berrehab* v. *the Netherlands* is an example of a case in which such an obligation was found.[176] Berrehab was born in Morocco, married a Dutch national and had been granted permission to stay in the Netherlands for the sole purpose of enabling him to live with his Dutch wife. They subsequently had

[168] Ibid at [47]. [169] Ibid at [45]. [170] Ibid at [47]. [171] Ibid at [49].
[172] Ibid at [50]. [173] Ibid at [50]. [174] Ibid at [51]. [175] Ibid at [52].
[176] *Berrehab* v. *the Netherlands* (1989) 11 EHRR 322.

a daughter in the Netherlands and shortly thereafter divorced, following which Berrehab was refused a residence permit. The ECtHR held that this violated Article 8 ECHR, emphasising that his situation was not the same as someone seeking admission for the first time, as he had lawfully lived there for several years, had a home, a job, and a child, and had not committed any offences.[177]

9.2.2.3.3 *Parent Allowed to Remain with Child Despite Breaching Immigration Law*

There are some highly exceptional cases in which the best interests of children have resulted in the finding of an obligation to admit, even though their parents had breached immigration law. An important example of this is *Jeunesse* v. *Netherlands*.[178] Jeunesse was a Surinamese national who had lived in the Netherlands for sixteen years with her husband and their three children. The ECtHR found removing her from the Netherlands would violate Article 8 ECHR, emphasising that she had resided in the Netherlands for sixteen years, had no criminal record and had repeatedly sought residency such that her presence was known and tolerated by the Dutch authorities.[179] In this respect the ECtHR cautioned that although States may allow individuals to remain, and they may establish ties during that time, this does not mean that the State is obliged to allow them to remain.[180] It went on, however, to note that her family members were all Dutch nationals and that she herself had Dutch nationality at birth, but had lost this when Suriname became independent, something which was outside of her control.[181] For this reason, the ECtHR determined that her status was not equivalent to someone who had never had Dutch nationality.[182] The ECtHR also noted that while it would not be impossible for her and her family to relocate to Suriname, that they would suffer hardship and the best interests of the children were not served by forced removal.[183] Consequently, the ECtHR determined that the Netherlands had not struck a fair balance.[184] Three judges dissented, arguing that this offers greater protection to those that enter or remain in a country illegally over those who respect entry conditions.[185] Moreover, they objected that the Court is 'drifting away from the subsidiary role assigned to it by the Convention, perhaps being guided more by what is humane, rather than by what is right'.[186]

The ECtHR also found a violation despite a breach of immigration law in *Rodrigues da Silva and Hoogkamer* v. *the Netherlands*, partly on the basis that the applicant had been entitled to lawful residency at an earlier point during her residency.[187] Consequently, the case was distinguished from other cases in

[177] Ibid at [29]. [178] *Jeunesse* v. *Netherlands* (n 117). [179] Ibid at [113]–[123].
[180] Ibid at [103]. [181] Ibid at [115]. [182] Ibid at [115]. [183] Ibid at [118]–[120].
[184] Ibid at [122]. [185] Ibid, joint dissenting opinion of Judges Villiger, Mahoney and Silvis.
[186] Ibid at [10].
[187] *Rodrigues da Silva and Hoogkamer* v. *the Netherlands* (2007) 44 EHRR 34 at [44].

which the persons concerned could not at any time reasonably expect to be able to continue family life in the host country.[188]

Yet while successful cases have generally concerned parents that either had lawful residency at some point or were entitled to it, *Nunez* v. *Norway* is an exceptional case in which the ECtHR found a positive obligation even though the applicant had never been entitled to residency.[189] On this occasion the ECtHR observed that whilst her breaches of immigration law weighed heavily in the balance, it had to consider the best interests of the children.[190] In this respect it emphasised that she was the primary carer for children who had lived their entire lives in Norway.[191] The ECtHR was also influenced by the fact that the authorities had tolerated her presence for four years.[192] Consequently, it held that this was an exceptional case, and it was not convinced that sufficient weight had been given to the best interests of the children. It thus concluded that the authorities had not struck a fair balance.[193]

In sum, what is evident from the case law is that the cases are highly fact specific and thus while the *M.A.* factors offer insight it can be difficult to predict outcomes. Nevertheless, the emphasis given to the ECtHR's subsidiary role means that provided States can demonstrate that sufficient consideration has been given at the domestic level to the principles highlighted in the ECtHR case law, the ECtHR is unlikely to intervene.

9.2.2.4 *Procedural Obligations when Processing Family Reunification Applications*

It might be expected that procedural obligations would come to the fore given the subsidiary role of the ECtHR in respect of the striking of a fair balance in relation to the substantive obligations. Yet while there are obligations pertaining to the processing of requests for family reunification, in particular, flexibility, promptness and effectiveness are required, the parameters of these obligations are still being established.[194] To date, the case law indicates that States have a margin of appreciation when it comes to waiting times but the breadth of this margin varies depending upon the status of the migrant, with

[188] Ibid at [43].

[189] *Nunez* v. *Norway* (2014) 58 EHRR 17 at [84]. Nunez had previously been deported from Norway and issued with a two-year prohibition on re-entry but had re-entered four months later under a false identity and married a Norwegian national. She subsequently divorced and cohabited with a settled non-national, with whom she had two daughters. In April 2005 the immigration authorities, who had been aware since 2001 that her residency was unlawful, decided she should be expelled again and prohibited from re-entering for two years.

[190] Ibid at [78]. [191] Ibid at [79]. [192] Ibid at [82]. [193] Ibid at [83-4].

[194] See *M.A.* v. *Denmark* (n 111) at [137]–[139] and *B.F.* v. *Switzerland* (n 113) at [90].

refugees[195] receiving a higher level of protection than migrants with subsidiary or temporarily protected status.[196] Judge Pinto de Albuquerque, writing extra-judicially, criticises the way in which the ECtHR validates 'a difference in treatment between refugees and other categories of protected persons based on the risk of ill-treatment in the state of origin, which, although justified in terms of the granting of status, is not very relevant in terms of family reunification';[197] commenting that '[i]t is difficult to see why the duration of such reunification should differ according to the risk suffered by the protected person'.[198]

In addition to the duration of the waiting period, an important consideration is whether there was a prospect of the applicant having an individualised assessment of the need for a shorter waiting period.[199] Yet while the ECtHR asserts that this is an important factor, it has been criticised for not adequately scrutinising whether there has in fact been such an assessment in practice.[200]

A further relevant issue in determining whether the procedural obligation has been met is the family relationship in question, as it appears that spouses receive a higher level of protection than a child–parent relationship where the child is close to the age of majority. This was apparent in *M.T.* v. *Sweden*, a case which also demonstrates how a weak approach to procedural obligations can leave applicants without any meaningful right to family reunification.[201] M.T. was a fifteen-year-old boy when he travelled from Syria to Sweden, applied for asylum and was granted temporary residence as a person eligible for subsidiary protection. His mother and brother sought to join him, but this was denied as Sweden had suspended family reunification for persons benefitting from subsidiary protection. In finding no violation, the ECtHR concluded that the suspension struck a fair balance, observing that M.T. had been affected for a period of less than eighteen months following which he came of age and was no longer entitled to family reunification.[202] The fact that suspension ran down the clock on his eligibility was not something which appeared to concern the Court. Moreover, the ECtHR in *M.T.* suggested that the margin of appreciation varies depending upon the family relationship in question. In particular, the ECtHR distinguished M.T. a teenage boy seeking to be reunited with his mother from *M.A.*, a case in which a husband sought to be reunited with his wife, suggesting that the latter was an 'essential cohabitation' and was thus more significant.[203] We thus see that even in the context

[195] *Tanda-Muzinga* v. *France*, App. No. 2260/10, 10/07/2014, *Mugenzi* v. *France*, App. No. 52701/09, 10/07/2014, *Senigo Longue and Others* v. *France*, App. No. 19113/09, 10/07/2014.

[196] *M.A.* v. *Denmark* (n 111).

[197] Pinto de Albuquerque and Dartigue (n 10).

[198] Ibid.

[199] *M.A.* v. *Denmark* (n 111) at [192]–[194].

[200] *M.T.* v. *Sweden* (2023) 76 EHRR 29, Judge Ktistakis.

[201] Ibid.

[202] Ibid at [72]–[84].

[203] Ibid at [81].

of procedural obligations the Court's view of the significance of the family ties calibrates the degree of protection accorded.

9.2.2.5 *Article 8 and 14 ECHR: Non-discrimination in Family Reunification*

Article 14 ECHR and the non-discrimination principle are considered in greater detail in Chapter 14. It is, however, important to note here that where a State confers a right of entry it must do so in a manner compatible with Article 14 ECHR. In this regard, we have already seen that the UK was found to have discriminated on the basis of sex, but not race in *ACB* v. *the United Kingdom.*[204] A violation was also found in *Hode and Abdi* v. *the United Kingdom* when more stringent provisions applied in respect of the spouses of refugees than for spouses of other persons with limited leave to remain such as students and workers.[205] Moreover, in *Biao* v. *Denmark*, the GC found a violation where more onerous reunification rules applied to those that had acquired Danish nationality as opposed to those that had Danish nationality from birth.[206] This constituted indirect discrimination based on race or ethnic origin, which the Government was unable to justify and thus a violation was found.[207] In his separate concurring opinion, Judge Pinto de Albuquerque observed the risk that Denmark may seek to address this by making family reunification more difficult:

> The *ratio* of the present judgment, which is to protect naturalised Danish citizens and Danish citizens of foreign ethnic origin, who are put in an extremely unfavourable position before the law, would evidently be frustrated if new legislation were to worsen the conditions for obtaining family reunification in Denmark, for instance by simply abolishing the exemption from the generally applicable 'attachment requirement'. A good-faith implementation of the present judgment warrants an overall reassessment of the legal framework concerning family reunification, including its 'attachment requirement'. I would thus also have indicated to the Danish Government under Article 46 of the Convention that the now 26-year rule should be amended, with the caveat that this should not in any way imply any retrogression in the legal protection of the right to family life of the potentially affected persons.[208]

9.2.3 Reflections on Article 8 ECHR

The role of Article 8 ECHR in immigration divides scholars. Some regard the recognition of these rights as a highly novel development, emphasising that

[204] *Abdulaziz, Cabales and Balkandali* v. *the United Kingdom* (n 122).

[205] *Hode and Abdi* v. *the United Kingdom* (n 20). See discussion in Chapter 14 (Non-Discrimination and Equality).

[206] *Biao* v. *Denmark* (n 21). [207] Ibid at [138]–[139].

[208] Ibid, concurring opinion of Judge Pinto de Albuquerque at [35].

the ECtHR was the first international court to extend human rights to non-nationals beyond forced migration.[209] Others criticise the ECtHR for allowing nationality to be a defining category and for being too deferential to States. In this respect, Dembour highlights the way in which the ECtHR commences its analysis with assertions of State sovereignty (rather than the Convention right), thus shifting the default position to one of State interest.

> The typical choice made by the European Court to start its reasoning in migrant cases with the principle that states have the prerogative to exclude migrants is thus bizarre, even if it has become such a staple of the Strasbourg case law that we tend to accept it as normal. When the Court examines criminal justice cases, it does not start its reasoning by saying that the state has the power to punish those who have offended; it starts with Article 6 ECHR which provides fair trial guarantees. One suspects that starting the reasoning in criminal cases with the power to punish rather than with Article 6 would shift the default position of the Court further towards the state and away from the claimant. The question arises: why does the Court not similarly start its reasoning in migrant cases with the relevant provision of the Convention (e.g. Article 8)?[210]

We have also seen throughout this chapter concerns about the way States are allowed to use deportation as an extra penalty against non-nationals, obligations on migrants to integrate, the limited prospects of success in the absence of family ties, and the Court's willingness to accept that family ties can be sustained from afar by the telephone and the internet. Consequently, scholars such as Dembour, emphasise that

> it has always been and continues to be extremely difficult – indeed too difficult – for migrants to have violations of their human rights recognised and denounced by the European Court of Human Rights ... Such a message flies in the face of the way the Strasbourg Court is portrayed by politicians and the media, especially in the UK.[211]

She suggests that the ECtHR has neutered its own role in this context.

> This position has become so normalised that it is perhaps important to clarify its implications. It means that European Convention law has nothing to say about the way in which state immigration laws force many families to live in a condition of dislocation by preventing family reunion and leaving the family 'dismembered' (as members are kept in different locations). It also pushes for a relocation of the whole family in a place which the family would not have considered primarily suitable, were it not for the restrictions they experienced under immigration laws (another form of dislocation).[212]

[209] See, for example, Daniel Thym, 'Residence as De Facto Citizenship? Protection of Long-Term Residence under Article 8 ECHR' in Ruth Rubio-Marin (ed), *Human Rights and Immigration* (Oxford University Press, 2014).

[210] Dembour (n 4), p.5. [211] Ibid, p.1. [212] Dembour (n 4), ch.4.

These concerns are not limited to scholars and have also been expressed by judges within the ECtHR itself.[213] While former Judge Pinto de Albuquerque has made the following extra-judicial comments:

> The slippery slope the Court is on will inevitably lead to more problems and less protection. Migration will not go away, and as we watch the world become increasingly more volatile, we must expect that waves of migrations will continue to bring many more vulnerable and desperate people to our shores. The Court will have to reflect on its role in protecting individuals who have come to Europe and managed to create a life here, only to have their lives upturned by arbitrary deportations. The Court will also have to consider its role in condoning an inhuman detention policy which treats migrants as disposable commodities. The Court is on a wrong path: one away from protection, and towards indifference. The implications of this are tragic, not only for individuals who have no other protection but the Convention, but also for the protection and development of human rights across Europe and the world.[214]

What then are the options for the ECtHR? Dembour suggests that the legal framework will always be biased in favour of either migrants or the State as 'a neutral position is an elusive goal when the individual and state interests at stake are constructed so differently from each other'.[215] She advocates a system that favours the migrant and suggests that in the future 'immigration control may come to be seen to be on par with the institutions of slavery and the incapacity of women, which were considered to make complete sense and were legally endorsed and organised before they became outlawed'.[216] The question that we need to ask, however, is whether such societal change can be driven by the ECtHR, or whether it has to wait for greater consensus, acknowledging that both seem unlikely in the current political climate.

9.3 INTRODUCTION TO THE UK LEGAL FRAMEWORK

For many years the Government's policy was explicitly to create a 'hostile environment' for migrants.[217] This ambition underpinned legislation such as

[213] See, for example: *Boughanemi* v. *France* (n 44), dissenting opinion of Judge Martens; *El Boujaïdi* v. *France* (2000) 30 EHRR 223, dissenting opinion of Judge Foighel; *Bouchelkia* v. *France* (n 49), dissenting opinion of Judge Palm; *Boujlifa* v. *France* (n 49), joint dissenting opinions of Judges Baka and Van Dijk; *Berisha* v. *Switzerland*, App. No. 948/12, 30/07/2013, dissenting opinion of Judges Jociene and Karakas; *Vasquez* v. *Switzerland*, App. No. 1785/08, 26/11/2013, dissenting opinion of Judge Pinto de Albuquerque; *Khan* v. *Germany*, App. No. 38030/12, 23/04/2015, dissenting opinion of Judge Zupančič. Note also, interesting separate concurring opinions in *A.S.* v. *Switzerland* (2017) 65 EHRR 12 and *Z.H. and R.H.* v. *Switzerland* (n 42).

[214] Paulo Pinto de Albuquerque and Guillaume Dartigue (n 10), pp.241–242.

[215] Dembour (n 4), p.8. [216] Dembour (n 4), p.31.

[217] On the hostile environment, see Shona York, 'The "Hostile Environment": How Home Office Immigration Polices and Practices Create and Perpetuate Illegality' (2018) 32(4) Journal of

the Immigration Act 2014, the Nationality and Borders Act 2022 and the Illegal Migration Act 2023. As human rights law was a potential impediment to this policy, it was a source of immense political consternation. In earlier chapters we saw that immigration was at the heart of calls to repeal the HRA and to withdraw from the ECHR. Some of this stems from Article 3 ECHR,[218] but there is also a long history of political opposition to Article 8 ECHR. A famous example of this arose in 2011 when Theresa May campaigned for the repeal of the HRA by highlighting the 'absurd' consequences of Article 8 ECHR. She stated:

> We all know the stories about the Human Rights Act. The violent drug dealer who cannot be sent home because his daughter – for whom he pays no maintenance – lives here. The robber who cannot be removed because he has a girlfriend. The illegal immigrant who cannot be deported because – and I am not making this up – he had a pet cat.

The inaccuracies in her statement prompted the Judicial Office at the Royal Courts of Justice to issue the following correction:

> This was a case in which the Home Office conceded that they had mistakenly failed to apply their own policy – applying at that time to that appellant – for dealing with unmarried partners of people settled in the UK. That was the basis for the decision to uphold the original tribunal decision – the cat had nothing to do with the decision.

Theresa May is not, however, alone in her attitude to Article 8 ECHR. Indeed, we will see later in this chapter that a desire to further restrict Article 8 ECHR was one of the driving forces behind the Conservative Government's proposal to repeal the HRA and replace it with a Bill of Rights.[219]

If we consider the nature of political discourse on immigration it is evident that much of it is fundamentally at odds with a human rights-based approach. One aspect of this is the ways in which dehumanising language is invoked to render migrants less 'human' and by implication less entitled to 'human rights'. Colin Yeo notes that this is more insidious and less direct than in the past as 'references to culture, values, traditions and solidarity have become proxies' for race.[220] It is, however, strikingly evident in the ways in which

Immigration Asylum and Nationality Law 363–384. On the devastating Windrush scandal, see House of Commons and House of Lords Joint Committee on Human Rights *Windrush Generation Detention,* Sixth Report of Session 2017–2019, HC 1034, HL Paper 160, 27 June 2018, Wendy Williams, *Windrush Lessons Learned Review* (March 2020), https://assets.publishing.service.gov.uk/media/5e7dd650e90e0706f7d69cc1/6.5577_HO_Windrush_Lessons_Learned_Review_LoResFinal.pdf and Amelia Gentleman, *The Windrush Betrayal: Exposing the Hostile Environment* (Guardian Faber Publishing, 2019).

[218] See Chapter 5. [219] See discussion at Section 9.3.1.4.

[220] Colin Yeo, *Welcome to Britain: Fixing Our Broken Immigration System* (Biteback Publishing, 2020), p.xxi.

'some politicians describe "migrants" in almost biblical language as a "flood" or "swarm" against which (not whom) existing residents need to be protected and shielded'.[221] Former Home Secretary Suella Braverman's references to an 'invasion' of migrants on the South Coast of England is one example of this.[222] Political discourse also marginalises migrants by invoking the pernicious immigration trope that migrants are criminals and terrorists. Suella Braverman also drew upon this in her statement in respect of those arriving by small boats.[223] Indeed, it is by depicting migrants as criminal and terrorists that they are presented as persons who are not worthy of human rights, but are instead threats to human rights. Yet, as Yeo observes, whilst 'major political figures continue to associate migrants with crime and terrorism', the evidence demonstrates that 'migrants commit fewer crimes than existing residents', and that 'major acts of terrorism on British soil have been carried out by British citizens born and brought up in the country'.[224]

A further aspect of the immigration debate that pulls us away from a human rights approach is the way in which migrants are depicted as either economic assets or liabilities. This portrays migrants not as humans entitled to rights, but as either assets to be exploited or worthless objects to be discarded, or even worse as parasites.[225] Underpinning this discourse is the assumption that immigration law must exclude outsiders that will claim an entitlement to the State's resources. The notion that the UK must safeguard its wealth from outsiders is challenged by scholars that highlight the role of immigration law and policy in perpetuating colonialist practices. For example, Nadine El-Enany argues that categorising people into those with and those without rights of entry and residence is a 'continuation of British colonial power' that 'sustains and reproduces colonial practices of racial ordering'.[226] She observes that those without a right to enter are predominantly the racialised poor and as such they are 'barred from accessing colonial wealth as it manifests in Britain today'.[227] This 'maintains the global racial order established by colonialism, whereby colonialized peoples are disproportionately disposed of land and resources within and outside Britain's borders'.[228]

Throughout this chapter we will encounter the ways in which this politics of immigration has shaped immigration policy, law and ultimately the

[221] Ibid.

[222] Andrew Sparrow, 'Suella Braverman condemned for claiming asylum seekers engaged in 'invasion' of South Coast', *The Guardian*, 31 October 2022, www.theguardian.com/politics/live/2022/oct/31/conservatives-roger-gale-migrant-centre-manston-suella-braverman-home-office-commons-rishi-sunak-uk-politics-live.

[223] Ibid. Braverman asserted that those arriving are 'facilitated by criminal gangs, some of them actual members of criminal gangs' and that we should 'stop pretending that they are all refugees in distress'.

[224] Yeo (n 220), p.xxi. [225] Ibid, p.xxii. [226] El-Enany (n 158), pp.17–18. [227] Ibid.

[228] Ibid.

application of Article 8 ECHR. Before we begin it is worth pointing out that immigration law is highly complex. There are numerous statutes and thousands of pages of Immigration Rules (statements of Government policy), as well as extensive guidance, the complexity of which led the Law Commission to recommend in 2020 a complete overhaul in order to promote accessibility, legal certainty and transparency.[229] This has yet to take place and the Supreme Court recently observed that the current poorly drafted Rules are creating difficulties and uncertainties which are resulting in expensive litigation.[230] They commented that 'it is highly desirable that the project to redraft the Immigration Rules to make them clearer should be carried forward to completion'.[231] The complexity of this means that a comprehensive account is impossible in a chapter of this length, hence, our focus is on key provisions that have been shaped by and themselves purport to shape Article 8 ECHR.

9.3.1 Automatic Deportation and Article 8 ECHR

In 2006 it was discovered that over a period of seven years, more than a thousand foreign national prisoners had been released without the Home Office considering whether a deportation order should be issued. This led to the resignation of then Home Secretary, Charles Clarke, and the introduction of automatic deportation. Consequently, s.3 of the Immigration Act 1971 which provides that a person is liable to deportation if the Secretary of State deems deportation to be conducive to the public good, is now supplemented by s.32 of the UK Borders Act 2007 which provides for automatic deportation of a foreign criminal (meaning a person who is not a British citizen) that is convicted of an offence in the UK and sentenced to a period of imprisonment of at least twelve months or an offence specified as a serious criminal offence. Section 32 UK Borders Act 2007 obliges the Secretary of State to make a deportation order in those circumstances unless deportation would violate Article 8 ECHR (s.33(2)(a) UK Borders Act 2007). The key question is thus whether deportation violates Article 8 ECHR and who makes that assessment.

9.3.1.1 Initial Judicial Determinations of the Role of the Human Rights Act 1998 and the Role of the Courts

In a series of cases, the House of Lords held that the courts and tribunals must determine whether deportation is compatible with Article 8 ECHR and not simply defer to the executive on this question. This was considered in *R (on the*

[229] Law Commission, *Simplification of the Immigration Rules: Report* HC14 Law Com No 388, 13 January 2020.

[230] *R (on the application of Afzal)* v. *SSHD* [2023] UKSC 46, [2023] 1 WLR 4593 at [91].

[231] Ibid.

application of Razgar) v. *SSHD* in which Lord Bingham explained that 'the reviewing court must . . . consider how an appeal would be likely to fare before an adjudicator, as the tribunal responsible for deciding the appeal if there were an appeal'.[232] Consequently, the court must determine whether Article 8 ECHR is applicable and whether the interference is justified under Article 8(2) ECHR.[233] The role of the judiciary was considered further in *Huang* v. *SSHD* in which the Lords observed that in enacting the HRA Parliament required Article 8 ECHR to be given effect as a matter of domestic law.[234] Amongst other things, this rendered it unlawful for a public authority (which includes immigration officers, the appellate immigration authority and the courts) to act incompatibly with a Convention right.[235] Consequently, the Lords in *Huang* held that when hearing an Article 8 ECHR appeal, the court's task is not limited to a reviewing function, it must make a determination of legality.[236] The Lords went on to state that in making that determination they must establish the relevant facts and consider and weigh the argument in favour of refusal of leave.[237] In *EB (Kosovo)* the Lords again reiterated the importance of a careful fact specific inquiry.[238]

9.3.1.2 Limiting Article 8 ECHR via Immigration Rules

The Government responded to this by setting out in Immigration Rules how Article 8 ECHR should be applied.[239] The effect of the rules was that persons sentenced to twelve or more months' imprisonment were liable to be deported unless they could satisfy one of three exceptions. The intention was that these rules would dictate the application of Article 8 ECHR such that if these thresholds were not met no further assessment would be made. This was, however, resisted by the Supreme Court in *SSHD* v. *Izuazu*, which observed that if the threshold specified in the rules is not met then an Article 8 ECHR assessment must still be made.[240] The Court emphasised that Parliament had not altered the legal duty in respect of Article 8 ECHR and there could be no assumption that the rules were conclusive of that assessment or that a fact-sensitive inquiry is not needed.[241] Moreover, it emphasised that if the Rules seek to restrict relevant and weighty considerations from being taken into account the courts will give less regard to the Rules in the assessment of proportionality.[242] Theresa May was furious and subsequently declared in an

[232] *R (on the application of Razgar)* v. *SSHD* [2004] UKHL 27, [2004] 2 AC 368 at [17].

[233] Ibid at [17]. [234] *Huang* v. *SSHD* [2007] UKHL 11, [2007] 2 AC 167 at [8].

[235] Section 6 of the HRA 1998. [236] *Huang* (n 234) at [11]. [237] *Huang* (n 234) at [16].

[238] *EB (Kosovo)* v. *SSHD* [2008] UKHL 41, [2009] 1 AC 1159.

[239] Statement of Changes to the Immigration Rules, 13 June 2012, HC 194.

[240] *SSHD* v. *Izuazu* [2013] UKUT 45 (IAC) at [41]. [241] Ibid at [59] and [67].

[242] Ibid at [67]–[69].

interview in the *Mail on Sunday* that she would legislate to compel the courts to abide.

I am therefore determined to introduce primary legislation that will specify that foreign nationals who commit serious crimes shall, except in extraordinary circumstances, be deported. Once this primary legislation has been enacted, it is surely inconceivable that judges in this country will maintain that it is they, rather than Parliament, who are entitled to decide how to balance the foreigner's right to family life against our nation's right to protect itself.[243]

We will look at the legislation that followed in a moment, but before we do, it is important to observe that in the interim both the domestic courts, and the ECtHR, found the Rules to be compatible with Article 8 ECHR. In *Hesham Ali* v. *SSHD*, Lord Reed (giving the majority judgment) observed that the idea that the new rules comprise a 'complete code' appeared to have been mistakenly interpreted in some cases as meaning that the Rules, and the Rules alone, govern appellate decision-making.[244] He held that this is not correct as the Rules are not law and therefore do not govern the determination of appeals, other than appeals brought on the ground that the decision is not in accordance with the Rules.[245] They are, however, a relevant and important consideration in determining appeals brought on Convention grounds, because they reflect the assessment of the general public interest made by the responsible Minister and endorsed by Parliament.[246] Thus, where the Secretary of State has adopted a policy in relation to the assessment of proportionality, which is set out in Rules endorsed by Parliament, the Upper Tribunal should give considerable weight to that policy.[247] Lord Kerr dissented. He observed that the ECHR case law does not permit states to limit or dictate the weight to be given to the *Boultif* factors, thus when those factors are relevant, they must be taken into account and given the weight that they deserve.[248] This dissent subsequently formed the basis for the applicant's submissions in *Unuane* v. *the United Kingdom* in which it was argued that the Rules precluded the domestic courts from applying Article 8 ECHR. The ECtHR rejected that argument.[249] It held that the domestic case law, in particular *Hesham Ali*, indicated that the Rules do not necessarily preclude the domestic courts from applying the *Boultif* criteria, and thus the Rules were not incompatible with Article 8 ECHR.[250]

[243] Theresa May, 'It's MY job to deport foreigners who commit serious crime – and I'll fight any judge who stands in my way, says Home Secretary', *Mail on Sunday*, 17 February 2013, www.dailymail.co.uk/debate/article-2279828/Its-MY-job-deport-foreigners-commit-crime–Ill-fight-judge-stands-way-says-Home-Secretary.html.

[244] *Hesham Ali* v. *SSHD* [2016] UKSC 60, [2016] 1 WLR 4799 at [52]. [245] Ibid at [53].

[246] Ibid. [247] Ibid at [46]. [248] Ibid at [120]. [249] *Unuane* v. *the United Kingdom* (n 83).

[250] *Unuane* v. *the United Kingdom* (n 83). For discussion, see Lewis Graham, 'Unuane v. United Kingdom: Does the Convention require "pure" proportionality?' Strasbourg Observers, 23 December 2020, https://strasbourgobservers.com/category/cases/unuane-v-united-

9.3.1.3 *Limiting Article 8 ECHR via Immigration Act 2014 (Section 117 Nationality Immigration and Asylum Act 2002)*

In 2014, Theresa May delivered on her promise when s.19 of the Immigration Act 2014 inserted provisions into Part 5 Nationality Immigration and Asylum Act 2002. This gave the force of primary legislation to the principles reflected in the Rules by requiring a court or tribunal, when determining whether a decision is in breach of Article 8 ECHR, to have regard to the public interest considerations as set out in the Bill.[251] Section 117A Nationality, Immigration and Asylum Act 2002 (NIAA) thus provides that where a court or tribunal is required to determine whether a decision made under the Immigration Acts breaches Article 8 and would be unlawful under s.6 HRA 1998, it must have regard to the considerations in s.117B NIAA in all cases, and in cases concerning the deportation of foreign criminals, to the considerations listed in s.117C NIAA.

In respect of foreign criminals, s.117C NIAA states that automatic deportation applies to those sentenced to twelve or more months imprisonment unless one of three exceptions is applicable. The *first exception* applies if the foreign national has been sentenced for a period of one–four years, has been lawfully resident for most of their life in the UK, is culturally integrated and there are *very significant obstacles to integration* in the country to which they would be deported. The *second exception* is applicable if the foreign national has been sentenced for a period of one–four years and the effect of deportation on a qualifying partner or child would be *unduly harsh*. The *third exception* is where there are *very compelling circumstances* over and above those applicable under exception 1 and 2. For those convicted and sentenced to a period of four or more years the third exception is the only applicable exception. Consequently, the legislation raises the bar by setting very high thresholds.

The severity of the thresholds is evident in the case law. The first exception '*very significant obstacles to integration*' was considered by the Upper Tribunal in *SSHD* v. *Treebhawon and Others* which observed that 'it is a self-evidently elevated threshold, such that mere hardship, mere difficulty, mere hurdles and mere upheaval or inconvenience, even where multiplied, will generally be insufficient in this context'.[252] The facts of *Sanambar* v. *SSHD* are indicative

kingdom/; and Alex Ewing, 'Deportation and Family Rights', UK Human Rights Blog, 10 December 2020, https://ukhumanrightsblog.com/2020/12/10/deportation-and-family-rights/.

[251] Explanatory notes, 10 October 2013 at [19].

[252] *SSHD* v. *Treebhawon and Others* [2017] UKUT 13, [2017] Imm. A.R. 790 at [37]. In respect of 'integration', note that the Court of Appeal in *SSHD* v. *Kamara* [2016] EWCA Civ 813, [2016] 4 WLR 152 at [14] observed that: 'The idea of "integration" calls for a broad evaluative judgment to be made as to whether the individual will be enough of an insider in terms of

of the severity of this threshold.[253] On that occasion the Supreme Court confirmed the Upper Tribunal's decision that the following obstacles to integration in Iran were not 'very significant'. First, Sanambar had not been in Iran since he was nine years old. Second, he did not read or write Farsi. Third, he was not aware of any relatives in Iran. Fourth, that he would have difficulties in obtaining employment and/or further education or training.[254] The Upper Tribunal held that the fact that he conversed in Farsi with his mother, he was academically able, and his mother had a friend in Iran that she had visited twice, were factors that could 'reasonably be said to afford the appellant some assistance in terms of integration'.[255] Thus it accepted that there 'was ample material to justify the conclusion of the tribunal that the obstacles to the appellant's integration into Iran were not very significant'.[256]

The threshold for the second exception, namely that the effect of the foreign criminal's deportation on a partner or child would be 'unduly harsh', is also high. This was considered by the Supreme Court in *HA (Iraq)*, which confirmed that

> 'unduly harsh' does not equate with uncomfortable, inconvenient, undesirable or merely difficult. Rather, it poses a considerably more elevated threshold. 'Harsh' in this context, denotes something severe, or bleak. It is the antithesis of pleasant or comfortable. Furthermore, the addition of the adverb 'unduly' raises an already elevated standard still higher.[257]

The severity of this was evident in *FN (Burundi)* v. *SSHD* in which the Court of Appeal held that the Upper Tribunal had not erred in concluding that the deportation of a mother would be harsh for her child, but not unduly harsh, despite the fact that there were allegations of domestic abuse against the father, and social services and the police had been involved.[258]

The third exception, which requires very compelling circumstances, over and above the other thresholds was considered by the Supreme Court in *HA (Iraq)*.[259] The Court of Appeal in *SSHD* v. *CT (Vietnam)* also explained that the national authorities have elected to impose a very high threshold with the scales tipped towards deportation.

> The starting point in considering exceptional circumstances is not neutral. Rather, the scales are heavily weighted in favour of deportation and something very compelling is

understanding how life in the society in that other country is carried on and a capacity to participate in it, so as to have a reasonable opportunity to be accepted there, to be able to operate on a day-to-day basis in that society and to build up within a reasonable time a variety of human relationships to give substance to the individual's private or family life.'

[253] *Sanambar* (n 99). [254] Ibid at [56]. [255] Ibid at [59].

[256] Ibid at [62]. See further, *NC* v. *SSHD* [2023] EWCA Civ 1379 at [26].

[257] *HA (Iraq)* v. *SSHD* [2022] UKSC 22, [2022] 1 WLR 3784 at [41]–[45].

[258] *FN (Burundi)* v. *SSHD* [2023] EWCA Civ 1350 at [33]. [259] *HA (Iraq)* (n 257) at [46]–[52].

required to swing the outcome in favour of a foreign criminal whom Parliament has said should be deported.[260]

This threshold was not met in *Akinyemi* v. *SSHD* even though Akinyemi was born in the UK and had never left.[261] It has, however, been met in very extreme cases of vulnerability.[262] For example, in *SSHD* v. *KE (Nigeria)* the threshold was met where

> the relevant offending resulted from his mental illness, namely paranoid schizophrenia; that illness is now controlled here, such that reoffending is unlikely; he has no relations or other support in Nigeria; without any support there, he will be unable to cope there and it is extremely likely that he will not have access to medication which will keep his paranoid schizophrenia in check; and, as a result, in a very real way, deportation would rob him of any sensible private life.[263]

The general approach that the courts should adopt to these provisions was considered by Lord Carnwath in *KO (Nigeria)* and was summarised and endorsed by the Supreme Court in *HA (Iraq)*.[264] First, it was observed that the legislation 'must be approached in the context of the history of attempts by Government, with the support of Parliament, to clarify the application of article 8 in immigration cases'.[265] In this respect they noted that 'the purpose of the changes was to promote consistency, predictability and transparency in decision making and to reflect the Government's and Parliament's view of how as a matter of public policy, the balance should be struck'.[266] Second, it was noted that the Rules were 'designed to change the previous position comprehensively by "reflecting an assessment of all the factors relevant to the application of article 8"'.[267] Third, that the legislation took that 'a stage further by expressing the intended balance of the relevant factors in direct statutory form'.[268] Finally, that the 'purpose was "to produce a straightforward set of rules, and in particular to narrow rather than widen the residual area of discretionary judgment for the court to take account of public interest or other factors not directly reflected in the wording of the statute"'.[269] In *NE-A (Nigeria)*, the Court of Appeal also distinguished the legislative provisions from the Immigration Rules finding that whilst the Rules could not offer a complete code for Article 8 ECHR, the legislative provisions provide a structured approach which ensures that all results are compatible with Article 8 ECHR. Thus, if there are no 'very

[260] *SSHD* v. *CT (Vietnam)* [2016] EWCA Civ 488 at [18].

[261] *Akinyemi* v. *SSHD* [2017] EWCA Civ 236, [2017] 1 WLR 3118.

[262] *SSHD* v. *JZ (Zambia)* [2016] EWCA Civ 116, [2016] Imm. A.R. 781.

[263] *SSHD* v. *KE (Nigeria)* [2017] EWCA Civ 1382, [2018] 1 WLR 2610 at [89].

[264] *HA (Iraq)* (n 257). See also *Gadinala* v. *SSHD* [2024] EWCA Civ 1410 at [35]–[47].

[265] Ibid at [18]. [266] Ibid. [267] Ibid. [268] Ibid. [269] Ibid.

compelling circumstances' the public interest requires deportation and this is compatible with Article 8 ECHR.[270]

The severity of the Rules is such that one leading practitioner has declared them akin to exile.[271] He suggests that 'statutory exceptions have deliberately been so narrowly drawn that virtually no one can rely on them' and that '[a]ny semblance of humane flexibility has been lost as a consequence'.[272] It has also been suggested that the role of the courts has shifted over the last twenty years as whilst the earlier HRA 1998 cases saw the courts engaging in full proportionality analysis, the more recent case law has seen a far more deferential approach. In this respect Christopher Rowe observes that:

> [S]enior judiciary have turned Article 8 related immigration law into a zone of extreme deference, with the courts selectively employing existing legal principles and ignoring binding precedent to assess the legality of the changes. Whilst it may be true that the UT was willing to uphold the constitutional principle that changes to the Immigration Rules and a House of Commons motion cannot override the domestic and Strasbourg Article 8 jurisprudence, the senior courts – almost unanimously – have shown no such backbone.[273]

9.3.1.4 Deportation and Proposals for Further Reform

Although domestic law has significantly curtailed Article 8 ECHR, there is enduring fierce political opposition to Article 8 ECHR. Indeed, part of the former Conservative Government's rationale for repealing the HRA was the extent to which the HRA precludes deportation.[274] Indeed, it asserted that reform was necessary because the courts have found thousands of deportations to be incompatible with human rights. An opposing view is that there are thousands of cases in which the Home Office would have violated human rights if the decisions had not been considered by the tribunals.[275] It is also noteworthy that they only identified three cases as indicative of the need for reform – one of which was in a redacted form such that it was not possible to make an assessment of the issues.[276]

[270] *NE-A (Nigeria)* v. *SSHD* [2017] EWCA Civ 239, [2017] Imm. A.R. 1077.

[271] Yeo (n 220), p.xxviii. [272] Ibid.

[273] Christopher Rowe, 'Falling into Line? The Hostile Environment and the Legend of the "Judges' Revolt"' (2022) 85(1) MLR 105, 107.

[274] Ministry of Justice, Human Rights Act Reform: A Modern Bill Of Rights – A Consultation To Reform the Human Rights Act 1998 (December 2021), p.45, www.gov.uk/government/consultations/human-rights-act-reform-a-modern-bill-of-rights.

[275] University of Cambridge, Centre for Public Law Submission to Human Rights Act Reform: A Modern Bill Of Rights – A Consultation To Reform the Human Rights Act 1998 (March 2022) at [377], research produced by Matilda Gillis, Bethan Hall and Darren Peterson played a vital role in the Centre for Public Law's submission on this point.

[276] Ibid.

Repeal of the HRA is not being pursued by the current Government, however, it has been reported that members of the Conservative party are pushing for an amendment to the Border Security, Asylum and Immigration Bill that would disapply the HRA in immigration cases.[277] It is also reported that the Labour Government is reviewing the operation of Article 8 ECHR in immigration cases and looking to other countries to see if a stricter approach to the right is possible.[278] It is expected that a white paper will be forthcoming which will set out how Article 8 ECHR should be interpreted.[279] In this respect, Yvette Cooper, the current Home Secretary, has stated that she believes 'it is possible to change the way in which Article 8 is being interpreted' and that 'too much has been left to ad hoc decisions by the courts'.[280] It has also been suggested that the UK might explore working within the Council of Europe to push for broader changes to the ECHR in this context.[281]

9.3.2 The UK Legal Framework on Family Reunification and Article 8 ECHR

As leading immigration barrister Colin Yeo explains, entry to the UK is 'governed by a cobbled-together conglomeration of incomprehensible and outdated laws, criteria that are set out in constantly shifting so-called "rules"'.[282] The complexity of the regime means that it is impossible to cover all aspects in this chapter, and in any event it is subject to frequent amendment.[283] Broadly speaking, Appendix FM (Family Migration) of the Immigration Rules provides certain 'routes' to entry depending upon the relationship between the person residing in the UK and the family member. Each route has a 'requirements' section; these requirements typically include Suitability, Relationship, Financial and English

[277] Francesca Gillett and Iain Watson, 'Tories say rights act should not apply to deportations', *BBC News*, 9 March 2025, www.bbc.co.uk/news/articles/c3rnv5l381eo.

[278] Charles Hymas, 'Migrants face curbs on using the ECHR to avoid deportation', *The Telegraph*, 14 March 2025, www.telegraph.co.uk/news/2025/03/14/migrants-echr-deportation-cooper-starmer-labour-europe/.

[279] Charles Hymas, 'Judges to get "common sense" guidance to stop migrants abusing human rights laws', *The Telegraph*, 29 April 2025, www.telegraph.co.uk/politics/2025/04/29/judges-common-sense-guidance-stop-migrants-abusing-human/.

[280] Ibid. [281] Hymas (n 278). [282] Yeo (n 220), p.xvii.

[283] The Rules were amended in February and March 2024 in line with a five-point plan set out by the Home Secretary in December 2023 intended to reduce net migration, Statement of changes to the Immigration Rules: HC 556, 19 February 2024 and Statement of changes to the Immigration Rules: HC 590, 14 March 2024. Those changes included a prohibition on care workers bringing dependents to the UK, restrictions on students bringing family members to the UK, as well as raising the minimum income rule. The minimum income requirement rose to £29,000 on 11 April 2024, and there were plans under the Conservative Government to increase it to £38,700 by early 2025. It is unclear at the time of writing whether the change of Government will affect this, however, a report published by the Migration Advisory Committee in June 2025 has advised against this increase, Migration Advisory Committee, *Family Route: Financial Requirements Review* (June 2025).

language, but they vary depending upon the type of application. One of the aims of Appendix FM is to 'unify consideration under the rules and Article 8 ECHR, by defining the basis on which a person can enter or remain in the UK on the basis of their family or private life'.[284] As discussed below, various legal challenges have been brought in respect of these Rules and Article 8 ECHR. To date, the courts have largely accepted that the rules can be applied in ways that are compatible with the Convention right and that where families are forced to live apart that this too may be compatible with Article 8 ECHR.

9.3.2.1 *Minimum Income Rule*

One of the most controversial aspects of Appendix FM is the minimum income requirement (MIR). This was one of the changes introduced in 2012 and it constituted a significant restriction when compared with previous policies. The earlier policy had required broadly that the parties would be able to maintain and accommodate themselves and any dependants adequately in the UK without recourse to public funds. Appendix FM introduced a minimum income threshold of £18,600 when applying for entry of a partner with no children.[285] In April 2024 this threshold was raised to £29,000.[286] It has been reported that when the minimum income rule was implemented, 47 per cent of the adult population in the UK would not have been able to meet the requirement.[287] The rule has thus been described as 'a flagrant, and arguably unprecedented, form of 'two-tier citizenship', with family reunification rights restricted to the affluent half of the population'.[288] It has also been suggested that it disproportionately affected' women and ethnic minorities with lower average earnings, whilst some suspected the policy had a racist intent targeting British citizens with South Asian backgrounds, with higher rates of marrying outside the UK'.[289] In addition to providing evidence that the minimum income threshold is met, evidence must also be provided of adequate accommodation. The rule applies to all, including British nationals who wish to bring their non-British partners to the UK. Writing in 2020, Colin Yeo highlighted the impact of these provisions:

> Families have been torn apart by these rules, with any spouse or partners earning less than £18,600 forced to make an invidious choice between emigrating, splitting apart

[284] Home Office, *Statement of Intent: Family Migration* (June 2012) at [31].

[285] If dependent children were involved, then the pre-2024 minimum income requirement was raised by a further £3,800 for the first child and £2,400 for additional children. A dependent child for these purposes is a non-British or settled person under the age of eighteen.

[286] Following the changes different threshold apply depending on whether the application was made before April 2024 and depending on whether the application is a new application. See further Home Office, *Family Migration: Appendix FM and Appendix HM Armed Forces – Minimum Income Requirement* (version 12.0, 12 March 2025).

[287] Wray (n 24), p.155. [288] Rowe (n 273), p.111. [289] Ibid, p.112.

> or living illegally in the UK. Around 40 per cent of the working population of the United Kingdom cannot afford a spouse visa, with women, ethnic minorities, the young, the old and those outside London particularly disadvantaged.[290]

While Rowe comments that 'the human consequences of the MIR for individuals' are 'plain – especially for citizens with partners from the poorest countries, where relocation is most likely to be unviable, the MIR might mean a lifelong separation, and the policy has been linked with a number of suicides'.[291]

It is perhaps not surprising then that the minimum income rule was challenged in *MM (Lebanon)* v. *SSHD* in which the applicants argued it violated Article 8 ECHR.[292] The Supreme Court rejected that argument. It observed that failure to qualify under the Rules was not conclusive as the Secretary of State retains a discretion to grant entry clearance outside of the rule in accordance with s.6 HRA. The Court held that this 'removes any substantial basis for challenging the new rules as such under the HRA'.[293] The Court then went on to observe that the fact that the rule may cause hardship to many does not render it unlawful as it has the legitimate aim of ensuring that applicants do not have recourse to welfare benefits and have sufficient resources to play a full part in British life.[294] Moreover, it observed that the minimum income requirement is rationally connected to this aim and the ECtHR allows states to set minimum income rules.[295] Consequently, the Supreme Court (SC) held that the minimum income rule is not inherently incompatible with Article 8 ECHR.[296] This has been subject to immense criticism by scholars who have highlighted the way in which the courts have raised the bar in immigration cases such that 'any legislative measure which would not inevitably lead to a Convention incompatible outcome in all or nearly all cases would be Convention compatible'.[297] Rowe suggests that this allows the senior courts to 'sidestep … controversial issues – [as] they did not have to, and did not, scrutinise whether the MIR was necessary or struck a fair balance, since it obviously satisfied the test',[298] whilst Wray suggests that the 'Court's clear aim was to deter further attacks on the Rules as a whole, rather than on individual decisions made under them'.[299] She observes that the impact of this is that Article 8 is 'not a way to challenge structurally unjust immigration policies but a remedy for occasional egregious unfairness'.[300]

There were, however, as Wray notes, some limited aspects of the judgment which were positive for migrants.[301] In respect of children, the SC held that the

[290] Yeo (n 220), p.xxiv. [291] Rowe (n 273), p.112.

[292] *MM (Lebanon)* v. *SSHD* [2017] UKSC 10, [2017] 1 WLR 771. [293] Ibid at [60].

[294] Ibid at [81]–[82]. [295] Ibid at [83]–[87]. [296] Ibid.

[297] Christopher Rowe, 'Challenges to Legislation under the Human Rights Act' (2024) PL 293, 313.

[298] Rowe (n 273), p.112. [299] Wray (n 24), p.157. [300] Ibid, p.157. [301] Ibid, p.157.

rules were inadequate in providing for the duty to safeguard and promote the welfare of children as they did not prescribe an approach in which the best interests of children are a primary consideration.[302] A further issue that was considered in *MM* was the impact of the rules regarding the type of evidence necessary to demonstrate compliance with the financial requirements as it meant that some applicants who were able to meet the minimum income requirement, were nevertheless unsuccessful because they could not provide the prescribed evidence. In *MM (Lebanon)*, the Court held that whilst the rules were lawful, where an application failed due to the evidence rules, this should be considered under Article 8 ECHR and a more flexible approach was needed. It indicated that the guidance and possibly even the Rules may need amending to clarify this,[303] following which the Home Office updated the Rules to allow other sources to be considered and to make it explicit that there needs to be consideration of Article 8 ECHR where the test is not met on the Rules.[304] This was, as Wray notes, a 'minimal response', which was all that the Supreme Court's judgment required.[305]

9.3.2.2 Language

Applicants under the partner or parent route must also satisfy the pre-entry language requirement, by providing evidence that they are a national of a majority English-speaking country, have passed a test with an approved provider or have a degree, Masters or PhD awarded by an educational establishment in the UK, or if outside the UK deemed to meet the standard in the UK and taught in English. The applicant will be exempt from this requirement if they are aged sixty-five or over, have a disability (physical or mental) which prevents them from meeting the requirement, or there are exceptional circumstances which prevent them from being able to meet the requirement prior to entry.

The pre-entry language requirement was unsuccessfully challenged in *Ali and Bibi* v. *SSHD*.[306] The appellants were UK citizens married to foreign nationals who were unable to satisfy the requirement. In Bibi's case her husband would have to relocate to another part of Pakistan for several months to complete the language requirement, which they could not afford. In Ali's

[302] *MM (Lebanon)* (n 292) at [88]–[92]. [303] Ibid at [93]–[100].

[304] On *MM (Lebanon)*, see also, Gemma Manning, 'The Minimum Income Requirement for Family Settlement: The Cost of Integration' [2019] PL 304–325; Michelle Yik Yu Wong, 'The Unequal Price of Love: A Critical Race Feminism Critique of the £18,600 Minimum Income Requirement for Family Reunification under Article 14 ECHR' (2019) 33(4) Journal of Immigration, Asylum and Nationality Law 302; Christopher Rowe, 'Family Reunification: The Minimum Income Requirements and the Welfare Myth' (2020) 34(1) Journal of Immigration, Asylum and Nationality Law 30.

[305] Wray (n 24), p.163. [306] *Ali and Bibi* v. *SSHD* [2015] UKSC 68, [2015] 1 WLR 5055.

case there was no test centre in Yemen. Although the SC expressed concern that there are countries and areas within countries where it may not be possible to obtain the necessary qualification, it nevertheless held that the rule did not breach Article 8 or Article 14 ECHR. Lady Hale suggested that the appropriate solution would be to amend the Guidance and grant an exemption where it is simply impracticable for a person to learn English, or to take the test in the country of origin, either because the facilities are non-existent, or because they are inaccessible due to the distance and expense involved.[307] The Government responded to this by amending the Rules so that if a refusal would breach Article 8 ECHR due to its 'unjustifiably harsh' consequences, the language requirement would be waived. Wray suggests that this is a 'grudging response' which 'benefited from the lack of specificity in the judgment and suggest[s] that exceptions [will] continue to be very rare'.[308]

9.3.2.3 *Adult Dependent Relatives*

Stringent provisions govern the admission of adult dependent relatives. Prior to the 2012 amendments, a parent or grandparent could qualify for immediate settlement in the UK, if he or she was over the age of sixty-five, wholly or mainly financially dependent on the sponsoring relative, had no other close relatives in their own country to turn to for financial support and could meet the maintenance and accommodation requirements. The Secretary of State's guidance in introducing the new rules made it plain that the new rules were intended to end the routine expectation of settlement for parents and grandparents. Two highly restrictive eligibility criteria must now be met, namely: (i) that the adult dependent must as a result of age, illness or disability require long-term personal care to perform everyday tasks; and (ii) that they must be unable, even with the practical and financial help of the sponsor, to obtain the required level of care in the country where they are living, either because it is not available and there is no person in that country who can reasonably provide it; or because it is not affordable. Until recently, these rules were contained in Appendix FM, but on 1 June 2023 they were moved to a separate Appendix, (Appendix Adult Dependent Relative). No substantive changes were made when the provisions were moved to the new Appendix.

The case of *Ribeli* v. *Entry Clearance Officer* illustrates the application of these rules.[309] *Ribeli* concerned a South African mother suffering from a degenerative disease who had been refused entry to join her daughter (who had acquired UK citizenship). It was determined that there was no disproportionate interference with Article 8 ECHR as the daughter could travel to South

[307] Ibid at [55] and [60]. [308] Wray (n 24), p.154.

[309] *Ribeli* v. *Entry Clearance Officer* [2018] EWCA Civ 611.

Africa to care for her mother. The following extracts highlight contrasting perspectives as to the significance of the applicant's life in the UK. First, the applicant articulated her experience as follows:

> From my perspective, the prospect of potentially having to leave the UK to care for my mother is extremely distressing. I have built a career here, made a home, formed friendships and relationships that I value greatly. I have a good life and I am happy and privileged to now call myself a citizen of this country. This country is my home.[310]

However, the Court, whilst accepting that she desired to remain, held that this could not establish a right of entry. It found that the 'crucial point' was that she could return to South Africa.

> The crucial point (and it is a powerful point as a matter of common sense as well as a matter of law) is that the Appellant's daughter could reasonably be expected to go back to South Africa to provide the emotional support her mother needs as well as to provide practical support.[311]

The adult dependent relative rules were challenged in *R (on the application of Britcits)* v. *SSHD* where it was argued that they were incompatible with Article 8 ECHR. In the High Court, Mitting J held that although the rules appeared to have had a much heavier impact on families than was acknowledged when approved by Parliament, the Court was bound by *MM Lebanon* to determine that the rules were not incompatible with Article 8 ECHR.[312] He went on, however, to observe that it was unsurprising that applicants have succeeded in demonstrating that individual decisions are incompatible with Article 8 ECHR and that this is likely to be replicated in many cases.[313] Moreover, he expressed scepticism as to the financial basis for the restrictions observing that 'estimates of the outcome have proved hopelessly amiss and do not take into account the potential loss to the UK Exchequer of sponsors who might leave the UK to avoid the hardship and loss imposed on their family members by the refusal of leave to enter for their elderly parents nor alternative methods of avoiding a burden on the NHS and social care'.[314] He thus stated that in the absence of the Supreme Court decisions he 'would not have hesitated to consider the lawfulness on the ground of proportionality of the rule and, if I had found it to be disproportionate and so unlawful, to declare it so'.[315]

On appeal, the Court of Appeal followed the rulings in *MM* and *Bibi* that the test for determining whether an immigration rule is compatible with Article 8 ECHR is whether the rule itself is incapable of being operated in a proportionate way and so is inherently unjustified in all or nearly all cases, that is to say that it is couched in a form which makes non-compliance in individual

[310] Ibid at [66]. [311] Ibid at [69].
[312] *R (on the application of Britcits)* v. *SSHD* [2016] EWHC 956 (Admin). [313] Ibid at [35].
[314] Ibid. [315] Ibid.

cases practically inevitable.[316] Applying this to the adult dependency rules, the Court of Appeal held that they did not fall foul of Article 8 ECHR.[317] Its reasoning was: (i) the right to respect for family life in Article 8 ECHR would not apply in all cases; (ii) regard must be had to the proportionality of the rules in relation to all dependents that can apply and not just parents and children; (iii) the applicants had failed to convince the Court that it was inevitable that the rules could not be fulfilled in the case of all parents, never mind all the categories of person to whom the rules could apply; and (iv) significant weight had to be given to the fact that these rules were the subject of prior consultation and parliamentary debate and received parliamentary approval.[318] The Supreme Court subsequently refused permission to appeal.

9.3.2.4 Exemptions and Exceptions

Finally, it is important to note that if an applicant cannot satisfy the requirements established in the Rules then they need to establish that refusal constitutes a disproportionate interference with family life. The Immigration Rules deal with this by reference to exceptions based upon demonstrating that there are insurmountable obstacles to family life continuing outside the UK or that refusal would result in unjustifiably harsh consequences for the applicant, their partner, a relevant child or another family member whose Article 8 ECHR rights would be affected by the refusal. The decision maker must take into account, as a primary consideration, the best interests of any relevant child. As to the threshold for these exceptions, Home Office guidance states that:

> The assessment of whether there are 'insurmountable obstacles' is a different and more stringent assessment than whether it would be 'reasonable to expect' the applicant's partner to join them overseas. For example, a British citizen partner who has lived in the UK all their life, has friends and family here, works here and speaks only English may not wish to uproot and relocate halfway across the world, and it may be very difficult for them to do so. However, a significant degree of hardship or inconvenience does not amount to an insurmountable obstacle. ECHR Article 8 does not oblige the UK to accept the choice of a couple as to which country they would prefer to reside in.

Thus, once more the thresholds are extremely high. It is striking in this respect to note that Colin Yeo observes he 'has lost count of the number of cases [he has] worked on where children were refused entry despite it being obviously in the child's best interests to join their parent in the UK'.[319] The severity of the threshold was also considered in *R (on the application of Agyarko)* v. *SSHD*, a case in which the applicants did not satisfy the requirements, nor the

[316] *Britcits* v. *SSHD* [2017] EWCA Civ 368, [2017] 1 WLR 3345 at [72]. [317] Ibid at [73]–[80].
[318] Ibid. [319] Yeo (n 220), p.94.

exceptions.[320] The Supreme Court observed that the ultimate question in Article 8 ECHR cases is whether a fair balance has been struck between the competing public and individual interests involved, and found that the Rules and Instructions do not depart from that position.[321] In particular, it held whilst the requirement of 'insurmountable obstacles' is a stringent test, and not merely one relevant factor to be taken into account, this does not make it incompatible with Article 8 ECHR.

9.4 CONCLUSION

We have seen throughout this chapter that while Article 8 ECHR provides some protection to migrants, there are significant limitations. On the international plane, States have been given considerable latitude in determining the balance to be struck between competing interests, and significant weight is accorded to State sovereignty, with the ECtHR adopting a subsidiary role. Meanwhile, domestically there has been a shift from the earlier days of the HRA in which the courts determined for themselves the Article 8 ECHR assessment to the present framework in which Immigration Rules and legislation dictate the manner in which Article 8 ECHR is to be evaluated and the thresholds that should apply. This bring to the fore the question of whether the courts, including the ECtHR, will regard ever more draconian restrictions as compatible with Article 8 ECHR. If the answer to that question is yes, then we need to ask what role human rights law and the courts play in protecting migrants. If the answer to that question is no, then we may need to consider whether greater protection of migrants will undermine the future of the HRA and membership of the ECHR.

[320] *R (on the application of Agyarko)* v. *SSHD* [2017] UKSC 11, [2017] 1 WLR 823.

[321] In reading *Agyarko*, ibid, it is important to note that until August 2017 some aspects of the provisions were provided for separately in the Immigration Directorate Instructions such that where individuals could not satisfy the Immigration Rules then the immigration instructions provided that Article 8 ECHR should be considered outside the Rules. Following the Supreme Court's decisions in *MM (Lebanon)* (n 292) and *Agyarko* (ibid) which endorsed the tests applied by the Immigration Rules and Instructions (albeit made some recommendations on other issues), the Immigration Rules were updated to incorporate those tests directly into the Appendix FM Rules. The result is that the same tests apply, but the tests now appear in the Rules themselves.

10 Privacy and Freedom of Expression

CONTENTS

10.1 INTRODUCTION

Prior to the HRA there was no general common law right to privacy in English common law, meaning that victims of press intrusions were usually left without a remedy.[1] This changed rapidly once the HRA came into force such that today a remedy is provided by the tort of misuse of private information, which is heavily shaped by Articles 8 and 10 ECHR. In this chapter we examine the obligations that arise under the ECHR and the ways in which the competing rights are balanced by the ECtHR. This offers insight into the role of Articles 8 and 10 ECHR in respect of private actors, the process of balancing rights and the subsidiary role of the ECtHR. In the second part of the chapter, we examine the impact of Articles 8 and 10 ECHR on the development of the tort of misuse of private information. Examining this tort sheds light on the impact of the HRA on the common law and on the relationship between private individuals. Finally, we conclude the chapter by considering calls for repeal of the HRA and a recalibration of privacy and freedom of expression. The recognition of a right to privacy in a legal system that had long accorded the press a free hand unsurprisingly fuelled press hostility towards the HRA, the ECHR and the ECtHR. As Lady Hale observed in reflecting upon the fate of the HRA in 2023:

> Certain sections of the media were, of course, upset that the courts were developing a tort of misuse of private information. The courts were public authorities. They had to act compatibly with the Convention rights, even in cases between private persons. So they had to balance a newspaper's right to freedom of expression against an individual's right to respect for her private life ... But the newspapers had got used to being able to publish all sorts of private information, whether about celebrities or about ordinary people, and did not like their activities being restrained. They began to refer to the 'hated Human Rights Act'.[2]

The power of the press was evident in the Bill of Rights proposed by the former Conservative Justice Secretary, Dominic Raab, which (amongst other things) sought to recalibrate the balance struck between privacy and freedom of speech, providing for 'a more restrictive application of [Article 8 ECHR] than Strasbourg' and 'limit[ing] an individual's ability to rely on other Convention rights when they are in competition with freedom of speech'.[3] As Fenwick observes, this was the latest example of a longstanding 'right-wing tendency in the UK to emphasise the creation of greater protection for free speech,

[1] For discussion, see Gavin Phillipson and Helen Fenwick, 'Breach of Confidence as a Privacy Remedy in the Human Rights Act Era' [2000] 63(5) MLR 660.

[2] Lady Brenda Hale, 'The Fate of the UK Human Rights Act' (2024) 3 EHRLR 212, 216.

[3] UK Government Bill of Rights: European Convention on Human Rights Memorandum (2022) at [11].

especially when in conflict with privacy, as a key basis for the revision or repeal of the Human Rights Act (HRA)'.[4]

10.2 ARTICLE 8 ECHR AND THE RIGHT TO PRIVACY

10.2.1 The Scope of Article 8 ECHR

The text of Article 8 ECHR provides that 'everyone has the right to respect for his private and family life, his home and his correspondence'. The European Court of Human Rights' HUDOC database indicates that over twenty thousand Article 8 ECHR decisions and judgments have been delivered by the Convention institutions. This is not suprising given that it is commonly acknowledged that of all the Convention rights Article 8 ECHR 'has by far the widest scope'[5] and that it is 'the least defined and most unruly' of the Convention rights.[6] As Harris et al. note, '[i]t is hard to argue with this appraisal: Article 8 places on states the obligation to "respect" a wide range of personal interests which embrace a number of overlapping and interrelated areas'.[7] There is no definition of 'private life' in the Convention, and the ECtHR has repeatedly stated that it is 'a broad term not susceptible to exhaustive definition'.[8] In this respect it has been observed that the provision reaches far beyond the 'anglo-saxon and French' notion of the right to privacy'.[9] This is reflected in the values that the ECtHR has identified as inherent in Article 8 ECHR which includes a right 'to establish and to develop relationships with other human beings, especially in the emotional field for the development and fulfilment of one's own personality',[10] 'physical and moral integrity' or 'physical and psychological integrity',[11] a 'zone of interaction of a person with others, even in a public context, which may fall within the scope of private

[4] Helen Fenwick, 'Raab's Bill of Rights and the Challenges Inherent in Attempting a Statutory Re-balancing of Articles 8 and 10 ECHR' (2023) 15(1) Journal of Media Law 1,1.

[5] Anthony Lester and David Pannick, *Human Rights Law and Practice* (3rd ed) (LexisNexis, 2009), p 359.

[6] *R (on the application of Wright)* v. *Secretary of State for Health* [2006] EWHC 2886 (Admin), cited with approval in the House of Lords [2009] UKHL 3 at [30].

[7] David Harris et al., *Law of the European Convention on Human Rights* (5th ed) (Oxford University Press, 2023), p.508.

[8] See, e.g., *Perry* v. *the United Kingdom*, App. No. 63737/00, 17/07/2003 at [36].

[9] *X* v. *Iceland* (1976) 5 DR 86, EComm HR. [10] Ibid.

[11] See, e.g., *X . and Y.* v. *Netherlands* (1986) 8 EHRR 235, 'physical and moral integrity' at [22]; *Mikulic* v. *Croatia* [2002] 1 FCR 720, 'physical and psychological integrity' at [53]; *Bevacqua and S* v. *Bulgaria* [2008] ECHR 498, 'physical and psychological integrity' at [65]; *Y.F.* v. *Turkey* (2004) 39 EHRR 34, 'physical and psychological integrity' at [33]; *Wainwright* v. *the United Kingdom* (2007) 44 EHRR 40, 'physical and moral integrity' at [43]; *Pfeifer* v. *Austria* [2007] ECHR 935, 'physical and psychological integrity' at [33].

life',[12] 'reputation',[13] and 'personal autonomy'.[14] Consequently Article 8 ECHR encompasses not only interferences with correspondence, State surveillance, wiretapping, police registers, recordings of conversations, searches of homes, strip searches, DNA databases, retention of fingerprints, registers of sex offenders and forced medical examinations; but also issues such as deportation, the criminalisation of homosexuality, the criminalisation of begging, gender recognition, euthanasia and assisted dying, in-vitro fertilisation treatment, restrictions on home births and restrictions on accessing abortion rights.[15] This is a non-exhaustive list. Indeed, as David Feldman has noted, the content of Article 8 ECHR is 'dynamic and continuous, so any account is only a snapshot of a developing process caught at a single moment'.[16]

This chapter focuses on just one of the many facets of Article 8 ECHR, namely the obligations on States which arise in respect of the publication of private information.[17] Although it was unclear for some years as to whether positive obligations arise under Article 8 ECHR in respect of the publication of private information by the press,[18] today there is no doubt that there are such obligations. A turning point in some respects was the tragic death of Princess Diana during a paparazzi car chase in Paris in 1997, following which the Council of Europe Parliamentary Assembly issued Resolution 1165 (1998). That Resolution called for Governments to introduce legislation to protect privacy from 'private persons or institutions, including the mass media'.[19] It also declared that the right to privacy under Article 8 ECHR and the right to freedom of expression under Article 10 ECHR 'are neither absolute nor in any hierarchical order, since they are of equal value'.[20] Although the Resolution itself was not binding, this position was subsequently adopted by the ECtHR in *Von Hannover* v. *Germany (Von Hannover (No.1))*.[21]

[12] See, e.g., *Peck* v. *the United Kingdom* (2003) 36 EHRR 41 at [57] and *Von Hannover* v. *Germany* (2005) 40 EHRR 1 at [50].

[13] See, e.g., *Chauvy* v. *France* (2005) 41 EHRR 29 and *Delfi AS* v. *Estonia* (2016) 62 EHRR 6.

[14] See, e.g., *Pretty* v. *the United Kingdom* (2002) ECHR 427 at [61].

[15] For broader discussion of the wide-ranging case law relating to Article 8 ECHR, see Harris et al. (n 7). See also, discussion and references in Kirsty Hughes, 'A Common Law Constitutional Right to Privacy: Waiting for Godot?' in Mark Elliott and Kirsty Hughes (eds), *Common Law Constitutional Rights* (Hart, 2020).

[16] David Feldman, *Civil Liberties and Human Rights in England and Wales* (2nd ed) (Oxford University Press, 2002), p 527.

[17] For broader discussion, see references at (n 15).

[18] *Winer* v. *the United Kingdom* (dec.), App. No. 10871/04, 10/07/1986; *Barclay* v. *the United Kingdom* (dec.), App. No. 35712/97, 18/05/1999; and *Earl Spencer* v. *the United Kingdom* (1998) 25 EHRR CD105.

[19] Parliamentary Assembly of the Council of Europe Resolution 1165 (1998) at [14].

[20] Ibid at [11].

[21] *Von Hannover* v. *Germany* (*Von Hannover (No.1)*) (2005) 40 EHRR 1. There were some hints that Article 8 ECHR was applicable in the earlier Commission decision in *Earl Spencer* v. *the United Kingdom* (n 18).

Von Hannover (No. 1) was the first in a series of cases concerning the publication of photographs of Princess Caroline von Hannover in magazines in Germany.[22] The Princess had spent more than ten years trying to establish her right to private life in Germany arguing that whenever she left her house she was hounded by paparazzi who followed her every movement, be it crossing the road, fetching her children from school, shopping, walking, engaging in sport or going on holiday.[23] Although she had partly succeeded in her litigation in Germany, a crucial limit was that the German courts had determined that figures of *par excellence* status, such as the Princess, were only entitled to privacy in secluded places.[24] Consequently, whilst photographs of her in secluded places could not be published, there were no restrictions on the publication of photographs of her in non-secluded places, including the images of her shopping, skiing, canoeing, and at a beach club. It was these photographs that formed the basis for her application to the ECtHR.

Before the ECtHR, Princess Caroline argued that the German law concept of a 'secluded place' was too narrow as it left her unprotected in many places. Moreover, she argued that that the German approach was unworkable as it required her to establish that on each occasion she had been in a secluded place. This meant that she had to keep a permanent record of her every movement, which was onerous and inconclusive as it was often impossible to determine the exact time and place at which the images had been taken.[25] She argued that this interfered with Article 8 ECHR and was not justified by the need to protect the right to freedom of expression in Article 10 ECHR. Although she accepted the importance of Article 10 ECHR where the press plays a vital role in a democratic society, she denied that the press was fulfilling such a role when they disseminated images of her; she suggested that in these circumstances they were simply profiting from satisfying readers' voyeuristic tendencies.[26] Germany refuted those arguments. It claimed that its legal framework contained sufficient safeguards and that its domestic courts had struck a fair balance between the right to privacy and freedom of the press. Germany also argued that a margin of appreciation should be accorded when balancing competing rights.[27]

In determining that Article 8 was applicable, the ECtHR identified the following points of principle:

(i) that the 'concept of private life extends to aspects relating to personal identity, such as a person's name or a person's picture';[28]
(ii) private life 'includes a person's physical and psychological integrity';[29]
(iii) 'the guarantee afforded by Article 8 of the Convention is primarily intended to ensure the development, without outside interference, of the

[22] *Von Hannover (No. 1)*, ibid. [23] Ibid at [44]. [24] Ibid at [23]. [25] Ibid. [26] Ibid.
[27] Ibid at [45]. [28] Ibid at [50]. [29] Ibid.

personality of each individual in his relations with other human beings';[30]

(iv) 'there is therefore a zone of interaction of a person with others, even in a public context, which may fall within the scope of "private life"';[31]

(v) 'in certain circumstances, a person has a "legitimate expectation" of protection and respect for his or her private life';[32]

(vi) 'as regards photos, with a view to defining the scope of the protection afforded by Article 8 against arbitrary interference by public authorities, the European Commission of Human Rights [has previously] had regard to whether the photographs related to private or public matters and whether the material thus obtained was envisaged for a limited use or was likely to be made available to the general public'.[33]

Having identified these general principles, it concluded that there was 'no doubt that the publication by various German magazines of photos of the applicant in her daily life either on her own or with other people falls within the scope of her private life'.[34] This was the first time that the ECtHR held that States have obligations in respect of press intrusion into privacy, and remarkably it held that those obligations extend to the publication of photographs of a public figure in a public place. This was a major development which significantly expanded the application of Article 8 ECHR. Yet, while *Von Hannover (No.1)* was groundbreaking, the Court's reasoning was cursory.[35] Indeed, the dearth of judicial reasoning meant that scholars were left working with breadcrumbs in seeking to understand its ramifications.[36] Part of the difficulty was identifying precisely when and why Article 8 ECHR was applicable. There are many different theories of privacy, but for present purposes we can focus upon three of the ways in which we might think about privacy in relation to Article 8 ECHR.[37] The first is a spatial conception: the idea that we are entitled to privacy in some places but not others. This was clearly rejected in *Von Hannover (No.1)* as the ECtHR refused to limit the right to private places and elected not to define the boundaries of the right to respect for private life by reference to public/private spaces. Yet, whilst it was evident that the ECtHR refused to limit the right to private places (or, to use the terminology of the German domestic courts, 'secluded places'), it was not clear whether Article 8 ECHR applied to the publication of *any* photograph or

[30] Ibid. [31] Ibid. [32] Ibid at [51]. [33] Ibid at [52]. [34] Ibid at [53].

[35] Helen Fenwick and Gavin Phillipson, *Media Freedom under the Human Rights Act* (Oxford University Press, 2006), p.672.

[36] See discussion in Kirsty Hughes, 'Von Hannover' in Paul Wragg and Peter Coe (eds), *Landmark Cases in Privacy Law* (Hart, 2023).

[37] There is a vast body of literature conceptualising privacy, but a good starting point is Daniel Solove, *Understanding Privacy* (Harvard University Press, 2008) and Beate Rössler, *The Value of Privacy* (Polity Press, 2005).

whether the applicability of Article 8 ECHR was limited to particular circumstances. The second way that we might think about privacy is in terms of the protection of personal or private information. This would be applicable if we perceive the publication of the photograph as something which triggers Article 8 ECHR on the basis that it reveals private information about the person concerned. Yet, the fact that the photographs in *Von Hannover (No.1)* consisted of images of the Princess engaged in everyday activities, suggested that the images did not have to be particularly intimate, nor sensitive.[38] Consequently, if Article 8 ECHR was applicable because the photographs constituted private information then this raised a further question, namely, whether *all* photographs are private, and thus whether all photographs engage Article 8 ECHR. A third way that we might think about privacy and Article 8 ECHR is as a state of human experience in which we wish to restrict the access of others to us.[39] If we consider *Von Hannover (No.1)* from this perspective, then one explanation for the Court's finding is that Article 8 ECHR was engaged because the Princess had been subjected to a climate of harassment by the paparazzi. Another possibility is that Article 8 ECHR was engaged by the act of taking the photographs because it was at this point that Princess Caroline was subjected to unwanted access which constitutes an intrusion regardless of whether she was harassed. Identifying the underlying conception of privacy is thus relevant to determining both *why* and *when* the right is applicable.[40] Yet, it was not clear in *Von Hannover (No.1)* precisely why and when the right was engaged and it was not apparent whether there was a threshold test for the applicability of Article 8 ECHR. This was because whilst the ECtHR 'used the terms "legitimate expectation" and "reasonable expectation" interchangeably, there was no explicit analysis of whether the applicant had a "reasonable or legitimate expectation of privacy"'.[41] As such *Von Hannover (No.1)* was seen by some as 'a radical extension of the court's jurisprudence'[42] that was lacking adequate 'justificatory reasoning'[43] and which left 'the contours of the "private" wholly undefined'.[44]

38 Contrast with *Hachette Filipacchi Associes* v. *France*, App. No. 71111/01, 14/06/2007, a case which concerned the publication of a photograph of the dead body of the murdered Prefect of Corsica in the days after his murder.

39 Kirsty Hughes, 'A Behavioural Understanding of Privacy and Its Implications for Privacy Law' (2012) 75(5) MLR 806.

40 Kirsty Hughes, 'Photographs in Public Places and Privacy' (2009) 1(2) Journal of Media Law 159.

41 Hughes (n 39), p.825.

42 Gavin Phillipson, 'The "Right" of Privacy in England and Strasbourg Compared' in A. Kenyon and M. Richardson (eds), *New Directions in Privacy Law* (Cambridge University Press, 2009), p.202.

43 Fenwick and Phillipson (n 35), p.672.

44 M. A. Sanderson, 'Is Von Hannover v. Germany a Step Backwards for the Substantive Analysis of Speech and Privacy Interests?' (2004) EHRLR 631, 643.

Since *Von Hannover (No.1)*, the ECtHR has received many more applications relating to the publication of personal information. It is evident that Article 8 ECHR applies to matters such as the publication of details of someone's sexual life,[45] sexual orientation[46] and medical information.[47] There is also a significant and developing body of case law concerning photographs,[48] in respect of which the ECtHR has stated that:

> [A] person's image constitutes one of the chief attributes of his or her personality, as it reveals the person's unique characteristics and distinguishes the person from his or her peers. The right to the protection of one's image is thus one of the essential components of personal development. It mainly presupposes the individual's right to control the use of that image, including the right to refuse publication thereof .[49]

It has also stated that while 'freedom of expression includes the publication of photos ... This is nonetheless an area in which the protection of the rights and reputation of others takes on particular importance, as the photos may contain very personal or even intimate information about an individual or his or her family'.[50] There is no doubt that Article 8 ECHR applies to the non-consensual dissemination of intimate images (or the threat thereof) (e.g. revenge pornography) and that in these cases the State's positive obligations require it to have an adequate legal framework and to conduct a thorough and prompt investigation.[51] In this context the ECtHR observed in *M.S.D.* v. *Romania* that 'the publication of intimate photographs of the victims, calculated to attract the attention of their family and friends in order to humiliate and degrade them' is a form of 'online violence'.[52] It went on to state that such 'online violence, or "cyberviolence", is closely linked with offline, or "real-life", violence and falls to be considered as another facet of the complex phenomenon of domestic violence'.[53] Consequently, States have 'a positive obligation to establish and

[45] *Mosley* v. *the United Kingdom* (2011) 53 EHRR 30 at [80].

[46] *Bazhenov and others* v. *Russia*, App. Nos. 8825/22 and 19130/22, 04/02/2025 at [71]: 'the Court finds it clear that the non-consensual disclosure by third parties of the applicants' private data – including their names, sexual orientation, the fact that they were in same-sex marriages, and photographs ... on the social media platform VK fell within the sphere of the applicants' private life under Article 8 of the Convention'. In that case the ECtHR found a violation of Article 14 taken in conjunction with Article 8 ECHR as the authorities failed to discharge their positive obligation to respond adequately to the non-consensual dissemination of the applicants' private data, including the information on their sexual orientation, by private individuals, and to investigate in an effective manner whether the dissemination of the data in question had been motivated by homophobic attitudes (at [78]).

[47] *Armoniene* v. *Lithuania* (2009) 48 EHRR 53 at [40].

[48] See European Court of Human Rights Press Unit, Fact sheet on Right to the Protection of One's Image, November 2023.

[49] *Von Hannover* v. *Germany* (No. 2) [GC] (2012) 55 EHRR 15 at [96]. [50] Ibid at [103].

[51] *M.S.D* v. *Romania*, App. No. 28935/21, 03/12/2024. [52] Ibid at [121]. [53] Ibid at [119].

apply effectively a system that punishes all forms of domestic violence, whether occurring offline or online, and to provide sufficient safeguards for and adequate protection measures in respect of the victims of domestic violence in the form of effective deterrence against serious breaches of their physical and psychological integrity'.[54] This positive obligation includes a duty to establish and apply in practice an adequate legal framework affording protection against violence by private individuals and the obligation to conduct an effective investigation into acts of violence.[55] Crucially it went on to state that in this context 'a civil-law remedy, which might constitute an appropriate remedy in situations of lesser gravity'[56] is not sufficient as a criminal law response is needed.[57] More generally, in respect of photographs, it is evident that the right is applicable at each stage within the life cycle of photography, namely the taking,[58] retention,[59] dissemination[60] and the publication[61] of photographs. The ECtHR has also confirmed that Article 8 ECHR may be applicable when a photograph is published even if the applicant initially consented to the taking of the photograph[62] and that systematic harassment is not a pre-requisite for the applicability of Article 8 ECHR. The latter was emphasised in *Dupate* v. *Latvia* when the ECtHR found a violation in respect of the publication of surreptitiously taken photographs of

[54] Ibid at [120]. [55] Ibid at [120]. [56] Ibid at [121]. [57] Ibid at [125]–[127].

[58] *Reklos and Davourlis* v. *Greece*, App. No. 1234/05, 15/01/2009, where a photographer took photographs of babies in a neo-natal unit in order to sell the images to the babies' parents. The applicants were the parents of one of the children. The ECtHR agreed that the taking and retention of the photographs violated Article 8.

[59] Ibid.

[60] In *MD* v. *Spain*, App. No. 36584/17, 28/06/2022, photographs of the applicants originating from a police database to which only the authorities had access were published in a newspaper. The way in which those photographs had been leaked had not been determined by the domestic investigation, but it was held that there was no explanation other than that the authorities permitted such a leak to be possible. The ECtHR held that when such an unlawful disclosure had taken place, the positive obligation inherent in the effective respect for private life implied an obligation to carry out effective inquiries. See also, *Khuzhin* v. *Russia*, App. No. 13470/02, 23/10/2008, in which it was held that the release of the applicant's photograph from the criminal file to the press had not pursued any of the legitimate aims in Article 8(2) and *Giorgi Nikolaishvili* v. *Georgia*, App. No. 37048/04, 13/01/2009, where the publication of the applicant's photograph on a wanted board was not in accordance with domestic law. Meanwhile in *Toma* v. *Romania*, App. No. 42716/02, 24/02/2009, a violation of Article 8 was found where the police contacted journalists and allowed them to film the applicant at the police station and in *Khmel* v. *Russia*, App. No. 20383/04, 12/12/2013, where the police invited journalists to the station and allowed them to film the applicant.

[61] *Sciacca* v. *Italy*, App. No. 50774/99, 11/01/2005.

[62] *Bogomolova* v. *Russia*, App. No. 13812/09, 20/06/2017. A single mother learnt that a photograph of her son had been reproduced on the cover of an adoption booklet without her authorisation or knowledge.

the applicant leaving a maternity ward with her newborn baby.[63] In coming to that determination, the ECtHR observed:

> With respect to the domestic courts' conclusion that the photographs were taken to illustrate a specific event and were not connected with following the applicant's everyday life the Court notes that there is nothing in its case-law to suggest that a violation of the right to private life could only occur if the person had been followed systematically.[64]

It is, however, still unclear as to whether the taking or publication of *any* photograph without consent triggers Article 8 ECHR. This is because whilst the ECtHR has generally found that Article 8 ECHR is applicable, there are some indications that there is a threshold for engaging Article 8 ECHR. For example, in *Couderc and Hachette Fillipachi Associés* v. *France* the ECtHR referred to the 'importance of assessing the seriousness of the intrusion into private life' in 'determining whether or not the publication of a photograph interferes with an applicant's right to respect for his or her private life'.[65] It identified a number of factors relevant to that assessment, including 'the manner in which the information or photograph was obtained', 'the importance of obtaining the consent of the persons concerned' and 'the more or less strong sense of intrusion caused by a photograph'.[66] This suggests that there is a threshold for engaging Article 8 ECHR, albeit that to date there is only one admissibility decision, *Vučina* v. *Croatia,* in which the ECtHR has held that Article 8 ECHR was not applicable.[67]

In *Vučina*, a magazine had published a photograph of the applicant at a music concert with a caption indicating that the photograph was of the wife of the Mayor. The applicant did not object to the publication of the photograph, but rather to being wrongly identified as the Mayor's wife. It was thus in respect of the caption that the Court concluded that 'the erroneous placement of the name of the Mayor's wife next to [the applicant's] photograph' did not give rise to an issue – neither in the context of the protection of her image nor her honour and reputation – under Article 8'.[68] Nevertheless in considering whether Article 8 ECHR was applicable, the ECtHR considered the factors identified in *Couderc* and suggested that the non-surreptitious taking of a photograph in a public place at a public event and its subsequent publication does not raise an issue under Article 8 ECHR.[69] Conversely, it indicated that Article 8 ECHR *will* be applicable where photographs are obtained 'covertly or by using some illicit means or subterfuge or taking advantage any form [sic] of vulnerable position'.[70] This suggests that there is a threshold for engaging

[63] *Dupate* v. *Latvia*, App. No. 18068/11, 19/11/2020. [64] Ibid at [72].

[65] *Couderc and Hachette Fillipachi Associés* v. *France* [GC] [2016] EMLR 19 at [86]–[87].

[66] Ibid. [67] *Vučina* v. *Croatia* (dec.), App. No. 58955/13, 24/09/2019. [68] Ibid at [50].

[69] Ibid at [35]–[36]. [70] Ibid at [35].

Article 8 ECHR in respect of photographs of 'public events in public places'. Yet, whilst this suggests a more nuanced approach to privacy in public places, we need to consider how this sits alongside the ECtHR's rejection of Germany's secluded places model in *Von Hannover (No. 1)*. We thus need further clarification as to what constitutes a 'public event in a public place' and what constitutes 'taking advantage of a vulnerable position'. It is therefore possible that there will be further case law in respect of the applicability of Article 8 ECHR to photographs taken in public places.[71]

One way of reconciling the dicta might be to develop a 'reasonable expectation of privacy' test for engaging Article 8 ECHR as this would allow for a contextual assessment. This is the way in which this is dealt with in domestic law in the UK, and as we will see later in this chapter this would be significant because domestic law has adopted a narrower approach to photographs taken in public places. For now, however, it is worth emphasising that while the ECHR case law hints at an implicit threshold for engaging Article 8 ECHR, this is not playing a significant role in the ECtHR's analysis in practice. Consequently, the ECtHR generally seems to be willing to assume that Article 8 ECHR is applicable and leave any evaluation to the second stage when dealing with the competing rights. This is similar to what we saw in the previous chapter in respect of 'private life' in the deportation context.

Finally, and before we consider the balancing exercise, it is worth noting that further issues arise in respect of the applicability of Article 8 ECHR to what is known as the 'right to be forgotten'. As the ECtHR acknowledged in *Hurbain*, whilst the 'great majority of cases' concern 'the initial publication of information about private aspects of the lives of individuals or their families', there are cases relating to the ongoing availability of information 'where the lawfulness of the initial publication is not disputed'.[72] This was the situation in *Hurbain* where the applicant, in his capacity as the editor of a newspaper, was issued with a civil order obliging him to anonymise an article in the newspaper's electronic archive. The article included the full name of G who had been convicted and sentenced for drink driving many years ago. The article

[71] See in this respect *Toth and Crişan* v. *Romania*, App. No. 45430/19, 25/02/2025 in which the ECtHR found that the level of severity was met, but when balancing the two competing rights found that the manner in which the photograph was obtained did not raise any issue under Article 8 ECHR. The applicants in that case were two police officers who complained of a violation of their right to respect for their private life and reputation because the domestic courts had allegedly failed to strike a fair balance between the competing interests at stake following an allegedly defamatory post uploaded by a private individual on Facebook. The photograph which accompanied the post had been taken by the private individual during a dispute with the police relating to a fine.

[72] *Hurbain* v. *Belgium* [GC] (2023) 77 EHRR 34.

first appeared in the print edition of the paper in 1994. In 2008, the newspaper created an electronic version of its archives making the article freely available online. Two years later, G applied to the newspaper asking that the article be anonymised or removed from the online archives. The request mentioned his profession as a doctor and the fact that the article immediately appeared when his name was entered into several search engines. The newspaper refused to remove the article from the archives, but informed G that it had notified the administrator of the search engine Google to de-reference the article. Following which G brought legal proceedings against Hurbain in the domestic courts and succeeded in obtaining an order that the article should be anonymised. Consequently Hurbain applied to the ECtHR arguing that the order to anonymise the article violated Article 10 ECHR. The case first went to a Chamber of the ECtHR which found no violation of Article 10 ECHR.[73] The Grand Chamber subsequently came to the same conclusion.[74] In coming to that determination the Grand Chamber observed that 'the protection of personal data is of fundamental importance to a person's enjoyment of his or her right to respect for private and family life as guaranteed by Article 8' ECHR[75] and that Article 8 ECHR 'provides for the right to a form of informational self-determination'.[76] It thus noted that for a number of years a

> growing number of persons have sought to protect their interests under what is known as the 'right to be forgotten'. This is based on the individual's interest in obtaining the erasure or alteration of, or the limitation of access to, past information that affects the way in which he or she is currently perceived. By seeking to have that information disappear, the persons concerned wish to avoid being confronted indefinitely with their past actions or public statements, in a variety of contexts such as, for instance, job-seeking and business relations.[77]

In this regard the ECtHR recognised that the publication of personal information may have 'a far-reaching negative impact on how the person concerned is perceived by public opinion' and that there is 'a risk of other harmful effects' including that it may create a fragmented and distorted reality and the person concerned may be faced with the constant threat and resulting fear of being unexpectedly confronted with their past at any time.[78] The ECtHR thus stated that it needed to determine 'whether Article 8 affords protection against these negative effects, and, if so, to what extent'.[79] In contemplating the ambit of the concept of a right to be forgotten it observed that it has many facets and that it is still under construction.[80] In particular, while the concept had first arisen in the context of national judicial practice it had since emerged in the context of digitisation of news articles, the impact of which had been

[73] *Hurbain* v. *Belgium*, App. No. 57292/16, 22/06/2021. [74] *Hurbain* v. *Belgium* (n 72).
[75] Ibid at [190]. [76] Ibid. [77] Ibid at [191]. [78] Ibid at [192]. [79] Ibid at [193].
[80] Ibid at [194].

magnified by the listing of websites in search engines.[81] Reflecting on how this is addressed within its case law, the ECtHR stated that

> from the standpoint of the Convention, the 'right to be forgotten online' has been linked to Article 8, and more specifically to the right to respect for one's reputation, irrespective of what measures are sought for that purpose (the removal or alteration of a newspaper article in the online archives or the limitation of access to the article through de-indexing by a news outlet).[82]

The ECtHR went on to declare that 'a claim of entitlement to be forgotten does not amount to a self-standing right protected by the Convention and, to the extent that it is covered by Article 8, can concern only certain situations and items of information'.[83] In this respect, the right to be forgotten case law follows the reputation case law in requiring that, 'in order for Article 8 of the Convention to come into play, an attack on a person's reputation must attain a certain level of seriousness'.[84] On the facts of *Hurbain*, the Grand Chamber accepted that Article 8 ECHR was applicable and, as discussed further below, it found that as the national courts had carefully balanced the rights, there was no violation of Article 10 ECHR.[85]

10.2.2 Balancing Articles 8 and 10 ECHR

In cases where Article 8 ECHR is applicable, the ECtHR has to consider whether the State has struck an appropriate balance between Articles 8 and 10 ECHR. Article 10 ECHR provides that everyone has the right to freedom of expression. It has the same structure as Article 8 ECHR, namely that it is a qualified right with the circumstances in which the right may be legitimately interfered with set out in Article 10(2) ECHR. The text of the Convention is silent as to the relationship between the two Convention rights, however, as noted above, Council of Europe Resolution 1165 states that 'the rights are neither absolute nor in any hierarchical order, since they are of equal value'.[86] In determining how to balance the two rights the ECtHR in *Von Hannover (No. 1)* declared that 'the decisive factor' lies 'in the contribution that the published photos and articles make to a debate of general interest'.[87] Applying this to the facts in *Von Hannover (No. 1)* it held that the publications made no contribution to a debate of general interest as the applicant exercised no official function and the photographs and articles related exclusively to details of her private life.[88] Accordingly, Germany had failed to strike the right balance and there had been a violation of Article 8 ECHR. In coming to this conclusion the ECtHR was criticised for failing to give States latitude to strike their own balance

[81] Ibid at [194]–[195]. [82] Ibid at [199]. [83] Ibid at [199]. [84] Ibid at [210].
[85] Ibid at [256]. [86] Council of Europe Resolution 1165 (n 19) at [11].
[87] *Von Hannover (No. 1)* (n 21) at [76]. [88] Ibid at [76].

between privacy and freedom of expression, particularly as the German courts had sought to strike a balance.[89] A further issue with *Von Hannover (No.1)* was the determinative role accorded to whether the publication 'contributed to a debate of general interest' which was held to be the 'decisive factor'.[90] This meant that the balance struck was dependent on the relevance, or, as in *Von Hannover,* the irrelevance, of Article 10 ECHR, without a corresponding evaluation of the significance of the intrusion into Article 8 ECHR. It was perhaps unsurprising then that when *Von Hannover* v. *Germany (No.2)* arrived at the Grand Chamber, it took the opportunity to recalibrate and expand the balancing exercise to include an evaluation of the intrusion into Article 8 ECHR, and a wider margin of appreciation for States.[91]

The background to *Von Hannover (No.2)* was that following *Von Hannover (No.1)*, Princess Caroline brought further proceedings in Germany in respect of photographs taken of her by the press during skiing holidays. The Federal Court of Justice had granted an injunction in respect of two photographs that did not contribute to a debate of general interest, but it had refused an injunction in respect of a third photograph, that accompanied an article relating to her father, concerning Prince Rainier's poor health. That decision was upheld by the Federal Constitutional Court. It held that the Federal Court of Justice had valid grounds for considering that the reigning Prince's health was a subject of general interest and that the press was entitled to report on the manner in which his children reconciled their obligations of family solidarity with the legitimate needs of their private life, among which was the desire to go on holiday. Princess Caroline subsequently applied to the ECtHR alleging that the failure to restrict the publication of the third photograph violated Article 8 ECHR. In considering her application, the Grand Chamber expanded the list of factors relevant to the balancing exercise as follows:

(a) Contribution to a debate of general interest;
(b) How well known is the person concerned and what is the subject of the report?;
(c) Prior conduct of the person concerned;
(d) Content, form and consequences of the publication;
(e) Circumstances in which the photographs were taken.[92]

Applying those criteria to the facts, the Grand Chamber held that the photograph, considered in the light of the article, contributed to a debate of general interest, and the domestic courts had carefully balanced the publishing companies' right to freedom of expression against the applicants' right to respect for their private life.[93] In particular, the Grand Chamber observed that the

[89] Sanderson (n 44), p.643. [90] *Von Hannover (No.1)* (n 21) at [76].
[91] *Von Hannover* v. *Germany (No.2)* (2012) 55 EHRR 15 [GC] at [108]–[113].
[92] Ibid at [103]–[113]. [93] Ibid at [124].

domestic courts had amended their approach following *Von Hannover (No.1)* and, considering the margin of appreciation enjoyed by the national courts, Germany had not failed to comply with Article 8 ECHR.[94] The ECtHR came to the same conclusion in *Von Hannover (No.3)*.[95]

The *Von Hannover (No.2)* balancing criteria continue to apply today, albeit that one further criterion applies where the applicant alleges that Article 10 ECHR has been violated. This stems from the Grand Chamber's judgment in *Axel Springer* v. *Germany*, which was handed down on the same day as *Von Hannover (No.2)*.[96] The facts in *Axel Springer* were that the applicant company had published a newspaper article revealing that an actor in a popular television series had been arrested at the Munich beer festival for possession of cocaine, following which the actor obtained an injunction restraining further publication and the applicant was ordered to pay a penalty. In the interim, the newspaper had published a second article reporting that the actor had been convicted of unlawful possession of drugs, and once more, the actor obtained an injunction and the newspaper was ordered to pay two further penalties. The applicant then applied to the ECtHR arguing that Germany had failed to give sufficient protection to freedom of expression.

Before the Grand Chamber in *Axel Springer* it was common ground that the injunctions and penalties interfered with Article 10 ECHR.[97] It was also common ground that the measures were prescribed by law and that they pursued the legitimate aim of protecting the reputation or rights of others.[98] The question for the Grand Chamber was thus whether the injunctions and penalties were necessary in a democratic society.[99] In making that assessment, the Grand Chamber applied the five *Von Hannover (No.2)* criteria and stated that it must also consider the severity of the sanction imposed.[100] This was not a substantive change from *Von Hannover (No.2)*; it simply reflected the fact that as no sanction had been applied in *Von Hannover (No.2)* the issue had not arisen in that case.[101]

Applying the criteria in *Axel Springer*, the Grand Chamber observed, first, that as the story concerned the arrest and conviction of an actor there was a degree of general interest.[102] Second, the actor was sufficiently well known to qualify as a public figure, he had been arrested in public, and he had previously sought the limelight by revealing details about his private life in interviews, which reduced any legitimate expectation that his private life would be protected.[103] Third, the information had been appropriately obtained and was reliable.[104] Fourth, the articles had not revealed details of his private life but had concerned the

[94] Ibid at [125]–[126]. [95] *Von Hannover* v. *Germany (No.3)*, App. No. 8772/10, 19/09/2013.
[96] *Axel Springer* v. *Germany* [GC] (2012) 55 EHRR 6 at [89]–[95]. [97] Ibid at [75].
[98] Ibid at [77]. [99] Ibid at [77]. [100] Ibid at [89]–[109].
[101] See, for example, *Hachette Filipacchi Associés* v. *France*, App. No. 7111/01, 14/06/2007.
[102] *Axel Springer* (n 96) at [96]. [103] Ibid at [97]–[99]. [104] Ibid at [102]–[107].

circumstances of his arrest and the outcome of the criminal proceedings.[105] Finally, in considering the severity of the sanction, the ECtHR observed that while the sanctions imposed were lenient, they could have a chilling effect and were not justified in the light of the other issues identified above.[106] Accordingly, the Grand Chamber held that the measures were not proportionate and there had been a violation of Article 10 ECHR.[107]

Before considering the role of the ECtHR in respect of the balancing criteria it should be noted that the Court has adopted a different approach for cases involving archives and the right to be forgotten. This was addressed in *Hurbain* (discussed above) where the Grand Chamber articulated the following bespoke set of balancing criteria:

(i) the nature of the archived information;
(ii) the time that has elapsed since the events and since the initial and online publication;
(iii) the contemporary interest of the information;
(iv) whether the person claiming entitlement to be forgotten is well known and his or her conduct since the events;
(v) the negative repercussions of the continued availability of the information online;
(vi) the degree of accessibility of the information in the digital archives; and
(vii) the impact of the measure on freedom of expression and more specifically on freedom of the press.[108]

In reflecting on those balancing criteria, the Grand Chamber observed that while in general Articles 8 and 10 ECHR 'are to be regarded as being of equal value, it does not follow that the criteria to be applied in conducting that exercise all carry the same weight'.[109] It went on to state that in this context:

> the principle of preservation of the integrity of press archives must be upheld, which implies ensuring that the alteration and, a fortiori, the removal of archived content is *limited to what is strictly necessary*, so as to prevent any chilling effect such measures may have on the performance by the press of its task of imparting information and maintaining archives.[110]

Consequently, in applying the relevant balancing criteria:

> particular attention should be paid to properly balancing, on the one hand, the interests of the individuals requesting the alteration or removal of an article concerning them in the press archives and, on the other hand, the impact of such

[105] Ibid at [108]. [106] Ibid at [109]. [107] Ibid at [110]–[111].

[108] *Hurbain* (n 72) at [205]. See also, *Biancardi* v. *Italy*, App. No. 77419/16, 25/11/2021 at [57]–[71].

[109] *Hurbain* (n 72) at [211]. [110] Ibid at [211].

requests on the news publishers concerned and also, as the case may be, on the functioning of the press.[111]

Provided, however, that the domestic authorities carry out the balancing exercise in accordance with those criteria, then the ECtHR will offer a margin of appreciation to the State and will only intervene if there are strong reasons to substitute its view.[112] This was the position adopted in *Hurbain* where the Grand Chamber found no strong reasons to intervene.[113] This was criticised by Judge Ranzoni who in a dissenting opinion joined by Judges Kūris, Grozev, Eicke and Schembri Orland argued that the Grand Chamber had viewed the 'case through the wrong prism and deal[t] with it using a set of instruments devised in different circumstances and ill-suited to the requirements of the modern communications era and the challenges posed by digital press archives and their accessibility'.[114] Judge Ranzoni proposed an alternative approach which would have emphasised press freedom and focused on proportionality and, under that approach, the anonymisation order did not satisfy the proportionality requirement of Article 10 ECHR.[115]

10.2.3 Margin of Appreciation

We have seen that the ECtHR's case law establishes the framework that domestic courts should follow in evaluating the weight to be accorded to the two competing Convention rights. Consequently, provided that the domestic authorities carry out that balancing exercise, the ECtHR regards its role as one of determining whether the domestic courts have struck a 'fair balance between the rights at stake and rules in accordance with the criteria established by it for that purpose'.[116] In such cases it will require 'strong reasons to substitute its views for that of the domestic courts'.[117] This margin of appreciation is evident in cases such as *Ruusunen* v. *Finland* where the ECtHR held that there was no violation of Article 10 ECHR where the former girlfriend of the Prime Minister of Finland was convicted for writing and publishing an autobiographical work which contained details of their relationship,[118] and in *Lillo-Stenberg* v. *Norway* where the ECtHR found no violation of Article 8 ECHR in respect of the publication of photographs of a well-known musician

[111] Ibid at [211]. [112] Ibid at [213]. [113] Ibid at [256].

[114] Ibid, dissenting opinion of Judge Ranzoni, joined by Judges Kūris, Grozev, Eicke and Schembri Orland at [3].

[115] Ibid, dissenting opinion of Judge Ranzoni, joined by Judges Kūris, Grozev, Eicke and Schembri Orland at [29].

[116] *Mediengruppe Österreich GmbH* v. *Austria*, App. No. 37713/18, 26/04/2022 at [54].

[117] *Von Hannover (No.2)* (n 49) at [107], *Axel Springer* (n 96) at [88], *Mediengruppe Österreich GmbH* v. *Austria* (n 116) at [52].

[118] *Ruusunen* v. *Finland*, App. No. 73579/10, 14/01/2014.

and actress in Norway,[119] as well as other cases in which the ECtHR has found no violation on the basis that the domestic courts have struck a balance between the competing rights.[120]

Yet, while the ECtHR affords a wide margin of appreciation, this does not mean that it has absolved itself of any supervisory role. On the contrary, the ECtHR clearly scrutinised whether a fair balance had been struck in *Couderc and Hachette* v. *France* and concluded that it had not.[121] The facts in *Couderc* were that a French court had awarded Prince Albert of Monaco 50,000 euros in respect of a publication that revealed that the Prince had secretly fathered a son, a measure which the publisher argued violated Article 10. In considering the balance struck between Articles 8 and 10 ECHR, the Grand Chamber found that while some aspects of the publication contributed to a debate of general interest, others did not, in particular, it held that the French courts should have distinguished between 'the core message of the article and the details of the article'. In this regard, while it was legitimate to publish the fact that the Prince had fathered a son, there were other details that fell outside the scope of what could be published, including 'elements which related solely to the private, or even intimate, life of the Prince and the boy's mother'.[122] As the French courts had prohibited the publication of even the core message and imposed a fine, this violated Article 10 ECHR.[123]

Equally, there are cases in which the ECtHR has found a violation of Article 8 ECHR. For example, in *Dupate* v. *Latvia*, a violation was found in respect of the publication of surreptitiously taken photographs of the applicant (the partner of a political figure) leaving a maternity ward with her newborn baby.[124] The ECtHR has also found violations of Article 8 ECHR in cases where, although there was a public interest in the story, the domestic authorities had not assessed whether there was a public interest in publishing or broadcasting the applicant's image without blurring or pixelating that image.[125]

[119] *Lillo-Stenberg* v. *Norway*, App. No. 13258/09, 16/01/2014.

[120] *Sihler-Jauch and Jauch* v. *Germany* (dec.), App. No. 68273/10, 24/05/2016; *Karl-Theodor zu Guttenberg* v. *Germany* (dec.), App. No. 14047/16, 25/06/2019; *Mediengruppe Österreich GmbH* v. *Austria* (n 116); *Küchl* v. *Austria*, App. No. 51151/06, 04/12/2012; *Rothe* v. *Austria*, App. No. 6490/07, 04/12/2012; *Axel Springer SE and RTL Television GmbH* v. *Germany*, App. No. 51405/12, 21/09/2017; *Bild GmbH & CO. Kg and Axel Springer AG* v. *Germany*, App. Nos. 62721/13 and 62741/13, 10/01/2019.

[121] *Couderc and Hachette Fillipachi Associés* v. *France* (n 65).

[122] Ibid at [59]–[60].

[123] Ibid at [74].

[124] *Dupate* v. *Latvia* (n 63).

[125] *Bremner* v. *Turkey*, App. No. 37428/06, 13/10/2015 at [83]–[85]; *Hájovsky* v. *Slovakia*, App. No. 7796/16, 01/07/2021. The ECtHR has also found violations of Article 8 ECHR in a number of cases concerning children. For example, in *Bogomolova* v. *Russia* (n 62), a violation was found when a photograph of the applicant's son was included on an adoption booklet. A violation was also found in *IVT* v. *Romania*, App. No. 35582/15, 01/03/2022, a case in which a minor had been included in a television interview following the death of a

10.2.4 Relevance of the Applicants' Characteristics

In considering the balance struck between the two competing rights, it is worth pausing to consider the way in which the ECtHR deals with different types of applicants. There is some evidence that the ECtHR is more willing to uphold the right to privacy of those that it regards as being in a state of vulnerability[126] and minors,[127] while at the same time there is some uncertainty as to whether public figures receive less protection. The case law is clear that public figure status is relevant as the ECtHR frequently states that a distinction has to be made between private individuals and persons acting in a public context. Yet, whilst the ECtHR has made it clear that public figure status is relevant, uncertainty surrounds both (i) who is affected and (ii) how this affects rights.

10.2.4.1 Who Is a Public Figure?

The ECtHR's position as to who is a public figure has evolved over time.[128] This is evident in the difference between *Von Hannover (No.1)*, where the ECtHR held that Princess Caroline was not a public figure as she did not exercise 'official functions',[129] and *Von Hannover* v. *Germany (No.2)*, where the Grand Chamber stated that 'it could not be claimed that the applicants [the Princess and her husband] who were undeniably very well known, were ordinary private individuals. They had to be regarded as public figures.'[130] Indeed, although the ECtHR initially limited the public figure concept to those exercising official functions, the doctrine now extends far beyond elected officials and even celebrities to include businessmen, journalists and lawyers, well-known academics, as well as other persons who have a 'position in society'.[131] The ECtHR has reasoned that while it 'vigorously defend[s] the privacy rights of individuals who have not consciously and intentionally submitted themselves to public scrutiny ... [t]he same degree of protection is not afforded to public figures'.[132] The doctrine has thus been extended to persons who, although not public figures, have 'consciously and intentionally submitted to

schoolmate, no parental consent had been sought and her identity had not been adequately protected.

126 *Egeland and Hanseid* v. *Norway*, App. No. 34438/04, 16/04/2009, concerned the publication of images of a woman leaving court after she had been convicted of murder. The ECtHR emphasised in particular the vulnerability of the convicted woman.

127 *Bogomolova* v. *Russia* (n 62) and *IVT* v. *Romania* (n 125).

128 For analysis, see Kirsty Hughes, 'The Public Figure Doctrine and the Right to Privacy' (2019) **78**(1) CLJ 70–99.

129 *Von Hannover (No.1)* (n 21) at [63].

130 *Von Hannover* v. *Germany (No.2)* (n 49) at [120].

131 *Verlagsgruppe (No. 2)* [2007] EMLR 13.

132 *Mitkus* v. *Latvia*, App. No. 7259/03, 02/10/2012 at [132].

the public scene'.[133] Consequently, although the ECtHR has held that children involved in high profile custody battles have not chosen to step into the public sphere,[134] it has held that applicants who have affairs with married politicians or engage in public disturbances *have* chosen to enter the public scene.[135] This seems to distinguish a category of rights-holders based upon assumptions about conduct and the relevance of such conduct to public life.

In many ways this broad, malleable approach is not surprising, as the societal concept of a public figure has evolved such that it is extremely difficult to pin down. Although in the past one's office or profession may have borne some correlation to the extent to which one was known to the public, these features have diverged radically such that those who are famous include some who hold public office, but many more who do not; the extent to which fame is transitory also raises further difficulties for identifying who is and who is not a public figure, yet whilst this may reflect the social reality, this is problematic if the concept is to be used as means of calibrating rights protection. Moreover, the role of public figure status as a tool of calibration raises questions about the universality of rights.[136]

10.2.4.2 Relevance of Public Figure Status

It is evident that public figure status does not automatically deprive public figures of all privacy rights as the ECtHR has upheld the rights of members of royal families, heads of state and celebrities.[137] The case law instead suggests a sliding scale in which those that exercise official functions receive the lowest level of protection; other public figures receive less protection than private individuals, but more than those with official functions; and private figures receive the highest level of protection. This is suggested by the ECtHR's determination that 'the right of public figures to keep their private life secret is, in principle, wider where they do not hold any official functions (even if, as members of a ruling family, they represent that family at certain events) and is more restricted where they do hold such a function'.[138]

These nuances are, however, somewhat lost in the broader uncertainty as to how public figure status affects rights. This partly arises from the fact that the

[133] *Standard Verlags GmbH* v. *Austria (No.3)*, App. No. 34702/07, 10/01/2012 at [37]; *News Verlags GmbH & Co.KG* v. *Austria* (2001) 31 EHRR 8 at [54]; *Verlagsgruppe (No. 2)* (n 131) at [36]; *Egeland and Hanseid* v. *Norway* (n 126) at [60]; *Flinkkilä* v. *Finland*, App. No. 25576/04, 06/04/2010 at [83]; *Eerikäinen and Others* v. *Finland*, App. No. 3514/02, 10/02/2009 at [66]; *Krone Verlag GmbH* v. *Austria*, App. No. 27306/07, 19/06/2012; and *Kurier Zeitungsverlagd und Druckerei GmbH* v. *Austria (No.2)*, App. No. 1593/06, 19/06/2012.

[134] *Krone Verlag GmbH* v. *Austria* (n 133) at [57]; and *Kurier Zeitungsverlagd und Druckerei GmbH* v. *Austria (No.2)* (n 133) at [59].

[135] *Flinkkilä* v. *Finland* (n 133) at [83]. [136] See Hughes (n 128). [137] Ibid.

[138] *Couderc and Hachette Fillipachi Associés* v. *France* (n 65) at [119].

case law suggests that public figure status is relevant to various aspects of the balancing criteria. As discussed earlier, Articles 8 and 10 should be balanced using the *Von Hannover (No.2)* criteria. Yet, if we examine those criteria, it appears that public figure status can come into play not only in criterion number (2) which examines 'how well known ... the person concerned [is]', but also when determining criterion (1) which asks whether the publication constitutes a contribution to a debate of general interest, and criterion (3) which examines the prior conduct of the person concerned. Depending upon the facts, it could also shape the ECtHR's analysis under (4) which concerns the content, form and consequences of the publication and (5) which considers the circumstances in which the photographs were taken. The balancing criteria thus allows public figure status to curtail and/or weaken the weight accorded to Article 8 ECHR, whilst simultaneously enhancing the weight accorded to Article 10 ECHR via multiple criteria. *Couderc and Hachette Filipacchi Associés* v. *France* is an example of this.[139] This can render it difficult to establish how the rights will be balanced which, when coupled with the margin of appreciation accorded to States, creates uncertainty for the various parties involved.

10.2.5 Remedies

We have already seen that in *Axel Springer* the Grand Chamber held that the severity of the sanction is relevant in determining whether an appropriate balance has been struck between the competing Convention rights; consequently there are cases in which the ECtHR has held that a domestic remedy for invasion of privacy violated Article 10 ECHR.[140] Equally, however, there are cases in which the ECtHR has held that a domestic remedy for invasion of privacy failed to adequately protect Article 8 ECHR.[141] This underscores the idea that the remedies awarded affect the substantive balance struck between privacy and freedom of expression. In this regard it is important to observe that it is often said that privacy cases are different from defamation cases, because in defamation cases reputation can be restored following a judgment in favour of the claimant, whereas privacy is 'inherently perishable and cannot be restored to the victim of the interference'.[142] The rationale here is that privacy (unlike reputation) is not well served by damages as privacy can only be preserved by an injunction.[143] In fact, not all claimants will

[139] Ibid.

[140] *Eerikäinen* v. *Finland* (n 133); *Krone Verlag GmbH & and Co KG* v. *Austria* (2003) 36 EHRR 57; *Verlagsgruppe News GmbH* v. *Austria* (No.2) (n 131); *Cumpana and Mazare* v. *Romania* (2005) 41 EHRR 14; *Karhuvaara and Iltalehti* v. *Finland* (2005) 41 EHRR 51; *Saaristo and others* v. *Finland*, App. No. 184/06, 12/10/2010.

[141] *Armoniene* v. *Lithuania* (n 47); *Khan* v. *Germany*, App. No. 16313/10, 17/03/2016.

[142] *Mosley* v. *the United Kingdom* (n 45) at [80].

[143] Mark Warby QC, Dr Nicole Moreham and Iain Christie (eds), *Tugendhat and Christie: The Law of Privacy and the Media* (Oxford University Press, 2016), 12.15 and 12.60-7.

pursue claims for damages in privacy cases because litigation tends to involve further publicity. Yet, whilst it is generally accepted that damages cannot 'restore' privacy, and that there are difficulties with a damages-based model, scholars differ as to whether we should accept that damages are a *satisfactory* remedy.[144]

It was the perceived inadequacy of damages, that was at the heart of *Mosley* v. *the United Kingdom,*[145] the background to which was the publication of photographs in a tabloid newspaper, the *News of the World,* of Max Mosley (a well-known British businessman, former racing driver and son of Oswald Mosley) engaging in secret sado-masochistic sex parties with professional dominatrices;[146] the images had been surreptitiously obtained and the newspaper initially alleged that there was a Nazi element to the activities. In *Mosley* v. *News Group Newspapers*, Eady J held that the details and images were private and that there was no proof of Nazi connotations and he awarded Mosley £60,000 damages for breach of confidence and/or the unauthorised disclosure of personal information.[147] Yet, whilst Mosley succeeded in having his Article 8 ECHR right upheld, he argued that this did not resolve matters. He applied to the ECtHR on the basis that Article 8 ECHR required the UK to oblige newspapers to inform the subject of a story before exposing details of their private life so that the person concerned had an opportunity to seek an injunction, arguing that the current system offers too little protection to the right to privacy. The UK opposed this arguing that States have a wide margin of appreciation and that this would be undermined if States were obliged to provide a pre-notification scheme.[148] They argued that there was no consensus across Europe that such a scheme is required, on the contrary, the consensus was against such a scheme.[149] They also emphasised the fact that a House of Commons Select Committee had recently considered and rejected the proposal,[150] and that it would be very difficult to put in place such a scheme.[151] The ECtHR agreed with

[144] Gavin Phillipson, 'Max Mosley Goes to Strasbourg: Article 8, Claimant Notification and Interim Injunctions' (2009) 1(1) Journal of Media Law 73; Andrew Scott, 'Prior Notification in Privacy Cases: A Reply to Professor Phillipson' (2010) 2(1) Journal of Media Law 49; Kirsty Hughes, 'Privacy Injunctions: No Obligation to Notify Pre-publication' (2011) 3(2) Journal of Media Law 179.

[145] *Mosley* v. *the United Kingdom* (n 45); for analysis see Hughes (n 144).

[146] In *Mosley* v. *News Group Newspapers* [2008] EWHC 1777, [2008] EMLR 20 Eady J observed at [121] that: 'some of the women were rather reluctant to accept the description "prostitute"'. (For the purposes of the Sexual Offences Act 2003, the term is defined by reference to providing "sexual services" in return for payment: s.51(2) of the Act.) Several of them offer a variety of services on their website (usually spanking or being spanked in various guises) but expressly warn that they do not offer specifically sexual services. They apparently made an exception in "Mike's" case and threw in a bit of sex, as it were, as an "extra" between friends. Indeed, sometimes they were not paid at all. As they liked the premises and found the atmosphere relaxing and congenial, things developed from there.'

[147] Ibid. [148] *Mosley* v. *the United Kingdom* (n 45) at [85]–[90]. [149] Ibid at [87].

[150] Ibid at [88]. [151] Ibid at [89].

the UK; it held that whilst the publication constituted a 'flagrant and unjustified invasion of the applicant's private life' this had been adequately remedied.[152] Beyond this it emphasised 'the importance of a prudent approach to the State's positive obligations' and the role of the margin of appreciation[153] and thus held that whilst Article 8 ECHR imposes a positive obligation on States to ensure effective protection, this does not mandate a pre-notification requirement.[154]

Another case in which the ECtHR has had to consider the scope of the State's margin of appreciation is *Green* v. *the United Kingdom*.[155] Green concerned the use of parliamentary privilege to disclose information that was the subject of a court order, the background to which was that a number of serious allegations of sexual harassment and bullying had been made against Green (a well-known businessman) which had been the subject of settlement agreements (non-disclosure agreements). As a journalist was intending to report the allegations, an injunction was sought by Green and others. In September 2018, the Court of Appeal granted an interim injunction and an anonymity order, following which the newspaper (*The Telegraph*) published a story detailing the nature of the information subject to the injunction but respecting the limits imposed by the court order. The following day, however, Lord Hain, a life peer in the House of Lords made a statement in Parliament naming Green as the individual in question. This rendered the court order redundant and Lord Hain's disclosure was protected by parliamentary privilege. Consequently, Green lodged an application with the ECtHR in which he argued amongst other things that the State has a positive obligation to ensure that parliamentary privilege cannot be used to circumvent a court injunction.[156] In particular, he argued that the absence of *ex ante* and *ex post* controls on the power to use parliamentary privilege to reveal confidential information subject to an injunction violates Article 8 ECHR.[157] In this regard he stated that he was not asking the ECtHR to impose an obligation on Parliament to implement controls, but instead wished for the Court to issue a declaration that the absence of such controls gives rise to a situation such as that in which Green's rights had been violated.[158] He accepted that the nature, design and implementation of those controls would then be a matter for Parliament.[159] The ECtHR recognised that there is a need for appropriate controls to be kept under regular review at the domestic level 'given the serious impact that the disclosure of such information may have on the privacy of the individual concerned, not to mention the implications for the rule of law and the separation of powers'.[160] However, it was reluctant to bring this under the supervision of the ECtHR observing that:

> in keeping with the well-established constitutional principle of the autonomy of Parliament … it is in the first instance for national parliaments to assess the need to

[152] Ibid at [104]. [153] Ibid at [107]. [154] Ibid at [118]–[132].

[155] *Green* v. *the United Kingdom*, App. No. 22077/19, 08/04/2025. [156] Ibid at [62].

[157] Ibid. [158] Ibid. [159] Ibid. [160] Ibid at [93].

> restrict conduct by their Members ... As the United Kingdom Parliament is aware of the problem of parliamentary privilege being used to frustrate injunctions and has addressed the need for further controls . . . the Court considers that for the time being it may be left to the respondent State, and Parliament in particular, to determine whether and to what extent *ex ante* and *ex post* controls might be necessary to prevent its Members from revealing information subject to privacy injunctions.[161]

It thus concluded that 'the rule on parliamentary privilege did not exceed the margin of appreciation afforded to the respondent State and there exist no sufficiently strong reasons to justify the Court substituting its view for that of Parliament and requiring it or the respondent State to introduce further *ex ante* and *ex post* controls on freedom of speech in Parliament'.[162]

10.2.6 Conclusion on Article 8 ECHR

The ECtHR has adopted a broad approach to Article 8 ECHR such that the right to private life is widely applicable. There is no sharp demarcation of public and private places, nor must an applicant demonstrate that they have been harassed by the press in order to engage the Convention right. Consequently, the focus of the ECtHR's analysis has been at the second stage at which it considers whether a fair balance has been struck between Articles 8 and 10 ECHR. Although there was some uncertainty in the early case law as to how to strike that balance, the applicable criteria have now been established for over a decade and provided the domestic courts apply those criteria, the ECtHR is likely to be deferential to the decision of domestic courts. Thus, while States have positive obligations to ensure that an appropriate balance is struck between privacy and freedom of expression, they have considerable latitude in implementing those obligations. With this in mind, we now turn to consider how the rights have shaped domestic law, via the law of misuse of private information and why this has been contentious.

10.3 DOMESTIC PRIVACY LAW

10.3.1 Privacy and the Common Law Prior to the HRA 1998

Prior to the HRA 1998, while the common law recognised some rights, such as the right to freedom of expression, there was no common law right to privacy in English law. Consequently, Article 8 ECHR and the HRA 1998 have played an important role as they formed the bedrock for the development of a common law tort of misuse of private information. The lack of a common law right to privacy was (as we will see below) significant, but it is also important to observe that its absence did not mean that there was no protection for privacy in English law prior to the HRA 1998. As Lord Neuberger explains

[161] Ibid. [162] Ibid.

We are sometimes led to believe that privacy has not in any way been protected in English law: that 1998 was for privacy, to use Larkin's famous words, what 1963 . . . was for sexual intercourse, "*the time when it all began*". Well, 1998 was no more when privacy began in English law than 1963 was when sexual intercourse began.[163]

In this respect it is important to acknowledge that English law has long protected some privacy-related interests; these include amongst other things trespass to the home, privilege and the equitable doctrine of confidentiality.[164] An important example of this is the famous case, *Entick* v. *Carrington*, in which the court found that there was no legal basis when the King's messengers broke into John Entick's home to search for seditious writings. Entick successfully sued for trespass as the court held that lawful executive power ended at Entick's door.[165] The common law has also long proffered other essential privacy-related rights such as the right to privilege.[166] The significance of which was evident in *SSHD, ex parte Daly*, when Daly successfully argued that a blanket policy, which precluded a prisoner from being present when their legally privileged correspondence was examined, infringed to an impermissible extent upon the common law right to legal professional privilege.[167] On that occasion Lord Cooke emphasised that it was of 'great importance that the common law by itself is being recognised as a sufficient source of the fundamental right', as 'the decision may prove to be in point in common law jurisdictions not affected by the [ECHR]'.[168] He went on to observe that in his opinion 'some rights are inherent and fundamental to democratic civilised society. [Thus] Conventions, constitutions, bills of rights and the like respond by recognising rather than creating them.'[169] Yet whilst the common law offered some significant fundamental rights, the courts repeatedly declined to recognise a general common law right to privacy in English law.[170] This refusal was said to be due to difficulties that judges would encounter in defining privacy and establishing necessary limits; a right to privacy was therefore deemed to be beyond the reach of the common law.[171] This was in stark contrast to freedom of expression, where there was a well-recognised common law right, albeit that as

[163] Lord Neuberger, *Privacy in the Twenty-first Century* (28 November 2012) speech at the UK Association of Jewish Lawyers and Jurists' Lecture.

[164] Ibid. [165] *Entick* v. *Carrington* (1765) 19 St Tr 1030.

[166] For discussion of the protection that the common law offered to privacy, see Feldman (n 16), Pt III and Hughes (n 15).

[167] *SSHD, ex parte Daly* [2001] UKHL 26, [2001] 2 AC 532, see Lord Bingham at [16]–[22].

[168] Ibid at [30] . [169] Ibid.

[170] For discussion of the absence of a right to privacy in domestic law and the piecemeal development of privacy laws, see D. Seipp, 'English Judicial Recognition of the Right to Privacy' (1983) 3 OJLS 325; Lord Neuberger (n 163) and Helen Fenwick, *Fenwick on Civil Liberties and Human Rights* (Routledge, 2017), pp. 689–690.

[171] The lack of protection for privacy and the difficulties of legislating were considered by *Committee on Privacy (Younger Committee), Report of the Committee on Privacy* (Cm 5012, 1972), *Committee on Privacy and Related Matters (Calcutt Committee), Report of the Committee on Privacy and Related Matters* (Cm 1102, 1990).

Rowbottom has suggested the significance of the common law right to freedom of expression has perhaps been overstated.[172]

The absence of a common law right to privacy was no mere oversight as prior to the HRA the courts had faced calls to recognise a right to privacy and consistently declined do so. For example, Sir Robert Megarry V-C, in the context of telephone tapping in *Malone* v. *Metropolitan Police Commissioner (No.2)*, famously refused to find a right on the basis that it would raise numerous definitional problems, and ultimately 'no new right in the law, fully-fledged with all the appropriate safeguards, can spring from the head of a judge deciding a particular case'.[173] The ECtHR subsequently found that the regime of telephone tapping breached Article 8 ECHR as it was not in accordance with law.[174]

In the context of press intrusion into privacy the shortcomings of the common law were also readily apparent with scholars such as Fenwick and Phillipson observing prior to the HRA that 'the lack of a clear legal remedy in respect of the non-consensual disclosure of personal information [wa]s one of the most serious lacunae in English law'.[175] This absence was most famously evident in *Kaye* v. *Robertson,* a case that arose prior to the HRA.[176] Gordon Kaye (an actor) had suffered a serious head injury after a piece of wood fell through his car windscreen during a storm and was in hospital following extensive surgery. Journalists gained access to his hospital room, 'interviewed' Kaye and took photographs of him. (Kaye's state of health during these events was such that shortly afterwards he had no recollection of the journalists' visit.) Following this intrusion a tabloid newspaper, *The Sunday Sport,* was intent on publishing the 'interview' and photographs, thus an injunction was sought on Kaye's behalf by his friend. Unfortunately for Kaye, the application was unsuccessful as there was no law that could prohibit the publication. Bingham LJ (as he then was) observed that the 'monstrous invasion' of privacy Kaye was forced to endure highlighted 'the failure of both the common law of England and statute to protect in an effective way the personal privacy of individual citizens'.[177]

> If ever a person has a right to be let alone by strangers with no public interest to pursue, it must surely be when he lies in hospital recovering from brain surgery and in no more than partial command of his faculties. It is this invasion of his privacy which underlies the plaintiff's complaint. Yet it alone, however gross, does not entitle him to relief in English law.[178]

Indeed in *Kaye* all three Court of Appeal judges deeply regretted the failure of the common law to deal with these 'monstrous violations'. Leggatt LJ noted

[172] Jacob Rowbottom, 'Freedom of Expression and the Right to Vote: Political Rights and the Common Law Constitution' in Mark Elliott and Kirsty Hughes, *Common Law Constitutional Rights* (Hart, 2020).

[173] *Malone* v. *Metropolitan Police Commissioner (No.2)* [1979] Ch 344.

[174] *Malone* v. *the United Kingdom* (1985) 7 EHRR 14.

[175] Phillipson and Fenwick (n 1), p.660.

[176] *Kaye* v. *Robertson* [1991] 18 FSR 62.

[177] Ibid, Bingham LJ at p.70.

[178] Ibid at p.70.

that the 'right has so long been disregarded here that it can be recognised now only by the legislature',[179] while Glidewell LJ declared that '[t]he facts of the present case are a graphic illustration of the desirability of Parliament considering whether and in what circumstances statutory provision can be made to protect the privacy of individuals'.[180]

Following *Kaye*, there were two further cases in which the House of Lords was asked to recognise a common law right to privacy and on both occasions it declined to do so. In 1997, the House of Lords in *R* v. *Khan (Sultan)* considered whether the law should recognise a right to privacy when the police fixed a listening device to the outside of the defendant's house;[181] on that occasion the Lords declined to determine the matter, concluding that even if such a right existed, the evidence obtained by the device would remain admissible. The fact that they did not outright reject a right to privacy perhaps suggests that they were more open to the prospect than Sir Robert Megarry V-C had been in *Malone.*[182] Certainly, Lord Nicholls expressed the view that he preferred to 'leave open for another occasion the important question whether the present, piecemeal protection of privacy has now developed to the extent that a more comprehensive principle can be seen to exist'.[183] A different note was, however, struck by Lord Nolan who noted that 'under English law, there is in general nothing unlawful about a breach of privacy'.[184] The case subsequently went to the ECtHR where the Strasbourg Court held that as there was no domestic law regulating the use of covert listening devices at the relevant time the interference was not in accordance with law and thus violated Article 8 ECHR.[185]

In *Wainwright* v. *Home Office* the Lords considered once more whether a potential invasion of privacy could be remedied under English law.[186] Although the proceedings took place in 2003, the incident had taken place prior to the HRA coming into force and thus the matter did not fall within the scope of the HRA. The case related to an incident in a prison during which Mrs Wainwright and her son Alan (who had physical and learning disabilities) were required to undergo a strip search in order to visit a prisoner (Patrick O'Neill, who was Mrs Wainwright's son and Alan's half-brother). It was determined by both the judge who heard the case in the County Court and by the Court of Appeal that there was no statutory authority for the strip search.[187] However, as Lord Hoffmann explained when the case went to the House of Lords, this was

[179] Ibid at p.71. [180] Ibid at p.66. [181] *R* v. *Khan (Sultan)* [1996] UKHL 14, [1997] AC 558.
[182] *Malone* (n 173). [183] *Khan* (n 181) at [582]. [184] Ibid at [581].
[185] *Khan* v. *the United Kingdom* (2000) 31 EHRR 45 at [26]–[28].
[186] *Wainwright* v. *Home Office* [2003] UKHL 53, [2004] 2 AC 406. [187] Ibid at [7].

> not enough to give the Wainwrights a claim to compensation. The acts of the prison officers needed statutory authority only if they would otherwise have been wrongful, that is to say, tortious or in breach of a statutory duty. People do all kinds of things without statutory authority. So the question is whether the searches themselves or the manner in which they were conducted gave the Wainwrights a cause of action.[188]

Consequently, the Wainwrights argued before the House of Lords that 'in order to enable the United Kingdom to conform to its international obligations under the Convention, the House should declare that there is (and in theory always has been) a tort of invasion of privacy under which the searches of both Wainwrights were actionable and damages for emotional distress recoverable'.[189] Lord Hoffmann reviewed the prior case law and concluded that he must 'reject the invitation to declare that since at the latest 1950 there has been a previously unknown tort of invasion of privacy'.[190] The other four Lords agreed and the appeal was unanimously dismissed. Lord Scott of Foscote added that

> whatever remedies may have been developed for misuse of confidential information, for certain types of trespass, for certain types of nuisance and for various other situations in which claimants may find themselves aggrieved by an invasion of what they conceive to be their privacy, the common law has not developed an overall remedy for the invasion of privacy.[191]

It is also worth observing that in *Wainwright*, the Lords expressed caution about pre-empting issues that would arise under the HRA:

> Furthermore, the coming into force of the Human Rights Act 1998 weakens the argument for saying that a general tort of invasion of privacy is needed to fill gaps in the existing remedies. Sections 6 and 7 of the Act are in themselves substantial gap fillers; if it is indeed the case that a person's rights under article 8 have been infringed by a public authority, he will have a statutory remedy. The creation of a general tort will, as Buxton LJ pointed out in the Court of Appeal, at [2002] QB 1334, 1360, para 92, pre-empt the controversial question of the extent, if any, to which the Convention requires the state to provide remedies for invasions of privacy by persons who are not public authorities.[192]

Wainwright subsequently ended up before the ECtHR and once more the Strasbourg Court held that the UK had violated Article 8 ECHR.[193] On this occasion, the ECtHR stated that while there was a legitimate aim behind the measure, namely the prevention of disorder or crime, it was

> not satisfied that the searches were proportionate to that legitimate aim in the manner in which they were carried out. Where procedures are laid down for the proper conduct

[188] Ibid at [7]. [189] Ibid at [14]. [190] Ibid at [35].

[191] Ibid at [62]. See also, Lord Hoffmann's analysis at [15]–[35]. [192] Ibid at [34]–[35].

[193] *Wainwright* v. *the United Kingdom* (2007) 44 EHRR 40.

of searches on outsiders to the prison who may very well be innocent of any wrong-doing, it behoves the prison authorities to comply strictly with those safeguards and by rigorous precautions protect the dignity of those being searched from being assailed any further than is necessary. They did not do so in this case.

Consequently, the Court finds that the searches carried out on the applicants cannot be regarded as 'necessary in a democratic society' within the meaning of Article 8 § 2 of the Convention. There has been, accordingly, a breach of Article 8 of the Convention in that regard.[194]

This brief look at privacy prior to the HRA reveals that the common law routinely failed to protect privacy as evidenced by the experiences of those who found themselves with no means of redress. Thus when the HRA was enacted, there was considerable interest amongst scholars and practitioners as to whether the HRA would lead to the development of a right to privacy in English law.

10.3.2 Privacy, the HRA 1998 and Horizontal Effect

It was observed in Chapter 2 that when the HRA was enacted there was uncertainty as to whether the legislation would apply to intrusions by private actors. This ambiguity arose from s.6 HRA as whilst private individuals and private organisations (such as newspapers) are not obliged to act compatibly with the Convention rights under s.6(1) HRA, the courts are bound by s.6(1) and s.6(3) HRA to act compatibly with Convention rights when applying the common law. Consequently, when the HRA was enacted, there was extensive debate as to whether s.6 HRA would lead to indirect horizontal application of the Convention rights in common law litigation. Some scholars argued that the HRA would only impose obligations on public authorities (vertical effect), others argued that the obligations created by the rights would apply horizontally to private actors (direct horizontal effect), and others argued that although the obligations would not apply directly to private actors that they would have some application (indirect horizontal effect).[195] It was the

[194] Ibid at [48]–[49].

[195] Murray Hunt, 'The Horizontal Effect of the Human Rights Act' (1998) PL 423; Basil Markesinis, 'Privacy, Freedom of Expression and the Horizontal Effect of the Human Rights Bill: Lessons from Germany' (1999) 115 LQR 47; Ian Leigh, 'Horizontal Rights, the Human Rights Acts and Privacy: Lessons from the Commonwealth?' (1999) 48 ICLQ 57; Gavin Phillipson, 'The Human Rights Act, "Horizontal Effect" and the Common Law: a Bang or a Whimper?' (1999) 62 MLR 824; Rabinder Singh, 'Privacy and the Media after the Human Rights Act' (1998) EHRLR 712. See also, Sir William Wade, 'The United Kingdom's Bill of Rights' in Ivan Hare and Christopher Forsyth (eds), *Constitutional Reforms in the United Kingdom: Practice and Principles* (Hart, 1998) who argued that there would be full horizontal effect, and Buxton LJ who argued that there would be vertical effect only in 'The Human Rights Act and Private Law' (2000) 116 LQR 48.

latter position that was adopted by Fenwick and Phillipson when they argued that whilst Article 8 ECHR would not be 'directly justiciable against the press, its reception into UK law will nevertheless provide an impetus for the notion of respect for privacy as an underlying legal value finally to find expression through the common law'.[196] They identified the law of breach of confidence as the common law vehicle by which the HRA would develop a right to privacy.[197]

Once the HRA came into force, it became apparent that whilst claimants cannot rely upon Article 8 ECHR directly against a private person or body, they can litigate based on the common law and that the courts interpret this in line with the Convention rights. This was articulated by Lady Hale in *Campbell* v. *MGN* as follows:

> The 1998 Act does not create any new cause of action between private persons. But if there is a relevant cause of action applicable, the court as a public authority must act compatibly with both parties' Convention rights.[198]

Consequently, the impact of the HRA was that the common law rapidly evolved providing a remedy for violations of privacy through what has become known as the tort of misuse of private information. This development occurred, as Fenwick and Phillipson predicted, by the courts developing the law of breach of confidence.[199]

196 Phillipson and Fenwick (n 1), p.661. 197 Ibid.

198 *Campbell* v. *MGN* [2004] UKHL 22, [2004] 2 AC 457, [2004] 2 WLR 1232 at [132]. For early judicial discussion of horizontal effect and the HRA, see *Douglas* v. *Hello! Ltd* [2001] QB 967, see also, Nicole Moreham, '*Douglas and others* v. *Hello! Ltd* the Protection of Privacy in English Law' (2001) **64** MLR 767.

199 For discussion of the evolution of breach of confidence and the law of misuse of private information, see Helen Fenwick, *Civil Liberties and Human Rights* (Routledge, 2016), ch.10, Fenwick and Phillipson (n 35), Nicole Moreham, 'Breach of Confidence and the Misuse of Private Information: How Do the Two Actions Work Together' (2010) **15** Media and Arts Law Review 265, Nicole Moreham 'The Protection of Privacy in English Common Law: A Doctrinal and Theoretical Analysis' (2005) **121** LQR 628, Gavin Phillipson, 'Privacy: The Development of Breach of Confidence – The Clearest Case of Horizontal Effect' in David Hoffman (ed), *The Impact of the UK Human Rights Act on Private Law* (Cambridge University Press, 2011), Gavin Phillipson, 'The Common Law, Privacy and the Convention' in Helen Fenwick et al. (eds), *Judicial Reasoning under the UK Human Rights Act* (Cambridge University Press, 2007), Gavin Phillipson, 'The Right of Privacy in England and Strasbourg Compared' in Andrew Kenyon and Megan Richardson (eds), *New Dimensions in Privacy Law: International and Comparative Perspectives* (Cambridge University Press, 2006). Gavin Phillipson, 'Judicial Reasoning in Breach of Confidence Cases under the Human Rights Act: Not Taking Privacy Seriously?' (2003) EHRLR **54**; Gavin Phillipson, 'Transforming Breach of Confidence? Towards a Common Law Right of Privacy under the Human Rights Act' (2003) **66**(5) MLR 726; Kirsty Hughes, 'Parliament Reports on Privacy and Injunctions' (2012) **4**(1) Journal of Media Law 17.

10.3.3 Developing Breach of Confidence into a Tort of Misuse of Private Information

The law of breach of confidence derives from equity and has a long history in English law.[200] Traditionally it has three elements: (i) the information must have the necessary quality of confidence about it; (ii) the information must have been imparted in circumstances importing an obligation of confidence; and (iii) there must have been an unauthorised use of the information to the detriment of the party communicating it.[201] It was the second requirement, namely circumstances importing an obligation of confidence, which was deemed to render the equitable doctrine ineffective as a privacy remedy. This was due to the fact that historically this second element required a pre-existing relationship of confidentiality between the parties, for example, employer–employee or marriage,[202] although even prior to the HRA the courts had shifted from requiring a strict pre-existing relationship towards recognising confidentiality as being imposed as a matter of conscience, induced by the circumstances of receiving information.[203] In this regard, Lord Goff famously observed *obiter* in *AG* v. *Guardian (No.2)* that an obligation of confidentiality exists where the information itself was obviously confidential:

> I realise that, in the vast majority of cases, in particular those concerned with trade secrets, the duty of confidence will arise from a transaction or relationship between the parties – often a contract, in which event the duty may arise by reason of either an express or an implied term of that contract. It is in such cases as these that the expressions 'confider' and 'confidant' are perhaps most aptly employed. But it is well settled that a duty of confidence may arise in equity independently of such cases; and I have expressed the circumstances in which the duty arises in broad terms, not merely to embrace those cases where a third party receives information from a person who is

[200] Tanya Aplin, Lionel Bently, Phillip Johnson and Simon Malynicz, *Gurry on Breach of Confidence* (2nd ed) (Oxford University Press, 2012), ch.2.

[201] *Coco* v. *A N Clark* [1969] RPC 41.

[202] *Argyll* v. *Argyll* [1967] Ch 302; *Woodward* v. *Hutchins* [1977] 1 WLR 760; *Lennon* v. *News Group Newspapers* [1978] FSR 573.

[203] The requirement of a 'pre-existing relationship of confidentiality' was replaced with the requirement that information was received on the basis that it is confidential in *Stephens* v. *Avery* [1988] Ch 449, where it was stated that: 'It is unconscionable for a person who has received information on the basis that it is confidential, subsequently to reveal that information ... the relationship between the parties is not the determining factor.' Consequently, the focus shifted from the nature of the relationship in general, to the nature of the relationship concerning the information. Subsequent cases clarified that it was not necessary for the expectation of confidentiality to be expressly stated as it may be implied from all the circumstances; see *Francome* v. *MGN* [1984] WLR 892 and *Shelley Films Ltd* v. *Rex Features Limited* [1994] EMLR 134, [1988] Ch 449. See analysis in Phillipson and Fenwick (n 1), p.671.

> under a duty of confidence in respect of it, knowing that it has been disclosed by that person to him in breach of his duty of confidence, but also to include certain situations, beloved of law teachers – where an obviously confidential document is wafted by an electric fan out of a window into a crowded street, or where an obviously confidential document, such as a private diary, is dropped in a public place, and is then picked up by a passer-by.[204]

Likewise, Laws J *obiter* in *Hellewell* v. *The Chief Constable of Derbyshire* suggested that an obligation of confidence would arise in the following scenario:

> If someone with a telephoto lens were to take from a distance and with no authority a picture of another engaged in some private act, his subsequent disclosure of the photograph would, in my judgment, as surely amount to a breach of confidence as if he had found or stolen a letter or diary in which the act was recounted and proceeded to publish it.[205]

Reflecting on these pre-HRA developments, Fenwick and Phillipson observed that while breach of confidence was evolving and offering greater protection to commercial information,[206] the courts were not applying breach of confidence to personal privacy cases.[207] Thus they argued that the HRA was needed to provide an organising principle around which uncertainties in the cause of action could be addressed.[208]

The HRA came into force in October 2000 and the privacy case law developed rapidly thereafter. An important early case was *Douglas* v. *Hello! Ltd* in which an injunction was granted in November 2000 prohibiting the magazine Hello! from publishing or republishing photographs of the wedding of actors Michael Douglas and Catherine Zeta-Jones. Prior to the wedding, the actors had entered into a contractual agreement with *Hello!*'s rival magazine (*OK!*) for exclusive coverage of photographs of the wedding and, in accordance with that agreement, guests had been prohibited from taking

[204] *AG* v. *Guardian (No.2)* [1990] 1 AC 109 (HL) 256.

[205] *Hellewell* v. *The Chief Constable of Derbyshire* [1995] 1 WLR 804, 807.

[206] *Shelley Films* v. *Rex Features Ltd.* (n 203), *Creation Records* v. *News Group Newspapers* [1997] EMLR 444, *Lion Laboratories* v. *Evans* [1984] 1 QB 530.

[207] Phillipson and Fenwick (n 1) were only able to identify one case at the interlocutory stage in which an obligation of confidentiality was imposed in respect of personal information without an express or implied promise of confidentiality and without a pre-existing relationship between the claimant and the defendant. This was *Francome* v. *Mirror Group Newspapers Ltd* (n 203), a case which concerned illegal phone tapping where an unknown person had tapped a jockey's phone calls and it was alleged that these calls revealed details of breach of rules. The Court found that all of the other surreptitious takings of information were commercial cases and that *Francombe* provided a fragile basis for identifying a general duty of confidence as the act of wiretapping was illegal, and publication could prejudice any criminal proceedings.

[208] Ibid.

photographs and employees had also signed agreements stating that they would not take photographs. Shortly after the wedding it became known that *Hello!* had obtained photographs of the event which they intended to publish. The claimants (the two actors and *OK!* magazine) were initially granted an interim injunction, but this was discharged in December 2000 by the Court of Appeal.[209] The sequence of proceedings which followed was complex with *OK!*'s claim ultimately ending up in the House of Lords,[210] however, the important point for present purposes is that less than two months after the HRA came into force Sedley LJ took the opportunity to reflect upon the relationship between confidentiality and privacy:

> What a concept of privacy does, however, is accord recognition to the fact that the law has to protect not only those people whose trust has been abused [as in confidence cases] but those who simply find themselves subjected to an unwanted intrusion into their personal lives. [211]

The role of the HRA in infusing privacy into breach of confidence was also explained by Lord Woolf in *A* v. *B* as follows:

> Under section 6 of the HRA, the court, as a public authority, is required not to act 'in a way which is incompatible with a Convention right.' The court is able to achieve this by absorbing the rights which articles 8 and 10 protect into the long-established action for breach of confidence.[212]

The common law rapidly evolved in the early years of the HRA and it was only four years after the HRA came into force that the House of Lords took the step of explicitly recognising a tort of misuse of private information in *Campbell* v. *MGN*.[213]

Campbell v. *MGN Ltd* was a landmark case which deserves close attention.[214] The defendant, MGN Ltd, was the publisher of the newspaper *The Daily Mirror*, which at the time of the events was published as *The Mirror*. In February 2001, it published details of supermodel Naomi Campbell's drug addiction, her treatment at a Narcotics Anonymous clinic and (surreptitiously obtained) photographs of her leaving that clinic. During the proceedings, Campbell conceded that the newspaper could publish the fact that she misused drugs, and that she was receiving treatment, as she had previously stated that unlike other models, she did not use drugs. Consequently, by the time the matter reached the Lords, the contested matters were whether the newspaper

[209] *Douglas* v. *Hello!* [2001] QB 967, [2001] 2 WLR 992. [210] [2007] UKHL 21, [2008] AC 1.

[211] *Douglas* (n 209), per Sedley LJ at [1001].

[212] *A* v. *B* [2002] EWCA Civ 337, [2002] 3 WLR 542. [213] *Campbell* v. *MGN* (n 198).

[214] For discussion of the significance of *Campbell*, see Gavin Phillipson, '*Campbell* v. *Mirror Group Newspapers* (2004)' in Paul Wragg and Peter Coe (eds), *Landmark Cases in Privacy Law* (Hart, 2023); Thomas D. C. Bennett and Daithí Mac Síthigh, *The Campbell Legacy: Reflections on the Tort of Misuse of Private Information* (Routledge, 2018).

could publish details of her treatment and the photographs. The Lords determined by 3:2 that MGN Ltd had misused her private information in publishing those details.

In contemplating the cause of action, Lord Nicholls observed that it had 'now firmly shaken off the limiting constraint of the need for an initial confidential relationship'.[215] In this regard, he went on to state that:

> [i]n doing so it has changed its nature. In this country this development was recognised clearly in the judgment of Lord Goff of Chieveley in Attorney-General v Guardian Newspapers Ltd (No 2) [1990] 1 AC 109, 281. Now the law imposes a 'duty of confidence' whenever a person receives information he knows or ought to know is fairly and reasonably to be regarded as confidential.[216]

He was not, however, content to leave matters there and instead went on to recognise that:

> Even this formulation is awkward. The continuing use of the phrase 'duty of confidence' and the description of the information as 'confidential' is not altogether comfortable. Information about an individual's private life would not, in ordinary usage, be called 'confidential'. The more natural description today is that such information is private. The essence of the tort is better encapsulated now as misuse of private information.[217]

The Supreme Court later reflected on these developments in *Bloomberg LP* v. *ZXC* (a case which is discussed further below), observing that the Lords in *Campbell* 'recognised that the values enshrined in articles 8 and 10 had become part of the cause of action for breach of confidence and that in relation to private information "the essence of the tort is better encapsulated now as misuse of private information"'.[218]

Having identified a new tort there were some differences between the Lords in *Campbell* as to the relevant test when determining the applicability of the law of misuse of private information, but both Lord Nicholls and Lady Hale referred to a reasonable expectation of privacy test.[219] Today it is apparent

[215] *Campbell* v. *MGN* (n 198). [216] Ibid. [217] Ibid.

[218] *Bloomberg LP* v. *ZXC* [2022] UKSC 5, [2022] AC 1158 at [45]. See also, *Douglas* v. *Hello! Ltd* [2007] UKHL 2, [2008] 1 AC 1; this was one of the very first HRA cases, but by the time it made its way to the House of Lords it was accepted by the Lords that there are now two causes of action (confidentiality and misuse of private information) protecting related but distinct interests: 'As the law has developed breach of confidence, or misuse of confidential information, now covers two distinct causes of action, protecting two different interests: privacy, and secret ("confidential") information. It is important to keep these two distinct' at [255]. See also, *Vidal-Hall* v. *Google* [2015] EWCA Civ 311, [2016] QB 1003 at [51].

[219] Lord Nicholls in *Campbell* (n 198) at [21]: 'Essentially the touchstone of private life is whether in respect of the disclosed facts the person in question had a reasonable expectation of privacy.' Lady Hale of Richmond in *Campbell* (n 198) at [137]: 'It should be emphasised that the "reasonable expectation of privacy" is a threshold test which brings the balancing exercise into play.'

that this is the test that the courts use when determining whether there has been a misuse of private information.

In considering the significance of *Campbell* it is important to note that when the Lords handed down the decision, the ECtHR had not yet delivered judgment in down *Von Hannover (No.1)*.[220] Thus as Phillipson observes:

> [r]emarkably . . . for a legal culture that has generally proved reluctant to do more than follow the caselaw of the [ECtHR], the decision was a very rare example of a domestic court anticipating Strasbourg on a point of major importance by finding that Article 8 did indeed require a cause of action between private parties for invasion of privacy.[221]

It is, however, also important to observe that when the *Von Hannover* judgment appeared a few months later it arguably afforded greater protection to privacy than the Lords had indicated in *Campbell*. As Phillipson notes, the pertinent passage is the following statement from Lady Hale in *Campbell* v. *MGN* in which she suggested that the photographs in question constituted a misuse of private information because they related to Campbell attending a drug rehabilitation programme:

> Publishing the photographs contributed both to the revelation and to the harm that it might do. By themselves, they are not objectionable. Unlike France and Quebec, in this country we do not recognise a right to one's own image: cf *Aubry v Editions Vice-Versa Inc* [1998] 1 SCR 591. We have not so far held that the mere fact of covert photography is sufficient to make the information contained in the photograph confidential. The activity photographed must be private. If this had been, and had been presented as, a picture of Naomi Campbell going about her business in a public street, there could have been no complaint. She makes a substantial part of her living out of being photographed looking stunning in designer clothing. Readers will obviously be interested to see how she looks if and when she pops out to the shops for a bottle of milk. There is nothing essentially private about that information nor can it be expected to damage her private life. It may not be a high order of freedom of speech but there is nothing to justify interfering with it.[222]

This contrasts with the ECtHR's willingness to prohibit the publication of photographs of Princess Caroline engaged in everyday activities in the street in *Von Hannover*.[223] Since *Campbell*, there has been considerable development of the misuse of private information case law, but the domestic courts have still not determined whether they would find a reasonable expectation of privacy on the facts of *Von Hannover*.

[220] Gavin Phillipson, 'Campbell v Mirror Group Newspapers (2004)' in Paul Wragg and Peter Coe (eds), *Landmark Cases in Privacy Law* (Hart, 2023), pp.159–186, 159.

[221] Ibid, pp.159–160. See also (n 1).

[222] *Campbell* (n 198) at [154]. For discussion, see Phillipson at (n 199) and (n 214).

[223] *Von Hannover (No.1)* (n 21) at [53].

10.3.4 The Two-Stage Approach to the Law of Misuse of Private Information

Having considered the origins of the law of misuse of private information and its relationship to Article 8 ECHR and the HRA, we now turn to consider how the law of misuse of private information operates. As the Supreme Court stated in *Bloomberg LP* v. *ZXC*, a two-stage test to the law of misuse of private information is now 'well established'.[224] At the first stage, the court determines whether the claimant had a reasonable expectation of privacy. If such an expectation is established then the court determines at the second stage whether that expectation is outweighed by the countervailing interest of the publisher's right to freedom of expression.[225] At the second stage the courts regard both rights as equally important and seek to evaluate the competing claims in accordance with the *Von Hannover (No.2)/Axel Springer* balancing criteria.

10.3.4.1 Stage 1: Was There a Reasonable Expectation of Privacy?

In determining whether the claimant had a reasonable expectation of privacy, the courts ask whether 'a reasonable person of ordinary sensibilities placed in the same position as the claimant and faced with the same publicity' would have an expectation of privacy.[226] This is a fact-specific question which must be addressed in every case,[227] albeit that 'general guidance can be found in the growing body of domestic legal precedent and also the jurisprudence of the European Court of Human Rights . . . on articles 8 and 10 which the court must take into account'.[228] In particular, the courts consider the issues which were identified in *Murray* v. *Express Newspapers* (and are known as the *Murray* factors).[229] *Murray* was a misuse of private information claim brought by the author J K Rowling on behalf of her infant son. The claim related to a series of photographs of Rowling, her partner and her son (who was in a pushchair at the time) walking down a street in Edinburgh, the images had been taken covertly and published in a newspaper. In contemplating whether the application for misuse of private information was likely to succeed, the Court of Appeal observed that:

> the question whether there is a reasonable expectation of privacy is a broad one, which takes account of all the circumstances of the case. They include the attributes of the claimant, the nature of the activity in which the claimant was engaged, the place at which it was happening, the nature and purpose of the intrusion, the absence of

[224] *Bloomberg LP* v. *ZXC* (n 218) at [47]. [225] Ibid at [47]. [226] Ibid at [49].

[227] Ibid at [144]. For earlier analysis of the test see Nicole Moreham, 'Unpacking the Reasonable Expectation of Privacy Test' (2018) 134 LQR 651.

[228] *Bloomberg LP* v. *ZXC* (n 218) at [48], Hughes (n 39).

[229] *Murray* v. *Express Newspapers* [2009] 1 Ch 481.

consent and whether it was known or could be inferred, the effect on the claimant and the circumstances in which and the purposes for which the information came into the hands of the publisher.[230]

It is important to make several observations. First, that the Murray factors are a non-exhaustive list. Second, that not all *Murray* factors are relevant in all cases. Third, that whilst each case requires a fact-specific assessment, there are 'certain types of information which will normally, but not invariably, be regarded as giving rise to a reasonable expectation of privacy so as to be characterised as being private in character'.[231] This means that the courts accept that for certain types or forms of information the starting point is that the information is likely to be private. This was acknowledged in *Douglas* v. *Hello!* where the Court of Appeal stated that 'the nature of the information, or the form in which it is kept, may suffice to make it plain that that information satisfies those criteria.[232] These presumptions were considered more recently by the Supreme Court in *Bloomberg LP* v. *ZXC* (discussed in more detail below) in which it was held that whilst the reasonable expectation of privacy threshold is a fact specific enquiry, there are general rules or 'legitimate starting points' in respect of certain types of information.[233] In this respect the Supreme Court observed that the most striking example of this is information relating to an individual's health which is widely considered to give rise to a reasonable expectation of privacy:

There can of course be exceptions even in relation to information concerning the state of an individual's health, but generally, details as to an individual's health are so obviously intimate and personal that a consideration of all the circumstances will result in that information being appropriately characterised as private under the stage one test unless there are strong countervailing circumstances.[234]

[230] Ibid at [36]. [231] *Bloomberg LP* v. *ZXC* (n 218) at [52].

[232] *Douglas* v. *Hello!* [2005] EWCA Civ 595, [2005] EMLR 609 at [83].

[233] *Bloomberg LP* v. *ZXC* (n 218) at [67] and [144]. See also, Stevie Martin, 'Mud Sticks: Publication of Information about Pre-charge Criminal Investigations and the Tort of Misuse Private Information' (2022) 81 CLJ 2.

[234] *Bloomberg LP* v. *ZXC* (n 218) at [72]. See also, *Campbell* v. *MGN* (n 198) and *McKennitt* v. *Ash* [2006] EWCA Civ 1714, [2008] QB 73 at [23], where it was stated that 'a person's health is in any event a private matter, as the Campbell case demonstrated'. The significance accorded to information related to health and mental health was also affirmed in *JQL* v. *NTP* [2020] EWHC 1349 (QB), a case concerning a Facebook post which referenced a niece/granddaughter's mental health problems. The defendants sought to strike the claim out as trivial, but this was rejected by the Court which held that '[t]his claim relates to very sensitive, confidential medical information, the disclosure of which is said to have caused significant prejudice to JQL's enjoyment of the right to respect for her private life'. The Court ultimately held that there was a misuse of private information and awarded £15,000 damages.

The Supreme Court in *Bloomberg LP* v. *ZXC* also identified a person's sexual orientation and the intimate details of personal relationships as types of information that are likely to give rise to a reasonable expectation of privacy.[235] Elsewhere the case law suggests that correspondence, telephone conversations, personal diaries and journals and information held on a personal computer may also be regarded as private for the purposes of the law of misuse of private information.[236]

Yet, while certain types of information are likely to be regarded as private, the Supreme Court in *Bloomberg LP* v. *ZXC* recognised that whether the information is in fact private might depend on the extent to which it is in the public domain, and that there are circumstances in which information may become so well known that it is no longer private.[237] The Supreme Court also emphasised that there is, even in relation to those types of information that are ordinarily presumed to be private, a threshold of severity and that 'in general, there will be no reasonable expectation of privacy in trivial or anodyne information'.[238] The extent to which there can be a reasonable expectation of privacy of anodyne information that is in the public domain has a particular significance of the context of photographs, as we saw in the *Von Hannover* litigation.

In domestic law, photographs are recognised as a special type of information that is perhaps more likely to be regarded as private. This was articulated as follows in *Douglas* v. *Hello!*:

> This action is about photographs. Special considerations attach to photographs in the field of privacy. They are not merely a method of conveying information that is an alternative to verbal description. They enable the person viewing the photograph to act as a spectator, in some circumstances voyeur would be the more appropriate noun, of whatever it is that the photograph depicts. As a means of invading privacy, a photograph is particularly intrusive. This is quite apart from the fact that the camera, and the telephoto lens, can give access to the viewer of the photograph to scenes where those photographed could reasonably expect that their appearances or actions would not be brought to the notice of the public.[239]

Yet, while special significance is accorded, this does not mean that all photographs will automatically be regarded as private. Certainly, there are cases in

[235] *Bloomberg LP* v. *ZXC* (n 218) at [52]. See also *Mosley* v. *News Group Newspapers* (n 146), *PJS* v. *News Group Newspapers* [2016] UKSC 26, [2016] AC 1081.

[236] Correspondence and telephone conversations fall within Article 8 ECHR. The contents of diaries have also been protected as private in *Lady Archer* v. *Williams* [2013] EWHC 1670, [2003] EMLR 38. See also, *HRH Prince of Wales* v. *Associated Newspapers* [2006] EWCA 1776 at [36], where the Court expressly stated that the form of the information would engage Article 8.

[237] *Bloomberg LP* v. *ZXC* (n 218) at [54]. For an application of this, see *Adams* v. *Amazon Digital UK Ltd* [2024] EWHC 3338 (KB) at [42].

[238] *Bloomberg LP* v. *ZXC* (n 218) at [55].

[239] *Douglas* v. *Hello!* (n 232) at [84].

which a reasonable expectation of privacy has been found in respect of photographs of children in public places even where they are engaged in anodyne activities. *Murray* is an example of this as the Court of Appeal held that the infant had an arguable case that he had a reasonable expectation of privacy which should be considered at trial.[240] Similarly in *Weller* v. *Associated Newspapers Ltd*, the court found that the children of the musician Paul Weller had a reasonable expectation of privacy in respect of photographs of them walking down the street and sitting outside a café.[241] On that occasion the Court observed that the photographs in *Weller* concerned a family activity and that 'this family element of the activity distinguishes it from Naomi Campbell's popping out to the shops for a bottle of milk'.[242] It was also accepted in *Ali* v. *Channel 5 Broadcasting* that the claimants had a reasonable expectation of privacy in respect of video footage taken from the street.[243] The facts of that case were that the defendants had broadcast a television documentary which featured the claimants being evicted from their home.[244] In determining that there had been a misuse of private information, the Court refused to separate the footage of the claimants captured in the street from the footage taken inside their home and regarded both as private.[245] Yet, whilst reasonable expectations of privacy have been found in respect of children in public as well as adults in situations of vulnerability in public, this does not mean that there are reasonable expectations of privacy in respect of all photographs in public. In this respect, Eady J commented as follows in *John* v. *Associated Newspapers Ltd* (a case in which he declined to issue an interim injunction in relation to a photograph of Sir Elton John standing with his driver in the street outside the gate to his home):

> In the present case there is no question of the photograph revealing information which touches upon or is relevant to Sir Elton John's health. Nor is there any information about social or personal relationships or, as sometimes happens in these cases, sexual relationships. Those are all matters in respect of which, to a greater or lesser extent, as with allegations about health, an individual has a reasonable expectation of privacy. Here it seems to me that the circumstances are much more akin to 'popping out for a pint of milk'. In other words, it is simply an individual leaving his car and going to his front gate.[246]

The principles were recently considered by the Court of Appeal in *Stoute* v. *NGN Ltd* which concerned photographs of the claimants taken by the paparazzi on a public beach in Barbados and published by *The Sun on*

[240] *Murray* v. *Big Pictures Ltd* [2008] EWCA 446, [2008] 3 WLR 1360.

[241] *Weller* v. *Associated Newspapers* [2014] EWHC 1163, [2014] E.M.L.R. 24.

[242] Ibid at [61]. [243] *Ali* v. *Channel 5 Broadcasting* [2019] EWCA Civ 677. [244] Ibid.

[245] See the High Court judgment *Ali* v. *Channel 5 Broadcasting* [2018] EWHC 298 (Ch) at [157]–[158].

[246] *John* v. *Associated Newspapers Ltd* [2006] EWHC 1611 (QB), [2006] EMLR 772 at [15].

Sunday.[247] The claimants (Mr and Mrs Stoute) own and run a company which supplies PPE to hospitals and they had achieved some notoriety due to certain beneficial Government contracts obtained during the Covid-19 pandemic. In this respect it is noteworthy that the photographs in question were published by the defendant newspaper alongside an article with the headline '£2BN PPE Couple Having a Laugh'.[248] The claimants sought an interim injunction to prohibit further publication of the images, which was refused by Johnson J on the basis that the claimants were not likely to establish that they had a reasonable expectation of privacy.[249] He held that the case law suggests that a reasonable expectation of privacy will be found where there 'is an additional element which renders information private even though it is obtained in a public place'.[250] He suggested that in 'the absence of that additional element, information that someone chooses to reveal in public is less likely to be recognised by the law as private'.[251] In particular, he noted that:

> public and private CCTV and the use of mobile phones to take photographs and record video is ubiquitous. Anyone venturing out in public may be captured by such cameras. The reasonable person knows that is the case. It follows that there is no general reasonable expectation of privacy in respect of information that is patent to anyone who happens to be in the same place at the same time.[252]

Applying this to the case in hand, Johnson J held that while the absence of consent and the use of highly magnified telescopic lenses in obtaining the photographs were relevant to whether or not the claimants had a reasonable expectation of privacy, those elements were not 'present to a degree or extent which make it likely that the court at trial would conclude that they had a relevant reasonable expectation of privacy'.[253] He thus determined that 'the degree of intrusion [wa]s far less than was present, for example, in the Princess Caroline of Monaco case: *Von Hannover* v. *Germany*'.[254] Consequently, he held that the claimants were not more likely than not to establish at trial that the photographs amounted to private information.

On appeal, the Court of Appeal held that the judge had made no error in concluding that it was unlikely that the claimants would be able to establish that they had a reasonable expectation of privacy.[255] In rejecting the appeal, the Court of Appeal observed that whilst 'photographs require special consideration' the domestic case law also establishes that 'a person is less likely to have a reasonable expectation of privacy with respect to a photograph if the photograph was taken in a public place than if it was taken in a private

[247] *Stoute* v. *NGN Ltd* [2023] EWCA Civ 523. [248] Ibid at [18].

[249] *Stoute* v. *NGN Ltd* [2023] EWHC 232 (KB).

[250] Ibid at [33]. Discussed in the Court of Appeal (n 247) at [52].

[251] *Stoute* (High Court) ibid at [33]. [252] Ibid. [253] Ibid at [34]. [254] Ibid.

[255] *Stoute* (Court of Appeal) (n 247) at [57].

place, but this is not a bright-line rule and depends on the circumstances'.[256] It observed that 'a person is more likely to have a reasonable expectation of privacy with respect to photographs taken by paparazzi, particularly photographs taken covertly from a distance using telephoto lenses, than in respect of photographs which do not involve such targeting, but again this is not a bright-line rule and depends on the circumstances'.[257] Consequently:

> If the domestic case law is compared with the case law of the European Court on this issue, it can be seen that the European Court is readier than the domestic courts to accept that Article 8 is engaged by the taking and publication of photographs of individuals, but nevertheless it places a strong emphasis on the need to balance publishers' Article 10 rights against applicants' Article 8 rights. In my view there is no reason to think that this slight difference in the two approaches leads to the overall balance being struck in a materially different way.[258]

Lady Hale's obiter dicta in *Campbell* that there would be nothing essentially private about photographs of Naomi Campbell popping out to the shops for a bottle of milk, thus appears to remain sound.

In considering the reasonable expectation of privacy test, it is also important to acknowledge that a particularly contentious issue has been the question of whether claimants have a reasonable expectation of privacy in relation to the fact that they are under police investigation.[259] This has been the subject of a number of cases which culminated in *Bloomberg LP* v. *ZXC* in which the Supreme Court confirmed that there *is* a reasonable expectation of privacy prior to charge.[260] The issue was first considered in *Richard* v. *BBC* when Mann J held that the BBC's reporting of the fact that Cliff Richard was under investigation for alleged sexual offences was unlawful.[261] In determining that there had been a misuse of private information, Mann J stated that 'as a matter of general principle, a suspect has a reasonable expectation of privacy in relation to a police investigation':[262]

> It seems to me that on the authorities, and as a matter of general principle, a suspect has a reasonable expectation of privacy in relation to a police investigation, and I so rule. As a general rule it is understandable and justifiable (and reasonable) that a

[256] Ibid at [36]. [257] Ibid at [46]. [258] Ibid at [47].

[259] Nicole Moreham, 'Privacy, Reputation and Alleged Wrongdoing: Why Police Investigations Should Not Be Regarded as Private' (2019) 11(2) Journal of Media Law 142; Robert Craig and Gavin Phillipson, 'Privacy, Reputation and Anonymity Until Charge: ZXC Goes to the Supreme Court' (2021) 13(2) Journal of Media Law 153.

[260] *Bloomberg LP* v. *ZXC* (n 218).

[261] *Richard* v. *BBC* [2018] EWHC 1837 (Ch), [2019] Ch. 169, [2018] 3 WLR 1715, see Jacob Rowbottom, 'Reporting Police Investigations, Privacy Rights and Social Stigma: Richard v. BBC' (2018) 10(2) Journal of Media Law 115.

[262] Ibid at [248].

suspect would not wish others to know of the investigation because of the stigma attached. It is, as a general rule, not necessary for anyone outside the investigating force to know, and the consequences of wider knowledge have been made apparent in many cases (see above). If the presumption of innocence were perfectly understood and given effect to, and if the general public was universally capable of adopting a completely open- and broad-minded view of the fact of an investigation so that there was no risk of taint either during the investigation or afterwards (assuming no charge) then the position might be different. But neither of those things is true. The fact of an investigation, as a general rule, will of itself carry some stigma, no matter how often one says it should not.[263]

Warby J adopted the same approach in *Sicri* v. *Associated Newspapers* after the Mail Online published an article stating that the claimant had been arrested in connection with the Manchester Arena bombing (the claimant was later released without charge and it was accepted by all that he had nothing to do with the terrorist attack).[264]

The applicable principles in the context of a police investigation were then considered by the Supreme Court in *Bloomberg* v. *ZXC*.[265] The facts were that the claimant, ZXC, was the chief executive of X Ltd a major international business that was under investigation by a UK law enforcement body in relation to possible offences including corruption and bribery. The defendant, Bloomberg, had obtained a copy of a confidential letter of request made by the law enforcement body to a foreign Government in which the law enforcement body sought assistance from the foreign Government with the investigation. Following which Bloomberg published an article based on the contents of that letter at a time when ZXC had not been charged with any offence. ZXC brought a claim for, amongst other things, misuse of private information and the defendant, Bloomberg, argued, amongst other things, that ZXC had no reasonable expectation of privacy.

In particular ZXC claimed that he had a reasonable expectation of privacy in relation to: (i) the fact that the law enforcement body had requested information relating to him in the context of its investigations, and (ii) the details of the matters that the law enforcement body was investigating in relation to him. The first instance judge held that Bloomberg had published private information that was in principle protected by Article 8 ECHR; and that in balancing ZXC's rights against those of Bloomberg under Article 10 ECHR, the balance favoured ZXC.[266] Bloomberg's appeal against that judgment was dismissed by the Court of Appeal.[267] Following which Bloomberg appealed to the Supreme Court arguing that the Court of Appeal was wrong

[263] Ibid. [264] *Sicri* v. *Associated Newspapers* [2020] EWHC 3541, [2021] 4 WLR 9.
[265] *Bloomberg* v. *ZXC* (n 218).
[266] *ZXC* v. *Bloomberg* [2019] EWHC 970 (QB), [2019] EMLR 20.
[267] *ZXC* v. *Bloomberg* [2020] EWCA Civ 611, [2021] QB 28.

when it held that there is a general rule, that was applicable in the present case, that a person under criminal investigation has, prior to being charged, a reasonable expectation of privacy in respect of information relating to that investigation.[268]

The Supreme Court held that the legitimate starting point is that prior to being charged a person under criminal investigation has a reasonable expectation of privacy in respect of information relating to that investigation.[269] It also held that in all the circumstances *Bloomberg* v. *ZXC* was a case in which there was a reasonable expectation of privacy[270] and that as there was no error in the Court of Appeal's approach there were no grounds for interfering with the judge's decision in relation to the balancing exercise (namely that the balance to be struck between Articles 8 and 10 ECHR came down in favour of the claimant).[271]

The Supreme Court's decision in *ZXC* was welcomed by some,[272] while others raised concerns about the ramifications for the demarcation of privacy and defamation[273] and whether the case should have been dealt with under breach of confidence instead of misuse of private information.[274] Concerns have also been raised as to whether *ZXC* is indicative of the ECHR jurisprudence having 'too much influence on English private law', something which they believe renders the tort vulnerable to legislative change.[275]

Thus far we have focused upon those types of information that may carry significant weight in determining whether there was a reasonable expectation of privacy. It is to be recalled, however, that in all cases the courts must carry out an assessment of the circumstances. One of the *Murray* factors that the courts consider is the attributes of the claimant. An important point to note here is that it is evident from the case law that the fact that someone is a public figure does not mean that they have no right to a private life. As Lord Phillips observed in the Court of Appeal in *Campbell*, 'the fact that an individual has

[268] Ibid at [63].

[269] *Bloomberg LP* v. *ZXC* (n 218) at [146]. Stevie Martin, 'Pre-charge Criminal Investigations and the Tort of Misuse of Private Information' (2022) **81**(2) CLJ 232; Nicole Moreham, 'Privacy and Police Investigations: ZXC v. Bloomberg' (2021) **80**(1) CLJ 5.

[270] Ibid. [271] Ibid at [157].

[272] Gavin Phillipson, 'Supreme Court Confirms Suspects' Privacy Rights: The Judgement Clarified, Two Criticisms Answered' (2022) **14**(2) Journal of Media Law 257; Robert Craig, 'Defendant Anonymity until Charge, the Presumption of Innocence and the Taxonomy of Misuse of Private Information' (2022) **14**(2) Journal of Media Law 266.

[273] Nicole Moreham, 'Privacy, Defamation and ZXC v. Bloomberg' (2022) **14**(2) Journal of Media Law 226, 236. See also, Jacob Rowbottom writing prior to this (n 261).

[274] Thomas D. C. Bennett, 'Confidence, Privacy and Incoherence' (2022) **14**(2) Journal of Media Law 245, for an opposing argument, see Phillipson (n 272). See also, Nicole Moreham, 'Police Investigations, Privacy and the Marcel Principle in Breach of Confidence' (2020) **12**(1) Journal of Media Law 1.

[275] Moreham (n 273), p.236.

achieved prominence on the public stage does not mean that his private life can be laid bare in the media'.[276] Equally in *Richard* v. *BBC*, it was stated that 'a public figure is not by virtue of that quality *necessarily* deprived of his or her legitimate expectations of privacy'.[277] Moreover, in *HRH The Duchess of Sussex* v. *Associated Newspapers Ltd*, Mr Justice Warby observed that 'it has long been established that a public figure does not, by joining that select group, give up her right to a private life, or open up every aspect of her private and family life or correspondence to examination in the press'.[278]

Yet, whilst public figures are not automatically deprived of the right to privacy, the courts have left open the possibility that public figure status may affect the assessment of whether there was a reasonable expectation of privacy. In this regard, defendants have tried to argue that public figures waived their right to privacy by disclosing or allowing disclosures of information relating to their private life in the past. The courts have rejected the argument that zones of private life are waived in this way and have held that each case is subject to a fact-sensitive evaluation.[279] They have also held that just because a person is known to the public or is connected to a public figure, this does not mean that they are a public figure for the purposes of the law of misuse of private information. For example, in *RocknRoll* v. *News Group Newspapers*, Briggs J held that the claimant (the partner of Kate Winslet) was not a public figure.[280]

In considering the attributes of the claimant, there is also some suggestion in the case law that children may be entitled to greater privacy protection than adults.[281] This is implicit in the fact that there are cases concerning photographs of children in public places where the courts have found a reasonable expectation of privacy, whilst it is not clear that they would have come to the same conclusion in respect of adults.[282] Yet, whilst children may be offered greater protection in some respects, it is also important to note that the case law suggests that children may have their rights to privacy waived by their parents. The origins of this can be found in *Murray* v. *Express Newspapers* when Patten J stated that one of the factors to be considered was 'the position

[276] *Campbell* v. *MGN* [2002] EWCA Civ 1373, [2003] QB 633 at [41].

[277] *Richard* v. *BBC* (n 261) at [256].

[278] *HRH The Duchess of Sussex* v. *Associated Newspapers Ltd* [2021] EWHC 273 (Ch), [2021] 4 WLR 35 at [71]. On appeal, the Court of Appeal stated at *HRH The Duchess of Sussex* v. *Associated Newspapers Ltd* [2021] EWCA Civ 1810, [2022] 4 WLR 81 at [81] that it agreed with Mr Justice Warby's analysis at [64]–[95] and that he had 'dealt in impeccable detail with each of the *Murray* factors'.

[279] *RocknRoll* v. *News Group Newspapers* [2013] EWHC 24 at [18]–[19].

[280] Ibid at [15].

[281] *Murray* v. *Big Pictures Ltd* (n 240), *Weller* v. *Associated Newspapers* (n 241) and *Ali* v. *Channel 5* (n 243) at [152]–[155].

[282] Kirsty Hughes, 'Publishing Photographs without Consent' (2014) 6(2) Journal of Media Law 180.

of the child's parents and the way in which the child's life as part of that family has been conducted'. He went on to state that the courts can 'attribute to the child reasonable expectations about his private life based on matters such as how it has in fact been conducted by those responsible for his welfare and upbringing'.[283] This was deployed in *AAA* v. *Associated Newspapers Ltd* where it was accepted 'that, in evaluating the strength of the claimant's reasonable expectation of privacy, the judge was entitled to take into account any relevant conduct of the mother'.[284] The claimant in *AAA* was an infant who had become the subject of media attention as it was alleged that her father was a prominent elected politician. The *Daily Mail* newspaper had pubished an article about the child and her paternity together with a photograph of the child being pushed in a pushchair by her mother. Eight further articles were published by the defendant, three of which included the photograph. At trial the child was awarded £15,000 in respect of the publication of the photograph but no damages were awarded in relation to the information relating to her paternity and no injunction was granted. The claim in respect of the private information failed on the basis that the child had a reduced expectation of privacy due to her mother's prior discussion of the child's paternity with a magazine editor at a country house party as well as in an interview published in a magazine; a determination that was upheld by the Court of Appeal.[285] Yet, as Hughes has argued elsewhere, it is unconscionable that the human right of one person can be waived by the conduct of another and there is no basis for departing from that simply because the claimant is a child; to suggest otherwise is to undermine the fact that the child has their own rights under international and domestic law.[286] Similarly, in the foreword to the book in which that view is expressed, Lady Hale writes:

> A children's rights analysis would not have held that the child's right to privacy was reduced because of her mother's indiscretion in talking about it; the child was a separate person from her mother; nor was the public interest in knowing about the alleged philandering of the politician a good reason to publish the child's name, which was not in her best interests.[287]

A further factor that the courts consider in determining whether there was a reasonable expectation of privacy is the place at which the intrusion occurred. Unsurprisingly, the home is accorded special protection,[288] yet, while it is

[283] *Murray* v. *Express Newspapers* (n 229) at [23].
[284] *AAA* v. *Associated Newspapers Ltd* [2013] EWCA Civ 554, [2013] WLR(D) 189 at [21].
[285] Ibid.
[286] Kirsty Hughes, 'Rewriting AAA v. Associated Newspapers' in Helen Stalford et al. (ed(s)), *Rewriting Children's Rights Judgments: From Academic Vision to New Practice* (Hart, 2017), p.204.
[287] Brenda Hale, 'Foreword', ibid, p.viii.
[288] *Ali* v. *Channel 5* (n 243) and *Richard* v. *BBC* (n 261).

evident that privacy is not limited to the home,[289] for the reasons noted above, it is not clear to what extent privacy in public is protected.

Another factor that the courts consider in determining whether there was a reasonable expectation of privacy is the nature and purpose of the intrusion. This was emphasised in *Murray* v. *Express Newspapers* and *Weller* v. *Associated Newspapers*,[290] with the Court observing that the photographs had been 'taken deliberately, in secret and with a view to their subsequent publication. They were taken for the purpose of publication for profit no doubt in the knowledge that the parents would have objected to them.'[291] Thus the surreptitious nature of the intrusion is a factor that is more likely to give rise to a reasonable expectation of privacy.

Finally, it is worth observing that the *Murray* factors require the courts to consider the effect of the disclosure, noting that whilst harm is not essential it will add weight to the claim.[292] In this regard the courts have considered the impact of the disclosure not only on the claimant but also on the claimant's children, who have their own privacy rights and interests.[293] This was evident in *PJS* v. *News Group Newspapers*, a case in which the Supreme Court had to consider whether to maintain an interim injunction which restrained publication of details of the claimant's sexual life.[294] PJS was a well-known individual in the entertainment business who was married to YMA and they had two young children. The editor of the *Sun on Sunday* newspaper which was published by the defendant had notified PJS that they were intending to publish details of PJS's extra-marital sexual relations. Following which, PJS had brought proceedings claiming that the publication would breach his rights to privacy and confidentiality protected by Article 8 ECHR. His application for an interim injunction had been refused by the High Court but was granted by the Court of Appeal. However, details of the sexual relationship and PJS' identity were subsequently published in the United States, Canada and Scotland. Those publications were restricted to print editions, whilst the online publication was geo-blocked meaning that internet users in England and Wales could not readily access the website. The detail of the publication was nevertheless published on other websites and social media. The defendant, News Group Newspapers, thus applied to have the interim injunction set aside on the ground that as the information was now in the public domain PJS was unlikely to obtain a permanent injunction at trial and the interim injunction could therefore no longer be justified. The Court of Appeal agreed that the injunction should be discharged, however, PJS appealed to the Supreme Court which allowed his appeal by a majority of 4:1. In making that determination, Lady Hale (with

[289] *Campbell* v. *MGN* (n 198), *Murray* v. *Big Pictures Ltd* (n 240) and *Weller* v. *Associated Newspapers* (n 241).

[290] *Murray* v. *Big Pictures Ltd* (n 240). [291] Ibid at [50]. [292] Ibid.

[293] *PJS* v. *News Group Newspapers* (n 235). [294] Ibid.

whom Lord Neuberger, Lord Mance and Lord Reed agreed) emphasised that children have their own privacy interests and rights under Article 8:

> It is simply not good enough to dismiss the interests of any children who are likely to be affected by the publication of private information about their parents with the bland statement that 'these cannot be a trump card'. Of course they cannot always rule the day. But they deserve closer attention than they have so far received in this case, for two main reasons. First, not only are the children's interests likely to be affected by a breach of the privacy interests of their parents, but the children have independent privacy interests of their own. They also have a right to respect for their family life with their parents. Secondly, by section 12(4)(b), any court considering whether to grant either an interim or a permanent injunction has to have 'particular regard' to 'any relevant privacy code'. It is not disputed that the IPSO Code, which came into force in January, is a relevant Code for this purpose. This, as Lord Mance has explained, provides that 'editors must demonstrate an exceptional public interest to over-ride the normally paramount interests of [children under 16]'.[295]

10.3.4.2 *Stage 2: Balancing Privacy and Freedom of Expression*

Once a reasonable expectation of privacy is established, the courts must balance the claimant's privacy right and the defendant's right to freedom of expression, in what the Supreme Court in *ZXC* referred to as the 'so-called "balancing exercise"'.[296] In reflecting upon the nature of this task they cited Lord Hoffmann in *Campbell* who stated:

> Both [rights] reflect important civilised values, but, as often happens, neither can be given effect in full measure without restricting the other. How are they to be reconciled in a particular case? There is in my view no question of automatic priority. Nor is there a presumption in favour of one rather than the other. The question is rather the extent to which it is necessary to qualify the one right in order to protect the underlying value which is protected by the other. And the extent of the qualification must be proportionate to the need.[297]

In evaluating the weight to be accorded to each right, the courts have emphasised that neither right has priority over the other and the assessment is inherently case-sensitive.[298] Lord Steyn in *Re S (A child)* set out the methodology for dealing with competing ECHR rights:

> First, neither article has *as such* precedence over the other. Secondly, where the values under the two articles are in conflict, an intense focus on the comparative importance of the specific rights being claimed in the individual case is necessary. Thirdly, the justifications for interfering with or restricting each right must be taken into account.

[295] *PJS* (n 235) at [72]. [296] *Bloomberg LP* v. *ZXC* (n 218) at [56].

[297] Ibid at [57], citing Lord Hoffmann in *Campbell* (n 198) at [55].

[298] *Douglas* v. *Hello!* (n 209), per Sedley LJ at [135], *Campbell* (n 198) at [55], *Re S* [2005] 1 AC 593 at [17].

Finally, the proportionality test must be applied to each. For convenience I will call this the ultimate balancing test.[299]

At this juncture, it is important to note the presence of s.12 HRA 1998. Section 12 applies if a court is considering whether to grant any relief which, if granted, might affect the exercise of the Convention right to freedom of expression (s.12(1)). Moreover, s.12(4) HRA 1998 provides that:

(4) The court must have particular regard to the importance of the Convention right to freedom of expression and, where the proceedings relate to material which the respondent claims, or which appears to the court, to be journalistic, literary or artistic material (or to conduct connected with such material), to–

(a) the extent to which–
  (i) the material has, or is about to, become available to the public; or
  (ii) it is, or would be, in the public interest for the material to be published;
(b) any relevant privacy code.

Yet, while s.12(4) HRA 1998 requires the courts to have 'particular regard' to the importance of freedom of expression, the courts have not interpreted this as meaning that they should prioritise freedom of expression. Sedley LJ famously neutered s.12 HRA in this respect in *Douglas* v. *Hello! Ltd* when he observed that having regard to Article 10 ECHR does not mean giving priority to it over other rights:

The case being one which affects the Convention right of freedom of expression, s.12 of the Human Rights Act requires the court to have regard to Article 10 (as, in its absence, would s.6). This, however, cannot, consistently with s.3 and Article 17, give the Article 10(1) right of free expression a presumptive priority over other rights. What it does is require the court to consider Article 10(2) along with 10(1), and by doing so to bring into the frame the conflicting right to respect for privacy. This right, contained in Article 8 and reflected in English law, is in turn qualified in both contexts by the right of others to free expression. The outcome, which self-evidently has to be the same under both articles, is determined principally by considerations of proportionality.[300]

The Supreme Court affirmed in *PJS* that even at the interlocutory stage 'neither article has preference over the other' and 'where their values are in conflict, what is necessary is an intense focus on the comparative importance of the rights being claimed in the individual case'.[301]

The non-hierarchical status of the rights and the factors relevant to the balancing exercise were also articulated by Mr Justice Warby in *HRH The Duchess of Sussex* v. *Associated Newspapers Ltd* as follows:

At stage two, the question is whether in all the circumstances the privacy rights of the claimant must yield to the imperatives of the freedom of expression enjoyed by

[299] *Re S* (n 298) at [17]. See also, *Bloomberg LP* v. *ZXC* (n 218) at [58].
[300] *Douglas* v. *Hello!* (n 209), per Sedley LJ at [137].
[301] *PJS* v. *News Group Newspapers Ltd* (n 235) at [20], see also at [51].

publishers and their audiences. The competing rights are both qualified, and neither has precedence as such. The conflict is not to be resolved mechanically, on the basis of rival generalities. The Court must focus intensely on the comparative importance of the specific rights being claimed in the particular case; assess the justifications for interfering with each right; and balance them, applying a proportionality test. The Court must have regard to the extent to which it is or would be in the public interest for the material to be published. The decisive factor at this stage is an assessment of the contribution which the publication of the relevant information would make to a debate of general interest. Other factors to be weighed in the balance are the subject-matter, how well-known the claimant is, the claimant's prior conduct, and editorial latitude. When examining the demands of free speech, the court should be slow to interfere in respect of matters of technique, form and detail; it should defer, to the extent appropriate on the facts, to the professional expertise and judgment of journalists and editors.[302]

Meanwhile in *ZXC* the Supreme Court highlighted the important public watchdog function of the press,[303] observing that whether a publication contributes to a debate of public interest is one of the *Von Hannover (No.2)/ Axel Springer* balancing criteria.[304]

It is thus evident that in determining the balance to be struck, the domestic courts adopt a similar approach to the ECtHR and apply the *Von Hannover (No.2)* and *Axel Springer* criteria.[305] In this respect it is important to observe that the domestic courts have emphasised that there must be a genuine debate of general interest, not just matters that happen to be of interest to the public.[306] This is significant because there are cases in which the press has advanced no public interest argument at all.[307] The courts have also made it clear that different types of expression are accorded different weight in this balancing exercise. For example, in *PJS*, the Supreme Court opined that:

it may be that the mere reporting of sexual encounters of someone like the appellant, however well known to the public, with a view to criticising them does not even fall within the concept of freedom of expression under article 10 at all. But, accepting that article 10 is not only engaged but capable in principle of protecting any form of expression, these cases clearly demonstrate that this type of expression is at the bottom end of the spectrum of importance (compared, for example, with freedom of political speech or a case of conduct bearing on the performance of a public office). For present purposes, any public interest in publishing such criticism must, in the absence of any

[302] *HRH The Duchess of Sussex* v. *Associated Newspapers* (n 278) at [31]. This was upheld on appeal, see (n 278) at [34] and [93].

[303] *Bloomberg LP* v. *ZXC* (n 218) at [61]. [304] Ibid at [62]. [305] Ibid at [62].

[306] *RocknRoll* v. *News Group Newspapers* (n 279) at [35].

[307] Kirsty Hughes, 'Parliament Reports on Privacy and Injunctions' (2012) 4(1) Journal of Media Law 17.

other, legally recognised, public interest, be effectively disregarded in any balancing exercise and is incapable by itself of outweighing such article 8 privacy rights as the appellant enjoys.[308]

Academic views differ as to precisely what happens at the balancing stage. For example, Wragg argues that whilst the courts say that they are engaged in a balancing of the competing rights, in reality there is 'usually little or no real comparison of the two' as the courts instead apply a rule the effect of which is that 'either the privacy claim fails because there is a public interest in publication, or it succeeds because there is no such public interest'.[309] This is disputed by Phillipson who argues that Wragg's critique is over-stated and that it neglects the fact that prior to *Campbell* the courts often did not evaluate the strength of the public interest in publication, but rather took it for granted.[310] He argues that *Campbell* and the cases that followed indicate that the courts evaluate the competing rights, but that it is unrealistic to look for a prescription as to the weight to be accorded to each right, such that it may be 'better and more honest in this regard to speak of "evaluating" the weight of each right, rather than "balancing" them'.[311] Others, such as Moreham, argue that importing the Strasbourg balancing criteria into the second stage of the tort creates uncertainty as to whether the courts should apply their own public interest approach, the Strasbourg factors or both.[312] She suggests that this creates overlap with the factors considered at stage 1 of the misuse of private information tort (when determining whether the applicant had a reasonable expectation of privacy) and that it distracts the courts from what should be the proper focus at the second stage, namely the audience's legitimate interest in receiving the information.[313] In this respect, she identifies four common law principles which she believes should underpin the analysis at the second stage: (i) where the private information raises questions about a person's fitness for a public role; (ii) where a claimant is peddling a false image; (iii) where the information contains evidence of harmful conduct or other serious wrongdoing; or (iv) where the information is disclosed to people with a particular interest in receiving it.[314] Moreham thus argues for a narrowing of the second stage of analysis and a retreat from the influence of Strasbourg allowing it to operate 'as high-level guidance about the shape of the private life interest, not a blueprint to be transplanted into the common law action directly'.[315] She also suggests amending the language for the second stage from one of 'public

[308] *PJS* v. *News Group Newspapers* (n 235) at [24].

[309] Paul Wragg, 'Protecting Private Information of Public Interest: Campbell's Great Promise, Unfulfilled' (2015) 7(2) Journal of Media Law 225, 226.

[310] Phillipson (n 214), p.174. [311] Ibid, p.180.

[312] Nicole Moreham, 'Privacy, Freedom of Expression and Legitimate Audience Interest' (2023) 139 LQR 412.

[313] Ibid. [314] Ibid. [315] Ibid.

interest' to 'legitimate audience interest' in order to accommodate situations in which disclosure is not to the public at large but to a more limited audience such as colleagues, spouses, friends or family.[316] Yet, while Moreham argues that common law principles should have greater prominence in the tort and that there should be less reliance on Strasbourg, she accepts that the ECHR provides 'high-level guidance' and thus the backdrop to the legal framework; as we will see others have pushed further and argued that a recalibration of the balance that is struck between privacy and freedom of expression is required.

10.3.5 The Compatibility of Domestic Law with the ECHR and Calls for Reform

We have seen that both the ECtHR and our domestic courts have developed a two-stage framework for protecting the right to privacy and balancing it against the right to freedom of expression. The ECtHR takes a broad approach to the applicability of Article 8 ECHR, such that whilst there is an implicit threshold of seriousness this remains almost entirely untested. This contrasts with the domestic tort of misuse of private information in which there is a far more developed threshold in the form of the reasonable expectation of privacy test. Yet, despite these differences, in most cases the reasonable expectation of privacy test seems to operate in line with the Article 8 ECHR case law such that the courts are not generally finding that there was no reasonable expectation of privacy in respect of something that would have triggered Article 8 ECHR. As we have already seen, one possible exception to this is in respect of photographs of adults engaged in everyday activities in public places (something that the ECtHR found fell within Article 8 ECHR in *Von Hannover*, but Lady Hale doubted fell within the tort of misuse of private information in *Campbell*). We may therefore see greater case law in respect of this issue.

Beyond this, it is evident that once a reasonable expectation of privacy is established, the domestic courts will balance privacy and freedom of expression in accordance with the *Von Hannover (No.2)* and *Axel Springer* criteria and that, provided they do, the ECtHR will be reluctant to intervene. Consequently, while the balancing exercise is replicated in the second stage of the domestic law of misuse of private information, it is unlikely that the ECtHR will find that a balance struck by our domestic courts is incompatible with the ECHR. Indeed, to date no violations have been found by the ECtHR in respect of the UK. Thus, in sum we can say that domestic privacy law has developed considerably following the introduction of the HRA and that it is broadly in line with the ECHR.

Given that position, it is interesting to note that there has been persistent opposition to domestic privacy law and ongoing calls for repeal of the HRA on

[316] Ibid, p.423.

the basis of its alleged deleterious impact on publishers. This is reflected in the ways in which tabloid newspapers have lambasted what they regard as oppressive privacy law with headlines such as 'Why the Law Is an ASS' and 'The Day Free Speech Drowned in a Paddling Pool of Olive Oil'.[317] There was also a period in which the politics surrounding privacy law was such that Members of Parliament (some might say opportunistically) invoked parliamentary privilege to publicly disclose in parliamentary proceedings information on matters, such as the identity of a footballer who had an affair, that they would not have been able to reveal outside Parliament as the information was protected by an injunction.[318] Much of the furore about privacy law has diminished in recent years, but the role of Article 8 ECHR in protecting privacy was part of the case advanced by the former Conservative Government in support of repealing the HRA and replacing it with a Bill of Rights.[319] In fact, as Fenwick notes, '[o]nce the Bill [of Rights] was introduced to Parliament, the enhancing of free speech was hailed in parts of the media, and by Raab [the Bill's proposer], as its most significant and welcome aspect – its flagship achievement'.[320]

These attempts to reconfigure privacy law give rise to two questions. First, given that the tort of misuse of private information emerged from the HRA, we have to consider whether the tort would survive repeal of the HRA and withdrawal from the ECHR? Second, assuming that the UK remains a party to the ECHR, could domestic legislation recalibrate the protection that is accorded to privacy and freedom of expression within the tort of misuse of private information?

In respect of the first question, while the HRA may have been a catalyst for the tort, it is probably not dependent upon the HRA for its survival.[321] It is true that misuse of private information embodies the same values as Article 8 ECHR, operates within a similar structure, and that the courts often tackle the common law and the Convention right in tandem, but this does not deny the independent existence of the common law cause of action. The fact that

[317] C. Duffin and I. Drury, 'Why the law is an ass: Part 3', *Daily Mail*, 9 April 2016, www.dailymail.co.uk/news/article-3530915/Why-law-ass-3-Man-took-threesome-says-celebrity-love-cheat-using-children-human-shields.html; T. Wells, 'The day free speech drowned in a paddling pool of olive oil . . . outrage at gagging verdict', *The Sun*, 20 May 2016, www.thesun.co.uk/news/1198394/the-day-free-speech-drowned-in-a-paddling-pool-of-olive-oil-outrage-at-gagging-verdict/ responding to the injunction granted in *PJS* (n 235).

[318] Hughes (n 307). See discussion earlier in this chapter of *Green* v. *the United Kingdom* (n 155) in which the ECtHR held that the operation of parliamentary privilege falls within the State's margin of appreciation.

[319] Ministry of Justice, Human Rights Act Reform: A Modern Bill of Rights – A Consultation to Reform the Human Rights Act 1998, December 2021, CP 588 at [206].

[320] Fenwick (n 4), p.2.

[321] Hughes (n 15).

there are two bodies of law was noted in *Richard* v. *BBC* where it was acknowledged that, strictly speaking, the complaint against the police was a direct complaint under the HRA whilst the complaint against the BBC was based in tort.[322] Consequently, although the two bodies of law are conjoined, the common law tort has an independent existence. This does not preclude the Government from legislating in respect of misuse of private information, but it does mean that the common law would not automatically be swept away in the event of repeal of the HRA.

Which brings us to the second question, assuming that the UK remains a party to the ECHR, could domestic legislation recalibrate the protection that is accorded to privacy and freedom of expression? This was the proposition that underpinned the Conservative Government's Bill of Rights, the impetus for which was set out in their Consultation document which stated that the 'case law of the Strasbourg Court has shown a willingness to give priority to personal privacy'.[323] There were several questionable aspects to the Conservative Government's proposals, not least that the notion that Strasbourg prioritises privacy is contradicted by the way in which the ECtHR has clearly and consistently stated that privacy and freedom of expression are of equal status.[324] Nevertheless, the Conservative Government's draft Bill of Rights included a clause that purported to recast the relationship between Article 8 and 10 ECHR as follows:

> When determining a question which has arisen in connection with the right to freedom of speech, a court must give great weight to the importance of protecting the right.[325]

That provision raised several questions.[326] First, whether 'giving great weight' would compel the courts to do something different from what they did with 'having particular regard to' under s.12 HRA?[327]Second, whether it is possible to give greater weight to freedom of expression whilst remaining a party to the ECHR where the rights are non-hierarchical? This is important because while the ECtHR accords a considerable margin of appreciation to States in striking the balance, the margin does not extend to allowing States to mandate that one right trumps the other or has a presumptive status.[328] At the time of writing, these challenges have been put into abeyance by the withdrawal of the Bill of Rights and the change of Government but they remain pertinent to

[322] *Richard* v. *BBC* (n 261) at [259].

[323] Ministry of Justice, Human Rights Act Reform (n 319) at [206].

[324] See discussion at Section 10.2.2 above.

[325] Bill of Rights Bill, Bill 117, 58/3, Clause 4.

[326] Centre for Public Law, Government Consultation to Reform the Human Rights Act 1998 Call for Submissions – Response, March 2022.

[327] Fenwick (n 4), p.18. See also, Jake Rowbottom, 'Will the Bill of Rights bill enhance the protection of free speech?' (Inforrm's blog, 29 June 2022), https://inforrm.org/2022/06/29/will-the-bill-of-rights-bill-enhance-the-protection-of-free-speech-jacob-rowbottom/.

[328] Fenwick (n 4), pp.11–12.

any future proposals to repeal the HRA or to legislate in respect of misuse of private information or freedom of expression.

The final point that is worth considering is whether the evolution of privacy law over the last two decades is such that our domestic courts would now be willing to recognise a common law right to privacy, a development that would in turn give rise to questions as to the ambit of such a right and its constitutional status.[329] Hughes has examined these questions elsewhere and concluded that whilst there may be some suggestions of a right to informational privacy there are no signs that the courts are eager to recognise a general constitutional common law right to privacy.[330] Moreover, even if they were willing to recognise such a right, it is likely that those rights would be more limited and less potent than their Article 8 ECHR counterpart.[331] Since then, the matter has been considered by the Scottish courts in the context of the use of off-duty police officers' Whatsapp messages. The messages in question were racist, sexist, ablist, homophobic and antisemitic in tone and were used as evidence in misconduct proceedings. The police officers unsuccessfully argued that this violated both their common law right to privacy and Article 8 ECHR. A preliminary question for the court during those proceedings was whether the common law of Scotland recognised a right of privacy.[332] Having contemplated this question, Lord Bannatyne opined in the Outer House that a common law right to privacy has developed in English law and thus stated that he considered that 'there is a nascent recognition of a common law right of privacy in the case law'.[333] In this respect he observed that 'if [the right] does not exist in Scots common law a very odd conclusion is reached that Scottish and English law in relation to this fundamental matter are entirely different'.[334] Lord Bannatyne's conclusion on the common law right was discussed on appeal where Lady Dorrian noted that it was 'unfortunate' that this issue had not been the subject of a cross appeal as this meant that 'the issue was not a live one for determination'.[335] She went on to observe that while she was unwilling to decide the matter without having the benefit of detailed submissions, she could not let the Lord Ordinary's conclusions on the matter pass without comment.[336] Considering the matter further, she concluded in respect of the common law in England that whilst '[t]here is no doubt that the law in this area continues to evolve, and that the scope of protection given to private information has

[329] See Hughes (n 15). [330] Ibid, pp.101–105. [331] Ibid, pp.107–112.

[332] *BC and others* v. *Chief Constable of the Police Service of Scotland and others* [2019] CSOH 48 at [8].

[333] Ibid at [124]. [334] Ibid at [116].

[335] *BC and* others v. *Iain Livingstone QPM, Chief Constable of the Police Service of Scotland and others* [2020] CSIH 61 at [75].

[336] Ibid at [75].

expanded considerably [she begged] leave to doubt that it has reached the absolute stage suggested by the Lord Ordinary'.[337]

10.4 CONCLUSION

In this chapter, we have seen how both the ECtHR and our domestic courts have developed the right to privacy. This chapter has therefore offered insight into the evolving nature of the Convention and the role of positive obligations. It raises questions about who and what the Convention is for, as whilst the right to privacy is pertinent to everyone, the claimants and applicants in many of these cases are oftentimes not those that are typically regarded as human rights victims. The development of obligations in this context might therefore be regarded as paradoxical when considered alongside the limits of the Convention in other contexts, such as the denial of socio-economic rights. An alternative view, however, is that the recognition of the right to privacy is entirely unrelated to the limits of other rights and that we all benefit from the recognition of a right to privacy. Thus, while it is inevitable that wealthier, high-profile, applicants will be the ones that have the resources to litigate, this establishes the legal principles that apply to everyone. We might also consider whether doctrines such as public figure status obfuscate the importance of the right to privacy, the vulnerability that a loss of privacy can entail and the universality of rights.[338] These questions as well as the challenges associated with identifying when Article 8 ECHR is applicable and when there is a reasonable expectation of privacy mean that there are ongoing conceptual challenges. Given the difficulties in identifying what is private, and the changing nature of society and technology, it is likely that there will be further questions that arise in this respect.

Once the right is engaged, then the criteria for balancing the competing rights appears to be fairly settled. The ECtHR is also willing to give Contracting States a wide margin of appreciation in striking that balance. We will consider in subsequent chapters other contexts in which rights conflict, and it is worth contemplating whether the ECtHR accords, and whether it should accord an equally wide margin of appreciation in those contexts, or whether distinct issues arise, which require a different approach. In any event, in this context, the breadth of the margin of appreciation afforded has not diminished calls for domestic reform, which perhaps illustrates the complexity of the challenges to the HRA and the ECtHR, or perhaps the nature of the voices that dominate the debate.

[337] Ibid at [86]. [338] Hughes (n 128).

11 Hate Speech

CONTENTS

11.1 INTRODUCTION

Article 10 of the ECHR protects the right to freedom of expression, but this right is not absolute, and it is well established that States can impose restrictions on expression, which may include prohibiting hate speech. Given the post-war origins of the ECHR it is perhaps not surprising that the Convention has been interpreted in ways that allow Contracting States to intervene in respect of expression that advocates violence or denies the Holocaust,[1] as well as expression that incites hatred.[2] There is, however, no definition of 'hate speech' in the Convention jurisprudence,[3] and while this arguably reflects and accommodates the context-specific nature of hate speech, the latitude that this

[1] Discussed at Sections 11.4.1–11.4.3.
[2] Discussed at Section 11.4.4.
[3] Discussed at Section 11.3.1.

may afford to States gives rise to concerns about the implications for democracy. Moreover, even assuming that States are acting in good faith, it is difficult to know where lines should be drawn between competing rights and interests and what role human rights law should play in this context.

We thus begin this chapter by considering the literature on freedom of expression and hate speech and why using law to tackle hate speech is contested. Following which we turn to the ECHR where we examine the way in which hate speech sits at the interface between several Convention rights, namely Articles 8, 10, 14 and 17 ECHR. We see that the initial question for the ECtHR was not *whether* States should prohibit hate speech, and if so *when* and *how*, but rather whether the restrictions that States had elected to impose were *justified* interferences with freedom of expression. The applicants (and thus victims) in those cases were therefore not those who were the target of hate speech, but rather those whose expression had been restricted. Consequently, the early hate speech case law was developed under Articles 10 and 17 ECHR. A more recent development has been the recognition of positive obligations under Articles 8 and 14 ECHR; obligations which require States to act in respect of hate speech. Although the existence of these obligations is not in doubt they are at something of an embryonic stage in the case law. These obligations raise several challenges, one of which concerns the absence of a definition of 'hate speech', as put simply it becomes more pressing to know what constitutes 'hate speech' if States are obliged to address it. We also need to know when the obligations are triggered as well as what they require from the State. This chapter examines the interlocking obligations and Convention rights and reflects upon the ways in which the hate speech jurisprudence might develop in the future.

The latter part of the chapter examines domestic law. It observes that unlike the right to privacy, which was the focus of the previous chapter, domestic hate speech laws existed long before the Human Rights Act 1998 (HRA) was enacted. Following the enactment of s.3 HRA, those provisions must be interpreted, as far as it is possible to do so, in line with the Convention rights; while s.6 HRA requires public authorities to act compatibly with the Convention rights. The parameters and operation of hate speech laws and policies have come under immense scrutiny in recent years in the context of alleged 'culture wars' in the UK, particularly following the rise of social media. Many of the domestic provisions have also been the subject of extensive review by the Law Commission, which considered amongst other things whether the provisions meet contemporary needs and whether they are compatible with Convention obligations.[4] This resulted in some significant proposals for reform, many of which are still pending at the time of writing.

[4] Law Commission, *Hate Crime Laws: Final Report*, HC 942, Law Com No 402 and Law Commission, *Modernising Communications Offences: A Final Report*, HC 547, Law Com 399, 20/07/2021.

11.2 ARGUMENTS FOR AND AGAINST HATE SPEECH RESTRICTIONS

There is a wealth of literature in respect of hate speech prohibitions exhibiting differences of opinion as to, on the one hand, the importance of freedom of expression and the extent to which it is threatened by hate speech laws; and on the other, the role of hate speech prohibitions in securing equality and dignity. If we consider, first, the literature on freedom of expression we see that a number of rationales are advanced as to the importance of freedom of expression and the dangers of restricting expression.[5] Eric Barendt in his classic book *Freedom of Speech* highlights four core arguments: (i) the importance of discovering truth; (ii) self-fulfilment; (iii) citizen participation in a democracy; and (iv) suspicion of government.[6] The first of those, the idea that unrestricted expression is vital to the pursuit of truth, is commonly attributed to John Stuart Mill,[7] but has also been traced back to Milton.[8] There are different versions of the truth thesis but the basic premise is that by allowing all possible views to be aired we are able to evaluate and determine what is true and what is false such that the truth will emerge. This view is reflected in the 'marketplace of ideas' metaphor famously articulated in *Abrams* v. *US* by Holmes J, who stated that 'the best test of truth is the power of the thought to get itself accepted in the competition of the market'.[9] There are, however, a number of criticisms of the truth thesis. Sticking with the marketplace of ideas metaphor, one of the objections to unrestricted expression is that the marketplace of ideas is susceptible to market failure, as false speech may flood the market, or powerful voices may capture the market and squeeze out others.

[5] For a good overview of free speech theory, see Part I of Adrienne Stone and Frederick Schauer (eds), *The Oxford Handbook of Freedom of Speech* (Oxford University Press, 2021); Eric Barendt, *Freedom of Speech* (2nd ed) (Oxford University Press, 2007), ch.1; and Jeffrey W. Howard, 'Freedom of Speech', in Edward N. Zalta and Uri Nodelman (eds), *The Stanford Encyclopedia of Philosophy* (Spring 2024 Edition), https://plato.stanford.edu/archives/spr2024/entries/freedom-speech/.

[6] Barendt (n 5). See also, Eric Heinze, 'Viewpoint Absolutism and Hate Speech' (2006) 69(4) MLR 489, 552–555 in which Heinze suggests the following taxonomy of defences of free speech: marketplace theories; peacekeeping; deontological theories; civic republicanism and what he terms coherency theory.

[7] J. S. Mill, *On Liberty* (1859) reprinted (Cambridge University Press, 2012).

[8] John Milton, *Areopagitica: A Speech for the Liberty of Unlicensed Printing* (1644) reprinted in John Milton *Areopagitica and Other Writings* (Penguin Classics, 2014). Eric Barendt observes the role of Milton in the truth thesis in *Freedom of Speech* (n 5), p.7.

[9] Holmes J, in *Abrams* v. *US*, 250 US 616, 630–631 (1919): 'But when men have realized that time has upset many fighting faiths, they may come to believe even more than they believe the very foundations of their own conduct that the ultimate good desired is better reached by free trade in ideas – that the best test of truth is the power of the thought to get itself accepted in the competition of the market, and that truth is the only ground upon which their wishes safely can be carried out.'

This feels particularly relevant in an era of fake news and deep fakes, but it is not unique to the digital era. Indeed it is frequently emphasised in the literature that the Nazis came to power in Germany in the 1930s even though there had been relatively free political discourse during the 1920s.[10] A second objection to the truth thesis states that as truthful expression can be harmful we may not wish to prioritise 'truth' (whatever 'truth' means) over all other values. Consequently, as Barendt explains, while Mill's thesis assumes that 'the publication of a possibly true statement is the highest possible good ... there are many situations where legal systems prefer to protect other values, and that choice seems defensible'.[11]

Other free speech theorists argue that freedom of expression is essential to individual self-development and self-fulfilment.[12] They argue that limiting freedom of expression restricts our personal growth and that we should resist allowing the State to have this power over us. Critics of this argument contend that there are many other rights that are equally important for self-development and self-fulfilment, some of which may clash with freedom of expression, and some of which may require the State's involvement, for example by providing education.[13] Critics thus challenge theories of freedom of expression which emphasise the importance of freedom of expression in fostering self-development and self-fulfilment over and above those other rights and interests.[14]

Another important aspect of the free speech literature is the relationship between freedom of expression and democracy. There are several versions of the democracy thesis, one of which is the idea of self-governance, namely that restrictions on expression limit the extent to which the electorate is informed and thus impinge upon our capacity to govern ourselves.[15] Other versions of the democracy thesis focus on the dangers of allowing States to regulate expression;[16] the concern here is that we cannot trust States to decide what can and cannot be said as allowing them to do this leaves us vulnerable to totalitarianism. Critics counterargue that we allow States to regulate other aspects of life and so they query why we should distrust States more in this context than in others.[17] A further version of the democratic account posits

[10] Barendt (n 5), p.9. For a different perspective, see Heinze (n 6), p.548 who suggests that by holding up the transition of Weimar Germany into fascism as an example of freedom run amok, we risk promoting a superficial and revisionist history, according to which Nazism came about as a result of 'too much' freedom.

[11] Barendt (n 5), p.7.

[12] Thomas Scanlon, 'A Theory of Freedom of Expression' (1972) 1(2) Philosophy & Public Affairs 204–226. See discussion in Barendt (n 5), p.13 and in Stanford Encyclopedia (n 5).

[13] Barendt (n 5), p.13. [14] Ibid.

[15] Alexander Meiklejohn, *Free Speech and Its Relation to Self-Government* (Harper Bros, 1948). For discussion, see Barendt (n 5), p.18.

[16] Frederick Schauer, *Free Speech: A Philosophical Enquiry* (Cambridge University Press, 1982).

[17] Barendt (n 5), p.22.

that public discourse 'must be safeguarded not only as an *individual right*, but as an essential *attribute of democratic citizenship*'.[18] Heinze thus argues that a State cannot be a democracy without guaranteeing the citizen's prerogative of expression within public discourse.[19]

Finally, it is important to note that values of tolerance and pluralism are sometimes advanced to oppose restrictions on expression. The liberal argument here is that we must respect each other's right to self-expression, and this is especially important if we dislike the way that the right is being exercised.[20] Scholars of this persuasion also argue that prohibiting hate speech 'might encourage people to believe the truth of the suppressed speech, which they would otherwise ignore or reject' if it were openly expressed.[21] They thus caution that it is 'dangerous to drive unpleasant ideas underground, for they may surface later in a more dangerous form'.[22] Conversely, critics argue that allowing hate speech does not encourage tolerance, but instead promulgates hatred and incites violence.

Having contemplated the main arguments advanced against restrictions on freedom of expression it is important to note that a dominant influence in free speech theory is the United States First Amendment, which provides strong constitutional protection to freedom of speech. This is different from the ECHR where Article 10 ECHR is a qualified right and where there is no doubt that tackling hate speech is one of the circumstances in which States may be able to restrict expression. Yet, the very fact that freedom of expression is one of several competing rights within the Convention framework means that we must consider why freedom of expression is important and what is lost when it is restricted. In this respect it is important to observe that the arguments that we have encountered from the free speech literature, namely truth, autonomy, democracy and tolerance, also appear in the way in which the ECtHR has articulated the values underpinning Article 10 ECHR. This can be seen in the following extract from the ECtHR's landmark judgment in *Handyside* v. *the United Kingdom*:

> Freedom of expression constitutes one of the essential foundations of ... a [democratic] society, one of the basic conditions for its progress and for the development of every man. Subject to paragraph 2 of Article 10, it is applicable not only to 'information' or 'ideas' that are favourably received or regarded as inoffensive or as a matter

[18] Eric Heinze, *Hate Speech and Democratic Citizenship* (Oxford University Press, 2016), p.4. See also Eric Heinze, *The Most Human Right: Why Free Speech Is Everything* (MIT Press, 2022) in which he argues that free speech is the fundamental right without which the concept of a right does not make sense.

[19] Heinze, *Hate Speech and Democratic Citizenship*, ibid, p.5.

[20] Lee Bollinger, *The Tolerant Society: Freedom of Speech and Extremist Speech in America* (Oxford University Press, 1986). For discussion, see Barendt (n 5), pp.30–31.

[21] Barendt (n 5), p.9. [22] Ibid.

of indifference, but also to those that offend, shock or disturb the State or any sector of the population. Such are the demands of that pluralism, tolerance and broadmindedness without which there is no 'democratic society'.[23]

Having considered the literature on freedom of expression, we now turn to the equality and dignity arguments advanced in respect of hate speech laws, observing that these values are invoked by both those who support, and those who oppose, hate speech restrictions. Scholars that oppose hate speech restrictions for reasons of equality include Ronald Dworkin who argued against hate speech laws on the basis that they undermine the legitimacy of other equality provisions.[24] He argued that we must protect 'women, homosexuals and minority groups from specific and damaging consequences of sexism, intolerance and racism' and that to do this 'we must not try to intervene further upstream by forbidding any expression of the attitudes or prejudices that we think nourish such unfairness or inequality'.[25] His reasoning was that if we want to have laws protecting equality, we need to allow people to express their views and opposition to those laws.[26] Consequently, he believed that if we 'intervene too soon in the process through which collective opinion is formed, we spoil the only democratic justification we have for insisting that everyone obey these laws, even those who hate and resent them'.[27] James Weinstein shares this view and argues that 'in some instances upstream restrictions on hate speech are so severe that they not only diminish but can potentially annihilate the legitimacy of downstream antidiscrimination laws'.[28]

Others, such as Jeremy Waldron, reject Dworkin and Weinstein's position on the relationship between equality and hate speech.[29] Waldron argues that the legitimacy argument advanced by Weinstein and Dworkin is flawed and he is sceptical as to both what 'legitimacy' means in this context, and the alleged relationship between hate speech laws and equality laws.[30] In contemplating what democracy needs, he states that:

in order to sustain a healthy working democracy, a society needs social peace and it is entitled to the assistance of citizens in maintaining that peace – or at least their assistance in not trying to disrupt it. Democracy requires trust among those of

[23] *Handyside* v. *the United Kingdom,* A 24 1979-80 1 EHRR 737 at [45].

[24] Ronald Dworkin, 'Foreword' in Ivan Hare and James Weinstein (eds), *Extreme Speech and Democracy* (Oxford University Press, 2009), p.viii.

[25] Ibid. See also James Weinstein's more detailed articulation of the legitimacy argument in James Weinstein, 'Hate Speech Bans, Democracy, and Political Legitimacy' (2017) 32 Constitutional Commentary 465.

[26] Dworkin (n 24). [27] Ibid. [28] Ibid, p.532.

[29] Jeremy Waldron, *The Harm in Hate Speech* (Harvard University Press, 2012).

[30] Jeremy Waldron, 'The Conditions of Legitimacy: A Response to James Weinstein' (2017) 32 Constitutional Commentary 697.

different views and different communities, and stirring up hatred is a way of undermining that trust.[31]

Waldron also denounces the liberal notion 'that I dislike what you say but I tolerate your right to say it' as a weak gesture advanced by those not affected by such speech.[32] He argues that we should instead think about what it is like to live in a society in which your position is constantly undermined, where you see racist signs every day. The voices and experiences of those targeted by hate speech have long been the focus of critical race theory. Scholars such as Mari Matsuda centre victims' experiences in arguing that racist hate messages cause real harm to real people, and legal systems that offer no redress for that perpetuate racism.[33] Matsuda thus argues that 'tolerance of hate speech is not tolerance borne by the community at large. Rather, it is a psychic tax imposed on those least able to pay.'[34] Others emphasise the ways in which hate speech silences those that are the target of such expression, thus advancing a *free speech* argument for restrictions on hate speech.[35]

It is important to note that not all aspects of the hate speech debate stem from differences of opinion as to whether the expression is morally repugnant.[36] On the contrary much of the dispute concerns how best to tackle hateful expression, as while some believe that the State should prohibit it (often using criminal law) others are of the opinion that we should tackle it in other ways e.g. through counter-speech and education.[37] In this vein some scholars query whether hate speech laws are effective in tackling the harms that they purport to address.[38] For example, C. E. Baker questioned whether

[31] Ibid, p.713. [32] Waldron (n 30), pp.3–4.

[33] Mari Matsuda, 'Public Responses to Racist Speech: Considering the Victim's Story' (1989) **87** Michigan Law Review 87, 2320–2381.

[34] Ibid, p.2323.

[35] See Caroline West, 'Words That Silence? Freedom of Expression and Racist Hate Speech in Speech' in Ishani Maitra and Mary Kate McGowan (eds), *Speech and Harm: Controversies over Free Speech* (OUP, 2012), as also discussed in Alon Harol, 'Hate Speech' in Stone and Schauer (eds) (n 5).

[36] Thomas Brudholm and Birgitte Schepelern Johansen (eds), *Hate, Politics, Law: Critical Perspective on Combatting Hate* (OUP, 2018).

[37] Alexander Brown, *Hate Speech Law: A Philosophical Examination* (Routledge, 2015); Judith Butler, *Excitable Speech: A Politics of the Performative* (Routledge, 1997); Richard Delgado and Jean Stefancic, *Understanding Words That Wound* (Westview Press, 2004); Hare and Weinstein (eds) (n 24); Heinze (n 18); Michael Herz and Peter Molnar (eds), *The Content and Context of Hate Speech: Rethinking Regulation and Responses* (Cambridge University Press, 2012); Maitra and McGowan (eds) (n 35); Matsuda (n 33); Alexander Tsesis, *Destructive Messages: How Hate Speech Paves the Way for Harmful Social Movements* (New York University Press, 2002); Waldron (n 29).

[38] In contemplating the effectiveness of counter-speech, Anjalee de Silva and Andrew Kenyon argue that it is important to also consider the positive dimensions of freedom of speech and not simply focus on concerns over State regulation, Anjalee de Silva and Andrew Kenyon,

there is any empirical evidence to support the argument that hate speech laws aid in preventing genocide.[39] He argued that allowing hate speech to be expressed is the only way to understand the real evil of it, whereas forcing it underground obscures its extent, antagonises racists, shifts their focus from politics to violence and diverts political attention away from more meaningful responses. Meanwhile, Eric Barendt suggests that scholars such as Waldron fail to adequately define the 'harm' of hate speech, in particular, whether hate speech *causes* harm or whether hate speech itself *constitutes* harm.[40] In this regard, he suggests that Waldron's approach is premised upon a general apprehension of the effects of hate speech, rather than empirical evidence. A converse view emerges from scholars such as Katherine Gelber and Luke McNamara who argue that their empirical findings indicate a close alignment between the experiences of victims of hate speech and the harms identified in the literature, which include negative stereotyping, normalising of racism, subordination, silencing, fear, victimisation, emotional symptoms, restrictions on freedom, lowering of self-esteem, maintenance of power imbalances, and undermining of human dignity.[41]

A different objection to hate speech prohibitions emerges from Eric Heinze, who, while recognising that hate speech is 'painful', suggests that whether it is harmful is not something which remains constant in nature but is dependent upon the political and social context.[42] According to Heinze hate speech laws are flawed as they involve deep contradictions that promote hypocrisy and discrimination and undermine the values of equality that they purport to promote.[43] In this respect he argues that the impact of hate speech prohibitions is that '[t]hey create two tiers, dividing society into those who may and those who may not, by law, be insulted, pitting one against the other in an unseembly battle of more-victim-than-thou'.[44] Consequently, he argues that hate speech restrictions which purport to combat discrimination 'tacitly promote it'.[45]

We have observed that both proponents and opponents of hate speech prohibitions alert us to harms that may follow from regulating or not regulating expression. Harol opposes these types of 'speculative empirical conjectures'.[46] He argues that those who support hate speech restrictions speculate as to the possible psychological effects and the prospect of violence, while those that oppose hate speech restrictions speculate as to the likelihood that political

'Countering Hate Speech in Context: Positive Freedom of Speech' (2022) **14**(1) Journal of Media Law 97, 98.

[39] C. Edwin Baker, *Human Liberty and Freedom of Speech* (Oxford University Press, 1993).

[40] Barendt (n 5).

[41] Katherine Gelber and Luke McNamara, 'Evidencing the Harms of Hate Speech' (2016) Social Identities **324**.

[42] Heinze (2016) (n 18), p.8. [43] Ibid. [44] Heinze (n 6), pp.567–568. [45] Ibid, p.555.

[46] Harol (n 35).

institutions will abuse power or regulate inappropriately.[47] He claims that we should move beyond this and focus upon foundational convictions:

> The debate concerning hate speech hinges, therefore, on fundamental disagreements concerning the nature of human beings, their ability to resist social pressures, and the degree of protection they need in order to preserve their dignity. It is ultimately these conflicting foundational premises rather than empirical conjectures which should dictate whether and how much to regulate hate speech.[48]

Yet, one might push back on at least one aspect of this by highlighting that the lived experiences of those writing within critical race theory and the voices of those represented in such scholarship are not speculative.

11.3 THE STRUCTURE OF THE ECHR FRAMEWORK

11.3.1 No Definition of Hate Speech in the ECHR

Although the ECtHR is increasingly drawing upon the concept of 'hate speech', there is, as the Grand Chamber noted in *Sanchez* v. *France*, 'no universal definition of "hate speech"' and there is no definition of hate speech within the ECHR case law.[49] Consequently, while inciting violence against others or denying the Holocaust are commonly designated 'hate speech', it is evident that 'hate speech' is broader than this. In this respect the ECtHR has opined:

> Inciting hatred does not therefore necessarily involve an explicit call for an act of violence, or other criminal acts. Attacks on persons committed by insulting, holding up to ridicule or slandering specific groups of the population can be sufficient for the authorities to favour combating xenophobic or otherwise discriminatory speech in the face of freedom of expression exercised in an irresponsible manner.[50]

The ECtHR is also attuned to the insidious nature of hate speech:

> Hate speech is not always openly presented as such. It may take various forms, not only through patently aggressive and insulting remarks that wilfully undermine the values of tolerance, social peace and non-discrimination ... but also implicit

[47] Ibid. [48] Ibid, p.476.

[49] *Sanchez* v. *France* [GC], App. No. 45581/1, 15/05/2023 at [169]. Examples of definitions of hate speech can be seen in Recommendation R (97) 20 of the Council of Europe's Committee of Ministers on hate speech, adopted on 30 October 1997; Council of Europe Recommendation CM/Rec(2022)16 on Combating Hate Speech, adopted on 20 May 2022; European Commission against Racism and Intolerance's General Policy Recommendation no. 15 on combating hate speech, adopted on 8 December 2015; UN Committee on Eliminating Racist Discrimination General Recommendation no. 35 of 26 September 2013, on combating racist hate speech.

[50] *Ibragim Ibragimov* v. *Russia*, App. Nos. 1413/08 and 28621/11, 28/08/2018 at [94]. See also, *Atamanchuk* v. *Russia*, App. No. 4493/11, 11/02/2020.

statements which, even if expressed guardedly or in a hypothetical form ... prove equally as hateful.[51]

The ECtHR is also aware that whether expression amounts to hate speech is context specific. Factors include: the content of the speech; the political and social context at the time the speech was made; the intention of the speaker; the speaker's role and status in society; the form of its dissemination; the manner in which the statements are made, and their capacity – directly or indirectly – to lead to harmful consequences, including imminence; the nature and size of the audience; the characteristics of the targeted group, for instance its size, its degree of homogeneity, its particular vulnerability or history of stigmatisation, and its position vis-à-vis society as a whole.[52] In respect of the latter the ECtHR has opined that it recognises the 'utmost importance' of 'combating racial discrimination in all its forms and manifestations',[53] while also acknowledging that 'discrimination based on sexual orientation is as serious as discrimination based on "race, origin or colour"'.[54] The concept of hate speech is therefore flexible and there is no hierarchy of hate speech based upon whom it targets. Yet, while this flexibility accords with the social reality of hate speech, it also accords greater latitude to States, which gives rise to concerns about the ramifications for freedom of expression.

11.3.2 Is Hate Speech 'Expression' for the Purposes of Article 10(1) ECHR?

Article 10 ECHR, the right to freedom of expression, is a qualified right. In line with the other qualified rights, Article 10(1) ECHR sets out the scope of the right, and Article 10(2) ECHR establishes the circumstances in which the State can justify interfering with the right. The ECtHR adopts a broad approach to what constitutes 'expression' for the purposes of Article 10(1) ECHR,[55] which covers not only speech and written expression, but also the display of flags or symbols,[56] and cartoons.[57] It includes a right to receive, as well as impart,

[51] *Sanchez* v. *France* (n 49) at [157].

[52] The Council of Europe's Explanatory Memorandum which accompanied its 2022 Recommendation to States on combatting hate speech summarises the factors that the ECtHR has considered in the case law. See also, *Sanchez* v. *France* (n 49) at [154] citing *Erkizia Almandoz* v. *Spain*, App. No. 5869/17, 22/06/2021 at [40]–[41].

[53] *Jersild* v. *Denmark* (1995) 19 EHRR 1.

[54] *Lenis* v. *Greece* (dec.), App. No. 47833/20, 27/06/2023.

[55] For discussion of the breadth of Article 10 and a wide range of the accompanying case law, see David Harris, Michael O'Boyle, Ed Bates and Carla M. Buckley, *Law of the European Convention on Human Rights* (Oxford University Press, 2023), ch.13. See also, the European Court of Human Rights, *Guide on Article 10 of the European Convention on Human Rights* (21 August 2022).

[56] *Fáber* v. *Hungary*, App. No. 40721/08, 24/07/2012.

[57] *Leroy* v. *France*, App. No. 36109/03, 02/10/2008.

information and ideas.[58] The ECtHR has also frequently stated that Article 10 ECHR protects expression which offends, shocks or disturbs, on the basis that this is a necessary part of the demands of 'pluralism, tolerance and broadmindedness without which there is no democratic society'.[59] Although, the extent to which the ECtHR protects such expression is questioned by scholars such as Jacob Mchangama and Natalie Alkiviadou who argue that the hate speech jurisprudence undermines the claim that Article 10 ECHR protects offensive, shocking or disturbing expression.[60]

11.3.3 When Is Hate Speech Excluded from Article 10 by Article 17 ECHR?

It is certainly true that at least some offensive, shocking and disturbing expression falls outside the ambit of Article 10 ECHR due to the application of Article 17 ECHR, the abuse of rights provision.[61] Article 17 ECHR provides that applicants cannot rely upon Convention rights to engage in activities aimed at destruction of the rights and freedoms provided for by the Convention. Consequently, in cases where Article 17 ECHR applies, the impugned expression falls outside the scope of Article 10 ECHR, the application will be declared inadmissible and there will be no requirement for the State to demonstrate that the legal safeguards embedded in Article 10(2) ECHR are met. The ECtHR has applied Article 17 ECHR to holocaust denial,[62] antisemitic remarks,[63] other forms of racial and religious hatred,[64] incitement of terrorism and violence,[65] idolatry of Nazism[66] and homophobic hate speech.[67] It is important to emphasise, however, that not *all* hate speech

[58] This was relevant in *Lowes* v. *the United Kingdom*, App. No. 13214/87, 09/12/1988 where the applicant, a prisoner, argued that his Article 10 ECHR right was violated when the prison authorities refused to allow him to receive an antisemitic publication. The Commission found that this was an interference with his right to receive information, but it was justified under Article 10(2) ECHR.

[59] *Handyside* v. *the United Kingdom* (n 23) at [49].

[60] Jacob Mchangama and Natalie Alkiviadou, 'Hate Speech and the European Court of Human Rights: Whatever Happened to the Right to Offend, Shock or Disturb' (2021) 21(4) HRLR 1008.

[61] On Article 17 ECHR, see the European Court of Human Rights, *Guide on Article 17 of the European Convention on Human Rights* (29 February 2024) and Harris et al. (n 55), pp.608–616 and 847–850.

[62] *Garaudy* v. *France*, App. No. 65831/01, 24/06/2003; *Witzsch* v. *Germany*, App. No. 7485/03, 13/12/2005; *M'Bala M'Bala* v. *France*, App. No. 25239/13, 20/10/2015.

[63] *Pavel Ivanov* v. *Russia*, App. No. 35222/04, 20/02/2007.

[64] *Glimmerveen and Haqenbeek* v. *the Netherlands* (1982) 4 EHRR 260, *Norwood* v. *the United Kingdom* (2004) 40 EHRR SE 111, *Belkacem* v. *Belgium*, App. No. 34367/14, 27/06/2017.

[65] *Roj TV A/S* v. *Denmark* (2018) 67 EHRR SE8.

[66] *B.H, M.W., H.P. and G.K.* v. *Austria* (dec.), App. No. 12774/87, 12/10/1989; *Nachtmann* v. *Austria* (dec.), App. No. 36773/97, 09/09/1998; *Schimanek* v. *Austria* (dec.), App. No. 32307/96, 01/02/2000.

[67] *Lenis* v. *Greece* (n 54).

(and not all of the aforementioned *types* of hate speech) are excluded via Article 17 ECHR.[68] Consequently, as the dissenting judges in the Grand Chamber in *Perinçek* v. *Switzerland* observed, a 'characteristic aspect of the Strasbourg approaches to Article 17 ECHR is that the Court has kept its options open. There is more than one tool in the box, to be used as the need is seen to arise in an individual case.'[69] One of the criticisms levelled at the ECtHR is thus that its approach to Article 17 ECHR is inconsistent and its reasoning is opaque.[70] In this respect it is noteworthy that the Council of Europe Recommendation to States on Combatting Hate Speech provides that States should 'pay due attention to the importance of clarifying *which types of expression fall outside* of the protection provided by freedom of expression'.[71]

Although there is uncertainty as to when the ECtHR will use Article 10 ECHR and when it will use Article 17 ECHR, there are several cases in which the ECtHR has sought to explain when Article 17 ECHR is triggered. An important case in this respect is the Grand Chamber's judgment in *Perinçek* v. *Switzerland* in which it articulated the threshold for Article 17 ECHR.[72]

The applicant in *Perinçek* (who was the chairman of the Turkish Workers' Party) had made a number of statements at various conferences during which he publicly denied that there had been any genocide of the Armenian people by the Ottoman Empire. Following his statements the Switzerland–Armenia Association lodged a criminal complaint against the applicant on account of his comments and the applicant was ordered to pay a fine and compensation. *Perinçek* thus lodged an application with the ECtHR in which he argued that these measures violated Article 10 ECHR.

Perinçek was initially considered by a Chamber of the Court which held by five votes to two that there had been a violation of Article 10 ECHR.[73] It was

[68] See Sections 11.4.1–11.4.4.

[69] *Perinçek* v. *Switzerland* [GC] (2016) 63 EHRR 6, Additional dissenting opinion of Judge Silvis, joined by Judges Casadevall, Berro and Kuris at [8].

[70] For analysis of the operation of Article 17 ECHR, see David Keane, 'Attacking Hate Speech under Article 17 of the European Convention on Human Rights' (2007) **25**(4) NQHR 641; Hannes Cannie and Dirk Voorhoof, 'The Abuse Clause and Freedom of Expression in the European Human Rights Convention: An Added Value for Democracy and Human Rights Protection?' (2011) **29**(1) NQHR 54; Antoine Buyse, 'Dangerous Expressions: The ECHR, Violence and Free Speech' (2014) **63**(2) ICLQ 491; Ulrich Wagrandl, 'The Prohibition to Abuse One's Human Rights: A Theory' (2019) **25**(6) European Law Journal 577.

[71] Council of Europe Recommendation CM/Rec(2022)16 of the Committee of Ministers to member States on combating hate speech (Adopted by the Committee of Ministers on 20 May 2022 at the 132nd Session of the Committee of Ministers), Recommendation 6(a) (emphasis added).

[72] *Perinçek* v. *Switzerland* [GC] (n 69).

[73] *Perinçek* v. *Switzerland* [Chamber], App. No. 27510/08, 16/12/2013. In their joint partly dissenting opinion, Judges Vučinić and Pinto de Albuquerque stated that they were of the view that the criminalisation of genocide denial and the punishment of the applicant for

then referred to the Grand Chamber at the Swiss Government's request and one of the issues that the Grand Chamber had to consider was whether Article 17 ECHR precluded the applicant from relying on Article 10 ECHR. Reflecting on the operation of Article 17 ECHR the Grand Chamber observed that Article 17 ECHR is 'only applicable on an exceptional basis and in extreme cases' and that 'it should only be resorted to if it is immediately clear that the impugned statements sought to deflect [Article 10 ECHR] from its real purpose by employing the right to freedom of expression for ends clearly contrary to the values of the Convention'.[74] In this regard it went on to state that the 'decisive point under Article 17' ECHR is 'whether the applicant's statements sought to stir up hatred or violence, *and* whether by making them he attempted to rely on the Convention to engage in an activity or perform acts aimed at the destruction of the rights and freedoms laid down in it'.[75] Applying this to facts it determined that, as it was not immediately clear that the decisive point was met, the question of whether Article 17 ECHR applied should be joined to the merits of the complaint under Article 10 ECHR.[76] At the merits stage (for reasons discussed further below) it found that there were no grounds for applying Article 17 ECHR and that there had been a breach of Article 10 ECHR.[77]

Perinçek thus established a high threshold for the applicability of Article 17 ECHR as the State must establish: (i) that the applicant's statements sought to stir up hatred or violence; and (ii) that in making those statements the applicant attempted to rely on the Convention to engage in an activity or perform acts aimed at the destruction of the rights and freedoms laid down in the Convention. This approach has largely been adopted by the ECtHR in the subsequent case law, albeit that some of the jurisprudence suggests that the two elements identified in *Perinçek* are not cumulative requirements.

A potential loosening up of the requirements can be seen in *Pastörs* v. *Germany* where the ECtHR stated (without suggesting that it was amending *Perinçek*) that Article 17 ECHR is applicable where *either* of the two elements is present.[78] The applicant in *Pastörs* was an MP who had given a speech in Parliament in which he denied the Holocaust, following which his inviolability from prosecution was revoked and he was convicted of offences of violating the memory of the dead and defamation. In his application to the ECtHR Pastörs argued that his conviction violated Article 10 ECHR, whilst Germany counter-argued that Article 17 ECHR applied.[79] In contemplating the applicability of Article 17 ECHR, the ECtHR cited *Perinçek* and reiterated:

denial of the Armenian genocide, in strict accordance with the law in force in the respondent State, did not breach Article 10 ECHR.

[74] *Perinçek* v. *Switzerland* (n 69) at [114]. [75] Ibid at [114]–[115] (emphasis added).

[76] Ibid at [115]. [77] Ibid at [281]–[282].

[78] *Pastörs* v. *Germany*, App. No. 55225/14, 03/10/2019 at [37]. [79] Ibid at [34].

> that Article 17 is only applicable on an exceptional basis and in extreme cases and should, in cases concerning Article 10 of the Convention, only be resorted to if it is immediately clear that the impugned statements sought to deflect this Article from its real purpose by employing the right to freedom of expression for ends clearly contrary to the values of the Convention.[80]

It went on, however, to state that:

> The decisive point when assessing whether statements, verbal or non-verbal, are removed from the protection of Article 10 by Article 17, is whether those statements are directed against the Convention's underlying values, for example by stirring up hatred or violence, *or* whether by making the statement, the author attempted to rely on the Convention to engage in an activity or perform acts aimed at the destruction of the rights and freedoms laid down in it.[81]

Subsequent cases suggest (contrary to what was set out in *Perinçek*) that Article 17 ECHR is applicable when either of the two elements is present.[82]

A further point that emerges from *Pastörs* v. *Germany* is the extent to which the application of Article 17 ECHR is context-specific. Although Holocaust denial is one of the contexts in which the ECtHR has been willing to deploy Article 17 ECHR, in *Pastörs* the ECtHR emphasised that even in this context 'whether the Court applies Article 17 directly ... or instead finds Article 10 applicable ... is a decision taken on a case-by-case basis and will depend on all the circumstances of each individual case'.[83] The need for a context-sensitive approach is evident from the facts of *Pastörs* in which aspects of the case pulled in opposite directions. These tensions are captured in the following reflections by the ECtHR:

> In the present case the Court considers, on the one hand, that the applicant's statements showed his disdain towards the victims of the Holocaust, which speaks in favour of the incompatibility *ratione materiae* of the complaint with the provisions of the Convention ... On the other hand, it has regard to the fact that the statement was made by a Member of Parliament during a Parliamentary session, such that it could warrant an elevated level of protection and any interference with it would warrant the closest scrutiny on the part of the Court.[84]

The Court was evidently torn in *Pastörs* between, on the one hand the strong protection that Article 10 ECHR typically affords to political speech,[85]

[80] Ibid at [37]. [81] Ibid at [37] (emphasis added).

[82] See *Wojczuk* v. *Poland*, App. No. 52969/13, 09/12/2021 at [43], *Mukhin* v. *Russia*, App. No. 3642/10, 14/12/2021 at [82], *Kilin* v. *Russia*, App. No. 10271/12, 11/05/2021 at [48]. Note that the cumulative *Perinçek* approach also appears in *Ibragim Ibragimov* v. *Russia* (n 50) at [63] and in the concurring opinion of Judge Lemmens in *Atamanchuk* v. *Russia*, App. No. 4493/11, 11/02/2020.

[83] *Pastörs* v. *Germany* (n 78) at [37]. [84] Ibid at [39].

[85] On the weight accorded to political expression in the case law, see Harris et al. (n 55), pp.616–620.

especially to elected representatives in their elected capacity, and on the other, the Convention's strong opposition to Holocaust denial (which ordinarily pulls towards the application of Article 17 ECHR). In *Pastörs* it thus reconciled this by considering Article 17 ECHR alongside Article 10 ECHR demonstrating how a context specific approach can accommodate the complexity of the issues and Convention rights at stake.[86] Applying this to the facts, the ECtHR ultimately concluded that there was no violation of Article 10 ECHR.[87]

The ECtHR offered further insight into the parameters of hate speech and the applicability of Article 17 ECHR in *Lilliendahl* v. *Iceland*.[88] The events in *Lilliendahl* stemmed from a proposal to strengthen education and counselling in schools 'on matters concerning those who identify themselves as lesbian, gay, bisexual or transgender'. This proposal had prompted substantial public discussion, which had included a debate on a radio show in which members of the public were able to phone in and express their views. After the radio show was broadcast, one of the authors of the proposal published an article online criticising the radio show for allowing people to phone in and express 'clear prejudice and hate speech' without any critical response from the show's host. The author also expressed their wish to participate on the show and respond to those views. The applicant, Lilliendahl, published homophobic comments on the article which ultimately led to him being convicted and fined for publicly threatening, mocking, defaming and denigrating a group of persons on the basis of their sexual orientation and gender identity. Lillendahl thus lodged an application with the ECtHR arguing that his conviction violated Article 10 ECHR.

In contemplating whether Article 17 ECHR was applicable in *Lilliendahl*, the ECtHR observed that the *Perinçek* threshold must be met.[89] Applying this to the facts, it found that the threshold was not met as while 'the comments were highly prejudicial . . . it [wa]s not immediately clear that they aimed at inciting violence and hatred or destroying the rights and freedoms protected by the Convention'.[90] The ECtHR thus considered the merits of the application, where it offered some further reflections on the nature of hate speech and the applicability of Article 17 ECHR.[91] In particular, the Court identified two categories of hate speech: (i) what it referred to as the 'gravest form' of harm speech, which is where the threshold for Article 17 ECHR is met; and (ii) a 'less grave' category of hate speech which falls for consideration under Article 10 ECHR. In respect of the latter it made the following observation:

> Into this second category, the Court has not only put speech which explicitly calls for violence or other criminal acts, but has held that attacks on persons committed by

[86] *Pastörs v. Germany* (n 78) at [46]. [87] Ibid at [49].
[88] *Lilliendahl* v. *Iceland* (dec.), App. No. 29297/18, 12/05/2020. [89] Ibid at [25].
[90] Ibid at [26]. [91] Ibid at [33]–[37].

insulting, holding up to ridicule or slandering specific groups of the population can be sufficient for allowing the authorities to favour combating prejudicial speech within the context of permitted restrictions on freedom of expression.[92]

This sheds some light on the Court's approach, yet the fact that 'explicit calls for violence' can fall into either of the two categories indicates that there is no clear boundary between them.[93] This is perhaps in part because (as we saw in *Pastörs*) whether Article 17 ECHR is applicable is not determined solely by what was said, but also who said it, to whom, when and where. The applicability of Article 17 ECHR thus remains context specific and cannot be predetermined by the content of the expression alone.

The significance of contextual elements was also apparent in *Lenis* v. *Greece* where the ECtHR (in determining that Article 17 ECHR applied) accorded significant weight to the fact that the statement was made by a senior official of the Church and disseminated online.[94] The facts were that Lenis (a Bishop in the Greek Orthodox Church) had published a homophobic statement on his personal blog which had led to his conviction for public incitement to violence or hatred against people because of their sexual orientation. In his application to the ECtHR, Lenis argued that the conviction violated Article 10 ECHR. The Greek Government opposed this, in part, by arguing that Article 17 ECHR applied. In determining that Article 17 ECHR was applicable the Court stressed that while 'criticism of certain lifestyles on moral or religious grounds is not in itself exempt from protection under Article 10 ECHR', 'when the impugned remarks go as far as denying LGBTI+ people their human nature, as in the present case, and are coupled with incitement to violence, then engagement of Article 17 of the Convention should be considered'.[95] In this respect the ECtHR distinguished *Lenis* from *Lilliendahl* on the basis that the statements in *Lenis* were made by a senior official of the Church, disseminated online and were coupled with incitement to violence.[96]

11.3.4 Justifying Hate Speech Restrictions under Article 10(2) ECHR

If the ECtHR does not exclude the impugned expression via Article 17 ECHR, then it will consider whether an interference is justified under Article 10(2)

[92] Ibid.

[93] See also *Minasyan and others* v. *Armenia*, App. No. 59180/15, 07/01/2025 at [66] where the ECtHR doubted that speech which 'incited intolerance and harmful discrimination against the LGBT community' could enjoy the protection accorded by Article 10 ECHR in the light of Article 17 ECHR. Ultimately, the Court did not consider it necessary to rule on this question definitively because, even assuming that the guarantees of Article 10 ECHR applied, the domestic courts had failed to balance the competing interests in accordance with the principles embodied in Articles 8 and 10 of the Convention, interpreted in the light of Article 17 of the Convention.

[94] *Lenis* v. *Greece* (n 54). [95] Ibid at [54]. [96] Ibid at [56].

ECHR. Article 10(2) ECHR provides that an interference is justified where it was (a) prescribed by law, (b) pursued a legitimate aim and (c) was necessary in a democratic society.

11.3.4.1 Interferences Must Be Prescribed by Law

The ECtHR famously elaborated as to what prescribed by law means in *Sunday Times* v. *the United Kingdom* (a case which concerned Article 10 ECHR but not hate speech specifically):

> a norm cannot be regarded as a 'law' unless it is formulated with sufficient precision to enable the citizen to regulate his conduct; he must be able, if need be with appropriate advice, to foresee to a degree that is reasonable in all the circumstances, the consequences which a given action may entail . . . [However] those consequences need not be attainable with absolute certainty: experience shows this to be unattainable . . . whilst certainly is highly desirable, it may bring in its train excessive rigidity and the law must be able to keep pace with changing circumstances. Accordingly many laws are inevitably couched in terms which, to a greater or lesser extent, are vague and whose interpretation and application are questions of practice.[97]

The continuing relevance of this approach to legality was affirmed by the Grand Chamber in *Perinçek* where it observed that 'the Court has, with minor variations in the formulation, consistently adhered to [the *Sunday Times*] position'.[98] In contemplating the need for what the ECtHR in *Sunday Times* called 'sufficient precision' the Grand Chamber in *Perinçek* acknowledged that even in cases concerning criminal penalties it is impossible to attain 'absolute precision in the framing of laws, especially in fields in which the situation changes according to the prevailing views of society'.[99] It thus stated that the ECtHR accepts that the 'need to avoid rigidity and keep pace with changing circumstances means that many laws are couched in terms which are to some extent vague and whose interpretation and application are questions of practice'.[100] In this regard it recognised that 'the mere fact that a legal provision is capable of more than one construction does not mean that it does not meet the requirement of foreseeability'[101] and that 'when new offences are created by legislation, there will always be an element of uncertainty regarding the meaning of this legislation until it is interpreted and applied by the criminal courts'.[102]

Yet whilst the ECtHR recognises the need for some flexibility, the Court is conscious of the risk of abuse of arbitrary power. Thus, criminal provisions must clearly and precisely define the scope of relevant offences to avoid a

[97] *Sunday Times* v. *the United Kingdom* (1979) 2 EHRR 245.

[98] *Perinçek* v. *Switzerland* (n 69) at [132]. [99] Ibid at [133]. [100] Ibid.

[101] Ibid at [135]. [102] Ibid.

situation where the State's discretion becomes too broad and potentially subject to abuse through selective enforcement.[103] This was important in *Selahattin Demirtas* v. *Turkey (No.2)* in which the GC held that the measure (a constitutional amendment to lift political immunity of opposition members) was not prescribed by law.[104] The applicant in *Selahattin Demirtas* v. *Turkey (No.2)* was an elected member of the National Assembly when an amendment was made to the Constitution whereby parliamentary immunity was lifted. Following this, the applicant was arrested on suspicion of membership of an armed terrorist organisation and inciting others to commit a criminal offence. Before the ECtHR, he argued, amongst other things, that the lifting of parliamentary immunity violated Article 10 ECHR as it was not foreseeable. The Grand Chamber agreed that the 'amendment created a situation that was not foreseeable for the members of parliament concerned'.[105] In this regard, it opined that it shared 'the view of the Venice Commission, that this was a one-off *ad homines* amendment that was unprecedented in Turkish constitutional tradition'.[106] Moreover, the measure was aimed expressly at specific statements by members of Parliament, particularly those of the opposition, which the Grand Chamber observed was contrary to the rule of law.[107] It also found that the amendment was a 'misuse of the constitutional amendment procedure'[108] and that 'bearing in mind Turkish parliamentary practice and tradition, a member of parliament could not reasonably expect that such a procedure would be introduced during his term of office, thereby undermining the freedom of expression of members of the National Assembly'.[109] It thus held that the interference with Article 10 ECHR was not prescribed by law as it did not satisfy the requirement of foreseeability; in particular it stated that 'in defending a political viewpoint, the applicant could legitimately expect to enjoy the benefit of the constitutional legal framework in place, affording the protection of immunity for political speech and constitutional procedural safeguards'.[110]

11.3.4.2 Pursuit of a Legitimate Aim

The legitimate aims are set out in Article 10(2) ECHR, and in hate speech cases, relevant aims might include national security, territorial integrity or public safety, the prevention of disorder or crime or the protection of the reputation or rights of others. In most cases it is straightforward for the State to point to at least one of these aims, but the ECtHR will not accept *any* legitimate aim

[103] *Savva Terentyev* v. *Russia*, App. No. 10692/00, 28/08/2018 at [85] and *Altuğ Taner Akçam* v. *Turkey*, App. No. 27520/07, 25/10/2011 at [93]–[94].

[104] *Selahattin Demirtas* v. *Turkey (No.2)* [GC], App. No. 14305/17, 22/12/2020.

[105] Ibid at [268]. [106] Ibid at [269]. [107] Ibid. [108] Ibid. [109] Ibid.

[110] Ibid at [270].

asserted by the State. For one thing the ECtHR has made it clear that the aim identified must have been the rationale for the measure.[111] This was relevant in *Perinçek* where the Grand Chamber held that while the criminal conviction and punishment of the applicant pursued the legitimate aim of protecting the rights of others it had not, contrary to what the State suggested, pursued the legitimate aim of preventing disorder.[112] This was not fatal in *Perinçek* as the State was able to rely upon the other legitimate aim, namely protecting the rights of others.

11.3.4.3 Interference Must Be Necessary in a Democratic Society

If the measure is in accordance with law and pursues a legitimate aim, then the ECtHR will consider whether it is necessary in a democratic society. In considering necessity, it is important to note that where there are competing rights (e.g., Articles 8 and 10 ECHR) the ECtHR will need to consider the balance struck between those rights; this is considered further below. It is, however, worth observing at this juncture that the degree of scrutiny that the ECtHR engages in depends upon the facts of the case. In particular that political expression by elected officials is given the strongest protection,[113] and the ECtHR will intervene where States are criminalising individuals for criticising State officials. Consequently, the ECtHR held in two cases concerning Spain (*Otegi Mondragon* v. *Spain* and *Stern Taulats and Roura Capellera* v. *Spain*) that convictions for insulting State officials violated Article 10 ECHR. [114] Yet while cases relating to political expression are marked by a more intense review of the restriction in question, this does not mean that a violation will always be found; see, for example, *Pastörs* v. *Germany* (discussed above).[115] In considering

[111] *Vereinigung Bildender Kunstler* v. *Austria* (2008) 47 EHRR 5; note the case concerned a sexually explicit, satirical painting censored by the Austrian courts following proceedings brought by a politician portrayed in the painting. The Court held that Austria could not rely upon 'protection of morals' as this was not the basis for the decision at the time.

[112] *Perinçek* v. *Switzerland* (n 69) at [154].

[113] *Castells* v. *Spain*, App. No. 11798/85, 23/04/1992 at [42].

[114] In *Otegi Mondragon* v. *Spain* (2015) 60 EHRR 7, the applicant was a representative of a Basque separatist political organisation. He was convicted after referring to the King of Spain as 'the supreme head of the Spanish armed forces, in other words, the person in command of the torturers, who defends torture and imposes his monarchic regime on our people through torture and violence'. The Court held that this violated Article 10 ECHR as it was disproportionate. In *Stern Taulats and Roura Capellera* v. *Spain*, App. Nos. 51168/15 and 51186/15, 13/03/2018, the applicants had been convicted for setting fire to a photograph of the King and Queen at a public demonstration during the King's Official visit to Girona. The Court held this violated Article 10 ECHR noting that this was political expression, which could not reasonably be construed as incitement of hatred or violence. The prison sentence was disproportionate.

[115] *Pastörs* v. *Germany* (n 78).

necessity, the ECtHR will also consider whether the domestic authorities correctly assessed the nature of the applicant's expression. In this respect the ECtHR will examine whether 'the statements, fairly construed and seen in their immediate or wider context, could be seen as a direct or indirect call for violence or as a justification of violence, hatred or intolerance'.[116] In making that assessment, the ECtHR is 'particularly sensitive towards sweeping statements attacking or casting in a negative light entire ethnic, religious or other groups',[117] while also remaining sensitive to the fact that hate speech can be subtle and insidious. In respect of the latter it observed in *Sanchez* v *France* that:

> Hate speech is not always openly presented as such. It may take various forms, not only through patently aggressive and insulting remarks that wilfully undermine the values of tolerance, social peace and non-discrimination ... but also implicit statements which, even if expressed guardedly or in a hypothetical form ... prove equally as hateful.[118]

This was emphasised in *Pastörs* where the ECtHR refused to accept the applicant's argument that the impugned speech had been taken out of context.[119] On this issue it observed that the domestic authorities had found that although large parts of the speech did not raise an inssue under domestic law:

> these parts of the applicant's speech could not mitigate, conceal or whitewash the qualified Holocaust denial that the applicant had uttered in a small part of the speech. It considered that the applicant had inserted that denial into the speech like 'poison into a glass of water, hoping that it would not be detected immediately'. [120]

In examining the approach adopted by the domestic authorities the ECtHR held that it could not accept 'the applicant's argument that the domestic courts wrongfully selected a small part of his speech, viewed it in isolation and based his conviction on that small part. The contrary is true. The Regional Court cited and assessed the applicant's speech in full'.[121]

Domestic courts are thus required to consider statements in context and the ECtHR will scrutinise their assessment, but neither the domestic courts, nor the ECtHR must accept the applicant's explanation of the meaning of the speech. The ECtHR will therefore consider the capacity of the statement to 'lead to harmful consequences' and that this may be shaped by the context in which the statement appeared.[122] For example, the ECtHR has stated that statements made on electoral leaflets may enhance the effect of the discriminatory and hateful message.[123] The ECtHR has also emphasised that interferences with expression may be more readily justifiable where the expression is directed at

[116] *Perinçek* v. *Switzerland* (n 69) at [206]. [117] Ibid at [206].
[118] *Sanchez* v. *France* (n 49) at [157]. [119] *Pastörs* v. *Germany* (n 78) at [43] and [44].
[120] Ibid at [43]. [121] Ibid at [44]. [122] *Perinçek* v. *Switzerland* (n 69) at [207].
[123] *Féret* v. *Belgium*, App. No. 15615/07, 16/07/2009 at [76].

those at an impressionable and sensitive age, for example, children.[124] Conversely, where statements are made in the course of a television debate in which a range of views are expressed this may reduce the negative effect of the impugned statement.[125]

11.3.5 Article 8 ECHR

Article 8 ECHR, the right to respect for private life, may be relevant at the Article 10(2) ECHR stage to an assessment of whether an interference with Article 10 ECHR is justified. Alternatively, in applications brought by the *targets* of hate speech in which it is alleged that the State has failed to intervene in respect of hateful expression and thus failed to protect their right to private life, the application will be based upon Article 8 ECHR, and at the Article 8(2) ECHR stage the ECtHR will have to consider the competing Article 10 ECHR right. In both contexts we therefore need to know when Article 8 ECHR is applicable and how to balance the two rights.

In terms of the applicability of Article 8 ECHR the ECtHR explained in *Aksu* v. *Turkey* that an individual's ethnic identity is an important aspect of Article 8 ECHR and that 'any negative stereotyping of a group, when it reaches a certain level is capable of impacting on the group's sense of identity and the feelings of self-worth and self-confidence of members of the group'.[126] It observed that in such contexts the expression may 'be seen as affecting the private life of members of the group'.[127] There were two applicants in *Aksu* who brought proceedings arguing that Turkey had breached Article 8 ECHR by allowing the publication of works that incited hatred against the Roma community. The applications related to different publications. The first application related to an academic book entitled *The Gypsies of Turkey*, which the applicant argued contained expressions and statements which offended his Roma heritage. The ECtHR observed that the domestic courts had sought to balance the 'conflicting fundamental rights' in line with the principles in the ECHR case law[128] and that the State had not exceeded its margin of appreciation.[129] In respect of the second application, which concerned two entries referring to 'Gypsies' in dictionaries, the ECtHR expressly stated that Article 8 ECHR was engaged, opining that as 'the applicant considered himself to be the victim of negative stereotyping on account of some of the entries contained in the impugned dictionaries. Article 8 of the Convention is therefore applicable'.[130] This suggests that the applicability of Article 8 ECHR is based

[124] *Vejdeland* v. *Sweden* (2014) 58 EHRR 15 at [56], statements had been made on leaflets left in the lockers of secondary-school students.

[125] *Gündüz* v. *Turkey*, App. No. 35071/97, 04/12/2003 at [43]–[44].

[126] *Aksu* v. *Turkey*, App. Nos. 4149/04 and 41029/04, 15/03/2012 at [58]. [127] Ibid at [58].

[128] Ibid at [74]. [129] Ibid at [77]. [130] Ibid at [81].

upon the victim's perception of the expression. Yet while Article 8 ECHR was held to be applicable, the ECtHR found no violation of Article 8 ECHR on the basis that the State had sought to balance the competing rights and had not exceeded its margin of appreciation. This was the subject of a dissent by Judge Gyulumyan who emphasised the vulnerability of the Roma community and the continuing stereotyping of that community and, accordingly, would have found a violation of the Convention.[131]

Since then the ambit of Article 8 ECHR has been considered in other cases in which the ECtHR has held that in addition to ethnic identity, the reputation and dignity of ancestors may also engage Article 8 ECHR.[132] For example in *Putistin* v. *Ukraine*, the ECtHR accepted that Article 8 ECHR was applicable where it was suggested that the applicant's father had collaborated with the Gestapo, albeit no violation was found on the basis that in the circumstances the level of impact on the applicant was quite remote and the domestic courts had struck an appropriate balance between competing rights.[133] Issues of dignity were pertinent in *Perinçek* where it was observed that Article 8 ECHR was engaged as the expression affected 'the rights of Armenians to respect for their and their ancestors' dignity, including their right to respect for their identity constructed around the understanding that their community has suffered genocide'.[134] Yet while the principles underpinning Article 8 were considered in some cases, there was often little discussion of the threshold for engaging the right. It was this issue that was addressed by the ECtHR in *Behar and Gutman* v. *Bulgaria*[135] and *Budinova and Chaprazo* v. *Bulgaria*.[136]

The applicants in *Behar and Gutman* were Bulgarians of Jewish ethnicity who brought proceedings against a politician in respect of antisemitic remarks. Their case was heard simultaneously with *Budinova and Chaprazo* v. *Bulgaria*, a case brought by two Bulgarians of Roma ethnicity in respect of anti-Roma remarks made by the same politician. In *Behar and Gutman*, it was observed that while the Grand Chamber in *Aksu* had stated that the negative stereotyping of the group must reach a 'certain level', it had not expressly articulated the factors which might come into play.[137] The ECtHR went on to observe that whether this 'certain level' is met 'can only be decided on the basis of the entirety of the circumstances of the specific case' and that it is 'necessary to spell out more explicitly the kinds of considerations which may

[131] Ibid, dissenting opinion of Judge Gyulumyan.

[132] See cases cited in *Perinçek* v. *Switzerland* (n 69).

[133] *Putistin* v. *Ukraine*, App. No. 16882/03, 21/11/2013.

[134] *Perinçek* v. *Switzerland* (n 69) at [227].

[135] *Behar and Gutman* v. *Bulgaria*, App. No. 29335/13, 16/02/2021.

[136] *Budinova and Chaprazo* v. *Bulgaria*, App. No. 12567/13, 16/02/2021.

[137] *Behar and Gutman* v. *Bulgaria* (n 135) at [60].

have a bearing on the assessment of that question'.[138] In this respect it stated that relevant factors include, but are not necessarily limited to:

(a) the characteristics of the group (for instance its size, its degree of homogeneity, its particular vulnerability or history of stigmatisation, and its position vis-à-vis society as a whole),
(b) the precise content of the negative statements regarding the group (in particular, the degree to which they could convey a negative stereotype about the group as a whole, and the specific content of that stereotype), and
(c) the form and context in which the statements were made, their reach (which may depend on where and how they have been made), the position and status of their author, and the extent to which they could be considered to have affected a core aspect of the group's identity and dignity.[139]

In contemplating those factors it observed that it 'cannot be said that one of those factors invariably takes precedence' as 'it is the interplay of all of them that leads to the ultimate conclusion on whether the "certain level" required under *Aksu* . . . has been reached', and therefore whether Article 8 ECHR is applicable.[140] The ECtHR also observed that 'the overall context of each case – in particular the social and political climate prevalent at the time when the statements were made – may also be an important consideration'.[141] Consequently, *Behar and Gutman* suggests that the threshold for Article 8 ECHR is not determined, as may have been indicated in *Aksu,* solely by 'whether the applicant considered himself to be the victim of negative stereotyping'.[142]

Applying this multi-factor approach in *Behar and Gutman*, the ECtHR observed that the impugned statements 'were virulently antisemitic' consisting of 'rehearsed timeworn antisemitic narratives'.[143] Thus it could 'hardly be in doubt' that they 'amounted to extreme negative stereotyping meant to vilify Jews and to stir up prejudice and hatred towards them'.[144] The statements were therefore 'capable of having a sufficient impact on the sense of identity of Jews in Bulgaria and on the feelings of self-worth and self-confidence of individual Jewish people', rendering Article 8 ECHR applicable.[145] A violation of Article 8 in conjunction with Article 14 ECHR was ultimately found on the basis that by refusing to afford redress to the applicants in respect of the discriminatory statements, the domestic authorities had failed to comply with their positive obligation to respond adequately

[138] Ibid at [65]. [139] Ibid at [66]. [140] Ibid at [67]. [141] Ibid at [67].
[142] *Aksu* v. *Turkey* (n 126) at [81]. [143] Ibid at [69].
[144] *Behar and Gutman* v. *Bulgaria* (n 135) at [71]. [145] Ibid at [73].

to discrimination on account of the applicants' ethnic origin and to secure respect for the applicants' private life.[146]

Applying the same principles in *Budinova and Chaprazo*, the Court noted that it 'has long acknowledged the disadvantaged and vulnerable position of Roma ... the need for their special protection' and 'the need to combat their negative stereotyping'.[147] Examining the statements in question, the Court found they were 'deliberately couched in inflammatory terms' and they 'visibly sought to portray Roma in Bulgaria as exceptionally prone to crime and depravity'.[148] The Court also noted that the overall thrust of the statements, 'conveyed bluntly and repeated many times over, was, in essence, that Roma were immoral social parasites who abused their rights, lived off the back of the Bulgarian majority, subjected that majority to systematic violence and crime without hindrance, and aimed to take over the country'.[149] The Court thus concluded it was 'beyond doubt that this amounted to extreme negative stereotyping meant to vilify Roma in Bulgaria and to stir up prejudice and hatred towards them'.[150] The Court also noted that the statements reached a wide audience given the many channels of communication used by the politician, who was a well-known figure and that 'his vehement anti-Roma stance appears to have constituted a core component of his party's political message'.[151] The Court thus held that Article 8 ECHR was applicable.[152] Thereafter, a violation of Article 8 in conjunction with Article 14 ECHR was found on the same basis as that which led to the finding of a violation on *Behar and Gutman*.[153]

In other cases the ECtHR has recognised that homophobic comments affect the 'psychological well-being and dignity' of applicants and therefore engage Article 8 ECHR.[154] For example, in *Beizaras and Levickas* v. *Lithuania* the ECtHR held that Article 8 ECHR was applicable when the applicants' Facebook pages were inundated with virulent homophobic comments.[155] The ECtHR ultimately found a violation of Article 14 ECHR in conjunction with Article 8 ECHR due to the failure of the domestic authorities to investigate in an effective manner whether the comments regarding the applicants' sexual orientation constituted incitement to hatred and violence.[156]

11.3.6 Balancing Articles 8 and 10 ECHR

Once the obligation under Article 8 ECHR arises, 'the chief question becomes whether the authorities have struck a proper balance between the aggrieved party's right to respect for [their] "private life" and the right of the author of

[146] Ibid at [106]. [147] *Budinova and Chaprazo* v. *Bulgaria* (n 136) at [64]. [148] Ibid at [65].
[149] Ibid at [65]. [150] Ibid at [65]. [151] Ibid at [67]. [152] Ibid at [68].
[153] Ibid at [95]. [154] *Beizaras and Levickas* v. *Lithuania* (2020) 71 EHRR 28 at [117].
[155] Ibid at [10]. [156] Ibid at [129].

the statements to freedom of expression'.[157] The Grand Chamber in *Perinçek* v. *Switzerland* articulated the general principles that apply when balancing Articles 8 and 10 ECHR:

(i) In such cases, the outcome should not vary depending on whether the application was brought under Article 8 by the person who was the subject of the statement or under Article 10 by the person who has made it, because in principle the rights under these Articles deserve equal respect.
(ii) The choice of the means to secure compliance with Article 8 in the sphere of the relations of individuals between themselves is in principle a matter that falls within the High Contracting Party's margin of appreciation, whether the obligations on it are positive or negative. There are different ways of ensuring respect for private life, and the nature of the obligation will depend on the particular aspect of private life that is in issue.
(iii) Likewise, under Article 10 of the Convention, the High Contracting Parties have a margin of appreciation in assessing whether and to what extent an interference with the right to freedom of expression is necessary.
(iv) The margin of appreciation, however, goes hand in hand with European supervision, embracing both the legislation and the decisions applying it, even those given by independent courts. In exercising its supervisory function, the Court does not have to take the place of the national courts but to review, in the light of the case as a whole, whether their decisions were compatible with the provisions of the Convention relied on.
(v) If the balancing exercise has been carried out by the national authorities in conformity with the criteria laid down in the Court's case law, the Court would require strong reasons to substitute its view for theirs.[158]

In respect of this latter requirement, the Grand Chamber in *Perinçek* noted that it had elaborated on this in *Aksu* where it had observed that the balance struck by the national authorities would be unsatisfactory if 'the importance or scope of one of the rights at stake was not duly considered' and that in such circumstances the margin of appreciation would be a narrow one.[159] It is thus evident from *Perinçek* that the onus is on the national authorities to carry out a balancing exercise in conformity with the criteria set out in the case law and that the national authorities must give due consideration to the importance and scope of the rights. This aligns with the approach taken to conflicts of Article 8 and Article 10 ECHR in the privacy context.[160] Following the approach in *Perinçek* and *Aksu*, we need to know what the relevant balancing

[157] *Budinova and Chaprazo* v. *Bulgaria* (n 136) at [89].

[158] *Perinçek* v. *Switzerland* (n 69) at [198]–[199]. [159] Ibid at [199].

[160] See discussion in Chapter 10.

criteria are and what is the 'importance and scope of the rights at stake'. In terms of the 'importance' of the rights we observed earlier in this chapter that the ECtHR has emphasised in respect of Article 10 ECHR values such as truth, self-fulfilment, democracy, and tolerance. Meanwhile, in *Perinçek* the Grand Chamber stated that dignity, ethnic identity and reputation are protected by Article 8 ECHR.[161] On that occasion it also stated that the following factors should be considered when balancing the two rights: (i) the context in which the interference occurred; (ii) the extent to which the expression affected the Article 8 ECHR rights of the affected group; (iii) the existence or lack of consensus among the High Contracting Parties on the need to resort to criminal-law sanctions in respect of such statements; (iv) the existence of any international-law rules bearing on this issue; (v) the method employed by the national courts to justify the applicant's conviction; and (vi) the severity of the interference.[162] There are some similarities here with the balancing criteria that are used in respect of privacy and freedom of expression.[163]

Applying these criteria in *Perinçek*, the Grand Chamber observed that where an interference with freedom of expression takes the form of a criminal conviction, then it is 'normally not sufficient that the interference was imposed because its subject matter fell within a particular category or was caught by a legal rule formulated in general terms; what is rather required is that it was necessary in the specific circumstances'.[164] On the facts, it determined that this balance had not been struck by the domestic courts and that the ECtHR therefore had to strike the balance for itself. In striking that balance it emphasised that

> the applicant's statements bore on a matter of public interest and did not amount to a call for hatred or intolerance, that the context in which they were made was not marked by heightened tensions or special historical overtones in Switzerland, that the statements cannot be regarded as affecting the dignity of the members of the Armenian community to the point of requiring a criminal-law response in Switzerland, that there is no international-law obligation for Switzerland to criminalise such statements, that the Swiss courts appear to have censured the applicant for voicing an opinion that diverged from the established ones in Switzerland, and that the interference took the serious form of a criminal conviction – the Court concludes that it was not necessary, in a democratic society, to subject the applicant to a criminal penalty in order to protect the rights of the Armenian community at stake in the present case.[165]

It thus found a breach of Article 10 ECHR.[166]

As noted above, the balancing criteria were also applied in *Behar and Gutman* and in *Budinova and Chaprazo* where the Court held that the

[161] *Perinçek* v. *Switzerland* (n 69) at [227]. [162] Ibid at [228].
[163] See discussion in Chapter 10. [164] Ibid at [275]. [165] Ibid at [280].
[166] Ibid at [281].

antisemitic and anti-Roma statements were entitled to no, or at best very limited, protection under Article 10 ECHR, read in the light of Article 17 ECHR, and the fact that the statements were made by a member of Parliament did not alter this. It thus held that the Bulgarian courts, which had ascribed considerable weight to freedom of expression and downplayed the effect of the statements on Jews and Roma, had failed to carry out the requisite balancing exercise.[167]

11.3.7 Margin of Appreciation

The ECtHR has consistently stated that its task is not to take the place of the competent national authorities but to review the decisions that they made under Article 10 ECHR.[168] It is thus primarily for the national authorities to assess whether there is a need that justifies the interference, and, to that end, they enjoy a certain margin of appreciation, albeit that this goes hand in hand with ECtHR supervision.[169] The scope of the margin of appreciation depends upon the nature of the interests at stake, for example, it is narrowed in respect of political expression.[170] The ECtHR has thus emphasised that interference with the freedom of expression of elected representatives 'calls for the closest scrutiny on the part of the Court'.[171] Yet it is important to note that the margin of appreciation is also calibrated by reference to competing rights. Consequently, the margin will be wider '[w]here the remarks in question incite violence against an individual or a public official or a sector of the population' or where the expression seeks 'to spread, incite or justify hatred based on intolerance, including religious intolerance'.[172] A further consideration in determining the breadth to be accorded to the margin of appreciation is the extent to which restrictions are justified by reference to the State's need to address political and social problems. Thus the ECtHR has held that 'the varying degrees of problems that States may face in the context of immigration and integration policies require that they be afforded a margin of appreciation that is broad enough to determine the existence and extent of the necessity of such interference'.[173] There are therefore a number of factors that govern the breadth of the margin of appreciation in any given case and the ECtHR will consider whether the 'decisions of the domestic courts were based on relevant and sufficient reasons'.[174]

[167] *Behar and Gutman* v. *Bulgaria* (n 135) at [105]–[106] and *Budinova and Chaprazo* v. *Bulgaria* (n 136) at [94]–[95].

[168] *Perinçek* v. *Switzerland* (n 69) at [196]. [169] Ibid.

[170] *Sanchez* v. *France* (n 49) at [146]. [171] Ibid at [147]. [172] Ibid at [156].

[173] Ibid at [157]. [174] Ibid at [209].

11.3.8 Article 14 ECHR

A further important component of the hate speech jurisprudence is Article 14 ECHR, the prohibition on discrimination. The use of Article 14 ECHR is considered further in Chapter 14. It is, however, worth noting that, as we have already seen in a number of cases, Article 14 ECHR may be applicable where it is argued that the State discriminated in failing to respond to hate. For example, in *Beizaras and Levickas* v. *Lithuania*, a violation of Article 14 coupled with Article 8 ECHR was found after the authorities failed to investigate homophobic hate speech posted on the applicants' Facebook pages.[175] A violation of Article 14 ECHR coupled with Article 8 ECHR was also found in *Association Accept* v. *Romania* where the authorities had failed to investigate homophobic hate speech directed at the applicants at a film screening to celebrate LGBT History month.[176] The ECtHR also found a violation of Article 14 ECHR taken in conjunction with Article 8 ECHR in *Bazhenov* v. *Russia*.[177] In *Bazhenov*, there had been non-consensual disclosure by third parties of the applicants' private data – including their names, sexual orientation, the fact that they were in same-sex marriages, and photographs – on a social media platform. The private data 'had been spread in homophobic public groups and personal accounts aimed at intimidating LGBTI activists and inciting intolerance, hatred and violence towards LGBTI people'.[178] Following which the domestic authorities engaged in only limited inquiries, refused to open criminal investigations and failed to inform the applicants of procedural decisions regarding their criminal complaints.[179] The ECtHR found that the authorities had failed to discharge their positive obligation to respond adequately to the nonconsensual dissemination of the applicants' private data, including the information on their sexual orientation, by private individuals, and to investigate in an effective manner whether the dissemination of the data in question had been motivated by homophobic attitudes.[180] The ECtHR thus held that the applicants had suffered discrimination on the grounds of their sexual orientation and therefore there had been a violation of Article 14 ECHR, taken in conjunction with Article 8 ECHR.[181]

A violation of Article 8 ECHR taken alone as well as in conjunction with Article 14 ECHR was found in *Minasyan and others* v. *Armenia* where the applicants had been the target of online homophobic hate speech.[182] The

[175] *Beizaras and Levickas* v. *Lithuania* (n 154). In the subsequent case *Valaitis* v. *Lithuania*, App. No. 39375/19, 17/01/2023 the ECtHR observed that following *Beizaras and Levickas* there had been a clear and positive shift in respect of prosecuting homophobic hate crime in Lithuania.

[176] *Association Accept* v. *Romania* (2022) 75 EHRR 15.

[177] *Bazhenov* v. *Russia*, App. Nos. 8825/22 and 19130/22, 04/02/2025.

[178] Ibid at [72].

[179] Ibid at [74]–[76].

[180] Ibid at [78].

[181] Ibid at [79].

[182] *Minasyan and others* v. *Armenia*, App. No. 59180/15, 07/01/2025.

events stemmed from the 2014 Eurovision Song Contest which was won by the artist Conchita Wurst. After the event, a press conference was held in which the Armenian jury members indicated that they had awarded the lowest points to Conchita Wurst because of their 'internal revulsion', adding that 'just like mentally-ill persons cause aversion, so do such phenomena'.[183] Many of the participants in the press conference, including the applicants, challenged the jury members, pointing out that their comments were discriminatory, hateful, intolerant, unconstitutional, inhumane and offensive to sexual minorities and persons with mental disabilities.[184] Following which an article was published on the website of an Armenian newspaper with the headline 'They Serve the Interests of International Gay Lobby: The Black List of Enemies of the Nation and the State'. The article referred to 'Homosexual rights lobbyists', 'the disgusting phenomenon called Eurovision', and described the Eurovision winner, Conchita Wurst as 'human waste', it also included links to the Facebook profiles of the applicants.[185] This was followed by a series of further articles in a similar vein.[186] The applicants who had been unsuccessful in their domestic proceedings lodged an application with the ECtHR in which they argued that the publications amounted to harassment and hate speech which interfered with their private life, and that the State had failed to provide protection in breach of the Convention.[187] The ECtHR found that by failing to address the discriminatory nature of the impugned statements the domestic courts had 'failed to comply with their positive obligation to respond adequately to the applicants' alleged discrimination on account of their perceived sexual orientation and association with the LGBT community, as required under Article 14' ECHR.[188] Accordingly there had been a violation of Article 8 ECHR taken alone and in conjunction with Article 14 ECHR.[189]

In cases where violence has taken place, Article 3 ECHR may be applicable. For example, in *Oganezova* v. *Armenia*, a violation of Article 3 ECHR taken in conjunction with Article 14 ECHR was found where the 'authorities failed to offer adequate protection to the applicant from homophobic attacks and hate speech and to conduct a proper investigation into the hate-motivated ill-treatment against her', which included an arson attack on the club that she owned and managed and where members of the LGBT community would meet to socialise.[190] The ECtHR also found a violation of Articles 3 and 8 ECHR taken in conjuction with Article 14 ECHR in *Hanovs* v. *Latvia*.[191] In *Hanovs*, the applicant and his partner were walking their dog to a local market when they were subjected to homophobic verbal attacks and threats of violence by two intoxicated men, which the police and the prosecutors subsequently

[183] Ibid at [6]. [184] Ibid. [185] Ibid at [8]. [186] Ibid at [10]–[18]. [187] Ibid at [34].
[188] Ibid at [70]. [189] Ibid at [76]. [190] *Oganezova* v. *Armenia* (2022) 75 EHRR 20 at [123].
[191] *Hanovs* v. *Latvia*, App. No. 40861/22, 18/07/2024.

declined to prosecute as a hate-motivated crime. The ECtHR found that this violated the Convention as the authorities had failed 'to provide adequate protection for the applicant's dignity and private life by ensuring the effective prosecution of the attack against him, while taking into account the hate motive behind the attack'.[192]

11.3.9 Positive Obligations

Thus far we have seen that States have obligations under Articles 8 and 14 ECHR in respect of those targeted by hate speech[193] and that this may have ramifications for Article 10 ECHR. Many of the cases concern a failure to investigate or prosecute hate offences that exist in domestic law, which raises questions as to the extent to which States are obliged to use criminal law measures in respect of hate speech. In this regard although the ECtHR indicates that criminal sanctions can only be invoked as an *ultima ratio* measure, and that it is 'careful not to hold that each and every utterance of hate speech must, as such, attract criminal prosecution and criminal sanctions',[194] it also states that in respect of 'serious offences ... directed against a person's physical or mental integrity, only efficient criminal-law mechanisms can ensure adequate protection and serve as a deterrent factor'.[195] The first question that arises is thus precisely *when* are States required to adopt criminal measures? Cases such as *Oganezova* v. *Armenia* and *Beizaras and Levickas* indicate that criminal law measures are required where violence is used or where there are calls for violence, but they also suggest that criminal law measures may be required where hateful expression attacks the applicant's 'mental integrity'.[196] The parameters are thus uncertain. A second question that arises is what *types* of hate must be prohibited by domestic law. In this regard the ECtHR observed, in finding a violation in *Oganezova,* that 'sexual orientation and gender identity [were] still not included in the characteristics of victims of the offence of hate speech despite the recommendations of the relevant international bodies in that respect'.[197]

[192] Ibid at [53].

[193] See in this respect, ibid at [38] where the ECtHR observed that the duty of the authorities to prevent hate-motivated violence by private individuals and to investigate any potential connection between a discriminatory motive and the violent act may fall under the procedural aspect of Article 3 or manifest as a positive obligation in Article 8. Additionally, it may be part of the authorities' obligations under Article 14 to uphold fundamental rights without discrimination or create an obligation under Article 13 to provide an effective domestic remedy for victims of discrimination.

[194] *Oganezova* v. *Armenia* (n 190) at [119]. [195] Ibid at [120].

[196] Ibid at [120] and *Beizaras and Levickas* v. *Lithuania* (n 154) at [110]–[111].

[197] *Oganezova* v. *Armenia* (n 190) at [121].

An interesting development in this context is the Council of Europe 2022 Recommendation to member States on Combatting Hate Speech which sets out a comprehensive and nuanced approach to tackling hate speech. It provides non-binding recommendations and defines hate speech as follows:

> For the purposes of this recommendation, hate speech is understood as all types of expression that incite, promote, spread or justify violence, hatred or discrimination against a person or group of persons, or that denigrates them, by reason of their real or attributed personal characteristics or status such as 'race', colour, language, religion, nationality, national or ethnic origin, age, disability, sex, gender identity and sexual orientation.[198]

That definition is broad and 'purposively open-ended' so that it can be 'interpreted in line with the evolutive nature of the rights of the Convention, notably Article 14' ECHR.[199] It is intended to cover intersectional hate speech, acknowledging that '[m]any persons (for example, black Muslims or lesbian Roma women) are targeted by hate speech on different, intersecting and cumulative grounds, which further worsens their situation'.[200] It is also intended that it will cover cases in which the targeted person 'is perceived or presumed to have a certain personal characteristic or status, whereas in reality this person does not have it'.[201]

The Recommendation advocates a comprehensive approach with a range of calibrated measures differentiating between: (i) hate speech that is prohibited under criminal law; (ii) hate speech that does not attain the level of severity required for criminal liability, but is nevertheless subject to civil or administrative law; and (iii) offensive or harmful types of expression which are not sufficiently severe to be legitimately restricted under the European Convention on Human Rights, but nevertheless call for alternative responses such as: counter-speech and other countermeasures; measures fostering intercultural dialogue and understanding, including via the media and social media; and relevant educational, information-sharing and awareness-raising activities.[202] The Recommendation thus provides that States should have a legal framework that consists of 'appropriately calibrated provisions of civil, administrative and criminal law' and that criminal law 'should only be applied as a last resort and for the most serious expressions of hatred'.[203] Moreover, in respect of criminal law it also provides that States should 'specify and clearly define in their national criminal law which expressions of hate speech are subject to criminal

198 Council of Europe 2022 Recommendation (n 71) at [2].

199 Explanatory Memorandum to Council of Europe Recommendation CM/Rec(2022)16 of the Committee of Ministers to member States on combating hate speech at [19].

200 Ibid at [8].

201 Ibid at [21].

202 Council of Europe 2022 Recommendation (n 71) at [3].

203 Ibid at [7].

liability'[204] and offers the following examples of types of expression which might be subject to criminal law:

a. public incitement to commit genocide, crimes against humanity or war crimes;
b. public incitement to hatred, violence or discrimination;
c. racist, xenophobic, sexist and LGBTI-phobic threats;
d. racist, xenophobic, sexist and LGBTI-phobic public insults under conditions such as those set out specifically for online insults in the Additional Protocol to the Convention on Cybercrime concerning the criminalisation of acts of a racist and xenophobic nature committed through computer systems (ETS No. 189);
e. public denial, trivialisation and condoning of genocide, crimes against humanity or war crimes; and
f. intentional dissemination of material that contains such expressions of hate speech (listed in a–e above) including ideas based on racial superiority or hatred.[205]

In addition to ensuring that there is a criminal law framework, the Recommendation provides that States should 'ensure that effective investigations are conducted in cases where there is reasonable suspicion that an act of hate speech punishable by criminal law has occurred'.[206] Meanwhile, in respect of civil and administrative law the Recommendation provides that States should ensure that effective legal protection against hate speech is provided in tort law, anti-discrimination law and administrative offences law.[207] States should also ensure that public authorities or institutions are required by law to actively prevent and combat hate speech and its dissemination and to promote the use of tolerant and inclusive speech.[208]

A further important point to observe is that the Recommendation is not limited to the legal framework, nor to investigations of potential criminal offences as it also provides that States should provide support for those targeted by hate speech including psychological, medical and legal assistance, awareness-raising and educational measures to ensure that persons targeted know their rights and how to obtain redress, facilitate reporting of hate speech,[209] monitor and analyse hate speech[210] and ensure national and international co-operation.[211]

The model adopted by the Recommendation is thus similar to the way in which we have seen positive obligations develop in respect of Articles 2, 3 and 4 ECHR.[212] The development of a more nuanced approach to hate speech is

[204] Ibid at [11]. [205] Ibid at [11]. [206] Ibid at [12]. [207] Ibid at [13].
[208] Ibid at [15]. [209] Ibid, Recommendation 5 at [55]–[57].
[210] Ibid, Recommendation 6 at [58]–[61]. [211] Ibid, Recommendation 7 at [62]–[63].
[212] See Chapters 4, 5 and 7.

also in line with the recognition of different categories of hate speech by the ECtHR and the requirements of proportionality under Article 10(2) ECHR. This may therefore lead States towards considering a wider range of measures short of prohibitions which has certain benefits but also certain risks. As Rowbottom observes:

> There are risks in treating hate speech as a matter of degree, as the category becomes more vulnerable to manipulation and expansion. Such a flexible definition increases the potential for government to characterise the speech that it disfavours as hate speech, and take such intermediate steps against it.[213]

Having considered the framework established in the Recommendation it is important to emphasise that this does not bind the ECtHR, but it will be interesting to see if the ECtHR is influenced by this in developing its case law on positive obligations, perhaps by reference to the more holistic positive obligations that it has developed elsewhere.[214]

11.4 ECHR CASE LAW IN RESPECT OF HATE SPEECH

Although the ECtHR does not adopt hard line rules based upon the type of hate speech, the following section provides examples of how the ECtHR has dealt with different types of hate speech. Overall, it is evident that *criminalisation* of Holocaust denial, incitement of terrorism, incitement of violence or hatred of another is compatible with the Convention, but that the Court will intervene, where there is no evidence that the applicant was inciting violence or hatred and where the State is seeking to suppress political opposition.

11.4.1 Genocide Denial

Article 17 ECHR has operated to preclude revisionists from relying on Article 10 ECHR *vis-à-vis* convictions for Holocaust denial.[215] In *Garaudy* v. *France*, the applicant, a former politician and writer, had been convicted of the offence

[213] Jacob Rowbottom, 'A Thumb on the Scale: Measures Short of a Prohibition to Combat Hate Speech' (2022) **14**(1) Journal of Media law 119, 137.

[214] See our earlier discussion in Chapter 7 (Modern Slavery and Human Trafficking).

[215] *Remer* v. *Germany* (dec.), App No. 25096/94, 06/09/1995 – Article 17 ECHR applicable where the applicant published statements that the gas chambers during the Nazi regime did not exist; *Honsik* v. *Austria* (dec.), App. No. 25062/94, 18/10/1995 – Article 17 applicable where the applicant wrote articles in a periodical denying the existence of gas chambers and the mass extermination of the victims of the Holocaust; *Marais* v. *France* (dec.) App. No. 31159/96, 24/06/1996 – Article 17 applicable where the applicant had written an article doubting the existence of gas chambers at Struthof-Natzweiler concentration camp; *Nachtmann* v. *Austria* (n 66) – applicant had published statements minimising and denying the atrocities of the Nazis.

of denying crimes against humanity in connection with a book that he had published which made a number of statements about the Holocaust. [216] The applicant argued that he was not a revisionist and that the main purpose of his book was to criticise the State of Israel's policies. He thus argued that his criminal convictions violated Article 10 ECHR. [217] The Government contested this, arguing that Article 17 ECHR rendered the application inadmissible, or at the very least Article 10(2) ECHR should be applied in the light of Article 17 ECHR. [218] In declaring the application inadmissible the Court held that 'there is a "category of clearly established historical facts – such as the Holocaust – whose negation or revision would be removed from the protection of Article 10 by Article 17"'.[219] It emphasised that denying the Holocaust is 'one of the most serious forms of racial defamation of Jews and of incitement to hatred of them ... Such acts are incompatible with democracy and human rights because they infringe the rights of others.'[220]

Similarly, in *M'Bala M'Bala* v. *France* the applicant (a comedian) argued that his Article 10 ECHR right was violated when he was convicted of the offence of proffering a public insult against persons of Jewish origin or faith after he invited a well-known revisionist to join him on the stage alongside an actor wearing a pair of striped pyjamas with a stitched-on star of David. [221] The Government argued that Article 17 ECHR was applicable as the applicant's remarks and acts clearly had a racist objective and sought to offend the memory of the Jewish people.[222] The ECtHR agreed that Article 17 ECHR was applicable, observing that in his antisemitic and revisionist 'comedy' show the applicant had sought to 'deflect Article 10 from its real purpose'.[223]

It is important to note that although Article 17 ECHR is often used in Holocaust denial cases, there are also cases involving Holocaust denial in which the ECtHR has examined Article 17 alongside Article 10 ECHR.[224] As noted above, an important factor in *Pastörs* was that the speech was made by an elected representative whose parliamentary immunity was removed. The importance attached to political expression in Parliament necessitated full Article 10 ECHR scrutiny, albeit that in carrying out that assessment the values of Article 17 ECHR remained relevant. In considering the relevance of Article 17 ECHR to that analysis the Court emphasised that the applicant planned the speech which evidenced an *intention* to use freedom of expression to promote ideas contrary to the Convention.[225]

[216] *Garaudy* v. *France* (n 62). [217] Ibid. [218] Ibid. [219] Ibid. [220] Ibid.

[221] *M'Bala M'Bala* v. *France* (n 62) at [41]. [222] Ibid at [26]. [223] Ibid at [41].

[224] *Pastörs* v. *Germany* (n 78).

[225] *Pastörs* v. *Germany* (n 78) at [46]. See also, discussion in *Williamson* v. *Germany* (2019) 68 EHRR SE9 where the Court emphasised 'that the applicant neither distanced himself from the content of those statements nor alleged a wrongful assessment of that content by the German courts'. Consequently, observing that the 'applicant sought to use his right to

The strong stance that the ECtHR takes on Holocaust denial requires us to consider whether it approaches the denial of other genocides in the same way. As noted earlier, this issue arose in respect of denial of the Armenian genocide in *Perinçek* v. *Switzerland. Perinçek* was first considered by a Chamber which held that a conviction for denying the Armenian genocide *violated* Article 10 ECHR.[226] In coming to that determination, it expressed doubt as to whether there was a general consensus that the events that could be characterised as genocide of the Armenian people,[227] it thus distinguished this from the Holocaust on the basis that the latter is a 'clearly established historical fact'.[228] At the request of the Swiss Government the case then went to the Grand Chamber which also found a violation of Article 10 ECHR, albeit for different reasons.[229] It determined that the relevant question was not whether the genocide was a 'clearly established historical fact', but rather the 'context of the interference', in relation to which it considered: (i) geographical and historical factors; and (ii) the time factor. In respect of the Holocaust and geographical and historical factors it observed that:

> its denial, even if dressed up as impartial historical research, must invariably be seen as connoting an antidemocratic ideology and anti-Semitism. Holocaust denial is thus doubly dangerous, especially in States which have experienced the Nazi horrors, and which may be regarded as having a special moral responsibility to distance themselves from the mass atrocities that they have perpetrated or abetted by, among other things, outlawing their denial.[230]

The Grand Chamber thus contrasted the Armenian genocide with the Holocaust observing that it had 'not been argued that there was a direct link between Switzerland and the events that took place in the Ottoman Empire in 1915 and the following years'.[231] It went on to comment that the only 'link may come from the presence of an Armenian community on Swiss soil, but it is a tenuous one'.[232] In evaluating the context of the interference the Grand Chamber also considered what it referred to as 'the time factor' observing that 'events of relatively recent vintage may be so traumatic as to warrant, for a period of time, an enhanced degree of regulation of statements relating to them, [but that] the need for such regulation is bound to recede with the passage of time'.[233] Applying this to the facts, the Grand Chamber stated that in

> the present case, the lapse of time between the applicant's statements and the tragic events to which he was referring was . . . about ninety years, and at the time when he

freedom of expression with the aim of promoting ideas contrary to the text and spirit of the Convention' and that this 'weighs heavily in the assessment of the necessity of the interference'.

226 *Perinçek* v. *Switzerland* (Chamber), App. No. 27510/08, 17/12/2013.

227 Ibid at [116]–[117]. 228 Ibid at [117]. 229 *Perinçek* v. *Switzerland* [GC] (n 69).

230 Ibid at [243]. 231 Ibid at [244]. 232 Ibid at [244]. 233 Ibid at [250].

made the statements there were surely very few, if any, survivors of these events. While in their submissions some of the third-party interveners emphasised that this was still a live issue for many Armenians, especially those in the diaspora, the time element cannot be disregarded.[234]

Several judges objected to this emphasis on local needs and temporal limitations. Judge Nussberger declared that she could not support it as States should be able to legislate to express solidarity with victims of genocide everywhere:

I cannot agree with this approach. For me it is not only 'laudable, and consonant with the spirit of universal protection of human rights, . . . to seek to vindicate the rights of victims of mass atrocities regardless of the place where they took place' (see paragraph 246 of the present judgment), but this is wholly sufficient to justify legislation of this kind. It is a 'choice of society' . . . which the Court must accept. Legislation expressing solidarity with victims of genocide and crimes against humanity must be possible everywhere, even if there are no direct links to the events or the victims, even if a long period of time has elapsed, and even if the legislation is not directly aimed at preventing conflicts. Each society must be free to settle the conflict between free and unrestricted debate on historical events and the personality rights of victims and their descendants in accordance with its vision of historical justice in the case of what is alleged to be a genocide.[235]

Judges Spielman, Casadevall, Berro, De Gaetano, Scilianos, Sivlis and Kūris also rejected the 'localism approach'.

Minimising the significance of the applicant's statements by seeking to limit their geographical reach amounts to seriously watering down the universal, *erga omnes* scope of human rights – their quintessential defining factor today . . . Drawing all the logical inferences from the geographically restricted approach apparently adopted by the majority, one might come to the view that denial in Europe of genocides perpetrated on other continents, such as the Rwandan genocide or the genocide carried out by the Khmer Rouge regime in Cambodia, would be protected by freedom of expression without any limits, or with scarcely any. We do not believe that such a vision reflects the universal values enshrined in the Convention.[236]

They also disputed the temporal element observing that if this was taken to its logical conclusion it would suggest that 'in twenty or thirty years' time, Holocaust denial itself might be acceptable in terms of freedom of expression'.[237]At present, however, there is no doubt that Holocaust denial is given very strong protection. This is also evident in the case law on the positive obligations under Article 8 ECHR where the ECtHR has firmly resisted

234 Ibid. 235 Ibid, partly concurring and partly dissenting opinion of Judge Nussberger.

236 Ibid, joint dissenting opinion of Judges Spielman, Casadevall, Berro, De Gaetano, Scilianos, Sivlis and Kūris.

237 Ibid.

the argument that States that were not as directly affected by the Holocaust have more limited obligations in tackling antisemitic speech.[238]

We have seen that the principles within the case law in respect of genocide denial largely reflect the ECtHR's attempts to tackle the dangers of allowing States to enact memory laws whilst recognising the origins of the ECHR and the values it promulgates.[239] Yet, sadly, atrocities are not always historic. Consequently issues may arise in connection with contemporary atrocities where courts will need to grapple with the ramifications of the ECtHR's case law, including the local needs approach promulgated in *Perinçek*.

11.4.2 Terrorism and Extremism

Given the historical context of the ECHR, it is hardly surprising that, for the same reasons that Holocaust denial is often excluded from the ECHR, totalitarian ideas that represent a threat to democracy, such as Nazi ideology, are also excluded by Article 17 ECHR.[240] Expressions of support or promotion of terrorist organisations may also be excluded by Article 17 ECHR.[241] The application of Article 17 ECHR is not automatic, hence there are cases in which the ECtHR has considered Article 17 ECHR alongside Article 10 ECHR.[242] For example, in two cases concerning a cartoon[243] and a T-Shirt[244] which glorified the 9/11 terrorist attacks, the ECtHR refused to apply Article 17 ECHR as the expression did not directly strike against the values underpinning the Convention, nor did it destroy the Convention rights and freedoms. It went on, however, to hold in both cases that the convictions were justified under Article 10(2) ECHR. In *Godenau* v. *Germany* the Court also considered the designation of an individual on a list of persons with connections to far-right parties under Article 10 ECHR (rather than declaring it inadmissible under Article 17 ECHR).[245] Godenau was a teacher whose name was included on a list of persons deemed unsuitable for appointment in public

[238] *Behar and Gutman* v. *Bulgaria* (n 135) at [95].

[239] Paolo Lobba, 'Testing the "Uniqueness": Denial of the Holocaust vs Denial of Other Crimes before the European Court of Human Rights' in Uladzislau Belavusau and Aleksandra Gliszczyńska-Grabias (eds), *Law and Memory: Towards Legal Governance of History* (Cambridge University Press, 2017).

[240] *Schimanek* v. *Austria* (n 66), *Nachtmann* v. *Austria* (n 66).

[241] In *Roj TV A/S* v. *Denmark* (n 65), the applicant was a television company that had promoted a terrorist party. The company was fined, and their licence was withdrawn, which they argued violated Article 10. The ECtHR held that Article 17 ECHR precluded them from relying upon Article 10 ECHR.

[242] *Herri Batasuna and Batasuna* v. *Spain*, App. Nos. 25803/04 and 25817/04, 30/06/2009; *Purcell* v. *Ireland* (dec.), App. No. 15404/89, 16/04/1991.

[243] *Leroy* v. *France* (n 57). [244] *ZB* v. *France*, App. No. 46883/15, 02/09/2021.

[245] In *Godenau* v. *Germany*, App. No. 80450/17, 29/11/2022.

schools because of her previous membership and affiliation to right-wing political parties and organisations with links to Neo-Nazi groups as well as her public statements in which she expressed such ideology. The ECtHR held that Germany's refusal to remove her name from the list was justified under Article 10(2) ECHR.[246]

Although the ECtHR supports States in criminalising terrorism and extremism, it is important to recall the challenges (as discussed in Chapter 8) associated with defining terrorism and extremism and the potential latitude that this can give to States. The ECtHR is aware of this and there are cases in which States have been unable to justify restrictions. For example, in *Ibragim Ibragimov* v. *Russia*, the State unsuccessfully sought to justify a ban on Islamic books on the basis that they advocated extremism.[247] The ECtHR held that Russia had not advanced relevant and sufficient reasons for the measure and the domestic proceedings were inadequate, the measure thus violated Article 10 ECHR.

11.4.3 Inciting Violence and Glorifying Violence

The position is similar in respect of inciting and glorifying violence, namely that in some cases Article 17 ECHR applies,[248] and in others the ECtHR has applied Article 10 ECHR before finding a measure justified under Article 10(2) ECHR.[249] It is important to observe that criminal measures may be justified even where the applicant did not themselves advocate violence. For example, in *Sürek* v. *Turkey (No.1)*, the Grand Chamber found no violation of Article 10 ECHR where the owner of a journal was convicted for publishing letters that advocated violence. The ECtHR observed that whilst he had not personally associated himself with those views, he 'provided their writers with an outlet for stirring up violence and hatred' and was liable for their publication.[250] Interferences may also be justified where the applicant glorified past violence, which was evident in *Altintas* v. *Turkey* where the Court found no violation in respect of a conviction for glorifying events in the 1970s when three British nationals working for NATO were abducted and executed by insurgents.[251] The ECtHR has also observed that statements expressing deep-seated and irrational hatred may be interpreted as likely to encourage violence.[252]

[246] Ibid at [52]–[61]. [247] *Ibragim Ibragimov* v. *Russia* (n 50).

[248] *Hizb ut-Tahrir* v. *Germany* (dec.), App. No. 31098/08, 12/06/2012; *Kasymakhunov and Saybatalov* v. *Russia*, App. Nos. 26261/05 and 26377/06, 14/03/2013; *Belkacem* v. *Belgium* (n 64).

[249] *Kilin* v. *Russia* (n 82); *Gündüz* v. *Turkey*, App. No. 35071/97, 04/12/2003.

[250] *Sürek* v. *Turkey (No.1)*, App. No. 26682/95, 08/07/1999 at [63].

[251] *Altintas* v. *Turkey*, App. No. 50495/08, 10/03/2020.

[252] *Dilipak* v. *Turkey*, App. No. 29680/05, 15/09/2015 at [62].

Again, it is important to emphasise that the ECtHR will scrutinise the State's claim that the applicant incited violence. Thus in *Gündüz* v. *Turkey*, the ECtHR held that the 'mere fact of defending Sharia without calling for violence to introduce it could not be regarded as "hate speech"'.[253] The Court is attune to the risk of States deeming those that oppose State policy to be inciting violence. This was evident in *Faruk Temel* v. *Turkey* where the ECtHR held that the applicant had not incited others to use violence and thus his conviction violated Article 10 ECHR.[254] The Court also held in *Stern Taulats and Roura Capellera* v. *Spain* that setting fire to a photograph of the royal couple did not amount to incitement of violence.[255] The Court will thus expect domestic courts to have scrutinised measures carefully and for there to be relevant and sufficient reasons for the measure. If domestic courts fail to examine statements in context or to provide applicants with an opportunity to contest evidence, then the State will find it difficult to justify the measure.

11.4.4 Inciting Hatred

Compared with the types of hate speech that we have considered so far, the threshold for Article 17 ECHR is less likely to be met by expression that incites hatred but does not incite violence. Thus, while there are cases in which Article 17 ECHR applies, the ECtHR will often apply Article 10 ECHR. This does not, however, mean that States are prohibited from criminalising expression that incites hatred. Indeed, in *Ibragim Ibragimov* v. *Russia*, the ECtHR observed that States may consider it necessary 'to sanction or even prevent all forms of expression which spread, incite, promote or justify hatred based on intolerance (including religious intolerance)' provided they comply with Article 10(2) ECHR.[256] It went on to observe that the ECtHR is 'particularly sensitive towards sweeping statements attacking or casting in a negative light entire ethnic, religious or other groups' as such statements contradict 'the Convention's underlying values, notably tolerance, social peace and non-discrimination'.[257] In this respect, although 'statements expressing deep-seated and irrational hatred towards identified persons may be interpreted as likely to encourage violence', inciting hatred does not 'necessarily involve an explicit call for an act of violence, or other criminal acts'.[258] Consequently, '[a]ttacks on persons committed by insulting, holding up to ridicule or slandering specific groups of the population can be sufficient for the authorities to favour combating xenophobic or otherwise discriminatory speech in the face of freedom of expression exercised in an irresponsible manner'.[259]

[253] *Gündüz* v. *Turkey* (n 249) at [51].

[254] *Faruk Temel* v. *Turkey*, App. No. 16853/05, 01/02/2011.

[255] *Stern Taulats and Roura Capellera* v. *Spain* (n 114).

[256] *Ibragim Ibragimov* v. *Russia* (n 50) at [94]. [257] Ibid. [258] Ibid. [259] Ibid.

In determining whether measures are justified, the ECtHR pays close attention 'to the manner in which the statements were made, and their capacity – direct or indirect – to lead to harmful consequences'.[260] Each case is therefore 'highly context-specific'[261] with the Court taking into account the wider political context, as well as the manner in which the statements were made.

11.4.4.1 *Racial Hatred and Hatred on Grounds of Ethnicity or Nationality*

The ECtHR emphasises the 'utmost importance' of 'combating racial discrimination in all its forms and manifestations'.[262] In some cases it has applied Article 17 ECHR,[263] while in other cases it has held that Article 17 ECHR does not exclude the expression entirely, but that the measures taken were justified under Article 10(2) ECHR. For example, in *Soulas and others* v. *France*, the ECtHR held that the applicants' convictions for inciting hatred and violence against Muslim communities from northern and central Africa were justified under Article 10(2) ECHR.[264] The convictions related to statements made in a book titled *The Colonisation of Europe*. The ECtHR observed that although the convictions were justified, the disputed passages in the book were not sufficiently serious to justify the application of Article 17 ECHR.[265] The ECtHR also found no violation of Article 10 ECHR in *Féret* v. *Belgium* when an MP was convicted for distributing racist leaflets during an election campaign.[266] Similarly, in *Le Pen* v. *France*, the ECtHR found no violation of Article 10 ECHR in respect of Jean-Marie Le Pen's conviction for incitement after he gave an interview with *Le Monde* asserting, among other things, that 'the day there are no longer 5 million but 25 million Muslims in France, they will be in charge'.[267] The ECtHR observed that those statements had been made in the context of a general debate on immigration and that considerable latitude should be left to the State in that context. The ECtHR has also found convictions justified in other contexts. For example, in *Šimunić* v. *Croatia*, the applicant (a footballer) had been convicted and fined approximately 3,200 euros after he took a microphone to the middle of the pitch, shouted a fascist slogan and gave a fascist salute.[268] The ECtHR noted that the fine was modest and determined that the courts had struck a fair balance between freedom of expression and society's interests in promoting tolerance and mutual respect at sports events as well as combating discrimination through sport.

[260] *Sanchez* v. *France* (n 49) at [207]. [261] Ibid at [208]. [262] *Jersild* v. *Denmark* (n 53).

[263] *Glimmerveen and Hagenbeek* v. *the Netherlands* (n 64).

[264] *Soulas* v. *France*, App. No. 15948/03, 10/07/2008.

[265] Ibid at [48]; author's own translation from French judgment.

[266] *Féret* v. *Belgium* (n 123). [267] *Le Pen* v. *France*, App. No. 18788/09, 07/05/2010.

[268] *Šimunić* v. *Croatia* (dec.), App. No. 20373/17, 22/01/2019.

11.4.4.2 *Religious Hatred*

Article 17 ECHR was applied to religious hatred in *Norwood* v. *the United Kingdom* where the Court declared that 'a general, vehement attack against a religious group, linking the group as a whole with a grave act of terrorism, is incompatible with the values proclaimed and guaranteed by the Convention, notably tolerance, social peace and non-discrimination'.[269] Norwood had been convicted and fined £300 for displaying in his window an Islamophobic BNP poster.[270] Article 17 ECHR was also applied in *Belkacem* v. *Belgium* where the applicant had been convicted following remarks he made in a YouTube video concerning non-Muslim groups.[271] The Court considered that the remarks had a markedly hateful content and that the applicant had attempted to use Article 10 ECHR for ends which were manifestly contrary to the spirit of the Convention.

In other cases, the ECtHR has applied Article 10 ECHR but found interferences justified under Article 10(2) ECHR. An example is *Zemmour* v. *France*, in which the applicant, a well-known journalist, was convicted and fined after he made statements on television that incited religious hatred against the Muslim community.[272]

A violation of Article 10 ECHR was, however, found in *Tagiyev and Huseynov* v. *Azerbaijan,* a case in which a writer and an editor, had been convicted for inciting religious hatred and hostility following the publication of an article.[273] The article in question made a number of statements about Europe and European values and was highly critical of Islam. The applicants argued that this could not be characterised as incitement to religious hatred and hostility as it had only sought to make a comparison between Islam and Christianity in the context of European and Eastern humanist values and human rights concepts.[274] The applicants also argued that the severity of the sanctions (three and four years' imprisonment respectively) was disproportionate.[275] Examining the content of the article, the Court observed that:

> although the article 'Europe and us' contained several remarks about Islam and its social and philosophical implications, it is clear from the reading of the whole text that the article mainly dealt with the comparison between Western and Eastern values, expressing the author's ideas about the role of religion in the formation of those values, as well as the impact of those values in the context of human rights and development in the world and in Azerbaijan. Therefore, the article should not be examined only in the context of a matter relating to religious beliefs, but also in the

[269] *Norwood* v. *the United Kingdom* (n 64). [270] Ibid. [271] *Belkacem* v. *Belgium* (n 64).

[272] *Zemmour* v. *France*, App. No. 63539/19, 20/12/2022.

[273] *Tagiyev and Huseynov* v. *Azerbaijan*, App. No. 13274/08, 05/12/2019. [274] Ibid at [27].

[275] Ibid at [28].

context of a debate on a matter of public interest, namely the role of a religion in society and its role in the development of society.

As regards the content of the impugned remarks characterised by the domestic courts as incitement to religious hatred and hostility, the Court notes that some of these remarks, in particular those concerning the Prophet Muhammad and Muslims living in Europe (see paragraph 42 above), may be seen by certain religious people as an abusive attack on the Prophet of Islam and Muslims living in Europe, capable of causing religious hatred. However, it is first of all for the national authorities to carry out a comprehensive assessment of the impugned remarks, putting forward relevant and sufficient reasons for justifying the interference and carefully balancing the applicants' right to freedom of expression with the protection of the right of religious people not to be insulted on the grounds of their beliefs.[276]

On the facts, the Court found that the national courts had not demonstrated that the conviction was necessary, they had not sought to examine the words in context, nor had they tried to balance the applicants' right to impart their views against the right of religious people to respect for their beliefs.[277]

11.4.4.3 *Hatred on Grounds of Sexual Orientation*

The ECtHR's jurisprudence in respect of hatred based on sexual orientation developed later than other aspects of its hate speech case law. In *Vejdeland* v. *Sweden*, the applicants were convicted for distributing leaflets in a school proclaiming that homosexuality was a 'deviant sexual proclivity', which had 'a morally destructive effect on the substance of society' and was responsible for the development of HIV and AIDS.[278] The ECtHR found no violation of Article 10 ECHR as the interference was reasonably regarded by the national authorities as necessary in a democratic society for the protection of the reputation and rights of others. However, several judges expressed concern about the lack of precision in the ECtHR's approach. Judge Spielmann and Judge Nussberger observed that whilst the statements were 'totally unacceptable' that to equate the content of the leaflets to hate speech required robust justification.[279] They agreed that there was no violation of Article 10 ECHR, emphasising that the leaflets were distributed in a school, but cautioned that

the offending statements should have been defined more precisely, bearing in mind that, by virtue of Article 17 of the Convention, 'hate speech', in the proper meaning of the term, is not protected by Article 10. A careful, in-depth analysis of the aim of the speech would have been necessary. As already indicated, the Supreme Court considered the aim (starting a debate) as being acceptable. However, the domestic courts

[276] Ibid at [45]–[46]. [277] Ibid at [47]–[50]. [278] *Vejdeland* v. *Sweden* (2014) 58 EHRR 15.
[279] Ibid, concurring opinion of Judge Spielmann, joined by Judge Nussberger at [4].

should have examined more thoroughly whether behind the apparent aim there was any hidden agenda to degrade, insult or incite hatred against persons or a class of persons on account of their sexual orientation. In the case at hand the Supreme Court, after having admitted that the applicants' actions had a legitimate purpose, namely starting a debate on a matter of public concern, characterised the impugned statements, not without contradiction, as being 'unnecessarily offensive.' It justified the interference by acknowledging the applicant's right to express his ideas, while at the same time stressing that freedoms and rights went hand in hand with obligations; one of which was 'to avoid, as far as possible, statements that are unwarrantably offensive to others, constituting an assault on their rights'.[280]

Meanwhile, Judge Yudkivska and Judge Villiger lamented the 'missed opportunity' to '"consolidate an approach to hate speech" against homosexuals'.[281] They observed that the impugned speech directly matched the definition of hate speech provided by Council of Europe Recommendation No.R (97) 20, and expressed concern that the majority of the Court seemed to be willing to impose a far higher threshold in which hate speech is protected by Article 10 ECHR until it threatens to give rise to imminent violence.[282] They argued that Europe, given its history, cannot afford the luxury of a US-style approach to freedom of speech,[283] the impugned expression was not in harmony with Convention values and thus should not be protected.[284]

The ECtHR had the opportunity to consider this further in *Lilliendahl* v. *Iceland*.[285] It will be recalled from the discussion earlier in this chapter that *Lilliendahl* sought to argue that his conviction and fine for posting homophobic comments online violated Article 10 ECHR and the Government opposed this in part by arguing that Article 17 ECHR was applicable. In determining that Article 10 ECHR was applicable, the ECtHR drew a distinction between the most serious forms of hate speech which fall within Article 17 ECHR and 'less grave' forms of hate speech,[286] finding that the comments in question fell into the second category of hate speech.[287] Yet while Article 10 ECHR applied, the Court saw no reason to disagree with the Icelandic Supreme Court's assessment that the comments were 'serious, severely hurtful and prejudicial' and that they promoted intolerance and detestation and thus that an interference was justified.[288] The Court also noted that the applicant had only been given a fine of 800 euros.[289] Consequently, the decision of the domestic court, which had been taken after an extensive balancing exercise, was found to be reasonable and justified.[290]

Although the ECtHR found no violation of Article 10 ECHR in *Lilliendahl*, its determination that the impugned speech fell within the less serious category of hate speech raised questions as to whether the ECtHR regards hate speech against

[280] Ibid. [281] Ibid, concurring opinion of Judge Yudkivska, joined by Judge Villiger at [2].
[282] Ibid at [4]–[6]. [283] Ibid at [6]. [284] Ibid at [8]. [285] *Lilliendahl* v. *Iceland* (n 88).
[286] Ibid at [34]–[35]. [287] Ibid at [26] and [39]. [288] Ibid at [38] and [45].
[289] Ibid at [46]. [290] Ibid at [47]–[48].

the LGBTQI+ community as less abhorrent than other forms of hate speech. An important development in this respect was the ECtHR's subsequent confirmation in *Lenis* v. *Greece* that Article 17 ECHR is applicable to some forms of homophobic hate speech.[291] Indeed, in *Lenis* it emphasised (as it had previously stated elsewhere) that 'discrimination based on sexual orientation is as serious as discrimination based on "race, origin or colour"'.[292] It will be recalled from the discussion earlier in this chapter that Lenis was a Bishop in the Greek Orthodox Church who published a homophobic statement on his personal blog. In determining that Article 17 ECHR applied, the Court stressed that whilst 'criticism of certain lifestyles on moral or religious grounds is not in itself exempt from protection under Article 10 ECHR, 'when the impugned remarks go as far as denying LGBTI people their human nature, as in the present case, and are coupled with incitement to violence, then engagement of Article 17 of the Convention should be considered'.[293] As discussed earlier, *Lenis* was also distinguished from *Lilliendahl* on the basis that the statements in *Lenis* were made by a senior official of the Church, disseminated online and coupled with incitement to violence.

If the ECtHR is going to use Article 17 ECHR at all then it is essential that it applies equally and that it does not distinguish, nor appear to distinguish, based upon protected characteristics. From this perspective the application of Article 17 ECHR in *Lenis* is a welcome development. One might, however, question whether the threshold for engaging Article 17 ECHR remains elevated in this context, recalling that in *Lenis* the ECtHR suggested that Article 17 ECHR applies where the expression 'go[es] as far as denying LGBTI people their human nature' *and* is 'coupled with incitement to violence'. Certainly, one might question whether these elements need to be cumulative and whether this is consistent with other case law in respect of Article 17 ECHR. In this regard one might also note that the statements in *Lilliendhal,* which the ECtHR held did not fall within Article 17 ECHR, met at least the first of those requirements.[294]

Finally, it is important to observe that although cases such as *Vejdeland, Lilliendahl* and *Lenis* concerned States that had sought to protect the LGBTQI+ community, there are also cases where States have failed to investigate homophobic hate speech and have thus violated the Article 8 and 14 ECHR rights of those who are the target of such expression, and in some circumstances even Article 3 ECHR.[295]

11.4.5 Journalism

The ECtHR is clear that a distinction should be made between persons making hateful statements and journalists reporting on such statements. This was

[291] *Lenis* v. *Greece* (n 54). [292] Ibid at [53]. [293] Ibid at [54].
[294] *Lilliendahl* v. *Iceland* (n 88). [295] See discussion at Section 11.3.8.

important in *Jersild* v. *Denmark*, a case concerning a documentary about an extreme right-wing group in which members of that group made racist remarks.[296] The journalist was convicted for aiding and abetting dissemination of racist remarks which he argued violated Article 10 ECHR. The ECtHR in finding a violation held that punishing a journalist for dissemination would seriously hamper the contribution of the press and should not be envisaged unless there are particularly strong reasons for doing so.[297] Accordingly, it held that his conviction violated Article 10 ECHR.[298]

11.4.6 Liability of Third-Party Intermediary Publishers

The liability of third parties is of growing importance in the digital age. A landmark case in this respect was *Delfi AS* v. *Estonia* in which the Grand Chamber held that an internet news portal could be held liable for user-generated comments.[299] In *Sanchez* v. *France*, the Grand Chamber had to consider whether the same approach applied in respect of racist comments made by third parties on the Facebook wall of a politician.[300] Sanchez was a politician running for a far-right party in France. During the election campaign he posted a message about a political opponent on his publicly accessible Facebook page to which third parties added comments expressing hatred towards immigrants from North Africa and those of Muslim faith. The third-parties were convicted for inciting hatred and Sanchez was convicted as the publisher for failing to act promptly to end dissemination of the comments. He argued that this violated Article 10 ECHR. The case was first heard by a Chamber which held that the State has a margin of appreciation, that the decision to convict was based on relevant and sufficient grounds and that it was necessary in a democratic society.[301] The case then went to the Grand Chamber which observed that 'the risk of harm posed by content and communications on the Internet to the exercise and enjoyment of human rights and freedoms, particularly the right to respect for private life, is certainly higher than that posed by the press'.[302] It went on to explain that this is because such expression 'can be disseminated as never before, worldwide, in a matter of seconds, and sometimes remain available online for lengthy periods'.[303] Consequently, there is a need to balance Articles 10 and 8 ECHR.[304] The ECtHR observed that in *Delfi AS* the Court had found that the domestic award of damages against the internet news portal for insulting comments posted on

[296] *Jersild* v. *Denmark* (n 53). [297] Ibid at [35].

[298] Ibid at [37]. Compare this with *Roj TV A/S* v. *Denmark* (n 65) where the television broadcasting company promoted terrorism.

[299] *Delfi AS* v. *Estonia* (2016) 62 EHRR 6. [300] *Sanchez* v. *France* (n 49).

[301] *Sanchez* v. *France*, Chamber, App. No. 45581/1, 02/09/2021.

[302] *Sanchez* v. *France* (n 49), [GC] at [161]. [303] Ibid at [162]. [304] Ibid.

its website by anonymous third parties had been justified, taking into account the extreme nature of the comments in question, amounting as they did to hate speech and speech inciting violence.[305] Applying this in *Sanchez*, the Grand Chamber examined (i) the context of the comments (including the nature of impugned comments, political context and applicant's specific liability in respect of comments posted by third parties), (ii) the steps taken by the applicant, (iii) the possibility of holding the authors liable instead of the applicant and (iv) the consequences of the domestic proceedings for the applicant.[306] Following which it held by thirteen votes to four that there had been no violation of Article 10 ECHR.[307] Several judges dissented on various grounds, including that the application of French law was not sufficiently foreseeable and did not satisfy the legality provision.[308] The expansion of liability in *Sanchez* to individuals in respect of posts made by third parties has serious ramifications for the use of social media, which will need to be further considered and developed in future cases.

11.4.7 Conclusion on ECHR and Hate Speech

It is evident that the ECtHR's case law on hate speech is evolving as it is confronted on a piecemeal basis with the challenges that come before it. Consequently, there are areas of considerable uncertainty as to the parameters of Article 17 and Article 10 ECHR and the extent to which States have, or should have, positive obligations under Articles 8 and 14 ECHR to take action to prohibit hate speech. At the backdrop of all of this are unresolved questions concerning what amounts to hate speech, the role of law (and particularly criminal law in responding to hate), and the role of the ECtHR in holding States to account.

11.5 DOMESTIC HATE SPEECH LAW

Freedom of expression was recognised as a common law right long before the HRA was enacted,[309] but the protection that the common law accorded was 'patchy and inconsistent'.[310] Thus as Rowbottom has highlighted, its 'historical foundation [was] more precarious than sometimes acknowledged and its

305 Ibid at [163]–[165]. 306 Ibid at [167]–[208]. 307 Ibid at [210].

308 Ibid, dissenting opinions.

309 *Reynolds* v. *Times Newspapers* [1999] UKHL 45, [2001] 2 AC 127, *R* v. *SSHD, ex parte Simms* [1999] UKHL 33, [2000] 2 AC 115.

310 See discussion in Jacob Rowbottom, 'Freedom of Expression and the Right to Vote: Political Rights and the Common Law Constitution' in Mark Elliott and Kirsty Hughes, *Common Law Constitutional Rights* (Hart, 2020).

content less than certain'.[311] The common law right to freedom of expression was also supplemented, even prior to the HRA, with Article 10 ECHR as whilst the Convention right did not form part of domestic law, the courts would take it into account in interpreting ambiguous legislation.[312] This was of limited effect when compared with the obligations that arise under the HRA. The enactment of the HRA was thus significant as it saw Articles 8, 10, 14 and 17 ECHR all included in Schedule 1 HRA rendering them applicable to the s.3 HRA obligation in interpreting legislation, the s.4 HRA declaration of incompatibility and the s.6 HRA obligation on public authorities. Consequently, the HRA and the ECHR rights now shape the development and application of domestic law, but it is important to note that in contrast to privacy, where prior to the HRA there was no law of misuse of private information, there were many hate speech provisions in domestic law long before the HRA. In fact, the offence of stirring up racial hatred was enacted as long ago as the Race Relations Act 1965. Moreover, prior to the HRA, criminal law provisions existed in respect of stirring up hatred, aggravated public order and communications offences.[313] Thus while the positive obligations within Article 8 ECHR indicate the need for a legal framework, which includes criminal law, there is no doubt that there is a legal framework for tackling hate speech in domestic law and that it includes the use of criminal law. The question that arises is thus whether the existing provisions are adequate. In particular whether the framework is sufficiently comprehensive, whether criminal law is used appropriately, and whether domestic law strikes the right balance between competing rights?

The hate speech provisions in domestic law were generally enacted as piecemeal responses to identified needs. This has resulted in different approaches meaning that greater protection is accorded to some groups than others. The broadest provisions tend to apply to racist hate speech, whereas narrower provisions typically apply to religious or sexual orientation-based

[311] Ibid, p.136.

[312] *Reynolds* v. *Times Newspapers* (n 309) and *R* v. *SSHD, ex parte Simms* (n 309).

[313] There are other offences that we will not consider in this chapter, for example, the offence of 'indecent or racialist chanting' under the Football (Offences) Act 1991 prohibits engaging or taking part in chanting of an indecent or racialist nature at a designated football match; s.3 Football (Offences) Act 1991. The Law Commission, *Hate Crime Laws: Final Report*, (n 4) (Chapter 11) considered whether this offence should be retained and whether it should be extended to cover hatred on the basis of other protected characteristics such as sexual orientation or disability. The Law Commission concluded that the offence should be retained and that it should not be extended. An important area of criminal law that we will also not consider in this chapter is *terrorism-related expression*. Examples of which include s.1 TA 2006 encouraging terrorism; s.11 TA 2000 professing membership of proscribed organisation; s.13 TA 2000 wearing, carrying, or displaying an item of clothing in support of a proscribed organisation; and s.2 TA 2006 dissemination of terrorist publications, as well as the operation of PREVENT. These were considered in Chapter 7.

hatred.[314] A further aspect of this is that we do not have hate speech provisions in respect of *all* protected characteristics across all four of the nations that comprise the United Kingdom.[315] Indeed, there are some protected characteristics such as sex, where there are no hate speech provisions at all.[316] The current provisions are therefore open to the criticism that Heinze advances in respect of hate speech laws, namely that they '[t]hey create two tiers, dividing society into those who may and those who may not, by law, be insulted'.[317] It is also questionable whether these provisions are compatible with the stance of the ECHR, namely that there should be no hierarchy of hatred.[318] The Law Commission of England and Wales has recommended amendments that would remove this hierarchy, but these have yet to be implemented.[319] In Scotland, the Hate Crime and Public Order (Scotland) Act 2024 covers a wider range of protected characteristics, but targets of racial-based hate speech still receive broader protection than those that are the targets of hate based on other protected characteristics.[320] At the time of writing, a common theme across England, Wales, Scotland and Northern Ireland is that there are no provisions which specifically target hatred based on sex, or hatred targeted at women; this has been the subject of review by a number of bodies and different conclusions have been drawn.[321]

One of the major challenges in respect of contemporary hate speech laws is the use of social media. Several statutory communications offences have existed in domestic law for many years but they were intended to deal with different forms of communication and different problems to those that arise today.[322] This was the subject of review by the Law Commission of England and Wales in *Modernising Communications Offences* (July 2021) and it made a number of recommendations for reform.[323] Some of those recommendations were implemented in the Online Safety Act 2023, a landmark new regulatory regime which places obligations on service providers, but other recommendations are still awaiting implementation.[324]

Domestic law has also not been immune from the challenges of identifying what constitutes hate speech, something which in recent years has been particularly contested in relation to gender critical views, especially, but not

[314] See discussion of stirring up hatred offences and aggravated public order offences at Sections 11.5.1 and 11.5.2.

[315] Ibid. [316] Ibid. [317] Heinze (n 18), pp.567–568.

[318] See discussion at Section 11.3.1.

[319] Law Commission, *Hate Crime Laws: Final Report* (n 4). See discussion at Sections 11.5.1.4 and 11.5.2.

[320] See discussion at Section 11.5.1.5.

[321] See discussion at Sections 11.5.2 and 11.5.1.4–11.5.1.6.

[322] See discussion at Section 11.5.3.

[323] Law Commission, *Modernising Communications Offences: A Final Report* (n 4).

[324] See discussion at Section 11.5.3.

exclusively on social media. This has implications not only for criminal law, but also for the reporting of non-crime hate incidents and employment law. This has given rise to legal proceedings in which arguments have been advanced based upon Convention rights, and in which some violations of the Convention have been found.[325] Another environment in which the parameters of freedom of expression have been hotly contested in recent years, is in universities, particularly in response to the cancellation of events and the dismissal of students and academics following the expression of views that may or may not fall within the parameters of protected beliefs and which may or may not amount to hateful expression. This led to the enactment (whilst the Conservative Government was in power) of the Higher Education (Freedom of Speech) Act 2023 which amongst other things placed duties to protect freedom of speech on registered higher education providers and students' unions. The Labour Government put the coming into force of these provisions on hold, but at the time of writing, it is reported that many of the provisions will come into force in August 2025.[326]

Domestic law is thus in a state of flux as attempts are made to tackle contemporary problems and establish the parameters of hate speech and freedom of expression by interpreting and applying existing provisions or developing new ones. The Convention rights and the principles developed by the ECtHR form the legal framework within which these solutions must be found.

11.5.1 Stirring Up Hatred Offences

The most serious public order offences are the stirring up hatred offences. Parts III and IIIA of the Public Order Act 1986 ('POA 1986') criminalise stirring up racial hatred, religious hatred, and hatred on the grounds of sexual orientation. The sentence for a stirring up offence is up to seven years' imprisonment, but the threshold for prosecution is high and the rate of prosecutions is very low. As the Law Commission explained in its Consultation Paper, 'the stirring up offences criminalise the incitement of something (racial hatred or hatred on grounds of religion or sexual orientation) which is not itself criminal (and which would rightly be considered a thought crime if it were)'.[327] The fact that they criminalise conduct that may not otherwise be unlawful distinguishes them from the aggravated offences and the offences subject to enhanced sentencing.[328] It also renders these offences controversial from the perspective

[325] See discussion at Sections 11.5.4, 11.5.5 and Chapter 14.

[326] HC Deb, 26 July 2024, vol. 752, col 31WS. See discussion at Section 11.7.

[327] Law Commission, *Hate Crime Law: A Consultation Paper*, Consultation Paper 250, 23/09/2020 at [18.3].

[328] See discussion at Sections 11.5.2 and 11.5.3.

of those that advocate stronger protection for freedom of expression. It is with this in mind that the Law Commission felt that it was vital to set out that they were of the opinion that the stirring up offences should be retained, even though repeal of those offences had not been part of its terms of reference. [329] They emphasised not only the important role of such offences, but also the fact that they had not received any evidence of the offences being *prosecuted* in a manner that amounted to an improper interference with freedom of expression.[330] On the contrary, they found that prosecution had almost invariably related to expression that would fall outside the protection of Article 10 ECHR altogether, or which amounted to encouragement of crime or violence.[331]

The three stirring up offences largely operate in similar ways, with the important caveat that stirring up racial hatred has a wider ambit than the other two offences. This emerges from the following features. First, that stirring up racial hatred encompasses '*threatening, abusive or insulting*' expression[332] whereas the religious and sexual orientation stirring up hatred offences only cover '*threatening*' expression.[333] Second, the stirring up racial hatred provisions apply when the defendant *intended* to stir up hatred or where in the circumstances it was *likely*.[334] The religious and sexual orientations stirring up hatred provisions only apply if the defendant *intended* to stir up hatred.[335] Third, there is no freedom of expression limitation to the racial hatred provisions, but there is in respect of religious hatred or hatred based on sexual orientation.[336]

The provisions are otherwise largely similar. The penalties are the same for all three offences,[337] and they all cover conduct ranging from using words and behaviour, to displaying and publishing images and written material, as well as recordings, broadcasts and theatrical productions.[338] *Hatred* is not defined in the POA 1986 in respect of any of the offences and there is little analysis of it in the case law. The Law Commission has suggested that it bears its ordinary meaning, is a stronger term than 'hostility',[339] and ultimately it is a question for the jury or magistrate as to whether the standard has been met.[340] An interesting question is to what extent a direction to the jury should ensure that hatred is given an Article 10 ECHR compatible meaning, bearing in mind that some hatred is excluded from the Convention by virtue of Article 17 ECHR.

All three offences can be committed in a public or a private place and an exception currently exists where the words or behaviour are used, or the

[329] Law Commission, *Hate Crime Laws: Final Report* (n 4) at [10.54]. [330] Ibid at [10.69].
[331] Ibid. [332] Sections 18–22 POA 1986. [333] Section 29B–F POA 1986.
[334] Sections 18–22 POA 1986. [335] Section 29B–F POA 1986.
[336] Section 29J and 29JA POA 1986. [337] s.27(3) and s.29L(3) POA 1986.
[338] Sections 18–22 and 29B-F POA 1986.
[339] Law Commission, *Hate Crime Laws: Final Report* (n 4) at [2.133]. [340] Ibid.

written material is displayed, by a person inside a dwelling and are not heard or seen except by other persons in that or another dwelling.[341] The Law Commission found this problematic as it protects a public meeting in a private house, but it does not protect a private conversation in a family's car. They thus propose amending the exception to one of 'private conversation'.[342] However, at the time of writing, the Government has yet to respond to this recommendation.

An important feature of the stirring up hatred offences is that consent of the Attorney General (AG) is required prior to prosecution.[343] Consequently, in the case of *R* v. *Lalchan*, a conviction was quashed where consent had not been sought prior to prosecution.[344] The Court of Appeal held that on ordinary statutory interpretation, consent was required and this could not be dispensed with by the court. One of the arguments advanced for the consent provision is that it is an important safeguard for freedom of expression as the AG is bound under s.6 HRA to act in accordance with Article 10 ECHR. The Law Commission considered the consent requirement whilst carrying out its review and concluded that it should be retained, albeit that it should shift from the AG to the Director of Public Prosecutions.[345] Again, the Government has yet to respond.

11.5.1.1 Stirring Up Racial Hatred

Stirring up racial hatred originated in s.6 of the Race Relations Act 1965, was amended by the Race Relations Act 1976, before being replaced by the Public Order Act 1986 (POA 1986). Section 17 POA 1986 provides that '*racial* hatred' means hatred against a group of persons defined by reference to 'colour, race, nationality (including citizenship) or ethnic or national origins'. A recent example of this is *R* v. *Adeyinka Shoyemi* where the defendant was convicted of attempting to stir up racial hatred between different ethnic groups in his home country of Nigeria, by posting videos on YouTube and by making posts on Facebook.[346]

The offence covers both conduct where the defendant *intends* to stir up racial hatred or where it was *likely* to be stirred up and includes public and private places (with exceptions for dwellings). There is no requirement to prove

[341] Section 18(2) POA 1986.

[342] Law Commission, *Hate Crime Laws: Final Report* (n 4) at [10.245]–[10.295]. In determining what constitutes a 'private conversation' they have proposed a reasonable expectation of privacy test following the same approach as in the law of misuse of private information.

[343] Sections 27 and 29L POA 1986.

[344] [2022] EWCA Crim 736, [2022] QB 680.

[345] Law Commission, *Hate Crime Laws: Final Report* (n 4), Recommendation 31.

[346] *R* v. *Shoyemi (Adeyinka)* Court of Appeal, Criminal Division, 16/11/2023, Case Nos 202201472/B1–202201774/B1.

either that racial hatred was stirred up, nor that distress was caused. The absence of a harm requirement is one of the elements that has given rise to concerns about freedom of expression. Yet the offences prosecuted to date suggest that the offence is used in extreme cases.[347] This is also reflected in the fact that inciting racial hatred has been charged alongside charges of soliciting murder.[348]

11.5.1.2 *Stirring Up Religious Hatred*

The Racial and Religious Hatred Act 2006 inserted Part IIIA into the POA 1986. It took six attempts over twelve years before the legislation was enacted. Part of the eventual impetus for the legislation were the actions of the British National Party (BNP) and the acquittal of their leader Nick Griffin. Griffin was acquitted by a jury after making a speech to BNP supporters at a pub in which he incited hatred against Muslims. The argument used by Griffin at trial was that he was only inciting against Islam and not against race and thus the stirring up racial hatred provisions did not apply. It was Griffin's exploitation of the race/religion distinction to attack Muslims which led to parliamentary support for an inciting religious hatred offence.[349]

Religious hatred is defined in s.29A POA 1986 as meaning 'hatred against a group of persons defined by reference to religious belief or lack of religious belief'. There is no definition of 'religious belief', but the Explanatory Note states that it is broad and is in line with Article 9 ECHR. Convictions for this offence have included the glorification of a stabbing and encouraging others to do the same.[350] As noted above, the religious hatred offences only cover *threatening* words or behaviour[351] and are only applicable where the defendant *intended* to stir up hatred, they are not applicable where stirring up hatred was *likely*. Moreover, s.29J POA 1986 provides a carve out from the offence to protect freedom of expression.

> Nothing in this Part shall be read or given effect in a way which prohibits or restricts discussion, criticism or expressions of antipathy, dislike, ridicule, insult or abuse of particular religions or the beliefs or practices of their adherents, or of any other belief system or the beliefs or practices of its adherents, or proselytising or urging adherents of a different religion or belief system to cease practising their religion or belief system.

[347] *R* v. *Sheppard* [2010] EWCA Crim 65, *R* v. *David Bitton* [2019] EWCA Crim 1372, *R* v. *Burns* [2017] EWCA Crim 1466.

[348] *R* v. *Abu Hamza* [2006] EWCA Crim 2918, [2007] QB 659 and *R* v. *El-Faisal (Abdullah Ibrahim)* (Reasons for Dismissal of Appeal) [2004] EWCA Crim 456.

[349] Kay Goodall, 'Incitement to Religious Hatred: All Talk No Substance' (2007) 70(1) MLR 89.

[350] *R* v. *Ahmad* [2012] EWCA Crim 959, [2013] 1 Cr. App. R. (S.) 17.

[351] The Government had sought to include abusive or insulting words or behaviour but had to drop this as the legislation passed through Parliament.

The Law Commission found it difficult to assess the practical effect of this provision as there are no reported cases in which s.29J has been interpreted, and prosecutions for stirring up religious hatred are rare. Ultimately, it concluded that the provision should be retained.[352]

11.5.1.3 Stirring Up Hatred on Grounds of Sexual Orientation

The Criminal Justice and Immigration Act 2008 amended Part IIIA of the POA 1986 to include an offence of stirring up hatred on the grounds of sexual orientation. This stemmed from a Law Commission report which found evidence of extreme examples of incitement to homophobic violence on a considerable scale.[353] The legislation provides that 'hatred on the grounds of sexual orientation' means hatred against a group of persons defined by reference to sexual orientation (whether towards persons of the same sex, the opposite sex or both).[354] The Law Commission has proposed that this should be amended to include protection of persons who are or are assumed to be 'asexual'.[355] As with the religious hatred provisions, *only threatening* words or behaviour is covered and the prosecution must prove that the defendant *intended* to stir up hatred. A further limitation is that s.29JA provides for an avoidance of doubt clause to give special recognition to freedom of expression.

29JA Protection of Freedom of Expression (Sexual Orientation)

(1) In this Part, for the avoidance of doubt, the discussion or criticism of sexual conduct or practices or the urging of persons to refrain from or modify such conduct or practices shall not be taken of itself to be threatening or intended to stir up hatred.
(2) In this Part, for the avoidance of doubt, any discussion or criticism of marriage which concerns the sex of the parties to marriage shall not be taken of itself to be threatening or intended to stir up hatred.

The Law Commission concluded that this provision should remain, noting that the classes of conduct covered reflect those that most respondents generally wished to see protected.[356] These limitations on the offence are, however, perhaps one of the reasons why the only reported example of a conviction

352 Law Commission, *Hate Crime Laws: Final Report* (n 4) at [10.483] and [10.486].
353 Law Commission, *Hate Crimes: Should the Current Offences Be Extended?* Law Com No. 348, Cm 8865, May 2014.
354 Section 29AB POA 1986.
355 Law Commission, *Hate Crime Laws: Final Report* (n 4), Recommendation 4 at [4.143]–[4.152].
356 Law Commission, *Hate Crime Laws: Final Report* (n 4), at [10.487].

for stirring up sexual hatred is *R* v. *Ali* where the defendants in the lead up to the Derby Gay Parade in 2010 distributed leaflets calling for the death penalty for homosexuals.[357]

11.5.1.4 *Law Commission: Reform of Stirring Up Offences*

One of the biggest problems identified by the Law Commission is the unequal protection afforded to different groups. There are several aspects to this. First, many groups are not protected. Second, the stirring up hatred offences have different requirements depending on the type of hatred expressed. The Law Commission concluded that this hierarchy 'is widely seen as unfair and sends a distinctly negative message to victims of hate crimes on the basis of disability, sexual orientation and transgender identity'.[358] One of its recommendations is thus to expand the stirring up hatred offences to include hatred based on 'disability', 'transgender or gender diverse identity', 'sex or gender'.[359]

The Law Commission's other recommendation relates to the thresholds for the offences. It observed that having different thresholds lacks a logical foundation, reinforces the idea of a 'hierarchy of hatred'; and reinforces the notion that whether a characteristic is mutable or immutable should have a bearing on the extent to which it is protected.[360] Consequently, they recommended a single test for all forms of hatred.[361] Under this test a person would be guilty of stirring up hatred if they used words or behaviour *intended* to stir up relevant hatred; or used *threatening or abusive* words or behaviour *likely* to stir up relevant hatred. This removes the 'insulting' aspect from racial hatred, whilst extending 'abusive' and 'likely to' elements to the other offences. For the 'likely to' limb of this test, the prosecution would have to prove that the person knew, or ought to have known, that the words or conduct were threatening or abusive, and knew, or ought to have known, that they were likely to stir up relevant hatred.[362]

As well as expanding the range of stirring up hatred offences and introducing a universal test, the Law Commission has made recommendations intended to offer greater protection to freedom of expression. These include amending the dwelling exception to one of 'private conversation'; retaining a consent filter for prosecution but shifting this from the AG to the Director of Public Prosecutions (DPP); and introducing a new 'neutral reportage' defence for journalists.[363] They have also made several recommendations in respect of types of expression. For example, while recommending extending the stirring

[357] *R* v. *Ali (Ihjaz), Ahmed (Kabir), R. Javed (Razwan)* Crown Court (Derby) (unreported), Judge Burgess.

[358] Law Commission, *Hate Crime Laws: Final Report* (n 4) at [8.69].

[359] Ibid, Recommendation 12 at [8.70].

[360] Ibid at [10.79].

[361] Ibid, Recommendation 21.

[362] Ibid.

[363] Ibid, Recommendations 24, 29–31.

up offences to cover hatred towards transgender or gender diverse people, they have also recommended that protection should be introduced for gender critical views.[364] In respect of the existing carve out for discussion and criticism of religious practices they suggest extending it to cover cultural practices.[365] Finally, they have recommended that a new provision should be introduced which protects discussion, criticism or expressions of antipathy, dislike, ridicule, insult or abuse of countries and their governments; and for discussion and criticism of policy relating to immigration, citizenship and asylum.[366]

At the time of writing, these recommendations have yet to be implemented.

11.5.1.5 *Scotland: Stirring Up Hatred Provisions*

In 2018, Lord Bracadale, a retired senior judge, led an independent review into hate crime in Scotland.[367] In respect of stirring up hatred it was observed that in Scotland, unlike England and Wales, there were only stirring up hatred offences in relation to race. He concluded that new stirring up hatred offences should be introduced in respect of each of the protected characteristics including any new protected characteristics and recommended revising the racial hatred provisions to bring them into line with the new provisions. Following further consultation,[368] the Hate Crime and Public Order (Scotland) Act 2021 was passed by the Scottish Parliament and implemented on 1 April 2024.

Section 4(1) of the Hate Crime and Public Order (Scotland) Act 2021 preserves the existing stirring up racial hatred provision. While s.4(2) and (3) of the Hate Crime and Public Order (Scotland) Act 2021 introduce a new stirring up hatred offence in respect of (a) age, (b) disability, (c) religion or, in the case of a social or cultural group, perceived religious affiliation, (d) sexual orientation, (e) transgender identity, (f) variations in sex characteristics. The s.4(2) offence is narrower than the stirring up racial hatred provision as the latter includes insulting behaviour and behaviour that is likely to stir up hatred (even if it was not intended). It is a defence under s.4(4) of the Hate Crime and Public Order (Scotland) Act 2021 in relation to either a s.4(1) or 4(2) offence to show that the behaviour was reasonable. This reasonable defence may have implicitly brought Article 10 ECHR into play, following the reasoning of the Supreme Court in *DPP* v. *Ziegler*,[369] but we do not need to go down this path as s.4(5) of the Hate Crime and Public Order (Scotland) Act 2021 leaves us in no doubt that Article 10 ECHR is applicable:

> For the purposes of subsection (4), in determining whether behaviour or communication was reasonable, particular regard must be had to the importance of the right to

[364] Ibid, Recommendation 29 at [10.539]. [365] Ibid at [10.537]. [366] Ibid at [10.538].

[367] Independent Review of Hate Crime in Scotland, Final Report, 31 May 2018.

[368] Scottish Government, *One Scotland: Hate Has No Home Here* (November 2018).

[369] *DPP* v. *Ziegler* [2021] UKSC 23, [2022] AC 408, see discussion in Chapter 12.

freedom of expression by virtue of Article 10 of the European Convention on Human Rights, including the general principle that the right applies to the expression of information or ideas that offend, shock or disturb.

Further protection is accorded to freedom of expression by s.9 of the Hate Crime and Public Order (Scotland) Act 2021 which provides that for the purposes of s.4(2) of the Hate Crime and Public Order (Scotland) Act 2021, behaviour or material is not to be taken to be threatening or abusive solely on the basis that it involves or includes:

(a) discussion or criticism of matters relating to (i) age, (ii) disability, (iii) sexual orientation, (iv) transgender identity, (v) variations in sex characteristics,
(b) discussion or criticism relating to, or expressions of antipathy, dislike, ridicule or insult towards – (i) religion, whether religions generally or a particular religion; (ii) religious beliefs or practices, whether religious beliefs or practices generally or a particular religious belief or practice; (iii) the position of not holding religious beliefs, whether religious beliefs generally or a particular religious belief;
(c) proselytising, or
(d) urging of persons to cease practising their religions.

The presence of s.4(4) and s.9 of the Hate Crime and Public Order (Scotland) Act 2021 has not, however, convinced everyone that the Act will not have a chilling effect on freedom of expression. On the contrary, the enactment of these offences prompted considerable furore on social media, particularly in relation to the implications for gender critical views. Others raised concerns about the role the legislation accords to the police and the use of criminal sanctions.

Much of the public discourse surrounding the potential impact of the 2021 Act on freedom of expression concerns the addition of a stirring up hatred offence based on transgender identity, which implicates public debates regarding a purported tension between transgender and women's rights, and the exclusion of sex as a protected characteristic. This discourse obscures the more significant free speech problem raised by these offences that, like broadly articulated hate speech offences in other jurisdictions, criminalise expression absent any evidence that hatred or violence resulted, or was likely to result. In so doing, they impose criminal sanctions on expression that falls well outside of traditional notions of incitement.[370]

Another contentious aspect is the fact that the 2021 Act does not include hate based on sex, albeit that s.12 of the Act empowers Scottish Ministers to add sex by regulation to various provisions including s.4(3). In 2022, the Working Group on Misogyny and Criminal Justice recommended a Misogyny and Criminal

[370] Eliza Bechtold, 'Scotland's New Hate Crime Act Imperils Freedom of Expression' (2022) 26(2) Edinburgh Law Review 250, 252. See also, Hannah Quirk, 'Hate Crime' (2024) (5) Criminal Law Review 285.

Justice (Scotland) Act which would include a stirring up hatred against women and girls offence.[371] In March 2023, the Scottish Government launched a consultation on the draft provisions.[372] The Scottish Human Rights Commission responded observing 'that human rights law provides substantive authority for further action to protect women and girls from gender-based violence',[373] but that the provisions 'must be sufficiently predictable and interference with freedom of expression must be proportionate to the need to respond to gender-based violence against women and girls, articulated as misogyny in the legislation'.[374] In May 2025, the Scottish Government announced that it would no longer bring forward a Misogny Bill as there was insufficient time to draft a bill before the next Holyrood election that could reflect the Supreme Court's recent judgment in *For Women Scotland Ltd* v. *The Scottish Ministers.*[375] It has been reported that the Scottish Government will instead seek to amend existing hate crime legislation to provide protections on the basis of sex.[376]

11.5.1.6 Northern Ireland: Stirring Up Hatred Provisions

Northern Ireland currently has stirring up hatred offences in relation to the characteristics of race, religion, disability or sexual orientation.[377] A major independent review overseen by Judge Marrinan recommended reforming the offences to include hatred based on all current and proposed protected characteristics.[378] The Stormont Assembly resumed in early 2024, after a two-year suspension, following which the Northern Ireland Assembly and Executive Justice Minister, Naomi Long, indicated that legislation will be forthcoming.[379] At the time of writing we await publication of a draft bill.[380]

[371] Scottish Government, *Misogyny: A Human Rights Issue*, March 2022.

[372] Scottish Government, *Reforming the Criminal Law to Address Misogyny: A Scottish Government Consultation*, March 2023.

[373] Ibid at [4]. [374] Ibid at [5].

[375] Phil Sim, 'Scottish government drops plans for new misogyny law', *BBC News*, 2 May 2025, www.bbc.co.uk/news/articles/crkx31my24ro. See Chapter 14 for discussion of *For Women Scotland Ltd* v. *The Scottish Ministers* [2025] UKSC 16 which concerned the definition of a 'woman' in the Equality Act 2010.

[376] Ibid. [377] Part III Public Order (Northern Ireland) Order 1987.

[378] Northern Ireland Department of Justice, *Hate Crime Legislation in Northern Ireland: Independent Review*, 1 December 2020.

[379] Northern Ireland Assembly, Written Ministerial Statement of Naomi Long, Department of Justice – Hate Crime Legislation, 9 September 2024, www.niassembly.gov.uk/assembly-business/official-report/written-ministerial-statements/department-of-justice–hate-crime-legislation/#:~:text=The%20model%20will%20become%20the,will%20be%20retained%20in%20legislation. See also Northern Ireland Executive, Justice Minister reflects on Past Year, 3 February 2025, www.northernireland.gov.uk/news/justice-minister-reflects-past-year.

[380] David Lowe, 'Hate Crime in Northern Ireland: The Need for Legislation and a Bespoke Version of the Prevent Strategy' (2024) **37**(2) Terrorism and Political Violence 1.

11.5.2 Aggravated Public Order Offences

A number of public order offences exist in an aggravated form in England and Wales in respect of hatred based upon race or religion, but not, at present, other protected characteristics. There is a hierarchy of public order offences in ss.4, 4A and 5 POA 1986 in relation to using threatening, abusive (or in some cases) insulting words or behaviour or displaying the equivalent in writing, a sign, or other visible representation.

- s.4 POA 1986 applies where the defendant intends to cause a person to fear violence or to provoke violence.
- s.4A POA 1986 applies where the defendant intends to cause a person harassment, alarm or distress.
- Under s.5 POA 1986 there is no requirement of intent and there is no need to cause a person harassment, alarm or distress, it is enough if the conduct takes place within the hearing or sight of a person likely to be caused harassment, alarm or distress.

Although all three provisions originally applied to threatening, abusive or *insulting* words, s.5 POA 1986 has since been amended to remove the reference to *insulting*.[381] This curtailed the scope of this provision, which was seen as encroaching too heavily upon freedom of expression. The racially aggravated form of the offences was introduced by s.31 Crime and Disorder Act 1998, while religious aggravation was added by the Anti-Terrorism, Crime and Security Act 2001.[382] Where a defendant is prosecuted with an aggravated public order offence the prosecution must prove both the underlying public order offence and that in committing the offence the defendant demonstrated, or the offence was motivated by, racial or religious hostility. It is sufficient that the victim was presumed by the offender to be a member of a particular group, even if that was not correct.[383] Moreover, the fact that the offender's hostility was based on other factors in addition to racist/religious hostility is irrelevant.[384]

Convictions for aggravated s.4 POA 1986 offences have included: shouting racist death threats;[385] shouting racially abusive comments and holding a fist in a woman's face on a train;[386] use of racist slurs during an altercation;[387] and shouting 'bloody foreigners' and 'go back to your own country' at three Spanish women in the street.[388] An aggravated s.4A POA 1986 conviction was handed down in *R* v. *Mark Connolly* after an altercation in a supermarket car

[381] Section 57(2) Crime and Courts Act 2013.

[382] Section 39 Anti-Terrorism, Crime and Security Act 2001.

[383] Section 28(1) Crime and Disorder Act 1998.

[384] *R* v. *Rogers* [2007] UKHL 8, [2007] 2 AC 62 and *DPP* v. *McFarlane* [2002] EWHC 485 (Admin).

[385] *R* v. *Jonathan Salter* [2010] EWCA Crim 2594.

[386] *R* v. *Clark* [2003] EWCA Crim 3143, [2004] 2 Cr. App. R. (S.) 1.

[387] *DPP* v. *McFarlane* (n 384). [388] *R* v. *Rogers* (n 384).

park in which the defendant used racist slurs and threatened to hit the victim,[389] whilst an aggravated s.5 POA 1986 offence was committed when a defendant shouted "Polish f****** b*******, f*** off!" within the hearing of their Polish next door neighbours.[390] In *R* v. *CF*, the defendant was also convicted of an aggravated s.5 POA 1986 offence after making a racially obscene remark to a police officer while being detained in a police cell.[391] Further examples of aggravated s.5 POA 1986 offences include racist comments made by a black defendant to two white parking attendants;[392] as well as racist slurs on a train.[393] A further case of note in relation to s.5 POA 1986 is *Ian Sleeper* v. *Commissioner of Police of the Metropolis* which concerned an applicant who had been arrested for a religiously aggravated s.5 offence in connection with two signs that he displayed outside Southwark Cathedral which stated 'Love Muslims Ban Islam the Religion of Terror!' and 'Love Muslims Hate Islam Jesus is Love + Hope'.[394] The Crown Prosecution Service subsequently decided not to prosecute and the applicant brought a claim against the Commissioner of Police of the Metropolis for false imprisonment.[395] This claim was dismissed by the County Court on the basis that the arrest was lawful as the arresting officer had a reasonable suspicion that the applicant has commited an offence and his belief that arrest was necessary was objectively reasonable.[396] The High Court agreed that the arrest and detention were lawful,[397] in particular it found that the County Court had recognised the applicant's Article 10 ECHR rights and engaged in a demonstrable balancing exercise.[398]

The Law Commission recommended extending the aggravated offences to sexual orientation, transgender and disability. They decided not to extend the provisions to sex or gender on the ground that it will be ineffective, and perhaps even counterproductive.[399] They also recommend that a conviction should be possible where the prosecution proves that the offence was motivated by, or the defendant demonstrated hostility towards 'one or more' protected characteristics.[400] At the time of writing there have been no amendments to the aggravated offences, however, in its 2024 election manifesto Labour declared that it will 'protect LGBT+ and disabled people by making all existing strands of hate crime an aggravated offence'.[401] We thus await further developments in this context.

389 *R* v. *Mark Connolly* [2018] EWCA Crim 3123.
390 *DPP* v. *D* [2017] EWHC 2244 (Admin), [2017] 4 WLR 177.
391 *R* v. *CF* [2006] EWCA Crim 3323, [2007] 1 WLR 1021.
392 *Johnson* v. *DPP* [2008] EWHC 509. 393 *DPP* v. *Smith* [2017] EWHC 3193.
394 [2025] EWHC 151 (KB). 395 Ibid at [4]. 396 Ibid at [6]. 397 Ibid at [145].
398 Ibid at [134]. 399 Law Commission, *Hate Crime Laws: Final Report* (n 4) at [5.5].
400 Ibid at [8.193]–[8.197], Recommendation 15.
401 Labour Party, *Change – Labour Party Manifesto 2024*.

11.5.2.1 Aggravated Offences in Scotland

The Hate Crime and Public Order (Scotland) Act 2021 maintained the existing legislative protections from crimes aggravated by prejudice towards race, religion, disability, transgender identity and sexual orientation while introducing new protections against offences aggravated by prejudice towards a person's age. It also updated the definition of transgender identity and created a separate characteristic of 'variations in sex characteristics'.

11.5.2.2 Aggravated Offences in Northern Ireland

There are currently no aggravated offences in Northern Ireland.[402] The independent review in Northern Ireland of hate crime thus recommended adding aggravated offences based on all current and proposed protected characteristics to all existing criminal offences.[403] However, David Lowe suggests that

> While ideally this should be the case, it is recommended that in drafting initial legislation the focus should be on public order offences, assaults, wounding, and criminal damage. Most of the hate crime offences recorded cover these categories of offences. If it is applied to sexual offences such as rape it will be more difficult to prove it was 'hate' related.[404]

As noted above, we wait to see what emerges from the Assembly.

11.5.3 Communications Offences

There are several offences in the Communications Act 2003 and the Malicious Communications Act 1988 applicable to hate speech. The Law Commission recommended repealing and replacing these provisions in July 2021.[405] The Malicious Communications Act 1988 had itself resulted from a Law Commission report in 1985,[406] however, as the Law Commission observed during its 2021 inquiry, technology and communications have fundamentally changed since then which necessitates the need for further reform:

> When we published our report in 1985 leading to the enactment of the Malicious Communications Act 1988, only 12.6% of UK households owned a home computer – and the internet wouldn't be invented for another four years. Even in 2003, when the Communications Act 2003 was passed, only 46% of UK households had internet

[402] Northern Ireland Department of Justice, *Hate Crime Legislation in Northern Ireland: Independent Review*, 1 December 2020 at [43].

[403] Ibid, Recommendation 2. [404] Lowe (n 380), p.3.

[405] Law Commission, *Modernising Communications Offences: A Final Report* (n 4).

[406] Law Commission, *Poisoned-Pen Letters* (1985) Law Com. No. 147.

access. It was another year before Facebook was released (and, even then, available only to select universities and colleges). Twitter was released in 2006. The first iPhone was not released until 2007, four years after enactment of the Communications Act. Nearly two decades later, in every single second that passes, nearly three million emails are sent, nearly ten thousand Tweets are posted, and over three quarters of a million WhatsApp messages are sent [which by late 2020 was actually 1.15 million per second], amongst the other c.95 terabytes of internet traffic per second.[407]

The 2021 recommendations were accepted by the Government and were included in the Online Safety Bill, however, one of the proposed recommendations was removed during the passage of the Bill. Consequently, some of the provisions that the Law Commission recommended repealing remain in force, whilst others have been replaced and supplemented by the Online Safety Act 2023.

11.5.3.1 Grossly Offensive Messages

There are two statutory provisions which criminalise the sending of grossly offensive messages. The first is section 1 of the Malicious Communications Act 1988 which was enacted to tackle the problem of 'poison pen' letters,[408] but was later extended to electronic communications or articles of any description which convey a message which is 'indecent or grossly offensive'. The second is s.127(1)(a) of the Communications Act 2003 which provides that it is an offence to send messages or other matters that are grossly offensive, indecent, obscene or of a menacing character by means of a *public electronic communications network*. In *DPP* v. *Collins*, Lord Bingham explained the roles of the two provisions:

> First, the object of section 127(1)(a) and its predecessor sections is not to protect people against receipt of unsolicited messages which they may find seriously objectionable. That object is addressed in section 1 of the Malicious Communications Act 1988, which does not require that messages shall, to be proscribed, have been sent by post, or telephone, or public electronic communications network. The purpose of the legislation which culminates in section 127(1)(a) was to prohibit the use of a service provided and funded by the public for the benefit of the public for the transmission of communications which contravene the basic standards of our society. A letter dropped through the letterbox may be grossly offensive, obscene, indecent or menacing, and may well be covered by section 1 of the 1988 Act, but it does not fall within the legislation now under consideration.[409]

[407] Law Commission, *Modernising Communications Offences: A Final Report* (n 4) at pp.1–2.

[408] Hansard, HC Deb 12 February 1988, vol 127 cc607–25 and Law Commission, *Report on Poison-Pen Letters* (n 406).

[409] *DPP* v. *Collins* [2006] UKHL 40, [2006] 1 WLR 2223.

11.5.3.1.1 *Section 127 Communications Act 2003*

Section 127(1)(a) of the Communications Act 2003 provides that it is an offence to send by means of a public electronic communications network messages or other matters that are grossly offensive, indecent, obscene or of a menacing character. In *DPP* v. *Collins*, a s.127 offence was committed when Collins left racially offensive telephone messages at the offices of his Member of Parliament.[410] The Lords stated that the standard for the offence is 'gross offensiveness' (not fear or apprehension), and that the offence is complete when the message was sent.[411] Section 127 offences were also established in *Cobban* v. *DPP* where the applicants (who were serving officers of the Metropolitan Police Service) had sent grossly offensive messages to each other in a private Whatsapp group.[412] On appeal the applicants argued that s.127 was not applicable to private consensual messages and thus that they should not have been convicted. This was rejected by the High Court.[413] The s.127 provision has also been used in cases where the defendant has disseminated Holocaust denial on the internet.[414] This is significant because although there is 'no crime of Holocaust denial in this jurisdiction',[415] Holocaust denial is a 'grossly offensive' message for the purposes of s.127. Thus, in *R* v. *Alison Chabloz,* the defendant was convicted of a s.127 offence in respect of the publication of various videos on YouTube in which she sang lyrics that consisted of antisemitic tropes and Holocaust denial set to the tunes of well-known Hebrew songs.[416] Meanwhile, in *Vincent Raynouard* v. *His Majesty's Advocate*, the Scottish High Court of Justiciary held that as dissemination of Holocaust denial online was contrary to s.127, the appellant could be extradited to France where he would be charged with offences relating to Holocaust denial. In coming to that determination, it observed 'that although it is not an offence to hold these views and, in certain contexts, to express them, it is a breach ofsection 127 of the 2007 Act to communicate them to the public on the internet'.[417]

The meaning of 'grossly offensive' was further considered in *R (on the application of Lynsay Watson)* v. *The Chief Constable of Greater Manchester* in which the applicant challenged the decision of the police to take no further action following a complaint about a number of posts on Twitter in the

[410] Ibid.

[411] Ibid at [8]. See also *Cobban* v. *DPP* [2024] EWHC 1908 (Admin) where the Court stated at [50] that: 'In our opinion, Lord Bingham's analysis in *Collins* as to the purpose and construction of section 127(1)(a) represents a binding decision of general application.'

[412] Ibid. [413] Ibid.

[414] *Vincent Raynouard* v. *His Majesty's Advocate* [2024] HCJAC 2, 2024 S.L.T. 179, 2024 S.C.C.R. 101.

[415] Ibid at [14]. [416] *R* v. *Alison Chabloz* [2019] EWHC 3094, [2020] 1 Cr. App. R. 17.

[417] *Vincent Raynouard* v. *His Majesty's Advocate* (n 414) at [29].

aftermath of the murder of a sixteen-year-old trans girl.[418] Hill J considered the legal framework under both s.127 CA and s.1 Malicious Communications Act 1988 and the applicable case law before rejecting the claimant's argument that 'the police had incorrectly applied the law in concluding that the posts were not "grossly offensive"'.[419] Hill J reasoned as follows:

> In my judgment the content of the posts illustrates that the Interested Party was doing two things.
>
> First, he was condemning the fact that, as he saw it, the tragic murder . . . was being 'weaponised' by activists in order to attack JK Rowling and other campaigners. This was a valid opinion that cannot conceivably be said to meet the 'grossly offensive' threshold set out in the case-law.
>
> Second, he was expressing the opinion that gender is biologically determined and cannot be changed, such that it is appropriate to refer to someone by pronouns which match their biological sex, including on their death certificate. This is a controversial matter of public interest in which many people share the view underlying the Interested Party's tweets. It has been specifically recognised that the Interested Party's opinion about gender is one that should be tolerated in a democratic society: as well as *Miller*, see *Forstater* v *CGD Europe* [2022] ICR 1 and *Higgs* v *Farmor's School* [2025] EWCA Civ 109 at [175](4).[420]

The judge thus determined that:

> the Defendant was entitled, and correct, to conclude that posts did not cross the threshold to be considered objectively 'grossly offensive', as interpreted by the case-law, by reference to the context of the posts and their content (irrespective of the Interested Party's state of mind). The Defendant's conclusion properly reflected society's fundamental values of free speech, including the need for tolerance of statements and opinions that some might find offensive or upsetting.[421]

The breadth of the offence and in particular the subjective nature of 'grossly offensive' has given rise to concerns as to its compatibility with Article 10 ECHR. For these reasons the Law Commission proposed repealing the provision and replacing it with a harmful communications offence.[422] This was intended to shift the focus from the *content* of the communication and towards its *potentially harmful effects*. They proposed a threshold of 'likely to cause harm', where the defendant *intends* to cause harm *without reasonable excuse*.[423] This was accepted by the Government and a clause appeared in an early version of the Online Safety Bill. The harmful communications offence

418 *R (on the application of Lynsay Watson)* v. *The Chief Constable of Greater Manchester* [2025] EWHC 954 (Admin).

419 Ibid at [36]–[48].

420 Ibid at [67]–[69].

421 Ibid at [73].

422 Law Commission, *Modernising Communications Offences: A Final Report* (n 4) at [2.257] and Recommendation 1.

423 Law Commission, *Modernising Communications Offences: A Final Report* (n 4).

was, however, removed from the Bill due to concerns about the impact on freedom of expression. Consequently, at the time of writing, s.127 of the Communications Act 2003 remains in force.[424]

11.5.3.1.2 *Section 1 of the Malicious Communications Act 1988*

Section 1 of the Malicious Communications Act 1988 covers letters, electronic communications or articles of any description which convey a message which is 'indecent or grossly offensive'. A person is guilty of an offence if their purpose, or one of their purposes, in sending it is to cause distress or anxiety to the recipient or to any other person to whom they intend that it or its contents or nature should be communicated.[425] The Law Commission expressed the same concerns about this offence (as the s.127 offence) namely that 'grossly offensive' is too vague which may render it incompatible with Article 10 ECHR.[426] Moreover, in the context of this offence the Law Commission stated that:

> the problem is compounded because the grossly offensive or indecent nature of the communication is relevant not only to the conduct element of the offence (the sending of a grossly offensive communication to a victim), but also to the mental element (the intention to cause a victim distress or anxiety). The nature of the communication may constitute evidence that one of the defendant's purposes was to cause the victim distress or anxiety. In other words, the prosecution would suggest to the jury that the communication is so grossly offensive that the defendant's purpose must have been to cause its recipient distress. Hence, the problem of vagueness and uncertainty arises in relation to both the conduct and the mental elements of the offence.[427]

Consequently, they recommended repealing s.1 MCA and replacing it with the harm-based offence.[428] However, as noted above, that provision did not make it into the Online Safety Act 2023.

[424] Note, that s.127(2) of the Communications Act which dealt with false messages was repealed in respect of England, Wales and Northern Ireland and replaced by the false communications offence in s.179 of the Online Safety Act 2023.

[425] See *R* v. *Casserly (Thomas)* [2024] EWCA Crim 25 in which a defendant successfully appealed against his s.1 Malicious Communications Act 1988 conviction in relation to an email that he sent to an elected town councillor. The Court of Appeal held at [52] that the conviction was unsafe as the 'jury should have been directed that the law protects freedom of speech because it is part of living in a free and democratic society. Whether a communication is so grossly offensive that it amounts to a criminal offence and loses the protection of freedom of speech, depends on its content, the context in which it was sent and the purpose(s) of the sender.'

[426] Law Commission, *Harmful Online Communications: The Criminal Offences – A Consultation Paper*, Consultation Paper 248, 11/09/2020 at [3.113] and [3.118].

[427] Ibid at [3.114].

[428] Law Commission, *Modernising Communications Offences: A Final Report* (n 4), Recommendation 1.

11.5.3.2 *Persistent Use of a Public Electronic Communications Network for the Purpose of Causing Annoyance, Inconvenience or Needless Anxiety to Another*

Section 127(2)(c) of the Communications Act 2003 (CA 2003) renders it an offence to persistently make use of a public electronic communications network for the purpose of causing annoyance, inconvenience or needless anxiety to another. The offence was initially concerned with protecting public communications networks and those involved in their operation, in particular there was a concern to address repeated hoax or vexatious or trivial calls to emergency services.

More recently, the High Court in *Scottow* v. *CPS* considered the provision in the context of social media posts.[429] Scottow had been tried in the Magistrates' Court at St Albans and convicted by District Judge Margaret Dodd of one offence of improper use of a public communications network, contrary to s.127(2)(c) of the Communications Act 2003.[430] The prosecution stemmed from complaints about messages posted by Scottow on social media. The complainant, Hayden, is a trans woman, with a public profile as an activist and advocate of transgender rights. Scottow describes herself as a radical feminist and has contrary views to Hayden. The complaint related to seventeen messages, sixteen were tweets which Scottow admitted making, and one was a message on Mumsnet, which she could not recall. It was accepted that the messages had been sent over a 'public telecommunications network'. The question for the Court was whether the messages represented the 'persistent' use of a network 'for the purpose of causing annoyance, inconvenience or needless anxiety' to Hayden within the meaning of s.127(2)(c) CA 2003. In interpreting the provision, Mr Justice Warby observed that 'the wording, legislative history, and context make it apparent that the mischief at which the offence … was aimed is not the communication of information or ideas that offend the recipient, or even the communication of messages that have offence as a purpose'.[431] Instead, its purpose is to prohibit the abuse of facilities afforded by a publicly funded network by repeatedly exploiting them for no other purpose than to annoy them, or cause them inconvenience, or needless anxiety. Consequently, the focus of the provision 'is not on the content of any communication, but rather its purpose and the way in which that purpose is put into effect'.[432] Warby J thus had no doubt the provision was intended to address prank calls, silent calls, heavy breathing, and other common forms of nuisance phone call. Although he resisted the argument that 'content will always be irrelevant' he found much force in the argument 'that what Parliament intended was to proscribe a course of persistent conduct the sole

[429] *Scottow* v. *CPS* [2020] EWHC 3421, [2021] 1 WLR 1828. [430] Ibid at [1].
[431] Ibid at [32]. [432] Ibid at [32].

purpose of which is to cause annoyance, anxiety or inconvenience by virtue of its persistence, rather than its informational content'.[433] He thus held the tweets did not constitute a persistent use of the network. Moreover, he went on to observe that s.127(2)(c) CA 2003 should, according to s.3 HRA, be read and given effect in a manner that is compatible with Article 10 ECHR as far as it is possible to do so.[434] He observed that the Judge had not given appropriate consideration to Article 10 ECHR as he appeared to have 'considered that a criminal conviction was merited for acts of unkindness, and calling others names, and that such acts could only be justified if they made a contribution to a "proper debate"'.[435] Warby J thus concluded that no convincing, relevant or sufficient reasons had been given for the decision to prosecute, there was no pressing social need, and the prosecution and conviction represented 'a grossly disproportionate and entirely unjustified state interference with free speech'.[436]

The Law Commission has since proposed repealing the provision and replacing it with an offence to address hoax calls to the emergency services.[437] At the time of writing, s.127(2)(c) CA 2003 has yet to be amended.

11.5.3.3 *Obligations on Providers of Internet Services*

The Online Safety Act 2023 received Royal Asset in October 2023. It imposes duties on organisations providing internet services such as user-to-user platforms and search engines.[438] Those duties include identifying, mitigating and managing the risks of harm from illegal content and activity. The obligations include risk assessment and preventative measures as well as the removal of illegal content. Specific duties relate to priority offences which include in Schedule 7 both the aggravated public order offences and the stirring up hatred offences. A new regulatory framework is created in which Ofcom is designated the online safety regulator and in December 2024 Ofcom issued its first Illegal Content Codes of Practice.[439] Penalties for breaching the Act include fines of up to £18 million or 10 per cent of global turnover (whichever is higher). It is also possible that an order of service cessation will be issued, which must be approved by the court. Only time will tell the impact that this legislation will have, but scholars have raised concerns, in part by looking at the operation of Germany's Network Enforcement Act, that it may result in platforms censoring more speech, 'and using the imposed "responsibility" as

433 Ibid at [32]. 434 Ibid at [33]. 435 Ibid at [43]. 436 Ibid at [47].

437 Law Commission, *Modernising Communications Offences: A Final Report* (n 4) at Recommendation 5.

438 Section 3 Online Safety Act 2023.

439 Ofcom Illegal Content Codes of Practice for User-to-User Services and Ofcom Illegal Content Codes of Practice for Search Services.

an excuse to censor speech that does not conform to their objectives'.[440] Indeed, Peter Coe argues that in creating legislation 'to protect the public from hate speech we may unintentionally open Pandora's Box by giving platforms a statutory justification to take more "control of the message"'.[441]

11.5.4 Non-crime/Non-criminal Hate Incidents

The police record 'non-crime hate incidents' (hate incidents that do not amount to criminal offences) in order to track incidents that could escalate into more serious harm or indicate heightened community tensions. The practice of recording 'non-crime hate incidents' stems from the Stephen Lawrence Inquiry which highlighted the need for the police to respond to racist incidents as well as crimes and thus to report, record and investigate with equal commitment.[442] This has been the subject of legal challenge based on Article 10 ECHR.

Responding to the Stephen Lawrence Inquiry Report, the Association of Chief Police Officers (ACPO) and the Home Office published documents in 2000 and 2005 which set out guidance on non-crime hate incidents. In 2014, the College of Policing updated that guidance which it published as the Hate Crime Operational Guidance. The Hate Crime Operational Guidance defined a non-crime hate incident as: 'any non-crime incident which is perceived by the victim, or any other person, to be motivated (wholly or partially) by a hostility or prejudice'. It provided that where any person reports a hate incident it must be recorded regardless of whether the person reporting it is the victim and irrespective of whether there is any evidence to identify the hate element.

It was the 2014 Hate Crime Operational Guidance and its application that was challenged in *R (on the application of Miller)* v. *College of Policing, CC of Humberside.*[443] The facts were that, Miller, a former police officer had posted numerous tweets relating to transgender issues. His tweets were reported to the police as transphobic and were recorded by the police as a non-crime hate incident; a police officer also went to Miller's place of work to speak to him, although Miller was not there at the time. Miller argued that this violated his Article 10 ECHR right to express himself on transgender issues. In particular, he challenged (i) the legality of the Hate Crime Operational Guidance and

[440] Peter Coe, 'The Draft Online Safety Bill and the Regulation of Hate Speech: Have We Opened Pandora's Box?' (2022) **14**(1) Journal of Media Law 50.

[441] Ibid.

[442] The Stephen Lawrence Inquiry, *Report of an Inquiry by Sir William Macpherson of Cluny*, Cm 4262-I, February 1999, Chapter 47 at [13].

[443] *R (on the application of Miller)* v. *College of Policing, CC of Humberside* [2020] EWHC 225 and *R (on the application of Miller)* v. *College of Policing, CC of Humberside* [2021] EWCA Civ 1926.

(ii) how the police dealt with him under that guidance. At first instance Knowles J rejected the argument that the Guidance was incompatible with Article 10 ECHR.[444] He offered two reasons for this. First, that the recording of a non-crime hate incident did not interfere with Article 10 ECHR.[445] Second, that even if it did interfere with Article 10 ECHR this was justified under Article 10(2) ECHR.[446] However, in respect of Miller's second argument (namely how the police had dealt with Miller), Knowles J found that the police had violated Article 10 ECHR.[447] This arose not from the recording of a non-crime hate incident, but rather from the fact that they had gone to his place of work and had warned him about the risk of prosecution if matters escalated.[448]

The Court of Appeal overturned the High Court's judgment on the first issue.[449] It held that not only was there was an interference with Article 10 ECHR,[450] but in fact there was a violation as this was not necessary in a democratic society.[451] This stemmed from the breadth of what may be deemed non-crime hate speech, the fact that incidents were recorded regardless of whether there was evidence that the speech was motivated by hostility, and the fact that there was no Guidance in respect of irrational complaints or those where there is no evidence of hostility.[452] The Court of Appeal also observed that the non-crime hate label 'is capable of unfairly stigmatising those against whom such a complaint is made', especially as there 'is no provision for proportionality to be applied to recording'.[453]

Since then, none-crime hate incidents have been put on a statutory footing in the Police, Crime, Sentencing and Courts Act 2022 (PCSCA) where they are referred to as 'non-criminal hate incidents'. Section 60 PCSCA 2022 provides that the Secretary of State may issue a Code of Practice provided a draft of the code is laid before and approved by a resolution of each House of Parliament (s.61). A new Code of Practice was laid before Parliament and came into force in 2023.[454] It provides that personal data may only be recorded if the event presents a real risk of significant harm to individuals or groups with a particular characteristic(s) and/or a real risk that a future criminal offence may be committed against individuals or groups with a particular characteristic(s).[455] If this threshold is not met, but all other criteria for recording are met, then an incident without personal data may be recorded instead.[456] The Code also specifies that a proportionate, necessary and common-sense approach is

[444] Ibid. [445] Ibid at [175]–[185]. [446] Ibid at [186]–[237]. [447] Ibid at [238]–[289].

[448] Ibid. [449] Ibid. [450] Ibid at [64]–[76]. [451] Ibid at [95]–[124]. [452] Ibid at [117].

[453] Ibid at [117].

[454] Code of Practice on the Recording and Retention of Personal Data in respect of Non-Crime Hate Incidents.

[455] Home Office, *Statutory Guidance: Non-Crime Hate Incidents – Code of Practice on the Recording and Retention of Personal Data*, 06/06/2023 at [21].

[456] Ibid at [23].

required.[457] In respect of proportionality, the Code states that recording without personal data should always be considered first as the least intrusive method.[458] The Code also specifies that 'special regard should always be given by the recording authority to the impact of NCHI recording on freedom of expression, including the potential risks of a record having a chilling effect on an individual's right to freedom of expression'.[459] The obligation to consider the impact on freedom of expression and to consider whether it is proportionate and necessary is, of course, in line with the HRA. It is difficult to see how the requirement to use 'common-sense' is to be interpreted. At the time of writing it is reported that the Conservative party are pushing for an amendment to be made to the Government's Crime and Policing Bill which would scrap the recording of non-crime hate incidents in most cases.[460]

11.5.5 Freedom of Expression, Hate Speech, Education and Employment

Finally, it is important to be aware that the expression of certain views has given rise to legal issues in respect of education and employment. Cases litigated under the Equality Act 2010 are addressed in Chapter 14. In the context of education, it is also important to note the case of *R (on the application of Ngole)* v. *University of Sheffield* in which a social work student was removed from his university course on fitness to practice grounds after posting a series of comments via Facebook in which he disapproved of homosexual acts. He argued that this violated Articles 9 and 10 ECHR. At first instance it was determined that the interference was justified,[461] however, this was overturned by the Court of Appeal.[462] It held that removing him from the course was disproportionate because the university's position precluded Ngole from expressing his views in any public space. Crucially, at no stage had the University made it clear that it was the *manner and language* in which Ngole had expressed his views that was the problem, nor had they discussed or offered him guidance as to how he might more appropriately and moderately express his views in a public forum and in a way in which it would be clear that he would never discriminate on such grounds or allow his views to interfere with his work as a professional social worker.[463] The Court of

[457] Ibid at [30]. [458] Ibid at [31 IV]. [459] Ibid at [44].

[460] Joshua Nevett, 'Tories push to ban recording of non-crime hate incidents', *BBC News*, 22 April 2025, www.bbc.co.uk/news/articles/c70zlgz4yjeo.

[461] *R (on the application of Ngole)* v. *University of Sheffield* [2017] EWHC 2669 (Admin), [2018] HRLR 1.

[462] *R (on the application of Ngole)* v. *University of Sheffield* [2019] EWCA Civ 1127.

[463] Ibid at [5].

Appeal thus determined that a less intrusive alternative would have been sufficient.[464]

Ngole was one of the cases cited by the Conservative Government in promulgating the Higher Education (Freedom of Speech) Act 2023. The Act reflected concerns about no-platforming and cancel culture on university campuses.

> The rise of intolerance and 'cancel culture' upon our campuses is one that directly affects individuals and their livelihoods. Students have been expelled from their courses, academics fired and others who have been forced to live under the threat of violence. These high profile incidents are but the tip of the iceberg. For every Ngole, Carl or Todd whose story is known, evidence suggests there are many more who have felt they had to keep silent, withheld research or believe they have faced active discrimination in appointment or promotion because of views they have expressed.[465]

The Higher Education (Freedom of Speech) Act 2023 placed duties to take steps to secure freedom of speech on higher education providers, constituent intuitions (such as constituent colleges) and students' unions. It also provided that civil claims may be brought in respect of breaches of those duties and established a free speech complaints system and sanctions which could include fines. The legislation thus provided for greater State interference in order to secure freedom of expression, which is at odds with many of the democratic 'minimal state' arguments for freedom of expression. The value accorded to freedom of expression by the Act also sat somewhat oddly with the Government's own Prevent strategy.[466] In July 2024 the newly elected Labour Government paused the coming into force of some of the legislation. At the time of writing it appears that some of the provisions will be brought into force in August 2025, but that other provisions including the introduction of a tort for breach of the statutory duty have been scrapped.[467]

11.6 CONCLUSIONS

The direction of travel in domestic law in respect of freedom of expression and hate speech is a complex one, which reflects both attempts to address

[464] Ibid.

[465] Department for Education, *Higher Education: Free Speech and Academic Freedom,* February 2021, CP 394, p.5.

[466] See Chapter 8.

[467] Department for Education, Office for Students and the Rt Hon Bridget Phillipson MP Press Release, 'Government reaffirmd commitment to free speech in universities', 15 January 2025, www.gov.uk/government/news/government-reaffirms-commitment-to-free-speech-in-universities.

contemporary problems, as well as political tensions. Some developments are intended to provide greater protection to freedom of expression, others are intended to address gaps in protection from hate speech. At the time of writing, while we await reform of the current hierarchy of hate speech, the enactment of the Online Safety Act 2023 has provided a new regulatory regime to address illegal and harmful content online. Only time will tell how this will operate in practice and its ramifications for freedom of expression.

One of the difficulties in addressing hate speech remains the contested nature of what constitutes 'hate'. This is particularly evident in discourse surrounding trans rights, gender identity and gender critical views, which is giving rise to litigation in a wide range of contexts stemming from criminal law to employment law. These challenges are unlikely to dissipate soon, and the courts will inevitably be faced with further cases in which they will have to determine where legal lines are drawn. They are not, however, the only ones who have to make determinations. The Online Safety Act 2023 places obligations on service providers while the Higher Education (Freedom of Speech) Act 2023 places obligations on higher education institutes. In this respect, legal responsibility for striking the balance between complex competing rights is increasingly taking place within the private sector, with far greater legal obligations and regulatory oversight than ever before.

12 The Right to Protest

CONTENTS

12.1 INTRODUCTION

Freedom to protest is an essential form of political expression that differentiates a democratic society from a totalitarian one.[1] As Eric Barendt observes for many people 'participation in public meetings or less formal forms of protest – marches or other demonstrations on the streets, picketing, and sit-ins – is not just the best, but the only effective means of communicating their views' to those in power, and the wider public.[2] There is also a recipient rationale for protecting protest as it is vital to democracy that we are aware of the views of others. Freedom to protest is not, however, solely concerned with democracy, nor is it solely concerned with expression, there is also the sense of autonomy, dignity, identity and community that is derived from forming and gathering in groups. As Abu El-Hak, Probert and Srinivasan explain, '[a]ssembly lies at the heart of our existence as social beings, at the foundation of our communities and polities, and at the core of our capacity to collectively begin anew to shape our lives and worlds', indeed, it is through assembling that 'people form senses of belonging and shape and nourish their identities'.[3] John Inazu also emphasises that a 'key aspect of the right of assembly is that it facilitates the formation of collective identity and belief within a social practice'.[4]

Yet while freedom to protest is valuable to individuals, groups and society, protests can be disruptive, annoying, offensive, harmful and violent. Moreover, any form of action or expression can be labelled a 'protest' by those engaged in it, including forms of criminal damage, violence, and as we

[1] The values underpinning freedom of expression and its relationship to democracy were considered in detail in Chapter 11.

[2] Eric Barendt, *Freedom of Speech* (Oxford University Press, 2005), p.268.

[3] Tabatha Abu El-Haj, Thomas Probert and Sharath Srinivasan, 'On Assembly' in Tabatha Abu El-Haj, Thomas Probert and Sharath Srinivasan (eds), *The Oxford Handbook of Peaceful Assembly* (Oxford University Press, 2025).

[4] John Inazu, 'Assembly, Pluralism and Identity' in Abu El-Haj, Probert and Srinivasan (eds), *The Oxford Handbook of Peaceful Assembly* (ibid). See also, John Inazu, *Liberty's Refuge* (Yale University Press, 2012).

saw in the last chapter, hate speech. This was evident in the summer of 2024 when hundreds of people were arrested in connection with violence at demonstrations organised by far-right groups following the murder of three children in Southport.[5] The Prime Minister, Keir Starmer, issued a statement in relation to those events declaring that: 'This is not a protest, it is organised, violent thuggery and it has no place on our streets or online.'[6]

There is clearly a line to be drawn between legitimate protest and violence and this is reflected in the ECHR which accords protection to 'peaceful assembly'. Yet while violent conduct does not warrant the protection of the Convention,[7] it may become more difficult to draw the line in respect of hateful or disruptive acts of protest.[8] Thus difficulties arise in determining where the line should be drawn between competing rights and interests. As David Feldman observes:

> In every society there is a tension between the desire of citizens to be free from annoyance and disorder and their wish to be free to bring to the attention of their fellow citizens matters which they consider to be important. The way in which any legal system resolves the tension, and the balance which it strikes between the competing interests, is indicative of the attitude of that society towards the relative value of different sorts of freedom. A society which tolerates a good deal of annoyance or disorder so as to encourage the greatest possible freedom of expression, particularly political expression, is likely to be one in which the public, political activities of citizens are regarded as making a useful contribution to the health of a democratic system. The citizens will enjoy a right, if not an obligation, to participate in political debate, and try to persuade other people to their point of view. The problem is that this inevitably collides with other people's right to be free of that sort of persuasion and of its accompanying annoyance and even offence. The job of the lawmakers is to determine when the interests of society in being free of unwanted persuasion and disorder outweigh the interest in free expression of opinions and persuasion.[9]

In a rights-based system we thus have to consider where those lines should be drawn and by whom. To what extent should an executive-dominated legislature determine the boundaries of protest? Should there be deference to those making decisions in real-time on the ground (i.e., the police)? And what role is there for the courts in upholding the freedom to protest? As we will see

[5] Thomas Mackintosh and Vicky Wong, 'Nearly 400 arrested after six days of violence', *BBC News*, 5 August 2024, www.bbc.co.uk/news/articles/cyvpp3e7mn4o.

[6] Prime Minister's Office, 10 Downing Street, The Rt Hon Sir Keir Starmer KCB, *Prime Minister Statement*, 4 August 2024.

[7] In addition to falling outside the ambit of 'peaceful assembly' which is protected by Article 11 ECHR, it may also fall foul of Article 17 ECHR; see discussion in this chapter as well as earlier discussion on Article 17 ECHR in Chapter 11.

[8] On peaceful and disruptive protest, see David Mead, *The New Law of Peaceful Protest: Rights and Regulation in the Human Rights Act Era* (Hart, 2010), chs.6 and 7.

[9] David Feldman, *Civil Liberties and Human Rights* (2nd ed) (Oxford University Press, 2002), p.1008.

throughout this chapter, the domestic and ECtHR case law reflects these tensions, with some cases leaning towards a more deferential approach and others establishing a more robust role for the courts.

12.2 PROTEST AND THE EUROPEAN CONVENTION ON HUMAN RIGHTS

The focus of this chapter is Article 11 ECHR, which provides a right to freedom of association and freedom of assembly.[10] It is important, however, to observe that the ways in which States deal with protesters may have implications for many other Convention rights, especially where they engage in use of force, unlawful detention, surveillance, or where they discriminate against particular groups of protesters. We thus commence this chapter by considering the ways in which protest cases raise issues which span the Convention rights.[11]

12.2.1 Article 2 ECHR

We considered Article 2 ECHR, the right to life, in detail in Chapter Four, noting that the Article imposes both substantive and procedural obligations on the State.[12] There are numerous cases in which the ECtHR has found a violation of those obligations in respect of protesters. For example, in *Boboc* v. *Republic of Moldova*, the ECtHR found a violation after the police beat a man to death while he was lying on the ground.[13] In several other cases, the ECtHR has held that while use of force may be justifiable, immediate recourse to lethal force is not acceptable. Consequently, in *Güleç* v. *Turkey*, a case in which the applicant's son was shot during a demonstration, the ECtHR held that it was incomprehensible and unacceptable that State agents had only been equipped with lethal weapons.[14] Similarly in *Şimşek* v. *Turkey*, a case in which officers shot directly at demonstrators without first having recourse to less life-threatening methods, the ECtHR held that the failure to provide necessary equipment was unacceptable.[15]

[10] See also, European Court of Human Rights, *Guide on Article 11 of the European Convention on Human Rights, Freedom of Assembly and Association* (Updated on 29 February 2024).

[11] See also, European Court of Human Rights, *Guide on the Case-Law of the European Convention on Human Rights, Mass Protests* (Updated on 29 February 2024). On the earlier case law, see Mead (n 8), ch.2.

[12] See Chapter 4.

[13] *Boboc* v. *Republic of Moldova*, App. No. 44592/16, 07/06/2022 at [49]–[51].

[14] *Güleç* v. *Turkey* (1999) 28 EHRR 121 at [71].

[15] *Şimşek* v. *Turkey*, App. No. 35072/97, 26/07/2005 at [104]–[133].

In considering the ambit of Article 2 ECHR it is important to recall the role of the 'honest belief' test, which was discussed in Chapter 4.[16] This was of paramount importance in *Giuliani and Gaggio* v. *Italy*, when a carabinieri shot and killed a man during demonstrations surrounding the G8 in Genoa. [17] In that case, the carabinieri had seen Giuliani lifting a fire extinguisher in a manner which suggested that he would use it as a blunt instrument to attack the three carabinieri who were trapped in a Jeep amidst a large crowd of violent protestors. The back window of the Jeep had been smashed and the carabinieri who fired the lethal shot was crouched in the back protecting himself on one side with a riot shield and suffering from the effects of the tear gas that had been discharged earlier. Before firing his weapon, the carabinieri displayed his gun and clearly warned the demonstrators, shouting at them to leave unless they wanted to be killed. The majority of the Grand Chamber found no violation on the basis that the carabinieri had an 'honest belief' that lethal force was absolutely necessary.[18]

The ECtHR has also found violations of the procedural obligation where the State has failed to provide a prompt and adequate investigation into deaths during protests.[19] For example, in *Association "21 December 1989" and Others* v. *Romania* a violation was found after the State failed for decades to investigate the use of lethal force against civilians during anti-Government demonstrations.[20]

12.2.2 Article 3 ECHR

The measures that a State takes in response to a protest may amount to a violation of Article 3 ECHR (freedom from torture or inhuman or degrading treatment or punishment).[21] In some cases, the severity of measures used has reached the threshold for torture. This was the case during the mass protests that took place in Ukraine between November 2013 and February 2014 (the so-called 'Euromaidan' or 'Maidan' protests) during which special police forces were mobilised to disperse protests, leading to violent clashes, and the authorities used non-State agents, who are alleged to have carried out numerous assaults, kidnappings and killings.[22] The ECtHR found multiple violations of Article 3 ECHR, including the torture provision.

[16] See Chapter 3. [17] *Giuliani and Gaggio* v. *Italy* [GC] (2012) 54 EHRR 10.

[18] Ibid at [189]–[191], [194]. [19] *Şimşek* v. *Turkey* (n 15).

[20] *Association "21 December 1989" and Others* v. *Romania*, App. No. 33810/07, 24/05/2011.

[21] For further analysis of Article 3, see Chapter 4.

[22] *Shmorgunov and Others* v. *Ukraine*, App No. 15367/14, 21/01/2021; *Lutsenko and Verbytskyy* v. *Ukraine*, App. Nos. 12482/14 and 39800/14, 21/01/2021; *Kadura and Smaliy* v. *Ukraine*, App. Nos. 42753/14 and 43860/14, 21/01/2021; *Dubovtsev and Others* v. *Ukraine*, App. No. 21429/14, 21/01/2021; and *Vorontsov and Others* v. *Ukraine*, App. No. 58925/14, 21/01/2021.

In other cases, the ECtHR has found violations of the inhuman and degrading treatment provisions of Article 3 ECHR. In *Pekaslan* v. *Turkey*, the applicants had taken part in International Women's Day celebrations during which they were kettled, sprayed with tear gas and hit, and their arms and legs were squeezed by male police officers whilst they were detained.[23] Medical reports corroborated their injuries and the Government failed to furnish convincing or credible facts justifying the degree of force used. The ECtHR thus found a violation of Article 3 ECHR. A violation of Article 3 ECHR was also found in *Navalnyy and Gunko* v. *Russia.*[24] In *Navalnyy*, there was video footage of the arrest of Aleksey Navalnyy at a demonstration, which revealed that the violent restraint that had been employed by the police had not been strictly necessary. The ECtHR held that the fact that this took place in public and was reported in the media was an aggravating factor; a determination that highlights the importance of dignity to Article 3 ECHR.[25] Moreover, the concept of dignity was expressly invoked in *Zakharov and Varzhabetyan* v. *Russia* where the applicants had been beaten with rubber truncheons.[26] The ECtHR held that although use of force is not prohibited, it has to be indispensable and not excessive. This was not the case in *Zakharov and Varzhabetyan* as the applicants had been engaged in a peaceful assembly; the use of force was not warranted by their own conduct and thus diminished their dignity.[27] The use of tear gas may also violate Article 3 ECHR, as while the ECtHR has held that tear gas is not prohibited,[28] it must be sufficiently regulated and subject to safeguards.[29]

In addition to these substantive obligations, States also have a procedural obligation to investigate alleged instances of ill-treatment. The significance of this was evident in the Maidan protest cases where the ECtHR found major shortcomings, including delays and omissions.[30] The ECtHR also found a violation in *Zakharov and Varzhabetyan* v. *Russia* due to the State's failure to investigate police brutality.[31] A further violation was found in *Chernega* v. *Ukraine* where the applicants argued that they had been assaulted during protests, that the police had done nothing to protect them and that no criminal proceedings had been instituted.[32] The ECtHR was unable to establish, to the required standard of proof, that the applicants had suffered ill-treatment reaching the threshold of Article 3 ECHR,[33] but it held that there had been a

[23] *Pekaslan* v. *Turkey*, App. Nos. 4572/06 and 5684/06, 20/03/2012.

[24] *Navalnyy and Gunko* v. *Russia*, App. No. 75186/12, 10/11/2020. [25] Ibid at [48].

[26] *Zakharov and Varzhabetyan* v. *Russia*, App. No. 35880/14, 13/10/2020. [27] Ibid at [71].

[28] *Oya Ataman* v. *Turkey*, App. No. 74552/01, 05/12/2006.

[29] *Abdullah Yaşa and Others* v. *Turkey*, App. No. 44827/08, 16/07/2013.

[30] See cases cited at (n 22). [31] *Zakharov and Varzhabetyan* v. *Russia* (n 26).

[32] *Chernega* v. *Ukraine* (2020) 70 EHRR 9. [33] Ibid at [155]–[156].

violation of the procedural limb as the authorities had consistently withheld information from the applicants.[34]

12.2.3 Article 5 ECHR

Applicants have argued in numerous cases that they have been detained, either prior, during, or as a consequence of a protest, in a manner that violates Article 5 ECHR. Article 5(1) ECHR provides that everyone has the right to liberty and that no one shall be deprived of their liberty except in accordance with a procedure prescribed by law and in circumstances which fall within one of the stated exceptions in Article 5 ECHR. In the context of protest, the State often seeks to invoke Article 5(1)(b) or Article 5(1)(c) ECHR. Article 5(1)(b) ECHR provides that there is no violation of Article 5 ECHR where detention constitutes 'the lawful arrest or detention of a person for non-compliance with the lawful order of a court or in order to secure the fulfilment of any obligation prescribed by law'. Article 5(1)(c) ECHR provides that there is no violation where the detention constitutes 'the lawful arrest or detention of a person effected for the purpose of bringing him before the competent legal authority on reasonable suspicion of having committed an offence or when it is reasonably considered necessary to prevent his committing an offence or fleeing after having done so'.

12.2.3.1 What Is a Deprivation of Liberty?

The first question that arises under Article 5 ECHR is whether there has been a deprivation of liberty. The ECtHR has stated on many occasions that the starting point is the applicant's 'concrete situation' and that 'account must be taken of a whole range of criteria such as the type, duration, effects and manner of implementation of the measure in question'.[35] Thus in determining whether or not there has been a violation, 'it is often necessary to look beyond the appearances and the language used and concentrate on the realities of the situation'.[36] In distinguishing between deprivation of liberty, which falls within Article 5 ECHR, and restriction of liberty, which does not,[37] the ECtHR has stated that the difference 'is merely one of degree or intensity,

[34] Ibid at [169].

[35] *Medvedyev and Others* v. *France* [GC], App. No. 3394/03, 29/03/2010 at [73]; *Creangă* v. *Romania* [GC] (2013) 56 EHRR 11 at [91]; *De Tommaso* v. *Italy* [GC] (2017) 65 EHRR 19 at [80].

[36] *Creangă* v. *Romania* (n 35) at [91].

[37] Restriction of liberty is covered by Protocol 4 (in particular Article 2) to the European Convention on Human Rights which has not been ratified by the UK: *Gillan and Quinton* v. *the United Kingdom* (2010) 50 EHRR 45 at [56].

and not one of nature or substance'.[38] It has also stated that the purpose underlying the contested measure is not decisive in determining whether there has been a deprivation of liberty;[39] although, as we will see, the ECtHR's approach to 'purpose' is arguably inconsistent in this context.

12.2.3.2 *Stop and Search*

As discussed in Chapter 7, a stop and search, even a brief one, may constitute a deprivation of liberty.[40] In *Gillan and Quinton* v. *the United Kingdom*, the applicants were both stopped on their way to a demonstration near an arms fair.[41] The first applicant was on his way to join the demonstration when he was stopped and searched under s.44 of the Terrorism Act 2000.[42] Nothing incriminating was found (although computer printouts giving information about the demonstration were seized by the police officers) and the applicant was allowed to continue to the demonstration after being stopped for roughly twenty minutes.[43] The second applicant was a journalist who was wearing a photographer's jacket.[44] She was also stopped and searched using the powers under ss.44 and 45 of the Terrorism Act 2000.[45] Again nothing incriminating was found and she was allowed to continue to the demonstration.[46] The applicant felt that she had been stopped for approximately thirty minutes, although the record of the search stated that she was stopped for five minutes.[47] Following the search, 'she felt so intimidated and distressed that she did not feel able to return to the demonstration although it had been her intention to make a documentary or sell footage of it'.[48] The ECtHR did not determine whether Article 5 ECHR was violated as it concluded that Article 8 ECHR had been violated, but it made some important comments in relation to Article 5 ECHR, in particular, that during the period in which the applicants were stopped, they were entirely deprived of any freedom of movement and this 'element of coercion' was 'indicative of a deprivation of liberty' within the meaning of Article 5(1) ECHR.[49]

12.2.3.3 *Kettling or Containment*

The suggestion in *Gillan and Quinton* that coercion is indicative of a deprivation of liberty sits uneasily with the ECtHR's subsequent determination in *Austin* v. *the United Kingdom*,[50] where it held that the applicants had not been

[38] *Medvedyev and Others* v. *France* (n 35) at [73].

[39] *Rozhkov* v. *Russia (No.2)*, App. No. 38898/04, 31/01/2017 at [74].

[40] *Gillan and Quinton* v. *the United Kingdom* (n 37), also discussed in Chapter 7 (Terrorism).

[41] Ibid. [42] Ibid at [8]. [43] Ibid at [8]. [44] Ibid at [9]. [45] Ibid at [9].

[46] Ibid at [9]. [47] Ibid at [9]. [48] Ibid at [9]. [49] Ibid at [57].

[50] *Austin* v. *the United Kingdom* [GC] (2012) 55 EHRR 14. See further, David Mead, 'Kettling Comes to the Boil before the Strasbourg Court: Is It a Deprivation of Liberty to Contain

subject to a deprivation of liberty when they were kettled by the police for many hours. Kettling or containment is a tactic which involves surrounding a crowd to restrict it to a particular area. Usually, those contained are kept in a small area, in uncomfortable conditions, for a lengthy period of time, until the police can disperse the crowd gradually. The applicants in *Austin* had been kettled at Oxford Circus during May Day demonstrations. The first applicant was a demonstrator who had been detained for a period of about seven hours, during which the police had refused to let her leave and she was unable to collect her eleven-month-old daughter from her crèche.[51] The second applicant was not a demonstrator but had been trapped while trying to go to a bookshop and was detained for seven hours.[52] The third and fourth applicants worked in the Oxford Circus area and were out on their lunch breaks when they became trapped; they were also detained for about six to seven hours.[53] The applicants argued that during this time they had been deprived of their liberty contrary to Article 5 ECHR.[54] This was rejected by the Grand Chamber. It reasoned that whilst the purpose behind a measure is not generally a factor to be taken into account when determining whether there has been a deprivation of liberty, it can consider the specific context and circumstances surrounding the restriction in cases other than the paradigm case of confinement in a cell.[55] The Grand Chamber thus distinguished between detention in a cell, where purpose is irrelevant, and other cases, where context is relevant.[56] It went on to observe that this is important as 'situations commonly occur in modern society where the public may be called upon to endure restrictions on freedom of movement or liberty in the interests of the common good'.[57] Consequently, it stated that it did not consider that:

> commonly occurring restrictions on movement, so long as they are rendered unavoidable as a result of circumstances beyond the control of the authorities and are necessary to avert a real risk of serious injury or damage, and are kept to the minimum required for that purpose, can properly be described as 'deprivations of liberty'.[58]

Applying this to the facts, the ECtHR thus held that the applicants had not been deprived of their liberty.[59] It is, however, important to note that the ECtHR observed that if it had not remained necessary for the police to impose and maintain the cordon to prevent serious injury or damage, the coercive and restrictive nature of the measure might have been sufficient to bring it within

Protesters en Masse?' (2012) **71**(3) CLJ 472, and Naomi Oreb, 'The Legality of "Kettling" after Austin' (2013) **76**(4) MLR 735. On the House of Lords judgment in *Austin*, see Helen Fenwick, 'Marginalising Human Rights: Breach of the Peace, "Kettling", the Human Rights Act and Public Protest' [2009] PL **737**.

[51] Ibid at [11]. [52] Ibid at [12]. [53] Ibid at [13]–[14]. [54] Ibid at [45]–[49].

[55] Ibid at [59]. [56] Ibid. [57] Ibid at [59]. [58] Ibid at [59]. [59] Ibid at [67].

Article 5 ECHR.[60] The ECtHR was therefore not willing to hold that all kettling falls outside the scope of Article 5 ECHR.

Three dissenting judges objected to the way in which the majority invoked purpose in *Austin*.[61] They observed that the majority had made no reference to *Gillan and Quinton* and that it had not dealt with the role of 'coercion' in determining that a measure constituted a deprivation of liberty.[62] They commented that this was particularly significant as the degree of coercion in *Austin* was far higher than that in *Gillan and Quinton*,[63] consequently, they would have found a deprivation of liberty.[64]

12.2.3.4 Preventative Detention

There are several cases in which the ECtHR has found that detaining demonstrators en route to a protest violates Article 5 ECHR. For example, in *Kasparov* v. *Russia*, the Court found a violation when the Russian chess champion, Garry Kasparov, was detained at an airport to prevent him from travelling to a rally opposing the Russian Government.[65] The Grand Chamber also found a violation of Article 5 ECHR in respect of the seven occasions when former Russian opposition leader Aleksey Navalnyy was arrested at peaceful demonstrations and the two occasions when he was placed in pre-trial detention.[66]

There is, however, no violation of Article 5 ECHR if – in accordance with a procedure prescribed by law – the deprivation of liberty falls within one of the stated exceptions. Those exceptions include preventative detention (Article 5 (1)(c) ECHR) when it is reasonably considered necessary to prevent the commission of an offence.

The ambit of lawful preventative detention was at the heart of *Eiseman-Renyard* v. *the United Kingdom*, a case concerning the arrest and detention of the applicants to prevent a breach of the peace during the Duke and Duchess of Cambridge's wedding.[67] There were three different cohorts of applicants in this case, most of whom had no previous convictions or cautions.

One of the applicants, Brian Hicks, had a long-standing involvement in republican politics and had previous convictions for minor offences committed over twenty years ago. He was intending to go to a 'Not the Royal Wedding' street party when he was stopped and arrested by a plain clothes

[60] Ibid at [68].

[61] Ibid, dissenting opinion of Judges Tulkens, Spielmann and Garlicki.

[62] Ibid, dissenting opinion at [13].

[63] Ibid, dissenting opinion at [13]–[14].

[64] Ibid, dissenting opinion at [15].

[65] *Kasparov* v. *Russia* (2018) 66 EHRR 21 at [35].

[66] *Navalnyy* v. *Russia* (2019) 68 EHRR 25 at [71]–[72]. In case reports, secondary sources and press reports that Aleksey Navalnyy's name appears in various different forms; this is common for Russian translated from Cyrillic. In this book we have adopted the spelling used in the ECHR case law to assist readers in locating the relevant cases.

[67] *Eiseman-Renyard* v. *the United Kingdom* (2019) 68 EHRR SE12.

police officer at 9.05am. He was taken to a police station where he was informed that he had been arrested to prevent a breach of the peace. He was strip searched and nothing of significance was found. Following which he was released at approximately 3.00pm and no further action was taken against him.[68]

The second cohort of applicants had no previous convictions or cautions. They were intending to participate in a 'zombie picinc' organised by the campaign group 'Queer Resistance' and were dressed accordingly. They were in a coffee shop on Oxford Street when a group of police officers arrived and arrested them to prevent a breach of the peace. The police were acting on information which stated that those dressed as zombies would attempt to gather at Westminster Abbey and throw maggots as confetti at the wedding procession. The applicants were taken to a police station where they were detained until approximately 3.45pm. No further action was taken.[69]

The third group of applicants were intending to attend a republican event when they were stopped at a train station by British Transport Police officers. The officers searched the applicants and found placards, a megaphone, a cycling or climbing helmet and a scarf. The applicants were held at the train station to prevent a breach of the police and then taken to the police station where there were detained until approximately 3.30pm.[70] No further action was taken.[71]

In considering the applications, the ECtHR observed that Article 5(1) requires

> that any deprivation of liberty should be in keeping with the purpose of protecting the individual from arbitrariness (see *S., V. and A. v. Denmark*, § 74). In the present context that means that the offence should be concrete and specific as regards, in particular the place and time of its commission and its victims and that the authorities must furnish some facts or information which would satisfy an objective observer that the person concerned would in all likelihood have been involved in the concrete and specific offence had its commission not been prevented by the detention.[72]

Applying this to the facts the ECtHR determined that

> the offence of breach of the peace which all the applicants were charged with was sufficiently concrete and specific in the circumstances. Against the factual background of the royal wedding in terms of crowd size and international interest, coupled with the threat level of 'severe' in the United Kingdom at the relevant time, the Court finds that an objective observer would be satisfied that the applicants would in all likelihood have been involved in the concrete and specific offence had its commission not been

[68] Ibid at [7]–[8]. [69] Ibid at [9]–[10]. [70] Ibid at [11]–[13].

[71] This is noted in the High Court judgment *Hicks and others* v. *Commissioner of Police of the Metropolis* [2012] EWHC 1947 (Admin) at [57].

[72] *Eiseman-Renyard* v. *the United Kingdom* (n 67) at [42].

prevented by their detention. Finally, it notes that the applicants were released as soon as the imminent risk had passed and in all cases their detention was for a matter of hours, which the Grand Chamber identified as broadly appropriate in the context of preventive detention.[73]

In finding no violation of Article 5 ECHR, the ECtHR also noted that the domestic courts had undertaken a comprehensive review of the facts and found that the arrests were necessary to prevent an imminent breach of the peace, taking into account the crowd size, international interest and the severe threat level on the day of the royal wedding.[74] The ECtHR also emphasised the fact that the applicants had been released as soon as the risk had passed and that in all cases their detention had only been for a matter of hours.[75] It therefore found that there were no convincing reasons for it to depart from the decisions of the domestic courts, which had struck a fair balance between the applicants' right to liberty and the public interest.[76] In fact, the ECtHR observed[77] that the approach of the domestic courts had informed the Grand Chamber's own judgment in *S. V. and A.* v. *Denmark* in which it had agreed with the UK Supreme Court[78] that preventive detention is compatible with Article 5 ECHR in certain circumstances.[79]

12.2.4 Article 6 ECHR

In several cases concerning proceedings brought against protesters, the ECtHR has found a violation of Article 6 ECHR, the right to a fair trial. In particular, the ECtHR held in *Kasparov* v. *Russia,* a case in which the applicants had been convicted for participating in an unauthorised protest, that the domestic court had accepted the police submissions unequivocally and denied the applicants any possibility of adducing evidence to the contrary.[80] The ECtHR found a violation of Article 6 ECHR in similar circumstances and for similar reasons in *Navalnyy* v. *Russia.*[81]

12.2.5 Article 8 ECHR

In two important cases concerning the UK, the ECtHR has been asked to consider whether stop and search powers and police databases of protesters violate Article 8 ECHR. We have already observed that in *Gillan and Quinton*

[73] Ibid at [43]. [74] Ibid at [46]. [75] Ibid at [43]. [76] Ibid at [45]–[46].

[77] Ibid at [46].

[78] *R (on the application of Hicks and others) (Appellants)* v. *Commissioner of Police for the Metropolis (Respondent)* [2017] UKSC 9, [2017] AC 256.

[79] *S. V. and A.* v. *Denmark*, App. Nos. 35553/12, 36678/12, 36711/12, 22/10/2018.

[80] *Kasparov* v. *Russia* (n 65). [81] *Navalnyy* v. *Russia* (n 66).

the ECtHR observed that Article 5 ECHR might be applicable to a stop and search but found that it was not necessary to determine this as there was a clear violation of Article 8 ECHR.[82] As discussed in Chapter 8, the ECtHR held that the suspicion-less stop and search power under s.44 Terrorism Act 2000 which empowered any constable in uniform to stop and search a pedestrian in any area specified by him within his jurisdiction if he considered it 'expedient for the prevention of acts of terrorism' was too broad and there were insufficient safeguards.[83]

Another important Article 8 ECHR judgment is *Catt* v. *the United Kingdom*.[84] In *Catt*, the ECtHR held that the retention of a peaceful campaigner's data on a police extremism database violated Article 8 ECHR. It is, however, important to observe that the ECtHR accepted that there was a pressing social need to *collect* the data and that the finding of a violation was limited to the indefinite retention of that data.[85]

12.2.6 Article 10 ECHR

The ECtHR has frequently commented on the close relationship between Articles 10 and 11 ECHR and their underlying values.[86] Moreover, in *Kakabadze* v. *Georgia*, the ECtHR explained that Article 11 ECHR should be considered in the light of the values underpinning Article 10 ECHR (freedom of expression and conscience).[87] Yet, while there is a close connection between the two rights, there are cases in which the ECtHR has considered protests under Article 10 ECHR directly. David Mead suggests that 'where protest takes a more symbolic form or is more obstructive and disruptive direct action, Article 10 is likely to come to the fore'.[88] Although, as he notes, nothing turns on the difference between the two rights as they tend to be analysed in the same way.

One example of this is *Tatár and Fáber* v. *Hungary* where the ECtHR considered a demonstration in which laundry was hung and displayed outside the Hungarian Parliament in Budapest.[89] The applicants stated that the symbolic meaning of this expression was 'to hang out the nation's dirty laundry'. In that case, the ECtHR declared that 'the mere fact that an expression occurs in the public space does not necessarily turn such an event into an assembly'.[90] The ECtHR thus applied Article 10 instead of Article 11 ECHR and

[82] See discussion at Section 12.2.3.2. [83] *Gillan and Quinton* (n 37) at [76]–[87].
[84] *Catt* v. *the United Kingdom* (2019) 69 EHRR 7. [85] Ibid at [108], [116] and [119]–[128].
[86] See, for example, *Ezelin* v. *France* (1992) 14 EHRR 362 at [37].
[87] *Kakabadze* v. *Georgia*, App. No. 1484/07, 02/10/2012 at [83].
[88] David Mead, *The New Law on Peaceful Protest* (Hart, 2010), p.64.
[89] *Tatár and Fáber* v. *Hungary*, App. Nos. 26005/08 and 26160/08, 12/06/2012.
[90] Ibid at [38].

found a violation on the basis that the authorities had not given relevant and sufficient reasons for the interference.[91] The ECtHR also turned to Article 10 ECHR when considering an application on behalf of the 'Naked Rambler' in which he argued that his repeated convictions and imprisonment for public nudity constituted a violation of the Convention.[92] The ECtHR recognised that the applicant chose to be naked 'in order to give expression to his opinion as to the inoffensive nature of the human body' and that this fell within the ambit of Article 10 ECHR.[93] Yet while the right was applicable the ECtHR found no violation, as the interferences were justified, in particular the Court observed that the reasons for the measures were 'relevant and sufficient' and the measures taken were not disproportionate to the legitimate aim pursued, namely prevention of disorder and crime.[94] *Women on Waves* v. *Portugal* is a further case in which the ECtHR applied Article 10 ECHR. In that case, a group of Dutch activists seeking to promote decriminalisation of abortion chartered a ship and set sail for Portugal. They were prohibited from entering Portuguese waters, which the ECtHR held violated Article 10 ECHR as the authorities could have resorted to other means of preventing disorder and protecting health, thus the interference in question had not answered a 'pressing social need' and could not be regarded as necessary in a democratic society.[95]

12.2.7 Article 14 ECHR

There is a growing body of case law in which applicants have successfully argued that their protest was prohibited or restricted on discriminatory grounds, violating Article 14 in conjunction with Article 11 ECHR. This has often involved prohibitions on demonstrations relating to LGBTQI+ rights. For example, in *Alekseyev* v. *Russia* the applicant was repeatedly refused permission to hold a Pride march, and the ECtHR found a violation of Article 11 and a violation of Article 14 in conjunction with Article 11 ECHR on the basis that the main reason for the ban was the authorities' disapproval of demonstrations which they considered to promote homosexuality.[96] In coming to that conclusion, the ECtHR refused to disregard the homophobic opinions that had been publicly expressed by the Mayor and the undeniable link between these statements and the ban.[97] The ECtHR also found a violation of Article 14 in conjunction with Article 11 ECHR for similar reasons in *Alekseyev* v. *Russia (No.2)*.[98]

[91] Ibid at [36]–[42].

[92] *Gough* v. *the United Kingdom*, App. No. 49327/11, 28/10/2014 at [150]. [93] Ibid at [150].

[94] Ibid at [176]. [95] *Women on Waves* v. *Portugal*, App. No. 31276/05, 03/02/2009.

[96] *Alekseyev* v. *Russia* [2010] ECHR 1562 at [109]–[110]. [97] Ibid at [109].

[98] *Alekseyev* v. *Russia (No.2)* (2019) 69 EHRR 16 at [21–[22].

The ECtHR also found a violation of Article 11 and 14 in conjunction with Article 11 ECHR ECHR in *GenderDoc-M* v. *Moldova*.[99] GenderDoc-M had sought permission for a demonstration aimed at encouraging the adoption of laws protecting sexual minorities from discrimination. This was refused and GenderDoc-M argued that it had been discriminated against 'due to the fact that it promoted the interests of the gay community in Moldova'.[100] The Government admitted a violation of Article 11 ECHR, but denied that the prohibition was discriminatory, arguing that they had been generally intolerant of *all* demonstrations.[101] This was rejected by the ECtHR as other assemblies had been permitted and the Government had argued before the domestic courts that the ban was justified because of the subject matter of the protest and the need to protect morals.[102]

The ECtHR has also emphasised that the State has positive obligations to protect demonstrators from violent counter-protesters and that LGBTQI+ protesters are particularly vulnerable.[103] The ECtHR clearly articulated this in *Berkman* v. *Russia*, where the applicant had attempted to take part in an annual LGBTI day, which had been violently disrupted by counter-demonstrators.[104] The police officers who outnumbered counter-demonstrators several times, had neither warned the latter against obstructing the meeting, nor attempted to secure a safe perimeter for the participants. The ECtHR found that the police had stepped in belatedly, only when a real risk of inflicting bodily injuries had appeared, and that the passive conduct of the police officers demonstrated that they had been concerned only with the protection of public order and had not considered it necessary to facilitate the meeting.[105] Crucially, the ECtHR held that the State's positive obligation has to be assessed in the light of the subject matter of the assembly.[106] In this context the positive obligation was of paramount importance because the participants belonged to a minority vulnerable to victimisation, particularly given the history of public hostility towards the LGBTI community in Russia.[107] There had thus been a violation of the respondent State's positive obligations under Article 11 taken alone and in conjunction with Article 14 ECHR.[108]

12.2.8 Article 18 ECHR

Finally, it is worth noting that in extreme cases the ECtHR has found a violation of Article 18 ECHR, which prohibits the limitation of rights for any reasons other than those permitted by the Convention. This threshold was reached in *Navalnyy* v. *Russia* on the basis that the repeated arrests of Russian

[99] *GenderDoc-M* v. *Moldova*, App. No. 9106/06, 12/06/2012. [100] Ibid at [43].
[101] Ibid at [42]. [102] Ibid at [52]–[54]. [103] See also discussion at Section 4.4 below.
[104] *Berkman* v. *Russia* (2021) 73 EHRR 3. [105] Ibid at [52]–[58]. [106] Ibid at [55].
[107] Ibid. [108] Ibid at [58].

opposition leader, Aleksey Navalnyy, were intended to suppress political pluralism.[109] The ECtHR found 'converging contextual evidence' that the authorities were becoming increasingly severe, and that his claim that he was a particular target was coherent in the context of a general move to bring the opposition under control.[110] It thus determined that there had been a violation of Article 18 in conjunction with both Article 5 and Article 11 ECHR.[111] In this respect it might be noted that two years later, in 2020, Navalnyy was hospitalised in Berlin for several weeks in an induced coma after reportedly being poisoned with a nerve agent. In March 2022 he was sentenced to nine years' imprisonment following a trial that was declared a sham by Amnesty International, and that in February 2024 Navalnyy died in a Russian prison.

12.3 ARTICLE 11 ECHR AND FREEDOM OF ASSOCIATION

One of the rights protected by Article 11 ECHR is freedom of association which includes the ability to form organisations and political parties. Dissolution or restrictions on associations that interfere with Article 11 ECHR may however be justified under Article 11(2) ECHR where the measure is prescribed by law and necessary in a democratic society for one of the aims stated in Article 11 (2) ECHR, namely, national security or public safety, the prevention of disorder or crime, the protection of health or morals, or for the protection of the rights and freedoms of others. Furthermore, if an organisation is engaged in activities contrary to Convention values (such as terrorism), the organisation may fall outside the ambit of protection accorded by Article 11 altogether by virtue of Article 17 ECHR.

12.3.1 ECHR Case Law on Freedom of Association

The ability to form political and non-governmental associations is vital as these are often the hub for finding, gathering, and identifying with like-minded people, developing and expressing ideas. As discussed in Chapter 8 (Terrorism), certain organisations are proscribed under domestic law and it is an offence to profess membership or support for such organisations. States may also dissolve associations that indirectly support, including through financing, terrorist organisations in other jurisdictions.[112] Given the challenges that arise in determining what should be labelled 'terrorist' and the scope this (potentially) affords to the State to suppress legitimate political

[109] *Navalnyy* v. *Russia* (n 66) at [163]–[176]. [110] Ibid at [172]. [111] Ibid at [176].

[112] *Internationale Humanitäre Hilfsorganisation e.V.* v. *Germany* [2023] ECHR 776. For further discussion, see Chapter 8.

opposition, the State's capacity to dissolve or prohibit organisations and to criminalise membership has the potential to severely curtail the rights protected by Article 11 ECHR. Clearly, if the State can regulate who can gather, it can limit opposition.

There are cases in which the ECtHR has held that the dissolution of a political association breaches Article 11 ECHR. For example, in *United Communist Party of Turkey* v. *Turkey*, it held that the dissolution of the United Communist Party of Turkey violated Article 11 ECHR.[113] Turkey (now officialy known as Türkiye) had argued that dissolution was justified, in part because the party used the word 'communist' in its name contrary to domestic law.[114] In determining that Article 11 ECHR had been violated, the ECtHR emphasised the 'essential' role of political parties in ensuring pluralism and a functioning democracy, concluding that States possess only a limited margin of appreciation in this context and that this goes hand-in-hand with Strasbourg's scrutiny.[115] Applying this to the facts, it held that the party's choice of name could not justify dissolution, in particular it observed that:

> a measure as drastic as the immediate and permanent dissolution [of the party] ordered before its activities had even started and coupled with a ban barring its leaders from discharging any other political responsibility, is disproportionate to the aim pursued and consequently unnecessary in a democratic society. It follows that the measure infringed Article 11 of the Convention.[116]

Socialist Party v. *Turkey* concerned the dissolution of a political party on the ground that the party had argued for the creation of an independent federated State (comprising separate States for Turks and Kurds).[117] In defending the dissolution the Turkish Government sought to distinguish this case from *United Communist* on the basis that the dissolution of the Socialist Party was motivated by its activities after formation (and not simply on its constitution and programme).[118] The ECtHR was not convinced. It found that there was no evidence that the group was inciting violence or infringing the rules of democracy.[119] Moreover, the statements made by the party were scarcely any different from those made by other political groups active in other Council of Europe States.[120] Consequently it determined that the dissolution violated Article 11 ECHR.[121] *Socialist Party* v. *Turkey* thus safeguarded the right of political parties to continue non-violent campaigns for political manifestos that challenge the basic ideologies and constitutional structures of their States, so long as the parties adhere to the Convention's idea of political democracy.

[113] *United Communist Party of Turkey* v. *Turkey* (1998) 26 EHRR 121. [114] Ibid at [20].
[115] Ibid at [25], [43] and [46]. [116] Ibid at [51]–[61].
[117] *Socialist Party* v. *Turkey* (1998) 27 EHRR 51. [118] Ibid at [38]. [119] Ibid at [46].
[120] Ibid. [121] Ibid at [54].

There are, however, cases in which dissolution has been found to be justified. For example, in *Refah Partisi (The Welfare Party) and Others* v. *Turkey*, the Grand Chamber unanimously found no violation in respect of the dissolution of a political party which supported fundamentalist Islamic views.[122] Frequent expression of extreme views contrary to recognised Convention values by leading members of Refah meant that the dissolution was compatible with Article 11(2) ECHR.[123] The Grand Chamber also noted that 'a State cannot be required to wait, before intervening, until a political party has seized power and begun to take concrete steps to implement a policy incompatible with the standards of the Convention and democracy, even though the danger of that policy for democracy is sufficiently established and imminent'.[124]

It is also important to note that while many of the cases have concerned political parties in Türkiye there are cases involving other States. For example, in *Herri Batasuna and Batasuna* v. *Spain* the dissolution of political parties connected with the Basque terrorist organisation ETA was found to be lawful under Article 11(2) ECHR.[125]

When it is being considered whether dissolution violates the Convention, the ECtHR is sometimes asked to consider whether Article 17 ECHR is applicable. As discussed in Chapter 11, Article 17 ECHR precludes an applicant from relying upon a Convention right for purposes contrary to Convention values. This is relevant because if an organisation is engaged in activities contrary to Convention values, the organisation may fall outside the ambit of protection accorded by Article 11 ECHR altogether. The Court applied Article 17 ECHR in *Kasymakhunov and Saybatalov* v. *Russia* in respect of the Hizb ut-Tahrir al-Islami (The Party of Islamic Liberation)[126] and in *Ayoub* v. *France* in respect of two extreme far-right organisations.[127] In *Vona* v. *Hungary*, the Hungarian Government unsuccessfully argued that the organisation (which expressed racial hatred) was precluded from relying upon the Convention right due to the operation of Article 17 ECHR. On that occasion the ECtHR declined to invoke Article 17 ECHR, but nevertheless held that the dissolution was justified under Article 11(2) ECHR.[128]

Freedom to associate is not limited to political organisations, and the dissolution of an NGO may also violate Article 11 ECHR. In *Tebieti Muhafize Cemiyyeti & Israfilov* v. *Azerbaijan* the dissolution of an environmental

[122] *Refah Partisi (The Welfare Party) and Others* v. *Turkey* (2003) 37 EHRR 1.
[123] Ibid at [132]–[136]. [124] Ibid at [102].
[125] *Herri Batasuna and Batasuna* v. *Spain*, App. Nos. 25803/04 and 25817/04, 30/06/2009.
[126] *Kasymakhunov and Saybatalov* v. *Russia*, App. Nos. 26261/05 and 26377/06, 14/03/2013.
[127] *Ayoub* v. *France*, App. No. 77400/14, 08/10/2020.
[128] *Vona* v. *Hungary*, App. No. 35943/10, 09/07/2013.

campaigning association violated Article 11 ECHR,[129] while in *Adana* v. *Turkey* the dissolution of an NGO that offered help and support to families of prisoners and convicts violated Article 11 ECHR.[130] Refusal to register an NGO may also violate Article 11 ECHR, thus in *Jafarov* v. *Azerbaijan* the ECtHR held that refusing to register a human rights organisation violated Article 11 ECHR,[131] and in *Zhdanov* v. *Russia* a refusal to register associations set up to promote and protect the rights of lesbian, gay, bisexual and transgender people violated Article 11 coupled with Article 14 ECHR.[132] It is important to note, however, that there are circumstances in which the State will be justified in dissolving an NGO, for example, where the organisation is involved in financing terrorist activity, indeed Article 17 ECHR may also be relevant in such cases.[133]

A further aspect of freedom of association is the right to become a member and profess membership of an organisation. Consequently, criminal convictions in respect of membership of an organisation may violate Article 11 ECHR. In *Gülcü* v. *Turkey* the ECtHR found that a conviction connected with membership of an organisation violated Article 11 ECHR as the domestic courts had failed to provide any reasons for the conviction when imposing a severe penalty on a fifteen year old.[134] A violation was also found in *Işikirik* v. *Turkey* on the basis that the applicability of the domestic provisions on membership of an illegal armed organisation was not foreseeable and thus the provisions were not sufficiently prescribed by law.[135] On that occasion the ECtHR observed that the domestic courts had 'interpreted the notion of "membership" of an illegal organisation' to include the 'mere fact of being present at a demonstration, called for by an illegal organisation, and openly acting in a manner expressing a positive opinion towards the organisation in question'.[136] It concluded that as this approach to membership was 'not "foreseeable" in its application … it did not afford the applicant the legal protection against arbitrary interference with his right under Article 11' ECHR.[137] The Court has also found a violation where applicants are convicted of an

[129] *Tebieti Muhafize Cemiyyeti & Israfilov* v. *Azerbaijan*, App. No. 37083/03, 08/10/2009.

[130] *Adana* v. *Turkey*, App. No. 59835/10, 21/07/2020.

[131] *Jafarov* v. *Azerbaijan*, App. No. 27309/14, 25/07/2019.

[132] *Zhdanov* v. *Russia*, App. No. 12200/08, 16/07/2019.

[133] In *Internationale Humanitäre Hilfsorganisation e.V.* v. *Germany* [2023] ECHR 776 (n 112) the ECtHR, whilst ultimately focusing on Article 11 and finding no violation, observed at [88] that associations which engage in activities contrary to the values of the Convention cannot benefit from the protection of Article 11 interpreted in the light of Article 17, and that Article 17 may also aid in the interpretation of Article 11(2) of the Convention so as to reinforce its conclusion on the necessity of the interference.

[134] *Gülcü* v. *Turkey*, App. No. 17526/10, 19/01/2016.

[135] *Işikirik* v. *Turkey*, App. No. 41226/09, 14/11/2017 at [63]–[70]. [136] Ibid at [63].

[137] Ibid at [70].

unrelated offence, but the real reason for the conviction is their active participation in a protest movement.[138]

12.3.2 Freedom of Association and Domestic Law

Association is generally unregulated under domestic law as there is no requirement to seek prior permission to establish a group. A group will, however, be prohibited if it is either (i) a quasi-military organisation (Public Order Act 1936) or (ii) a proscribed organisation (Terrorism Act 2000). The provisions on quasi-military organisations were introduced as a response to Fascist marches in the 1930s, whereas the proscribed organisation provisions are aimed at terrorist organisations.

In respect of quasi-military organisations, s.2 of the Public Order Act 1936 (POA 1936) prohibits political groups that seek to use or display physical force in promoting a political object. This legislation was enacted to deal with the threat of Oswald Mosley's British Union of Fascists (BUF) which embraced Nazi-style antisemitism and was involved in violent clashes. The BUF had a quasi-military structure, with members having a rank and being taught military drill and some members even lived in 'Barracks' under military discipline. In October 1936 there was a riot following a BUF march in a Jewish part of London ('Battle of Cable Street'), following which the Public Order Act 1936 received royal assent. In the 1960s and 1970s, s.2 POA 1936 was used against members of the Irish Republican Army, Free Wales Army and a far-right Nazi movement called Spearhead.[139] Today, however, prosecutions are more likely to be brought under the terrorism legislation (see below and Chapter 8). Section 1 POA 1936 also created an offence of wearing a uniform signifying association with any political organisation or with the promotion of any political object in a public place or at a public meeting. This was intended to address the wearing of Blackshirts by the BUF, but it has since been used to prosecute members of the KKK wearing white robes and hoods. It was also used in several cases (prior to the Terrorism Act 2000) in relation to the IRA,[140] and has more recently been used in relation to far-right political organisation Britain First.

As discussed in Chapter 8, s.3 of the Terrorism Act 2000 (TA 2000) empowers the Home Secretary to proscribe organisations and once an organisation is proscribed it is an offence to be a member, or to profess membership or invite support for the organisation.[141] These provisions do not cause

[138] *Jhangiryan* v. *Armenia*, App. No. 44841/08, 08/10/2020.

[139] *R* v. *Jordan and Tyndall* [1963] Crim. L.R. 124.

[140] *O'Moran* v. *DPP* [1975] QB 864, [1975] 2 WLR 413; *Whelan* v. *DPP* [1975] QB 864, [1975] 2 WLR 413.

[141] Sections 11–12 Terrorism Act 2000.

difficulties for groups unless they are proscribed, but given that the Secretary of State only needs to believe that the organisation is concerned in terrorism and the fact that terrorism has a very broad definition under s.1 TA 2000, there is the possibility that non-violent protest groups could be brought within these provisions. In this respect it is worth noting that the police sought to list Extinction Rebellion as an extremist ideology alongside terrorist organisations in its guidance on Prevent. If a group is prohibited then expressing support for that group is a criminal offence. The strict liability offence under s.13 TA 2000 of wearing clothing or displaying an item capable of arousing suspicion of support or membership of a proscribed organisation covers items such as badges and flags, that would not otherwise fall within the meaning of uniform in s.1 POA 1936.[142]

12.4 ARTICLE 11 AND FREEDOM OF PEACEFUL ASSEMBLY

The right to freedom of peaceful assembly, like freedom of association, is a qualified right under Article 11 ECHR and is subject to the same exceptions under Article 11(2) ECHR, i.e. where the measure is prescribed by law and necessary in a democratic society for one of the aims stated in Article 11(2) ECHR, namely, national security or public safety, the prevention of disorder or crime, the protection of health or morals, or for the protection of the rights and freedoms of others.[143]

12.4.1 Scope of Right to Peaceful Assembly

The ECtHR takes a broad approach to the definition of an 'assembly' for the purposes of Article 11 ECHR and does not distinguish between static assemblies, moving processions or occupations. In *C.S.* v. *Germany*, it accepted that a sit-in may constitute an assembly.[144] It also appears that while very small protests (such as one-person protests) are more likely to be considered under Article 10 ECHR, there is no minimum number of persons required to constitute an assembly for the purposes of Article 11 ECHR. A further question that has arisen is whether the duration of a protest can affect whether it is deemed to be as assembly for the purposes of Article 11 ECHR. This was important in *Cissé* v. *France* where the ECtHR rejected the French Government's argument that an occupation of several months was not an 'assembly'.[145] Thus the

142 *Pwr* v. *DPP* [2022] UKSC 2, [2022] 1 WLR 789. See discussion in Chapter 7.

143 On Freedom of Assembly, see Mead (n 8) and Orsolya Salát, *The Right to Freedom of Assembly: A Comparative Study* (Hart, 2015).

144 *C.S.* v. *Germany* (dec.), App. No. 13858/88, 06/03/1989.

145 *Cissé* v. *France* (dec.), App No. 51346/99, 16/01/2001.

ECtHR does not attach a temporal limit to the meaning of an assembly. Of course, this does not mean that the duration of an assembly is irrelevant; it may well be relevant to the question of whether the State has been tolerant of an assembly such that an interference is justified, but, the mere fact that an assembly has continued for some time will not take it outside the scope of Article 11(1) ECHR altogether. A further point to observe is that the right belongs both to those who organise and those who take part in an assembly.[146] While further breadth is accorded through the ECtHR's recognition that it includes social as well as political gatherings, albeit that less protection is afforded to social gatherings.[147]

12.4.1.1 'Peaceful' Assembly

After comtemplation of the breadth of an assembly, it is important to observe that Article 11 ECHR expressly refers to a *peaceful* assembly. Consequently, if an assembly is deemed 'non-peaceful' it may fall outside the scope of Article 11 ECHR. This was important in *C.S.* v. *Germany* in which the Commission stated that the right is 'secured to everyone who organises or participates in a peaceful demonstration' and will not apply 'where the organisers and participants have violent intentions which result in public disorder'.[148] The ECtHR will, however, assume that the protesters' intentions were peaceful unless there is evidence to the contrary and the 'burden of proving the violent intentions of the organiser . . . lies with the authorities'.[149] An issue that sometimes arises is that an assembly becomes violent because it is hijacked by a third party. Here the case law suggests that what matters is the intention of the organisers and participants. This was apparent in *CARAF* v. *the United Kingdom* where the Commission emphasised that:

> the possibility of violent counterdemonstrations, or the possibility of extremists with violent intentions, not members of the organising association, joining the demonstration cannot as such take away that right. Even if there is a real risk of a public procession resulting in disorder by developments outside the control of those organizing it such procession does not for this reason alone fall outside the scope of Article 11.[150]

Consequently, arresting someone purely because they are wrapped up in what has become a violent demonstration is an interference and it cannot be

[146] *Christians Against Racism and Fascism* v. *the United Kingdom* (dec.), App. No. 8440/78, 16/07/1980.

[147] *Friend and The Countryside Alliance and others* v. *the United Kingdom* (dec.), App. No. 16072/06, 24/11/2009.

[148] *C.S.* v. *Germany* (n 144).

[149] *Christian Democratic Party* v. *Moldova (No.2)*, App. No. 25196/04, 02/02/2010 at [23].

[150] *Christians Against Racism and Fascism* v. *the United Kingdom* (n 146).

justified solely on the basis that that person has lost the protection of Article 11 ECHR.[151]

A further issue is whether disruptive, but non-violent, assemblies fall within the parameters of Article 11 ECHR. This is important because arguably all mass protests are disruptive in some way, moreover disruption is inherent in direct action. In some cases, the ECtHR has applied Article 10 ECHR to direct action. For example, in *Steel and Others* v. *the United Kingdom* the ECtHR applied Article 10 ECHR to protesters who disrupted a grouse shoot and to protesters who attempted to disrupt building works on a motorway.[152] In other cases, particularly, where a larger number of people were involved, the ECtHR has applied Article 11 ECHR. An example of this is *Balçik* v. *Turkey* in which it was alleged that the protesters had blocked a tram line.[153] In *Balçik*, the ECtHR observed that 'where demonstrators do not engage in acts of violence, it is important for the public authorities to show a certain degree of tolerance towards peaceful gatherings if the freedom of assembly guaranteed by Article 11 of the Convention is not to be deprived of all substance'.[154] Applying this to the facts, the ECtHR was 'struck by the authorities' impatience in seeking to end the demonstration'.[155] Yet, while *Balçik* emphasised the need for tolerance, the Grand Chamber in *Kudrevicius* v. *Lithuania* found no violation of Article 11 ECHR where a peaceful blockade of farmers were charged as rioters.[156] The farmers had blocked several roads for two days to protest against falling milk prices. The ECtHR, initially sitting in a Chamber formation, found that the riot charge was disproportionate, in part because there was no violence.[157] However, the Grand Chamber later held that as there was serious intentional disruption, the intervention fell within the scope of the State's margin of appreciation, and that 'the Contracting States enjoy a wide margin of appreciation in their assessment of the necessity in taking measures to restrict such conduct'.[158] In this regard it distinguished between 'serious intentional disruption' and disruption to ordinary life and traffic which is a side-effect of a demonstration held in a public place, observing that the former 'might be considered a "reprehensible act" within the meaning of the Court's case-law' and that '[s]uch behaviour might therefore justify the imposition of penalties, even of a criminal nature'.[159] Indeed, on the facts it found that the measures in question fell within the State's margin of appreciation and thus there had been no violation of Article 11 ECHR.[160]

[151] *Ezelin* v. *France* (n 86) at [53].

[152] *Steel and Others* v. *the United Kingdom* (1999) 28 EHRR 60.

[153] *Balçik* v. *Turkey*, App. No. 25/02, 29/11/2007. [154] Ibid. [155] Ibid.

[156] *Kudrevicius* v. *Lithuania* [GC] (2016) 62 EHRR 34.

[157] *Kudrevicius* v. *Lithuania*, App. No. 37553/05, 26/11/2013 at [67], [82]–[84].

[158] *Kudrevicius* v. *Lithuania* [GC] (n 156) at [156] and [175]. [159] Ibid at [170] and [173].

[160] Ibid at [182]–[183].

The meaning of a peaceful assembly was also considered in *Laurijsen* v. *Netherlands*, a case that related to a demonstration against the eviction of squatters.[161] On the day of the intended eviction approximately 150 participants gathered outside the building where the squatters resided. They danced, played loud music and instruments, chanted slogans, and displayed banners. The street was obstructed with seats and tables, as well as some air mattresses. Approximately an hour after the demonstration commenced, the police commissioner ordered them to disperse. The participants refused to do so and when the police attempted to disperse, some of the participants threw beer bottles and a crate at the police. Several smoke bombs were set off and a small fire broke out. All demonstrators were informed that they were under arrest on suspicion of participating in an unlawful gathering or otherwise disturbing public order. The applicants were later charged with participating in an unlawful gathering or otherwise disturbing public order and failing to comply with a police order to disperse. In the ensuing legal proceedings one of arguments that was ultimately put by the protesters was that the demonstration was a 'peaceful assembly' within the meaning of Article 11 ECHR.[162] This was unsuccessful with the domestic court stating that Article 11 ECHR does not protect 'a demonstration where the organizers and participants have violent intentions'.[163] The applicants then applied to the ECtHR, arguing that their Article 11 ECHR rights had been violated as the interferences lacked a legal basis and were disproportionate.[164] In particular, they argued that the gathering was intended to be a peaceful assembly and that this was evident from the messages advertising the gathering and the initial atmosphere at the demonstration. The Government counter-argued that Article 11 ECHR did not apply as neither the organisers' intentions nor their actions were peaceful.

The ECtHR reiterated that Article 11 ECHR applies to all gatherings except those where the organisers and participants incite violence or otherwise reject the foundations of a democratic society.[165] It went on to state that in determining the applicability of Article 11 ECHR, the ECtHR considers:

(i) whether the assembly was intended to be peaceful or whether the organisers had violent intentions;
(ii) whether the applicant demonstrated violent intentions when joining the assembly; and
(iii) whether the applicant inflicted bodily harm on anyone.[166]

In this regard the ECtHR observed that in cases where both sides – demonstrators and police – were involved in violent acts, it is sometimes necessary to

[161] *Laurijsen* v. *Netherlands*, App. Nos. 56896/17, 56910/17, 56914/17, 56917/17, 57307/17, 21/11/2023.

[162] Ibid at [18]. [163] Ibid at [20]. [164] Ibid at [40]–[42]. [165] Ibid at [48].

[166] Ibid at [49].

examine who started the violence.[167] It also reiterated that applicants do not lose the protection of Article 11 ECHR as a result of sporadic violence or other punishable acts committed by others if the individual in question remains peaceful in his or her own intentions or behaviour.[168] Finally, it emphasised that the burden of proving violent intentions lies with the authorities.[169] The ECtHR was thus clear that even obstructive demonstrations fall within the ambit of Article 11 ECHR if they are peaceful.[170] This does not, however, mean that they receive the same level of protection as other types of demonstrations. In this regard the ECtHR observed that 'physical conduct purposely obstructing traffic and the ordinary course of life in order to seriously disrupt the activities carried out by others is not at the core of that freedom as protected by Article 11' ECHR.[171] Consequently, the obstructive nature of the demonstration 'may have implications for any assessment of "necessity" to be carried out under Article 11(2)'.[172]

Applying this to the facts, the ECtHR held that even if it was foreseeable that the eviction would be impeded and even if this was what the applicants intended, Article 11 ECHR remained applicable.[173] No violent intentions or behaviour could be inferred from the message that had been published by the organisers calling for people to gather, nor from the personal conduct of the applicants.[174] They were therefore entitled to rely upon Article 11 ECHR.[175] Indeed, the ECtHR then went on to determine that there had been a violation of Article 11 ECHR as the domestic court had 'failed to give relevant and sufficient reasons for the interference' and 'thus failed to convincingly establish the necessity for such restrictions'.[176] The ECtHR thus determined that the requirements of Article 11 ECHR 'were not met because the analysis of applicability of that provision – and, consequently, the assessment of the justification of the interference – were not carried out at the domestic level in a manner consistent with the Convention and the Court's case-law'.[177]

Finally, it is worth noting that 'peaceful' has an autonomous Convention meaning and is not governed by whether the assembly was lawful in domestic law. This was important in *Cissé* v. *France* when the French Government argued that because the occupation was unlawful under domestic law it was not a peaceful assembly.[178] The ECtHR disagreed and held that Article 11 ECHR continued to apply.[179] The ECtHR also refused to accept in *Obote* v. *Russia* that a flash mob of seven people standing in silence with their mouths sealed with adhesive tape and holding blank sheets of paper fell outside the scope of a peaceful assembly, even if its intention was to provoke conflict with the authorities.[180]

[167] Ibid at [49]. [168] Ibid at [50]. [169] Ibid at [51]. [170] Ibid at [55].
[171] Ibid at [52]. [172] Ibid. [173] Ibid at [54]. [174] Ibid at [56]. [175] Ibid at [59].
[176] Ibid at [66]. [177] Ibid. [178] *Cissé* v. *France* (n 145) at [35]. [179] Ibid at [40].
[180] *Obote* v. *Russia*, App. No. 58954/09, 19/11/2019.

12.4.2 What Constitutes an Interference with Freedom of Assembly?

There are multiple ways in which a State may interfere with freedom of assembly. These include but are not limited to punishing organisers and participants, prohibiting the assembly, requiring the protester to seek permission and authorisation, imposing restrictions on the assembly, and arresting participants or ending an assembly.

12.4.2.1 Criminal Convictions and Civil Penalties

Criminal convictions clearly interfere with Article 11 ECHR, as does arrest even if there is no subsequent charge.[181] The ECtHR has also found an interference where applicants were prosecuted and convicted of unrelated offences, but the impetus for the prosecution was participation in a protest.[182] Punishment outside the criminal justice system can also interfere with Article 11 ECHR. For example, in *Ezelin* v. *France,* the formal disciplining of a lawyer for participating in a protest constituted an interference even though the punishment was civil in nature.[183] Equally it was held in *Sadrettin Güler* v. *Turkey* that a disciplinary warning constitutes an interference with Article 11 ECHR.[184]

12.4.2.2 Prohibitions, Authorisation Systems and Refusals of Permission

Prohibiting assemblies even if only temporarily also constitutes an interference.[185] Moreover, whilst States have sometimes sought to argue that there is no interference if a protest goes ahead in the face of a prohibition, the ECtHR rejected this in *Baczkowski* v. *Poland* on the basis that a ban puts the applicants at risk and can have a chilling effect.[186] Equally, refusing to grant permission for a particular assembly constitutes an interference, although it is important to observe that this does not mean that systems of prior notification and authorisation are themselves automatically incompatible with Article 11 ECHR.[187] In *Ziliberberg* v. *Moldova*, the ECtHR explained that authorisation procedures can be compatible with Article 11 ECHR as they aid the authorities in facilitating peaceful assemblies.[188] The ECtHR thus distinguishes between the need for authorisation, which is generally not an interference and penalising someone for failing to obtain authorisation, which will violate the

181 *Steel and Others* v. *the United Kingdom* (n 152).

182 *Jhangiryan* v. *Armenia* (n 138). See also, *Smbat Ayvazan* v. *Armenia*, App. No. 49021/08, 08/10/2020, which was handed down on the same date.

183 *Ezelin* v. *France* (n 86).

184 *Sadrettin Güler* v. *Turkey*, App. No. 56237/08, 24/04/2018.

185 *Christians Against Racism and Fascism* v. *the United Kingdom* (n 146).

186 *Baczkowski* v. *Poland* (2009) 48 EHRR 19.

187 *Ziliberberg* v. *Moldova*, App. No. 61821/00, 04/05/2004.

188 Ibid.

Convention if it is not proportionate. In *Rai and Evans* v. *the United Kingdom*, a challenge to the UK notification system concerning protests around Parliament was therefore declared inadmissible.[189] Yet, while notification systems are permissible, States must be tolerant in circumstances where it is not possible to comply with an authorisation procedure. This was important in *Bukta* v. *Hungary* where a protest was dispersed on the basis that the applicants had not given three days' notice in circumstances in which it was impossible to comply with this requirement.[190] The ECtHR held that in the circumstances failure to give notice alone could not justify disbanding the assembly.[191] The ECtHR also held in *Navalnyy* v. *Russia* that if the police interrupt a peaceful, albeit unnotified, protest, without considering whether it is necessary to do so, then this will violate Article 11 ECHR.[192] This has been significant as there have been a number of Russian cases in which the police have shut down protests simply on the basis that they have not been authorised.[193]

12.4.2.3 *Restrictions on Mode of Assembly*

Restrictions on the mode of the assembly may also constitute an interference and the ECtHR has stated that the applicant has a right to choose the time, place and manner of an assembly.[194] Thus, where the State relocates protesters to remote locations this is likely to constitute a violation. An important case in this respect was *Lashmankin* v. *Russia*, a case concerning fifteen separate applications originating in different parts of Russia.[195] All of the applicants had faced bureaucratic obstacles trying to organise peaceful assemblies and many of the applicants had been compelled to hold their protest in a remote suburb or industrial estate. This stemmed from the Russian Public Events Act which conferred wide powers on the authorities to change the location of an assembly. The applicants complained that this gave the authorities excessive discretion and that there was no effective judicial control. In determining that there had been a violation of Article 11 ECHR the ECtHR held that allowing an assembly to take place only at a location 'which is not within sight and sound of its target audience and where its impact will be muted, is incompatible with the requirements of Article 11' ECHR.[196] Yet while restrictions on locations will constitute an interference with Article 11 ECHR that needs to be justified, the ECtHR also stated that 'in the sphere of restrictions on the location, time or

[189] *Rai and Evans* v. *the United Kingdom* (dec.), App. Nos. 26258/07 and 26255/07, 17/11/2009; see also, *Novikova* v. *Russia*, App. No. 25501/07, 26/04/2016.

[190] *Bukta* v. *Hungary* (2010) 51 EHRR 25.

[191] Ibid at [35]–[37].

[192] *Navalnyy* v. *Russia* (n 66).

[193] See, for example, *Kasparov* v. *Russia (No.2)* (2018) 66 EHRR 20.

[194] *Sáska* v. *Hungary*, App. No. 58050/08, 27/11/2012.

[195] *Lashmankin* v. *Russia*, App. No. 57818/09, 07/02/2017.

[196] Ibid at [426].

manner of conduct of an assembly the Contracting States must be allowed a wider margin of appreciation'.[197]

In *Pleshkov and others* v. *Russia*, the ECtHR held that when it comes to assessing the suitability of locations, States have a wide margin of appreciation, but this margin is not unlimited and the ECtHR must examine whether the decision-making processes were fair.[198] *Pleshkov* concerned two assemblies where the applicants had been refused permission to gather in their proposed location. The first applicant wished to organise an assembly outside the Russian Parliament protesting against the increase in the state pension age.[199] Permission was refused on the basis that it was unsafe, and the authorities offered an alternative location 3km away. The applicant opposed this arguing that it was crucial to protest in front of Parliament to make parliamentarians aware of their objections.[200] The second applicants were human rights activists.[201] They wished to gather in Pushkin Square in central Moscow to mark the anniversary of the first post-war political protest that was held in that square in 1965.[202] They also wished to assemble near the authorities to urge them to respect rights to freedom of expression and assembly.[203] Permission was refused on the basis that another public event was scheduled to take place in the square on the same day and the authorities proposed that the assembly should be held 8km away. The second applicants challenged this highlighting the symbolic importance of Pushkin Square and the fact that the alternative location was far away from the public authorities to whom they wished to direct their message.[204] The ECtHR found a violation of Article 11 in respect of both applications.

In respect of the first application in *Pleshkov*, the ECtHR observed that the authorities' 'categorical exclusion of such a high-profile location as being unsuitable for public events for safety reasons ... imposed a substantial burden of justification on the national authorities, including the domestic courts' and yet there was 'no indication in the domestic courts' decisions that the security concerns clearly outweighed the adverse impact of such an exclusion on the event organiser's interests'.[205] A further factor emphasised by the ECtHR was that the domestic courts were obliged to assess whether the alternative location would enable the applicant's picket 'to have a meaningful impact'.[206] Yet 'the domestic courts [had] paid little attention to the importance of the event's intended location, instead broadly stating that "[the applicant] was offered an alternative location accessible to the public"'.[207] They had also 'failed to examine whether holding the "picket" in Lermontov Park would have fundamentally altered the character of the protest due to its

[197] Ibid at [417].

[198] *Pleshkov and others* v. *Russia*, App. Nos. 29356/19 and 31119/19, 21/11/2023 at [57].

[199] Ibid at [5]–[12]. [200] Ibid at [7]. [201] Ibid at [13]–[23]. [202] Ibid at [15].

[203] Ibid. [204] Ibid. [205] Ibid at [63]. [206] Ibid at [64]. [207] Ibid.

distance from the target audience'. Consequently, the ECtHR held that the domestic courts had not applied the standards inherent in Article 11 ECHR to strike a fair balance.[208]

Turning to the second application in *Pleshkow*, the ECtHR observed that the location had a 'special significance' in commemorating a historical event and that close proximity to the authorities was also important in order to urge them to respect freedom of expression and assembly.[209] It held that the authorities, including the domestic courts, had failed to propose acceptable alternative arrangements and had failed to provide 'relevant and sufficient reasons' to justify the restrictions imposed.[210] In such circumstances, these restrictions were not necessary in a democratic society.

12.4.2.4 Use of Force

Finally, it is important to note that in addition to raising issues in respect of other Convention rights (as noted above), use of force may also constitute an interference with Article 11 ECHR. Thus, in *Disk and Kesk* v. *Turkey* the ECtHR found that Article 11 ECHR was interfered with when the police used gas bombs, paint sprays and water cannons in respect of protesters.[211]

12.4.3 Justifying an Interference with Freedom of Peaceful Assembly under Article 11(2) ECHR

If there is an interference with Article 11(1) ECHR the ECtHR will consider whether this is justified under Article 11(2) ECHR. This involves the same tripartite approach used for other qualified rights, that is, legality, legitimacy and necessity.

12.4.3.1 Prescribed by Law

The first question is whether the interference is prescribed by law and there are cases in which a violation has been found on this basis. This can arise in several ways. First, if there was no legal regime at all authorising the interference.[212] Second, where there was a legal framework, but there was an unforeseeable application of those provisions.[213] Third, where the legal framework was vague or unclear.[214] Fourth, where there has been improper domestic

[208] Ibid at [65]. [209] Ibid at [66]. [210] Ibid at [69].

[211] *Disk and Kesk* v. *Turkey*, App. No. 38676/08, 27/11/2012.

[212] *Adali* v. *Turkey* (dec.), App. No. 38187/97, 31/01/2002 at [271]–[275].

[213] *C.S.* v. *Germany* (n 144) and *Karakaya and Piroglou* v. *Turkey* (dec.), App. Nos. 36370/02 and 37581/02, 02/05/2006.

[214] *Hashman and Harrup* v. *the United Kingdom* (dec.), App. No. 25594/94, 26/06/1996.

application of the provisions.[215] Finally, the ECtHR may determine that the powers conferred on the authorities were so broad that they lacked legal safeguards (as was the case in *Gillan and Quinton* v. *the United Kingdom* discussed above and in Chapter 8).[216] The lack of legal safeguards was also the basis for the finding of a violation in *Lashmankin*.[217]

12.4.3.2 *Legitimate Aim*

States can usually satisfy at least one of the legitimate aims in Article 11(2) ECHR, hence cases do not generally turn on this point. Perhaps the most frequently advanced aim is 'prevention of disorder'. In this regard the Grand Chamber observed in *Navalnyy* v. *Russia* that it is usually fairly easy for States to point to a legitimate aim.

> Respondent Governments normally have a relatively easy task in persuading the Court that the interference pursued a legitimate aim, even when the applicants cogently argue that it actually pursued an unavowed ulterior purpose. The Court has indeed itself recognised that in most cases it deals with the point summarily. Cases in which the Court has voiced doubts about the cited aim without ruling on the issue or has rejected one or more of the cited aims were few and far between, and the cases in which it has found a breach of the respective Article purely owing to the lack of a legitimate aim are rarer still. The real focus of the Court's scrutiny has rather been on the ensuing and closely connected issue: whether the restriction is necessary or justified, that is, based on relevant and sufficient reasons and proportionate to the pursuit of the aims or grounds for which it is authorised. Those aims and grounds are the benchmarks against which necessity or justification is measured.[218]

This does not, however, mean that the ECtHR will never determine that the measure did not pursue a legitimate aim. This was significant in *Navalnyy* v. *Russia* itself where the Grand Chamber found that some of the impugned measures had not pursued the legitimate aims of prevention of disorder or crime and the protection of the rights and freedoms of others, as claimed by the Government.[219] In respect of other impugned measures it expressed serious doubts that any legitimate aim provided for in Article 11(2) ECHR was pursued, but determined that there was no need to reach a firm conclusion on this point as the interferences were in any event not 'necessary'.[220]

Another aim that is often advanced is 'protection of the rights of others'.[221] An important aspect of the case law here is the ECtHR's rejection of the

[215] *Steel and Others* v. *the United Kingdom* (n 152).

[216] *Gillan and Quinton* v. *the United Kingdom* (n 37).

[217] *Lashmankin* v. *Russia* (n 195).

[218] *Navalnyy* v. *Russia* (n 66) at [120].

[219] Ibid at [126].

[220] Ibid at [124]–[126].

[221] *Éva Molnár* v. *Hungary*, App. No. 10346/05, 07/10/2008 at [34].

argument advanced by some States that 'protection of morals' justifies restricting LGBTQI+ demonstrations.[222]

12.4.3.3 *Necessary in a Democratic Society*

As with other qualified rights, the final and often most important aspect of Article 11(2) ECHR is the question of whether the interference was necessary in a democratic society. The ECtHR's approach here is based on proportionality analysis tempered by the margin of appreciation.[223] Thus, the ECtHR states that its task is not to substitute its view for that of the relevant national authorities but to review the way the decision was taken. This review does not, however, mean that the ECtHR simply determines whether the authorities acted in good faith; it must look at whether the interference was proportionate to that aim and whether the reasons adduced to justify it are relevant and sufficient. It therefore 'has to satisfy itself that the national authorities applied standards which were in conformity with the principles embodied in Article 11 and, moreover, that they based their decisions on an acceptable assessment of the relevant facts'.[224] In making that assessment, the intensity of the ECtHR's scrutiny will vary depending upon the circumstances. The ECtHR has not set out a list of criteria, but the following factors seem to affect its approach.

In general, the ECtHR will subject content-based prohibitions, blanket bans and severe penalties to a higher level of scrutiny. In respect of content-based prohibitions it is important to note that Article 11 ECHR protects assemblies even if the views advanced may annoy or cause offence to others. Consequently, if an assembly is prohibited simply on the basis that the ideas are shocking to others then this is likely to constitute a violation of Article 11 ECHR, unless the assembly is inciting violence or rejection of democratic principles. Content-based restrictions are therefore subject to the most serious scrutiny by the ECtHR.[225]

States often seek to prohibit assemblies not because of the views advanced, but because of public order concerns. In these circumstances a general prohibition (or blanket ban) will fall foul of the necessity test if it is disproportionate to the risk, including where authorities could have used other less restrictive means. The authorities also need to consider the impact of a prohibition on all demonstrations, including those that do not pose a risk to public safety.[226]

The nature and severity of any penalties imposed are important factors in considering whether there has been a violation. Criminal sanctions require particular justification and peaceful demonstrations should not be subject to

[222] *Bayev and Others* v. *Russia* [2017] ECHR 572 at [66]–[69].

[223] *Stankov* v. *Bulgaria*, App. No. 29221/95, 29/06/1998 at [87].

[224] Ibid at [87].

[225] *Navalnyy* v. *Russia* (n 66) at [136].

[226] *Christians Against Racism and Fascism* v. *the United Kingdom* (n 146).

the threat of a criminal sanction and deprivation of liberty.[227] Moreover, criminal convictions and lengthy sentences for those that have had only a minor role in a protest that has become hostile are likely to be disproportionate.[228] Criminal sanctions may, however, be justified where the protest is obstructive and the applicant has refused to obey a police order. Thus, in *Chernega* v. *Ukraine* the ECtHR held that a ten-day custodial sentence was not disproportionate where the applicant had refused to leave a construction site.[229] Civil sanctions may also be found to be incompatible with Article 11 ECHR.[230]

The nature of the protest will also affect the proportionality analysis. The ECtHR expects States to show a degree of tolerance and if authorities swiftly end a peaceful protest, this is likely to constitute a violation.[231] If, however, the protest is seriously obstructive, the State will have a wider margin of appreciation.[232] States also benefit from a wider margin of appreciation where public safety is affected.[233] If protesters have been able to exercise their views for some time before authorities intervene then it is more likely that the intervention will be justified. For example, in *Tuskia* v. *Georgia* the applicants had been allowed to protest for months before the intervention.[234] The ECtHR thus concluded that the interference was proportionate. Where force is used to disperse a peaceful protest, especially without prior warning, this is more likely to constitute a violation.[235]

In all cases, the ECtHR will find a violation if the State is unable to provide adequate reasons for an interference. In *Zakharaov and Varzhabetyan* v. *Russia*, the Government had not submitted any explanation for the use of force.[236] Whilst in *Chernega* v. *Ukraine*, the domestic courts had not provided sufficient reasons for their decision to impose custodial sentences of such severity.[237]

Striking a fair balance between competing rights and interests is of vital importance. This was emphasised in *Christian Democratic People's Party* v. *Moldova*:

> although individual interests must on occasion be subordinated to those of a group, democracy does not simply mean that the views of the majority must always prevail: a

[227] *Razvozzhayev* v. *Russia*, App. No. 75734/12, 19/11/2019.

[228] *Yaroslav Belousov* v. *Russia*, App. No. 2653/13, 04/10/2016.

[229] *Chernega* v. *Ukraine* (n 32). [230] *Ezelin* v. *France* (n 86).

[231] *Balçik* v. *Turkey* (n 153) at [51]–[52]. See also *Bukta* v. *Hungary* (n 190) and *Kortvelyessy* v. *Hungary*, App. No. 58274/15, 03/10/2017.

[232] *Drieman* v. *Norway* (dec.), App. No. 33678/96, 04/05/2000.

[233] *Rassemblement Jurassien*, App. No. 8191/78, (1979) 17 DR 93.

[234] *Tuskia* v. *Georgia*, App. No. 14237/07, 11/10/2018.

[235] *Laguna Guzman* v. *Spain*, App. No. 41462/17, 06/10/2020 at [54].

[236] *Zakharaov and Varzhabetyan* v. *Russia*, App. Nos. 35880/14 and 75926/17, 13/10/2020 at [90].

[237] *Chernega* v. *Ukraine* (n 32) at [256].

balance must be achieved which ensures the fair and proper treatment of minorities and avoids any abuse of a dominant position.[238]

The need for a fair balance was also apparent in *Karaahmed* v. *Bulgaria* where the domestic authorities had to balance Articles 9 and 11 ECHR in respect of clashes between demonstrators and worshippers outside a Mosque during prayer time.[239] On that occasion the ECtHR held that there had been a violation of Article 9 ECHR and elaborated on the balancing exercise. Observing that Articles 9, 10 and 11 ECHR are all qualified rights and there is no hierarchy between those rights, the ECtHR stated that the rights must be balanced in a manner which recognises their importance in a society based on pluralism, tolerance and broad-mindedness.[240] It went on to articulate three principles that follow from this. First, the State is obliged to ensure, insofar as is reasonably possible, that both rights are protected, and this obligation applies regardless of whether the acts in question are carried out by private individuals.[241] Second, there must be an effective legal framework to safeguard rights from third parties and to take effective measures.[242] Third, the task of the ECtHR is 'to verify whether the authorities struck a fair balance' and in making this assessment the ECtHR 'should not act with the benefit of hindsight'.[243] It should not 'simply substitute its view for that of the national authorities who, in any given case, are much better placed to assess where the appropriate balance lay and how best to achieve that balance'.[244] This suggests that provided the domestic authorities can establish that they sought to strike a fair balance the ECtHR will not intervene.

Conversely, the ECtHR will intervene if the domestic authorities have not demonstrated that they have struck a fair balance. This was the outcome in *Öllinger* v. *Austria.*[245] The facts of that case were that the applicant, Öllinger, had been prevented from holding a meeting in the Salzburg municipal cemetery on All Saints Day, in order to commemorate the Salzburg Jews killed by the SS during the Second World War. A meeting of Comradeship IV (SS soldiers) was scheduled at the same time and in the same location.[246] The domestic authorities prohibited Öllinger's meeting on the ground that it would endanger public order and security.[247] They stated that the disruption of the commemoration ceremonies was likely to offend the religious feelings of members of the public visiting the cemetery and would be regarded as disrespectful towards the dead soldiers of both world wars and thus as an unbearable

[238] *Christian Democratic People's Party* v. *Moldova* (n 149) at [64].

[239] *Karaahmed* v. *Bulgaria*, App. No. 30587/13, 24/02/2015 at [92]. [240] Ibid at [92].

[241] Ibid at [93]. [242] Ibid at [94]. [243] Ibid at [95]. [244] Ibid at [95].

[245] *Öllinger* v. *Austria* (2008) 46 EHRR 38. See also, David Mead, 'Strasbourg Discovers the Right to Counter-Demonstrate: A Note on Öllinger v. Austria' [2007] (2) EHRLR 133. See also, Mead (n 8), pp.111–114.

[246] Ibid at [8]. [247] Ibid at [10].

provocation.[248] Accordingly, there was a risk of protests by visitors to the cemetery which could degenerate into open conflict between them and those participating in the assembly.[249] After his domestic challenges to the prohibition were unsuccessful, Öllinger lodged an application with the ECtHR arguing that the prohibition violated Article 11 ECHR . The ECtHR observed that the case concerned competing fundamental rights as '[t]he applicant's right to freedom of peaceful assembly and his right to freedom of expression have to be balanced against the association's right to protection against disruption of its assembly and the cemetery-goers' right to protection of their freedom to manifest their religion'.[250] It noted that the 'domestic authorities had regard to the various competing Convention rights' and that the ECtHR's task was therefore to examine whether the domestic authorities 'achieved a fair balance between [the rights]'.[251] In respect of the applicant's Article 10 and 11 ECHR rights the ECtHR stated that 'the unconditional prohibition of a counter-demonstration is a very far-reaching measure which would require particular justification, all the more so as the applicant, being a member of parliament, essentially wished to protest against the gathering of Comradeship IV and, thus, to express an opinion on an issue of public interest'.[252] It was not disputed by the parties that protecting the gathering of Comradeship IV did not provide sufficient justification for the contested prohibition the question for the ECtHR was thus 'whether the prohibition was justified to protect the cemetery-goers' right to manifest their religion'.[253] Here the ECtHR identified a number of factors which indicated that the measure was disproportionate to the aim. First, it observed that the assembly was not directed against the cemetery-goers' beliefs, nor the manifestation of them.[254] Second, the applicant expected only a small number of peaceful participants and had explicitly ruled out the use of chanting or banners.[255] Third, although the authorities feared that heated debates might arise, it was not alleged that any incidents of violence had occurred on previous occasions.[256] Consequently, the ECtHR stated that it was 'not convinced by the Government's argument that allowing both meetings while taking preventive measures, such as ensuring police presence in order to keep the two assemblies apart, was not a viable alternative'.[257] Overall, it found that the domestic authorities had attached 'too little weight to the applicant's interest in holding the intended assembly and expressing his protest against the meeting of Comradeship IV, while giving too much weight to the interest of cemetery-goers in being protected against some rather limited disturbances'.[258] Consequently the ban constituted a disproportionate interference with Article 11 ECHR.[259]

[248] Ibid at [12]. [249] Ibid at [12]. [250] Ibid at [34]. [251] Ibid at [42].
[252] Ibid at [44]. [253] Ibid at [46]. [254] Ibid at [47]. [255] Ibid. [256] Ibid.
[257] Ibid at [48]. [258] Ibid at [44]. [259] Ibid at [49].

12.4.4 Positive Obligations

Article 11 ECHR also includes positive obligations, an important aspect of which is the State's role in safeguarding the effective enjoyment of the right where there are counter-demonstrators. This was considered in *Plattform Arzte fur das Leben* v. *Austria.*[260] The applicants were doctors campaigning for changes to Austria's abortion laws who argued that the police had failed to adequately protect their protests from counter-demonstrators. The applicants had held two events that had been disrupted by counter-demonstrators shouting; moreover, during the second event, the counter-demonstrators had thrown eggs and clumps of grass at the applicants.[261] At the end of the event 'when tempers had risen to the point where physical violence nearly broke out, special riot-control units – which had until then been standing by without intervening – formed a cordon between the opposing groups'.[262] The ECtHR observed that 'while it is the duty of Contracting States to take reasonable and appropriate measures to enable lawful demonstrations to proceed peacefully, they cannot guarantee this absolutely and they have a wide discretion in the choice of the means to be used'.[263] Consequently, the obligation is one 'as to measures to be taken and not as to results to be achieved'.[264] Applying this to the facts, the ECtHR held that the authorities had not failed to take reasonable and appropriate measures.[265]

The proactive and pre-emptive aspect of the positive obligation was significant in *Frumkin* v. *Russia* where the ECtHR held that States have an obligation to communicate with organisers of assemblies to ensure the peaceful conduct of an assembly.[266] This was breached in *Frumkin* as the police had not complied with even the minimum requirements of their duty to communicate with the organisers.[267] The importance of planning was also evident in *Kudrevičius* v. *Lithuania* where the Grand Chamber stated that the obligation includes taking appropriate measures to ensure the 'peaceful conduct and the safety of all citizens' including 'ensuring the presence of first-aid services'.[268]

The fact that States have an obligation to facilitate a peaceful assembly can justify limiting counter-demonstrations, but the ECtHR has emphasised that States cannot intervene too readily. This was significant in the above-mentioned case of *Öllinger* v. *Austria.*[269] Equally in *Stankov and the United Macedonian Organisation Ilinden* v. *Bulgaria*, it was recognised that 'if every probability of tension and heated exchange between opposing groups during a demonstration were to warrant its prohibition, society would be faced with

[260] *Plattform Arzte fur das Leben* v. *Austria* (1991) 13 EHRR 204. [261] Ibid at [12].
[262] Ibid at [13]. [263] Ibid at [34]. [264] Ibid. [265] Ibid at [39].
[266] *Frumkin* v. *Russia* (2016) 63 EHRR 18. [267] Ibid at [129].
[268] *Kudrevičius* v. *Lithuania* (2016) 62 EHRR 34 at [158]–[160].
[269] *Öllinger* v. *Austria* (n 245) at [44].

being deprived of the opportunity of hearing differing views on any question which offends the sensitivity of the majority opinion'.[270]

There are also signs that the ECtHR is increasingly emphasising the importance of the positive obligation for persons holding unpopular views or belonging to minorities that are more vulnerable to victimisation.[271] As observed earlier, this was of paramount importance in *Berkman* v. *Russia* where the ECtHR found that the State had failed to provide adequate policing for an LGBTI assembly.[272] Equally, a violation was found in *Promo Lex* v. *Moldova* where the police had offered no assistance to a demonstration attacked by masked men.[273] It is important to observe that the obligation in this context does not simply include responding to events, but also imposes an obligation to actively promote tolerance. This was emphasised in *Identoba* v. *Georgia* where it was stated that where authorities know or should know of the risk of tensions they are 'under an obligation to use any means possible, for instance by making public statements in advance of the demonstration to advocate, without any ambiguity, a tolerant, conciliatory stance'.[274] On the facts, the ECtHR found that the domestic authorities had not used the nine days' notice that they had been given prior to an LGBT march 'for careful preparatory work' and that 'given the attitudes in parts of Georgian society towards the sexual minorities, the authorities knew or should have known of the risk of tensions associated with the applicant organisation's street march to mark the International Day Against Homophobia'.[275] In such circumstances, the Court held that the authorities were 'under an obligation to use any means possible, for instance by making public statements in advance of the demonstration to advocate, without any ambiguity, a tolerant, conciliatory stance ... as well as to warn potential law-breakers of the nature of possible sanctions'.[276] They also held that 'it was apparent from the outcome of the LGBT procession, that the number of police patrol officers dispatched to the scene of the demonstration was not sufficient, and it would have been only prudent if the domestic authorities, given the likelihood of street clashes, had ensured more police manpower by mobilising, for instance, a squad of anti-riot police'.[277] The ECtHR therefore held that the 'domestic authorities failed to ensure that the march ... could take place peacefully by sufficiently containing homophobic and violent counter-demonstrators' and '[i]n view of those omissions, the authorities fell short of their positive obligations under Article 11 taken in conjunction with Article 14 of the Convention'.[278]

[270] *Stankov and the United Macedonian Organisation Ilinden* v. *Bulgaria* (n 223) at [107].
[271] *Baczkowski* v. *Poland*, App. No. 1543/06, 03/05/2007 at [64].
[272] *Berkman* v. *Russia* (n 104). [273] *Promo Lex* v. *Moldova*, App. No. 42757/09, 24/02/2015.
[274] *Identoba* v. *Georgia*, App. No.73235/12, 12/05/2015 at [99]. [275] Ibid at [99].
[276] Ibid. [277] Ibid. [278] Ibid at [100].

A further issue to consider in respect of positive obligations is whether Article 11 ECHR entails a right to access private land.[279] This is important for two reasons. First, because privatisation of land means that there is less and less public space available in which to protest, and many quasi-public forums such as town centres, shopping centres and railways stations are now privately owned. The second is that protests are often directed at the activities of private organisations and thus proximity is important. The approach taken by the ECtHR is that there is no right of access to private land. This issue arose in *Appleby* v. *the United Kingdom* where the applicants had been refused permission to set up a stall and distribute leaflets at the local shopping centre, which had previously been public property but was now privately owned.[280] The applicants wished to oppose local development plans and they felt that the shopping centre was the best forum in which to interact with residents. The ECtHR declined to find that the UK was required to provide access to private property but it accepted that there are positive obligations in respect of Article 10 ECHR. Indeed, the ECtHR observed that if a

> bar on access to property has the effect of preventing any effective exercise of freedom of expression or it can be said that the essence of the right has been destroyed, the Court would not exclude that a positive obligation could arise for the State to protect the enjoyment of the Convention rights by regulating property rights. A corporate town where the entire municipality is controlled by a private body might be an example.[281]

Nevertheless, it noted that here the applicants had alternative means of communicating their ideas.[282] Thus, '[b]alancing the rights in issue and having regard to the nature and scope of the restriction in this case', the Court did not find 'that the respondent State failed in any positive obligation to protect the applicants' freedom of expression'.[283] *Appleby* has been criticised for failing to address the erosion of public space through privatisation and the impact that this has on freedom of assembly.[284] In the two decades that have followed *Appleby*, there has been considerable privatisation of key locations within city centres, vastly beyond what was in dispute in *Appleby*, consequently it may be time for the ECtHR to revisit this.

12.4.5 Conclusion: Article 11 ECHR and Peaceful Assembly

Pre-2000, Helen Fenwick concluded that there would be effective rights of peaceful protest only if domestic judges disregarded much of the Strasbourg

[279] See Jacob Rowbottom, 'Property and Participation: A Right of Access for Expressive Activities' [2005] (2) EHRLR 186, Mead (n 8), ch.4, Salát (n 143), ch.8.

[280] *Appleby* v. *the United Kingdom* (2003) 37 EHRR 38. [281] Ibid at [47]. [282] Ibid at [48].

[283] Ibid at [49]. [284] Rowbottom (n 279).

case law.[285] In 2007 David Mead's research indicated that out of sixty-six protest cases taken to Strasbourg, only thirty-three had been declared admissible and only thirteen had resulted in a finding of violation.[286] Since then, there have been far more cases brought before the ECtHR, and the Court has found many violations. Yet whilst it is evident that the Convention rights provide some protection for those that may be deemed 'peaceful' protesters, the extent to which disruptive protest is protected remains uncertain. This is an issue that is likely to be of growing importance, given that, as we will see in the next section of this chapter, domestic legislation has expanded the circumstances in which restrictions can be placed on noisy or disruptive protests.

12.5 FREEDOM OF PEACEFUL ASSEMBLY IN DOMESTIC LAW

The HRA 1998 (HRA) gave further effect to Convention rights, including Article 11 ECHR, in domestic law. Consequently it is unlawful under s.6 HRA for public authorities (which includes the police and the courts) to act in a way which is incompatible with Article 11 ECHR. Moreover, s.3 HRA requires that, so far as it is possible to so do, primary and subordinate legislation must be read and given effect in a way which is compatible with Article 11 ECHR. It is, however, important to note that even prior to the HRA the common law had long recognised rights of freedom of expression and freedom of assembly. This can be seen in *R* v. *Roberts (Richard)* where the Court of Appeal held that the 'long-established recognition in the United Kingdom of the value of peaceful protest ... is a manifestation of the importance attached by the common law to both the right to protest and free speech'.[287] Given the significance attached to freedom of assembly by the common law, we might therefore question whether the HRA and the ECHR have added anything to domestic law. However, Gavin Phillipson, having reviewed the record of the common law, concludes that 'the difference between the common law and the HRA-ECHR approaches ... [is] so profound that loss of the HRA-ECHR scheme would radically diminish the potential for judicial application'.[288] In particular, he observes that 'common law thinking in this area has barely progressed beyond the traditional approach whereby 'rights' of association or assembly figure as mere negative liberties – aspects of

285 Helen Fenwick, 'The Right to Protest, the Human Rights Act and the Margin of Appreciation' (1999) 62 MLR 513.

286 David Mead, 'The Right to Peaceful Protest under the European Convention on Human Rights: A Content Study of Strasbourg Case Law' [2007] (4) EHRLR 345–384.

287 *R* v. *Roberts (Richard)* [2018] EWCA Crim 2739, [2019] 1 WLR 2577 at [37].

288 Gavin Phillipson, 'Searching for a Chimera? Seeking Common Law Rights of Freedom of Association and Assembly' in Mark Elliott and Kirsty Hughes, *Common Law Constitutional Rights* (Hart, 2020).

the general freedom to do that which the law does not forbid'.[289] Indeed, it was the fact that the pre-HRA common law provided a civil liberty rather than a right which led Sedley LJ to herald the HRA 1998 as ushering in a 'constitutional shift' in the law of protest.[290] Yet, since then, while there have been landmark cases in which the courts have relied upon the Convention rights in upholding freedom of assembly, it is questionable whether there has been the constitutional shift that Sedley LJ anticipated. Consequently, a decade after the HRA came into force Keith Ewing argued that the contribution of the HRA 'has been little more than a mirage'.[291]

One of the reasons for scepticism is that the post-HRA period has seen the enactment of far wider legislative restrictions on protest than had existed previously. Indeed, there has been no abeyance of the long-standing tradition in domestic law of enacting legislative provisions to deal with threats or perceived threats to public order.[292] This is evident from the fact that in the last few years alone we have seen the enactment of the Police, Crime, Sentencing and Courts Act 2022 (PCSCA 2022), the Public Order Act 2023 (POA 2023) and the Public Order Act 1986 (Serious Disruption to the Life of the Community) Regulations 2023.[293] All of which are a response to protests by groups such as Extinction Rebellion, Insulate Britain and Just Stop Oil. Environmental activism and direct action are, however, far from new and there were already extensive police powers available.[294] The case for expanding police powers by creating new offences and by lowering thresholds and widening the circumstances in which existing police powers can be deployed has been advanced by reference to the cost of policing such protests and the scale of disruption. To date, it is reported that the cost of policing Just Stop Oil protests stands at over £20 million, while the cost of policing Extinction Rebellion's protests between April and October 2019 alone was £37 million.[295] This prompted Her Majesty's Inspectorate of Constabulary and Fire and Rescue Service (HMICFRS) to report in 2021 that the police were not

[289] Ibid.

[290] *Redmond Bate* v. *DPP* [1999] Crim. L.R. 998. For further discussion of civil liberties see Chapter 2 at Section 2.2.1.

[291] Keith Ewing, *Bonfire of the Liberties* (OUP, 2010), p.135.

[292] The POA 1936 was a response to fascism, whilst the Public Order Act 1986 (POA 1986) was enacted under the Thatcher Government as a response to riots and miners' strikes.

[293] See Richard Martin, 'The Protest Provisions of the Police, Crime, Sentencing and Courts Bill: A "Modest Reset of the Scales"?' (2021) 12 Criminal Law Review 1008 for comments on some of the proposals when they were in draft form.

[294] In the 1990s direct action by environment protesters prompted the Criminal Justice and Public Order Act 1994 (CJPOA 1994) which criminalised various forms of trespass.

[295] Vikram Dodd, 'Extinction Rebellion protests cost Met police £37m so far', *The Guardian*, 22 October 2019, www.theguardian.com/uk-news/2019/oct/22/extinction-rebellion-protests-cost-met-police-37m-so-far. HMICFRS, *Getting the Balance Right? An Inspection of How Effectively the Police Deal with Protests* (March 2021).

striking the right balance, that the balance was too readily tipping in favour of protesters, and that 'a modest reset of the scales is needed'.[296] The legislation that followed was heavily contested in Parliament, some provisions were enacted in the PCSCA 2022, others were rejected during the passage of that Act, only to later reappear in the Public Order Act 2023. Further provisions were rejected by Parliament during the passage of the POA 2023 but were then controversially put into regulations by the Secretary of State via the Public Order Act 1986 (Serious Disruption to the Life of the Community) Regulations 2023.[297] At the time of writing the Crime and Policing Bill currently before Parliament also contains provisions that will introduce further offences relating to processions and assemblies and will make some further amendments to police powers in relation to processions and assemblies.[298]

In addition to new legislation, there have been concerns about legislative creep where provisions that were intended for matters such as national security, anti-social behaviour or harassment are used against protesters. The interface between political activism and terrorism has given rise to significant concern in this respect. The 'war on terror' climate following the 9/11 and July 2007 bombings saw the enactment of both the Serious Organised Crime and Police Act 2005 and the Police Reform and Social Responsibility Act 2011 which restricted protest around Parliament, while the Counter-Terrorism Act 2008 criminalised taking photographs of police officers. More generally, as discussed in Chapter 8, the changed landscape of political 'extremism' and the wide definition of terrorism under s.1 of the TA 2000 has the potential to lead to some forms of protest being labelled as 'terrorism' thereby engaging the panoply of terrorism powers available to authorities. Other national security legislation has also been invoked in respect of direct action, and while there are circumstances in which the terrorism label can legitimately be attached to violent political protests, concerns arise where national security laws are invoked in respect of peaceful direct action. An example of this is the case of the Stansted 15, a group of peaceful protesters that surrounded a plane and locked themselves together to prevent the Home Office from forcibly deporting people. The Stansted 15 were initially charged with aggravated trespass under the CJPOA 1994, but it was later decided that they should be prosecuted for a security offence under the Aviation and Maritime Security Act 1990, which can attract a maximum sentence of life imprisonment. The Court of Appeal quashed that conviction and held that the protesters should not have been prosecuted for a security

[296] HMICFRS (n 295).

[297] This has been the subject of legal challenge; see *R (on the application of National Council for Civil Liberties)* v. *Secretary of State for the Home Department* [2025] EWCA Civ 571, discussed at Section 12.1.5.3.

[298] Crime and Policing Bill, Bill 235 (2024–2025).

offence.[299] During these events, UN Human Rights experts also wrote to the Government urging them not to prosecute protesters under security and terrorism legislation.[300] Subsequent cases have been prosecuted using other provisions and in some cases hefty sentences have been handed down in respect of non-violent but disruptive climate protesters.[301]

Further concerns arise from the growing surveillance of protesters, including not only the use of stop and search powers, but also undercover policing, facial recognition technology, extremism databases; as well as the use of force during the policing of demonstrations.[302] The Crime and Policing Bill currently before Parliament will also create a new offence of concealing identity at protests.[303]

Finally, it is important to note that as the right to protest is usually contingent upon having access to somewhere in which to protest there are concerns about restrictions on protests in specific locations, the growing use of injunctions, as well as the impact of privatisation of land on the right to protest. In particular, the privatisation of city centres raises the question of whether there is sufficient space in which to protest.

The remainder of this chapter will examine the ways in which public order legislation regulates protest (Section 12.5.1), restrictions on specific locations (Section 12.5.2), policing of protests (Section 12.5.3), surveillance of protesters (Section 12.5.4), offences that may be committed by protesters (Section 12.5.5), and injunctions and preventative orders (Section 12.5.6). In addition to considering whether these measures individually curtail freedom of assembly, it is also important to reflect on the extent to which the sheer breadth and complexity of the regime itself undermines freedom of assembly.

12.5.1 Prohibiting, Regulating and Restricting Protests

The POA 1986 provides that the police can, in certain circumstances, prohibit a procession or an assembly or issue directions imposing conditions upon a procession or an assembly. It distinguishes between processions and assemblies and has separate provisions in respect of each of them. This reflects the fact that from 1936 to 1986 only processions were subject to statutory

[299] *Thacker & Ors* v. *R.* [2021] EWCA Crim 97, [2021] QB 644, [2021] 2 WLR 1087 at [113].

[300] UN Press Release, *UK must stop disproportionate use of security laws after conviction of Stansted 15, say UN rights experts*, 06/02/2019.

[301] *R* v. *Hallam and others*, Sentencing Remarks of HHJ Christopher Hehir, 18/07/2024, available at www.judiciary.uk/judgments/rex-v-hallam-and-others/ (last accessed 12 August 2024) and *R* v. *Hallam (Julian Roger)* [2025] EWCA Crim 199 in which some of the sentences awarded by HHJ Christopher Hehir were quashed and substituted with lower sentences. On the relevance of conscientious motive to sentencing in protest cases see *R* v. *Trowland (Morgan)* [2023] EWCA Crim 919, [2024] 1 WLR 1164.

[302] See Sections 12.5.3 and 12.5.4.

[303] Crime and Policing Bill 235 (2024–2025).

provisions. The statutory powers introduced by the POA 1936 had dealt only with processions; static meetings were not subject to statutory control, but were subject to the common law powers in respect of breach of the peace.[304] When the POA 1986 was enacted it contained provisions for both processions and assemblies but there were differences between them. This reflected the position taken in the 1985 White Paper that preceded that legislation in which it was stated that 'meetings and assemblies are a more important means of exercising freedom of speech than are marches'.[305] Consequently, an important distinction is that s.11 POA 1986 requires written notice to be given prior to holding a procession, but there is no equivalent requirement for assemblies. There are also different provisions in respect of when processions or assemblies can be prohibited (s.13 and s.14A POA 1986). Meanwhile, s.12 and s.14 seperately provide for the circumstances in which a senior police officer can impose conditions on a procession or an assembly. Those provisions have been significantly amended by recent legislation which has lowered the threshold and expanded the range of circumstances in which conditions can be imposed on both processions and assemblies.

12.5.1.1 *Prohibiting Protests*

12.5.1.1.1 *Prohibiting Processions*

Section 13(1) POA 1986 empowers the chief officer of the police to apply to the relevant council for an order prohibiting the holding of all public processions in any district (or part thereof) for a period not exceeding three months in circumstances in which the chief officer reasonably believes that imposing conditions will not be sufficient to prevent serious public disorder.[306] Once an order is made it is an offence to organise or participate in a procession, knowing that it is prohibited, or to incite another to commit such an offence.[307]

12.5.1.1.2 *Prohibiting Assemblies*

When the POA 1986 was enacted it did not include a power to prohibit assemblies as at that time 'there was no strong request from the police for a power to ban'.[308] This changed when the CJPOA 1994 inserted s.14A into the POA 1986. Section 14A POA 1986 empowers the chief officer of the police to

[304] In addition to the power to arrest in respect of breach of the peace see *Kamara* v. *Director of Public Prosecutions* [1974] AC 104 in respect of crime of unlawfully assembling in such a manner as to disturb the public peace.

[305] Review of Public Order Law (Cmnd. 9510, 1985).

[306] Section 13(1) POA 1986.

[307] Section 13(7)–(9) POA 1986.

[308] Review of Public Order Law at [5.3].

apply to the council of the district for an order prohibiting trespassory assemblies, for a period of no more than four days, and in an area which does not exceed a five mile radius.[309] This applies to assemblies of twenty or more persons on land in the open air to which the public has no or only a limited right of access.[310] Once a ban is in place, s.14B POA 1986 provides that it is an offence to organise or participate in a prohibited assembly, or to incite another to commit such an offence. Section 14C of the POA 1986 also provides the police with the power to issue an order directing a person not to proceed in the direction of an assembly within the area to which an order under s.14A applies. Failure to comply with that direction is an offence (s.14C(3) POA 1986).

In an important pre-HRA decision, *DPP* v. *Jones*, the courts examined the scope of trespassory assemblies and thus the reach of a s.14A order.[311] The facts were that Jones and others had participated in a peaceful, non-obstructive demonstration on part of the highway near Stonehenge whilst a s.14A order was in place, for which they were arrested and subsequently convicted. The question on appeal was whether the assembly, which had taken place on the public highway, had exceeded the public's right of use of the highway. If the assembly was within the public's right of use of the highway then Jones and others had not commited a trespass, there was no trespassory assembly, and no offence had been committed. The convictions were quashed by the House of Lords which held that a public highway is a place where any activity which is reasonable, which does not involve a public or private nuisance and does not obstruct the highway should not be regarded as a trespass. Consequently, a peaceful, non-obstructive assembly on the highway amounted to a reasonable use, was not a trespassory assembly and they had committed no offence.[312] The case was heralded at the time as an 'important vindication of a fundamental civil liberty'.[313]

12.5.1.2 *Notice Requirement for Processions*

Section 11 POA 1986 requires organisers to give written notice six days before the date when a public procession is to be held unless it is not reasonably practicable to do so. It is an offence to organise a procession without giving notice,[314] and it is also an offence if the date, time or route differs from that

[309] Section 14(A)(6) POA 1986.

[310] Note that the definition of an assembly for s.14A POA 1986 (i.e. twenty or more persons) is provided in s.14A(9) POA 1986 and it is different to the definition of public assembly used in s.16 POA 1986 in respect of the other provisions (two or more persons).

[311] *DPP* v. *Jones* [1999] 2 AC 240, [1999] 2 WLR 625.

[312] Ibid.

[313] For discussion, see Gina Clayton, 'Reclaiming Public Ground: The Right to Peaceful Assembly' (2000) 63(2) MLR 252, 252.

[314] Section 11(7)(a) POA 1986.

specified in the notice.[315] An important exception is that written notice is not required where the procession is one commonly or customarily held in the police area (or areas) in which it is proposed to be held.[316]

Separate provisions apply in respect of Northern Ireland where the Public Processions (Northern Ireland) Act 1998 (PP(NI) Act 1998) places responsibility in the hands of the Parades Commission. The PP(NI) Act 1998 makes it a criminal offence to organise or participate in a procession if notification has not been given. This was considered by the Supreme Court in *DB* v. *Chief Constable of Police Service of Northern Ireland*.[317] The case concerned the flag parades in Belfast, the background to which was that after Belfast City Council decided to stop flying the Union flag over Belfast City Hall every day, there was a wave of protests by loyalists marching from East Belfast to Belfast City Hall through a nationalist area. No notification was made in respect of those protests, the parades continued for months, and the police believed that they had no power to stop a parade that had not been notified. During this time '[t]here was substantial violence and disorder as the parade went through that nationalist area. Sectarian abuse was directed at the residents of Short Strand; stones and other objects were thrown at them; and their homes were attacked'.[318] The appellant, DB, was resident in Short Strand and his and his neighbours' homes were attacked during the parades that took place during December 2012 and January 2013.[319] Thus, DB brought proceedings, arguing that the police should have intervened to stop the parades.

The Supreme Court, in a unanimous judgment handed down by Lord Kerr, held that while there could be 'no reasonable suggestion ... that the police failed to treat the control of parades and demonstrations with sufficient seriousness',[320] the police were wrong to believe that they were obliged by Article 11 ECHR to facilitate 'peaceful protests even if they were "technically illegal"'.[321] They found that the police in fact had an 'inescapable duty to prevent, where possible, what were plainly illegal parades from taking place and to protect those whose rights under article 8 of the ECHR were in peril of being infringed'.[322] The Supreme Court recognised that '[m]eeting those obligations had to be tempered by operational constraints' and that '[s]topping the parades without taking account of what further violence that might provoke was not an option'.[323] Nevertheless, it emphasised that the police 'had to have a clear-sighted appreciation of their available powers'[324] and that dispersing a

[315] Section 11(7)(b) POA 1986.

[316] Section 11(2) POA 1986; see, *Kay* v. *Commissioner of Police of the Metropolis* [2008] UKHL 69, [2008] 1 WLR 2723, where the Lords held that notice was not required for the monthly Critical Mass Cycle Ride in London even if the route was not predetermined.

[317] *DB* v. *Chief Constable of Police Service of Northern Ireland* [2017] UKSC 7, [2017] N.I. 301.

[318] Ibid at [12]. [319] Ibid. [320] Ibid at [2]. [321] Ibid at [61]. [322] Ibid at [62].

[323] Ibid. [324] Ibid.

procession that had not been lawfully notified would not have infringed Article 11 ECHR.[325] Yet while there may have been grounds for intervention in *DB*, it is questionable whether the blanket statement that the police should disperse a protest simply for failure to notify is compatible with the ECtHR case law canvassed above.

12.5.1.3 *Imposing Conditions on Protests*

12.5.1.3.1 *Conditions on Processions*

Section 12 of the POA 1986 empowers a senior police officer to impose conditions on processions that appear to them to be *necessary* to prevent disorder, damage, disruption, impact or intimidation. This includes conditions as to the route, which may include prohibiting the procession from entering a specified public place.[326] The legislation provides considerable discretion as to what conditions can be imposed, but they must appear to be 'necessary' to the senior police officer, and the officer is required by s.6 HRA to act compatibly with Articles 10 and 11 ECHR.[327] Where conditions are imposed, it is an offence for an organiser or participant to fail to comply with a condition that they knew or ought to have known was imposed, unless they can establish that the failure arose from circumstances beyond their control.[328] The s.12 POA 1986 power to issue a direction is applicable even to processions that are not subject to the requirement to give notice under s.11 POA 1986.[329]

The s.12 POA 1986 power was significantly extended by the PCSCA in 2022, before being extended further by the Public Order Act 1986 (Serious Disruption to the Life of the Community) Regulations 2023. Under the original s.12 POA 1986, conditions could only be imposed when it was reasonably believed that the procession may result in *serious public disorder, serious damage to property, serious disruption to the life of the community*, or that those organising intended to intimidate others with a view to compelling them

325 Ibid at [60]–[62]. 326 Section 12(1) POA 1986.

327 See, for example, *R (on the application of the English Defence League)* v. *Commissioner of Police of the Metropolis* [2013] EWHC 3890 in which restrictions were imposed on an EDL march in Tower Hamlets, residence of the largest Muslim population in the country. EDL sought judicial review of the conditions imposed on the route. The Court held that the conditions were a proportionate restriction on the right to protest, in part due to the applicants' intention to intimidate the local community and the risk of serious public disorder. See also, discussion of s.6 HRA in Chapter 3.

328 Section 12(4) and (5) POA 1986. See also, *Jukes* v. *DPP* [2013] EWHC 195 (Admin) where participants in a procession of which s.12 had been imposed, which designated the route of the procession, were found to be in breach of those conditions when they diverted from the route to join another protest as they remained part of the original procession.

329 *Powlesland* v. *DPP* [2013] EWHC 3846 (Admin), [2014] 1 WLR 2984.

not to do an act they have a right to do, or to do an act they have a right not to do.[330] Section 73 of the PCSCA 2022 inserted s.12(2A) into the POA 1986 which provides that *serious disruption to the life of the community* includes *significant delay to the delivery of a time-sensitive product to consumers or prolonged disruption of access to any essential goods or services.* Section 73 of the PCSCA 2022 also expanded the range of circumstances in which conditions can be imposed. Thus conditions can be imposed where the noise generated by a procession may result in serious disruption to the activities of an organisation carried on in the vicinity.[331] In the case of a procession in England and Wales conditions may also be imposed where the noise generated may have an impact on persons in the vicinity, and that impact may be significant.[332] This vastly expanded the scope for conditions, as whilst the original s.12 POA 1986 power focused on serious public disorder and intimidation, it now includes precluding disruption and even impact. Sections 12(2C)–(2E) POA 1986 provide insight into how the new noise provisions should be interpreted and applied.

The PCSCA 2022 also empowered the Secretary of State (SofS) to amend s.12 POA 1986 by regulation and to make further provisions in respect of the meaning of serious disruption to an organisation in the vicinity, or serious disruption to the life of the community.[333] This includes defining any aspect of expression and giving examples of cases in which a procession is or is not to be treated as resulting in such disruption.[334] It was this power that the SofS deployed when creating the Public Order Act 1986 (Serious Disruption to the Life of the Community) Regulations 2023 (POA Regulations 2023) in order to further extend the power to impose conditions under s.12 POA 1986. The POA Regulations 2023 achieve this by lowering once more the threshold for imposing conditions. As noted above, under the PCSCA 2022 the standard was one of *significant delay* to the delivery of a time-sensitive product to consumers or *prolonged disruption*. Yet, under the Regulations serious disruption to the life of the community now includes *hindrance*, *delay* or *disruption* that is *more than minor*. The POA Regulations 2023 also specify that the senior police officer can take into account 'cumulative disruption' in determining whether to make an order and the meaning of community for the purposes of assessing 'serious disruption to the life of the community' is 'any group of persons that may be affected by the procession, whether or not all or any of those persons live or work in the vicinity of the procession'. All of which arguably gives the senior police officer a wider basis on which to intervene.

The POA Regulations 2023 were highly contentious because the SofS brought in, via secondary legislation, provisions that had been rejected by

[330] Section 12 POA 1986. [331] Section 12(1)(ab) POA 1986. [332] Ibid.
[333] Section 12(12) POA 1986. [334] Section 12(13) POA 1986.

Parliament during the passing of the POA 2023. The use of secondary legislation to usher in via the backdoor what Parliament had rejected was regarded by many as not only egregious, but also potentially unconstitutional. The House of Lords Secondary Legislation Scrutiny Committee expressed its concerns about both the process and the fact that the SofS had provided no reasons for doing this.[335] The Committee pointedly observed that it was not aware of any previous occasions on which measures were brought in as secondary legislation so soon after they were rejected in primary legislation. It also observed that the Explanatory Memorandum which accompanied the Regulations had made no mention of the defeat of the measures during the passage of the POA 2023. Indeed, in the section of the Explanatory Memorandum that asks whether there were any matters of special interest to Parliament, the response was simply 'none'. It was therefore no wonder that the Committee decided that the Explanatory Memorandum was not satisfactory.[336] Yet, while the Committee concluded that the Regulations raised constitutional issues that the House may wish to consider, in the end neither the Commons nor the Lords refused to approve the Regulations. This was perhaps because, as Tom Hickman and Gabriel Tan noted at the time, 'it is more difficult and hazardous for the House of Lords to reject statutory instruments than amendments to Bills' and the last time they did (in 2015) it prompted a mini-constitutional crisis and a review of the powers of the House of Lords.[337] Hickman and Tan thus alluded to the prospect of legal challenge to the POA Regulations 2023 while noting that although there is an argument that the Regulations reverse the policy agreed by Parliament in the POA 2023, 'the underdeveloped jurisprudence on the operation and limits of Henry VIII powers provides thin gruel for an argument along these lines'.[338] That said, they observed that the inadequacies of the consultation process (which had been a one-sided process) was more clearly open to challenge.[339] Liberty subsequently commenced legal proceedings in respect of the POA Regulations 2023 and the Divisional Court found that the Regulations were unlawful on both the ultra vires and the flawed consultation grounds.[340] On appeal, the Court of Appeal held that the Regulations were ultra vires,

[335] House of Lords Secondary Legislation Scrutiny Committee, 38th Report of Session 2022–2023 (HL Paper 189), 11/05/2023.

[336] In fact, the explanatory memorandum indicated that there were no matters of special interest to Parliament in the Regulations and that the Regulations are compatible with the Convention rights.

[337] Tom Hickman and Gabriel Tan, 'Reversing Parliamentary Defeat by Delegated Legislation: The Case of the Public Order Act 1986 (Serious Disruption to the Life of the Community) Regulations 2023', UK Const. L. Blog (22 May 2023).

[338] Ibid. [339] Ibid.

[340] *R (on the application of National Council for Civil Liberties)* v. *Secretary of State for the Home Department* [2024] EWHC 1181 (Admin).

but declined to uphold the Divisional' Court's decision that the regulations were unlawful for the further reason that the consultation process was procedurally unfair.[341]

12.5.1.3.2 *Conditions on Assemblies*

Section 14 of the POA 1986 empowers a senior police officer to impose conditions on assemblies. When s.14 POA 1986 was enacted, 'public assembly' was defined in s.16 POA 1986 as 'an assembly of 20 or more persons in a public place which is wholly or partly open to the air'. This was amended by the Anti-social Behaviour Act 2003 to reduce the number of people from twenty to two or more. The legislation provides considerable discretion as to what conditions can be imposed but, as with s.12 POA 1986 conditions, the police are obliged to act compatibly with Articles 10 and 11 ECHR under s.6 HRA 1998 and the conditions must appear 'necessary' to them.[342] It is an offence for an organiser or participant to fail to comply with a condition that they knew or ought to have known was imposed, unless they can establish that the failure arose from circumstances beyond their control.[343]

An important limitation on exercising the s.14 POA 1986 power was, however, identified in *R (Jones)* v. *Commissioner of Police of the Metropolis.*[344] The case arose from the Extinction Rebellion Autumn Uprising (XRAU) which consisted of multiple site protests between 7–19 October 2019. At the time, the Commissioner of the Police concluded that the Uprising was an assembly that may result in serious disruption to the life of the community. He thus purported to exercise the s.14 POA 1986 power and imposed a condition that the assembly must cease by 9pm, 14 October 2019. The applicants were activists and politicians that had been arrested for breach of that condition. They argued that the Uprising was not *one* 'public assembly' but was in fact *many* public assemblies, consequently as there was not *a* public assembly at the scene of which the Superintendent was present, there was no power to impose a condition under s.14 POA 1986. In interpreting the ambit of s.14 POA

[341] *R (on the application of National Council for Civil Liberties)* v. *Secretary of State for the Home Department* (n 297).

[342] See *R (on the application of the English Defence League)* v. *Commissioner of Police of the Metropolis* (n 327) where it was held that neither s.12, nor s.14 conditions were disproportionate.

[343] Section 12(4) and (5) POA 1986. See also, *Jukes* v. *DPP* (n 328) where participants in a procession of which s.12 had been imposed which designated the route of the procession were found to be in breach of those conditions when they diverted from the route to join another protest as they remained part of the original procession.

[344] *R (Jones)* v. *Commissioner of Police of the Metropolis* [2019] EWHC 2957, [2020] 1 WLR 519, for discussion, see Stevie Martin, 'The Meaning of "Public Assembly": Policing Protest in the Twenty-First Century' (2020) **79** CLJ 1.

1986, the Court held that 'separate gatherings, separated both in time and by many miles, even if co-ordinated under the umbrella of one body, were not one public assembly within the meaning of section 14(1)'.[345] The decision to impose the condition was thus unlawful because there was no power to impose it under s.14(1) POA 1986.[346]

Section 14 POA 1986 was also significantly extended by the PCSCA 2022 and the POA Regulations 2023 in a manner that mirrors the changes to s.12 POA 1986. The circumstances in which a direction can be given are set out in s.14(1) POA 1986. It provides that a senior police officer, having regard to the time or place at which and the circumstances in which any public assembly is being held or is intended to be held may give a direction if they reasonably believe:

(a) it may result in serious public disorder, serious damage to property or serious disruption to the life of the community,
(aa) in the case of an assembly in England and Wales, the noise generated by persons taking part in the assembly may result in serious disruption to the activities of an organisation which are carried on in the vicinity of the assembly,
(ab) in the case of an assembly in England and Wales–
   (i) the noise generated by persons taking part in the assembly may have a relevant impact on persons in the vicinity of the assembly, and
   (ii) that impact may be significant, or
   (b) the purpose of the persons organising it is the intimidation of others with a view to compelling them not to do an act they have a right to do, or to do an act they have a right not to do.

Section 14(1A) POA 1986 provides that the senior police officer may give directions imposing on the persons organising or taking part in the assembly –

(a) in the case of an assembly in England and Wales, such conditions as appear to the officer necessary to prevent the disorder, damage, disruption, impact or intimidation mentioned in subsection (1);
(b) in the case of an assembly in Scotland, such conditions as to the place at which the assembly may be (or continue to be) held, its maximum duration, or the maximum number of persons who may constitute it, as appear to the officer necessary to prevent the disorder, damage, disruption or intimidation mentioned in subsection (1)(a) or (b).

Akin to the provisions in respect of processions, the impact of the POA Regulations 2023 is that s.14(2A) POA 1986 now provides 'serious disruption

[345] Ibid. [346] Ibid at [71].

to the life of the community' includes, in particular, where it may, by way of physical obstruction, result in:

(i) the prevention of, or a hindrance that is more than minor to, the carrying out of day-to-day activities (including in particular the making of a journey),
(ii) the prevention of, or a delay that is more than minor to, the delivery of a time-sensitive product to consumers of that product, or
(iii) the prevention of, or a disruption that is more than minor to, access to any essential goods or any essential service.

Sections 14(2C)–(2E) POA 1986 set out the circumstances in which the noise provisions of s.14(1)(aa) and s.14(1)(ab)(i) POA 1986 will be met. The s.14 POA 1986 provision also mirrors the s.12 POA 1986 provision in that in considering whether a public assembly in England and Wales may result in serious disruption to the life of the community, the senior police officer must take into account all relevant disruption, and may take into account any relevant cumulative disruption. A further point to observe is that s.14 POA 1986 has also been amended by the POA 2023 to empower the British Transport Police and the Ministry of Defence police to set conditions on assemblies.[347] Moreover, the PCSCA 2022 has introduced a power to impose conditions on noisy one-person assemblies under s. 14ZA POA 1986.

12.5.1.4 *Restrictions during COVID-19*

During the COVID-19 pandemic, significant restrictions were placed on movement and interaction which affected freedom of assembly. The regulations that applied during the first lockdown were challenged in the case of *R (on the application of Dolan)* v. *Secretary of State for Health and Social Care*.[348] The applicants in that case argued that the regulations 'imposed sweeping restrictions on civil liberties which were unprecedented and unlawful'.[349] One of their many grounds of challenge was that the regulations violated a number of Conventions rights guaranteed in domestic law under the HRA 1998, which included Article 11 ECHR. In particular, that regulation 7, which imposed

[347] Section 16 POA 2023. Section 15 POA 2023 also amended s.14 POA 1986 to provide that in London the Metropolitan Police Commissioner or City of London Police Commissioner can delegate functions to an officer of the rank of Commander, this placed the provisions on the same footing as those that existed in respect of policing outside London. The Explanatory Notes to the POA 2023 at [86] state that this was necessary to relieve Assistant Commissioners of the heavy burden of attending court to provide first-hand evidence whenever the lawfulness of a condition attached to a protest is contested.

[348] *R (on the application of Dolan)* v. *Secretary of State for Health and Social Care* [2020] EWCA Civ 1605, [2021] 1 WLR 2326.

[349] Ibid at [1].

restrictions on gathering by permitting only six people to gather outdoors and two people indoors, breached Article 11 ECHR. The Court of Appeal observed that on the face of it '[r]egulation 7 as originally enacted in March 2020 might be thought to have taken away this right [Article 11 ECHR] altogether', however the Court went on to observe that regulation 9(1)(a) provided a general defence of 'reasonable excuse'.[350] Consequently, it was not the case that the regulations were incompatible with the right as they could be interpreted compatibly by virtue of the reasonable excuse exception.

> In our view, the regulations cannot be regarded as incompatible with article 11 given the express possibility of an exception where there was a reasonable excuse. It may well be that in the vast majority of cases there will be no reasonable excuse for a breach of regulation 7 as originally enacted. There were powerful public interests which lay behind the enactment of regulation 7, given the gravity of the pandemic in late March.[351]

They also observed that there were 'powerful arguments that the restrictions, time limited and subject to review as they were, were in any event proportionate'.[352]

Yet while *Dolan* held that the regulations (which were no longer applicable by the time of the Court's judgment) could be read in such a way that freedom of assembly could be assessed as part of the reasonable excuse exception, it was arguably unclear to the public that protest was not outright prohibited. This was commented on by the JCHR, which reported that the frequently changing regulations during COVID-19 had created substantial confusion as to whether participating in a protest was illegal.[353] The JCHR concluded that the regulations had left 'too much subjective interpretation and discretion to the police'.[354]

In addition to the question of whether the regulations satisfied the requirement of legal certainty, it has also been queried whether they were a proportionate interference with Articles 10 and 11 ECHR or whether alternatives could/should have been explored. In this regard the JCHR noted that in some periods of lockdown, other activities that seem to pose similar public health risks such as picketing and gathering for worship were permitted whilst protest was not explicitly permitted.[355] A further concern was whether the prohibitions were impartially and proportionately policed.[356] This was of particular concern in relation to protests relating to the Black Lives Matter

[350] Ibid at [101]. [351] Ibid at [103]. [352] Ibid.

[353] Joint Committee on Human Rights, *Government Response to Covid-19: Freedom of Assembly and the Rights to Protest*, HC 1328, HL Paper 252 (19 March 2021) at [45].

[354] Ibid, p.3. [355] Ibid at [81]–[83].

[356] Joint Committee on Human Rights, *Government Response to Covid-19: Human Rights Implications*, HC 265, HL Paper 125 (21 September 2020) at [63].

movement during the summer of 2020 (following the death of George Floyd in May 2020).[357]

The events surrounding the Sarah Everard vigil also highlighted uncertainty for both the police and protesters as to what was permissible, and problems with policing of demonstrations. In March 2021, Sarah Everard was abducted in Clapham, London, raped and murdered by a Metropolitan Police officer. A peaceful gathering, intended 'to channel the collective grief, outrage and sadness in our community', was proposed to take place on Clapham Common on Saturday, 13 March 2021. The organisers contacted the Metropolitan Police in advance to ensure that the event could safely and legally take place. The police did not approve the event and so the organisers issued legal proceedings to establish whether the lockdown restrictions prohibited all gatherings for protest. In *Leigh* v. *Commissioner of the Metropolitan Police*, the High Court indicated that the applicable regulations had to be read compatibly with Articles 10 and 11 ECHR.[358] The regulations provided a defence of 'reasonable excuse' and it was accepted that this gave effect to the Convention rights.[359] The result was that whilst a given protest on its facts could/might be restricted, it would be inappropriate to treat the regulations as if they gave rise to a blanket prohibition.[360] The Court was not, however, asked to determine whether the Sarah Everard vigil should go ahead.[361] The police subsequently refused to confirm to the organisers that the event could go ahead lawfully, and as each of the organisers would be at risk of receiving a fine of £10,000 for breaching the restrictions on gatherings, the official event was cancelled.

In *Leigh (No.2)*, the High Court ruled that the Metropolitan Police acted unlawfully in respect of the proposed vigil.[362] The Court held that in dealing with the request, the police interfered with the claimants' Convention rights as their decisions had a chilling effect.[363] Moreover, the police were under a duty to make a proportionality assessment and had to weigh up the competing considerations; they were not entitled to simply look at the regulations and determine that any gathering would pose a serious risk to health.[364] In this regard the Court found that 'the practical burden of applying the proportionality principle ha[d] been considerably overstated' by the police.[365] The police were not entitled in law to ignore altogether the question of what the available evidence might show about the gravity of current public health risks.[366] Consequently, the claimants had been deprived of a decision by the police which was in accordance with the law and they were entitled to a decision from the Court which vindicated their position in relation to the

[357] Ibid. [358] *Leigh* v. *Commissioner of the Metropolitan Police* [2021] EWHC 661 (Admin).

[359] Ibid at [13]–[14]. [360] Ibid at [17]. [361] Ibid at [19].

[362] *Leigh* v. *Commissioner of the Metropolitan Police (No.2)* [2022] EWHC 527 (Admin), [2022] 1 WLR 3141.

[363] Ibid at [76]. [364] Ibid at [80]. [365] Ibid at [81]. [366] Ibid at [82].

unlawfulness.[367] It is, however, important to note that the Court held that it would be inappropriate for it to carry out the proportionality exercise itself.[368] Thus, the Court did not find that the police should have allowed the vigil to go ahead.

It is also worth noting that although the official event was cancelled, many people gathered on Clapham Common on the evening of 13 March. Confrontations broke out between the police and members of the public and police officers were filmed using force to restrain women and remove them from the event. In July 2021, the All Party Parliamentary Group on Democracy and the Constitution found failings in the policing of the vigil which included disproportionate use of force.[369]

12.5.2 Statutory Restrictions on Specific Locations

In addition to the POA 1986 which enables the police to impose conditions that may include restrictions on the location of an assembly or procession, there are also other statutory provisions dealing with specific locations.

12.5.2.1 Protesting in the Vicinity of Parliament

A natural place for protesters to gather is close to Parliament, but there are some restrictions when protesting in its vicinity. In 2005, (now repealed) provisions of the Serious Organised Crime and Police Act 2005 (SOCPA) required protesters to obtain authorisation for a demonstration within the designated area around Parliament. The impetus for that legislation was Brian Haw's long-term protest in Parliament Square against the war in Iraq. In *Evans and Others* v. *DPP*, two protesters who had been convicted for demonstrating without SOCPA authorisation were unsuccessful in arguing that this violated the Convention.[370] They subsequently applied to the ECtHR, arguing that their convictions violated Article 11 ECHR, but their case was declared inadmissible on the basis that although the authorisation requirement was an interference with the right it could not be considered to be disproportionate.[371]

The SOCPA provisions were later repealed and replaced by the Police Reform and Social Responsibility Act 2011 (PRSRA) which seeks to tackle long-term protests in Parliament Square Gardens by prohibiting camping and the use of amplified noise equipment. It also gives the police powers to issue directions, failure to abide by which is an offence. Measures taken under these

[367] Ibid at [107]. [368] Ibid.

[369] All Party Parliamentary Group on Democracy and the Constitution, *Police Powers and the Right to Peaceful Protest*, July 2021.

[370] *Evans and Others* v. *DPP* [2006] EWHC 3209. [371] *Rai and Evans* (n 189).

provisions were unsuccessfully challenged in *R (on the application of Gallastegui)* v. *Westminster City Council*[372] and *R (on the application of Barda)* v. *Mayor of London on behalf of GLA*.[373] The PRSRA provisions were later extended by ss.76–77 PCSCA which expand the parameters of the controlled area and render it an offence to obstruct the passage of vehicles entering and exiting certain areas.[374] Section 77 PCSCA also empowers the SoS to specify other areas as controlled areas by regulation.

12.5.2.2 *Abortion Clinics*

Until recently there was no legislation specifically dealing with protests in the vicinity of abortion clinics. This changed in respect of Northern Ireland with the enactment of the Abortion Services (Safe Access Zones) (Northern Ireland) Act 2023,[375] and in England and Wales where s.9 of the POA 2023 was brought into force in October 2024. Both Acts render it an offence to interfere with access to or provision of abortion services. There is no reasonable excuse defence in respect of these offences. Provisions also apply in Scotland following the entry into force of the Abortion Services (Safe Access Zones) Act 2024 in September 2024.

Prior to this legislation protests in the vicinity of individual abortion clinics had sometimes been addressed by local authorities via a Public Service Protection Order (PSPO). Section 59 of the Anti-social Behaviour, Crime and Policing Act 2014 (Anti-social Behaviour Act 2014) provides that a local authority may make a PSPO if it is satisfied on reasonable grounds that two conditions are met. The first condition is that activities carried on (or likely to be carried on) in a public place within the authority's area have had (or are likely to have) a detrimental effect on the quality of life of those in the locality. The second condition is that the effect, or likely effect, of the activities: (a) is, or is likely to be, of a persistent or continuing nature; (b) is, or is likely to be, such as to make the activities unreasonable; and (c) justifies the restrictions imposed by the notice.

In 2018 a PSPO was made by the London Borough of Ealing prohibiting anti-abortion protests in the immediate vicinity of Marie Stopes UK West London Centre. This was challenged by a pro-life campaigner in *Dulgheriu & Anor* v. *The London Borough of Ealing*.[376] The applicant, Dulgheriu, argued that the local authority had no power to issue a PSPO where the activity

[372] *R (on the application of Gallastegui)* v. *Westminster City Council* [2013] EWCA Civ 28, [2013] 1 WLR 2377.

[373] *R (on the application of Barda)* v. *Mayor of London on behalf of GLA* [2015] EWHC 3584 (Admin), [2016] 4 WLR 20.

[374] Section 76(3)(a) PCSCA 2022.

[375] See also, discussion in Chapter 5.

[376] *Dulgheriu & Anor* v. *The London Borough of Ealing* [2019] EWCA Civ 1490, [2020] 1 WLR 609.

regulated impacts only or primarily on the quality of life of occasional visitors to the locality rather than on those who reside or work there or visit regularly. She also argued that the restrictions were incompatible with Articles 9, 10 and 11 ECHR. Turner J dismissed both those arguments finding (i) that that the requirements for issuing a PSPO were met, and (ii) that although the PSPO interfered with the applicant's Convention rights, the measure was a justified intereference, given the impact of the protests on the Article 8 ECHR rights of the service users.[377] The Court of Appeal rejected her appeal.[378] It concluded that the judge had been correct to find that the protests had a detrimental effect within the meaning of the statute and that a PSPO could be used. In respect of the Convention rights, it held that the rights were applicable, but found that they were outweighed by the competing Article 8 ECHR rights of those wanting to access the clinic. Thereafter the Supreme Court refused permission to appeal. Convention rights challenges to PSPOs have also been rejected in other cases brought by anti-abortion protesters.[379]

As discussed in Chapter 6, abortion was illegal in Northern Ireland under the Offences Against the Person Act 1861, but since 2019 is now lawful in certain circumstances. This has raised many questions as to how to ensure that there is effective access to abortion services, one aspect of which relates to protests in the vicinity of abortion clinics. In 2022, the Northern Ireland Assembly sought to address the problem of protests in the vicinity of clinics by passing the Abortion Services (Safe Access Zones) (Northern Ireland) Bill which would render it a criminal offence to engage in certain conduct in these locations. The Attorney General for Northern Ireland asked the Supreme Court to determine whether this would be outside the legislative competence of the Northern Ireland Assembly, on the basis that the offence constitutes a disproportionate interference with protestors' Articles 9, 10 and 11 ECHR rights. Consequently, in *Abortion Services (Safe Access Zones), REFERENCE by the Attorney General for Northern Ireland*, the Supreme Court considered whether the legislation implementing 'safe access zones' in Northern Ireland was compatible with the rights protected under the HRA 1998.[380] It held that clause 5 of the Abortion Services (Safe Access Zones) (Northern Ireland) Bill (as it then was), which criminalises specific conduct in the vicinity of premises from which treatment, advice or counselling relating to the lawful termination of a pregnancy is provided, is compatible with those rights. Clause 5 creates an offence of

[377] *Dulgheriu & Anor* v. *The London Borough of Ealing* [2018] EWHC 1667 (Admin) at [90]–[97].

[378] See (n 376).

[379] *Tossici-Bolt* v. *Bournemouth, Christchurch and Poole Council* [2023] EWHC 3229 (Admin), *R (on the application of Hacking)* v. *Stafford Magistrates Court* [2022] EWHC 2733 (Admin).

[380] *Abortion Services (Safe Access Zones), REFERENCE by the Attorney General for Northern Ireland* [2022] UKSC 32, [2023] AC 505. See Stevie Martin, 'Proportionality and Protest-Related Offences' (2023) 82 CLJ 2.

intentionally or recklessly influencing a person (either directly or indirectly), preventing or impeding access by a protected person, or causing harassment, alarm or distress to a protected person, within a safe access zone. A protected person is a person who is accessing treatment or advice, accompanying such a person, or who works in or provides services to the protected premises. In respect of clause 5 the Supreme Court held that there is no need for a court to consider whether, on the specific facts of the case before it, the defendant's conviction is a proportionate interference with their ECHR rights, '[t]hat is because either the defendant's conduct will not engage articles 9 to 11 ECHR, for example because it is violent, or, if rights under those articles are engaged, the proportionality balance has been struck by the legislation'.[381]

12.5.2.3 *Places of Worship*

At the time of writing, it is intended that the Crime and Policing Bill currently before Parliament will amend the POA 1986 to make further provisions for imposing conditions on protests in the vicinity of places of worship in circumstances where the protest may intimidate persons of reasonable firmness with the result that those persons are deterred from: (i) accessing that place of worship for the purpose of carrying out religious activities, or (ii) carrying out religious activities at that place of worship. These provisions have been introduced following concerns about protests at synagogues and mosques.

12.5.3 Policing a Protest

12.5.3.1 *Statutory Powers*

We have already seen in respect of the POA 1986 that the police have extensive statutory powers which allow them to issue directions imposing conditions during a procession or assembly. [382]

12.5.3.2 *Breach of the Peace*

Alongside statutory powers there is a common law power to intervene to prevent suspected and/or imminent breaches of the peace. In *Steel* v. *the United Kingdom* it was argued that this common law power is too ill-defined to satisfy the quality of law requirements of Article 11 ECHR, however the ECtHR held that it is sufficiently precise for the purposes of the Convention right.[383]

Although there are, as was discussed earlier, extensive statutory powers, the common law power remains significant because it was accepted in

[381] Ibid at [155]. [382] See above Section 12.5.1.3.

[383] *Steel* v. *the United Kingdom* (n 152) at [55].

Wright v. *Commissioner of Police for the Metropolis* that even if conditions cannot be given under the POA 1986, the police may still be able to impose restrictions under the common law power to prevent a breach of the peace.[384]

One of the most important cases in respect of the common law power to intervene to prevent breach of the peace is *R (on the application of Laporte)* v. *CC Gloucestershire* in which the House of Lords clarified that the power may only be exercised where a breach of the peace is *imminent.*[385] The applicant, Laporte, was a passenger in one of three coaches travelling to an RAF base to protest against the war in Iraq when the coaches were stopped by the police. The background to which was that the police had received evidence that a group of protesters known as the 'Wombles' were travelling on the coaches and that they were carrying items and equipment to disrupt the protest and gain entry to the air base. In the proceedings that followed, it was reported that the Chief Superintendent had directed the police to stop the coaches on the M25, but that the protestors were not to be arrested to prevent a breach of the peace as at that time the Chief Superintendent did not consider there to be an imminent breach of the peace.[386] However, the protestors were to be warned that if articles were found on the coaches and they arrived at Fairford, he would consider them to be there intent on causing disruption and a breach of the peace and they may find themselves arrested. The coaches were stopped by the police at a lay-by and during a search of the coaches the police found some dust and face masks, three crash helmets, hoods, five hard hats, overalls, scarves, a can of red spray paint, two pairs of scissors and a safety flare. In the luggage compartment of the first coach, the police found five polycarbonate home-made shields.[387] All these articles were seized. Following which the Chief Superintendent directed that the coaches and passengers be escorted by the police back to London.[388] The coaches were thereafter driven to the motorway, where police motorcycle outriders prevented them from stopping on the hard shoulder or turning off to motorway services, even to allow passengers to relieve themselves. Some suffered acute physical discomfort and embarrassment as a result.[389] The Chief Superintendent explained to the court that he decided not to allow the coaches to proceed to the protest, as the evidence suggested that upon arrival at RAF Fairford a breach of the peace would have occurred.[390] The question for the House of Lords was whether this was a lawful exercise of the power of breach of the peace given that the point at which the police intervened was some distance away from the protest,

[384] *Wright* v. *Commissioner of Police for the Metropolis* [2013] EWHC 2739 (QB).

[385] *R (on the application of Laporte)* v. *CC Gloucestershire* [2006] UKHL 55, [2007] 2 AC 105. See A. T. H. Smith, 'Protecting Protest: A Constitutional Shift' (2007) **66**(2) CLJ 253 and Fenwick (n 50).

[386] *R (on the application of Laporte)* v. *CC Gloucestershire,* ibid at [10]. [387] Ibid at [11].

[388] Ibid at [12]. [389] Ibid. [390] Ibid at [13].

meaning that a breach of the peace was not imminent. Lord Bingham concluded that it was not a lawful exercise of the power. He opined that the police had interfered with the protesters' Convention rights and that this interference was not prescribed by law as the necessary condition for exercising the power of breach of the peace was not met.[391] Lord Mance emphasised that in addition to a breach not being imminent, the decision to turn back all of the protesters was disproportionate.[392]

The requirement that a breach of the peace must be imminent before it can be exercised is significant. Yet while the facts of *Laporte* meant that it could not be said to be imminent in that case, in subsequent cases it appears that the police retain considerable latitude and courts are reluctant to intervene with decisions made in respect of events unfolding on the ground. For example, in *Wright* v. *Commissioner of Police for the Metropolis* the Court held that in deciding to pen a group protesters, it was clear that the police officers honestly believed that a breach of the peace was about to occur and that there were reasonable grounds for that belief.[393] Equally in *R (on the application of Moos and McClure)* v. *Commissioner of the Police of the Metropolis*, a case concerning the legality of kettling during a G20 demonstration, the Court of Appeal held that the High Court had wrongly formed its own assessment of whether breach of the peace was imminent, rather than considering the reasonableness of the apprehension of the police of an imminent breach of peace.[394] The Court of Appeal held that there was no justifiable basis for concluding that the apprehension of the police that such a breach was imminent was unreasonable.[395] A further case in which the court deferred to the police was *R (on the application of Hicks)* v. *Commissioner of Police of the Metropolis*.[396] *Hicks* concerned the arrest and detention of a number of individuals on the day of the wedding of the Duke and Duchess of Cambridge in order to prevent an imminent breach of the peace. The applicants, who had all been arrested on this basis, argued that this violated Article 5 ECHR. The Administrative Court,[397] Court of Appeal[398] and the Supreme Court all held that the arrests and detention were lawful. In contemplating both the scope of Article 5 ECHR and the common law power of breach of the peace, the Supreme Court stated

391 Ibid at [50]–[56].
392 Ibid at [152]–[155].
393 *Wright* v. *Commissioner of Police for the Metropolis* (n 384).
394 *R (on the application of Moos and McClure)* v. *Commissioner of the Police of the Metropolis* [2012] EWCA Civ 12.
395 Ibid at [90] and [93].
396 *R (on the application of Hicks)* v. *Commissioner of Police of the Metropolis* [2017] UKSC 9, [2017] AC 256.
397 *R (on the application of Hicks)* v. *Commissioner of Police of the Metropolis* [2012] EWHC 1947 (Admin), [2012] ACD 102.
398 *R (on the application of Hicks)* v. *Commissioner of Police of the Metropolis* [2014] EWCA Civ 3, [2014] 1 WLR 2152.

that 'an appreciation of the reality and practical implications is central to the principle of proportionality, which is not only embedded in article 5 but is part of the common law relating to arrest for breach of the peace'. [399] The Court went on to determine that:

> In this case there was nothing arbitrary about the decisions to arrest, detain and release the appellants. They were taken in good faith and were proportionate to the situation. If the police cannot lawfully arrest and detain a person for a relatively short time (too short for it to be practical to take the person before a court) in circumstances where this is reasonably considered to be necessary for the purpose of preventing imminent violence, the practical consequence would be to hamper severely their ability to carry out the difficult task of maintaining public order and safety at mass public events.[400]

As discussed earlier in this chapter the applicants application to the ECtHR was also unsuccessful.[401]

12.5.3.3 *Kettling*

The courts have often found that kettling is a proportionate and thus justifiable interference with the Convention rights.[402] We also saw earlier in this chapter that the ECtHR found no violation of Article 5 ECHR in *Austin* v. *the United Kingdom* where the applicants were kettled for many hours in Oxford Circus. Note, however, that the High Court identified some limits to kettling in *Mengesha* v. *Commissioner of Police of the Metropolis* where, although it was accepted that kettling was justified, it held that it was unlawful to require each individual to provide their name, address and date of birth and to be filmed doing so as the price for being released from the containment.[403]

12.5.3.4 *Use of Force*

Section 3 of the Criminal Law Act 1967, s.117 Police and Criminal Evidence Act 1984 (PACE) and the common law allow the police to use force in preventing crime, making an arrest or protecting themselves or others. The police must act compatibly with the HRA 1998 and thus are subject to Articles 2 and 3 ECHR. As discussed in Chapter 4, Article 2 ECHR requires that use of force is limited to no more than absolutely necessary for one of the listed aims. There have been numerous examples of police brutality in the context of

[399] *R (on the application of Hicks)* v. *Commissioner of Police of the Metropolis* (SC) (n 396) at [30].

[400] Ibid at [31].

[401] See discussion at Section 12.2.3.4.

[402] *Wright* v. *Commissioner of Police for the Metropolis* (n 384) and *R (on the application of Moos and McClure)* v. *Commissioner of the Police of the Metropolis* (n 394).

[403] *Mengesha* v. *Commissioner of Police of the Metropolis* [2013] EWHC 1695 (Admin).

demonstrations, perhaps the most famous of which was the death of newspaper vendor Ian Tomlinson during the 2009 G20 protests. Tomlinson was on his way home from work on 1 April 2009 during the G20 demonstrations when he was struck from behind by a police baton and pushed by a police officer causing him to fall. As a result, Tomlinson suffered internal bleeding, which led to his collapse and subsequent death. An inquest found that at the time of the strike and the push, Tomlinson was walking away from the police line,[404] he was complying with police instructions to leave the area, and he posed no threat. The jury returned a verdict of unlawful killing.[405] After the inquest verdict, PC Simon Harwood, the police officer who struck Tomlinson, was prosecuted for manslaughter and acquitted in 2012.[406] He was dismissed from the Metropolitan Police Service after a disciplinary hearing. Tomlinson's family brought civil proceedings against the Metropolitan Police, which were settled following receipt of an undisclosed sum in August 2013 and an apology.[407]

Concerns about use of force have also arisen in other contexts. For example, in 2011 the Independent Police Complaints Commission determined that excessive force had been used when the police dragged across a road a disabled student protester whom they had removed from his wheelchair and struck with a baton.[408] The findings of a Netpol report on policing during Black Lives Matter protests also raise very serious concerns about use of force and institutional racism.[409]

12.5.3.5 *Protection of Journalists*

Section 17 of the POA 2023 provides for an important limitation on the exercise of police powers in respect of journalists. It provides that a constable may not exercise a police power either:

(1) for the *sole* purpose of preventing a person from observing or reporting on a protest; or

404 'Ian Tomlinson inquest verdict', *The Guardian*, 3 May 2011, www.theguardian.com/uk/blog/2011/may/03/ian-tomlinson-inquest-verdict-live-blog.

405 Ibid.

406 Peter Walker and Paul Lewis, 'Ian Tomlinson death: Simon Harwood cleared of manslaughter', *The Guardian*, 19 July 2012, www.theguardian.com/uk/2012/jul/19/simon-harwood-not-guilty-ian-tomlinson.

407 Matthew Taylor, 'Ian Tomlinson's family win apology from Met police over death in 2009', *The Guardian*, 5 August 2013, www.theguardian.com/uk-news/2013/aug/05/ian-tomlinson-apology-met-police.

408 Independent Police Complaints Commission, Annual Report and Statement of Accounts 2011/12, HC 292.

409 The Network for Police Monitoring, 'Britain is not innocent': A Netpol Report on the policing of Black Lives Matter protests in Britain's towns and cities in 2020, November 2020, https://netpol.org/black-lives-matter/#.

(2) for the *sole* purpose of preventing a person from observing or reporting on the exercise of a police power in relation to a protest-related offence, a protest-related breach of an injunction, or activities related to a protest.

12.5.4 Surveillance of Protesters

12.5.4.1 Stop and Search Powers

There are both suspicion-based and suspicion-less stop and search powers that may be used in respect of protesters.

Section 10 POA 2023 amends the existing *suspicion-based* stop and search power under s.1(8) PACE to include the power to stop and search where there is suspicion of an offence of wilful obstruction, intentionally or recklessly causing public nuisance or some of the new offences under the POA 2023.

Suspicion-less stop and search powers are highly controversial and give rise to serious concerns about arbitrariness and discrimination. As noted above and in Chapter 8, in *Gillan and Quinton* v. *the United Kingdom* the ECtHR determined that the suspicion-less power in s.44 TA 2000 violated Article 8 ECHR. This power was repealed and replaced with s.47A TA 2000 which provides senior police officers with the power to authorise searches without suspicion in a specific area. Section 60 CJPOA 1994 also gives police the right to search people without reasonable suspicion when they reasonably believe that serious violence will take place. The discriminatory impact of stop and search powers on persons of colour is well documented.[410] The introduction of a further *suspicion-less* stop and search power was thus one of the most contested aspects of the POA 2023. Section 11 of the POA 2023 provides for suspicion-less stop and search in relation to protest activity. It applies where 'a police officer of or above the rank of inspector reasonably believes' that one of the offences specified in s.11(1)(a) POA 2023 may be committed in any locality within the officer's police area, or that persons are carrying prohibited objects (as defined in s.11(2) POA 2023) in any locality within the officer's police area. Those offences are wilful obstruction, intentionally or recklessly causing public nuisance or some of the new offences under the POA 2023. Section 11(4) POA 2023 states that in order to exercise the power under s.11 POA 2023 the police officer must reasonably believe that: (a) the authorisation is necessary to prevent the commission of offences within subsection (1)(a) or the carrying of prohibited objects (as the case may be); (b) the specified locality is no greater than is necessary to prevent such activity; and (c) the specified period is no longer than is necessary to prevent such activity. Provided those conditions are met, then s.11(2) POA 2023 provides that the police officer may

[410] House of Common Home Affairs Committee, *The Macpherson Report: Twenty-Two Years On*, Third Report of Session 2021–2022, HC 139, 30 July 2021, Ch.6 especially at [301]–[311].

give an authorisation that the powers conferred by this section are to be exercisable: (a) anywhere within a specified locality within the officer's police area; and (b) for a specified period not exceeding twenty-four hours. The authorisation must be given in writing, specify the grounds on which it is given and specify the locality in which and period during which the powers are exercisable.[411] The effect of authorisation is that any constable in uniform will then have the power: (a) to stop any person and search them or anything carried by them for a prohibited object; and (b) to stop any vehicle and search the vehicle, its driver and any passenger for a prohibited object.[412] No grounds for suspicion are required.[413] It is an offence to intentionally obstruct a constable in the exercise of this power.[414] Section 11(5) POA 2023 provides that if it appears to a police officer of or above the rank of *superintendent* that it is *necessary* to do so to prevent the commission of offences within subsection (1)(a) or the carrying of prohibited objects, the officer may direct that the authorisation is to continue in force for a further period not exceeding twenty-four hours. This direction must be given in writing or where it is not practicable to do so must be recorded in writing as soon as it is practicable to do so.[415]

12.5.4.2 *Undercover Investigations of Protesters*

Undercover police officers have infiltrated protest groups, formed sexual relations and in one case even fathered a child as part of an attempt to crack down on protest groups. The practices of undercover police officers were examined in *Kate Wilson* v. *The Commissioner of Police of the Metropolis, National Police Chiefs' Council* where the Investigatory Powers Tribunal (IPT) found that Wilson had been deceived into a sexual relationship by an undercover police officer, Mark Kennedy, between November 2003 and February 2005 and had been subject to covert surveillance by Kennedy and at least five other undercover officers over a period of more than ten years.[416] The police conceded that Kennedy's conduct amounted to degrading treatment of Wilson contrary to Article 3 ECHR, and also conceded breaches of Article 8 and Article 10 ECHR.[417] They denied, however, that more senior officers knew of or acquiesced in the relationship, and maintained that their training, supervision and safeguarding was generally adequate.[418] As discussed in Chapter 5, the IPT found that the police violated Article 3 ECHR and 8 during these operations.[419] The IPT also found breaches of Articles 10, 11 and 14 ECHR.[420] The

[411] Section 12(2) POA 2023. [412] Section 11(6) POA 2023. [413] Section 11(7) POA 2023.

[414] Section 14 POA 2023. [415] Section 12(3) POA 2023.

[416] *Kate Wilson* v. *The Commissioner of Police of the Metropolis, National Police Chiefs' Council* [2021], Case No: IPT/11/167/H. See also, discussion in Chapter 5.

[417] Ibid at [3] and [14]–[15]. [418] Ibid at [179]. [419] Ibid at [234]–[235].

[420] Ibid at [325], [332]–[336], [341]–[342].

UN Special Rapporteur on Peaceful Assembly also condemned these practices,[421] and in 2015 substantial undisclosed sums were paid by way of compensation.[422]

12.5.4.3 *Facial Recognition Technology*

The use of facial recognition technology in respect of protesters has been the subject of legal challenge. In *R (on the application of Bridges)* v. *CC of South Wales Police*, a civil liberties campaigner sought judicial review of the use of automated facial recognition technology by the police (AFR).[423] The technology had been used by the police in a pilot project which involved deployment of surveillance cameras to capture digital images of people, which were then processed and compared with images of persons on police watchlists. If no match was made, the image was immediately and automatically deleted. The appellant challenged the lawfulness of AFR generally, and specifically two occasions when his own image had been captured. The High Court held that there was no violation of the Convention as there was a common law basis for the measures and the interference with Article 8 ECHR was justified.[424] However, the Court of Appeal subsequently held that the interference was not in accordance with the law as there was no clear guidance on where AFR could be used and who could be put on a watchlist and the discretion afforded was too broad to meet the standard required by Article 8(2) ECHR.[425] The Court also stated, however, that had the interference been in accordance with the law, it would have been a proportionate interference.[426]

12.5.4.4 *Databases of Protesters*

Protesters have also been documented in extremism databases held by the police. This was challenged in *R (on the application of Catt)* v. *Association of Chief Police Officers of England, Wales and Northern Ireland* by a ninety-one-year-old peace activist living in Brighton.[427] Catt had been arrested twice

[421] United Nations General Assembly, *Report of the Special Rapporteur on the rights to freedom of peaceful assembly and of association, Maina Kiai, Mission to the United Kingdom of Great Britain and Northern Ireland*, A/HRC/23/39/Add.1 at [24]–[28].

[422] Rob Evans, 'Police apologise to women who had relationships with undercover officers', *The Guardian*, 20 November 2015, www.theguardian.com/uk-news/2015/nov/20/met-police-apologise-women-had-relationships-with-undercover-officers.

[423] *R (on the application of Bridges)* v. *CC of South Wales Police* [2020] EWCA Civ 1058, [2020] 1 WLR 5037 at [143].

[424] *R (on the application of Bridges)* v. *CC of South Wales Police* [2019] EWHC 2341 (Admin), [2020] 1 WLR 672 at [68]–[78] and [98]–[108].

[425] *Bridges* (Court of Appeal) (n 423) at [130].

[426] Ibid at [134]–[144].

[427] *R (on the application of Catt)* v. *Association of Chief Police Officers of England, Wales and Northern Ireland* [2015] UKSC 9, [2015] AC 1065.

for demonstrations obstructing the highway but had never been convicted of an offence. In March 2010, Catt made an access request under the Data Protection Act 1998 for information relating to him. Sixty-six entries from nominal records for other individuals and information reports which incidentally mentioned him were disclosed to him. Those records were held on a police database known as the 'Extremism database', which at the relevant time was under the responsibility of the National Public Order Intelligence Unit of the police. In the vast majority of cases, the information recorded about Catt was his name, presence, date of birth and address. In some cases, his appearance was also described. A photograph of Catt taken at a demonstration in September 2007 was also disclosed. He asked for the entries to be deleted but this was refused and a further subject access request in 2015 - disclosed additional entries. Catt thereafter commenced legal proceedings in which he argued that the retention of the data violated Article 8 ECHR. The Supreme Court held that there had been no violation of Article 8 ECHR as this was not a disproportionate interference with his private life.[428] Lady Hale indicated that if the police had retained a nominal record collecting together all the information that they currently hold on Catt then she would have been inclined to hold that it could not be justified.[429] However, as the 'the nominal record relating to Catt had been deleted' and all that 'remained, until recently, were the incidental references to his presence at certain demonstrations in information reports about those demonstrations and nominal records relating to other people' she agreed that this was not a disproportionate interference.[430] Catt subsequently applied to the ECtHR. [431] In examining his application, the ECtHR expressed doubts as to the legal basis for the collection and indefinite retention of the data and therefore whether this was in accordance with law for the purposes of Article 8(2) ECHR.[432] It did not, however, decide that point as it elected to instead consider the necessity of the interference determining that although there was a pressing need to collect the data there was no pressing need to retain the data indefinitely.[433]

12.5.4.5 *Offence of Concealing Identity at a Protest*

The police have the power to direct people to remove face coverings in designated areas and to seize face coverings where they reasonably believe people are wearing these wholly or mainly for the purpose of concealing their identity. However, the police have reported concerns that while individuals may follow the direction of an officer to remove their face covering, they may

[428] Ibid. [429] Ibid at [51]. [430] Ibid at [52]. [431] *Catt* v. *the United Kingdom* (n 84).
[432] Ibid. [433] Ibid at [117]–[128].

then move to a new area and put the face covering back on.[434] The Crime and Policing Bill that is currently before Parliament thus contains provisions which, if enacted, will render it an offence for a person in a designated public place to wear or otherwise use an item that conceals their identity or another person's identity. The stated purpose of the new offence is to prevent protesters from concealing their identity for the purpose of avoiding conviction for criminal activity in the designated area.[435] A public place will be designated for these purposes if the police reasonably believe that a protest is or may take place, that the protest activity is likely to involve, or has involved, the commission of offences and that the designation would prevent or control the commission of offences. The offence will carry a maximum penalty of one month imprisonment, a £1,000 fine, or both. The draft provisions contain a defence if the item is used for a purpose relating to health of the person or others, for religious observance, or for a purpose relating to the person's work.

12.5.5 Offences Committed by Protesters

12.5.5.1 Is It Necessary to Prove That Prosecution and Conviction Is a Proportionate Interference with the Convention Rights?

There are numerous offences that can be committed by protesters, and an important question is whether it is necessary to prove that a prosecution and conviction is a proportionate interference with the Convention rights. The courts have been grappling with this issue since the Supreme Court's judgment in *DPP* v. *Ziegler* in which it was stated that 'determination of the proportionality of an interference with ECHR rights is a fact-specific enquiry which requires the evaluation of the circumstances in the individual case'.[436]

Ziegler related to two protests at the Defence and Security International weapons fair at the Excel Centre. In the first protest four defendants lay in the middle of a road leading to the Excel Centre, locking their arms onto a bar in the middle of a box. One carriageway was entirely blocked and they were removed after around ninety minutes. During the second protest, four defendants suspended themselves by ropes from a bridge above carriageways close to the Excel Centre. The police closed the road for safety reasons, and the defendants were removed seventy-eight minutes later. All defendants were charged under s.137 Highways Act 1980, but were acquitted on the basis that

[434] Home Office and Ministry of Justice Policy Paper, *Crime and Policing Bill: Public Order Factsheet* (25 February 2025), www.gov.uk/government/publications/crime-and-policing-bill-2025-factsheets/crime-and-policing-bill-public-order-factsheet#:~:text=Introduce%20a%20new%20criminal%20offence%20which%20prohibits%20the%20possession%20of,to%20a%20£1%2C000%20fine.

[435] Ibid.

[436] *Director of Public Prosecutions* v. *Ziegler* [2021] UKSC 23, [2022] AC 408 at [59].

their actions fell within the 'lawful excuse' defence. The DPP appealed. The High Court, relying on s.3 HRA 1998, interpreted the 'without lawful excuse' aspect of s.137 Highways Act 1980 by reference to Articles 10 and 11 ECHR. It explained that the provisions interact as follows:

> The way in which the two provisions can be read together harmoniously is that, in circumstances where there would be a breach of Articles 10 or 11, such that an interference would be unlawful under section 6(1) of the HRA, a person will by definition have 'lawful excuse'. Conversely, if on the facts there is or would be no violation of the Convention rights, the person will not have the relevant lawful excuse and will be guilty (subject to any other possible defences) of the offence in section 137(1).[437]

Consequently, the High Court held that if the removal of the defendants violated Article 10 or 11 ECHR then this would provide a defence to the charge of wilfully obstructing the highway.[438] On the facts, however, the Court concluded that their removal had not violated their rights and therefore they did not have a lawful excuse.[439]

The case then leapfrogged to the Supreme Court which agreed that 'lawful excuse' should be given a Convention-compliant interpretation and that a defendant charged with wilful obstruction whilst exercising their rights will have a lawful excuse unless prosecution is shown to be necessary in a democratic society.[440] A crucial aspect of the Supreme Court's judgment was the way in which it distinguished between arrest and conviction; even if removal is justifiable, *conviction* may not be proportionate.[441] Lord Sales and Lord Hodge dissented.

The Supreme Court's approach in *Ziegler* has been controversial. David Feldman deemed the distinguishing of removal from conviction as 'nuanced and principled'.[442] However, it is evident that courts have been retreating from a broad application of *Ziegler*. Thus, in *R* v. *Brown*, a case in which the defendant superglued his hand to an airplane and was convicted of public nuisance, the Court of Appeal observed:

> We shall say little more about *Ziegler* in this case. The exact ramifications of the decision of the Supreme Court will call for exploration in other cases where they arise directly in any of three jurisdictions of the United Kingdom and possibly by the Supreme Court once more. The decision appears to have been misunderstood by some as immunising peaceful protesters from arrest and from the operation of the criminal law in broad circumstances, which on any view it does not.[443]

[437] Ibid at [62]. [438] Ibid. [439] Ibid at [111]–[117].

[440] *Ziegler* (Supreme Court) (n 436). [441] Ibid at [57].

[442] David Feldman KC, 'Applying Convention Rights to Statutory Defences' (2021) 80(3) CLJ 433–436.

[443] *R* v. *Brown* [2022] UKCA Crim 6, [2022] 1 Cr. App. R. 18.

The scope of *Ziegler* was further considered by the High Court in *Cuciurean*,[444] the background to which was that Cuciurean had been charged with an aggravated trespass offence after he dug a tunnel on land which was to be used for the HS2 train line. He was subsequently acquitted after the Deputy District Judge accepted Cuciurean's submission that before she could convict, the prosecution had to satisfy the court that a conviction is a proportionate interference with Articles 10 and 11 ECHR.[445] The prosecution appealed, arguing, amongst other things, that a conviction for the offence of aggravated trespass is

> intrinsically and without the need for a separate consideration of proportionality in individual cases – a justified and proportionate interference with those rights. The decision in *Ziegler* did not compel the judge to take a contrary view and undertake a *Ziegler*-type fact-sensitive assessment of proportionality.[446]

The High Court agreed, it held that

> it is impossible to read the judgments in *Ziegler* as deciding that there is a general principle in our criminal law that where a person is being tried for an offence which does engage articles 10 and 11, the prosecution, in addition to satisfying the ingredients of the offence, must also prove that a conviction would be a proportionate interference with those rights.[447]

Applying this to the facts, the High Court held that the offence of aggravated trespass is not incompatible with Articles 10 or 11 ECHR and that neither *Ziegler* nor s.3 HRA require a new ingredient to be inserted into the offence which entails the prosecution proving that a conviction would be proportionate in Convention terms.[448] The case was thus remitted to the Magistrates' Court with a direction to convict the respondent of the offence.[449]

A year after *Ziegler*, the Supreme Court in *Abortion Services (Safe Access Zones)* considered the argument that a 'fact-specific' approach is needed in all cases in the context of draft legislation in Northern Ireland.[450] It will be recalled that the legislation implemented 'safe access zones' around clinics providing reproductive services (including abortions) and the question for the Supreme Court was whether this was compatible with the rights protected under the HRA 1998.[451] The Supreme Court held that the proposed offence was compatible with those rights. In coming to that determination it made it clear that the statement in *Ziegler* that proportionality determinations are

444 *DPP* v. *Cuciurean* [2022] EWHC 736 (Admin), [2022] QB 888 at [67].
445 Ibid at [2].
446 Ibid at [4].
447 *DPP* v. *Cuciurean* (n 444) at [67].
448 Ibid at [81].
449 Ibid at [90].
450 *Abortion Services (Safe Access Zones), REFERENCE by the Attorney General for Northern Ireland* [2022] UKSC 32, [2023] AC 505. See Stevie Martin, 'Proportionality and Protest-Related Offences' (2023) 82 CLJ 2.
451 Ibid.

'fact-specific' is not a principle that is applicable in all cases involving offences emanating from protests.[452] Instead, the Supreme Court held that such questions may often be 'decided as a matter of general principle, rather than on an evaluation of the circumstances of each case'.[453] In particular, it held that '[i]t is possible for a general legislative measure in itself to ensure that its application in individual circumstances will meet the requirements of proportionality under the Convention, without any need for the evaluation of the circumstances in the individual case'.[454] The Court thus rejected the notion that *Ziegler* 'established that every criminal conviction of protesters involved a restriction upon their Convention rights, and must be proved to be justified and proportionate on the basis of an assessment of the particular facts'.[455] Moreover, it stated that '[i]t is important not to make the mistake of supposing ... a reference to lawful or reasonable excuse in the definition of an offence necessarily means, in cases concerned with protests, that an assessment of proportionality can or should be carried out. The position is more nuanced than that'.[456] This is in part because Convention rights are not applicable in all cases. If the conduct in question is violent, then it will not constitute a peaceful assembly and Article 11 ECHR will not be applicable. Equally, where Article 17 ECHR applies it will preclude defendants from relying upon the Convention rights.[457] The Court went on to observe that in cases where the Convention rights are applicable, we have to consider 'whether the offence is one where the ingredients of the offence themselves strike the proportionality balance, so that if the ingredients are made out, and the defendant is convicted, there can have been no breach of his or her Convention rights'.[458] In circumstances where 'the offence is so defined as to ensure that any conviction will meet the requirements of proportionality, the court does not have to go through the process of verifying that a conviction would be proportionate on the facts of every individual case'.[459] The offence under the Abortion Services legislation was held to be a provision of this kind, namely, one where the proportionality balance had been struck by the legislation'.[460] Further examples of these types of offences include failing to comply with a condition imposed on a protest and aggravated trespass. Richard Martin has suggested that this 'offence-centric' approach puts 'domestic courts at odds with a clear line of Strasbourg authority that necessitates greater judicial scrutiny of protest-related convictions, anchored in a fact-specific proportionality assessment'.[461]

[452] *Abortion Services (Safe Access Zones)* (n 450) at [28]–[29]. [453] Ibid at [29].
[454] Ibid at [34]. [455] Ibid at [42]. [456] Ibid at [53]. [457] Ibid at [54].
[458] Ibid at [55]. [459] Ibid. [460] Ibid.
[461] Richard Martin, 'Convicting Peaceful Protesters: Proportionality's Proper Place at Criminal Trial' (2024) **44**(2) OJLS 342, 366.

In cases where the conduct in question falls within the scope of the Convention rights and proof of the ingredients of the offence does not in itself ensure the proportionality of a conviction, then the possibility arises that a conviction might be incompatible with the Convention rights. The Supreme Court in *Abortion Services (Safe Access Zones)* held that in such cases it may be possible to read the provision compatibly with the Convention right, for example by requiring a proportionality analysis as part of a defence of lawful or reasonable excuse.[462] Thus, in cases where the Convention rights *are* applicable and where the offence itself does not strike the balance between the rights, then a proportionality assessment may take place within the defence of reasonable excuse or lawful excuse defence. Offences which contain a reasonable excuse or lawful excuse defence include the offence of obstruction of the highway, the statutory public nuisance provision, minor or temporary criminal damage, expression offences under s.4A and s.5 POA 1986 and offences under the POA 2023. However, the question remains as to whether the offence *itself* strikes the balance between the rights or whether the offence does not such that a proportionality assessment is required.

In this regard, the Court of Appeal's recent decision in *R* v. *Sarti (Chiara)* suggests that the offences under the POA 2023, namely locking-on, tunnelling, obstruction of major transport works and interference with use or operation of key national infrastructure may not require a proportionality assessment. [463] This is despite the fact that the ECHR Memorandum which accompanied the Bill stated that '[t]he 'reasonable excuse' defence will permit a fact-specific enquiry by a court, and enable consideration of the exercise of Convention rights'.[464] One may therefore have assumed, following the *Abortion Services* reasoning, that in cases where the Convention rights were applicable (ie where the protest was peaceful) that a proportionality analysis would apply when dealing with the 'reasonable excuse' defence to the POA offences. That approach was rejected by the Court of Appeal in *R* v. *Sarti (Chiara)* which held that no additional proportionality analysis applies in relation to the POA 2023 offence of interfering with use or operation of key national infrastructure.[465] In determining that the legislation itself strikes the right balance the trial Judge had observed that:

The POA 2023 had been enacted specifically to criminalise particular forms of protest; and it would be "remarkable" if Parliament had intended persons charged under it to be able to rely on the fact that they were protesting as a defence.[466]

[462] *Abortion Services (Safe Access Zones)* (n 453) at [57].

[463] *R* v. *Sarti (Chiara)* [2025] EWCA Crim 61.

[464] Home Office, *Public Order Bill: European Convention on Human Rights Memorandum.*

[465] *R* v. *Sarti (Chiara)* (n 463). [466] Ibid at [16].

On appeal the Court of Appeal agreed that no proportionality analysis was required.[467]

Consequently, at present it appears that where offences are enacted specifically to deal with protest, the courts may determine that the balance has been struck by the legislature and that no additional proportionality analysis is required. This may well give rise to difficult questions as to (i) whether the legislative provisions are compatible with the Convention if there is no scope for proportionality analysis and (ii) whether the courts are complying with their s.3 duty under the HRA 1998.

Having considered the question of whether a proportionality analysis is needed we will now look at some examples of the various offences.

12.5.5.2 *Breach of a Condition or a Prohibition Imposed under the POA 1986*

It is an offence for an organiser or participant to fail to comply with a condition that they knew or ought to have known was imposed, unless they can establish that the failure arose from circumstances beyond their control.[468] A question that has arisen for the courts is whether the courts should engage in a further proportionality assessment beyond the threshold for issuing a direction in the POA 1986. This was considered in *James* v. *Director of Public Prosecutions* where the defendant had been convicted for failing to comply with a s.14 POA 1986 direction in relation to a protest blocking the road outside the Royal Courts of Justice.[469] James had sought to argue that the court needs to determine whether the decision to prosecute was proportionate. In rejecting James' appeal, the High Court observed that provided the statutory tests for making a condition under s.14 POA 1986 are met this should establish that the condition satisfies the proportionality requirements of Articles 10 and 11 ECHR.[470] Accordingly, 'the proportionality of [a s.14] direction and condition for the purposes of Articles 10 and 11 ECHR can be raised through testing of the reasonableness of the beliefs which necessarily underpin [the s.14 direction and condition]'.[471] This was acknowledged in passing in *Bennett* v. *DPP* where the High Court held that the Crown Court had not erred in upholding the convictions of members of Extinction Rebellion for failing to comply with a s.14 POA 1986 condition which required them to relocate to a different site.[472] In considering whether the condition was proportionate, the Court observed that 'the starting point is that it is well-established in law that satisfaction of the stringent statutory test for making a condition under section 14 will *in itself* establish that the measure satisfies the ECHR standard

[467] Ibid. [468] Section 14(4) and (5) POA 1986.

[469] *James* v. *Director of Public Prosecutions* [2015] EWHC 3296 (Admin), [2016] 1 WLR 2118.

[470] Ibid. [471] Ibid at [42]. See also, *Bennett* v. *DPP* [2022] EWHC 1822 at [21].

[472] *Bennett* v. *DPP* ibid.

of proportionality'.[473] This was not contested and the Court held that the condition was reasonably necessary and proportionate to prevent serious disorder and that it had not impermissibly prohibited future assemblies.[474] The Court also held that there was nothing in s.14 POA 1986 which precluded the police from imposing a condition which required the protesters to move to a location which was not within the 'scene' of the existing protest.[475] This arose as it had been argued by the appellant that s.14 POA 1986 restricts the senior officer present at the 'scene' to imposing conditions on movement only within the 'scene' of the existing protest.[476] The Court found that there was nothing in the statutory provisions, the case law or the Convention rights which required this.[477]

Following the Supreme Court judgment in *Ziegler*, the approach taken in *James* and *Bennett* was challenged in *DPP* v. *Eastburn*.[478] The background to which was that Eastburn had sat down in Parliament Street as part of an Extinction Rebellion protest. She was told by a police officer that this was unlawful because a direction had been given under s.14 of the POA 1986 that the assembly had to be confined to Parliament Square Gardens. She remained seated in Parliament Street. Consequently, she was arrested and charged with the offence of failing to comply with the direction.[479] She was acquitted at the City of London Magistrate's Court on the basis that it had not been proven that a conviction would be a proportionate interference with her Article 10 and 11 ECHR rights. The DPP appealed against that acquital.[480] The High Court examined *Ziegler* as well as the subsequent case law, including the Supreme Court's judgment in *In re Abortion Services (Safe Access Zones)*. It held that s.14 POA 1986 is not a *Ziegler*-type provision but is like the provision in *In re Abortion Services (Safe Access Zones)*, 'an example of an offence-creating statute where the ingredients of the offence in themselves ensure the compatibility of a conviction with the defendant's rights under Articles 10 and 11'.[481] The High Court thus concluded that as the ingredients of the offence were proved, 'the judge should have convicted the Respondent without further consideration. His finding that she had caused very little disruption can properly be reflected in the level of any penalty to be imposed.'[482] The case was remitted to the Magistrates' Court with a direction to convict.[483]

The prevailing position is thus that there is no additional requirement for the prosecution to prove that a conviction for breaching a condition or direction would be a proportionate interference with those rights.[484] As this

[473] Ibid at [21]. [474] Ibid at [24]. [475] Ibid at [29]–[32]. [476] Ibid. [477] Ibid.

[478] *DPP* v. *Eastburn* [2023] EWHC 1063 (Admin). See Neil Parpworth, 'Public Assembly Offence: Does a Conviction Need to Be a Proportionate Interference with Convention Rights' (2023) **87**(3) Journal of Criminal Law 231.

[479] Ibid at [1]. [480] Ibid at [2]. [481] Ibid. [482] Ibid at [25]. [483] Ibid at [26].

[484] Ibid at [25].

was prior to the recent expansion of the powers to impose conditions, it is possible that we will see cases being brought in respect of the exercise of the revised provisions in which questions as to the compatibility of directions with the Convention rights will arise again.

12.5.5.3 *Offences under the Public Order Act 1986*

The actions of protesters may amount to an offence under other provisions of the POA 1986. This includes serious offences such as riot, violent disorder and affray, as well as at the lower end of the spectrum expression offences. For example, a protester will commit an offence under s.4 POA 1986 if with intent to cause a person harassment, alarm or distress, they (a) use threatening, abusive or insulting words or behaviour, or disorderly behaviour, or (b) display any writing, sign or other visible representation which is threatening, abusive or insulting, thereby causing that or another person harassment, alarm or distress. Moreover, s.5 POA 1986 renders it an offence to use threatening or abusive words or behaviour, or disorderly behaviour, or display any writing, sign or other visible representation which is threatening or abusive, within the hearing or sight of a person likely to be caused harassment, alarm or distress thereby.[485] This offence is complete even if no-one is actually caused harassment, alarm or distress.

Where the protesters' Convention rights are engaged, then a proportionality assessment should be made in establishing whether the reasonable conduct defence is met.[486] In *DPP* v. *Manchester City Magistrates' Court*, the Divisional Court held that the judge had been right to conduct a fact-sensitive proportionality assessment in respect of conviction for a s.4A Public Order Act 1986 offence where the defendant has relied on Articles 10 and 11 ECHR in respect of the reasonable conduct defence under s.4A(3)b.[487] The background to the case was that the defendants had shouted 'Tory Scum' at Iain Duncan Smith at a protest. They were prosecuted with a s.4A public order offence but found not guilty as the Chief Magistrate had found that Articles 10 and 11 ECHR were applicable and that the prosecution had not proved that it would be proportionate to convict them.

12.5.5.4 *Aggravated Trespass*

Section 68 of the CJPOA 1994 criminalises trespass where there is an intent to intimidate, obstruct or disrupt lawful activity. This was intended to deal with hunt saboteurs, ravers and the travelling community, but in *DPP* v. *Chivers* it

[485] See *Ian Sleeper* v. *Commissioner of Police of the Metropolis* [2025] EWHC 151 (KB).

[486] See discussion in *Munim Abdul* v. *DPP* [2011] EWHC 247 at [49].

[487] *DPP* v. *Manchester City Magistrates' Court* [2023] EWHC 2938 (Admin).

was confirmed that 'land' for the purposes of this provision includes inside buildings, rendering aggravated trespass applicable to those engaged in direct action inside buildings.[488] Consequently, in *Edward Bauer & Ors* v. *DPP* the defendants were charged with aggravated trespass in respect of a protest inside Fortnum and Mason.[489] The High Court in *Bauer* observed that s.68 CJPOA 1994 could not be challenged as contrary to Articles 10 and 11 ECHR[490] and that once the prosecution had established an offence under s.68 CJPOA 1994 'it does not have to prove ... that the prosecution was proportionate'.[491] In *DPP* v. *Cuciurean* the Court reconsidered this in the light of *Ziegler* and reaffirmed that:

> section 68 ... is not incompatible with articles 10 or 11 of the Convention. Neither the decision of the Supreme Court in *Ziegler* nor section 3 of the [HRA] 1998 ... requires a new ingredient to be inserted into section 68 which entails the prosecution proving that a conviction would be proportionate in Convention terms.[492]

12.5.5.5 *Obstruction of the Highway*

Section 137(1) Highways Act 1980 provides that if a person, without lawful authority or excuse, in any way wilfully obstructs the free passage along a highway, he is guilty of an offence. Protesters are frequently charged with this offence.

The ambit of s.137 Highways Act 1980 was considered in *Westminster City Council* v. *Haw* when the local authority sought an injunction restraining Brian Haw from obstructing the pavement in Parliament Square with placards protesting the war in Iraq.[493] The Court observed that the placards encroached on the pavement, that this was not de minimis and that it represented an obstruction that was deliberate, and thus wilful.[494] However, it then went on to determine that s.137 Highways Act 1980 only precludes obstructions that are unreasonable, and that this obstruction was not unreasonable.[495] In this respect the Court observed that while Haw's protest had been ongoing for some fifteen months, his aim of influencing the Government was a reasonable one, the pavement on which the placards had been displayed was little used and there was no evidence of any pedestrians being obstructed.[496] In addition, Haw had been exercising his Article 10 ECHR right in relation to a political issue. In this respect the judge stated that while Article 10 ECHR is not a trump card, it 'is a significant consideration when assessing the reasonableness of

[488] *DPP* v. *Chivers* [2010] EWHC 1814 (Admin), [2011] 1 WLR 2324.
[489] *Edward Bauer & Ors* v. *DPP* [2013] EWHC 634 (Admin), [2013] 1 WLR 3617.
[490] Ibid at [39]. [491] Ibid at [40]. [492] *DPP* v. *Cuciurean* (n 444) at [81].
[493] *Westminster City Council* v. *Haw* [2002] EWHC 2073 (QB). [494] Ibid at [16].
[495] Ibid at [17]–[25]. [496] Ibid at [21].

any obstruction to which the protest gives rise'.[497] Applying this to the facts, he was not satisfied that there was 'any pressing social need to interfere with the display of placards so as to protect the right of others to pass and re-pass'.[498]

The lawful excuse component of the offence was, as noted above, considered in *Ziegler.*[499] As discussed in detail above, the Supreme Court held in *Ziegler* that 'lawful excuse' should be given a Convention-compliant interpretation and that a defendant charged with wilful obstruction whilst exercising their rights will have a lawful excuse unless prosecution is shown to be necessary in a democratic society.[500]

12.5.5.6 *Obstruction or Interference with Major Transport Works or Key National Infrastructure*

Sections 6 and 7 POA 2023 create offences in respect of obstruction or interference with major transport works[501] or key national infrastructure.[502] The s.6 POA 2023 offence is established where the defendant obstructs or interferes with the matters set out in s.6(1) POA 2023. The s.7 POA 2023 offence is established if the defendant does an act which interferes with the use or operation of any key national infrastructure in England and Wales *and* they *intend* that act to interfere with the use or operation of such infrastructure *or* are *reckless* as to whether it will do so. In respect of both offences there is a reasonable excuse defence.[503] The Explanatory Notes to the Bill state that for the s.6 POA 2023 offence, the burden of proof for the reasonable excuse defence is on the defendant and that the standard of proof is the balance of probabilities. There is no reference to the burden and standard in respect of the s.7 POA 2023 offence, although it is presumably the same as for the s.6 POA 2023 offence.

The applicability of Articles 10 and 11 ECHR to the s.7 POA 2023 offence was addressed in *R* v. *Sarti (Chiara),* a case where the defendants had been

[497] Ibid at [22]–[25]. [498] Ibid at [24]–[25].

[499] *DPP* v. *Ziegler* [2019] EWHC 71 (Admin), [2020] QB 253.

[500] *Ziegler* (Supreme Court) (n 436).

[501] Major transport works are defined in s.6(6) POA 2023 as meaning either (a) works in England and Wales relating to transport infrastructure, and the construction of which is authorised directly by an Act of Parliament, or (b) works the construction of which comprises development within subsection (7) that has been granted development consent by an order under section 114 of the Planning Act 2008.

[502] Key national infrastructure is defined in s.7(6) POA 2023 and s.8 POA 2023 and includes: road transport infrastructure; rail infrastructure; air transport infrastructure; harbour infrastructure; downstream oil infrastructure; downstream gas infrastructure; onshore oil and gas exploration and production infrastructure; onshore electricity generation infrastructure; or newspaper printing infrastructure.

[503] Section 6(2) and s.7(2) POA 2023.

convicted of a s.7 POA 2023 offence following their actions during a Just Stop Oil protest,[504] which had involved slow marching and blocking a main road in London.[505] At trial, the judge, having heard argument on the issue, ruled 'the elements of the offence created by s. 7 POA 2023 were such as to guarantee that a conviction would be proportionate'.[506] In particular he observed that 'Parliament had provided that the offence would apply only to interference with main roads (and the road here was one of London's principal traffic arteries); the prosecution had to prove significant delay had been caused (it had); and the maximum penalty (12 months' imprisonment) was low'.[507] He also observed that the

> POA 2023 had been enacted specifically to criminalise particular forms of protest; and it would be 'remarkable' if Parliament had intended persons charged under it to be able to rely on the fact that they were protesting as a defence.[508]

He thus concluded that the elements of the offence were sufficient in themselves to ensure that a conviction was proportionate interference with the rights.[509] The Court of Appeal subsequently rejected the defendants' appeal. It distinguished the s.7 POA 2023 offence from the s.137 Highways Act offence in *Ziegler* on the basis that the former is 'materially narrower' and 'leaves protestors with a wider variety of ways in which to make their protest lawfuly'.[510] It found that s.7 POA 2023 stuck a fair balance that was within the State's margin of appreciation[511] and that

> once the ingredients of the s. 7 offence are made out, s. 7(2)(a) does not require a court to consider whether a conviction would be a proportionate interference with the defendant's Article 10 or 11 rights. The judge was right in his conclusion to this effect, as he was right to conclude that the defence of reasonable excuse did not arise on the facts of this case.[512]

In determining that no separate proportionality analysis is required, it is interesting to observe that in *Sarti* the defendants had sought to rely on the Home Office Memorandum on the compatibility of the legislation with the ECHR. The Memorandum stated in relation to the POA provision that '[t]he "reasonable excuse" defence will permit a fact-specific enquiry by a court, and enable consideration of the exercise of Convention rights'.[513] However, in *Sarti* the Crown counter-argued that this statement was 'no more than a statement by the relevant Minister, which cannot be ascribed to Parliament'.[514] The Court of Appeal agreed; it held that 'contrary to the (unexplained) view expressed in the ECHR Memorandum, once the ingredients of the s.7 offence are made out, s.7 (2)(a) does not require a court to consider

[504] *R* v. *Sarti (Chiara)* (n 463). [505] Ibid at [4]–[14]. [506] Ibid at [16]. [507] Ibid.
[508] Ibid. [509] Ibid. [510] Ibid at [73]. [511] Ibid at [75]. [512] Ibid at [76].
[513] Ibid at [37]. [514] Ibid at [49].

whether a conviction would be a proportionate interference with the defendant's Article 10 or 11 rights'.[515]

12.5.5.7 *Locking On Offences*

Section 1 of the POA 2023 provides that a person commits the offence of locking on if the following three conditions are met. First, that they (i) attach themselves to another person, to an object or to land, (ii) attach a person to another person, to an object or to land, or (iii) attach an object to another object or to land. Second, that this act causes, or is capable of causing, serious disruption to two or more individuals, or an organisation, in a place other than a dwelling. And, third, that they intend that act to have that consequence or are reckless as to whether it will have such a consequence. There is a reasonable excuse defence. There is also an offence of being equipped for locking on. This offence is committed if the person has an object with them in a place other than a dwelling with the intention that it may be used in the course of or in connection with the commission by any person of the locking on offence.

12.5.5.8 *Offences Relating to Tunnelling*

Sections 3–4 POA 2023 create offences of causing serious disruption by tunnelling or being present in a tunnel. These offences are subject to a reasonable excuse defence. Section 5 POA 2023 creates an offence of being equipped for tunnelling, which replicates the equivalent offence in respect of being equipped for locking on.

12.5.5.9 *Public Nuisance*

Section 78 PCSCA 2022 abolished the common law offence of public nuisance and created a statutory offence, which came into force from 28 June 2022. Per s.78(1) PCSCA 2022, the offence is committed where a person does an act, or omits to do an act required by any enactment or rule of law, and the act or omission: creates a risk of, or causes, serious harm to the public or a section of the public, or obstructs the public or a section of the public in the exercise or enjoyment of a right that may be exercised or enjoyed by the public at large, and the person intends that their act or omission will have one of the above consequences, or is reckless as to whether it will have such a consequence.[516] Section 78(2) PCSCA 2022 provides that 'serious harm' means death, personal

[515] Ibid at [76].

[516] On the interpretation of the provision, see *R* v. *Smith (Joshua)* [2024] EWCA Crim 1040, [2025] 2 WLR 215.

injury, or disease, loss of, or damage to, property, or serious distress, serious annoyance, serious inconvenience, or serious loss of amenity.[517] There is a reasonable excuse defence under s.78(3) PCSCA 2022.

12.5.5.10 *Criminal Damage*

Section 1 of the Criminal Damage Act 1971 provides that it is an offence to intentionally or recklessly destroy or damage property belonging to another. There is a defence of lawful excuse to this provision. Section 3 of the Criminal Damage Act 1971 also renders it an offence to be in possession of something with intent to destroy or damage property. This is also subject to a lawful excuse defence. Section 5 of the Criminal Damage Act provides examples of what might constitute a lawful excuse defence but this is not exhaustive.

The operation of the lawful excuse defence was considered in *Attorney General's Reference No. 1 of 2022*.[518] In June 2020, during a Black Lives Matter protest, a monument of seventeenth-century slave trader Edward Colston was pulled down from its plinth and tossed into Bristol Harbour. Four of those involved were charged with criminal damage. There were several lawful excuse arguments made during the trial by the defence, and the defence also argued that Convention rights might provide the basis for a lawful excuse defence. The protesters were found not guilty by the jury but we do not know on what basis. The Attorney General subsequently sought the opinion of the court as to whether the Convention rights could provide the basis for the lawful excuse defence. The Court of Appeal opined that the answer was not simply yes or no as it depended upon the type of damage that was caused. In this respect it drew a distinction between offences of significant damage and offences of minor or trivial damage. Prosecution and conviction for causing significant damage to property falls outside the protection of the Convention rights either because the conduct in question was violent or not peaceful, or alternatively because (even if it was theoretically a peaceful protest) prosecution and conviction would clearly be proportionate.[519] Thus, in cases concerning significant damage, no proportionality assessment would be required.[520] Where the damage was, however, minor or temporary, a conviction may not be a proportionate response.[521] In such cases, the Court held that the Strasbourg case law suggests that there would need to be a

[517] The M25 Gantry climbers in *R* v. *Hallam (Julian Roger)* [2025] EWCA Crim 199 (n 301) were convicted of a s.78 PCSCA 2022 offence. On sentencing and the s.78 offence, see *R* v. *Trowland (Morgan)* (n 301).

[518] *Attorney General's Reference No. 1 of 2022* [2022] EWCA Crim 1259, [2023] 2 WLR 651. For discussion, see Alex Benn, 'Criminal Damage: The "Colston Four", Proportionality and the Concerns that Linger – *Attorney General's Reference (No.1 of 2022)*' (2023) **87**(1) Journal of Criminal Law 61.

[519] Ibid at [115]. [520] Ibid. [521] Ibid at [116].

case-specific assessment of the proportionality of conviction at least in connection with damage to public property.[522] The Court stated that it would expect that such prosecutions would not be launched because they too would be a disproportionate reaction to the conduct in question.[523] It gave the example of scrawling a message on a pavement using water soluble paint, which might technically be sufficient to sustain a charge of criminal damage, but to prosecute or convict for doing so as part of a political protest might well be a disproportionate response.[524]

Reflecting on the facts that had led to the application, the Court observed that the circumstances in which the statue was damaged did not involve a peaceful protest.[525] The toppling of it was violent.[526] Moreover, the damage to the statue was significant.[527] The Court thus concluded that the prosecution was correct in its submission that the conduct in question fell outside the protection of the Convention.[528] Thus, the proportionality of the conviction was not a matter that should be considered by the jury.[529] The Court emphasised that this did not mean that the defendants were in fact guilty of the offence of criminal damage as the jury had to consider a range of defences.[530]

Following the enactment of s.50 PCSCA 2022, criminal damage to memorials is now exempt from the rule that criminal damage that is valued at less than £5,000 must be tried by a Magistrates' Court. Thus, even 'low value' damage cases may now be heard by the Crown Court. Moreover, the Crime and Policing Bill currently before Parliament contains a provision that will render it an offence to climb on a specified war memorial.[531]

12.5.6 Injunctions and Serious Disruption Prevention Orders

12.5.6.1 Anti-social Behaviour Injunctions

Section 1 of the Anti-social Behaviour, Crime and Policing Act 2014 provides that a court may grant an injunction against a person aged ten or over if two conditions are met. The first condition is that the court is satisfied, on the balance of probabilities, that the respondent has engaged or threatens to engage in anti-social behaviour. The second condition is that the court considers it just and convenient to grant the injunction for the purpose of preventing the respondent from engaging in anti-social behaviour. This provision was at the heart of *Birmingham City Council* v. *Afsar,* a case in which the Council applied for injunctions to restrict protests outside a primary school in relation to the content of the curriculum taught to their children.[532] For seven months, there had been regular protests about the content of the

[522] Ibid. [523] Ibid. [524] Ibid. [525] Ibid at [123]. [526] Ibid. [527] Ibid.
[528] Ibid. [529] Ibid. [530] Ibid. [531] Crime and Policing Bill, Bill 235 (2024–2025).
[532] *Birmingham City Council* v. *Afsar* [2019] EWHC 3217, [2020] 4 WLR 168.

school's curriculum in relation to same-sex relationships and other LGBTQ+ issues. In upholding the injunction, Warby J accepted that it interfered with the defendants' Article 10 and 11 ECHR rights, but found this was justified given the school children's right to an education, the private lives of staff, and the right to respect for local residents' homes and family lives. It was also noted that the injunction did not target the content of the defendants' speech, but merely imposed an exclusion zone around the school.

12.5.6.2 *Occupations: Order for Possession and Injunction*

Occupations are a form of direct action in which participants seek to reclaim space. *City of London* v. *Samede* concerned the Occupy London camp next to St Paul's Cathedral which had been ongoing for months when the local authority sought possession and an injunction.[533] The High Court judge found that the local authority's application was subject to the applicants' rights under Article 10 and Article 11 ECHR, but that the local authority's arguments easily outweighed these rights.[534] The applicants sought to appeal, arguing that the order was an unjustified interference with their Convention rights and, in the alternative, that the judge should have made more limited orders. The Court of Appeal refused permission to appeal. Although it accepted that Articles 10 and 11 ECHR were engaged, it held that the applicants' argument amounted to saying that their rights mandated the court to allow the camp to continue for the foreseeable future.[535] The Court stated that the limits to the right are fact-sensitive and that relevant factors include the extent to which the protest would breach domestic law, the importance of the precise location to the protesters, the duration of the protest, the degree to which the protesters occupied the land and the rights of others, including the property rights of the owners of the land, and the rights of any members of the public.[536] It was also appropriate to take into account, as the judge had, the fact that the applicants were expressing views on important issues and strongly believed in the views they were expressing.[537] In dismissing the application, the Court emphasised that whilst St Paul's is an important prominent location, the order did not prevent the applicants from protesting anywhere else.[538] Moreover, the camp had been trespassing for three months, substantially interfering with the public's right of way and the rights of those who wished to worship in the cathedral, it had also strained public health facilities, and caused some damage to local businesses.[539] Finally, the Court observed that if the applicants wanted more limited orders, it was for them to formulate a specific proposal.[540] The

[533] *City of London* v. *Samede* [2012] EWCA Civ 160, [2012] 2 All ER 1039 and *City of London* v. *Samede* [2012] EWHC 34 (QB).

[534] Ibid. [535] Ibid, Court of Appeal judgment at [37]. [536] Ibid at [39]. [537] Ibid at [41].

[538] Ibid at [42]. [539] Ibid at [43]–[44]. [540] Ibid at [51]–[55].

applicants had not put forward such a proposal and the Court was doubtful whether any proposal could realistically be formulated.[541]

12.5.6.3 *Injunctions*

A rapidly growing area of law concerns the issuing of injunctions against protesters. In this respect, Lord Carnwath has commented that 'there is no other area of law moving so fast'.[542] Injunctions are increasingly sought by both local authorities and private organisations. Injunctions are often sought where there is an underlying tort, including but not limited to, trespass to land, nuisance or protection from harassment; the claimant may rely upon economic torts if they have no right to occupy the land.[543] The Privy Council has also recently stated that the court has the power to grant an injunction when it is just and equitable to do so, and thus no underlying cause of action is needed.[544] Both interim injunctions and final injunctions may be sought.

Where an injunction relates to private land, claimants may have rights under Article 1 of Protocol 1 ECHR to peaceful enjoyment of their possessions, whilst protesters will usually not have applicable Article 10 and 11 ECHR rights when they are trespassing on private land.[545]

Where an injunction relates to public land, although core public authorities cannot be victims for the purposes of s.7 HRA 1998, the courts will evaluate rights and competing public interests when determining whether to issue an injunction.[546]

If the protesters are engaged in violence or have violent intentions, their Convention rights will not be applicable, but where they engage in peaceful direct action Articles 10 and 11 ECHR may be applicable.

Where Convention rights are applicable, the court will need to consider whether the injunction constitutes a proportionate interference.[547] In particular, the courts are cautious about broadly construed injunctions. In contemplating the proportionality of the measure, a further complexity has arisen in the environmental context where Dexter Dias J held in *Shell UK Ltd* v. *Persons Unknown* that the Aarhus Convention is relevant to cases

541 Ibid at [51]–[55].

542 Lord Carnwath's preface to Yaaser Vanderman, *Manual on Protest Injunctions: Practice, Procedure and Persons Unknown* (Landmark Chambers, 2023).

543 *Shell UK Oil Products Ltd* v. *Persons Unknown* [2022] EWHC 1215, *Esso Petroleum* v. *Breen* [2022] EWHC 2664. See Vanderman (n 542).

544 *Broad Idea International Ltd* v. *Convoy Collateral Ltd* [2021] UKPC 24, [2023] AC 38.

545 *DPP* v. *Cuciurean* (n 444) at [40]–[50] and *Appleby* v. *the United Kingdom* (n 280).

546 *HS2* v. *Persons Unknown* [2022] EWHC 2360.

547 On the factors that the courts consider, see Vanderman (n 542) at [8.31]–[8.32].

involving environmental protestors.[548] The facts were that a number of companies in the Shell Group had sought final injunctions against persons unknown and a number of named environmental protestors. The protestors argued that the granting of a final injunction would be in breach of the Aarhus Convention, which the UK ratified in 2005. Article 3(8) of the Aarhus Convention states: 'Each Party shall ensure that persons exercising their rights in conformity with the provisions of this Convention shall not be penalized, persecuted or harassed in any way for their involvement.' Thus in *Shell UK* v. *Persons Unknown*, Dexter Dias J was asked to consider whether the acts of the defendants were protected by the Aarhus Convention, and if so, in what way.[549] In examining this issue he concluded that the Aarhus Convention (as an unincorporated treaty)

> is relevant to the court's assessment of interferences with the Convention rights of protesters under the ECHR and proportionality analyses. It consequently has relevance for the court's equitable discretion confirmed by section 37 of the Senior Courts Act 1981.[550]

Nevertheless, on the facts he held that the granting of the injunctive relief sought was necessary and proportionate.

It is important to note that many of the injunctions in respect of protesters are sought in respect of persons unknown as often the claimant cannot identify all of the defendants. The courts have expressed caution about granting injunctions against persons unknown.[551] The fifteen factors that must be taken into account when considering an injunction against persons unknown were set out in *Valero Energy Limited and others* v. *Persons Unknown*, one of which is that the court must taken into account the balancing exercise set out in *Ziegler*.[552] This is important as whilst claimants argue that they cannot identify the defendants, an order against persons unknown means that no-one is served and that protesters may not be represented in challenging the injunction. The Court of Appeal in *Canada Goose UK Retail Limited* v. *Persons Unknown* thus stated that injunctions against persons unknown can only be justified for as long as it is practically impossible to identify alleged wrongdoers.[553] Persons unknown must be defined by

[548] *Shell UK Ltd* v. *Persons Unknown* [2024] EWHC 3130 (KB). On the inappropiateness of sentencing judges taking into account the Aarhus Convention, see *R* v. *Hallam (Julian Roger)* [2025] EWCA Crim 199 (n 301).

[549] Ibid at [6]. [550] Ibid at [167].

[551] *Boyd* v. *Ineos Upstream Ltd* [2019] EWCA 315 at [31], *Bromley* v. *Persons Unknown* [2020] EWCA Civ 12, [2020] 4 All ER 114 at [34].

[552] *Valero Energy Limited and others* v. *Persons Unknown* [2024] EWHC 134 (KB) at [58]. See also, *Shell UK Ltd* v. *Persons Unknown* (n 548) at [200].

[553] *Canada Goose UK Retail Limited* v. *Persons Unknown* [2020] EWCA Civ 303, [2020] 1 WLR 2802.

reference to their conduct which is alleged to be unlawful.[554] In *Canada Goose* the Court of Appeal also stated that 'invoking the civil jurisdiction as a means of permanently controlling ongoing public demonstrations ... is not appropriate' and that 'private law remedies are not well suited to the task'.[555] This was, however, rejected by the Supreme Court in *Wolverhampton CC* v. *London Gypsies and Travellers:*

> We are also unpersuaded by the court's observation that private law remedies are unsuitable 'as a means of permanently controlling ongoing public demonstrations by a continually fluctuating body of protesters' (para 93). If that were so, where claimants face the prospect of continuing unlawful disruption of their activities by groups of individuals whose composition changes from time to time, then it seems that the only practical means of obtaining the relief required to vindicate their legal rights would be for them to adopt a rolling programme of applications for interim orders, resulting in litigation without end. That would prioritise formalism over substance, contrary to a basic principle of equity ... [T]here is no overriding reason why the courts cannot devise procedures which enable injunctions to be granted which prohibit unidentified persons from behaving unlawfully, and which enable such persons subsequently to become parties to the proceedings and to seek to have the injunctions varied or discharged.[556]

In that case, the Supreme Court confirmed that newcomer injunctions (i.e. injunctions against those who have not yet committed or threatened to infringe any right or duty which the claimant seeks to enforce but may do so at a later date) are a wholly new form of injunction, which are granted without prior notice against persons who cannot be known at the time the order is made.[557] They therefore potentially apply to anyone in the world. However, a court should only exercise this power in circumstances where there is a compelling need to protect civil rights or to enforce public law that is not adequately met by any other available remedies.[558] In addition, newcomer injunctions should only be made subject to procedural safeguards designed to protect newcomers' rights.[559] The injunctions should also be constrained by both territorial and temporal limitations so as to ensure, as far as practicable, that they neither outflank nor outlast the compelling circumstances relied upon.[560]

An interesting recent injunction case is *University of Cambridge* v. *Persons Unknown* where an interim injunction for a period of approximately four months was granted in order to prevent protestors from entering, interfering

[554] On the specificity that this entails, see Vanderman (n 542) at [7.5]–[7.17].

[555] *Canada Goose* (n 553) at [93].

[556] *Wolverhampton CC* v. *London Gypsies and Travellers* [2023] UKSC 47, [2024] 2 WLR 45 at [138].

[557] Ibid, see also discussion of protest cases at [235]–[236]. [558] Ibid at [167]. [559] Ibid.

[560] Ibid.

with access to or erecting structures at two specified locations within the university.[561] The injunction was sought on the basis that there was a real and imminent risk of direct action affecting graduation ceremonies (previous direct action had disrupted graduations for thousands of students and their guests). In granting the injunction, Soole J found that there was a compelling need for the grant of an injunction as there was an imminent and real risk of the occurrence of the conduct and consequent substantial harm.[562] Indeed, Soole J concluded that without an injunction 'there [was] a strong probability that this will otherwise occur'.[563] In relation to the defendants' Article 10 and 11 ECHR rights, he proceeded on the assumed basis that they were engaged, but found the interference justified as necessary.[564] In particular, he stated that the

> suggested alternative means of reliance on police powers and the provisions of criminal offences such as for aggravated trespass and unreasonable obstruction of the highway; and/or through deployment of the University's internal disciplinary processes . . . do not meet the problem which the University faces. This is in particular because they are essentially focused on dealing with disruptive events as and after they happen, whereas the fully justified concern of the University is to prevent their occurrence. I do not accept that prior letters to students from the University or warnings from the police would be a sufficient alternative to the remedy which the civil law provides if (as here) the Court otherwise thinks it just to grant such relief.[565]

He was thus satisfied that the proposed injunction struck a fair balance between the rights of all parties.[566] Reasoning that '[t]he protesters and the campaign are left with ample opportunities and ability to protest their cause in Cambridge; and the University is enabled to carry on its administrative and ceremonial work in these core buildings and spaces'.[567]

Breach of an injunction is contempt of court. Importantly, in *Cuadrilla*, the Court of Appeal held that the fact that protesters disobeyed a court order as part of a peaceful protest is relevant in assessing culpability for the purpose of sentencing.[568] Whilst the motives of a protester are not a licence to flout court orders with impunity, there are reasons for showing greater clemency in response to non-violent acts of civil disobedience done with the aim of bringing about a change in law or policy. The Court reasoned that there is a moral difference between such acts, generally committed by otherwise law-abiding citizens, and those of ordinary law-breakers. It is therefore often appropriate to suspend the operation of the sanction in such cases. Note, however, that in *Cuciurean* the Court of Appeal held that this does not mean

[561] *University of Cambridge* v. *Persons Unknown* [2025] EWHC 724 (KB).
[562] Ibid at [47] and [81]. [563] Ibid at [81]. [564] Ibid at [87]–[89]. [565] Ibid at [89].
[566] Ibid at [90]. [567] Ibid at [90].
[568] *Cuadrilla Bowland Ltd & Ors* v. *Lawrie & Ors* [2020] EWCA Civ 9, [2020] 4 WLR 29.

that there is 'some sort of guideline sanction from which a reduction, to a greater or lesser extent, then needs to be made to reflect the decision in *Cuadrilla*. What matters is that the judge reaches a proportionate sanction in all the circumstances of the case, including the culpability of the contemnor.'[569] The Court thus observed that where a defendant had not behaved with a sense of proportion, or had caused excessive harm, or had not accepted the penalties imposed, their culpability would be much higher and there would be little or no basis to expect corresponding restraint from the courts.[570] The Court also emphasised that where there is 'a serial contemnor . . ., where the court has concluded that dialogue is no longer possible, the fact that the underlying protest was non-violent and a matter of conscience may be of no or negligible weight in the balancing exercise. That is because the whole thrust of *Cuadrilla*, and the subsequent cases, is about the importance of dialogue.'[571] It thus declared that:

> A protestor, no matter how conscientious he or she believes themselves to be, cannot keep ignoring the court's orders, and then expect some sort of discount in the sanction to be applied every time they are dealt with for contempt. That would be contrary to principle and the two-way nature of the process.[572]

12.5.6.4 *Secretary of State Injunction*

The POA 2023 empowers the SofS to bring civil proceedings where they consider it expedient in the public interest to do so in respect of protest activities. At the time of writing, these provisions have yet to be brought into force. The power will apply where the SofS reasonably believes that one or more persons are carrying out, or are likely to carry out, activities related to a protest, and either of the following conditions are met.[573] The first condition is that the Secretary of State reasonably believes that the activities are causing, or are likely to cause, serious disruption to:

(a) the use or operation of any key national infrastructure in England and Wales, or
(b) access to any essential goods, or to any essential service, in England and Wales.[574]

The second (and alternative) condition is that the SofS reasonably believes that the activities are having, or are likely to have, a serious adverse effect on public safety in England and Wales.[575] The SofS must consult with such persons (if any) as the SofS considers appropriate, having regard to any

[569] *Cuciurean* v. *Secretary of State for Department* [2022] EWCA Civ 1519 at [71].
[570] Ibid at [73]. [571] Ibid at [74]. [572] Ibid at [75]. [573] Section 18(1).
[574] Section 18(2). [575] Section 18(3).

persons who may also bring civil proceedings in relation to those activities.[576] Moreover, the bringing of proceedings by the SofS does not affect the ability of any other person to bring civil proceedings in relation to those activities.[577] If the court grants an injunction in proceedings brought by the SofS, it may, in certain circumstances, attach a power of arrest to any provision of the injunction.[578]

12.5.6.5 *Serious Disruption Prevention Order*

Part 2 of the POA 2023 establishes Serious Disruption Prevention Orders (SDPO) which can be made on conviction (s.20 POA 2023) or on application to the Magistrates' Court by a chief officer of police, Chief Constable of the British Transport Police, Civil Nuclear Constabulary or Ministry of Defence Police (s.21 POA 2023). The SDPO is a new type of order which will allow courts to place requirements or prohibitions on an individual aged eighteen or over which they consider necessary and proportionate to prevent that individual from causing serious disruption. An SDPO can be sought on the basis of at least two occasions of particular behaviour. These provisions were brought into force in April 2024.[579] Various requirements may be imposed by a SDPO, including prohibiting the individual who is the subject of the order from being in or entering a particular place, being with particular persons, participating in particular activities, and having particular articles with them.[580] The court making the order must think that the restrictions are necessary for a purpose specified in the relevant provisions of the POA.[581] A SDPO must be for a fixed period of not less than a week and not more than two years;[582] it may be renewed but it cannot be renewed more than once.[583] It is an offence to breach a SDPO without reasonable excuse.[584] The SofS has the power to issue guidance on SDPOs and must lay a draft of the guidance before Parliament.[585] Statutory guidance was accordingly issued in April 2024.[586]

12.6 CONCLUSION

We have seen in this chapter that freedom of assembly is subject to a vast (and ever-expanding) body of common law and statutory restrictions. There are also numerous cases relating to protesters in which courts have had to

576 Section 18(5). 577 Section 18(6). 578 Section 19(2).

579 The Public Order Act 2023 (Commencement No.4) (England and Wales) Regulations 2024, S.I. 2024/472.

580 Section 22(4) POA 2023. 581 Section 22(1) POA 2023. 582 Section 25 POA 2023.

583 Section 28 POA 2023. 584 Section 27 POA 2023. 585 Section 30 POA 2023.

586 Home Office, *Serious Disruption Prevention Orders: Statutory Guidance*, 5 April 2024.

consider whether decisions taken under the extensive statutory provisions and common law powers are compatible with human rights. While there have been some important successes for protesters, in particular the House of Lords' decision in *Laporte* and the Supreme Court's decision in *Ziegler,* other cases suggest that the courts are more willing to defer to police decisions made during a demonstration. Moreover, given the ever-growing body of legislative provisions restricting protest, the Supreme Court's determination in *Abortion Services (Safe Access Zones)* that it is possible for a general legislative measure to meet the requirements of proportionality, without any need for an evaluation of the circumstances of the individual case, raises questions as to the extent to which the courts will engage with rights in this context in the future and whether this will be in line with Strasbourg.

13 Freedom of Thought, Conscience and Religion

CONTENTS

13.1 INTRODUCTION

Millions of Jews were persecuted and murdered during the Holocaust; consequently when the ECHR was enacted in the post-war period, the right to freedom of thought, conscience and belief (Article 9 ECHR) was of profound and grave importance. Article 9 ECHR contains two rights: an absolute right to hold a belief; and a qualified right to manifest a belief. These rights are important to individuals of all faiths – and none – as well as groups and society more generally. Consequently, while Article 9 ECHR is 'primarily a matter of individual conscience' it includes the freedom to manifest one's religion in community with others and within the circle of those whose faith one shares.[1] This communal component reflects the significance of Article 9 ECHR to group identity, perhaps particularly minority group identity. Meanwhile, the societal value of the right is encapsulated in the ECtHR' declaration that 'the pluralism indissociable from a democratic society, which has been dearly won over the centuries, depends on' Article 9 ECHR.[2]

The volume of Article 9 ECHR case law is relatively low when compared with some other Convention rights, however, over the last fifteen years the case law has expanded significantly. One of the factors that has contributed to this is 'the increasing importance of religion and related matters in socio-political discourse'.[3] This is particularly pertinent to the jurisprudence on State restrictions on religious clothing where the ECtHR has been the subject of immense criticism, in particular its case law on Islamic clothing has given rise

[1] *Bayatyan* v. *Armenia* [GC], (2012) 54 EHRR 15 at [119].

[2] *Kokkinakis* v. *Greece* (1994) 17 EHRR 397 at [31].

[3] European Court of Human Rights, *Guide on Article 9 of the European Convention on Human Rights* at [9].

to scepticism as to whether Article 9 ECHR is protected in practice and whether the ECtHR has succeeded in protecting the pluralism that it deems indissociable from a democratic society.[4]

More generally, the Court has been criticised for failing to engage sufficiently with the question of why religious freedom is important, leaving the right vulnerable in the face of other rights and interests.[5] In this respect Evans makes the following observation:

> The Court has spoken vaguely of pluralism and the importance of religion to the individual believer, but has not reflected on the way in which these concepts affect their interpretation and application of Article 9. Unless a coherent philosophical justification underlies all the cases dealing with Article 9, then the result is likely to be inconsistency and unfairness as the judges move from one rationale to another to justify their intuitions about the right outcome for a particular factual scenario.[6]

Indeed, in the absence of adequate engagement with the values that underpin Article 9 ECHR, it is difficult to see how the right can be balanced against other competing rights and interests. In this regard, Evans suggests that the right should be 'perceived as an essential component of self-identity' such that an interference is 'an attack on the autonomy of the individual'.[7] An absence of a normative foundation for the right may also leave it open to critics querying whether such a right is needed given that other Convention rights, including the right to life, freedom from torture, freedom of expression and freedom of association protect those of faith from persecution, and Article 14 ECHR prohibits discrimination.[8]

Despite the limitations of Article 9 ECHR, the enactment of the HRA 1998 was significant as prior to this there was no explicit right to freedom of religion in domestic law. The case law that has followed has been mixed as while Article 9 ECHR has been upheld on some occasions, the courts have also adopted a narrow approach to the question of what constitutes an interference with the right, it is thus questionable whether the current approach is in line with the Strasbourg approach to interpreting Article 9 ECHR.[9] It is therefore likely that there will be further case law on what constitutes an interference with Article 9 ECHR, the necessity analysis which applies when there is an interference, and the process of balancing rights where there are competing rights at stake.

[4] See Section 13.5.5 below.

[5] Carolyn Evans, *Freedom of Religion under the European Convention on Human Rights* (Oxford University Press, 2001). The early case law was criticised for failing to establish effective guiding principles; see Malcolm D. Evans, *Religious Liberty and International Law in Europe* (Cambridge University Press, 2010), ch.11.

[6] Ibid, p.33. [7] Ibid, p.32.

[8] On the importance of a right to freedom of religion, see Silvio Ferrari, 'Who Needs Freedom of Religion?' in Frank Cranmer et al., *The Confluence of Law and Religion* (Cambridge University Press, 2016).

[9] See, in particular, the narrow approach accorded to Article 9 ECHR in *R (on the application of Soltany)* [2020] EWHC 2291 (Admin) discussed at Section 13.5.4.4 below and in *R (on the application of TTT)* v. *Michaela Schools Trust* [2024] EWHC 843 discussed at Section 13.5.2 below.

The issues underpinning these cases are of growing significance, such that as Christopher McCrudden observes, the 'tensions arising between resurgent religion and human rights cannot be considered a transitional issue'.[10] He cautions that they will 'increase and fester if not addressed', observing that '[r]eligions are a problem for human rights, and human rights are a problem for religions'.[11] He identifies three ideological reasons behind these rising tensions and conflicts: (i) significant developments in human rights doctrine that have resulted in religious practices coming more into conflict with human rights; (ii) significant developments within particular religions that have resulted in more 'fundamentalist' approaches to religious doctrine being adopted; and, (iii) religious issues increasingly becoming of renewed geopolitical significance, in some ways replacing, in other ways exacerbating other ideological tensions.[12] He suggests that increased migration is also a 'significant part of the ideological story' as the 'ideological conflicts' he identifies 'become more salient due to migration'.[13]

As noted above, religious dress is one context in which legal challenges are arising, another context is in respect of conflicts between religious beliefs and the rights of the LGBTQI+ community (a group that was also persecuted and killed during the Holocaust). The growth of equality law and non-discrimination law (as discussed in Chapter 14) means that such challenges are inevitable, some of which play out in employment law, for example where an individual is dismissed for refusing to provide services to members of the LGBTQI+ community, or for expressing religious beliefs on social media which attack the LGBTQI+ community. To date the ECtHR has offered limited insight into how such cases should be resolved by the domestic authorities and further challenges are likely. A further context in which courts are asked to consider the applicability of Article 9 ECHR is where individuals seek to rely upon Article 10 ECHR to espouse views critical of faith and those of particular faiths.

Given contemporary political discourse across Contracting States, the breadth of contexts in which these issues arise, and the lack of clarity within the case law as to the applicable principles, it is likely that there will be further case law in the future.

13.2 FREEDOM OF RELIGION IN THE UK PRIOR TO THE HRA

The relationship between law and religion in the UK is a complex one which has been shaped over centuries.[14] In particular it is important to note that the 'law did not begin from the starting-point that people had a right to freedom

[10] Christopher McCrudden, *Litigating Religions: An Essay on Human Rights, Courts and Beliefs* (Oxford University Press, 2018), p.4.

[11] Ibid. [12] Ibid, p.21. [13] Ibid.

[14] On the legal position of religious groups in the UK, see Russell Sandberg, *Law and Religion* (Cambridge University Press, 2012), ch.4.

of religion'.[15] Nor from the position that all faiths are equal, or even that they should be tolerated.

Today, socially and culturally, the UK is a diverse nation encompassing many faiths. Munby LJ reflected upon this in *R (on the application of Johns)* v. *Derby City Council*:

> Although historically this country is part of the Christian west, and although it has an established church which is Christian, there have been enormous changes in the social and religious life of our country over the last century. Our society is now pluralistic and largely secular. But one aspect of its pluralism is that we also now live in a multicultural community of many faiths. One of the paradoxes of our lives is that we live in a society which has at one and the same time become both increasingly secular but also increasingly diverse in religious affiliation.[16]

Institutionally, the 'current relationship between religion, law and society is characterised by a number of complexities, confusions and contradictions'.[17] In this regard Sandberg suggests that 'it cannot be said with conviction that Britain is a Christian or a secular country'.[18] Certainly the residual role of Christianity in key institutions means that the UK is not a wholly secular State[19] and a 'distinction is often made between the legal position of the Church of England on the one hand and all other religious groups on the other'.[20] Indeed, there is a long tradition of Christianity receiving special recognition and provision in the UK. The Church of England is an established church (meaning that it has a special relationship with the State) and the Monarch, as the supreme governor of the Church of England, must be in communion with the Church of England and must swear to preserve the Church of England and the Church of Scotland.[21] The Church of Scotland is a national church but whether it is an established church is a matter of some debate.[22] Meanwhile, twenty-six places in the House of Lords are reserved for archbishops and bishops of the Church of England. Faith, and particularly Christian faith, is also reflected in schooling with around a third of all State-funded schools in England designated as faith schools of which Church of England schools are the most common, followed by Roman Catholic schools, whilst non-Christian

[15] Ibid, p.36.

[16] *R (on the application of Johns)* v. *Derby City Council* [2011] EWHC 375 (Admin) at [38].

[17] Ibid.

[18] See also, Russell Sandberg, *Religion, Law and Society* (Cambridge University Press, 2014).

[19] Ibid. [20] See Sandberg (n 14), p.59.

[21] Act of Settlement 1701. Until 2013 the Monarch could not marry a member of the Roman Catholic church, reformed by Succession of Crown Act 2013.

[22] David Torrence, 'Is the Church of Scotland Established?', House of Commons Library, 16 May 2024, https://commonslibrary.parliament.uk/is-the-church-of-scotland-established/. See also House of Commons Library, *The Relationship between Church and State in the United Kingdom*', Briefing Paper Number CBP8886, 14 September 2023.

faith schools make up less than 1 per cent of all State-funded mainstream schools.[23] Significantly, until 2008 Christianity also received special protection under the common law offence of blasphemy.[24] As Alderson B directed in *R* v. *Gathercole*:

> a person may, without being liable to prosecution for it, attack Judaism, or Mahomedanism [Islam], or even any sect of the Christian Religion (save the established religion of the country); and the only reason why the latter is in a different situation from the others is, because it is the form established by law, and is therefore a part of the constitution of the country.[25]

The special protection that the common law accorded to Christianity was apparent in *R* v. *Chief Metropolitan Magistrate, ex parte Choudhury* when a magistrate refused to issue a summons in respect of Salman Rushdie's *The Satanic Verses* on the basis that blasphemy protected only Christian beliefs (and not Islamic beliefs).[26] The offence of blasphemy was later abolished and has not been replaced with a broader offence of offending religious freedom.[27]

As discussed in Chapter 2, prior to the enactment of the HRA the position at common law was one of civil liberties, namely that in the absence of a legal prohibition, people were permitted to do as they wished. In the context of religious freedom this meant that it was generally 'protected negatively rather than positively'.[28] Moreover, whilst judges explicitly referred to a common law right of freedom of expression, it is hard to find explicit acknowledgement of a common law right of freedom of religion.[29] A rare reference to a common law right can be found in Goddard J's judgment in the 1936 case, *Cole* v. *Police Constable*, in which he suggested that the common law may protect a right of a parishioner to attend his parish church:

> It is clear, and it is agreed on all hands, that a parishioner has a right to attend his parish church, but the magistrate in this case, and, indeed, some writers, have expressed the view that the right to attend is limited to those who have by statute the duty to attend divine service. In other words, it is said that the right to attend divine service in the parish church is merely correlative to the duty which is imposed by the

[23] House of Commons Library, *Faith Schools in England: FAQs*, Briefing Paper Number 06972, 20 December 2019, p.17.

[24] The abolition of blasphemy was recommended in the Law Commission Working Paper No 79 'Offences against Religion and Public Worship' (1981). This recommendation was not taken up and a subsequent Law Commission report, Offences against Religion and Public Worship (LC Working Paper No.145) (1985), was split, with the majority of commissioners recommending outright abolition whilst others recommended replacing the offence with an offence of offending religious freedom.

[25] *R* v. *Gathercole* (1838) 2 Lew. CC 237 at 254.

[26] *R* v. *Chief Metropolitan Magistrate, ex parte Choudhury* [1991] 1 QB 429, [1990] 3 WLR 986.

[27] Criminal Justice and Immigration Act 2008. [28] Sandberg (n 14), p.36.

[29] On the common law right to freedom of expression, see Chapter 11.

> Act of Uniformity of Edw. VI. and the Act of Uniformity of Elizabeth to attend divine service at the parish church on Sundays and holy days. I cannot think, however, that the right of the parishioner to attend his parish church depends only upon that statutory obligation. I think that it must be of far more ancient origin, and that it may be described as a common law right. The church, by being dedicated to sacred uses, is being dedicated to the use of the parishioners to be there for worship, and it seems to me, therefore, that the right of the parishioner to attend his church, which is indeed regarded by all writers upon the subject as clear, depends not upon the statute law but upon the older and wider common law.[30]

Such statements are, however, rare, and the narrow ambit of the right that he identified is indicative of the questions that would arise in seeking to rely upon the common law, in particular in identifying what religious freedoms give rise to such rights. A nod towards the role of the common law in protecting freedom of religion can perhaps also be found in Laws LJ's judgment in *McFarlane* v. *Relate Avon Ltd*:

> In a free constitution such as ours there is an important distinction to be drawn between the law's protection of the right to hold and express a belief and the law's protection of that belief's substance or content. The *common law* and ECHR Article 9 offer vigorous protection of the Christian's right and every other person's right to hold and express his or her beliefs, and so they should.[31]

In this regard Sandberg is correct to conclude that 'while religious freedom may have long been implicitly protected by the common law' the HRA 1998 marks a substantial shift in explicitly promoting religious freedom as a positive right'.[32]

Finally, in considering the pre-HRA position it is important to note that prior to the enactment of the HRA the Court of Appeal considered the extent to which domestic legislation should be interpreted compatibly with Article 9 ECHR in *Ahmad* v. *Inner London Education Authority*, a case which concerned the question of whether a Muslim teacher had the right to take time off for worship every Friday afternoon.[33] Ahmad argued that s.30 of the Education Act 1944 provided for this[34] and that s.30 should be interpreted in the light of Article 9 ECHR. In considering how the legislative provision

[30] *Cole* v. *Police Constable* [1937] 1 KB 316, p.333, [1936] 3 All ER 107.

[31] *McFarlane* v. *Relate Avon Ltd* [2010] EWCA Civ 880 at [21], emphasis added.

[32] Sandberg (n 14), p.31.

[33] *Ahmad* v. *Inner London Education Authority* [1978] QB 36, [1977] 3 WLR 396.

[34] Section 30 Education Act 1944 stated as follows:

> Subject as hereinafter provided, no person shall be disqualified by reason of his religious opinions, or of his attending or omitting to attend religious worship, from being a teacher in a county school or in any voluntary school, or from being otherwise employed for the purposes of such a school; and no teacher in any such school shall be required to give religious instruction or receive any less emolument or be deprived of, or disqualified for, any promotion or other advantage by reason of the fact that he does or does not give religious

should be interpreted Denning LJ observed that 'whilst the Convention is no part of our English law ... we will always have regard to it',[35] but he also cautioned that Article 9 ECHR was 'drawn in such vague terms that it can be used for all sorts of unreasonable claims and provoke all sorts of litigation'.[36] He ultimately rejected the argument that the legislative provision should be read in a manner that would provide Ahmad with a right to worship.

I venture to suggest that it would do the Muslim community no good – or any other minority group no good – if they were to be given preferential treatment over the great majority of the people. If it should happen that, in the name of religious freedom, they were given special privileges or advantages, it would provoke discontent, and even resentment among those with whom they work. As, indeed, it has done in this very case. [sic] and so the cause of racial integration would suffer. So, whilst upholding religious freedom to the full, I would suggest that it should be applied with caution, especially having regard to the setting in which it is sought. Applied to our educational system, I think that Mr. Ahmad's right to 'manifest his religion in practice and observance' must be subject to the rights of the education authorities under the contract and to the interests of the children whom he is paid to teach. I see nothing in the European Convention to give Mr. Ahmad any right to manifest his religion on Friday afternoons in derogation of his contract of employment: and certainly not on full pay.[37]

Scarman LJ dissented. He observed that the courts must construe legislation

not against the background of the law and society of 1944 but in a multi-racial society which has accepted international obligations and enacted statutes designed to eliminate discrimination on grounds of race, religion, colour or sex. Further, it is no longer possible to argue that because the international treaty obligations of the United Kingdom do not become law unless enacted by Parliament our courts pay no regard to our international obligations. They pay very serious regard to them: in particular, they will interpret statutory language and apply common law principles, wherever possible, so as to reach a conclusion consistent with our international obligations.[38]

Applying this to the facts he held that a narrow construction of the legislative provision should be rejected.

A narrow construction of the section would mean that a Muslim, who took his religious duty seriously, could never accept employment as a full-time teacher, but must be content with the lesser emoluments of part-time service. In modern British

instruction or by reason of his religious opinions or of his attending or omitting to attend religious worship :

Provided that, save in so far as they require that a teacher shall not receive any less emolument or be deprived of, or disqualified for, any promotion or other advantage by reason of the fact that he gives religious instruction or by reason of his religious opinions or of his attending religious worship, the provisions of this section shall not apply with respect to a teacher in an aided school or with respect to a reserved teacher in any controlled school or special agreement school.

[35] *Ahmad* (n 33), p.41. [36] Ibid. [37] Ibid. [38] Ibid, p.48.

society, with its elaborate statutory protection of the individual from discrimination arising from race, colour, religion or sex, and against the background of the European Convention, this is unacceptable, inconsistent with the policy of modern statute law, and almost certainly a breach of our international obligations. Unless, therefore, the language of section 30 forces one to adopt the narrow construction, I would think it wrong to do so.[39]

13.3 FREEDOM OF RELIGION AND THE HRA

The HRA 1998 gave further effect to Article 9 ECHR in domestic law meaning that public authorities must act compatibly with the right by virtue of s.6 HRA, and legislation should, as far as is possible to do so, be read compatibly with the right by virtue of s.3 HRA. An important point to note here is that religious groups will generally not be regarded as public authorities for the purposes of the HRA and thus will not be subject to the s.6 HRA duty themselves.[40]

The HRA also incorporated Article 2 of Protocol 1 ECHR which provides that no person shall be denied the right to education, and that in the exercise of any functions which it assumes in relation to education and to teaching, the State shall respect the right of parents to ensure such education and teaching in conformity with their own religious and philosophical convictions. Article 14 ECHR (non-discrimination) was also brought into domestic law, a provision that is a double-edged sword for some as whilst it prohibits religious discrimination it also prohibits discrimination based on sexual orientation.

Reflecting upon these changes (and the development of equality law) in extrajudicial comments, Lady Hale observed that:

Once we stop giving preference to a State religion, and accord equal respect and protection to all religions and beliefs, all sorts of difficult questions begin to arise. There may be laws which conflict with particular religious beliefs or practices; there may be requirements imposed, most notably by employers, which conflict with particular religious beliefs or practices; and there may be other forms of discrimination against people because of their religion or beliefs; but in this case there is also the problem that some religious beliefs may lead people to want to discriminate against people with some other characteristic to which the law gives protection, such as their race, their sex or, most notably these days, their sexual orientation.[41]

[39] Ibid, pp.50–51.

[40] *Aston Cantlow and Wilmcote with Billesley Parochial Church Council* v. *Wallbank* [2003] UKHL 37, [2004] 1 AC 546.

[41] Lady Hale Annual Human Rights Lecture for Law Society of Ireland, 'Freedom of Religion and Belief' (13 June 2014), p.2.

These are the very tensions and conflicts that we will see arising throughout this chapter, as well as in Chapter 14, the Equality and Non-discrimination chapter.

In contemplating potential conflicts between those rights, it is important to observe that s.13 HRA 1998 requires courts to 'have particular regard to the importance' of Article 9 ECHR when deciding cases that 'might affect the exercise by a religious organisation (itself or its members collectively) of the Convention right'. At first glance it might be thought that this creates a hierarchy of rights such that religious freedom takes priority over other rights, including non-discrimination. However, whilst there is very little s.13 HRA case law, it is evident that it does not have this effect. In *H* v. *Secretary of State for the Home Department* the Upper Tribunal stated that the function of s.13 HRA is to expressly protect a right for the benefit of the religious organisation *itself* which is distinct from Article 9 ECHR.[42] The impact of s.13 HRA was further considered by the Outer House, Court of Session in *Philip and others* v. *Scottish Ministers*, which rejected the argument that s.13 requires courts to accord special weight to Article 9 ECHR.

> The requirement to have particular regard to a factor does not entail that the factor in question is to be accorded any more weight than any other factors. In a case where the very issue is whether the right has been unjustifiably interfered with, it is axiomatic that the court would in any event be paying particular regard to the importance of the right. What section 13 does do, is to underscore, if any underscoring be needed, that the rights under article 9 are important, but the section cannot be read as meaning that they are any more important than any other Convention right.[43]

Thus, s.13 HRA does not affect the weight accorded to Article 9 ECHR *vis-à-vis* other rights or interests, but simply emphasises that the courts have a duty to pay attention to the importance of the right. In this sense, s.13 HRA is limited in the same way that s.12 HRA is in the context of freedom of expression.[44]

When contemplating the relationship between religious freedom and non-discrimination, it is also important to observe that another fundamental part of the domestic legal framework is the equality legislation where 'religion or belief' is a protected characteristic. This was previously covered in regulations but was subsequently replaced by the Equality Act 2010 (EA 2010). The EA 2010 implemented EU Directive 2000/78 which prohibits discrimination by public and private employers, providers of goods and services, and others, on the basis of protected characteristics. Section 10(1) EA 2010 states that 'religion' means any religion and a reference to religion includes a reference to a lack of religion, whilst section 10(2) states that 'belief' means any religious or

[42] *H* v. *Secretary of State for the Home Department* [2016] UKUT 286 (IAC) at [25].

[43] *Philip and others* v. *Scottish Ministers* [2021] CSOH 32, 2021 S.L.T. 559 at [85]–[86].

[44] *Douglas* v. *Hello!* [2001] QB 967, [2001] 2 WLR 992, per Sedley LJ.

philosophical belief and a reference to belief includes a reference to a lack of belief. It is important to note, however, that 'religion or belief' is only one of the protected characteristics and that those protected characteristics also include sexual orientation. This is relevant in cases where it is alleged that upholding religious beliefs gives rise to discrimination against others in relation to their protected characteristics. It is also important to note that the EA 2010 does not apply in Northern Ireland, which is instead governed by the Fair Employment and Treatment (Northern Ireland) Order 1998. These provisions are considered further in Chapter 14.

As noted above, another context in which courts are asked to consider the applicability of Article 9 ECHR is where individuals seek to rely upon Article 10 ECHR to espouse views critical of faith and those of particular faiths. Within domestic law, as observed in Chapter 11, expressions of 'hatred against a group of persons defined by reference to religious belief or lack of religious belief' may constitute a public order offence, including the stirring up religious hatred offence, or may form the basis for an aggravated offence. It is, however, important to note that s.29J POA 1986 protects expression which challenges the *religion itself* as opposed to expressions of hatred against the person.[45] Similarly, it is important to observe, when considering whether the expression of religious beliefs amounts to stirring up hatred based on *sexual orientation*, that s.29JA POA 1986 states that 'discussion or criticism of sexual conduct or practices or the urging of people to refrain from or modify such conduct or practices shall not be taken of itself to constitute threatening or intending to stir up hatred on the grounds of sexual orientation'. Section 29JA also states that 'any discussion or criticism of marriage which concerns the sex of the parties to marriage shall not be taken of itself to be threatening or intended to stir up hatred'.

13.4 THE STRUCTURE AND SCOPE OF ARTICLE 9 ECHR

Article 9 ECHR – Freedom of Thought, Conscience and Religion

1. Everyone has the right to freedom of thought, conscience and religion; this right includes freedom to change his religion or belief and freedom, either alone or in community with others and in public or private, to manifest his religion or belief, in worship, teaching, practice and observance.

[45] Nothing in this Part shall be read or given effect in a way which prohibits or restricts discussion, criticism or expressions of antipathy, dislike, ridicule, insult or abuse of particular religions or the beliefs or practices of their adherents, or of any other belief system or the beliefs or practices of its adherents, or proselytising or urging adherents of a different religion or belief system to cease practising their religion or belief system.

2. Freedom to manifest one's religion or beliefs shall be subject only to such limitations as are prescribed by law and are necessary in a democratic society in the interests of public safety, for the protection of public order, health or morals, or for the protection of the rights and freedoms of others.

Article 9 ECHR protects two rights. The right to hold a belief and to change one's beliefs is absolute. The right to manifest that belief is not absolute – it is a qualified right – hence the State may justify an interference in accordance with Article 9(2) ECHR.[46] We will examine the operation of the two rights in a moment, but first we must consider the role of secularism in Article 9 ECHR and what beliefs are protected by Article 9 ECHR.

13.4.1 The Role of Secularism in Article 9 ECHR

It is perhaps surprising that we would commence our discussion of Article 9 ECHR – the right to freedom of thought, conscience and religion – by contemplating secularism, but this is a concept that is frequently invoked either explicitly or implicitly in the case law.[47] In particular, a place for secularism is secured by the role that the ECtHR accords to the State, which it tasks with being 'the neutral and impartial organiser of the exercise of various religions, faith and beliefs', a role that the ECtHR regards as 'conducive to public order, religious harmony and tolerance in a democratic society'.[48]

In contemplating what secularism means, it is important to observe that there are different versions of secularism. One approach is 'neutral pluralism', according to which the State does not afford priority to one faith over another, nor between religious and non-religious belief systems that are equivalent to religion. Neutral pluralism purports to cement democracy by guaranteeing an equal status for all in society. Maclure and Taylor explain this in the following terms.

In a society where there is no consensus about religious and philosophical outlooks . . . the state must avoid hierarchizing the conceptions of the good life that form the basis of citizens' adherence to the basic principles of their political association. In the realm of core beliefs and commitments, the state, to be truly everyone's state, must remain "neutral." This implies that the state should adopt a position of neutrality not only toward religions but also toward the different philosophical conceptions that stand as the secular equivalents of religions.[49]

[46] On the drafting of Article 9, see Malcolm D. Evans (n 5), Carolyn Evans (n 5), ch.3, and Samuel Moyn, 'Too Much Secularism? Religious Freedom in European History and the European Court of Human Rights' in Nehal Bhuta (ed), *Freedom of Religion, Secularism and Human Rights* (Oxford University Press, 2019), especially at pp.117–121.

[47] On secularism and Europe, see chapters in Bhuta (ed) (n 46).

[48] *Bayatyan* v. *Armenia* (n 1) at [120].

[49] Jocelyn Maclure and Charles Taylor, *Secularism and Freedom of Conscience* (Harvard University Press, 2011), p.13.

An alternative understanding of secularism emerges in the form of *laïcité*. This goes further than neutral pluralism in separating religion from the State and confining religion to the private sphere. It is *laïcité* that is often at the heart of arguments that religious dress should not be worn in public places. Eoin Daly explains this as follows:

> Laïcité has been re-formulated as embracing a regulative role for private religious expression, as an imperative of national and social cohesion, and thus as requiring public discretion in religious practice. It is increasingly seen as requiring a deeper privatization of religion, on the sociological and personal, as well as institutional planes.[50]

Both forms of secularism are apparent in the Article 9 ECHR case law. Neutral pluralism is present in cases such as *Eweida* v. *the United Kingdom* where the ECtHR stated that: 'the State's duty of neutrality and impartiality is incompatible with any power on the State's part to assess the legitimacy of religious beliefs or the ways in which those beliefs are expressed'.[51] Neutral pluralism was also evident in *Lautsi* v. *Italy,* a case where the applicants unsuccessfully argued that the display of crucifixes in Italian State school classrooms violated Article 9 ECHR and the right to education under Protocol 1 Article 2 ECHR.[52] In rejecting that claim, the Grand Chamber observed that Article 9 ECHR 'imposes on Contracting States a "duty of neutrality and impartiality"'[53] and that Italy did not oppose the display of other religious symbols at school.[54]

Yet whilst those cases suggest an approach premised upon neutral pluralism, the fact that the ECtHR accepts that States have different constitutional structures and accords them a wide margin of appreciation, means that it has also accommodated *laïcité*. This is reflected in the Court's observation that '[w]here questions concerning the relationship between State and religions are at stake, on which opinion in a democratic society may reasonably differ widely, the role of the national decision-making body must be given special importance'.[55] The use of a wide margin of appreciation has prompted concern as to whether the ECtHR adequately protects Article 9 ECHR, particularly in the context of Islamic religious clothing.[56] An important case to consider here is *Leyla Şahin* v. *Turkey* in which the Grand Chamber held that prohibiting the wearing of Islamic headscarves in university did not violate Article 9 ECHR.[57]

[50] Eoin Daly, 'The Ambiguous Reach of Constitutional Secularism in Republican France: Revisiting the Idea of Laïcité and Political Liberalism as Alternatives' (2012) 32(3) OJLS 583, 583–588.

[51] *Eweida* v. *the United Kingdom* (2013) 57 EHRR 8.

[52] *Lautsi* v. *Italy* (2012) 54 EHRR 3.

[53] Ibid at [60].

[54] Ibid at [72] and [74].

[55] *Leyla Şahin* v. *Turkey* (2007) 44 EHRR 5 at [109].

[56] On the use of the margin of appreciation doctrine in general in the Article 9 case law, see Konstantina Alexopoulou, 'The Margin of Appreciation in Freedom of Thought, Conscience, and Religion under Article 9 of ECHR' (2022) 11(2–3) Oxford Journal of Law and Religion 220.

[57] *Leyla Şahin* v. *Turkey* (n 55).

In *Leyla Şahin* the Government argued that the headscarf had taken on a particular political meaning in Türkiye as extremist movements were seeking to impose their religious way of life,[58] and that the ECtHR had to recognise the legitimacy of efforts to maintain secularism as a fundamental principle of the Turkish State as interpreted by the Turkish Constitutional Court.[59] This was accepted by the ECtHR which held that the principle of secularism was 'in harmony with the rule of law and respect for human rights' and that it 'may be considered necessary to protect the democratic system in Turkey'.[60]

We will examine the case law relating to religious clothing in greater detail later in this chapter, but at this juncture it suffices to observe that in other cases the ECtHR has accepted prohibitions in schools, places of employment and even public places as compatible with Article 9 ECHR, and this has been the subject of immense criticism. It has brought to the fore the question of whether the ideology surrounding secularism (whether invoked explicitly or implicitly), or at least forms of secularism such as *laïcité*, are in fact neutral. Critics argue it is not, as it is premised upon an assumption that certain ways of living are 'neutral', a perspective that neglects the impact of structural bias.[61]

13.4.2 What Beliefs Are Protected?

Article 9 ECHR has a broad scope that is not limited to specified religions, faiths or beliefs. Religion is not defined in the text of the Convention, nor in the case law, and in practice Article 9 ECHR has been applied to a wide range of faiths.[62] The ECtHR has also made it clear that 'Article 9 would be highly theoretical and illusory if the degree of discretion granted to States allowed them to interpret the notion of religious denomination so restrictively as to deprive a non-traditional and minority form of a religion of legal protection'.[63] Another important attribute of Article 9 ECHR is that it is not limited to religious freedom. This is reflected in the text of Article 9(1) ECHR which states: 'Everyone has the right to freedom of *thought, conscience* and religion'

[58] Ibid. [59] Ibid. [60] Ibid at [114].

[61] Stephanie Berry, 'A "Good Faith" Interpretation of the Right to Manifest Religion? The Diverging Approach of the European Court of Human Rights and the UN Human Rights Committee' (2017) 37(4) Legal Studies 627–694, 694.

[62] Russell Sandberg, 'Clarifying the Definition of Religion in English Law; The Need for a Universal Definition' (2018) 20 Ecclesiastical law Society 132. The right has been applied to faiths including: Christianity; Islam; Hinduism; Buddhism; Judaism; Sikhism; Taoism; Alevism; Mormonism, or the Church of Jesus Christ of Latter-Day Saints; Neo-Paganism; Jehovah's Witnesses; Bhagwan Shree Rajneesh movement, known as Osho movement; Reverend Sun Myung Moon's Unification Church; Aumism of Mandarom; the Raëlian Movement and Santo Daime: see, European Court of Human Rights, *Guide on Article 9 of the European Convention on Human Rights* (31 August 2022) at [17].

[63] *İzzettin Doğan and others* v. *Turkey* [GC] (2017) 64 EHRR 5 at [114].

and that this 'includes the freedom to change one's religion or *belief*' (emphasis added).[64] Accordingly, the ECtHR recognises that whilst the right 'in its religious dimension, [is] one of the most vital elements that go to make up the identity of believers and their conception of life ... it is also a precious asset for atheists, agnostics, sceptics and the unconcerned'.[65] A further consequence of this is that as the right covers 'beliefs' there is no need to determine whether a particular belief is a religious one. In contemplating the breadth of the provision, it is worth observing that the following convictions have been found to fall within the scope of Article 9 ECHR:[66] pacifism;[67] principled opposition to military service;[68] veganism and opposition to the manipulation of products of animal origin or tested on animals;[69] opposition to abortion;[70] a doctor's opinions on alternative medicine, constituting a form of manifestation of medical philosophy;[71] the conviction that marriage is a lifelong union between a man and a woman and rejection of homosexual unions;[72] and secularism.[73]

The parameters of 'belief' are thus broad, certainly in relation to the right to hold a belief (as compared to the right to manifest that belief).[74] In fact, an early Commission case implied that even 'Nazism' could fall within the scope of Article 9 ECHR. In that case it was determined that criminal convictions in respect of neo-Nazi activities were justified under Article 9(2) ECHR, an outcome which implies that Nazi ideology fell within Article 9(1) ECHR in the first instance.[75] The applicability of Article 9 ECHR to such heinous ideology raises similar questions to those which arise in the context of hate speech, namely whether such beliefs (and in the Article 10 ECHR context – expression) should be recognised at all for the purposes of Convention rights, or whether they should be excluded by Article 17 ECHR.[76] The current position appears to be that they will be excluded from the ambit of the Convention, because in a more recent case, *Kasymakhunov and Saybatalov* v. *Russia*, the ECtHR held that Article

[64] On freedom of thought, see Sjors Ligthart et al., 'Rethinking the Right to Freedom of Thought: A Multidisciplinary Analysis' (2022) 22 HRLR 1.

[65] *Kokkinakis* v. *Greece* (n 2) at [31].

[66] See European Court of Human Rights, *Guide on Article 9 of the European Convention on Human Rights: Freedom of Thought, Conscience and Religion* (updated on 29 February 2024), p.8.

[67] *Arrowsmith* v. *the United Kingdom* (dec.) (1981) 3 EHRR 218 at [69].

[68] *Bayatyan* v. *Armenia* (n 1).

[69] *W* v. *the United Kingdom* (dec.), App. No. 18187/91, 10/02/1993.

[70] *Knudsen* v. *Norway* (dec.) (1986) 8 EHRR CD63; *Van Schindel* v. *Netherlands* (dec.), App. No. 30936/96, 10/09/1997.

[71] *Nyyssönen* v. *Finland* (dec.), App. No. 30406/96, 15/01/1998.

[72] *Eweida* v. *the United Kingdom* (n 51).

[73] *Lautsi* v. *Italy* (n 52) at [58]; *Hamidović* v. *Bosnia and Herzegovina*, App. No. 57792/15, 05/12/2017 at [35].

[74] See discussion at Sections 13.4.3 and 13.4.4.

[75] *X* v. *Austria* (dec.), App. No. 1747/62, 13/12/1963.

[76] See Chapter 11.

17 ECHR prohibited the applicants from relying upon Article 9 ECHR to engage in activities contrary to the text and spirit of the Convention.[77]

A further limitation that arises in respect of the right to manifest one's belief is that the belief must meet a minimum threshold of conviction in order to argue that there has been an interference with a *manifestation* of that belief.[78] In *Campbell and Cosans* v. *the United Kingdom* the ECtHR stated that belief under Article 9 ECHR embraces 'views that attain a certain level of cogency, seriousness, cohesion and importance'.[79] The House of Lords in *R (on the application of Williamson)* v. *Secretary of State for Education and Employment* also held that when the right to manifest a belief is invoked, that 'belief must satisfy some modest, objective minimum requirements'.[80] *Williamson* involved a group of parents who sought to oppose legislation prohibiting corporal punishment of school children on the basis that it violated the parents' protected beliefs.[81] The case failed on the basis that the children's rights needed to be safeguarded, but in coming to that conclusion the Lords had to consider whether Article 9 ECHR was applicable. One of the arguments put forward by the Secretary of State was that Article 9 ECHR did not apply as the parents' beliefs were not religious in nature. The House of Lords rejected this on the ground that the right embraces both religious and non-religious beliefs provided it 'relate[s] to an aspect of human life or behaviour of comparable importance to that normally found with religious beliefs'.[82] It stated that Article 9 ECHR protects manifestations of non-religious beliefs if the belief satisfies 'some modest, objective minimum requirements'.[83] Relevant factors include whether the belief is consistent with basic standards of human dignity or integrity; relates to matters more than merely trivial (possessing an adequate degree of seriousness and importance); and is coherent in the sense of being intelligible and capable of being understood.[84] Applying this in *Williamson*, the Lords found that authorising a school to administer corporal punishment was a manifestation of the parents' beliefs, such that the legislation interfered with Article 9 ECHR, but that the interference was necessary in a democratic society for the protection of the rights and freedoms of the children.[85] Lady Hale later observed extra-judically

[77] *Kasymakhunov and Saybatalov* v. *Russia*, App. Nos. 26261/05 and 26377/06, 14/03/2013 at [113].

[78] Ibid.

[79] *Campbell and Cosans* v. *the United Kingdom* (1991) 13 EHRR 441 at [36]. On this dictum and the subsequent case law, see Tim Wolff, 'Cogency, Seriousness, Cohesion, and Importance: Assessing the Strasbourg Case-Law on Religion or Belief' (2022) 11(2–3) Oxford Journal of Law and Religion 177.

[80] *R (on the application of Williamson)* v. *Secretary of State for Education and Employment* [2005] UKHL 15, [2005] 2 AC 246, [2005] 2 WLR 590.

[81] Ibid. [82] Ibid at [24]. [83] Ibid at [23]. [84] Ibid at [23].

[85] It is worth noting that in respect of children's rights Lady Hale commented as follows, ibid at [71]: 'This is, and has always been, a case about children, their rights and the rights of their

that while '[i]t would have been very tempting to interrogate that belief and to demonstrate that the parents and teachers were mistaken in thinking that the Bible required them to beat their children. We could only examine whether that belief was genuinely held'.[86]

Two cases in which courts were reluctant to find that a belief fell within the ambit of Article 9 ECHR are *Pretty* v. *the United Kingdom* and *Whaley* v. *Lord Advocate*. In *Pretty* it was implied (although not definitively determined) that Pretty was unable to establish that her belief in assisted dying was one that was protected by Article 9 ECHR.[87] In *Whaley* the House of Lords rejected the argument that hunting with hounds is a 'belief' comparable to a religious belief.[88] Lord Hope held that it is not a 'belief' as 'hunting with hounds is carried on mainly for pleasure and relaxation for those who take part in it'.[89] He held that the 'jurisprudence does not support the proposition that a person's belief in his right to engage in an activity which he carries on for pleasure or recreation, however fervent or passionate, can be equated with beliefs of the kind that are protected by article 9'.[90] He went on to observe that '[i]t would be surprising if it did so, as it would be hard in that event to set any limits to the range of beliefs that would be opened up for protection'.[91] A subsequent application to the ECtHR based on Article 9 ECHR was rejected as manifestly ill-founded.[92]

An important case in respect of the limits of Article 9(1) is the ECtHR's determination in *de Wilde* v. *Netherlands* that 'Pastafarianism' is not a religion or belief within the meaning of Article 9 ECHR.[93] The facts were that de Wilde had applied for a new driving licence and identity card with a photograph that showed her wearing a colander on her head. In submitting her application she stated that she was a committed Pastafarian and that she was therefore entitled on religious grounds to avail herself of the exception to the requirement that the head should be uncovered on identity photographs.

The idea of 'Pastafarianism' is rooted in a broader political discourse which originated in a decision in Kansas, United States, to introduce the doctrine of

parents and teachers. Yet there has been no-one here or in the courts below to speak on behalf of the children. No litigation friend has been appointed to consider the rights of the pupils involved separately from those of the adults. No non-governmental organisation, such as the Children's Rights Alliance, has intervened to argue a case on behalf of children as a whole. The battle has been fought on ground selected by the adults. This has clouded and over-complicated what should have been a simple issue.'

[86] Brenda Hale, 'Religious Freedom and the Law' in Frank Cranmer et al., *The Confluence of Law and Religion* (Cambridge University Press, 2016).

[87] *Pretty* v. *the United Kingdom* (2002) ECHR 427. For further discussion of this case, see Chapter 5.

[88] *Whaley* v. *Lord Advocate* [2007] UKHL 53. [89] Ibid at [18]. [90] Ibid at [18].

[91] Ibid at [18]. [92] *Friend* v. *the United Kingdom* (dec.) (2010) 50 EHRR SE6.

[93] *de Wilde* v. *Netherlands* (2023) 76 EHRR SE4.

'intelligent design' alongside the theory of evolution into the school curriculum. Following that decision, a physics graduate wrote an open letter suggesting that the creator of the universe was in fact a Flying Spaghetti Monster and demanding that corresponding doctrine should be taught alongside the theories of evolution and intelligent design. This received considerable attention which culminated in the argument that Pastafarianism is a religion and that there is a 'Church of the Flying Spaghetti Monster'. It was this movement which formed the crux of de Wilde's argument that she should be exempt from the identity card requirement. Her application was, however, rejected by the authorities in the Netherlands on the basis that the Church of the Flying Spaghetti Monster was a parody intended to call into question the position of religion in contemporary society and was not properly a religion.

De Wilde argued before the ECtHR that the domestic authorities were wrong to conclude that Pastafarianism cannot be considered a religion or belief with the meaning of Article 9 ECHR.[94] The ECtHR rejected her application. In considering the ambit of Article 9 ECHR it observed that the right 'would be highly theoretical and illusory if the degree of discretion granted to States allowed them to interpret the notion of religious denomination so restrictively as to deprive a non-traditional and minority form of a religion of legal protection',[95] but that this 'does not mean that all opinions or convictions are to be regarded as such'.[96] In this respect it reiterated that 'the right to freedom of thought, conscience and religion denotes only those views that attain a certain level of cogency, seriousness, cohesion and importance'.[97] The ECtHR observed that the domestic authorities had applied these standards and there was no reason for the ECtHR to depart from a decision that 'appears carefully measured and does not seem in any way arbitrary or illogical'.[98] The ramifications of deference to the State on this question of whether Article 9 ECHR is applicable have, however, been highlighted by critics as a potential shortcoming of the judgment.[99]

13.4.3 Absolute Right to Hold a Belief

The right to hold a belief ensures that States cannot dictate what a person believes, nor can they take coercive steps to make an individual change their beliefs. There is very little case law on the right to hold a belief as most interferences involve restrictions on manifestations, but it was important in *Ivanova* v. *Bulgaria.*[100] Ivanova had been dismissed from her position in a school on the basis of her religious beliefs with the pretext that she was no

[94] Ibid at [49]. [95] Ibid at [50]. [96] Ibid at [51]. [97] Ibid at [51]. [98] Ibid at [53].

[99] Wojciech Brzozowski, 'Did Pastafarians Lose in Strasbourg, After All? (2021) 10 Oxford Journal of Law and Religion 3, 487–494.

[100] *Ivanova* v. *Bulgaria* (2008) 47 EHRR 54.

longer qualified for the post.[101] The ECtHR found that Ivanova had been pressured by two government officials to renounce her religious beliefs in order to keep her job and that this constituted a violation of Article 9 ECHR.[102] In coming to that determination, it explained the structure of Article 9 ECHR:

> Unlike the second paragraphs of Arts 8, 10 and 11 of the Convention, which cover all the rights mentioned in the first paragraphs of those Articles, that of Art.9 of the Convention refers only to 'freedom to manifest one's religion or belief'. In so doing, it recognises that in democratic societies, in which several religions coexist within one and the same population, it may be necessary to place restrictions on this freedom in order to reconcile the interests of the various groups and ensure that everyone's beliefs are respected. At the same time, it emphasises the primary importance of the right to freedom of thought, conscience and religion and the fact that a state cannot dictate what a person believes or take coercive steps to make him change his beliefs.[103]

Beyond *Ivanova* there is very little case law on the right to hold a belief, although it can be difficult to draw a sharp line between holding a belief and manifesting a belief. A significant case in this respect is *Mockutė* v. *Lithuania* in which it was held that Article 9 ECHR was violated when the applicant (who had been held unlawfully at a psychiatric hospital) was unable to practice meditation and doctors tried to 'correct' her by persuading her to abandon her religion, which they considered 'fictitious'.[104]

13.4.4 The Article 9 ECHR Right to Manifest a Belief

Given the breadth of beliefs, there are countless ways in which they may be manifested. These include, amongst other things, the act of worship either individually or in community with others, the wearing of religious dress, the observance of religious practices, and the right not to be obliged to manifest one's beliefs. Later in this chapter we will examine case law in respect of some of the principal types of manifestation, but first we need to consider the relationship between manifestation and belief.

13.4.4.1 Relationship between the Manifestation and the Belief

Manifestations mandated by a religion will clearly fall within Article 9 ECHR, but it is important to observe that applicants are not required to establish that a manifestation is *mandatory*.[105] As Lady Hale notes, '[t]hat is undoubtedly good news for members of the Church of England and indeed of the Church of

[101] Ibid. [102] Ibid at [84]. [103] Ibid at [79].
[104] *Mockutė* v. *Lithuania*, App. No. 66490/09, 27/02/2018. [105] See also *Williamson* (n 80).

Ireland, which impose so few mandatory requirements'.[106] Yet whilst a practice does not have to be mandatory, it does not mean that any act that the applicant asserts is motivated by a belief will be regarded as a manifestation. Indeed, there must be some limits because if applicants were free to argue that any conduct is a manifestation this would vastly expand the application of Article 9 ECHR, especially when coupled with the broad range of beliefs protected by Article 9 ECHR. This raises the thorny question of how we determine what constitutes a manifestation.

In examining this issue in *Eweida*, the ECtHR explained that what is needed is a sufficiently close and direct nexus between the act and the underlying belief and this must be determined on the facts of each case:

> Even where the belief in question attains the required level of cogency and importance, it cannot be said that every act which is in some way inspired, motivated or influenced by it constitutes a 'manifestation' of the belief. Thus, for example, acts or omissions which do not directly express the belief concerned or which are only remotely connected to a precept of faith fall outside the protection of Article 9 § 1… In order to count as a 'manifestation' within the meaning of Article 9, the act in question must be intimately linked to the religion or belief. An example would be an act of worship or devotion which forms part of the practice of a religion or belief in a generally recognised form. However, the manifestation of religion or belief is not limited to such acts; the existence of a *sufficiently close and direct nexus* between the act and the underlying belief must be determined on the facts of each case. In particular, there is no requirement on the applicant to establish that he or she acted in fulfilment of a duty mandated by the religion in question.[107]

Consequently, in *Eweida* the ECtHR held that wearing a cross *is* a manifestation of Christian faith even if it is not mandatory.[108] The Court has also accepted that Muslim parents are entitled to exempt their daughters from compulsory mixed swimming lessons even though the Koran only requires that the female body be covered from puberty.[109] Similarly accepted is that a Muslim man's wish to wear a skullcap, while not a strict religious duty, is protected by Article 9 ECHR.[110]

UK domestic courts have also considered the relationship between a belief and a manifestation. See, for example, *R (on the application of Haq)* v. *Walsall Metropolitan Borough Council* where it was accepted that the claimant had a sincere religious belief that 'people should not step onto his father's grave'[111]

[106] Lady Hale, *Annual Human Rights Lecture for Law Society of Ireland 'Freedom of Religion and Belief'* (13 June 2014), p.14.

[107] *Eweida* v. *the United Kingdom* (n 51) at [82]. Emphasis added.

[108] Ibid.

[109] *Osmanoğlu and Kocabaş* v. *Switzerland*, App. No. 29086/12, 10/01/2017 at [42].

[110] *Hamidović* v. *Bosnia and Herzegovina* (n 73) at [30].

[111] *R (on the application of Haq)* v. *Walsall Metropolitan Borough Council* [2019] EWHC 70 (Admin).

and that his wish to have marble edging around the grave was sufficiently linked to that belief to constitute a manifestation.[112] Meanwhile, in *Halcrow* v. *CPS* the High Court accepted that presence in the stone circle at Stonehenge was a necessary manifestation of the Druids' religious beliefs.[113]

13.4.4.2 *State's Obligation to Refrain from Interfering with a Manifestation of a Belief*

There are countless ways in which a State may interfere with a manifestation of a belief.[114] These include (amongst other things): the application of a criminal or administrative penalty; dismissal or non-renewal of a contract;[115] a disciplinary sanction;[116] psychological pressure to abandon beliefs;[117] physical obstacles to exercising rights such as the interruption of meetings by the police;[118] dissolution of a faith organisation;[119] denial of authorisation, recognition or approval which impedes the exercise of rights;[120] denial of official status which gives rise to difficulties;[121] and the use of pejorative expressions in connection with a religious community in official state documents.[122]

As the right to manifest a belief is a qualified right the State may justify an interference if the measure is prescribed by law, pursues a legitimate aim and the means chosen to achieve the aim are necessary in a democratic society.

In respect of the legitimate aim component of the justification analysis, Article 9(2) ECHR provides that the State can intervene in pursuit of public safety, the protection of public order, health and morals, or the protection of the rights and freedoms of others. There are various examples of States relying upon these aims within the case law. For example, the protection of health was invoked in *Surayanda* v. *The Welsh Ministers* where a Krishna group's ceremonial bullock was slaughtered to prevent the spread of bovine

[112] Ibid at [61]. [113] *Halcrow* v. *CPS* [2021] EWHC 483, [2021] 2 Cr App R 1 at [46].

[114] See European Court of Human Rights' Case Guide on Article 9 at (n 3).

[115] *Kokkinakis* v. *Greece* (n 2); *Ivanova* v. *Bulgaria* (2008) 47 EHRR 54; *Masaev* v. *Moldova* (2013) 57 EHRR 6; *Ebrahimian* v. *France*, App. No. 64846/11, 26/11/2015; *Taganrog LRO and Others* v. *Russia*, App. No. 32401/10, 07/06/2022 at [269].

[116] *Korostelev* v. *Russia* (2022) 75 EHRR 17 at [50].

[117] *Mockutė* v. *Lithuania* (n 104) at [123]–[125].

[118] *Boychev and Others* v. *Bulgaria*, App. No. 77185/01, 27/01/2011.

[119] *Jehovah's Witnesses of Moscow and Others* v. *Russia*, App. No. 302/02, 10/06/2010 at [99]–[103]; *Biblical Centre of the Chuvash Republic* v. *Russia*, App. No. 33203/08, 12/06/2014 at [52].

[120] *Metropolitan Church of Bessarabia and Others* v. *Moldova* (2002) 35 EHRR 13; *Vergos* v. *Greece* (2005) 41 EHRR 41.

[121] *İzzettin Doğan and Others* v. *Turkey* [GC] (n 63) at [95].

[122] *Leela Förderkreis e.V. and Others* v. *Germany*, App. No. 58911/00, 06/11/2008 at [84]; *Centre of Societies for Krishna Consciousness in Russia and Frolov* v. *Russia*, App. No. 37477/11, 23/11/2021 at [38].

tuberculosis.[123] It was also accepted by all parties (albeit reluctantly) in *Philip* v. *Scottish Ministers* that the Covid-19 lockdown restrictions on religious organisations pursued the legitimate aim of public health.[124]

Akin to other qualified Convention rights, the list of legitimate aims set out in the text of Article 9 ECHR is said to be an exhaustive list. This was confirmed by the Grand Chamber in *S.A.S.* v. *France* in which it was also stated that the specified aims should be interpreted restrictively.[125] Yet having advocated a restrictive approach, the Grand Chamber immediately undermined this by stating that the measure must 'pursue an aim that can be *linked* to one of those listed in this provision'.[126] This is a significant loosening of the strict interpretation requirement. Indeed, as we will see later in this chapter, the breadth accorded by the Grand Chamber to the legitimate aim of the rights of others in *S.A.S.* resulted in the Court finding that the prohibition on the face veil in France was justified under Article 9(2) ECHR.[127] This has been heavily criticised by critics as a misuse of the 'rights of others' aim.[128]

In line with other qualified rights, the State must also demonstrate that the impugned measure was necessary in a democratic society in order to justify the interference. The ECtHR has repeatedly stated that this does not mean merely 'useful' or 'desirable'.[129] The domestic courts have also confirmed that the *Bank Mellat* principles apply, namely: (i) whether the aim was sufficiently important to justify interference with a fundamental right; (ii) whether there was a rational connection between the means chosen and the aim in view; (iii) whether there were less restrictive means available to achieve that aim; and (iv) whether there was a fair balance between the rights of the individual and the general interest of the community, including the rights of others.[130] The approach taken to proportionality will depend upon the context and the rights and interests at stake. For example, in *Williamson* Lord Nicholls observed that Parliament was entitled to conclude that a universal ban on corporal punishment was necessary 'because this issue is one of broad social policy. As such it is pre-eminently well suited for decision by Parliament' as 'the legislature is to be accorded a considerable degree of latitude in deciding which course should be selected as the best course in the interests of school children as a whole'.[131] Meanwhile in *R (on the application of Begum)* v. *Denbigh High School* (an important case concerning a school uniform policy which is discussed later in

[123] *Surayanda* v. *The Welsh Ministers* [2007] EWCA Civ 893.

[124] *Philip* v. *Scottish Ministers* (n 43) at [99].

[125] *S.A.S.* v. *France* (2015) 60 EHRR 11 at [113]. [126] Ibid at [113]. Emphasis added.

[127] Ibid at [141]–[142]. [128] See discussion below at Section 13.5.5.

[129] *Svyato-Mykhaylivska Parafiya* v. *Ukraine*, App. No. 77703/01, 14/06/2007 at [116].

[130] See, for example, *Halcrow* v. *CPS* (n 113) at [37], *Philip* v. *Scottish Ministers* (n 43), *Michaela Schools Trust* (n 9) at [156].

[131] *R (on the application of Williamson)* v. *Secretary of State for Education and Employment* (n 80) at [50]–[51].

this chapter), Lord Hoffmann commented that 'a domestic court should accept the decision of Parliament to allow individual schools to make their own decisions . . . and it is there that an area of judgment, comparable to the margin of appreciation, must be allowed to the school'.[132] Conversely, the 'least restrictive means' requirement was prominent in Lord Braid's reasoning in *Philip* v. *Scottish Minister* that COVID-19 regulations closing places of worship in Scotland were incompatible with Article 9 ECHR as the respondents had not established why less restrictive means had not been adopted.[133]

The requirement for a fair balance is evident in a number of cases. For example, in *R (on the application of Adath Yisroel Burial Society and Anor)* v. *Inner North London Senior Coroner*[134] the claimant challenged a coroner's policy of not prioritising any death on the basis of the religion of the deceased or family. The effect of the policy was that no priority was given to adherents of Judaism or any other faith for which it is an important principle that the funeral should take place as soon as possible, ideally on the day of death itself. The Court held that 'what Article 9 requires is not that there should be any favouritism, whether in favour of religious belief in general or in favour of any particular religious faith, but that there should be a fair balance struck between the rights and interests of different people in society'.[135] It went on to determine that the fundamental flaw in the defendant's policy was that 'it fails to strike any balance at all, let alone a fair balance'.[136] Conversely, the fact that a fair balance had been struck was determinative in *Halcrow* where the High Court held that restricting access to Stonehenge struck a fair balance between the important rights of the individual appellants and the general interest of the community to see Stonehenge preserved for present and future generations.[137]

13.4.5 Positive Obligation: State Obligation to Protect

Thus far we have been focusing upon the negative obligation, but it is important to note that States also have positive obligations in respect of Article 9 ECHR. Moreover, in a similar fashion to other Convention rights, the ECtHR has observed that the boundary between positive and negative obligations is not susceptible to an exact definition and that the applicable principles are comparable.[138]

[132] *R (on the application of Begum)* v. *Denbigh High School* [2006] UKHL 15, [2007] 1 AC 100 at [64]. This dicta was also considered and applied in *Michaela Schools Trust* (n 9) at [158]–[168].

[133] *Philip* v. *Scottish Minister* (n 43).

[134] *R (on the application of Adath Yisroel Burial Society and Anor)* v. *Inner North London Senior Coroner* [2018] EWHC 969 (Admin), [2019] QB 251.

[135] Ibid. [136] Ibid at [107]. [137] *Halcrow* v. *CPS* (n 113) at [49].

[138] *İzzettin Doğan and Others* v. *Turkey* (n 63) at [96].

One element of the positive obligations is that the State is required to provide an effective and accessible means of protecting the rights guaranteed under Article 9 ECHR, including both the provision of a regulatory framework of adjudicatory and enforcement machinery protecting individuals' rights and the implementation, where appropriate, of specific steps.[139] For example, in *Savda* v. *Turkey* it was held that the State was obliged to provide the applicant with an effective and accessible procedure that would have enabled him to establish whether he was entitled to conscientious objector status.[140]

Positive obligations may also oblige the State to facilitate the right in other ways. For example, in *Jakóbski* v. *Poland* the ECtHR considered that the State's failure to provide a vegetarian diet to a Buddhist prisoner was best analysed in terms of a positive duty to take reasonable and appropriate measures to secure the applicant's rights.[141] Whilst in *Abdullah Yalçin* v. *Turkey (No.2)* the ECtHR found a violation of the positive obligation where the State had failed to demonstrate that it had weighed the competing interests at stake when it refused to allocate a room to prisoners for congregational Friday prayers.[142]

States also have a positive obligation to protect individuals and ensure that 'competing groups tolerate each other'.[143] This was important in *Members of the Gldani Congregation of Jehovah's Witnesses* v. *Georgia* as the applicants had been attacked, humiliated and severely beaten during their congregation by 'Orthodox believers', their religious literature had been confiscated and burnt and one of the applicants had his head shaved to the sound of prayers as a punishment.[144] The ECtHR held that the authorities' total indifference and failure to act violated Article 9 ECHR as they had failed to take the necessary measures to ensure that the applicants could exercise freely their rights to freedom of religion.[145] Similarly, the ECtHR found a violation in *Karaahmed* v. *Bulgaria*, where the applicants were subjected to egg-throwing, use of loud-speakers to drown out the call to prayer at their Mosque, the attempted burning of prayer mats and physical assaults.[146] On that occasion the ECtHR held that the Bulgarian authorities had not done all that could reasonably have been expected of them.

The scope of the positive obligation may also be relevant where there are competing Convention rights. For example, where a third party opposes the belief or practices of a religious community, that third party may also have Article 10 or 11 ECHR rights that need to be evaluated. In *Karaahmed* v.

[139] *Osmanoğlu and Kocabaş* v. *Switzerland* (n 109) at [86].

[140] *Savda* v. *Turkey*, App. No. 42730/05, 12/06/2012 at [98].

[141] *Jakóbski* v. *Poland* (2012) 55 EHRR 8 at [46]–[47].

[142] *Abdullah Yalçin* v. *Turkey (No.2)*, App. No. 34417/10, 14/06/2022.

[143] *Members of the Gldani Congregation of Jehovah's Witnesses* v. *Georgia* (2008) 46 EHRR 30 at [132].

[144] Ibid. [145] Ibid at [134]. [146] *Karaahmed* v. *Bulgaria*, App. No. 30587/13, 24/02/2015.

Bulgaria the ECtHR set out the applicable principles in such cases.[147] It observed that there is no hierarchy of these rights within the Convention and thus they must be balanced against each other 'in a manner which recognises the importance of these rights in a society based on pluralism, tolerance and broad-mindedness'.[148] It identified three further principles that follow from this:

> First, it is incumbent upon the State to ensure that – insofar as is reasonably possible – both sets of rights are protected. This duty applies equally when acts which may impinge upon one of the two rights are carried out by private individuals …
>
> Second, to do so, the State must ensure that a legal framework is put in place to safeguard those rights from third parties and to take effective measures to ensure that they are respected in practice …
>
> Third, as is always the case when a Contracting State seeks to protect two values guaranteed by the Convention which may come into conflict with each other, in the exercise of its European supervisory duties, the Court's task is to verify whether the authorities struck a fair balance between those two values … In doing so, the Court should not act with the benefit of hindsight. Nor should it simply substitute its view for that of the national authorities who, in any given case, are much better placed to assess where the appropriate balance lay and how best to achieve that balance.[149]

We will consider at a later point in this chapter the case law that has arisen in respect of provocative portrayals of religious veneration and expression that is offensive to religious sensibilities. It is, however, worth observing at this juncture that whilst there have been a number of Article 10 ECHR cases in which the ECtHR has upheld domestic restrictions on expression, this does not mean that in such cases there was a positive obligation within Article 9 ECHR which obliged the State to take such measures.[150] In this respect the ECtHR has observed that the State cannot be held responsible for a failure to offer protection against acts by private individuals unless they exercise their right to freedom of expression in a manner causing serious prejudice to the enjoyment by the applicant of another right protected by the Convention.[151]

13.4.6 Non-discrimination: Article 14 ECHR

In addition to the protection accorded by Article 9 ECHR, applicants may also argue that they were discriminated against because of their religious beliefs, relying upon Article 14 ECHR. In cases where Article 14 is raised, the ECtHR will consider whether there was discrimination and if so whether it was justified. This is considered further in Chapter 14.

[147] Ibid. [148] Ibid at [92]. [149] Ibid at [93]–[95].

[150] See discussion at Section 13.6 below.

[151] *Centre of Societies for Krishna Consciousness in Russia and Frolov* v. *Russia* (n 122) at [31].

13.5 IMPORTANT CONTEXTS IN WHICH ARTICLE 9 ECHR IS INVOKED

Having examined the applicable framework, we now consider specific contexts in which Article 9 ECHR is invoked.

13.5.1 State Prohibits or Refuses to Recognise a Religious Organisation

In some jurisdictions, religions must be formally registered with the State, and the ECtHR has found that refusal to register a religion violates Article 9 ECHR.[152] This issue does not arise in the UK where there is no such registration requirement.[153]A similar interference may, however, arise if a group is dissolved. For example, a State may argue that a religious institution is in fact a terrorist organisation and that this justifies dissolution.[154] We saw in Chapter 8 that this is provided for in the UK by domestic terrorism legislation in respect of proscription of organisations; the concerns raised in that chapter regarding the potential breadth of those powers are of evident significance in this context.[155] States may also seek to dissolve a religious organisation that promotes harmful beliefs. Russia sought to rely on this when it argued that Jehovah's Witnesses could be prohibited on the basis that they refuse to accept blood transfusions.[156] The ECtHR rejected this, observing that as the right to refuse a blood transfusion is protected by Articles 8 and 9 ECHR it cannot serve as justification for dissolution.[157]

13.5.2 Restrictions on Worship and Places of Worship

The right to manifest one's belief via worship 'implies freedom to manifest one's religion not only alone and in private but also in community with others,

[152] *Kimlya* v. *Russia* (2013) 57 EHRR 27 at [84].

[153] There is domestic legislation governing officially registering a place of worship and registering places for the solemnisation of marriage, but it is possible for a congregation to worship in a building that has not been recorded.

[154] See for example, *Taganrog* v. *Russia* (n 115) in which multiple violations of Article 9 and other rights were found after Russia dissolved Jehovah's Witnesses on the basis that they were an extremist organisation.

[155] See Chapter 8.

[156] *Jehovah's Witnesses of Moscow and Others* v. *Russia* (n 119). See also, *Taganrog* v. *Russia* (n 115).

[157] *Jehovah's Witnesses of Moscow and Others* v. *Russia* (n 119) at [131]–[144]. On blood transfusions and Jehovah's Witnesses see also *Pindo Mulla* v. *Spain*, App. No. 15541/20, 17/09/2024 and *Lindholm and the Estate after Leif Lindholm* v. *Denmark*, App. No.25636/22, 05/11/2024 where the ECtHR held that the right to respect for private life Article 8 ECHR is applicable in these cases and that the religious aspect of the complaint can be adequately accommodated by interpreting and applying Article 8 in the light of Article 9 ECHR.

in public and within the circle of those whose faith one shares'.[158] Article 9 ECHR thus protects a right to gather to worship.[159] This in turn means that restrictions on places of worship interfere with the right. There are numerous cases relating to refusals to register official places of worship as well as restrictions on the construction of religious buildings.[160] Other restrictions include preventing people from travelling to places of worship. For example, in *Cyprus* v. *Turkey* the Grand Chamber found violations of Article 9 ECHR when Greek Orthodox Cypriots residing within the Turkish Republic of Northern Cyprus were prevented from leaving their villages to attend places of worship.[161] A violation has also been found in cases in which the State has dispersed groups that have gathered for worship.[162]

Yet whilst there is a right to gather to worship, this does not mean that there is a right to gather wherever the applicants wish.[163] Consequently, the Commission found no violation when Stonehenge was closed during midsummer solstice.[164] It also refused to find a violation when applicants were fined for entering the premises of an abortion clinic and praying in the corridor.[165] The Court of Appeal in England and Wales came to the same conclusion in *Dulgheriu* v. *London Borough of Ealing.*[166]

The right to gather for worship was also invoked in challenges to COVID-19 restrictions. During the first lockdown, a case was brought in respect of the closure of a mosque in England; on that occasion it was determined that there was no prospect of success as the infringement of Article 9 ECHR was not disproportionate.[167] However, in *Philip* v. *Scottish Ministers* it was held that the closure of churches in Scotland during a subsequent lockdown was contrary to Article 9 ECHR as it had not been demonstrated that it was the least restrictive means.

158 *Guler and Ugur* v. *Turkey*, App. No. 31706/10, 02/12/2004.

159 *The Church of Jesus Christ of Latter-Day Saints* v. *the United Kingdom* (2014) 59 EHRR 18; *Cumhuriyetçi Eğitim ve Kültür Merkezi Vakfi* v. *Turkey*, App. No. 32093/10, 02/12/2014 at [41].

160 See, for example, *Religious Denomination of Jehovah's Witnesses in Bulgaria* v. *Bulgaria*, App. No. 5301/11, 10/11/2020, *Religious Denomination of Jehovah's Witnesses of Kryvyi Rih's Ternivsky District* v. *Ukraine*, App. No. 21477/10, 03/09/2019.

161 *Cyprus* v. *Turkey* [GC] (2002) 35 EHRR 30 at [243]–[246].

162 For example, a Jehovah's Witnesses service, a Muslim prayer meeting held in a private house (*Masaev* v. *Moldova* (n 115)), and a gathering of adherents of the Reverend Moon's Unification Church (*Boychev and Others* v. *Bulgaria* (n 118)).

163 *Pavlides and Georgakis* v. *Turkey* (dec.), App. Nos. 9130/09 and 9143/09, 02/07/2013 at [29].

164 *Chappell* v. *the United Kingdom* (dec.) (1988) 10 EHRR CD510; see also, *Pendragon* v. *the United Kingdom* (dec.) (1999) 27 EHRR CD179.

165 *Van Schindel and Others* v. *the Netherlands* (dec.), App. No. 30936/96, 10/09/1997.

166 *Dulgheriu* v. *London Borough of Ealing* [2019] EWCA Civ 1490, [2020] 1 WLR 609 at [81]. See discussion in Chapter 11.

167 *R* v. *Hussain* [2020] EWHC 1392.

The right to worship at school has recently been litigated in the domestic courts in the high-profile case *R (on the application of TTT)* v. *Michaela Schools Trust.*[168] The Michaela Community School was established a decade ago in a converted office block in Wembley, it has exceptionally good academic results and is heavily over-subscribed.[169] For a secondary school it also has a high media presence, having been labelled as the 'strictest school in Britain' and its Headteacher Katharine Birbalsingh as the 'strictest headteacher';[170] Birbalsingh was also for a period the Chair of the Social Mobility Commission. There are two main aspects to the ethos of the school: a disciplinary ethos and a 'team ethos', which Birbalsingh explained to the court in *Michaela Schools Trust* means that pupils must do their duty and that the success of the school 'depends on minimising the distinctions and divisions between the children and promoting social and cultural integration between them'.[171] It was argued in *Michaela Schools Trust* that this ethos justified the restrictions that the school placed on worship at school.

Michaela Schools Trust related to a decision of the school's governing body to prohibit pupils from performing prayer rituals on the school premises. The policy stemmed from incidents that arose in March 2023 when pupils started praying in the school yard and brought prayer mats into school which was contrary to school rules. This led to a confrontation with a teacher, and two pupils were excluded from the school for two days, following which matters escalated further both within and outside the school, where online abuse, including highly racist abuse was levelled at the teacher who had intervened, and there were threats of violence and death threats. The school also received abusive phone calls and emails, and an email was sent to the school stating that bombs had been planted in the school. The Head of the school also gave evidence to the Court that the situation had created division within the school, which 'was undermining the School's culture of all races and religions mixing and being friends with each other'.[172] Following these events, the Headteacher decided to ban prayer rituals and confirmed her decision with the Governing Body thereafter. In May 2023 the Governing Body met to review the decision and voted to continue the prohibition on prayer rituals for the time being.

The restriction applied to all prayer religions, regardless of faith, but there was no evidence that pupils of any religion other than Islam wished to perform prayer rituals during the school day.[173] TTT wished to pray during the lunch break in order to complete the '*Duhr* or *Zuhr* prayer, which is required to be undertaken in a window of time from when the sun passes its highest point in the day to the opening of the window for the next of the five prayers: the *Asr* prayer'.[174] During the autumn/winter months, the window for performing

[168] *Michaela Schools Trust* (n 9) . [169] Ibid at [47]–[49]. [170] Ibid at [49].
[171] Ibid at [58]. [172] Ibid at [106]. [173] Ibid at [3]. [174] Ibid at [4].

Duhr overlapped with the school lunch break and TTT wished to use twenty-five minutes of this break to perform *Duhr.*[175] She argued that the school policy which prohibited her from doing this violated Article 9 ECHR (Ground 1).[176] She also argued that it indirectly discriminated against Muslims contrary to the Equality Act 2010 and that in introducing the policy the school failed to have due regard to the need to eliminate discrimination, to advance equality of opportunity and to foster good relations between Muslims and non-Muslims, contrary to the public sector equality duty under s.149 of the Equality Act 2010 (Grounds 2 and 3).[177] The claimant's Article 9 ECHR and Equality Act arguments failed. There were further arguments in respect of the procedure that applied when the claimant had been excluded from the school, one of which was upheld (Ground 4).[178]

The relevant ground for the purposes of this chapter is the first ground, namely the Article 9 ECHR ground. The school contested this ground; it argued that the policy did not interfere with the Applicant's freedom to manifest her religion and in any event, it argued that any interference was justified. In respect of the first issue, Linden J agreed with the school concluding that he 'did not accept that there had been an interference with the Claimant's Article 9 rights'[179] observing that

> this may appear to some to be a surprising conclusion but in my view it is consistent with the pre *Eweida* caselaw of the Strasbourg Court, which reflects the fact that Article 9 protects 'freedom' to manifest religious beliefs rather than conferring an absolute right to do so.[180]

In coming to this conclusion, he was influenced first by the fact that the 'Claimant at the very least impliedly accepted, when she enrolled at the School, that she would be subject to restrictions on her ability to manifest her religion'.[181] He highlighted the fact that she knew the school was secular, that long before the policy was introduced she had believed that prayer was not permitted at school and she had made up for prayers at home, and that she had not raised any objection until she was the best part of the way through Year 9.[182] Second, by the fact that the Claimant had not shown that there would be 'undue hardship or inconvenience' if she were to move to a different school which permitted her to pray during the school day.[183] In this respect he clarified that he did not mean to suggest that there would be 'no adverse consequences' but that the degree of hardship was not sufficient for there to be an interference with Article 9 ECHR.[184] He opined that either of these first two points were sufficient for the Article 9 ECHR claim to fail before noting that in

175 Ibid. 176 Ibid at [5].
177 Grounds 2 and 3 of the claimant's case at [5] and pp.45–51 and pp.51–65.
178 Ground 4, ibid at [6] and pp.65–71. 179 Ibid at [175]. 180 Ibid at [175].
181 Ibid at [176]. 182 Ibid at [176]. 183 Ibid at [177]. 184 Ibid at [178].

addition to those arguments there was evidence that Qada was available to mitigate the failure to pray during the lunch break.[185] Qada prayers are prayers which compensate for missed prayers and there were differences of opinion in the proceedings as to when these prayers could be used and the status of such prayers. The Claimant argued that Qada was not available 'where the adherent wilfully or voluntarily chooses not to pray during the allotted time. In any other case, such as where there would be a clash with lessons or family lunch, it is available'.[186] Conversely, the school argued that if Qada is available where there is a good reason to miss a prayer then it should also be available where the adherent is in a location or subject to a regime where prayer is prohibited.[187] It was the school's argument that was accepted by Linden J and he concluded that this meant that TTT was able to manifest her beliefs in accordance with Islamic teaching, notwithstanding the school policy 'albeit in a modified and less satisfactory way'.[188] He thus concluded that there was no interference with Article 9 ECHR but went on to consider (in the event that he was wrong on that point) whether any interference would be justified.[189]

In relation to Article 9(2) ECHR, the school argued that the continuation of the policy had a number of aims: preserving the ethos, policies and practices of the school; promoting pupils' compliance with the school behaviour policy; protecting the school from threats of abuse; avoiding logistical disruption and detriments to other school activities which would be caused by accommodating prayer rituals within the school; and avoiding detriment to pupils' education and to social cohesion within the school which would occur if they were permitted to opt out of the important period of socialising during the lunch break.[190] The school also argued that if there was any interference it was 'slight at most' for the reasons considered in respect of the Article 9(1) ECHR argument and that a lesser or different measure was not possible.[191] Finally, the school emphasised that the decision was not permanent and it could be reviewed in the future.[192]

The Claimant argued that the school bore the burden of proof of establishing that the policy was justified. She accepted that 'avoiding detriment to education and social cohesion through opting out of socialising during the lunch-break, and avoiding logistical disruption, were both legitimate aims' which were rationally connected to the policy.[193] However, she argued that

(i) Insofar as reliance on the ethos of the School meant removal of any distinction between pupils based on religion, rather than teaching other pupils to respect and tolerate each other's differences, this was not a legitimate aim ... Nor was preservation of the inclusive ethos of the

[185] Ibid at [180]. [186] Ibid at [180]. [187] Ibid at [180]. [188] Ibid at [180].
[189] Ibid at [182]. [190] Ibid at [183]. [191] Ibid at [184]–[185]. [192] Ibid at [185].
[193] Ibid at [186].

School rationally connected with the total banning of prayer given that the School permits certain signs of religious difference, including the wearing of headscarves and allowing pupils to observe Ramadan . . .[194]

(ii) The [prohibition on prayer rituals] is not rationally connected to the aim of promoting compliance with the School's behaviour policy. It is not rational to rely on experience from when there were no rules regulating permitted prayer to predict that there would be similar difficulties even if there were such rules . . .[195]

(iii) The concerns about a repetition of the abuse and threats directed at the School in March 2023 were only rationally connected to prayer outside in the school yard.[196]

The Claimant also argued that it had not been established that a less intrusive measure had been considered.[197] Finally, she argued that a fair balance had not been struck between the severity of the effects of the policy on Muslim pupils and the importance of the aims behind the policy.[198]

In finding that if there was an interference it was justified, Linden J found that there was a rational connection between the policy and the aim of the school to promote inclusivity and social cohesion. He recognised that the school permitted some signs of religious observance but found that 'the question is one of degree' and that allowing Muslim pupils to go into school for these purposes takes 'the identification of Muslim pupils as such significantly further'.[199] He also accepted that there were logistical difficulties in facilitating this and that the school did not have to demonstrate that it would be impossible.[200] He opined that the school was 'entitled to say that, taken with the other considerations as to the effect on its ethos etc, the level of effort and the cost in terms of use of the School's resources would be such that it would not be proportionate to make the arrangements which would be necessary'.[201] He thus accepted that there were legitimate aims for the purposes of Article 9(2) ECHR.[202] He then considered whether a less intrusive measure could have been introduced without unacceptably compromising these aims and found that it could not.[203] Finally, in respect of balancing, he found that a fair balance had been struck and emphasised the following: (i) prayer had not been raised as an issue prior to March 2023; (ii) the policy only affected Muslim pupils during winter months and Qada is available when it does; and (iii) the claimant and her fellow pupils or at least their parents had chosen the school and chosen to remain there notwithstanding the policy.[204] He thus concluded that the pursuit of the legitimate aims outweighed the adverse effects on the rights of Muslim pupils.[205]

194 Ibid at [186]. 195 Ibid at [186]. 196 Ibid at [186]. 197 Ibid at [187].
198 Ibid at [188]. 199 Ibid at [199]. 200 Ibid at [200]. 201 Ibid at [200].
202 Ibid at [201]. 203 Ibid at [202]. 204 Ibid at [204]–[205]. 205 Ibid at [206].

The position taken by Linden J in respect of Article 9(1) ECHR is one which significantly narrows the application of the Convention right and is difficult to square with the position adopted in *Eweida* by the Strasbourg Court in respect of the workplace where it opined that it:

> considers that, where an individual complains of a restriction on freedom of religion in the workplace, rather than holding that the possibility of changing job would negate any interference with the right, the better approach would be to weigh that possibility in the overall balance when considering whether or not the restriction was proportionate.[206]

Linden J considered this dictum in *Michaela Schools Trust* but it was accepted by all that he was bound to follow the House of Lords in *Begum* v. *Denbigh High School* on this issue.[207] As we will see later in this chapter, the position adopted by the majority of the House of Lords in *Begum* v. *Denbigh High School*, which was prior to *Eweida*, was that there is no interference with Article 9(1) ECHR 'where a person has voluntarily accepted an employment or role which does not accommodate that practice or observance and there are other means open to the person to practise or observe his or her religion without undue hardship or inconvenience'.[208] There was some discussion in *Michaela Schools Trust* as to what this meant in practice. The Claimant argued that for *Begum* v. *Denbigh High School* to apply, there must be both voluntary acceptance and other means open to manifest the religious belief without undue hardship or inconvenience and that on these facts this was not a voluntary acceptance case.[209] Linden J determined that the principle was not as narrow as this. He opined that:

> In my view, the essence of this aspect of the principle identified at [23] of Lord Bingham's Opinion is that voluntary acceptance of the rules or the regime of an institution may mean that the individual has expressly or impliedly agreed to limitations being placed on their freedom to manifest their religious beliefs and therefore cannot subsequently complain when such limitations become an issue. This may be so whether or not the precise limitations are known to the claimant at the moment of joining, and whether or not limitations which are known at the time of joining only become an issue later on as a result of decisions which the claimant takes after joining.[210]

Moreover, he concluded that

> The essence of this aspect of the principle identified in *Begum* is that if the individual has a genuine choice (see Lord Scott at [87] of *Begum*, above) to manifest their beliefs elsewhere there will be no interference with their Article 9 rights.[211]

206 *Eweida* v. *the United Kingdom* (n 51) at [83].
207 *Michaela Schools Trust* (n 9) at [147].
208 *Begum* v. *Denbigh High School* (n 132) at [23].
209 *Michaela Schools Trust* (n 9) at [148]–[149].
210 Ibid at [151].
211 Ibid at [155].

Applying this to the facts, he concluded that there was no interference. It is, however, worth noting, as discussed below, that in *Begum* v. *Denbigh High School* the Lords were divided on this issue[212] and that the decision in *Begum* v. *Denbigh High School* was prior to *Eweida*.

13.5.3 Restrictions on Teaching

13.5.3.1 Proselytism

The text of Article 9 ECHR expressly refers to a right to manifest one's religion or belief through 'teaching'.[213] Restrictions on proselytising may therefore violate Article 9 ECHR.[214] It is important to observe that the ECtHR has distinguished here between 'bearing Christian witness' (self-evidently not a neutral term) and 'improper proselytism':

> First of all, a distinction has to be made between bearing Christian witness and improper proselytism. The former corresponds to true evangelism, which a report drawn up in 1956 under the auspices of the World Council of Churches describes as an essential mission and a responsibility of every Christian and every Church. The latter represents a corruption or deformation of it. It may, according to the same report, take the form of activities offering material or social advantages with a view to gaining new members for a Church or exerting improper pressure on people in distress or in need; it may even entail the use of violence or brainwashing; more generally, it is not compatible with respect for the freedom of thought, conscience and religion of others.[215]

'Improper proselytism' was found in *Larissis* v. *Greece* on the basis that it had taken place within a military structure which may render an individual more vulnerable.[216]

13.5.3.2 Restrictions on Religious Literature

Restrictions or prohibitions on religious texts may interfere with Article 9 (and Article 10) ECHR. For example, in *Ibragim Ibragimov* v. *Russia* it was held that a ban on books by a well-known Muslim theologian, allegedly on the basis that they constituted extremist literature, violated Article 10 read in the light of Article 9 ECHR.[217] And in *Tsartsidze* v. *Georgia* a violation of Article 9 ECHR was found when religious literature was confiscated from Jehovah's Witnesses and burnt in the street.[218]

[212] See discussion at Section 13.5.5.1 below.

[213] *Kokkinakis* v. *Greece* (n 2). On autonomy and proselytism, see Farrah Ahmed, 'The Autonomy Rationale for Religious Freedom' (2017) 80(2) MLR 238.

[214] Ibid. [215] Ibid at [48]. [216] *Larissis* v. *Greece* (1999) 27 EHRR 329.

[217] *Ibragim Ibragimov* v. *Russia*, App. No. 1413/08, 28/08/2018.

[218] *Tsartsidze* v. *Georgia*, App. No. 18766/04, 17/01/2017.

13.5.3.3 *Restrictions on Public Expression of Religious Views*

There are several cases in which the domestic courts have held that expression of religiously motivated views may not constitute a *manifestation*, but rather an act *motivated by belief.* The impact of this is that such expression is not protected by Article 9 ECHR, but is instead considered within Article 10 ECHR. This was significant in *Ngole* in which a student was dismissed from his course after he posted biblically inspired homophobic statements on Facebook.[219] The High Court held that his posts were not a protected manifestation of religion, but that the religious element was relevant when considering Article 10 ECHR. This was accepted by the Court of Appeal.[220] See also the earlier case of *R (on the application of Raabe)* v. *SSHD* in which the High Court held that the claimant's highly offensive homophobic views were not a 'manifestation' of a religious belief, thus whilst they were 'motivated' by the claimant's beliefs this was not protected by Article 9 ECHR.[221]

13.5.4 Restrictions on Practice and Observance

13.5.4.1 *Religious Days and Dates*

Requiring individuals to work on religious days or dates may also constitute an interference with Article 9 ECHR. In *Sessa* v. *Italy* it was accepted that requiring a lawyer to participate in a hearing on a religious holiday constituted an interference,[222] but on the facts this was justified due to the importance of the right to proper administration of justice, the fact that the lawyer should have expected this, and he could have arranged to have been replaced at the hearing. The same is true in respect of discrimination law; see in this regard, *Mba* v. *Merton Borough* where the Court of Appeal held that it was proportionate for the Claimant's Employer to require her to work on Sundays.[223]

13.5.4.2 *Religious Confidentiality*

Another important part of the case law relates to the principles on which individuals interact with leaders of their faith, in particular obligations of confidentiality. In *Lancashire CC* v. *E and F* it was observed that whilst 'religious confidentiality' is a protected manifestation, it may need to be set aside in particular contexts.[224] Two Jehovah's Witness Elders (ministers of religion) sought to resist witness summons in respect of a child sex abuse case

[219] *Ngole* v. *Sheffield University* [2019] EWCA Civ 1127. [220] Ibid at [61].

[221] *R (on the application of Raabe)* v. *SSHD* [2013] EWHC 1736 (Admin) at [250].

[222] *Sessa* v. *Italy* (2015) 60 EHRR 32.

[223] *Mba* v. *Merton Borough* [2013] EWCA Civ 1562, [2014] 1 WLR 1501.

[224] *Lancashire CC* v. *E and F* [2020] EWHC 182, [2020] 4 WLR 133.

involving a former member of their congregation. They argued that participating as witnesses would compel them to breach obligations of confidentiality that they owed in respect of information that had been disclosed to them in the course of confidential spiritual counselling. This was rejected by the Court which held that '[i]t could not be more obvious that a freedom to manifest one's religious beliefs must give way to the need to protect a child from sexual abuse'.[225] The Court went on to express deep concern as to the extent which the Elders had known of the allegation, their failure to report this to the police and their failure to take effective steps to protect a young child within their community.[226]

13.5.4.3 *Ritual Slaughter*

In many jurisdictions, including the UK, it is a requirement that animals are stunned prior to being slaughtered to ensure that the animal is unconscious and to minimise the risk of the animal experiencing pain, stress or fear.[227] A requirement that the animal is stunned is contrary to the practices of some faiths where animals must be slaughtered via exsanguination, which usually entails the animal's throat being cut and the animal being bled out. Consequently, there are sometimes religious exemptions to requirements for stunning, including in the UK where licensed slaughterhouses can kill animals without stunning where the meat is for consumption by persons practising Muslim and Jewish faiths.[228] Animal welfare groups are, however, campaigning for States to dispense with exemptions for ritual slaughter in a number of European States, including in the UK.[229] Others call for States to restrict the number of animals killed without stunning by using permitted systems.[230]

There have been two cases before the ECtHR concerning restrictions on ritual slaughter. In *Cha'are Shalom Ve Tsedek* v. *France*, a Jewish association argued that France violated Articles 9 and 14 ECHR when it refused to grant them approval to access slaughterhouses for the purposes of performing ritual

225 Ibid at [45]. 226 Ibid at [12].

227 EU Council Regulation (EC) No. 1099/2009 of 24 September 2009 on the protection of animals at the time of killing. The Regulation is directly applicable in all EU Member States. In the UK the regulation is applicable as Retained EU law, it is implemented by the Welfare of Animals at the Time of Killing Regulations (England) 2015, Welfare of Animals at the Time of Killing Regulations (Wales) 2014, Welfare of Animals at the Time of Killing Regulations (Scotland) 2012, Welfare of Animals at the Time of Killing Regulations (Northern Ireland) 2014.

228 Ibid.

229 See, for example, the RSPCA (Royal Society for the Prevention of Cruelty to Animals) and PETA (People for the Ethical Treatment of Animals).

230 See, for example, the British Veterinary Association.

slaughter.[231] France counter-argued that as Judaism did not impose a requirement that the applicants slaughter the animals themselves there was no interference with Article 9 ECHR.[232] The ECtHR agreed that there would only be an interference if the prohibition had made it impossible for them to obtain 'glatt' meat and, as it did not, the Court held that there was no interference with Article 9 ECHR.[233]

Ritual slaughter came before the ECtHR again in *Executief van de Moslims van België* v. *Belgium*.[234] This case concerned legislation in Belgium's Wallonia and Flanders regions which prohibited slaughter without the use of stunning. The applicants, who were Jewish and Muslim organisations, argued that this violated Articles 9 and 14 ECHR. On this occasion, the Court accepted that the legislation interfered with Article 9 ECHR.[235] This was significant because, as discussed above, in *Cha-are Shalom* the ECtHR had accepted that there would be an interference only if the measure made it possible to obtain meat. If this approach had been applied here, then Article 9 ECHR would not have been applicable. (The prohibition only applied to two regions in Belgium and it was not impossible for the applicants to obtain meat.) The ECtHR's approach in *Executief van de Moslims van België* thus gives a broader ambit to Article 9(1) and leaves questions of accessibility to the proportionality stage of the analysis. Having determined that Article 9 ECHR was applicable, the ECtHR then considered whether the interference was justified. It held that there was a legal basis for the measure, and it pursued a legitimate aim, namely the 'protection of public morals', which it stated, 'could not be understood as being intended solely to protect human dignity in the sphere of relations between individuals'.[236] It thus held that the Court was 'entitled to take into account the growing importance attached to the protection of animal welfare'.[237] Having identified this legitimate aim, the Court then considered whether the measure was necessary. Here it emphasised that the margin of appreciation is not a narrow one, that the legislation had been the subject of an extensive parliamentary process and there had been considerable judicial scrutiny by both the domestic courts and the Court of Justice of the European Union (CJEU).[238] Consequently, it held that the ban fell within the State's margin of appreciation and did not violate Article 9 ECHR.[239] The application based on Article 9 coupled with Article 14 ECHR also failed.[240]

[231] *Cha'are Shalom Ve Tsedek* v. *France* [GC], App. No. 27417/95, 27/06/2000. See also, discussion of non-discrimination arguments in Chapter 14.

[232] Ibid at [64]. [233] Ibid at [83].

[234] *Executief van de Moslims van België* v. *Belgium*, App. Nos. 16760/22, 16849/22, 16850/22 et al., 13/02/2024. Judgment is only available in French; a legal summary is available in English. See also, discussion in Chapter 14.

[235] Ibid at [88]. [236] Ibid at [95]. [237] Ibid at [100]. [238] Ibid at [103]–[124].

[239] Ibid at [124]. [240] Ibid at [151]. For further discussion of Article 14 ECHR, see Chapter 14.

The ECtHR's reasoning in *Executief van de Moslims van België* is a major breakthrough for animal welfare, but from the perspective of religious freedom a number of criticisms have been levelled at the Court's approach.[241] First, its procedural focus; some scholars have argued that focusing heavily on parliamentary and judicial processes means that the Court disengages from questions of principle. This is particularly problematic when cases concern the protection of the rights of minorities who are more likely to lose out if weight is given to a democratic parliamentary process. Second, the ECtHR allows animal welfare to be prioritised over the rights of religious minorities which is not provided for by the Convention. In this vein, it is argued that it is hypocritical to protect animal welfare vis-à-vis ritual slaughter while still allowing battery farming. In this respect, Iddo Porat argues that we should adopt a 'starting at home' principle in ritual slaughter cases meaning that members of a minority have a right not to be subjected to more stringent moral criteria than the majority is willing to subject itself to.[242] Applying this to ritual slaughter, Porat argues that there are several factors which indicate that bias is at play: (i) the number of exceptions for killing without stunning where it is part of 'small-scale' or 'home' slaughter, he argues that this is discriminatory as ritual slaughter is invariably done in commercial abattoirs and thus cannot benefit from the exemptions;[243] (ii) commercial methods for killing chickens and pigs involve substantial pain;[244] (iii) other practices which involve pain and suffering for animals are not prohibited, such as dehorning, castration and branding, and the fact that hunting is permitted.[245] Porat thus argues that concentrating campaigns against religious minority practices rather than against majority practices which result in much greater harm to a greater number of animals is an indication of majority-based bias. It is worth noting that Porat concludes that if we had a society that fully committed itself to not hurting animals for human benefit that he would accept that religious minorities would not have a right to claim an exception to that. His reasoning being that if society fully commits itself to such a principle there is no special reason to suspect that it is motivated by bias.

[241] Elien Verniers, 'Executief van de Moslims van Belgie and others v Belgium: The ECtHRs Perspective on Balancing Animal Welfare with Religious Freedom' Strasbourg Observers, 8 May 2024; Harriet Ní Chinnéide and Dr Cathérine Van de Graaf, 'Prohibition of Religious Slaughter in Executief van de Moslims van Belgie and others v. Belgium: Process-Based Review and a New Legitimate Aim', Strasbourg Observers, 26 April 2024; Gerhard van der Schyff, 'Five Remarks on Freedom of Religion and Ritual Slaughter: Executief van de Moslims van België and Others v. Belgium' and Sian Devriendt and Carla M. Zoethout, 'Animal Welfare and the Evolution of Public Morality: Requirement to Stun Animals Prior to Ritual Slaughter is Convention-Proof' *EJIL:Talk!*, 26 April 2024.

[242] Iddo Porat 'The Starting at Home Principle: On Ritual Animal Slaughter, Male Circumcision and Proportionality' (2021) 41(1) OJLS 30.

[243] Ibid, p.46. [244] Ibid, p.47. [245] Ibid, pp.47–48.

The ritual slaughter case law raises many points for consideration, and it is likely that there will be further jurisprudence based on the principles developed in *Executief van de Moslims van België*. For now, however, the Grand Chamber has refused to hear an appeal from the Chamber's judgment so we will not have the benefit of a fuller judgment any time soon.

13.5.4.4 *Restrictions while in Detention*

There are numerous cases relating to restrictions on manifestations of belief during detention, particularly restrictions on worship. For example, in *Korostelev* v. *Russia*, the ECtHR held that reprimanding a Muslim prisoner for performing acts of worship at night violated Article 9 ECHR.[246] The ECtHR accepted the importance of prison discipline, but did not accept that this warranted a formalistic approach, which did not strike a fair balance between the competing interests. A violation of Article 9 ECHR was also found in *Abdullah Yalçinn* v. *Turkey (No.2)* where no provision had been made for communal Friday prayers in a high security prison.[247] The violation in that case was found on the basis that the authorities had failed to demonstrate that they had weighed the competing interests at stake and considered possible options for facilitating the prayers.[248] The courts have emphasised that while the positive obligation to facilitate worship requires the striking of a fair balance between competing interests, it does not mandate that provision must be made for all prisoners on every possible occasion. Consequently, in *Abdullah Ahmed Ali* v. *SSHD* it was held that there was no violation when weekly prayers were generally facilitated but were not offered on fourteen occasions over an eight month period.[249]

The conditions in which a prisoner has to carry out acts of worship in detention may also violate Article 9 ECHR. For example, in *R (on the application of Hussein)* v. *SSHD* it was determined that a lock-in regime at an immigration centre, under which practising Muslims who wished to adhere to mandatory prayer times had to do so in their rooms, in the presence of other detainees and close to a lavatory cubicle without a door, breached Article 9 ECHR.[250] However, in a later case, *R (on the application of Soltany)* v. *SSHD*, the High Court judge declined to follow *Hussein* on the basis that more extensive evidence had been put before his Court and he was not bound by the earlier conclusion.[251] He held that there was no interference with Article 9 ECHR, or in the alternative that any interference was justified in the context of

246 *Korostelev* v. *Russia* (2022) 75 EHRR 17.

247 *Abdullah Yalçinn* v. *Turkey (No.2)*, App. No. 34417/10, 14/06/2022.

248 Ibid at [31]–[36]. 249 *Abdullah Ahmed Ali* v. *SSHD* [2024] EWHC 2829 at [38]–[39].

250 *R (on the application of Hussein)* v. *SSHD* [2018] EWHC 213 (Admin).

251 *R (on the application of Soltany)* v. *SSHD* [2020] EWHC 2291 (Admin).

the lockdown.[252] The background to *Soltany* was that during lockdown, detainees were locked in their rooms between 9pm and 8am. This was a longer and more restrictive lock-in than in other detention centres which led to several complaints, but the one that is relevant here is that Muslim detainees were required to perform prayers in their room during the lock-in. In some cases, this meant that they had to face the toilet whilst they prayed, whilst in every case they were in very close proximity to the toilet. The High Court held that this did not completely prevent them from manifesting their religion or go against the very essence of their freedom and thus there was no interference.[253] In any event, the Judge went on to conclude that even if there was an interference, it was justified as it 'was within the scope of the Defendant's lawful discretion'.[254] This approach arguably conflicts with the least restrictive means approach to proportionality that was evident in *Philip* v. *Scottish Ministers.*[255] There are various parts of the reasoning in *Soltany* which are deeply concerning and difficult to reconcile with the values of respect and dignity, in particular, the Judge's determination that there was no interference because 'if a roommate chose to use the toilet whilst a Muslim detainee was praying, or if there were particularly strong odours emanating from the toilet, the Muslim detainee could pause in his prayers until the roommate had finished and/or the worst of the odours had dissipated'.[256]

Cases have also arisen in respect of dietary requirements during imprisonment. As noted above, in *Jakóbski* v. *Poland* the ECtHR held that failure to provide a vegetarian diet to a Buddhist prisoner violated Article 9 ECHR.[257] The fact that States may be obliged to cater for such diets brings to the fore the question as to how States can establish the genuineness of the applicant's beliefs.[258] This arose in *Neagu* v. *Romania* in which the ECtHR held that requiring 'documentary proof of adhering to a specific faith' went beyond the level of substantiation of genuine belief that could be required.[259]

13.5.4.5 *Right Not to Practice Religion and Not to Reveal Religion*

Thus far we have been considering the right to practice and observe a religion or belief, but it is important to note that Article 9 ECHR also includes the right not to belong to a religion and not to practice it. The Grand Chamber has therefore held that a requirement to take an oath on the Gospels is tantamount to being required to swear allegiance to a particular religion, which is not compatible with Article 9 ECHR.[260] Article 9 ECHR also prohibits the State

[252] Ibid at [374]–[375]. [253] Ibid at [375]. [254] Ibid at [369].

[255] *Philip* v. *Scottish Ministers* (n 43). [256] R (*on the application of Soltany*) (n 251) at [370].

[257] *Jakóbski* v. *Poland* (n 141). [258] Ibid.

[259] *Neagu* v. *Romania*, App. No. 21969/15, 10/11/2020.

[260] *Buscarini* v. *San Marino* [GC] (2000) 30 EHRR 208.

from requiring an individual to reveal their beliefs.[261] The ECtHR has thus held that a 'religion' box on an identity card violates Article 9 ECHR on the basis that leaving the box blank would have specific connotations.[262] Equally the Court has held that a birth certificate revealing the parents' choice not to christen their child violated the right.[263]

13.5.5 Restrictions on Religious Clothing

An important manifestation for some religions is the practice of wearing religious clothing. In this regard the ECtHR has recognised that the right to manifest one's belief through clothing is vital to both the individual and to society because a 'healthy democratic society needs to tolerate and sustain pluralism and diversity'.[264] This right is not, however, absolute and there are various contexts in which the ECtHR has accepted that restrictions can be imposed either directly on the wearing of religious clothing or indirectly by prohibiting, for example, face coverings. Consequently, as we will see in this section, the ECtHR has allowed States to impose stringent restrictions in a number of contexts, most notably educational contexts, public services and public places. Some of these restrictions are temporary, for example, a requirement to remove a head covering during an airport security check, while others are continuous, for example a prohibition on wearing a religious headscarf in a school, university or public hospital. The most expansive restrictions are those that are permanent and apply in all public places. Indeed, in recent years there has been a rise in legislation across European States prohibiting the wearing of clothing that covers the face in public places. This has particularly affected some members of the Islamic faith and the issues raised by such restrictions has given rise to one of the most controversial cases in the ECtHR's jurisprudence, *S.A.S.* v. *France*, which resulted in the ECtHR being criticised for failing to protect Islam.

13.5.5.1 Educational Context

States enjoy a wide margin of appreciation when imposing restrictions on the wearing of religious clothing in State educational settings. These restrictions can apply to both teachers and students.

One of the arguments advanced by States when justifying the imposition of restrictions on teachers is that wearing such clothing in the classroom can

[261] *Stavropoulos* v. *Greece* (2021) 72 EHRR 5.

[262] *Sinan Isik* v. *Turkey*, App. No. 21924/05, 02/02/2010.

[263] *Stavropoulos* v. *Greece* (n 261).

[264] *Eweida* v. *the United Kingdom* (n 51) at [94].

have a proselytising effect on students.[265] The ECtHR accepted this rationale in *Dahlab* v. *Switzerland* and held that there was no violation of Article 9 ECHR when a primary school teacher was prohibited from wearing an Islamic headscarf. In coming to that conclusion, the ECtHR controversially stated that:

> it cannot be denied outright that the wearing of a headscarf might have some kind of proselytising effect, seeing that it appears to be imposed on women by a precept which is laid down in the Koran and which, as the Federal Court noted, is hard to square with the principle of gender equality. It therefore appears difficult to reconcile the wearing of an Islamic headscarf with the message of tolerance, respect for others and, above all, equality and non-discrimination that all teachers in a democratic society must convey to their pupils.[266]

The ECtHR's interpretation of the Koran and its relationship to gender equality is contentious. Moreover, concerns as to the ECtHR's stance on Islam are compounded by the fact that whilst the ECtHR held that the headscarf may have a proselytising effect in *Dahlab*, in *Lautsi* it held that a crucifix in a classroom was a passive symbol.[267] This raises concerns as to the ECtHR's approach to different faiths and their traditions.

A further point to observe is that whilst the ECtHR found the restrictions in *Dahlab* justified on the basis that the headscarf may have a proselytising effect on *young children*, in other cases it has accepted restrictions in the context of higher education. For example, in *Kurtulmuş* v. *Turkey* the ECtHR found no violation when a disciplinary sanction was imposed on an associate professor at a State university for wearing the Islamic headscarf in the performance of her teaching duties.[268] The rationale advanced, and accepted in that case was that a State is entitled to require its public servants to be loyal to the constitutional principle of secularism. Consequently, there are two aims that may be drawn upon to justify restrictions in educational settings, proselytism and secularism.

States have also advanced secularism as a justification for prohibiting *students* from wearing religious clothing. For example, as discussed earlier in the chapter, the ECtHR accepted in *Leyla Şahin* v. *Turkey* that the constitutional principle of secularism justified restrictions on university students.[269] Meanwhile, in *Köse and Others* v. *Turkey*, the ECtHR accepted that prohibiting secondary school students from wearing the Islamic headscarf was justified by the need to preserve the neutrality of secondary education for teenagers liable to be exposed to a risk of pressure.[270]

Both those cases concerned Turkey (now known as Türkiye), but French law also prohibits the wearing of clothing manifesting religious affiliation in

[265] *Dahlab* v. *Switzerland* (dec.), App. No. 42393/98, 15/02/2001. [266] Ibid.

[267] *Lautsi* v. *Italy* (n 52). [268] *Kurtulmuş* v. *Turkey*, App. No. 65500/01, 24/01/2006.

[269] *Leyla Şahin* v. *Turkey* (n 55).

[270] *Köse and Others* v. *Turkey* (dec.), App. No. 26625/02, 24/01/2006.

schools. In a series of cases the ECtHR has accepted that this is justified by the constitutional principle of secularism.[271] It is worth contrasting that stance with that of the UN Human Rights Committee which found a violation of the right to freedom of religion (Article 18 ICCPR) when a Sikh student was prohibited from wearing a turban at a French public school.[272]

In the UK there are no national laws restricting the wearing of religious clothing in schools, but issues have arisen in respect of individual school uniform policies. A famous example of this is the case of *R (on the application of Begum)* v. *Denbigh High School* where it was argued that a school uniform policy which prohibited the wearing of the jilbab violated Article 9 ECHR.[273] It is important to observe that Denbigh High School had not prohibited the wearing of all religious dress; on the contrary, it had formulated a uniform policy in consultation with the Imams of local mosques and three uniform options were available, one of which was the shalwar kameeze, no objections had been raised during the consultation process to the shalwar kameeze, and no suggestion had been made that it failed to satisfy Islamic requirements. For two years Shabina Begum wore the shalwar kameeze, but at the start of her third year Shabina (then aged nearly fourteen) went to the school with her brother and another young man who insisted that Shabina must wear a jilbab. They argued that this was the only garment which met her religious requirements because it concealed, to a greater extent than the shalwar kameeze, the contours of the female body. The headteacher subsequently wrote to the family stating that Shabina must attend school and must wear the school uniform. Shabina's brother replied stating that he would not allow her to attend unless she wore the jilbab.

Legal proceedings followed in which it was argued that the uniform policy violated Article 9 ECHR. The case went to the House of Lords and the Lords were split on the question of whether the policy interfered with Article 9 ECHR.[274] Lord Bingham, after considering the Strasbourg jurisprudence, determined that there is no interference with Article 9 ECHR if the claimant has voluntarily accepted a role which gives rise to an obligation that conflicts with their beliefs and there are other means open to them to manifest their beliefs without undue hardship or inconvenience.[275] Applying this to the facts, he observed that Shabina freely chose the school, that there were three other schools in the area where she could have worn the jilbab, and that she could have easily changed school.[276] That view was shared by Lord Hoffmann and Lord Scott.[277] It was not, however, welcomed by commentators who observed

[271] *Gamaleddynv* v. *France* (dec.), App. No. 18527/08, 30/06/2009; *Aktas* v. *France* (dec.), App. No. 43563/08, 30/06/2009; *Ranjit Singh* v. *France* (dec.), App. No. 27561/08, 30/06/2009; *Jasvir Singh* v. *France* (dec.), App. No. 25463/08, 30/06/2009.

[272] *Bikramjit Singh* (CCPR/C/106/D/1852/2008).

[273] *Begum* v. *Denbigh High School* (n 132).

[274] Ibid.

[275] Ibid at [23]–[25].

[276] Ibid.

[277] Ibid at [50]–[51] and [89].

that '[a] finding of "no interference" . . . constitutes a poor basis on which to determine Miss Begum's case'.[278] It is worth pausing at this juncture to observe that at the time Lord Bingham's approach was grounded in ECHR case law but since then the ECtHR has changed its approach such that it will no longer find that there is no interference with Article 9 ECHR if a measure can be circumvented.[279]

In *Begum* v. *Denbigh High School*, Lady Hale and Lord Nicholls reached a different (and preferable) conclusion on the first question as they felt that there may have been an interference with Article 9 ECHR.[280] In this regard, Lady Hale emphasised that as it is usually a child's parents that choose a school, she was uneasy with assuming that Shabina had voluntarily accepted this.[281] Consequently, as the Lords were split on the question of whether there was an interference, consideration was given to whether any interference could be justified. On this question the Lords all agreed that any interference was justified. They observed that the school had 'taken immense pains to devise a uniform policy which respected Muslim beliefs . . . in an inclusive, unthreatening and uncompetitive way'.[282] Consequently, they held that it would be 'irresponsible of any court, lacking the experience, background and detailed knowledge of the head teacher, staff and governors, to overrule their judgment on a matter as sensitive as this'.[283] Lady Hale in particular observed that the school policy was 'a thoughtful and proportionate response to reconciling the complexities of the situation'[284] and that girls at the School had 'expressed their concern that if the jilbab were to be allowed they would face pressure to adopt it even though they do not wish to do so'.[285]

13.5.5.2 Public Services

Another important aspect of the case law relates to the wearing of religious clothing in public establishments such as ministries, courts, local authorities

[278] Nicholas Gibson, 'Faith in the Courts: Religious Dress and Human Rights' (2007) **66**(3) CLJ 657, 669. See further, criticism in Mark Hill and Russell Sandberg, 'Is Nothing Sacred? Clashing Symbols in a Secular World' (2007) PL **488**. For further analysis of this approach, see also Sheldon Leader, 'Freedom and Futures: Personal Priorities, Institutional Demands and Freedom of Religion' (2007) **90**(5) MLR 713.

[279] *Eweida* v. *the United Kingdom* (n 51) at [83].

[280] *R (on the application of Begum)* v. *Denbigh High School* (n 132) at [41] and [92]–[93].

[281] Ibid at [92]–[93].

[282] Ibid at [34]. For discussion and critique of the deference to local knowledge, see Anastasia Vakulenko, 'Islamic Dress in Human Rights Jurisprudence: A Critique of Current Trends' (2007) **7**(4) HRLR 717, Gareth Davies, 'The House of Lords and Religious Clothing in *Begum* v. *Head Teacher and Governors of Denbigh High School*' (2007) **13**(3) European Public Law 423.

[283] *R (on the application of Begum)* v. *Denbigh High School* (n 132) at [34].

[284] Ibid at [98].

[285] Ibid.

and public hospitals. In respect of State representatives and employees working in public services, the ECtHR has accepted that States can justify restrictions as necessary to the State's secular constitutional model. In this respect the ECtHR has accepted that strict religious neutrality may be necessary in order to protect the rights and interests of public service users, especially where the latter are in a vulnerable situation. The ECtHR has thus held that restrictions in State hospitals are justified on the basis that patients are entitled to enjoy equal treatment without distinction based on religion.[286] It therefore found no violation when a Muslim woman's contract was not renewed following her refusal, after receiving a warning, to remove her Islamic headscarf whilst working in a French hospital.[287] On that occasion the ECtHR observed that the measure was underpinned by the need to ensure respect for the religious beliefs of the patients with whom she was in contact and reassure them that as users of a public service they were treated on an equal footing by the State, whatever their own religious beliefs.[288] An alternative perspective is that it may have been reassuring to patients to be treated in a multicultural environment as this would have assured them of equality.

As users of public services are not State representatives, they are not bound by a duty of discretion in the public expression of their religious beliefs.[289] The general rule is therefore that users of public services are free to express their religious beliefs inside a public building or in their dealings with the public authorities. This freedom is not absolute and the ECtHR has accepted that in some cases a court may be able to order a witness to remove a religious symbol in a courtroom.[290] However, in the case of *Hamidović* v. *Bosnia and Herzegovina* a violation was found where a witness was fined for refusing to remove his skullcap when testifying.[291] The ECtHR considered that the State had overstepped the wide margin of appreciation afforded to it as the applicant was not a public official; he had been required to testify on pain of sanction; his attitude had been clearly inspired by his sincere religious belief that he should wear his skullcap at all times; he had had no secret intention of disrupting or making a mockery of the trial; and he had appeared in court and stood up when requested, making it clear that he respected the State's laws and courts.[292] The ECtHR adopted the same approach in *Lachiri* v. *Belgium* in finding a violation in respect of a Muslim woman who had been expelled from a courtroom for refusing to remove her headscarf.[293] The ECtHR emphasised that she had in no way been disrespectful or threatened the proper conduct of the hearing.[294] In England and Wales the Equal Treatment Bench-Book

[286] *Ebrahimian* v. *France* (n 115) at [53]. [287] Ibid. [288] Ibid.

[289] Ibid at [64]; *Lachiri* v. *Belgium*, App. No. 3413/09, 18/09/2018 at [44].

[290] *Hamidović* v. *Bosnia and Herzegovina* (n 73) at [41]. [291] Ibid. [292] Ibid.

[293] *Lachiri* v. *Belgium* (n 289). [294] Ibid.

observes that the wearing of the veil in court is a very sensitive matter, in this regard it strives to provide some general guidance, while also observing that the wearing of the veil in court remains very much a matter of judicial discretion, unless and until an appellate court gives guidance.[295]

13.5.5.3 Workplace

Thus far, we have seen that restrictions on State employees may be justified by reference to secularism, but what about employees of private organisations? Can commercial organisations mandate a neutral image for their business? These questions arose in *Eweida* v. *the United Kingdom*, a case in which the first applicant, Eweida, was prohibited from wearing a cross while working as a British Airways flight attendant.[296] In this respect the ECtHR held that whilst an employer may wish to project a specific commercial image and that this can sometimes lead to restrictions on the wearing of religious symbols, those interests are not absolute and must be weighed against the individual's right to manifest their religion.[297] On the facts the ECtHR found that the policy violated Article 9 ECHR, as whilst Eweida had been prohibited from displaying a Christian cross, other religious symbols such as the turban or hijab were permitted.[298]

Having considered restrictions based upon secularism and brand identity, it is important to note that there may be other reasons for prohibiting the wearing of certain items in the workplace. An example of this can be seen in the case of the second applicant in *Eweida*, Chaplin, who was also prohibited from wearing a cross at work. Chaplin was a nurse who worked for the NHS, and was thus a State employee. It is important to note, however, that she was prohibited from wearing the cross at work *not* because of State secularism, but because of concerns that the cross posed a risk of infection across patients. Chaplin had thus been offered the option of securing her cross and chain to the lanyard which held her identity badge, with a requirement that she remove it when performing close clinical duties (again to minimise the risk of infection); however, she had refused to do this. In considering whether there had been a violation of Article 9 ECHR, the ECtHR recognised that whilst this was an important manifestation of her Christian faith, the protection of health and safety on a hospital ward was an important competing interest. Moreover, it went on to state that this is a field where the domestic authorities must be allowed a wide margin of appreciation as the hospital managers were better placed to make decisions about clinical safety than a court, particularly an

[295] Judicial College, *Equal Treament Bench Book,* July 2024 at [14].

[296] *Eweida* (n 51).

[297] Ibid at [94].

[298] Ibid at [94]–[95]. The ECtHR held that it was not necessary to examine separately her complaint under Article 14 taken in conjunction with Article 9.

international court which had heard no direct evidence; it thus held that it was unable to conclude that the measures were disproportionate. It followed that the interference with her freedom to manifest her religion was necessary in a democratic society and that there was no violation of Article 9 ECHR. It also rejected her application based on Article 9 coupled with Article 14 ECHR for similar reasons.

13.5.5.4 Public Places

The ECtHR has consistently held that compulsory temporary removal of religious clothing for safety reasons or security reasons is justifiable. It is therefore legitimate for a State to impose a fine on a Sikh for refusing to wear a crash helmet on a motorcycle.[299] It is also legitimate for the State to require the removal of a turban when passing through the walk-through scanner at an airport,[300] or the removal of a veil during an identity check at a consulate.[301] Obligations to appear with the head uncovered in identity photographs have also been upheld in relation to Muslim and Sikh applicants.[302]

Yet whilst those cases concerned temporary removals, cases have also arisen in respect of permanent prohibitions on the wearing of religious clothing in public places. In *Ahmet Arslan and Others* v. *Turkey* the ECtHR found a violation of Article 9 ECHR when the applicant was convicted for wearing certain religious dress in public,[303] as on that occasion the ECtHR found that the necessity of the measure had not been established.[304] However, in the landmark case, *S.A.S.* v. *France*, the Grand Chamber held that there was no violation when France prohibited wearing clothing designed to conceal one's face in public.[305] The ECtHR distinguished this from *Ahmet Arslan* on the basis that the prohibition in France related only to the covering of the face and was not explicitly based on the religious connotation of the clothing.[306]

S.A.S. v. *France* is a case which requires close examination. The applicant argued that French law prohibited her from wearing the Islamic face veil in public and that this violated Article 9 ECHR. She explained that she wore the burqa and niqab to live in accordance with her religious faith, culture and personal convictions.[307] She added that she wore this of her own accord in public and in private, that she was content not to wear it in certain circumstances but she wished to be able to wear it when she chose to do so.[308] There

[299] *X* v. *the United Kingdom* (dec.), App. No. 7992/77, 12/07/1978.

[300] *Phull* v. *France* (dec.), App. No. 35753/03, 11/01/2005.

[301] *El Morsli* v. *France* (dec.), App. No. 15585/06, 04/03/2008.

[302] *Karaduman* v. *Turkey* (dec.), App. No. 16278/90, 03/05/1993; *Araç* v. *Turkey* (dec.), App. No. 69037/01, 21/09/2006; *Mann Singh* v. *France* (dec.), App. No. 24479/07, 13/11/2008.

[303] *Ahmet Arslan and Others* v. *Turkey*, App. No. 41135/98, 23/02/2010.

[304] Ibid.

[305] *S.A.S.* v. *France* (n 125).

[306] Ibid at [151].

[307] Ibid at [11].

[308] Ibid at [12].

were also certain times (for example, during religious events such as Ramadan) when she believed that she ought to wear it to express her religious, personal and cultural faith.[309] She argued that the ban meant that she had to either refrain from dressing in accordance with her beliefs or refuse and face criminal sanctions.[310]

The Government argued that whilst the law prohibited her from wearing such clothing in public this was justified as the restriction was necessary for public safety, and the protection of the rights and freedoms of others.[311] The ECtHR accepted that the measure pursued the legitimate aim of public safety.[312]

In respect of the legitimate aim of protecting the rights of others, France advanced three arguments. First, France argued that covering the face broke social ties and manifested a refusal of the principle of 'living together'.[313] Second, it argued that the ban sought to protect equality between men and women.[314] Third, it argued that it was a matter of respect for human dignity since 'the women who wore such clothing were ... "effaced" from the public space'.[315]

S.A.S. strongly opposed the gender equality and human dignity arguments. She contended that feminist argument supports the wearing of the veil as the 'wearing of the veil often denote[s] women's emancipation, self-assertion and participation in society'.[316] Consequently 'as far as she was concerned, it was not a question of pleasing men but of satisfying herself and her conscience'.[317] She also found it ironic that an abstract idea of gender equality could run counter to the profoundly personal choice of women who decided to wear veils, and contended that imposing legal sanctions exacerbated inequality.[318] Moreover, she argued that the French Government was advancing arguments based on stereotyping and chauvinistic logic and the assumption that women who wore veils were 'effaced'.[319] S.A.S.'s arguments were supported by studies provided by third party interveners which indicated that women who wore the veil did so voluntarily and that those who had given up the practice had done so mainly as a result of public hostility.[320] The Government disputed those studies arguing that they were based on a small, unreliable sample.[321]

Ultimately, S.A.S. was successful in convincing the ECtHR to reject the Government's gender equality. On this issue it stated that:

> a State Party cannot invoke gender equality in order to ban a practice that is defended by women – such as the applicant – in the context of the exercise of the rights enshrined in those provisions, unless it were to be understood that individuals could

[309] Ibid at [12]. [310] Ibid at [69] and [76]–[80]. [311] Ibid at [81]–[85].
[312] Ibid at [115]. [313] Ibid at [82]. [314] Ibid at [82]. [315] Ibid at [82].
[316] Ibid at [77]. [317] Ibid at [77]. [318] Ibid at [77]. [319] Ibid at [77].
[320] Ibid at [77]. [321] Ibid at [82].

be protected on that basis from the exercise of their own fundamental rights and freedoms.[322]

The ECtHR also rejected the Government's 'dignity' rationale:

> however essential it may be, respect for human dignity cannot legitimately justify a blanket ban on the wearing of the full-face veil in public places. The Court is aware that the clothing in question is perceived as strange by many of those who observe it. It would point out, however, that it is the expression of a cultural identity which contributes to the pluralism that is inherent in democracy. It notes in this connection the variability of the notions of virtuousness and decency that are applied to the uncovering of the human body. Moreover, it does not have any evidence capable of leading it to consider that women who wear the full-face veil seek to express a form of contempt against those they encounter or otherwise to offend against the dignity of others.[323]

Yet whilst the ECtHR rejected both the gender and dignity arguments, the Court's suggestion that the veil is 'perceived as strange' set the scene for the most controversial aspect of *S.A.S.*, in which it accepted that covering the face breaks social ties and manifests a refusal of the principle of 'living together'.[324] The essence of France's argument here was that the face plays an important role in social interaction and that wearing the veil breaches the right of others to live in a space of socialisation which makes living together easier. The ECtHR accepted that this was a legitimate aim which could justify the prohibition.[325]

Thus, having accepted that the ban pursued the legitimate aims of public safety and living together, the ECtHR then turned to the question of necessity. In respect of public safety, it held that a blanket ban could only be justified where there was a general threat to public safety and France had not shown this to be the case.[326] In the absence of such a threat, the objective of public safety could be achieved by an obligation to show one's face where a risk had been established. It could not therefore be said that the ban was necessary, in a democratic society, for public safety.[327]

However, in respect of the living together argument, the ECtHR found that the ban was justified.[328] It observed that the question of whether it should be permissible to wear the full-face veil in public was a choice for society and that the ECtHR had a duty to exercise restraint in its review since this would lead it to assess a balance that had been struck by means of a democratic process.[329] Consequently, a wide margin of appreciation should be conferred and having regard to the breadth of that margin the ban was proportionate.[330]

322 Ibid at [119]. 323 Ibid at [120]. 324 Ibid at [121]. 325 Ibid at [121]–[122].
326 Ibid at [139]. 327 Ibid at [139]. 328 Ibid at [140]–[158]. 329 Ibid at [154]–[155].
330 Ibid at [156]–[157].

The ECtHR also found that there was no violation of Article 14 ECHR coupled with either Article 8 or Article 9 ECHR.[331]

It is worth emphasising that the ECtHR was split 15:2. In their strongly dissenting judgment, Judges Nussberger and Jaderblom opposed what they regarded as the sacrifice of 'concrete individual rights guaranteed by the Convention to abstract principles'.[332] They rejected the 'living together' argument as 'far-fetched and vague' and noted that it stems from the ways in which the veil is perceived by others, interpretations that had been called into question by the applicant.[333] They also observed that even assuming those interpretations were correct, 'there is no right not to be shocked or provoked by different models of cultural or religious identity'.[334] Nor is there a right to enter into contact with other people in public places against their will.[335] Consequently, they found that there were no concrete rights that can be inferred from the abstract principle of living together.[336] In coming to that conclusion they highlighted the irony of the Court referring to the importance of pluralism, tolerance and broadmindedness whilst justifying a State restricting pluralism.[337]

Having rejected living together as a legitimate aim, they also challenged the conclusion that the measure was necessary in a democratic society. First, they rejected the idea that the State had a wide margin of appreciation given that the prohibition directly impacted religious faith and personal identity.[338] Second, they argued that there was clear European consensus that a ban was not needed as at the time forty-five of the forty-seven Contracting States did not prohibit the face veil in public.[339] Third, they contended that the ban would not liberate women but would only exclude them from society.[340] Fourth, they found that the Government had not demonstrated that it was impossible to adopt less restrictive means – for example awareness-raising and education.[341] Consequently, they concluded that the prohibition was disproportionate.

S.A.S. has been the subject of considerable academic criticism.[342] For example, Jill Marshall argues that the purpose of human rights law is 'to

331 Ibid at [159]. See also, Chapter 14 (Equality and Non-discrimination).

332 Ibid , joint partly dissenting opinion at [2]. 333 Ibid at [5]. 334 Ibid at [7].

335 Ibid at [8]. 336 Ibid at [10]. 337 Ibid at [13]–[14]. 338 Ibid at [15]–[24].

339 Ibid at [19]. 340 Ibid at [21]. 341 Ibid at [24].

342 See, for example, John Adenitire, 'SAS v. France: Fidelity to Law and Conscience' (2015) 1 EHRLR 78, John Adenitire, 'Has the European Court of Human Rights Recognised a Legal Right to Glance at a Smile?' (2015) 131 LQR 43, Shu-Perng Hwang, 'Margin of Appreciation in Pursuit of Pluralism? Critical Remarks on the Judgments of the European Court of Human Rights on the "Burqa Bans"' (2020) 20 HRLR 361, Kati Nieminen, 'Eroding the Protection against Discrimination: The Procedural and De-contextualised Approach to S.A.S. v. France' (2019) International Journal of Discrimination and Law 69. See also, Eva Brems (ed), *The Experiences of Face Veil Wearers in Europe and the Law* (Cambridge University Press, 2014).

empower individuals, recognizing and protecting their identities' and the ECtHR should not 'interpret concepts within the ECHR as constraining identities'.[343] Nor should it 'focus on how "others" perceive a person's personality and ban practices for that reason'.[344] A further criticism is offered by Kimberly Brayson who posits the prohibition as a form of colonial assimilation.[345] She argues that the whole debate concerning Islamic dress is subject to 'shifting legal justifications of gender oppression and national security [which] simultaneously obfuscate and enact a strategy of cultural and colonial assimilation that controls and regulates Islamic bodies in public space'.[346] She thus argues that the 'living together' doctrine results in 'structural discrimination against Muslim communities',[347] while secularism (in particular *laïcité*) creates 'the political space for the French state to suppress colonial narratives and pursue an assimilationist agenda through law'.[348]

S.A.S. nevertheless remains the current position of the ECtHR and it was followed in *Dakir* v. *Belgium*[349] and *Belcacemi and Oussar* v. *Belgium*,[350] when the ECtHR upheld a similar prohibition in Belgium.[351] Since then, there has been a rise in restrictions on the wearing of face coverings in public places in other Contracting States, a move which would now lend greater weight to the argument that there is a consensus on the need for such restrictions. Yet the necessity of such provisions also needs to be considered in the light of COVID-19 measures, which resulted in a situation in which compulsory face masks were required in France alongside the general legislative prohibition on face coverings. This brings to the fore the fact that the legislation, whilst not framed as such, was clearly directed towards religious dress. The intentions behind the legislation are also evident in calls in France to go further in restricting the wearing of religious dress in public places. Indeed, there have been some calls led by far-right political parties for restrictions on the wearing of the hijab.

13.5.6 Conscientious Objection

Article 9 ECHR refers to the right to freedom of conscience, but it does not explicitly state that there is a right to conscientious objection. Thus far the

For a contrary view, see Stéphane Mechoulan, 'The Case against the Face-Veil: A European Perspective' (2018) 16(4) International Journal of Constitutional Law 1267–1292.

343 Jill Marshall, '*SAS* v. *France: Burqa Bans and the Control or Empowerment of Identities*' (2015) 15 HRLR 377.

344 Ibid, p.378.

345 Kimberley Brayson, 'Of Bodies and Burkinis: Institutional Islamophobia, Islamic Dress and the Colonial Condition' (2019) 46(1) Journal of Law and Society 55.

346 Ibid, p.57. 347 Ibid, p.58. 348 Ibid, p.60.

349 *Dakir* v. *Belgium*, App. No. 4619/12, 11/07/2017.

350 *Belcacemi and Oussar* v. *Belgium*, App. No. 37798/13, 11/07/2017.

351 See Brems (n 342).

ECtHR has recognised a right to conscientious objection in the military context, but in other contexts there is considerable uncertainty as to whether, and if so to what extent, an individual can claim a right to conscientious objection under Article 9 ECHR.[352]

13.5.6.1 *Conscientious Objection in the Military Context*

Initially, the ECtHR refused to recognise a right to conscientious objection under Article 9 ECHR,[353] however, in *Bayatyan* v. *Armenia* the Court recognised such a right.[354] Bayatyan concerned a pacifist Jehovah's Witness who had been convicted for refusing to serve in the military. The applicant informed the authorities that he refused to serve and offered to carry out alternative civil service. There was, however, no alternative civil service and so when he was summoned he failed to report for duty and temporarily left his home for fear of being forcibly taken to the military. He was charged with draft evasion, sentenced to two and a half years' imprisonment and released on parole after serving about ten and a half months of his sentence.

The ECtHR held that, contrary to the jurisprudence of the Commission, Article 9 ECHR protects the right to conscientious objection in the military context.[355] This departure was justified by the Grand Chamber, inter alia, on the basis that 'the Convention is a living instrument which must be interpreted in the light of present-day conditions and of the ideas prevailing in democratic States today'.[356] After reviewing many European and international authorities, it found that almost all Contracting States and several international instruments, including the ICCPR and the EU Charter of Fundamental Rights, recognised a right to conscientious objection in the military context.[357] Hence, in line with the living instrument doctrine, it recognised a right within Article 9 ECHR and found that the imposition of a criminal sanction, where no allowance was made for the applicant's religious beliefs was not necessary in a democratic society.[358] The ECtHR reached the same conclusion in *Mushfig Mammadov* v. *Azerbaijan*.[359] It also found a violation in *Adyan* v. *Armenia* on the basis that whilst civilian service had been introduced, the system was not sufficiently distinguished from the military.[360]

[352] On the right to conscientious objection, see John Adenitire, *A General Right to Conscientious Objection: Beyond Religious Privilege* (Cambridge University Press, 2020).

[353] *Grandrath* v. *Germany* (dec.), App. No. 2299/64, 12/12/1966. *GZ* v. *Austria* (dec.), App. No. 5591/72, 02/04/1973. See also, *Khan* v. *Royal Air Force Summary Appeal Court* [2004] EWHC 2230 (Admin) in which it was held that there was no right to conscientious objection when a Muslim sought to object to participating in the Iraq war on the basis that his religious beliefs prohibited him from killing other Muslims.

[354] *Bayatyan* v. *Armenia* (n 1). [355] Ibid. [356] Ibid at [102]. [357] Ibid at [105]–[109].

[358] Ibid at [118]–[128].

[359] *Mushfig Mammadov* v. *Azerbaijan*, App. No. 14604/08, 17/10/2019.

[360] *Adyan* v. *Armenia*, App. No. 75604/11, 12/10/2017.

Recognising a right to conscientious objection inevitably requires consideration of whether States can require proof of belief. In *Dyagilev* v. *Russia*, the ECtHR held that if an individual requests exemption 'it is not oppressive or in fundamental conflict with freedom of conscience to require some level of substantiation of genuine belief and, if that substantiation is not forthcoming, to reach a negative conclusion'.[361] In this respect it is also important to note that whilst many of the cases concern Jehovah's Witnesses, the ECtHR has also found violations in respect of pacifists without religious beliefs.[362] Thus, an applicant does not have to adhere to a religion in order to be recognised as a conscientious objector.[363]

13.5.6.2 *Conscientious Objection and Abortion*

The ECtHR has refused to uphold a right to conscientious objection in respect of abortion in several cases. For example, in an early case the Commission held that an applicant who was opposed to abortion could not refuse to pay a percentage of the tax used for funding abortions.[364] In another case, the Commission determined that joint owners of a pharmacy could not refuse to sell the contraceptive pill on the grounds of their religious beliefs.[365] More recently the Court held in *Grimmark* v. *Sweden* that refusing to employ midwives who will not carry out abortions does not violate Article 9 ECHR.[366]

In England, Wales and Scotland, conscientious objection is provided for by s.4 of the Abortion Act 1967, while in Northern Ireland it is provided for by s.12 of the Abortion (Northern Ireland) (No.2) Regulations 2020. The scope of conscientious objection under the 1967 Act was considered by the Supreme Court in *Greater Glasgow Health Board* v. *Doogan (Scotland)*, a case which concerned two midwives of Roman Catholic faith who argued that their entitlement to conscientious objection extended to a refusal to delegate, supervise and/or support staff to participate in and provide care to patients throughout the termination process.[367] This was rejected by the Supreme Court which held that s.4 of the Abortion Act 1967 should be given a narrower reading.[368] In coming to that determination Lady Hale observed that

> it is a feature of conscience clauses generally within the health care profession that the conscientious objector be under an obligation to refer the case to a professional who

[361] *Dyagilev* v. *Russia* (2020) 71 EHRR 18 at [62].

[362] *Savda* v. *Turkey* (n 140); *Tarhan* v. *Turkey*, App. No. 9078/06, 17/07/2012.

[363] *Papavasilakis* v. *Greece*, App. No. 66899/14, 15/09/2016.

[364] *Bouessel du Bourg* v. *France* (dec.) (1993) 16 EHRR CD49.

[365] *Pichon and Sajous* v. *France* (dec.), App. No. 49853/99, 02/10/2001.

[366] *Grimmark* v. *Sweden* (dec.), App. No. 43726/17, 11/02/2020.

[367] *Greater Glasgow Health Board* v. *Doogan (Scotland)* [2014] UKSC 68, [2015] AC 640.

[368] Ibid at [37]–[41].

does not share that objection. This is a necessary corollary of the professional's duty of care towards the patient. Once she has assumed care of the patient, she needs a good reason for failing to provide that care. But when conscientious objection is the reason, another health care professional should be found who does not share the objection.[369]

Arguments were advanced during the proceedings that the provision should be read in line with Article 9 ECHR, but the Supreme Court deemed this to be a distraction as the question of whether an interference with Article 9 ECHR is proportionate is a context-specific question.[370] The Supreme Court also recognised that aside from s.44 of the Abortion Act 1967, there may be an argument that either under the HRA or the Equality Act the midwives' employers should have made reasonable adjustments to the requirements of their job to cater for their religious beliefs, but the Court held that this would depend upon issues of practicability which were better suited to resolution in the employment tribunal proceedings than in the judicial review proceedings that were before the Supreme Court.[371]

13.5.6.3 *Conscientious Objection and Non-discrimination*

A highly contentious aspect of the case law concerns claims by members of a faith that they have a right to conscientious objection in respect of provision of services to members of the LGBTQI+ community. These claims raise questions as to whether there is a right to conscientious objection in such circumstances and, in the event that there is, whether that right can be upheld if it conflicts with the rights of others not to be discriminated against. In domestic law, these claims are addressed through the Equality Act which is covered in further detail in Chapter 14. Consequently, while the focus here will be on the Article 9 ECHR arguments, this should be read in conjunction with that chapter.

Earlier in this chapter, we considered *Eweida* in respect of the first two applicants, who challenged restrictions on wearing religious items in their place of work;[372] there were, however, two other applicants, Ladele and McFarlane, who argued that Article 9 ECHR was violated when they were dismissed by their employers for refusing to provide services to same-sex couples. Ladele was a publicly employed marriage registrar, whilst McFarlane was a privately employed sex counsellor. Both applicants argued that their refusal to provide the services was based upon their religious beliefs and that their dismissal violated the Convention. Ladele argued that it violated Article 9 coupled with Article 14 ECHR, whilst McFarlane primarily focused on Article 9 ECHR. The ECtHR accepted in both cases that the applicants' conduct

[369] Ibid at [40]. [370] Ibid at [23]–[24]. [371] Ibid at [24].
[372] *Eweida v. the United Kingdom* (n 51).

was motivated by their faith and that Article 9 ECHR was applicable. In respect of Ladele, the ECtHR held that there was no violation of Article 9 coupled with Article 14 ECHR as the State was pursuing a legitimate aim and the measure was a proportionate one which fell within the State's margin of appreciation.[373] In respect of McFarlane, the Court observed that the State has positive obligations under Article 9 ECHR, but the State has a wide margin of appreciation in deciding where to strike the balance between McFarlane's right and the employer's interest in securing the rights of others.[374] In all the circumstances, the ECtHR held that the margin of appreciation had not been exceeded.

The finding of no violation in respect of Ladele was the subject of a vociferous dissent by Judges Vučinić and de Gaetano.[375] They argued that this was a matter of conscience and that this right is not subject to the limitation in Article 9(2) ECHR. Consequently, they asserted that once

> a *genuine* and *serious* case of conscientious objection is established, the State is obliged to respect the individual's freedom of conscience both positively (by taking reasonable and appropriate measures to protect the rights of the conscientious objector and negatively (by refraining from actions which punish the objector or discriminate against him or her).[376]

They went on to state that it was 'a combination of back-stabbing by her colleagues and the blinkered political correctness of the Borough of Islington (which clearly favoured "gay rights" over fundamental human rights) [that] eventually led to her dismissal',[377] a statement which has a distinct homophobic tone.

The dissenting judges were not, however, the only ones who opposed the way in which the ECtHR handled Ladele's case. Ian Leigh and Andrew Hambler argue that the ECtHR should have found a violation as it would have been possible to exempt Ladele without affecting the availability of registrars for same-sex civil partnerships.[378] They assert that as there would be no reduction of services the only harm that would have been caused is one of offence, which is not protected under the Convention. Consequently, they argue that Ladele's beliefs should have been accommodated.

An alternative and more multifaceted perspective grounded on substantive equality is offered by Sandra Fredman.[379] She argues that there is a distinction between claims of conscience that are not complicity based and those that are.

[373] Ibid at [106]. [374] Ibid at [109]–[110].

[375] Ibid, joint partly dissenting opinion of Judges Vučinić and de Gaetano.

[376] Ibid, joint partly dissenting opinion of Judges Vučinić and de Gaetano at [3] (emphasis in original).

[377] Ibid, joint partly dissenting opinion of Judges Vučinić and de Gaetano at [5].

[378] Ian Leigh and Andrew Hambler, 'Religious Symbols, Conscience and the Rights of Others' (2014) 3(1) Oxford Journal of Law and Religion 2–24.

[379] Sandra Fredman, 'Tolerating the Intolerant: Religious Freedom, Complicity and the Right to Equality' (2020) 9 Oxford Journal of Law and Religion 305.

> Whereas the former can be accommodated without imposing costs on specifically identified third parties, complicity-based claims 'are oriented towards third parties who do not share the claimant's beliefs about the conduct in question. For this reason, their accommodation has distinctive potential to impose material and dignitary harm on those the claimants condemn'.[380]

In these complicity cases she suggests that neither tolerance, nor State neutrality are determinative as these are both value judgments which disguise a hierarchy of values. She thus argues that 'in the context of complicity claims, there should be a hierarchy of values which places the right to substantive equality above the values attached to tolerance and neutrality respectively'.[381] The concept of substantive equality that she offers examines how to

> redress disadvantage (the distributive dimension); address stigma, stereotypes, prejudice, and violence (the recognition dimension); facilitate participation, voice, and social inclusion (the participative dimension) and accommodate difference, including through structural change (the transformative dimension).[382]

Another way of considering these challenges is the harm-centred approach offered by Farrah Raza.[383] She identifies four broad categories of harms which include: (i) endangering the health and safety of others; (ii) impeding access to rights, goods and services; (iii) constituting violations of dignity; and (iv) posing excessive practical costs.[384] Fredman and Raza consider the application of their approaches to a wide range of cases such as those that we consider in this section.

In the UK's domestic courts, there have been two high-profile cases concerning conscientious objection arguments that need to be considered. Both cases went to the Supreme Court and concerned the application of equality law; those elements are considered further in Chapter 14. The first case, *Bull* v. *Hall*, concerned B&B owners who refused to provide a double bed to a same-sex couple in a civil partnership on the basis that this was contrary to their Christian beliefs.[385] The couple, Preddy and Hall, successfully argued that the B&B owners had discriminated against them contrary to the Equality Act (Sexual Orientation) Regulations 2007 (these provisions have since been replaced by the Equality Act 2010). Non-discrimination is discussed in more detail in Chapter 14, but for now it is sufficient to note that the Regulations prohibited direct or unjustified indirect discrimination. In their appeal to the Supreme Court, the Bulls argued that they had not discriminated against the claimants as they had not differentiated on the basis of sexual orientation but rather on marital status (as they would not allow anyone who was not married to share a double bed). The Bulls also argued that the Regulations had to be

[380] Ibid, pp.306–307. [381] Ibid, p.306. [382] Ibid, p.312.

[383] Farrah Raza, *Religious Accommodation and Its Limits* (Hart, 2023). [384] Ibid.

[385] *Bull* v. *Hall* [2013] UKSC 73, [2013] 1 WLR 3741.

applied compatibly with their right to manifest their religious beliefs under Article 9 ECHR.

The Supreme Court unanimously dismissed their appeal. Three judges – Lady Hale, Lord Kerr and Lord Toulson – held that the policy constituted direct discrimination on grounds of sexual orientation, while Lord Neuberger and Lord Hughes considered that the policy constituted indirect discrimination which was not justified. All of the judges held that although the Regulations engaged Article 9 ECHR that this was a justified and proportionate restriction of the right of others in line with Article 9(2) ECHR such that there was no need to read down the Regulations.[386] In coming to that determination, Lady Hale held first that the Regulations were in pursuit of a legitimate aim, namely the rights of others, which includes not only Convention rights but also non-discrimination rights under ordinary law.[387] In considering whether the interference was necessary, Lady Hale reflected on whether an argument could be made that the measure was disproportionate on the basis that it obliged the B&B owners to provide a double bed when perhaps a compromise would have been to have provided a twin room.[388] Lady Hale rejected that position as follows:

> The legitimate aim was the protection of the rights and freedoms of Mr Preddy and Mr Hall. Whether that could have been done at less cost to the religious rights of Mr and Mrs Bull by offering them a twin bedded room simply does not arise in this case. But I would find it very hard to accept that it could.[389]

In this respect it is important to observe that she acknowledged that fundamental to the weight that should be accorded in any proportionality analysis is the importance of sexual orientation to identity and dignity:

> Heterosexuals have known this about themselves and been able to fulfil themselves in this way throughout history. Homosexuals have also known this about themselves but were long denied the possibility of fulfilling themselves through relationships with others. This was an affront to their dignity as human beings which our law has now (some would say belatedly) recognised. Homosexuals can enjoy the same freedom and the same relationships as any others. But we should not underestimate the continuing legacy of those centuries of discrimination, persecution even, which is still going on in many parts of the world. It is no doubt for that reason that Strasbourg requires 'very weighty reasons' to justify discrimination on grounds of sexual orientation. It is for that reason that we should be slow to accept that prohibiting hotel keepers from discriminating against homosexuals is a disproportionate limitation on their right to manifest their religion.[390]

[386] Ibid at [41]–[55]. [387] Ibid at [44]. [388] Ibid at [50]. [389] Ibid at [51].
[390] Ibid at [53].

She also firmly rejected the argument that the Regulations replaced legal oppression of one community (homosexual couples) with that of another (religious communities):

> If Mr Preddy and Mr Hall ran a hotel which denied a double room to Mr and Mrs Bull, whether on the ground of their Christian beliefs or on the ground of their sexual orientation, they would find themselves in the same situation that Mr and Mrs Bull find themselves today.[391]

Ilios Trispiotis commenting on the case agrees and concludes that the Bulls were:

> wrong when they were arguing that the courts should leave space for the 'alternative' lifestyles of devout people, who wish to live honouring their most important commitments in life. Strong protection for anti-discrimination legislation is not meant to constrict alternative lifestyles, but to achieve the exact opposite: to allow different, unconventional lifestyles to arise and flourish.[392]

Another important case is *Lee* v. *Ashers Baking Co Ltd*.[393] In this case the Supreme Court had to consider whether the Christian owners of a bakery, who refused to bake a cake with a slogan 'support gay marriage', had discriminated on the basis of sexual orientation. The bakery owners (the McArthurs) offered a service by which customers could request images or inscriptions to be iced onto a cake. In May 2014, Lee, a gay man, wished to take a cake to an event organised by campaigners for same-sex marriage in Northern Ireland. He placed an order for a cake with a depiction of Sesame Street characters 'Bert and Ernie' and the words 'Support Gay Marriage'. Mrs McArthur initially took the order, but later advised Lee that she could not in conscience produce such a cake and gave him a refund.

Lee brought proceedings arguing direct and indirect discrimination on grounds of sexual orientation, contrary to the Equality Act (Sexual Orientation) Regulations (Northern Ireland) 2006 (the SORs) and/or on grounds of religious belief or political opinion, contrary to the Fair Employment and

[391] Ibid at [54].

[392] Ilios Trispiotis, '"Alternative Lifestyles" and Unlawful Discrimination: The Limits of Religious Freedom in Bull v. Hall' (2014) EHRLR **39**, 48.

[393] *Lee* v. *Ashers Baking Co Ltd* [2018] UKSC 49, [2020] AC 413. There has been extensive analysis of this case including Christopher McCrudden, 'The *Gay Cake Case*: What the Supreme Court Did, and Didn't Decide in *Ashers* (2020) **9**(2) Oxford Journal of Law and Religion 238; Ilana Hirschberg, '*Lee* v. *Asher's Bakery*: The Final Tier' (2019) **8**(2) Oxford Journal of Law and Religion 422; Mariëtta D. C. van der Tol, 'Conscience and Cakes: Reaffirming the Distinction Between Institutional Duties and Individual Rights' (2020) **9**(2) Oxford Journal of Law and Religion 372; Rex Ahdar and Jessica Giles, 'The Supreme Courts' Icing on the Trans-Atlantic Cakes' (2021) **10**(1) Oxford Journal of Law and Religion 155 and Richard Moon, 'Conscientious Objection and the Politics of Cake-Making' (2020) **9**(2) Oxford Journal of Law and Religion 329.

Treatment (Northern Ireland) Order 1998 (FETO). His claim was supported by the Equality Commission for Northern Ireland. The district judge in the County Court found that this was direct discrimination on all three grounds. The McArthurs appealed to the Court of Appeal, arguing that this was incompatible with their Convention rights. The Court of Appeal dismissed that appeal, holding that Lee had suffered direct discrimination on grounds of sexual orientation and that it was not necessary to interpret the SORs to take account of the Convention rights.[394] The case then went to the Supreme Court.

The Supreme Court allowed the McArthur's appeal. Lady Hale handed down the unanimous judgment in which the Supreme Court held that this was not direct discrimination as the objection was to the message, not to the customer.[395] In respect of Article 9 ECHR, Lady Hale explained that it includes a right not to be obliged to manifest beliefs one does not hold.[396] Thus, while the McArthurs could not refuse to provide a cake to Lee they were not obliged to supply a cake with a message with which they profoundly disagreed.[397] Consequently, the applicable domestic provisions were not to be read or given effect in a way that would compel the McArthurs to do this, unless justification was shown, and the Court found that justification was lacking.[398]

In a postscript to her judgment, Lady Hale observed that after the Supreme Court hearing, but whilst the judgment was being prepared, the Supreme Court of the US had handed down *Masterpiece Cakeshop Ltd* v. *Colorado Civil Rights Commission*.[399] She distinguished the UK and US cases, emphasising that *Masterpiece Cakeshop* had concerned a Christian baker who refused to create a wedding cake for a gay couple because of his opposition to same-sex marriage and that there was no message on the cake. She emphasised that there is a clear distinction between refusing to produce a cake conveying a particular message and refusing to produce a cake because of the customer's characteristics.[400]

Scholars have been divided on *Lee* v. *Ashers*. Sarah Fraser-Butlin welcomes the decision as a 'vital affirmation of the fundamental importance of freedom of conscience and of speech'.[401] She notes that many would 'disagree with the stance of the McArthurs', but argues that the judgment 'represents an important waymark in the equality project, achieving a difficult balance between protecting minority groups from discrimination and ensuring religious freedom'.[402] She suggests that 'this balance is essential if we are to live in a truly

[394] *Lee* v. *Ashers Baking Co Ltd* [2016] NICA 39.

[395] *Lee* v. *Ashers Baking Co Ltd* (Supreme Court) (n 393) at [34]. [396] Ibid at [50].

[397] Ibid at [55]. [398] Ibid at [56].

[399] Ibid at [59], referring to *Masterpiece Cakeshop Ltd* v. *Colorado Civil Rights Commission* (2018) 138 s Ct 1719.

[400] Ibid at [62]. [401] Sarah Fraser Butlin, 'Cakes in the Supreme Court' (2019) **78**(2) CLJ 280.

[402] Ibid.

plural and diverse society'.[403] However, others such as Steve Foster argue that this 'does not address the issue of how the two opinions can be reconciled and balanced in practice, and what weight is to be placed on each view in conducting that balancing exercise'.[404] He argues that the Supreme Court 'ignore[d] the opportunity to set out the criteria for any balancing exercise in these cases, and instead assumed that there was no good reason for restricting the shop owners religious views and free speech, other than that their views conflicted with another's political opinions'.[405] In considering how these conflicts should be addressed, others have argued that different weights should be accorded to these interests. For example, Kenneth Norrie argues against what he regards as an 'unfortunate undercurrent throughout the Supreme Court's decision ... that all protected characteristics are of equal weight':

> Some characteristics are in need of more protection than others because of a long history of discrimination; some characteristics demand more protection because they are immutable (race, for example, and sexual orientation); others are chosen but not necessarily based on rational choice (political beliefs, religious beliefs). Opinions can change but skin colour cannot.[406]

His suggestion that faith is a choice is contentious, but there is no doubt that there is a long history of, as well as ongoing oppression of, the LGBTQI+ community. In this respect Jonathan Cooper QC argued that:

> [t]he *Ashers* judgment is more than a wasted opportunity to bolster the status quo. It is grim. Its implications cannot be underestimated and are more worrisome than the judgment itself. Our defences have been breached. Can we shore them up? Social media is already ablaze with those set to exploit it. There will be case after case seeking to use religious freedom to trump LGBTI equality. Can we have confidence in the ability of the Supreme Court to do the mental gymnastics to make sense of it all? Probably, but what about the rest of us? A new era has been ushered in and LGBTI people's mental health will pay the price.[407]

Following the Supreme Court's judgment, Lee applied to the ECtHR arguing that the UK had violated his Convention rights.[408] This application was declared inadmissible on the basis that he had not exhausted domestic

[403] Ibid, p.283.

[404] Steve Foster, 'Accommodating Intolerant Speech: Religious Free Speech Versus Equality and Diversity' (2019) 6 EHRLR 609–625, 614.

[405] Ibid.

[406] Kenneth Norrie, 'Lee v. Ashers Baking Co Ltd' (2019) 1 Juridical Review 88, 95. See also, Kenneth Norrie, 'What Level of Respect Does Opposition to Same-Sex Marriage Deserve in a Democratic Society?' (2023) **74**(3) NILQ 417.

[407] Paul Johnson, 'The Love of Law, and the Law of Love: Jonathan Cooper and LGBT Human Rights Advocacy' (2022) 1 EHRLR 33.

[408] Ibid.

remedies as he had failed to litigate the Convention rights issue before the domestic courts. The details of Lee's application, and the criticisms which have been levelled at the ECtHR's decision are considered further in Chapter 14 in the context of our analysis of non-discrimination. It is, however, worth emphasising one point here, which is that in *Lee* v. *the United Kingdom* the ECtHR stated that due to the 'heightened sensitivity of the balancing exercise in the particular national context [Northern Ireland] the domestic courts were better placed ... to strike the balance between the competing Convention rights'.[409] A statement that suggests that the ECtHR is willing to accord a wide margin of appreciation to States where issues relating to faith raise political challenges. Yet while the ECtHR often accords a wide margin of appreciation where two rights conflict, this is usually contingent upon the domestic authorities demonstrating that they have applied balancing criteria identified by the ECtHR. The problem in this context is that the ECtHR has not identified the criteria that the domestic authorities should be considering.

13.6 FREEDOM OF RELIGION VS. FREEDOM OF EXPRESSION

A final question that arises is whether the protection that is accorded to Article 9 ECHR justifies prohibiting the exercise of views that are critical of a religion or belief. This is important as the expression of views that are critical of a religion or belief may itself be protected by Article 10 ECHR, the right to freedom of expression. Consequently, in these cases Article 9 ECHR may conflict with Article 10 ECHR, and we need to determine where the balance should be struck between the two competing rights. Where such expression attacks not just the faith but members of that faith, then in certain circumstances this may amount to hate speech, which we have already considered in Chapter 11. Accordingly, in this chapter we focus on the expression of views that critique the faith or aspects of beliefs themselves (as opposed to the individual). In domestic law, historically this would have fallen within the ambit of the common law offence of blasphemy which applied in respect of Christianity and was abolished in 2008. However, other ECHR Contracting States have criminal offences in respect of disparaging religious precepts and this has given rise to case law before the ECtHR.

The ECtHR famously dealt with this in *Otto-Preminger Institute* v. *Austria*, a case that concerned the seizure and forfeiture of a satirical film found to be offensive on religious grounds.[410] The applicant, an art-house cinema, publicised the proposed showing of a film, giving a clear indication of its contents

[409] *Lee* v. *the United Kingdom* (dec.), App. No. 18860/19, 07/12/2021 at [76].

[410] *Otto-Preminger Institute* v. *Austria* (1995) 19 EHRR 34.

and prohibiting under seventeens from attending. The local Catholic church complained, criminal proceedings were brought, and the film was seized. Before the ECtHR the applicants argued that this violated Article 10 ECHR, but this was rejected by the Court which held that the interference was legitimate, not just to protect morals, but also to protect the right to religious freedom. In this regard it observed that whilst those who choose to exercise the freedom to manifest their religion 'cannot reasonably expect to be exempt from all criticism' the 'manner in which religious beliefs and doctrines are opposed or denied is a matter which may engage the responsibility of the State, notably its responsibility to ensure the peaceful enjoyment of the right guaranteed under Article 9'.[411] It went on to state that:

> respect for the religious feelings of believers as guaranteed in Article 9 ... can legitimately be thought to have been violated by provocative portrayals of objects of religious veneration; and such portrayals can be regarded as malicious violation of the spirit of tolerance, which must also be a feature of democratic society.[412]

Accordingly, it held that the seizure pursued the legitimate aim of the protection of the rights of others under Article 10(2) ECHR and that 'a certain margin of appreciation is ... to be left to the national authorities in assessing the existence and extent of the necessity of such interference'.[413]

Otto-Preminger was heavily criticised.[414] Moreover, the dissenting judges argued that contrary to what the Court had determined, the Convention does not 'guarantee a right to protection of religious feelings' and that such a 'right cannot be derived from the right to freedom of religion, which in effect includes a right to express views critical of the religious opinions of others'.[415] They accepted that protecting the religious feelings of certain members of society against criticism and abuse may be a legitimate aim for the purposes of Article 10(2) ECHR and that it may be 'necessary in a democratic society' to set limits to the public expression of such criticism or abuse, but not that there was a right under Article 9 ECHR. Consequently, they argued that whilst intervention may be justified in some circumstances a complete ban is only acceptable 'if the behaviour concerned reaches so high a level of abuse, and comes so close to a denial of the freedom of religion of others, as to forfeit for itself the right to be tolerated by society'.[416] On the facts, they found that this threshold was not met. This is important because if there is such a right to protection of religious feelings within Article 9 ECHR then this raises the

411 Ibid at [47]. 412 Ibid at [47]. 413 Ibid at [50].

414 See, e.g. David Pannick, 'Religious Feelings and the European Court' (1995) PL 7.

415 *Otto-Preminger Institute* v. *Austria* (n 410), joint dissenting opinion of Judges Palm, Pekkanen and Makarczyk at [6].

416 Ibid.

question as to when the State has a positive obligation to provide such protection.

Otto-Preminger was handed down in 1994 and so there was a considerable period of time in which it was uncertain as to whether the ECtHR would revisit this approach, and whether this approach would be applied in the context of other faiths. In 2018 the ECtHR returned to the issue in *E.S.* v. *Austria*, which concerned a criminal conviction for disparaging religious precepts in relation to Islam.[417] The applicant held seminars advertised as 'Basic information on Islam' at the far right-wing Freedom Party Education Institute, at one seminar (which was attended by an undercover journalist who later reported E.S. to the authorities), E.S. made disparaging remarks about the Prophet. Following this, E.S. was convicted of disparagement of religious precepts and sentenced to pay a fine of EUR 480 or serve sixty days' imprisonment in the event of default. E.S. argued that this violated Article 10 ECHR.

The ECtHR followed its reasoning in *Otto-Preminger* and held that there was no violation of Article 10 ECHR. It observed that Article 10(2) ECHR carries duties and responsibilities, which includes a 'duty to avoid as far as possible an expression that is, in regard to objects of veneration, gratuitously offensive to others and profane'.[418] It went on to state that where such expression goes beyond the 'limits of a critical denial of other people's religious beliefs' and 'is likely to incite religious intolerance, for example in the event of an improper or even abusive attack on an object of religious veneration' then a State may legitimately consider such expression 'to be incompatible with respect for the freedom of thought, conscience and religion and take proportionate restrictive measures'.[419] It also noted that expression that seeks 'to spread, incite or justify hatred based on intolerance, including religious intolerance' does not enjoy the protection afforded by Article 10 ECHR.[420] In this respect it noted that the nature of the impugned seminar was misleading and that the applicant could have anticipated that persons may be present who might be offended:

> The applicant's intervention was entitled 'Basic information on Islam' and was meant to be a critical analysis of Islamic doctrine, allowing for a discussion with the participants of the seminars. The title gave the – in hindsight misleading – impression that the seminars would include objective information on Islam. It appears that anyone interested was able to enrol; there was no requirement to be a member of the Freedom Party. The applicant therefore could not assume that there would only be like-minded people in the room who would share her very critical views of Islam, but had to expect that there could also be people among the audience who might be offended by her statements. It is of little relevance that only thirty people attended on average. The applicant's statements were in fact recorded by a journalist, who had participated in the seminar, and whose employer subsequently reported them to the public prosecutor.[421]

[417] *E.S.* v. *Austria* (2019) 69 EHRR 4. [418] Ibid at [43]. [419] Ibid. [420] Ibid.
[421] Ibid at [51].

The ECtHR went on to conclude that the domestic courts had comprehensively assessed the wider context of the applicant's statements, and carefully balanced the competing rights. They had regarded these statements as an abusive attack on Islam, which were capable of inciting prejudice, they had put forward relevant and sufficient reasons for this conclusion, and they had not overstepped their margin of appreciation.

Like *Otto-Preminger* before it, *E.S.* has been the subject of considerable criticism; Marko Milanovic argues that the Court's 'reasoning lacks rigour and fetishizes the national margin of appreciation'.[422] Moreover he argues that the:

> judgment will likely do nothing to promote religious tolerance in Europe, but will only help to further the narrative of Islamophobic closet neo-Nazis (who are, by the way, already in power in Austria, and not for the first time) that they are free speech martyrs, victimized in their own country by horrible minorities, elites and human rights lawyers.[423]

Yet Stijn Smet, whilst also criticising some aspects of the judgment, suggests that it was inevitable given the earlier *Otto-Preminger* judgment:

> the only major difference between both cases was the 'targeted' group. *Otto-Preminger* involved alleged offence to the religious feelings of the Christian majority. In *E.S.*, by contrast, the supposedly offended believers were Muslims, a religious minority in an Austria that is now (though not at the time of the facts) led by a right-wing populist government that targets Islam. Given this constellation, distinguishing *E.S.* or using it as an occasion to overrule *Otto-Preminger* would surely have opened the Court up to renewed claims of prejudice against Islam.[424]

Indeed, it is important to consider the broader context in which *E.S.* arose, namely that the impugned statement formed part of a far-right attack on Islam. From this perspective the judgment might be considered in the context of the ECtHR's developing hate speech case law and the difficulties that can arise in distinguishing between attacks on faiths and attacks on individuals of that faith. In this respect it is important to observe that in *Tagiyev* v. *Azerbaijan* the ECtHR held that a criminal conviction for inciting religious hatred and hostility violated Article 10 ECHR.[425] In *Tagiyev* it was held that whilst the content of the articles might be seen as an abusive attack on the Prophet of Islam and on Muslims living in Europe, capable of causing religious hatred, the domestic courts' decisions had given no explanation as to why the particular remarks had constituted incitement to religious hatred and hostility.

422 Marko Milanovic, 'Legitimising Blasphemy Laws through the Backdoor: The European Court's Judgment in *E.S.* v. *Austria*', *EJIL:Talk!*, 29/10/2018.

423 Ibid.

424 Stijn Smet, 'Free Speech versus Religious Feelings, the Sequel: Defamation of the Prophet Muhammad in *E.S.* v. *Austria*' (2019) 15 European Constitutional Law Review 158, 170.

425 *Tagiyev* v. *Azerbaijan* (2020) 71 EHRR 15.

The domestic courts had also failed to consider the public interest and the intention of the author and had not even attempted to balance freedom of expression with the protection of the right of religious people not to be insulted on the grounds of their beliefs. This was particularly important given that prison sentences of three and four years had been imposed.

Yet whilst the ECtHR increasingly requires States to demonstrate that they have balanced the competing interests, it provides limited insight into the criteria that they should use in doing so, especially when compared with the criteria that it has established in other contexts.[426] There is also considerable uncertainty as to when the State will have positive obligations under Article 9 ECHR, in a similar fashion to the uncertainty that prevails in respect of the positive obligation under Article 8 ECHR in the hate speech context. We may therefore anticipate further case law on these issues.

13.7 CONCLUSIONS

In this chapter we have seen that Article 9 ECHR protects both religious and non-religious beliefs and that there are two rights: a right to hold a belief and a right to manifest a belief. Although freedom to hold a belief is absolute, the right to manifest a belief is a qualified right. In principle, no special advantage is given to any particular religion or belief and the State should remain neutral in matters of religious and non-religious beliefs. Yet 'neutrality' takes different forms, from neutral pluralism (which accommodates diverging religious and non-religious beliefs) to *laïcité* (which seeks to confine religious expression to the private sphere), this is reflected in the case law and the latitude that is accorded to States. One of the consequences of this is that the ECtHR's case law in respect of religious clothing suggests that Islam does not fare well when compared to other religions. Thus, whilst in principle Article 9 ECHR protects religious freedom, we have to consider whether it provides adequate protection. Related to this is the question of what constitutes an interference with Article 9 ECHR and whether the conservative approach to this issue that is evident in some of the domestic case law is compatible with the Convention. Finally, it is apparent that difficulties arise when Article 9 ECHR conflicts with other competing rights, and in the absence of further guidance from the courts as to how this balance should be struck, it is likely that there will be further case law on these issues in the future.

[426] See, for example, the criteria that the ECtHR has developed in the context of deportation as discussed in Chapter 9 and in cases concerning privacy and freedom of expression as discussed in Chapter 10.

14 Non-discrimination and Equality

CONTENTS

14.1 INTRODUCTION

Human rights instruments in jurisdictions throughout the world assert the right to equality and non-discrimination. These principles lie at the heart of human rights. The first recital to the UDHR recognises their significance by confirming 'the equal and inalienable rights of all'. Moreover, the first two articles of the Declaration provide that 'All human beings are born free and equal in dignity and rights' and that '[e]veryone is entitled to all the rights and freedoms set forth in this Declaration, without distinction of any kind, such as race, colour, sex, language, religion, political or other opinion, national or social origin, property, birth or other status'.[1] The importance accorded to the equal enjoyment of rights is also reflected in the ECHR in which Article 1 ECHR states that the High Contracting Parties shall secure to *everyone* within their jurisdiction the rights and freedoms defined in Section I of this Convention. Meanwhile, Article 14 ECHR, which prohibits discrimination, provides that the enjoyment of the rights and freedoms set forth in this

[1] Other international treaties incorporate similar non-discrimination clauses. The International Covenant on Civil and Political Rights (ICCPR) art 26 and the International Covenant on Economic, Social and Cultural Rights (ICESCR) art 2.2. Some treaties have also directly dealt with specific facets of discrimination, e.g. the International Convention on the Elimination of All Forms of Racial Discrimination (CERD), the Convention on the Elimination of All Forms of Discrimination Against Women (CEDAW) and the Convention on the Rights of Persons with Disabilities (CRPD).

Convention shall be secured without discrimination on any ground such as sex, race, colour, language, religion, political or other opinion, national or social origin, association with a national minority, property, birth or other status. In many States, domestic constitutional provisions protect equality and non-discrimination, but in the UK, it is the Equality Act 2010 (EqA) which has transformed the piecemeal provisions against discrimination into a more coherent framework while the Human Rights Act 1998 has also extended domestic law.[2]

This chapter proceeds as follows. Section 2 of the chapter considers the meanings of equality and non-discrimination. Section 3 examines equality and non-discrimination in the context of Article 14 of the ECHR and considers race, religion, sex and gender as examples to illustrate the applicability of Article 14 ECHR to specific protected categories. Section 4 examines the application of Article 14 ECHR in domestic UK law. Section 5 examines the UK EqA and the complexities raised by competing equality claims.

14.2 MEANINGS OF EQUALITY AND NON-DISCRIMINATION

The meanings of equality and non-discrimination are 'elusive'[3] and highly contested.[4] How do we decide who should be protected and how this protection should be conceptualised in the legal framework? In what circumstances should equality defer to other priorities, such as conflicting freedoms or costs? This section looks at formal and substantive notions of equality and the concept of vulnerability.

[2] Note, *Matadeen* v. *Pointu* [1999] 1 AC 98, [1998] 3 WLR 18. Equality is not regarded as a free-standing principle of common law. Colm O'Cinneide, 'Equality: A Core Common Law Principle, or "Mere" Rationality?' in Mark Elliott and Kirsty Hughes (eds), *Common Law Constitutional Rights* (Hart, 2020); See also, Aileen McColgan, *Discrimination, Equality and the Law* (Hart, 2014), pp.10–13; Sandra Fredman, 'From Deference to Democracy: The Role of Equality under the Human Rights Act 1998' (2006) 122 LQR 53.

[3] Nicholas Bamforth, 'Conceptions of Anti-discrimination Law', (2004) 24(4) OJLS 693–717,704.

[4] See further in Sandra Fredman, *Discrimination Law* (3rd ed) (Oxford University Press, 2022), ch.1; Shreya Atrey and Sandra Fredman (eds), *Exponential Inequalities*, Introduction, (Oxford University Press, 2021); Sandra Fredman, 'Substantive Equality Revisited' (2016) 14 ICON 712; Catherine A. MacKinnon, 'Substantive Equality Revisited: A Reply to Sandra Fredman' (2016) 14 ICON 739; Sandra Fredman, 'Substantive Equality Revisited: Rejoinder' [2016] 15(4) ICON 747; Elizabeth Anderson, 'What Is the Point of Equality?' (1999) 109(2) Ethics 287; Catherine Albertyn, 'Contested Substantive Equality in the South African Constitution: Beyond Social Inclusion towards Systemic Justice' (2018) 34(3) South African Journal on Human Rights 441.

14.2.1 Concepts of Equality and Non-discrimination

Equality in an Aristotelian formulation requires that like cases are treated alike.[5] The notion of formal equality resonates with this: it requires that all persons in the same situation should be accorded the same treatment, and that people should not be treated differently because of individualised characteristics such as race, gender or religion. According to this understanding, provided that there is consistency in treatment, there will be no discrimination. For many years, the jurisprudence of the ECtHR adopted an Aristotelian or formal understanding of equality. The formal notion of equality contrasts with the substantive notion of equality which is concerned with addressing treatment that tends to reinforce inequality. Although the origins of the ECtHR's jurisprudence are founded on the formal concept of equality, the ECtHR has more recently moved towards a more substantive understanding of equality.[6] This move demonstrates an awareness of the idea that if pre-existing disadvantages exist, formal equal treatment will exacerbate an inequality of outcome.

A substantive concept of equality may require the State to provide or facilitate an 'equality of opportunity' and/or 'equality of results or outcomes'.[7] In this regard Sandra Fredman argues that 'a substantive conception [of equality] resists capture by a single principle'.[8] Consequently, she proposes a four-dimensional approach to substantive equality which includes: redressing disadvantage; addressing stigma, stereotyping, prejudice and violence; enhancing voice and participation; and accommodating difference and achieving structural change. Underpinning this approach is the idea that 'the right to equality should be located in the social context, responsive to those who are disadvantaged, demeaned, excluded or ignored'.[9]

The shift to a more substantive understanding of equality has also encouraged the development of the legal concept of indirect discrimination. This concept recognises that laws or policies which appear neutral on their face may have a deleterious effect on a certain group. Yet if we examine these important developments in the Strasbourg case law, through the lens of Fredman's multi-dimensional framework, it is evident that the ECtHR and the concept of indirect discrimination still fails to address all aspects of substantive equality. Indeed, Fredman has suggested that while the recognition of indirect discrimination has made some headway in relation to redistribution, recognition and participation, it has not achieved structural change.[10]

[5] For further discussion, see Daniel Moeckli, 'Equality and Non-Discrimination' in Daniel Moeckli et al. (eds), *International Human Rights Law* (4th ed) (Oxford University Press, 2022).

[6] Fredman, 'Substantive Equality Revisited' (n 4). [7] Ibid, p.714. [8] Ibid, at p.713.

[9] Ibid, at p.738.

[10] Sandra Fredman, 'Emerging from the Shadows: Substantive Equality and Article 14 of the European Convention on Human Rights' (2016) 16 HRLR 273, 274.

In more recent years, the ECtHR has, however, taken steps in some arenas which may remedy this lacuna. For example, in the jurisprudence concerning the education of Roma[11] children, the ECtHR has shifted its attention to remedying segregation and has demanded the speedy implementation of appropriate desegregation measures.[12]

14.2.2 Vulnerability

A further significant development in the case law is that the ECtHR increasingly emphasises 'vulnerability' or 'vulnerable groups', which may also prove to be consistent with a 'thick' or substantive concept of equality.[13] Vulnerability can operate as a critical tool that enables the Court to navigate inequality in a more substantive way. The concept of vulnerability was first used in relation to Roma people[14] but it has been extended to, for example, HIV patients,[15] people with mental disabilities,[16] and asylum seekers.[17]

In relation to disability discrimination, the concept of vulnerability has also played a part in the Court's analysis.[18] An example is *Çam* v. *Turkey* which concerned a blind student who had successfully passed a competitive musical examination for the Turkish National Music Academy performing on the baglama.[19] She was also given a medical report certifying her fitness to study

[11] Roma, Romani, Romany and Traveller are often used interchangeably. As observed in Council of Europe Strategic Action Plan for Roma and Traveller Inclusion (2020–2025), approved by the Committee of Ministers on 22/01/2020, the term 'Roma and Travellers' is used at the Council of Europe to encompass the wide diversity of the groups covered by the work of the Council of Europe in this field: on the one hand a) Roma, Sinti/Manush, Calé, Kaale, Romanichals, Boyash/Rudari; b) Balkan Egyptians (Egyptians and Ashkali); c) Eastern groups (Dom, Lom and Abdal); and, on the other hand, groups such as Travellers, Yenish, and the populations designated under the administrative term 'Gens du voyage', as well as persons who identify themselves as Gypsies. This is not an exhaustive definition of Roma and/or Travellers. In this book, Roma is used as the umbrella term.

[12] *X and others* v. *Albania* (2022) 75 EHRR 26 at [87]. See also, *Elmazova and Others* v. *North Macedonia*, App. Nos. 11811/20 and 13550/20, 13/12 /2022; *Szolcsán* v. *Hungary*, App. No. 24408/16, 30/03/2023. Merel Vrancken, 'Segregation in Education and a Duty of Desegregation under the ECHR' [2024] 2 EHRLR 112.

[13] Lourdes Peroni and Alexandra Timmer, 'Vulnerable Groups: The Promise of an Emerging Concept in European Human Rights Convention Law' (2013) 11 ICON 1056.

[14] *Chapman* v. *the United Kingdom*, App. No. 27238/95, 18/01/2001. *Chapman* was the first case to use the term vulnerability. See also, *DH* v. *the Czech Republic* [GC] (2008) 47 EHRR 3 at [181].

[15] *Kiyutin* v. *Russia* (2011) 53 EHRR 26.

[16] *Alajos Kiss* v. *Hungary*, App. No. 38832/06, 20/05/2010 at [42]; and *Kiyutin* v. *Russia* (n 15) at [74].

[17] *M.S.S.* v. *Belgium and Greece* [GC] (2011) 53 EHRR 2.

[18] See also, *V.I.* v. *the Republic of Moldova*, App. No. 38963/18, 26/03/2024 at [170].

[19] *Çam* v. *Turkey*, App. No. 51500/08, 23/02/2016 at [7]–[8]. The baglama is a small Turkish lute.

but was denied admission to the music school on account of her blindness. A violation of Article 14 ECHR read with Article 2 of Protocol 1 (Right to Education) ECHR was found. The ECtHR observed that Article 14 ECHR should guarantee rights that are practical and effective and it should therefore be read in the light of the emerging consensus and international human rights standards on disability which required the State to adopt 'reasonable accommodation' measures that help 'to correct factual inequalities which are unjustified and therefore amount to discrimination'.[20] On the facts, no attempt had been made by the State 'to identify the applicant's needs or to explain how her blindness could have impeded her access to a musical education'. In this respect it observed as follows:

> [T]he Court takes the view that it is important for the States to be particularly careful in making their choices in this sphere, having regard to the impact of the latter on children with disabilities, whose particular vulnerability cannot be overlooked. It consequently considers that discrimination on grounds of disability also covers refusal to make reasonable accommodation.[21]

Many academic commentators have welcomed this development of the Court's jurisprudence on vulnerability but some fear potential drawbacks if there is a failure 'to attend to the stigmatizing, essentializing and stereotyping risks associated to the concept'.[22] There are also concerns that greater clarification is required as to which groups should be included and who should be included within an identified vulnerable group.

14.3 NON-DISCRIMINATION AND EQUALITY WITHIN EUROPEAN HUMAN RIGHTS LAW

14.3.1 Scope and Ancillary Nature of Article 14 ECHR and Protocol 12

Article 14 ECHR applies to discrimination in respect of '[t]he enjoyment of the rights and freedoms set forth in [the] Convention'. This means that it is not a free-standing right with an independent existence from the other Convention rights and can only be invoked with one of the other provisions of the ECHR or its Protocols. This has led to commentators describing this provision as a 'parasitic' or a 'Cinderella'[23] provision.

[20] Ibid at [65]. [21] Ibid at [67] and [68].

[22] Peroni and Timmer (n 13), p.1067. See also Alexandra Timmer, Moritz Baumgartel, Louis Kotze, Lieneke Slingenberg, 'The Potential and Pitfalls of the Vulnerability Concept for Human Rights' (2021) 39(3) NQHR 190.

[23] Rory O'Connell, 'Cinderella Comes to the Ball: Art 14 and the Right to Non-discrimination in the ECHR' (2009) 29 LS 211.

The Court has developed a significant role for non-discrimination despite its ancillary nature.[24] Importantly, the principle of non-discrimination forms an integral part of *each right* set out in the ECHR.[25] Every right in the Convention must be read as including a principle of non-discrimination. The applicability of Article 14 ECHR does not 'presuppose the violation of one of the substantive rights protected by the Convention'[26] and to this extent it is autonomous.[27] The Court has expanded the role of Article 14 ECHR through finding that the 'material scope' of its application is not restricted to that of the substantive protected right.[28] Article 14 ECHR can apply if the facts of the case 'fall within the ambit' of one of the substantive provisions. Thus, a claim may fall '*within the ambit*' of a Convention right, even though an applicant cannot demonstrate or even claim a breach of a substantive Convention right. The flexible '*ambit*' test renders Article 14 ECHR applicable to many areas such as social security,[29] education,[30] paternity,[31] and right to an effective investigation.[32]

Of special relevance to the applicability of Article 14 ECHR is where a State has chosen to provide additional rights. In these circumstances, these additional rights may fall within the scope of a protected Convention right and the State must ensure that they are administered without discrimination. An example of this can be seen in *E.B.* v. *France* which concerned adoption.[33] According to the Grand Chamber, there was no need to decide whether adoption rights fell within Article 8 ECHR taken alone as France had gone beyond its Article 8 ECHR obligations in legislating expressly to grant single persons the right to apply for adoption. Consequently where the applicant, who was in a same-sex relationship with another woman, was denied approval to adopt a child, the Grand Chamber, by majority, concluded that there was a violation of Article 14 of the Convention on the grounds of sexual orientation taken in conjunction with Article 8 ECHR. As the Grand Chamber clearly stated:

> The prohibition of discrimination enshrined in Article 14 thus extends beyond the enjoyment of the rights and freedoms which the Convention and the Protocols thereto

[24] Fredman (n 10).

[25] *Case 'Relating to Certain Aspects of the Laws on the Use of Languages in Education in Belgium'* v. *Belgium*, known as the *Belgian Linguistics Case (No 2)* (1979–80) 1 EHRR 252 at [9]; *Marckx* v. *Belgium*, App. No. 6833/74, 13/06/1979 at [32].

[26] *EB* v. *France* [GC] (2008) 47 EHRR 21 at [47].

[27] *Sidabras and Dziautas* v. *Lithuania* (2017) 65 EHRR 11 at [38].

[28] See European Court of Human Rights, Guide on Art 14 ECHR and Article 1 of Protocol 12 to the Convention (31/08/2024) at [1.4].

[29] *Stummer* v. *Austria* [GC] (2012) 54 EHRR 11.

[30] *DH* v. *the Czech Republic* (n 14); *Oršuš* v. *Croatia* [GC] (2011) 52 EHRR 7; *Ponomaryovi* v. *Bulgaria*, App. No. 5335/05, 21/06/2011.

[31] *Rasmussen* v. *Denmark* (1985) 7 EHRR 371.

[32] *Nachova* v. *Bulgaria* [GC] (2006) 42 EHRR 43; *Opuz* v. *Turkey* (2010) 50 EHRR 28; *B.S.* v. *Spain*, App. No. 47159/08, 24/07/2021.

[33] *EB* v. *France* (n 26).

require each State to guarantee. It applies also to those additional rights, falling within the general scope of any Convention Article, for which the State has voluntarily decided to provide.[34]

In many cases, the Court considers it unnecessary to examine the complaint under Article 14 ECHR if a violation of a substantive provision has been found. For example, in *Airey* v. *Ireland*, the Court held that once a violation is found of another substantive right, 'it is not generally required' to examine the complaint under Article 14 ECHR unless 'a clear inequality of treatment in the enjoyment of the right in question is a fundamental aspect of the case'.[35] In practice, the Court tends to address discrimination if the difference of treatment forms an integral part of the case, but its approach is not always consistent. In *Lacatus* v. *Switzerland*, the Court found that the criminalisation of begging was a violation of Article 8 ECHR but did not find it necessary to consider the Article 14 ECHR claim.[36] The applicant, who was Roma, complained that she had been the victim of discrimination on the grounds of her social and financial status and of her origins. Two judges, who partly concurred and partly dissented with the majority, considered a separate examination of the complaint of discrimination was warranted.[37] Judge Ravarani expressed regret that indirect discrimination against the Roma population was not tackled by the Court. In his view the question of the discriminatory effects of the 'legislation prohibiting begging was different from that of the applicant's individual ability to beg'.[38] *Lacatus* is an important decision for the protection of an individual who is 'extremely poor, illiterate and unemployed' but the reluctance of the Court to consider discrimination, once a separate breach of a normative Article has been found, inhibits the development of Article 14 ECHR.[39]

In other cases, the Court has decided to deal with applications solely under Article 14 ECHR in conjunction with a substantive provision and has thus elected not to consider the case under the substantive provision alone. The facts of the case and the nature of the allegations will determine whether the non-discrimination issue will be dealt with separately.[40] For example, in *Çam* v. *Turkey* the Court found that as the discriminatory treatment was the

[34] Ibid at [48].

[35] *Airey* v. *Ireland* (1981) 2 EHRR 592 at [30]. See also, *Lavida* v. *Greece*, App. No. 7973/10, 30/05/2013 at [62]; *Dudgeon* v. *the United Kingdom* (1982) 4 EHRR 149 at [67]; *Chassagnou and others* v. *France* [GC] (2000) 29 EHRR 615 at [89]; and *Timichev* v. *Russia*, App. Nos. 55762/00 and 55974/00, 13/12/2005 at [53].

[36] *Lacatus* v. *Switzerland*, App. no. 14065/15, 19/01/2021. The Court also failed to address the alleged violation of Article 10. See Chapter 10.

[37] Ibid, Judge Lemmens and Judge Ravani.

[38] Ibid, partly concurring and partly dissenting opinion of Judge Ravarani at [17].

[39] Ibid at [58]. Judge Ravarani suggested that that there is a principle of procedural economy in deciding not to engage with the Article 10 and Article 14 issues.

[40] *Makhashevy* v. *Russia*, App. No. 20546/07, 31/07/2012 at [139].

essence of her complaint, it was assessed under Article 14 ECHR.[41] The Court found a violation of Article 14 ECHR in conjunction with Article 2 of Protocol 1 ECHR (Right to Education).

In recognition of the ancillary nature of Article 14 ECHR, the Council of Europe has developed Protocol No. 12 ECHR.[42] It deliberately avoids the accessory character of Article 14 ECHR and contains an independent and autonomous non-discrimination guarantee. The idea underlying the new Protocol is to strengthen the protection against discrimination through this independent prohibition.[43] The Protocol entered into force on 1 April 2005 but it has not received widespread support. To date, less than half of the Member States of the Council of Europe have ratified the Protocol and the UK is not one of the ratifying States. Few cases concerning the Protocol have been examined by the ECtHR but it has been held that Article 14 ECHR and the Protocol should be interpreted in a similar way.[44]

14.3.2 Prohibited Grounds of Discrimination

Article 14 ECHR lists the following prohibited grounds of discrimination: 'sex, race, colour, language, religion, political or other opinion, national or social origin, association with a national minority, property, birth'. This list is not exhaustive, as Article 14 ECHR states 'such as' before listing the protected grounds and also concludes with the term 'or other status'. The Court has thus recognised grounds not specifically mentioned in Article 14 ECHR, including disability,[45] remand and convicted prisoners,[46] and sexual orientation.[47] The ECtHR has also confirmed that 'other status' is not limited to characteristics that are personal in the sense that they are innate or inherent, such as gender, ethnic origin or age.[48] The words 'other status' in Article 14 ECHR have generally been given a broad meaning and it has been applied, for example, to discrimination between large and small landowners,[49] possessors of fishing rights,[50] and place of residence.[51]

41 *Çam* v. *Turkey* (n 19) at [55].

42 Council of Europe, European Treaty Series 177, 04/11/2000.

43 See Explanatory Report to Protocol No. 12 CETS No.177, 04/11/2000.

44 *Sejdić and Finci* v. *Bosnia Herzegovina* [GC] [2009] ECHR 2122 at [55].

45 *Glor* v. *Switzerland*, App. No. 13444/04, 30/04/2009; *Enver Sahin* v. *Turkey*, App. No. 23065/12, 30/11/2018.

46 *Laduna* v. *Slovakia*, App. No. 31827/02, 13/12/ 2011.

47 *Sutherland* v. *the United Kingdom* (Commission) (1997) 24 EHRR CD 22 at [51].

48 *Kiyutin* v. *Russia* (n 15) at [56]; *Clift* v. *the United Kingdom*, App. No. 7205/07, 13/07/2010 at [56]. Guide on Art 14 ECHR and Article 1 of Protocol 12 to the Convention (n 28) at [166].

49 *Chassagnou and Others* v. *France* [GC] (n 35) at [90] and [95].

50 *Alatulkkila* v. *Finland* (2006) 43 EHRR 34 at [70].

51 *Carson and Others* v. *the United Kingdom* (2010) 51 EHRR 13 at [70]–[71].

The ground of discrimination may influence the intensity of the review of the Court. A very stringent test of justification has been applied to certain 'suspect' categories, such as sex, race, ethnicity and gender: discrimination based solely on these grounds will never be acceptable. The State will also be required to provide 'weighty reasons' to justify differences of treatment of vulnerable people.[52] This stringent test is in sharp contrast to the more deferential approach applied to differences of treatment based on for example, place of residency.[53]

14.3.2.1 *Direct and Indirect Discrimination*

There is no definition of what constitutes discrimination in Article 14 ECHR and thus we need to look at the jurisprudence of the Court to determine the meaning. The concept of direct discrimination is premised on the principle that likes should be treated alike. Under Article 14 ECHR, direct discrimination occurs if there is a 'difference in treatment of persons in analogous, or relevantly similar situations' and 'based on an identifiable characteristic, or "status" protected by Article 14'.[54] Direct discrimination also covers harassment and instruction to discriminate.[55]

In addition, the ECtHR has recognised 'the right not to be discriminated against ... is also violated when states without an objective and reasonable justification fail to treat differently persons whose situations are significantly different'.[56] In the gound-breaking decision of *Thlimmenos* v. *Greece*, the Greek Institute for Chartered Accountants had refused admission to the applicant because he had a prior criminal conviction. The applicant, a Jehovah's Witness, argued that his criminal conviction for a refusal to wear a military uniform should be distinguished from other convictions as it arose from the exercise of his religious beliefs. The Court unanimously concluded that the failure of the Institute to treat the applicant differently was disproportionate and did not pursue a legitimate aim.[57] The Court thus found a breach of Article 14 taken in conjunction with Article 9 ECHR. An examination to determine a violation of Article 9 taken on its own was considered unnecessary.

[52] *Alajos Kiss* v. *Hungary*, App. No. 38832/06, 20/05/2010 at [236].

[53] *Carson and Others* v. *the United Kingdom* (n 51).

[54] See, e.g., *Biao* v. *Denmark* [GC] (2017) 64 EHRR 1 at [89]; *Burden* v. *the United Kingdom* [GC] (2008) 47 EHRR 38 at [60].

[55] See *Bączkowski and others* v. *Poland* (2009) 48 EHRR 19 and *Oganezova* v. *Armenia* (2022) 75 EHRR 20. Guide on Art 14 ECHR and Article 1 of Protocol 12 to the Convention (n 28) at [34].

[56] *Guberina* v. *Croatia* (2018) 66 EHRR 11 at [70].

[57] *Thlimmenos* v. *Greece* (2000) 31 EHRR 15. See also discussion below, Section 14.3.2.4 (Positive Action).

The concept of indirect discrimination refers to measures or decisions which though couched in neutral terms, or appear neutral on their face, in practice have a discriminatory effect on a particular group. It was not until 2008 that the ECtHR found a breach of Article 14 ECHR based specifically on indirect discrimination.[58] Earlier decisions had suggested that such a claim would be possible,[59] and notably in *Jordan* v. *the United Kingdom* the Court had stated that discrimination may arise where prejudicial effects of a general policy, measure or rule, even though worded in neutral terms, has 'disproportionately prejudicial effects on a particular group … notwithstanding that it is not specifically aimed or directed at that group'.[60]

It was, however, the seminal decision of *DH* v. *the Czech Republic* that led to the first finding of indirect discrimination. The facts of *DH* were that a disproportionate number of Roma children had been transferred to 'special' schools for children with learning disabilities in the Czech Republic. The tests used to assess all children's learning abilities had been designed to suit the mainstream Czech population and 'the results were not analysed in the light of the particularities and special characteristics of the Roma children who sat them'.[61] Moreover children placed in the 'special' schools suffered a significant disadvantage. Statistical evidence submitted by the applicants, and accepted by the Court, found that these tests, used to evaluate the intellectual capacities of the children, led to indirect discrimination of the Roma children. According to the Court 'there is a danger that the tests were biased … In these circumstances, the tests in question cannot serve as justification for the impugned difference in treatment'.[62] The Grand Chamber found that there was indirect discrimination on the ground of ethnic origin. Indirect discrimination does not require any discriminatory intent.[63] Moreover indirect discrimination can occur even though the general policy or measure was not specifically aimed at a particular group or intended to have any prejudicial effects on them.

In recent years indirect discrimination has also been deployed in contexts beyond education. The Court made a significant finding of indirect discrimination in *Biao* v. *Denmark*,[64] where it considered a statutory requirement enshrining a difference in treatment between Danish citizens and those of non-Danish origin for the purposes of granting family reunification. The Court concluded that this requirement had a disproportionately prejudicial effect on

[58] *DH* v. *the Czech Republic* (n 14).

[59] In the *Belgian Linguistics Case (No 2)* (n 25) at [4], the Court had referred to the 'aims and effects' of discriminatory measures.

[60] *Jordan* v. *the United Kingdom* (2003) 37 EHRR 2 at [154].

[61] *DH* v. *the Czech Republic* (n 14). For further discussion, see Sina Van den Bogaert, *Segregation of Roma Children in Education* (Brill, 2019), ch.9.

[62] *DH* v. *the Czech Republic* (n 14) at [201].

[63] Ibid at [184].

[64] *Biao* v. *Denmark* (n 54). See also discussion in Chapter 9.

persons who acquired Danish nationality later in life and were of a different ethnic group. This treatment constituted a violation of Article 14 read in conjunction with Article 8 ECHR.[65] In the landmark judgment of *Opuz* v. *Turkey*,[66] involving domestic violence against women, the Court observed that the Turkish law in force did not explicitly distinguish between men and women in the enjoyment of rights and freedoms. The discrimination at issue was not based on the legislation itself, 'but rather resulted from the general attitude of the local authorities, such as the manner in which the women were treated at police stations when they reported domestic violence and judicial passivity in providing effective protection to victims'.[67] This created a climate conducive to domestic violence against women and led the Court to find a violation of Article 14 read in conjunction with Articles 2 and 3 ECHR.

Indirect discrimination has also recently been addressed in the context of State border management practices which is discussed below in Section 14.3.5.3 (Racial Profiling).

14.3.2.2 *Burden of Proof in Indirect Discrimination*

In *DH* v. *the Czech Republic*, the Court explained its approach to handling indirect discrimination complaints.[68] The usual evidentiary test applied by the Court is that the applicant must prove his or her allegation. In recognition of the potential difficulties for applicants complaining of indirect discrimination, the Court has modified the evidentiary requirements. The applicant must establish a prima facie case of indirect discrimination by persuading the Court that an apparently neutrally formulated law or policy affects a disproportionate number of members of a group characterised by a 'suspect' ground and, as a consequence, places them at a significant disadvantage. It may be difficult for applicants to gather the evidence proving discriminatory treatment. In order to ensure the effective protection of rights, the Court has applied less strict evidential rules in cases of alleged indirect discrimination.[69] The Court is prepared to accept 'reliable and significant' statistical evidence,[70] reports from non-governmental or international organisations.[71]

Where an applicant establishes a prima facie case that the measure or its effect is discriminatory, the burden then shifts to the State, which can discharge the burden by showing that the indirect difference in treatment is not discriminatory. For example, the State could demonstrate that the difference in the effect of the measure is a consequence of objective factors and unrelated to discrimination on the ground claimed. The ECtHR has noted that 'it would

[65] See also *Zarb Adami* v. *Malta* (2007) 44 EHRR 49.

[66] *Opuz* v. *Turkey* (n 32). Note also, *SAS* v. *France* [GC] (2015) 60 EHRR 11 at [161].

[67] *Opuz* v. *Turkey* (n 32) at [192]. See further Section 14.3.5.7.1.

[68] *DH* v. *the Czech Republic* (n 14). [69] Ibid at [186]. [70] Ibid at [187]. [71] Ibid.

be extremely difficult in practice for applicants to prove indirect discrimination without such a shift in the burden of proof'.[72] If the State is unable to put forward compelling or very weighty reasons, there will be a violation of Article 14 ECHR.[73]

14.3.2.3 *Discrimination by Association*

Discrimination by association occurs when a person is treated less favourably because of the characteristics of another person with whom they are associated. The concept of dignity underpins the development of this form of discrimination. In 2008 the European Court of Justice (ECJ) (as it was known at the time) pointed out that targeting third persons who are closely associated with individuals belonging to a certain protected group is one way to undermine the dignity and autonomy of individuals. In the ECJ's view this subtler form of discrimination should be covered by anti-discrimination legislation.[74]

The idea that discrimination may affect more than just the individual with the particular or protected characteristic was confirmed by the ECtHR in *Guberina* v. *Croatia*.[75] The applicant requested a tax exemption on the purchase of a new property specifically adapted to the needs of his severely disabled child. Without taking into account the disabled child's needs, the authorities refused as the applicant was already in possession of a suitable place to live. The ECtHR found that the discriminatory treatment of the applicant, on account of the disability of his child for whom he provides care, was a form of disability-based discrimination covered by Article 14 ECHR.[76] In *Molla Sali* v. *Greece*, the Grand Chamber addressed the principle of discrimination by association. The facts concerned a will that was drawn up in accordance with the Greek Civil Code, by a testator of Muslim faith. On account of the testator's Muslim faith, Sharia law had been applied to the inheritance which was less advantageous to the applicant wife. The Court found that the difference of treatment suffered by the wife, in which Sharia law had been applied to an inheritance dispute contrary to the will of the testator, had no objective or reasonable justification.[77]

14.3.2.4 *Positive Action*

Article 14 ECHR does not contain a specific reference to positive action or, as it was sometimes previously called, affirmative action or reverse discrimination.

[72] Ibid at [189]. [73] *Biao* (n 54) at [114].

[74] *Coleman* v. *Attridge Law*, EU C-303/06 (17/07/2008), AG12 [2008] ICR 1128. This concept is covered in the EqA in s.13. See *Abrams* v. *EAD Solicitors LLP* [2016] ICR 380.

[75] *Guberina* v. *Croatia* (n 56). See also, *Škorjanec* v. *Croatia* (2018) 66 EHRR 14 at [55] and *Weller* v. *Hungary*, App. No. 44399/05, 31/03/2009.

[76] Ibid at [79]. [77] *Molla Sali* v. *Greece* [GC] (2019) 69 EHRR 2 at [161].

As outlined above, there will be discrimination if a person or group is treated less favourably than another, without justification. A finding of discrimination may vary according to the personal characteristic associated with the discrimination and the context in which the discrimination takes place. The ECtHR's interpretation of 'discrimination' has indicated that the concept is not necessarily a symmetric one that prohibits all differences in treatment. In the *Belgian Linguistics Case*, the Court concluded that not all differences will be discriminatory.

> Article 14 does not forbid every difference in treatment in the exercise of the rights and freedoms recognised. . . . The competent national authorities are frequently confronted with situations and problems which, on account of differences inherent therein, call for different legal solutions; moreover, certain legal inequalities tend only to correct factual inequalities.[78]

In contrast to EU and domestic UK law, the ECtHR allows justification for direct discrimination as an absolute refusal to allow justification could prohibit positive action. Article 14 ECHR does not prohibit treating groups differently in order to correct 'factual inequalities' between them. In *Stec* v. *the United Kingdom*, the ECtHR recognised that a package of measures had been adopted to ameliorate prior disadvantage.[79] The case concerned differences in pensionable ages between men and women in the UK. The rationale for the difference was to mitigate a situation of financial hardship for women who traditionally carried out unpaid caring roles in the home. Although sex discrimination falls within one of the categories that are particularly difficult to justify, a less demanding approach was adopted, requiring that the State's discriminatory measure not be 'manifest without reasonable foundation'.[80] This is because, according to the Court, national authorities are better placed to decide on social and economic matters.[81] This important decision which is intended to correct 'factual inequalities' between men and women is analysed in greater detail in the section below on gender discrimination.[82] The ECtHR in *Andrle* v. *the Czech Republic* also upheld that State's preferential treatment of women concerning pension eligibility.[83] The differential treatment between men and women was objectively and reasonably justified as it was designed to compensate for the inequality and hardship generated by the expectation that women would work full-time, as well as taking care of the children and the household.

In a later decision, the ECtHR went even further suggesting that Article 14 ECHR may demand, and not simply allow, differential treatment to

[78] *Belgian Linguistics Case (No 2)* (n 25) at [10]. This section was also quoted in the Opinion of the ECtHR on draft Protocol 12 ECHR (adopted at the plenary administrative session of the Court on the 6 December 1999) Doc. 8608, 5 January, 2000 at [5].

[79] *Stec* v. *the United Kingdom* [GC] (2006) 43 EHRR 47. [80] Ibid at [52]. [81] Ibid.

[82] Ibid at [61]. See Section 14.3.5.7. [83] *Andrle* v. *the Czech Republic* (2015) 60 EHRR 14.

ameliorate disadvantage. In *Thlimmenos* v. *Greece*, the ECtHR found that the State was required, in operating a ban on those with a criminal conviction from joining the profession of chartered accountants, to distinguish between persons convicted of offences committed because of their religious beliefs (conscientious objection to military service) and persons convicted of other offences.[84] Later cases have confirmed that 'in certain circumstances a failure to attempt to correct inequality through different treatment may in itself give rise to a breach of the article'.[85]

14.3.2.5 *Intersectionality*

Tackling discrimination from the perspective of a single category or ground may fail to address the complex manifestations of unequal treatment. The Court has considered situations of discrimination that have involved multiple and overlapping grounds of discrimination at the same time.[86] As Article 14 ECHR prohibits discrimination on a non-exhaustive number of grounds, this has opened the space for an analysis that acknowledges the interlocking nature of discrimination.[87] Radhika Coomaraswamy, who was at the time the UN Special Rapporteur on Violence against Women, set out a working definition of the concept:

> The idea of 'intersectionality' seeks to capture both the structural and dynamic consequences of the interaction between two or more forms of discrimination or systems of subordination. It specifically addresses the manner in which racism, patriarchy, economic disadvantages and other discriminatory systems contribute to create layers of inequality that structures the relative positions of women and men, races and other groups.[88]

There have been some notable examples of the ECtHR adopting intersectionality as an analytical tool to address multidimensional discrimination.[89]

[84] *Thlimmenos* v. *Greece* (n 57) at [44]. See also *Horváth and Kiss* v. *Hungary* (2013) 57 EHRR 31 at [104].

[85] *JD and A* v. *the United Kingdom* [2019] ECHR 753 at [86] and *Sejdić and Finci* v. *Bosnia and Herzegovina* (n 44) at [44].

[86] Multiple discrimination refers to discrimination that occurs on the basis of several grounds operating separately.

[87] Kimberlé Crenshaw, 'Demarginalizing the Intersection of Race and Sex: A Black Feminist Critique of Antidiscrimination Doctrine, Feminist Theory and Antiracist Politics' (1989) 1 *U. of Chicago Legal Forum* 139–167; Aileen McColgan, 'Reconfiguring Discrimination Law' [2007] 1 PL 74; Iyiola Solanke, 'Putting Race and Gender Together: A New Approach to Intersectionality' (2009) **72** MLR 723. See also, Shreya Atrey, *Intersectional Discrimination* (Oxford University Press, 2019). See comments of the third party intervenors in *BS* v. *Spain* (n 32) at [56].

[88] United Nations General Assembly, 'Review of reports, studies and other documentation for the preparatory committee and the world conference', A/CONF.189/PC.3/5, 21 July 2001 at [23].

[89] Colm O'Cinneide, "The Potential and Pitfalls of Intersectionality in the Context of Social Rights Adjudication" in Shreya Atrey and Peter Dunne (eds), *Intersectionality and Human Rights Law* (Hart Publishing, 2020), pp.59–82.

In *B.S.* v. *Spain*,[90] the applicant was an African prostituted woman who claimed that the failure of the domestic authorities to investigate allegations of racist police ill-treatment, both physically and verbally, was a violation of Article 14 ECHR in conjunction with Article 3 ECHR. The Court found a breach of Article 3 ECHR due to a failure to investigate the alleged racist ill-treatment. It also considered the applicability of Article 14 ECHR. The Court highlighted the applicant's 'particular vulnerability' arising from both her ethnic origin, gender and the fact that she was prostituted.[91] Article 14 ECHR was used as a vehicle to acknowledge the effect of these intersecting factors and in a manner that was particularly sensitive to her vulnerability.

A further example is provided by *JD and A* v. *the United Kingdom*,[92] where the UK authorities had deducted housing benefits from a woman occupying accommodation that exceeded by one bedroom, the number to which she was entitled. The applicant had been a victim of serious domestic violence and the additional room had been modified through a 'Sanctuary Scheme' designed specially to allow women to remain safely in their homes. In finding a violation of Article 14 ECHR in conjunction with Article 1 of Protocol 1 of the Convention, the Court concluded that States have a duty to protect the physical and psychological integrity of individuals in the context of domestic violence.[93] Colm O'Cinneide suggests that this illustrates how the 'developing strand of the Court's case law is potentially able to accommodate intersectionality, in situations of clear "group vulnerability" at least'.[94]

Unfortunately, however, the Court does not always take cognisance of intersectionality or the importance of Article 14 ECHR. A significant example of this is *NB* v. *Slovakia*[95] which concerned the forced sterilisation of a Roma woman, who claimed discrimination on grounds of race, ethnic origin and sex. In finding a violation of Articles 3 and 8 ECHR, the Court surmised that 'the practice of sterilisation of women without their consent affected vulnerable individuals from various ethnic groups'.[96] While acknowledging that the applicant is a member of the vulnerable Roma community, the Court nevertheless held that it was not necessary to consider separately the Article 14 ECHR claim presumably because violations of Articles 3 and 8 ECHR had already been found. Nevertheless, the failure to address Article 14 ECHR was a disappointment and a missed opportunity to address the structural issues behind the individual claims of vulnerable women from ethnic minorities.

Another important case in this respect is *Garib* v. *the Netherlands,* in which the applicant, a single mother of two children, was refused a permit to move to

[90] *BS* v. *Spain* (n 32). [91] Ibid at [62]. [92] *JD and A* v. *the United Kingdom* (n 85).

[93] Ibid at [105].

[94] O'Cinneide (n 89), p.65. See also, *Yocheva and Ganeva* v. *Bulgaria* (2021) 73 EHRR 21 and *Carvalho Pinto de Sousa Morais* v. *Portugal* (2018) 66 EHRR 25.

[95] *NB* v. *Slovakia*, App. No. 29518/10, 12/06/2012. [96] Ibid at [121].

a new flat in an area of Rotterdam as she failed to meet the necessary income requirement or the prerequisite of six years of residence.[97] She unsuccessfully claimed a violation of her freedom to choose her residence (Article 2 of Protocol 4) and of discrimination under Article 14 ECHR. Disappointingly, the Grand Chamber did not consider the intersection of poverty-related discrimination with other human rights issues. Judge Pinto De Alberquerque delivered a highly critical dissenting judgment commenting that '[b]ehind Dutch housing policy hides a more serious problem of discrimination against individuals on account of their socially precarious situations'.[98] He added:

> the concept of 'intersectional discrimination', which represents a reality that has been virtually disregarded to date by the European system, has been increasingly acknowledged in international law. It is now indispensable to take this phenomenon into consideration in order to reach a global and comprehensive understanding of the various discrimination situations and thus guarantee the effectiveness of the Convention rights.[99]

14.3.3 The Test of Discrimination

When deciding cases of discrimination, the Court will apply the following test:

1. Only differences in treatment based on an identifiable characteristic or 'status' are capable of amounting to discrimination.
2. An issue under Article 14 arises if there is a difference in treatment of persons in (i) analogous or relevantly similar situations – or (ii) a failure to treat differently persons in relevantly different situations.
3. The difference in treatment – or absence of treatment – is discriminatory if it has no reasonable and objective justification:
   (i) Does it pursue a legitimate aim?
   (ii) Is there a reasonable relationship of proportionality between the means employed and the aim sought to be realised?[100]

14.3.3.1 What Constitutes Discrimination for the Purposes of Article 14 ECHR?

14.3.3.1.1 Difference in Treatment

Article 14 ECHR lists protected characteristics which may result in a conclusion that differential treatment is discriminatory. The use of the term 'other status' in Article 14 ECHR means that the guarantee is not restricted solely to

97 *Garib* v. *the Netherlands* [GC] (2018) 66 EHRR 2.
98 Ibid, dissenting opinion of Judge Pinto De Alberquerque joined by Judge Vehabović at [22].
99 Ibid at [34].
100 Guide on Article 14 (n 28) at [55]; *Carson* (n 51) at [61]; *R (on the application of SC)* v. *Secretary of State for Work and Pensions* [2021] UKSC 26 at [37].

the listed protected characteristics. The Court has given a broad interpretation to 'other status' as discussed above. Some protected characteristics, in particular those specifically listed in Article 14 ECHR, will be assessed by a more intense standard of review at the justification stage. As discussed below, difference of treatment solely on the basis of sex /gender, race or ethnicity, birth and sexual orientation (and perhaps other categories) may be incapable of justification.

There must be a difference in treatment for a finding of discrimination. 'The difference in treatment – or failure to treat differently – can result in any of the forms of discrimination … such as direct and indirect discrimination, and discrimination by association.'[101] On occasions, there is a dispute as to whether there has been any difference in treatment at all and the ECtHR will determine whether or not there has been a difference.[102] In other cases, the Grand Chamber has accepted that Article 14 ECHR might require differential treatment of people in relevantly different situations.[103] It is possible for States to treat groups differently in order to correct factual inequalities as discussed in Section 14.3.2.4 above.

14.3.3.1.2 *Situation Must Be Analogous*

The person or group of persons to whom an applicant is compared is referred to as the comparator. In a case of direct discrimination there must be an actual difference between comparable cases based on at least one prohibited ground of discrimination. Determining who or which group is an appropriate comparator is not always easy or straightforward. Aileen McColgan comments that the comparative evaluation 'creates conceptual and practical difficulties. Conditioning equal treatment on "likeness" however defined, functions so as to grant less privileged actors access to the benefits enjoyed by the more privileged only to the extent that the former can prove "sameness" with the latter.'[104]

One example is *Carson* v. *the United Kingdom*[105] which concerned applicants who were former residents of the UK and who now lived abroad. The dispute concerned the payment of pensions and whether they could be adjusted annually to allow for inflation. Applicants who resided in countries

[101] Guide on Article 14 (n 28) at [64]. [102] *E.B.* v. *France* (n 26) at [88].

[103] *Thlimmenos* v. *Greece* (n 57) at [44]. The Greek Institute for Chartered Accountants had refused to appoint the applicant because he had a prior conviction. The applicant, a Jehovah's Witness, argued that his conviction for insubordination (refusing to wear military uniform) should be distinguished from other convictions, as it stemmed from the exercise of his religious beliefs. The Court concluded that the failure of the Institute to treat the applicant differently was disproportionate and did not pursue a legitimate aim. The Court thus found a breach of Article 9 with Article 14.

[104] McColgan (n 2), p.102. [105] *Carson* v. *the United Kingdom* [GC] (n 51).

with which the UK had reached reciprocal arrangements received annual pension adjustments while those who did not, had pension payments frozen upon their retirement. The applicants claimed that the differential treatment was a breach of their Article 14 ECHR rights taken with Article 1 of Protocol 1 (right to property) ECHR. These claims failed before the Grand Chamber who concluded that the 'complex and interlocking system makes it impossible to isolate the payment of National Insurance contributions as a sufficient ground for equating the position of pensioners who receive up-rating and those, like the applicants who do not'.[106] The outcome was that the Court did not find that the payment of National Insurance contributions placed the applicants in a relevantly similar position to all other pensioners, as the system is designed primarily to serve the needs of UK residents.[107] As a consequence, the applicants were found not to be in a relevantly similar position to residents of the UK or residents of countries which are a party to an agreement with the UK.

In *Burden* v. *the United Kingdom*[108] cohabiting sisters, who had shared a home during the whole of their adult life, were found not to be in a comparable position to spouses or civil partners for the purpose of inheritance tax. By assigning primacy to the question of whether persons are 'similarly situated', the burden of proof will often not shift to the State to establish and justify the reason for the difference in treatment. Lady Hale, commenting on this judgment, observed that 'unless there are very obvious relevant differences between the two situations, it is better to concentrate on the reasons for the difference in treatment and whether they amount to an objective and reasonable justification'.[109] In her view, the most appropriate time to assess these differences is at the justification stage where the burden is placed on the discriminator to – at the very least – put forward the aims pursued, rather than leaving it to the claimant to second-guess them.[110]

Although it is necessary to show a difference in treatment of persons in an analogous situation, this requirement does not mean that the comparator groups must be identical. In *Fábián* v. *Hungary*, the Grand Chamber elucidated on the comparator requirement noting that 'the elements which characterise different situations, and determine their comparability, must be assessed in the light of the subject-matter and purpose of the measure which makes the distinction in question'.[111] In *Fábián*, civil servants and private employees were not found to be comparable: the terms and conditions of employment including the eligibility for employment-linked social benefits cannot be assumed to be similar in these two categories of employees. In contrast, in

[106] Ibid at [84]. [107] Ibid at [85]. [108] *Burden* v. *the United Kingdom* (n 54).

[109] *AL (Serbia)* v. *Secretary of State for the Home Department* [2008] UKHL 42, [2008] 4 All ER 1127 at [25].

[110] Ibid. [111] *Fábián* v. *Hungary* (2018) 66 EHRR 26 at [121].

Yocheva and Ganeva v. *Bulgaria*, the applicants, single mothers, were refused a family-allowance payment for families 'with only one living parent'.[112] They successfully argued that they were in a similarly situated position to both widowers and widows with children, as well as to single mothers whose children had a father who had recognised them before dying, all of whom could access the payment. The Court found a violation of Article 14 ECHR taken in conjunction with Article 8 ECHR.

14.3.3.2 Justifying Discrimination

Differential treatment of a protected right will be discriminatory if it 'has no objective or reasonable justification'.[113] In the circumstances of a *Thlimmenos*-type discrimination, it is the lack of or failure to make a different rule for those who are adversely affected which needs to be justified. In relation to indirect discrimination, the measure giving rise to the differential or disparate impact must be justified. As not every difference in treatment is prohibited, the justification for the impugned distinction is of great importance. In determining justification, the Court has developed a two-stage test. It is necessary to determine (a) whether the discriminatory treatment pursues a legitimate aim; and then, (b) whether there is a reasonable relationship of proportionality between the means employed and the aim sought to be realised. It is the discrimination itself that must be justified and not a broader scheme of which it is part. Once an applicant has demonstrated a difference in treatment, any reliance upon justification should be carefully scrutinised and the burden of proof of establishing it rests with the respondent state.[114] It is possible to justify both direct and indirect discrimination under the Court's Article 14 ECHR jurisprudence.

14.3.3.2.1 Legitimate Aim

For a State to justify a difference of treatment in the exercise of a protected right it must be able to show that it is in pursuit of a legitimate aim. The justification provided must have a rational basis: the State must demonstrate 'a link' between the legitimate aim and the differential treatment claimed by the applicants.[115] The policy aims submitted by governments are often

112 *Yocheva and Ganeva* v. *Bulgaria* (n 94).

113 *Abdulaziz, Cabales and Balkandali* v. *the United Kingdom* (1985) 7 EHRR 471 at [72]; *Molla Sali* v. *Greece* (n 77) at [135].

114 *Molla Sali* v. *Greece* (n 77) at [137]; *Vallianatos and Others* v. *Greece* [GC] (2014) 59 EHRR 12 at [85]; and *DH* v. *the Czech Republic* (n 14) at [177].

115 Guide on Art 14 (n 28) at [66].

accepted as legitimate, but it will not automatically follow that the difference in treatment can necessarily be justified.[116]

In several cases, the Court has accepted differential treatment as pursuing a legitimate aim. In the *Belgian Linguistics Case* the aim of effectively implementing a policy of linguistic unity was accepted.[117] Legal certainty of completed inheritance tax arrangements,[118] restoration of peace,[119] protection of women against gender-based violence, abuse and sexual harassment in the prison environment have all been considered legitimate aims.[120]

In earlier jurisprudence the Court considered the aim of supporting and protecting the family in a traditional sense as a legitimate reason to justify a difference in treatment.[121] In more recent years, the Court has reconsidered the traditional concept of the family. In *Taddeucci and McCall* v. *Italy*, the applicants, a same-sex couple, were refused a residence permit as under Italian law, a cohabiting status did not satisfy the Italian statutory requirement of 'spouse'.[122] Their application had been treated in the same manner as unmarried heterosexual couples, even though such couples could marry and obtain legal recognition of their relationship in domestic law, whereas same-sex couples did not have this option available. The Court stated that 'applying the same restrictive rule ... to heterosexual couples who had not regularised their situation and to homosexual couples, with the sole aim of protecting the traditional family ... subjected the applicants to discriminatory treatment'.[123]

In *Abdulaziz* v. *the United Kingdom*, the legitimate aim put forward by the Government was successfully challenged. The Government's claim that the Immigration Rules, distinguishing between men and women, was necessary to protect the domestic labour market was found to be unconvincing.[124] The Court concluded that there was direct discrimination and found a breach of Article 14 taken together with Article 8 ECHR on the ground of sex. The Court had not yet developed its indirect discrimination jurisprudence thus it was not surprising, albeit disappointing, that it rejected the further claim that the Rules in practice operated to disadvantage those from the 'New Commonwealth and Pakistan' and were therefore racially motivated.[125]

[116] David Harris et al., *Harris, O'Boyle and Warbrick: Law of the European Convention on Human Rights* (5th ed) (Oxford University Press, 2023), pp.781–782. See *Abdulaziz, Cabales and Balkandali* v. *the United Kingdom* (n 113); *Eweida and Ors* v. *the United Kingdom* (2013) 57 EHRR 8 at [105].

[117] *Belgian Linguistics Case* (n 25), p.293 [A7]. See Harris et al. (n 116), p.782.

[118] *Fabris* v. *France* [GC] (2013) 57 EHRR 19 at [56].

[119] *Sejdić and Finci* v. *Bosnia and Herzegovina* (n 44) at [137].

[120] *Khamtokhu and Aksenchik* v. *Russia* [GC] (2017) 65 EHRR 6 at [82]. Guide on Article 14 (n 28) at [59].

[121] *Marckx* v. *Belgium* (n 25) at [40] and *Karner* v. *Austria* (2004) 38 EHRR 24 at [40].

[122] *Taddeucci and McCall* v. *Italy*, App. No. 51362/09, 30/06/2016.

[123] Ibid at [94].

[124] *Abdulaziz* (n 113) at [78].

[125] Ibid at [85]–[86]. *DH* v. *the Czech Republic* (n 14) was the first decision decided by the Court on indirect discrimination.

In a number of European States, the poor education provision and segregation of the Roma minority has led to consideration of Article 14 ECHR. In *Oršuš and Others* v. *Croatia*, the Grand Chamber concluded that the temporary placement of Roma children in a separate class, due to inadequate language familiarity, was not automatically contrary to Article 14 ECHR.[126] However, disproportionate measures or those that exclusively affect members of an ethnic group will only be legitimate if appropriate and effective safeguards are implemented. The Court's role is to examine whether safeguards existed at each stage and the efficacy of such measures.[127]

The Court's recent jurisprudence in accepting the protection of 'constitutional identity' as a legitimate aim pursuant to Article 14 ECHR is controversial. The background to these cases is the unlawful annexation of the Baltic States into the USSR in 1940. In 1991, the Latvian authorities declared full independence but there remains tension between Latvia and Russia, which has increased since the invasion of Ukraine. In *Savickis and Others* v. *Latvia*,[128] the Grand Chamber considered the issue of discriminatory treatment in the calculation of pensions between Latvian citizens and the applicants who were 'permanently resident non-citizens'. The applicants, a minority in Latvia, were denied recognition of their period of employment accrued in other USSR States in their State pension calculations whereas Latvian citizens could enjoy this benefit. The Grand Chamber relied on the undeveloped notion of 'protection of constitutional identity' as a legitimate aim to justify the differential treatment in pension entitlement.[129] This troubling decision was further confirmed in cases concerning the education of Russian-speaking minorities who sought to be taught in their native language.[130]

14.3.3.2.2 *Proportionality*

The concept of proportionality comprises the second limb of the test of whether different treatment can be justified on objective and reasonable grounds. Even when shown that the alleged discriminatory treatment pursues

[126] *Oršuš* v. *Croatia* (n 30) at [157]. [127] Ibid at [157].

[128] *Savickis and Others* v. *Latvia* [GC] (2022) 75 EHRR 21.

[129] Ibid at [198]. Note also the joint dissenting opinion of O'Leary, Grozev and Lemmens who characterised the case as a 'difference in treatment based exclusively on grounds of nationality'. Very weighty reasons for the different treatment should be submitted by the State even though the matter concerned economic and social policy for which the State is usually accorded a wide margin of appreciation (at [8]).

[130] *Valiullina and Others* v. *Latvia*, App. No. 56928/19, 14/09/2023; *Dzibuti and Others* v. *Latvia*, App. Nos. 225/20 and others, 16/11/2023. See Ignatius Yordan Nugraha, 'Protection of Constitutional Identity as a Legitimate Aim for Differential Treatment' (2023) 19(1) European Constitutional Law Review 141–162; Merel Vrancken, 'Schools as the Battlefield for Enhancing National Unity: Curtailing Minority Language Rights in Education' [2024] *EHRLR* 185–189.

a legitimate aim, Article 14 ECHR is violated if there is no 'reasonable relationship of proportionality between the means employed and the aim sought to be realised'.[131] The Court assesses whether the differences in treatment 'strike a fair balance between the protection of the interests of the community and respect for the rights and freedoms safeguarded by the Convention'.[132]

The Court has also identified certain forms of discrimination where the State's margin of appreciation will be reduced. The ECtHR distinguishes between differences of treatment on certain grounds. Certain special categories identified by the Court echo to an extent the 'inherently suspect categories' developed in US constitutional law jurisprudence. Any differences of treatment based on race, ethnic origin, religion, sex/gender, nationality, sexual orientation/gender identity and birth can only be justified by very strong or weighty reasons, or cannot be justified at all in relation to race and ethnic origin.[133] The more significant the difference of treatment, the greater the rationale required from the State to justify it. In these circumstances, the Court will be demanding 'very weighty reasons' in its proportionality assessment.

The Court in the *Belgian Linguistics Case* also acknowledged that the public interest may provide a justification for some distinctions in treatment.[134] This is linked to the margin of appreciation whereby States have a certain leeway in assessing whether and to what extent differences in similar situations justify different treatment. According to the Court, the scope of the margin of appreciation 'will vary according to the circumstances, the subject-matter and its background'.[135] This is a matter of some complexity.

A relevant factor may be the extent of the existence of common ground among the Contracting States, and the Court will have regard to whether a consensus exists across Europe. The living instrument doctrine ensures that the Court will consider emerging values and changing standards. For example, in *Markin* v. *Russia*,[136] the facts concerned a divorced military serviceman who had custody of three young children. The applicant sought three years of parental leave which was denied, as only female military personnel could have the extended parental leave. The Grand Chamber noted that the advancement of gender equality is a major goal in Europe and that traditional and

[131] *Belgian Linguistics Case* (n 25) at [10]; *Molla Sali* v. *Greece* (n 77) at [135].

[132] *Belgian Linguistics Case* (n 25) at [7].

[133] See *Abdulaziz, Cabales and Balkandali* v. *the United Kingdom* (n 113) at [78]; *Markin* v. *Russia* [GC] (2013) 56 EHRR 8 at [127]; *Schalk and Kopf* v. *Austria* (2011) 53 EHRRR 20 at [97].

[134] *Belgian Linguistics Case* (n 25) at [10]. Harris et al. (n 116), p.782.

[135] *Molla Sali* v. *Greece* (n 77) at [136]; *Stummer* v. *Austria* (n 29) at [88]; *Burden* v. *the United Kingdom* (n 54) at [60]; *Carson* v. *the United Kingdom* (n 51) at [61].

[136] *Markin* v. *Russia* (n 133).

stereotypical assumptions in a particular country could not be a sufficient justification for a difference in treatment.[137]

The margin of appreciation accorded to States usually remains wide in circumstances concerning general measures of economic or social strategy.[138] It is assumed that the national authorities are in a better position to judge societal needs than an international law judge or institution. The domestic Governments' policy choice will generally be respected unless it is 'manifestly without reasonable foundation'.[139]

The Court has also identified certain forms of discrimination where the State's margin of appreciation will be reduced. The more significant the difference of treatment, the greater the rationale required from the State to justify it. In these circumstances, the Court will be more demanding in a proportionality assessment for the State to show that a fair balance has been struck. Very strong or weighty reasons must be provided, especially in those categories that the Court has deemed 'suspect', to justify any difference of treatment. [140] The Court is sensitive to the context and there is no hard and fast rule.

14.3.4 States' Obligations in Respect of Article 14 ECHR

Article 14 ECHR jurisprudence has been slow to develop in comparison to many other Convention rights. Too often the ECtHR, on finding a breach of the substantive right, did not see the need to consider Article 14 ECHR and discrimination. However, the *Belgian Linguistics Case* in 1968 marked a significant shift.[141] The applicants submitted that the Belgian linguistic legislation relating to educational provisions for their children violated their rights to Article 8 in conjunction with Article 14 ECHR and Article 2 of Protocol 1. According to the ECtHR, if the facts fall within the ambit of a Convention right or protocol, an Article 14 ECHR analysis is relevant and the opportunities for the Court to consider discrimination are extended. Thus the prohibition of discrimination reaches beyond the protection of Convention guarantees that

[137] Ibid at [127].

[138] *Belli and Arquier-Martinez* v. *Switzerland*, App. No. 65550/13, 11/12/2018 at [94]; *Mamatas and Others* v. *Greece*, App. Nos. 63066/14, 64297/14 and 66106/14, 21/07/2016 at [88]–[89]; *Stummer* v. *Austria* (n 29) at [89]; *Andrejeva* v. *Latvia* [GC] (2010) 51 EHRR 28 at [83]; *Burden* v. *the United Kingdom* (n 54) at [60]; *Stec* v. *the United Kingdom* (n 79) at [52].

[139] *Carson and Others* v. *the United Kingdom* [GC] (n 51) at [61]. *JD and A* v. *the United Kingdom* (n 85); *TC* v. *Italy* (2022) 75 EHRR 24 at [43].

[140] See *Abdulaziz, Cabales and Balkandali* v. *the United Kingdom* (n 113) at [78]; *Markin* v. *Russia* (n 133) at [127]; *Schalk and Kopf* v. *Austria* (n 133) at [97]. Note the summary of the Strasbourg jurisprudence by Lord Reed in *R (on the application of SC)* v. *Secretary of State for Work and Pensions* [2021] UKSC 26 at [115]–[116] and [142].

[141] *Belgian Linguistics Case* (n 25).

the State is required to protect and applies 'to those additional rights, falling within the general scope of any Convention Article, for which the State has voluntarily decided to provide'.[142] As a consequence, the ECtHR's Article 14 ECHR jurisprudence has overcome the limitation of its ancillary nature and there is evidence of a framework developing, recognising a substantive right to equality in certain areas. The Court's recognition of substantive equality is increasingly evident in relation to cases addressing stereotyping and vulnerability.[143] Violence against women is a further arena where the Courts have acknowledged the equality issues at stake.[144] The acknowledgment that discrimination can manifest itself in an indirect form has also enhanced its efficacy. These issues are analysed below.

One troubling aspect of Article 14 ECHR jurisprudence has been the approach of the Court to ethnically motivated violence. The ECtHR has emphasised that racist violence is an equality issue. It is puzzling however, that the ECtHR has focused on the subjective intent of the perpetrators in its discrimination assessment even though this is so difficult to prove. While the Courts have often found violations of Articles 2 and 3 ECHR, both substantive and procedural, especially in cases concerning violence against the Roma community, this has often not translated into a finding of a breach of Article 14 ECHR.

The Court has been inconsistent in its approach where the question of intentional racial discrimination has played a seminal part in the violations of rights.[145] In *Anguelova* v. *Bulgaria*, Judge Bonello in a perspicacious dissenting opinion had argued that by avoiding the Article 14 ECHR assessment, the systemic discrimination involving the Roma community was disregarded.[146] It is striking that fewer cases than would be expected have dealt with the substantive aspects of racial violence in conjunction with Article 14 ECHR. The Court's jurisprudence concerning racial violence is thus out of step with the evolution that can be seen in relation to, for example, educational segregation.[147] Ruth Rubio-Marín and Mathias Möschel have observed:

> Looking for evidence of specific motives has prevented the Court from asking generally whether, in view of the evidence before it, it can simply accept that certain ethnic minorities are more likely than others to be victims of police, state or private violence

[142] See *E.B.* v. *France* (n 26) at [48].

[143] *Markin* v. *Russia* (n 133).

[144] See *Opuz* v. *Turkey* (n 32).

[145] See e.g. *V.C.* v. *Slovakia* (2014) 59 EHRR 29; *N.B.* v. *Slovakia*, App. No. 29518/10, 12/06/2012; *I.G.* v. *Slovakia*, App. No. 15996/04, 13/11/2012 concerning the sterilisation of Roma women.

[146] *Anguelova* v. *Bulgaria* (2004) 38 EHRR 31, partly dissenting opinion of Judge Bonello at [2].

[147] E.g., *DH* v. *the Czech Republic* (n 14) and *Opuz* v. *Turkey* (n 32) concerning gender violence as a form of discrimination.

and probably from finding violations of Article 14 more easily once it is faced with a concrete case of relevant indicia.[148]

A number of scholars have attempted to explain the discrepancies in the Court's approach to racist violence. Marie-Bénédicte Dembour posits that the explanation lies in the Court's failure to recognise the historical relevance of empire and (post-)colonialism. She includes the anti-Roma violence decisions in her post-colonial analysis.[149] Rubio-Marín and Möschel have suggested an alternative explanation, the hypothesis of the 'Holocaust Prism'. According to these authors, the trauma of the Holocaust has shaped the Court's approach to State-sponsored violence.[150] This powerful connection invites a 'Gestalt shift whereby those standards that were developed as a response to the Holocaust experience, articulated mostly around the definition of genocide and crimes against humanity, become predominant'.[151] They conclude:

> The problem is that having genocide in the back of one's mind when analysing racial violence cases will make it extremely hard to find an Article 14 violation, not only because of the ECtHR's understandable reluctance to act as a criminal law court[69] but also in view of the seriousness of the accusation and the political reactions that may ensue from accused state parties. Ironically then, the closer the forms of discriminatory violence resemble those that actually occurred under the Holocaust (physical abuse by state officials, systematic killings and forced sterilizations, including of Roma people), the less likely the Court is to be inclined to denounce the practice.[152]

There is likely to be no one rationale to explain the Court's approach to racial violence but it has been disappointing, given the advances in other arenas concerning race and ethnicity in Strasbourg. It has also systematically led to the underdevelopment of Article 14 ECHR in important arenas. These issues are discussed in further detail below.

14.3.5 Examples from the Article 14 ECHR Jurisprudence

This section examines race and ethnicity, religion, sex/gender and sexual orientation, gender identity and sex characteristic categories as a way of demonstrating how the Court's Article 14 ECHR case law has developed in significant ways.

[148] Ruth Rubio-Marín and Mathias Möschel, 'Anti-discrimination Exceptionalism: Racist Violence before the ECtHR and the Holocaust Prism' (2015) 26(4) EJIL 881, 890.

[149] Marie-Bénédicte Dembour, 'Postcolonial Denial: Why the European Court of Human Rights Finds It So Difficult to Acknowledge Racism' in K. Clarke and M. Goodale (eds), *Mirrors of Justice: Law and Power in the Post Cold-War Era* (Cambridge University Press, 2009), p.45. Cited in Rubio-Marín and Möschel (n 148).

[150] Rubio-Marín and Möschel (n 148), p.893. [151] Ibid. [152] Ibid.

14.3.5.1 *Race and Ethnicity*

The European Commission against Racism and Intolerance (ECRI), established by the Council of Europe in 1993, acts as an independent human rights monitoring mechanism focusing on questions of racism and intolerance in Europe. Its most recent report is sobering.[153] Despite the existence of legal prohibitions on racist discrimination over many years, the evidence remains that people from racial minorities continue to suffer discrimination and disadvantage. The recent trends observed by the ECRI included the situation of people displaced by war and other emergencies, the rise in anti-Semitism because of the current conflict in the Middle East and the continuing atmosphere of suspicion against Muslims in Europe.[154] The experience differs between, and even within, these minority communities. For example, the report notes that while the millions of people displaced from Ukraine because of the war have been accommodated in Europe, there are cases of discrepancy of treatment based on ethnicity, particularly Roma with Ukrainian citizenship.[155] The Council of Europe Commissioner of Human Rights, Michael O'Flaherty, has stated that 'Roma continue to suffer from widespread anti-gypsyism. This specific racism takes several forms ranging from daily anti-Roma discourse by ordinary citizens, politicians and the media to the most heinous ones such as hate crimes targeting Roma.'[156] He urges Member States to make the plight of Roma a top priority: 'The discrimination experienced by Roma and Travellers in Europe and the scale of human rights violations that they face is shocking and calls for firm action.'[157]

'Race' and 'colour' are listed as discriminatory grounds in Article 14 ECHR. Discrimination that is associated with 'race' or 'colour' is often considered under the category of 'ethnic' origin or 'ethnicity'.[158] National and social origin are also prohibited categories, and these too may also serve as a substitute for 'race'. The international human rights system still refers to 'racism' and 'racial discrimination.' The ECtHR, when interpreting the category of 'race', has referred to the definition of 'racial discrimination' in

[153] Council of Europe, Annual Report on ECRI's Activities covering the period from 1 January 2023 to 31 December 2023.

[154] Ibid, pp.7–8. [155] Ibid, p8.

[156] Council of Europe Commission for Human Rights, 'The protection of the human rights of Roma and Travellers must become a top priority in our member states', Strasbourg, 05/04/2024.

[157] Ibid. On antigypsyism, see ECRI General Policy Recommendation N°13 revised on combating antigypsyism and discrimination against Roma – adopted on 24/06/2011 and amended on 01/12/ 2020.

[158] William Schabas, *The European Convention on Human Rights: A Commentary*, (Oxford University Press, 2015) p. 577.

Article 1 of the International Convention on the Elimination of All Forms of Racial Discrimination:

In this Convention, the term 'racial discrimination' shall mean any distinction, exclusion, restriction or preference based on race, colour, descent, or national or ethnic origin which has the purpose or effect of nullifying or impairing the recognition, enjoyment or exercise, on an equal footing, of human rights and fundamental freedoms in the political, economic, social, cultural or any other field of public life.[159]

Racial discrimination has been described in the Strasbourg jurisprudence as a 'particularly invidious kind of discrimination and, in view of its perilous consequences, requires from the authorities special vigilance and a vigorous reaction'.[160] The ECtHR has viewed discrimination on these grounds in strict terms:

where a difference in treatment is based on race or ethnicity, the notion of objective and reasonable justification must be interpreted as strictly as possible . . . The Court has also held that no difference in treatment which is based exclusively or to a decisive extent on a person's ethnic origin is capable of being objectively justified in a contemporary democratic society built on the principles of pluralism and respect for different cultures.[161]

Racism is multidimensional. In the ECtHR's explanation of the concepts of race and ethnicity, it has held that language, religion, nationality and culture may be inextricably linked. In *Timishev* v. *Russia*, the ECtHR explained the interrelationship of ethnicity and race:

Ethnicity and race are related and overlapping concepts. Whereas the notion of race is rooted in the idea of biological classification of human beings into subspecies according to morphological features such as skin colour or facial characteristics, ethnicity has its origin in the idea of societal groups marked by common nationality, tribal affiliation, religious faith, shared language, or cultural and traditional origins and backgrounds.[162]

The Court has also held that it is not possible to justify objectively a difference of treatment based exclusively or to a decisive extent on a person's ethnic origin as this would be contrary to a 'contemporary democratic society built on the principles of pluralism and respect for different cultures'.[163] Indeed, in

[159] Ibid; UN GA (1966) International Convention on the Elimination of All Forms of Racial Discrimination (1966) UNTS Vol. 660, p.195.

[160] *DH* v. *the Czech Republic* (n 14) at [176]; *Nachova* v. *Bulgaria* [GC] (n 32) at [145]; *Timishev* v. *Russia* (2007) 44 EHRR 37 at [56]; *Sampanis* v. *Greece*, App. No. 32526/05, 5/06/2008 at [69].

[161] *Sejdic and Finci* v. *Bosnia Herzegovina* (n 44) at [44]. See also, *DH* v. *the Czech Republic* (n 14) at [196].

[162] *Timishev* v. *Russia* (n 160) at [55].

[163] *DH* v. *the Czech Republic* (n 14) at [176].

some circumstances race or ethnic discrimination could reach the level of severity to be considered a violation of Article 3 ECHR.[164]

14.3.5.2 *Violence and Racism*

In *Nachova* v. *Bulgaria*, a case concerning ethnically motivated violence against persons of Roma origin, the Grand Chamber stated: 'Racial violence is a particular affront to human dignity and, in view of its perilous consequences, requires from the authorities special vigilance and a vigorous reaction.'[165] Given this strong statement, it is perhaps surprising then that the ECtHR has focused on the subjective intent of the perpetrators in its discrimination assessment. The proving of a 'racial motivation' is often very difficult and this has limited the efficacy of Article 14 ECHR.

The burden of proof in the discrimination arena is variable. The burden initially falls on the applicant to show that there is a difference in treatment and if this is established, the burden shifts to the Government to establish that the measure in question is justified. In circumstances where the claim is that ill-treatment is the result of conduct motivated by a prohibited ground, the applicant is required to establish more than the existence of differential treatment. Some further demonstration of the discriminatory conduct of the authorities must be demonstrated before the burden of proof will shift to the Government to disprove an alleged claim of discrimination. This has proved to be a controversial issue.

An important example of this is in *Nachova*.[166] The case concerned two young Roma men, aged twenty-one years, who were shot dead by the military police. They were both unarmed and non-violent men.[167] Violations of Article 2 ECHR were found on the basis of unlawful death and failure to investigate effectively. It was, however, alleged that there was evidence of racist verbal abuse by one officer involved in the shooting of the victims and that prejudice and hostile attitudes towards persons of Roma origin had played a role in the deaths. Consequently, the Grand Chamber was also asked to decide whether these unlawful deaths disclosed a violation of Article 14 in conjunction with Article 2 ECHR.

The Grand Chamber noted various reports of allegations of discrimination against Roma including an ECRI report which expressed concern about racially motivated police violence, particularly against Roma, in several

[164] *East African Asians* v. *the United Kingdom*, ECommHR, App. Nos. 4403/70 and 30 others, 14/12/1973 at [207].

[165] *Nachova* v. *Bulgaria* (n 32) at [145]. Harris et al. (n 116) have an extensive discussion on racial violence, pp.788–792.

[166] *Nachova* (n 32) at [103]. [167] Ibid at [103].

countries including Bulgaria.[168] However, the Grand Chamber was not prepared to alter its usual approach to the standard of proof and shift the burden to the Government in relation to the alleged violation of Article 14 ECHR.[169] According to the Court, 'its sole concern [was] to ascertain whether in the case at hand the killing of [the deceased] was motivated by racism'.[170] The Chamber concluded that there was no violation of Article 14 in conjunction with Article 2 ECHR as there was insufficient evidence that the events leading to the death of the two young men constituted an act of racial violence.

In the Grand Chamber's opinion, where it is alleged that a violent act was motivated by racial prejudice, adopting a shift in the burden of proof 'would amount to requiring the respondent Government to prove the absence of a particular subjective attitude on the part of the person concerned'.[171] Judge Bratza, in his concurring judgment, expressed concern that this passage suggested that the evidential difficulties which a Government would face meant that it would rarely be appropriate to shift the burden of proof.[172] In this regard, it is important to note that in the later decision of *Stoica* v. *Romania*, the Court assumed that the Grand Chamber in *Nachova* had left open the possibility of reversing the burden of proof in certain circumstances.[173] The facts in *Stoica* concerned an alleged racially motivated serious assault on a Roma minor during a day of racist tension and violence between the police and members of a village largely populated by Roma. After considering the factual evidence, the Court concluded that 'clear' racial motives behind the police officers' actions were indicated.[174] The burden of proof was then shifted to the respondent Government to show that the serious attack on the applicant, which violated Article 3 ECHR (his injuries were the result of inhuman and degrading treatment), was not racially motivated. As neither the prosecutor nor the Government could provide an explanation showing that the incidents were racially neutral, the Court found a violation of Article 14 in conjunction with Article 3 ECHR.[175]

In *Nachova* v. *Bulgaria*, a further question that arose was whether the authorities had complied with the procedural obligation in Article 14 ECHR. The applicants claimed that 'the authorities had failed in their duty to investigate possible racist motives' in the killings.[176] As noted above, the Court had already found a violation of Article 2 ECHR, as the Bulgarian authorities had failed to conduct a meaningful investigation into the deaths of the two Roma men.[177] Nevertheless, the Court decided that it would still examine separately

[168] Ibid at [51]. [169] Ibid at [157]. [170] Ibid at [155]. [171] Ibid at [157].

[172] Ibid. Concurring opinion of Judge Sir Nicholas Bratza.

[173] *Stoica* v. *Romania*, App. No. 42722/02, 04/03/2008 at [126] and [127]. See also, *Antayev* v. *Russia*, App. No. 37966/07, 03/07/2014.

[174] *Stoica* (n 173) at [131]. [175] Ibid. [176] Ibid at [124].

[177] *Nachova* (n 32) at [114]–[119].

the issue of the failure to investigate a possible link between alleged racist attitudes and the lethal shootings.[178] The Grand Chamber endorsed the Chamber's analysis in *Nachova*, in particular:

> [W]here there is suspicion that racial attitudes induced a violent act it is particularly important that the official investigation is pursued with vigour and impartiality, having regard to the need to reassert continuously society's condemnation of racism and ethnic hatred and to maintain the confidence of minorities in the ability of the authorities to protect them from the threat of racist violence.[179]

The Grand Chamber further approved the observations of the Chamber that the authorities must 'take all reasonable steps to unmask any racist motive and to establish whether or not ethnic hatred or prejudice may have played a role in the events'.[180] In their view, failing to distinguish between cases which have racist overtones and those that do not would be 'to turn a blind eye' to these acts which are particularly destructive of human rights.[181] There was also an acknowledgement that proving racist motivations may be difficult in practice. Nevertheless, there is an obligation on the State to use 'best endeavours' and the authorities must do 'what is reasonable in the circumstances' in relation to the investigation.[182]

On the facts of the *Nachova* case, the authorities had 'plausible information' of discriminatory attitudes, including allegations of racist verbal abuse by a member of the military police who had carried out the shooting. According to the Court, any understanding of the context of the events had to be 'seen against the background of the many published accounts of the existence in Bulgaria of prejudice and hostility against Roma'.[183] The Court found that the authorities had omitted to question witnesses or check the background of the police officer, who allegedly used racist abuse, to see whether there was a history of anti-Roma sentiment. The Court concluded that the investigations failed to take all possible steps and that there was a violation of Article 14 of the Convention taken in conjunction with Article 2 ECHR in its procedural aspect.[184]

Following the Grand Chamber decision in *Nachova*, the Court has found numerous violations of the procedural aspect of Articles 2 and 3 in conjunction with Article 14 ECHR.[185] Positive obligations on the authorities to

[178] The Court noted the interplay between the investigative obligations in Articles 2 and 14 and said that it would be dependent on the facts as to whether a case would be examined under one of the two provisions, or under both Articles. Ibid at [161].

[179] Ibid at [160], endorsement of the Chamber decision at [157].

[180] Ibid, endorsement of the Chamber decision at [158].

[181] Ibid.

[182] Ibid, endorsement of the Chamber decision at [159].

[183] Ibid at [163].

[184] Ibid at [168].

[185] See, e.g., *Fedorchenko and Lozenko* v. *Ukraine*, App. No. 387/03, 20/09/2010.

investigate will arise under Article 14 ECHR if there is any evidence of a possible link between acts of violence and discriminatory motives.[186] The Court has emphasised that in investigations of violent incidents, the States' authorities have the additional duty to take all reasonable steps to expose any discriminatory motive and to establish whether discrimination was a catalyst in the impugned conduct.[187] The additional duty on States still applies even where the actual treatment contrary to Articles 2 and 3 ECHR was perpetrated by private individuals.[188]

In addition to the cases that arise in respect of Articles 2 and 3 ECHR coupled with Article 14 ECHR, issues relating to discriminatory intent have also arisen in relation to Article 8 in conjunction with Article 14 ECHR. In contrast to earlier judgments,[189] the Court has found a violation of Article 8 ECHR in conjunction with Article 14 ECHR in *Paketova and Others* v. *Bulgaria.*[190] The applicants, of Roma origin, were forced to leave their homes because of repeated anti-Roma marches in their village. They were subsequently prevented from returning to their homes by the opposition of officials. They claimed that the authorities had refused them protection in an environment of racially based hostility and that they continued to fear for their safety. The Court concluded that there was a violation of Article 8 ECHR read with Article 14 ECHR as the applicants were unable to enjoy their home and family life and the authorities failed to provide the required protection.[191] The Article 8 ECHR issues which arise in respect of hate speech were considered in greater detail in Chapter 11,[192] which includes a detailed discussion of the cases, heard simultaneously, of *Budinova and Chaprazov* v. *Bulgaria*[193] and *Behar and Gutman* v. *Bulgaria.*[194] Both cases were examined in the light of Article 14,

[186] *Bekos and Koutropoulos* v. *Greece* (2006) 43 EHRR 2; *Abdu* v. *Bulgaria*, App. No. 26827/08, 11/03/2014; *Angelova and Iliev* v. *Bulgaria* (2008) 47 EHRR 7; *Members of the Gldani Congregation of Jehovah's Witnesses and Others* v. *Georgia*, App. No. 71156/01, 03/05/2007; *Virabyan* v. *Armenia*, App. No. 40094/05, 02/10/2012; *Talpis* v. *Italy* [2017] ECHR 224; *Škorjanec* v. *Croatia* (2018) 66 EHRR 14; *Kreyndlin* v. *Russia* (2023) 77 EHRR 14; *Georgian Muslim Relations and others* v. *Georgia* (2024) 79 EHRR 12.

[187] See, for example, *Ognyanova and Choban* v. *Bulgaria* (2007) 44 EHRR 7 at [145]; *Abdu* v. *Bulgaria* (n 186) at [44]; *Eremia and Ors* v. *the Republic of Moldova* (2014) 58 EHRR 2 at [85]; *Members of the Gldani Congregation of Jehovah's Witnesses and Others* v. *Georgia* (n 186) at [14]; *Virabyan* v. *Armenia* (n 186) at [218]; *Kreyndlin* v. *Russia* (n 186) at [58].

[188] *Šečić* v. *Croatia*, App. No. 40116/02, 31/08/2007 at [67]; *Abdu* v. *Bulgaria* (n 186); *Fedorchenko and Lozenko* v. *Ukraine* (n 185).

[189] *Yordanova and Others* v. *Bulgaria*, App. No. 25446/06, 24/04/2012.

[190] *Paketova and Others* v. *Bulgaria*, App. Nos. 17808/19 and 36972/19, 04/10/2022.

[191] Ibid at [167]. [192] See pp. 541–581.

[193] *Budinova and Chaprazov* v. *Bulgaria*, App. No. 12567/13, 04/03/2021.

[194] *Behar and Gutman* v. *Bulgaria*, App. No. 29335/13, 04/03/2021.

which enhanced the victims' right to challenge hateful racist speech. In this respect the Court stated:

> Since the statements in respect of which the applicants sought redress were . . . prima facie discriminatory in intent as regards Roma, in the present case that analysis [of the balance between Articles 8 and 10] must also be coloured by the duties stemming from Article 14 of the Convention – in particular the duty to combat racial discrimination, which includes discrimination on account of someone's ethnic origin.[195]

14.3.5.3 *Racial Profiling*

The ECRI's General Policy Recommendation No. 11, on combatting racism and racial discrimination in policing, states that racial profiling is 'the use by the police, with no objective and reasonable justification, of grounds such as race, colour, language, religion, nationality or national or ethnic origin in control, surveillance or investigation activities'.[196] It generates a feeling of humiliation and injustice among those groups that are subjected to it, results in their stigmatisation, negative stereotyping and alienation, and hinders good community relations.[197] Many international organisations have raised issues with racial and ethnic profiling, but it is not explicitly prohibited in any binding international human rights instrument.[198] Numerous studies and reports indicate that this phenomenon remains widespread across Europe.[199]

The Court has addressed racial profiling in the context of police powers in *Timishev* v. *Russia*[200] (a ban imposed on Chechens crossing an administrative

[195] *Budinova* (n 193) at [91].

[196] ECRI General Policy Recommendation No. 11 at [1] adopted on 29/06/2007, https://rm.coe.int/ecri-general-policy-recommendation-no-11-on-combating-racism-and-racia/16808b5adf.

[197] ECRI, Statement on Racist Police Abuse, including Racial Profiling, and Systemic Racism, Adopted at its 82nd plenary meeting (30 June–2 July 2020), https://rm.coe.int/statement-of-ecri-on-racist-police-abuse-including-racial-profiling-an/16809eee6a.

[198] UN Committee on the Elimination of Racial Discrimination (CERD), the Council of Europe Commissioner for Human Rights, the UN Special Rapporteur on Racism, the UN Special Rapporteur on Countering Terrorism, the Office of the High Commissioner for Human Rights (OHCHR), the OSCE High Commissioner on National Minorities, and the European Commission against Racism and Intolerance (ECRI) have produced a plethora of recommendations and guidelines on preventing racial profiling in law enforcement and the European Parliament, has condemned this practice as discriminatory and called upon States to take measures to tackle it.

[199] See Commissioner for Human Rights, *Ethnic Profiling: A Persistent Practice in Europe*, 2019; Parliamentary Assembly of the Council of Europe, *Ethnic Profiling in Europe: a Matter of Great Concern*, 2020; EU Fundamental Rights Agency, *Your Rights Matter: Police Stops*, 2021. See Olivier De Schutter and Julie Ringelheim, 'Ethnic Profiling: A Rising Challenge for European Human Rights Law' (2008) **71** MLR 331.

[200] *Timishev* v. *Russia* (n 160).

border) and *Lingurar* v. *Romania*[201] (a police operation targeting a Roma village). A breach of Article 14 ECHR was found in both cases. More recently and for the first time, the ECtHR has confronted the issue of alleged racial profiling in 'routine' police identity checks in public places. In two cases decided by the Court on the same day, both applicants alleged that they had been stopped and subjected to an identity check based on their race, ethnicity or skin colour.

Muhammad v. *Spain* concerned an identity check of a Pakistani national on a street in Barcelona.[202] The submission of international reports of racially motivated profiling in Spain was found to be irrelevant as the Court's 'sole concern in the case at hand' was to determine whether the identity check of the applicant was 'motivated by racism'.[203] The Court held by a thin majority of four to three that there was no violation of Article 14 in conjunction with Article 8 concerning either the grounds for the police check or arrest or due to a failure to carry out an effective investigation. The second decision on profiling, *Basu* v. *Germany*, concerned the stop and search of a German national of Indian origin on a train.[204] The Court found a procedural violation of Article 14 ECHR because of the failure of the authorities to carry out an effective investigation into the applicant's allegation of racial discrimination.

Drawing on the caselaw concerning racist violence, in particular *Nachova* v. *Bulgaria*[205] and *B.S.* v. *Spain*,[206] the Court focused on the 'racist motives' of the police officials.[207] The burden of demonstrating the presence of racist motivations lay entirely on the applicants and not on the State. The Court has determined that once an applicant has an arguable claim to have been subject to an identity check or stop and search on the basis of race or ethnicity, the State has a duty under Article 14 ECHR to conduct an effective and independent investigation to ascertain whether the agent was motivated by discrimination. Yet in both *Muhammad* and *Basu*, the Court chose not to engage with a critical assessment of the frameworks in Spain and Germany to investigate whether the police power to carry out an identity check has adequate protections to prevent racial profiling.[208] This was the case even though the issue was raised by the applicants.

This lacuna was even more disappointing given the Court's willingness to assess whether there had been an effective investigation in these particular cases. In *Basu*, the Court found that State authorities had failed to comply with

201 *Lingurar* v. *Romania*, App. No. 48474/14, 16/04/2019.

202 *Muhammad* v. *Spain*, App. No. 34085/17, 18/10/2022.

203 Ibid at [100].

204 *Basu* v. *Germany*, App. No. 215/19, 18/10/2022.

205 *Nachova* (n 32) at [160]–[161].

206 *B.S.* v. *Spain* (n 32) at [58].

207 *Muhammad* (n 202) at [102] and *Basu* (n 204) at [36].

208 This was criticised by Judge Pavli in *Basu* (n 204) at [9]–[12] and in the dissenting opinion of Judge Krenc in *Muhammad* (n 202).

their duty to investigate the incident. First, the internal investigation carried out by the German Federal Police could not be deemed independent. Second, the administrative courts which handled the applicant's complaint had not taken the necessary evidence and had rejected the complaint on formal grounds, denying that the applicant had a legitimate interest in a decision on the lawfulness of his identity check.[209] The ECtHR concluded that, owing to the lack of such an investigation, it was 'unable to make a finding' whether there had been a substantive violation of the prohibition of discrimination.[210] Judge Pavli, in a partly dissenting opinion, strongly criticised this conclusion as providing 'perverse incentives' to national authorities to sweep cases of racial profiling under the carpet. It also greatly limits the chances of victims being able to demonstrate discrimination in identity checks.[211] In *Muhammad*, the ECtHR found no violation of the State's procedural obligation under Article 14 ECHR. This conclusion is odd for many reasons. For example, the applicant and the police had given entirely diverging accounts of the incident but the administrative courts which examined the applicant's complaint for discrimination relied exclusively on the statements of the police officers. In their dissenting opinions, both Judge Zünd and Judge Krenc strongly criticised this aspect of the judgment.

These judgments also raised questions concerning the appropriate burden of proof. In a concurring opinion in *Muhammad*, Judges Elósegui and Serghides submitted:

> that the relevant evidential rule which is adopted in the judgment, namely that the burden of proof can be shifted to the authorities *only* when there is a prima facie case of discrimination brought by the applicant, is an aspect of the principle of effectiveness ... The principle of effectiveness ... should, in our view, also apply in making the evidential rules concerning these rights practical and effective ... Without the existence of the requirement for the applicant to make a prima facie case of discrimination before the burden of proof is shifted to the authorities, the task of the authorities in performing their duties would become excessively difficult, because they would have to prove in every case that every step or action on their part was taken without any discrimination.[212]

Yet proving racial profiling is difficult, especially as the police often enjoy wide discretionary powers in laws regulating identity checks. Moreover, police officers will rarely admit that they have acted because of racial or ethnic prejudice. In his dissent in *Basu*, Judge Pavli points out, 'discrimination in this context may not be driven necessarily by a police officer's *individual and conscious* attitude or hostility against a particular racial or ethnic group; it

[209] *Basu* (n 204) at [37]. [210] Ibid at [38].
[211] Ibid, see dissenting opinion of Judge Pavli at [4] and [18].
[212] *Muhammad* (n 202), a joint concurring opinion of Judges Elósegui and Serghides at [37].

may also be the result of biased (or at least permissive) internal police guidelines, practices or attitudes, whether formalized or merely tolerated by the hierarchy'.[213] In *Basu* and *Muhammad*, the Court recognised that the applicants had an 'arguable claim' of having been subject to racial profiling. The applicants submitted evidence of international institutions and NGOs reports highlighting the prevalence of profiling practices by the police in Germany and Spain and arguably indicating a systemic pattern in both countries. The Court however refused to accept this evidence as establishing a presumption of discrimination. In his strong partly dissenting opinion, Judge Pavli argued that where an arguable claim of direct discrimination on racial or ethnic grounds has been made, the burden of proof should be reversed. Where only the State had the ability to establish the relevant facts, it was up to the authorities to show that the identity check had an objective and reasonable basis.[214]

The issue of racial profiling came before the Courts again in *Wa Baile* v. *Switzerland*.[215] The facts concerned Mohamed Wa Baile, a Swiss citizen of Kenyan origin, who was stopped by the municipal police in the Zurich train station while on his way to work. According to the police officer in charge, he stopped Wa Baile because of his behaviour, which appeared suspicious as Wa Baile looked away when he realised that he was a police officer. From the perspective of the police, there were grounds to suspect him of an offence against Swiss immigration law. Wa Baile refused to produce an ID card, arguing that he was weary of being stopped because of the colour of his skin. His appeal against the fine for failing to comply with a police order was turned down by the criminal courts. Wa Baile also initiated administrative proceedings, resulting in a decision of the cantonal administrative court finding that the identity check had not been justified under the cantonal domestic law. However, the Court refused to rule on his discrimination claim.

The ECtHR ruled that the identity check of Mohamed Wa Baile amounted to racial profiling in violation of Article 14 in conjunction with Article 8 ECHR. According to the Court, where an arguable claim of discrimination is lodged with the national authorities, they have an obligation under Article 14 ECHR to examine that claim effectively. Unlike in *Basu*, the identity check in *Wa Baile* had been reviewed by several domestic courts. The cantonal administrative court concluded that no objective grounds could justify the check, but it did not specifically address the question of the racist intentions of the police. The ECtHR concluded that the right to the procedural limb of Article 14 ECHR was violated.

In a dramatic turnabout given the recent decisions of *Basu* and *Muhammad*, the ECtHR ruled unanimously that the substantive limb of Article 14 read with

[213] *Basu* v. *Germany* (n 204), dissenting opinion of Judge Pavli at [7].

[214] Ibid, dissenting opinion of Judge Pavli at [4].

[215] *Wa Baile* v. *Switzerland* App. Nos. 43868/18 and 25883/21, 20/02/24.

Article 8 ECHR was also violated. The Court essentially adopted the approach suggested by Judge Pavli in *Basu* and sidestepped the evidentiary hurdles in racial profiling cases to reverse the burden of proof.[216] In the Court's view, the resulting lack of an adequate legal and administrative framework was liable to give rise to discriminatory identity checks.[217] In contrast to its approach in *Muhammad*, the Court in *Wa Baile* relied heavily on the recommendations and findings of international human rights organisations regarding racial profiling in its assessment of Article 14 ECHR.[218] It also included observations by Amnesty International, which intervened as a third party, to substantiate a presumption of racial discrimination among the Swiss police.[219] Finally, reliance was placed on the finding of the cantonal administrative court that had decided that there were no objective grounds for the identity check.[220] The Court concluded that the identity check was discriminatory.[221] The burden of proof was reversed and it was now up to Switzerland to provide a convincing explanation for the reason Mr Wa Baile had been stopped.[222] Switzerland, the Court found, failed to discharge this burden. The authorities could neither produce figures or information demonstrating that other persons were also stopped in Zurich that day[223] nor overall statistical figures on identity checks.[224]

Whether it can be declared that *Wa Baile* is a 'revolutionary' decision will depend on a number of factors. In *Wa Baile,* the cantonal administrative Court in Switzerland had concluded that the identity check was unlawful, and this gave rise to a strong presumption that the police request was discriminatory. This factual scenario was different from *Muhammad* and *Basu*. If this is the essential reason why the ECtHR adopted a different approach, it is uncertain whether the ECtHR will follow this decision, if the facts of future cases vary. It is worth remembering the concern expressed by Judges Elósegui and Serghides in their concurring opinion in *Muhammad* that 'the task of the authorities in performing their duties would become excessively difficult, because they would have to prove in every case that every step or action on their part was taken without any discrimination'.[225] Nevertheless, the Court's reliance on the submissions and recommendations of international bodies must be welcomed as it can support evidence of a systemic problem. It may be that the Court will infer a prima facie case of discrimination if the State's legal and administrative framework is inadequate for prohibiting racially discriminatory police practices and there is some proof of racially discriminatory police practice in the State. In these circumstances the burden of proof would shift to the respondent State.

[216] Judge Pavli was a member of this Chamber. [217] *Wa Baile* v. *Switzerland* (n 215) at [130].
[218] Ibid at [130] and [135]. [219] Ibid at [135]. [220] Ibid at [134]. [221] Ibid at [136].
[222] Ibid at [132]. [223] Ibid at [134]. [224] Ibid at [135].
[225] *Muhammad* (n 202), joint concurring opinion of Judges Elósegui and Serghides at [37].

In a further important decision of *Memedova and others* v. *North Macedonia*, the Court extended, for the first time, the concept of indirect discrimination to border checks.[226] In this case, the applicants were stopped at the border and subject to an identity check by the authorities on public policy grounds. The background to these checks was that an increasing number of nationals from North Macedonia were seeking asylum in EU States. This was an abuse of the visa-free agreement with Schengen Treaty Member States and thus a new system of stronger border controls was introduced for groups of citizens wishing to cross the border and who could be potential asylum seekers. Although there was no direct evidence that instructions had been issued that border controllers should prevent Roma nationals from crossing the border, it was evident that the enhanced controls had the effect of preventing a disproportionate number of such nationals from crossing.[227] Both the United Nations and Council of Europe bodies had expressed concerns about ethnic profiling, especially of Roma persons, even prior to the case being bought.[228] The five applicants in *Memedova* were persons of Roma origin who were prevented from leaving by crossing the border. They claimed violations of Article 2 of Protocol No. 4 (right to freedom of movement), as well as the prohibition of discrimination under Article 14 ECHR read in conjunction with Article 2 of Protocol No. 4.[229] The Court found a prima facie case of indirect discrimination as the practice of the border police had 'resulted in a disproportionate number of Roma being prevented from travelling abroad'.[230] The impact of this was that the State had to establish that the practice had an 'objective and reasonable justification'. The Government did not present any evidence to the Court to refute the applicant's claims that they were discriminated against because of their Roma origins and a violation was duly found.[231] Vandita Khanna explains why extending indirect discrimination to border controls is significant.

> According to states, the effective exercise of this right includes distinguishing between citizens and non-citizens. This 'assumed legitimacy of discrimination' clouds the ability of international and domestic human rights law to cut through discriminatory regimes in migration control. The statist assumption has typically meant that the Court too has remained highly deferential to states on such politically sensitive questions ... *Memedova* shows how the Court *can* address certain border management practices in discrimination law.[232]

[226] *Memedova* v. *North Macedonia* (2024) 79 EHRR 3. [227] Ibid at [94]. [228] Ibid at [91].

[229] The applicants had also bought a claim under Protocol 12 but the Court chose to characterise the facts as one concerning Article 14 and not Article 1 of Protocol No. 12.

[230] *Memedova* (n 226) at [100].

[231] Ibid at [97]. One applicant did not succeed on the facts of the case.

[232] See Vandita Khanna, 'Racial Profiling as Indirect Discrimination' [2024] 2 EHRLR 181, pp.182–183 (footnote from quote omitted).

Memedova is also the first time that the Court has addressed racial profiling within indirect discrimination. Khanna acknowledges that this is a significant development, but she suggests that dealing with these cases on an individual basis, bypasses the systemic problem that racial profiling is pervasive.[233] In this respect *Wa Baile* is a promising judgment in which the ECtHR was prepared to correct the individual-oriented approach to racial profiling that it had initially adopted in *Basu* and *Muhammad*. There is therefore still considerable uncertainty about accommodating racial profiling within the existing Article 14 ECHR framework, but the Strasbourg jurisprudence is increasingly recognising the harm of this type of discriminatory behaviour and that it is a structural problem.

14.3.5.4 Immigration

Article 14 ECHR and the principle of non-discrimination are also relevant in the context of immigration. As observed in Chapter 9, Article 8 ECHR does not guarantee an obligation on the State to allow family reunification. Nevertheless, if a State confers a right of entry, it must do so in a manner compatible with Article 14 ECHR. Consequently, in *Abdulaziz, Cabales and Balkandali* v. *the United Kingdom*, the ECtHR found that there was sex discrimination where immigration laws had the effect that it was far easier for a man to be joined by his non-national wife, than for a woman to obtain such permission for her spouse. This difference of treatment was not disputed. In the context of sex discrimination, the applicants were able to show that the reason presented by the State to justify the differential treatment of men and women, that there was a different impact on the labour market, was without factual basis and not a legitimate aim.[234]

The Court rejected the applicants' claim that the immigration rules were racially motivated. According to the Court, most immigration policies differentiate on the basis of nationality and indirectly on race, ethnic origin and possibly colour and this did not amount to racial discrimination. It concluded that there was no evidence of an actual difference of treatment on grounds of race. Nevertheless, there was a strong suspicion that the effect of the immigration policy was to prevent immigration from the new Commonwealth and Pakistan but this was not accepted by the Court.[235] This case was decided before the ECtHR had developed its indirect discrimination jurisprudence.

More recently in an important decision, *Biao* v. *Denmark*, the Court considered a statutory requirement that imposed differential treatment between Danish citizens and those of non-Danish origin for the purposes of granting

[233] Ibid, p.184.

[234] *Abdulaziz, Cabales and Balkandali* (n 113) at [78]–[79]. See also the discussion in Chapter 9.

[235] Ibid at [84].

family reunification.[236] The Court found a violation of Article 14 read with Article 8 ECHR as this requirement had a disproportionately prejudicial effect on persons who acquired Danish nationality later in life and were of a different ethnic group.[237]

14.3.5.5 *Discrimination against Roma and Educational Segregation*

Many of the cases which come before the ECtHR dealing with racism relate to the prejudice and abuse directed at Roma. The Council of Europe has recognised that Roma are one of the most discriminated and disadvantaged groups in Europe.[238] The Court has established that:

> [A]s a result of their turbulent history and constant uprooting, the Roma have become a specific type of disadvantaged and vulnerable minority. They therefore require special protection. Their vulnerable position means that special consideration should be given to their needs and their different lifestyle both in the relevant regulatory framework and in reaching decisions in particular cases.[239]

We have seen already that the first case decided by the ECtHR on indirect discrimination, *DH* v. *the Czech Republic*, concerned the segregation of Roma children through the enrolment of a disproportionate number of them in schools for pupils with learning disabilities.[240] Since *DH*, there have been many decisions in which the ECtHR has found indirect discrimination in the education and desegregation arena.[241] The Court has recognised that general policies or measures that have disproportionately prejudicial effects on a particular group may be considered discriminatory notwithstanding that they are not specifically aimed at the group.[242] In relation to the burden of proof, the Court held that once the applicant has been able to demonstrate a difference in treatment, the burden falls to the State to show that such treatment was justified.[243] One example is the case of *Sampanis* v. *Greece* concerning a group of Roma children who were placed in classes at a regular school.[244] Following complaints and a blockade of the school by about two hundred parents of non-Roma children, approximately fifty Roma pupils were placed

236 *Biao* v. *Denmark* (n 54). 237 See also, *Zarb Adami* v. *Malta* (2007) 44 EHRR 49.

238 Council of Europe, The Roma – Europe's Forgotten People, www.coe.int/en/web/portal/the-roma-europe-forgotten-people; UNICEF, Roma Children, www.unicef.org/eca/what-we-do/ending-child-poverty/roma-children; European Union Agency for Fundamental Rights.

239 *Horváth and Kiss* v. *Hungary* (n 84) at [102].

240 *DH* v. *the Czech Republic* (n 14), see Section 14.3.2.1 Direct and Indirect Discrimination.

241 See e.g. *Oršuš and Others* v. *Croatia* (n 30); *Horváth and Kiss* v. *Hungary* (n 84); *Sampani* v. *Greece*, App. No. 59608/09, 11/12/2012.

242 See discussion of indirect discrimination above at Section 14.3.2.1.

243 *DH* v *the Czech Republic* (n 14) at [175]–[177].

244 *Sampanis* v. *Greece*, App. No. 32526/05, 05/06/2008.

in special preparatory classes in an annexe to the main school building. The declared objective of these special classes was to facilitate the integration of the Roma pupils into the ordinary classes. After two years of schooling no student had been integrated into ordinary school classes and there was a failure to establish an adequate system of testing. Although the behaviour of the non-Roma parents could not be imputed to the Greek authorities, it was assumed that these incidents of a racist nature influenced the decision to segregate the Roma pupils.[245] The State failed to show that this difference in treatment was the result of objective factors unrelated to the Roma ethnic origin of the children. The Court held that there was discrimination in conjunction with Article 2 of Protocol 1 ECHR.

Indirect discrimination has been used by the ECtHR to condemn these serious human rights violation but the Court's approach to segregation has continued to evolve.[246] For the purposes of the indirect discrimination test, the focus is on the *actual effect* of a legal measure or policy. In the earlier Court decisions on segregation, the Court had required proof of an additional negative effect, apart from the segregation itself. However, there remained some ambiguity about whether the issue lay with the separation of pupils and their lack of inclusion in mainstream schools, or the inferior educational experience, or both.[247] In *Lavida* v. *Greece*, the applicants attended a Roma-only school but there was no difference between the level of the educational programme between the Roma school and mainstream ones.[248] While the authorities had acknowledged the problem of segregation and the need to end it, the proposed policies to remedy the situation were met with hostility from non-Roma parents and never implemented.[249] The Court found a violation of Article 14 ECHR together with Article 2 of Protocol 1 ECHR. Interestingly, the Court did not use the term indirect discrimination in its judgment.[250] This decision suggested that educational segregation was viewed by the Court as a special concept of discrimination as the existence of the segregation established a prima facie case of discrimination. The burden of proof then falls on the respondent State to show that the difference in treatment is justified.[251]

The Court clarified its approach in *X* v. *Albania*[252] and *Elmazova* v. *North Macedonia*,[253] where the Court acknowledged that segregation is a distinct form of discrimination which requires an objective justification.[254] In both *X*

[245] Ibid at [81]. [246] Vrancken (n 12). [247] Ibid, p.117.

[248] *Lavida and Others* v. *Greece*, App. No. 7973/10, 30/05/2013. [249] Ibid at [68]–[69].

[250] Ibid at [32] contains the only mention of indirect discrimination. The Court was discussing the International Convention for the Elimination of All Forms of Racial Discrimination, General Recommendation 27 of 16/08/2000.

[251] Ibid at [72]. [252] *X* v. *Albania* [GC], App. nos. 73548/17 and 45521/19, 31/05/2022.

[253] *Elmazova* v. *North Macedonia* (n 12). [254] Ibid at [73] and [78].

and *Elmazova*, the differential treatment of ethnic minority children was not the result of intentional discrimination by the authorities. In *X* the segregation could be linked to a programme of free school meals that led to the over-representation of Roma and Egyptian pupils.[255] While in *Elmazova*, the State authorities did not end the segregation because of the opposition of non-Roma parents to enrolling their children in the 'Roma school'.[256] Even in the absence of any discriminatory intent by the authorities, the Court found that educational segregation cannot be objectively and reasonably justified by any legitimate aim. In *X* the State was required under Article 46 ECHR to implement desegregation measures in the school attended almost exclusively by Roma and Egyptian children. The Court has also been willing to provide practical solutions aimed at ending segregation.[257]

Where evidence exists of ethnic segregation, the State's positive obligations require it to take swift appropriate measures to ensure the desegregation for all pupils.[258] The Court has emphasised the State's positive obligation to 'undo a history of racial segregation'.[259] In effect, this is a duty of collective desegregation. In *Szolcsán* v. *Hungary*, the Court addressed the connected issue of ending the educational segregation of an individual pupil in circumstances where court judgments ordering desegregation of Roma children had not been implemented.[260] The applicant attended an almost exclusively Roma school and his request to be transferred to a non-segregated school was rejected by the authorities. His argument before the Court was twofold: first, the refusal of the transfer violated his 'right to a racially inclusive education' and was contrary to Hungary's positive obligations.[261] The second argument alleged that the refusal to transfer him was 'racially discriminatory'.[262] Under the domestic law, anyone had a right to apply to a school outside their catchment area. The applicant argued that the reasons provided by the authorities to prevent his transfer could not serve as valid ones to prevent the transfer, rather their purpose was to keep the Roma children at the segregated school. The Court's judgment largely bypassed the first of these claims. In relation to the second claim, the Court, drawing on the previous case law, concluded that the failure to take adequate measures to rectify the discriminatory situation was incompatible with the State's obligation not to discriminate on the grounds of race or ethnicity.[263] The Court found a violation of Article 14 ECHR read with Article 2 of Protocol 1 ECHR.

[255] *X* v. *Albania* (n 252) at [3] and [89]. [256] *Elmazova* v. *North Macedonia* (n 12) at [72].
[257] *X* v. *Albania* (n 252) at [86].
[258] *Horváth and Kiss* v. *Hungary* (n 84) at [102] and *X* v. *Albania* (n 252) at [84].
[259] *Horváth and Kiss* v. *Hungary* (n 84) at [116].
[260] *Szolcsán* v. *Hungary*, App. No. 24408/16, 30/03/2023 at [28] and [36]. [261] Ibid at [36].
[262] Ibid at [37]. [263] Ibid at [57].

The first claim, concerning a right to racially inclusive education, was not successful. As the applicant was unable to point to 'any concrete evidence or statistical data' the Court could not conclude that the transfer request was refused because of his Roma ethnicity.[264] This decision has been criticised for failing to engage with individual desegregation measures which could provide an effective and speedy remedy. As education is limited to a few years, time is of the essence and the implementation of collective measures, albeit important, may not assist an individual pupil until it is too late.[265]

Overall, these decisions have established a strong duty of collective desegregation specifically addressing structural discrimination. As Merel Vrancken surmises: 'These cases could be a first step towards a European Court of Human Rights that considers not only individual, seemingly incidental instances of (in)direct discrimination, but which instead recognises the structural issues behind those "incidents" and requires states to address those structures to create a more equal society for all.'[266]

14.3.5.6 *Religion*

The non-discrimination principle in Article 14 ECHR expressly lists religion as a protected ground. In this regard, the ECtHR has stated that differential treatment based on religion will only be compatible if very weighty reasons exist.[267] The rationale for making this a 'suspect ground' is the close link between the importance of the rights enshrined in Article 9 ECHR and personal self-fulfilment.[268] The Court has thus found violations of this provision in respect of violence based on the victims' faith[269] as well as discrimination in relation to parental rights.[270] Freedom of religion does not require the State to create a legal framework to grant religious communities a special status but if the State has done so then it must ensure that the criteria are applied in a non-discriminatory manner.[271]

Where a State displays preferential treatment of one religion over another, the Court usually finds a violation. In *O'Donoghue* v. *the United Kingdom*,[272]

[264] Ibid at [51]. [265] Vrancken (n 12), pp.125–126. [266] Ibid, p.126.

[267] *Vojinty* v. *Hungary*, App. No. 2961/07, 12/02/2013 at [36]. [268] Ibid.

[269] *Members of the Gldani Congregation of Jehovah's Witnesses and Others* v. *Georgia*, App. No. 71156/01, 03/05/2007; *Milanovic* v. *Serbia* (2014) 58 EHRR 33; *SAS* v. *France* (n 66) at [55].

[270] *Hoffman* v. *Austria* (1994) 17 EHRR 293 at [36] concerning the refusal to grant parental rights because the parent was a Jehovah's Witness, the Court stated 'a distinction based essentially on a difference in religion alone is not acceptable. See also, *Vojinty* v. *Hungary* (n 267).

[271] *Ancient Baltic Religious Association 'Romuva'* v. *Lithuania*, App. No. 48329/19, 08/06/2021 at [126].

[272] *O'Donoghue and Others* v. *the United Kingdom* (2011) 53 EHRR 1.

the applicants complained that the requirement for persons subject to immigration control to obtain a 'Certificate of Approval' and pay a fee to marry, other than those marrying according to the rites of the Church of England, was discriminatory. The Court acknowledged that the applicants were not hindered in their right to practise their religion and thus there was no violation of Article 9 ECHR standing alone. As the facts of the case fell within the ambit of Article 9 ECHR, the Court considered Article 14 ECHR. As the Government failed to adduce reasons that could provide an objective and reasonable justification for the difference in treatment, the Court found a violation of Article 14 ECHR read with Article 9 ECHR.[273]

The Court draws a distinction between 'discrimination with respect to the enjoyment of a right based on religion and discrimination concerning the manifestation or enjoyment of the right to freedom of religion itself'.[274] The margin of appreciation may come into play in the Article 9 ECHR assessment concerning the manifestation of the right. In *Cha'are Shalom Ve Tsedek* v. *France*, the applicant, an Orthodox Jewish association, considered that the meat slaughtered by an existing Jewish organisation no longer conformed to the strict precepts associated with kosher meat.[275] The applicant association sought authorisation from the State to conduct its own ritual slaughter in accordance with the religious prescriptions they considered applicable. This was refused. The applicants claimed that the French authorities had infringed in a discriminatory way its right to manifest its religion through observance of the rites of the Jewish religion. The GC stated that there would be interference with the freedom to manifest one's religion only if it was impossible for ultra-orthodox Jews to eat meat from animals slaughtered according to their prescriptions, but this was not the case. The GC added that regard must be had to the State's margin of appreciation, 'particularly with regard to establishment of the delicate relations between the Churches and the State'.[276] In relation to the discrimination claim, the GC concluded that the difference of treatment had been limited in scope, pursued a legitimate aim and that there was a reasonable relationship of proportionality between the means employed and the aims sought to be achieved. There was no violation of the applicant association's rights pursuant to Article 14 ECHR.[277] The margin of appreciation also came into play in *Executief van de Moslims van Belgie and others* v. *Belgium* concerning the obligation to stun animals before ritual slaughter.[278] The Court found that the State had properly taken into account the difference between the applicants, Muslim and Jewish believers, and other members of

[273] Ibid at [108]–[110]. [274] Harris et al. (n 116), p.787.

[275] *Cha'are Shalom Ve Tsedek* v. *France* [GC], App. No. 27417/95, 27/06/2000.

[276] Ibid at [84]. [277] Ibid at [87].

[278] *Executief van de Moslims van België and Others* v. *Belgium*, App. Nos. 16760/22, 16849/22, 16850/22 et al., 13/02/2024.

the population who did not have religious dietary requirements. The adoption of this law, for the protection of animal welfare, was not overstepping the margin of appreciation.[279]

The controversial decision of *SAS* v. *France* is discussed in detail in Chapter 13. In addition to the applicant's complaint of a breach of Articles 8 and 9 ECHR, SAS also argued that the measure prohibiting the wearing of the full-face veil in public was indirectly discriminatory to Muslim women. The Grand Chamber confirmed that a policy may be discriminatory if it has a disproportionately prejudicial effect on a group, even where the policy is not aimed specifically at the group and there is no discriminatory intent. The Grand Chamber acknowledged that while the full-face veil ban had specific negative effects on Muslim women who wished to cover their face for religious reasons, the measure pursued an objective and reasonable justification.[280] The reasons put forward by the Grand Chamber mirrored their rationale for finding no breach of Article 9 ECHR.[281] Unfortunately, the question of indirect discrimination against a minority group was not tackled directly by the Court. It would also have been preferable if the GC had addressed the intersectionality of gender and religion in an Article 14 ECHR analysis.

In the *Eweida* case, which is also discussed at length in Chapter 13,[282] four separate applicants claimed a breach of Article 9 in conjunction with Article 14 ECHR. Mrs Eweida was the only successful applicant. She was a Christian employed by British Airways who was not permitted to wear a discreet cross as it did not conform to British Airways' dress code. The Court found that the treatment constituted discrimination based on religion but it did not find it necessary to consider the complaint under Article 14 ECHR. It is also worth noting that in this case there was no reference to a very weighty reasons test. It may be that religion warrants a high level of protection 'if the discrimination is essentially based on religious convictions rather than on religious expression'.[283]

14.3.5.7 *Sex and Gender*

Women remain at a significant disadvantage in Europe.[284] The Council of Europe's factsheet publication on Equality between men and women emphasises that despite some progress, 'gender inequalities, traditional gender roles

[279] Ibid at [123]. [280] *SAS* v. *France* (n 66) at [161].

[281] Ibid, the GC referred back to [144]–[159].

[282] *Eweida and Ors* v. *the United Kingdom* (n 116).

[283] Pieter Van Dijk et al. (eds), *Theory and Practice of the European Convention on Human Rights* (5th ed) (Intersentia, 2018), p.1028.

[284] The term 'sex' is used in Article 14 ECHR but the term has gradually been replaced by 'gender'.

and gender stereotypes persist in all walks of life, notably at home, in education, in the media and in the justice system'.[285] Violence against women in its different forms remains the most widespread violation of women's human rights in Europe.[286] Women often face multiple and intersecting forms of discrimination and violence.[287]

The findings of the most recent EHRC report on equality and human rights in the UK notes that although the employment gap between men and women has narrowed owing to the improvements in educational attainment, the gender pay gap has narrowed only slightly. The 'motherhood penalty' is identified as the key cause of the gender pay gap. Over the last decade, women have also experienced higher rates of poverty than men, and households headed by women were more overcrowded than households headed by men.[288] The disproportionate impact of poverty and financial vulnerability on women is evident from this statement in the report:

> Households headed by women may find it harder to move into more suitable housing because, relative to their earnings, mortgages and private rent are less affordable to women. For example, in 2018 there was no region in England where a woman could privately rent at the median rate without it absorbing more than a third of median earnings, whereas a man could offer to rent in every region but London.[289]

Although the gendered nature of poverty and discrimination in the labour force is a primary focus of women's inequality, the rights protected in the Convention have not always proved capable of addressing these structural equality issues. Recent years, however, have seen an increased willingness of the Court to step in, even in relation to employment issues. The Court has consistently stated that differences based exclusively on sex must have 'particularly weighty and convincing reasons' of justification[290] and the margin of appreciation will be narrow.[291] However, the scope of the margin will vary in relation to economic and social matters: the policy choices of the State will be respected unless it is 'manifestly without reasonable foundation'.[292]

As discussed below, the Court has rejected the notion that stereotypical gender roles can justify a difference of treatment.[293] The Court has also extended its review to the employment context. This is an important extension as women have traditionally faced inequality in the workplace. The Court has accepted that discrimination in the course of employment may fall within the

[285] Council of Europe, Factsheets, *Equality between Women and Men*, p.3. [286] Ibid.

[287] Ibid, p.5.

[288] Equality and Human Rights Commission, Equality and Human Rights Monitor, (November 2023).

[289] Ibid. [290] *Jurčić* v. *Croatia* (2021) 73 EHRR 10 at [65].

[291] *X and Others* v. *Austria* [GC], App. No. 19010/07, 19/02/2013 at [99]; and *Vallianatos and Others* (n 114) at [77].

[292] *Stec* v. *the United Kingdom* (n 79) at [52]. [293] See Section 14.3.5.7.2.

ambit of Article 8 ECHR or Article 1 of Protocol 1 ECHR, thus permitting Article 14 ECHR to be considered. In *Emel Boyraz* v. *Turkey*,[294] a woman was dismissed from her position as a security officer in the public sector because she was a woman. The Turkish Government contended that neither Article 8 nor Article 14 ECHR were relevant, as any right to employment was not secured by the Convention. The Court gave short shrift to this point stating that her dismissal from work on account of her sex would have adversely affected both her material well-being, sense of self-esteem and relations with others. This treatment fell within the ambit of Article 8 ECHR. The State tried to justify her exclusion from the position on the grounds that the job would require her to handle weapons, work during the day and night and use physical force in case of an attack. No explanation had been provided as to why women were incapable or unqualified to meet the requirements of the job. The Court concluded that 'the mere fact that security officers had to work night shifts and in rural areas and might be required to use physical force and firearms under certain conditions could not in itself justify the difference in treatment between men and women'.[295] The Court found that there was no legitimate aim to justify the difference.[296] Disappointingly, the Court did not specifically mention the stereotypical assumptions underlying the dismissal. The decision has thus been criticised for not tackling head-on the outdated gender assumptions and only taking issue with the Government's claim that the nature of the work was unsuitable for women, on the ground that it was insufficiently substantiated.[297]

Jurčić v. *Croatia*[298] is an important decision in the employment arena on the issue of discrimination on the grounds of pregnancy. The applicant had undergone invitro fertilisation (IVF) and took sick leave on account of pregnancy-related complications. As she had entered employment ten days after she had undergone IVF, it was suspected that her reason for seeking employment must have been to enable her to claim the benefit. As a consequence, her health insurance application was reassessed and rejected. The Court emphasised 'that a woman's pregnancy as such cannot be considered fraudulent behaviour'.[299] The Court held that the difference in treatment would amount to direct sex discrimination unless it could be justified.[300] In assessing the justification, the Court, referring to EU law, stated that 'the protection afforded to a woman during pregnancy cannot be dependent on whether her presence at work during maternity is essential for the proper

[294] *Emel Boyraz* v. *Turkey* (2015) 60 EHRR 30. [295] Ibid at [54].

[296] See also, *Hulya Ebru Demirel* v. *Turkey*, App. No. 30733/08, 19/06/2018.

[297] Alexandra Timmer, 'Of Firearms and Weak Women: Sex Discrimination in Hulya Ebru Demirel v. Turkey' (July 2018) Strasbourg Observers, https://strasbourgobservers.com/2018/07/31/of-firearms-and-weak-women-sex-discrimination-in-hulya-ebru-demirel-v-turkey/.

[298] *Jurčić* v. *Croatia* (n 290). [299] Ibid at [73]. [300] Ibid at [69].

functioning of her employer, or by the fact that she is temporarily prevented from performing the work for which she has been hired'.[301] The Court also critiqued the implication that pregnant women, or where there was even a possibility of pregnancy, should not seek employment. In the Court's view, such gender stereotyping 'presents a serious obstacle to the achievement of real and substantive gender equality' and is at odds with international gender equality standards.[302] This decision is important for broadening protection by critiquing the gendered assumptions that perpetuate stereotypes deriving from the ascription to women of reproductive roles in the employment arena.[303]

In cases concerning Article 1 Protocol 1 ECHR and discrimination regarding financial benefits, the Court has confirmed a wide margin of appreciation is given to States in the field of economic and social strategy. In *Stec and Others* v. *the UK*, the Court assessed whether the underlying difference in treatment between men and women in the State pension scheme was justifiable under Article 14 ECHR.[304] The applicants had suffered work-related injuries and received reduced earnings allowances (REA), a form of compensation, for an impairment in earning capacity. In 1986, it was decided that REA should not be given to claimants who would no longer be in paid employment due to their age. Eligibility for REA payments ended by reference to the ages used by the statutory age pension scheme which was sixty-five for men and sixty for women. Legislation had been introduced to increase progressively the pensionable age of women and by 2020 the pensionable age of men and women would be equalised at age sixty-five. The applicants argued that it was illegitimate to introduce sex-based discrimination into the REA scheme by linking the cut-off date to the variable pension age. The Grand Chamber held that the difference of treatment in the pension scheme was justified as it was intended to correct the historically disadvantaged economic position of women; the benefit was intended to compensate for reduced earning capacity during a person's working life.[305] While measures were gradually being taken to remove this difference in treatment by increasing the age of retirement for women, the inequality was not so manifestly unreasonable as to exceed the wide margin of appreciation. In the opinion of the Court, it was 'impossible to pinpoint any particular moment when the unfairness to men caused by differential pensionable ages began to outweigh the

[301] Ibid at [76]. [302] Ibid at [83].

[303] In contrast, in *Napotnik* v. *Romania*, App. No. 33139/13, 20/10/2020, the Court concluded that the early termination of the applicant's diplomatic posting was justified and there was no discrimination. Further employment cases include *Nurcan Bayraktar* v. *Turkey*, App. No. 27094/20, 27/06/2023; and *Moraru and Marin* v. *Romania*, App. Nos. 53282/18 and 31428/20, 20/03/2023.

[304] *Stec and Others* v. *the UK* (n 79). The GC concluded that non-contributory, as well as contributory, social security benefits were within the ambit of Article 1 of Protocol 1.

[305] Ibid at [66].

need to correct the disadvantaged position of women'.[306] The Grand Chamber concluded that there was no breach of Article 14 ECHR taken in conjunction with Article 1 of Protocol 1 ECHR. Although the difference between pension ages of men and women was originally put in place to mitigate financial inequality of women, the operation of the REA payments, linking the cut-off age for REA to the State pensionable age, did not benefit women. In fact, it placed at a financial disadvantage women who had suffered work-related injuries in comparison to men injured at work because women were forced to retire earlier than men. Women were thus denied the higher REA payment at age 60. *Stec* established an important principle; it was possible to correct the historical financial disadvantages and hardship to women without violating the principle of non-discrimination. However, in this instance, the result was disadvantageous for women. The Court adopted a less rigorous approach, the manifestly without reasonable foundation test, to this sex discrimination case. In his dissenting opinion, Judge Loucaides considered that at the time of this complaint, it was no longer possible to provide an objective and reasonable justification for this discriminatory outcome. In his view, the slow measures taken by the UK to introduce remedial legislation should not be invoked under the doctrine of the margin of appreciation as an excuse for not acting in time to avoid a discriminatory result.

14.3.5.7.1 Gender-Based Violence

In the Strasbourg jurisprudence concerning violence against women, the Court recognises the 'gendered nature' of domestic abuse and the need for the Convention to be interpreted in a manner that ensures that victims of domestic abuse are provided with 'effective protection and safeguards'.[307] Recognition of specific gender discrimination against domestic violence victims was first seen in the landmark decision of *Opuz* v. *Turkey* in 2009,[308] where the Court clearly aligned itself with the international human law rights approach to gender-based violence (GBV).[309] The Court drew upon General Recommendation 19 of the Committee on the Convention on the Elimination of All Forms of Discrimination Against Women (CEDAW), which defines discrimination against women to include 'gender-based violence, that is, violence that is directed against a woman because she is a woman or that affects women disproportionately'. Viewing domestic violence through an equality prism, the Court held that the failure to give women appropriate protection against GBV, even if unintentional, constituted sex discrimination.

[306] Ibid at [62].

[307] See, for example, *Kurt* v. *Austria* [GC] (2022) 74 EHRR 6 at [137] and [161].

[308] *Opuz* v. *Turkey* (n 32).

[309] The Court cited CEDAW and the UN Commission of Human Rights. Ibid at [184]–[191].

In the *Opuz* case, which involved a long history of serious violence against the applicant and her mother, the applicant's partner murdered his mother-in-law. The Court found a breach of Articles 2 and 3 ECHR but importantly the Court was prepared to consider GBV as a form of discrimination against women and a violation of Article 14 ECHR.[310] The Court observed that 'the general and discriminatory judicial passivity in Turkey [to domestic violence against women] created a climate that was conducive to domestic violence'.[311] The Court was also sensitive to the circumstances of the woman at risk: 'The great majority of these women [who were victims of GBV] were of Kurdish origin, illiterate or of a low level of education and generally without any independent source of income.'[312] In recognition of the hurdles faced by women victims, including the unhelpful attitude of the police and other authorities, the Court stated that 'the State's failure to protect women against domestic violence breaches their right to equal protection of the law and that this failure does not need to be intentional'.[313] Moreover, in a case of GBV, it is sufficient for the applicant to provide the Court with adequate elements to make a prima facie allegation of discrimination, which will 'shift the burden of proof to the respondent State to show what remedial measures it has taken to redress the disadvantage associated with sex'.[314]

Unfortunately, the ECtHR has been called upon to consider many cases on GBV and inaction on the part of authorities. In *Eremia* v. *Moldova*,[315] the Court concluded that the domestic authorities had failed to take adequate measures to protect the applicant and her family from GBV and that this demonstrated 'not a simple failure or delay in dealing with violence against the first applicant, but amounted to repeatedly condoning such violence and reflected a discriminatory attitude towards the first applicant as a woman'.[316]

In some cases, the Court has found that the domestic legal regime was so deficient and displaying such large scale structural bias in dealing with GBV that the system itself was discriminatory against women.[317] In *Volodina* v. *Russia*, the Court unanimously found a violation of Article 14 ECHR taken in conjunction with Article 3 ECHR and concluded that '[b]y tolerating for many years a climate which was conducive to domestic violence, the Russian authorities failed to create conditions for substantive gender equality that would enable women to live free from fear of ill-treatment or attacks on their physical integrity and to benefit from the equal protection of the law'.[318] These

310 *Opuz* v. *Turkey* (n 32) at [74], [187] and [199]. 311 Ibid at [198]. 312 Ibid at [194].

313 Ibid at [191]. 314 Guide to Article 14 (n 28) at [109].

315 *Eremia and Ors* v. *Moldova* (2014) 58 EHRR 2. 316 Ibid at [89].

317 Harris et al. (n 116), p.796.

318 *Volodina* v. *Russia*, App. No. 41261/17, 09/07/2019 at [132]. For a gender-sensitive interpretation of the ECHR, see the separate opinion in *Volodina* of Judge Pinto de Albuquerque, joined by Judge Dedov.

findings were repeated in *Tunikova* v. *Russia* where the Court found that the continued failure to adopt legislation to combat GBV and to create conditions for substantive equality amounted to a structural bias and a systemic defect in Russian law.[319] Pursuant to Article 46 ECHR, the Court indicated the type of general measures that would be needed to put an end to GBV, which included developing 'a comprehensive and targeted response encompassing all areas of State action including legislation, public policy, programmes, and institutional frameworks and monitoring mechanisms'.[320] Further measures to protect women victims of GBV should be made available immediately and the authorities should put in place a plan for altering the public perception of GBV against women.[321]

In many GBV judgments, the Court's application of Article 14 ECHR situates the experiences of the victims within the context of much wider societal patterns of GBV and, indeed, systemic obstacles to women seeking protection. In *Tkhelidze* v. *Georgia*, the Court criticised 'the general and discriminatory passivity of the law-enforcement' which was exacerbated by the 'systemic problem' of violence against women, discriminatory gender stereotypes and entrenched patriarchal attitudes.[322] The Court found a breach of Article 2 ECHR under its substantive and procedural limbs in conjunction with Article 14 ECHR, as the domestic authorities had failed to take preventive measures to protect the victim and to investigate the police inaction.[323] In the recent decision of *Gaidukevich* v. *Georgia*, the victim committed suicide as a consequence of a long period of severe GBV. In finding a violation of the positive obligation to protect under Article 2 ECHR, taken together with Article 14 ECHR, the Court took into account 'the repeated failure of the Georgian authorities to prevent and to stop violence against women'.[324]

The situation is not entirely bleak, however, and the Court has lauded changes in some Contracting States influenced by previous judgments of the Court on GBV. In *Landi* v. *Italy*[325] the Court observed that Italy had taken many steps to implement the Istanbul Convention concerning violence against women.[326] The Court found that there was no evidence of passivity towards the victims of domestic violence or discriminatory measures.[327]

[319] *Tunikova* v. *Russia* (2022) 75 EHRR 1 at [129]. [320] Ibid at [152].

[321] Ibid at [157]–[158]. See also Chapter 4.

[322] *Tkhelidze* v. *Georgia*, App. No. 33506/17, 08/07/2021 at [56].

[323] See also, *A and B* v. *Georgia*, App. No. 73975/16, 10/02/2022; *A.E.* v. *Bulgaria*, App. No. 53891/20, 23/05/2023 at [120]–[122].

[324] *Gaidukevich* v. *Georgia*, App. No. 38650/18, 15/06/2023 at [174].

[325] *Landi* v. *Italy*, App. No. 10929/19, 07/04/2022.

[326] Council of Europe on preventing and combating violence against women and domestic violence (CETS No. 210).

[327] The Court found that Italy had improved its response to GBV since the earlier decision of *Talpis* v. *Italy* (n 186). See also, Council of Europe's 2022 High Level Report, Chapter E which

The fact that the ECtHR has been receptive to addressing GBV as an equality issue, emphasising the stereotypical and prejudicial attitudes towards women has contributed to a more sophisticated understanding of this problem. Unfortunately, greater awareness of the scale of the problem has not been successful in reducing the vast numbers of victims of abuse.

14.3.5.7.2 *Stereotyping*

The Court has frequently emphasised the importance of gender equality and that its advancement is 'a major goal of the Member states of the Council of Europe'.[328] In *Markin* v. *Russia* (discussed above), the Grand Chamber was not prepared to accept assumptions based on stereotypes:

> [R]eferences to traditions, general assumptions or prevailing social attitudes in a particular country are insufficient justification for a difference in treatment on grounds of sex. For example, States are prevented from imposing traditions that derive from the man's primordial role and the woman's secondary role in the family.[329]

This critique of stereotypical assumptions was further developed by the Grand Chamber in *Beeler* v. *Switzerland*.[330] The applicant challenged the termination of his widower's pension when his youngest child reached eighteen. He had given up his job and brought up his daughters alone on the death of his wife. In contrast, a widow in the same position would retain the pension. The Swiss Government argued that the difference in treatment was necessary as widows still needed a 'slightly higher level of protection' than widowers,[331] to 'compensate for the less favourable situation of women on the labour market and the persisting unequal distribution of household tasks'.[332] The Grand Chamber concluded that the applicant had been a victim of discrimination pursuant to Article 14 in conjunction with Article 8 ECHR. Even though the case touched upon the field of social welfare where a State usually has a wide margin of appreciation, the Grand Chamber concluded that reliance upon the 'male breadwinner model' was not a reasonable or objective justification. The Court observed that 'references to traditions, general assumptions or prevailing social attitudes in a particular country are insufficient justification for a difference in treatment on grounds of sex, whether in favour of women or men'.[333] This decision is a powerful statement that the Court will not accept as

focused on violence against women. The Group noted that Chapter E was specifically included in light of the backlash affecting the Council of Europe Convention on Preventing and Combating Violence against Women and Domestic Violence (the Istanbul Convention).

[328] *Markin* v. *Russia* (n 133) at [65].

[329] Ibid at [127]. *Yocheva and Ganeva* v. *Bulgaria* (n 94) at [102].

[330] *Beeler* v. *Switzerland* [GC] (2023) 76 EHRR 33. [331] Ibid at [89]. [332] Ibid at [91].

[333] Ibid at [110].

justification the gendered roles ascribed to men and women. An approach assigning parenting obligations predominantly to women, reinforces the assumption that women are primarily responsible for child care. In the Court's view, the Swiss legislation contributed to 'perpetuating prejudices and stereotypes regarding the nature or role of women in society and is disadvantageous both to women's careers and to men's family life'.[334] Real substantive equality can only be achieved if stereotypes about both men and women are challenged and transformed.

The ECtHR has also rejected stereotyping in judicial decisions. In *Carvalho Pinto de Sousa Morais* v. *Portugal*, the applicant complained of age and sex discrimination.[335] The Portuguese court had reduced her damages award for medical negligence after a surgical procedure which had caused her serious pain, depression and negatively affected her sexual relations. The ECtHR identified and rejected the stereotypical assumptions: 'The question at issue here is not considerations of age or sex as such, but rather the assumption that sexuality is not as important for a fifty-year-old woman and mother of two children as for someone of a younger age. That assumption reflects a traditional idea of female sexuality as being essentially linked to child-bearing purposes and thus ignores its physical and psychological relevance for the self-fulfilment of women as people.'[336] The Court found a violation of Article 14 in conjunction with Article 8 ECHR.

14.3.5.8 *Sexual Orientation, Gender Identity and Sex Characteristics*

The ECtHR has acknowledged sexual orientation, gender identity and sex characteristics as concepts protected by Article 14 ECHR and falling under 'any ground such as' or 'other status'. Members of these communities have faced legal problems in having their identities recognised in law, their relationships legally accepted and respected in the family law context. Many cases turn on the lack of recognition, especially in official documents which serve to highlight the issues faced by this community, including prejudice, stereotyping, stigma, discrimination and violence. Gender information presented in official documents does not solely reflect legal status but also influences, often negatively, an individual's social status.[337] Discrimination on this ground strikes at the heart of an individual's identity and personality: it is a denial of dignity and equality. There is overlap between discrimination based on sexual orientation, gender identity and sex characteristics but it also raises distinct issues, and for that reason, each will be dealt with separately.

[334] Ibid at [113]. [335] *Carvalho Pinto de Sousa Morais* v. *Portugal* (n 94). [336] Ibid at [52].

[337] Lena Holzer, 'Legal Gender Recognition in Times of Change at the European Court of Human Rights' (2022) 23 ERA Forum 165–182 at 167.

14.3.5.8.1 *Sexual Orientation*

Earlier decisions of the Court routinely characterised sexual orientation as falling under substantive provisions of the Convention, especially Article 8 ECHR, rather than as an equality issue.[338] The approach of the Court today is that any differentiation based on grounds of sexual orientation requires convincing and weighty reasons by way of justification.[339] According to the Court's jurisprudence, differences based solely on considerations of sexual orientation will never be acceptable under the ECHR.[340] Moreover, discrimination based upon sexual orientation is as serious as discrimination based on 'race, origin or colour'[341] and the State's margin of appreciation is accordingly narrow.[342] The living instrument principle has played an important role in developing the jurisprudence in this area. Yet despite these principled statements, the Court has applied Article 14 ECHR in cases concerning sexual orientation in an inconsistent manner limiting 'the potential of the ECHR to raise the standards of protection of the human rights of gay and lesbian people throughout the 46 States of the Council of Europe'.[343]

In considering the meaning of equality in this context, the Court has considered important cases concerning sexual orientation in conjunction with the right to private life and family life under Article 8 ECHR. In 1999, in *Salgueiro da Silva Mouta* v. *Portugal*,[344] the Court found for the first time a violation of Article 14 in conjunction with Article 8 ECHR on the grounds of sexual orientation in a case concerning parental rights. The applicant's sexual orientation was 'a factor which was decisive' in determining the decision of the domestic court to award parental responsibility of his daughter to his former wife.[345] The Court concluded that considerations based on the applicant's sexual orientation, is 'a decision which is not acceptable under the Convention'.[346]

Since 1999,[347] the Court has made decisions based on the grounds of sexual orientation in a number of contexts including criminal law,[348] tenancies,[349]

[338] *Dudgeon* v. *the United Kingdom* (1983) 5 EHRR 573 and *Smith and Grady* v. *the United Kingdom* (2001) 31 EHRR 24.

[339] *Salguiero da Silva Mouta* v. *Portugal* (2001) 31 EHRR 47.

[340] *Vallianatos and Others* v. *Greece* (n 114).

[341] *Vejdeland and Others* v. *Sweden* (2014) 58 EHRR 15 at [55].

[342] *Kozak* v. *Poland* (2010) 51 EHRR 16 at [92].

[343] Paul Johnson, 'Sexual Orientation Discrimination and Article 14 of the European Convention on Human Rights: The Problematic Approach of the European Court of Human Rights' [2023] 6 EHRLR 548–563 at 549.

[344] *Salgueiro da Silva Mouta* v. *Portugal*, App. No. 33290/96, 12/12/1999. Note also the Commission decision in *Sutherland* v. *the United Kingdom* (n 47) at [66]–[67].

[345] Ibid at [35]. [346] Ibid at [36]. [347] See Guide to Article 14 (n 28).

[348] *L and V* v. *Austria* (2003) 36 EHRR 55.

[349] *Karner* v. *Austria* (n 121); *Kozak* v. *Poland* (n 342).

social insurance,[350] adoption[351] and protection from homophobic speech or acts of violence.[352] Nevertheless, the Court's approach to the use of Article 14 ECHR is inconsistent. In a recent decision, concerning restrictions on a fairy tale book depicting same-sex relationships, where limitations were imposed on access by children under the age of fourteen, the Grand Chamber found a violation of Article 10 ECHR but found no need to consider Article 14 ECHR.[353] An excoriating dissent by five judges observed that as the case demonstrated 'discriminatory attitudes against the LGBTI community', it should have been brought within the ambit of protection against discrimination and addressed directly under Article 14 ECHR.[354] Again in *Fedotova* v. *Russia*, in a case concerning the lack of recognition of same sex relationships, the Court saw no need to analyse this under Article 14 ECHR.[355] The Court had no hesitation in finding a breach of Article 8 ECHR but declined to consider Article 14 ECHR. This led to a partly dissenting opinion criticising the failure to address discrimination and the equal enjoyment of rights.[356] The dissent stresses that: 'the applicants' sexual orientation was *the sole basis* for denying them any form of legal recognition or protection of their bond as couples in committed relationships'.[357] They add that laws 'help shape a society's moral views . . . They tell their beneficiaries that they are not invisible, that they are seen and valued as equal members of that society, irrespective of their differences.' Conversely, States that discriminate 'tend to reinforce prejudice and social segregation, causing harm that goes above and beyond the violation of particular individuals' Article 8 rights'.[358]

Although there is a growing body of case law dealing with same-sex relationships, the Court has stopped short of recognising a right to same-sex

[350] *P.B. and J.S.* v. *Austria* (2012) 55 EHRR 31.

[351] *E.B.* v. *France* (n 26); *Gas and Dubois* v. *France*, App. No. 25951/07, 15/03/2012.

[352] Recent cases include *Nepomnyashchiy and Others* v. *Russia*, App. Nos. 39954/09 and 3465/17, 30/05/2023; *Oganaezova* v. *Armenia*, App. Nos. 71367/12 and 72961/12, 17/05/2022; *Genderdoc-M and M.D.* v. *the Republic of Moldova*, App. No. 9106/06, 12/06/2012; and *Karter* v. *Ukraine*, App. No. 18179/17, 11/04/20. See also, Guide to Article 14 (n 28).

[353] *Macate* v. *Lithuania* [GC], App. No. 61435/19, 23/01/2023. Compare *Bayev* v. *Russia*, App. No. 67667/12, 20/06/2017 which found a violation of Article 10 and Article 14 in conjunction with Article 10: '[D]ifferences based solely on considerations of sexual orientation are unacceptable under the Convention' at [89]. The usual term is LGBTIQ+ but we adopt the variation of the term used in the judgment that is under discussion.

[354] *Macate* v. *Lithuania*, ibid, joint partly dissenting opinion of Judges Yudkivska, Lubarda, Guerra Martins and Zünd joined by Judge Kūrisat [19]. These judges also stated: 'the ground on which the individual is treated less favourably is not a protected *personal* characteristic' at [10].

[355] *Fedotova* v. *Russia* [GC], App. Nos. 40792/10, 30538/14 and 43439/14, 17/01/2023.

[356] Ibid, partly dissenting opinion of Judge Pavli, joined by Judge Motoc. [357] Ibid at [4].

[358] Ibid at [5]. See also, *Przybyszewska* v. *Poland*, App. No. 11454/17, 12/12/2023. The Court declined to consider Article 14.

marriage as protected pursuant to the Convention. In *Schalk and Kopf* v. *Austria*, the Court recognised 'a rapid evolution of social attitudes towards same-sex couples'.[359] In view of this emerging consensus, the Court stated that it was artificial to assume that, in contrast to a different-sex couple, a same-sex couple cannot enjoy family life for the purposes of Article 8 ECHR. Thus 'a cohabiting same-sex couple living in a stable *de facto* partnership, falls within the notion of "family life", just as the relationship of a different-sex couple in the same situation would'.[360] The Court, however, was unprepared to find that same-sex couples had a right to marry under either Article 12 ECHR or under Article 14 ECHR in conjunction with Article 8 ECHR.[361] It held that there was insufficient consensus for this as only a small number of States provide for it and States enjoy a margin of appreciation.[362]

The Court has taken a more robust line regarding civil partnerships. In *Vallianatos* v. *Greece*, the Court was unprepared to accept the Greek Government's contention that same-sex couples were not disadvantaged in legal terms by being prevented from entering into civil partnerships available to opposite-sex couples. The Court emphasised, 'the civil partnerships provided for by [the relevant law] as an officially recognized alternative to marriage have an intrinsic value for the applicants irrespective of the legal effects, however narrow or extensive, that they would produce'.[363] In the breakthrough decision of *Oliari* v. *Italy*, a positive step was taken towards full legal recognition of same-sex relationships in Europe.[364] The applicants contended that the failure to make available legal recognition under Italian domestic law, which was needed for residence purposes, was discriminatory. The couple were in a stable same-sex relationship and had been married abroad. The Court found that Italy had breached the positive duty under Article 8 ECHR by failing to provide a form of recognised civil partnership.[365] Given the violation of Article 8 ECHR, the Court found it unnecessary to analyse Article 14 ECHR. In contrast, discrimination was specifically addressed in *Taddeucci and McCall* v. *Italy*[366] concerning immigration and Italian laws aimed at protecting the traditional family. The applicants (an EU and non-EU citizen) were in a long term same-sex couple relationship and sought residency in Italy. The non-EU citizen was unable to obtain a residence permit as a 'family member' as he did not meet the Italian statutory criteria, which required him to be a 'spouse' and not a cohabitant. Neither unmarried opposite-sex couples nor same-sex couples were eligible for the residence permit under Italian law. In the

359 *Schalk and Kopf* v. *Austria* (n 133) at [93]. 360 Ibid at [94]. 361 Ibid at [108]–[109].

362 Ibid at [105].

363 *Vallianatos* v. *Greece* (n 114) at [81]. See also *Maymulakhin and Markiv* v. *Ukraine*, App. No. 75135/14, 01/06/2023.

364 *Oliari* v. *Italy* (2017) 65 EHRR 26. 365 Ibid at [185].

366 *Taddeucci and McCall* v. *Italy*, App. No.51362/09, 30/06/2016.

Court's opinion, however, these couples were not in an analogous position. Same-sex couples had no legal means which would give them the necessary status as 'family member', whereas heterosexual couples could marry and obtain a residence permit for family reasons. The Court adopted a more substantive equality approach and found that the discrimination was without any legitimate aim. It observed: 'the fact that [the applicants] were not treated differently from unmarried heterosexual couples, who alone had access to a form of regularisation of their partnership, had no objective and reasonable justification'.[367] The 'significant trend' around the world recognising the status of same-sex partners and their right to live together was also noted by the Court.[368] The Court thus found a violation of Article 14 ECHR in conjunction with Article 8 ECHR.[369] In *Pajic* v. *Croatia*, an applicant applied for a residence permit on the basis of family reunification.[370] The request was refused as the domestic law excluded such a possibility for same-sex couples. The ECtHR found that the State had not put forward any justification or convincing reasons to justify the difference in treatment between same-sex and different-sex couples and thus a violation was found. A difference of treatment based solely on the applicant's sexual orientation can never be justified.

14.3.5.8.2 *Gender Identity*

Issues concerning the 'right to gender identity' have come before the Court on numerous occasions, although often without a separate examination under Article 14 ECHR.[371] In *Hämäläinen* v. *Finland*,[372] the applicant, a married transgender woman, sought to obtain legal recognition of her female identity. The Finnish authorities refused her request because the applicant was, according to national law, still married: under Finnish law, a person's new gender could not be registered unless they were unmarried, or their spouse gave consent to change their marriage into a registered civil partnership. The applicant and her wife were unwilling, for religious reasons, to end the marriage or to convert their marriage into a civil partnership, as permitted under Finnish law. The applicant argued that the legal situation was discriminatory as she was forced to choose between obtaining full recognition of her preferred gender or the preservation of her marriage. She claimed that she had

[367] Ibid at [96]. [368] Ibid at [97]. [369] See also *Przybyszewska* v. *Poland* (n 358).

[370] *Pajic* v. *Croatia* (2018) 67 EHRR 12.

[371] See *Rees* v. *United Kingdom* [1987] 9 EHRR 56, the first case where the Court was asked to decide on a change of legal gender; *Goodwin* v. *United Kingdom* [GC] (2002) 35 EHRR 18, where the Court recognised a right to change the legal gender on a birth certificate. Note also the Gender Recognition Act 2004.

[372] *Hämäläinen* v. *Finland* [GC], App. No.37359/09, 16/07/2014.

been treated less favourably than cisgender individuals, who obtained legal gender recognition automatically at birth and without running the risk of 'forced' divorce as in the applicant's case. At the time of the legal proceedings, Finland had not recognised same-sex marriage equality and any approval of marriage continuing after a legal gender change would, in practice, allow it.[373]

The Grand Chamber concluded that there had been no violation of the Convention. The Chamber highlighted that since Articles 8 and 12 ECHR do not impose upon Contracting States the obligation to provide marriage equality, nor does Article 8 ECHR in conjunction with Article 14 ECHR establish the obligation to grant same-sex couples a right to remain married.[374] As to the prohibition of discrimination, the Chamber concluded that the applicants' situation was not 'sufficiently similar' to that of cisgender individuals and the Chamber did not proceed to consider whether the Finnish law was objectively and reasonably justified.[375] The decision is disappointing: without identity cards which corresponded to her actual gender, the applicant was frequently placed in compromising situations. The decision has been widely criticised as reverting to a formal notion of equality as requiring that likes be treated alike,[376] exposing cisnormativity in the law[377] and underlining the fact that 'legal gender assignment has functioned as a tool to safeguard marriage as a heterosexual union', at the expense of transgender and same-sex partnerships.[378]

The ECtHR has recently considered the issue of non-binary people and their legal documents in *Y* v. *France*.[379] The applicant in this case, an intersex person, complained about the domestic courts' refusal to grant his request to have the word 'neutral' or 'intersex' entered on his birth certificate. The Court considered this case under Article 8 ECHR. Article 14 ECHR was not invoked. Giving the State a wide margin of appreciation, the Court found no violation of Article 8 ECHR.

Transphobic violence is a growing concern, and the ECtHR has delivered a number of judgments addressing this issue. The Court has consistently confirmed that Article 14 ECHR imposes a positive duty on States to protect transgender individuals from transphobic violence.[380] The positive duty also extends to enabling them to participate in public demonstrations. The Court has found breaches of Article 14 ECHR taken together with Articles 3 and 11 ECHR where the authorities failed to take measures to protect the applicants

[373] The GC had recently decided that there was no right to same-sex marriage. See *Schalk and Kopf* v. *Austria* (n 133).

[374] *Hämäläinen* v. *Finland* (n 372) at [87]. [375] Ibid at [112]. [376] Fredman (n 10), p. 297.

[377] Damian Gonzalez-Salzberg, *Sexuality and Transsexuality under the European Convention on Human Rights: A Queer Reading of Human Rights Law* (Hart, 2019).

[378] Holzer (n 337), p.175. [379] *Y* v. *France*, App. No. 76888/17, 31/01/2023.

[380] *Aghdgomelashvili and Japaridze* v. *Georgia*, App. No. 7224/11, 8/10/2020.

from transphobic violence, to conduct an effective investigation or to ensure that an LGBT demonstration took place peacefully.[381] Exploring these violations through an equality assessment allows the Court to examine and, if necessary, condemn motives of the authorities.

14.3.5.8.3 *Sex Characteristics*

A landmark decision of the ECtHR has found for the first time that discrimination based on a sex characteristic may violate Article 14 ECHR. *Semenya* v. *Switzerland* concerned a discrimination complaint by a highly successful South African professional athlete Mokgadi Caster Semenya.[382] The applicant is an intersex woman with natural levels of testosterone that exceed those of most other women athletes. In order to ensure competitive fairness, World Athletics[383] adopted a new set of regulations. The applicant refused to comply with the regulations as it required her to undergo hormone treatment to lower her natural testosterone levels. Her refusal meant that she was unable to compete in certain international competitions. After unsuccessfully challenging the regulations before the Court of Arbitration for Sport (CAS) and an appeal to the Swiss Federal Tribunal, she took her case to Strasbourg. The Court had no hesitation in determining that the applicant's sexual characteristics were protected by Article 14 ECHR.[384] The Court observed that Switzerland had a positive obligation to provide adequate institutional and procedural safeguards to ensure an efficacious examination of the applicant's discrimination claim.[385] As the different treatment was based upon sex and sexual characteristics, the margin of appreciation was narrow and could only be justified by very weighty reasons.[386] The Court determined that there were insufficient institutional and procedural safeguards in Switzerland for an effective examination of her substantiated and credible discrimination claim and thus there was a violation of Article 14 ECHR taken in conjunction with Article 8 ECHR. The Court relied on the same reasoning for also finding a violation of Article 13 ECHR (right to effective remedy) in conjunction with Article 14 ECHR. The GC delivered judgment in July 2025. The Court found that the complaints under Articles 8, 13, and 14 ECHR were inadmissible. The Court concluded that there was a violation of Article 6(1) ECHR (Right to a Fair Hearing).[387] Nevertheless, the Chamber judgment is important as it analyses the discrimination experienced by intersex persons through the prism of equality. The Court also recognises for the

[381] *Women's Initiatives Supporting Group* v. *Georgia*, Apps. Nos. 73204/13, 74959/13, 16/12/2021.

[382] *Semenya* v. *Switzerland*, App. No. 10934/21, 11/07/2023.

[383] The International Association of Athletics Federation.

[384] *Semenya* v. *Switzerland* (n 382) at [158]. [385] Ibid at [166]. [386] Ibid at [169].

[387] *Semenya* v. *Switzerland* App. No. 10934/21, 10/07/2025.

first time that discrimination based on sex characteristics is covered by Article 14 ECHR under the grounds of 'sex' or 'genetic characteristics' and that differential treatment on this basis can only be justified by very weighty reasons.

14.3.6 Article 14 ECHR in Domestic UK Courts

Article 14 ECHR is one of the scheduled rights that was introduced into domestic law by the Human Rights Act 1998 (HRA). The inclusion of Article 14 ECHR is important as the EqA prohibits discrimination in particular contexts, namely: access to goods, services and facilities and the exercise of public functions; premises; work; education; and associations.[388] Article 14 ECHR complements and enhances the principles of equality and non-discrimination. Discrimination-related claims brought under the HRA have included the recall of prisoners on licence,[389] prison sentences,[390] bereavement benefits,[391] birth registration,[392] funding for abortion in Northern Ireland,[393] immigration and student loans,[394] and adoption and fostering agencies.[395]

The test that the domestic courts apply when considering whether there is a breach of Article 14 ECHR is similar to the questions considered by the ECtHR but there is no one accepted formulation of the test. Indeed, the courts have warned that 'a rigidly formulaic approach is to be avoided'.[396] The test has been given slightly different formulations by judges[397] but, in essence, the

388 EqA pts 3–7. 389 *R (Hilland) (Northern Ireland)* [2024] UKSC 4.

390 *R (Clift)* v. *Secretary of State for the Home Department* [2006] UKHL 54, [2007] 1 AC 484; *R (Khan)* v. *Secretary of State for Justice* [2020] EWHC 2084 (Admin), [2020] 1 WLR 3932; *R (Stott)* v. *Secretary of State for Justice* [2018] UKSC 59, [2018] AC 51.

391 *R (McLaughlin) (Northern Ireland)* [2018] UKSC 48, [2018] 1 WLR 4250; *R (Jackson & Ors)* v. *Secretary of State for Work and Pensions* [2020] EWHC 183 (Admin), [2020] 1 WLR 1441.

392 *R (McConnell and Anor)* v. *Registrar General for England and Wales* [2020] EWCA Civ 559, [2020] 3 WLR 683.

393 *R (A and B)* v. *Secretary of State for Health* [2017] UKSC 41, [2017] WLR 2492. Note the strong dissenting judgments of Lord Kerr and Lady Hale.

394 *R (Tigere)* v. *Secretary of State for Business, Innovation and Skills* [2015] UKSC 57, [2015] WLR 3820.

395 *R (Cornerhouse (North East) Fostering and Adoption Services)* v. *Ofsted* [2021] EWCA Civ 1390, [2022] 2 All ER 516. It is worth noting the important decision of *R* v. *Immigration Officer at Prague Airport* [2004] UKHL 55, [2005] 2 AC 1, where the House of Lords unanimously held that British immigration officers working at Prague Airport had discriminated against Roma wishing to travel from the airport to the United Kingdom. The system operated by the British immigration officers was found to be systemically discriminatory on racial grounds against Roma and contrary to the Race Relations Act 1965. (The legislation then in force which has now been replace by the EqA.) Lady Hale's judgment provides an insightful discussion of direct and indirect discrimination. See [73]–[75].

396 *Ghaidan* v. *Godin Mendoza* [2004] UKHL 30, [2004] 2 AC 557 at [133]–[134].

397 See *R (DA and Ors)* v. *Secretary of State for Work and Pensions* [2019] UKSC 21, [2019] 1 WLR 3289 at [136], per Lady Hale.

courts address justification with four questions: is there a legitimate aim; is there a rational connection between the means and the aim; could the aim be achieved by measures which would intrude less upon the fundamental right in question; and has a fair balance been struck between the ends and the means? The determination of the appropriate intensity of review varies and will depend upon context. The Supreme Court has stated:

> It is more useful to think of there being a range of factors which tend to heighten, or lower, the intensity of review. In any given case, a number of these factors may be present possibly pulling in different directions, and the court has to take them all into account in order to make an overall assessment.[398]

Many Article 14 ECHR claims involve social and economic rights in the field of welfare benefits and pensions. In these cases, the courts have usually adopted a lower intensity review and afforded the decision maker considerable deference or margin of appreciation.[399] In the past, the courts have sometimes suggested that intervention is only appropriate where a measure is 'manifestly without reasonable foundation'.[400] Some caution should be exercised with the use of this phrase. According to the Supreme Court, this phrase is one way of referring to a wide margin of appreciation and suggests that the focus should be on whether a wide margin is appropriate given the context of the case.[401] There is further discussion of this issue in the section on welfare benefits and socio-economic rights.[402]

14.3.6.1 *Domestic Court Judgments Concerning Article 14 ECHR*

Soon after the HRA came into force, the House of Lords was asked to consider the compatibility of anti-terrorist measures with Convention rights in *A and Ors* v. *Secretary of State for the Home Department* (the *Belmarsh* case).[403] The Anti-terrorism, Crime and Security Act 2001 was passed in response to the events of 9/11. Section 23 of the Act provided for indefinite detention without trial of non-nationals who were suspected of terrorist activity. The Government claimed that the internment of non-nationals was an immigration control measure. The House of Lords, however, decided to assess for itself the relevance of the protected characteristic to the underlying aim or purpose of the legislation. According to the majority, anti-terrorist measures may be

[398] *R (SC, CB and 8 children)* v. *Secretary of State for Work and Pensions* [2021] UKSC 26, [2021] 3 WLR 428 at [99].

[399] Ibid at [144] and note also *Stec* v. *the United Kingdom* (n 79).

[400] *R (DA and Ors)* (n 397) at [55]–[66], [110]–[118], [125].

[401] *R (SC, CB and 8 children)* (n 398) at [160]–[161].

[402] See Section 14.3.6.1.3.

[403] *A and Ors* v. *Secretary of State for the Home Department* [2004] UKHL 56, [2005] 2 AC 68. See the discussion of the *Belmarsh Case* in Chapters 3 and 8.

justified but where such measures discriminate against non-nationals, that discrimination must be justified. Lady Hale clearly set out the issue:

> The Government knew about certain foreign nationals presenting this problem [of terrorism], because they were identified during the usual immigration appeals process. But there is absolutely no reason to think that the problem applies only to foreigners. Quite the reverse. There is every reason to think that there are British nationals living here who are international terrorists within the meaning of the Act; who cannot be shown to be such in a court of law; and who cannot be deported to another country because they have every right to be here. Yet the Government does not think that it is necessary to lock them up. Indeed, it has publicly stated that locking up nationals is a Draconian step which could not at present be justified. But it has provided us with no real explanation of why it is necessary to lock up one group of people sharing exactly the same characteristics as another group which it does not think necessary to lock up.[404]

She astutely highlighted the difficulty with the Government's discriminatory treatment in this passage.

> No one has the right to be an international terrorist. But substitute 'black', 'disabled', 'female', 'gay', or any other similar adjective for 'foreign' before 'suspected international terrorist' and ask whether it would be justifiable to take power to lockup that group but not the 'white', 'able-bodied', 'male' or 'straight' suspected international terrorists. The answer is clear.[405]

In 2004, in *Ghaidan* v. *Godin-Mendoza*,[406] the House of Lords held that it was contrary to Article 14 ECHR in conjunction with Article 8 ECHR for a tenant's opposite-sex unmarried partner, but not a same-sex partner, to succeed to a statutory tenancy following the tenant's death. The court said that this difference in treatment came within the ambit of Article 8 ECHR, because it concerned a home,[407] and that same-sex couples were in an analogous position to unmarried opposite-sex couples. Given the high level of scrutiny demanded in cases concerning sexual orientation, the difference in treatment could not be justified. The Court proceeded to use the interpretative obligation in s.3(1) HRA to read the legislative provision in a Convention-compatible manner to include same-sex partners.

R (Steinfeld and Keidan) v. *Secretary of State for International Development* is another significant Article 14 ECHR judgment.[408] A heterosexual couple, in a committed and long-term relationship, were genuinely ideologically opposed to marriage and wished to enter into a civil partnership instead.

[404] Ibid at [228]. [405] Ibid at [238].

[406] *Ghaidan* v. *Godin-Mendoza* (n 396). See also Chapter 2 for a discussion of this case in the context of s.3 HRA.

[407] Ibid at [135].

[408] *R (Steinfeld and Keidan)* v. *Secretary of State for International Development* [2018] UKSC 32, [2020] AC 1.

They were prevented from doing so by the Civil Partnership Act 2004, which was only available as an option to same-sex couples. Under the UK law at the time, same-sex couples had a choice of marriage or a civil partnership whereas couples of different sexes could choose only marriage. The Government claimed that a longer period of time to collect information was needed to ensure a confident policy decision about the future of civil partnerships. According to Lord Kerr, with whom the other members of the Supreme Court agreed, there was no legitimate aim[409] that justified the inequality of treatment.

> To be legitimate, therefore, the aim must address the perpetration of the unequal treatment, or . . . the aim must be intrinsically linked to the discriminatory treatment. In this case it does not and is not. The respondent does not seek to justify the difference in treatment between same sex and different sex couples. To the contrary, it accepts that that difference cannot be justified. What it seeks is tolerance of the discrimination while it sorts out how to deal with it. That cannot be characterised as a legitimate aim.[410]

Lord Kerr further observed that even if the appellant's rights 'could be regarded as being in pursuit of a legitimate aim', a fair balance had not been struck. While the interests of the community in denying different sex couples the opportunity to enter a civil partnership were 'unspecified and not easy to envisage', a denial to form a civil partnership could have serious fiscal disadvantage for couples.[411] Lord Kerr relied upon s.4 HRA 1998 and issued a declaration of incompatibility. Consequently, the Civil Partnership Act 2004 was amended to enable opposite-sex couples to form a civil partnership.[412]

14.3.6.1.2 *Judgments on Non-gendered Identity*

The legal recognition of non-gendered identity has also been addressed in the Supreme Court. In *R (Elan-Cane)* v. *Secretary of State for the Home Department*,[413] the policy of HM Passport Office that a passport can only be issued with a recorded gender of either female or male was challenged. The appellant was assigned female at birth but identified as having no gender and sought to have this recognised by an 'X' marker on their passport. Lord Reed, giving judgment for the Court, rejected a claim based on Article 14 ECHR read in conjunction with Article 8 ECHR. While it was accepted that there is a difference in treatment between those who identify as female and male, and

[409] Ibid. The Supreme Court followed the justification test set out in *R (Quila)* v. *Secretary of State for the Home Department* [2011] UKSC 45, [2012] 1 AC 621 cited in *Steinfeld*, ibid at [41].

[410] *Steinfeld* (n 408) at [42]. [411] Ibid at [52].

[412] Civil Partnership (Opposite-sex Couples) Regulations 2019/1458.

[413] *R (Elan-Cane)* v. *Secretary of State for the Home Department* [2021] UKSC 56, [2023] AC 559.

those who identify as non-gendered, the difference could be justified: public interest considerations such as the need to maintain a coherent approach to recognising gender categories across government practice outweighed the appellant's interests.[414]

A more recent case dealing with non-gendered identity was heard in the High Court. In *R (Castellucci)* v. *Gender Recognition Panel*,[415] the claimant challenged the refusal by the Gender Recognition Panel (GRP) to issue them a Gender Recognition Certificate (GRC) which would certify their acquired gender as 'non-binary'. As a US national, the claimant has legal recognition of their non-binary gender on all their official US documents, including their Californian birth certificate and US passport. The Gender Recognition Act 2004 (GRA)[416] states that the GRP must grant an application for a GRC if the place where the applicant's gender has been legally recognised is on the approved list. California, where the applicant gained legal gender recognition, is on the approved list. The claimant argued that they had received less favourable treatment than transgender persons. The non-binary yet legally acquired gender is not recognised in the GRA, whereas a transgender woman, whose acquired gender had been recognised in California, would obtain automatically a GRC in the female gender. The Court accepted that 'non-binary' was a protected status under Article 14 ECHR and the complaint fell within the ambit of Article 8 ECHR.[417] It was accepted that the claimant and the comparator were in an analogous situation. The claimant also argued that as Parliament had chosen to recognise some foreign law changes of gender in the GRA, it must act in a non-discriminatory way, and also recognise non-gender.[418] Given the sensitive and moral issues surrounding gender identity, the Court assumed 'that very weighty reasons are required to justify the difference of treatment of which they complain'.[419] However, on the basis of legal and administrative coherence and cost, the Court found that the discriminatory treatment was justified.[420] There is no doubt that this issue raises

414 Ibid at [50]–[54] and [66]. The HRA did not extend to give judges a right to find breaches of Convention rights where the Convention would not do so. See Lewis Graham, 'Taking Strasbourg Jurisprudence into Account' [2022] 2 EHRLR 163.

415 *R (Ryan Castellucci)* v. *Gender Recognition Panel and Minister for Women and Equalities* [2024] EWHC 54 (Admin), [2024] 2 WLR 1201.

416 The Gender Recognition Act 2004 was enacted in response to *Goodwin* v. *the United Kingdom* [GC] (2002) 35 EHRR 18 and *Bellinger* v. *Bellinger* [2003] UKHL 21, [2003] 2 AC 467 concerning discrimination against transgender persons. The legislation is premised on the basis of gender as a binary concept.

417 Note, *Taylor* v. *Jaguar Land Rover Ltd* (ET) Case 1304471/2018.

418 *Castellucci* (n 415) at [103]. The Court distinguished the *Elan-Cane* judgment as it concerned self-identification while the claimant in *Castellucci* relies on the recognition of non-binary by a foreign State.

419 *Castellucci* (n 415) at [128]. The Court assumed this point without deciding on it.

420 Ibid at [130].

important and highly sensitive elements concerning an individual's identity and the Court's conclusion seems at variance with the recognition that weighty reasons are needed to justify discrimination. The test of objective and reasonable justification asks the Court to consider whether the means bear a 'reasonable relationship of proportionality' to the aims sought to be realised. Accepting a 'foreign' non-binary gender would result in the recognition of this category for all purposes in domestic law. It would involve significant bureaucratic and legal changes as many laws such as the Equality Act, and institutions, for example prisons, are gendered.[421]

There is growing recognition of non-binary or non-gender as a legal status around the world, especially in common law jurisdictions. There are eleven states worldwide, including Australia, Argentina, Canada (some provinces) India, New Zealand and the USA (some states) and four member states of the Council of Europe which recognise non-binary or non-gender as a legal status. The pressure for legal change in the UK is thus likely to continue.

14.3.6.1.3 *Judgments on Welfare Benefits and Social and Economic Rights*

Social welfare policies have also been challenged using Article 14 ECHR and the HRA.[422] Many of these cases are controversial. Recent changes to the welfare systems have had a disproportionate impact on the poorest and most vulnerable in society: women, disabled people, ethnic minorities, children and single parent families. In 2019, these issues were highlighted by the UN Special Rapporteur on Extreme Poverty and Human Rights, Philip Alston.[423] He observed that 'the philosophy underpinning the British welfare system has changed radically since 2010'[424] and that there are 14 million people living in poverty, even in families where all adults work full time.[425] Since 2021, the UK has experienced inflation, especially in relation to food and energy, outstripping both wages and benefits and leading to a fall in disposable incomes.[426] The poverty rates are likely to have increased since the 2019 Alston report.[427]

[421] See also, *Y* v. *France* (n 379).

[422] The entitlement to all State benefits are considered 'possessions' for the purposes of Article 1 Protocol 1 ECHR, which protects property rights. See also *Lacatus* v. *Switzerland* (n 36) discussed above in Section 14.3.1.

[423] Report of the UN Special Rapporteur on Extreme Poverty and Human Rights, Visit to the UK and Northern Ireland, A/HRC/41/39/Add.1, 23 April 2019 (Alston Report).

[424] Ibid at [95].

[425] Ibid at [28]. See also EHRC, Is Britain Fairer? The State of Equality and Human Rights, www.equalityhumanrights.com/sites/default/files/is-britain-fairer-accessible.pdf.

[426] EHRC, Equality and Human Rights Monitor (2023), p.20.

[427] See e.g. Lalitha Try, 'Analysis of the impact of the two-child limit and benefit cap', Resolution Foundation (31 January 2024), www.resolutionfoundation.org/publications/catastophic-caps/.

According to Lady Hale, '[E]quality is the most complicated and difficult of all the fundamental rights, even without the delicate context of entitlement to welfare benefits.'[428] Judicial assessment in this 'delicate context' raises constitutional separation of powers issues: it has not proved to be an easy task for the judiciary to navigate the relationship between the Government, Parliament and the courts. There is a tension that is evident in welfare judgments. On the one hand, where the difference in treatment is based on the specially protected characteristics, any discretion should be narrow, and such differences in treatment can only be justified by very weighty reasons. On the other, courts often adopt a lower intensity review and considerable discretion is given to public authorities when dealing with social or economic policies.

In previous judgments of the Supreme Court, the majority had held that the test of justification in circumstances where differential treatment was the result of social and economic policies, was 'manifestly without reasonable foundation'.[429] This test is not difficult to satisfy as it requires little more than a rational relationship between means and ends. A later judgment of the ECtHR found that this less stringent test was only appropriate where an alleged difference in treatment was the consequence of transitional measures, correcting an inequality.[430] In their view, weighty reasons are still needed to justify differences in treatment based on specially protected characteristics, regardless of the context.

The Supreme Court considered this Strasbourg jurisprudence for the first time in *R (SC)*.[431] The Supreme Court modified its previous approach and directly addressed the tension between the intensity of the domestic court's review and the 'discretionary area of judgment' afforded to the decision maker. According to the Court, this is a flexible and nuanced question which depends on several factors.[432] The Court confirmed that 'a low intensity of review is generally appropriate . . . in cases concerned with judgments of social and economic policy in the field of welfare benefits and pensions, so that the judgment of the executive or legislature will generally be respected unless it is manifestly without reasonable foundation'.[433] The phrase 'manifestly without reasonable foundation' is used by the ECtHR to describe a wide margin of appreciation but in domestic cases, the Court suggested that 'it is more fruitful to focus on the question whether a wide margin of judgment is appropriate in the light of the circumstances of the case'.[434] The intensity of a review of a

[428] *R (DA and Ors)* (n 397) at [132].

[429] Ibid at [66]; *R (Carmichael)* v. *Secretary of State for Work and Pensions* [2016] UKSC 58, [2016] 1 WLR 4550.

[430] *JD and A* v. *the United Kingdom* (n 85) at [87]–[89].

[431] *R (SC, CB and 8 children)* v. *Secretary of State for Work and Pensions* (n 398); Lord Reed delivered the judgment with whom Lord Hodge, Lady Black, Lord Lloyd-Jones, Lord Kitchin, Lord Sales and Lord Stephens agreed.

[432] Ibid at [100]–[159]. [433] Ibid at [158]. [434] Ibid at [161].

domestic court and 'the discretionary area of judgment' afforded to decision makers will depend on a number of factors. The Court observed that 'the intensity of review will usually be correspondingly high, if a difference in treatment on a "suspect" ground is to be justified'.[435] Other factors include the impact on the best interests of children which may inform the interpretation of Article 14 ECHR;[436] whether the measure in question is a general measure of social and economic strategy;[437] and whether legislation is applied to correct an historical inequality. The Court will also give appropriate weight to the decision maker. If Parliament has made a judgment on the issues that are relevant to the Court's assessment, the Court will be more likely to accept Parliament's decision, and if the issue of discrimination were raised during the legislative process, then a broader margin of discretion would be appropriate.[438] Nevertheless, the decision maker cannot rely on a broad margin of appreciation if there is inadequate concrete evidence to show how the decision is connected to the suggested justification.[439]

In spite of this more flexible and nuanced approach, the Supreme Court, in a unanimous judgment, decided that legislation which restricted child tax credit (a non-contributory benefit intended to provide financial support to families with children) to two children was compatible with Article 14 ECHR.[440] The Court concluded that the rule limiting child tax credit to two children was indirectly discriminatory against women as it affects more women than men.[441] This rule was also directly discriminatory against children in families with more than two children.[442] The Government was successful in showing that the discrimination was justified in both circumstances: the measures pursued the legitimate aims of reducing expenditure and protecting the economic wellbeing of the country by contributing to reducing the fiscal deficit. It was inevitable that there would be a disproportionate impact on women, since more women than men are responsible for bringing up children. The Court questioned whether the inevitable impact on women outweighed the importance of the aims pursued and concluded that Parliament had decided to pursue these aims, notwithstanding a disproportionate impact on women.[443] In relation to the alleged discrimination against children, there was found to be a rational connection between the objectives pursued by legislation and Parliament's decision to limit child tax credit to two children. Savings in

435 Ibid.

436 Ibid at [158]. The Supreme Court rejected the argument that the UN Convention on the Rights of the Child is part of domestic UK law at [76]–[96].

437 Ibid at [159]–[161], [208].

438 Ibid at [180]–[183].

439 *De Smith's Judicial Review* (9th ed) (2023), 14.024.

440 Welfare benefits fell within the ambit of Article 8 ECHR. Ibid at [41] and Article 1 Protocol 1 ECHR at [42].

441 *R (SC, CB and 8 children)* (n 398) at [44]–[46].

442 Ibid at [70]–[72].

443 Ibid at [199].

public expenditure and a reduction of the fiscal deficit would be achieved by this measure and a difference in treatment based on the number of children in a household was unavoidable if the aim was to be achieved. According to the Court:

> The assessment of proportionality, therefore, ultimately resolves itself into the question as to whether Parliament made the right judgment. That was at the time, and remains, a question of intense political controversy. It cannot be answered by any process of legal reasoning. There are no legal standards by which a court can decide where the balance should be struck between the interests of children and their parents in receiving support from the state, on the one hand, and the interests of the community as a whole in placing responsibility for the care of children upon their parents, on the other.[444]

This is a disappointing conclusion. The Supreme Court may have claimed to have moved away from the 'manifestly without reasonable foundation' test but this has failed to make any real difference to their analysis. Even though the Court unanimously agreed that there was discrimination against women, a 'suspect ground', the intensity of review was not respectively high, and the Government's fiscal priorities were given deference. In fact, this decision strongly suggests that the proportionality assessment will, in most circumstances, always vindicate the economic financial decision of the relevant public authority.

In writing about earlier benefit decisions, Meghan Campbell points out that these 'cases bring together intersecting status vulnerabilities (gender and reproductive care) with economic vulnerabilities (poverty)'. Until the courts are willing to tackle these 'multifaceted inequalities' the balancing stage is skewed and the courts 'myopically analyse these benefit cut claims through the lens of one type of inequality: economic'.[445] She adds that in undertaking a balancing exercise that fully interrogates the inequalities of both sides of the scale, 'the court is not overstepping its role, but asking searching questions to ensure the government upholds its commitment to equality and non-discrimination'.[446]

The hurdles remain very high for Article 14 ECHR claimants to show that discrimination is unjustified, but there have been some successful benefit challenges. In *Burnip* v. *Birmingham City Council*, discrimination and the award of housing benefit was considered by the Court of Appeal.[447] Due to severe disabilities, the applicants required extra bedrooms to accommodate their special needs, but their housing benefits were calculated based on what

[444] Ibid at [208].

[445] Meghan Campbell, 'The Austerity of Lone Motherhood: Discrimination Law and Benefit Reform' (2021) 41 OJLS 1197–1226.

[446] Ibid. [447] *Burnip* v. *Birmingham City Council* [2012] EWCA Civ 629.

would reasonably be required for an able-bodied person. Two of the appellants were severely disabled and needed overnight carers: thus they required two-bedroom flats. They received housing benefit but only on the basis of entitlement to a one-bedroom flat. The third appellant lived with his wife and three children, including two severely disabled daughters in a four-bedroomed flat. He argued that it was inappropriate for them to share a bedroom in the way in which able-bodied sisters of a young age could be expected to do so. He was provided housing benefit on the basis of a three-bedroomed flat. They successfully established their claim based on Article 14 ECHR. Relying on *Thlimmenos* v. *Greece*, the Court concluded that the defendant's failure to make allowances for the fact that the claimants needed larger properties due to their, or their children's, disabilities, resulted in the bedroom tax disadvantaging them and to a finding of discrimination.

14.4 EQUALITY ACT 2010

The EqA is a fundamental part of the domestic legal framework. It replaced the disparate and often inconsistent, domestic statutory provisions regulating discrimination into a single Act. The Explanatory Notes to the EqA describe its two main purposes as to harmonise discrimination law and to strengthen the law to support progress on equality. Although the EqA was primarily concerned with consolidation, it also included several substantive changes such as the extension of positive duties on public authorities in respect of eliminating discrimination and advancing equality of opportunity.

The first statement in the Preamble of the EqA is: 'An Act to make provision to require Ministers of the Crown and others when making strategic decisions about the exercise of their functions to have regard to the desirability of reducing socio-economic inequalities.'[448] The socio-economic duty is set out in s.1 EqA. The Explanatory Notes state that this duty requires those public bodies, 'when making strategic decisions such as deciding priorities and setting objectives, to consider how their decisions might help to reduce the inequalities associated with socio-economic disadvantage'.[449] This is a specific recognition of the interaction between socio-economic disadvantage and discrimination. The duty has been implemented in Scotland[450] and Wales[451]

[448] EqA, Preamble. [449] EqA s.1, Explanatory Notes at [23].

[450] Equality Act 2010 (Authorities subject to the Socio-economic Inequality Duty) (Scotland) Regulations 2018 SI 2018/101, which came into force on 1 April 2018. Regulation 2 lists the public authorities subject to the duty.

[451] Equality Act 2010 (Authorities subject to a duty regarding Socio-economic Inequalities) (Wales) Regulations 2021 SI 2021/295 were brought into force in 2021. Regulation 2 lists to which public authorities the duty applies.

but not yet in England, although a number of English local authorities such as Newcastle City Council and the North of Tyne Combined Authority have adopted the duty voluntarily. It is hoped that this important pillar of the EqA will eventually be implemented throughout England.

The EqA does not apply in Northern Ireland which has its own legislative provisions.[452] This chapter does not undertake a comprehensive analysis of the EqA, which is a specialism in its own right, but rather focuses on cases where HRA arguments have been advanced.[453]

14.4.1 Protected Characteristics

The EqA regulates and extends protection across the 'protected characteristics'.[454] These are age,[455] disability,[456] gender reassignment,[457] marriage and civil partnership,[458] race,[459] religion and belief,[460] sex[461] and sexual orientation.[462] It is also prohibited to discriminate on grounds of pregnancy and maternity.[463] The EqA provides that for the purpose of this legislation, race comprises four categories: colour; ethnic origins; nationality; and national origins.[464] The protected characteristic of religion and belief includes a lack of religion or belief.[465]

The ambit of protected characteristics is not always straightforward. The recognition of 'belief' as a protected characteristic is one area which has raised controversial issues. The threshold criteria for determining whether a belief qualifies for protection was set out initially in *Grainger Plc* v. *Nicholson* by the Employment Appeal Tribunal (EAT).[466] This case turned upon whether asserting a philosophical belief about anthropogenic climate change and the environment was capable of being a belief for the purposes of the Employment Equality (Religion or Belief) Regulations 2003, which regulated this area of the law prior to the EqA. In *Grainger* it was stated that in order to qualify as a protected characteristic: '(1) the belief must be genuinely held; (2) it must be a

[452] The primary legislative provisions in Northern Ireland are: The Northern Ireland Act 1998; The Human Rights Act 1998; The Employment Equality (Age) Regulations (Northern Ireland) 2006; The Disability Discrimination Act 1995; The Equal Pay Act (NI) 1970; The Sex Discrimination (NI) Order 1976; The Maternity and Parental Leave etc. Regulations (NI) 1996; The Employment Equality (Sexual Orientation) Regulations (NI) 2003; Equality Act (Sexual Orientation) Regulations (NI) 2006. See also, discussion of *Lee* v. *Ashers* in Chapter 13 on Religion.

[453] For a comprehensive account of the Equality Act 2010 and discrimination law, see Aileen McColgan KC, *Discrimination Law: Text, Cases and Materials* (Hart, 2023).

[454] EqA s.4. [455] EqA s.5. [456] EqA s.6. [457] EqA s.7. [458] EqA s.8.

[459] EqA s.9. [460] EqA s.10. See also Chapter 13. [461] EqA s.11. [462] EqA s.12.

[463] EqA ss.17 (non-work related) and 18 (work related). [464] EqA s.9.

[465] EqA s.10(1) and (2).

[466] *Grainger Plc* v. *Nicholson* [2009] UKEAT 219_9_311, [2010] 2 All ER 253.

belief and not ... an opinion or viewpoint based on the present state of information available; (3) it must be a belief as to a weighty and substantial aspect of human life and behaviour; (4) it must attain a certain level of cogency, seriousness, cohesion and importance; (5) it must be worthy of respect in a democratic society, be not incompatible with human dignity and not conflict with the fundamental rights of others'.[467] The claim that 'beliefs' protected by the EqA must be 'worthy of respect' as set out in (5) above was a laudable attempt to avoid giving beliefs, such as holocaust denial or white supremacy, a 'protected characteristic' for the purposes of the EqA.[468] This criteria, however, does not specifically engage with Article 9 ECHR which is unusual in that it combines absolute protection in relation to the holding of all beliefs, with a qualified right to manifest them.[469]

In *Forstater* v. *CGD Europe*,[470] the claimant, Mrs Forstater, had carried out consultancy work for the respondents but after posting tweets on transgender issues, her contract was not renewed. The respondents' staff had found her tweets to be transphobic and offensive. She brought proceedings alleging direct discrimination because of her gender-critical beliefs: the belief that biological sex is immutable and is distinct from gender or gender-identity. She had argued that her beliefs were a protected 'philosophical belief' under s.10 of the EqA. Section 10(2) states that: 'Belief means any religious or philosophical belief and a reference to belief.' The Employment Tribunal (hereafter ET) found that her beliefs did not satisfy the fifth *Grainger* criteria.

On appeal, the EAT (Employment Appeals Tribunal) found that the claimant's views constituted a 'philosophical belief' under s.10 of the EqA.[471] According to the EAT, qualification for protection does not depend on the quality or open-mindedness of the belief.[472] Beliefs must be protected pursuant to Article 9 and Article 10 ECHR unless they fall outside the scope of protection by virtue of Article 17 ECHR.[473] Although these beliefs might be considered 'offensive or abhorrent' to some, the claimant's statements of her beliefs did not seek 'to destroy the rights of trans people'.[474] The Tribunal also noted that the gender-critical belief is widely shared[475] and that these beliefs are consistent with our common law.[476] The EAT acknowledged the trauma

[467] Ibid at [24]. [468] See McColgan (n 2) for a fuller discussion at pp.152–156.

[469] Note also the effect of Article 17 ECHR. See also Chapter 13.

[470] *Forstater* v. *CGD Europe* [2021] UKEAT 0105_20_1006, [2022] ICR 1.

[471] The EAT considered the criteria for determining whether a belief qualifies for protection as set out in *Grainger Plc* v. *Nicholson* (n 466). In addition, s.10 EqA must be interpreted in a way that is Convention compatible, s.3 HRA 1998.

[472] *Forstater* (n 470) at [86].

[473] At the preliminary stage, the analysis was confined to determining whether the belief qualified for protection pursuant to Art 9 ECHR. There is no balancing exercise between competing rights at this stage. *Forstater* (n 470) at [102].

[474] Ibid at [111]. [475] Ibid at [113]. [476] Ibid at [115].

and distress faced by trans persons, but also observed that the Gender Recognition Act 2004 does not compel a person to believe something that they do not in a private or non-legal context.[477] The EAT remitted the case to the ET to decide whether the treatment complained of was because of, or related to, her beliefs. Two complaints of direct discrimination and one of victimisation were upheld.[478] There is strong protection for philosophical beliefs under the EqA and the ECHR and even beliefs which are shocking, offensive or disturbing to others are protected.

14.4.2 Prohibited Conduct

The EqA regulates direct discrimination (less favourable treatment because of a protected characteristic);[479] indirect discrimination (unjustified application of a provision, criterion or practice, the effect of which is to disadvantage disproportionately members of groups defined by reference to a protected characteristic);[480] victimisation (unfavourable treatment because of an allegation or complaint of discrimination);[481] and harassment (unwanted conduct connected with a protected characteristic, the purpose or effect of which is to violate dignity or create an 'intimidating, hostile, degrading, humiliating or offensive environment' for the person complaining of it).[482] The EqA does not prohibit all discrimination associated with the protected characteristics; it prohibits discrimination in particular contexts, namely: access to goods, services and facilities and the exercise of public functions; premises, which provides wide protection in the housing field; work; education; and associations.[483]

Section 13 EqA sets out some circumstances where different treatment does not constitute direct discrimination. For example, in the context of age, different treatment that is justified as a proportionate means of meeting a legitimate aim is not direct discrimination.[484] If disability is the protected characteristic, it is not discrimination to treat a disabled person more favourably than a person who is not disabled.[485] In contrast, racial segregation will always be discriminatory.[486]

If the discriminatory treatment falls outside the EqA, however, it may still be considered discrimination pursuant to the HRA and Article 14 ECHR or it may be possible to bring a challenge under the common law.

14.4.3 Direct and Indirect Discrimination

In contrast to Article 14 ECHR, there is no general justification defence in *direct* discrimination claims under the EqA, save in relation to age and

[477] Ibid at [99]. [478] Ibid. See also *Bailey* v. *Stonewall Equality Ltd* [2024] EAT 119.
[479] EqA s.13. [480] EqA ss.19 and 19A. [481] EqA s.27. [482] EqA s.26.
[483] EqA pts 3–7. [484] EqA s.13(2). [485] EqA s.13(3). [486] EqA s.13(5).

disability.[487] As a result of this important difference, direct and indirect discrimination must be separated. As explained by Lady Hale:

> Direct and indirect discrimination are mutually exclusive. You cannot have both at once . . . The main difference between them is direct discrimination cannot be justified. Indirect discrimination can be justified if it is a proportionate means of achieving a legitimate aim.[488]

In a direct discrimination claim there must be a link between the treatment and the reason for it. Section 13(1) EqA provides; 'A person (A) discriminates against another (B) if, because of a protected characteristic, A treats B less favourably than A treats or would treat others.' Thus, direct discrimination is less favourable treatment *because of* a relevant protected characteristic.

Indirect discrimination focuses on impact. It is intended to prohibit practices which may be fair in form but operate in a discriminatory fashion. Indirect discrimination in the EqA is thus characterised as: 'A person (A) discriminates against another (B) if A applies to B a provision, criterion or practice which is discriminatory in relation to a relevant protected characteristic of B's.'[489] The concept is further explained in s.19(2) EqA through the provision of examples of indirect discrimination. Unlike direct discrimination, indirect discrimination can be justified if it is 'a proportionate means of achieving a legitimate aim.'[490]

Lady Hale explains the difference between direct and indirect discrimination in the following terms in the context of race discrimination (though the same observations apply with respect to each of the protected characteristics):

> The basic difference between direct and indirect discrimination is plain . . . The rule against direct discrimination aims to achieve formal equality of treatment: there must be no less favourable treatment between otherwise similarly situated people on grounds of colour, race, nationality or ethnic or national origins. Indirect discrimination looks beyond formal equality towards a more substantive equality of results: criteria which appear neutral on their face may have a disproportionately adverse impact upon people of a particular colour, race, nationality or ethnic or national origins.[491]

The courts, however, have not always found it straightforward to distinguish between the reason for the differential treatment and a justification for that treatment, which is not relevant in a direct discrimination assessment. One way around this is to restrict any consideration of motive or intention. This approach was approved by the House of Lords in a case bought by the Equal Opportunities Commission in respect of a local council policy which had set

[487] EqA s.13(2) and s.13(3) and protection on grounds of marriage/civil partnership, s.13(4).

[488] *R (E)* v. *Governing Body of JFS & Anor* [2009] UKSC 15, [2010] 2 AC 728 at [57].

[489] EqA s.19(1). [490] EqA s.19(d).

[491] *JFS* (n 488) at [56]. See also, *Essop and Others* v. *Home Office (UK Border Agency)* [2017] UKSC 27, [2017] 1 WLR 1343 at [25], per Lady Hale.

the pass mark higher for girls than boys in the '11 plus test' which was used to select children for secondary schools. The reason being that the local council had fewer grammar school places for girls than for boys.[492] The Court confirmed that there was no requirement to show that the Council was motivated by a prohibited ground. As Lord Goff explained:

> The intention or motive of the defendant to discriminate ... is not a necessary condition of liability ... [I]f [it were] it would be a good defence for an employer to show that he discriminated against women not because he intended to do so but (for example) because of customer preference, or to save money, or even to avoid controversy.[493]

This approach has led to some blurring of the distinction between direct and indirect discrimination and some decisions have 'slipped over the boundary between differential *treatment on the ground of* a protected characteristic and differential *impact*'.[494] Sandra Fredman argues that if the perpetrator's motive is irrelevant, the notion of direct discrimination is severed 'from its moral anchor in fault and responsibility of the perpetrator, and instead makes A responsible for putting in motion a series of steps which have a detrimental *effect* on B, thus crossing the border between direct and indirect discrimination'.[495]

14.4.4 Public Sector Equality Duty

An important facet of the EqA is the imposition of the Public Sector Equality Duty (PSED).[496] The PSED requires that public authorities (and private bodies exercising public functions)[497] must have 'due regard' to several statutory needs. There are three equality objectives set out in the PSED and '*due regard*' must be given to each of them. These needs are to eliminate unlawful discrimination, to advance equality of opportunity and to foster good relations between persons defined by reference to protected characteristics.[498] This PSED is a different class of provision from those which prohibit discrimination. The idea underlying the duty is 'to bring about a culture change so that

[492] *R (Equal Opportunities Commission)* v. *Birmingham City Council* [1989] UKHL 8, [1989] AC 1155.

[493] Ibid at [175]. Note also, *R (European Roma Rights Centre)* v. *Immigration Officer at Prague Airport* [2004] UKHL 55, [2005] 2 AC 1.

[494] Sandra Fredman, *Discrimination Law* (2nd ed) (OUP, 2011), p.204 (emphasis in original). She refers to *James* v. *Eastleigh BC* [1990] UKHL 6, [1990] 2 AC 751 and *JFS* (n 488). See also, Sandra Fredman, 'Direct and Indirect Discrimination: Is There Still a Divide?' in Hugh Collins and Tarunabh Khaitan (eds), *Foundations of Indirect Discrimination Law* (Hart, 2018).

[495] Fredman, *Discrimination Law* (n 494), p.205 (emphasis in original) and Sandra Fredman, *Discrimination Law* (3rd ed) (Oxford University Press, 2023), ch.5. See also Colin Campbell and Dale Smith, 'Distinguishing between Direct and Indirect Discrimination' (2023) **86**(2) MLR 307.

[496] EqA s.149. [497] EqA s.149(2). [498] EqA ss.149(1)(a), 149(1)(b) and 149(1)(c).

promoting equality becomes part of public bodies' core business'.[499] The obligation should be understood not as one of results, but of procedure: the public authority is required to take into account equality-related needs in reaching decisions.[500] If a policy formulation has taken place without regard to the PSED, there is a high risk that any consideration will be too late to ensure substantive compliance with the duty. Any claim for breach of a PSED is by way of an application for judicial review. Two recent cases are discussed below which have found a breach of the PSED.

A violation of the PSED was found in *R (DXK)* v. *SSHD* concerning the system of allocation of asylum accommodation as it related to pregnant and new-mother asylum seekers under the Immigration and Asylum Act 1999.[501] 'Pregnancy and maternity' and 'age' are protected characteristics under the EqA. Pregnant and new-mother asylum seekers and their infants had a need for longer-term and self-contained accommodation that was not shared by other asylum seekers or failed asylum seekers who did not share either protected characteristic. The claimants argued that the Secretary of State could not provide evidence that the PSED was discharged as its failure to collect and monitor statistical data meant that no assessment was possible as to whether the system is working, or new solutions are required. In finding the Government had acted unlawfully, the Court stated: 'Equality evidence, including "hard statistical data" is at "the root of effective compliance with the general equality duty" . . . [it] is the "key means by which to identify and correct failure and to inform change" and "the foundation of ensuring that [his] duty is met."'[502]

The PSED was also considered, amongst other claims, in a case that arose out of the 'Windrush scandal'. It concerned a decision of the Secretary of State not to introduce two of the thirty recommendations made in an independent assessment of the events leading up to the Windrush scandal.[503] The two recommendations were Recommendation 9 (the introduction of a Migrants' Commissioner) and Recommendation 10 (the role and remit of the Independent Chief Inspector of Borders and Immigration).[504] The Claimant was born in Jamaica in 1955. He came to the UK in 1967 and resided there

[499] Government Equalities Office (2009) Equality Bill; Making It Work. Policy Proposals for Specific Duties at [3.3] quoted in Bob Hepple, *Equality: The Legal Framework* (2nd ed) (Hart, 2014), p.163.

[500] Aileen McColgan, *Discrimination Law: Text Cases and Materials* (Hart, 2023) p.169.

[501] *R (DXK)* v. *Secretary of State for the Home Department* [2024] EWHC 579 (Admin), [2024] 4 WLR 46.

[502] Ibid at [154].

[503] *R (Donald)* v. *Secretary State Home Department* [2024] EWHC 1492 (Admin), [2024] 4 WLR 46.

[504] Independent Review by Wendy Williams, 'Windrush Lessons Learnt Review', HC 93 (March 2020).

continuously until 2010 when he travelled to Jamaica for his mother's funeral. He was denied permission to re-enter the UK and his visa applications were refused for approximately nine years. In relation to the PSED requirement, the Court found that in the absence of any clear evidence that the Secretary of State had appreciated the likely benefits of implementing those recommendations or the equality implications of not implementing them, the duty had not been fulfilled.[505] The Secretary of State's decision was also found unlawful as it had breached a procedural legitimate expectation (failure to consult with stakeholders including the Windrush community) and indirectly discriminated against the Windrush community. Given the devastating impact of the Windrush scandal and the profound effect that it had on many victims, membership of the Windrush community was a relevant status for Article 14 ECHR[506] and the issue fell within the ambit of Article 8 ECHR.[507] The Government had not shown that these policy decisions were a proportionate means of achieving a legitimate aim, given the very limited evidence as to the basis of its decision-making.[508]

The PSED has expanded the 'toolkit' available to claimants to challenge failures to comply with human rights standards and to ensure accountability of public authorities. These decisions strongly indicate that the PSED principles have legal clout. These principles, however, can only go so far. It was noted in *Hackney LBC* v. *Haque* that 'the concept of due regard is to be distinguished from a requirement to give the PSED considerations specific weight. It is not a duty to achieve a particular result.'[509]

14.4.5 Equality Act Case Studies

In order to highlight and examine in greater detail issues that arise in discrimination disputes, four case studies follow. The first considers specific contexts where protected characteristics are relied upon by both litigants. A feature of claims under the EqA is that they can raise competing human rights claims. These cases are examined from the perspective of discrimination, but they have also been discussed in Chapter 13. The second concerns cases in the employment context. The third, is a case study on discrimination in the educational environment. Finally, the Supreme Court has recently concluded that the characteristic of 'sex', 'woman' and 'man' for the purposes of the EqA refer to biological sex.[510] This judgment also examines the relationship between the EqA and the Gender Recognition Act 2004.

[505] *R (Donald)* (n 503) at [277]–[288]. [506] Ibid at [130]. [507] Ibid at [124].

[508] Ibid at [237]–[242] and [256]–[263].

[509] *Hackney LBC* v. *Haque* [2017] EWCA Civ 4, [2014] HLR 14 at [23], per Briggs LJ.

[510] *For Women Scotland* v. *Scottish Ministers* [2025] UKSC 16.

14.4.5.1 *Discrimination, Sexual Orientation and Religious Belief*

In *Bull* v. *Hall*, which was discussed in Chapter 13, devout Christian B&B keepers had a policy of denying a room with a double bed to unmarried couples (regardless of sexual orientation).[511] A same-sex couple in a civil partnership were not aware of this policy and on arrival at the hotel, they were refused a double room. They brought proceedings against the owners claiming that the refusal to accommodate them amounted to unlawful discrimination on grounds of sexual orientation. The claim was based on the Equality Act (Sexual Orientation) Regulations 2007 (now replaced by the EqA) which made it unlawful for persons concerned with the provision to the public of services to discriminate on grounds of sexual orientation directly or indirectly. The owners argued that they had not discriminated against the couple on the ground of sexual orientation but because they were not married to one another. They emphasised that they would have also denied a double bed to a heterosexual unmarried couple and that it is not unlawful to discriminate against the unmarried.[512] This case involved a clash between parties, all of whom have 'protected characteristics'.[513]

The Supreme Court initially addressed whether the difference in treatment amounted to direct or indirect discrimination, with Lady Hale commenting that 'the distinction is by no means easy to draw, as this case illustrates all too clearly'.[514] The Supreme Court unanimously agreed that the owners had unlawfully discriminated against the couple. By a 3:2 majority the Court found that the treatment amounted to direct discrimination, albeit with differing reasoning.

Lady Hale concluded that discrimination between a married person and a civilly partnered person cannot be anything other than direct discrimination on grounds of sexual orientation. Marriage was (at this time) only available to heterosexual couples and civil partnerships only available to same-sex couples. She stated:

> The principal purpose of each institution is to provide a legal framework within which loving, stable and committed adult relationships can flourish. I would therefore regard the criterion of marriage or civil partnership as indissociable from the sexual orientation of those who qualify to enter it. More importantly, there is an exact correspondence between the advantage conferred and the disadvantage imposed in allowing a double bed to the one and denying it to the other.[515]

Lady Hale discerned that the owners were not only applying a criterion that couples must be married but also that the legal relationship should be between a man and a woman. They would have turned away not only civil partners but

[511] *Bull* v. *Hall* [2013] UKSC 73, [2013] 1 WLR 3741. [512] Ibid at [17]. [513] Ibid at [4].
[514] Ibid at [16]. [515] Ibid at [29].

also same-sex married couples from jurisdictions in which it was lawful for same-sex couples to marry. Indeed, a later amendment to their policy made that even clearer. The requirement that the married couple comprise a man and a woman was direct discrimination on grounds of sexual orientation as much as a requirement that married couples be over the age of thirty to hire a double room would be direct discrimination on grounds of age.[516] In her view, she had the 'greatest difficulty' in seeing how this could be other than direct discrimination on grounds of sexual orientation.[517]

Although all the justices were unanimous in the view that the couple had been subject to unlawful discrimination because of their sexual orientation, Lord Neuberger and Lord Hughes would have characterised this matter as unjustified indirect discrimination. Lord Neuberger explained:

> Parliament's purpose in introducing civil partnerships was to enable homosexual couples to enjoy the same rights as heterosexual couples. However, that is not, in my view, either as a matter of logic or as a matter of policy, a reason for holding that the discrimination in this case was direct, given that it would have been indirect if Mr Preddy and Mr Hall had not been in a civil partnership.[518]

Lee v. *Ashers Baking Company Ltd*[519] is another case concerning sexual orientation discrimination, which was also discussed in Chapter 13. The claimant, Lee, was a gay man who volunteered for QueerSpace, an LGBT organisation supporting the campaign for same-sex marriage in Northern Ireland. Asher's Bakery was run by a Christian couple who believed sincerely that gay marriage was inconsistent with Biblical teaching. Lee placed an order for a cake with Asher's bakery to be iced with the QueerSpace logo, a coloured picture of 'Bert and Ernie' and the words 'Support Gay Marriage'. Mrs McArthur, a Director of Asher's, who had originally accepted the order, telephoned Lee and informed him that the order could not be fulfilled as the bakery was a 'Christian business' and she should not have accepted the order. He was given a refund.

Mr Lee brought a discrimination claim against the Appellants under Northern Ireland legislation alleging unlawful discrimination on the grounds of sexual orientation,[520] political opinion or religious belief.[521] (The EqA is slightly different: s.10 protects religious and philosophical beliefs but there is no explicit mention of political opinion.) His claim was also supported by the Equality Commission of Northern Ireland. The claims of unlawful

[516] Ibid at [30]–[31], per Lady Hale. [517] Ibid at [29].
[518] Ibid at [80]. See also Lord Hughes at [89].
[519] *Lee* v. *Ashers Baking Company Ltd* [2018] UKSC 49, [2020] AC 413.
[520] Equality Act (Sexual Orientation) Regulations NI 2006.
[521] Fair Employment and Treatment (NI) Order 1998.

discrimination were successful in both the County Court and the Court of Appeal.[522] He was, however, unsuccessful in the Supreme Court.

Lady Hale delivered the judgment of the Supreme Court on the discrimination issues. In a significant decision, the Supreme Court held that Asher's Bakery did not directly discriminate against Lee on the grounds of sexual orientation. In the Court's view, support for gay marriage was a political belief: '[t]he objection was to the message and not to any particular person or persons'.[523]

Lady Hale discussed the findings of the District Judge who had questioned 'whether the criterion used by the bakery was "indissociable" from the protected characteristic and had held that support for same sex marriage was indissociable from sexual orientation'.[524] According to Lady Hale, this was a misunderstanding of indissociable and direct discrimination. Indissociable is relevant when the express criterion used as the reason for the less favourable treatment is not the protected characteristic, but a proxy for it. She used the decision of *James* v. *Eastleigh Borough Council*[525] to explain: the criterion to allow free entry for swimming was not the protected characteristic of sex but the statutory retirement age, which was at age sixty for women, and sixty-five for men. There was, however, an exact correspondence between the criterion of the statutory retirement age and sex. Women aged sixty to sixty-four could swim for free while no man of this age could do so. In the *Bull* v. *Hall* judgment discussed above, letting rooms with double beds to married couples but not to civil partners was 'directly discriminatory because marriage was (at that time) indissociable from hetero-sexual orientation'.[526] Lady Hale distinguished the situation in *Lee* v. *Ashers* on the facts. In her view, support for gay marriage was not a proxy for sexual orientation: 'People of all sexual orientations, gay, straight or bi-sexual, can and do support gay marriage.'[527]

The Court of Appeal had considered that this was an example of associative discrimination as Lee had been less favourably treated because of his association with the gay community and the protected characteristic was the sexual orientation of that community.[528] Lady Hale found no factual evidence to suggest that Ashers' refusal to supply the cake was because Lee would associate with gay people. 'The reason was their religious objection to gay marriage.'[529] In her conclusion, Lady Hale acknowledged the real problem of discrimination against gay people and the humiliation and affront to dignity of being denied a service because of personal characteristics. But in the opinion of the Supreme Court that was not the situation here and 'it does

[522] *Lee* v. *Ashers Baking Company Ltd* [2016] NICA 39.

[523] *Lee* v. *Ashers Baking Company Ltd* (UKSC) (n 519) at [34].

[524] Ibid at [25].

[525] *James* v. *Eastleigh Borough Council* [1990] UKHL 6, [1990] 2 AC 751.

[526] *Bull* v. *Hall* (n 511).

[527] *Lee* v. *Ashers Bakery Company Ltd (UKSC)* (n 519) at [25].

[528] Ibid at [28].

[529] Ibid.

the project of equal treatment no favours to seek to extend it beyond its proper scope'.[530]

Protection against direct discrimination on grounds of political opinions and religious beliefs has constitutional status in Northern Ireland.[531] The nexus between the political message supporting gay marriage and Lee was 'such that it could be argued that they are "indissociable" for the purpose of direct discrimination on the ground of political opinion'.[532] It was therefore necessary to consider the McArthurs' Articles 9 and 10 ECHR rights. Lady Hale acknowledged that the bakery would not be able to refuse to provide Lee a cake because he was gay or because he supported gay marriage. However, the McArthurs were entitled 'to refuse to supply a cake with a message with which they profoundly disagreed'.[533]

Despite the acknowledgement, by Lady Hale, of the discrimination faced by the gay community, this judgment has been perceived as controversial, especially by those in the LGBTQI+ community.[534] Norrie argues:

> [Ashers's] belief in their own heterosexual superiority may justly be described as homophobic, and as harmful to those who do not share their sexuality. *Lee v Ashers Baking Company Ltd* may not have been about an act of discrimination against someone because of their sexual orientation, but it was fundamentally about the extent to which homophobic belief was worthy of respect in a democratic society. Though obscured by the Supreme Court's focus on the defendants' right not to express a belief that they did not actually hold, the defendants were in essence asserting their right to deny the equal worth of homosexuality and heterosexuality as aspects of the human condition . . . This is no different from the claim to racial superiority that lies at the heart of racism, and courts often point to homophobia and racism being regarded in the same light, and as equally unworthy of respect.[535]

As noted in Chapter 13, Lee unsuccessfully applied to the ECtHR.[536] Jonathan Cooper QC, together with Paul Johnson, provided a third-party intervention in support of Lee. They argued that the Supreme Court failed to uphold Parliament's intent that a person, when seeking commercial goods and services, should be protected from discrimination on grounds of sexual orientation. The Supreme Court had adopted a very narrow approach to equality which did not 'sufficiently appreciate the clear intention of the law to root out anti-gay hostility in certain aspects of social life, such as commercial activity'.[537] They also argued that the Supreme Court had not adequately taken into

[530] Ibid at [35]. [531] Ibid at [37]. [532] Ibid at [48]. [533] Ibid at [55].

[534] See Chapter 13.

[535] Kenneth Norrie, 'What Level of Respect Does Opposition to Same-Sex Marriage Deserve in a Democratic Society?' (2023) **74** NILQ 417, pp.427–428.

[536] *Lee* v. *the United Kingdom*, App. No. 18860/19, 06/01/2022.

[537] Paul Johnson 'The Love of Law, and the Law of Love: Jonathan Cooper and LGBT Human Rights Advocacy' (2022) 1 EHRLR 33, p.44.

account the context in which this occurred 'both in terms of the hostility often experienced by gay people in Northern Ireland – hostility that is fuelled by the beliefs of many in religious communities – and the importance of securing the right to same-sex marriage as a mechanism for challenging that hostility'.[538] Finally, in developing their argument, they compared the campaign for same-sex marriage in Northern Ireland to campaigns against laws prohibiting interracial marriages in the US. Advancing a hypothetical scenario in which a bakery refused to provide a cake with a message saying 'support multi-racial marriage', they suggested that:

> The message on that cake would be inextricably linked to the identities and race of those who were not permitted to marry. It would not matter who is seeking to purchase this particular hypothetical cake. To deny the cake with its iced message would be to discriminate on grounds of race, which can never be justified. The faith arguments to justify the outlawing of inter-racial marriage [should] be given no weight.[539]

As Paul Johnson explained in later writing, they thought it was important to make this argument because they felt that the analogies that had been used in the Supreme Court's judgment in *Ashers*, namely support for living in sin, support for a particular political party, support for a particular religious denomination, trivialised the issues involved.[540] A further aspect of their intervention was their critique of the Supreme Court's 'selective and limited engagement with the human rights issues relevant to the case'.[541] They argued that concepts such as 'fair balance' had been ignored and that the Supreme Court had failed to adequately grapple with the competing rights.

In rejecting the complaint, the ECtHR declared that Lee had not exhausted domestic remedies as he had failed to litigate the Convention rights in the domestic courts. You may recall from Chapter 13 that Paul Johnson observes that this 'is problematic because it appears to place "blame" on Mr Lee, rather than the [Supreme Court], for failing to appropriately consider the relevance of his ECHR rights to the issues in dispute'.[542] Johnson thus regards this a dereliction of the ECtHR's role as it was its duty to 'assess whether the domestic courts had met their obligation to secure Mr Lee's ECHR rights and freedoms, not to assess the extent to which Mr Lee had explicated those rights and freedoms'.[543] Indeed, if we look at how the ECtHR has approached other applications, it is evident that the ECtHR's stance is difficult to reconcile with

[538] Ibid.

[539] Ibid. *Lee* v. *the United Kingdom*, Joint Third-Party Intervention by Mr Jonathan Cooper OBE and Prof. Paul Johnson at [22].

[540] Ibid at [45].

[541] Ibid. This criticism is probably misplaced. The Supreme Court does not raise entirely new arguments of their own motion, especially when the respondent is represented by the Equality Commission for Northern Ireland and senior counsel.

[542] Ibid. [543] Ibid.

its practice elsewhere. For example, in Chapter 7 we saw that in the case of *Chowdury* v. *Greece*, a human trafficking case, the Greek Government sought to have the case declared inadmissible for failure to exhaust domestic remedies on the basis that 'at no stage of the domestic proceedings had they clearly referred to one of the rights guaranteed by the Convention and in particular the right – invoked by the applicants in their application to the Court'.[544] Yet on that occasion the Court held:

> Without expressly relying on Article 4 of the Convention, the applicants found arguments in domestic law and international law by which they clearly complained of an infringement of the rights guaranteed by that provision of the Convention. They therefore provided the judicial authorities with an opportunity to avoid, or provide redress for, the alleged violations, in accordance with the purpose of Article 35 of the Convention. Accordingly, the Government's objection must be rejected.[545]

The basis for declaring Lee's case inadmissible is thus questionable.

A further aspect of the ECtHR's judgment in *Lee* that has given rise to concern is its statement that it was 'not self-evident that the facts of the present case … fall within the ambit of Article 8, 9 or 10 of the Convention' and that it was 'not immediately apparent how the findings of the Supreme Court and the consequences of those findings for [Lee] either constitute one of the modalities of or are linked to the exercise of a right guaranteed by any of those Articles'.[546] Although it is important to observe here that the ECtHR did not determine that the facts *could* not fall within the ambit of the rights, Johnson argues that 'for the Court to conclude that it was not self-evident or immediately apparent how the judgment of the [Supreme Court] impacted on Mr Lee's ECHR rights is extremely concerning' as discrimination on the grounds of sexual orientation 'has long been recognised by the European Court of Human Rights as falling within the ambit of art.8'.[547] Indeed, the only way that this would be possible is if the ECtHR accepted that the refusal related only to the message and had no broader implications at all, but this would be a narrow approach to Article 8 which does not tally with either the broad approach that is taken to the applicability of that right in general, nor the strong protection that the ECtHR has accorded in the context of discrimination on the basis of sexual identity.

14.4.5.2 *Discrimination, Employment and Competing Rights*

The prohibition of discrimination often leads to tensions or direct clashes with other protected Convention rights or those protected characteristics under the

[544] *Chowdury* v. *Greece* [2017] ECHR 300 at [62]. See also, *S.M.* v. *Croatia* [GC] (2021) 72 EHRR 1.

[545] *Chowdury*, ibid at [68].

[546] *Lee* v. *the United Kingdom* (n 536) at [73] cited in Johnson (n 537), p.46.

[547] Ibid.

EqA.[548] This has arisen in the context of employment rights. In Chapter 13 we saw that this issue arose in respect of Ladele and MacFarlane in *Eweida* v. *the United Kingdom*.[549]

The case of *Forstater* was discussed above.[550] It is important to note that while Forstater's gender-critical beliefs are protected under the EqA, trans persons are also protected against discrimination and harassment. According to the EAT, 'this judgment does not mean that those with gender-critical beliefs can "misgender" trans persons with impunity.'[551] For example, in *Mackereth* v. *Department of Work and Pensions*,[552] the claimant, in line with his Christian beliefs, held gender-critical views. He left his position as a health and disabilities adviser with the Department for Work and Pensions after refusing to agree that he would comply with a policy which required him to refer to transgender persons by their preferred pronouns. On appeal, the EAT found that his gender-critical beliefs were protected but that no direct or indirect discrimination had taken place. In the view of the EAT, any employee, regardless of their beliefs, who refused to address service users by their preferred pronouns would be treated in the same manner and the measures adopted by the respondents were necessary and proportionate to meet the needs of potentially vulnerable service users.[553] Thus while gender-critical beliefs are protected under the EqA, the manner in which such beliefs manifest themselves may not be protected.[554]

The knotty question of manifestation of beliefs and its restrictions was directly addressed by the EAT in *Higgs* v. *Farmor's School*.[555] This case also dealt with expressions of gender critical beliefs and whether there was direct discrimination under s.13 EqA. Higgs, a Christian, was a pastoral administrator and work experience manager at Farmour's School. She was dismissed from her employment after the school received a complaint concerning social media posts that she had made criticising the nature of sex education in schools and the teaching of 'gender fluidity'.[556] The school was concerned that she may be perceived as hostile towards the LGBTQ+ community, and especially, transgender people. The ET found that her dismissal was not discrimination based on her religious beliefs: while her beliefs were protected under the EqA, she was dismissed because of the school's concerns that she held homophobic and transphobic views. The EAT allowed the appeal as the ET

[548] Section 4, EqA sets out the protected characteristics.

[549] *Eweida* v. *the United Kingdom* (n 116).

[550] *Forstater* v. *CGD Europe* (n 470).

[551] Ibid at [118].

[552] *Mackereth* v. *Department of Work and Pensions* [2022] EAT 99, [2022] IRLR 721.

[553] Ibid at [138].

[554] See *Page* v. *NHS Trust Development Authority* [2021] EWCA Civ 255, [2021] WLR(D) 125 in relation to the manifestation of religious beliefs.

[555] *Higgs* v. *Farmor's School* [2023] EAT 89, [2023] ICR 1072.

[556] Ibid at [4]–[10].

had failed to 'engage with the question whether this was ... because of, or related to, the claimant's *manifestation* of her beliefs'.[557] In determining whether her social media posts were a manifestation of her beliefs the tribunal relied on the Strasbourg decision in *Eweida*. Eady J in the EAT stated:

> If the claimant's actions have a sufficiently close and direct nexus to an underlying religion or belief, such that they are properly to be understood as a manifestation of that religion or belief, any limitation would need to be such as is prescribed by law and necessary, in one of the ways identified under article 9(2).[558]

Thus the right to express beliefs, even offensive ones, is protected in a democratic society but the right to manifest religion or belief and expression are qualified rights.[559] These rights should only be interfered with if there is a legal basis and the requirements of legitimate aim (is there a link between the legitimate aim pursued and the differential treatment), necessity in a democratic society and proportionality are satisfied.[560] Whether a restriction can be objectively justified will always be context-specific.

Eady J added that 'a danger can arise from any attempt to lay down general guidelines ... [as] the issues arising from the exercise of rights to freedom of religion and belief, and rights to freedom of expression, are invariably fact-specific'.[561] Nevertheless, in the context of an employment dispute, the EAT laid down some considerations which are likely to be relevant when assessing the proportionality of any interference. They are:

> (i) the content of the manifestation; (ii) the tone used; (iii) the extent of the manifestation; (iv) the worker's understanding of the likely audience; (v) the extent and nature of the intrusion on the rights of others, and any consequential impact on the employer's ability to run its business; (vi) whether the worker has made clear that the views expressed are personal, or whether they might be seen as representing the views of the employer, and whether that might present a reputational risk; (vii) whether there is a potential power imbalance given the nature of the worker's position or role and that of those whose rights are intruded upon; (viii) the nature of the employer's business, in particular where there is a potential impact on vulnerable service users or clients; (ix) whether the limitation imposed is the least intrusive measure open to the employer.[562]

The guidance set out in *Higgs* was followed by the ET in *Miller* v. *University of Bristol*.[563] David Miller, a sociology professor, was dismissed by the University after he was accused of antisemitic comments. The hearing in this case took

[557] Ibid at [81]. Direct discrimination is defined as less favourable treatment because of the protected characteristic.

[558] Ibid at [81].

[559] See Chapter 13.

[560] The four-stage proportionality analysis set out in *Bank Mellat* v. *HM Treasury (No 2)* [2013] UKSC 38, [2014] AC 700.

[561] *Higgs* v. *Farmor School* (n 555) at [93].

[562] Ibid at [94].

[563] *Miller* v. *University of Bristol*, Employment Tribunal, Case No. 1400780.2022, 31/01/2024.

place just after the October 7 attack in Israel which was the catalyst for the war in Gaza. However, these debates on university campuses are not new and issues surrounding anti-Zionism, antisemitism and its definition have been ongoing for many years. The ET in *Miller* concluded that the claimant's anti-Zionist views qualified as a philosophical belief and as a protected characteristic pursuant to s.10 EqA. The claimant succeeded in his claim of direct discrimination against the University for his dismissal although his award will be somewhat reduced as the ET found that the claimant's actions had contributed to his dismissal.

These decisions deal with highly sensitive issues where beliefs such as anti-Zionism clash with race equality, as seen in the *Miller* dispute. Some religious beliefs promote patriarchal views which are incompatible with gender equality, while others lead to hostility to notions of gender identification and gender fluidity even though this is offensive and, perhaps even threatening, to the transgender community. The strong protection afforded to religion and beliefs under the EqA and the ECHR, however, does not provide a rationale to engage in gender or racist discrimination or 'misgendering' behaviour, all of which are also protected grounds.

14.4.5.3 *Discrimination, Education and Religion*

The EqA prohibits direct (s.13) and indirect discrimination (s.19). The protected characteristics include religion, race and ethnicity. The relevant legislation concerning education is in Part 6 of the EqA. EqA, s.85, makes it unlawful for school authorities to discriminate against a pupil or prospective pupil in relation to the terms on which it offers him or her admission, by not admitting him or her, or in the way it treats the pupil once admitted. Prior to the EqA, the Race Relations Act 1976 (RRA)was a separate statute dealing with discrimination based on race and ethnicity. The Supreme Court decision in *R (E)* v. *Governing Body of JFS*[564] was decided under the RRA but it and the new legal framework in the EqA are similar. Under both the RRA and the EqA, schools cannot lawfully discriminate against pupils because of their race or ethnicity. The second case discussed below, the *Al-Hiraj School*, concerns segregation of male and female pupils on the basis of gender, also a protected characteristic. The final case, *R (TTT)* v. *Michaela Community Schools Trust*, concerns the prohibition of ritual prayer at school.[565]

An important case concerning ethnicity and school admissions was addressed by the Supreme Court in *R (E)* v. *Governing Body of JFS*.[566] Faith schools are exempted from the prohibition of religious discrimination but not

[564] *JFS* (n 488).

[565] *R (TTT)* v. *Michaela Community Schools Trust* [2024] EWHC 843 (Admin), [2024] HRLR 9.

[566] *JFS* (n 488).

from discrimination based on race/ethnicity. The JFS (formerly the Jewish Free School) is a voluntary aided Jewish school. The claimant, E, wished to send his son to the JFS but the child failed to gain a place because he was not recognised as a Jew. The central question addressed by the Court in *JFS* was whether it constituted direct racial discrimination under s.1(1)(a) of the RRA (now covered by the EqA) to impose a criterion for admission to the JFS that the child applicant concerned be recognised as being Jewish by the Office of the Chief Rabbi of the United Congregation of the Commonwealth (OCR). The admissions criterion seeks to discriminate between Jewish and non-Jewish children. This is a distinction which is permissible if made on religious grounds but unlawful if made on racial/ethnic grounds.

A particular difficulty of this case concerned the question of who is a Jewish person – an issue which remains controversial among the Jewish community. According to the Orthodox view and that of the OCR, whose rules the JFS followed in their admission criteria, a Jewish person is one who is the child of a Jewish mother (the matrilineal test) or a person who has become Jewish by conversion. Thus the JFS' admission criteria gave preference to children whose mothers satisfied the matrilineal test or who were Jews by conversion by Orthodox standards. In this case, the father of the child seeking admission was Jewish and his mother had undergone a course of conversion, but it was not one recognised by the OCR. The family practised the Jewish faith and worshipped at a Masorti Synagogue. As the child's mother was not recognised as Jewish by the OCR, the child was not given the preference accorded to children whose mothers were recognised.

The majority concluded that the question whether any less favourable treatment was 'on grounds' of ethnic origins is to be decided by a simple factual enquiry: why was the victim treated as they were? Or as framed by Lady Hale, does 'the criteria used by JFS to select pupils for the school treat people differently because of their "ethnic origins"?'.[567] The criterion applied in this child's case was one which depended upon ethnic origins. According to Lord Phillips, '[O]ne thing is clear about the matrilineal test; it is a test of ethnic origin.'[568] The Court found that this differentiation was unlawful notwithstanding the theological motive for the OCR's definition of Jewishness. Thus, the refusal of the JFS to admit the child applicant was less favourable treatment of him on racial grounds. A Jewish faith school can give preference to Jewish applicants, but eligibility must depend on faith, and not on ethnicity.

The Court noted that the statutory scheme provided that no justification of direct discrimination is possible. The RRA and the other anti-discrimination enactments, including under the EqA, instead enact a formalistic and

[567] Ibid at [54]. [568] Ibid at [45], per Lord Phillips.

symmetrical concept of discrimination and inequality. As Lady Hale observed, 'Parliament might have adopted a model of substantive equality, allowing distinctions which brought historically disadvantaged groups up to the level of historically advantaged groups. But it did not do so. It adopted a model of formal equality.'[569] Thus it does not allow for the justification of objectively beneficial forms of discrimination. Nor was the motivation for the discrimination relevant. This means that, however positive or benign an act of direct discrimination, unless specially exempted, it will violate the RRA. (Under the EqA, direct discrimination cannot be justified, apart from the few exceptions provided for in the Act, and the motive is immaterial.)

A number of the judges were at pains to express some sympathy with the JFS and to emphasise that the treatment in issue in this case could in no way be described as 'racist' in the way that expression is popularly understood.[570] Nevertheless these distinctions can be invidious. In the Court of Appeal, Lord Justice Sedley made this interesting analogy:

> M was refused admission to JFS because his mother, and therefore he, was not regarded as Jewish. The school has been perfectly open in giving this as the ground of non-admission. There are of course theological reasons why M is not regarded as Jewish, but they are not the ground of non-admission: they are the motive for adopting it. If it were otherwise, a person who honestly believed, as the Dutch Reformed Church of South Africa until recently believed, that God had made black people inferior and had destined them to live separately from whites, would be able to discriminate openly without breaking the law. The reason why it is not so is that the ground of any such discrimination would be that the victim was black; its religious motive would be immaterial.[571]

Sandra Fredman is critical of this decision as divorcing motive from direct discrimination. She believes that there is a loss of moral condemnation when the motive is irrelevant for the purpose of the discrimination.[572] In her view, focusing on the effect of the perpetrator's action falls within the province of indirect discrimination.[573] If the issue was considered as a form of indirect discrimination and consequently justifiable, consideration could be given to the real reason for the discrimination and the proportionality of the admissions policy assessed.[574]

[569] Ibid at [67], per Lady Hale. [570] Ibid at [9], per Lord Phillips and at [54], per Lady Hale.

[571] *R (E)* v. *Governing Body of JFS and United Synagogue Intervening* [2009] EWCA Civ 626, [2009] 4 All ER 375 at [30]–[31], per Lord Justice Sedley. See Lord Clark in *JFS* (n 488) at [150].

[572] Sandra Fredman, *Discrimination Law* (2nd ed) (OUP, 2011), pp.208–210.

[573] Ibid, pp.208 and 210–214. [574] Ibid, p.211.

In *HM Chief Inspector of Education, Children's Services and Skills* v. *The Interim Executive Board of Al-Hijrah School & Ors*,[575] the Court of Appeal was asked to consider whether it is discriminatory for the purposes of s.13 EqA (direct discrimination) and s.85 EqA (it is unlawful for the responsible body of a school to discriminate against a pupil) for a school to have complete segregation of male and female pupils. Al-Hijrah School is a voluntary aided faith school for girls and boys aged between four and sixteen. The school has an Islamic ethos and for religious reasons believes that separation of the sexes from Year 5 onwards is obligatory. Complete segregation of boys and girls in the age range of nine to sixteen for all lessons, breaks, school clubs and trips was one of the defining characteristics of the school. The school's argument was that separate but equal treatment by reason of gender could not be unlawful discrimination as, even if it was detrimental, there was no discrimination as both sexes suffered the same detriment. The Court of Appeal unanimously rejected the school's argument, finding that the segregation constituted direct discrimination and holding that the motive for discrimination (adherence by the school to applicable tenets of Islam) was irrelevant.[576] Sir Terence Etherton and Lord Justice Beatson explained:

> We do not consider that s.13(5) EqA is of any material assistance in the present case.[577] We do not find that there is discrimination in the present case merely because of the fact of segregation. So far as concerns the School, in the context of section 85(2), we find that the strict segregation by gender is a detriment which involves less favourable treatment because it diminishes the quality of education that the girl pupils and the boy pupils would receive but for their respective sex. It is not the mere fact of segregation which gives rise to discrimination, as would be the situation under section 13(5) in the case of race, but rather it is the impact on the quality of education which the pupils would receive but for their respective sex.[578]

All the judges agreed that there was unlawful discrimination by the school, but Lady Justice Gloster delivered a separate robust judgment and went further than the other two members of the Court. She would have held that the segregation itself amounted to direct discrimination pursuant to s.13 EqA. In her view, gender segregation gave rise to a greater detriment for girls for two interrelated reasons. First, the girls at this school were subject to a practical detriment as the evidence (which included references to books in the school library espousing conservative religious views about the role of women and in some cases even condoning violence against them) indicated that a gender segregation policy was likely to reinforce misogynist attitudes.

[575] *HM Chief Inspector of Education, Children's Services and Skills* v. *The Interim Executive Board of Al-Hijrah* [2017] EWCA Civ 1426, [2018] 1 WLR 1471.

[576] Ibid at [81]. [577] EqA s.13(5) provides that racial segregation is always discriminatory.

[578] *Board of Al-Hijrah School & Ors* (n 575) at [80].

Secondly, it also subjected them to 'expressive harm'.[579] It was particularly 'discriminatory against girls in that it reinforces the different spaces – private and public – that men and women must occupy, and their respective stereotyped roles which accord them differential and unequal status'.[580] She also observed:

> Before a girl has reached adulthood, any school she attends has an obligation to enable and support her to make free and informed choices, as to the role she wishes to undertake as an adult in a democratic British society, whether it be in the workplace or in the home. Such choices may well reflect her cultural, religious and community background – but they should not be predicated by it. And segregation on grounds of sex in a mixed sex school does just that.[581]

Lady Justice Gloster's judgment reflects a more nuanced conception of equality rights which appreciates that a system (effectively) endorsing traditional gender stereotypes promotes male power and economic dominance. Her views are closer to an understanding of substantive equality rights.

The final example is *R (TTT)* v. *Michaela Community Schools Trust*, which concerned the prohibition of ritual prayer on the school's site.[582] The Court found that there was no interference with the pupil's right to Article 9 ECHR. This aspect of the decision has been analysed in Chapter 13. The pupil also claimed indirect discrimination (s.19 EqA) and a breach of s.85(2)(d) EqA which requires that a pupil is not discriminated against by not affording 'access to a benefit, facility or service' and s.85(2)(f) EqA by not subjecting the pupil to any other detriment. The Court concluded that the disadvantage to Muslim pupils was outweighed by the aims which the prohibition on the prayer ritual seeks to promote on behalf of all the school pupils.[583] The judge's conclusions in finding no indirect discrimination were the same as those given for finding no breach of Article 9 ECHR.[584] Nor did the Court find any breach of the PSED pursuant to s.149 EqA.

14.4.5.4 *The Equality Act and the Definition of the Words Used to Protect Women and the Trans Community*

In April 2025, the Supreme Court decided the controversial appeal, *For Women Scotland* v. *the Scottish Ministers,*[585] concerning the interpretation to be given to 'sex', 'man' and 'woman' in the EqA. The appellant, For Women Scotland, is a women's voluntary organisation that campaigns to strengthen women's and children's rights in Scotland. They brought a judicial review of the Scottish

[579] Ibid at [154]. [580] Ibid at [170]. [581] Ibid at [171].

[582] *Michaela Community Schools Trust* (n 565). [583] Ibid at [232].

[584] Ibid and the judge also referred back to [192]–[207].

[585] *For Women Scotland* v. *Scottish Ministers* (n 510).

Government's definition of the term 'woman' in the statutory guidance of the Gender Representation on Public Boards (Scotland) Act 2018.[586] This statute created gender representation targets to enhance the number of women on public boards in Scotland. The guidance stated that for the purposes of the Gender Representation on Public Boards (Scotland) Act 2018, the definition of a 'woman' is the same as that in the EqA[587] and included trans women who had obtained a GRC under the Gender Recognition Act 2004 (GRA). For Women Scotland challenged the lawfulness of the guidance arguing that it misstated the law as the definition of 'man', 'woman' and 'sex' in the EqA refers to 'biological sex'. This challenge was dismissed by both the Outer House[588] and on appeal to the Inner House of the Court of Session.[589] The Inner House concluded that 'women' and 'sex' can refer to biological sex in some sections and certificated sex under the GRA in others.[590] In contrast, the Supreme Court unanimously allowed the appeal and held that the terms 'woman', 'man' and 'sex' in the EqA refer to biological sex: that is the sex assigned at birth and recorded on the original birth certificate. The Supreme Court did not specifically spell out a definition of 'biological sex' but this inference can be drawn from their decision. Nor did they address the fact that 'biological sex' may not always be as distinct as they assumed. [591]

The judgment turned on statutory interpretation and the interaction between section 9 of the GRA and the EqA.[592] Section 9(1) of the GRA establishes that trans people with a GRC become 'for all purposes' the acquired gender. Thus 'if the acquired gender is the male gender, the person's sex

[586] FWS had successfully challenged the even broader definition of women initially included in the Act in the Inner House on devolution grounds. It was held that creating a definition of women for implementing equality law fell outside the legislative competence of the Scottish Parliament. *For Women Scotland Ltd* v. *Lord Advocate* [2022] CSIH 4, [2022] S.C. 150. New statutory guidance was issued on the meaning of 'woman' in the legislation which is the subject of this appeal.

[587] EqA s.212. [588] [2022] CSOH 90, [2023] S.C. 61. [589] [2023] CSIH 37, [2024] S.C. 117.

[590] Ibid at [62].

[591] 'Biological sex' assigned at birth is usually uncontroversial. In some circumstances, however, the position is not so clear cut. Not all individuals are born with unambiguous external genitals and the sex determined by doctors and parents/carers may not correspond to the individual's chromosomal sex makeup. We recognise and acknowledge this diversity. In circumstances where cases, reports and academic material to which we refer use the term 'biological sex' to refer to the binary female and male distinction, we also use that terminology for consistency with the source material.

[592] The Court examined the legal background and concluded that the Sex Discrimination Act 1975 (SDA) used the words 'man' and 'woman' to refer to biological sex. The SDA was repealed and replaced by the EqA, a consolidating statute. In the Court's assessment, there is no indication that the terms 'man' and 'women' were modified by the EqA. See *For Women Scotland* v. *Scottish Ministers* (n 510) at [162]–[164]. In the EqA, the protected characteristics on the basis of which discrimination is generally prohibited include sex and gender reassignment. Ibid [113]–[116].

becomes that of a man and, if it is the female gender, the sex becomes that of a woman'.[593] Section 9(3) contains an exception to that rule: 'Subsection (1) is subject to provision made by this Act or any other enactment'. The central question for the Court was deciding the test to apply when determining whether other legislation displaces the application of s.9(1). There was no requirement in s.9(3) that legislation expressly disapply s.9(1) or that disapplication would arise by necessary implication.[594] The Court determined that s.9(3) will 'apply where the terms, context and purpose of the relevant enactment show that it does, because of a clear incompatibility or because its provisions are rendered incoherent or unworkable by the application of the rule in section 9(1)'.[595] The Supreme Court noted that the EqA does not address 'the effect (if any) which section 9(1) of the GRA 2004 has on the definition of "sex" or the words "woman" or "man"'.[596] As the EqA does not expressly disapply the rule in s.9(1), the Supreme Court undertook 'a close analysis' of the EqA to determine whether s.9(3) applies and displaces the rule in s. 9(1) as regards the EqA.[597] In the view of the Court, the EqA would be 'incoherent and unworkable' if the rule in s.9(1) GRA were to be applied.[598] For example, it made no sense to the Court that sex-based rights and protections under the EqA would be regulated 'by reference to categories that can only be ascertained by knowledge of who possesses a (confidential) certificate'.[599] The effect of a certificated sex interpretation would be to create inequality within subgroups giving trans people who possess a GRC greater rights than trans people who do not, even though there may be no obvious way to distinguish between them.[600] The Court also referred to the provisions concerning pregnancy and maternity discrimination.[601] In their view, as it is only biological women who can become pregnant, the protection is limited to biological women.[602] The Court also noted the practical implications for lesbians should a wider definition of 'sex' and 'woman' be adopted, including the impact it would have on lesbian clubs and associations.[603] If the GRC altered the meaning of sex under the EqA, according to the Court, the 'concept of sexual orientation [a protected characteristic under the EqA] towards members of a particular sex in section 12 is rendered meaningless.'[604]

[593] GRA s.9(1). [594] *For Women Scotland* v. *Scottish Ministers* (n 510) at [99]–[104].

[595] Ibid at [156]. [596] Ibid at [158]. [597] Ibid at [161]. [598] Ibid at [264].

[599] Ibid at [173]. This term, 'sex-based rights', had not been recognised as a legal term before the judgment. The language of sex-based rights refers to 'exceptions' to the general prohibition of discrimination on the basis of sex in relation to the single-sex provisions in the EqA.

[600] Ibid at [203]. Further impracticalities would arise concerning the operations of provisions relating to single-sex associations and charities, women's participation i n sport, the operation of the public sector equality duty and the armed forces, [229]–[246].

[601] EqA ss.13(6), 17 and 18. [602] *For Women Scotland* v. *Scottish Ministers* (n 510) at [177].

[603] Ibid at [207] and [34]. [604] Ibid at [206].

The Court commented upon the importance in the EqA of 'clarity and consistency' to protect those with rights and also those who have duties imposed on them by the EqA.[605] The Court concluded that the exception in s.9(3) applied and the terms 'sex', 'man' and 'woman' in the EqA refer to biological sex.[606] As a consequence, a trans woman with a GRC does not fall within the definition of a 'woman' under the EqA and therefore the statutory guidance issued by the Scottish Ministers was incorrect.[607] The Court stressed that a biological sex interpretation of the EqA does not disadvantage or remove protection from trans people, with or without a GRC, as they are protected from discrimination under the protected characteristic of gender reassignment under the EqA.[608]

The judgment has been received with dismay from the trans community. Although the focus of the judgment was narrow, (it applies directly to those trans people with GRCs) it will have profound ramifications for all trans people. The Court commented upon the written and oral interventions that were submitted. [609] Particular praise was given to Sex Matters, an association who believe that 'ideas and behaviours promoted in the name of gender ideology are misguided and harmful. They are morally and scientifically wrong, irrational and damaging'.[610] The Court was clearly influenced by this intervenor, stating that it 'gave focus and structure to the argument that 'sex', 'man' and 'woman' should be given a biological meaning'.[611] The trans community was indirectly represented by the Scottish Ministers arguing in support of their legislation and Amnesty International who made a written intervention setting out their position on legal gender recognition grounded on international human rights standards.[612] The fact that no trans voices were heard directly by the Court has led to criticism of the decision.[613] A further legal critique of the judgment focuses on the Supreme Court's failure to address whether an interpretation of 'sex' as biological would be consistent with the human rights of trans people. Crash Wigley has argued that as 'a trans-exclusionary interpretation of sex would breach the Article 8 rights of trans people' she has questioned why the Court failed to use the interpretative power under s.3(1) HRA to read the legislation compatibly with the Convention rights of trans persons. [614] Michael Foran contests this

605 Ibid at [151]–[154]. The EqA imposes duties on individuals and organisations not to discriminate unlawfully. This is achieved through the regulation of the day-to-day conduct of, for example, employers, service-providers and others [152].

606 Ibid at [264]. 607 Ibid at [266]. 608 Ibid at [248]. 609 Ibid at [34].

610 See https://sex-matters.org/posts/updates/being-clear-about-our-beliefs/.

611 (n 510) at [35]. 612 Ibid at [34].

613 Good Law Project, 'The Supreme Court ignored trans voices. I'm ashamed of what our law has become', 16 April 2025, https://goodlawproject.org/the-supreme-court-ignored-trans-voices-im-ashamed-of-what-our-law-has-become/.

614 C. Wrigley, 'For Women Scotland: A case of significant silences", UK Const. L. Blog (6 May 2025), available at https://ukconstitutionallaw.org/.

interpretation as neither party argued that s.3 should be applied to the interpretation of the EqA.[615] He concludes: 'This being the case, one can hardly blame the Supreme Court for not ruling on a claim which was not advanced before it and which was not one of the issues to be determined'.[616]

Amnesty International's written intervention[617] in the Supreme Court emphasised that the the GRA was enacted in response to a decision of the ECtHR in *Goodwin* v. *the United Kingdom*[618] in which the ECtHR stated: 'the unsatisfactory situation in which post operative [trans people] live in an intermediate zone [as] not quite one gender or the other is no longer sustainable'.[619] Many trans people sense that this judgment means that their lives have once more fallen into the 'intermediate zone', with potentially profound implications for their day-to day lives. It is puzzling that the Court did not analyse in any depth the Article 8 ECHR rights of trans people as set out by Amnesty International in their written statement. The ECtHR in *Goodwin* established that state parties must provide an avenue for the legal recognition of the new sexual identity of post-operative trans people. The GRC was the framework chosen to achieve this but the Supreme Court's decision in For Women Scotland has the potential to undermine the scheme. It is possible, of course, that even after grappling with Article 8 ECHR and the Strasbourg jurisprudence, the Court's decision would have remained the same but the omission is unsettling. The Supreme Court sought to bring clarity to the EqA but new uncertainties have now emerged.

The EqA makes provision for single sex/separate services.[620] A person with the protected characteristic of gender reassignment may be lawfully excluded from such services where that exclusion is a proportionate means of achieving a legitimate aim.[621] On April 25 2025, the Equality and Human Rights Commission (EHRC) published 'an interim update on the practical implications of the UK Supreme Court judgment'[622] which seem to go further than the requirements set out in the EqA Schedule 3. This update interpreted the judgment as creating obligations on workplaces and services to exclude trans women from women's facilities and trans men from men's facilities. It added that trans people should not be put in a position where there are no facilities

[615] M. Foran, 'For Women Scotland: Is legal recognition of biological sex a violation of human rights?' UK Const. L. Blog (15 May 2025).

[616] Ibid.

[617] Amnesty International UK, Written Intervention in *For Women Scotland* v. *Scottish Ministers* at [10].

[618] (2002) 35 EHRR 18.

[619] Ibid at [90]. The Supreme Court referred to this passage from *Goodwin* (n 510) at [65] and discussed the human rights implications at [63]–[68] and [73].

[620] EqA paragraphs 26 and 27 of Schedule 3.

[621] EqA paragraph 28 of Schedule 3.

[622] EHRC, 'An interim update on the practical implications of the UK Supreme Court judgment' 25 April 2025.

for them to use. Unsurprisingly, many trans people are left fearful that where unisex facilities are not provided, they may be left without access to any services, or they may be placed in danger when doing so.[623] Lord Sumption, a former Justice of the Supreme Court, considers that the Supreme Court's judgment has been misunderstood: while many have taken the ruling to mean that service providers are obliged to provide single-sex spaces based on biological sex, the ruling meant that excluding transgender people from single-sex spaces was allowed, and not a breach of the 2010 Equality Act. . . . I think it's quite important to note that you are allowed to exclude trans women from these facilities. But you are not obliged to do it.[624]

Concern about the approach taken by the EHRC in response to the Supreme Court judgment has been expressed by the Chairs of the JCHR and the Women and Equalities Committee (WEC). Lord Alton, Chair of the JCHR, has written to the Chair of the EHRC, concerning the legal status of the interim guidance, the limited consultation period (two weeks) and the failure of the guidance to address the Supreme Court's statement about the rights of trans people. [625] The Chair of the (WEC), Sarah Owen MP, has also written in a similar vein. She requested information from the EHRC about steps to ensure that the Code of Practice is 'supportive of the rights of all people' and 'whether the Code of Practice will clarify rights of trans people, for example around strip searching by police officers'.

In May 2025, the EHRC launched a consultation on updates it has made to its code of practice for services, public functions and associations which largely follow those published in the interim update. The updated content sets out that a GRC does not change a person's legal sex for the purposes of the EqA.[626] Circumstances are envisaged where it may be necessary to request a birth certificate, especially where service providers exercising public functions need to discharge their legal obligations under the EqA. Where there is genuine concern about the accuracy of information provided about birth sex, a birth certificate could be requested. The Code then notes that a person

[623] Jess O'Thomson, 'The UK Supreme Court's ruling on sex has brought only doubt', *Prospect*, 28 April 2025. The Good Law Project has sent a judicial review pre-action letter indicating a challenge will be brought concerning the interim update. https://goodlawproject.org/wp-content/uploads/2025/05/Letter-to-the-Equality-and-Human-Rights-Commission-16-May-2025_Redacted.pdf.

[624] David Maddox, 'No obligation to exclude trans women under "misunderstood" Supreme Court ruling, former top judge says', *Independent*, 18 April 2025, www.independent.co.uk/news/uk/politics/lord-sumption-trans-biolgical-woman-supreme-court-b2735828.html.

[625] Lord Alton, Chair of the JCHR, letter to Baroness Faulkner, Chair of the Equality and Human Rights Commission, 1 May 2025, https://committees.parliament.uk/publications/47703/documents/249228/default/.

[626] EHRC, 'Code of practice consultation 2025: Changes that apply across the code' (20 May 2025), ch.2.1.

who has a GRC may have an amended birth certificate in their acquired gender and the Code suggests that additional requests may be necessary, 'such as confirmation as to whether a person has a GRC.'[627] This is suggested even though, according to the Supreme Court, a GRC is confidential. It adds that requests 'should be made in a proportionate way which is discreet and sensitive'.[628] Services that are open to the public must be defined by biological sex if they are claiming to be single-sex spaces. Requiring trans people to 'out' themselves if they need to use facilities, such as toilets, in public is an unsatisfactory situation. Further litigation on these difficult and sensitive issues is highly likely.

14.5 CONCLUSION

Over the last twenty-five years, the Strasbourg jurisprudence concerning the prohibition of discrimination has evolved: it has become a more responsive and effective tool to address stigma, stereotype and violence based on prejudice. In the context of, for example, gender and gender-based violence, the Court has made important headway. *Opuz* v. *Turkey* which defines discrimination against women to include 'gender-based violence, that is, violence that is directed against a woman because she is a woman or that affects women disproportionately' was a landmark decision. The development of indirect discrimination and the accompanying shift in the burden of proof has made this evolution possible, along with the modification of the evidentiary requirements and the willingness of the Court to assess statistical evidence. The importance of discrimination through violence has also been recognised in relation to race and ethnic origin, religion and sexual orientation. Nevertheless, the 'heavily proceduralised' approach to racial violence in the Court's jurisprudence has been disappointing.[629]

Given the inherent limitations of Article 14 ECHR, the receptive approach by the Court to expanding the categories protected and the 'ambit test' have been welcome. However, the development of Article 14 ECHR jurisprudence continues to be hindered by the many non-discrimination cases which the Court decides without any examination of the Article 14 ECHR complaint. This perplexing situation creates an opaque hurdle for applicants as the Court does not explicitly expound on why a consideration of non-discrimination is unnecessary. The analogous or comparator test has posed conceptual and practical difficulties. It has led, on occasions, to the application of a restrictive comparator test encouraging the Court to return to a more formal understanding of equality.[630]

[627] Ibid, ch.2.2.8. [628] Ibid. [629] See, e.g., *Nachova* v. *Bulgaria* (n 32).
[630] *Hämäläinen* v. *Finland* (n 372).

This approach permits States to circumvent providing objective and reasonable justifications for discriminatory treatment. In addition, the inconsistency of the Court's interpretation, as highlighted in the jurisprudence on sexual orientation, has restricted the effective enhancement of Article 14 ECHR. The Article 14 ECHR analysis, underlining discriminatory treatment, should be used consistently by the Court to stress that unacceptable prejudice will not be tolerated and that it will act to redress disadvantage.

In the UK, consideration of Article 14 ECHR has led to some important changes in domestic law. The ECtHR's decision in *JD* v. *the United Kingdom* has been instrumental in altering the undemanding test of justification in circumstances where differential treatment is the result of social and economic policies.[631] Consequently, the 'manifestly without reasonable foundation' criteria applied by the UK domestic courts is no longer the accepted test. Nevertheless, the Supreme Court in *R (SC and Others)* v. *Secretary of State for Work and Pensions* adopted a highly deferential approach in its analysis of the justification for the acknowledged disparity in treatment and discrimination.[632]

The EqA is concerned with status equality, that is the relationship between a limited number of particular characteristics and the treatment afforded to individuals or groups to which they belong. Litigation under the EqA is ongoing and the courts continue to wrestle with the knotty issues concerning competing protected characteristics. In *For Women Scotland* v. *The Scottish Ministers*, the Supreme Court's decision that 'sex' in the EqA means 'biological sex' has led to a heated and ongoing debate, especially concerning the operation of single-sex facilities.[633]

Overall equality law has, however, been a disappointment for those who had hoped it would respond more sensitively to socio-economic disadvantage. Income inequality stubbornly persists in the UK and systemic differences in economic outcomes exist between men and women, between different ethnic groups and those living in disadvantaged and other areas. Social disadvantage is a highly complex problem with many causes, and equality law is only one form of response to disadvantage and unfairness. The EqA and the HRA have widened the scope for 'positive action' in some contexts but have also represented only partial solutions. Although law alone will never lead to a transformation of society, law retains the capacity to protect human rights and to draw public and political attention to social injustices.

[631] *JD* v. *the United Kingdom* (n 85).

[632] *R (SC, CB and 8 children)* (n 398).

[633] See (n 510).

INDEX

For EU product safety concerns, contact us at Calle de José Abascal, 56–1°,
28003 Madrid, Spain or eugpsr@cambridge.org.

www.ingramcontent.com/pod-product-compliance
Lightning Source LLC
LaVergne TN
LVHW060006210926
848481LV00013B/3662
* 9 7 8 1 0 0 9 0 9 5 4 5 7 *